P9-CQT-371

St MARTIN'S
TRUE CRIME
CLASSICS

Jill had the rare ability to spot vulnerabilities in a man, and she focused in on their weaknesses like a hungry cheetah surveying a herd of wildebeest to pick out a prey animal that was too young or too old, lame or sick. Men were her prey, and when she was on a blood scent she didn't deviate from her target. She was a sultry temptress who could addle male minds with her sexual charisma, serve as a charming dinner companion, or chat knowledgeably about sports cars, guns or business.

Poisoned Vows

Clifford L. Linedecker

St. Martin's Paperbacks

POISONED VOWS

Copyright © 1995 by Clifford L. Linedecker.

Cover photograph by Marc Witz.

ISBN: 0-312-95513-8

Printed in the United States of America

St. Martin's Paperbacks edition/September 1995

10 9 8 7 6 5 4 3

Acknowledgments

Books dealing with true events do not come into being solely through the efforts of the authors, but are the result of the active assistance and cooperation of many people. This is especially true when the primary subject of the book was so peripatetic, who crisscrossed the country and repeatedly settled in one state and then another.

Some of the individuals and organizations the author wishes to thank for assistance in tracking Jill Billiot-Coit around the country and unraveling her story include:

In New Orleans: Jeannine Macaluso and Irvin L. Magri, Jr.

In Houston: Ed Wendt of Texas Media Services; and B. B. McCurdy.

In Indiana: Carl V. Steely; Worth Weller of *The News-Journal* in North Manchester; and a number of friendly folks in North Manchester, Plymouth, and Culver who shared personal recollections with me and helped dig through dozens of documents and files.

In Steamboat Springs: The helpful staff at the *Steamboat Pilot* and *Steamboat Today,* especially reporter Joanna Dodder; staff at the Routt County Courthouse; and the waitresses, clerks, shoppers, and others who willingly shared experiences and stories with me.

My special thanks to the Reverend and Mrs. Charles Coit of Orange Park, Florida, who were so helpful in passing on recollections of their brother and brother-in-law, William Clark Coit, Jr.

Finally, thanks go to my editor at St. Martin's Press, Charles Spicer, and to my agent, Tony Seidl of T. D. Media, for their encouragement and support.

Author's Note

This book is totally nonfiction. Nothing has been made up. The events happened, and they are recounted here as accurately and faithfully as it is within the ability of the author to do so. No names have been changed. Conversations and quotes are taken from the recollections of law-enforcement officers; other participants who were interviewed by the author; journalists and other news sources; statements in legal files; or testimony from court proceedings. In cases where accounts or recollections conflict with each other, I have used the story that is most plausible or presented both, while pointing out the sources so the reader can decide for him- or herself. In a few instances, accounts are given slightly out of chronological order for the purposes of smoothing out the narrative and making the story more readable.

October 1994

Contents

Introduction

It's not news that society in the United States is violent. At this writing, according to the latest statistics available, the FBI's annual Uniform Crime Reports show that approximately 24,500 people were murdered in this country during 1993.

And through the early months of 1994 there was no indication of any significant let-up in the rate that Americans and occasional visitors to this country, shoot, stab, strangle, poison, and beat each other to death. Violent crime in the United States has shot up a mind-boggling 560 percent during the past thirty years, according to US Justice Department figures.

The unwary, unlucky, and sometimes grossly foolish, can become murder victims in myriad ways.

Drug deals go bad and turn into violent shootouts; women and children of both sexes are murdered by rapists; serial killers troll for male and female prostitutes, barroom pickups, or hitchhikers; longtime drinking buddies kill each other in drunken brawls; men and women are shot down for a few dollars after making withdrawals at ATM machines; other die in coldly-calculated, carefully-planned executions; and family members are turning on each other with increasing frequency.

It is a continual struggle between good and evil that provides plotlines for countless movies, television series, newspapers, and books. There is a fascination with murder that is unequalled by any other crime. And the obsession with homicide is especially keen when the accused killer is a woman.

Women aren't supposed to do such things. They create and nurture life. It is the testosterone-driven male with his naturally-aggressive, competitive, and territorial instincts who most often kills on the battlefields during wars between nations or during the ongoing war that rages on America's streets and in its homes.

When a woman abandons her more traditional function in the deadly game of homicide as victim, survivor, or observer and assumes the role of killer, it's especially disturbing—and sensational. Even then, her behavior is often linked to ties with a homicidal male companion that gives their crimes a Bonnie-and-Clyde patina.

They are women like Judith Ann Neely, who was barely fifteen when she ran off to marry husband, Alvin, and began to make babies and murder anyone unlucky enough to stray into their path during a rape, robbery, and murder spree in Alabama, Georgia, and Tennessee; of Debra Brown, who joined boyfriend Alton Coleman in a savage orgy of sex and murder that linked them to the slayings of more than a half-dozen men, women, and children in the Midwest. Both murder teams went about their bloody work in the early 1980s.

Women with homicide on their mind also tend to look for a man to do the dirty work for them. Or they use poison to do the job themselves. Any crime historian worth his or her salt can compile a long list of "Arsenic Annies," who have inflicted agonizing deaths on unsuspecting victims with poisons. Cyanide and strychnine are other lethal compounds that are sometimes used by both female and male poisoners.

Occasionally, homicidal females freelance on their own, but with rare exceptions such as serial killer Aileen Wuornos, a hitchhiking prostitute now on Florida's death row, their victims are people who have been dependent on their care in hospitals and nursing homes—or family members. When women kill, the victim is likely to be someone who knows and trusts them, or did trust them at one time. It's a tragic fact that a disproportionate number of women who kill tend to murder boyfriends, husbands, and former mates.

The woman who is the subject of this book fits neatly into that mold. Jill Coit has been described by a private investigator as a "black widow," a lethal creature who murders her mate then feeds off his corpse.

That term, when applied to humans, is usually reserved for women who have killed a series of husbands. At this writing, Jill was charged with a single murder of an ex-husband who was shot to death with a .22 caliber pistol in Steamboat Springs, Colorado. But an earlier husband she was feuding with in Houston died in disturbingly similar circumstances.

Jill has had a lot of husbands. And the fact she was married multiple times, to nine different men, was a big factor in my decision to examine her life and try to figure out what makes this particular woman tick.

It was a bit of serendipity when I began checking into her tumbleweed travels around the country and learned that three of her husbands live within a forty-mile radius of my small hometown in Indiana. In fact her most bitter divorce was fought out in the Marshall County Courthouse in Plymouth, the bucolic farming community where I grew up.

But it became quickly obvious to me that regardless of whether or not she was living in a small town like Culver, Indiana, or Steamboat Springs, or in a big city like Houston or New Orleans, Jill was one of those women who had the ability to attract boyfriends and husbands almost at will. And she held on to them until she was ready to cut them loose and move on.

Jill wasn't a woman with a reputation for stealing other women's men. She didn't prowl back alleys looking for husbands locked into boring or unhappy marriages who were ripe and ready for plucking. With one exception, none of her men were married to other women when she became involved with them. Her husbands were men who were lifelong bachelors or were already divorced when she met them. She was too intelligent to get herself into situations where she had to waste valuable time and energy fighting another woman over a man.

She was a charming woman, an engaging Lorelei who wore her many marriages like trophies, continuing to hold on to the loyalty of some of her husbands and enlist their help in her various personal and business ventures long after they were divorced. Her husbands represent a richly diverse range of professions and activities that include a bricklayer, student, lawyer, auctioneer, engineer, educator, merchant, Marine officer, and retired Navy chief petty officer. At one time or another, they all fell under her spell.

Some were luckier than others.

Clifford L. Linedecker
October 1994

"But before this, you could ask any of my husbands and they would tell you I was an excellent wife."

Jill Coit
Interview with
Rocky Mountain News

Prologue

Debbie Fedewa didn't like the looks of the two heavily-bundled-up strangers loitering in the neighborhood. It was about nine o'clock Thursday morning on October 21, 1993, and she was leaving her house with her son to go to a health club when she first noticed them wandering along West Hillside Court with their hands stuffed in their pockets.

There were no strange vans or trucks parked nearby, and they weren't wearing uniforms to indicate they were there to deliver or repair appliances or furniture. Considering their weird get-ups, it was also obvious that they weren't door-to-door salesmen. They didn't look like the type of characters anyone would willingly open their door for.

That was one of the bothersome aspects of their disturbing appearance in the quiet, small-town neighborhood. They weren't recognizable as people who lived in any of the nearby homes, and they didn't appear to have any special business in the area.

They looked so menacing and alarming, in fact, that Debbie turned her car around, returned to the house, and locked the doors. It was something she didn't usually do, even when she was home alone. But one of the characters had turned and glanced at her as she drove past them. There was something about the furtive look that was intensely disturbing.

So it was a relief when they drove away down the street after a few minutes. But by about two o'clock in the afternoon they were back again wearing the same ludicrous outfits and once more cruising slowly and aimlessly through the neighborhood. Their outlandish getups were downright weird, almost like something for a Halloween party.

But Halloween was still more than a week away. It was a typical early Autumn day in the Rockies, and temperatures were pleasantly invigorating. It was still far too warm during the daylight hours to be as heavily dressed as the strangers were, and people were still wearing T-shirts outside. Winter wouldn't officially settle in with its bone-chilling winds and heavy snows for a couple of months.

From the top of the ragged ridge the neighborhood was built along, the scarred face of Mount Werner could be clearly seen looming with its dull-green criss-cross of ski trails extending from Storm, Sunshine, Thunderhead, and Christie Peaks, as well as lower levels cut out through the stands of fir and pine. In late October the trails were still empty, and it would be several weeks yet before they filled with hardy locals and vacationers plummeting down the steep slopes and slogging along cross-country trails. For now, the pace of life in Steamboat Springs, Colorado, was comfortably slow and relaxed. The vans, pickup trucks, passenger cars, and rugged utility vehicles that navigated the roughly seven-block-long downtown area on Lincoln Avenue were mostly filled with locals.

The drivers and passengers lived in the ski town, or in the growing clutter of suburbs, trailer parks, and one-horse Routt County hamlets with names like Hahn's Peak, Milner, Oak Creek, and Hayden. Most of them had come to work, shop, or relax in the retail outlets with names like Go-Fer Foods, the Steamboat Smokehouse, F. M. Light & Sons, Boggs Hardware, and other businesses and restaurants that lined the main drag.

All that would change during the season, when the tourists showed up in full force to ski, snowboard, snowmobile, and take advantage of other winter sports. Steamboat's resort hotels, motels, bed and breakfasts, and condominiums would fill up with visitors. The winter resort would then come into its own as "Ski Town USA," and Lincoln Avenue (US Route 40) would be snow-lined and clogged with vehicles.

But for now, Steamboat's roughly 5,000 year-round residents were taking a breather and enjoying the brief respite and relative privacy that settles over the community between the winter and summer sports and tourist seasons. Strangers were a rarity.

That was one of the reasons the curiously-dressed couple was so disturbing.

Ms. Fedewa lived in a quiet, private, upper-middle-class neighborhood of two- and three-story terraced homes built into the rugged hillsides. For the most part, the people who lived on Hillside Court were members of families headed by merchants and professional men who knew each other. During the summer the streets were spotted with adults and children on bicycles, and during the winter months the bike racks atop Jeeps and Broncos were replaced with skis and other cold-weather toys suitable for the snow country.

It was a neighborhood where strangers, even well-dressed strangers, were immediately noticed. And this couple wasn't well dressed. They stuck out like a sore thumb.

It was fairly obvious that the shorter of the two strangers was a woman dressed like a man. Her bulky jacket couldn't completely hide the generous breasts, and the hips were definitely feminine. Her rear-end was palpably flat. When she walked it wasn't with the confident stride or easy lope of a male, but with the more fluid, graceful movements and the feminine rolling of the hips of a woman.

The conspicuously odd cross-dresser was about five-foot, five-inches tall. An absurd and obviously false mustache was plastered over her upper lip. It was much darker than the hair on her head. The mustache and the ponytail dangling from the cap were so ridiculous it was frightening.

Her companion was bigger: an athletically-slim man who appeared to be at least six feet tall, perhaps more. He was wearing a brightly-colored cap over a thicket of light-colored hair, a tan canvas-like rancher's jacket, and blue jeans. Both he and his companion were white and appeared to be between thirty-five and forty-five-years old.

The strangers didn't look like the kind of people anyone would want lurking around the neighborhood when local kids returned home from school. By the time children began bursting noisily through front doors and heading for kitchen refrigerators or bathrooms after school, however, the disturbing mystery couple was gone.

Gerald William Boggs didn't show up for work on Friday and he hadn't been in touch with any of his family or friends since he left the Boggs Hardware Store at about one PM, the previous day. That wasn't at all like the tall, fifty-two-year-old merchant and lifetime resident of Steamboat Springs.

"Gerry" to his friends and family, he was athletic and adventurous and traveled frequently to indulge his passions of scuba diving and undersea and outdoor photography. Photography was only a hobby, but Gerry was good at it, and he set up a darkroom in his house where he developed his own film and made prints after trips into the mountains or forays farther afield to islands or offshore Pacific reefs.

He and his brother, Douglas, had grown up with the Boggs Hardware Store, and they took their responsibilities seriously at the business their father, William Harold Boggs, founded more than a half-century earlier. Gerry wouldn't let down his brother and their partner, Bob McCullough, by cavalierly skipping out on the job without at least telephoning to say he wouldn't be in to work that day. But he didn't call, and he didn't answer when other people tried to telephone him to ask about his bewildering and troubling out-of-character absence and see if he was okay.

Doug was worried about his brother. Gerry was healthy as a horse, and he took good care of himself. He wasn't a problem boozer, and he ate right and got plenty of exercise. Summer and winter, he was either working or outdoors enjoying the clear mountain air and taking advantage of the recreational opportunities.

But he had been living alone since he and his wife had had their marriage annulled a couple of years earlier, after barely nine months as man and wife. Gerry agreed to an annulment after he learned his wife hadn't bothered to divorce her previous husband. Their split followed an ugly confrontation over their personal lives and business matters.

Failing to get a divorce before remarrying was an inexcusable oversight, because if anyone should have known better, Jill Lonita Steely should have. She already had more experience with marriages and divorce than almost anyone, except Hollywood queen Elizabeth Taylor and longtime USO entertainer Martha Raye. When Jill and Gerry linked up she had been married to seven different husbands.

When word got out around Steamboat about Jill and Gerry's marital shoot-out, some of the local comedians, titillated by the development affecting one of the community's oldest and most prominent families, joked that the former Mrs. Boggs changed husbands almost as often as she changed her panty hose.

But the star-crossed union was no joke to Gerry or other members of his family. In recent months the dispute between Jill and him had turned especially nasty and was becoming embarrassingly public, while they clawed at each other in Routt County Court with a rush of motions, depositions and writs. The smalltown merchant was visibly wilting under the pressure. Douglas Boggs climbed into his car and steered toward his brother's house at 870 West Hillside Court.

After parking in the drive and approaching the house, Doug found his brother curled up dead on the floor of a utility room just off the kitchen. His high forehead was a smear of scarlet. Blood was everywhere, splattered on the floor and smeared on the white wall and the kitchen door a few inches behind Gerry's head. The kitchen door was unlocked, as it usually was, but it was blocked by Gerry's body.

Lying on his left side, he was dressed warmly in a flannel shirt, blue jacket, pants, and heavy shoes, as if he had either just come into the house from outside or was about to leave. Curiously, the handle of a dust mop was balanced at a forty-five-degree angle on his right hip, with the business end resting on the floor. There wasn't the slightest sign of life.

ONE

Jill and Larry

Jill Lonita Billiot and her only sibling, Marc, weren't exactly the Smothers Brothers, but at least as far as she was concerned they shared a common experience with television's famous singing comedy team: sibling rivalry. She was jealous of her baby brother and convinced that her parents loved him more than their only daughter.

Eventually, as an adult with children of her own, she would confide to a reporter for Denver's *Rocky Mountain News:* "I was raised that women were to entertain, to get married, and have babies."

Jill's father, Henry Albert Billiot, was a New Orleans-area towboat captain who worked the waterways of the world's largest and busiest port city. He was owner and operator of his own business, Billiot Tug Boat. Her father traces his ancestry to the Houma Indians. Billiot is an especially common name around New Orleans and Houma (population 30,000), seat of local government in Terrebonne Parish, fifty miles southwest of New Orleans in the middle of the Louisiana Bayou country. In fact, seven bayous converge in the town, and there are so many canals and bridges that tourism promoters and many locals call it the "Venice of America."

Established in 1834, only nineteen years after the
Battle of New Orleans, the bustling seafood-packing
and shipping center's name is taken from the Houma
tribe, which is now settled in Terrebonne and La-
Fourche parishes in southeast Louisiana. The name of
the small tribe and the closely-related Chakchiuma
homma can be translated as the "Red Crawfish (People)."

Although Jill's father's family roots are sunk deeply
into Louisiana's crawfish and alligator country, her
mother is a native Midwesterner from a state that
proudly touts itself on license plates and tourism bro-
chures as the "Crossroads of America."

She grew up as Juanita Engelman, and traced her
ancestry to hardy Germans who settled in the rich, fertile farm country of northern Indiana. Some family
members and other acquaintances who were on a
friendly basis with her shortened her first name when
addressing her and called her "Nita." When her children were born Nita Billiot was a full-time New Orleans housewife.

By her own admission, after Jill matured and began
her marrying ways, she altered her birth-date, gradually advancing it a year or two at a time into the early
1950s. But she was probably born during one of the
most momentous periods of America's history, while
World War II was raging, either on June 11, 1943, or
on the same day and month a year later in 1944.

The little dark-haired, dark-eyed girl was as brown
and feisty as one of the crawfish that prowled the Louisiana bayous and canals, but she arrived too late to
remember the war years and homefront hardships like
ration books and shortages of gasoline, tires, and silk
stockings. By the time she was old enough to begin
elementary school, the American economy was experiencing the immediate post-war boom years and the

country was already confronting the Soviet Union in the Cold War.

Jill was far too young to worry about such convoluted problems as the economy and the Cold War, however. Her world was smaller, more warm and secure. And until the arrival of her brother, Marc, it appeared she was at the center of her parents' world as well.

Before and after the squalling interloper made his appearance however, Jill's world was filled with the odor of spicy Cajun cooking, as well as with fried chicken and dumplings prepared Indiana-style. She learned early how to crack the shell of a blue crab or snap open a crawfish steamed bright red before sucking out the sweet pale meat and juices. As she grew up she was also taught in Sunday school about Jesus and the Ten Commandments; she grappled with the three R's; played with dolls; and competed for attention with a younger brother she may not have liked at all.

Her home was in one of the most colorfully exotic locations in the country. Despite its catchy nicknames such as the "Queen City of the South" and the "Crescent City," (because of the way it's snuggled between the scythe-shaped shoreline of Lake Pontchartrain and lazy loops of the Mississippi River) New Orleans has a bawdy history that few cities can match. Since the 1987 release of Hollywood's sexy crime thriller, *The Big Easy,* which was set there, New Orleans has become more firmly attached to its most popular modern nickname. Somehow, in many ways, the "Big Easy" seems more appropriate today than its longtime predecessors.

The city of a half-million people sprawls between the huge lake and the serpentine meanderings of the country's grandest river as it nears the end of its journey in the Gulf of Mexico. Tourism authorities would prefer that potential visitors associate their community

with positive images like the fine seafood and other
savory cuisine epitomized by the famous chef, Paul
Prudhomme and his colleagues, along with standard
local favorites like black iron skillet corn bread, blackened redfish, Cajun seafood jambalaya, turtle soup,
and Louisiana pecan pie.

The history of jazz in New Orleans is another source
of civic pride and the city sponsors an annual Jazz Fest
that attracts enthusiasts from all over the world. One
of America's most captivating and enduring music
forms, jazz was born on Basin Street and adjoining
arteries in what is now the French Quarter. The
Queen City has produced or nurtured the careers of a
long line of musical geniuses ranging from pianist Jelly
Roll Morton (Ferdinand LeMenthe) to Joseph "King"
Oliver with his hot cornet; from the famous trumpeter
and scratch-voiced vocalist Louis "Satchmo" Arm-
strong to fellow trumpet player Al Hirt.

The unique colonial and antebellum architecture,
which includes some of the most elegant examples of
wrought-iron courtyard gates and iron-lace balconies
and balustrades in the world, is yet another aspect of
the city that local movers and shakers are especially
proud of. Even the otherworldly shadowland of the
above-ground cemeteries, with their historical tombs
laid out in blunt, flat, simple slabs and their showpiece
elaborate sculptured monuments draw tourists with
curiosities whetted by the unique blend of the artistic
and the macabre.

New Orleans earned a reputation for wet graves
centuries ago because of its high water table. Many
early settlers buried their dead only after boring holes
in the coffin then lowering it into the moist ground
where a couple of slaves stood on it until it filled with
water and settled into its final resting place.

Wealthier residents of the old city, repulsed at the
idea of after-death immersion, began burying their

loved ones in wall vaults and stone sepulchres anchored only a few inches into the ground. Sealed in stone, the corpses didn't share the wet graves of their predecessors. Under the hot southern sun, they baked inside their stone ovens instead.

For decades, the unique burial vaults in century-old graveyards like the Garden District's Lafayette Cemetery Number One were a huge tourist attraction. Spontaneous tours of some of the more notable graveyards have been stifled in recent years, however, by hoodlums from nearby public housing projects who have taken to mugging and raping unwary tourists wandering around the ancient burial grounds.

The Mardi Gras in New Orleans, of course, is famous throughout the world. The annual celebration attracts thousands of tourists to the city and surrounding communities before its raucous windup on Shrove Tuesday, or Fat Tuesday, the final day before the beginning of Lent.

But mention New Orleans and serious historians as well as many other people are likely to think of Storyville, which was the Queen City's notorious official red-light district for roughly twenty years before it was closed by the US Department of the Navy in 1917 and absorbed by the rough-and-tumble *Vieux Carré*, the French Quarter. The exotic old neighborhood is synonymous with New Orleans as the slightly sinister playground of generations of flatboatmen, sailors, and tourists.

Voodoo was a part of the New Orleans mystique even before Storyville. The mysterious and menacing blend of West African animism and shamanism with Roman Catholicism is the stuff of legend as well as religion in New Orleans. And no historical character has been so closely related with the mystical rites, magic, and lore of voodoo than a series of menacing priestesses collectively known as Marie LaVeau.

The original Marie, a beautiful free mulatto who worked as a hairdresser for elegant white ladies and arranged sex orgies for rich white men when she wasn't concocting magical spells, is believed to be buried at the foot of Basin Street in Cemetery Number One. A few years after she passed the mantle of voodoo queen on to a successor, the occupants of the city's ubiquitous brothels and crib houses were still doing such big business with the spell peddlers that members of a so-called benevolent association of madams got together and officially agreed not to use the voodoo women against each other.

The Crescent City's dark side has been well chronicled in literature, film, and song, much more so than its record of positive accomplishments. Director Louis Malle's blockbuster movie, *Pretty Baby,* starred young Brooke Shields as a child prostitute in a Storyville brothel and the movie launched her career. A few years earlier, country music crooner Bobby Bare scored big with a hit single that was a comic version of a Marie LaVeau story penned by former *Playboy* cartoonist, author, and composer Shel Silverstein.

The New Orleans that Jill grew up in had undergone massive changes since the days of Storyville and the birth of jazz, but they weren't all necessarily improvements. New Orleans was still a rough-and-tumble rivertown populated by people whose appetites were often too big and their tempers too short for their own good. Although the brothels and crib houses of Storyville closed long ago, prostitutes of both sexes were still more easily available than parking spaces on many of the streets. The opium that Storyville whores and their clients smoked in private had been replaced by heroin—later cocaine—that was openly available from street peddlers in the same neighborhoods.

As late as 1993, when Jill was having serious trouble of her own with the law, her hometown was tagged with the unofficial title, "Murder Capital USA." New Orleans took the title from Washington, DC, which had held the dubious distinction as the nation's most violent city for four years in a row.

New Orleans eased the nation's capital out of the top spot for cities of 250,000 population or more by recording 389 homicides. According to the FBI statistics and the most recent census figures, that worked out to 78.2 murders per 100,000 people. Most of the slayings occurred in and around public housing projects, and a large number involved narcotics.

Washington, DC, which is a larger city and actually had more slayings, 467, came in a close second, with 76.6 homicides per 100,000 of population. Detroit ran a distant third. By mid-1994, a concerned bar owner in the French Quarter was keeping a public tally sheet comparing homicides in New Orleans with those in Boston, a city with approximately the same population. The kill rate in New Orleans was running more than five to one ahead of homicides in Boston.

But when Jill was a girl growing up in the New Orleans area, it was not nearly as violent. When she was fifteen years old and her family was living on Yetta Avenue in Metairie, a bedroom community of 172,000 snuggled between the New Orleans International Airport and the western edge of the Crescent City between Lake Pontchartrain and the river, she moved out of her family home. The teenager traveled north to live with her maternal grandparents in northwest Indiana's tranquil farm country.

The Englemans lived just outside Servia, an unincorporated village at the intersection of Nehr and Klutz roads about a ten-minute drive southeast of North Manchester. Servia is a smattering of a half-dozen or so houses surrounded by farm fields and cow pastures that makes the bucolic North Manchester look like a metropolis by comparison.

North Manchester, which became the new center of Jill's school and social life, is a quiet little farming community and college town that is about as different from New Orleans as it can be. Once the site of a village of Potawatomi Indians, and roamed even earlier by Miami tribesmen, the area welcomed its first white settlers in 1834. That was barely eighteen years after the state, which English settlers named for the "Land of the Indians," was admitted to the union.

Many of the families living in North Manchester when Jill arrived still traced their ethnic roots to Great Britain and Germany. The ancestors of most were hardy farmers who made their living by tilling the soil. Dairy cattle, hogs, and poultry are important elements of the local agricultural industry.

During the growing season Wabash County fields are filled with wheat, hay, oats, corn, sorghum, soybeans, and a variety of other crops. Many farmers double-crop, planting and harvesting wheat and other grains early in the season, then sneaking in fast-growing yields of sunflowers that successfully resist early frosts for late-season harvests.

The town of roughly 5,000 people is also a center for the Church of the Brethren and its immediate offshoots, including the United Brethren Church. The United Brethren founded a seminary in 1816, which eventually became Manchester College, and was operated by the Church of the Brethren. Today it hosts about 1,400 students and is one of six Brethren-related co-educational colleges of liberal arts and sciences. The Brethren also sponsor a graduate school, Bethany Theological Seminary, in Illinois.

The Brethren organized in 1708 in Schwarzenau, Germany, after breaking away from the Lutheran Church. Within roughly twenty years almost all of them had emigrated to the United States. Also referred to in their early days as "Dunkers" or

"Dunkards," because of their practice of baptizing members by threefold immersion, they are one of the historic peace churches along with the Quakers and the Mennonites. Even during World War II, many young Brethren men refused military service as conscientious objectors. Some of the more pious still refuse to press lawsuits.

The quiet and unadorned lifestyle followed by some of the more conservative members of the Brethren and German Baptist neighbors is still obvious in North Manchester. German Baptist women lend an Old World charm to the community as they attend church services, do their shopping, and tend to other activities and chores dressed in simple blue or white ankle-length dresses set off with delicate plain white bonnets.

North Manchester's most famous citizen was Thomas R. Marshall, governor of Indiana from 1909 to 1913, and vice-president of the United States from 1913 to 1921. Marshall served with Woodrow Wilson during the first World War.

Many of Jill's new schoolmates in the junior class at North Manchester High School were farm kids who did the chores in the mornings before boarding buses and heading for school. In the afternoon and evening after returning home they did more chores. They fed, watered, milked, and cleaned up after cows; slopped hogs; gathered eggs; pitched hay; and helped out with the cooking and cleaning. On weekends and during spring and summer breaks, children drove tractors, hauled combines, or maneuvered shovels and hoes in the fields alongside brothers and sisters and parents.

For fun, they paired off and dated at nearby drive-in theaters, went on hayrides, and skated at area rinks. But the most popular recreation for North Manchester teenagers was provided by the high-school basketball and football teams. There was little that could compare with packing the stands around the football field on a crisp late September or October night to cheer on the Squires while chewing on popcorn or hot dogs and sipping fresh, sweet apple cider.

During the fierce northern Indiana winters the Squires moved indoors and exchanged their bulky football gear for T-shirts and shorts to test their prowess on the basketball court against prep squads from Cherubusco, Columbia City, Rochester, Tippecanoe Valley, Wabash, and other nearby communities. Once or twice a year the Squires squared off against one of the big-town high schools in Fort Wayne. The schoolmates of the players, along with many of the town's adults, filled the gymnasium with their cheers.

On winter weekends, if Manchester College was playing home games, they could also assemble to watch the Spartans match their football and basketball skills against teams from other small Midwest schools such as the Rose Hulman Institute in Terre Haute, Ball State in Muncie, and Rockford College in Illinois.

North Manchester High was a small school in a small town, and Jill didn't slip in unnoticed by the other teenagers. She exploded on the high-school dating scene like a rocket. Although she was not necessarily prettier, or more attractive than most of the other girls, there was something about the combination of teenage charm, vivaciousness, her Southern accent, and the exotic locale of her former home that made the local teenage males sit up and pay attention. "All the boys were attracted to her like a magnet, and of course most of the girls hated her for that reason," Nancy Reed, her best friend from those high-school days, recalled years later.

When Jill posed for her junior picture in the 1961 edition of the school yearbook, *The Crest,* her dark curly hair was swept back from her forehead and was well above her shoulders. The features in her oval face were even, and her high, full cheekbones gave her a slightly plump appearance that was misleading.

Her photo was the last picture in the second row of the first page showing the junior class. The photos were arranged alphabetically, and her picture and name appeared between those of classmates Nancy Bickel and Allen Bitzell. Judging by the pictures of the neatly-dressed, well-groomed boys and girls, they represented a good cross section of wholesome Midwest American teenagers. There was nothing about any of the photos to indicate any of the juniors were destined to become especially famous—or notorious.

Jill's photo didn't appear with her classmates at North Manchester High School during their senior year. By the time the 1962 edition of *The Crest* was distributed and the graduating class began passing personal copies around to friends for autographs, Jill had interrupted her formal education to get married.

She eloped with Larry Eugene Ihnen, a rural North Manchester boy with a freshly-scrubbed handsomeness who graduated a year ahead of her with the class of '61. Larry's last name was pronounced "Ee-nan." His senior appearance in the 1961 edition of *The Crest* was unique. Other graduating seniors had lists of extracurricular activities with everything from football, basketball, and track, to the student council, class play, dance band, speech, Spanish and science clubs, or the National Honor Society. After four years of high school, Larry didn't have a single entry. Jill, apparently, was his primary extracurricular activity, at least during much of his senior year.

Judging solely by the photographs, he might easily have passed for the youngest of all the students in the graduating class. Wearing a light-colored sports jacket with a dark bow tie for his senior photo, the baby-faced schoolboy with the neatly trimmed dark hair could have been mistaken for a fourteen- or fifteen-year-old.

The young couple were joined in holy matrimony by the Reverend William A. Nangle, pastor of the United Methodist Church in the county seat town of Wabash about fifteen miles almost due south of North Manchester. It was July 24, a couple of months after the groom's high-school graduation.

Jill wore street clothes for the ceremony. She explained to a Denver newspaper reporter years later that she didn't have a big wedding and wear a white gown because white was for virgins. And she didn't qualify.

On the couple's application for a marriage license, Jill listed "student" as her occupation. Larry indicated he was an apprentice bricklayer. The eighteen-year-old groom's parents were divorced, and his mother, Donas L. Armey, signed her consent for the marriage. In the space on the application for consent of parents or guardian, Jill indicated that her father and mother were also divorced. There was no consent signature for the seventeen-year-old bride.

Like Jill, Larry was born under the sign of the twins, Gemini. His birthday was May 28, 1943, just less than one year and two weeks before hers. According to people who put store in such things, the birthdays of the bride and the groom indicated that they would be ambitious, alert, intelligent—and temperamental.

The teenage wedding may or may not have been fated by the stars to occur, but it was virtually unnoticed back in North Manchester. Page-one stories in the town's local newspaper, *The News-Journal* were devoted to a tornado that ripped through the nearby communities of Tippecanoe Lake and Goshen; high-school journalism students attending a workshop at Indiana University; a new budget adopted by the North Manchester Church of the Brethren; and a national story about President John F. Kennedy threatening Russia over the Cuban missile crisis.

There wasn't a word about the wedding that day in that issue of the paper, or in any subsequent editions.

The teenagers quietly moved into a mobile home at Cleveland's Trailer Court on the outskirts of Manchester. Larry went to work laying bricks. Jill found herself a job at the Heckman Bindery, one of North Manchester's most dependable and largest employers.

Whether or not it was moodiness or crabbiness on the part of the young bride, the groom, or both, the ill-fated marriage quickly shattered. The teenagers lived together less than a year before breaking up in March 1962. Larry moved in with his mother on Packerton Road in an area a mile or so out of town known as Damrod Heights. Jill continued to live in the trailer. Represented by a local law firm, Plummer & Plummer, she obtained a restraining order on March 7, preventing her husband from bothering her at her home or elsewhere. Wabash Circuit Court Judge John W. Beauchamp signed the order.

In her petition for divorce filed in the circuit court in Wabash, Jill also asked that her husband be directed to pay her attorney fees and half of the approximately $280 the couple had in a joint savings account with the Indiana Lawrence Bank & Trust company in North Manchester. She noted that she was a housewife and factory worker and said she had no funds to pay for the cost of the divorce.

Jill accused her husband of the catch-all offense of cruel and inhuman treatment and said it was no longer possible for them to live together as husband and wife. She also asked for restoration of her maiden name, Billiot.

Larry filed a cross-complaint claiming it was he who was the victim of cruel and inhuman treatment. He was represented by attorney Sarah Kelton Browne of

North Manchester, and he agreed that he and his wife could no longer live together.

On June 12, a couple of weeks after the graduation of Jill's former classmates at North Manchester High School, her marriage was formally dissolved. Jill dropped her complaint and the divorce was granted to her husband. Her maiden name was restored. The young couple had been married a few weeks short of a year.

Like the hurried wedding, the divorce of the former high-school sweethearts attracted little more than a whisper of attention from their neighbors and acquaintances. For awhile, Jill hung onto her job at the bindery while she put her disappointing marriage behind her. But she wasn't going to settle for very long for the life-numbing existence of a high-school dropout who lived in a trailer and worked at a dead-end job in a factory.

She was barely eighteen, single again, and just beginning to burst into the full bloom of her beauty and power as a mature woman. She was ready for challenge, romance, and adventure.

TWO

Steven and Clark

For your hands are defiled with blood, and your fingers with iniquity; your lips have spoken lies, your tongue hath muttered perverseness.

Isaiah 59:3

It was a typical Saturday night in the French Quarter: the tiny nightclubs, bars, and eateries were moist, sultry, and overcrowded with neighborhood regulars moving or seated elbow-to-elbow in the twilight darkness with a smattering of adventure-seeking tourists. They listened to the vagabond jazz riffs of a mellow sax, or a modern-day descendant of Storyville's old whorehouse professors tickling the ivories, enjoying the atmosphere while sipping idly at drinks and sharing the conviviality and sticky gloom. Ceiling fans droned overhead, slapping listlessly at the tobacco smoke and stale air.

William Clark Coit, Jr., was relaxing with a martini after another long day in the marshes when he got his first look at Jill.

She was a stunningly beautiful woman with long legs, exquisitely-swelling breasts that were shown off with a provocatively low-cut blouse, and a tiny waist that complimented the smooth feminine flare of her hips. Her long, dark hair was pulled back to accentuate the dramatic planes of her oval face.

Jill knew how to use clothes and cosmetics to enhance her natural loveliness and make the most of her sensuous shape, smoldering brown eyes, and fine, high cheekbones. Her makeup was perfectly applied, with just enough accent to complement her dusky complexion, the inquisitive brightness of her big eyes, and the stark sensuality of her full lips. Clark was enchanted by the alluring temptress.

A lanky thirty-five-year-old bachelor, who had spent the past decade working his way up through the ranks with the Tennessee Gas Transmission Company and Tennessee Gas Pipeline Company, he was a rolling stone. By the time he began loping through French Quarter jazz joints and watering holes, he was already on the fast track at Tennessee Gas and was in charge of all the company's construction in southern Louisiana. It was such a massive responsibility that he had his own company-assigned float plane and pilot so he could inspect and examine potential pipeline sites in the bountiful marshes and gummy shallows of the tidewater.

The job he was working would eventually involve the laying of an intricate network of more than 300 miles of pipe through the swamps and across the Mississippi River. Company bigwigs as well as the men in the field referred to the job as the Muskrat Line because of the proliferation of the fecund little rodents in the marshes. They may have as easily and appropriately named it the Nutria, Blue Heron, or the Alligator Line.

After the pipelines were connected, natural gas was pumped through them and across the country to customers as far away as the Midwest, New England, and New York.

Clark wasn't a ladies man, and it was especially difficult for him to develop a serious relationship with a woman. After fifteen years of moving around the country from job to job and living in temporary apartments, he was more experienced at casual short-term, hit-and-run romance. In large part, it was the nature of the job. There wasn't much of an opportunity to lay down solid roots.

But in other ways, it was exactly what he wanted. He didn't busy himself pursuing waitresses, barmaids, and other women he met on his travels like many of his colleagues did. He was quiet and professional on the job, and those characteristics marked his personal life as well.

He was midway into his thirties, however, and it was a time when even longtime holdouts like Clark were beginning to consider finding a girl and settling down. Jill was young, dark, beautiful, charming, intelligent, and had a tiny waist that would fit perfectly between his big, rough engineer's hands. She was everything that a man like Clark could wish for, or so it seemed.

The attraction appeared to be mutual. Clark was tall and as rawboned as a cowboy. He was also blond, lonely, and had an excellent job with a high income and even greater future earning potential. He was just what Jill wanted in a man.

The morning after meeting Jill, Clark telephoned his pilot and asked if he minded taking him on a rare Sunday flight over the marshes. The pilot said it wouldn't be a problem. Clark was a popular man among his fellow employees, and people did things for him because they liked him. All he had to do was ask.

When he showed up for the flight, his sexy companion from the previous evening was with him. She looked as sensuous and enticing in the bright light of the late Sunday morning as she had looked the evening before when she was shielded by the protective blue gray haze of the French Quarter. At twenty-one, there were no bothersome wrinkles to cover up. Her face and body were flawless, and when the pontoon plane took off for the rare Sunday morning inspection tour she was seated snugly inside with Clark and the pilot.

Clark was already falling under the spell of the enchanting woman beside him. But despite her youth she was a ruthlessly ambitious and complex individual with a life that was already rapidly filling with awkward secrets.

She was still married to her second husband, and was the mother of an infant son. And she was already, or would soon become, a woman who was reputed to be capable of monstrously greedy acts.

Jill was never cut out for production-line work or life in a trailer home. She had left the flat Indiana corn and soybean country with its barnyard odors to return to New Orleans a few months after her divorce from the teenage swain she left school to marry. She came alive as she drove along the canals and levees, dined on delectable seafood, and strolled past the walled gardens and terraces that sheltered brilliant splashes of blooms and smells from jasmine, camellias, magnolias, and sweet olives.

She returned to her interrupted studies and quickly completed work for her high-school diploma. In 1963 she signed up for a single course, British literature, during the fall term at Tulane University. Tulane is the fulcrum of a trio of colleges whose campuses are lined with magnolia trees and flower beds stretched along the eastern shore of the Mississippi. Newcomb College and Loyola University of New Orleans are the neighboring schools.

Early in the new year, Jill traveled north to enroll at Northwestern State University of Louisiana in Natchitoches, one of the oldest schools of higher learning in Louisiana. The university was established in 1884. This time she committed herself to a more ambitious class load.

The oldest settlement in the Louisiana Purchase, Natchitoches is solidly anchored in an area known as the "crossroads country," where the rich French and Spanish traditions of the southern part of the state meet with the stolid values of the old cotton plantations and modern-day sugarcane fields and dirt farmers. Natchitoches is four years older than New Orleans. The popular comedy, *Steel Magnolias,* was written in Natchitoches by local playwright, Robert Harling, and the 1989 movie starring Dolly Parton, Sally Field, and Herbert Ross was filmed there.

Back on her home ground in the Pelican State, Jill was confident, ambitious, and full of energy. She was a gifted student with a talent for entrepreneurism. Her mind soaked up information, then sifted through it, analyzed it, and figured out how her newfound knowledge could be put to the best use to further her dreams of luxury and wealth.

Among the business and other down-to-earth classes designed to prepare students for their pragmatic workaday future, Jill managed to jam in an acting course. She was a natural actress, who had always shown a gift for drama and comedy. She could turn on and turn off emotions as quickly as flicking her long eyelashes.

Any baby fat she may have retained or expanded on while she was living in Indiana dining on a traditional Midwestern diet of mashed potatoes, dumplings, gravies, and pork roasts was quickly trimmed off her lithesome five-foot, six-inch frame after she returned to Louisiana.

The confidently-poised and charming beauty didn't go unnoticed by the male students when she strolled with other coeds among the magnolia trees, lofty spires, and gothic arches on the Northwestern State campus. She was always pert, bright, and impeccably dressed. She was already perfecting her skills at dealing with men in business and on a more personal level. She didn't denigrate or overlook her own attributes and accomplishments, but she knew how to make a man feel like he was the most important person in the world.

Jill had an innate sense of the delicate art of seduction, a natural understanding of how and when to send out sexual signals. She knew how to fix a man with a long, smoldering glance that attracted his attention and signaled that she might be interested. She knew the dynamics of silent communication between the sexes.

Steven Moore, a handsome student from downstate was one of the most impressed and persistent of her suitors. Casual campus dates soon developed into intimate *tête-à-têtes,* then mushroomed into a full-blown love affair. On May 5, 1964 when the gardenias were in full bloom, Jill took her second plunge into matrimony. The couple first married in a civil ceremony in Mississippi, and the following October, they had a religious ceremony in Abbeville, Louisiana, in marshy Vermilion Parish, midway between New Orleans and the Texas state line.

Jill's demanding schedule and busy life became even more complicated a few weeks after the marriage, when she realized she was pregnant. On March 28, 1965, she gave birth to her first child, Steven Seth Moore.

By that time her new marriage had already broken down, and she had been separated from her husband for several months. She was too much of a party girl and had too many independent interests for the union to have much of a chance of surviving.

Steven Seth was still in diapers when she met Clark. The rugged construction engineer was an easy conquest. He was bowled over by the dark-eyed temptress who was so well-versed in the delicate art of seduction.

Jill didn't waste much time attempting to maintain a balancing act between the husband she was still tied to, the new man in her life, and her infant son. She was a formidable woman who had a robust lust for living and charged head-on at life. Along with her beauty and sexual charisma, she was smart, focused, and tireless. To many of her acquaintances, and to others who knew her more intimately, it appeared that she never ran out of energy and enthusiasm.

On August 27, 1965, she filed a petition for divorce in the Jefferson Parish Courthouse in Gretna, across the river from New Orleans. It is an odd fact about the southern Louisiana parishes in and around New Orleans that although the lion's share of the population has settled north of the Mississippi, the courthouses and seats of local parish government are all located on the more marshy and isolated south side of the river. Moore was served with the divorce papers at his Fig Street home in Harvey. He filed his own cross-action divorce suit a hundred miles or so west of New Orleans in Vermilion Parish.

Jill moved into Clark's apartment in the French Quarter. The lonely engineer thought he was the luckiest man in the world, and as he enmeshed himself further into the relationship, he plunged deeply and irretrievably in love. Jill also enrolled once more at Tulane, taking classes during the fall term of 1965 in US history, the history of public address, and in astronomy. And she kept in touch with Nancy, her close friend from high school in North Manchester.

In November, 1965, eight months after the birth of her son, Jill and her boyfriend flew from New Orleans to Cleveland where he showed her off to his family during the Thanksgiving holiday. Jill was her usual charming self when the family gathered around the dinner table at the house in the comfortable upscale bedroom community of Gates Mills just outside the east edge of the city. Neither Clark nor his girlfriend mentioned that she was the mother of an infant son, left behind in New Orleans.

Jill was attractive and pleasant, and Clark was as proud as a peacock. She seemed to settle into the warm, friendly rhythm of the close family group with a minimum of awkwardness. She had a delightful sense of humor, and her table manners were refined. If there were any warnings in her behavior that she might not be exactly the genuinely sincere young woman she appeared to be, the signals were either too subtle to be picked up by anyone or they were simply overlooked because of the happiness of the occasion.

Clark was too stunned by her tantalizing sexiness to notice or care about the possibility of any defects of character or moral blemishes. His pride in his companion was obvious. He was attentive and courteous, pulling out her chair to help her seat herself and taking special pains to include her in the conversation.

Because William C. Coit Sr., had already laid claim to the names William and Bill, family members and many of his friends and acquaintances called Jill's boyfriend by his middle name, Clark. It avoided mix-ups. Clark was one of two children, and his brother, Charles H., was three years older. The small family was close. William C. Coit Sr., made a good living, and his wife, Anna Dix-Coit, made a good home for her little brood. During most of his working career William Sr. was a salesman, peddling everything from real estate to cars, although he worked in an aircraft plant in Cleveland during WWII helping to build bombers.

Despite the gap in ages, his sons were close while they were growing up in suburban Cleveland. They played and roughhoused and tangled with each other in occasional spats as most siblings do. Years later, Charles recalled that he quit fighting with his brother when Clark got too big to handle. It was also about that time when the family stopped calling the younger son "Clarkie" and settled into use of the more grown-up "Clark."

As the boys grew up and approached full manhood, Charles went off to theological school. A few years later, Clark traveled catty-corner across the state to the college town of Athens where he enrolled in classes at Ohio University.

Clark continued dating in college as he had in high school, but unlike his older brother, who married and fathered three children, he never took the plunge. Even after graduating and going to work for a friend of his father's who was a land buyer for Tennessee Gas, he tenaciously hung onto his bachelorhood. He was enthusiastic about his job and quickly began working himself up in the giant multi-national business that today has interests in everything from natural gas and chemicals to packing and farm products.

He traveled from state to state working in the field on major construction sites and was project manager on various operations in the Midwest and elsewhere before he moved up to his job in oil-rich southern Louisiana and a position as head of construction on field projects. One of the earliest and most challenging jobs he oversaw was the Ohio River Crossing Project, laying pipes during the winter of 1963. Despite his traveling and constantly-shifting location, he maintained his close emotional ties to his family.

The brothers kept in touch by telephone and by mail while Clark worked his way up the company ladder, and Charles ministered to the congregations of Episcopal churches closer to home in Ohio. A few years after the Thanksgiving gathering, when both his parents, William Sr. and Anna Dix-Coit were seriously ill, even though he was in Houston some 3,000 miles away from Gates Mills at the time, he shouldered his share of responsibility along with his older brother for their care. He had a strong sense of family.

Clark was also a loving and attentive uncle to his brother's two boys and one girl. He loved children, and during family get-togethers he showered them with toys and with exciting yarns about his travels around the country. He was a good storyteller, and if he embellished a few details now and then to make the tales more exciting for his nephews and niece it merely added to their enjoyment and affection for their uncle.

As Clark moved up to increasing levels of responsibility he was in and out of the company headquarters in Houston. He loved the east Texas metropolis. Once nicknamed the "Bayou City" before most of the bayous were covered in a blanket of skyscrapers, cement parking lots, streets, and highways, Houston was a vibrant, exciting place to live.

Houston is as well known as a hub for national and multi-national businesses as for any of its other accomplishments.

With its deep-water Houston Ship Channel giving it easy access to Galveston Bay and the Gulf of Mexico, Houston is one of America's busiest centers of commerce. Billion dollar businesses like Tenneco, with its various subsidiaries, are headquartered and thrive in Houston. Tenneco is only one of a glittering number of major multi-national corporations with headquarters there.

Clark quickly adopted many of the characteristics and much of the lifestyle of longtime residents of Texas and other states in the far South and Southwest. He was outdoors much of the time when he was on the job and when he was relaxing. He bought hmself a pair of pointy-toe cowboy boots and began collecting a little Western art. But he never took to ten-gallon hats, and he usually made his pipeline rounds wearing the same beat-up, faded old beige porkpie hat to shield his head and face from the blistering sun.

He made friends easily and was a good party guest or host. He had a good ear for music and taught himself to play the piano without ever taking a lesson. But once he met Jill, Clark's bachelor days, if not all his carefree playboy ways, were numbered.

A couple of months after the Thanksgiving dinner, he telephoned his brother to make a surprise announcement.

"We're married," he said.

The development was about as unexpected as it could be. There had been no forewarning to the family and no invitations to the wedding. The longtime bachelor had simply driven west across the Louisiana border to Orange County, Texas, with his girlfriend, and on January 29, 1966, they were united in a simple ceremony. Clark was thirty-six years old, and Jill was twenty-two.

His older brother reflected years later, "He was no spring chicken. I mean he was beyond the age of the first juices running."

Clark's behavior in shutting his family out of one of the most important events in his life was out of character for William and Anna Coit's youngest son. His brother was an Episcopal priest, and it wouldn't have been either surprising or inappropriate for him to have been asked to officiate at the ceremony. But he wasn't. In fact, the family couldn't even figure out exactly where the marriage took place. Clark and his new bride never told them. Nevertheless the news was more pleasing than distressing. It was about time Clark settled down and began raising a family of his own.

The Coits didn't know that cutting families out of her marriages was Jill's style. It was a pattern she would follow for three decades, slipping off to marry

men in quiet little ceremonies performed in courthouses, wedding chapels, or churches without bothering to invite members of her family or those of her
grooms.

Clark and his puzzled family were unaware that the
bride hadn't yet bothered to legally divorce her former
husband. Jill's divorce from Moore didn't become final
until March 23, 1967. By that time she had already
been married bigamously to the laid-back, fun-loving
engineer for more than fourteen months.

For awhile after their marriage, the couple rented
an apartment in the town of Harvey, on the south
bank of the Mississippi River just across from New
Orleans. Clark's company was occupied in a big offshore drilling project there. The first summer the couple were together in Harvey, Clark's brother and
sister-in-law visited them. Charles tagged the little
town with the personal nickname, the "Big Pookah,"
for the Pulitzer prize-winning Broadway play and
blockbuster 1950 movie *Harvey,* starring Jimmy Stewart. Stewart was cast as a likeable tippler with a six-
foot rabbit sidekick named Harvey, only he could see.
The rabbit was a "pookah," a friendly otherworldly
entity who came and went with the ease of a Cheshire
cat's smile.

Clark brought his family to Ohio once to visit Gates
Mills and the Findlay area where Charles was pastor
of a church. Jill also took her husband back to North
Manchester one Christmas to show him off to relatives
and to Nancy and her other friends.

While Clark was roaming the marshlands of Jefferson, Plaquemines, and LaFourche parishes exploring,
taking soil samples and running lines to the offshore
drilling rigs, he learned how insular and protective of
their territory some of the Cajuns and other locals
could be. They were suspicious of outsiders and let
him know they didn't like him poking around in their

swamps and wetlands. He stuck around anyway and completed his job, but he was careful.

After nearly two years in the New Orleans area, Clark moved to the company's home offices in Houston, where Tenneco occupied an imposing structure that covered an entire city block in the downtown area. The building loomed more than thirty stories high and in those years before construction of the Houston National Bank building and other skyscrapers, it was the third tallest structure in the city. Although the Bayou City became his home base, he continued to take assignments to jobs throughout the South and the Midwest that lasted months at a time.

A friend, B. B. McCurdy, was already working at the home office. Like Clark, McCurdy was an engineer and the two men had become friends when their paths crossed at various times while they were pipelining during their early years with the company. But they didn't work together until they both wound up in Houston, and that was when their friendship began to bloom in earnest. McCurdy was a native of the little oil-rig town of Ranger, near Abilene in west Texas.

McCurdy and his wife, Virginia, "Ginny" to her family and friends, were about the first people from the Tenneco "family," whom Clark introduced to Jill. Ginny McCurdy, a former Georgia peach who met her husband while he was pipelining in Monroe, Louisiana, liked Clark as much as her husband did. It was difficult for anyone who worked with him or spent any time around him not to be captivated by his boyish enthusiasm and charm.

Men enjoyed him for his rowdiness and camaraderie; and many women thought he was adorable. He had a high, prominent forehead with blue eyes that had a hint of leprechaun orneriness about them and diverted attention from the slightly-noticeable cleft lip that was the only flaw in his leathery-faced handsomeness.

The McCurdys were happy for their friend when he introduced Jill. "We just felt good for him when we first saw her and he married her, because she was so beautiful," McCurdy later recalled. "He had waited this long in his life, then he married this beauty." Clark was proud as he could be, and he could hardly stop grinning.

For awhile the couple rented an apartment in the Sharpstown area of southwest Houston, four or five blocks from the McCurdy home. It was large enough to provide a separate bedroom for young Steven Seth. Then they put a down payment on a single-story, four-bedroom, white-brick home at 8923 Sharpcrest about two-and-a-half miles away in the same development and moved in. The house had a two-car garage but no basement. Basements are rare in Houston residences because of the moist gumbo-like earth, and most builders simply pour huge slabs of concrete on a housing site and build the structure on top.

During the late 1960s and early 1970s when Clark settled his family into the spacious house, a bride could hardly have asked her husband for a nicer home in a more attractive neighborhood. Several Tenneco families bought homes there, and at that time, Sharpstown was one of the most prosperous and affluent neighborhoods in the city. The comfortably attractive subdivision even had its own country club, and along with communities with names like Tanglewood and River Oaks it was part of the Silk Stocking congressional district where George Bush got his start in politics. Houston, like many southern cities, was a longtime Democratic stronghold, and Bush breathed life into the local Republican party. From 1966 to 1968, when Clark and Jill were setting up housekeeping together, the World War II hero Navy pilot and future president was their congressman.

Clark and his pal, whom he called "Mac," about as often as he called him "B. B.," worked hard, and when it was time for recreation, they played hard. The two couples visited back and forth, and they were such close friends they didn't need invitations to show up at one another's house.

McCurdy loved Thunderbirds, and he had two 1957 models that he kept in perfect running condition and glossed to such glistening high sheen that they would have satisfied a Marine Corps drill sergeant. Clark fell in love with his buddy's Thunderbirds and decided he had to have one of the high-performance machines for his own to tool around in.

Eventually McCurdy heard about someone who had a 1957 T-Bird to sell, and the two pals drove over to the owner's house for a look. It was a beauty. Clark and the owner dickered for awhile, made a deal, and the engineer drove the sleek, black sportscar home. It ran perfectly, but one of the first things he did was take it in for a new paint job. He had it painted bright red.

With the exception of Jill, the Thunderbird was the love of his life. He kept the car washed and polished until it glittered so brightly he could have used the reflection to shave in. The elegantly designed and engineered little T-bird was his passion, and he enjoyed wheeling around Houston. It wasn't at all unusual on a Saturday or Sunday afternoon to hear the roar of the engine as the T-Bird whipped down the street and screeched to a stop in front of the house. When they went to the door, Clark and Jill would be outside in the car with the fiberglass top removed and a martini precariously balanced on the dashboard.

"Hi, B. B. Hi, you guys," Clark would call out. "Just thought I'd come over and pay you a little visit." Clark had been in the Lone Star State long enough and enjoyed it enough to pick up the raw east Texas nasal twang and rhythm.

During one of the more memorable visits, Clark brought another of his toys with him: a miniature steel cannon about eight or ten inches long that could fire. It worked like a muzzle loader. The men trooped out to McCurdy's big backyard, and Clark poured a load of powder in the cannon, stuffed in some wadding, and fired it. After a couple of dish-rattling explosions, McCurdy suggested to his pal that maybe they should quit. Neighborhood kids were already hanging over the fences, and he was worried one of the neighbors was going to call the police.

"Well, then, I guess we better stop," Clark agreed. He called off the noisy demonstration, packed up the cannon, and went inside the house to mix a fresh martini. He was easy to get along with.

Clark and McCurdy were members of a local Thunderbird club, and their wives shared in the activities. One year, Jill served as the club secretary and recorded minutes of meetings and took care of the paperwork. She also loved the T-Bird, but it was her husband's toy. The club, which was nameless at first but eventually evolved into the Classic Thunderbirds of Houston, sponsored rallies and joined with other groups for shows, picnics, and parades. There was a very active club in San Antonio, and every year several members from the Houston group drove there to appear in the St. Patrick's Day Parade. Other car owners drove in from Dallas and Fort Worth for the event. Yet another group of T-Bird owners from Arkansas and Louisiana met in Shreveport and invited the Houston club to many of their events.

An annual picnic is held in the little town of Katy—about ten miles west of Houston—for owners of sports cars, Model-T's, and just about any vintage Ford vehicle that catches the eye of a driver or collector.

Every September, Clark, McCurdy, and colleagues from Tenneco went off for a rowdy boys-only jaunt to south Texas and Mexico for a weekend of bird-hunting or golfing and all-around carousing. Contractors who dealt with the company had developed the custom of treating some of Tenneco's top talent to the trips. One of the contractors established a golf tournament at a course near Brownsville and named it the Martini Open. It was rumored that to compete, the golfers had to drink a martini at every hole.

Clark played a little golf, but he liked the annual September whitewing parties the best. Sponsors of the hell-raising forays paid for almost everything, including the leasing of ten or twenty acres of the orange groves where the doves congregated.

One of the contractors provided a bus outfitted with a big stock of beer and liquor and gobs of man-sized sandwiches and other food for the trips to the border. The old bus was painted bright orange and white, the colors of the University of Texas. During those years, McCurdy assumed an important role as one of the designated drivers. He and the other driver stayed sober and made sure that the party animals got safely to and from the marathon frolics along the Rio Grande. They usually followed US Route 59 to Victoria, where they dropped down to the city of Alice about fifty miles inland from the curving Gulf Coast, then cut a straight line south to the orange, lemon, and grapefruit groves in Hidalgo and Cameron counties near McAllen and Brownsville.

"Wasted Days and Wasted Nights," "Raindrops Keep Fallin On My Head," and a variety of other Tex-Mex, hard country, and Texas Outlaw tunes blasted non-stop from the stereo, while the rowdy passengers partied, drank, and played gin rummy all the way

downstate. Native Texas crooners Freddy Fender and
B. J. Thomas were riding high on the country and pop
charts in those days.

There wasn't much that was exciting to see during
the last hundred miles or so of the trip, except dry,
desolate scrub land and mesquite trees, until they
reached the Lower Rio Grande Valley. Irrigation
brought the previously sun-parched valley to life with
graceful palm trees, fields of lettuce, tomatoes, and cu-
cumbers, and huge orchards filled with row after row
of orange, lemon, grapefruit, and lime trees. South
Texans and visitors today sometimes refer to the area
as the "Magic Valley" because of its fertility and the
abundant crops produced there.

McCurdy knew the area well. One year he and a
crew just completed a surveying job around Edinburg
a few days before Christmas. Their boss told them to
take a few days off, then get up to Zanesville, Ohio to
begin a new project. After working in the balmy
weather of the Valley, they spent the worst months of
the winter in the ice and snow of east central Ohio.
That was standard operational procedure for the men
like McCurdy, Clark, and their colleagues when they
were working the pipelines. It was a gypsy life.

The citrus groves near McAllen and Edinburg were
teeming with a flutter of whitewing doves. The tiny
game birds didn't make easy targets, especially for a
hunter with a few drinks under his belt. When white-
wings were flushed from the groves, they took off fast,
skimming low over the tops of the trees with the swift-
ness of a World War II Japanese kamikaze. At the first
flustered rustle of wings, the Texans started blazing
away.

Sparrows, crows, starlings, and an occasional wild
parakeet were sometimes blasted into oblivion or dis-
patched in a scatter of feathers and pinwheeling death
dives along with the real targets of the hunt. When the

birds were flushed, it was shoot first and ask questions later. McCurdy had developed a hobby as an amateur photographer into a professional skill and he took pictures of the hunters with their trophies. One year Clark mailed one of the photos to his brother in Ohio, showing him standing outside an orange grove with a drink in one hand and a tiny feathered trophy in the other. It looked about the size of a hummingbird, but Clark was proud of it.

The hunters stayed in local motels, and men were hired there to pick and clean the birds.

After a day of hunting, McCurdy loaded his rowdy charges into the bus and drove them across the border to Matamoros for some serious carousing. Just about any male who has grown up or spent much of his youth and young manhood in or near south Texas, has at one time or another checked out Boys' Town—the utilitarian name for the red-light districts—in Matamoros, Reynosa, Nuevo Laredo, Juarez, and other cities or villages that hug the Texas border. As politically incorrect as it may be today, for generations of south Texans the practice has been followed as a virtual rite of manhood.

Not everyone headed straight for Boys' Town; some of the restless men settled for the noisy cantinas where they tipped one icy longneck bottle of Corona and Dos Equis after another or squared off in friendly contests to see who could drink the most tequila, lick the most salt, and crunch and swallow the largest number of the fat little cactus worms embalmed in alcohol and curled up inside the bottles.

The girls and the madams at the cathouses in Boys' Town knew McCurdy by his first name. He usually made his appearance, still stone sober, at two or three o'clock in the morning, solely to round up his hell-raising sidekicks for the trip back across the border. One night he drove through three or four miles of narrow streets and alleys before he was satisfied with his final head count. Some of his charges were very important people with the company, and McCurdy was determined to get them safely back.

Despite his enjoyment of the whitewing parties, Clark wasn't a big gun collector. He knew how to use and care for a gun, but he never developed the same obsession with them as he did for his T-Bird. Shotguns were provided by the sponsors or loaned by friends for the hunts. At the end of the hunt a company aircraft flew down to pick up most of the weary revelers and save them the long trip back to Houston by bus.

Wives went along on other outings that were more subdued, and Clark and Jill once posed for a photo with another engineer and his wife while they were dining on a trip to Mexico. Jill was pregnant.

While she was tending to her duties as a new housewife, belatedly divesting herself of her marital ties to Moore in Louisiana, and building on her relationship with her new husband, she was also marking up other important milestones in her life.

On Veterans Day, November 11, 1966, she gave birth to another boy. He was named William Andrew. The tiny newcomer had Clark's blond hair, and as he grew up friends described him as looking like a carbon copy of his father with the same distinctive features. On March 1, 1968, a third son was born. The baby of the family was named William Clark Coit III, after his father and paternal grandfather. With two boys in the family sharing the same name, the middle son was called Andrew or Andy. Like his grandfather, the youngest Coit was called William, Billy, or Bill. Jill's dark-haired oldest son used his middle name, Seth. It would be the only portion of the name given to him at birth that survived.

The birth of William Clark Coit III also reportedly marked the end of his mother's childbearing years.

Doctors are said to have performed a partial hysterectomy on her at the time of his birth. Jill claimed years later however she did not have a hysterectomy, although she conceded some cancerous cells were removed from her cervix during the operation. At any rate, she was no longer capable of giving birth.

During the first few years of the marriage, the couple got along well together. Clark was a man with a ready sense of humor, and he enjoyed his bride's quick wit and zest for life. She was not only the kind of beauty who stopped men in their tracks, she was fun. He was proud of the boys and was generous with toys and presents. During good weather he hauled out the barbecue grill, and cooked hot dogs, hamburgers, chicken, or steak.

Gradually, however, their relationship began to change, and admiration turned to suspicion and doubts. Jill was a shameless narcissist who was hung up on her good looks, and she tended to be overly dramatic. She was also an outrageous flirt, and men who didn't know Clark well and weren't his close friends usually responded to her come-ons. Her behavior was embarrassing to Clark and to the couple's friends. It was creating serious strains on the marriage.

As the 1960s drew to a close and the messages of love from flower children were giving way to the violence and easy slogans of Vietnam War protests, the Coits' marriage was in serious trouble, despite the birth of two sons.

Disturbing stories about Jill were circulating among Tenneco couples at the home office, linking her to a series of tawdry affairs with other men.

One summer when she and Clark temporarily settled in Lexington, Kentucky, in the center of the bluegrass and thoroughbred country while he was working on a job there, Jill took riding lessons. She was a natural equestrienne, and she easily learned to ride and jump her mounts. Within weeks however, the story was being whispered around that she was having a romance with her riding instructor.

Shortly after Clark was sent to Syracuse on another job, the rumor mill began buzzing again about a torrid liaison she was reputedly having with a doctor who had treated one of the boys.

Jill and Clark were back in Houston when she began taking scuba-diving lessons, and a new round of stories started circulating. This time she was said to be having an affair with her diving teacher. She was flaunting her infidelities and almost deliberately inviting attention, as if she enjoyed being at the center of the feast of spicy gossip.

B. B. McCurdy didn't like what he was hearing. None of the company gossips seemed to have any real evidence to back up the stories, but they were troubling, nevertheless. There were so many of them, and how, he wondered, did they start? Furthermore, if the nasty tales were untrue they were grossly unfair and damaging to his friends. And if they were true, Jill's behavior was a tragedy of major proportions for Clark, who was as deeply in love with his wife as he was when they married.

It was Jill herself who crushed any doubts McCurdy may have had about the stories that she was cuckolding her husband.

Clark and Jill were hosting a Christmas party for some of their friends from Tenneco, and McCurdy was in the kitchen by himself mixing a drink when she opened the back door and slipped inside, according to his recollections. A bitter wind, which locals call a "Canadian Norther" was sweeping across the prairie.

Despite the frigid weather outside, Jill didn't have a coat on. She had a reputation for wearing flashy, revealing outfits that showed a lot of skin, especially her

long legs and breasts. The cold clung to her body like
an envelope as she moved up close to McCurdy.

"Has anybody missed me?," she asked in her velvet
voice.

McCurdy hadn't expected the question, but he
wasn't really surprised. Nothing about Jill Coit was
surprising anymore.

"Well, I don't know. Where the hell have you
been?" He couldn't have asked a question she was
more anxious to answer. She was steaming mad, and
she spit out more information than McCurdy really
wanted to hear.

"That sonofabitch I'm taking scuba lessons from.
He knew I had to run this party tonight," she snarled.
She had called him a bit earlier from the telephone in
a back bedroom and suspected from the way he talked
to her that he wasn't alone. So she drove over to his
home to take a look for herself.

"I just went over there and caught him shacking up
with somebody," she said. "That sorry sonofabitch."

Any image of a sweet Southern belle Jill may have
planned to maintain for her friend that night, had exploded into a nasty torrent of jealousy and vitriol. It
seemed nobody hates a cheater as much as another
cheater.

Jill spent a lot of time away from home on her own.
A fledgling modeling career and public relations work
she was doing were taking up big chunks of her time.
Her boys were being looked after by professional
baby-sitters or accommodating friends. After awhile
she began taking overnights, weekends, and then
breaks of a week or two at a time to deal with her busy
business affairs. Sometimes she headed back to New
Orleans.

Another Tenneco couple were close friends with
Clark and kept the boys a few times while Jill was on
one of her trips. They later told McCurdy that one day

they found ugly bruises on one of the boys where Jill had whipped him with a belt buckle.

When the boys were picked up, the woman who had been taking care of them had a little talk with Jill. She made it plain that if she ever saw evidence again on one of the boys that they had been beaten, Jill was going to be in big trouble. She was a woman who wouldn't stand for permitting children to be abused.

She and Clark began an on-again, off-again series of separations and reconciliations. Clark was embarrassed by his wife as she played out her bold ritual of betrayal. The relationship quickly turned from warm and exciting to cool and bleakly ominous.

She openly boasted about her lovemaking skills. Stunningly lovely, Jill had a keen sense of the power of her beauty and femininity to go along with a convenient set of elastic morals. She was a sassy, sexy temptress, and she had no difficulty—or compunctions about—attracting admirers and lovers.

She knew how close McCurdy was to her husband, and perhaps that's why she tried to tease him with boasts of her erotic skills and accomplishments. One time she confided to him that it was too bad he wasn't a blond or she would already have had him in bed, he recalled. He joshed back that he guessed he would have to dye his hair. But Jill responded that wouldn't help anyway. The blond hair had to be natural.

She loved to boast, and he figured she thought it was safe to use him as her sounding board because he was too loyal to break Clark's heart by saying anything to him. But B. B. didn't want to hear that kind of talk from his friend's wife, and he told her so.

"Jill, don't tell me any more about your exploits," he finally told her. "Honey, I just don't want to know it."

That was too bad, Jill reputedly said, because she gave the best blow job on earth.

By now Clark was humiliated and his self-confidence and sense of manhood were being hopelessly smothered. The effect of Jill's reputation for runaway infidelity in the marriage was devastating. He stepped up his boozing. His tippling grated on his wife's nerves and made things worse. She was basically a teetotaler and preferred going out for a nice meal in a fancy restaurant to spending an evening draining a bottle of fine wine or stronger spirits.

The couple broke up the first time on October 10, 1969. Jill filed in the Court of Domestic Relations in Harris County for divorce. She accused her husband of almost non-stop boozing during his time off from work.

According to her complaint, Clark would begin drinking "on many occasions" after returning home from work and continue boozing late into the night. There was more of the same on weekends, despite her abhorrence of his habit. He made matters worse by badgering her with "unpleasant invectives" that kept her "continuously upset and nervous," she added. Jill claimed his behavior was so troubling they could no longer live together.

"Plaintiff would show that while married to Defendant she conducted herself with propriety and attempted at all times to do everything possible to please Defendant," she declared. Clark filed a reply denying the accusations made against him.

Jill asked for custody of the boys, an unspecified amount for their temporary support, community property, and $1,500 in attorney fees. The requested lawyer fees had gone up considerably since her divorce from Ihnen, when the Indiana court ordered him to pay filing costs and $75 in preliminary attorney fees.

The second page of the petition contained a statement that, if true, would have made her ripe fodder for the supermarket tabloids. She noted that two children were born of the marriage, listing Andrew's birthdate as November 11, 1967 and Billy's as March 11, 1968. If the birthdays were correct and Jill was the mother of both boys, it would have meant that they were born four-months apart. If correct, it was a feat for the record books, but it was more likely a simple oversight or typographical error.

A few weeks after the divorce action was filed, the couple reconciled. In May, Jill dropped her petition for divorce and moved back into her Sharpstown home with her husband and boys. Clark earned a good salary, and he was a good provider who was generous with his money. And he loved the boys. Much of the time, Jill had a Mexican-American maid to help take care of them and the house while she and her husband were at work.

After four years of the still-shaky marriage, Clark formally adopted Seth. Jill also petitioned the District Court in Houston to have her oldest son's name changed. Steven Seth Moore became Jonathan Seth Coit. Seth's mother stated on the petition that her son had lived in the household of his stepfather for more than four years. He was expected to enter school within the next year and wished to begin classes with the new name, she said.

In accordance with Texas law, the adoption file was closed. No one bothered to inform the child's natural father in Louisiana of his boy's adoption or name change.

Seth was a bright, inquisitive, and energetic child. Nevertheless, he wasn't in school long before he became aware that he may have had a problem. He was eventually diagnosed with dyslexia, a condition usually reflected in reading difficulties. Dyslexia often reveals itself by causing victims to see mirror images of words or to mix up the letters.

For whatever reason, perhaps because he was her

first child, or because he was dyslexic, Seth grew up with an especially close and enduring attachment to his mother. Jill claimed she also suffered from a mild form of the disorder.

Even with Seth officially becoming a Coit, however, the household on Sharpcrest still wasn't one big happy family. Despite efforts to make the truce work and heal the corrosive wounds steadily eating away at the marriage, they weren't getting along well. It was difficult for the ambitious young woman, juggling tasks of public-relations executive, model, wife, and mother of three healthy little boys. She repeatedly complained that the kids were driving her up a wall, according to Clark.

The troubled couple temporarily joined forces in court however after Jill was involved in a rear-end collision while she was driving in the 4600 block of the Southwest Freeway. She was at the wheel of her new 1970 Mercury when she slowed for a line of cars ahead and a vehicle driven by an employee of the Floyd West & Co., hit the car immediately behind her, knocking it forward into her vehicle, according to her account.

Jill was treated at a nearby hospital and ultimately claimed in court that she suffered a whiplash that left her with frequent headaches, pain in the shoulders and upper back, dizziness, and nervous shock. In a lawsuit filed against the company and the driver by the same attorney who represented her in the divorce action, she was identified as a twenty-five-year-old woman who was employed as a model and in public-relations work, earning approximately $800 per month. She complained she had been unable to work since the accident and asserted that unless her condition improved, work in her profession and in her job as a housewife would be carried out under the handicap of pain and suffering.

Jill asked for $50,000 for pain, suffering, and cost of

medical care. As part of the same suit, Clark asked that the defendants be ordered to pay for the cost of repairing the car. The defendants claimed the mishap was an unavoidable accident and that Jill had neglected to exercise ordinary care.

The lawsuit was eventually settled in January 1972 without a trial when a compromise was worked out by the court. But the litigation helped set a precedent for a flurry of divorce actions, civil lawsuits, and criminal charges that Jill would be involved in for the next twenty-five years of her life.

By the time the damage suit was settled, Jill and Clark had been separated again for four months. On September 7, 1971, Clark returned from work to find the boys alone in the house with the maid. His wife had cleared out and left without a word about where she was going or when she would return. Jill was back in New Orleans again, where she was said to be taking flying lessons. New stories were already making the rounds at Tenneco that she was having a torrid affair with her flying instructor.

Clark did his best to meet the challenge of his sudden role as a single parent. He made arrangements with the maid to care for the boys while he was at work in the city and during periods when he was on business away from Houston. Once while he was playing bachelor father he took a couple of weeks off from work, loaded the boys into an old Greyhound bus that had been converted into a motor home and drove to Ohio. He and the boys visited with his parents in Gates Mills, then drove back south with Charles and his wife, Alma, to Fostoria to stay the rest of the weekend. Charles was pastor of the Trinity Episcopal Church there and he hooked up the bus's electrical system to the church so his brother and nephews would have power Saturday night. Clark talked about some of his domestic problems to his brother and sister-in-law, but didn't mention his wife's reputed infidelities.

His troubles were waiting for him back home. It was only 350 miles from the Big Easy through Baton Rouge, past the sugar cane fields, bald cypress, and Cajun country bayous of southern Louisiana, across the Texas line at Beaumont, all the way to Houston.

Jill was a long way from being permanently out of her husband's hair. In those days the drive could be made along Interstate 10 in about seven hours. And a flight from the New Orleans International Airport to one of the Bayou City's two major airports, Houston Intercontinental on the far northside or William P. Hobby at the southern edge of town could be made in little more than an hour.

Jill returned to Texas a few times to see the children, but continued for several months to leave them in the care of her husband and the maid. Then on February 22, 1972, she returned to the house again while he was at work. When Clark returned, he discovered that much of the furniture had been carried out of the house and the boys were nowhere to be seen.

He was still trying to figure out what to do when he heard a child crying. It was Billy, his youngest, who was three years old. Clark later said the three brothers were in a car with their mother when she told Billy to get out. He wasn't going along with his older brothers. Clark also claimed his mother-in-law had helped Jill while his furniture was loaded into a truck and hauled away.

Two days later, Jill returned to the house, removing almost all the rest of the furniture. This time she also took little Billy along with her. Jill was back in New Orleans with the furniture and the boys.

Clark confided in his older brother during their telephone calls, telling him about his troubles. Charles asked him if he had cancelled his credit cards, and

Clark said he planned to. But it was too late; his wife was continuing to rachet up the pressure. About the time he learned that his boys and furniture were gone, he was informed that Jill had run up a whopping $1,800 bill at Foley's Department Store, one of the classiest stores in Houston.

Clark's life was suddenly plunging out of control, and he was facing financial ruin and personal disaster. Alone, with Jill and his boys gone, the disconsolate husband continued drinking more than was good for him. He confided to a couple of friends from Tenneco at different times that he thought someone was planning to kill him, but he didn't name names.

On March 1, his youngest son's fourth birthday, Clark filed a petition for divorce in the Harris County domestic relations court, accusing his wife of abandoning her husband, home, and family. The subsequent raids on the house to take the boys and the furniture were carefully detailed in the complaint.

The complainant described himself as a man who was a good and dutiful husband, father and provider who conducted himself properly during the marriage. But his wife's personality had changed so radically and the marriage relationship was so badly damaged, the couple could no longer maintain any reasonable expectation of reconciliation, he claimed.

Clark asked for custody of the three children, and a fair division of the community property. Curiously, the petition cited a different set of birthdays for the two younger boys from the dates provided with the divorce action previously filed by their mother. The date of Andrew's birth was listed as November 11, 1966, and Billy's was given as March 1, 1968. None of the three divorce petitions filed over two-and-a-half years cited the same combination of birthdays for the younger boys.

Two weeks after Clark filed his divorce petition, Jill

cross-filed against him. It appeared that just about everything that could turn sour in Clark's personal life had, but he was still hopeful of salvaging enough of his property and savings to start over. He told his friends that his wife was doing her best to clean him out of everything he owned.

McCurdy was concerned about his friend. Clark was going through a rough time, and with his brother three thousand miles away in Ohio, he was pretty much enduring it alone. When he wasn't working, he was in the quiet, spartanly-furnished house with just himself and the bottle. About the only furniture Clark had in the place was a narrow cot and a twelve-inch television set.

Despite all the ugliness and hurtful things that had happened, Clark bared his heart to his friend and talked about how much he still wanted his wife back. "Mac, it's very simple," he confessed one night. "I just love the woman." He was helpless when it came to Jill.

But Jill was keeping the pressure on, and Clark was beginning to wilt. The stress and heartbreak were wearing him down. After work Tuesday evening, March 28, Clark, McCurdy, and some of their colleagues from Tenneco trooped across the street to the Normandy, one of their favorite watering holes, to tip a few cool ones. It was Seth's seventh birthday, but he was in New Orleans with his mother and brothers and Clark wouldn't have an opportunity to share the occasion with him. The troubled engineer reluctantly conceded to his friends that it seemed to be inevitable that he and Jill would be divorced, and he had given up trying to salvage the marriage.

She was so determined to clean him out financially, that he withdrew $10,000 from the company credit union that day, he said. "At least she won't get this away from me," he glumly told his audience. Everyone was doing their best to cheer him up, but after awhile McCurdy decided it was time to head for home.

"Clark, I'm goin' on home now. Goddamnit, don't stay out here too late," he told his friend.

There wasn't anything waiting for Clark at home except loneliness and an empty house, and he was in no hurry to leave. But he assured his pal that he wouldn't hang around the bar drinking all night.

"I'll be on home, don't worry," he said. "I'll call you when I get there." One of the Tenneco secretaries stuck around and had another drink or two with him, and he showed her the wad of money he had withdrawn from the credit union a few hours earlier. She stared in surprise at the stack of $100 bills for a moment, then with an intake of breath she cautioned: "Clark you shouldn't be carrying that much money around."

"Don't worry, I'm goin' on home," he assured his friend. "But this is one bunch of money that she won't get her hands on." A few minutes later he walked out of the Normandy, climbed in his old station wagon, and headed for Sharpstown.

About 10 o'clock that night, McCurdy telephoned his friend at the house. "You okay?" he asked when Clark picked up the telephone. "Yep, everything's fine," Clark replied. "Gonna take a little nap, and I'll see you in the morning."

According to McCurdy, another, more curious telephone call was accepted by the wife of one of Clark's fellow engineers in Houston roughly a half-hour earlier that night. She was the same woman pictured with her husband and the Coits in the photograph taken during the trip to Mexico. Her husband was on business in St. Louis when she answered the phone and a woman posing as a long-distance operator said she was trying to reach him or a Mr. Coit. Her husband was out of town, the Houston woman replied.

"Well, how about Mr. Coit then?" the caller asked.

"So far as I know, he's in town," the housewife replied.

The next time she talked with her husband she told him a funny thing had happened. Jill Coit called while he was gone, pretending to be a long distance operator and asking for him or Clark. The housewife wasn't fooled by the transparent ruse. She had been around Jill too many times not to recognize her on the telephone. Jill's soft, sexy voice, with its distinctive hint of a Louisiana accent was unmistakable.

The official workday for most of the employees in Tenneco's main office began at 8 AM, but many of the engineers and executives came in early, especially if they were involved in a construction project or dealing with people in the field. Clark was usually in his office by 7:15 or 7:30. At about eight that morning, McCurdy dialed his friend's extension for a quick checkup to make sure Clark was okay.

One of Clark's co-workers answered the call and said he hadn't showed up yet. That was out of character for him. Despite all his troubles he was too serious about his work to allow his personal difficulties to affect his performance at Tenneco. He already held down an important position with the company, and appeared to have a brilliant future. He never shirked his responsibilities.

He didn't have any business appointments elsewhere in Houston or out of town that colleagues at Tenneco knew about, and he hadn't telephoned to say he would be late or taking a day off. He wasn't a man who missed work without a good reason. But no one answered the telephone when co-workers tried to contact him at his house.

McCurdy was alarmed and sincerely concerned about his friend. Clark's drinking had become especially heavy since Jill left, and his chum was afraid he might have had a heart attack. The possibility of suicide even crossed McCurdy's mind. But he didn't really believe Clark would kill himself. He loved the three boys too much to run out on them that way.

McCurdy telephoned his wife and explained that their friend hadn't shown up for work and he was worried about him.

"Sweetheart, get in the car and go over to Clark's house and see if he's okay," he told her. "Now if his old station wagon's parked out there, don't go inside. You either go to a pay phone, or you go home and call me." Clark kept his prized Thunderbird in the garage.

Ginny was a gentle, steady woman who raised a fine family and made a good home for her little brood. She was devoted to her family and friends, and she was especially fond of Clark. Her husband didn't want her walking in on some grisly situation that would leave her with unpleasant memories.

In late March there was still an east Texas chill in the air, and she slipped on a light jacket before climbing into her car and beginning the twenty-minute drive to Sharpcrest. The big 1966 station wagon was standing in the driveway. Ginny parked her car and rang the bell at the front door. There was no answer, so she rapped on it a couple of times with her knuckles. The door didn't open, no one called out, and there were no sounds of activity inside, so she walked around to the back entrance.

She knocked at the back door, and when there was still no reply she tried the knob and realized it was unlocked. Cracking the door open a few inches, she called out Clark's name. The house was silent. Ginny appreciated her husband's concern for her and his caution not to enter the house, but she couldn't resist checking out the situation for herself. She was worried about their friend, and she eased inside. Entering a small alcove where the washer and dryer were kept, she walked through the kitchen into the den and peered into the hallway.

Clark was lying on the floor in his blue boxer shorts and a T-shirt. Blood was all over the place. His trunk and underclothes were soaked in it. Blood was gathered in pools under his head and upper body, and ugly smears stained the walls.

Ginny took one horrified look and retreated to the kitchen. She called her husband from the wall phone and told him something terrible had happened to their friend.

"I-I don't know if he's dead or not," the shaken woman stammered. "But there's blood all over, and he's laying in the hall."

McCurdy's first thought was getting help for his friend as quick as possible. He might still be alive.

"Honey, you call an ambulance. The first thing you call is an ambulance, and call the police, and get out of there," he instructed his wife. It was still a few years before the 911 system was initiated in most cities. In those days, he says, "You just dialed zero and begin to holler."

As soon as his wife hung up the phone, McCurdy dialed Clark's office and talked with Reavis L. Maggard, one of the men who worked with him.

"There's something wrong at Clark's house and I'm goin' down there," he said.

"I'm going with you," Maggard responded.

Minutes later the two men were in McCurdy's car, pulling out from the company-owned parking garage across the street from the Tenneco building. McCurdy's mind was racing, trying to figure out what had happened. He was scared to death that Clark had fallen in the shower, cut himself on broken glass and staggered into the hallway where he bled to death.

It took the men about twenty minutes to negotiate their way through the early morning traffic and reach

Sharpcrest. Clark's house was only two blocks from
the corner, and his friends could see an ambulance
and a couple of police cars clustered in and around
the driveway.

McCurdy stopped behind a parked squad car, and
he and his companion hurried along the driveway to
the back door. He hardly noticed Clark's old Suburban
station wagon sitting in the drive. A Houston Police
Department uniform officer was standing just outside
and asked them who they were and what they wanted.

"Well, I'm a real close friend of Mr. Coit's," Mc-
Curdy replied. "And my wife was the one that came
over here and found him. She called me."

The cop motioned them inside. McCurdy and Maggard walked through the utility room and kitchen into
the den and stopped about eight feet from the body of
their friend. Clark was crumpled face-down in the
hallway leading to the bedroom area, with his body
turned at a slight angle against the wall. The head was
toward the kitchen. He was still in the same position
he had been lying in when McCurdy's wife found him
there.

It didn't require the training of a homicide detective
or a medical examiner to recognize the ugly gunshot
wounds on the body. Clark had been shot from behind. McCurdy and Maggard didn't stick around and
try to count the wounds. They took one quick, ago-
nized look and retreated from the house as quickly as
they could. Several homicide investigators and evidence technicians were busy at the scene, and they
wouldn't have been permitted to stick around much
longer anyway. It was no place for civilians—or for
close friends of the victim.

Evidence technicians were inside and outside of the
house dusting carefully-selected objects for possible
latent fingerprints, shooting photographs from a variety of angles, taking measurements, studying the blood

spatter-pattern, and scrutinizing the crime scene for trace evidence and potential clues. A detective interviewed Virginia McCurdy later at her home, and she described her discovery of the body.

There was no sign in the house of the $10,000 Clark had withdrawn from the credit union the previous day or of his billfold with the $500 to $600 pocket money he usually carried around with him. Two rings he wore were still on his fingers.

A prized .41 caliber Magnum, which he recently bought, was also missing from the little wooden case he kept it in. Models of the high-muzzle-velocity revolver had been on the market less than ten years and were used by several police departments around the country. Clark admired the sleek, powerful firearm for its stopping power and wouldn't have considered getting rid of it.

For awhile after police found some new wood and other signs of recent repair around the front door lock, they puzzled over the possibility of an earlier break-in. The door appeared to have been jimmied open and a new lock installed. The old lock, a hammer, and screwdriver were on a table in the front room. But McCurdy cleared the matter up and saved wasted time and effort for the investigators when he laid the blame for the damage on the home owner. Clark rambled home drunk one night and couldn't find his key, so he kicked the door in. Then he had to buy and install a new lock.

Several other suspicious holes were observed in the door, the door casing, and in the walls of the hallway that appeared to have been caused by bullets.

Early on the same afternoon, only three hours after Clark's body was found, the forty-two-year-old engineer was wheeled into the Harris County Morgue for an autopsy. There, among the cold, sterile surroundings of the morgue, Assistant Medical Examiner Ethel

E. Erickson performed a classic autopsy. Chief Medical Examiner Joseph A. Jachimczyk witnessed the procedure. The first step in the process was to make a close visual observation of the corpse to observe the condition of the body and record the presence of external injuries or other unusual marks. Then Clark was weighed and measured. He was seventy-inches long, just under six feet, and weighed 167 pounds. The body was stiffened with rigor mortis.

The pathologists observed lacerations of the upper right scalp, and a gunshot entrance-wound in his left temple. There were no powder burns or stipling to indicate the barrel of the gun may have been held within a few inches of his head when he was shot. A small inch-long abrasion also marked his right forehead.

Another bullet had grazed his jaw on the left side of his face. The path of the bullet was in line with three superficial grazing wounds extending from his left shoulder toward the left side of his neck. Two more entry wounds were found in Clark's back, one on the right side and one on the left.

The pathologist opened Clark's chest and abdomen by making a Y-shaped incision and peeling back the flesh. Small-caliber bullets like .22s can do more damage to someone's insides than slugs fired from more powerful weapons. A shot from a .45 can blast a hole straight through flesh and bone, but the smaller .22s may bounce around inside, richocheting off bones while zig-zagging through tissue and organs. Clark suffered dreadful internal damage. One of the bullets passed completely through the left ventricle of his heart; his liver was slashed in two places; his left lung was pierced in two places; and the second rib on the left side was fractured.

Dr. Erickson removed a small caliber, copper-jacketed slug from the left side of the victim's chest. It was the bullet fired into the left side of his back. The other bullet fired into his back was also recovered just under the tenth left rib. Like the first slug, it was marked and placed in a separate special evidence container. X-rays of his skull disclosed that the bullet shot into his forehead shattered into small bits. The fragments were recovered from Clark's brain and packaged as evidence.

Laboratory tests and other observations indicated Clark was a healthy, middle-aged man before the fatal assault. Blood tests for barbiturates and narcotics were negative. His blood-alcohol level was 0.164 percent. The formula for determining legal intoxication varies in different states at different times. But .08 or .10 are usually in the ballpark, and people have been arrested for alcohol levels as low as .05. Clark had tipped quite a few drinks before he was shot.

"It is our opinion that the decedent, William Clark Coit, Jr., came to his death as a result of gunshot wounds (1) of head and (2) of back—Homicide," the pathologists concluded in their autopsy report.

Clark wasn't shot with his .41 caliber pistol, or with a .38 caliber handgun that he also owned. The slugs recovered from his body and from the house were all fired from a .22. The murder weapon wasn't recovered.

One of the police detectives theorized Clark was lying in bed watching television Tuesday night or early Wednesday morning when he went to the back door to let someone inside and was attacked. The television was still turned on and playing in the master bedroom when police arrived. The sheets on the bed were rumpled.

McCurdy thought that was probably an accurate reconstruction of what happened. He figured Clark got out of bed to admit someone into the house, then was shot in the back after he turned around to lead them further inside or toward the front door. And he fig-

ured the bushwhacker had to be someone Clark
trusted.

Clark's missing billfold was found several days after
his murder, tossed into a ditch a few miles north of the
city limits near the Intercontinental Airport. There
wasn't so much as a single dollar bill inside, but the
discovery sparked suspicions about why it was dis-
carded at that particular location. Did Clark's killer
leave town via the airport right after the murder?

A detective asked McCurdy if Clark would have
agreed to let Jill come to the house or would have
driven to the airport to pick her up if she had telephoned and said she was in town and wanted to see
him.

"Yes, he would have done it," McCurdy replied.
"He would have picked her up at the airport, or he
would have said, 'Yeah, you can come inside.'"

The investigation began to bog down almost as soon
as it began. In the early 1970s when the Tenneco engineer was murdered, the Houston Police Department
was already developing a spotty reputation that would
make it at least as well known for its failures as its
triumphs.

When Clark Coit was shot to death in his house by a
mystery killer, teenage boys from a shabbier neighborhood across town were being slaughtered by a vicious
gang of sex-and-torture slayers. The murders of boys
from the Heights had been going on since 1970. But
worried parents couldn't work up much interest from
the police in solving the mystery of their missing teenagers. The youngsters were disappearing one and two
at a time, but when parents tried to enlist law enforcement officers to investigate the strange vanishings they
were put off with suggestions the boys were probably
runaways.

Houston police busied themselves with other matters while the killings continued. On August 8, 1973,

the serial-murder case involving the missing boys finally resolved itself. Nineteen-year-old Elmer Wayne Henley telephoned police in suburban Pasadena and blurted out that he had just shot his friend to death.

The friend was Dean Corll, a thirty-three-year-old former candy-maker and mastermind of the murder ring. Henley had brought a thirteen-year-old neighborhood girl along with a teenage boy intended as a victim to Corll's house, setting off the fatal confrontation. Eventually the remains of twenty-seven victims were recovered from three burial sites, although one was later said to represent an unrelated homicide. Corll was a native Hoosier, who grew up just outside Fort Wayne, Indiana, about a half-hour drive from Wabash County where Jill married her first husband.

In the early 1970s, serial murder wasn't an everyday event in the United States, and the story flashed around the world, setting off a flurry of shock and outrage ranging from the Vatican to the Soviet government's official Communist press organ, *Izvestia*. Commentators for the party newspaper seized the opportunity to blast the Houston Police Department for cruel unconcern and crippling bureaucracy.

In Houston parents of the murdered boys were saying many of the same things. Some Houston police were defending themselves by blaming the boys, muttering that they were prostitutes who knew about the sex and paint-sniffing orgies at Corll's home and got into trouble because of their willingness to play for pay. The police department came in for additional criticism for reputedly cutting the search for bodies off short. The critics theorized that the search ended when it did because the people of the Heights were without significant political power, and the police weren't overly anxious for Houston to set a long-standing record for serial killing.

But Clark was murdered in a neighborhood where

the residents had plenty of political power and knew how to use it. The house on Sharpcrest was surrounded by comfortable up-scale homes of important people and respected well-to-do professionals like himself: teachers, lawyers, accountants, dentists, and engineers. On the rare occasions when a murder occurred in Sharpstown, concerned neighbors expected the police department to take a close look at the evidence and make a determined effort to bring the killer to justice. Sharpstown wasn't a neighborhood where there was a longstanding pattern of unsolved murders.

But for one reason or another the investigation of the engineer's slaying broke the pattern. Police couldn't find the murder weapon, they couldn't find a witness, and they never had a sit-down discussion with Jill about her stormy relationship with her late husband and his perplexing murder. The homicide probe quickly fizzled and lost steam.

About a week after the slaying, the *Houston Post*, one of the city's two major daily newspapers, offered a $4,000 reward as part of its "Public Protector" program for information leading to the arrest and conviction of the killer. Rewards in the same amount were posted in twelve other homicide cases and $2,000 was offered for help in the arrest and conviction of a stickup man, but the writer opened the major crime roundup with Clark's slaying. Along with everything else, Houston was also a violent city.

The anonymous author of the story observed that police believed robbery might be the motive for the slaying. The reward for help solving Clark's slaying was never claimed. And the paperwork compiled during investigation of his murder began gathering dust alongside others in the Houston Police Department's unsolved case files.

THREE

Major Brodie &
Daddy Johansen

Clark's violent death and the gruesome scene at the house were fiercely traumatic, and McCurdy was badly shaken when he returned to Tenneco and reported the tragedy to company administrators.

The somber group of executives agreed among themselves that someone had to notify Jill. Since McCurdy was one of Clark's closest friends and had a pretty good idea of where to find her in New Orleans, he drew the unenviable task of passing along the message about the shooting to the widow.

A year or two earlier when McCurdy flew into New Orleans International on business, he had driven the few miles from the airport to visit Jill's parents in Metairie, and he still had their address and telephone number.

He figured the home on Yetta Avenue was a good place to begin looking for her. When he dialed the number Jill was there.

She sounded a bit surprised, but was friendly and responded with a standard greeting:

"Hi, Mac. How are you?"

Speaking softly and struggling to suppress the lump in his throat, he replied he had bad news. "Clark has been killed."

"What? How?" Jill demanded.

"He was shot!"

Jill hesitated for a moment or so, before gasping, "Who would want to do that to Clark? Oh, Clark . . ."

It was a good question, one that would still be unanswered twenty years later, except for rumors and suspicions that somehow were never quite pinned down. But McCurdy wasn't an interrogator; he was a messenger with bad news, and he listened patiently and sympathetically while Jill apparently began to lose her composure.

She was reacting with the expressions of shock and agony that could be expected of any normal person in her position, considering the circumstances.

A couple of days later, McCurdy took a telephone call at his office from a man in New Orleans who identified himself as Louis A. DiRosa. He was Jill's lawyer, and he wanted to know about company death benefits and any other proceeds that might be coming to his client. McCurdy had not only been Clark's chum, but he was also Tenneco's manager of employee benefits for all the pipelines. He handled all the paperwork involved with the death or disabilities of pipeline employees and mailed out the checks to survivors. He was the right man to call.

Clark was killed twenty days after Jill cross-filed for divorce, and she was still his wife and next of kin. Tenneco had a generous package of death benefits and other extras for its employees. Clark had a hefty retirement policy and a company insurance policy with a double-indemnity clause for accidental death. Death by gunshot, if the victim wasn't shooting back at someone, was covered by the special provision.

Jill eventually wound up with roughly $156,369.41, solely from her husband's company benefits. The package included funds from a retirement plan, life insurance, and a company savings program in which he had 689 shares of Tenneco stock. At the time it was worth $24 per share, but the value doubled over the next decade. A portion of the estate of Clark's parents also eventually fell into her hands through $150,000 trust funds set up for each of the boys. The total estate was also shared with the other grandchildren.

The young widow collected a small fortune after everything was totalled. In 1972 when fast-track engineers like Clark were earning between $25,000 and $30,000 annually, she had come into a tremendous amount of money.

McCurdy wound up mailing most of the checks from the retirement policy to Jill at the Tower Advertising Company, which she had formed and operated in New Orleans. Jill's company offices were next door to those of her lawyer in the Pere Marquette Building. But Clark's old friend also turned over some checks and documentation directly to DiRosa in Houston. The high-powered New Orleans lawyer was in town within a couple of days or so of Clark's death, looking after his client's welfare and affairs.

DiRosa was an experienced attorney who was a member of a politically powerful New Orleans family. His older brother, Joseph V. DiRosa, was a longtime member of the seven-member city council, who held one of two at-large seats voted on in all precincts of the city. For awhile Joseph was council president and mayor pro tem.

The younger DiRosa was a shrewd and resourceful legal technician who understood politics and the subtle intricacies of the law. He was a skilled professional who knew how to get everything for his sexy client that was coming to her from her late husband's estate.

One of the first things DiRosa did when he got to the Bayou City, was sweep into the Houston Police Department homicide headquarters and begin going over records of their investigation into the murder. He also talked with B. B. about the company's survivor benefits. One time DiRosa drove around the block until B. B. rode the elevator down from his office and walked out to the curb to hand over benefits documents to the lawyer in his car.

DiRosa's client was safely back in New Orleans, where she checked herself into a psychiatric hospital for treatment of acute hysteria after slashing her wrists. She was desperately worried about how she would raise three little boys without her husband, she claimed. But she was convinced at the hospital that she had to put those feelings behind her and go on with her life for the sake of the children.

While she was in the hospital, she was conveniently removed from the direct attentions of homicide investigators in Houston. Under the circumstances, as a patient hospitalized for hysteria and emotional distress, the fragile state of her mental health and her well-being were too important to risk by submitting her to questioning by inquisitive lawmen.

"We wanted to talk to her but she hid behind attorneys," Houston Detective Sgt. Jim Binford told the *National Enquirer* twenty years later. Binford was also quoted as saying Jill was the only suspect.

While DiRosa was collecting information and familiarizing himself with his client's tangled affairs and Jill was coping with her grief in the hospital, Charles Coit was tending to funeral arrangements for his only brother.

Charles had been home alone at five o'clock Wednesday afternoon when he answered the telephone. A man on the other end of the line identified himself as an officer with the Houston Police Department. The policeman asked if he was the brother of William Clark Coit. A sick feeling of apprehension was already sweeping over Charles when he replied affirmatively.

"Well, he's been shot," the officer said.

Charles dreaded the question he had to ask, but it couldn't be avoided.

"Is he dead?"

"Yes," the policeman confirmed.

Charles was standing up with the telephone in his hand, and his legs suddenly felt like strings of cooked spaghetti. He sat down on the floor. He asked the officer if his parents had been notified and was told they weren't.

"Well, don't tell them then," he said. "I will."

He was still sitting in a half-daze on the floor a minute or two later after hanging up the telephone, when his wife returned home from work. Alma Coit was filled in on the heartbreaking news. Then the couple began making arrangements to leave for Gates Mills to carry out one of the saddest tasks of their lives.

They had just broken the dreadful news to Charles's parents when the telephone rang and his father, William Coit, picked up the receiver. He was still shaken from the disclosure of Clark's violent death, and his face blanched. Charles asked who was on the line. It was Jill.

Charles picked up another phone and told his father to hang up, then took over the conversation. Jill said she just telephoned to tell them Clark was dead.

A few minutes later, the brief conversation ended. Then Charles and Alma began the long, mournful 150-mile drive back to their home in Findlay. Distraught and shaken, Charles notified his bishop at the diocese headquarters in Cleveland about Clark's murder. It was Holy Week, the most solemn and one of the busiest times of the year for the church, but Charles found it impossible to concentrate on his pastoral duties. He also had a funeral coming up for one of his parishioners, and the next day he telephoned his bishop again and said he needed help. He simply wasn't functioning as he should be.

A half-hour later a substitute pastor for the church was knocking at his door. The substitute handled the funeral. On Maundy Thursday, the two priests filed into Charles's church, Trinity Episcopal, in Fostoria, where he informed the congregation of his personal tragedy. Then his fellow priest conducted the services.

On Good Friday, Charles boarded an airliner and flew to Houston. His wife stayed in Findlay to care for their children. His parents also remained behind. The elder Coits simply weren't up to the trip. A Tenneco vice president arranged for Charles to be met at the airport and driven to a house where he spent the night. The next morning he talked with a company lawyer, who advised him that he was being made executor of his brother's estate.

No one had been able to find a will, and since Clark was estranged from his wife and she was in New Orleans, Charles was the obvious choice for the role. His brother's body had been transferred from the coroner's office to the George H. Lewis & Sons Funeral Home, and Charles arranged to have his brother cremated. He directed the morticians to ship the ashes back to Ohio.

The bishop in Cleveland had arranged through a counterpart in Texas to have an Episcopal priest from Houston conduct the funeral service. Charles sat in the front row at the church, flanked by close friends and colleagues of his brother during the somber ceremony. Jill didn't attend the funeral.

As they walked out of the church following the service, Charles told his companions that he needed a drink. But they had one more stop to make first. The company executive took Charles to the funeral home, where the mortician asked if he wanted to see his brother one last time.

"He's in the box isn't he?" Charles asked, nodding toward the closed coffin.

The mortician assured him that was the case. "Well, then I don't want to see the body," Charles responded. He preferred to remember his baby brother as he had been in life, and had no desire to inspect the results of the mortician's skilled efforts to smooth over the terrible damage to Clark's shattered face and ruined jaw.

Charles had his drink at the home of one of his brother's friends, where his friends and colleagues from the company gathered for an old-fashioned wake. They swapped stories about the easy-going, fun-loving engineer, and they mourned. The next day, Charles attended Easter services at a Presbyterian church with friends of his brother.

After returning to Ohio, he scattered Clark's ashes over the Chagrin River, a few miles from the home in Gates Mills where they spent their boyhood together. A few months later, in October, Anna Dix-Coit's ashes were sprinkled over the same river. About a year after that, the ashes of William Clark Coit Sr. were also consigned to the tranquil waters.

A few days after Charles left Houston, Clark's will was found in a safety-deposit box at a local bank. Clark had made out the will and signed it on March 14, 1967, when William Andrew was still an infant and about a year before the birth of his namesake, William Clark Coit III. He left everything to his wife. She was also named executrix in the document.

He stipulated that he was leaving nothing to either Seth, who was then twenty-three months old and hadn't yet been adopted, or to William Andrew, or to any future children of his. He did so because he was ". . . conscious of the fact that the well-being, upbringing, and the education of my said children is the primary concern of my beloved wife, Jill Lonita Coit, to whom I leave all of my estate as above stated."

In the event that he and Jill died together in an accident, or she failed to survive him by thirty days, his estate was to be used for the care and education of his children and the remainder should be equally divided among them at the time the youngest of them reached the age of thirty. Another Houston friend of Clark's was named to oversee the trust account that would be set up for them. Jill's mother, who at that time was living in Harvey, was named as the alternate trustee and as guardian for the children in the event his wife didn't survive him.

The will did not specifically mention Clark's considerable company-related benefits, except for $756.36 remaining in his Tenneco Credit Union account and $2,525 in wages and vacation pay due to him at the time of his death. But it included the house on Sharpcrest, which had a cancellation policy that paid off the mortgage in the event of the death of the primary wage earner. With his death, the house in the Sharpstown County Club Terrace became free and clear for the widow. It was worth roughly $30,000.

Also listed in the will were a $6,000 cashier check from the Houston National Bank payable to W. C. Coit Jr.; $1,081 in a checking account at the Houston National Bank; fifty shares of the Philadelphia Life Insurance Company worth a total of $928 at that time; and one share of Midwestern Gas Transmission Company stock worth $121.

Personal property included furniture and personal effects worth $1,260; escrow refunded on a repaid loan at the First Mortgage Company of Texas of $556; a federal income tax refund of $205; the 1966 Ford station wagon valued at $350; a 1967 Ford two-door valued at $200; a 1970 Mercury two-door valued at $2,250; and a 1967 Ford two-door valued at $200.

Clark did not have a 1967 Ford two-door, but he had the 1957 T-Bird which, considering the excellent condition it was in, would have been worth at that time about $8,000 to $10,000.

When a Houston lawyer had the will probated for the executrix on January 26, Jill's address was given as 9809 Joel Street in Harahan, Louisiana. DiRosa signed as notary public on a statement she signed in New Orleans appointing attorney William M. Schultz to represent her in the proceedings in Houston. It was also noted that all the debts against the estate had been paid, including several doctor bills, $1,250 to Foley's, and $1,632.79 to the mortuary for Clark's funeral. B. B. swore out a deposition in probate court confirming Clark's death, former residence in Harris county, and the fact that to his knowledge the will was never revoked.

With his role as executor cut short, Charles returned to Houston to sign more legal papers. He remained there long enough to be interviewed by homicide detectives, then returned again to Ohio. More than twenty years after he made the sad journey, the grieving brother still hadn't heard another word from the Houston Police Department about the investigation into his brother's murder. And he talked directly only once more with his brother's widow. Jill telephoned him in Fostoria and asked where he had interred the ashes.

Charles told her he scattered them over the river, where the brothers had played as boys.

"You mean there's no place where we can go and put a stone?" she asked.

"No," Charles replied. "Because this is what Clark wanted."

They didn't talk again. Jill eventually paid for Clark's name and the dates of his birth and death to be inscribed in a niche on a memorial at a cemetery in

New Orleans. A few years later one of Clark's friends
visited the memorial, and was shocked at the dismal
condition it was in. When a complaint was lodged with
a cemetery employee the response was laconically
blunt.

"Well, don't worry about it," the employee said.
"There's nothing in there, anyway." Charles thought
creation of the memorial was an odd thing to do. But
people who knew Jill had learned to expect unortho-
dox behavior. It was in perfect character for her.

Houston police probably didn't contact Charles after their interview because they had nothing positive
to report about the investigation. Efforts to solve the
mystery began bogging down before the victim was
even put to his final rest.

The *Post's* "Public Protector" program reward offer
of $4,000 for information helping to solve the slaying
was never claimed.

In the meantime, DiRosa obtained affidavits stipu-
lating that Jill was attending a birthday party in New
Orleans on the night her husband was murdered. Seth
had just turned seven years old. One of the statements
was from a guest at the party who claimed to have
seen her at 7:30 PM. Another was from a guest who
stated he saw her there around midnight.

The affidavits were impressive, but they still left a
four-and-a-half-hour gap in her whereabouts that was
unexplained. Homicide detectives checked out flights
between Houston and New Orleans on the night of
Clark's death, but if they learned anything suspicious
they kept a tight lip about it with the public.

Jill made good use of the telephone while she was in
the hospital, frequently talking with B. B. in Houston.
She asked her old friend if he knew where Clark's
T-Bird was. It was still in the garage at the house.

"Now, Mac, I want you to have that car," she said.
B. B. conceded that he loved the car and would like to

buy it because it had belonged to his friend. He insisted he wouldn't take it as a gift, and would only accept it if he could pay her the fair market price. Jill was equally insistent. She wanted to give it to him. The ultimate fate of the car remained a standoff, and neither of the two shifted their position when they discussed it during subsequent calls.

DiRosa also talked to McCurdy about his client's determination to sign over the title to the Thunderbird to him, according to the Texan. As soon as the estate was settled, the lawyer reportedly said, the Thunderbird would be signed over to him. Several times DiRosa telephoned him to discuss Jill's company benefits or other matters, and invited him to come by New Orleans for a visit. The lawyer said he would pick up some tickets for the Saints' games and McCurdy could watch some professional football as a guest of his and Jill's. The Tenneco executive was just as stubborn and determined as she was. There was no way he would accept the car as a gift. After one of his telephone talks with Jill at the hospital, he was more convinced than ever that he had made the right decision.

She might need a friend in Houston sometime who would be willing to talk about what a good person she was, he says she told him. But nobody was going to buy a glowing character reference from the engineer, by giving him Clark's Thunderbird—no matter how much he wanted it.

"Jill, I want the car and I'll buy it," he told her. "As far as anything I could tell about you, I don't know anything for a fact." He pointed out that although she had bragged to him a few times, he couldn't tell anyone he thought she was evil. The time would come however, when he would revise that opinion and became convinced she was about as bad as could be.

Three years after McCurdy started looking after the car, he finally had enough and dropped it off at a local auto storage which specialized in T-Birds. Then he wrote registered letters and mailed them to DiRosa at his office, to Jill at the Tower Advertising Agency, and a third copy to her at her parents' address in Metairie. He advised them where the car was and said he was washing his hands of the matter.

DiRosa telephoned him about two weeks later and asked what was going on. "Well, the letter explains it. You're a lawyer," McCurdy pointed out. He said he was sick and tired of the game-playing and the car was no longer his responsibility. DiRosa wanted to know what the storage fees were.

"I don't know, and I don't care," the crusty engineer replied. "I don't have to pay it."

DiRosa sent a young man to pick up the car from the garage and drive it back to New Orleans. Coincidentally, the driver's uncle was a vice president with Tenneco, and the youth mentioned meeting a beautiful woman in New Orleans whose late husband was with the company. He said her name was Jill Coit. The executive told his nephew to stay as far away from the woman as he could.

Soon after the Thunderbird was delivered to Jill in New Orleans, she obtained a personalized license plate for it with the slogan, "Q. T. BIRD."

Long before the matter of the Thunderbird was settled, it appears authorities in Houston never got anywhere in bringing the Tenneco engineer's killer or killers to justice, and the investigation died on the vine. The McCurdys still mourned their friend, but they had accepted his death and their loss. Ginny never failed to remember Clark on the anniversary of his death, however, and she always had a memory or observation to dredge up and share with her husband. Charles Coit also telephoned every year about that time to chat with the McCurdys and reminisce about his brother and their friend.

Jill finally walked out the doors of the hospital, presumably cured of her suicidal depression. She was refreshed and primed for new adventure. She had enough of New Orleans and Houston for awhile, so she collected her sons and headed west to seek her fortune in California.

The boys were told that their father had died of a heart attack. The thought of their father dying a quiet, natural death was less traumatic than forcing their young minds to cope with the idea of murder.

About the time Jill arrived on the West Coast and was settling down in the Los Angeles area, back in Houston the divorce suits she and her late husband had filed against each other were dismissed by the Harris County Court of Domestic Relations. With Clark's death, the matter of the divorce and the promise of bitter legal wrangling over the couple's property and the boys had become a moot point.

By that time two new men had emerged in Jill's life.

Edwin Bruce Johansen was a wealthy, older retired businessman who lived on Barrows Drive in Los Angeles. There are two versions of how the lives of this odd couple crossed. Jill claims they met when Johansen sold her a warehouse, that she was sorry for the old man and helped care for him for two or three years. Other sources indicate Johansen was a longtime acquaintance of her and her family when they crossed paths again in California.

Whatever may have sparked the relationship, Johansen was apparently as enchanted with Jill as so many younger men were. The frail eighty-nine-year-old man traveled to New Orleans, and on July 20, 1973, signed a document signifying his wish and intention to adopt Jill.

DiRosa handled the legal procedures and paperwork for the adoption. Jill loved to drive, and after moving to California she frequently made the trip by

car back to New Orleans to visit with her family and
follow up on her various interests there. She stayed in
close touch with her lawyer there. He was the man she
went to when she needed legal advice.

According to the act of adoption subsequently filed
with the clerk of the court in Jefferson Parish, which
lies due south of the western end of New Orleans, Johansen had not remarried after the death in 1969 of
his wife, the former Mary Taney, and he had no surviving close relatives. The adoption was being carried out
in Louisiana because Jill's residence at that time was
in Jefferson Parish, according to the legal document.

The would-be adopted daughter added her consent
to the procedure and both she and her prospective
new parent declared that it was their wish that her
name be legally changed at the same time from Jill
Billiot-Coit to Jill Coit-Johansen. Jill, Johansen, and
two witnesses signed the document. DiRosa added his
signature and stamp as a notary public in the Parish of
Orleans, state of Louisiana. Jill had observed her thir-
tieth birthday five weeks earlier.

But she wasn't the only woman who was showing
intimate concern for the lonely, sometimes cantankerous old widower. Ann H. Schwartz, the wife of his
longtime accountant, Morris Schwartz, was also dem-
onstrating a strong personal interest in helping him
wind up his financial affairs during his final days. On
October 10, less than three months after he adopted
Jill, Johansen made out a will leaving his total estate
to his accountant's wife. She was also designated as
the executrix.

Johansen was a devoted Mason, and he specified
that in the event of Mrs. Schwartz's death, his entire
estate would go to the Masonic Lodge #381 F&AM,
in Oceanside, California.

His newly-adopted daughter wasn't even mentioned
by name in the will, but it was carefully worded to

specifically disinherit anyone claiming to be his "heir-at-law."

"If any person whether or not related to me in any way shall either directly or indirectly attempt to oppose or set aside the probate of this will or to impair or invalidate any of the provisions hereof and such person shall establish a right to any part of my estate, I give and bequeath to such person the sum of $1 only and no further interest whatsoever in my estate," the document stated. There seemed to be no question about it; Jill was cut out of any inheritance from her adoptive father. But the tug-of-war was just beginning.

On November 29, the old man again picked up a pen, and in his shaky handwriting, signed a new will leaving his entire estate after funeral and burial expenses to Jill. She was also named executrix. Similar to a stipulation in the earlier will, the new document carried a declaration that anyone challenging the provisions would be left with $1 and no further interest in the estate.

The will was witnessed by Louis A. DiRosa and an Oceanside, California, man, Noel L. Mares. In both wills, Johansen stipulated his wishes to be cremated and for his remains to be placed next to those of his wife in Santa Monica's Woodlawn Cemetery.

That was apparently the last of the wills, but the struggle over the disposition of his estate hadn't even gotten really started yet. Johansen died a peaceful, apparently-natural death on August 1, 1974, shortly after observing his ninetieth birthday. According to his wishes, he was given a Masonic funeral, cremated, and interred next to his wife. Then the fireworks began exploding in a three-way money squabble that would spark accusations that were incredibly bizarre even for California. Their echoes could still be heard around the court almost twenty years later.

Ann Schwartz filed for probate of the will naming

her as heir and executrix a month after Johansen's death. On November 25, Jill filed a petition in the Los Angeles County Superior Court seeking revocation of the action. Identifying herself as Johansen's adopted daughter, she said the document admitted to probate was not his final will. She produced a copy of the will naming her as heir and executrix. Although Jill was represented by a different attorney, she listed the Pere Marquette Building in New Orleans where DiRosa had his law offices, as her address.

By early the following year, relatives of the old couple had surfaced. Led by a niece of Mrs. Johansen, they were also becoming embroiled in the fray. In her own petition for revocation of the probated will, Frances Young Getze, of Newport Beach, accused the Schwartzs of taking grossly unfair advantage of a senile old man who was paranoid, belligerent, confused, and suffered from loss of memory. He was in such awful condition he didn't know what he was doing when he signed the purported will leaving his estate to Mrs. Schwartz, the niece contended.

The couple took advantage of Morris Schwartz's confidential relationship with Johansen and the old man's deteriorated mental health to ingratiate themselves with him and persuade him he was obligated to reward them, she said in the petition.

They allegedly convinced him he and Mrs. Schwartz were reincarnated souls who knew each other in a prior life. She was a queen and he was her slave, whom she had treated with kindness and consideration. Consequently, he owed her a debt for that kindness.

As 1975 neared its end, several additional distant relatives, including first and second cousins, had joined in the dispute to challenge both wills. Neither of them were valid because of Johansen's alleged senility and other mental problems at the time they were made out, they claimed. They also charged that Jill was not in fact his adopted daughter. And if he indeed made out a will naming her as his heir, he executed the document shortly before his death while he was "obviously sick in mind with a progressively deteriorating condition and . . . was easily influenced and controlled by anyone seeking to take advantage of him . . ."

When Jill filed her version of Johansen's will for probate in 1977, it was challenged by Mrs. Getze, just as the documents held by Mrs. Schwartz were.

The full story of the titanic struggle and its conclusion is still hidden in the awesome maze of the Los Angeles County Court system archives. But as recently as January 1990, a declaration for final discharge and order was filed releasing Ann Schwartz as executor of the estate. The document indicated she was the "sole distributee." Another document filed in superior court the previous year awarded a balance remaining in the estate of approximately $7,000 to Mrs. Schwartz after payment of a small amount of attorney and court fees.

So what happened to the rest of the estate? Despite later published denials by Jill that she didn't profit financially, according to her youngest son, she wound up with a considerable inheritance that included about $60,000 in cash, three or four houses, and some other property.

Jill didn't simply cool her heels while resolution of the dispute over Johansen's estate was being slowly played out in the courts. She had never been a woman known for letting grass grow under her feet, and she obviously would not be happy living the single life for long.

She had already changed her name again a few weeks before Johansen was bundled off to New Orleans to sign her adoption papers. On November 3,

1973, she tied the knot with a rugged thirty-three-year-old major in the US Marine Corps. Her married name wasn't really "Coit" when she was adopted. She was Mrs. Donald Charles Brodie.

The ceremony was conducted by a Lutheran clergyman, the Reverend Donald J. Fisher, in the city of Orange, a far suburb at the southwest edge of Los Angeles. Gerald and Mary Ellen Soma of Santa Ana stood up for the couple.

Jill indicated on her marriage license that she had been married only once before, and that her previous husband had died. She signed her name on the marriage certificate as Jill Lonita Coit and listed her date of birth as June 11, 1946, either two or three years after her true birth date. According to the information in the marriage certificate, she was twenty-seven years old, more than five years younger than the groom. Brodie had been married once previously, and was divorced in August 1969. He listed his occupation as the "USMC" and the kind of industry or business he was in as the "US Government." Jill gave her occupation as "model," and her industry or business as "advertising agency."

Both the bride and groom indicated they had sixteen years of formal education and listed the same address on South Ditmar Street in Oceanside, San Diego County. The picturesque coastal city of approximately 77,000 people is roughly midway between Los Angeles and San Diego at the southern edge of the sprawling Camp Pendleton US Marine Corps Base.

A native Hoosier and military career man, Major Brodie may have been as susceptible to his bride's sexual allure and mesmerizing charms as his predecessors. But he was no pushover when it came to handling the couple's finances and personal property. He was a strong man, and his reputed refusal to go along with his wife's demands was a surefire formula for serious trouble in the marriage.

Jill wasn't a woman who could live with her wings clipped and a crimp put on her high-flying ways. That wasn't her style, and any effort to restrict her freedom wasn't something she would put up with for long. It amounted to a declaration of war. She had her own business and other interests, and many other personal affairs were still centered half a continent away in New Orleans and even more exotic locales.

Back home in California, the honey in Jill's relationship with the marine officer rapidly turned to acid, corroding feelings, sensibilities, and emotions. Unhappy with the role of military wife, and blocked from getting her way, Jill packed up her sons and cleared out of Southern California.

Jill and the boys returned to New Orleans, the city of voracious mosquitoes, persistent mildew, distinctive colors, aromas, and tastes—and just enough of the hint of madness, brash dreams and opportunity about it to be irresistible. It was her childhood home, and it was perfect for her. She settled with her boys into a temporary domicile in the 9800 block of Joel Street in Harahan. A separate town of about 11,000 people in Jefferson Parish, Harahan is just below Metairie and it bulges snugly into one of the loops of the north bank of the Mississippi. It is a working-class town where rusty tugboats and fishing skiffs are tied to the piers and docks.

The new address would merely prove to be a stopping-off place where she parked the boys for awhile. A handy baby-sitter was nearby: their grandmother. And Jill's lawyer friend was no longer a half-continent away. The law offices of DiRosa & DiRosa, at 812 Pere Marquette Building, were a fast twenty-minute drive from Harahan. The sturdy old brick structure, only one block off Canal Street, New Orleans' main shopping thoroughfare, was about fifteen floors high, and in those days before the construction boom of the 1980s and 1990s it was one of a handful of buildings that dominated the skyline. It was a modern landmark.

FOUR

Louis

When Jill left California she was ready to embark on imaginatively challenging ventures and to hammer strong new links into her long, ongoing relationship with Louis DiRosa.

In some ways, the wealthy forty-seven-year-old lawyer was the perfect partner for her. He was knowledgeable, with legal and political savvy that could be invaluable to someone with Jill's hungry obsession for wealth.

He had already helped smooth her passage through some fretful times, and it wasn't easy keeping up with the legal and personal needs of a woman like Jill. Some of her enterprises were as quixotically off-the-wall as they were ingenious.

She hadn't lived very long with Brodie, certainly nowhere near the six years she spent with Clark Coit. But actions she took after returning to her hometown indicated the ill-fated union had lasted long enough for her to produce another son.

Jill claimed she was pregnant when she left California, and at 2 AM, on October 18, 1974, gave birth to a boy at 864 Roosevelt Place in New Orleans. She lived in Apartment B, and it appeared that delivery of her fourth son was a home birth.

The child was named Thadius John Brodie, according to a certificate of live birth authenticated by the Louisiana State Registrar. Boxes on the certificate for identification of the birth attendant by profession were checked off both for "MD" and "Other." A box to indicate the presence of a midwife was left blank. The name "T. Kisla" was signed in the space for the signature of the attendant. It was a name that would show up in different variations at other time's in the "mother's" adventuresome life.

Neither Brodie, nor it appears anyone else, ever saw Thadius. There was a good reason for that. There never was a Thadius John Brodie born at the New Orleans apartment building. The entire affair was a hoax.

DiRosa was having personal problems of his own by that time. His marriage of more than twenty-five years was crumbling.

Louis Anthony DiRosa and Marie Buffa were married on September 8, 1948, at the altar of the St. Louis Cathedral in the French Quarter. The stately basilica is one of the oldest active cathedrals in America and easily the most famous structure in New Orleans. For nearly two centuries, the famous as well as the little-known have attended mass and worshipped together at the cathedral and its predecessor.

Constructed on Chartres Street in 1849 after its predecessor was razed, the famous old cathedral faces St. Anthony's Square, where high-spirited Creole dandies, wealthy gentlemen, and military officers at one time fought bloody duels with *colche-mordes* (sword canes) or pistols over sloe-eyed New Orleans belles and matters of honor.

In more recent times the one-time *Place d' Armes,* or military parade ground, is better noted for the amateur and professional artists who sketch, paint, and peddle their work there; for peanut vendors; leftover hippies; beggars; lovers; casual passersby; and office workers on lunch breaks who share its simple enjoyments.

The wedding in the historic cathedral was an auspicious beginning for the couple's life together, and while Louis was busy building a successful career, Marie was providing him with a handsome family of two boys and two girls spaced nearly fifteen years between the first and the last. Claire Frances was born on November 29, 1950; Denise Marie on December 2, 1953; Louis Anthony DiRosa Jr., on October 18, 1956; and Daniel Anthony on March 20, 1963.

The family home was on Robert E. Lee Boulevard, in a suitably genteel and upscale neighborhood in the far north area of the city, only a few blocks from the scoop-shaped shoreline of Lake Pontchartrain. Through his successful law practice and other investments, DiRosa was able to provide well for his family, presenting them with a nice home and good educations for the children. As 1974 was drawing to a close he had accumulated community property valued at nearly $2 million and was earning about $300,000 annually, according to information in legal documents.

The documents were part of a divorce petition filed on December 6, by his wife. Marie accused her husband in the action of adultery, mental harassment, and abandonment. And she pointed her finger squarely at Jill as the other woman involved in the breakup of the marriage.

Marie claimed her husband and Jill had been carrying on an adulterous affair for roughly four years, and they used aliases at times to help cover up their activities and behavior. According to the documents filed in Civil District Court for the Parish of Orleans, Louis used the alias "Ladd DiRosa" and Jill used the name "Sandra Kelly."

If the allegations about a long-running affair were

true, the romance spanned the last, rocky years of Jill's marriage to Clark, her adoption by Edwin Bruce Johansen, her marriage to Brodie, and the years since her return to greater New Orleans. Jill was already carrying on her dalliance with the lawyer while she was leaving her husband and children behind in Houston to take off on business trips, and when Clark was murdered, if the time frame outlined in the divorce petition was correct.

Marie Buffa DiRosa didn't simply manufacture the information to back up her allegations out of thin air. She hired a private detective to check into the activities of her husband and the stunning woman who was spending so much time with him in business dealings and other activities the suspicious homemaker believed to be of a much more personal nature.

The choice of a private investigator was a good one, even though it could hardly have been further from the classic image of a crusty, hard-smoking, hard-drinking, woman-chasing gumshoe. She was no Mike Hammer.

Glenda Imburgia was a middle-aged, matronly woman, a real-life Jessica Fletcher with more meat on her bones. Her ordinary appearance was perfect cover for her profession. She was also bulldog tenacious, a quiet, serious professional who paid attention to detail and understood the most basic requirement of the job, one recognized by any sleuth worth his or her salt: legwork pays off. She searched through courthouse records, examined business dealings, looked through old newspaper files—and knocked on doors.

One of the doors she knocked on was at B. B. and Ginny McCurdy's house in Sharpstown. She talked with them at their home on two different occasions before she extracted enough information to satisfy her. One time she brought her mother along with her from New Orleans, and the women took the McCurdy's out to dinner. The PI told the couple she was working for Marie and trying to pin down how much family money DiRosa had invested in real estate or other business projects he and Jill were involved in. She also wanted to know how much money Jill had contributed to the joint ventures, and how much she received from Clark's Tenneco-related benefits.

One day after the private investigator had already spent months tracking Jill and DiRosa's movements and purchase of properties through Texas, Louisiana, and California, McCurdy telephoned her in New Orleans. The PI's mother answered the telephone and broke the bad news. Her daughter had died. But a good portion of her investigative work was reflected in documents filed with her client's divorce suit.

DiRosa was served with the divorce papers at his law offices in the Pere Marquette Building and retained attorney Sydney J. Parlongue to represent him. His wife was represented by another prominent attorney, J. Harrison Henderson III. Neither side in the domestic dispute was willing to simply roll over and give in.

Marie claimed her husband lived with Jill at a home in the 2100 block of Cleary Street in Metairie from January 7, 1971 through October 1974. At the end of October they reputedly moved to an apartment in the 3800 block of Dumaine, and an apartment at 864 Roosevelt Place, both in New Orleans. The apartment at Roosevelt Place was the location of Thadius's reputed birth. Both properties were owned by the Tower Advertising Agency, in which Jill was an incorporator and the majority stockholder.

The petition also claimed Jill was still married to Clark, but that was an error. At the time the divorce was filed, the Tenneco engineer had been dead more than two-and-a-half years.

Jill eventually bought a bundle of properties around

New Orleans. In documents identifying her as the widow of William C. Coit Jr., Jill took out a $255,000 mortgage on nineteen lots known as the Mid-City Baptist Church property on June 1, 1973.

A couple of months before buying the church property she had arranged to have herself named as the natural tutrix of her three boys, a legal maneuver that expanded her powers over the normal responsibilities of guardianship for her minor sons and their estates. At the time of the appointment in the Twenty-fourth Judicial District Court in Jefferson Parish, the total property said to be owned by the boys was appraised at a measly $4,666.66.

Peering at the legal strategem from the outside, it appears to be a curious action to take. But the hidden motivations and Machiavellian finagling that lurked behind Jill's surface behavior were seldom easy to figure out.

The divorce was quickly settled at a hearing on March 10, 1975. It was barely three weeks short of the third anniversary of Clark's death. After considering the pleadings and evidence offered by both parties and listening to the arguments of their attorneys, Judge Henry J. Roberts found for the plaintiff. He granted a divorce to Mrs. DiRosa and continued a previously-issued preliminary injunction, blocking her former husband or anyone acting with him or on his behalf from selling or otherwise disposing of or tieing up any of the community property. It was a broad-ranging order that applied to real estate, stocks, bonds, bank accounts, partnership interests, and other property they shared ownership in.

Exceptions were made for some personal and office bank accounts at several New Orleans banks for DiRosa and some personal accounts in the name of his ex-wife. The law practice remained with Louis.

Mrs. DiRosa was given custody of their last remaining minor child, Daniel Anthony, with visitation rights granted to his father. The newly-divorced lawyer was ordered to pay permanent monthly alimony of $250 to his ex-wife, and $750 per month in child support. The $1,000 total was to be paid in increments of $500 each on the first and the fifteenth of each month. DiRosa was also ordered to make mortgage payments, and to pay taxes, insurance, and electricity bills on the family home, as well as school tuition for Daniel.

Although the divorce itself was quickly settled, the contest over related matters dragged on for months, becoming a nasty marathon of accusations and denials.

Louis had taken a good shot in court, and the acrimony wasn't over yet, but the way was clear for the next act in the business and romantic saga he was playing out with Jill. On October 11, 1976, eighteen months after Marie obtained her divorce, Louis and Jill slipped off to Mississippi to tie the knot.

When she was a little girl, Jill may or may not have dreamed of marrying in the majestic St. Louis Cathedral, but it's unlikely she even considered that for her union with the lawyer. The Cathedral was for white dresses and at least the appearance of virginal brides, and Jill hadn't qualified at any of her weddings.

Temperatures in Louisiana were hovering in the high sixties, and the banana leaves and the ginger lilies were just beginning to turn brown when the couple drove northwest past Baton Rouge, then continued on through the plantation country and on across the Mississippi state line to Wilkinson County. There, in the quiet town of Woodville in the middle of nowhere, they repeated their vows in front of the Reverend O. B. Beverly. The ceremony was simple, as they tended to be at Jill's weddings. The bride gave her age as thirty-three. The groom was fifty.

Unsurprisingly for a couple who were so familiar with the workings of the courts, divorces, and such weighty matters as alimony and property rights, they signed a prenuptial agreement before repeating their "till-death-do-us-parts." The pact waived the Louisiana community-property laws and declared their property to be separately owned.

DiRosa knew his way around the divorce courts because it was his business to know, and he had recent personal experience as well. But Jill was no babe in the woods when it came to the marriage game either. She had logged in more experience than most brides and divorcees, and she knew how to protect her financial interests.

Her proximity and intimate relationship to the experienced lawyer was also adding to her knowledge of how to use the legal system to her advantage. She was alert, attentive, and eager to learn, and she acquired a smattering of knowledge about some of the convolutions and ambiguities that are such puzzling aspects of the law to most.

It was just enough knowledge to smooth the way for some of her business deals—or to get her into a peck of trouble if she became too ambitious and made a misstep. But Jill understood that her spouse was the lawyer in the family.

Looking back on the marriage years later, Nancy Reed, her longtime friend in North Manchester, observed: "She was attracted to men who could teach her lots about life." Nancy was impressed by the two of Jill's several husbands she had met, and thought they were nice, interesting people.

Jill helped arrange for her former high-school friend to move to New Orleans for awhile, and the young woman from North Manchester worked for Louis while she lived in the Crescent City.

When the tugboat captain's daughter drove home with her new husband after the wedding in Mississippi, she probably felt that she had at last acquired the credentials to move into a strata of New Orleans society where she had belonged all along. It was a world of personal prestige, power, money, and all the trappings of flash and luxury that go with it.

She wasn't a woman who got terribly excited about fixing a dinner at home, and she loved to eat out. New Orleans was perfect for that and offered nights of fine dining in a city where it may well be argued that its unique culinary arts are surpassed nowhere in the world, not even in Paris. Fine restaurants with world-renowned chefs, and smaller, more intimate eateries that were off the beaten path offered gourmet specialties with everything from Creole favorites like *crawfish étouffée* and gumbo to blackened redfish and rich desserts of pecan pie. There was always shrimp, prepared in a variety of manners, of course, and other fresh seafood appetizers of raw oysters, clams, and scallops.

Jill bought and wore exciting clothes and exquisite jewelry, drove sleek and powerful automobiles, and rubbed shoulders with male and female companions whose social skills were finely polished. Jill may not have vaulted all the way to the top of New Orleans society, and she and her husband weren't about to pull up stakes and leave Louisiana for a Palm Beach mansion, but she was living an exciting life. And she was accumulating more knowledge and wealth with every marriage. She was on the fast track. Doors of opportunity previously closed to her were opening, and she wasn't shy about continuing to pound at those that were still closed. The sky was the limit.

On September 19, 1977, almost exactly eleven months after the quiet Mississippi wedding, Jill and Louis married again. The reason? Jill loved wedding ceremonies. This time the early evening nuptials were performed in marshy St. Bernard Parish which curls under Lake Borgne at the southeastern edge of the Crescent City. The vows were repeated in the town of

Chalmette before Michael D. Roig, a justice of the peace. The bride's name on the marriage certificate was listed as Jill Billiot (Coit.)

The bride listed the address in the 3800 block of Dumaine Street, as her home. The groom listed 864 Roosevelt place as his domicile. Jill also identified the birthplace of her mother as Louisiana, rather than Indiana, and indicated on the license that she had completed four years of college. Her husband stated on the form that he had "5 +" years of college.

Jill indicated it was her second marriage, and that her previous union had ended in death. DiRosa also indicated it was his second marriage, and his first marriage ended in divorce.

Chalmette is best known as the site where advancing British troops were slaughtered by a rag-tag army of American frontiersmen including Tennessee sharpshooters led by General Andrew Jackson and a corps of ragged Baratarian pirates headed by swashbuckling buccaneer Jean Lafitte during the Battle of New Orleans. Tragically, the bloody confrontation occurred a few days after a peace treaty was signed between the American and British governments, officially ending the War of 1812. But because of the primitive system of communications at that time, the combatants didn't learn the war had ended until after the battle.

It's doubtful that Jill and her husband wasted any thoughts that night on the role of Chalmette in America's military or political history. They were concerned with more personal struggles and challenges. And, in fact, when they repeated their vows for the second time, their own history together was already rapidly nearing an end.

Less than four months later, according to court documents filed by the groom, the couple separated. Jill had kept busy buying up valuable property almost to the last minute, and a few weeks before the separation she took out a $100,000 mortgage and purchased another.

On February 1, 1978, however, she left behind her lawyer husband, the enticing business opportunities, and the sultry, moist heat that produces ugly tempers and prickly red blotches on the skin. Once more she headed north to Indiana, and the bleak, frozen, midwinter farm country of Wabash County. Her friend, Nancy, had already returned home, and Jill had other close ties there, as well.

FIVE

Eldon

Although Jill may have slipped relatively quietly into North Manchester when she was a teenager, she played out a complete reversal when she returned to the bucolic farm community ten years later. She blew back into town with all the subtlety of a hand grenade with the pin pulled out. And she didn't try to get her old job back at the book bindery.

By most local standards the former North Manchester High School dropout had metamorphosed into an accomplished woman of the world; an exotic and sexually-magnetic siren who had crisscrossed half the country and carried a passport stamped with the names of glamorous foreign locales (in those days) like Port-au-Prince in Haiti and Tegucigalpa, Honduras.

But she was a single mother with three sons, and she behaved like she was serious about putting down some strong new roots in the close-knit little community. She told friends she wanted to raise her boys in a safer, more wholesome environment than New Orleans.

Jill backed up her words by buying a farm a few miles northwest of town and began putting together a menagerie of animals there for the boys. She planted a garden, harvested the crops, and canned and froze the fresh produce. She also proved that she could put together an impressive meal. She was a fantastic cook, according to her friend Nancy.

Once she was back home, Jill renewed and cemented old friendships and made new ones. She was generous, and frequently surprised people she liked or wished to impress with fine gifts. She was charming, a great storyteller who had wonderful tales to spin about her travels, experiences, and husbands. An exciting air of mystery seemed somehow to always cling to her.

At the time, she was between husbands—sort of. During the winter of 1977 to 1978, when she swept back into North Manchester, she was still legally married to DiRosa, although divorce proceedings were already filed.

But she wasn't a woman willing to settle for being without a special man in her life for very long. As oldtimers in Indiana say, the flamboyant, effervescent beauty with the exquisite café-au-lait complexion was the kind of woman whose smoldering gaze could make a man's eyeballs sizzle.

She had barely swept back onto the scene in North Manchester with her boys, her flashy, expensive jewelry, and her snazzy red classic T-Bird before she attracted the eye and earnest attention of one of the community's most eligible bachelors.

Eldon Duane Metzger was a highly respected local farmer and businessman who had managed to hold onto his bachelorhood for thirty-seven years before his path crossed with Jill's. Various branches of the extensive Metzger family in Wabash County and other nearby northern Indiana communities had produced lawyers, teachers, doctors, nurses, secretaries, truck drivers, and practitioners of a host of other professions. The Metzgers sprung from solid, taciturn German Baptist stock, and when Eldon brought Jill along to family get-togethers, she livened up the normally-subdued, proper affairs.

Metzger was best known in North Manchester for his dual professions as an auctioneer and realtor. The Metzger Auction & Realty Company was a fixture in North Manchester. And just about every weekend when the weather was good, and often when it wasn't so good, Metzger could be tracked down in front of a local home in town or a Wabash County barnyard auctioneering household goods, farm equipment, real estate, and animals.

Metzger Realty helped her purchase a store building in Laketon, another little settlement of about 500 people a few miles southwest of North Manchester. It was known locally as Mary's Sundries and was a popular local hangout. Jill turned it into a luncheonette. Years later she dropped the luncheonette idea, and opened a noodle factory in the building. The boys helped their mother with the noodle-making, she said. Local residents remembered the noodle venture differently, however, and claim that except for being involved in a real estate transaction for the building, she had almost nothing to do with the business.

She was working hard to build up new businesses, however, and she was also occupied with more personal matters—building a relationship with the new man in her life.

Jill had the rare ability to spot vulnerabilities in a man, and she focused in on their weaknesses like a hungry cheetah surveying a herd of wildebeest. Men were her prey, and when she was on a blood-scent she didn't deviate from her target. She was a sultry temptress who could addle male minds with her sexual charisma, serve as a charming dinner companion, or chat knowledgeably about sports cars, guns, or business.

On March 14, 1978, Jill and the auctioneer drove across the Ohio line to the Allen County seat of Lima and filed an application in the probate division of the common pleas court for a marriage license. The bride identified herself to the license clerk as Jill Coit-Johansen, and stated that her union with Metzger would be her first marriage. Spaces on the form for listing of prior marriages and minor children were left blank. Her birth date was listed as June 11, 1943, her birthplace as Iberia, Louisiana, and her profession as secretary. In the blanks on the form for the name of her father and the maiden name of her mother, she stated they were Edwin Johansen and Mary Taney.

Metzger entered his birth date as July 14, 1940, his birthplace as Wabash County, Indiana, and his occupation as "farming." He identified his parents as Orville E. Metzger and the former Ellen Niccum. Curiously, both the prospective bride and groom gave their residence as Route 4, Manchester, in Jacob County, Kentucky. The tiny Cumberland mountain settlement of 1,800 people in the Bluegrass State is more than three hundred miles from North Manchester, in the Daniel Boone National Forest near the tri-state border with Tennessee and Virginia. And it is in Clay County. Manchester is adjacent to Jackson County, but there is no Jacob County in Kentucky.

Such minor inconsistencies in the filling out of personal details on legal documents weren't anything new when Jill was involved. The couple drove back to North Manchester to wait out the next few days until they could be married. A week later they returned to the old courthouse in Lima for the ceremony. Each of them signed their names—his as "Eldon D. Metzger" and hers as "Jill C. Johansen"—under a statement certifying that they were legally free to marry, according to Ohio laws. The statement read: "That neither of the said parties is an habitual drunkard, imbecile, or insane, and is not under the influence of any intoxicating liquor or narcotic drug, that neither has syphilis which is communicable or likely to become so and they have complied with the Ohio serological test. Said parties are not nearer of kin than second cousins, and there is no legal impediment to their marriage."

In the state of Ohio, as in other states, a former marriage that has not yet been legally dissolved constitutes a legal impediment to a new marriage.

But Common Pleas Court Judge Richard D. Heeter was obviously unaware that the bride was still married to a husband in New Orleans, and he performed the civil ceremony. This time when the couple drove back to Indiana, they returned as bride and groom. Jill's marriage to Metzger marked the second time she had committed bigamy.

She didn't get around to making an effort to officially cut her conjugal ties to DiRosa until she had already been married to Metzger for nearly eight months. In November she and DiRosa boarded flights to Port-au-Prince to obtain a Haitian divorce. The process required little more than Jill appearing before a civil court official on November 4 with a French and English translator and signing a one-page statement signifying she and her husband were incompatible and wished to be divorced.

The statement dissolving the fourteen-month union two days later specifically referred to the marriage on September 19, 1977 in St. Bernard Parish. The wife's name on the document was entered as Mrs. Jill J. Coit-DiRosa, and her domicile was entered as 864 Roosevelt Place, Apartment B, New Orleans. Her husband's domicile was listed as 812 Pere Marquette Building, New Orleans. It was the address of his law office.

The civil court functionary also ruled, "that the lady has the right to use again her former married name: COIT."

When the divorced couple left Haiti and flew back

to the United States, nothing had been entered on record in Port-au-Prince about Jill's marriage to DiRosa in Mississippi or about her latest marriage to Metzger.

The auctioneer got along well enough with Jill's boys, but she had other priorities that sometimes conflicted with her role as a mother. In her wanderings around the country while she flitted from husband to husband, the boys were a necessary burden. If she didn't exactly operate according to the old saying, "out of sight, out of mind," she sometimes came close. At least once she fixed up the basement of her home, so her sons could live downstairs most of the time, out of the way and out of sight of adults.

"It was always a different person, a different man," her youngest son, William III recalled years later. "She just . . . kept us in a little closet."

Jill was a busy woman, and she had to have help raising the boys and with her housekeeping. She liked the Old Order Amish and hired some of the plain, unassuming young women to help out with the homemaking. At one time she also arranged for a woman who was a Central American refugee to live with her and take care of the house. When the housekeeper worried about a child she left behind, Jill brought the youngster to live with them in Indiana.

It was that kind of generous behavior that endeared Jill to her friends in Indiana. Jill was a woman who seemed never to forget a card or a present for the anniversary or birthday of a friend. She worked hard at being a friend. Even then, though, some of her friends had second thoughts about her motivations for some of the things she did.

Nancy Reed later recalled in an interview with the hometown newspaper that Jill was the sharpest businesswoman she ever met. She was constantly "wheeling and dealing" and striving to get ahead. Reed said there was always a sense, however, that Jill wasn't being completely upfront. "She had so many stories, she had been so many places, done so many things, that after awhile you couldn't keep up and didn't ask all the questions that came to mind, because you knew you wouldn't get answers."

When the younger boys became old enough, she arranged for their education away from home in boarding schools or military academies. She squeezed every dime she could get out of the trust estates left by her former in-laws, the Coits, with pleas for money she said was needed to pay for the boys' educations.

Seth grew up closer to his mother than his younger brothers did, and as they gradually drew away from her, he seemed to grow closer. When he was thirteen, about the time his mother married Metzger, he began helping out at the office of a Manchester veterinarian. He held onto the job for several years, and as he grew older he also obtained experience in farming.

By the time he was twenty-one he was working in the little farming town of Nappanee at the edge of the Amish and Mennonite country in nearby Elkhart County at Holiday Rambler as an insulator and roof assembler.

Soon after their mother settled again in Wabash County, the two younger boys were enrolled at the Culver Military Academies, roughly fifty miles west of North Manchester along the north shore of Lake Maxinkuckee.

Maxinkuckee is the second largest natural lake in Indiana. The town of Culver, a popular summer resort of about 1,600 year-round residents, curls around the northwest shoreline where bathers congregate at a fine public beach during the warm summer months. But the Marshall County locale is best known nationally for CMA, the Culver Military Academies—Culver Military Academy, the Culver Girls Academy, and the Culver Summer Camps. Established in 1894 as the

Culver Military Academy for boys only, the expanded
program now draws both male and female students to
the 1,500-acre lakeside campus from throughout the
country and from foreign nations as far away as the
Republic of Korea, Thailand, India, Japan, Israel, Slo-
venia, France, and Spain for its fine prep-school educational opportunities and summer camping activities.
About twenty percent of the student body is from foreign countries.

Students at the tradition-steeped institution can
train for private pilot ratings at Fleet Field, the academy's own twin-runway airfield; learn sailing skills
aboard the *R. H. Ledbetter,* a three-masted sailing ship
or smaller watercraft; or become an accomplished
equestrian and polo player, along with mastering
traditional academics. Culver has the largest equestrian school in the United States, and since 1897 has
been home to the Black Horse Troop that has ridden
at ten presidential inaugurations beginning with the
presidency of Woodrow Wilson, and his vice-president,
North Manchester's famous son, Thomas Marshall.
The troop led the inaugural parade for President
Jimmy Carter.

Costs of obtaining an education at Culver are not
cheap. By the beginning of the 1994 school year, the
total for basic tuition and board at CMA and CGA
was $16,950. Hefty additional charges are tacked on
for special programs such as pilot instruction, the
Black Horse Troop, and the sister program for girls,
"equitation" (horsemanship).

But Jill's sons were enrolled at one of the premier
prep schools in the nation, with alumni who made
names for themselves in everything from politics, business, and the media to the entertainment industry and
the military. Michael Huffington, US Congressman
then an unsuccessful US Senate candidate from California; Will Van Rogers Jr., movie actor, congressman,

Battle of the Bulge tank commander, and son of famous humorist Will Rogers Sr.; actor Hal Holbrook; New York Yankees owner George Steinbrenner; and Pulitzer-Prize winning producer and director Joshua Logan are a few of the better-known graduates.

While her boys were at CMA being looked after by someone else or looking after themselves, Jill kept busy pursuing her quest for wealth. She collected and hoarded expensive toys, baubles, and easily-negotiable possessions like the T-Bird and diamonds. She stashed South African gold Krugerrands into three and four-foot lengths of two-inch metal pipe then sealed them by capping the ends. The valuable coins were a perfect fit.

"She was money mad, money mad," says McCurdy. A few years after Jill arrived back in Wabash County she had approximately $100,000 invested in certificates of deposit, and $150,000 in cash in addition to diamonds and gold and silver coins in her safety-deposit box.

She bought a used 1976 Mercedes to drive when she wasn't tooling around in the T-Bird, and added a Lincoln, two Porsches, a U-Haul truck and an Airstream trailer to her growing fleet of vehicles.

She also scanned legal advertisements in the *News-Journal,* the *Plain Dealer* in Wabash and in other area newspapers, and checked at the courthouses for tax-sale properties she could invest in. Other people's failures and disappointments turned into her opportunities and accomplishments. Eventually she acquired a house in North Manchester, two houses in Wabash, two farms, including one spread that was fifty acres, and approximately thirty pieces of tax-sale property in northern Indiana. She owned other pieces of real estate in Louisiana and Texas, including an $8,000 property in Austin.

Most of the properties were purchased under Tower

Advertising or other corporate names. Seth moved into the North Manchester house, which was purchased under the Nei Mar Corporation A few years later she made him an equal partner in the corporation.

Jill was a natural saleswoman and entrepreneur. She had a keen eye and ear for business and the personal charisma of a successful evangelist. She was also a devoted collector of licenses, diplomas, and certificates of accomplishment. She was credential-driven, and licenses and similiar documents were essential elements of her freedom and mobility. With the right license she could go almost anywhere and do almost anything.

If she wasn't out somewhere buying properties, she was attending night school or some other class in order to equip herself with new skills or hone old ones to a greater degree of proficiency. One of the schools she attended was sponsored by State Farm Insurance to train its agents.

While Jill was attending the school she shared a motel room with another woman. One evening after returning from classes Jill walked into the room and dumped the contents of her purse on her bed. Her roommate was shocked when a little pearl-handled pistol tumbled out onto the bedspread.

"What are you doing with that pistol?" the woman gasped.

Jill stared at her as if she was insane for asking such a question.

"You mean you don't have a pistol?" she asked. "Every woman should have a gun. How are you going to defend yourself?"

Jill's companion found herself apologizing for not carrying a gun and trying to hide her embarrassment. She had grown up in a small town where the streets were safe, and private homes were secure sanctuaries. Jill was from New Orleans, a big and violent city where people locked their doors at night and were as likely as not to barricade their windows with metal bars.

The way Jill explained it, packing a gun in her purse made a lot of sense. She had a way of turning things around, so that her eccentricities seemed suddenly not so curious anymore and anyone who didn't share them appeared to be the one who was out of step.

One of her girlfriends from her high-school days in North Manchester was visiting at her house once when Jill opened a dresser drawer. It was crammed full of handguns.

The same year Jill was licensed as a State Farm agent, she obtained a real-estate license, an auctioneer license, a nursery-dealer's license, and a health-food license. She began attending school to obtain a travel-agent's license but dropped out. Her health failed her, she explained.

In 1981 she took a trip to North Carolina where she got herself a gun license. She used the name Terri Kisla, a variation of "T. Kisla," the name used for the doctor or paramedic on the bogus birth certificate for Thadius Brodie. Jill also bought a tract of tax-sale property while she was in North Carolina.

Back home she ran ads in the *News-Journal* encouraging insurance shoppers to: "See me for car, home, life, health, and business insurance." A photograph run with the advertisement showed Jill's hair pulled away from her face and piled high in a bun. Large circular earrings dangled from her ears, and she was wearing a business-suit jacket with a tasteful high-necked blouse and a knotted scarf. Jill ran the busy agency from a yellow house on West Street, just off the main drag.

She was a hard worker, and a decade later she was receiving monthly checks from the company for more than $1,600 in residuals from policies she sold during her brief career in insurance. Jill often opened the doors at six-thirty in the morning to take care of business with factory workers before they checked in at their jobs. It wasn't at all unusual for her to stay on the job until seven or eight o'clock at night.

Eventually, during her travels around the country she collected driver's licenses from more than a dozen states, usually in one of her married names. She acquired a North Carolina driver's license, however, in the name of Jill Theressa Kisla. She also obtained an Alaskan voter-registration card.

Jill lived in some of the states where she acquired driver's licenses, such as Louisiana, Indiana, and Texas for years. In others—Arizona, California, Georgia, Kentucky, New York, New Mexico, and North Carolina—she stayed for only a few weeks or for a few months.

If Jill is to be believed, however, after she settled down in rural North Manchester tending to her duties as homemaker, mother, and businesswoman, a painful tragedy intruded on her busy life. She claimed to have given birth to another baby, and it died.

When stories first began circulating around town that Jill was pregnant and Eldon was going to become a father, it was considered good news. Jill's boys were growing up, and townspeople who knew the couple speculated that it would be about the best thing that could happen to the marriage to have a new baby in the house. At the time she was living in a farmhouse west of town, and she fixed up one of the rooms as a nursery. She showed the nursery off to her friend Nancy, along with baby clothes for the anticipated newcomer.

Jill, it seemed, was a woman who didn't gain much weight, even in an advanced state of pregnancy. She explained to her friend she never showed.

When the time came for the baby to arrive, however, Jill was out of town. She returned after a few weeks without the baby, and quickly resumed her normal routine looking as slim and feisty as ever. When people began asking questions, she explained the baby was afflicted with serious congenital defects and had to stay behind in a hospital incubator. One day when Worth Weller, the local newspaper publisher, ran into Metzger on the street, the newshound told the auctioneer how sorry he was to hear the tragic news about the baby.

"He just gave me a blank look," Weller recalled later.

According to Weller, a few days later his weekly newspaper, the *News-Journal* ran an obituary for Tinley Metzger, who it appeared had died in a hospital halfway across the country without ever drawing a breath in Indiana.

It was true that Jill had been back in New Orleans again, but she didn't go there to have a baby. She was still involved in legal wrangling involving DiRosa and his former wife, Marie. Jill was in New Orleans to provide a deposition, a legal term for testimony or a statement given under oath outside a courtroom.

Some of the questions asked at the December 14, 1978, confrontation were merely curious, others were exceedingly odd. "Have you used the name Jean or Gene Remington?," she was asked. "Are you related to the Rockefeller family?," and "Are you presently living with Elton Metsker?" The auctioneer's first and last name were spelled phoenetically by the court reporter.

Her attorney, Harry R. Cabral, Jr., refused to permit her to answer the questions, claiming Marie was merely attempting to humiliate his client. However, according to the records, she did state that she was not married at that time and was currently living in Princeton, Indiana. Princeton is more than 200 miles catty-cornered across the state from North Manchester, and the town of approximately 9,000 is in Gibson County near Evansville. Jill did not say anything about how she happened to settle so far from her more usual haunts in the northeastern area of the state. Another smaller Indiana town named Pierceton is only a few miles from North Manchester in adjoining Kosciusko County, however, leaving the question open that her statement may have been misunderstood during transcribing of the deposition tape.

Jill also didn't say anything during the deposition hearing about being pregnant with or giving birth to the auctioneer's child. The Metzger baby was another phantom, like Thadius, as difficult to grasp and pin down as the putative mother.

Early in 1979, Marie Buffa-DiRosa filed a lawsuit against Jill and her New Orleans lawyer, Cabral, accusing them of defamation of character. Cabral represented Jill in the divorce suit between DiRosa and Marie. Curiously, among the information filed with the suit, three separate Social Security numbers were listed for Jill.

The first Mrs. DiRosa sought a total of $300,000 from the two defendants for humiliation and mental suffering allegedly caused by a petition for injunction that Cabral filed in the Orleans Parish courts accusing her of making threats against the lives of Jill and her children. Cabral asked the court to issue an order prohibiting Marie from interfering with Jill Coit-DiRosa or her family in any matter whatsoever.

Through her attorney, Marie denied threatening or harassing Jill and contended the allegations were made in order to damage her character and reputation. She claimed the petition exposed her to "disrepute and ridicule and has lowered her in the opinion of her friends and family by picturing her as a jealous wife who would go to any extreme to cause harm to Jill Coit-DiRosa . . ."

In filing the petition for injunction, Cabral "acted recklessly, maliciously, and in wanton disregard of the truth," it was claimed in the lawsuit. Breaking down the requested judgment, Marie's lawyers asked for $100,000 for injury to her reputation in the eyes of her friends, $100,000 for injury to her reputation in the eyes of her relatives, and $100,000 for injury due to embarrassment and mental anguish caused by filing of the injunction petition.

The Jefferson Parish-based lawyer and Jill apparently avoided any serious damage from Marie DiRosa's spirited defense of her character. At her request, the suit was dismissed in August, less than four months after it was filed.

Seth was a teenager while Jill was coping with phantom pregnancies, depositions, and a Haitian divorce, and he was experiencing some troubles of his own. He was named in a paternity suit filed in the Kosciusko County Courthouse in neighboring Warsaw.

Jill was undaunted by all the fuss about babies. She was on a roll, frenetically collecting licenses, educational credits, and properties. She was obsessed with money and all its trappings, and was constantly scheming, plotting and mapping out new ways to accumulate more wealth. In 1980 she bought a three-year-old Porsche.

She also managed an amicable breakup with her husband and took up with another local man. He was the grown son of a well-to-do Wabash County farmer, and they were involved with each other after Jill moved out of her husband's farm home and into a historic home near North Manchester's downtown area. But Jill didn't invest too much of her time on the farmer's son before that relationship, like her marriage to the auctioneer, ended.

Other business and romantic interests were already developing a few miles west of North Manchester in an area of small farming communities that were very much like those in Wabash.

Wabash County is known for its scenic namesake river that winds southwesterly to Terre Haute where it dips almost due south and defines Indiana's western border with Illinois until it flows into the Ohio River at the tri-state juncture with Kentucky.

Jill was busily shuttling between North Manchester and Marshall County, where the best-known body of water is the 1,854-acre spring-fed Lake Maxinkuckee. The town of Culver and the Culver Military Academies are located on it's shores.

SIX

Carl

"I had some of the best training that the world has to give. . . . I think in terms of mental and emotional toughness, was the Marine Corps. If you're gonna lead marines you need to be more than just physically tough. You have to be mentally and emotionally tough. And I was prepared for that. But I wasn't prepared for the likes of her."

Carl Victor Steely,
Interview with author

The pace in Culver, Indiana, was slow, and the people were friendly.

A huge chunk of the local economy was geared to visitors attracted to the academies and to vacationers who settled into rental cottages and boarding houses or motels to take advantage of the recreational activities provided by the lake. For generations, Maxinkuckee's cool waters have offered opportunities to swim, fish, boat, water-ski, or simply sunbathe and shake off the pressures of the workaday world for awhile.

Little more than a half-century ago, in the days before electricity transformed refrigeration, harvesting of lake ice was still a major commercial wintertime undertaking. One year shortly after the turn of the centruy, robust ice-gangs harvested an incredible 40,000 tons of ice from Maxinkuckee. Some of the workmen were paid in gold from a local bank for their frigid labors.

Historians agree the lake's name is a Potawatomi Indian word, but translators have never quite settled on the exact meaning. Some have translated "Max-inkuckee" to mean "clear waters." Others believe "peaceful waters" is the correct translation, and still others say "high land and good water" is the proper meaning.

Civil War general Lew Wallace, a native Hoosier, wrote part of his epic historical novel, *Ben Hur*, at a popular Culver lakeside hostelry, Allegheny House. Broadway director and composer Joshua Logan at-tended elementary school in Culver, and Buffalo Bill and World War I General John J. "Blackjack" Per-shing, who later chased Pancho Villa, visited the resort community. The Potawatomi were long gone by those days, broken in spirit and decimated in numbers after being sent off in 1838 to a reservation in Kansas in a forced march that became known as the "Trail of Tears."

The attention of modern citizens of the town is fo-cused on happier events, and each July back to back weekend celebrations, the Culver Lakefest, and the Corn Roast and Firemen's Festival draw huge crowds of people from surrounding communities to the small town.

But when Jill wheeled into the postcard-pretty little lakeside town to check on her two younger sons at Culver Military Academy she wasn't looking for festi-vals, good neighbors, or a picturesque new home.

New surroundings meant new business opportuni-ties. And if the timing and situation were right, they might also lead to a new romance and a pliable new man in her life.

Carl Victor Steely was the commandant at CMA, and he was just the kind of man she needed to fill the recent void in her life. Except for one glaring deficiency, a lack of property or ready cash, he was excellent husband material.

A tall, spare, ramrod-straight man with glasses, penetrating blue eyes, and thinning hair cut military-close and doorknob-smooth, Steely had recently undergone some dreadful personal and financial reverses. He was at a low point economically. He had gone through a painful divorce and had to close down a flying school he operated in Florida with several partners that left him deeply in debt.

But he had a responsible job at CMA, and as Jill quickly learned when she glided into his life, he was an only child who anticipated a hefty inheritance when his aged mother in Kentucky died.

After lonely months of bachelorhood, the commandant suddenly found himself making the dating scene once more, strolling the lush, heavily-wooded academy campus, sharing long drives around Marshall County in a sporty red T-Bird, and dining out with a delightfully entertaining and lovely companion. Culver residents became used to seeing them holding hands as they pedalled twin 10-speed bicycles side-by-side along the tree-lined streets of the resort town.

Jill was cultured and intelligent. She told the commandant she was a graduate of the exclusive Newcomb College, an all-girls' school with a campus that adjoins that of Tulane University in New Orleans. It was there, while she was studying drama at Newcomb, that she met her late husband, "W. C.," she said. Jill had taken long ago to calling her late husband by his initials; there was something classy about it. Jill, of course, had attended Tulane, not Newcomb.

At first, there were long, serious discussions about her sons. She was concerned one of the boys wasn't doing well enough with his studies and needed additional help. But the conversations quickly became more intimate and turned to personal interests they shared like horseback riding, sports cars, traveling, flying, and skiing.

Steely was an athletic man and a licensed pilot. He bicycled, rode motorcycles, and perhaps most importantly, was an avid skier. Skiing was a sport Jill also shared a healthy interest in. During winter breaks around the Christmas and New Year's holidays, Steely liked to board an airliner and fly to Colorado to spend a few days or a week on the slopes of one of the ski resorts clustered in the Rocky Mountains. About the only major ski resort in the state he had missed was Steamboat Springs, a picturesque community of about 6,000 people nestled in the fertile Yampa Valley a drive of only an hour or so from the Wyoming state line. He was determined to try out the slopes there at the first opportunity.

But one of the most appealing characteristics to Steely about the sexy woman he was squiring around Culver, was her ability to discuss the Bible so knowledgeably and with such insight. The CMA commandant was a former Southern Baptist minister who had once pastored his own church in Kentucky about twenty miles up and across the Ohio river from Cincinnatti. Jill told him that she too was raised as a Southern Baptist, and she could match him word for word and thought for thought when it came to quoting verses of the Bible or analyzing parables and lessons. They began attending church services together.

"That's what really drew us together," he says.

The son of Arthur Dilman Steely, a family doctor in Kentucky, and Thelma Christine Steely, a homemaker, the lanky young man felt a sincere calling for the ministry. He enjoyed his work, but he was troubled that he was too young and didn't have the experience to counsel members of his tiny flock about such intimate matters as problems with their marriages and other troubles.

"I realized, in the ministry, I was trying to counsel people about their problems, and I really led a very sheltered life . . . I really didn't understand people's problems."

He decided a good way to gain experience, while seeing the world, was to join the Marine Corps. As far as matters of personal safety were concerned, Steely's timing was fortunate. The Korean War was winding down, and the the US military wasn't yet bogged down in the war in southeast Asia. Steely began his brief military career as a second lieutenant, serving at the US Marine Base at Quantico, Virginia, before he was given a duty assignment to Camp Fuji, the US Marine Corps Base at the foot of Mount Fuji in Japan. He wound up his four-year Marine Corps enlistment at the Parris Island Marine Corps Recruit Depot just outside Beaufort, South Carolina.

Older, more experienced, and presumably wiser, after his stint in the marines Steely shifted gears and entered what he now calls "the ministry of education." A former marine friend he knew at Parris Island told him about an opening on the faculty of the Florida Military School in Deland, a few miles inland from Daytona Beach.

Steely stayed there for seven years. He also got together with some business acquaintances and formed the Piper Acceptance Corporation. The group established a flying school at nearby Sanford on Lake Monroe and the St. John River. Initially, they also sold airplanes but eventually decided to concentrate on teaching other people to fly. It was more profitable.

Things began turning sour at the flying school, about the time a new federal statute was passed permitting the Drug Enforcement Administration and other law enforcement agencies to seize cash, real estate, and other property including cars, boats, and airplanes purchased with drug profits or used in drug trafficking. As the DEA cracked down on smugglers in the Miami area, some of the drug-runners began to move their operations further north. Steely says he and his partners realized they had almost no protection against the possibility that one of their instructors might use one of their aircraft to make a drug run. Students or pilots who rented their aircraft could also bring the law down on them, and they could lose their small fleet of Pipers and everything they owned. They wouldn't even be able to get insurance.

Then they learned that one of their pilots may have already been involved in drug-running, Steely says. According to the forfeiture law, the government doesn't have to prove that the owner is a criminal, only that the property was used in commission of a crime or bought with crime-generated funds. Steely and his partners reluctantly decided to fold their business.

In 1966 when a job opportunity became available at CMA he left the Florida Military School and moved to Culver. He was an energetic man, and while attending to his duties at CMA, he added to his collection of degrees by earning a Masters in Business Administration from the University of Notre Dame. The Notre Dame campus is a thirty-five-mile drive northeast of Culver.

Less than a week into the new year, on January 6, 1983, the couple were married on the campus inside the stately Culver Memorial Chapel. CMA Chaplain David R. Pitt conducted the ceremony. It was a typically frigid northern Indiana midwinter day, and a few hundred yards outside the chapel, the bulky figures of hardy fishermen dotted the lake where they huddled over holes chopped in the ice and angled for fat crappie, yellow perch, bluegill, and an occasional catfish or pike.

Jill may have still been married to two or three men at that time. Many aspects of her intricate life are murky, and a decade later private investigators, legal authorities, and journalists were still trying to sort them out. There was difficulty locating any records showing she and Metzger had divorced, and the auctioneer was keeping a tight lip on the subject although he eventually told a local reporter his marriage was dissolved.

But there was no question the Haitian divorce from DiRosa was invalid. She was committing bigamy for the third time, and may have been married simultaneously to three men.

Jill and DiRosa still hadn't gotten around to obtaining a legal US divorce that would stand up in the American courts. Less than a month before she and Steely stood together at the altar in the academy chapel, a judge in the Civil District Court, Parish of Orleans, declared the Haitian divorce to be invalid.

The pre-marital agreement signed before the weddings in Mississippi and in St. Bernard Parish appeared to be at the heart of the belated legal move initiated by DiRosa. The New Orleans lawyer filed a petition for declaratory judgement to invalidate the divorce. He stated that he and Jill were both residents of the United States and travelled to Haiti for the sole purpose of obtaining a divorce. Consequently it should be declared invalid, and the prior marriage recognized, DiRosa stated. He asked that the pre-marital contract waiving community assets and providing instead for institution of separate property rights be confirmed by the court.

On December 14, 1982, Judge Henry J. Roberts Jr., issued an order complying with the request. Jill, who was named defendant in the action, once again wound up apparently married to two husbands at the same time—DiRosa and Metzger. Three weeks later she added Steely to the roster.

DiRosa didn't obtain an American divorce from Jill until the summer of 1985. He represented himself in the proceeding filed in the Civil District Court, Parish of Orleans. At that time Jill had been married to Steely more than two years, and may have still been married to Metzger as well.

Nevertheless, a few weeks after the ceremony on the Culver campus, the bride and groom visited Carl's mother in Louisville and reaffirmed their marriage by again repeating their vows in a church. This time they were taken with the Reverend Carmen Sharp officiating.

The marriage, followed by the reaffirmation, marked a break from the tradition Jill had established of out-of-town rituals conducted quickly and quietly. For her initial marriage to Steely, however, she didn't even bother slipping off to another state to obtain a license. They drove fourteen miles to the Marshall County Courthouse in Plymouth for their license. Judge Michael D. Cook waived the usual waiting period for the couple.

On the application for marriage license, both the bride and the groom listed a post-office box at Culver Military Academy as their address. Jill named her three sons, Jonathan Seth and the two Williams, as dependent children. There was no mention of Thadius, or of a child born to her while she was living with Metzger.

Steely had experienced his own problems, including the 1982 divorce from his wife of ten years, Jody Hollowell MacGregor-Steely. His earlier union produced four children. The three girls and a boy were scattered around the South, two in Florida and one each in Virginia and Georgia. Jill stated that her last marriage ended in the death of her husband. She also indicated her parents were living in Texas.

Steely gave the date of his birth as September 8, 1930, and his birthplace as Kentucky. Jill listed her birthday as June 11, 1944. It was the same date used for her marriage to Ihnen. But it was one year later than on documents for her previous marriages to DiRosa and Metzger and three years earlier than the date provided when she married Brodie. Her birthplace was given as Louisiana, and she signed her name as Jill Coit.

There was no mention of Metzger, DiRosa, or any of her other previous husbands, except for the late engineer in Houston, whose last name she was still using.

Jill hadn't cut all her ties to Wabash County, and for several months she continued making the roughly forty-five-mile drive between the two communities several times a week to take care of her varied business interests in North Manchester.

New crops were already springing green and sturdy from the rich loam of Wabash County, and farmers were in their fields on tractors breaking up the soil to prepare it for planting when she reported to the North Manchester Police Department that she had been assaulted and robbed at knifepoint in her State Farm Insurance Office.

Armed robbery is not a crime that commonly shows up on the police blotter in the quiet farming community. Petty thefts, public intoxication, occasional minor hell-raising by exuberant teenagers after a big game, and physical violence or threats between spouses are more likely to be logged as offenses. North Manchester even has an occasional murder; but armed robbery? No! Nevertheless, despite the local rarity of such a serious crime, when hometown journalist Worth Weller made his routine police-beat check there was nothing on the blotter to tip him off to the reported robbery.

Weller and the *News-Journal* didn't know anything about the report of a major felony occurring on West street, a five-minute walk from their offices, until they read about it in a competing newspaper. The *Plain Dealer* in nearby Wabash ran a story about the robbery report.

Weller and his wife were near Jill's age, and they had a friendly relationship. Like the State Farm slogan says, Jill was a "good neighbor," and she had bought gifts for the Weller children. The small-town journalist was embarrassed and outraged. He stormed across the street and down the block to confront the police chief and find out how he was scooped and what was going on. The local police were usually cooperative and as open as law enforcement ethics and good sense would allow, but they were strangely reticent to talk about the report.

According to Jill's account, she was working late at her offices on May 23, 1983, when a man telephoned and said he wanted to buy some life insurance. She had withdrawn $1,600 from the nearby Francis Slocum State Bank earlier that day to buy a graduation present for one of her sons, and still had the money with her when the stranger showed up about seven PM.

Preparing to fill out the paperwork, she asked who would be making the payments for the insurance. At that time the customer pulled out a knife and growled, "You are."

Jill reported that he took the $1,600, forced her to slip a ring off her finger and give it to him, then threw her on her back, kicked her several times, and tied her up. After freeing herself from the rope, she was driven to the Wabash County Hospital where she was treated for a bump on the head and a bruised rib. Jill told police she had never seen the man before, and didn't recognize the name he used. It was assumed the name was an alias.

Weller left the police headquarters with the firm impression that the local lawmen were so uncharacteristically quiet about the case because they were suspicious about the legitimacy of the report. A decade later the current police chief, who was a patrolman when the report was filed, still didn't want to talk about it.

The *News-Journal* ran the story in its May 30 edition. Although it appeared near the top of the front page with the headline "Suspect At Large After Armed Robbery," it was about as short as it could be: two paragraphs of one sentence each. Police Chief Buddy Hittmansperger was quoted as saying the robber was known to police but hadn't yet been located. That was the end of the news coverage of the chilling downtown knifepoint stickup.

Curiously, however, at some time after the reputed armed robbery, the incident was somehow transposed into a rape when Jill discussed it with acquaintances. One of her closest female friends visited to comfort her while she was in bed recovering from what the insurance agent described as a violent sexual assault. Years later the incident would be referred to in court by two attorneys as a reputed rape rather than as a robbery.

Jill's trauma over the dreadful assault was ultimately eased with monthly disability payments from State Farm and from Social Security, based on her reported head injury. Characteristically, even years later State Farm authorities were close-mouthed about the incident. Claim records are confidential, they pointed out.

In Culver, Jill's life with her new husband was proceeding in more orderly, less traumatic fashion. But an exact rundown on the intimate details of the married life of the one-time Kentucky preacher and the fast-stepping Southern belle depends on whose recollections are tapped.

In legal documents filed at the courthouse in Plymouth, Jill claims that from the beginning the couple had a platonic relationship. Her descripton of the marriage indicates it was purely a business deal that included her agreement to advance her husband thousands of dollars in interest-free loans over a period of years to bridge the gap between his earnings and his expenditures.

Jill says it didn't bother her that Carl was broke, "because he was a Christian and [that] he would never take from me. After all," she added, "he told me he was a former Baptist minister."

According to her account, she wanted him to help her youngest son. At that time Steely was in debt and living by himself in a $75-per-month room at the Culver Inn on the Academy campus. He was still saddled with payments stemming from his flying-school venture. And his only personal possessions were a sofa and his clothing. Even the vehicle he was driving, "an old beat up green car, about a 1976 Chevy," belonged to his mother, she claimed. By contrast, Jill was a woman of considerable means.

Consequently, in return for his assistance with her son she agreed to help him live the lifestyle expected of a senior member of the CMA faculty. Steely earned roughly $30,000 annually at the Academy, but his income was eventually expanded by another approximate $2,000 from nearby Ancilla College where he began teaching geology and other courses part-time in the late 1980s.

The worth of Jill's possessions and income from the properties she owned, stock earnings, her work in real estate and insurance sales and other earnings amounted to considerably more. One of her farms in Wabash county brought in about $600 per month. Her income also included combined disability payments totalling approximately $1,200 per month from Social Security and State Farm for a brain injury reputedly suffered during the reported robbery/rape in North Manchester. The Social Security payment was $520.

Residuals from past insurance sales boosted her monthly income by almost $1,000 more, so her total checks from State Farm alone amounted to $1,644. The disability payments from both sources were tax free.

The money reportedly borrowed from Carl's new wife was to be paid back within six months of the time his mother died and he came into his inheritance. The old woman's estate was expected to be worth in the neighborhood of $400,000. As part of the agreement, Jill said she expected Carl to provide her with dental and medical insurance, and after he obtained his inheritance to loan her money if she needed it.

A document Jill identified as a promissory note dated December 31, 1983 and carrying signatures with the names of herself and her husband indicates she loaned him or paid out money for his bills and other expenses amounting to $30,000. Another note dated on December 20, 1984 was for $40,000 she claimed was advanced to Steely during the second year of their marriage.

But Steely claims the marriage was much more than a loveless, business deal. It was a normal romantic marriage, in which sexual relations played a traditional role. He says that he and Jill were husband and wife in every way. He also denied signing a special pact outlining proposed living arrangements and signing the promissory notes.

Steely was aware that Jill had a partial hysterectomy when William Clark III was born or shortly thereafter and could not have any more children. There were never any female sanitary items around the house, and if she had the need for such things she wouldn't have made a secret of it, he says. She wasn't shy about matters of that type.

She did keep several handguns around the house, however. Jill hadn't broken off her love affair with guns, and her husband was aware that she carried a small pistol in her purse. As a former marine, he was familiar with firearms, and her affection for guns didn't bother him at all. He was proud of her knowledge of weapons, and pleased that she knew how to use them.

Steely recalls that Jill told him one time soon after their marriage that she was afraid of Charles Coit because he believed she murdered his brother. Don't ever answer a knock or a ring at the door by simply opening it up; always make sure you know first who's outside, she cautioned him. "He's after me." Steely had never met Charles Coit, but he knew he was an Episcopal priest. It seemed difficult to believe he was such a threatening or violent man that Jill would be afraid of him.

The commandant's new wife was full of surprises. Just about a week short of their first wedding anniversary, the couple flew to Port-au-Prince and obtained a quickie Haitian divorce. The papers were signed and the divorce was granted on December 29, 1983 and validated by a government functionary in front of a French and English translator. Jill stated that "an incompatibility of temperament" existed between her spouse and herself. She claimed they had separated the previous June.

Civil Registrar Emeran Cineas added once again, as another Haitian bureaucrat had done five years earlier: ". . . the lady has the right to use again her maiden name: COIT."

According to Steely, Jill explained the paper divorce was necessary for tax purposes. The couple returned to Culver from their brief trip to the Caribbean in time to celebrate the New Year, and carried on their married lives just as they had before the divorce. Looking back on the curious proceeding a few years later, Steely, described the Haiti trip as a honeymoon.

Despite, or perhaps because of the perplexing quirks in her behavior, Jill was an exciting and entertaining woman to be married to. Steely was impressed by her keen business sense, and he loved her humor and her energy. She was an exciting woman of the world, who told wonderful stories, and could concoct dramatic epics from the most miniscule incidents.

She also confided that her late husband, W. C., was chairman of the board at Tenneco, Carl later recalled. Furthermore, her lawyer husband from New Orleans was a federal judge. It's true today that DiRosa eventually moved up to the bench. But when he made the move, it was as an elected member of the civil district court, a position that falls far short of the responsibilities and prestige that goes with appointment to a seat on the federal bench.

The couple settled into a large tree-shaded two-story house at 203 Lakeshore Drive in Culver, a casual ten-minute walk from the public beach. Neatly-tended flower beds that bloomed with peonies, Indiana's state flower, and other brightly colored blossoms, sprouted in the back yard and decorated the approaches to the house. Jill bought the attractive neo-colonial style home in June for approximately $70,000 with proceeds from the sale of her house in North Manchester. Ownership was listed under the Nei Mar Corporation.

They also upgraded the diverse fleet of vehicles Jill had brought to the marriage. In 1984 she traded in her 1977 Porsche on a rugged new utility vehicle, a Toyota 4-Runner. They bought their own U-Haul truck, an Airstream Trailer, and spent about $7,700 at a dealership in South Bend to have a new transmission and new engine installed in Jill's 1976 Mercedes.

The couple jointly purchased a forty-acre parcel of North Carolina mountain property worth more than $20,000. Jill was the sole owner of another property there valued at more than $5,000. She also continued to scan area newspapers for tax sales and occasionally submitted a bid but didn't make any additional local real estate purchases. While she was in North Carolina she also obtained a driver license, using the name, "Jill Theressa Kisla." She gave her birthday as June 11, 1946, and signed the license in her distinctive straight-up-and-down script.

Tower Advertising was already registered in Indiana, and she used the company for her earlier tax sale purchases. But she also formed a new corporation, Coit International, and plunged into a couple of challenging businesses in the lakeside community. One was a cab company. A woman acquaintance who lived at the Academy came up with the idea for the venture, and they went into the business as equal partners, according to Jill. The taxi service was established exclusively for transporting students and families at CMA to and from area airports, usually either to the Plymouth Municipal Airport or thirty-five miles to the Michiana Regional Airport in South Bend. The South Bend airport is the closest facility to Culver that was served by commercial airlines.

When her partner moved to Turkey, Jill brought Seth in to operate the taxi business, she says. He had left Holiday Rambler at Nappanee and was employed for a year at the Dollar General store in Plymouth, spent a few months teaching water safety to summer school students at CMA, and worked at a lumber yard before going on the payroll at Culver Taxi.

Jill was the sole owner of the other business she opened. The Culver Bed and Breakfast was operated out of her home, and she set it up exlusively for Academy-connected guests. She claims she started the bed-and-breakfast because friends of her husband were taking advantage of their hospitality for frequent overnight stays, and she decided she might as well put things on a paying basis. The inn was listed in a booklet published by the Marshall County Convention and Tourism Commission, and included in other material recommending accommodations for visitors to the area.

Jill's darkly-handsome oldest son also pitched in and assumed a key role in operation of the bed-and-breakfast. Seth kept in good physical condition, and he was constructed like a body builder, with big shoulders, a barrel chest and heavily-muscled upper arms. He moved into the house, where he cooked, baked, and functioned as the general manager. Jill and Seth were close, and he became somewhat of a confidant for her.

The other boys, who spent most of their time in prep school, didn't form the same strong emotional ties with their mother. It was difficult to become firmly attached for very long to any of the men in their mother's life, either. There was such a parade of them. The boys looked at her husbands, the various men she was involved with, simply as their mother's friends, according to Jill's youngest son, Billy, years later. It seemed there was always a different man around.

For awhile Seth attended Vincennes University a couple of hundred miles downstate from Culver. The two-year college is in the historic city where British forces surrendered Fort Vincennes to George Rogers Clark in 1779 during the Revolutionary War. The school has a strong agriculture and pre-veterinary program, but Seth obtained an associate degree in business in 1987. Later he returned to Northern Indiana and enrolled in courses at Ancilla College where Carl taught part time. Jill also attended some general business courses at the independent two-year community college and took additional classes at Indiana University Extension Campus in South Bend. Her youngest son, William Clark III, was shipped off to upper Michigan to complete his prep-school education.

"Jill is a very bright woman, very bright. She's an entrepreneur who likes to start businesses, get things going, and then move on to something else," Steely recalled.

The prep-school educator's personal and professional financial fortunes weren't improving, and a few years after the marriage he moved from the position of commandant to a job as a dean. Later he became assistant director of admissions. But he also formed a corporation of his own.

Despite the setback, the couple continued to live their affluent lifestyle. Jill was no longer as enthusiastic about cooking as she had been when she first returned to North Manchester, and her husband didn't have an opportunity to sample any Cajun or south Louisiana dishes whipped up in their own kitchen. Although she could still put together a tasty basic meal if it was necessary, they usually dined out, sampling the menus at some of the finer restaurants in Marshall County or in nearby Starke, Pulaski, and St. Joseph counties. South Bend was only about a fast hour's drive away.

They continued to maintain the fleet of cars. Jill dressed in flashy and expensive clothes. During the long summer vacation period at the Academy, the couple took the opportunity to make frequent trips around the United States and out of the country together. "We skied the world," Carl later recalled.

During their travels they collected passport stamps from Curaçao, Argentina, Ecuador, Australia, New Zealand, Luxembourg, and Switzerland. Jill browsed in some of Europe's toniest shops. But she also bought two fur coats on separate trips to Zurich from a used-clothing store that one of her sons discovered. One of the furs cost $140 and the other $107, in American money.

Closer to home, Steely made frequent trips with his wife to North Manchester and other locations in Wabash County where she had property. The prep-school educator was impressed with the friendship that seemed to still exist between Jill and Metzger. He later remarked to a news reporter that they seemed to be better friends after their divorce than they were before. Jill said she divorced her husband in North Manchester and Steely believed her. But like many things related to Jill's life and associations, locating records of her divorce from Metzger was difficult to do.

Two days before Christmas 1985, Thelma Steely died. She left an estate valued at $151,000, far less than half the amount her son and his wife had anticipated. There would be enough to repay the $70,000 worth of promissory notes, with some to spare. But it was already December, and it would be several weeks, perhaps months, before the estate was finally settled. A week after his mother's death, according to documents on file at the Marshall County Courthouse, Carl signed another $50,000 promissory note with his wife. The authenticity of the documents would be seriously questioned.

The elderly widow also left Carl antique furniture, including a cherry canopy pencil-post bed, a Queen Anne swing-leg game table, and a mahogany Martha Washington chair, as well as other personal property. Many of the old woman's antiques were sold to a dealer in Louisville for a total of $14,795.

After the death of Steely's mother in Kentucky, the intricate personal and business dealings of the couple in Culver became even more elaborately complicated than before. They plunged into a baffling maze of legal complexities.

With the easing of Carl's financial difficulties after his mother's death, the couple apparently settled whatever financial accounts that existed between them. Jill wrote "paid in full" across the documents purported to be promissory notes from her husband. Remaining funds from the estate were deposited in a Teachers Credit Union account that he shared with Jill.

Carl also dug $22,000 from his pocketbook and presented his wife with a 1988 Suburban as a birthday present, according to Jill. That marked only the second time during the more than six years of their relationship up to that time that he had given her a gift, she says. The first present was a pair of cloth earrings, according to her account. On August 8, a couple of months after her birthday, the couple flew to Las Vegas, obtained another marriage license and were wed once again. This time they exchanged vows in one of the glitter city's quickie wedding chapels.

Steely recalls the ceremony as merely a "reaffirmation" of their earlier vows, a practice many couples share on dates that are important to them such as five or ten, twenty-five and fifty year anniversaries. But few of those couples, if any, bother with a new marriage license. Carl and his two-time bride obtained a Nevada license at the Clark County Courthouse in Las Vegas.

The license contained true, false, and a confusing mix of information put together from various marriages and other important events and players in Jill's busy life. The bride gave her name as Jill Johansen-Coit, and indicated her father was Edwin Johansen and her mother's maiden name was Juanita Engleman. She said she married once before, and the union ended in 1972 with a Haitian divorce. In a space under her name asking for "her address," she indicated her home was in Harvey, Louisiana. Her birthday was listed as 6-11-1944 and her age as forty-four.

A couple of curious entries also appeared among information on the document provided for the groom's background. In the space set aside to indicate the number of marriages, "1st" was typed in. And in the space set aside under Steely's name for listing of the city or town where he lived, the words "Liberty, Texas" appeared. Liberty is an east Texas town of about 8,000 people along US Route 90 midway between Houston and Beaumont.

Reflecting on his life with Jill, Steely says he believes the marriage, or marriages, began to go bad after she lost her temper one time in front of him and one of her boys. She tried to enlist him in a scheme to kill her brother, because Marc had informed William III that he was old enough to handle his trust himself, Steely says. Jill was furious at the prospect of losing control over the money.

He says he chuckled when Jill brought up the subject of murder. "We thought she was just having a little temper tantrum or something," he says.

"I think her past caught up with her when her brother blew the whistle on her to her younger son . . . and she knew I was going to find out about it, and that's when she began conniving against me. Because there was none of that during most of our marriage. She was married to me the longest of anybody. And I really think that we got along well. Until the last year, when things fell apart." The marriage lasted nine years, including the final two years when they no longer lived together.

But when Jill brought up the subject of murder, he figured she was merely joking or overreacting. She was a natural-born comedienne who was outlandishly dramatic and exaggerated everything. Jill talked at different times to her husband about studying drama at Newcomb College, and he was used to outrageous outbursts or behavior that might alarm someone who didn't know her as well as he did.

It appears more likely, however, that the tangled financial maneuvers between the entrepreneur and the educator had more to do with their final parting of the ways.

The storm clouds began to form after Steely suggested to Jill they take a trip to Steamboat Springs to ski and find a house to settle down in. Early in 1990 he was fifty-nine years old and rapidly nearing the age when he was looking forward to going into semi-retirement, relaxing and catching up on his skiing. It was early spring and the snow on the slopes was excellent.

One of Jill's knees was hurting her, so while Carl skied, she looked for a place to live. She found the Oak Street B&B, which, depending on how the main house was partitioned, could be set up with more than a dozen rental units. She was also nearing the half-century mark, and after giving birth to three children and developing some health problems, she was receptive to the idea. Running a bed-and-breakfast in the popular resort town seemed to fit perfectly into the plan. It appeared the timing might be especially good because the resort was catching on with affluent skiers from Japan.

Jill has a different version, however, of how she came to set her sights on going into business as an innkeeper in Steamboat Springs. She claims it was all her idea, and her husband was dead set against it.

The story is still being sorted out, but certain facts are known. Jill began to marshal her financial resources to meet a $230,000 purchase price on the inn.

She sold a farm in North Manchester; cashed an IRA for about $19,000; withdrew her $15,000 retirement fund; cashed $15,000 in certificates of deposit

from the Bippus State Bank in the hamlet of Bippus a
few miles south of North Manchester; and at last sold
most of the shares of Tenneco stock she inherited as
part of Clark's estate. The stock had appreciated considerably during the eighteen years she held onto it
and brought in $46,581 to apply to purchase of the
business in Steamboat Springs.

Steely also reportedly provided $47,000 toward the
purchase price. He sold off $30,000 worth of Exxon
stock his mother had left him, and withdrew money
from an IRA and his retirement fund. Jill says it was a
loan, and she signed a promissory note to repay the
money. She swapped him a tax-sale property in return
for an agreement to make the loan interest-free for
five years, she added. If the money was not repaid by
June 15, 1995, he would become owner of her tax-sale
properties in Indiana, Louisiana, and Austin, Texas.
She bought the Austin property in 1974 for $8,000.

Her husband co-signed a note on another loan of
more than $70,000 using the combination home and
bed-and-breakfast as collateral. In return for the favor,
she wrote him a $3,000 check on the new account set
up for the Oak Street Bed & Breakfast, she says.

He stayed at the resort only a week before catching
a flight back to the Midwest in order to finish up the
current school term running through April and May.
Later he would have to prepare for the new class reg-
istering at the academies for the fall school term. According to his account, they agreed he would remain
at the academies for one more term before retiring
and joining her in Steamboat Springs. His salary would
come in handy getting their new business started. Jill
stayed behind to complete details of the purchase, do
some redecorating, and make other changes in the
B&B.

Jill sold the bed-and-breakfast in Culver for
$120,000 to Conley B. Phiffer, Jr., and his wife, Mary

Jane, acquaintances she and Carl knew from the church they attended. Earlier, the same couple had taken over the taxi operation.

Since the house was sold and Carl had a new school term coming up at CMA, he moved out of the bed-and-breakfast over the Labor Day weekend and into an apartment. He never considered applying for a leave of absence. Borrowing a Suburban from friends, he made several trips back and forth with his clothes and other possessions. The furniture and most of his wife's personal property were loaded into a truck and sent to her in Steamboat Springs.

When he left Jill in Steamboat Springs it marked the beginning of the end of their connubial life, however. Their comfortable union seemed to spoil virtually overnight, souring like fresh milk left unattended on a back porch. Carl says Jill began talking about him hanging onto his job at the school for a year, not for merely one more semester. And when he tried telephoning her in Steamboat Springs, she was never available for the calls.

In early summer, after the end of the school term, he flew to Denver, then caught a commuter flight to the Steamboat Springs Airport on Elk River Road. His reunion with Jill was disappointing. Among other things, he learned he wasn't even named as a co-owner of the bed-and-breakfast. Seth and his mother were the co-owners. The vibrations were all bad, and a few days after arriving in the resort community, Steely packed up his clothes and returned to the Midwest, alone.

The seven-year marriage was suddenly slipping away in a morass of bitter accusations of scheming, cheating, thieving, and betrayal. Steely found himself in one of the few legal fights of his life. On August 7, 1990, he filed a petition for divorce at the Marshall County Courthouse in nearby Plymouth. In the petition his wife was referred to simply as "Jill Steely," with no mention of a middle name, married name, or any of the other names she had been known by during the past quarter of a century.

They had been separated since July 12 and the marriage was irretrievably broken, Steely asserted. Significantly, he also stated: ". . . the parties have acquired real and personal property subject to division." Steely was represented by attorney Peter L. Rockaway, a partner in the Plymouth law firm of Rockaway and Shorter-Pifer.

A few weeks later Jill cross-filed, asking through her attorney for a decree of divorce from the Marshall Circuit Court, a decree distributing marital assets, restoration of her pre-marital surname of Coit, costs of the suit, and any other relief the court considered to be just. The petitioner was identified as "Jill Coit-Steely." She concurred with her estranged husband's assessment of the marriage, and stated it had irretrievably broken down. That was one of the few things they agreed on anymore. Jill was represented by attorney John C. Hamilton of Doran, Blackmond, Ready, Hamilton & Williams in South Bend.

Although the legal action surrounding the divorce was played out in the Marshall County Circuit Court, it ultimately involved lawyers, witnesses, or depositions from South Bend, Culver, Steamboat Springs, and Plymouth. The court was showered with a flurry of interrogatories, affidavits, writs, motions, and other legal papers that fell like confetti at a wedding.

Nevertheless, teams of judges and lawyers worked for two years to sort out the tangled marital and business affairs of the feuding couple. It was a nasty divorce, filled with incredible amounts of acrimony, spite, and bizarre accusations.

Obviously, falling in love with Jill was an experience that was fraught with dangers. But each of the combatants, the much-married entrepreneur, as well as the prep-school educator, had grasped a tiger by the tail. Once Steely slipped the gloves off, he was a formidable and determined fighter. Neither of them dared to let go.

Jill depicted Carl as a miserably impoverished fortune hunter, who preyed on her because she was a wealthy woman. "His first wife tried to warn me, but I would not believe her, that he was only marrying me for money," she complained. "When I look at how much money we went through during the years we were in contact, I realize she was right. His promise to me that he would never try to take any of my property sure was a lie."

According to Jill's calculations, she contributed about $41,000 to the couple's living expenses, and her husband contributed approximately $15,000 during the first year of their marriage.

The following year, 1984, she contributed about $66,000 to their expenses. "Carl's directed deposit was $626 every two weeks," she said. She computed the amount: "$1,252 × 12 = $15,024. If you take out the $200 per month he had to pay every month for his bad-debt loan, that reduces his contribution to $12,614 for the year."

In 1985, Jill's initial estimate of her contribution was $74,000, with her husband pitching in only $18,000. Running through the arithmetic in more detail, however, she dropped the amount he contributed to an even more anemic $14,760.

In 1986, the first year after her husband's mother died and his financial situation eased somewhat, she came up with $68,000 for their expenses. Jill said Carl's take-home pay from his primary employer was about $19,000 that year but he had probably begun his part-time teaching at Ancilla and his new source of income was enough to offset the monthly cost of paying off his old debt.

Jill claimed they signed a ten-year living-arrangement agreement prior to their marriage. She produced a document to back up the assertion.

According to the pact, she says she agreed to buy a house in Culver within one year for them to live in and attend social functions with him together, so long as he contributed $200 per week. He could also use her cars if he helped maintain them. Whether or not they married, Jill agreed to behave in public as if they were. But there was to be an understanding that he was not to expect her to submit to sexual relations, and he would not claim any interest in her cars, stocks, or other property she already owned or acquired in the future, even if they later decided to marry.

She also produced a document dated May 1, 1990, to back up her insistance that her husband was never a part owner or would-be partner in the bed-and-breakfast in Steamboat Springs. The document stated:

"I, Carl V. Steely, acknowledge the fact that I have no interest in the property Jill Coit is intending to buy in Steamboat Springs, Colorado. I have advised her against the purchase and want no part of it. I think it will not succeed. I do not want to be liable for any debts she might incur. I have never, except for one in North Carolina, been a partner to her purchases, a forty-acre track (sic) we bought together. She is disabled and I do not feel that even with her son being a partner, this enterprise will be successful."

Jill continued pecking away at her husband's story and his reputation. She accused him of taking a hoard of loose diamonds that were squirrelled away in a storage container in the attic of the Culver house and of digging up and making off with gold and silver coins in an ammunition box that was buried in a crawl space. Carl responded that he never saw the treasure after his wife left town. At the beginning of the marriage there was approximately $10,000 worth of diamonds and thousands of dollars' worth of gold and silver coins as well, he said.

Jill also claimed she had a pair of phony identification documents he overlooked in a dresser drawer with his passport, a sweater, and some underwear when he left their Steamboat Springs home for the last time. In turn, she accused him of keeping her tax-sale and other business and banking records when he loaded the truck with her belongings to be transported to Colorado. He also reputedly kept her keys to safety deposit boxes at the Bippus State Bank and in the NorCen bank in Culver.

Carl said in an interrogatory that Jill had their income-tax records. And he clawed back at his estranged wife with all the feisty ferocity of a cornered possum, targeting her with a flurry of hurtful accusations of his own.

In remarks independent of the bitterly-contested divorce suit, he indicated he believed his wife twice attempted to kill him or to have him murdered.

One morning she didn't leave for her college class as she usually did. Instead she stuck around the house and made coffee for him, according to his account. A short time later while he was teaching his first-period class at the Academy, he passed out as he was standing at the blackboard and struck his head. Tests run a few days later were inconclusive, he said.

Another time he was pedaling along the street on his bicycle, his long, lanky form looking like Ichabod Crane with a crew cut, when a motorist tried to run him down. Since that time he has told more than one person he believes he is lucky to be alive. Jill labeled the intimations or accusations of attempted murder as absurd.

In documents filed as part of the divorce suit, Steely

branded the promissory notes as bogus. She used pho-
tocopies of his signature to forge the documents, he
claimed. "This came as no surprise to me because on
previous occasions she thought that she was very
clever in cutting and taping documents to make them
read as she wanted," he said.

Steely said he believed the house in Culver, as well
as the new business in Steamboat Springs were titled
jointly in the names of himself and of his wife,
". . . but I am finding that is not correct." And in
statements outside the court suit, he said he was surprised when he learned he wasn't listed as a part
owner and that Seth was listed as Jill's partner. He
also claimed an equitable interest in the remaining
house in Wabash because of repairs he said were fi-
nanced in part with his income. He contributed to repairs on the Oak Street Bed & Breakfast as well,
according to his account.

Steely accused his absent wife of receiving monthly
disability payments based on bogus claims of a head
injury received in a feigned accident. In a statement
labeled "Wife's proposed findings and conclusions,"
that was submitted to the court, Jill responded
through her attorney:

"Carl acknowledged on the basis of his allegation of
Jill's engagement in a campaign of fraud of having
been both a witness to, and participant in, Jill's alleged
misconduct, including his presence with her at Rush
Presbyterian Hospital where, according to Carl, her
fraudulent endeavor was pursued with apparent success. Carl also acknowledged having received some of
the benefits of the alleged fraud in the form of Jill's
ongoing disability payments."

The statement was couched in classic legal language, but it sounded as if her lawyer was saying she
didn't do it, or at least no one had yet proven she did
it. But if she did do it, her accuser himself was up to

his ears in the fraud. It was the kind of statement that is made in American courtrooms every day.

A bit further along in the document, Hamilton remarked that it was "more probable than not that Jill did suffer a disabling injury in 1983," and asked that Carl be made liable for her support in the event that at some future date the disability left her unable to support herself.

A representative from the State Farm Insurance Company headquarters in Bloomington, Illinois, eventually filed a handwritten request with the circuit court clerk asking for a complete transcript of the divorce case. The transcript was provided to the company, as requested. A State Farm investigator also talked with Steely. Jill had collected a small fortune in disability payments related to her reputed injury while she was representing the company in North Manchester.

Hamilton took a swipe at Steely for reputedly painting himself as someone who didn't know much about business and was unsophisticated in financial matters. The attorney pointed out in the "proposed findings" that the educator had several college degrees, including a Master of Business Administration, and had once established his own corporation in Florida that apparently included issuance of stock.

If Jill's husband was indeed trying to give a false impression that he was a naive babe in the woods when it came to business dealings, she was playing a bit of the same game: Jill Coit-Steely an innocent girl who had hardly any education and was being taken to the cleaners by a conniving man.

Steely complains it took years to drag her into court, and when his attorneys finally got her there, she tried to get the judge's sympathy by saying she had never graduated from college. "Whatever she thinks is going to get the desired effect, that's what she's gonna say." Whenever she was caught in inconsistencies, she simply backpedaled out of it, and she did it gracefully. "She was really good at backpedaling, and you know, making you laugh," he says.

Considering all the years she had devoted to study on college campuses, attending the State Farm school, gathering licenses, buying up real estate, and her myriad other business dealings, it seemed difficult to believe she would err so fundamentally as to execute promissory notes with her husband for loans involving tens of thousands of dollars and not bother to have the documents witnessed.

She was also apparently very good at winning delays in the proceedings. One time when she was supposed to fly to Indiana for an appearance in the divorce proceeding, she claimed she suffered a "seizure" at the airport in Denver, Steely reported. "Throughout the seven years of our marriage Jill talked at length about how easy it was for her to 'beat the system' in this way by faking a medical disability."

In a final argument, Rockaway claimed his client entered the marriage trusting that "we shall be open and loving and share everything." He also scoffed at the crude pre-nuptial agreement Jill claimed she and Carl entered into prior to their marriage.

". . . this woman is far too clever not to have had a legitimate pre-nuptial agreement drawn up if she wanted one. Instead she wants us to believe that these two people looking forward to marriage in several days are signing a document that says one is a poor wretch who is divorced, living in a one-room motel unit with debt and no money whereas the other one will build up his image by buying a house, etc.," the lawyer declared. "I suspect that this document was written somewhere in October 1991, and not in January of 1983."

Rockaway made similar observations about the promissory notes. "This is patently an attempt to justify Jill in her grabbing her husband's inheritance so that she can then say that he was paying her back the debt he owed her," he asserted. "It has the same ring of falsity as does her other exhibit that supposedly Carl was against buying the Colorado property and that this was strictly her business endeavor."

The small-town divorce lawyer's argument was sprinkled with colorful remarks like: ". . . no Johnny-come-lately to manipulating money," "This is a cunning mind at work," "There is no need for this Byzantine cloak-and-dagger stuff," and "he didn't know that his wife had secrets which the heart is not prone to disclose." Rockaway has a definite flair for the dramatic, a knack with words that would have made great sound bites for television, if the electronic media had been covering the divorce trial.

He requested the court award his client a money judgment of about $130,000. "It's not much to ask for a man reaching the end of his working life," Rockaway added in what for him was couched in rather plebian language. In a note to Hamilton, the Plymouth lawyer stated his client had left the couple's financial matters to his wife to handle and consequently didn't know how all of the funds were expended.

"Apparently a lot of the moneys were moved in and out of different banks—foreign corporations were utilized, etc.," he wrote.

Tracing some of the couple's expenditures during the ill-fated marriage, Steely said his wife bought new cars for each of her sons. And despite Jill's claims she didn't continue to buy tax-sale properties during their marriage, he said she drew from their Teachers Credit Union account to make new purchases. The withdrawals included at least $20,000 for tax-sale investments in Colorado, he said.

Asked on an interrogatory if he contended his remarriage to Jill in Las Vegas either didn't happen or was invalid, Steely said he didn't know what the legalities were. "I have assumed that Jill and I have been continuously married since the date of our first marriage, and that any terminations in that were only for purposes of tax necessity, which she had indicated," he said.

The contest played out over nearly eighteen months before Judge Cook at last brought it to a conclusion. He was the same judge who waived the waiting period prior to the marriage nearly nine years earlier. Jill flew back to Indiana, and Carl drove the fourteen miles along the narrow, winding, bumpy asphalt trail that is State Road 17, for the hearing in Plymouth.

The slate-gray, early winter skies outside were overcast and a brisk wind was whipping through the bare black branches of the maples and oaks that dotted the lawn of the Marshall County Courthouse when the estranged couple and their lawyers assembled before the judge for the final time.

Judge Cook ordered the marriage dissolved. He further decreed that the respondent's premarital name, Jill Coit, be reinstated. It wasn't the first time, nor the last, that she would regain her late husband's name.

It was December 23, 1991, the sixth anniversary of Thelma Christine Steely's death. It was also just under eight years since Jill and Carl obtained their paper divorce in Haiti. But the Plymouth judge's decree was no paperwork quickie or exercise in voodoo law; this time the divorce was for real, as legitimate and binding as it can be. Both parties wanted it that way. They were serious about a permanent parting.

Judge Cook observed that the former man and wife had agreed in most part about how their property should be distributed.

"The actual financial circumstances of the respondent (Jill) are not fully understood by the Court, inasmuch as a total accounting of the respondent's assets was not made available to the Court," he added.

Considering the convoluted nature of Jill's business dealings and financial affairs, it was an observation that would be difficult for almost anyone familiar with them to disagree with. It sounded like an understatement.

The jurist observed that during the marriage Jill contributed a disproportionately large amount to their financial upkeep, and that they both lived "a rather extravagent lifestyle" in view of the modest income of the petitioner (Steely). Judge Cook declared, however, that he did not believe notes and documents submitted as evidence were valid.

He also noted the conflicting accounts concerning the whereabouts and ultimate fate of the diamonds and coins left at the house in Culver. Jill claimed Carl made off with them. He said he never saw them again after she left Culver for Colorado. The judge left it at that, without adding any remarks of his own about which one of the accounts he may have found more believable. Carl's accusations about Jill's disability claim were handled in the same manner.

"The Petitioner (Carl) also contends that the Respondent's (Jill) disability is the result of a feigned accident and brain injury and that he in fact, has participated in that deception." If there were to be any follow-up investigation related to Jill's disability claim, it wasn't a problem that would be sorted out in Judge Cook's court.

Cook did point out however, that Jill acknowledged she owed her husband $47,000, and that Steely was asking for $130,000 from her as the balance due him from his mother's inheritance. The CMA faculty member acknowledged expenditure of $35,000 from the inheritance while supporting his and Jill's lifestyle.

Consequently, the judge ordered that the Oak Street Bed & Breakfast, the house in Culver (already sold), the tax-sale properties in Louisiana and Texas, in Wabash County, Indiana, and the remaining tract in North Carolina were all Jill's and that Steely would have no further claim on them. Additionally, the vehicles, including the Thunderbird, Mercedes, Suburban, Toyota 4-Runner, U-Haul Truck, the Airstream trailer, a computer worth about $600, and diamonds and gold and silver coins that were her pre-marital property went to Jill. The Porsches and the Lincoln had already been disposed of, and the other vehicles were in Colorado. The Suburban had been sold to Seth, and even the T-Bird was mortgaged, Jill claimed.

Steely wound up with a laptop computer worth about $900, a VCR worth an estimated $300, personal property such as his clothing, and ski and motorcycle equipment, along with diamonds and gold and silver coins as his share of the personal property. No estimate of the value on the gems or valuable coins was given for either Jill or Steely.

Perhaps the Marshall County jurist's most significant decision in regard to splitting up the couple's assets, was an order that Jill pay her ex-husband $100,000. He specified that the payment was to be made on or before January 1, to prevent a lien from being placed on her real estate. Jill had barely one week to come up with the money.

For one of the first times in her adult life, she was suddenly facing a critical money crunch. With the whopping judgment favoring her ex-husband, piled on top of debts she had already incurred to finance purchase and renovation of the bed-and-breakfast in Colorado, she was seriously overextended financially. Everything she had built up could come tumbling rap-

Jill Coit being escorted into the Routt County Courthouse in Steamboat Springs for a hearing. This was shortly after her return from Greeley. (*John F. Russell*, Steamboat Pilot)

Michael O. Backus, Jill's co-defendant, being escorted into the Routt County Courthouse for a hearing with Jill. (*John F. Russell,* Steamboat Pilot)

Jill and husband Gerald "Gerry" W. Boggs at the social event of the season, the annual Ski Ball in Steamboat Springs in December 1980. (*John F. Russell,* Steamboat Pilot)

The alpine home of Gerry Boggs on the day his body was discovered inside. (*John F. Russell,* Steamboat Pilot)

Childhood photo of William Clark Coit II (taken about 1931), Jill's first husband to be shot to death with a .22-caliber pistol. Clark grew up in Gates Mills, Ohio, a well-to-do suburb of Cleveland. (*Reverend Charles Coit*)

Walter P. Bruning
Prooss
Kenmore 1683

Jill with William Clark Coit II (*right*), and his brother, Reverend Charles Coit, during a trip to meet the family in Gates Mills, Ohio at Thanksgiving, 1965. This was while she was still married to college student Steven Moore, and shortly after the birth of her oldest son. A few weeks later, she and Clark married in what was her first bigamous marriage. (*Reverend Charles Coit*)

Jill with her three sons: Seth, the oldest, to her right; middle son William Andrew, to her left; and William Clark III in the foreground. (*Reverend Charles Coit*)

William Clark Coit with his mother, Anna Dix Coit, and his and Jill's youngest son, William Clark Coit III, during a visit in 1967. (*Reverend Charles Coit*)

From left to right: Jill and her oldest son, Seth; the middle son, William Andrew, who everyone said was his father's double; and the youngest, William Clark Coit III. (*Author's collection*)

William Clark Coit II on one of the pipeline projects he engineered for Tenneco. (*Reverend Charles Coit*)

Jill's first bed and breakfast in Culver, Indiana. Photo taken in the summer of 1994, when it was under new ownership. (*Author's collection*)

Below: The Oak Street Bed & Breakfast on the corner of 7th and Oak Streets in Steamboat Springs, one block from the town's main street, and one block from Boggs Hardware Store. (*Author's collection*) *Right:* Brochure from the Oak Street Bed & Breakfast.

Oak Street
Bed & Breakfast

corner of Oak & 7th

Telephone & Fax
(303) 870-0484

Features:

Downtown Location
Private Baths
Cable Television & VCR
1 and 2 Bedroom Suites
On City Bus Route

Rates include a savory breakfast with homemade breads, meats, eggs, fresh fruit, and more.

We hope you will visit us soon

Julie & Seth Coit   *Jill Coit*

P.O. Box 772434 • Steamboat Springs • CO • 80477

CLARK COUNTY, NEVADA
CERTIFIED ABSTRACT OF MARRIAGE

GROOM: STEELY CARL VICTOR

BRIDE: COIT JILL JOHANSEN

DATE OF MARRIAGE: JULY 03, 1988

RECORDED: JULY 13, 1988 **BOOK:** 880713 **INSTRUMENT:** 92804

APPLICATION: C063873

This is to certify that this document is a true abstract of the
marriage record filed with the County Recorder of Clark County, Nevada.

Joan L. Swift
Clark County Recorder

This copy is not valid unless prepared on an engraved form,
impressed with the raised seal of the Clark County Recorder.

ANY ALTERATION OR ERASURE VOIDS THIS CERTIFICATE

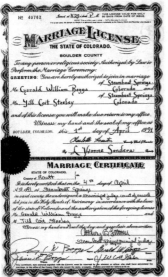

Above: Certificate of marriage for Jill Coit and Carl Victor Steely. *Left*: Marriage license and certificate of marriage for Jill Coit Steely and Gerald Boggs. *Below*: Birth certificate for Jill's first "phantom" baby, Thadius Brodie.

Evidence from the trial, including a picture of Gerry Boggs as he was found slumped on his utility room floor after the murder. (*Author's collection*)

idly down, and the thought of starting all over again had to be a frightening prospect.

Jill was in a pressure situation with a potential for disaster that neither Judge Cook nor the attorneys appearing before him could have foreseen.

SEVEN

Gerry

"I sleep with them, I marry them, okay? I could just sleep around."

Jill Lonita Coit
Deposition, January 30, 1993

There was a new man in Jill's life! She met him while she was fixing up her new business, before her breakup with Steely, and months before the divorce.

When Jill assumed ownership of the Oak Street Bed & Breakfast, she launched herself into the enterprise with her usual energy and enthusiasm.

Once her husband was back in Culver she worked quickly to wind up the paperwork finalizing the sale, so she could turn her full attention to renovating and redecorating the B&B to meet her own specifications of what it should look like.

Seth tagged along with her and apparently invested somewhere between $53,000 and $106,000, most of it from his trust fund, to become a partner. Different versions were eventually given of exactly how much of his money went into the B&B.

They shared the work as well as the financing. Jill cooked, cleaned, handled the books, and ran the office, making reservations and welcoming guests. Seth mowed lawns, did most of the repairs and handled the day-to-day maintenance. Neither mother nor son were lazy.

The business partnership between them was a business decision that Steely bitterly complained he had been unaware of.

"I didn't even know my name wasn't on the paperwork when the trouble started," he says.

In Steamboat Springs, Jill was busy launching the new business. The B & B at the corner of Oak and Seventh Streets occupies a large lot with a string of single story wooden motel guest units painted brown and arranged in an L-shape. A two-story brown, woodframe house constructed at the intersection of the streets, which sits back across the driveway and parking spaces from the center of the "L" has five additional guest rooms in the upstairs area.

Across an alley behind the ground-floor L-shaped units, there was also a small house and four additional parking spaces that were included in the purchase. Jill and her son rented the house to tenants.

A small single-story wooden building at the side of the main house in the motel complex was set up as the dining room, where guests were served a varied menu of breakfasts featuring selections from eggs cooked to order, with bacon, sausage, and ham, to delectable French toast or pancakes and hot or cold cereals. Guests were provided with endless pots of steaming coffee, fruit juice, and a selection of fresh breads and rolls, jams, and jellies and fruit—everything served family style at place settings arranged with linen napkins.

But Jill's taste perhaps was most obvious in her decoration of the guest rooms. They were small, snug, and cozy. Perhaps above all, they were decorated with a feminine appreciation for design and comfort.

The one-bedroom units were dominated by huge, high brass beds that sat in the middle of the rooms, made up with thick, fluffy comforters with bright floral patterns. Pillows were almost big enough to serve as beds themselves. Another patterned quilt used as a wall hanging covered one side of the rooms. A large cradle-shaped wicker basket on the floor filled with fluffy towels and washcloths decorated with bright floral patterns to match the decor of the room, brass-based lamps and a couple of small tables—one accommodating a television set—comprised the remainder of the furnishings. Narrow walkways surrounded the bed on three sides, and a tiny bathroom about the size of an average closet accounted for the remainder of the space.

The low ceilings were barely high enough to accommodate a six-footer without bending his head, but rather than being a negative aspect, they merely added to the cozy atmosphere of the rooms. They conserved heat and made it easy to imagine returning from a cold winter day on the slopes, and burrowing into the warmth and snug security of the little bungalows. Crisp white lace curtains were hung at the windows, and a couple of healthy green plants completed the decorating motif.

Inside the house, the living room was sparsely furnished with antiques, including a few pieces retained from the estate of the late Thelma Steely. The brightly-polished hardwood floors and stairway bannisters were stained or varnished in their natural color to show the grain. A fireplace was built into one wall. The upstairs accommodations were also small, and a hallway bathroom was set up to be shared by the guests in two of the rooms. There were also a few two-bedroom units.

With all the renovations, Jill and her son were able to offer guests rooms ranging from $90 to $125 nightly during the ski season. The location, a few minutes' walk from the shops, restaurants and taprooms along Lincoln Avenue and the side streets, was prime. Jill fixed up one of the upstairs units in the house for herself.

Seth and his girlfriend, Julie A. English, lived in one of the apartments in the L-shaped units. Another unit was set aside as a laundry room, leaving eight for rentals. Julie was an industrious and solidly-built young woman from Georgia who skied and enjoyed bicycling, gardening, and other outdoor activities. She also liked to travel, and she worked for awhile as a cashier at the Hard Rock Cafe in London, England, and as a travel coordinator and receptionist for a firm in Melbourne, Australia.

Seth began to look into the possibilities of adding a 500-square-foot greenhouse with dormer windows and French doors onto the central building, making preliminary enquiries with a builder and discussing city-zoning requirements with an attorney. He also talked about putting in a hot tub and spiffing up the driveway.

But the renovating and redecorating didn't occur overnight or without a lot of hard work, and Jill found herself making regular buying trips around the corner to the Boggs Hardware store.

Boggs Hardware is a downtown landmark in Steamboat Springs. It is one of the oldest family-owned businesses in the resort town. And it occupies the ground floor of a two-story, red-brick building at 730 Lincoln Avenue, facing on the north side of the main drag, which is also US Route 40 and defines the little resort town's six or seven-block-long central business district. Longtime residents refer to the structure simply, as the "Boggs Building."

Surrounded by restaurants, taprooms, curio and souvenir stores, and T-shirt and ski shops that cater heavily to the tourist trade, Boggs Hardware was only a few minutes from the B & B. It was a trip Jill made frequently, and more often than not, of all the busy clerks and salesmen she was waited on, she was most often served by one of the co-owners, Gerald William Boggs. Family members and almost everyone else called him Gerry.

In 1989 when Jill bought the B & B, Gerry was a tall and husky lifetime bachelor a few days away from his forty-eighth birthday. He had rapidly balding dark hair, wore a heavy but neatly trimmed mustache and dark-framed glasses. He and his younger brother, Douglas W. Boggs, were the children of William Harold Boggs, who started the business in Steamboat Springs in 1939. A half-century later ownership had passed to the two sons and to another partner, Bob McCullough.

The Boggs brothers were native Coloradoans, but the oldest son was born in Burlington in Kit Carson County a few miles west of the Kansas border. At about the time WWII broke out in Europe, the family moved further west across the Front Range of the Rockies to Steamboat Springs in the fertile Yampa Valley. It was a nice place to live for a young family, with parents who were independent, hardy, and energetic enough to thrive in and endure the fierce winters.

Even in those early days, the vibrant little community already had a reputation as a resort town, although it is also the center of commerce for scores of other families who make their living as ranchers, farmers, miners, or railroaders. Many of the people who drove into Steamboat Springs to shop lived in other even smaller towns nearby.

But Steamboat Springs was the commercial center. And it has always drawn tourists. As recently as the early nineteenth century, nomadic Indians still made annual treks to the valley to live off the local bounty, while soaking in the profusion of hot sulphur springs that bubble up throughout the area. They believed the springs were sacred and the Great Spirit lived below them, hidden deep in the earth.

The Indians found the springs rejuvenating and visited them when they were exhausted, ill, or after battles with their enemies. Most of the visitors were bands of Arapaho or northern Utes, mountain Indians who pursued deer and elk in the high timber country and fiercely defended their Rocky Mountain domain against occasional hunting or war parties from Shoshone, Cheyenne, Kiowa and other neighboring tribes. The Arapaho and Utes clashed frequently over the lush hunting ground.

Most of the Utes who visited the roughly 150 natural mineral springs in what is now Routt County during the summer belonged to the Yamparika, or Yampa, band. Related Utes called them root-eaters, because of their fondness for the succulent carrot-like yampa root that was as much a part of their diet as wild game. They dressed in buckskin decorated with feathers and beads and lived during the deadly cold winters in teepees made of buffalo hide.

The tribal name of a group of their smaller, more primitive and weaker Piute cousins, the Uintahs, which fished and foraged farther west in the sunparched desert plateau near Great Salt Lake, was eventually adapted to coin a name for the state of Utah.

The most memorable of the thermal springs once visited by the Yampa Utes is Black Sulphur Spring. It was the churning roar of the unique spring that led to the community's current name. According to early storytellers, French trappers made their way into the valley in the mid-1800's when they heard the sound of chugging, and assumed the noise was caused by an approaching steamboat. The mountain men were wrong. The noise was made by Colorado's only geyser, chugging and gushing water into the air.

If the trappers had been in the area awhile longer and paid closer attention, they would have realized there was no way a steamboat could have negotiated the swift-moving shallow water of the rocky Yampa River at that point. Although there may have been periods of heavy snow-melt or other conditions a century ago when the river swelled, even then it's still highly unlikely that anything with a deeper draft than a raft or a canoe could have safely skimmed over the rocks and boulders. Cold and clean, with deep pools scattered here and there, it was near perfect for breeding trout, but it wasn't a stream that was formed to handle commerce or passenger boats.

Hot springs still bubble from the earth in the settlement today, but the geyser and chugging are long gone. The underground foundation was disturbed when the railroad was constructed through the valley. There are still more natural springs in the immediate area than any other location in the world, however. And residents share their habitat with a surprising variety of wild animals that have survived the encroachment of civilization. Mule deer show up in back yards, foxes raid chickenhouses and spook dogs, raccoons pilfer cat food from pet dishes, and rare bald eagles still occasionally screech overhead.

It wasn't long before people realized the potential of winter sports for tourist revenue, and skiing became an important local business as well as an avocation. In the meantime, world competitors were developing on the slopes as males and females trained and vied in everything from cross-country and downhill skiing to slalom and jumping.

By the time Jill and Seth bought the Oak Street Bed & Breakfast, the even smaller town of Vail surrounded by the White River National Forest miles to the south, was the Rocky Mountain ski resort of choice for most of Hollywood's celebrities for winter vacationing. But buoyed by the attraction of Mount Werner, which peaks at 10,585 feet and is named after a legendary family of world and Olympic skiers, Steamboat is becoming more popular every year. Storm Peak and Sunshine Peak are only 300 feet lower than the crest of Mount Werner, and with Thunderhead Peak, Christie Peak, and Rendezvous Saddle, they offer a glistening white powder crisscross of ski slopes and trails for everyone from beginners to world class competitors.

Winter tourists begin showing up in full force with the first deep snowfall to ski, snowmobile, dogsled, hunt, and take advantage of other winter sports. Steamboat's resort hotels, motels, bed-and-breakfasts, and condominiums fill up with visitors, and the winter resort comes into its own as "Ski City USA." The population of the town of 5,000 nearly doubles.

Gerry spent his formative years there, and returned to live out his life as an adult. He graduated from the local high school in 1959, then matriculated to the University of Colorado. He majored in political science, with a minor in Russian language.

Graduating in 1964, he enlisted in the Army and successfully applied for military-intelligence training. By the fall of 1965 he was in Vietnam as a member of the First Cavalry Division and helped set up the huge base at An Khe in the central highlands. He was assigned to a helicopter unit. After completing his one-year tour of duty he returned to Steamboat Springs for a thirty-day furlough, then went back to Vietnam as a volunteer for a second tour. He was awarded a Bronze Star for his service, and in 1967 was given an honorable discharge.

Although he joined the family business, his adventurous life didn't end after returning home from the military service. He took advantage of a government program to learn to fly and eventually qualified to pilot multi-engine aircraft. And he became an excellent scuba diver and undersea and outdoor photographer, using his vacation time to travel to Pacific Ocean diving locations at least once or twice a year.

Like so many of his Rocky Mountain neighbors, he was a devoted outdoorsman. But he was also careful to make time for the academic and intellectual side of his personality and was an avid reader. He continued to take classes at the University of Colorado, served as a museum tour guide, and became a very good amateur archeologist and anthropologist.

He had a special fondness for mind-games, cryptograms, and anything that challenged the intellect. He liked movies and was a regular patron at local theaters, the Chief Plaza III across Lincoln Avenue from the hardware store, and the Times Square Cinema among the shops and restaurants scattered at the foot of Mount Werner. He frequently rented videos to watch at home, as well.

Gerry also loved children, showering the offspring of family and friends with attention and presents. He was "Uncle Gerry" to many youngsters, and became the godfather of the son of his business partner, Bob McCullough. He was a regular visitor at the McCullough home and on Christmas and birthdays, children could count on "Uncle Gerry" to show up with an armload of presents. He was a caring and loyal friend, and McCullough's wife once remarked to her husband that if anything ever happened to him she knew she would have Gerry to lean on.

His friends were devoted to him, as he was to them. But if there was one thing he had missed out on in his busy life it was heavy dating experience or serious relationships with women. He was simply too busy, or too shy, to chase after them.

He was the kind of man Jill was especially successful with. And he looked like excellent husband material. He owned his own $90,000 home, earned a good salary of $2,500 a month with take-home pay of about $1,900, and had no large debts.

She could hardly have been more charming during their brief encounters at Boggs Hardware. According to Jill, she eventually spent nearly $19,000 at the store during her renovation project at the B&B. Her relationship with the quiet bachelor didn't progress beyond small talk over her purchases at the store, however, until a warm day in the late spring or early summer of 1990—Jill was later unable to remember more exactly—when they chanced on one another outside the City Market Food & Pharmacy in Central Park Plaza at the edge of town. Gerry was with his father when they stopped in the parking lot to chat about her T-Bird. It was warm and she had removed the top.

The sports car was perfectly cared for and it was shining like new. Gerry remarked that he would love to drive it. He invited her out to dinner.

As Jill later recalled the incident, she told him that if he wanted to take her T-Bird for a spin it was okay with her. Later she dropped off a note for him at the hardware store. It was typewritten in cursive style on a word processor and, although her name was typed on the note, typical of her, it wasn't signed. By Jill's own admission, her handwriting was atrocious and she typed almost all of her written communications on a word processor, usually in cursive letters. And throughout her relationship with the Steamboat Springs merchant, she began his first name with a "J" rather than a "G."

Gerry took her out, and he drove the T-Bird. He headed west on Route 40 past the Yampa Valley Regional Airport to a little restaurant in the town of Hayden, which developed after the railroad arrived as a cattle-shipping center for surrounding ranches.

After their first date, the couple got together a cou-

ple of times a week, usually driving somewhere for
dinner dates or simply meeting for lunch at the Para-
dise Grill and Saloon, the Fifth Street Cafe, Anderson
& Friends Good Earth Restaurant, or some other
eatery near the hardware store. The people who live
and visit in Steamboat Springs tend to be active and
outdoorsy, and tourists are lured during the more tem-
perate seasons with a variety of festivals and other
events. Although snow sports and attractions are what
Steamboat Springs is most famous for, they are far
from the only game in town.

Jill and Gerry, like their neighbors, had year-round
local entertainment choices. June featured marathon
footraces, a music festival, the Yampa River Festival,
and the Western Weekend with a huge chili-cooking
contest, cowboy poetry reading, a rodeo, and an Old
West gunfighter competition. On the Fourth of July,
children and adults joined in a downtown parade
along Lincoln Avenue. There was Cowboy Roundup
Days for rodeo fans, the Summer Jubilee, and the dramatic and colorful Rainbow Week featuring a "hot-air
balloon rodeo." A softball tournament and more ro-
deos were offered for entertainment in August. In
September there was Motorcycle Week to look forward to; they could view the annual Vintage Auto
Race and *Concours d'Elegance,* or enjoy the Vintage
Aircraft Fly-in.

But Jill and Gerry shared more personal pleasures,
as well. They were both avid bibliophiles and they
talked about books they had read and collected. One
day she surprised him with a present of a Nordic-
Track, which was set up in an area of the house used
as an exercise room. She had a stationary exercise bike
which also wound up in the room, alongside weight-
lifting devices and other workout equipment. Jill believed in keeping fit, and in addition to her lifelong
avoidance of smoking and drinking, exercise was an

important part of her healthy lifestyle. She and Gerry sometimes rode a tandem bicycle around the neighborhood. It was Jill's.

By the time of the Christmas holidays, Jill had virtually moved out of her upstairs quarters at the bed-and-breakfast and into Gerry's home at 870 West Hillside Court, on a steep ridge overlooking the town. Early the next year, Jill and Gerry slipped off to Boulder and obtained a marriage license. It was April Fools' Day.

Three days later they were quietly married in a private civil ceremony in Steamboat Springs by a municipal court judge. The bride had told her groom she was married twice before: to William Clark Coit, and to Carl V. Steely. She was once-widowed, and once-divorced.

She gave her name on the application as Jill Coit-Steely, and indicated that she was divorced in 1983 in Haiti. Her birthday was entered on the form as June 11, 1944, and her place of birth as New Orleans. She used a post-office box number for her current address. The groom indicated his father was William Harold Boggs and his mother was Edith (Parke) Bullock, who was deceased. The elder Boggs had been married to his wife, Sylvia, for years.

There were no formal wedding announcements, and no photos of the happy couple in *The Steamboat Pilot.* Their friends and relatives learned about the marriage a few at a time. No fuss, no muss. Jill liked it that way, and Gerry was agreeable. He was a private man who had never sought out attention. Seth, his mother's faithful confidant and shadow, didn't even attend. Gerry's brother and sister-in-law, Jan, joined the newly-married couple in celebrating the wedding with a big feed at the Old West Steakhouse a few blocks down Lincoln Avenue from the store.

Months later, the bride complained that two weeks

after the wedding her new husband went off by himself on a scuba diving trip to Belize when he should have been with her on their honeymoon. He told her he couldn't spend two weeks in a confined area with one person, she said. So she cancelled out and her husband went on the Central American scuba-diving adventure by himself.

The lifelong bachelor probably never should have gotten married in the first place, Jill groused. She married him for his intellect. Most of the eligible men in Steamboat Springs were ski bums, she explained.

Despite the irritation of the separate honeymoon, even if Jill's version of the odd event is indeed true, the first months of the marriage were nearly idyllic. The energetic couple took weekend trips and occasional longer journeys together around Colorado or nearby states, usually staying in bed-and-breakfasts. Operators of many of the hostelries banded together to swap complimentary rooms and meals, and the couple took advantage of the cost-saving opportunity to travel.

About the time Gerry went off on his diving trip, an insurance claim was filed for major water damage at the house. The loss was eventually estimated at more than $17,400. Jill blamed the incident on Gerry. He insisted on remodeling his garage just about the time the season's heavy snowfalls were about to begin, she said. Even though he had been warned about the bad timing, he undertook the project for her so there would be room to park her car in the garage alongside his Jeep. Another version of exactly why Gerry was remodeling the garage would be told later.

The claim, nevertheless, included damage to the drywalls, replacement of carpet from the upstairs hallway, bedroom, bath, and stairs, and major remodeling. Georgia A. Taylor, one of the few woman acquaintances in Steamboat Springs that Jill sometimes lunched with, was the claims adjuster. According to Jill, Seth pitched in to help out with the repair work, putting in more than thirty hours and charging for only a fraction of his time.

Jill drove all the way to Denver to shop and save money on appliances for the house. She bought a black leather sofa for the living room, replaced kitchenware, and shored up the supply of towels and linens. Even before the water damage occurred, Gerry's house was sparsely furnished with a combination of treasured longtime possessions and cast-offs passed on to him by friends or relatives. He lived bachelor style. His new wife enjoyed upgrading things and giving the home a feminine touch.

Despite the damage, Jill moved most of the rest of her possessions into her husband's house, and assumed the role of the new Mrs. Boggs. She already knew her father-in-law, William, and his wife, Sylvia; her brother-in-law and his wife, Jan. She met nieces and nephews and cousins; and she met the Boggs family attorney, Vance E. Halvorson.

She later recalled that shortly after Gerry introduced them, the lawyer soberly advised her that she was now a Boggs and should conduct herself as a Boggs. The implication was clear: her new role carried important obligations and responsbilities.

Now that he was married to Jill, Gerry had less time for private hours of reading, playing intellectual games, and poking around with hobbies like archeology and anthropology. For the first time, he attended the annual ski ball sponsored by the Steamboat Springs Winter Sports Club. It was the central event of the local social season. During all his years of living in the resort town, Gerry had never attended a major social event, and a photographer for the local newspaper, the *Steamboat Pilot,* snapped a picture of the prominent retailer, gussied up in a handsome, dark suit with his beautiful wife on his arm. Dressed in the suit and tie, Gerry looked more stiff and uncomfortable than entertained. But Jill, wearing her hair cut Audrey Hepburn-close, with dangling oval earrings and a white formal gown, was smiling and radiant as she walked into the glittering ballroom at the Sheraton Steamboat Resort with her husband.

When Jill's middle son, William Andrew, got married, Gerry traveled with Jill to Jackson, Mississippi, to attend the nuptials. Andrew and his bride, Lynn, settled in Denver.

Gerry met Jill's parents, Henry and "Nita" Billiot at the wedding. The first thing Mrs. Billiot asked her new son-in-law was about his religious beliefs. It was a surprising question, and he was a bit taken aback.

"I'm sort of a Heinz Fifty-seven variety-type religion," he replied. Gerry wasn't a regular churchgoer and religion wasn't a big part of his life, but he was tolerant of the beliefs of others including some non-Christian traditions. Judging by the query, he figured Mrs. Billiot to be a woman of strong religious faith. The question was obviously important to her.

William Clark III also married. The youngest son and his wife eventually settled in Manhattan Beach, California, where he assumed a management position overseeing the operation of three stores for a national retail chain. When Gerry's niece married, Jill attended the wedding with him, and some of the out-of-town guests stayed at the bed-and-breakfast. Suddenly, Gerry's days and nights were filled with social events and family activities, many of them organized or arranged by his bride.

As they always had, cars continued to play an important role in Jill's life. She loved them and she loved driving. She also resumed her zealous pursuit of education. Jill signed up for college classes at two schools in Greeley, the town laid out and settled east of the

Rocky Mountains at the confluence of the South Platte and Cache LaPoudre rivers more than a century earlier.

She took psychology, education, and Asian history classes at the University of Northern Colorado, and geography and US history classes at Aims Community College. Jill attended UNC full-time during the summer and fall terms in 1991, and eventually continued through the fall term of 1992 and the spring term of 1993. She was especially interested in acquiring the proper education and credentials to counsel people who were suicidal. She was combining studies at two schools so she could graduate more quickly, and told people back in Steamboat Springs she was working for a master's degree.

For most people perhaps, regularly making the grueling two-hundred-fifty-mile round-trip jaunts over the Continental Divide between Steamboat Springs and Greeley might be a prospect that was more discouraging than attractive for a successful businesswoman and homemaker who was already in late middle age. But Jill wasn't intimidated, and she easily found accommodations in Greeley where she could stay during the week. She and her husband took turns driving to visit with each other on alternating weekends. One weekend he drove to Greeley or some other town where they could stay together at a bed-and-breakfast, and the next weekend she did the driving. Often their get-togethers were a hundred miles or more from either Steamboat Springs or Greeley. They went wherever they had a complimentary room, and they had an opportunity to visit areas of the state they hadn't seen or spent much time in before.

At that time, Gerry owned a 1984 Toyota Jeep and a 1976 Toyota 4-Runner he had bought from his niece, Carlynn Taylor. Gerry usually drove the Jeep, and he fretted that it wasn't good for the 4-Runner to sit around idle, so Jill borrowed it for some of her trips.

One weekend he borrowed Jill's Mercedes to drive to Evergreen, just outside the southwest edge of Denver to stay with her at a bed-and-breakfast. He picked up the car from Jill's son, who had some diesel-mechanic training. Seth checked the oil and drove the car to a gas station where he filled the tank before turning it over to Gerry. Before his stepfather drove away in the car, Seth explained a few basics about its operation, such as how to gas it up, and how to buckle the seat belts. He cautioned that if motor oil was added, Gerry should use diesel.

Nevertheless, when Gerry was still miles from Evergreen the oil pressure trouble light flicked on. By the time he got to the bed-and-breakfast the engine was ruined. Seth drove down the next day in the Suburban with a mechanic and they hauled the car back to Four Star Repair in Steamboat Springs. Jill was upset, and let her husband know she blamed him for the expensive repair.

Gerry offered to pay for the repairs, but according to his later account, Jill refused. She planned to pawn the damaged car off on Carl Steely as part of her settlement with him. Jill denied she had any such intent. "I think it's a joke because Carl would not accept a broken-engine car," she scoffed.

The vehicle was the same car taken to a South Bend Mercedes dealer to replace the engine and transmission a couple of years earlier. Estimates for replacing the engine once again varied from $5,000 to $7,000, depending on who was making the calculations and whether or not a junkyard Mercedes could be found and cannibalized for the expensive part. The *Blue Book* value was only $2,800. A professional insurance adjuster eventually appraised the total value of the Mercedes at much less than that: $1,001.23.

Although Jill had a way of making a mountain out of a molehill, it appeared at the time that the bad luck with the Mercedes had caused only a minor glitch in the happiness of the marriage. She had another, more positive and happier revelation to spring on the couple's acquaintances and friends.

Jill was either forty-six or forty-seven—depending on which year of birth, 1943 or 1944, is correct—when she began confiding to various people in Steamboat Springs that she was pregnant with Gerry's baby. She told Georgia Taylor, and she told William and Sylvia Boggs. The prospective parents made an appointment with a local obstetrician-gynecologist, and discussed home birthing and the possibility of home delivery. But Jill never returned to the doctor for follow-up prenatal care.

Gerry was ecstatic. His heart was set on becoming a parent, and he especially wanted a little girl that he could raise and spoil. He even picked a name for their child: Lara. Jill disclosed to close friends of the couple that she underwent an ultrasound, which confirmed the baby was a girl.

Gerry's friends in Steamboat Springs and elsewhere were thrilled at the news and happy for the couple. Barbara Smith, who had known Gerry since 1968, later recalled how excited he was about his impending fatherhood. He laughed and joked, and they decided to set up a college fund so Lara could attend Harvard. Gerry was obsessed with his daughter and speculated endlessly about how she would be raised and about her future.

He had the Boggs family attorney draw up a new will for him naming Jill and their unborn child as beneficiaries of his estate. Gerry explained to Halvorson that his wife also planned to have her lawyer, Bruce Jarchow, draft a new will for her.

The Thanine (Thane) Gillilands, a couple from the western Denver suburb of Westminster, who were especially close and longtime friends of Gerry, gave the expectant parents a crib, a stroller, and clothing left by their own little girl who had died. They were gifts from the heart, and Gerry appreciated their importance and special meaning to his friends. Mrs. Gilliland helped Jill shop for other baby clothes.

The expectant parents kept busy preparing for the arrival of the child.

Gerry had a $19,500 addition built onto his house for the baby. He bought books and audiotapes on child rearing and a car-seat baby carrier, and he promised he would arrange to pick up a high chair at the store, where he got a discount. Children's books, including copies of *Grimm's Fairy Tales, If I Ran The Circus, Aesop's Fables, Sneches* and *Six By Seuss,* were collected, along with video movies: *Treasure of the Lost Lamp, The Jungle Book,* and *Fantasia.* A stuffed animal collection was started for the baby, with a large pink panther and a small dinosaur. Gerry was even given a card signed, "To Daddy, from Lara."

Jill came home with armloads of baby clothes. "I bought gobs of clothes. . . . Everywhere I went. Any time there was a sale. I'm basically cheap. I bought lots of clothes," she later recalled. Jill watched for sales at stores like Steamboat Kids and bought little girl baby clothes from infancy up to the age of four.

She explained she was seeing a doctor in Greeley to monitor the health of herself and the baby. But when Gerry asked who the doctor was, she was evasive. Eventually she gave him the name of a doctor at a womens' clinic. The birth was expected in September, but the due date was eventually set back by several weeks.

Nonetheless, Jill inquired at a Steamboat Springs dentist's office about making an appointment for a checkup after Lara cut her baby teeth. And she talked to a hairdresser about making an appointment to have the infant's hair done. Lara was still apparently

months away from making her appearance, but her
mother was arranging a busy schedule for her. Nothing about her future welfare was being neglected.

Jill was gone from Steamboat Springs for weeks at a
time, attending classes and hitting the books in Greeley or taking care of business affairs. It worried her
husband terribly. He was concerned about his pregnant wife being away on her own so much and doing
all that driving over treacherous mountain roads while
she was carrying their baby. The child was the only
thing he talked about when he telephoned or visited
with his friends the Gillilands.

Despite his suspicions about Jill's curious pregnancy
and odd behavior, he asked his friend, Gilliland, for a
professional opinion: Was Jill really pregnant? Gilliland was a Certified Physician's Assistant (PAC). He
was a highly-trained medical journeyman who was pro-
fessionally and legally qualified to perform many, although not all, of the functions of a physician. Gerry
cast him in multiple roles and at various times he was
asked to be doctor and medical advisor, father confes-
sor, and most important of all perhaps, trusted friend.

At that time, according to Jill, her pregnancy was in
the seventh month. On the rare occasions lately when
Gerry saw her, she didn't look pregnant to him, but he
didn't trust his own observations. Although his brother
and sister-in-law had a couple of children, and he was
a godfather to another child, he hadn't spent much
time around pregnant women. He wasn't quite sure
how they behaved, or if a woman could carry a baby at
that late stage without showing more physical signs
than Jill was exhibiting. She was supposedly in her
third trimester.

She wore bulky clothes, but that wasn't unusual for
anyone, man or woman, pregnant or not, who lived in
the Rocky Mountain ski community during the late

fall or early winter season. Jill was still pert, still full of energy, and looked as healthy as a whole-grain muffin.

Gilliland told his friend the only thing he could, considering the circumstances. Jill had dropped in for a visit with the Gillilands the previous week, but Thane hadn't examined her. He said he simply didn't know.

Gerry's chum didn't let matters drop at that, however. He telephoned the clinic in Greeley and asked for the doctor Jill had named as her obstretrician. No one there had been monitoring a pregnancy for Jill Boggs.

While Jill was replaying the old phantom baby game with her prominent Steamboat Springs husband, pressure was building on her from the divorce court judgment in Plymouth, Indiana. She owed Steely $100,000, and the deadline set by Judge Cook had long ago come and gone. Steely wanted his money. But coming up with the purchase price of the Oak Street Bed & Breakfast, costs of renovations and other expenses, had depleted most of her ready cash and other negotiables and plunged her deep into debt for loans from banks, family members, personal acquaintances, and ex-husbands.

In North Manchester, Metzger had indicated he would help out with a $50,000 loan. She was counting on an acquaintance in Mississippi, R. L. Goodwin, to provide more money. And the First National Bank of Steamboat Springs agreed to float a $50,000 loan to Jill and Seth.

Just about the time it looked as if she was about to work herself out of her financial morass, Steely filed a suit against her for $250,000. She and Seth were anxious to build the greenhouse and make other improvements at the bed-and-breakfast. But she was suddenly back in the soup, plunged even deeper than before into a money mess and left with hardly any room for necessary financial maneuvering.

She had tapped just about every possible source of loans she could think of, and she was still dreadfully short of money. Jill advertised the bed-and-breakfast for sale. An ad in the *Steamboat Pilot* on April 11, 1991 announced: "OAK STREET BED & BREAKFAST. Recently renovated, nine-unit plus five-bedroom house, charming antique decor in this turnkey operation." No price was quoted.

Another ad in a giveaway real estate publication, however, pitched the B&B for $750,000. This time the copy specified a total of thirteen "professionally-decorated" rooms, one less than the newspaper listing indicated. A later ad in a different real estate booklet listed the "charming B&B located in the heart of Old Town" for $650,000. The ad carried a picture of the inn, and also stipulated thirteen rooms.

Jill also went to her new husband for help. She said she needed to borrow $100,000.

As later recounted by Jill in depositions, Gerry agreed to take out a loan from the Yampa Valley National Bank in Hayden where his brother was a member of the board of directors. Then he would pass the money on to her, in return for a personal note or deed of trust on the bed-and-breakfast. Jill signed over a partial deed of trust and settled back to wait for the loan.

Seth also recalled discussing the loan with his mother's husband a couple of times—once during Burger Night at the Old Town Pub & Restaurant and another time during Taco Night at the Old West Steakhouse. "Gerry Boggs mentioned it to me that he was going to help us out," Seth remembered, "because I was really stressed out about it. Gerry was going to help us out. Loan us $100,000."

Like so much about Jill's life and business affairs,

explanations and surface appearances don't always tell
the whole story about what was really going on, however. For one thing, Gerry firmly denied in depositions
that he ever agreed to try to use his brother's influence
in any way to obtain a loan from Yampa Valley National. He also denied talking with Seth at the restaurants and telling him he was going to loan the young
man and his mother $100,000.

Gerry provided a startling different version of Jill's
motivations for signing over the deed of trust to him.
She explained she wanted to give him the deed of trust
in order to protect the Oak Street Bed & Breakfast for
their child, he said. Jill didn't want Carl Steely coming
to town and seizing the business to satisfy the whopping financial judgment ordered by the Indiana court.

That version of the affair sounds especially believable in view of the fact that Jill never got the $100,000
loan Gerry supposedly promised to arrange for her.

Jill may have been concerned by the threat to the
financial bulwark she had built for herself. But neither
that nor baby Lara slowed the pace of her frenetic life.
While all the talk and commotion was going on about
the mysterious new member of the Boggs family, other
more ominous matters that Jill and her husband were
initially unaware of were already set in motion that
were about to shatter her latest masquerades. Ghosts
from her past were lurking just offstage, and were
about to make their appearance.

The Boggs brothers were close, and Douglas was
troubled by ugly suspicions about the real background
and character of the perplexing woman who had
charmed his longtime bachelor brother. All the mystery and intrigue over the baby simply didn't make any
sense, and other aspects of Jill's behavior were troubling. She was pestering him to help her out financially, and there seemed to be reason to believe that

both Gerry's welfare and that of the hardware store could be damaged.

The concern mushroomed after Carl Steely traveled back to Steamboat Springs to ski and to talk with the local lawyer who was working with him to collect the divorce judgment from Jill. Attorney William C. Hibbard was also a skier, and the two men spent some time together on the slopes, mixing business with pleasure. Hibbard reportedly told Douglas Boggs that Jill's husband was in town and he wanted to settle up matters with his wife. He was planning to file a lawsuit against her. The news was a bombshell. Douglas is said to have told his brother about the planned lawsuit —and that Jill was still married to a man in Indiana.

She was furious when she heard the story. Hibbard's office was on Oak Street only a couple of blocks from the Bed & Breakfast, and she stormed inside to read the riot act. She was outraged because Gerry's brother learned about the impending suit. "I went in and told Bill Hibbard, number one, he shouldn't be putting my business on the street before he did something," she later explained.

Among other things, she was also angry because some of Hibbard's business associates or clients sometimes stayed at the B&B, and he had agreed to represent Carl. She considered the combination of the two to constitute a betrayal.

But the cat was out of the bag. Douglas Boggs talked by telephone with Steely. The Indiana educator had some hair-curling stories to tell about his onetime helpmate.

Douglas Boggs hired a private investigator from Denver to check into the life of the merry widow and divorcee who had breezed into town and married his brother after a whirlwind courtship. Judy Prier-Lewis had been a close friend of Gerry's for twenty years and a private investigator for more than half that time. She turned to the task at hand with quiet determination. It didn't take long to confirm that her friend, the brother of her client, was married to a bigamist.

As the investigation broadened the industrious PI learned that the new Mrs. Boggs had many other secrets hidden in her background. When the investigation turned for help to Houston, the private detective called on Stan Lewis Associates, a firm headed by a fellow sleuth in the Bayou City area. The two Lewis's were no relation through either blood or marriage, but she had done work for him in the past. Stan Lewis, his colleagues, and Judy Prier-Lewis quickly collected an alarming package of information.

Jill Boggs was a woman who had been married to four different men before tying the knot with Gerry. It would still be awhile before Gerry learned she was wed to almost twice that number of men before she charmed her way into his life. A deposition was eventually filed in Routt County Circuit Court stating: "Four of the prior marriages overlapped and were either bigamous or polygamous."

The investigators ultimately inspected court records, records of property sales, interviewed a string of men and women, and conducted surveillances. They determined Jill had used a fistful of names, including aliases that had no connection to the surnames of her various husbands. Perhaps most disturbing of all, one of her husbands had died in an unsolved shooting nearly twenty years earlier that occurred only twenty days after she filed for divorce. And despite police efforts to question her in the baffling case, she had avoided all personal contact with homicide investigators.

Gerry was crushed when he learned that his wife was still married to Carl Steely. Jill said she was merely confused about her marital status, and had made an honest mistake. She had believed she was divorced.

Jill went to a Greeley attorney, Elizabeth Strobel, and explained her problem, or at least part of it. She applied for declaration of invalidity of her marriage to Gerry, a legal ruling and terminology that amounted to an annulment. He was agreeable to permitting Jill to handle the matter with an out-of-town lawyer, and in an out-of-town court. He hadn't done anything wrong, but it was embarrassing none the less, and he could see no reason to make the marriage muddle a public affair in Steamboat Springs. He didn't even tell his family lawyer, until the annulment procedure was already a done deal.

The settlement was affirmed by the Logan County District Court in Sterling, more than one hundred miles northeast of Greeley on December 3. It wasn't likely that a snoopy reporter from either Steamboat Springs or from Greeley would hear about it, and if a Sterling journalist stumbled onto the file he or she would have no interest in the case. There wasn't much chance anyone outside the courtroom knew either Jill or Gerry or cared if they had obtained an annulment. The town and the court in the far northeast corner of Colorado less than an hour drive from the Nebraska state line was about as isolated from Steamboat Springs and Boggs Hardware as it could be.

A decree of invalidity of marriage was issued by Judge Steven E. Shinn. The jurist noted the couple believed at the time of their marriage that Jill's previous union to Steely was already dissolved. When she attempted to obtain a copy of her decree of dissolution of marriage from the Indiana educator, however, she learned that it hadn't yet been issued. She was still married to him.

"It is therefore ordered, adjudged, and decreed that the marriage of the parites in this matter is void, *ab initio,* and the Court declares this marriage to be invalid," he wrote.

The judge observed that the couple indicated they hadn't incurred any joint debts during the union, and agreed they had no joint marital property. Jill had indicated she was a student at the University of Northern Colorado, and was self employed as an owner of the Oak Street Bed & Breakfast. She listed monthly earnings of $2,000, including $1,500 in take-home pay. Her total income listed on the previous year's federal income tax was approximately $24,000. She also indicated on an affidavit of financial affairs supplied to the judge, ownership of a single vehicle, the 1984 Toyota 4-Runner.

In an accompanying document in a space referring to custody of minor children, she declared that no children were born of the marriage. There were no references on the paper to the possibility that she was pregnant.

The matter of the annulment was handled quietly by the couple. Jill appeared at the final hearing with her attorney. Gerry didn't make the long, exhausting drive across the front range for the hearing. The mess wasn't the kind of personal Boggs family business that would lend special luster to their reputation in the community. After the annulment was concluded, they continued their rather odd relationship and living arrangements for awhile. They told the judge they planned to remarry once the legalities of her relationship to Steely were finally sorted out.

Jill's sordid marital background had been exposed, however, and the handwriting was on the wall. In early December she packed up some of her clothes, cosmetics, and a few other small personal possessions and stormed out of Gerry's house for good. They had locked in a nasty quarrel that Jill claimed was sparked when Gerry's brother tipped off his parents about the annulment.

Gerry spent Christmas Day with Douglas and the

rest of the Boggs family. He didn't know where Jill was or who she spent the holiday with, but he couldn't turn off the worry—because she had advised him three days earlier that he was a new father.

She talked to him by telephone and told him she had given birth to their daughter in Denver, alone and unattended at about eleven o'clock, Saturday night, December 21. She was at her son William Andrew's home, but claimed she convinced him and his wife to go ahead with plans for a holiday visit with Lynn's family in Mississippi. Gerry never saw his daughter; Jill never brought the baby home to show to him.

He became more despondent than ever, and Gilliland's concern for his old friend mounted. He tried to talk Gerry into consulting a friend of his who was a psychiatrist. But Gerry was a proud man who was used to dealing with his own problems and had always been able to work his way out of whatever troubles were bothering him. He turned his thumbs down on the proposal.

Sometimes when he was especially desperate to get away from all the trouble for a while, he drove to the Gilliland home to stay over the weekend. He was embarrassed, frustrated, and so depressed he could barely function. Gerry fretted about Jill, about Lara, and about the effect his troubles were having on his parents and on the family business.

He was unsure of himself. His eyes were hollow, his hands shook, and he had been making mistakes at the store. He had trouble sleeping, his memory was shot, and it was beginning to look like he would never be able to work his way out of the mess he was in.

Gilliland suggested a couple of more times that he seek professional psychiatric help, but Gerry stuck to his guns. His troubles were something he would have to work out for himself. One time Gilliland talked with Douglas Boggs about arranging to have the troubled man hospitalized, but the discussion concluded with a decision to wait awhile longer.

As Gerry's frustration and torment increased, Jill continued living life to the fullest, with the seemingly limitless energy she had possessed since childhood. Neither the baby, nor any of her mounting troubles seemed to slow her down. She was Gerry's nemesis, and she pestered him by telephone at the house on Hillside Court, until he told her not to call him anymore.

"Don't call me. Call my lawyer," he snapped.

Seth helped his mother remove more of her possessions from the house. Gerry wasn't at home. He had packed her things and dragged them into the garage near the door where she could pick them up without moving any further inside. She and Seth loaded two cars, then came back for a second trip to pick up books and a few other things they hadn't had room for the first time around. Jill had a big collection of books. Seth wanted to take his mother's stationary bike, but it was locked in the exercise room.

She still owned the U-Haul, but it was being used for storage and it would have taken too long to unload. Jill wasn't at all pleased, and her son also complained that Gerry apparently tossed everything down the stairs into the basement, before moving them into the garage.

In an angry note, she complained to Gerry's lawyer that her ex-husband deliberately destroyed her things. "Did you advise him to trash my possessions?" she demanded. She charged that Gerry scratched her oak furniture and tossed breakable items into boxes with other effects to deliberately cause breakage. He was hanging onto her good china, twenty-four-karat gold-rimmed goblets and purple wine glasses, and she simply wouldn't stand for it, she warned.

She identified a long list of items she wanted returned, that included everything from five skillets and a coin ring to a Nikon camera, a gold bracelet, and a leather notebook she had planned to give Gerry for Christmas. Their relationship didn't survive until the holiday, she said, so she wanted the notebook back.

"He is trying to force me to be mean and do something nasty so that he can retaliate."

Halvorson countered the accusations by declaring his client hadn't intentionally or accidentally damaged any property of Jill's that was left at the house. If any damage occurred, he indicated, it was her own fault because she deliberately left possessions there so she could remove them in dribs and drabs in order to provide an excuse for continuing to pester Gerry.

"Mr. Boggs does not wish to retain personal effects of hers to the extent they have been left behind by her, but he doesn't want her coming and going for her stuff on a repetitive basis," the lawyer declared.

Jill fussed over everything. Nothing, it appeared, was too petty to pester Gerry and the lawyers with. She complained about the damaged Mercedes, but eventually agreed Gerry had offered to have it repaired and the offer was repeatedly refused. And Gerry claimed through his lawyer the engine was defective before he drove it, and Jill knew it. So she assumed the risk of the car being further damaged when she decided to drive it and to allow Gerry to drive it in a defective condition.

One day while Gerry was away from home, someone took the hand-held electronic garage door opener from his Jeep and used it to get inside the house. The intruder left a business card on his pillow so he would know someone had been there. Months later when a lawyer asked Jill about the incident, she denied having anything to do with it. She had no idea who might have done such a thing. It was an absolute mystery.

Regardless of whoever was responsible for the incident, it was part of a pattern of harassment that Gerry was subjected to for months. There seemed to be little question that Jill had a hand in most, if not all, of the dirty work.

As for Gerry, he could never completely relax. Just when he was about to take a deep breath, and try to convince himself he could see the light at the end of the tunnel, something new happened to upset him. He had taken over financial responsibility for the investigation, and eventually paid an estimated $6,000 in PI and lawyer fees while tracking his former wife's trail of deceit and connubial flim-flam through Indiana, Texas, and Colorado.

He even enlisted the help of another Plymouth lawyer, Roy D. Burbrink, to collect information from court records and from witnesses in Indiana. Metzger was one of the witnesses called to the law offices of Stevens, Travis, Fortin, Lukinbill and Burbrink in the center of the Indiana town's business district to give a deposition.

After the year-end holidays, Jill resumed her classes in Greeley, moving into a two-story house she bought. And the storytelling about the baby and other aspects of her life with Gerry turned extremely ugly.

She continued to commute between Greeley and Steamboat Springs, and when she was back in the Routt County resort town she spread false stories that Gerry was a closet homosexual. He managed to keep his guilty secret all those years because he traveled to other towns when he felt the urge for intimate male companionship, she asserted.

Jill was a passionate letter writer. The letters were almost always undated, and when they were inspected months after composition it was difficult to tell when they were really written. But they were convenient building blocks that always backed up her version of the relationship between herself and Gerry. Like the dental and hairdressing appointments for Lara and the stories about the pregnancy and birth, they provided ammunition for whatever Jill felt at the time would throw the most suspicion on Gerry and cast her in the best light.

She seemed at times to be operating as if she had taken to heart an old Indiana farm axiom, "If you toss enough fresh manure against a barn door, some of it's bound to stick." She flung a lot of verbal cow flops.

In an undated letter she addressed to Gerry, Jill berated him for drinking too much one time while they were soaking in a hot tub. She criticized him for what she said was his inability to love and be a friend to people. She referred in the note and in other statements to what she claimed was a traumatic event in his childhood when he was sexually abused by a male teacher. She accused him of belittling her because she was half American Indian, because she was Southern, and treating her as if she were stupid. She was maintaining a 3.5 grade-point average, while carrying at least twenty-one hours each semester, she defended.

In one letter, Jill was angry because he had wanted her to go to San Francisco with him for "one last fling," she wrote. "Are you nuts?" Elsewhere in the angry missive, Jill complained she paid for his flight with her credit card, and he expected to use her paid hotel accommodations as well. (During their last days together she purchased a two-for-one airline ticket, permitting one passenger to pay and her companion to fly free. But they broke up before the scheduled date of the trip.)

Despite her claim in one letter that she was sensitive because of her cultural heritage, Jill was showing about as much compassion and understanding for her ex-husband's feelings as a Lucrezia Borgia.

In another earlier note apparently written while they were still together, Jill complained he refused to have sex with her and used sex as a weapon. Because of her classes they were only able to see each other on weekends, and even then he wouldn't touch her. Jill demanded to know if it was because he thought she was ugly.

Perhaps the most bizarre letter of all, however, was addressed to her husband's attorney, Halvorson, at his office suite. This time there was a postmark with a date: Humble, Texas, January 6, 1992. Humble is a little town about the same size as Steamboat Springs, just outside the north edge of Houston. The letter was a ten-page diatribe aimed at convincing him she had given birth to a baby and was caring for it.

She apologized for choosing Gerry as the father of her child, but accepted the blame on herself. She claimed she got pregnant before they were married. She said she made him deny the pregnancy to his friends, because that was the question they all asked immediately after the marriage. At first, she also denied the pregnancy.

She concluded that the whole marriage was based on a lie. But, despite all the efforts at a cover-up, Jill said, "I still ended up giving birth to an illiagamatee [sic] child."

The long letter was generally composed with good sentence structure and proper grammar, but she made a few glaring spelling errors such as her trouble with "illegitimate." Another word she had a surprising bit of trouble with, considering her unique marital history, was "marrying." She spelled it "marring"—and perhaps that was closer to the truth than the traditional spelling.

Jill rambled on about what she claimed was her parents' opposition to the possibility of giving Gerry joint custody of Lara. She claimed he never wanted a child, but she desperately wanted a little girl—and should have gone to a sperm bank instead of depending on a husband who didn't love her and was a reluctant dad.

She promised to never file a paternity suit or seek child support. She promised not to try and get in touch with the elder Boggs couple even though she had already told them they could visit with their new grandchild. She referred to them as "Mother and Father Boggs."

Repeating her accusation that Gerry kicked her out of the house, she claimed he told her to go to the bed-and-breakfast where Seth could take care of her until the baby was born. He wanted the child born at Routt Memorial Hospital in Steamboat Springs, but she insisted on returning to Greeley for the birth even though the due date was only about a week away.

Jill said Gerry may have been feeling a little guilty the morning after their titanic squabble because he helped her load some clothing for herself and the baby in her car before she started the long, arduous drive to Greeley. He even offered to permit her to stay at the house until she gave birth. She was uncomfortable and her back was killing her, but she gamely declined the last-minute offer of a reprieve. She also refused to ask her son to take care of her.

Jill said when she got to Greeley she became frightened because it was the semester break and her student neighbors were gone. So she drove to her son Andrew's house in Denver. But he and his wife, Lynn, left for a visit to Mississippi, after she assured them that if she needed help she could call Gerry.

He telephoned her the next morning and screamed and threatened that if she refused to go to a doctor with him and his friend, Thane, he wouldn't continue supporting her through her troubles with Carl, and he wouldn't recognize the baby as his, according to the account.

Jill was drawing a tragic picture of a woman

hounded by a cold and vicious man who drove her from his house only days before she was to give birth. She worried that she would be arrested for bigamy and Lara would wind up with a child protective-services agency. And she fussed and fretted because he told people he wasn't even sure she was pregnant.

How could he wonder about that when her breasts had swollen from size 34D to 34EE, and her belly had grown about ten inches, she asked the lawyer in apparent amazement? Gerry had rubbed her back and gone through false labor with her; and then had the gall to say that maybe she wasn't pregnant, that she was just getting fat.

Jill wrote about her lonely ordeal delivering Lara by herself at her son's house about twelve hours after suffering through the abusive telephone call. It was an easy delivery; the baby practically dropped out, she said.

Lara had Gerry's temper, and yelled so loud for her one o'clock breast feeding a couple of hours later that one of the neighbors across the hall asked her whose baby was squalling.

After noting that she had expended her "emotional enema," Jill wrote, "so I leave you alone." Then she typed four more pages.

According to Jill, her real friends, who knew her character, were lining up in her support.

She claimed her lawyer in New Orleans whom she didn't name but identified as a "personal friend," told her to forget about Gerry. She didn't need the emotional stress and financial drain of another fight with someone, in addition to her ongoing legal troubles with Steely.

Her banker, who also was unnamed, also reputedly assured her she was a good person, a good mother, and a sound businesswoman.

She returned to Culver to see her friends there and

seek out their moral support. They advised her to forget about Gerry and about Steamboat Springs.

Only her clergyman told her it was her own fault for getting herself into the mess, and if she was sincere when she took her vows she was married "until death do us part." Jill noted she was concerned about her daughter's religious upbringing because Gerry believed as much in Buddha, which she spelled "Buda," as much as he believed in Jesus. He believed equally in all gods.

Jill also couldn't resist taking a few more potshots at Gerry's sexuality, claiming he was homosexual and married her only to provide cover for his secret life.

She also claimed he had what she described with typical college-classroom psychobabble as "a seasonal affective [sic] disorder," that made him depressed and negative. He didn't want to be around people.

Jill told the lawyer she could be contacted at the address in Humble for about a week. (She was staying with a relative.) She didn't know where she and little Lara would be after that. The lawyer had been around the legal merry-go-round for a few years and had talked to Jill a few times. If he believed there was anything to her story about little Lara, it didn't show.

In early December a bulletin from the Steamboat Springs Evangelical Free Church which Jill attended made hazy reference to problems in her personal life. Under a column titled "Prayer Concerns," the first listing asked the congregation to: "Pray for our family of the week, Gerald Boggs." Other prayer pleas printed on the same missive were made for a family that had lost two girls to a traffic accident and for the success of a church remodeling project.

Jill told people in Steamboat Springs and other Colorado communities, including an acquaintance in Boulder, that Gerry kicked her out of their house a few days before Christmas. Lara was her little girl by

Gerry Boggs, but he refused to recognize her as his, she explained to the hairdresser. Lara was never brought into the shop for the appointment, however.

According to some reports, Jill showed up in Steamboat Springs at least once with a warmly-bundled-up baby. It was little Lara, she claimed. After the probe of Jill's background and activities, investigator Judy Prier-Lewis arrived at a different theory about the infant that was shown around: the would-be mom paid someone to borrow a baby. Reporter Joanna Dodder of the *Steamboat Pilot*, speculated in a private discussion that she suspected the baby may have been a bundled up doll.

The terrible stories Jill was spreading about Gerry could be extremely damaging to someone who had been such an important part of the local business community for so long. The Boggs name, after all, was etched in the stone of one of the oldest and most impressive buildings in the very heart of the town's downtown shopping area.

Gerry was devastated by what was happening to him, embarrassed for his family, and troubled by the nagging possibility, dim though it was, that Jill really had given birth to a daughter. He served two tours in Vietnam and acquitted himself with integrity and courage. But he had never dealt with someone like Jill and what appeared to be her hateful determination to ruin him and drag his family name through the mud.

The former Mrs. Boggs actually seemed to gather new vigor and energy from the marathon bickering. She was growing stronger and more cantankerous all the time. But the vicious wrangle was taking a dreadfully savage toll on her onetime husband's self-confidence and emotions. He wanted it settled and over with.

"At the time I believed there was no child, and yet every time Jill came to Steamboat she would go around telling people that she had given birth and that I kicked her and the child out of my home," he said in a deposition. "And needless to say, this upset me greatly, and I guess maybe that since hope springs eternal, I thought, well maybe she did have a child."

Intellectually, Gerry found it hard to believe there was really a baby, but emotionally he still wasn't sure. He was being cruelly whipsawed by his emotions, suspicions, and doubts. He talked a few times by telephone with Steely, and the Indiana educator assured him Jill had undergone a hysterectomy. It didn't seem likely she could give birth to a baby, no matter how much she might wish to. Gerry observed that she had shown a baby, or what appeared to be a baby, around town, and even if she had adopted a baby, he would feel a responsibility.

"She really knows how to pull my chain," he groaned. At other times he walked around, or stood shaking his head and muttering to himself, "What a fool! What a fool!"

Now working at Gerry's request, his friend Judy Prier-Lewis beat the bushes in three states looking for a baby no one really expected her to find. She tracked Jill in Colorado, Indiana, and Texas. Jill had drifted back to the Lone Star State and was shuttling between the Houston area and Greeley.

The investigator checked with one of Jill's ex-husbands in Indiana, and asked if he thought the Billiots might be taking care of the baby. He didn't. By that time, Henry Billiot was living in the little farming and onetime glass-manufacturing community of Greentown just outside the east edge of Kokomo. Judy Prier-Lewis passed the information on to Gerry, and he telephoned his former in-laws to ask if they had the baby. He talked to both parents.

"Did Jill have a child by me?" he asked. They seemed to be taken completely by surprise. They said

they didn't know of any new grandchild. Jill hadn't
given birth to another baby.

Gerry was satisfied he had been told the truth. "I
felt if anybody on the face of the earth wouldn't lie to
me about this it would be her parents," he remarked.

At last his depression and uncertainty turned to anger. He had been lied to, made a fool of, and almost
driven into a mental hospital. He was still worried that
his former wife might find some awful new way to revenge herself on him by hurting his parents, but he
decided it was time to strike back. He revoked the will
he had prepared the previous year naming Jill and
their expected child as beneficiaries.

And when Jill got word to him she wanted the deed
of trust returned, Gerry refused to meekly hand it
over. He was determined to hold onto it until he was
absolutely convinced he was not the father of a daughter Jill had hidden away somewhere. It was his most
important bargaining chip.

"I find out she had been married numerous times
and didn't tell me about it. She had been pregnant and
not had this child, and things of this nature certainly
led me to believe that I was not going to sign any document and give it to her," Gerry reflected. "I think she
knew perfectly well she was still married when we got
married, when she married me. For reasons like that, I
was not going to give her a signed document and let
her walk off with it except in the presence of my attorney."

The deed of trust was a powerful lever, the key element in Gerry's defensive arsenal. Jill wasn't a person
who could stand for things to remain static in her life,
especially anything related to her financial affairs.
Money and property were to be used to make more
money. But almost everything she owned, in real estate, other solid material goods, and on paper, was
tied up in the Oak Street Bed & Breakfast. Gerry had

her in a bind, and financial institutions wouldn't consider taking new mortgages or liens on the bed-and-breakfast until the property was free and clear of the deed of trust.

Although Gerry had never provided the actual cash for the $100,000 loan to her, he had a legal document that said he did. And as long as he held onto it, he had a financial stranglehold on Jill. Seth's investment was tied up as well.

Gerry wasn't a cheat, and he didn't want Jill's money or Seth's. There were other considerations he insisted she meet, however, before releasing his hold over her finances. And he wanted everything spelled out in firm, indisputable legal terms before he budged. It wasn't a matter that Jill could any longer settle with idle verbal promises or softly uttered pillow talk.

When Gerry at last dug his heels in Jill responded with a new torrent of anger and abuse. She telephoned him so often at his house that he began taping the calls. Jill did most of the talking, but when he had a chance to get a word in he assured her he was willing to return the deed of trust once he knew for an absolute certainty there was no baby.

Jill filed a civil suit in the District Court of Routt County for return of the deed of trust and to settle other elements of the dispute. Seth was a co-plaintiff with his mother in the civil action over the deed. Jill was represented by attorneys Randall W. Klauzer and J. Richard Tremaine. The offices of their law firm, Klauzer & Tremaine were on Lincoln Avenue.

Gerry struck back by filing a counterclaim. In the document prepared by his attorney, he accused Jill of false representation, infliction of emotional distress, defamation, extreme and outrageous conduct, and asked for an unspecified amount of damages.

The defendant in the suit was named as "Jill Steely aka Jill Coit aka Jill Coit-Steely," but referred to in

the body of the document by the first of the names, Jill
Steely. She was no longer referred to as Boggs, the
name she had proudly laid claim to for such a short
time. Once more, Jill and a man she had married
found themselves and their lawyers in a nasty court
fight.

Through his attorney, Gerry stated that Jill was living at an unknown location in Texas and was planning
to remove a material portion of her property in Routt
County in order to make it unavailable to her creditors.

On a more personal level, he accused her of lying to
him about being a single woman available for marriage and of later lying about being pregnant and giving birth to a daughter he had conceived. He
complained he had justifiably relied on her word, with
the result being that he suffered damage and loss in
time expended, effort, and money preparing for the
birth of the daughter who never was.

He asserted that she told him and others he was not
a good father to the child and caused him great
shame, distress, and a baker's list of other emotional
damages and embarrassments.

Supporting the charge of defamation, he declared:
"That since January 1992 to the present, Steely (Jill)
has told numerous parties that Steely had a baby by
Boggs and that Boggs disowned Steely and the baby.
She and the baby had been thrown out by Boggs and
ordered out of town and/or words to similar effect
which gave the listener the understanding that Boggs
was a bad and neglectful father . . ."

It was a mouthful, and it was couched in a typically
awkward run-on sentence, but the message was clear.
Jill was a baldfaced liar, who had been going around
badmouthing Gerry. She was depicting him to friends
and acquaintances as a rotten father who disowned his
own infant daughter and threw his pregnant wife out

of his house. Gerry invested considerable time and money in lawyers, investigators, and travel expenses in order to determine if he was, indeed, the father of a child, it was added.

He asked in the countersuit for a decree from the court stating that no child was born of the relationship between Gerry and Jill, as well as an order for a cash award.

Halvorson charged $140 an hour as his normal rate for services. Meeting his fee could translate into a whopping amount of sales of paint, nails, tools, and plumbing supplies at the hardware store. He put in a lot of hours working to sort out the legal morass his friend and client had gotten himself into.

Even before the suits were filed, the lawyers set to work exchanging a busy dither of telephone calls and legal papers—letters, proposed agreements, releases, drafts, and suggestions for a non-disturbance pact. At one point during the summer of 1992, Klauzer wrote to Halvorson and pointed out Jill was in Alaska, and he would deal with the issue of the non-disturbance agreement as soon as he could. She bought some real estate and picked up an Alaskan voter registration there.

On the subject of the non-disturbance agreement, Klauzer said he planned to modify the proposal to make it "somewhat more bilateral in its application." Gerry wanted Jill to leave him alone.

He insisted she promise to no longer use the Boggs name. She was to confirm either that no child was born as a result of their union, or if a child was indeed born, that she would provide visitation, (in a more formal version, she was to acknowledge she never became pregnant by Gerry, nor had a child by him). She was to refrain from contacting him in person, by telephone, mail, or through members of his family, in any manner except through his lawyer. She was to agree that she, her heirs, or anyone representing her had no claims against him for money, property, support or inheritance. Finally, each of them would agree not to disturb the tranquility of the other, and agree not to enter the other's residential or business properties.

The non-disturbance pact was central to obtaining the release of the deed of trust. It was Gerry's position that one agreement was linked inextricably to the other.

Klauzer didn't see it that way. He argued to Halvorson that the issues weren't related. If the question of a child was truly an issue for Gerry, then that problem was a matter to be worked out by the Logan County District Court which handled the annulment, which he referred to in proper legal terms as the "invalidity action."

"This issue is clear-cut. I cannot in good faith agree that they should be interrelated," he wrote. Klauzer repeated his earlier request, that Halvorson send him a signed release for the deed of trust. Jill's lawyer probably wasn't at all shocked, when Gerry's lawyer failed to comply with the request. Halvorson wrote in part in his reply:

> "I further find it amazing that you have failed to confirm that there is a baby yet you assert that we can bring paternity proceedings. If paternity proceedings are appropriate, they are customarily brought by the mother and she has not done so to date. Indeed, such is one more fact which convinces us that there was no baby and any claims to the contrary were deceitful and outrageous."

He also assured his legal adversary that Gerry preferred to minimize or avoid the stress and expense of litigation by reaching an amicable solution to the dispute with Jill.

The wish expressed in Halvorson's letter to reach an amicable solution without resorting to litigation wasn't to be realized. A few weeks later the lawyers broke off their efforts to settle matter by mutual agreement and filed the lawsuits.

Accompanied by her lawyer, Jill went to Halvorson's offices in the Norwest Bank Building at 320 Lincoln Avenue early in January 1993 where she and Seth were scheduled to answer questions in depositions. A couple of weeks earlier, in the middle of December, Jill drove over the Continental Divide from Greeley to meet with her lawyer in Steamboat Springs and prepare for the proceeding. She stayed overnight, then made the exhausting return trip.

Seth was the first to be interrogated.

At the very beginning of the session, just after Seth was sworn in, he was asked what he did at the bed-and-breakfast. "I do everything," he replied.

"You do everything? What is the nature of the duties you perform?"

"Cleaning toilets and fix breakfast."

Taking Seth's deposition was a trying process that was made even more difficult by Jill's frequent interruptions. From time to time she broke into her son's testimony to prompt him or to make remarks including: "He didn't understand what you mean, Vance," "What does litigation mean?" and "That was a guess, Vance. We were estimating it."

Halvorson finally became fed up and asked Tremaine to keep his client quiet until it was her turn to talk. If that couldn't be done, he was going to ask Jill to leave. Tremaine apologetically agreed that he understood the other attorney's position. Jill quieted down, squinting and furrowing her eyebrows occasionally, but managed to hold her peace throughout most of the remainder of the process.

Significantly, when Seth was asked if he had siblings

and what their names were, he replied that he had two. "Andy and Billy."

"Do you happen to know whether or not your mother became pregnant during the course of her relationship with Gerry Boggs?" Halvorson asked.

"She's too mature to be doing something like that," Seth replied. "No. No."

"Okay, she didn't," Halvorson acquiesced. "And how do you know that?"

"Because I think they usually swell at the belly." Seth could respond to certain questions in a manner as disconcertingly neutralizing or peevish as his mother.

Seth indicated he and his mother never discussed the possibility of her having children with Gerry, and she never said anything to him to make him believe she was pregnant during the period she was with Gerry. "She has not had a child since 1968," he said.

Although the lawyer didn't go into the matter of the earlier phantom children, Seth's statement would indicate there was no Thadius Brodie and no Tinley Metzger—as well as no Lara Boggs. Jill's only children were Seth and the two Williams.

At one point when Halvorson was trying to learn the name of the girl in Indiana who filed the paternity suit against Seth, he pleaded that he was having trouble understanding some of the questions because of his dyslexia. His difficulties were audio-visual, and he sometimes had trouble with big words or round-about questions. "Just go right to it," he suggested.

At another time when Halvorson was discussing possible fears that Steely would try and attach the Oak Street B&B to satisfy the court judgment in Plymouth, he asked if Seth had employed a lawyer.

"For my mental . . . ?"

"Pardon?" Halvorson appeared surprised at the answer, but he didn't follow up on the possible implications. Instead, Seth quickly recovered and explained in an obvious reference to Klauzer and Tremaine that they had. "Richard and Randy." The local lawyer team had represented him and his mother in their business matters as long as they had known them.

Seth painted Gerry as a man who could be cruel and made his mother cry and said she used her money to meet the couple's expenses. "My mom would spend money, Gerry would not." He said their relationship was erratic. "Gerry has a different beat, a different drummer, a different attitude towards women. Up and down. Cold!" Seth didn't know his mother's friends. It wasn't his business who they were. He had other things to do, he said.

The husky young man conceded he didn't attend his mother's wedding when she married Gerry. Halvorson asked if he approved of Gerry.

"My mom's a big girl. She can do what she wants," he said. But he agreed he didn't like the way his mother was treated by the hardware store owner.

Continuing to respond to the lawyer's questions, Seth indicated he didn't want to sell the bed and breakfast. He had gotten to understand the business and to be comfortable with it, and he liked it. "I have people drive by and wave at me," he said. "So I'm pretty happy where I'm at."

Seth agreed the business may have been listed for sale at one time since he and his mother bought it; he wasn't sure. But he didn't want to sell it, and in fact he had bought his mother's interest. Halvorson wanted to know how much he paid for Jill's share of the inn, but Seth couldn't provide him with an exact figure. He explained that she just took whatever she needed.

"Whatever she needs?" Halvorson asked in what appeared to be understandable surprise.

"Uh-huh!" Seth agreed.

"What was the amount that you have agreed that she needed?"

"She just—I just let her take whatever she wants," Seth repeated.

It was a curious, and it would seem, a dangerously sloppy way to operate a business. It was especially strange for someone who was such an experienced businesswoman as Jill, and Halvorson asked if she took money out of the till on a regular or on an occasional basis. Seth said he wasn't sure. He didn't keep track.

When it was his mother's turn to testify, she announced she wasn't going to cooperate and stalked out. Halvorson later asked the court to order her to repay his client's attorney fees for the lost time, and to force her to submit to the deposition.

Jill had a way about her of delaying the legal process when it was time to give depositions.

When Jill finally gave her deposition about three weeks later, it was a tedious and trying process. As Halvorson struggled to pin down specific information, Jill bobbed and weaved, pleading for an opportunity to check her records at some other time or cited problems with her memory. Her affliction with dyslexia made it difficult for her to keep numbers in her head, she explained.

Obtaining a clear picture of her financial arrangements concerning the Oak Street Bed & Breakfast was especially difficult and trying. Jill agreed she got a $47,000 loan from Carl, but said it wasn't recorded. Some of the amounts she borrowed were recorded and some were not.

Halvorson observed she had said she got $135,000 from the First National Bank and $50,000 from Eldon Metzger. "It was [$60,000]," she corrected him on the Metzger loan.

"Well, that's true. Then why does this say [$50,000]

here?" the lawyer asked, pointing the sum out on a list.

"I don't know. But it was [$60,000]," she insisted.

"And Henry Billiot, $20,000?" Halvorson asked, as he consulted the same list. "I think it was $35,000."

"It was [$35,000]," she responded.

Later in the deposition process, Jill said she gave her father the T-Bird in return for the money he turned over to her. It was worth $35,000 in the condition it was in, she said. "To me it was worth a million."

Halvorson wanted to know about other loans.

"Jules English," he queried. "It says $20,000?"

"Okay, don't touch it. Don't correct it. I'm sorry . . ." Jill stammered.

"What was that loan?"

"I don't know. I'll have to check the record," she replied. Jill was having as much trouble keeping the amounts of her loans straight as she would later have explaining the dates of marriages and divorces with her husbands. It was all very confusing. Even the names of her creditors were turning out to be sources of confusion.

Halvorson said he assumed "Jules English" referred to Julie English, the maiden name of Seth's wife. It wasn't. He didn't even have the gender right. Jules and Julie were two different people, Jill said.

"Oh, this is somebody else?," Halvorson asked.

"Yes, sir."

"Okay. Jules English. Who is Jules English?"

"A male," Jill replied.

"Pardon?" The deposition wasn't going as smoothly as it might have. Jill seemed determined to make the lawyer work for his information and wasn't giving anything up easily.

"It's a male. It's not a female," she said. If the lawyer wanted information, he was going to have to squeeze it out of her. Jill may or may not have been able to give a precise definition of obfuscation, but she knew how the process worked. She was expert at slowing down a line of questioning.

She agreed again in response to another question, that Jules English was a male, not a female. "Then tell me, what is your relationship to Jules English?" Halvorson persisted.

"He is related to Julie English," Jill said. How were they related? "A relative!" Jill replied. That wasn't the kind of answer likely to earn her a favorable mark in one of her college classes, but the lawyer wasn't about to give up. He tried again to determine just exactly who the mysterious Mr. English was.

"Father? Son? Brother?"

"No, not father. She doesn't have any brothers. I don't know the exact relationship, but I will find out the exact one . . ."

Halvorson was still reluctant to surrender and admit he was proceeding down a dead-end path with the line of questioning. He asked if Jill could pin down her benefactor's age a bit and speculate whether or not he was closer to twenty or fifty. Jill didn't know. He was simply someone who had agreed to loan her money, and she wasn't even sure about where he lived. She had a post-office box number for an address.

Twenty thousand dollars was an awful lot of money for someone to loan to a stranger, and Halvorson's puzzlement over the odd transaction was understandable. But Jill either couldn't or wouldn't provide the answers he was looking for.

The lawyer at last dropped the subject of Mr. English, and asked if there was anyone else to whom she owed money.

"Oh, I owe lots of money," she bubbled. Jill listed a few more loans ranging from $10,000 to $25,000, including $10,000 she said she obtained from her middle son, Andrew. Asked if she took out a note for $50,000 from R. L. Goodwin, Jill said she was going to get money from him but the loan was never concluded.

"Who was this Goodwin, R. L.?" Halvorson asked, sounding a bit like a military drill instructor barking names off the roster of his platoon.

"That's a friend of mine in Mississippi."

Halvorson asked if she sent Goodwin letters, and she replied that she did not. The lawyer abstained from further questions about her Mississippi friend before the exchange could deteriorate into the same kind of frustrating morass he got himself entangled in over Jules English.

Instead, he turned the questioning to more personal matters linked to her relationship with Gerry. Did Jill understand Gerry was remodeling his house in order to make more room for the baby? No, Jill said. That wasn't her understanding.

"This comes as a surprise to you?" he asked as if her response was a shock to him. It was an eyebrow-raiser.

Jill told the story about Gerry undertaking the remodeling project so she would have room to park her car inside the garage. He had been keeping his weight-lifting equipment in there, but "a garage is for parking," she said.

Halvorson asked if she was saying Gerry remodelled the garage to accommodate her, not because he wanted the room for a child they were expecting.

"I don't know why he was building a garage. I don't know his mind. But it stands to reason, so I would be able to park in the garage."

Halvorson asked her about a notation indicating a purchase made at Moonflower Birthing in Louisville, Colorado. Jill replied that when she and Gerry were in Boulder he bought a floral backpack. The lawyer wanted her to be more specific. "For a child?"

"Right," Jill said. "I think it's the only thing he

really purchased for a child. When I was with him, anyway."

"It wasn't a home delivery kit, or anything of that nature, was it?"

Jill didn't appear to be bothered by the very personal turn the questioning had taken. "I don't know. I thought, to my recollection, it was a weird-looking floral thing. I thought it was rather feminine-looking, but it wasn't for me. I usually brought presents, not Gerry."

The question-and-answer session began to bog down again when the lawyer drew closer to her claims of pregnancy. Jill blamed the stories about being pregnant with a daughter on Gerry. And she used the opportunity to fire another salvo at what she continued to claim was his secret homosexuality.

He asked if during their life together she became pregnant.

"I was not pregnant with Gerry Boggs."

The lawyer ignored the obfuscation and patiently established that she was not pregnant by anyone. He asked if she had claimed to be pregnant.

She agreed she had—because it was what Gerry wanted. Jill seemed to be trying to draw a picture of a compliant, loving woman who was manipulated by her husband into living a lie. She did it to help him create the virile, masculine, heterosexual image he wished to project for his neighbors. It made him happy.

Jill claimed at another time during the lengthy statement that although she had undergone what she termed "a partial hysterectomy" in New Orleans to have some abnormal cells removed from her uterus, she was still capable of becoming pregnant. She said she and Gerry used condoms when they had sexual relations to avoid the possibility of a tubular pregnancy. She even volunteered the brand name of the devices for her questioner.

Halvorson asked her about an earlier statement she made saying: "Anyway I am to blame. I slept with him and got pregnant before we were married."

Jill replied that was what her husband wanted her to say. "But I did sleep with him, but I was not pregnant," she added.

"So, basically this is a false statement. It's a true statement that you slept with him, but it's a false statement that you got pregnant before you got married? Is that a fair statement?"

A lot of references to "statements" were being bounced around the room, and Jill's attorney, Tremaine, objected that she had already answered the question. Halvorson didn't pursue it any further at that time and instead turned to questions about some of her business and banking dealings in Culver and Plymouth.

Jill became understandably confused at one point while Halvorson was grilling her about the judge's order in Plymouth awarding Carl $100,000 and subsequent matters relating to the Indiana educator's efforts to collect. Jill said she had attended a hearing with her husband, and Halvorson asked exactly when the hearing was.

"I have a question," Jill said. "What hearing and what husband are we talking about?"

Her confusion was understandable to the lawyer. "That's true. They're hard to follow, aren't they?" he commiserated.

"I sleep with them, I marry them, okay?" Jill shot back. "I could just sleep around."

At another point in the grueling session, Jill said she repeated her vows with DiRosa about four times. "You married DiRosa four times?" Halvorson echoed in astonishment.

"Uh-huh! Every time we went away to an island we got remarried. I'm sorry, that's just the way it was. I

married W. C. six times." She followed the amazing
statement up with several remarks about her respect
for DiRosa as an attorney and as an individual.
"Whatever he sent me, I signed, okay. There were no
hard feelings. I liked the man as a person. . . . I'm
sure that—because he's an attorney, whatever he's
done is legal."

Halvorson asked if she read things that were printed
above her signature, or if she simply signed whatever
he sent her without reading it.

"Can I say something?" she responded. "Right now
if he sent me something I would sign it. This man is
not trying to screw me in any way." DiRosa had
brought presents to her children, she said. Just because their marriage didn't work out there was no reason to be enemies. They were friends.

While discussing the promissory notes that surfaced
during the process of the bitter divorce in Plymouth,
Halvorson asked if Carl accused her of fabricating
them.

"He accused me of fabricating everything in the
whole world," she snapped.

Halvorson observed that there was some whiteout
on one of the promissory notes produced as an exhibit
in the Indiana divorce trial and asked if she could ex-
plain why it was there. She couldn't—but she had a
suggestion: "Let's scratch it off and see what's under
it?" No one scratched off the whiteout, and the deposition interview turned to other matters.

Jill and her former husband's attorney clashed over
a journal which Gerry had kept during their marriage.
She said it included remarks about his thoughts, opin-
ions and what she described as his shortcomings and
failures—matters that disturbed him.

The journal was discovered to be missing from the
house after she left. Halvorson included the journal
among other documents he asked to inspect before

permitting his client to give his own depositions. Jill agreed she took the journal with her when she left, and Halvorson's plea to inspect it was a perfectly proper request to make as part of the discovery process. But Jill said she couldn't turn it over just then, because it was apparently in luggage misplaced by Continental Airlines while she was traveling between Colorado and Houston.

Halvorson asked if she had a tag on her luggage, and she said she had one which she slid her business card into. She was careful to stress that it was "a pretty tag." For a moment, she was Jill the pussycat. The Jill who was always intensely and happily feminine. It was a persona that was much more appealing and pleasant than some of the other Jills that Gerry, Carl, Clark, and other husbands had glimpsed at one time or another.

Jill had filed a claim with the airline over the luggage. And in response to a query from Halvorson, she agreed she once worked in the airline industry for six weeks. She knew a bit about the system of claims and payment for lost luggage. Jill was a woman who knew a lot about a few things and a little about a lot of things. An impressive amount of the knowledge seemed to somehow revolve either around husbands or money.

She apologized that although she couldn't produce the journal just then, she promised if and when she recovered it she would be sure to make it available to Gerry's lawyer. Halvorson wasn't about to buy that story, and he made it plain in written remarks how he felt about Jill's reputed difficulty keeping track of the journal. He wrote: "Alas, a shell game defense to discovery, first we have it, now we can't find it, so you still can't have it. But just wait because we might find it and then use it. But if it turns out that it supports your client, it probably won't ever be found." The lawyer said his client's deposition should be held off until the journal and other information were supplied to him.

The court agreed and ruled that Gerry wouldn't be forced to give his deposition until Jill had complied with the discovery process.

At long last, Jill's deposition session was ended. But she wasn't through with Gerry Boggs. Many traditional marriage ceremonies in this country incorporate the words, "till death us do part." The maxim would eventually prove to have tragic application to the mean and spiteful quarrel between Jill and her onetime husband.

It's unlikely that either Gerry, his lawyer, or Gerry's family and close friends were unaware that the bitterness and acrimony were a long way from being over. It's also doubtful any of them could have realized just how filled with anger and hate the quarrel between him and Jill had become. Unimaginable fury and savagery were about to forever blight their lives.

EIGHT

Roy and Michael

Jill was forty-eight years old and a single woman again.

Being unmarried wasn't a condition she would put up with for very long.

On Friday, February 7, 1992, about six weeks after her divorce from Carl Steely at last became final, she walked into a small wedding chapel in Las Vegas and married her ninth husband.

Roy C. Carroll was a retired US Navy chief petty officer and businessman who lived at the north edge of Houston. He was sixty-seven years old and was embarking on what was very likely the most bizarre adventure of his life. The North Carolina-born widower had exchanged vows in a marriage that was doomed to failure.

Of course he didn't know that at the time. That was the way it was with the men who walked down the aisle with Jill Lonita Billiot-Ihnen-Moore-Coit-Brodie-DiRosa-Metzger-Steely-Boggs-Carroll. On the document prepared for the quiet wedding with the retired sailor, the bride indulged her taste for fudging important information on her marriage applications and licenses.

She boosted her birthday forward to June 11, 1951,

neatly trimming seven or eight years off her real age.
In the space for her mother's maiden name, she used
her birth mother's first name, Juanita. Taney, the
maiden name of Edward Bruce Johansen's long-dead
wife, was used for the surname. A similar disregard for
the truth was used in identifying her father, who was
named as Henry Johnson. Jill's handwriting was jerky
and scratchy. It wasn't pretty to look at, but she had a
deft hand when it came to filling out marriage licenses.

She indicated she was married only once before and
was widowed. The information would become chillingly prophetic when it was compared months later
with her signature on the document. She signed her
name as Jill Boggs.

Carroll's marriage probably had even less chance of
success than those of his predecessors. That was because Jill was already playing house with a handsome
hunk of a man who was nearly twenty years younger
than the unsuspecting groom. According to some descriptions the boyfriend's hair was light brown, or
"dishwater blond." That was close enough for Jill. She
had always had a weakness for blond-haired men. It
was one of the things that attracted her to Clark more
than twenty years earlier.

Michael O. Backus was a slender, hard-bodied,
forty-eight-year-old equipment maintenance man and
troubleshooter for US West Communications, the
telephone company that serves Greeley, Steamboat
Springs, and other communities in Colorado. He was
six-foot, one-inch tall and weighed about one hundred
seventy-five pounds. Outdoor work and a fondness for
outdoor recreation helped keep him in good shape.

Like four of his girlfriend's former husbands,
Backus had strong Indiana connections in his background. He was born in Evansville, on September 9,
1945. Michael, like Gerry, was also a Vietnam veteran,
although he served his single hitch there with the US

Air Force instead of the Army. After four years of active duty from 1963 to 1967, he returned to the Evansville area and served a year with the Indiana National Guard. In Evansville, he worked with the Indiana Bell Telephone Company.

After moving to Fort Collins in 1984 and going to work for US West, he enlisted in the Colorado National Guard and began building an impressive record as a non-commissioned officer in Company C of the 140th Signal Battalion. the National Guard unit was headquartered seventy-five miles south of Fort Collins in the east Denver suburb of Aurora, but he was meticulously loyal about his attendance at evening or weekend meetings and drills and summer encampments. His duties involved the installation, operation, and maintenance of wire and cable communication systems, a vital element for making any military operation work.

One time in September 1988 when danger suddenly developed from what his supervisors referred to as "a hot shelter," he quickly shooed the men under his command away and troubleshooted the problem himself. "Staff Sgt. Backus is a good NCO and he demonstrates the principles of NCO leadership by taking care of his troops," an evaluator observed. Michael loved his work with the National Guard.

Glowing reports from a superior described him on an annual enlisted evaluation report thus: "Sgt. Backus has displayed sound judgment, initiative, and technical skills when dealing with his subordinates and peers. Sgt. Backus was a major contributing factor to the success of the switching section they now enjoy. I would recommend Sgt. Backus for any position or career field he may want to persue [sic]."

A year later an evaluator had this to say: "Sgt. Backus is s key NCO within the unit. He has distinguished himself through a consistent record of high

NCO standards including appearance, leadership, effective communication with subordinates, and being dependable to complete all assignments regardless the conditions."

His employers and fellow workers at US Communications West seemed to share much the same high regard for him. He was a dependable, hard-working, patriotic American who loyally served his country and had apparently never been in trouble with the law in his life.

He was also divorced from his wife, Kathy, and was the father of an eight-year-old girl when he met Jill. His daughter, Erin, lived in Fort Collins with her mother.

Michael was looking for a place to live in Greeley when he learned about an apartment in a house at 1309 Eleventh Avenue. Jill owned the house, and soon after he rented the downstairs apartment he fell under her spell. A short time later he moved upstairs with his lonesome landlady. She rented her boyfriend's former apartment to a young man, Rick Mott.

They were living there when Jill flew to Las Vegas to tie the knot with the retired CPO. Curiously, with her marriage to Carroll and her live-in relationship with Michael, she had completed a near-clean sweep of America's armed services, all of which were served by the main men in her life. Two were Marine corps, one was Army, one was Navy, and the other had served in the Air Force and in the National Guard of two states. Only the Coast Guard was left out.

The new Mrs. Carroll and her groom didn't waste much time honeymooning in Las Vegas before returning to Houston. While the groom attended to business and began planning a move to Colorado, his wife busily shuttled back and forth between Houston and Greeley. Even though she was away from Carroll's home in Houston much of the time, the vivacious, attractive, and smartly dressed younger woman had brought a sense of happiness and pride to his life.

Jill was as busy as a hummingbird, playing out an exhausting balancing act between two men: a husband in Texas and a live-in boyfriend in Greeley. Somehow she also made time between her roles as wife, sweetheart, full-time college student, and businesswoman to regularly make the arduous, nearly three hundred-mile round-trip drive over the Continental Divide between the "All American City" in Weld County and "Ski City USA" in Routt County to keep track of affairs at the Oak Street Bed & Breakfast and to meet with her lawyers on matters relating to Gerry and Carl.

She still had her trademark vibrant personality and driving ambition. But keeping her energy level up wasn't the piece of cake it had once been. She had lived nearly five decades, been married to nine husbands, given birth to and raised at least three children, formed or operated several businesses, and traveled much of the United States and the rest of the world.

The old silhouettes of the lithesome model's shape that helped her win photo assignments and a beauty crown were being blurred by extra pounds. Crows feet and wrinkles were taking their inevitable toll on her once-flawless, high-cheekboned face. Even her butternut-brown skin didn't have its former healthy glow and elasticity.

She had to reach for a pair of reading glasses when she was looking at small print, and she was having serious problems with her right hip. Another physician was treating her for degenerative arthritis, and she was taking cortisone shots for pain. Even her soft, silky, Southern drawl was fading, and when she got emotional or angry her voice could be as raw and scratchy as a cigarette smoker's cough. There was no avoiding it; Jill wasn't a sexy, saucy woman-child anymore. Age, an arthritic hip, and flab were ruining her beauty.

Gerry had finally released the deed of trust after being convinced beyond the shadow of a doubt he hadn't fathered a child. Jill admitted that in front of her lawyer and in front of Gerry when she finally gave her deposition. But they were still locked in a legal battle over her demands that he pay for the damage to the engine of the Mercedes and pay attorney fees and his counterclaim for defamation and demand that she repay him for remodeling the house and other expenses he incurred preparing for the birth of a daughter.

And, of course, there was the ongoing mess with Carl and his $250,000 lawsuit. The emotional pressure on her was intense, and if later accusations are to be believed, dark thoughts were running through her mind. She was still intent on making as much trouble for Gerry as she could.

Jill talked in front of her daughter-in-law about using stolen money orders to cause trouble for Gerry with the law, Julie later told law-enforcement authorities. She figured she could get him in hot water by signing his name and cashing some of them.

Gerry was deathly afraid of snakes, and Jill reportedly speculated about slipping a snake into his car or Jeep while he was working at the store or inside his house.

She also told Julie that Gerry was homosexual and talked about putting an advertisement in the personal columns of one of Colorado's daily newspapers with statewide circulation, *The Denver Post* or the *Rocky Mountain News,* to embarrass him. The ad would invite gay men to telephone or stop in Boggs Hardware when they were in Steamboat Springs looking for company and advise them to ask for Gerry in order to get a ten percent discount.

Steamboat Springs was a small town. The residents were curious and chatty and possibly less likely to show the same easy acceptance of homosexuality generally found in larger urban centers like New York, Chicago, or San Francisco.

Gerry began receiving mysterious telephone calls, including one from a man who claimed to have had sex with him. The voice wasn't familiar to him, and he taped that call and others.

Ridiculing and harassing Jill's ex-husband wasn't the worst thing Jill had in store for him, according to her oldest son, his wife, and several other people. They say Jill wanted Gerry killed. If sworn statements from family members and acquaintances are to be believed, Jill had made up her mind to employ a bloody solution to her problems. Gerry had to die, quickly and violently.

Jill telephoned Seth more than once and asked him to do a favor for his mother: murder Gerry.

Her new boyfriend had fallen under her siren spell, as so many other men had done before him. And he was apparently as determined as she was to see to it that Gerry was murdered, according to Seth's account. "We're only doing this for you kids," Michael was quoted as saying.

Statements by Jill's son weren't the only ones to place Michael squarely in the middle of a ruthless scheme to murder the Steamboat Springs merchant.

The telephone company employee did a lot of talking with one of his buddies who worked with him at US Communications West. He reportedly asked Troy Giffon at least five times to carry out a contract hit on Jill's ex and offered to pay thousands of dollars for the job. Like Michael, Giffon was a veteran of Vietnam and the shared experience helped cement their friendship.

According to Giffon's later statement to a police in-

vestigator, Michael pestered him for a couple of weeks
during the early summer in efforts to enlist him in a
murder conspiracy. Jill's boyfriend stopped at his
friend's house four times and talked once with him by
telephone about the need to get rid of the Steamboat
Springs businessman because he was blocking the sale
of the bed-and-breakfast. Somehow, as Michael explained it, sale of the inn had become a million-dollar
deal. His girlfriend would have access to that amount
after the sale was concluded, and he was lined up for a
big piece of the action once the troublemaking merchant was out of the way.

Michael was telling people at the telephone company that he had been cut in as a ten percent owner of
the bed and breakfast by his wealthy sweetheart. He
confided a similar story to a friend from Evansville,
whom he had worked with at Indiana Bell.

He offered Giffon $3,500 to do the dirty work for
him. Giffon wasn't a killer and wasn't interested. But
Michael wasn't ready to give up. He wheedled and
promised and eventually more than doubled the
bounty to $7,500. Giffon still wasn't buying. But their
disagreement didn't shoot down their friendship, at
least not immediately. He continued opening his door
to his buddy when Michael dropped by the house, and
he continued to listen.

Michael had been roaring over the Divide to Steamboat Springs on his Harley-Davidson or making the
drive with Jill in one of her cars, and they were both
too well known in the little town to carry out the murder themselves, he explained. Someone else had to be
found who would do it for them.

As Jill had done with others, Michael painted a sordid picture of the target of their bloodthirsty scheming, according to Giffon's continuing account. Gerry
was a twisted bisexual who enjoyed watching his wife
have sex with other men before joining in the action,

Michael confided. Because of his respected position in the business community, he traveled outside Steamboat Springs to find male company. So when he was murdered, police suspicion would focus on one of his secret gay lovers.

Gerry's own allegedly intricately-hidden sex life would deflect the investigation and send police off on a wild goose chase, providing a perfect cover for the homicide. At least it seemed from Michael's glib explanation, that was the way the problem would be resolved.

At times, Michael called his girlfriend's former husband filthy names, especially concentrating on crude descriptions of homosexual activity. Giffon's wife, Teri listened while her husband's friend lambasted Gerry as a "son of a bitch," "faggot," and even nastier words because he was preventing Jill from selling the bed-and-breakfast. All he talked about while he was at the house was marrying Jill, selling the bed-and-breakfast and making enough money to retire, she told investigators.

She thought it was odd that he had never hung around their house before, then all of a sudden for a two-week period he was dropping by every three or four days. "Man, he must really hate Jill's ex-husband," Troy's wife remembered him saying to her one day a few minutes after Michael left. "He wants to kill the guy."

Giffon didn't want anything to do with the lunatic proposal. Michael wondered out loud if he might be able to find someone from Greeley's so-called Latin Quarter to carry out the murder for him.

It seems he never tried to follow up on that idea, or if he did, he ran into the same lack of cooperation he was faced with in his efforts to enlist Giffon. Michael left Greeley later in the summer, on assignment from the company after persistent rains and a massive flood that roared through much of the Midwest. Michael was one of thousands of skilled journeymen and technicians rushed to the area from around the country to repair damage and restore vital services.

Events in Steamboat Springs were continuing to move rapidly, however, and early in June an effort to solve the dispute out of court at a mediation hearing fell through. The Colorado Judicial Department's Office of Dispute Resolution set up a hearing at the NorWest Banks Building where the opposing attorneys had their offices. The first session was canceled because Gerry hadn't produced some necessary documents. For whatever reason, the attempt at mediation failed.

With the failure of the mediation attempt, the long-awaited trial on the suit and countersuit was at last ready to be heard in the Routt County District Court. Three days were set aside on the court calendar for the proceedings, July 28, 29 and 30.

Jill begged off. The timing was awful, and it would be a terrible burden on her if she was forced to appear in court for the scheduled proceedings, she complained through her attorneys.

She underwent total replacement of her right hip on June 23 at the Northern Colorado Medical Center in Greeley, and her attorneys explained she needed about three months to recover. Her mobility was extremely limited and she asked the trial be put back until early the next year. The motion for continuance was signed by Tremaine on June 23, the same day of the scheduled surgery.

The lawyers submitted letters from several doctors in Greeley and in Houston confirming the seriousness of Jill's medical condition and her need for a hip replacement operation. A letter from Dr. Patricia Mayer on letterhead of the North Colorado Arthritis Clinic was dated May 17 and indicated the physician had seen "Ms. Coit-Carroll" in follow-up consultation dealing with degenerative arthritis of her right hip. Dr. Mayer wrote that over a period of time Jill was treated with multiple injections of cortisone, and given anti-inflammatories but none of the efforts eliminated the pain for very long. X-rays revealed severe degenerative arthritis of the hip, and Dr. Mayer concluded that the only option "for lasting relief" was hip replacement.

Another orthopedist in Houston wrote he saw Jill on June 2 after she was referred to him for a second opinion, and x-rays revealed degenerate joint damage of the right hip. Jill was quoted as saying she didn't know why she developed osteoarthritis, but she had been in an auto accident about twenty years earlier and suffered hip pain. The doctor concluded that total hip replacement would be proper treatment.

Dr. Barry A. Nelms, also a Houston orthopedic surgeon, wrote he saw Jill Carroll in his office on June 3 and concurred that she would benefit from total replacement of her right hip. X-rays revealed osteoarthritis. The letter also disclosed Jill was on her current husband's health-care plan.

She had suffered muscle spasms and agonizing pain. The message was clear, Jill's condition had left her no viable choice except to submit to an operation to cope with the pain and to halt the rapidly continuing degeneration of her hip.

Gerry and his lawyer strongly opposed the continuance nevertheless. Halvorson argued she had built up a history of acting to delay the proceedings and presented a deposition from Steely describing Jill's timely seizure at the Denver airport. The lawyer also claimed a delay would give Jill an opportunity to get rid of her Colorado real estate, making any judgment against her uncollectible.

The B&B was still on the market, and the price was

recently dropped by about twenty-five percent to
$200,000 in order to make a quick sale, he added. In
1991, the property was being offered for $850,000, was
then reduced to $750,000 and most recently at
$650,000 before taking the latest nosedive.

Gerry's attorney also pointed out William Harold
and Sylvia Boggs, who were expected to be called to
testify at the trial, made it a practice to leave the area
in the fall and spend the cold-weather months in Arizona. If the trial was put off three or four months the
elderly couple would have to testify by deposition,
rather than appear in court in person.

Reluctantly, Judge Rebecca Kourlis rescheduled the
trial, setting aside three days on the court calendar
beginning on Wednesday, October 27, 1993. There
really wasn't much choice. Jill had undergone the operation, and it seemed obvious that she needed time
to recover from such a serious surgical procedure. The
ailing woman had pulled off a timely *fait accompli.*

At Gerry's request, the jurist made it a condition of
the continuance, however, that Jill would again be re-
strained from selling or in any other way, encumbering
her real estate owned in Routt County. A legal hold
was back in place, once more preventing sale of the
bed-and-breakfast. It would ensure her appearance at
the civil trial. Nothing was said in the order about her
holdings in Greeley or Alaska, but Jill's legal troubles
were expanding, rather than improving. The continuance merely bought her some time, but not much.

Tremaine remarked in a motion document that his
client was "optimistic that she can withstand the travel
to Steamboat Springs and a trial in late October . . ."

In the meantime, the ailing woman went to Iowa
with her boyfriend. She had a job to do: find herself a
hired killer.

When Michael packed up his tools, extra work
clothes, and other personal effects, Jill loaded her own

bags with traveling clothes and necessities for the long trip. They set up temporary housekeeping in Ottumwa, a Des Moines River town of about 25,000 people. An agriculture and meat-packing center, Ottumwa is about an hour-long drive from the Missouri border, and it was water-soaked and reeling from recent storms.

While Michael was dealing with generators, fuse boxes, and a tangle of fallen telephone lines, Jill presented herself in Ottumwa as a psychologist. She was a curious kind of psychologist, who did her best to talk an acquaintance into a bigger mess than the troubled Iowa woman would have dreamed of, according to a later statement to a law-enforcement investigator.

Jill asked R. Mohee Hanley to murder a businessman in Colorado for her. It was a weird request for a psychologist to make of anyone. In the personal experience of most Midwesterners like Ms. Hanley, contract murder was a matter that was confined to what they read in books or watched on television shows and in movies. Asking someone to assassinate another person wasn't something expected to come up in casual conversation. The professional-appearing woman she met at a gay and lesbian meeting in Ottumwa was nevertheless urging her to commit a horrific crime. Jill wanted her to travel a thousand miles or so and murder a man she didn't know and had never heard of before.

Jill didn't blurt out the murder proposal all at once. She was more subtle, according to the story recounted by the Ottumwa woman. Jill claimed to be a bisexual who counselled gays and lesbians, Ms. Hanley said. Jill reportedly counselled her once a week for three or four weeks, and during one of the early sessions Ms. Hanley expressed strong feelings about the behavior of rapists.

"How would you feel if someone raped your daughter?" Jill asked her.

"I'd kill him."

Jill could hardly have created a better opening to bring up the subject of a revenge murder.

During their next counseling session, Jill explained she had a lover who was killed in a traffic accident. The dead man had a daughter who was about five years old, living with an aunt, and being sexually abused by a close male relative. It was a tragic and nasty situation to contemplate, and Jill continued to build on the story during subsequent meetings.

She described the child molester as a man who was in his mid-forties, was tall and stockily built, with dark hair and a mustache. He was the owner of a hardware store in a brick building and lived by himself in Colorado. Ms. Hanley later couldn't recall if Jill said he lived in Steamboat Springs or Greeley.

Unfortunately, the hardware-store owner was bound to get away with his disgusting abuse of the little girl because he was such a prominent member of the community. No one in authority would call him to task for his crimes, Jill reportedly explained.

Mohee Hanley had a dislike for rapists and sexual abusers of children, but murder for hire or for any other reason was something else. Jill would have to look elsewhere if she wanted someone killed, even if the grossly-detestable stories she was telling about the target of her bloodthirsty fantasies were true.

Jill asked if Ms. Hanley knew where she could buy a clean untraceable gun. Ms. Hanley didn't want anything to do with helping her strange counselor find an untraceable gun, any more than she wanted to commit a murder for her. The answer was no.

After returning to Greeley with Michael, Jill was right back where she had started when they left for Iowa. If the stories related to investigators were true, she and Michael had struck out in efforts to find someone who would agree to kill Gerry in a murder-for-hire scheme—or as a humanitarian gesture to prevent the continuing sexual abuse of a child. The trial had been rescheduled, and it was unlikely that the judge could be convinced to agree to yet another continuance.

Jill telephoned Ms. Hanley in Ottumwa, and during a series of calls, eventually offered her $1,000 to carry out the murder, the Iowa woman recounted. Jill reportedly volunteered to take an active role in the killing, and explained she knew how to get into the would-be victim's house through the back door. She also suggested he could be ambushed while he was getting out of his car. Jill would drive by while Mohee could shoot him from the passenger seat. In her final call, Jill offered to take care of Ms. Hanley's travel costs and send her airline tickets.

Ms. Hanley wouldn't budge. She wasn't going to kill anyone for Jill Coit. By late September or early October, according to the Ottumwa woman, Jill was increasingly frantic. She reportedly responded to the stubborn refusal with a statement that she was bound to find a way to have the man killed. If she couldn't find someone to do it for her, she would do it herself.

The leaves on the trees lining the UNC campus were already turning to brilliant yellows and reds when Jill walked into Bizarbor, a beauty shop on Ninth Street. She asked hair-stylist Mary Weber if she could borrow a blond wig that was on display in the shop window. Jill explained that she wanted to go to Steamboat Springs in disguise and follow her boyfriend to see if he was cheating on her.

Jill was a regular customer, and the hair stylist consented to the odd request. The next weekend, Jill returned the wig, as good as new. Nothing happened in

Steamboat Springs, she explained, because her boyfriend was sick.

According to Seth, his mother continued to keep after him to help with the killing. When he continued to refuse to kill Gerry or to help her do the job, she asked him for advice about how she could get into the house. She also asked him to pick up and get rid of the body. She could stuff it in plastic bags and leave it in a ditch near the house for him, Jill suggested, according to his statements to investigators. Then he could load the corpse into the back of Gerry's car, drive it to the airport, and dump it.

Understandably, Seth was reluctant to get involved in a murder. He had worked with her in legitimate business enterprises, and respected her for her industry. But murder was altogether a different kettle of fish.

At one point, however, he advised: "If you do anything stupid, wear gloves." It was October 8, 1993.

Jill hadn't left her daughter-in-law alone either. She once confided to Julie that she had found someone to "take care of Gerry," the young woman later reported. Jill didn't say who the mystery person was or exactly how Gerry was to be taken care of.

Jill telephoned her frequently from Greeley or Texas; Julie didn't always know where the calls originated from. Almost every time Jill called, she asked Julie to check on Gerry to find out if he was at work or at the house. When Jill was in Steamboat Springs, she had Julie drive by Gerry's house with her to see if he was at home. Jill kept herself well informed about her ex-husband's normal daily routine.

Julie recalled that Michael roared across the mountains from Greeley on his Harley one day and took her to lunch at the Steamboat Yacht Club on the riverfront. He groused about all the money Jill was losing because of Gerry and how unfair it was that she was

being sued. When he dropped Julie off back at the
bed-and-breakfast, he told her he was going to ride by
Gerry's house. He didn't say why, and she didn't ask.

During their brief meeting, Michael also mentioned
how quickly he made the trip across the mountains.
He kept the pedal to the metal on his bike and was
behaving as if he was as obsessed as Jill was with
bringing a sudden end to the angry conflict with Gerry.

Events were moving fast and time was running out.
The rescheduled date of the trial with Gerry was only
nineteen days away.

In Manhattan Beach, California, Jill's youngest son
received a telephone call from someone he later described only as "a relative." The caller was worried
about Gerry Boggs's safety, fearful that the merchant
was in serious danger from Jill. William didn't take the
call too seriously. He ignored it, according to his later
recollection. By that time, the trial date was little more
than a week away.

In Indiana, Steely and Metzger had already replied
to subpoenas. Metzger was ordered to report to the
law offices in downtown Plymouth of Stevens, Travis,
Fortin, Lukenbill & Burbrink and produce a virtual
armload of legal documents tied to his domestic and
business relationship with Jill. Copies of marriage applications, marriage certificates, divorce pleadings, final divorce dissolution documents, and any legal
papers related to the Oak Street Bed & Breakfast
were among the material he was directed to produce.

On a deposition Carl gave, he stated that he and Jill
had what he thought was a close marriage, and they
spent all their free time together and didn't even quarrel. "I was utterly devastated to learn that the high
ideals of marriage which we shared had been so bla-
tantly violated," he said. "It became evident from her
own deposition that Jill had been plotting from the
very first year of our marriage to do me in financially."

Then he added, a bit loftily but perhaps in typical pedagogic fashion: "In the words of Thomas Jefferson, 'We are not afraid to follow truth wherever it may lead, nor to tolerate any error so long as reason is left free to combat it.'"

The two ex-husbands were learning the sad truth of another pithy aphorism: "True loves and new loves may come and go, but an ex is forever." Closer to home, the trouble shooter from Four Star Repair, Inc., on West US Highway 40, was also among probable witnesses who were subpoenaed so he would be available for questioning about the damaged Mercedes.

The pressure on Gerry hadn't eased off very much, if at all, and he was anxious to at last settle the acrimonious two-year squabble. He told his friend, Barbara Smith, on Wednesday, October 20, that although he was nervous about seeing his former wife in court he was also looking forward to the confrontation.

"I still have to know there was no baby," he told her.

Despite the findings of the private investigation carried out by Judy Prier-Lewis and her colleagues, Gerry's telephone conversation with Jill's parents, and her sworn statement at the deposition declaring she had not been pregnant and there was no baby Lara, he wanted to hear the denial of his reputed fatherhood in court from her own lips. He wanted to watch and listen as she admitted there was no baby.

On Thursday, October 21, he checked out the receipts in his cash register at about one o'clock in the afternoon, said good-bye to his fellow workers, and left for the rest of the day.

Although Friday is usually a busy time at the store because it's payday for so many people and householders are getting ready to take advantage of their weekends off to make home repairs, Gerry never showed up for work. He didn't telephone, and he

hadn't said anything to anyone Thursday about taking
the day off. Even through what appeared to have been
the worst period of his long-going troubles with Jill, he
had always managed to either keep to his work schedule or at least to let his brother and others know when
he didn't expect to be on the job.

Douglas Boggs knew it wasn't at all like Gerry to
simply sleep in or go off somewhere on his own and
forget about his responsibilities at the store. Douglas
was worried about his older brother. Gerry didn't answer repeated attempts to reach him by telephone.
When Douglas went to the house to check on his
brother, he walked onto a scene in his older brother's
kitchen that was sickening and primitively savage.
Gerry was dead on the kitchen floor.

The prophecy that was so ominously implicit in the
entry on Jill's marriage application for her wedding to
Roy Carroll was realized. She had come as close as it
was possible, to becoming "the Widow Boggs."

Steamboat Springs Police Department Patrolman
Kevin Parker arrived at the house a few minutes later
in response to a telephone call indicating a possible
suicide had occurred. The uniform officer barely had a
chance to take a look at the crumpled body and peek
around to see if there were any others, before he was
asked by Detective Rick Crotz if the victim was still
alive. Crotz had pulled up in his police car only moments behind the patrolman. Parker said the man on
the floor was dead.

Crotz was a fourteen-year law-enforcement veteran,
who spent the first part of his career with the San
Diego Police Department, and he learned his job well
while moving up the ranks. He was efficient, but pro-
fessionally cautious. He checked out the body to confirm for himself that Parker's observation was correct
and the man on the floor was dead. There was no
question the diagnosis was on target. Gerry's body was

cadaver-cold, there was no pulse, and his eyes were glazed over.

The corpse was blocking the back door. A ragged, scarlet gash that appeared as if it might have been caused by a gunshot, creased his high forehead. A small hole in the back of his heavy blue parka also appeared to have been made by a gunshot.

Exposed areas of the man's warmly-bundled body were also marked with ugly lacerations and bruises, including an injury to his right cheek. A huge pool of blood had formed next to the head, and other splatters extended at least ten feet away. The nearby walls were marked with more ugly rust-colored smears. A plastic bag near the body, and a small metal lump that appeared to be the slug from a small-caliber cartridge were also blood-smeared. The kitchen looked like a slaughterhouse.

Crotz took another quick look around for additional bodies or anyone who might be injured or hiding. Outside the immediate kitchen area there wasn't much to see. There were no lurking killers with a gun, no bodies, no blood, no overturned furniture, or other indications of violence or a struggle. Everything seemed to be in place, except for the answering machine on the telephone. The lid that permits the audiotape to be slipped in or out was open and there was no cartridge inside. On the surface, there was nothing especially alarming about that. It would not be very long, however, before the missing audiotape took on more significance in the investigation.

That was in the near future, however. For the present, Crotz and the uniform officer retreated outside for a war council with police department colleagues and an assistant Routt County district attorney. The street, driveway, and yards outside the attractive bi-level house on West Hillside Court were becoming very busy.

Assistant DA Kerry St. James and patrolman Jerry Stabile were among the newcomers. It was quickly agreed by St. James and Crotz that there would not be a comprehensive inspection of the interior of the house until a search warrant could be obtained from a judge. Murder is a serious crime whenever and wherever it occurs, but it wasn't something that happened in Steamboat Springs every day. Not even every year. Authorities at the scene were determined to see that no aspect of the investigation was botched.

There wasn't much of a mystery about the last previous murders that occurred in the city almost two years earlier. In September 1991, William Coleman gunned down his ex-wife Jan and her friend, Luke McKee. Coleman killed himself the next day. Crotz played an important role in investigation of the tragedy and during his career had probed several other homicides as well.

This time police were faced with a completely different kind of challenge. So far there was one dead man, and based on their cursory observation, it was obvious he was killed by someone else. Gerry didn't commit suicide. There were no other bodies in the immediate area, so it seemed to be an excellent bet that his killer was still very much alive and on the loose.

No one wanted a slick defense attorney somewhere down the line getting critical evidence tossed out of court because it had been discovered and seized without a warrant authorizing search of the house. St. James and police investigators played it safe and secured the immediate area inside and around the house to preserve the integrity of the crime scene and wait for the warrant. For the time being the interior of the house was off-limits to police, neighbors, and the press.

Reporter-photographer Brad Bolchunos from *Steamboat Today,* the sister publication to the *Pilot,* snapped pictures from the street of the house and the small group of law-enforcement officers conferring or standing just outside.

Officers dialed Routt County Coroner Dayle D. Hammock at a minute or two after four PM, and told him to get in touch with Captain J. D. Hays at the police department about a death. Hammock drove to the police headquarters, conferred with Hays for a few minutes, then hurried to the house with his deputy, Douglas Allen.

Crotz explained to him that the crime scene was secured, and after discussing the matter with St. James as well, the coroner decided to defer making an official pronouncement of death. The detective assured him the victim was dead, and Hammock chose to hold off on going inside until the search warrant was obtained.

The position taken by the police, the assistant DA and the coroner was a carefully considered good-faith decision, but it opened them to a spate of second guessing and eventually led to serious problems determining the approximate time of death.

Exactly how damaging or critical the delay would eventually become was a matter to be worked out much later before a judge and a jury. But there was no question it would make the job of police and prosecutors much more difficult in some respects. Valuable information provided by conditions such as lividity and body temperature was either already lost or soon would be. Lividity is the discoloration that occurs when the heart stops beating and gravity causes the blood to settle to the lowest areas of the body. The process of lividity stops in about two hours, or less, when the blood coagulates.

Although those factors can be a big help, even they are not sure-fire indicators of the precise time of death. Under average conditions, bodies begin to cool after the first hour or two following death. They start to feel cold to the touch after about twelve hours, and after twenty-four hours even the internal organs have usually reached the same temperature as the outside surroundings. Other elements can lead to critical variations in the speed at which a body cools, however, and must be taken into consideration in making final calculations.

Bodies cool at different rates, based on the build, how the limbs are arranged, and temperatures or weather conditions where they are found. Other conditions such as health, and how warmly someone is dressed can also be important factors. The bodies of heavier people cool at a slower rate than those of thinner people. And someone who had a fever would have a higher temperature to begin with and it would take more time for the body to reach the same cool state as a healthy person.

Skillful detectives, coroners, or pathologists must take all those possibilities and many other factors into consideration when working to arrive at a time of death. But getting a good lock on an approximate time can be critical to an investigation. Every minute of uncertainty about an exact time confronts police, prosecutors, and defense attorneys, with a wider window of time in which the murder may have been committed.

Other factors, of course, were still available to help narrow the time gap. Gerry's stomach contents could, and almost certainly would be, examined to determine approximately when and what he had last eaten. Although the rate of digestion varies with different people and can be affected by such things as anger or fear, the condition of food found in the stomach often provides valuable clues to helping pin down the time of death.

Witnesses would also be located and interviewed to determine the time he was last seen alive. Witnesses are important, but again they provide less-than-perfect tools for crime investigators. Every homicide cop knows witnesses aren't infallible. Far from it. Two witnesses describing the same individual might differ with one estimating the height and weight at six-foot and 200 pounds, and the other insisting the subject was five-foot-eight-or-ten and 145 pounds. Or one person might describe a car as a gray Ford Escort, and another will say it was a red Pontiac Sunbird.

Usually, although not always, being able to cite a close approximation of the time of death is not so helpful to defense attorneys—especially if their client is guilty.

Crotz and his colleagues didn't simply cool their heels for half a day waiting for a warrant. Not by any means. Most professionals in the field agree that the first forty-eight-hours are crucial to a homicide investigation. After that amount of time the trail begins to grow cold.

Police officers began drifting through the neighborhood, knocking on doors and talking with residents. Footwork is a tedious job, but it is a staple element of almost any homicide investigation. If anyone in the normally-quiet neighborhood saw anything unusual or suspicious on their street or around the home of the dead businessman in the last day or so, it was important for police to gather the information as quickly as possible.

Other officers got busy on the telephone, calling family members and acquaintances of Gerry's. SSPD Detective Robert DelValle talked with Thane Gilliland, who told him about a surprising discovery made during the summer of 1992 when he was trying to adjust the front seat of Gerry's red Isuzu for Jill. Two pistols were under the driver's seat. One was a .45 caliber semi-automatic handgun in a leather holster. The other was described as a small "palm gun," possibly a .25 caliber or .32 caliber blue-steel semi-automatic.

During another interview a few weeks later, Gilliland turned over a box of .22 caliber long-rifle ammunition to Colorado Bureau of Investigation, (CBI), agent Susan Kitchen. He explained Gerry told him that after the breakup with Jill he took the hollowpoint and round-nose bullets out of a car she had been driving. Gerry gave the ammunition to his friend because he couldn't use it. He didn't own a .22.

Crotz talked with Douglas Boggs. So did Detective DelValle and Stabile. The dead man's brother had discussions with all three officers during the first twenty-four hours of the probe. Boggs telephoned his lawyer's office and broke the dreadful news to Sharon Halvorson that Gerry was dead and he was with the police and about to be questioned. She passed the word to her husband, and he hurried to the SSPD headquarters. The attorney hovered protectively near his shaken friend and client as he was interviewed.

Police investigators were forced by the unhappy circumstances to ask some painful questions and carry out some unpleasant functions. The grieving brother wound up having his hands swabbed for gunshot residue, hair and blood samples were taken, and he may even have been strip searched, according to a later report in the local press.

At that stage of an investigation, a good homicide detective has to consider practically everyone who has anything to do with the victim as a potential suspect, even when he is a close family member, prominent member of the business community, and a former county government office-holder. Douglas was a one-time Routt County Commissioner. Law-enforcement officers are especially aware that there is nothing unusual about family members turning on each other, and in fact family murders are all too common. It's still more the rule than the exception, even in these days of drive-by gang shootings and drug wars, that victims are killed by someone they know.

Boggs told the officers about Gerry's marriage, the annulment and long-running quarrel with Jill, her outrageously-checkered marital background, and the approaching civil trial. He also advised them about the harassment and mysterious telephone calls. Douglas said Halvorson told his brother to save the tapes of the harassing calls from Jill and from the mystery man recorded on his answering machine. They could be important evidence in the approaching civil court proceeding.

The open lid on the empty answering machine was suddenly an aspect of the investigation that warranted a very close look.

Other, unforeseen contacts made during the sweep of the neighborhood were also turning up important gems of information, however. Stabile talked with Girl Scouts Andrea Thorne and Lisa Re and learned they had stopped at Gerry's house about four o'clock Thursday after school, hoping to sell fund-raising nuts. Although Lisa noticed vehicles parked inside the garage while she was climbing the stairs to the front door, no one answered when she rang the bell. The girl's description of the vehicles matched those of Gerry's Isuzu and his Jeep.

Debbie Fedewa was also contacted, and told DelValle about the suspicious characters she noticed lurking around the neighborhood Thursday. She described the couple who were in such inappropriate warm clothing in the balmy, early fall weather; the woman dressed as a man with the obviously false mustache and pony tail, and her tall athletically-built male companion.

Meanwhile, after conferring with the assistant DA, Steamboat Springs police called for help from the

CBI. Although the Steamboat Springs Police Department was composed of experienced and well-trained law-enforcement professionals, certain crimes sometimes occurred that strained the capabilities of a small-town organization. They didn't have the sophisticated crime laboratory or trained technicians to conduct all the ballistics, serology, and other forensic operations and tests that were so vital to a successful investigation.

The CBI also had trained crime-scene technicians who could help in the gathering of evidence and homicide detectives who had probed scores or hundreds of murders around the state. Summoning the CBI was no reflection on the professionalism of the local police department. It was a good call.

A few minutes after midnight, almost nine hours after Gerry's body was discovered, Steamboat Springs Detective Ross Kelly showed up at the house with the search warrant. Detective Kelly at last walked back into the house, accompanied by a few other hand-picked colleagues from the SSPD, St. James, and a forensics team from the CBI.

Police officers fanned out to make a thorough search of the house, while forensics technicians from the CBI moved methodically through the utility room and kitchen snapping photographs, tracking, measuring and collecting samples of blood smears, and gathering trace evidence such as hair, fiber, and dirt. Photos of the back entrance were also taken immediately before the homicide team walked inside. The coroner joined the small squad of grim-faced men minutes later.

Hammock was first elected to his job as coroner in 1987. Before that he was with the police department in Austin, Texas, for four years, then served six years from 1976 to 1988 as Routt County Sheriff.

Like many of his current colleagues in other thinly-populated counties in Colorado, he had taken advantage of professional courses sponsored by the state for coroners. He had limited medical training and knew some first aid. Although he had crime-scene training during his law-enforcement career, he wasn't a forensic pathologist.

Under the circumstances, the small-town coroner did what was expected of him: the best job he could. He made a close visual inspection of the heavily-bundled body on the kitchen floor. A ragged, bloody hole was plainly visible in the victim's parka covering the upper right portion of his back, that appeared to have been caused by a gunshot. At 1:20 AM, three minutes after walking into the house, the county coroner made the official pronouncement of death.

Hammock had known Gerry Boggs for years and he recognized the dead man, but his report was properly dispassionate and professional. On a form titled "Routt County Coroner's Office Report For Case No. 93-33," he recorded the time of entry, location and position of the body, and other pertinent information. Interestingly, in a space labeled "SPOUSE," the words "Never married" were typed in.

Hammock observed that the single bloody bullet on the floor about five feet from the corpse appeared to have been discharged from a firearm "of approximately .25 caliber." The wooden handle of a shovel lying a few feet from the body, was also covered with red smears that appeared to have been left by bloody fingers.

Elsewhere in the silent, night-shrouded structure that had been Gerry's home, police were gathering a collection of articles as possible evidence. Gerry had a modest collection of weapons, and investigators took a loaded .357 Smith & Wesson pistol from his nightstand, along with thirty-one extra rounds of ammunition in a bullet wallet and dump pouch, and another handgun and two rifles from a closet.

One of the more intriguing discoveries was made in the attached garage. Several cassette tapes, a compass, trash bags, and a Denver map were collected from the top of his car. Each of the weapons and the other items were meticulously packaged or marked separately with tags identifying the location, the date, the time, and the initials of the officer in charge of the evidence at that stage. When technicians had completed their immediate work with the bloody shovel and other items found near the body or taken from Gerry's pockets, those were also carefully tagged and added to the growing mound of evidence.

After confirming his law-enforcement colleagues were satisfied with their picture-taking, studies, and inspection of Gerry's body, Hammock carefully rolled the victim over onto his back. The coroner observed what appeared to be another gunshot wound when he lifted Gerry's right arm. A third ragged bullet hole was found in the front of the parka. The slug had smashed into the victim's chest. Gunpowder spackles around the holes in his clothing and the entry wounds indicated he was shot at close range.

Gerry was savagely beaten as well as shot. The bloody shovel was obviously the weapon used as a bludgeon. The victim's forehead was marked with a curved four-inch long gash that was so raggedly deep and ugly it was initially taken by Crotz to be a possible gunshot wound. Gerry had other injuries on his nose, cheek, right temple, knee, and all over the trunk of his body. His right hand was cut and bruised with injuries that appeared to be defense wounds.

While the coroner went about his grim task of moving the body, inspecting it, and probing for information, a CBI photographer took pictures of every step of the process.

At last Hammock removed a worn black billfold from Gerry's right rear pocket. A driver's license, other identification and personal papers, and a single $10 bill was inside. A brown wallet containing $260 was removed from Gerry's left front pocket, and a leather packet of keys was taken from his pants pocket. Then Allen helped Hammock roll Gerry's cold corpse into a body bag and seal it up.

Although a few porch lights in the neighborhood were on earlier in the evening, and residents peeked for awhile through cracked curtains or stood on front porches to stare curiously toward the house, by the time Gerry's body was at last loaded into a waiting ambulance nearby residents had finally settled down for the night. The only activity was inside and immediately around the house. Even the most persistently curious snoops had given up and gone to bed, and there wasn't so much as the faint light from a television set showing in neighboring houses when the friendly hardware-store owner was driven away from his troubled home on West Hillside Court for the last time.

Gerry's body was transported to the Shearon Funeral Home on Sixth Street, but the respite was only temporary. Hammock took a short rest, cleaned up, had some coffee and a few bites of breakfast, then drove back through the crisp, early morning gloom to the funeral home.

He was met there by his deputy, who helped him load the gurney holding the dead man into a hearse. They began the long drive over the mountains, across Rabbit Ear Pass to the Jefferson County Coroner's Department in Denver. The autopsy was performed there by a team of investigators under the direction of forensic pathologist, Dr. Mike Dobersen. Jefferson County Deputy Coroners Triena Harper and John Jaungclaus, along with Tim Garner, a district attorney's office investigator, made up the rest of the team.

After x-rays were taken and photographs were snapped by both Hammock and Garner, the gurney holding Gerry's body was wheeled into the autopsy room. Dressed in crisp white smocks, and with their mouths and noses covered by white gauze masks, the forensic experts gathered around the stainless-steel slab holding the body.

More color photographs were taken. Gerry's body was weighed and measured. He was a sturdy six-foot, one-inch tall, and weighed a hefty 195 pounds. The autopsy team then made a close visual study of the body, recording the observations of Dr. Dobersen, including the location and nature of the injuries, on audiotape. The tape would be transcribed later. Samples were collected of blood, urine, other body fluids, and tissue. Hair samples were taken from Gerry's mustache, pubic area, and from different areas of his head. Variations in color often occur, especially with someone of Gerry's age, whose dark hair is frequently just beginning to turn to white. The dead man's fingers and thumbs were also inked and rolled on fingerprint cards. Scrapings were taken from under his fingernails, a critically important procedure in case he had managed to scratch an assailant and tear away tissue or blood.

Precise analyses would be made later by forensic toxicologists at the CBI laboratory on the samples, including scans for the presence of alcohol, prescription, and over-the-counter drugs. The hair samples could possibly become valuable later to match against loose hairs that may have been collected from the body or elsewhere at the crime scene and compared with those of suspects. Garner labeled and packaged the evidence, carefully signing his name or initials on each of the samples. Everyone who handled the samples from that point on would add their own initials or signatures in order to maintain the chain of evidence, a procedure that would be vital when the legal process moved into the courtroom.

As Hammock and investigators in Steamboat Springs observed earlier, Gerry was shot three times, once where his chest bones curved under his right arm and twice in the back. When Gerry's body was opened, the chief pathologist and his assistants were able to follow and determine the trajectory of the low-caliber bullets and recover two slugs.

The bullet hole on the right side of Gerry's chest a few inches away from his arm was an exit wound, made by one of the bullets fired into his back. The other bullet that sliced into his back was high and to the left of his spine and traveled along the rib cage to the soft tissue under his left arm where it was stopped. That bullet, along with one of the others, was recovered from the body. The final slug was picked up earlier from the floor during the initial search of the crime scene.

The path of the bullets indicated the killer fired from right to left, leading investigators to surmise the gunman was right-handed. The bullets also coursed slightly upward through the body. Gerry was either standing up and the shooter was shorter than he was, or he was lying down and the killer fired as he or she stood over him.

If he was lying down when all three shots were triggered, he would have had to have rolled over—or been rolled over by the killer or killers for the bullets to be fired both into his chest and in his back.

At the conclusion of the autopsy, Dr. Dobersen reported the cause of death was multiple gunshot wounds to the chest.

Hammock and Allen again loaded the body into the hearse, and drove it back to Shearson Funeral Home in Steamboat Springs. The coroner filled out the death certificate and provided copies to the police and prosecutor. This time, "Divorced," was typed in the space designated for information about the marital status of the deceased. More significantly, "Undetermined" was typed in both for the date of death and the time of death. The time and date of the pronouncement of death was filled in however, as 1:20 AM, October 23. Hammock checked a box labeled "Pending Investigation," for the manner of death.

Earlier, while police were waiting for a search warrant, news of the shocking tragedy was beginning to filter out among Gerry's friends, neighbors, and acquaintances in Steamboat Springs.

One of Jill's attorneys in the civil suit, Klauzer, was about ready to wind up business for the day and leave when a lawyer acquaintance, Ralph A. Cantafio, walked into his office. Cantafio said he had heard Gerry Boggs was dead. Klauzer telephoned his client the next day. When he wasn't able to reach her, he left an urgent message for her to call him back.

Late the next day the Boggs family attorney and his wife had an exceedingly strange experience. Vance Halvorson and his wife, Sharon, had just left the Douglas Boggs home on Routt County Road 38-A and were turning onto Strawberry Park Road when a bright-red sportscar approached them from the opposite direction.

Sharon Halvorson could hardly believe her eyes. She had seen the sports car, or its twin, before. It was either Jill's car or one just like it. But the most startling thing about the approaching vehicle was the driver. As the cars passed, Mrs. Halvorson was certain the driver was Jill. The lawyer's wife said both she and her husband saw Jill in the car and was later quoted in the hometown newspaper as saying the driver was "wearing a big, fat bushy mustache and wearing a baseball cap turned backwards." The cap was gray and the phony mustache was black.

The next day the lawyer's wife was startled by what appeared to be another Jill sighting. Mrs. Halvorson was at the Shearon Funeral Home where Douglas Boggs was making final arrangements for his brother. The lawyer's wife watched in amazement as the red Toyota Paseo cruised by the funeral home with a woman at the wheel who looked exactly like Jill. Mrs. Halvorson drew Doug's attention to the car, and as they watched, the driver peered intently at the mortuary. This time there was no phony mustache. Boggs told police he was "ninety-nine percent sure" the driver of the car was Jill.

Seth confirmed during an interview with Officer David Deschant that his mother owned a red Paseo. Jill, it was obvious, changed cars often. And she loved red.

In Manhattan Beach, William took a telephone call from his mother. Gerry Boggs was dead, she told him. Someone murdered him. It was chilling news. William was scared.

While grieving family members and morticians at the funeral home prepared for the popular merchant's last rites and burial, Steamboat police detectives and agents from the CBI were pulling together the early threads of their investigation. On Sunday, two days after Gerry's body was discovered, Detectives Crotz, DelValle, Kelly, Officer Deschant, Hammock, St. James, and DA's investigator Tim Garner met with CBI agents Robert C. Sexton and Kitchen at the police department to share information and discuss their battle plan.

They had been busy looking up people who knew Jill and Gerry for interviews. They were especially anxious to talk to Jill—when the time was right.

For the time being, police were necessarily keeping a tight lip with the local and state press. They refused to comment to reporters about a motive for the murder or possible suspects and said nothing about the strong focus the investigation was taking on the activities of the former Mrs. Boggs and her handsome boyfriend.

Douglas Boggs and Halvorson had already informed them that the civil trial was scheduled for Wednesday. It was less than a week away. As it turned out, that was one day after Gerry's family, friends, neighbors, and fellow employees from the store gathered at the United Methodist Church at Eighth and Oak streets, only three blocks from the courthouse and two blocks due west of Jill's bed-and-breakfast, to remember him and to mourn at his final rites.

When they assembled for the two PM funeral service, the pews were filled. Some time later most of the mourners joined in the grim procession of vehicles that followed the hearse carrying Gerry's body to the local cemetery for burial.

Boggs Hardware was closed. A message on letterhead stationery, advised in large black type:

> "In memory of Gerry Boggs.
> We are closed today for funeral
> services."

At the request of his family, memorials were made to the Yampa Valley Foundation Hospice Fund in Steamboat Springs.

When Jill returned Klauzer's call he informed her that Gerry was dead, and she told him she would be in Steamboat Springs Sunday and stop in at his office Monday morning. She spent a big portion of Monday with her lawyer conferring about the mysterious slaying of her former husband and the effect of the murder on the civil trial that was to begin Wednesday. It would obviously have to be postponed once more, but that was a problem to be worked out between the attorneys and the judge.

Jill indicated she was going to drive to Denver, but promised to stay in touch. She kept her word, and talked with Klauzer by telephone at least once a day on Tuesday, Wednesday, Thursday, and Friday. Judge Kourlis postponed the trial as expected. There really wasn't any other viable alternative.

A week to ten days after Jill talked with her lawyer at his office she telephoned and asked if authorities investigating Gerry's murder had placed any travel restrictions on her that would prevent her from taking a previously planned trip. Klauzer said he didn't know of any.

In that event, Jill responded, she would be away traveling for awhile. But she promised to keep in touch through the mails with Klauzer, and through the law office with her son, Seth, in order to take care of business matters.

When investigators from the Steamboat Springs Police Department and the CBI were finally ready to look up Jill Coit-Boggs-Carroll for a long, serious talk about her ex-husband's murder it was too late.

NINE

John Law

Solving the shocking slaying of the local merchant was top-priority business in the Steamboat Springs Police Department, among the CBI agents assigned to assist them, and Assistant DA St. James.

The law enforcement officers moved fast and cast a wide net in their search for the killer or killers who had bushwhacked Gerry Boggs in his home. Investigators began snooping through courthouse records in Steamboat Springs and questioning people in Colorado towns and cities from the Routt County seat to Denver, Westminster, Fort Collins, and Greeley.

They contacted Judy Prier-Lewis, who shared information with them collected during the investigation she conducted for her friend. Very quickly, the law enforcement sleuths expanded their probe far outside the boundaries of the Centennial State to Texas, Indiana, Louisiana, and Iowa.

Much of the early activity was focused on Greeley, where the odd couple who had rapidly become the principle suspects in the dreadful crime was living. After checking in with local Greeley police and enlisting their cooperation to avoid stepping on jurisdictional toes, DelValle interviewed the tenants who rented the downstairs portion of Jill's house. The young men described their landlady and her live-in boyfriend as best they could for the officer.

Michael was described by Rick Mott as being in his middle-to-late thirties, between five-foot, eleven-inches and six-foot, one-inch, with a slim build, dish-water-blond hair and no beard or mustache. Steve Giamberdine told the detective Michael was about forty years old, six-foot-tall, and had his blond hair cut short. There was no beard or mustache.

Mott said his landlady was in her early forties, with large breasts, big hips, and dark brown hair almost to her shoulders. Giamberdine described her as about five-foot, seven-inches or five-foot, eight-inches tall, with brown shoulder-length hair, a "flat rear" and "kind-of-wide-in-the-hips." Interestingly, both men's description of their landlady's "flat rear" fit in per-fectly with Debbie Fedewa's observation about the oddly-flat bottom of the strange cross-dresser lurking outside Gerry's house.

After the interview on the Tuesday following the slaying, Michael telephoned Mott and said Jill wanted to talk with him. Mott conversed with his landlady for a few minutes, and she said she was coming to the house to pick up some clothes. She walked up to the house about five minutes later, and they greeted each other while he stood on the front porch. Mott didn't see her red Paseo parked anywhere nearby. Jill didn't want to go inside the house after all. She preferred to take a walk with her young tenant and have a little talk.

While they strolled slowly down the quiet street a few moments later, Jill peppered Mott with questions. She wanted to know what the police officer said to him, and exactly what information the investigators were after. As Mott recounted the odd encounter to yet another detective, Don Eyer of the Greeley Police Department, Jill cautioned that the lawmen were try-

ing to harass him and advised him not to talk with
them. He should get himself a lawyer, she said.

Why should he hire a lawyer, Mott asked? He
hadn't done anything wrong. But Jill insisted he
needed legal representation. Her former husband was
a homosexual who only married her to put up a front,
she explained. But she was involved in a divorce and
lawsuit with him, and several of his friends killed him
in order to avoid personal embarrassment at the approaching trial.

It was a weird story that was difficult to swallow.
The entire matter was very strange, in fact, like a children's game of cops and robbers or an exceedingly-
poorly written mystery yarn. Mott didn't take his landlady's suggestion that he find himself an attorney or
avoid police. In fact, he disclosed one other especially-
important fact to the same Greeley detective. He saw
Jill about nine o'clock Friday morning, October 22,
when she knocked on his door. That was only a bit
more than six hours before Gerry's body was discovered.

There was no question that Jill and her boyfriend
were feeling intense pressure from the fast-moving police investigation. It was becoming more intense every
day, and the stress was getting to them. The fallout
from the savage slaying was also getting to other people, according to a story passed on by *Houston Chronicle* reporter Susan Bardwell to Worth Weller in North
Manchester.

Houston police reportedly opened Clark's old case
file after an anonymous woman caller began telephoning them to inquire about the two-decades-old murder. Police pulled the file and traced the call. Then
they telephoned the Oak Street Bed & Breakfast and
Jill Coit answered the phone. In a follow-up call, the
Houston police spoke with Julie Coit. When she was
confronted and accused of being the mystery caller,

she told the police her mother-in-law's ex-husband in Steamboat Springs had just been murdered.

In Steamboat Springs, police descended on the Oak Street Bed & Breakfast with a search warrant. Among the items collected in the sweep were a cashier's check with the name "William Clark Coit" on it and another paper with the name "Jill C. Metzger." Another warrant was served on U S West Communications, which turned over Jill's telephone records. Eventually more than a dozen search warrants would be issued and served during the rapidly-broadening probe.

On the Tuesday after Gerry's death, Michael was summoned to the US West Communications offices a few miles outside Greeley in unincorporated Weld County. A CBI agent wanted to talk with him, he was advised by Neil Wilson, manager of US West's Network & Technology Services in Greeley and Michael's immediate supervisor. Robert Sexton was waiting at the office to discuss a murder in Steamboat Springs. Michael told the CBI investigator he wasn't talking; any questions about the affair should be directed to Jill's attorney.

Sexton told him he had been seen, and it was already "a done deal!" The agent also pointedly observed that it was obvious Michael was wearing new boots. The telephone-company worker wouldn't budge however. He wasn't talking to the CBI about a murder.

Michael had walked into a tense confrontation, but he stuck by his guns. Before Michael left the office his boss informed him the company was keeping the US West truck he usually drove. A different truck would be provided for him later. Being temporarily without company wheels wasn't the problem for Michael. It was obvious why his truck was taken away. The CBI had a search warrant and was planning to comb it for evidence.

About eight-thirty the next morning, Michael telephoned his friend, Troy Giffon, and asked for a lift to work. He explained that police had his company vehicle tied up. On the way to work he pulled his wallet from his pocket, opened it up, ripped out a handful of papers and tossed them outside the window of the truck. He was becoming an emotional basket case, and Giffon was alarmed.

Michael had continued to show up for work, but he was jumpy, erratic, and his distraction was obvious. He told his friend that Jill's ex-husband had been found dead of multiple gunshot wounds the previous Friday. Giffon reminded Michael about his efforts that summer to talk him into killing, or helping to murder the victim. "I was hoping you'd forget that," Michael said. "This is the only thing that could hang me."

Did anyone else know about the hit, Giffon asked? Michael said there was someone in Ottumwa, Iowa, and police were pretty sure to talk with the individual because the name was written down in the vehicle investigators were searching. At times while he was talking about the murder and the interest of police in him and his girlfriend, Michael choked up. Tears formed in his eyes.

Firmly gripping Giffon's shoulder, he soberly advised: "Vietnam buddies don't rat off their buddies." Although it went unsaid, Gerry Boggs was also a Vietnam veteran, twice over, and he had suffered a much more terrible betrayal.

After the appeal to Giffon's loyalty as a fellow veteran, Michael launched into a spirited explanation of the alibi he and Jill had for the period immediately surrounding the time of Gerry's death. They went camping at Kelly Flats between Greeley and Steamboat Springs the Wednesday night before Gerry was found dead at the house. Michael said the campground was empty, and he filled out an envelope, wrote their name on it, and dropped it into a collection box along with a $4 fee.

He didn't learn of the murder until after he and Jill had temporarily gone off in separate directions, and she telephoned him from Steamboat Springs to leave a message on his answering machine, Michael said. When he checked his messages Sunday, he heard Jill's voice telling him, "Something's happened at Steamboat. Don't talk to anybody about anything."

According to Giffon's account to investigators, his friend was concerned about how accurately it was possible for law-enforcement authorities to pin down the exact time of death. Giffon said he thought they could figure it out to within about an hour and that got his pal upset.

"They can't tie me to the murder. I wasn't there," he declared. Several times he repeated that he didn't own a light-tan jacket. Giffon listened, and for the most part, kept his own counsel while his friend rambled on. He knew that despite what Michael was saying, he had indeed owned such a jacket with a corduroy collar and details. He might not still have the jacket at that very moment, but he had owned one, and not very long ago.

Michael reportedly said the murderer would be bound to have blood on his shoes and could be "burned" if they weren't disposed of. The killer, whoever that might be, would definitely destroy the shoes.

"There's no way anyone could have evidence against me," he was quoted. "I wouldn't hide the stuff, and I wouldn't save the stuff."

Giffon glanced at Michael's feet. The shaken man was wearing a pair of workboots that were sparkling new. Michael explained he needed new boots and bought them during the weekend.

The two men discussed which foreign countries had criminal extradition treaties with the United States and which ones would refuse to extradite. Giffon thought Argentina and Brazil would refuse to send someone back.

Michael was behaving as if he was going through a checklist in his mind about the evidence in the murder investigation. At one point, in mid-afternoon, he seemed to lose control and his emotions overwhelmed him. He was raving and waving around a knife he used on the job. Michael was "livid and going nuts," according to Giffon, and begged him to slap and punch him, to beat him up. Giffon figured Michael's conscience was bothering him, and he wanted to be punished.

He didn't beat Michael up. He listened. When he got home, he told his wife about his unsettling day with Michael and about the camping alibi. They agreed the story was ludicrous. Later, when Susan Kitchen met with the couple, he told the CBI agent about the disturbing conversation. The Giffons also told her, in considerable detail, about Michael's earlier efforts to enlist Troy as a hit man.

CBI Agent Scott Mundine talked with US West worker Bern Barry Boker while he was on the job. Boker, whose friends usually called him "Bud," had known Michael since 1991 and never noticed him with a tan jacket. Michael referred to Jill's father as his father-in-law and talked about owning ten percent of the bed-and-breakfast, a share that was worth a whopping $100,000, Boker recalled.

Michael never once talked in front of him about murdering Jill's former husband in Steamboat Springs, Boker said. When he talked about wanting to kill someone, it was his ex-wife, Kathy who was named as the potential target. Sometimes when Michael talked about wanting to find someone to kill Kathy his anger was obvious. At other times he discussed it calmly.

In other discussions Michael said Jill would only

stay at B&B's when the couple was driving around Colorado, Boker revealed. She wasn't the camper type. Michael's reported remarks fit in with Jill's history; she liked cleanliness and comfort and wasn't known as a woman who looked forward to roughing it in the mountains or a woodland campsite.

As lead investigator, Rick Crotz was assuming much of the responsibility for coordinating the fast-moving probe. While interviews were conducted and other aspects of the investigation were carried out by CBI agents and other law-enforcement officers from cooperating police departments, reports were typed and filed with the Steamboat Springs detective. Somehow Crotz made time to conduct his own interviews while he and Captain Hays fought to keep up with the flurry of paperwork and information that was flooding in.

One of the people Crotz talked to was Sue Heiser, a Greeley manicurist who works out of her home. She told the SSPD detective a woman telephoned her about eleven AM on Friday, October 22, identified herself as Jill Coit, and asked for an appointment. The client showed up about three PM. Ms. Heiser described the woman as nervous and chatty. While her nails were being filed and polished, she confided that she was on her way to Steamboat Springs where she owned a B&B, and had to go to court Monday morning because her ex-husband was suing her for slander. The woman, who identified herself as Jill, added that she had gotten her marriage annulled after learning her husband was a homosexual.

Just before leaving, she asked Ms. Heiser if she knew a good lawyer. The manicurist recommended a local attorney and offered to permit her client to telephone him from there. The woman declined and said she needed to make the call from a public phone. She left the manicurist's home about four PM.

That was about twenty minutes after Douglas Boggs

reported finding his brother dead. Two people, Mott and the manicurist, had reported seeing Jill in Greeley on the day her former husband's body was discovered, one in the morning and one in the afternoon.

If investigators expected to show that Jill was either the killer or was present when Gerry was murdered in Steamboat Springs, developing a close determination of the time of death was absolutely imperative. Her alibi for Friday was growing stronger as the investigation progessed. Judging from the way the situation was shaping up, she was more than a hundred miles away from Steamboat Springs on the day the murder was discovered. If Gerry died on Thursday however, she would have a big time-window to account for.

While investigators were developing new leads and sorting out such details, Crotz and Hays were continuing to deal with the shower of information and the steadily-rising mound of paperwork. Some of the most important aspects of the paperwork they were concerned with was tied to search warrants.

As searches were being conducted of the house the couple shared in Greeley and of his work vehicle, Michael asked his supervisor for a day off on Thursday so he could talk with his attorney in Steamboat Springs. Wilson was agreeable and told his troubled employee he could also have Friday off if he wished. Michael agreed that was a good idea and added that he might decide to take a vacation the following week, beginning November 1. His supervisor told Michael to be sure and let him know if he decided definitely on taking the work break.

In Denver, CBI laboratory ballistics experts determined that the bullet recovered at the crime scene and one of the slugs taken from Gerry's body were .22 caliber round-noses, with copper color coating. Tests were still being conducted on the other bullet.

Also downstate, Detective Tim Palmer of the Fort

Collins Police Department interviewed Michael's daughter and his ex-wife, Kathy Backus at the elementary school in Wellington. Eight-year-old Erin Backus was a student there. The school girl told Palmer she was with her father from six o'clock Friday night, October 22, until six o'clock Sunday night. Jill was with them from about the time it began to get dark on Saturday night, and they drove to William Andrew Coit's house in Denver, she added. Jill and Andrew left in a small, new red car.

A few days later when Detective Crotz interviewed Andrew in the office of the Denver apartment complex where the young man lived and worked as manager, he heard a different story. Andrew said he hadn't even seen his mother since sometime before Gerry Boggs was killed, although he talked to her by telephone a few times after the slaying. So far as he knew, his mother's red sportscar wasn't parked anywhere near the apartments, and he didn't see her on that weekend.

The conflicting stories told by Michael's daughter and Jill's son, were typical of the frustrating discrepancies investigators often run into when conducting interviews with different people. The inconsistencies posed a problem to be worked out in subsequent talks, sworn statements—or in a courtroom.

Investigators were faced with other problems. Michael didn't return to work after his long weekend. The first couple of weeks of November came and went and there was still no sign of him—or of Jill. In Steamboat Springs, rumors spread that the couple was out of the country. The stories were right on target.

She was in Mexico. Jill's youngest son, William Clark Coit III and his wife Robin were new parents. On her flight south of the border, Jill had a layover in California, and she telephoned William at his home in Manhattan Beach. William drove to the airport with his four-month-old son, so his peripatetic mother could see her first grandchild.

On November 9, Jill was at the US Embassy in Mexico City where she signed a document giving power of attorney to Seth so he could sell the B&B and the house in Greeley.

Two days later Michael telephoned his boss at US West and left a message asking for a two-year leave of absence. In two years he would be eligible for retirement and a pension. He was a bit tardy making the call. After he failed to return to work on time and didn't get in touch as he had promised, Wilson advised a labor-union representative that the missing employee was going to be fired. But Michael had always been a dependable worker who compiled an excellent attendance record until his recent troubles. Wilson began looking into the matter of the leave of absence for him.

Robert DelValle executed a warrant for the search of one of the three Toyota 4-Runners Jill had driven at various times. One was black, one pewter-gray, and the other red. Her constantly changing fleet of vehicles during that period also included the red Paseo and a red Ford pickup truck. DelValle searched the first of the rugged, boxy, utility vehicles for a false mustache, hairs and fibers, and a pair of blue jeans. Nothing that appeared to be blood stains was observed by the detective and evidence technicians when they looked through the vehicle. And there was no false mustache or blue jeans.

On November 20, Crotz had a long talk with Ms. Hanley, and the Iowa woman recounted her story of Jill's repeated efforts to talk her into carrying out a murder in Colorado. Incriminating evidence was piling up.

There was even more reason for police to be pleased over the way the investigation was shaping up.

They received a tip that Jill and her boyfriend were returning to Greeley. The tipster was Jill's youngest son. When his mother telephoned him from Mexico to say she was coming home, William quietly passed on the message to police. He was afraid she would get away.

Jill's sons were shaken by the news of the brutal slaying in Steamboat Springs and the realization their mother was a principle suspect. William III telephoned his uncle, Charles Coit, to talk and to ask questions. Jill had raised her sons to believe that Clark died of a heart attack. The Episcopal minister, who was in semi-retirement in Orange Park, Florida, at the south edge of Jacksonville, knew better than that. But he wasn't anxious to be the bearer of bad news.

"I was beating around the bush," he says of the talk with his nephew. But as he later recounted, William was persistent. He wanted to know what happened to his father, and he continued to press his uncle for the truth. According to Charles the young man asked:

"My mother did it, didn't she?"

The clergyman reluctantly confessed what he knew about the story. William's father was shot to death in his home in a murder that was never solved. The Reverend Coit was so emotionally rattled by the developments, he went into therapy for awhile. He said his nephew did the same.

The tip was just what police were hoping for, and they began closing in on the couple. On November 22, Fourteenth Judicial District Judge Richard P. Doucette issued arrest warrants for Jill and Michael. They were ordered picked up on suspicion of first-degree murder for the gunshot slaying of Gerald W. Boggs.

The bulky twenty-three-page documents related the manner of Gerry's death, the way his body was found, the witness's sighting of strangers lurking in the neighborhood, and detailed some of the background of the bitter lawsuit fought out between him and his former wife. Significantly, the warrants indicated the date of death was Thursday, October 21. But they also noted the murder weapon, a .22 caliber handgun, was not recovered.

Sixteen names by which Jill was believed to have been known by at one time or another were listed on her arrest warrant. She was identified as: Jill Coit, aka Jill Johansen-Coit, Jill Lonita Billiot, Jill Steeley, Jill Steely, Jill Coit-Steely, Jill Boggs, Jill Johanson, Jill Carroll, Jill Kisla, Jill Billiot, Jill Ihnen, Jill Brodie, Jill Metzger, Jill Moore and as Jill DeRosa (sic). Although Jill had used Michael's surname at least a time or two, it did not appear on the list. There were three dates of birth, all June 11, in 1944, 1946, and 1950.

Her companion's arrest warrant was less exotic. He was named simply as Michael O. Backus, and a single birthday was listed, September 9, 1945. He was described as a white male, about six-foot, one-inch, 175 pounds, with brown eyes and blond hair.

At dusk Monday night, November 22, a cadre of law-enforcement officers from the Steamboat Springs and Greeley police departments and the CBI positioned themselves at various locations in the neighborhood surrounding the two-story house at 1309 Eleventh Avenue. Jill's pewter-gray, 1993 4-Runner was parked in the driveway.

Ten hours later, around four AM, a couple drove slowly down the street in a car recognized by the license plates as a rental vehicle. A tall, bearded man and a woman were inside. As they got almost in front of the house, the waiting stakeout team pounced. Two police cars pulled up behind, the spotlights trained on the rental vehicle.

In moments, Michael and Jill were outside with their hands on the roof of the rental car and their legs spread while they were patted down by police. Moments later they were handcuffed, advised they were under arrest, and helped into separate police vehicles. Jill was carrying her passport. The couple also were carrying $3,000 with them. The arrests occurred just more than a month after the murder was discovered.

While they were driven to the Weld County Jail on Tenth Avenue and locked up on suspicion of first-degree murder and conspiracy to commit first-degree murder, the Toyota and the rental car were towed to the Greeley Police Department Auto Pound at 1300 A Street.

This time, authorities had Jill and her newly-bearded boyfriend solidly in custody. She wouldn't be running to New Orleans and committing herself to a psychiatric hospital.

The police officers moved fast to take every bit of advantage of the situation they could, and by seven AM they were sitting down to an interview with her at the jail. It had already been a long, exhausting night for her and for the detectives. The gray late autumn sky that was just beginning to show slivers of light over the eastern horizon would have a bright mid-morning glow before she returned to her cell.

Jill had invited the interrogation team, Sexton and DelValle, inside the cell, but they insisted on using the interview room. They weren't there for a five-minute chat about the accommodations.

It was Jill's decision whether or not to talk with the officers, and she agreed to the tape-recorded procedure. But simply reading her the obligatory Miranda Warning which advises criminal suspects of their constitutional rights against self-incrimination was an ordeal. Jill repeatedly interrupted DelValle's recitation with questions and comments.

Through the first ten minutes or so of the interview, she peppered the lawmen with questions and remarks including: "What is the fastest way to get me to trial so that I can get out?" "Okay, I don't want to talk to you. I was gonna ask you one question though" "I don't sign anything. That's what Randy says" "Okay, and I get to ask questions, too?"

Jill apparently wanted to ask questions more than she wanted to avoid answering them. After a period of fitful starts and stops, DelValle finally completed the reading and wound up with Jill's consent to the interview. She had always been a woman who liked to talk.

The lawmen began the deadly-serious procedure on a light note, joshing with the suspect and establishing as friendly an atmosphere as they could, considering the grim job ahead. Jill was still smarting from the coldly-efficient process of the arrest and booking and pleaded with Sexton and DelValle not to treat her "like the other cops."

She complained about her bad hip and the fact that she almost ended up at the hospital the previous night because of her reputed rough treatment during the arrest.

Jill was also concerned about publicity that was so sure to be sparked by her arrest back in Steamboat Springs. "I want to get this over with as quickly as possible because the Steamboat paper is gonna come out and they're gonna say I've been arrested," she announced. "And it's gonna be on the front page. And when I am released it's gonna be on the little bitty back page so nobody will notice it."

Klauzer advised her on the Saturday after the murder not to talk to police until she knew what time Gerry died, she said. For awhile the woman and the police officers verbally fenced over the subject. But the detectives couldn't quote an exact time when it was believed Gerry died. They didn't know. If the accusations made in the warrant for her arrest were correct, she knew more about it than they did.

She talked about her annulment, and she repeated

her accusations that Gerry was bisexual or gay. All of
a sudden, because Gerry was dead, he was suddenly
no longer bisexual, Jill scoffed. "One of the main reasons why Gerry hated me was because of me getting—
when we finally broke up, okay, people were going
around saying he was gay. That's the only reason
Gerry married me. Gerry didn't marry me because he
loved me. It was all surface."

In Jill's version of the story, it was other people who
were spreading tales that Gerry was gay. Other people
who heard the stories, however, were pointing their
fingers at her as the originator. Sexton pointed out she
hadn't answered the question: Did she get the annulment because Gerry was gay?

"For double fold," she said. Although Jill never provided a complete explanation, she claimed to have obtained the annulment because Gerry was gay, and she
was still married.

Moments later the suspect had the interrogators on
the defensive. She accused them of being out to get
her. She was an easy target because she had been married so many times. Sexton tried to get the message
across that multiple marriages weren't the point "Hey,
we're talking murder, not bigamy," he said.

Suddenly, the interview veered back to the question
of an alibi. "Let me tell you what. I have enough witnesses that are normal people that saw me there.
There's no way in hell I could have killed him Thursday or Friday," Jill declared.

DelValle asked if she was saying the witnesses would
confirm her story. Just give her attorney the time of
death, she said. He took depositions from her witnesses.

DelValle asked if it was correct that it took four
hours to get from Greeley to Steamboat Springs. Jill
replied that was what she had figured, but her lawyer
told her someone could make the trip by air in an

hour and return in two hours. "So there's one four-hour period that I'm not covered."

The SSPD detective asked exactly when that four-hour period was, but Jill didn't fall into the trap. "No, see, that's what I'm not telling you because that's when Gerry had died."

Sexton asked if Michael could account for his whereabouts during the critical time period. Jill said he was with her part of the time and other people part of the time. DelValle asked if it was true she and Michael went camping. She agreed they camped out at Kelly Flats on Thursday, October 21.

Later in the interview, Jill flatly denied killing Gerry or asking anyone to murder him for her. "I was out of the country. I came back to clear up this shit," she snapped.

Her irritability flared again when the subject turned back to her domestic relationships. "You know what was in the paper, okay, that I'm a bigamist? That I was living with two men! I wasn't living with two men," she declared. "Give me a break, okay?"

"You're married to Roy Carroll and you're living with Mike Backus," Sexton pointed out.

"I have a question. I'm living . . ." Jill began, before starting over. "How do you know I lived with Roy Carroll? How do you know I even slept with him?"

"You're married to Roy Carroll," the CBI agent repeated.

"Just answer your question. Answer my question," she demanded. Once more the suspect and the police officers were tilting over who was controlling the interview. Who was there to ask questions and who was there to answer them?

"Can I say something?" Jill asked.

"When I knocked—" the CBI agent began.

Jill was steaming and she interrupted him before he

could finish the sentence. "You're probably fucking wrong."

Sexton ignored the profanity and pointed out that when he looked her up earlier for a talk he knocked on her cabin door and Carroll was inside with her. Jill agreed. He was in Colorado for her civil trial, which at that time was scheduled only three days away.

A bit later, Jill veered back to Gerry's sexuality, asking if police had checked out any of his former lovers. DelValle answered the question with a query of his own. Who were the dead man's former lovers? Did she have names?

Jill told him to look in Gerry's address book. What names should they look for? DelValle asked. He pointed out there might be hundreds of names in an address book. Look for entries with initials and telephone numbers, she suggested.

The suspect claimed a family member of Gerry's told her he was sexually abused by a teacher when he was in high school. "How many psychologists would put two and two together?" she asked. "If a person can only have sex from the rear, with the lights out, the person that I didn't want [undecipherable word] here." Jill said she had long hair when she first came to Steamboat Springs, and Gerry made her cut it off so she would look like a boy. "Totally like a little boy."

It must have been difficult to believe that the big-breasted woman who spent a lifetime exploiting her femininity could ever be mistaken for a boy. Even with the lights out.

Before Gerry had her cut her hair it was so long she wrapped it around her head, she said. "I'm French. I've always had long hair." No one bothered to bring it up, or perhaps it simply wasn't considered important enough, but she had claimed at least one time in Steamboat Springs that she was being picked on because she was an American Indian. On the other side of the family, her mother's maiden name was Engleman. If the surname was French, it had an oddly Germanic sound to it.

During a return to the question of alibis, Jill disclosed another ailment to her interrogators. She said she left her bed "super early" in the mornings. "By six o'clock in the morning I am wide awake. Wide awake, okay?"

"Okay." Sexton was already convinced, or at least he seemed to be.

"Wide awake because I have to have food. I have hypoglycemia. If I don't eat from the time of midnight to six o'clock, if I don't have food in my mouth by six o'clock I get shaky and can't function," she blurted.

Jill complained that while she was standing with her hands on top of her car one of the policemen suddenly kicked her legs out to spread them further apart.

"Immediately I went down," she said. There was just time for mental images to form of a helpless woman recovering from a major hip operation knocked to the ground, when she asked, "Well, you know how you're the nice guy and he's the bad?" When she said "nice guy," she looked at DelValle. She glanced at his companion when she said "he's the bad."

Sexton sputtered, in mock surprise, "I'm the bad guy? I thought I was the nice guy."

"Yeah," Jill soberly confirmed. "You're the one who is supposed to. Nice guy, bad guy."

DelValle protested that they didn't play that game. Jill began to resume her story about the policeman kicking her legs out when Sexton interrupted. "I'm too tired to hear this," he groaned. He heard it anyway.

"Don't do that. I've had hip surgery," Jill recalled saying to the roughneck lawman. That was when another officer stepped in and stopped the leg-kicking.

Jill then proceeded to tie the story about the arrest

and the trouble with her hip to her claim of innocence
in the brutal attack on Gerry. "Because that's the reason I couldn't have killed him. Because the paper—
Jan Boggs told the manicure lady that he was beaten,
okay? Either by the fist or with a shovel or something,
okay? And something about abrasions and stuff. If you
so much as push me hard you would knock my hip out.
The total hip surgery took a solid year, because the
first six months if I even step in a hole, my hip popped
out." Jill said it would have been impossible for her to
have fought a 200-pound man.

It was an interesting scenario, but in drawing the
picture for her interrogators, Jill had unwittingly offered a wide opening to follow up. She seemed to
know an awful lot about the brutalities of the slaying.
"Who told you that the guy was beat up?" Sexton
asked.

Jill stammered for a moment, but eventually managed to put together a reply that pointed the finger at
her onetime sister-in-law. Jan Boggs told a manicurist
in Steamboat Springs. That was Jill's story. "That's the
gossip around town, is that Gerry was beat up," she
added.

"Okay," Sexton said.

"And that he was either beat up with a fist or a
shovel. And he was cut up with a knife or something.
Okay? And he was shot. Okay, I'm guilty, you know. I
said I am capable." Jill wasn't stammering anymore.
She had turned to sarcasm.

Sexton moved the interrogation to the question of
handguns, asking what kind of gun she carried in her
purse. Jill replied that she had a .45, but she didn't
even carry a purse. "Do you have a chrome Derringer
with pearl handles?" the CBI agent asked. She said
she didn't know; her gun was a .45.

She also said she didn't know if she had a .22, when
she was asked. Her interrogators knew Gerry was shot

with a .22, and they pressed her for more information. Sexton pointed out she had a box of .22 shells in her car.

"In my car? Twenty-two?" she responded in surprise.

"Uh-huh," Sexton said, nodding his head.

Jill said she didn't have a .22. "My gun is at—the gun that I use, and would use in case of anything is a great big .45," she said. "Because that way if I shoot you, you're not moving."

"That's probably true," DelValle agreed.

Jill said she had a gun dealer's license and knew how to shoot a .45. DelValle wanted to know how she received her firearms training.

It was the result of being raped, she replied. The rape was also tied into the hip surgery, she related. "Yeah, I was raped and beaten approximately ten or eleven years ago," she continued. "The guy did not get an erection . . . and so he proceeded to kick the shit out of me. I had a concussion . . . I had damage, uh, broke the ribs, did damage to my hip."

The dreadful attack was bad enough, but apparently she was still suffering repercussions according to her tale. She confided she had a bad hip ever since and sometimes had seizures. She cautioned the two lawmen not to touch her in case she had a seizure while they were with her.

"Just leave you go?" DelValle asked.

"Yeah," she said, "because it only lasts for . . . It's going to be grand mal. It's three minutes. If you touch me, if I fight, if I fight with this hip I'm in a body cast for six months. So please, I mean, I know you would want to help me," she pleaded. "But I won't die. Just don't let anybody touch me."

The officers were presented with a sobering thought. No one wanted the suspect flopping around helplessly on the floor with a grand mal seizure. For someone who was so frenetically active, however, it seemed Jill had suffered from a bewildering cornucopia of ailments; she had everything from a degenerative hip and grand mal to hypoglycemia and dyslexia. It was a virtual medical miracle that she was able to lead such an active life.

While tracing her ailments, Jill became so caught up in the subject she forgot what they had been discussing a few moments before. "What were we talking about?" she asked.

"The training, after the rape," DelValle prompted.

Jill said she took firearms training after the rape, "a policeman's course." Later she took additional instruction with Captain Hays in Steamboat Springs, she explained. (Months later, Carl Steely would testify in court that she attended a paramilitary school in Georgia. She boasted that the training made her "more conniving," he said.)

Sexton tried to slip in a quick change-of-pace question. "Can I ask you: Who is Thadius Brodie?"

If Jill was caught off-guard, she didn't show it. "You don't want to know," she said.

"Why don't I want to know?"

"Because I'm not telling you."

With the subject of Thadius so firmly disposed of, the officers returned to the subject of firearms. If she was going to shoot someone, she would use her .45 caliber, she remarked at one point. "I would, too," DelValle agreed.

"Okay, what caliber of gun was it? You can't tell me what caliber of gun was used," she asked. "Okay, no, if I was going to shoot somebody it [would] be with my .45."

The two experienced officers weren't interrogating the suspect in order to provide her with information about what they knew about the investigation. She was there to answer questions, not to ask them. DelValle responded with a cautiously neutral "uh-huh." If Jill was the shooter, or present when the shooting occurred, it was obvious that she knew the caliber of the gun that was used anyway.

Sexton asked what kind of .38 caliber pistol she owned. Jill replied that she thought she had a .38 in her safety-deposit box, and when the CBI agent asked where that was she snapped, "You know where it is. It's all over the *Pilot* from Steamboat." Jill clearly didn't appreciate the storm of publicity that had erupted since the murder.

She wasn't sure about the location of the .38, however, and suggested that Seth might have it. If he didn't have the pistol, then it would be in the safety-deposit box, she said. "Was he [Gerry] shot with a .38?"

"Where is the .45?", DelValle asked in response. Neither he nor the CBI agent were there to spar with Jill over word games. She said the .45 was in her house, then hesitated and said she wasn't sure. A moment later she switched direction again, and accused her interrogators of already knowing where the pistol was. Police saw the gun when they served the search warrant on her house. DelValle and Sexton claimed they didn't go in the house. But Jill had been reminded of something that got her dander up.

"Okay, the people laid my dildo next to my .45 to be funny," she accused. Jill was properly offended.

Sexton reacted with apparent shock to the outrageous accusation. "Somebody do that?" he asked as if in disbelief.

Jill didn't think the low-class antic was at all funny "Yeah," she said.

Both officers denied again they were even at the house when it was searched. DelValle said they were across Oak Street from the B&B in front of the Bell

Telephone Company building. Sexton agreed. They weren't at the house.

The suspect's pique at the crude prank seemed to subside, and she veered away from the subject. Her girlfriend was also standing across the street watching the activity at the house during the search, she said. Jill had asked her to see what was going on, after being advised by her lawyer that the search warrant was going to be executed. Jill complained about officers rummaging through her desk and taking a pair of Seth's blue jeans. It was illegal to take the jeans, she claimed.

Jill conceded that she didn't blame the two officers for what went on at the bed-and-breakfast. DelValle agreed. They were down at US West, he said. The remark opened a brand new can of worms.

"Oh," Jill responded. "Then it must of been you guys that told one of the people that . . . if they couldn't pin it on me, they were gonna pin it on Michael."

Michael was telling her a bunch of nonsense, DelValle replied. Sexton said it wasn't their job to pin anything on anybody.

Jill asked if Klauzer had provided them with her alibi. "He doesn't tell us anything, you have to," Sexton said.

"Okay, then I have to tell you till after y'all charge me, because as soon as you charge me and I provide my alibi, then y'all can never harass me again?" she asked. "Is that right?" The officers said it was up to her, that she didn't have to tell them anything.

"The only thing is that the alibi, if you got a good alibi . . ." DelValle began.

"I've got nine alibis," Jill shot back, chuckling at her own awkward joke.

Her mood changed abruptly a few moments later when Sexton asked if she ever solicited anyone to murder her husband. Jill had enough. "Let's stop the question, okay?," she snapped. "No, I did not." The question was ridiculous and tacky, she declared. The question wasn't tacky at all, Sexton defended. "That is tacky," she insisted.

The interrogation was almost concluded when one of the most startling moments occurred. Jill seemed to have a woeful misconception of just how much trouble she was in and how slowly it took the wheels of justice to grind out a conclusion to a matter as serious as she was faced with. Observing that she was already in jail, Jill said she figured she had seventy-two hours to be formally advised of the charges against her and another three weeks to wait until the trial. "So I'm looking at one month," she concluded.

Both lawmen were taken aback by the naive assumption. It was an astounding remark.

"Ho, Jill, it's not gonna come to trial in three weeks," DelValle corrected.

It was a disappointing revelation, but Jill rolled with the punch. "Well, I guess I'll be a bit longer than a month in jail," she said. Sexton told her "a speedy trial" takes about six months. It went unsaid that although criminal suspects have a right by law to a speedy trial, it is usually their own attorneys who drag out the process. Long delays are generally much more advantageous to the defense than to the prosecution, as memories fade, witnesses die or drift away, or evidence is misplaced.

Six months didn't go down as well with Jill.

"Okay, then I'm looking at six months in jail," she conceded. "Am I allowed to have my glasses and reading material? Or do I just have to sit in this fucking jail?" The two lawmen surmised she would be permitted to keep her glasses with her.

"Well, good, as long as I can have my glasses and

carry my computer, then I'm in good shape," Jill said. "I can spend six months in jail."

Before the matter of her guilt or innocence was decided in court, she would mark hundreds of days off her calendar. She had far more than six months in local jails to anticipate while awaiting trial. There was the grim possibility of years behind bars—or execution by lethal injection—if she was convicted of the murder.

Jill had apparently been back in Colorado with her boyfriend at least a day or so before they were apprehended and one or both of them had already been in the house. Mott gave police a photograph of Jill he found on the floor near an overturned garbage bag after Backus was inside cleaning up. Several bags were filled with refuse. Michael also sold his motorcycle back to a Harley-Davidson dealer in Fort Collins and cashed the check the Saturday before the arrest.

Police tracked the fast-moving couple's movements to a rented room at Lowry Air Force Base at the east edge of Denver between the Mile High City and suburban Aurora. Jill and Michael stayed in Room C232 in Building 1400 of the Mile High Lodge, which was set aside for rental to visiting families and civilian dependents of military men and women.

Base Commander Major General Jay D. Blume Jr., signed a search warrant for the room. Jill's 1992 red Paseo, parked behind the three-story brick building, was also searched.

Considering Jill's later claims that she and Michael returned to Colorado to face the music and straighten out the mess over Gerry's murder when they were suddenly thrown in jail, the couple's temporary living and driving arrangements were exceedingly strange. They had at least two of their own cars available to them, as well as a house in Greeley. Yet they rented a car to drive, and also rented at room a Lowry AFB. It was curious behavior for someone who wasn't trying to hide something.

Special Agent Richard Griffith, of the Air Force Office of Special Investigation at the base, was in charge of the searches, which were carried out at night. Air Force authorities pointed out that civilian private investigators had been snooping around the lodge trying to get into the room.

The searches at Lowry yielded a plastic bag containing two wigs, one brown and one a darker brown; two pairs of surgical gloves; maps of Mexico and Europe; a hotel receipt from Cancun, Mexico; two Aero Mexico tickets for trips to Spain; EuroRail passes which would permit each of them to travel through Europe fast and cheap; a Continental Airline employee ID issued to Jill Boggs; a MasterCard issued to Jill C. Backus; an Alaska voter-registration card issued to Jill Boggs-Coit; a US Embassy document from Mexico giving power of attorney from Jill Coit Steely to Seth J. Coit; the military dependent ID card issued to Jill Coit-Brodie; a photocopy of a military ID card issued to Chief Petty Officer Roy C. Carroll; an empty envelope addressed to Jill Coit-Backus; and a pair of international driving permits.

Jill's international license was issued on November 1, 1993 at Heathrow, Florida. It was signed "Jill Coit (Boggs)." Jill was behaving strictly in character, utilizing a confusing combination of names on important documents.

She may have known her way around the jet-set world, but if reports about her behavior are true, Jill didn't know a crucially-important rule of behavior for people who are locked up in prisons or jails. Never talk about your troubles with the law or reveal your personal business to your cellmates.

Two women inmates who were locked up with her passed on information to police about conversations

with Jill while they were locked up together in Weld
County jail. One said Jill claimed she established an
alibi for the time of Gerry's slaying by writing checks
at different businesses in Greeley. The other said Jill
posed a rhetorical question about how she could be in
Steamboat Springs at two o'clock if she was somewhere else. At that time, police had not told Jill the
date or time frame when they believed Gerry was murdered.

The suspects appeared at a brief court hearing in
Greeley where they were formally advised of the
charges against them. Each was charged with first-degree murder and with conspiracy to commit murder.
The homicide charges carried maximum penalties of
execution in Colorado's death chamber or life in
prison with no parole. The conspiracy counts carried a
maximum prison sentence of forty-eight years. They
were also liable to fines totalling nearly $1.5 million
each on the charges.

Colorado is one of thirty-seven states with the death
penalty, and specifically permits execution by lethal injection for first-degree murder, felony murder, and
kidnapping when the death of the victim occurs.

On Saturday, Jill and her co-defendant were driven
back across the mountains to Steamboat Springs in
separate Routt County Sheriff's Department cars, the
possibility of the death penalty looming ominously
over them.

Before being led to their cells in the Routt County
Detention Center, they were run through the booking
process, posing for mug shots and standing quietly
while their fingers and thumbs were inked and rolled
onto fingerprint cards. Jill's SSPD booking number
was 934966A. Michael's was 934966B. The couple also
exchanged their civilian clothes for baggy orange jail-
issue jumpsuits.

As accused killers, they were locked in maximum

security areas of the jail, and held on temporary bail of $5 million each.

Jill's shoulder-length, reddish brown hair was curly, but news reporters who later wrote about her appearance seemed to be more impressed with her eyebrows. She was described in nationally-distributed press reports as "stocky" and "heavy-eyebrowed." Michael's hair, beard, and mustache were cut short and neat. Sometimes he wore glasses, and at other times he didn't.

The same law firm Jill had depended on to handle most of her legal matters during the past two years continued to represent her immediately after her arrest. But Klauzer and Tremaine had built their practice with strong focus on civil law. Criminal matters, especially when such critical charges as first-degree murder were involved, were another thing altogether.

The talk in taprooms, coffee shops, and courthouse corridors began to speculate that Jill would call in a big-time criminal lawyer. Staff at *The Steamboat Pilot* and the *Steamboat Today* were pestered for collections of news clips on the story by journalists from other cities and by lawyers whom Dodder described as "name-brand attorneys."

Michael didn't have any property or cash to speak of. Even his Harley was gone. And in an application for a court-appointed attorney, he stated he was on leave without pay from his job at US West. Judge James Garrecht appointed Deputy State Public Defender William S. Schurman to represent him.

Schurman was in his corner when Michael and Jill appeared in court on the Monday morning after their arrival back in Steamboat Springs for an advisement hearing. At the proceeding, Judge Garrecht soberly explained to the defendants the charges against them and the possible penalties. About twenty people witnessed the brief hearing, including five sheriff's deputies.

Bob McCullough was also among the spectators for the appearance of the couple accused in the slaying of his longtime friend and business colleague at Boggs Hardware. He was astonished when Jill turned to look at him and said, "Hi."

A request by Schurman and Klauzer asking that their clients be released on their own recognizance was denied. The motions were based on claims the defendants were not formally charged within seventy-two hours of their arrest as the law required. Garrecht disagreed, pointing out the court appearance in Weld County the previous Friday. It was one of those go-through-the-motion motions, and it seemed doubtful anyone really expected it to succeed.

The pair wore their bright orange jail jumpsuits and were handcuffed during the hearing. The roomy rear-end of the suit on the woman who had once impressed acquaintances in Indiana with her fashionable clothes slumped into a weary mass of wrinkles. The defendants didn't look at each other during the hearing, or if they did it wasn't noticed by most observers.

Before the proceeding concluded, Judge Garrecht set Thursday morning, December 16, 1993 for the preliminary hearing to determine if there was sufficient probable cause to continue the prosecution. Unable to even come close to raising the staggering $5 million bail, both defendants were returned to the detention center. They traveled the same way they were transported from the center to the court, handcuffed in the back of separate sheriff's cars.

In the meantime, Detective Eyer, and other officers and technicians had already searched the impounded 4-Runner. According to the warrant, they were looking for .22 caliber firearms and ammunition, bloodstains, body fluid and tissue, footwear, false mustaches or false-mustache hairs and adhesive, baseball caps, including a cap with a ponytail, a light canvas rancher's jacket, camping gear, maps, soil and vegetation, and other items.

They came up with a treasure trove of potential evidence, including an Omega stun gun. Stun guns come in different varieties and have different shapes, but the job they are designed to do is the same. They stop and temporarily incapacitate people or animals they are used on. Contact of only three or four-seconds from one of the more powerful stun guns can shock nerves and muscles with up to 4,700 volts of electricity and deliver a blow like a horse's kick.

They were initially developed to provide police and corrections officers with a non-lethal means for subduing unruly or dangerous criminal suspects or convicts. Inevitably, stun guns spread from law-enforcement and corrections agencies to the civilian market where they can be legally purchased by anyone. Police also seized a stun gun from Seth. Discovery of the weapons were significant to investigators because marks on Gerry's body appeared to have been inflicted with a stun gun. No fingerprints from the stun gun found in the car or the package it was in, could be traced to Jill or to Michael.

The search team recovered a wealth of less dramatic items from the vehicle that were of interest nonetheless. Texaco and Chevron credit cards issued to Roy G. Carroll, a photo of Jill, and a vehicle registration made out to Jill Coit were taken from the glove compartment. The Colorado license tag was also issued in Jill Coit's name. A floor mat was tagged, and hair, fiber, and other debris were carefully vacuumed from the front and back, then placed in nine marked envelopes.

No firearms or ammunition were found, and there were no obvious bloodstains, although laboratory analysts would make the final determination after concluding their examinations.

While police continued to press their investigation and Jill and Michael cooled their heels at the jail, important changes were being made in their legal representation. The earlier speculation was right on target.

Jill's local lawyers bowed out of her criminal case, and were replaced by one of the best-known defense lawyers in Colorado. Joseph Saint-Veltri took over the defense chores after Klauzer and Tremaine left. Saint-Veltri was a grizzled twenty-five-year veteran of the legal wars who had a reputation for defending clients hauled into federal court on various drug charges.

At the time Saint-Veltri's entry into the sensational murder case was publicly disclosed, Joanna Dodder wrote a piece in the *Steamboat Pilot* based on an interview with a pair of noted Colorado trial lawyers and law partners, Walter Gerash and Scott Robinson. Referring to Gerash as the man Saint-Veltri called his "mentor," the reporter quoted him as saying the Denver law firm was considering taking on Backus as a client.

The big-time city lawyers had compiled a glittering record of murder acquittals, including that of former policeman James King, accused of killing four guards during a holdup of the Mile High City's United Bank in 1991. Robinson was quoted as saying the firm was contacted by Backus's family, and the lawyers expected to take the case if they could work out the details.

"I like Michael Backus. He seems like a decent guy. I'm hard-pressed to see him as a murderer," Robinson added.

Jill's longtime Steamboat Springs lawyer also pulled out of the civil case after Tremaine explained to Judge Kourlis he wasn't being paid. The judge gave Jill until the middle of the following month to get herself a new lawyer or else she would have to defend herself in the continuing dispute with the Boggs family. Douglas Boggs was executor of his brother's estate and was working with Halvorson to defend against Jill's lawsuit and to continue to press Gerry's claims.

Money was rumored to be the bait reputedly used to lure Jill and her boyfriend back to Colorado and interrupt a planned trip from Mexico to Europe. She was forced to return to try and free some of her money or possibly pick up valuables that were stashed away and could be converted to cash.

Significantly, during the same hearing where Jill's former lawyers were permitted to step out of the civil case, Judge Kourlis refused to release the restraining order preventing sale of the bed-and-breakfast. Speaking for his clients, Halvorson argued vociferously against lifting the ban. If the Boggs family won the countersuit, he declared, the B&B might be needed to pay off the award. The lawyer added that although some of the allegations in the countersuit were now void because of Gerry's slaying, it was possible a wrongful-death suit might be lodged.

The development meant Saint-Veltri was taking a chance Jill wouldn't be able to pay him for his work. She needed the money from the sale for her defense. Judge Garrecht warned the high-powered criminal defense lawyer that if things went the wrong way for his client in her efforts to sell the B&B, Saint-Veltri might wind up as her court-appointed attorney. That would mean, of course, that his normal fee would probably be drastically reduced.

Saint-Veltri didn't talk in open court about his exact fee schedule, but it seemed safe to assume it was somewhere between the $140-per-hour that was the going rate for Steamboat Springs lawyers practicing civil law and the whopping $475-per-hour commanded by big-time Washington lawyer Robert Bennett for defending President Clinton in the Paula Jones sex-harassment case. But when a complicated and long-drawn-out defense like Jill's promised to be was at hand, even fees based on the lower end of that spectrum could be staggering.

After all the years Jill spent accumulating wealth, it seemed the orderly transfer of her riches to lawyers was inevitably underway. And her already desperate situation was becoming even more complicated.

Her new criminal defense attorney's entry into the fray added another odd element into the equation as well. For people who concern themselves with such matters, there promised to be an interesting matchup in the courtroom, if for no other reason, because of the similarities in the surnames. St. James would be on one side of the courtroom, and Saint-Veltri would be on the other. St. James was a recent arrival in Colorado from Palm Beach county, Florida, where he was also an assistant district attorney. In one of his more high-profile cases there, he assisted in the successful prosecution of members of a gang of contract killers who advertised in *Soldier of Fortune Magazine,* and of a boatyard owner who hired them to murder his wife. But there was more at stake than idle interest in surnames. St. James's boss, District Attorney Paul McLimans, joined his subordinate and began assuming an increasingly important role in shaping the prosecution's case.

Michael also changed lawyers, dropping his public defender. But he didn't sign on with Gerash and Robinson. He replaced Schurman instead, with Leonard E. Davies, another Denver-based lawyer with a respected record in Colorado for criminal defense. In the 1960s and 1970s, Davies drew considerable attention to himself in Colorado for his work in several high-profile civil-rights cases, and he was author of a book dealing with cross-examination. Details of the financial arrangements were not publicly disclosed, but stories circulated that members of Michael's family were providing money for his defense.

Settling down with a pair of experienced criminal-defense lawyers would appear to have been a plus for the defendants in their efforts to make their pleas of not guilty to the horrible charges against them stand up. On the negative side, perhaps the most discouraging development occurred about as close to home as possible. After talking in early January with Agent Kitchen, Jill's son, Seth, and daughter-in-law, Julie, agreed to a deal with authorities to testify as prosecution witnesses at the trials. In return for their cooperation, they would be given immunity from prosecution. The immunity pact was not further identified publicly by St. James or by police at that time.

The first public notice of the drastic turn taken in the case occurred less than three weeks into the new year when the preliminary hearing for Jill and Michael was postponed. They had already been led into the Routt County Courtroom for the proceeding when St. James disclosed that two new witnesses had surfaced with evidence that was tremendously damaging to the defendants.

St. James didn't identify the witnesses during the hearing, and it was a few days before the names came to light through public documents. The prosecutor also declined to identify the nature of the information, but he did reveal the witnesses were given immunity from prosecution.

The development was so recent, the prosecutor wasn't yet able to provide the defense with transcripts of the statements by the new witnesses. That was a necessary legal requirement as part of the discovery process, which according to American rules of law requires sharing of information developed by the prosecution with the defense. The process is governed by strict rules, and prosecutors can't hand the information over at the last moment in order to take the defense by surprise. Discovery is one of those elements of the system that provides a distinct advantage for the defense, but is so necessary to ensure a fair trial. It is in keeping with the long-established legal reality of the American system of criminal justice which requires that the burden be on the prosecution to prove guilt, not on the defense to prove innocence.

The defense had already been complaining that the prosecution was slow in complying with the discovery process. "Mr. St. James won't even tell me when Gerald Boggs died," Davies complained. "How am I supposed to determine an alibi without the time of death? I'm flabbergasted not to be told this. A preliminary hearing should be to determine probable cause, not a trial by ambush."

Davies pointed out that information available at that time left a glaring twenty-six-hour window between one PM Thursday when Gerry was last seen alive leaving the store and about three PM Friday when his body was discovered. Saint-Veltri asserted that the prosecutor could do better than that. Forensic science was sufficiently sophisticated to pin down the time of death within an hour, he claimed.

The assistant DA disagreed. "It is the state's theory that only three people know when Gerald Boggs died," he responded. "Jill Coit, Michael Backus and Gerald Boggs." Nevertheless, the legal fallout over the failure or inability to be more exact was already beginning to be felt.

The defense lawyers also appealed to the judge to permit their clients to appear at hearings without their shackles.

"My client is brought in here shackled like he's a convicted criminal. I think it's highly prejudicial," Davies carped. "Mr. Backus must be presumed innocent, and we must preserve that."

The judge denied the motion. He pointed out that Routt County Sheriff's Department officers considered the shackles to be a necessary security measure. Later, when a trial or trials began and a jury was present, the defendants would appear in civilian clothes without handcuffs, ankle, or belly restraints. Judges are not as likely as juries to be swayed or impressed by defendants who appear in court in cuffs and chains.

The exchange was one more replay of a contest that occurs in courtrooms throughout the United States practically every day, when defendants are involved who are charged with major felonies. Jurists usually rule as Judge Garrecht did. The wishes of the defendants to appear unshackled at preliminary hearings must give way to security requirements as decided by the local sheriff or other experienced and knowledgeable law-enforcement and judicial authorities.

Judge Garrecht postponed the hearing until the middle of February to give defense attorneys an opportunity to examine the new information. Jill and her co-defendant were driven back to the detention center where she was marking time reading and studying languages and psychology.

When the preliminary hearing finally occurred on schedule a few weeks later, Kitchen's testimony about her conversation with Seth and Julie was devastating.

Between three-thirty and four PM, a couple of hours or so after Gerry was last seen alive, she said, Seth received a telephone call from a woman whose voice he recognized as his mother's. The caller relayed a message that was chillingly blunt, according to the testimony, and advised, "Hey, baby, it's over, and it's messy."

It was a critical statement, that if accepted as true, could become a vital element in helping the prosecu-

tion pin down the time of Gerry's death. The time
window between one PM when he was seen leaving the
hardware store, and three-thirty or four PM, was considerably less than the twenty-six hours investigators
were previously faced with. There would be a time period of only a few hours on Thursday, October 21, for
proving the whereabouts of the defendants that would
be crucial to both sides facing off in the courtroom
shootout.

The CBI agent recounted the other conversations
between Jill and Michael and the younger couple that
were tied to the alleged murder plot against Gerry
sparked by the civil dispute. Seth told her Michael
claimed to have an untraceable .22 caliber pistol, the
witness said. She also quoted Julie as talking about
watching her mother-in-law trying on scarves and a
wig she planned to use as disguises.

During cross-examination, Saint-Veltri quickly followed up on disclosure that Seth and Julie claimed to
have known in advance that Gerry's murder was being
plotted, then kept quiet about their knowledge for
months after the slaying.

"If what they told you is true, they both knew an
impending murder was going to take place in Steamboat Springs," he observed of the couple. "Did they
tell you what benefit they stood to gain?"

Kitchen said Seth and Julie would never be prose-
cuted for any role they may have played in the murder, and were also given immunity for an alleged
insurance scam. No details were provided about the
affair involving the insurance. Julie was also planning
to write a book about the case, the witness added.

Agent Kitchen also testified about the statements by
Giffon, tying Michael to the alleged murder scheme
through a $7,500-offer for a contract hit and other re-
marks.

Members of the Boggs family crowded into the

courtroom with scores of Gerry's friends and other spectators. It was an ordeal, and some of the testimony was especially agonizing. When a police photo of Gerry's body was introduced and described by a witness as "messy," although the picture was shielded from the audience, William Harold and Sylvia Boggs leaned against each other in horror and pain. Douglas Boggs cried.

Jill watched the proceedings from the defense table, and frequently smiled.

When it was Rick Crotz's turn to testify, he brought up the statements by Ms. Hanley in Iowa about Jill's reputed efforts to talk her into killing a man in Colorado. But the lead detective on the case ran into stiff cross-examination from the defense. He had to concede no physical evidence had yet been turned up that positively linked either of the defendants to the crime scene.

The defense lawyers established that police did not have a murder weapon, blood-stained clothing, or identifiable fingerprints or footprints, despite the execution of at least thirteen search warrants. And once again, they criticized initial handling of the investigation that led to the difficulties establishing a more exact time of death.

Two other law enforcement officers and Sharon Halvorson also testified at the hearing. Mrs. Halvorson recounted her two sightings of the red Paseo in the days immediately following Gerry's murder, including observation of the weirdly-costumed woman both she and her lawyer husband recognized as Jill at the wheel.

St. James and his team of law officers were constructing a solidly-impressive case. With Seth's devastating revelation, so far the prosecutor had three people lined up who were ready to testify they were solicited by either Jill or Michael to carry out the murder. And circumstantial evidence was piling up from the searches, laboratory tests, and other sources.

The assistant DA told the judge that statements from the witnesses about being solicited to carry out the slaying was proof the crime was premeditated. It was not a crime of passion, a spur-of-the-moment act. "Each of these defendants had a long-standing desire to kill Gerald Boggs or to have him killed," St. James declared. "They had motive, opportunity, and method, and the evidence confirms the great premeditation of this act, the premeditation of two evil minds."

Saint-Veltri passed on his opportunity to make a closing statement. Davies, however, claimed there was a woeful lack of evidence against his client. He insisted there was nothing in Michael's background to indicate he would commit such a "heinous act," and he called the case against the bearded defendant "singularly circumstantial." Davies asked the court to dismiss the charges.

Judge Garrecht didn't comply with the defense attorney's proposal for dismissal. At the conclusion of the tedious six hour proceeding, he declared that the prosecution had established its case and bound the matter over for trial. There would be no quick or easy out for Jill and Michael, not that anyone really expected there to be. They were one big step closer to a first-degree murder trial.

TEN

Lady Justice

The arrest of Jill and her boyfriend as suspects in the grisly murder of the prominent hardware store owner was big news in Steamboat Springs. Jill had been an exceedingly busy woman during the past three decades of her life, and the dreadful accusations were also big news around the country.

At various times she lived in a half-dozen states or more, married nine different men, romanced others, obtained divorces in the United States and in Haiti, was adopted once, raised three sons, and made loyal friends and bitter enemies.

Her myriad romantic and domestic entanglements and business dealings left a trail that was untidy at best. At worst, it was a nightmare for any investigator to follow, whether law-enforcement officer, private detective, journalist, or author. The path she took was twisted, and diffused into an impenetrable fog like a haze of smudged fingerprints. Some of the questions about Jill and her life will probably never be fully answered.

People who knew her and the men and women she interacted with, reacted with a mixture of emotions ranging from anger and disgust to pity and relief.

Private eye Stan Lewis bestowed on her a classic

nickname that is commonly used for women who are suspected of murdering their husbands.

"She's a psychotic, vicious, ruthless black widow," he told a reporter. "She takes a sadistic, fiendish delight in preying on well-meaning men to facilitate her ultimate goal of furthering her financial welfare."

Lewis had delivered a solid verbal spanking, but he hadn't yet exhausted his descriptive repertoire. "She was very manipulative and knew how to press the right buttons. She's no doubt a psychopath and a very sick person," he added to *Steamboat Pilot* reporter Joanna Dodder.

Dodder was quoted, in turn, in an interview with *The News-Journal* in North Manchester. "Everyone here is saying she did it . . . It's really bizarre. Everyone kept coming to us with all kinds of stories, and now we are finding out a lot of them are true."

"I think she got to the point after twenty years of scams, she got this false sense of security of what she could get away with," Judy Prier-Lewis, the Denver P.I. remarked to another journalist.

"She was able to turn men's brains to mush," *Chronicle* reporter Bardwell told Weller of the accused murderess.

In Ottumwa, reporter Alan Pierce of the *Chronicle*, hurried to Mohee Hanley's house after learning of the local connection to the bizarre story. The house was locked up and it sounded like a big dog was raging inside. He left and didn't go back.

"I'm thankful to be alive," said Carl V. Steely in Culver. "If you were to meet her and talk to her, you'd think she's just the greatest person you ever met. Why would all these people marry her if she weren't that way?" he added in another statement.

"She's a master of dirty tricks," he told the author in additional remarks. "I mean it was so funny, the things she'd think to do, you wouldn't take her seriously."

"The Houston murder was my brother and I've always thought that she did it," said Charles Coit. "She's ruined a lot of lives, whole families."

"He grabbed his chest like he was going to have a heart attack," Houston Police Department Detective Sgt. Binford said of Roy Carroll's response when he was told about the trouble his wife was in. "He's in total shock." After his first stunned reaction, the retired Navy chief reportedly clammed up and responded to police efforts to interview him by telling them to talk to his attorney.

In New Orleans, Judge DiRosa was "unavailable for comment," according to a report in *The Times-Picayune*. He ducked inside a house when he was tracked by television cameras.

"She was a beautiful damn woman, and cold clear through," added B. B. McCurdy in Houston.

Twenty years of fast living had apparently changed that, according to the observations of a woman at the North Manchester Library after seeing a picture of a frizzy-haired Jill being led away in handcuffs by police. "She was so dramatic and beautiful when she was in business here. Then people saw her on television after her arrest and the reaction was: 'Oh my. She didn't age well!'"

Even Eldon Metzger spoke out, and when he at last broke his silence, it was to defend the woman he was once married to. He complained to *The News-Journal* the information compiled by private investigators in Colorado was slanted against her. "Most people didn't really know Jill. There was a side to her that isn't being reported that was very kind," he said. ". . . She gave, and gave and gave."

"I just can't believe she had in her whatever it takes

to be a murderer," said her friend, Nancy Reed, the North Manchester town clerk.

Michael's longtime friend from US West also joined in. Troy Giffon telephoned Denver's Channel 4 news and reported he had received a threatening telephone call after talking with police. He wouldn't let the threat keep him from testifying at the trial, he insisted, however. When reporter Rick Sallinger asked what he was doing to protect himself, Giffon replied, "Guns, caution, watching. The Greeley police will take care of it." He accused Jill of being responsible for a "river of tears."

Greeley police confirmed they were investigating a call that contained what Sgt. Carl Alm described as "moderately threatening language." He refused to be more precise, and added that police couldn't confirm it was specifically related to the murder case. The police department refused to release a report on the incident, and another sergeant said there weren't even any officers assigned to investigate it.

The news coming out of Steamboat Springs and Houston was an astounding story, even without occasional inaccuracies in some reports that gave the slightly erroneous impression Jill was married at various times to ten or eleven different men. Some early reports indicated Michael was her tenth husband.

To most men and women who may have been married once or twice, she was a record setter.

Throughout her life, Jill managed to be many different women to many different people. As the year-end holidays of 1993 approached, she was still playing multiple roles.

To the prosecutor and police, she was a ruthless woman who was accused of the grisly murder of her husband in Steamboat Springs—and was a strong suspect in the disturbingly similar murder of another spouse in Houston twenty years earlier.

Police in Houston responded to queries from news agencies and other interested parties about the status of the investigation into Clark's murder, however with oddly divergent statements.

During a telephone call to the Houston Police Department, Joanna Dodder says she was told it was too late to reopen the investigation. The file on the case was lost. The small-town reporter was astounded by the statement.

"You mean you lost the file?" she asked again, in disbelief.

"Well," the anonymous Houston PD spokesman explained, "we have lots of homicides here."

DelValle told *The News Journal* in North Manchester he talked with Houston police and reported they might re-open the old murder case there.

Months after Jill's arrest when the Houston Police Department was petitioned through the Texas Open Records Act for information about the case for this book, the request was forwarded to the City Legal Department. The legal department passed it up the ladder to Texas State Attorney General Dan Morales in Austin for an opinion. The city's legal experts stated in their letter to Morales they believed the request should be exempted from the act because "the case has remained open" and was "now under active investigation by the Homicide Division of HPD due to new information . . ."

Disclosure of the information could interfere with the investigation into Clark's slaying and potential prosecution of the suspect in the case. The Steamboat Springs Police Department had also asked the investigative file be kept confidential while the SSPD established the case against their suspect.

The opinion was pending as the murder charges against Jill and Michael were about to go to trial in Colorado.

Twenty years after leaving Houston, following his brother's funeral, Charles still hadn't heard anything from police about the matter. "I don't know why they won't open the case," he says.

The behavior of Houston police department bigwigs is curious for people with nothing to hide. There were various reasons that would seem to justify reopening the investigation and actively seeking information. The telephone calls to the Houston police department that were traced back to Jill's bed and breakfast in Steamboat Springs were one. The similarities in the manner of Clark's murder and Gerry's slaying were another.

In Colorado, the Steamboat Springs Police Department, the Greeley Police Department, the CBI, and other cooperating law-enforcement agencies conducted a sparklingly professional investigation they could be proud of. Of course, the investigation didn't end with the arrests.

While St. James and defense attorneys began the demanding task of preparing for one of the most dramatic, sordid and highly-publicized criminal trials in the history of Colorado's Fourteenth Judicial District, investigators still had much work to do. New witnesses were contacted, and people already interviewed were talked to again. Every lead had to be followed up.

A few weeks after the arrests, Judge Doucette imposed a gag order on police, prosecutors, defense attorneys, and others involved in an official capacity with the case. The court order didn't slow the rush of publicity, however, and stories about the lurid affair were prominently featured as far away as London, England, where the popular tabloid, the *Sunday Mirror* printed a photograph of Jill in custody, and a major story headlined, "Murder Cops Unravel Real Black Widow's Deadly Web." The article predicted a quickie Hollywood film would be made on the subject.

Jill helped fuel the firestorm of publicity by giving a

few carefully-selected interviews. She talked to a reporter for the TV tabloid show, *A Current Affair,* and she did a far-ranging interview with Denver's *Rocky Mountain News.*

When she met at the jail with a reporter for the tabloid TV show, Jill had trouble keeping straight the dates she married and divorced her husbands, and was occasionally forced to consult a crib sheet she brought with her for the interview. One matter she was firmly consistent about, however, was her insistence she never murdered anyone.

Ignoring twenty-year-old divorce records, she denied there was any trouble in her marriage with Clark before his murder. She was waiting in New Orleans with the boys where the family was planning to relocate when she learned the dreadful news he was dead, she said.

Her youngest son, as well as the Reverend Coit and B. B. McCurdy also appeared in the two-part television presentation. Coit spent about three hours hanging around for the interview and appeared for a couple of minutes on the show. McCurdy was on for a longer period. But with the exception of his mother, William was the most dramatically-riveting appearance on the show.

Jill's youngest son vowed to have no more to do with his mother if it was proven she was involved in his father's murder. "This is my mother. People are calling her the black widow, the most poisonous spider there is," he said. "Maybe it's true."

When Jill chatted with a reporter for the *Rocky Mountain News,* she apologized for the way she looked. She was dressed in the usual baggy orange trousers and a gray sweatshirt with the words "ROUTT COUNTY JAIL" stenciled on the back in ugly black capital letters. Her current appearance wasn't the real Jill, she explained. The real Jill Coit had class.

During the talk, she traced some of her background and insisted she didn't kill Gerry. She explained she married him because of his intelligence, despite hearing stories he was bisexual. He stood out in Steamboat Springs because most of the available men there were "ski bums," she explained.

She agreed she was not pregnant while she was married to him, but begged off going into much detail about the matter because the civil suit was still pending. She hinted, however, that plans for an adoption of a child may have been involved. Her new attorney in Denver had wisely counseled that some subjects were, by necessity, off-limits.

Jill took a verbal potshot at Steely, whom she referred to as "the ugly part," and scoffed at his intimation she may have tried to kill him or to have him killed.

Stories circulated in Steamboat Springs and elsewhere that Jill was charging for interviews, and was paid thousands of dollars for the television appearance. Although Klauzer and his partner were no longer working for Jill in her criminal or civil case, the Steamboat Springs lawyer was representing her in efforts to peddle her story to television and movie producers and book publishers.

Douglas Boggs called reports of her efforts to sell broadcast, movie, and book rights to her story "bizarre." In written remarks, the murder victim's relatives declared: "The Boggs family is extremely disappointed that Jill Coit and her lawyers are seeking to profit from the sensationalism of either this case, the death of Gerry Boggs, or the events of her life. We are confused about why her attorneys withdrew from her case, yet they continue to represent her in the film, book rights, and the story of her life."

When Worth Weller telephoned the SSPD from Indiana, Rick Crotz explained he couldn't talk because a defense request for a gag order had been approved. The detective suggested the reporter talk to someone at *The Steamboat Pilot,* according to Weller. The enterprising Indiana reporter and newspaper publisher did that. He also drove to Steamboat Springs and interviewed Jill at the detention center.

They barely had time to settle down on opposite sides of a heavy clear-glass barrier in the sparkling clean, brightly-lighted room and begin to talk through telephones, before she boasted about how she was losing weight on the jail food. It wasn't very good or very plentiful, she said, as she stood up and patted her hips to show how she had slimmed down.

Getting down to more serious talk, she traced her version of her troubles with Gerry Boggs and firmly denied she had anything to do with his murder. At the trial, her attorney would either pinpoint the real killers or at least provide details about the type of people they were and reveal their motive, she claimed. Jill complained she was being picked on because she was an outsider in a close-knit community run by people close to the Boggs family.

When Weller asked about the reports she tricked Gerry into believing she was pregnant by him, Jill explained it away by saying they were planning to adopt a child. "We were very happy about that," she told the reporter. "I don't do fake pregnancies. I have real children. You know who they are."

At the conclusion of the hour-long sit-down, Jill said she expected to be back in North Manchester in March, after the trial, to visit with her mother and friends who have stood by her.

The baptism of fire for the defense attorneys and the prosecutor occurred weeks before the *News-Journal* interview when they at last squared off at the downtown courthouse in a preliminary hearing before Routt County Judge James Garrecht.

The most devastating testimony came second-hand from Seth, when CBI Agent Kitchen recounted her interview with him. The CBI agent quoted him as telling her about the efforts to enlist him in Gerry's murder and in the disposal of the body. Seth was called to the witness stand for brief questioning by the defense and conceded he was granted immunity from prosecution in return for his testimony in the case.

Although Seth appeared in court, as far as reporters were concerned it seemed he and his wife had gone underground. They cleared out of the Oak Street Bed & Breakfast, and workers there refused to reveal where the couple was or to answer any other questions. For awhile, at least, they were reportedly in Atlanta where Julie's parents lived. Roy Carroll also pulled up stakes in Houston for awhile and went to Gulfport, Mississippi.

Investigators continued interviewing witnesses and collecting new evidence well into the new year. Steamboat Springs police served a warrant and opened a bank safety-deposit box rented by Jill and found several handguns inside. None of them were the .22 caliber pistol they were looking for, however, and none of them were seized.

Other warrants were served to: the American Telephone & Telegraph Company in Denver for records of calls made on an AT&T calling card made out to Jill Backus; the NorWest Bank in Greeley for Michael's personal banking records; and the J. C. Penny Credit Service Center in Littleton for an account in the name of Jill Coit.

A .22 pistol surfaced from an unexpected location hundreds of miles away about that time, however. The couple who bought the bed-and-breakfast in Culver found the firearm in a box of possessions left behind when Jill and Carl split up. They turned it over to Culver Town Marshal Steve Michael, who telephoned

Steamboat Springs police and told them about the discovery. The weapon, which was believed to belong to Jill, was old.

Initially, a detective in Colorado talked about flying to Indiana to pick up the unregistered weapon, but later advised the town marshal to contact authorities in Houston where another husband of Jill's was also shot to death in an unsolved slaying. The pistol was at the bed-and-breakfast in Culver at least two years or more, and couldn't possibly have been used in the Steamboat Springs homicide. Marshal Michael wound up packaging the handgun and mailing it to the Houston Police Department, which had ballistics tests conducted on it.

Small caliber firearms such as .22s have a history of being difficult for ballistics experts to work with, but recent advances have made the job easier. Nevertheless, the tests on the pistol found in Culver reportedly failed to show a matchup with the bullets recovered after Clark's murder.

Back in Colorado, Crotz and Kitchen paid another call on the Giffons, this time carrying an audiotape along with them. It was the telephone message left by the mystery male caller who claimed to be Gerry's homosexual lover. After Agent Kitchen and the husband left the room, Crotz played the tape for Mrs. Giffon and asked if she recognized the caller's voice. She didn't. Before the tape was played for her husband, however, she told the detective about his frightening brushes with Michael riding to work and on the job with him after Gerry's murder.

After Mrs. Giffon left the room, her husband was brought inside and the tape was played for him. He was a bit hesitant when he was asked if he recognized the voice, but told the detective it sounded like Mike Backus.

On another front, Judge Kourlis finally released the

restraining order preventing sale of the Oak Street Bed & Breakfast, freeing up Jill's assets to pay for her defense. The hostelry wound up being sold for a fraction of the amount she and Seth originally sought.

At the request of Gerry's family, the civil trial itself was put on hold until the murder case was decided. Through their attorney, the Boggses argued that publicity over the civil lawsuit might prejudice the murder trial. Police and prosecutors also had custody of the files in the civil suit. Jill was representing herself in the case, since her previous attorneys were given court approval to pull out.

In the criminal case, the defendants publicly disclosed their alibis through documents filed in the middle of May. They claimed they were together at the national forest campground in Poudre River Canyon during a critical four-hour period on the Thursday afternoon of the day Gerry was most likely believed to have been slain. They said they checked into Kelly Flats about one PM, but left about four hours later and drove to Fort Collins, then to Thornton where they stopped at the Cactus Moon nightclub. They stayed at the club for about a half-hour from ten to ten-thirty PM, before driving to the house they shared in Greeley.

According to their account they were together at the house from about eleven-thirty PM until six-thirty the next morning when Michael left for work. He attended a training class until about ten AM then worked the rest of the day.

Jill talked with Ricky Mott downstairs about eight AM and left approximately forty-five minutes later to meet with a State Farm Insurance agent. She was back home again by nine-fifteen, then left at ten-thirty for the law offices of Greeley lawyer William Cresher. By eleven AM, she was beginning an hour-long class at UNC, and was back home again by twelve-fifteen. She left home about three PM to get the manicure from Mrs. Heiser.

The couple had an impressive array of witnesses to back up their account of their activities on Friday, October 22. But during the crucial hours the previous afternoon and evening there was a glaring lack of witnesses. Their attorneys were reportedly looking for someone who might have seen the pair at the Cactus Moon or elsewhere Thursday night or earlier in the afternoon.

Mott also threw a damper on the alibi when he told DelValle he thought it was odd that Jill left a note for him Thursday, advising him that she and Michael were camping. Michael had a nasty cold, and Jill was still on the mend from her hip surgery, and neither of them indicated before that they were camping enthusiasts, Mott related. The tenant thought Jill was making a special effort to be noticed at the house when she dropped in on him Friday morning.

Dozens of motions were filed and considered in the criminal case against Jill and Michael. A request by the defense to separate the trials was rejected. So was a move to suppress evidence and another defense request to dismiss the charges because investigators hadn't more closely pinpointed the time of death. Judge Doucette stated there was no evidence of bad faith involved in the delay because investigators were waiting for a search warrant. "The danger of going into the house without a warrant is that all of the evidence obtained may have been suppressed," he pointed out.

But a motion for a change of venue because of the pervasive publicity, the victim's prominence in the community, and the reputed inability to select an impartial jury was granted by the court. Saint-Veltri cited an opinion poll conducted by the defense indicating forty-three percent of potential jurors in the district believed Jill was guilty.

The decision was only a partial victory for the defense, which had asked for the trial to be moved completely out of the Fourteenth Judicial District which embraces Routt, Moffat, and Grand counties. Jurisdiction remained in the district, but Judge Doucette moved the proceedings seventy miles southeast of Steamboat Springs to the Grand County Courthouse in Hot Sulphur Springs on the other side of the 9,426-foot high Rabbit Ears Pass. (The pass gets its name from a geological formation that gives it the appearance of a *Playboy* magazine logo.) Pretrial hearings continued to be held in Steamboat Springs, but it was a convenient move for the jurist, nevertheless. Both he and District Attorney McLimans lived in Grand county.

Jill's hope of getting the show on the road and disposing of the trial within six months was not to be realized. The trial was originally set to begin on July 13, then set back to August 29, but even the later effort to comply with her desire for a speedy trial was hopelessly ambitious. When Judge Doucette moved the trial out of Steamboat Springs, he also rescheduled it to begin at 8:30 AM on February 6, 1995. He set aside four weeks on his court calendar for the proceeding. Once more, summonses were mailed out to expected witnesses in the case. Carl Steely was looking forward to the trip back to Colorado. He planned to take his skis along.

In October 1994, almost a year from the day Gerry's body was found at his house, a large two-column display advertisement appeared in the *Pilot* with the headline: "INFORMATION WANTED." A private investigator working for lawyers for one of the defendants was looking for information to help identify the killer or killers, the ad stated. An 800 number was provided for callers.

The defendants continued to wait out the long process at the Routt County Detention Center still held under $5 million bail each. Jill was keeping occupied with her books, helping other prisoners study for GED examinations, and reading her news clippings. Outside the jail, the man whose life they were accused of ruthlessly snuffing out, was still being mourned by his family and friends.

Inside Boggs Hardware, a framed photograph of Gerry was hung as a tribute. An inscription by his friend, Judy Prier-Lewis, read: "A practical man with a heart of gold leaves much behind. He leaves memories and a place in the hearts of each of us who were touched by his gentle hand."

ELEVEN

Guilty

Jill and Michael were found guilty of twin charges of first-degree murder and of conspiracy to commit first-degree murder after a six-week trial extending from early February to the middle of March 1995.

All three of Jill's sons testified as prosecution witnesses during the grueling proceedings in the Grand County Courthouse in Hot Sulphur Springs. Each of them said their mother had talked of killing Gerry.

But the nine men and seven women making up the jury, and four alternates, never heard about Jill's sordid string of marriages, some of them bigamous. Defense objections to the efforts of prosecutors to detail her many marriages and divorces to the jury with a chart were upheld by Judge Doucette.

The judge also refused to allow the prosecution to enter into evidence the tape of the 911 telephone call made by Douglas Boggs after finding his brother's body at the house. Douglas accused her of the crime during the call, and Judge Doucette ruled out the tape because he didn't want to prejudice the jury.

The influx of reporters from newspapers around the country and tabloid television shows previously expected to descend on the quiet little mountain town for the trial never materialized.

There were plenty of empty seats for spectators in the small courtroom gallery. The County Seat Restaurant, the only public eatery in the little mountain town, was a bit more crowded than usual but the staff managed to get everyone served quickly enough for them to get to court on time for the morning and afternoon sessions. Hot Sulphur Springs is busier during the annual hunting seasons.

The attention of much of the nation's conventional and tabloid media had been diverted from the reputed "black widow" and her co-defendant to Los Angeles and the O. J. Simpson trial. After attracting widespread interest at the time of the arrests, the trial of Jill and Michael raised scarcely a ripple among the press outside Colorado.

District Attorney Paul McLimans used his opening statements to paint Jill as a scheming woman who manipulated Gerry and others in order to realize her own aims. Gerry was killed after showing "a resolute commitment to steer his own course," the prosecutor declared.

Defense attorneys claimed, however, their clients were nowhere near the location of the shooting and added that investigation of the crime scene was so woefully bungled that the real killer may never be found.

Saint-Veltri declared that a "massive, intense, panoramic investigation" produced hundreds of items, and none of them could be tied to the defendants. The murder weapon was never found.

Although his brothers also testified, Jill's oldest son, who had moved with his wife to Idaho, was the star witness. Seth said his mother became increasingly angry over her civil-court dispute with Gerry during the last summer of his life and began talking about having the businessman murdered.

A week before Gerry was shot to death, both Mi-

chael and Jill made separate trips to Steamboat
Springs, Seth continued. He said his mother stayed at
the bed-and-breakfast and before leaving she instructed him not to clean the room because she was
planning to return.

Seth also recounted taking the telephone call from a
woman whose voice he recognized as his mother's,
telling him, "Hey, baby, it's over, and it's messy." He
ordered her not to talk to him and slammed the receiver down. The call occurred between three-thirty
and four PM, October 21, according to the witness.

Continuing his testimony, Seth said he told his wife
about the call and they went out to a restaurant to eat
that night. "We wanted people to see us," he explained.

He also checked Room 7, which his mother had ordered him not to clean. "I just had a feeling she had
been there," he said. There was an unpleasant odor in
the room, and the sink was spotted with drops of
blood.

Seth testified that he sopped up the blood with towels, and washed and bleached them. Asked why he
cleaned the room, he replied, "I don't know. I related
it to the Boggs murder."

That Sunday, his mother telephoned and demanded
to know what questions he was asked by police, the
witness added. "She kept asking if they knew when the
time of death was. She said she did not have a seven-
hour alibi and a three-hour alibi. "I was scared!"

A surprise witness later provided testimony for the
defense that seriously questioned the timetable Seth
laid out in his statements about the "hey baby" call.
Jan Bertrand said she waited on Gerry at the Pilot
Computer and Office Supply Store in Steamboat
Springs during the time period Seth gave for receiving
the call.

Prosecutors, however, produced sequential sales

tickets showing that Gerry made his purchase at the store closer to one PM.

During cross-examination of Seth, Davies attempted to tie the the witness to the murder instead of his own client.

"I submit to you that when it became evident that Mr. Backus would not participate in the killing of Gerald Boggs, it was in your best interest to kill him," the lawyer declared.

"You're wrong," Seth calmly replied.

"Isn't that true?" the lawyer persisted, pointing his finger at the witness.

"No," the husky young man responded.

During William's testimony, Jill's youngest son said his mother discussed Gerry's death with him during her brief stopover in Southern California and told him not to talk to police about it. They were driving to his home from the airport when he advised her he had already talked to police, and she became enraged and started hitting him, he testified.

William said his mother ordered him not to continue on to his house in Manhattan Beach because she was afraid police already had it under surveillance, so he drove her and Michael to a motel. He said his mother was still upset later in the day when they met at a mall, and she carried her four-month-old grandson under her arm like she was lugging a sack.

Steely also flew in to testify at the trial and take advantage of the opportunity to get in a little skiing. He told the jury Jill had bragged of taking mercenary training that made her "more conniving."

Some of the most intriguing testimony, however, revolved around the contention of prosecutors that Gerry was attacked with a stun gun before he was murdered. Investigators testified that injuries found on Gerry's body were consistent with those that could be caused by a stun gun. And a stun gun was found in Jill's car twelve days after his death.

Defense attorneys countered that police didn't test the gun to determine if it was fired. They argued that no fingerprints from the weapon itself or from the package it came in were traced to either Jill or Michael.

The lawyers also pointed out that Seth owned a stun gun and offered into evidence a weapon seized from him by police.

Dr. Robert Stratbucker, an Omaha, Nebraska, cardiologist, testified as a prosecution witness to back up the state's contention Gerry was assaulted with a stun gun before he was killed. Dr. Stratbucker, considered one of the nation's leading experts on stun-gun injuries, stated that testing the weapon taken from Jill's car may not have revealed anything of use.

Stun guns are tested at the factory where they are manufactured, he pointed out. They do not have individual signatures (such as the rifling inside the barrels of firearms), so testing the weapon wouldn't have revealed if it was used in the attack.

During summations, McLimans said the defendants killed Gerry after he had threatened to open a "closet door" that would reveal the secrets of Jill's past. "And that closet was brim-full of skeletons," the district attorney declared.

After all the testimony was over and the summations delivered, the jury deliberated only five hours before returning verdicts against both defendants of guilty to all counts.

"She picked the wrong town, she picked the wrong man, and she picked the wrong family," Douglas Boggs told reporters of his former sister-in-law after the verdicts were revealed.

Jan Boggs described Michael, whom family members said they believed was a willing participant in the murder but who was duped by his co-defendant, as Jill's final victim.

The Boggs family, including Gerry's heartbroken parents, his brother and sister-in-law, faithfully attended each day of the trial. Family members of Jill's and Michael's also made the trip to the little Colorado town and attended the proceedings.

In Culver, Carl Steely said he was relieved the ordeal was over and that he believes justice was served. "I feel sorry for her. I pity her for what she's going to have to go through, but she certainly had to be stopped," he said.

Gerry's persistence in pressing the civil suit against Jill wasn't motivated by money, Steely observed. The businessman was determined to stop her from continuing to prey on other men, the Indiana educator added.

Reflecting on his own star-crossed relationship with Jill, Steely remarked, "I think I was more bewitched—love is too strong a word. I was very vulnerable at that time. She told me all the things I wanted to hear."

In Houston, Sgt. Binford told reporters that police had gathered volumes of information about Jill, and he or some of his colleagues expect to eventually meet with her in prison to discuss Clark Coit's unsolved slaying. The meeting wasn't expected to be set up for several months, sometime later after the appeals process ran out on her conviction.

Although at this writing sentencing hearings were still a few weeks away, there was apparently no question that Jill and Michael would be ordered to spend the rest of their lives behind bars. Life in prison without the possibility of parole is the mandatory sentence for conviction of first-degree murder in cases where the prosecution did not seek the death penalty.

Jill was expected to be sent to the Colorado Prison for Women at Canyon City. It is not a prison with a reputation as a country club. The cunning woman with the talent for business and the sordid history of obsessively misusing the men in her life can be expected to live out the rest of her days amid the harsh surroundings of one of the nation's toughest prisons for female felons.

There will be no ski trips, scuba-diving expeditions or sports cars for Jill at the grim fortress-like prison at Canyon City.

APPENDIX

A Celebration of Men

Jill Lonita Billiot changed her name many times during the first half-century of her life. She married nine different husbands, some of them more than once. This is a list of her husbands with the date of marriage and the date the marriage was dissolved by divorce, annulment or death. The name of her co-defendant, whom she lived with, also appears on the list.

LARRY IHNEN, apprentice bricklayer.
Married 7-24-61 in Wabash, Indiana.
Divorced 6-12-62 in Wabash.

STEVEN MOORE, college student.
Married 5-5-64 in Mississippi.
Divorced 3-23-67 in Louisiana.

WILLIAM CLARK COIT, JR., Tenneco engineer.
Married 1-29-66 in Orange County, Texas.
Shot to death 3-28-72 in Houston.

DONALD CHARLES BRODIE, US Marine Corps major.
Married 11-3-73 in Orange, California.
Divorced 7-8-75 in California.

LOUIS A. DIROSA, lawyer (later a New Orleans civil district court judge).
Married 10-11-76 in Wilkinson County, Mississippi.
Divorced 11-4-78 in Haiti; divorced again 7-26-85 in New Orleans.

ELDON DUANE METZGER, auctioneer and realtor.
Married 3-27-78 in Lima, Ohio.
Divorced ?

CARL V. STEELY, prep-school teacher and administrator.
Married 1-6-83 in Culver, Indiana.
Divorced 12-29-83 in Haiti; divorced again 12-23-91 in Plymouth, Indiana.

GERALD W. BOGGS, merchant.
Married 4-4-91 in Steamboat Springs, Colorado.
Annulment 12-3-91 in Sterling, Colorado.

ROY C. CARROLL, retired US Navy chief petty officer and businessman.
Married 2-7-92 in Las Vegas, Nevada.

MICHAEL O. BACKUS, telephone company maintenance and repairman.
Met in late 1991 or early 1992 and lived with Jill in Greely, Colorado. Reports they were married are apparently untrue, although Jill is known to have used his last name.

P9-CQL-769

CODES
AND
CHEATS

Vol. 1 2013

Prima Games
An Imprint of Random House, Inc.
3000 Lava Ridge Court, Suite 100
Roseville, CA 95661
www.primagames.com

The Prima Games logo is a registered trademark of Random House, Inc., registered in the United States and other countries. Primagames.com is a registered trademark of Random House, Inc., registered in the United States.

Code Compiler: Michael Knight
Product Manager: JJ Zingale
Layout: Melissa Jeneé Smith, Jamie Knight Bryson, Rick Wong

All products and characters mentioned in this book are trademarks of their respective companies.

Please be advised that the ESRB Ratings icons, "EC," "E," "E10+," "T," "M," "AO," and "RP" are trademarks owned by the Entertainment Software Association, and may only be used with their permission and authority. For information regarding whether a product has been rated by the ESRB, please visit www.esrb.org. For permission to use the Rating icons, please contact marketing at esrb.org.

Important:
Prima Games has made every effort to determine that the information contained in this book is accurate. However, the publisher makes no warranty, either expressed or implied, as to the accuracy, effectiveness, or completeness of the material in this book; nor does the publisher assume liability for damages, either incidental or consequential, that may result from using the information in this book. The publisher cannot provide any additional information or support regarding gameplay, hints and strategies, or problems with hardware or software. Such questions should be directed to the support numbers provided by the game and/or device manufacturers as set forth in their documentation. Some game tricks require precise timing and may require repeated attempts before the desired result is achieved.

Australian warranty statement:

This product comes with guarantees that cannot be excluded under the Australian Consumer Law. You are entitled to a replacement or refund for a major failure and for compensation for any other reasonably foreseeable loss or damage. You are also entitled to have the goods repaired or replaced if the goods fail to be of acceptable quality and the failure does not amount to a major failure.

This product comes with a 1 year warranty from date of purchase. Defects in the product must have appeared within 1-year, from date of purchase in order to claim the warranty.

All warranty claims must be facilitated back through the retailer of purchase, in accordance with the retailer's returns policies and procedures. Any cost incurred, as a result of returning the product to the retailer of purchase - are the full responsibility of the consumer.

AU wholesale distributor: Bluemouth Interactive Pty Ltd, Suite 1502, 9 Yarra Street, South Yarra, Victoria, 3141. (+613 9646 4011)

Email: support@bluemouth.com.au

ISBN: 978-0-307-89680-3   **ISBN: 978-0-307-89681-0**   **ISBN: 978-0-307-89702-2**

Printed in the United States of America

NEW CODES

ALL CODES

4

CONTENTS ◄

►CONTENTS

CONTENTS

CONTENTS ◄

►CONTENTS

▶CONTENTS

NEW!

007 LEGENDS (PLAYSTATION 3)

TROPHIES

UNLOCKABLE	HOW TO UNLOCK
00 Agent (Bronze)	Public Match: Reach level 50 (00 Agent Grade 0).
007 (Gold)	Complete all levels on a 'Classic' difficulty.
A Farewell to Arms (Silver)	Multiplayer: Enter 00 Specialization.
Above and Beyond a 00 (Silver)	Complete three of the '007' level trials.
All That Glitters (Silver)	Earn a 3 star rating in any mission of the Challenges mode.
All the Time in the World (Silver)	Public Match: Play for more than 24 hours.
Around the world one more time (Bronze)	Get 100% collection rating for 'Moonraker'.
Boys with Toys (Bronze)	Campaign: Buy all of the attachments for one weapon class.
Challenger (Bronze)	Earn a 1 star rating in each mission of the Challenges mode.
Clandestine (Silver)	Campaign: Collect 100% of all organization intel.
Counter-Sniper (Bronze)	Public Match: Kill 50 players while they are aiming down the scope of a sniper rifle.
Danger! High Voltage (Bronze)	Public Match: Get 25 electrocution kills as Zao or Gustav Graves.
Die Another Day (Bronze)	Complete the 'Die Another Day' mission.
Disarmed and Dangerous (Bronze)	Public Match: In Escalation demote an enemy who is armed with the RPG.
Distracting (Bronze)	Distract an enemy.
Everything or Nothing (Silver)	Complete all of the trials on any one level.
Extended Operative (Bronze)	Complete eight of the 'Operative' level trials.
Fascination with all things gold (Gold)	Get 100% of all available stars in the Challenges mode.
Goldfinger (Bronze)	Complete the 'Goldfinger' mission.
Happy Snapper (Bronze)	Campaign: Take a photograph of the crocodile.
Hold the Line (Bronze)	Public Match: Win a Data Miner match without being killed.
I expect you to die (Bronze)	Get 100% collection rating for 'Goldfinger'.
Laser Eraser (Bronze)	Public Match: Win a match using only laser-based weapons.
Legend (Platinum)	Unlock all trophies.
Licence To Kill (Bronze)	Complete the 'Licence To Kill' mission.
Making it Personal (Silver)	Campaign: Collect 100% of all character bio intel.
Master at Arms (Bronze)	Make an elimination with every weapon class.
Midas Touch (Bronze)	Public Match: Win a match on Main Vault, Smelting Room and Loading Bay.
Moonraker (Bronze)	Complete the 'Moonraker' mission.
More Than an Agent (Silver)	Complete six of the 'Agent' level trials.

A
B
C
D
E
F
G
H
I
J
K
L
M
N
O
P
Q
R
S
T
U
V
W
X
Y
Z

CODES & CHEATS

Never happened to the other guy (Bronze)	Get 100% collection rating for 'O.H.M.S.S.'
O.H.M.S.S. (Bronze)	Complete the 'O.H.M.S.S.' mission.
Omega Virus (Bronze)	Public Match: As Blofeld, kill everyone else in the match.
One small step for a man (Bronze)	Experience zero-g.
People Power (Bronze)	Campaign: Collect 30% of all character bio intel.
Positively shocking! (Bronze)	Take out two enemies with one shock dart.
Return to Sender (Bronze)	Public Match: In Bomb Defuse disarm the bomb and plant it at enemy base without getting killed.
Scream if you want to go faster (Bronze)	Campaign: Overload the gyroscopic training machine in the Space Port.
Secret Agent (Silver)	Complete all levels on 'Agent' difficulty or higher.
Shaken, but not Stirred (Bronze)	Public Match: Survive 50 explosions while using Reactive Armor.
Shooting Star (Bronze)	Get 30% of all available stars in the Challenges mode.
Signature (Bronze)	Campaign: Reach level three weapon proficiency with the P99.
Spend the money quickly Mr. Bond (Silver)	Campaign: Be awarded a total of 10,000 XP.
Standards of Physical Perfection (Bronze)	Campaign: Acquire all of the MI6 training modules.
Star Struck (Bronze)	Get 60% of all available stars in the Challenges mode.
Unlocked and Loaded (Bronze)	Public Match: Reach level 6 (Midshipman).
Very novel Q (Bronze)	Campaign: Upgrade a gadget to its highest level.
Vodka martini, plenty of ice... (Bronze)	Get 100% collection rating for 'Die Another Day'.
Web of Intrigue (Bronze)	Campaign: Collect 30% of all organization intel.
With or Without Q (Bronze)	Reach Grave
You prepare for the unexpected (Bronze)	Get 100% collection rating for 'Licence To Kill'.

UNLOCKABLES

UNLOCKABLE	HOW TO UNLOCK
Bond Moonranker Suit (Splitscreen)	Password at Cheat Codes: astr0b0y

007 LEGENDS (XBOX 360)

ACHIEVEMENTS

UNLOCKABLE	HOW TO UNLOCK
00 Agent (30)	Public Match: Reach level 50 (00 Agent Grade 0).
007 (50)	Complete all levels on a 'Classic' difficulty.
A Farewell to Arms (50)	Multiplayer: Enter 00 Specialization.
Above and Beyond a 00 (30)	Complete three of the '007' level trials.
All That Glitters (10)	Earn a 3 star rating in any mission of the Challenges mode.
All the Time in the World (40)	Public Match: Play for more than 24 hours.
Around the world one more time (20)	Get 100% collection rating for 'Moonraker'.
Boys with Toys (10)	Campaign: Buy all of the attachments for one weapon class.
Challenger (20)	Earn a 1 star rating in each mission of the Challenges mode.

Clandestine (10)	Campaign: Collect 100% of all organization intel.
Counter-Sniper (25)	Public Match: Kill 50 players while they are aiming down the scope of a sniper rifle.
Danger! High Voltage (10)	Public Match: Get 25 electrocution kills as Zao or Gustav Graves.
Die Another Day (15)	Complete the 'Die Another Day' mission.
Disarmed and Dangerous (20)	Public Match: In Escalation demote an enemy who is armed with the RPG.
Distracting (10)	Distract an enemy.
Everything or Nothing (5)	Complete all of the trials on any one level.
Extended Operative (20)	Complete eight of the 'Operative' level trials.
Fascination with all things gold (60)	Get 100% of all available stars in the Challenges mode.
Goldfinger (15)	Complete the 'Goldfinger' mission.
Happy Snapper (10)	Campaign: Take a photograph of the crocodile.
Hold the Line (30)	Public Match: Win a Data Miner match without being killed.
I expect you to die (20)	Get 100% collection rating for 'Goldfinger'.
Laser Eraser (15)	Public Match: Win a match using only laser-based weapons.
Licence To Kill (15)	Complete the 'License To Kill' mission.
Making it Personal (10)	Campaign: Collect 100% of all character bio intel.
Master at Arms (20)	Make an elimination with every weapon class.
Midas Touch (15)	Public Match: Win a match on Main Vault, Smelting Room and Loading Bay.
Moonraker (15)	Complete the 'Moonraker' mission.
More Than an Agent (25)	Complete six of the 'Agent' level trials.
Never happened to the other guy (20)	Get 100% collection rating for 'O.H.M.S.S.'
O.H.M.S.S. (15)	Complete the 'O.H.M.S.S.' mission.
Omega Virus (15)	Public Match: Kill an enemy who has completed the campaign or who already has this Achievement.
One small step for a man (0)	Experience zero-g.
People Power (10)	Campaign: Collect 30% of all character bio intel.
Positively shocking! (12)	Take out two enemies with one shock dart.
Return to Sender (35)	Public Match: In Bomb Defuse disarm the bomb and plant it at enemy base without getting killed.
Scream if you want to go faster (10)	Campaign: Give someone an exciting training experience.
Secret Agent (50)	Complete all levels on 'Agent' difficulty or higher.
Shaken, but not Stirred (10)	Public Match: Survive 50 explosions while using Reactive Armor.
Shooting Star (20)	Get 30% of all available stars in the Challenges mode.
Signature (7)	Campaign: Reach level three weapon proficiency with the P99.
Spend the money quickly Mr. Bond (20)	Campaign: Be awarded a total of 10,000 XP.
Standards of Physical Perfection (30)	Campaign: Acquire all of the MI6 training modules.
Star Struck (40)	Get 60% of all available stars in the Challenges mode.
Unlocked and Loaded (5)	Public Match: Reach level 6 (Midshipman).
Very novel Q (10)	Campaign: Upgrade a gadget to its highest level.

NEW!

A B C D E F G H I J K L M N O P Q R S T U V W X Y Z

CODES & CHEATS

Vodka martini, plenty of ice... (20)	Get 100% collection rating for 'Die Another Day'.
Web of Intrigue (10)	Campaign: Collect 30% of all organization intel.
With or Without Q (16)	Reach Grave's plane without using any in-car gadgets.
You prepare for the unexpected (20)	Get 100% collection rating for 'License To Kill'.

ANARCHY REIGNS (PLAYSTATION 3)

TROPHIES

UNLOCKABLE	HOW TO UNLOCK
All of the Lights of Anarchy (Bronze)	Complete White Side stage 3 on hard difficulty.
Anarchist's Tomato Cookbook (Bronze)	Defeat 50 enemies with the Rifle. (Campaign Mode)
Anarchy Carrier (Bronze)	Complete White Side stage 2 on hard difficulty.
Anarchy Clockwork Drone (Bronze)	Defeat 5 enemies by throwing a self-destructing Drone before they explode. (Campaign Mode)
Anarchy Coast Guard (Bronze)	Complete Black Side stage 2 on normal difficulty.
Anarchy in the Calamari (Gold)	Defeat the Kraken within 5 minutes. (Campaign Mode)
Anarchy in the Dunes (Bronze)	Complete Black Side stage 4 on hard difficulty.
Anarchy in the Navy (Bronze)	Complete Black Side stage 2 on hard difficulty.
Anarchy is a Killer Weapon (Bronze)	Defeat 50 enemies with Killer Weapon attacks. (Campaign Mode)
Anarchy Recognizes Anarchy (Bronze)	Unlock all player characters in the game.
Anarchy Reigns is an Oxymoron (Silver)	Starting on Black Side, complete the Campaign on hard difficulty.
Anarchy Traning Complete (Bronze)	Complete all tutorials.
Anarchy's Executioner (Silver)	Defeat all the bosses with your Killer Weapon. (Campaign Mode)
Backyard Barbeque (With Anarchy) (Bronze)	Fry 50 enemies with the Flying Platform. (Campaign Mode)
Bari Shur Loves Anarchy (Bronze)	Complete White Side stage 4 on hard difficulty.
Baron von Anarchy (Bronze)	Defeat 50 enemies while riding a Helicopter Drone. (Campaign Mode)
Big Combo Anarchy (Silver)	Defeat an enemy with a combo of 100 hits or longer. (Campaign Mode)
Bright Side of Anarchy (Bronze)	Complete White Side stage 3 on normal difficulty.
Broken Bottles of Anarchy (Bronze)	Complete White Side stage 1 on hard difficulty.
Burnt Out Anarchy (Silver)	Defeat all the bosses while in a Rampage. (Campaign Mode)
Chasing Anarchy (Bronze)	Starting on Black Side, complete all Campaign and free missions on any difficulty. (Stage Select OK)
Dead Anarchy (Bronze)	Starting on White Side, complete the Campaign on normal difficulty.
Defending Coastal Anarchy (Bronze)	Complete White Side stage 2 on normal difficulty.

Drunken Anarchy (Bronze)	Complete White Side stage 1 on normal difficulty.
Dual of the Anarchies (Bronze)	Counter 5 enemy attacks. (Campaign Mode)
Elite Force of Anarchy (Bronze)	Starting on White Side, complete all Campaign and free missions on any difficulty. (Stage Select OK)
Ending Anarchy is Endless (Bronze)	Starting on Black Side, complete the Campaign on normal difficulty.
Filling Dark Souls with Anarchy (Bronze)	Complete Black Side stage 3 on normal difficulty.
Frozen in Time for Anarchy (Bronze)	Defeat a frozen enemy. (Campaign Mode)
Guy Dead Missile Anarchy (Bronze)	Destroy a Helicopter Drone by throwing its missile back at it. (Campaign Mode)
In Anarchy, Timing is Everything (Bronze)	Evade 10 times. (Campaign Mode)
Knockdown, Drag Out Anarchy (Bronze)	Complete Black Side stage 1 on hard difficulty.
Lake of Fire? Lake of Anarchy! (Bronze)	Defeat 5 enemies at once with an incendiary grenade. (Campaign Mode)
Machine Gun Anarchy (Bronze)	Defeat 15 enemies with the Gatling gun. (Campaign Mode)
Mad Anarchy (Silver)	Starting on White Side, complete the Campaign on hard difficulty.
Massage with an Anarchy Ending (Bronze)	Evade 5 throws. (Campaign Mode)
Max Anarchy (Gold)	Complete the game without using retries on any difficulty.
Meet the Anarchy Butcher (Bronze)	Kill 20 mutants via the mutant execution technique. (Campaign Mode)
Minefield of Anarchy (Bronze)	Shock 3 enemies at once with a Supercharged Trap. (Campaign Mode)
Path of the Weak isn't Anarchy (Bronze)	Defeat 30 enemies with throw attacks. (Campaign Mode)
Platinum Anarchist (Platinum)	Obtain all Trophies.
Pub Crawl Anarchy (Bronze)	Complete Black Side stage 1 on normal difficulty.
Rage! Rampage! Anarchy? (Bronze)	Defeat 50 enemies while in Rampage mode. (Campaign Mode)
Sandstorm of Anarchy (Bronze)	Complete White Side stage 4 on normal difficulty.
Shining a Light on Anarchy (Bronze)	Complete Black Side stage 3 on hard difficulty.
Someone Set Up Us The Anarchy! (Bronze)	Defeat 10 enemies by throwing an explosive Pyro Killseeker before they explode. (Campaign Mode)
The Best Defense is Anarchy (Bronze)	Defend against an enemy attack 10 times. (Campaign Mode)
The Plural of Ninja is Anarchy (Bronze)	Throw 10 enemies from behind using stealth. (Campaign Mode)
The Rude Sandstorm of Anarchy (Bronze)	Complete Black Side stage 4 on normal difficulty.
Throw The Anarchy Already! (Bronze)	Defeat 20 enemies with thrown objects. (Campaign Mode)
Ultimate Weapon of Anarchy (Gold)	Defeat Cthulhu within 5 minutes. (Campaign Mode)

NEW!

A
B
C
D
E
F
G
H
I
J
K
L
M
N
O
P
Q
R
S
T
U
V
W
X
Y
Z

UNLOCKABLES

UNLOCKABLE	HOW TO UNLOCK
Gargoyle	Reach level 22 in multiplayer or beat both Jack and Leo's Red Side in the Campaign

ANARCHY REIGNS (XBOX 360)

ACHIEVEMENTS

UNLOCKABLE	HOW TO UNLOCK
All of the Lights of Anarchy (15)	Complete White Side stage 3 on hard difficulty.
Anarchist's Tomato Cookbook (20)	Defeat 50 enemies with the Rifle. (Campaign Mode)
Anarchy Carrier (15)	Complete White Side stage 2 on hard difficulty.
Anarchy Clockwork Drone (15)	Defeat 5 enemies by throwing a self-destructing Drone before they explode. (Campaign Mode)
Anarchy Coast Guard (10)	Complete Black Side stage 2 on normal difficulty.
Anarchy in the Calamari (60)	Defeat the Kraken within 5 minutes. (Campaign Mode)
Anarchy in the Dunes (15)	Complete Black Side stage 4 on hard difficulty.
Anarchy in the Navy (15)	Complete Black Side stage 2 on hard difficulty.
Anarchy is a Killer Weapon! (15)	Defeat 50 enemies with Killer Weapon attacks. (Campaign Mode)
Anarchy Recognizes Anarchy (30)	Unlock all player characters in the game.
Anarchy Reigns is an Oxymoron (30)	Starting on Black Side, complete the Campaign on hard difficulty.
Anarchy Training Complete (10)	Complete all tutorials.
Anarchy's Executioner (40)	Defeat all the bosses with your Killer Weapon. (Campaign Mode)
Backyard Barbeque (With Anarchy) (15)	Fry 50 enemies with the Flying Platform. (Campaign Mode)
Bari Shur Loves Anarchy (15)	Complete White Side stage 4 on hard difficulty.
Baron von Anarchy (15)	Defeat 50 enemies while riding a Helicopter Drone. (Campaign Mode)
Big Combo Anarchy (40)	Defeat an enemy with a combo of 100 hits or longer. (Campaign Mode)
Bright Side of Anarchy (10)	Complete White Side stage 3 on normal difficulty.
Broken Bottles of Anarchy (15)	Complete White Side stage 1 on hard difficulty.
Burnt Out Anarchy (40)	Defeat all the bosses while in a Rampage. (Campaign Mode)
Chasing Anarchy (20)	Starting on Black Side, complete all Campaign and free missions on any difficulty. (Stage Select OK)
Dead Anarchy (20)	Starting on White Side, complete the Campaign on normal difficulty.
Defending Coastal Anarchy (10)	Complete White Side stage 2 on normal difficulty.
Drunken Anarchy (10)	Complete White Side stage 1 on normal difficulty.
Duel of the Anarchies (15)	Counter 5 enemy attacks. (Campaign Mode)
Elite Force of Anarchy (20)	Starting on White Side, complete all Campaign and free missions on any difficulty. (Stage Select OK)
Ending Anarchy is Endless (20)	Starting on Black Side, complete the Campaign on normal difficulty.
Filling Dark Souls with Anarchy (10)	Complete Black Side stage 3 on normal difficulty.

Frozen in Time for Anarchy (15)	Defeat a frozen enemy. (Campaign Mode)
Guy Dead Missile Anarchy (20)	Destroy a Helicopter Drone by throwing its missile back at it. (Campaign Mode)
In Anarchy, Timing is Everything (10)	Evade 10 times. (Campaign Mode)
Knockdown, Drag Out Anarchy (15)	Complete Black Side stage 1 on hard difficulty.
Lake of Fire? Lake of Anarchy! (20)	Defeat 5 enemies at once with an incendiary grenade. (Campaign Mode)
Machine Gun Anarchy (15)	Defeat 15 enemies with the Gatling gun. (Campaign Mode)
Mad Anarchy (30)	Starting on White Side, complete the Campaign on hard difficulty.
Massage with an Anarchy Ending (15)	Evade 5 throws. (Campaign Mode)
Max Anarchy (60)	Complete the game without using retries on any difficulty.
Meet the Anarchy Butcher (20)	Kill 20 mutants via the mutant execution technique. (Campaign Mode)
Minefield of Anarchy! (20)	Shock 3 enemies at once with a Supercharged Trap. (Campaign Mode)
Path of the Weak isn't Anarchy (15)	Defeat 30 enemies with throw attacks. (Campaign Mode)
Pub Crawl Anarchy (10)	Complete Black Side stage 1 on normal difficulty.
Rage! Rampage! Anarchy? (15)	Defeat 50 enemies while in Rampage mode. (Campaign Mode)
Sandstorm of Anarchy (10)	Complete White Side stage 4 on normal difficulty.
Shining a Light on Anarchy (15)	Complete Black Side stage 3 on hard difficulty.
Someone Set Up Us The Anarchy! (15)	Defeat 10 enemies by throwing an explosive Pyro Killseeker before they explode. (Campaign Mode)
The Best Defense is Anarchy (10)	Defend against an enemy attack 10 times. (Campaign Mode)
The Plural of Ninja is Anarchy (20)	Throw 10 enemies from behind using stealth. (Campaign Mode)
The Rude Sandstorm of Anarchy (10)	Complete Black Side stage 4 on normal difficulty.
Throw The Anarchy Already! (15)	Defeat 20 enemies with thrown objects. (Campaign Mode)
Ultimate Weapon of Anarchy (60)	Defeat Cthulhu within 5 minutes. (Campaign Mode)

UNLOCKABLES

UNLOCKABLE	HOW TO UNLOCK
Gargoyle	Reach level 22 in multiplayer or complete the campaign mode twice, once starting as White and once starting as Black.

ASSASSIN'S CREED III (PLAYSTATION 3)

TROPHIES

UNLOCKABLE	HOW TO UNLOCK
A Complete Set (Silver)	See all the optional characters settled at the Homestead.
Abstergo Entertainment (Silver)	Reach level 20 in the multiplayer mode.
All Washed Up (Silver)	Complete all Naval Missions aboard the Aquila.
An Extraordinary Man (Bronze)	Complete the Encyclopedia of the Common Man.
Blowing in the Wind (Bronze)	Retrieve every page for one of Ben Franklin's Almanacs.
Bring Down the House (Bronze)	Explore Fort Wolcott.

By Invitation Only (Bronze)	Be invited to join a Club.
Caged Wolf (Bronze)	Complete Sequence 8.
Circus Act (Bronze)	Kill 15 guards with a single cannon shot.
Completionist (Silver)	Complete ALL progress tracker grid entries.
Coureur des Bois (Bronze)	Exchange undamaged pelts at all different general stores.
Criss Cross (Bronze)	Complete Present - Skyscraper.
Daddy Dearest (Bronze)	Complete Present - Stadium.
Difficult End (Bronze)	Complete Sequence 11.
Entrepreneur, not Pirate! (Bronze)	Complete all 12 Privateer Contracts.
Eye Witness (Bronze)	Witness a predator killing an enemy.
Fin (Silver)	Complete each of the epilogue missions unlocked after the credits roll.
Grim Expectations (Bronze)	Complete Sequence 10.
Head in the Cloud (Silver)	Find all pivots and sync the Animus to the Cloud.
Heroes are Born (Bronze)	Complete Sequence 4.
House Party (Bronze)	Recruit any of the Artisans and see them settled on the Homestead.
How D'ya Like Them Apples (Bronze)	Complete Sequence 3.
Hunter/Killer (Bronze)	Reach sequence 10 in a map on Wolfpack multiplayer mode.
In Good Standing (Silver)	Complete all challenges for any of the Clubs.
Jager Bomb (Bronze)	After becoming fully Notorious, kill 10 Jagers before losing your notoriety.
Kidd Gloves (Bronze)	Uncover the mystery of Oak Island.
Magna cum Laude (Bronze)	Have a Trainee reach the Assassin Rank.
Man of the People (Silver)	Liberate all districts in Boston OR New York.
Master Assassin (Platinum)	Get every trophy.
Monopoly Man (Bronze)	Send a convoy to Boston, New York and the Frontier.
Multitasking (Bronze)	Complete 50% of the Progress Tracker entries.
Mystery Guest (Bronze)	Complete Sequence 1 & 2.
No Good Deed Goes Unpunished (Silver)	Open the Temple Door and learn Desmond's fate.
Original Gamer (Bronze)	Win a game of Fanorona, Morris and Bowls on the Homestead.
Patent Not Pending (Bronze)	Craft one of Franklin's inventions to decorate your Manor.
Perfectionist (Silver)	Complete 100% of all main mission constraints.
Personalized (Bronze)	Customize your multiplayer Profile and Character.
Predator (Bronze)	Hang 5 enemies by using rope darts.
Prince of Thieves (Bronze)	Loot a convoy without killing any of its guards.
Rude Awakening (Bronze)	Re-Enter the Animus.
Spit Roast (Bronze)	Perform a double assassination using a musket.
Tea is for Englishmen (Silver)	Complete Sequence 6.
The Day the Templars Cried (Bronze)	Complete Sequence 5.
The End is Nigh (Silver)	Complete Present - Abstergo.
The Sum of Truth (Gold)	Complete Sequence 12.
The Truth Will Out (Silver)	Unlock a hacked version of one of the Abstergo videos in the story quest.

The Whites of Their Eyes (Silver)	Complete Sequence 7.
Tumblehome (Bronze)	Upgrade the Aquila.
Two if by Sea (Silver)	Complete Sequence 9.
Whit's fur ye'll no go by ye! (Bronze)	Block a firing line 5 times by using a human shield.
Winning Team (Bronze)	Be on the winning team at the end of a multiplayer game session.

ASSASSIN'S CREED III (XBOX 360)

ACHIEVEMENTS

UNLOCKABLE	HOW TO UNLOCK
A Complete Set (20)	See all the optional characters settled at the Homestead.
Abstergo Entertainment (10)	Reach level 20 in the multiplayer mode.
All Washed Up (40)	Complete all Naval Missions aboard the Aquila.
An Extraordinary Man (10)	Complete the Encyclopedia of the Common Man.
Blowing in the Wind (20)	Retrieve every page for one of Ben Franklin's Almanacs.
Bring Down the House (20)	Explore Fort Wolcott.
By Invitation Only (20)	Be invited to join a Club.
Caged Wolf (20)	Complete Sequence 8.
Circus Act (10)	Kill 15 guards with a single cannon shot.
Completionist (50)	Complete ALL progress tracker grid entries.
Coureur des Bois (10)	Exchange undamaged pelts at all different general stores.
Criss Cross (20)	Complete Present - Skyscraper.
Daddy Dearest (20)	Complete Present - Stadium.
Difficult End (20)	Complete Sequence 11.
Entrepreneur, not Pirate! (20)	Complete all 12 Privateer Contracts.
Eye Witness (10)	Witness a predator killing an enemy.
Fin (30)	Complete each of the epilogue missions unlocked after the credits roll.
Grim Expectations (20)	Complete Sequence 10.
Head in the Cloud (20)	Find all pivots and sync the Animus to the Cloud.
Heroes are Born (20)	Complete Sequence 4.
House Party (10)	Recruit any of the Artisans and see them settled on the Homestead.
How D'ya Like Them Apples (20)	Complete Sequence 3.
Hunter/Killer (20)	Reach sequence 10 in a map on Wolfpack multiplayer mode.
In Good Standing (30)	Complete all challenges for any of the Clubs.
Jager Bomb (20)	After becoming fully Notorious, kill 10 Jagers before losing your notoriety.
Kidd Gloves (30)	Uncover the mystery of Oak Island.
Magna cum Laude (20)	Have a Trainee reach the Assassin Rank.
Man of the People (20)	Liberate all districts in Boston OR New York.
Monopoly Man (10)	Send a convoy to Boston, New York and the Frontier.
Multitasking (20)	Complete 50% of the Progress Tracker entries.
Mystery Guest (20)	Complete Sequence 1 & 2.
No Good Deed Goes Unpunished (20)	Open the Temple Door and learn Desmond's fate.

A
B
C
D
E
F
G
H
I
J
K
L
M
N
O
P
Q
R
S
T
U
V
W
X
Y
Z

Original Gamer (20)	Win a game of Fanorona, Morris and Bowls on the Homestead.
Patent Not Pending (10)	Craft one of Franklin's inventions to decorate your Manor.
Perfectionist (50)	Complete 100% of all main mission constraints.
Personalized (10)	Customize your multiplayer Profile and Character.
Predator (10)	Hang 5 enemies by using rope darts.
Prince of Thieves (10)	Loot a convoy without killing any of its guards.
Rude Awakening (10)	Re-Enter the Animus.
Spit Roast (20)	Perform a double assassination using a musket.
Tea is for Englishmen (20)	Complete Sequence 6.
The Day the Templars Cried (20)	Complete Sequence 5.
The End is Nigh (20)	Complete Present - Abstergo.
The Sum of Truth (50)	Complete Sequence 12.
The Truth Will Out (20)	Unlock a hacked version of one of the Abstergo videos in the story quest.
The Whites of Their Eyes (20)	Complete Sequence 7.
Tumblehome (10)	Upgrade the Aquila.
Two if by Sea (20)	Complete Sequence 9.
Whit's fur ye'll no go by ye! (10)	Block a firing line 5 times by using a human shield.
Winning Team (20)	Be on the winning team at the end of a multiplayer game session.

ASSASSIN'S CREED III: LIBERATION (PLAYSTATION VITA)

TROPHIES

UNLOCKABLE	HOW TO UNLOCK
Bayou Fever (Silver)	Complete every Bayou Fever mission
Business Woman (Silver)	Complete every Business Rivals mission
Buy All Dressing Chambers (Bronze)	Buy every Dressing Chamber
Charming (Bronze)	Charm 50 NPC's
Climber (Bronze)	Climb 8848 meters
Complete 100% of all Mission Constraints (Silver)	Achieve 100% Synchronization in all Sequences
Complete Aveline's Story (Silver)	Complete the game (fake ending)
Completionist (Silver)	Reach the maximum player level in the multiplayer
Deadly Haystack (Bronze)	Kill 50 enemies from haystacks using the Blowpipe
Diarist (Bronze)	Collect every diary page
Disguised (Bronze)	Change your persona 50 times
Egg Hunter (Bronze)	Collect every alligator egg
Fighter (Bronze)	Participate in 100 fights in multiplayer
Hanger (Bronze)	Hang an enemy on the gibbet at the Place d'Armes
Hangman (Bronze)	Perform 10 predator moves using the Whip
Human Shields (Silver)	Block 10 firing lines with a human shield
Liberation (Silver)	Complete every Free Slaves mission
Machete (Silver)	Kill 5 guards in 15 seconds using only the Sugarcane Machete (without using the Chain Kill)
Mushroom Queen (Bronze)	Collect all the mushrooms collectibles
My 1st Dressing Chamber (Bronze)	Buy your 1st Dressing Chamber

Notorious (Bronze)	Move through New Orleans for 10 minutes in the Assassin Persona
Persona Collector (Silver)	Collect every persona-specific collectible
Pirates (Silver)	Complete every Pirates mission
Platinum Trophy (Platinum)	Collect all other 44 Trophies for this Trophy
Poison (Silver)	Use berserk poison to force an enemy to kill 5 enemies
Power master (Bronze)	Complete 30 economic missions in multiplayer
Predator (Bronze)	Kill an enemy from a tree, with the blowpipe, while using eagle vision
RHP Master (Bronze)	Synchronize all viewpoints
Sequence 1 (Silver)	Complete Sequence 1
Sequence 2 (Silver)	Complete Sequence 2
Sequence 3 (Silver)	Complete Sequence 3
Sequence 4 (Silver)	Complete Sequence 4
Sequence 5 (Silver)	Complete Sequence 5
Sequence 6 (Silver)	Complete Sequence 6
Sequence 7 (Silver)	Complete Sequence 7
Sequence 8 (Silver)	Complete Sequence 8
Shipmaster (Bronze)	Buy the maximum number of ships (8)
Statuette Collector (Bronze)	Collect every Mayan statuette
Survivor (Bronze)	Survive 5 alligator encounters
Swamp Queen (Bronze)	Tree Run for 10 branches without touching the ground
The Truth (Gold)	Kill all Citizen E and experience the true ending
Thief (Silver)	Pickpocket 5000 écu
Tree ninja (Bronze)	Complete 15 Air Assassinations from trees
Umbrella (Bronze)	Kill 25 enemies with the Parasol Gun
What is she doing? (Silver)	Kill 7 guards on rooftops in the Lady Persona

BORDERLANDS 2 (PLAYSTATION 3)

TROPHIES

UNLOCKABLE	HOW TO UNLOCK
A Road Less Traveled (Bronze)	Completed the mission "The Road To Sanctuary"
Always Improving (Silver)	Reached level 25
An Angel's Wish (Silver)	Completed the mission "Where Angels Fear To Tread"
An Old Flame (Bronze)	Completed the mission "Hunting The Firehawk"
Arctic Explorer (Bronze)	Discovered all named locations in Three Horns, Tundra Express, and Frostburn Canyon
Better Than Money (Bronze)	Purchased 5 items from the black market
Better Than You Were (Bronze)	Reached level 10
Blight Explorer (Bronze)	Discovered all named locations in Eridium Blight, Arid Nexus, and Sawtooth Cauldron
Bombs Away (Silver)	Completed the mission "Toil And Trouble"
Borderland Defender Round Two (Platinum)	Unlocked all Borderlands 2 trophies
Bounty Hunter (Bronze)	Completed 20 side missions
Build Buster (Bronze)	Killed a Constructor without it ever building another bot.

A
B
C
D
E
F
G
H
I
J
K
L
M
N
O
P
Q
R
S
T
U
V
W
X
Y
Z

Can See My House From Here (Bronze)	Completed the mission "Bright Lights, Flying City"
Capped Out…For Now (Silver)	Reached level 50
Challenge Accepted (Gold)	Completed level 1 of all non-level-specific challenges with a single character
Cool Story, Bro (Gold)	Defeated Jack
Cute Loot (Bronze)	Killed a Chubby
Decked Out (Bronze)	Had Purple-rated gear or better equipped in every slot
Definitely An Italian Plumber (Bronze)	Killed Donkey Mong
Did It All (Silver)	Completed all side missions
Dragon Slayer (Bronze)	Completed the mission "Best Minion Ever"
Farewell, Old Girl (Bronze)	Completed the mission "Wildlife Preservation"
Feels Like The First Time (Bronze)	Opened the chest at the bus stop in Fyrestone
First One's Free (Bronze)	Completed the mission "My First Gun"
Friendship Rules (Bronze)	Revived someone from "Fight for Your Life!" that is on your friends list
Goliath, Meet David (Bronze)	Allowed a Goliath to level up four times before killing him
Got The Band Back Together (Bronze)	Completed the mission "The Once and Future Slab"
High-Flying Hurler (Bronze)	Killed a flying enemy with a thrown Tediore weapon
Highlands Explorer (Bronze)	Discovered all named locations in The Highlands, Thousand Cuts, and Wildlife Exploitation Preserve
How Do I Look? (Bronze)	Unlocked 10 customization items
Identity Theft (Silver)	Completed the mission "The Man Who Would Be Jack"
Knowing Is Half The Battle (Silver)	Completed the mission "Data Mining"
New In Town (Bronze)	Completed the mission "Plan B"
No Man Left Behind (Bronze)	Completed the mission "A Dam Fine Rescue"
Not Quite Dead (Bronze)	Reached level 5
Phased and Confused (Bronze)	Phaselocked 100 enemies
Sabre Rattler (Bronze)	Killed 100 enemies with the Sabre turret
Sky's The Limit (Bronze)	Completed the mission "Rising Action"
So Much Blood! (Bronze)	Gunzerked continuously for 90 seconds
Sugar Daddy (Bronze)	Tipped Moxxi $10,000
Thresher Thrashed (Silver)	Defeated Terramorphous the Invincible
Token Gesture (Bronze)	Redeemed 25 tokens
Tribute To A Vault Hunter (Bronze)	Got an item from Michael Mamaril
Unseen Predator (Bronze)	Remained in Zero's Deception mode for ten seconds straight
Up High, Down Low (Bronze)	Gave Claptrap a high five
Urban Explorer (Bronze)	Discovered all named locations in Sanctuary, Opportunity, and Lynchwood
Well That Was Easy (Bronze)	Completed the mission "Shoot This Guy in the Face"
Went Five Rounds (Bronze)	Completed Round 5 of any Circle of Slaughter
What does it mean? (Bronze)	I can't even capture it on my camera
Wilhelm Screamed (Bronze)	Completed the mission "A Train To Catch"
World Traveler (Silver)	Discovered all named locations

BORDERLANDS 2 (XBOX 360)

ACHIEVEMENTS

UNLOCKABLE	HOW TO UNLOCK
A Road Less Traveled (20)	Completed the mission "The Road To Sanctuary"
Always Improving (25)	Reached level 25
An Angel's Wish (25)	Completed the mission "Where Angels Fear To Tread"
An Old Flame (20)	Completed the mission "Hunting The Firehawk"
Arctic Explorer (15)	Discovered all named locations in Three Horns, Tundra Express, and Frostburn Canyon
Better Than Money (15)	Purchased 5 items from the black market
Better Than You Were (10)	Reached level 10
Blight Explorer (15)	Discovered all named locations in Eridium Blight, Arid Nexus, and Sawtooth Cauldron
Bombs Away (20)	Completed the mission "Toil And Trouble"
Bounty Hunter (25)	Completed 20 side missions
Build Buster (20)	Killed a Constructor without it ever building another bot
Can See My House From Here (20)	Completed the mission "Bright Lights, Flying City"
Capped Out…For Now (50)	Reached level 50
Challenge Accepted (30)	Completed level 1 of all non-level-specific challenges with a single character
Cool Story, Bro (30)	Defeated Jack
Cute Loot (15)	Killed a Chubby
Decked Out (25)	Had Purple-rated gear or better equipped in every slot
Definitely An Italian Plumber (15)	Killed Donkey Mong
Did It All (40)	Completed all side missions
Dragon Slayer (20)	Completed the mission "Best Minion Ever"
Farewell, Old Girl (20)	Completed the mission "Wildlife Preservation"
Feels Like The First Time (10)	Opened the chest at the bus stop in Fyrestone
First One's Free (10)	Completed the mission "My First Gun"
Friendship Rules (10)	Revived someone from "Fight for Your Life!" that is on your friends list
Goliath, Meet David (15)	Allowed a Goliath to level up four times before killing him
Got The Band Back Together (20)	Completed the mission "The Once and Future Slab"
High-Flying Hurler (10)	Killed a flying enemy with a thrown Tediore weapon
Highlands Explorer (15)	Discovered all named locations in The Highlands, Thousand Cuts, and Wildlife Exploitation Preserve
How Do I Look? (25)	Unlocked 10 customization items
Identity Theft (20)	Completed the mission "The Man Who Would Be Jack"
Knowing Is Half The Battle (20)	Completed the mission "Data Mining"
New In Town (20)	Completed the mission "Plan B"
No Man Left Behind (20)	Completed the mission "A Dam Fine Rescue"
Not Quite Dead (5)	Reached level 5
Phased and Confused (20)	Phaselocked 100 enemies

Sabre Rattler (20)	Killed 100 enemies with the Sabre turret
Sky's The Limit (20)	Completed the mission "Rising Action"
So Much Blood! (20)	Gunzerked continuously for 90 seconds
Sugar Daddy (10)	Tipped Moxxi $10,000
Thresher Thrashed (30)	Defeated Terramorphous the Invincible
Token Gesture (20)	Redeemed 25 tokens
Tribute To A Vault Hunter (15)	Got an item from Michael Mamaril
Unseen Predator (20)	Remained in Zero's Deception mode for ten seconds straight
Up High, Down Low (15)	Gave Claptrap a high five
Urban Explorer (15)	Discovered all named locations in Sanctuary, Opportunity, and Lynchwood
Well That Was Easy (10)	Completed the mission "Shoot This Guy in the Face"
Went Five Rounds (25)	Completed Round 5 of any Circle of Slaughter
What does it mean? (15)	I can't even capture it on my camera
Wilhelm Screamed (20)	Completed the mission "A Train To Catch"
World Traveler (50)	Discovered all named locations

CABELA'S HUNTING EXPEDITIONS (PLAYSTATION 3)

TROPHIES

UNLOCKABLE	HOW TO UNLOCK
20 Lever Action Hunts (Silver)	Hunt 20 animals with Lever Action firearms
20 Semi-Auto Hunts (Silver)	Hunt 20 animals with Semi-Auto firearms
25 Flags (Silver)	Collect 25 Flags from the vehicle hunts
All Flags (Gold)	Gather all the Flags from the vehicle hunts
Backbone (Bronze)	Hunt 8 attacking animals
Big Five (Silver)	Hunt one Cape Buffalo, Elephant, Leopard, Lion and White Rhino
Complete Lever Action Collection (Silver)	Unlock all the Lever Action firearms
Complete Rifle Collection (Gold)	Unlock all the Rifles
Complete Semi-Auto Collection (Silver)	Unlock all the Semi-Auto firearms
Experience is Piling Up (Gold)	Reach 500,000 XP
Far, Far Away... (Bronze)	Hunt 5 Trophies from at least 200 yards away
Fearless Hunter (Bronze)	Hunt 3 attacking animals in a single mission
First Five Flags (Bronze)	Collect the first 5 Flags from the vehicle hunts
First of Many (Bronze)	Hunt the First Trophy
Gold Rush (Bronze)	Obtain all the Gold medals
Grand Master Hunter (Platinum)	Unlock all Trophies in the game
Gun Master (Silver)	Unlock all the gun parts
High Score (Silver)	Earn 25,000 XP from a single Trophy
Hunter Vision (Bronze)	Mark 10 Trophies in Strategic View
Hunting Expertise (Bronze)	Finish the first hunting mission
Know Your Target (Bronze)	Mark 20 big game animals
Master Hunter (Gold)	Reach the highest level possible
Move on Hands and Knees (Bronze)	Activate 15 Shooting Rests
Optimal Shot (Bronze)	Shoot a Trophy from optimal distance
Overlooking (Bronze)	Activate 20 Hilltop Spotting locations

Pursuing the Hunt (Silver)	Find 50 animal tracks
Quick Hunt Expert (Silver)	Claim more than 20 animals in Quick Hunt
Quick Hunt Pro (Silver)	Claim an animal on all Quick Hunt levels
Quick Hunt Rookie (Bronze)	Claim an animal on 5 Quick Hunt levels
Shiny New Firearm (Bronze)	Unlock your first firearm
Shooting Proficiency (Bronze)	Earn 180 GP in one hunt
Skill Shot (Silver)	Hunt a big game animal from at least 70 yards away
Skillful Hunter (Silver)	Hunt 10 small game animals
Steadiness (Bronze)	Hunt 15 Trophies from a Shooting Rest
Step on the Gas (Silver)	Hunt 4 animals in the vehicle hunts

CABELA'S HUNTING EXPEDITIONS (XBOX 360)

ACHIEVEMENTS

UNLOCKABLE	HOW TO UNLOCK
20 Lever Action Hunts (30)	Hunted 20 animals with the Lever Action firearms
20 Rifle Hunts (30)	Hunted 20 animals with rifles
20 Semi-Auto Hunts (30)	Hunted 20 animals with Semi-Auto firearms
25 Flags (40)	Collected 25 Flags from the vehicle hunts
All Flags (30)	Gathered all the Flags from the vehicle hunts
Backbone (25)	Hunted 8 attacking animals
Big Five (30)	Hunted one Cape Buffalo, Elephant, Leopard, Lion and White Rhino
Complete Lever Action Collection (30)	Unlocked all the Lever Action firearms
Complete Rifle Collection (30)	Unlocked all the Rifles
Complete Semi-Auto Collection (30)	Unlocked all the Semi-Auto firearms
Experience is Piling Up (40)	Reached 500,000 XP
Far, Far Away... (20)	Hunted 5 Trophies from at least 200 yards away
Fearless Hunter (25)	Hunted 3 attacking animals in a single mission
First Five Flags (20)	Collected the first 5 Flags from the vehicle hunts
First of Many (20)	Hunted the First Trophy
Gold Rush (40)	Obtained all the Gold medals
Gun Master (30)	Unlocked all the gun parts
High Score (30)	Earned 25,000 XP from a single Trophy
Hunter Vision (25)	Marked 10 Trophies in Strategic View
Hunting Expertise (25)	Finished the first hunting mission
Know Your Target (40)	Marked 20 big game animals
Master Hunter (50)	Reached the highest level possible
Move on Hands and Knees (25)	Activated 15 Shooting Rests
Optimal Shot (20)	Shot a Trophy from optimal distance
Overlooking (25)	Activated 20 Hilltop Spotting locations
Pursuing the Hunt (30)	Found 50 animal tracks
Quick Hunt Expert (30)	Claimed more than 20 animals in Quick Hunt
Quick Hunt Pro (25)	Claimed an animal on all Quick Hunt levels
Quick Hunt Rookie (25)	Claimed an animal on 5 Quick Hunt levels
Shiny New Firearm (25)	Unlocked the first firearm
Shooting Proficiency (25)	Earned 180 GP in one hunt
Skill Shot (25)	Hunted a big game animal from at least 70 yards away

NEW!

A
B
C
D
E
F
G
H
I
J
K
L
M
N
O
P
Q
R
S
T
U
V
W
X
Y
Z

CODES & CHEATS

Skillful Hunter (30)	Hunted 10 small game animals
Steadiness (20)	Hunted 15 Trophies from a Shooting Rest
Step on the Gas (25)	Hunted 4 animals in the vehicle hunts

CALL OF DUTY: BLACK OPS II (PLAYSTATION 3)

TROPHIES

UNLOCKABLE	HOW TO UNLOCK
Art of War (Silver)	Successfully assassinate SDC Chairman Tian Zhao.
Back in Time (Bronze)	Use a future weapon in the past.
Big Leagues (Silver)	Win 5 multiplayer League Play games after being placed in a division.
Black Ops II Master (Bronze)	Complete the campaign on Hardened or Veteran difficulty.
Blind Date (Bronze)	Successfully rescue HVI.
Dance On My Grave (Bronze)	In Green Run, acquire your Tombstone.
Dead or Alive (Bronze)	Jailor or executioner.
Death from Above (Silver)	Stop Menendez once and for all.
Deep Cover (Bronze)	Capture Menendez.
Defender (Bronze)	Successfully defend FOB Spectre from incursion.
Desert Storm (Bronze)	Successfully escort the VIPs to safety.
Dirty Business (Bronze)	Listen and think before you shoot.
Don't Fire Until You See (Bronze)	In TranZit, have all doors opened without being set on fire.
Driven by Rage (Bronze)	Take down Menendez and his operation.
False Profit (Bronze)	Capture Manuel Noriega and bring him to justice.
Family Reunion (Bronze)	There are two futures.
Fuel Efficient (Bronze)	In TranZit, use an alternative mode of transportation.
Futurist (Silver)	Complete all future levels in veteran.
Gathering Storm (Bronze)	Investigate the jungle facility.
Giant Accomplishment (Gold)	Complete all challenges in Black Ops II.
Good Karma (Bronze)	Crack the celerium worm.
Gun Nut (Bronze)	Complete a level with customized loadout.
Happy Hour (Bronze)	In TranZit, buy 2 different perks before turning on the power.
Hey Good Looking (Bronze)	Plastic surgery avoided
High IQ (Bronze)	Collect all intel.
I Don't Think They Exist (Bronze)	In TranZit, kill one of the denizens of the forest while it is latched onto you.
Just Gettin' Started (Bronze)	Complete 1 challenge in any level.
Late for the Prom (Bronze)	Escort the president to the secure location in downtown LA.
Man of the People (Bronze)	Stop the brutality inflicted by the PDF.
Mission Complete (Silver)	Complete all challenges in a level.
No Man Left Behind (Bronze)	Rescue Woods.
Old Fashioned (Silver)	Complete "Pyrrhic Victory", "Old Wounds", "Time And Fate", and "Suffer With Me" in Veteran.
Party Animal (Bronze)	Win 10 multiplayer games while playing in Party Games playlists.
Platinum (Platinum)	Awarded when all other trophies have been unlocked
Shifting Sands (Bronze)	Gather intel on Raul Menendez from Mullah Rahmaan.
Ship Shape (Bronze)	Reinforcements on the way.

Showdown (Bronze)	A duel between rivals
Singapore Sling (Bronze)	Successfully neutralize the SDC freighter at Keppel Terminal.
Sinking Star (Bronze)	Interrogate Menendez.
Standard Equipment May Vary (Bronze)	In TranZit, acquire 4 different equippable items in 1 game.
Ten K (Bronze)	Minimum score 10k in every mission.
The Lights Of Their Eyes (Bronze)	In Green Run, pacify at least 10 zombies with 1 EMP.
Tower of Babble (Silver)	In TranZit, obey the voices.
Trained Up (Bronze)	Win 10 multiplayer games while playing in Combat Training playlists.
Ultimate Sacrifice (Bronze)	Only one can survive.
Undead Man's Party Bus (Bronze)	In TranZit, complete all additions to the bus in 1 game.
Waterlogged (Bronze)	Gather information on Raul Menendez' suspected terrorist plot.
Welcome to the Club (Bronze)	Reach Sergeant (Level 10) in multiplayer Public Match.
Welcome to the Penthouse (Gold)	Prestige once in multiplayer Public Match.
What Happens in Colossus... (Bronze)	Find the Karma weapon.
You Have No Power Over Me (Bronze)	In TranZit, defeat "him" without being attacked by "him".

CALL OF DUTY: BLACK OPS II (XBOX 360)

ACHIEVEMENTS

UNLOCKABLE	HOW TO UNLOCK
Art of War (25)	Successfully assassinate SDC Chairman Tian Zhao.
Back in Time (10)	Use a future weapon in the past.
Big Leagues (20)	Win 5 multiplayer League Play games after being placed in a division.
Black Ops II Master (15)	Complete the campaign on Hardened or Veteran difficulty.
Blind Date (15)	Successfully rescue HVI.
Dance On My Grave (5)	In Green Run, acquire your Tombstone.
Dead or Alive (15)	Jailor or executioner.
Death from Above (50)	Stop Menendez once and for all.
Deep Cover (20)	Capture Menendez.
Defender (15)	Successfully defend FOB Spectre from incursion.
Desert Storm (15)	Successfully escort the VIPs to safety.
Dirty Business (15)	Listen and think before you shoot.
Don't Fire Until You See (30)	In TranZit, have all doors opened without being set on fire.
Driven by Rage (20)	Take down Menendez and his operation.
False Profit (20)	Capture Manuel Noriega and bring him to justice.
Family Reunion (10)	There are two futures.
Fuel Efficient (10)	In TranZit, use an alternative mode of transportation.
Futurist (50)	Complete all future levels in veteran.
Gathering Storm (20)	Investigate the jungle facility.
Giant Accomplishment (50)	Complete all challenges in Black Ops II.

A
B
C
D
E
F
G
H
I
J
K
L
M
N
O
P
Q
R
S
T
U
V
W
X
Y
Z

Good Karma (20)	Crack the celerium worm.
Gun Nut (10)	Complete a level with customized loadout.
Happy Hour (10)	In TranZit, buy 2 different perks before turning on the power.
Hey Good Looking (10)	Plastic surgery avoided
High IQ (20)	Collect all intel.
I Don't Think They Exist (10)	In TranZit, kill one of the denizens of the forest while it is latched onto you.
Just Gettin' Started (10)	Complete 1 challenge in any level.
Late for the Prom (20)	Escort the president to the secure location in downtown LA.
Man of the People (15)	Stop the brutality inflicted by the PDF.
Mission Complete (10)	Complete all challenges in a level.
No Man Left Behind (20)	Rescue Woods.
Old Fashioned (50)	Complete "Pyrrhic Victory", "Old Wounds", "Time And Fate", and "Suffer With Me" in Veteran.
Party Animal (10)	Win 10 multiplayer games while playing in Party Games playlists.
Shifting Sands (20)	Gather intel on Raul Menendez from Mullah Rahmaan.
Ship Shape (10)	Reinforcements on the way.
Showdown (15)	A duel between rivals
Singapore Sling (15)	Successfully neutralize the SDC freighter at Keppel Terminal.
Sinking Star (20)	Interrogate Menendez.
Standard Equipment May Vary (25)	In TranZit, acquire 4 different equippable items in 1 game.
Ten K (15)	Minimum score 10k in every mission
The Lights Of Their Eyes (5)	In Green Run, pacify at least 10 zombies with 1 EMP.
Tower of Babble (75)	In TranZit, obey the voices.
Trained Up (10)	Win 10 multiplayer games while playing in Combat Training playlists.
Ultimate Sacrifice (15)	Only one can survive.
Undead Man's Party Bus (15)	In TranZit, complete all additions to the bus in 1 game.
Waterlogged (20)	Gather information on Raul Menendez' suspected terrorist plot.
Welcome to the Club (10)	Reach Sergeant (Level 10) in multiplayer Public Match.
Welcome to the Penthouse (50)	Prestige once in multiplayer Public Match.
What Happens in Colossus... (20)	Find the Karma weapon.
You Have No Power Over Me (15)	You Have No Power Over Me

CARRIER COMMAND: GAEA MISSION   (XBOX 360)

ACHIEVEMENTS

UNLOCKABLE	HOW TO UNLOCK
5 Finger Discount (10)	Capture the enemy Stockpile
Air Strike MK.I (5)	Destroy 1 Walrus using a Manta
Air Strike MK.II (10)	Destroy 100 Walruses using a Manta
Air Strike MK.III (25)	Destroy 1000 Walruses using a Manta
Balls Of Steel MK.I (25)	Capture 1 island with a Deadly defense
Balls Of Steel MK.II (50)	Capture 10 islands with a Deadly defense

Balls Of Steel MK.III (75)	Capture 25 islands with a Deadly defense
Barricade Blaster MK.I (5)	Destroy 1 Turret from Direct Control
Barricade Blaster MK.II (10)	Destroy 100 Turret from Direct Control
Barricade Blaster MK.III (25)	Destroy 1000 Turret from Direct Control
Blueprint Collector (25)	Locate and acquire all available Blueprints
Bug Crusher MK.I (5)	Destroy 1 Walrus from Direct Control
Bug Crusher MK.II (10)	Destroy 100 Walruses from Direct Control
Bug Crusher MK.III (25)	Destroy 1000 Walruses from Direct Control
Bunker Buster MK.I (10)	Capture 1 island with a Very Strong defense
Bunker Buster MK.II (25)	Capture 10 islands with a Very Strong defense
Bunker Buster MK.III (50)	Capture 25 islands with a Very Strong defense
Captain (10)	Successfully commandeer an enemy Carrier
Conqueror Of The Dead Zone (50)	Capture all enemy islands in the Dead Zone
Damsel in distress (10)	Rescue Captain Aurora from the APA
Fence Off (10)	Defeat the enemy Carrier in naval combat
Fly Swatter MK.I (5)	Destroy 1 Manta from Direct Control
Fly Swatter MK.II (10)	Destroy 100 Mantas from Direct Control
Fly Swatter MK.III (25)	Destroy 1000 Mantas from Direct Control
Hammers And Nails (25)	Produce over 1000 items
Hardcore MK.I (10)	Capture 1 island without using load
Hardcore MK.II (25)	Capture 3 islands without using load
Hardcore MK.III (50)	Capture 5 islands without using load
Iron Fist MK.I (10)	Capture 1 island with a Strong defense
Iron Fist MK.II (25)	Capture 10 islands with a Strong defense
Iron Fist MK.III (50)	Capture 50 islands with a Strong defense
Island Hopper (50)	Capture over 250 islands
Kali (10)	Unleash the Lord of Death within you, eliminate Fulcrum's facilities
Lean Mean Green Machine (25)	Locate all Green Laser research files
Lost Friends (10)	Restore contact with Captain Aurora
Manhattan project (10)	Reassemble the Hammerhead Nuclear Missile system
Millionaire (25)	Mine over 1 million in resources
Relentless (10)	Shoot down Shin's Manta
Revenge Is Sweet (75)	Execute Dr. Mao Shin
Road Kill MK.I (5)	Run over 1 enemy infantry unit
Road Kill MK.II (10)	Run over 50 enemy infantry units
Road Kill MK.III (25)	Run over 100 enemy infantry units
Silent Heroes (10)	Locate survivors from the Dead Zone drop
Titanic (20)	Sink the enemy Carrier
To Protect, To Destroy (10)	Decommission the Geothermal power plants

DANCE CENTRAL 3 (XBOX 360)

ACHIEVEMENTS

UNLOCKABLE	HOW TO UNLOCK
Beat Down (10)	Earned at least 450,000 points in a single round of Keep the Beat.
Best Practices (15)	Beat your high score on a song immediately after practicing it in Rehearse.
Beyond Flaw (20)	Earned "Flawless" on at least 1,000 moves.
Boogie Woogie Woogie (15)	Earned 5 stars on "Electric Boogie."

A
B
C
D
E
F
G
H
I
J
K
L
M
N
O
P
Q
R
S
T
U
V
W
X
Y
Z

Consistent Performers (15)	Earned the same move rating as your partner 5 times in a row.
Custom-Made (15)	Played through a Custom Playlist at least 15 minutes in length.
Daily Grind (20)	Played Dance Central 3 every day for at least 7 days in a row.
DCI's on the Prize (30)	Earned 5 stars on all 9 of DCI's songs on any difficulty.
Dig In Deep (10)	Changed the sorting options on the Song Select screen.
Do It... (15)	Earned 5 stars on "The Hustle."
First-degree Burn (15)	Burned at least 100 calories in any mode.
Flash Back (30)	Earned 5 stars on all 9 of Flash4wrd's songs on any difficulty.
Go Shorty (15)	Performed "In Da Club" with a character on that character's birthday.
GOOOAAALLL! (20)	Set a weekly fitness goal and achieved that goal.
Hi-Definitely (30)	Earned 5 stars on all 9 of Hi-Def's songs on any difficulty.
Just Pick Something! (10)	Skipped 5 songs in Party Time.
Keep It Old School (20)	Performed a song with both dancers in matching Crew Look outfits.
Let 'Em Know (20)	Flaunted at least 5 scores to your Friends List.
Lost in the Shuffle (15)	Earned 5 stars on "Cupid Shuffle."
Master Mimic (10)	Earned "Flawless" on every move your opponent created in Make Your Move.
Minor Skirmish (15)	Finished a Crew Throwdown with two single-player teams competing.
Movin' Up in the World (10)	Earned at least 1,500,000 points in a single round of Make Your Move.
Nice Moves (20)	Earned "Nice" on at least 1,000 moves.
OMG Indeed! (100)	Earned 5 stars on "OMG" on Hard difficulty.
Party Planner (20)	Started a Party with a Custom Playlist.
Playing Favorites (25)	Danced with the same character at least 20 times.
Que Soy Bueno (15)	Earned 5 stars on "Macarena."
Really Nice Moves (30)	Earned "Nice" on at least 10,000 moves.
Rematch! (15)	Replayed a Crew Throwdown with the same teams.
Rippin' It Up (30)	Earned 5 stars on all 9 of Riptide's songs on any difficulty.
Same Gold Story (20)	Earned Gold stars on a song.
Shut 'Em Down (20)	Won every round of a Crew Throwdown.
So Lu$h (30)	Earned 5 stars on all 9 of Lu$h Crew's songs on any difficulty.
Ten Large! (40)	Earned "Flawless" on at least 10,000 moves.
Th3Glitt3rati is online (20)	Completed Story mode and watched through the Credits. Thank you!
Top Agent (15)	Deciphered a Craze on your first try in Story mode.
Unique Technique (15)	Created a move in Make Your Move that your opponent cannot match.
Up All Night (25)	Started a Party before midnight and played 'til morning.
Up to the Challenge (20)	Won a Player Challenge.
Walk-In Closet (75)	Performed a song with every character in every unlockable outfit.
We're Friends, Right? (20)	Linked Dance Central 3 to your Facebook account.

Weekend Warrior (20)	Played Dance Central 3 on three weekends in a row.
What a Scream (15)	Earned 5 stars on "Scream."
Where Have You Been?? (20)	Played 10 songs with D-Coy.
Worth a Thousand Words (15)	Shared a Photo online.

DARKSIDERS II (XBOX 360)

ACHIEVEMENTS

UNLOCKABLE	HOW TO UNLOCK
A Stroll In The Demonic Park (30)	Complete the game on any difficulty setting
A True Horseman (90)	Complete the game on APOCALYPTIC
Abracadabra (30)	Open all Death Tombs
All You Can Eat Buffet (30)	Complete Sticks and Stones
Antiquing (30)	Complete Lost Relics
BFA (10)	Unlock Everything
Bravo Old Chap (20)	Defeat Wicked K
By Your Command (10)	Collect the Interdiction Stone
City of the Dead (10)	Complete City of the Dead
Clipped Wings (20)	Defeat Archon
Crow Carrion (20)	Defeat the Crowfather
Death Will Tear Us Apart (10)	Collect the Soul Splitter
Diamond Geezertron (10)	Unlock the final skill in either skill tree
Dust to Dust (20)	Defeat the Guardian
Epic! (10)	Death Reaches Level 30
Feeding Time (20)	Level Up Your 1st Possessed Weapon
Fire of the Mountain (10)	Complete Fire of the Mountain
Four My Brother (90)	Complete the game on NORMAL
Full Potential (30)	Unlock All Combat Moves & Upgrades
Gnomad (40)	Complete GnoMAD
Grim Reaping (30)	Unlock Reaper Form
Heart of the Mountain (10)	Complete Heart of the Mountain
I Can Has Cake? (10)	Collect the Voidwalker
I've Brought You A Gift (30)	Defeat the Soul Arbiter
Is There Anyone Else? (30)	Complete The Crucible
It's Not Over (20)	Defeat Samael
Like a Noss (30)	Defeat the four creatures named by Thane
Looks Familiar (10)	Collect Redemption
Lord of the Black Stone (10)	Complete Lord of the Black Stone
Mass Ruckus (10)	Equip elite items to all slots
Pathfinder (10)	First use of Fast Travel
Pay It Forward (10)	Gift An Item To A Friend
Respec Yourself (20)	Your First Respec
Soul Crushing (20)	Defeat The Wailing Host
Stains of Heresy (10)	Complete Stains of Heresy
Tearing Time A New One (10)	Collect the Phasewalker
Tears of the Mountain (10)	Complete Tears of the Mountain
The Big Boss (20)	Defeat Absalom
The Book of the Dead (10)	Complete The Book of the Dead
The Court of Bones (10)	Defeat Basileus
The Lord of Bones (10)	Complete The Lord of Bones

A
B
C
D
E
F
G
H
I
J
K
L
M
N
O
P
Q
R
S
T
U
V
W
X
Y
Z

The Mad Queen (10)	Complete The Mad Queen
The Rod of Arafel (10)	Complete The Rod of Arafel
The Root Of Corruption (10)	Open The Well Of Souls
The Secondary Adventure (50)	Complete all Secondary Quests
The Spectral Touch (10)	Collect Deathgrip
The Toll of Kings (10)	Complete The Toll of Kings
The Triple Lindy (10)	Complete 3 different high dives in the Foundry
To Move a Mountain (10)	Complete To Move a Mountain
Tree of Life (10)	Complete Tree of Life

DEAD OR ALIVE 5 (PLAYSTATION 3)

TROPHIES

UNLOCKABLE	HOW TO UNLOCK
A Fight to Remember (Bronze)	Save a replay.
Ahhh, Memories (Bronze)	View your photos in the Album.
Akira Yuki (Bronze)	Unlock Akira.
Anybody, Anytime, Anywhere (Silver)	Fight 50 people through invitations.
Arcade Cleared (Bronze)	Clear 1 course in Arcade mode.
Arcade Master (Silver)	Clear all courses in Arcade mode.
Blow 'Em Away (Bronze)	Successfully land a Power Blow.
Cliffhanger Comeback (Bronze)	Successfully block an opponent's attack during a Cliffhanger.
DOA5 Is My Life (Gold)	Fight online 1000 times.
DOA5 Master (Platinum)	Unlock all trophies.
Down You Go (Bronze)	Successfully attack during a Cliffhanger.
Exercise Newbie (Bronze)	Perform all moves for all characters in Command Training.
Failure Teaches Success (Bronze)	See all characters' losing poses.
Fighter, Know Thyself (Bronze)	View your results in Fight Record.
Fighting Entertainment (Bronze)	Have your first fight outside of Training or Versus modes.
Fighting For Real (Bronze)	Play a Ranked match.
Fighting in Style (Gold)	Unlock all costumes.
First Tag Team (Bronze)	Play Tag Battle.
First Throwdown (Bronze)	Send a Throwdown Challenge to someone in your Fighter List.
Fledgling Fighter (Bronze)	Fight 10 Versus matches.
Gesundheit! (Bronze)	Trigger the Special Danger Zone in The Show.
Get out there and Fight! (Bronze)	Play a Lobby match.
How Do I Fight Like a Pro? (Bronze)	Display the Move Details.
How Do I Fight? (Bronze)	Display the Move List.
I Read Every Move (Bronze)	Win without taking any damage.
Insomniac (Bronze)	Watch all movies in Story mode without skipping any of them.
Jump In (Bronze)	Play a Simple match.
My Fight, My Rules (Bronze)	Create your own online lobby.
On the Edge of Your Seat (Bronze)	Play Spectator mode.
Rival Rampage (Silver)	Fight online 100 times.
Rival Rumble (Bronze)	Fight online 10 times.
Rivals (Bronze)	Register 5 fighters in your Fight List.

Safety First (Bronze)	Turn Danger Zones off on the Stage Select screen.
Sarah Bryant (Bronze)	Unlock Sarah.
Say Cheese! (Bronze)	Take a photo in Spectator mode.
Survival Cleared (Bronze)	Clear 1 course in Survival mode.
Survival Master (Silver)	Clear all courses in Survival mode.
Tango Kilo November (Bronze)	Trigger the Special Danger Zone in Hot Zone.
The Fight Never Ends (Silver)	Fight 100 Versus matches.
The Power of Two (Silver)	Perform 50 kinds of character-specific tag throws.
Time Attack Cleared (Bronze)	Clear 1 course in Time Attack mode.
Time Attack Master (Silver)	Clear all courses in Time Attack mode.
Training Hard (Bronze)	Play Training mode for 1 hour.
You Asked for It! (Bronze)	Fight 10 people through invitations.

UNLOCKABLES

UNLOCKABLE	HOW TO UNLOCK
Character System Voice	Complete a character command training in training mode
Legend Courses	Clear the Master course in Arcade mode, survival mode, or time attack modes.
Master Courses	Clear the True Fighter course in Arcade mode, survival mode, or time attack mode.
System voices	Clear command training in training mode with each character.
True Fighter Courses	Clear the champ course in Arcade mode, survival, or time attack mode.
Akira Yuki	Defeat Akira in Story Mode
Alpha-152	Obtain 300 titles
Gen Fu	Clear Eliot's Story Mode Chapter
Pai Chan	Obtain 100 titles
Sarah Bryant	Defeat Sarah in Story Mode
Christie Swimsuit	Clear the Legend course (solo match) in time attack mode with Christie without using a continue.
Kasumi Black Suit	Clear the True Kasumi chapter in Story Mode.
Kasumi Kimono	Clear the Kasumi vs. Christie battle in the True Kasumi chapter of story mode.
Lisa Swimsuit	Clear the Legend course (solo match) in survival mode with Lisa.
Tina Swimsuit	Clear the Legend course (solo match) in Arcade mode with Tina, without using a continue.

DEAD OR ALIVE 5 (XBOX 360)

ACHIEVEMENTS

UNLOCKABLE	HOW TO UNLOCK
...And Then THIS Happened! (30)	Clear all chapters in Story mode.
A Fight to Remember (10)	Save a replay.
Ahhh, Memories (10)	View your photos in the Album.
Akira Yuki (20)	Unlock Akira.
Anybody, Anytime, Anywhere (30)	Fight 50 people through invitations.
Arcade Cleared (10)	Clear 1 course in Arcade mode.
Arcade Master (30)	Clear all courses in Arcade mode.
Blow 'Em Away (10)	Successfully land a Power Blow.
Cliffhanger Comeback (10)	Successfully block an opponent's attack during a Cliffhanger.

DOA5 Is My Life (50)	Fight online 1000 times.
DOA5 Master (100)	Unlock all achievements.
Down You Go (10)	Successfully attack during a Cliffhanger.
Exercise Newbie (20)	Perform all moves in Command Training.
Failure Teaches Success (20)	See all characters' losing poses.
Fighter, Know Thyself (10)	View your results in Fight Record.
Fighting Entertainment (10)	Have your first fight outside of Training or Versus modes.
Fighting For Real (10)	Play a Ranked match.
Fighting in Style (50)	Unlock all costumes.
First Tag Team (10)	Play Tag Battle.
First Throwdown (20)	Send a Throwdown Challenge to someone in your Fighter List.
Fledgling Fighter (20)	Fight 10 Versus matches.
Gesundheit! (20)	Trigger the Special Danger Zone in The Show.
Get out there and Fight! (10)	Play a Lobby match.
How Do I Fight Like a Pro? (10)	Display the Move Details.
How Do I Fight? (10)	Display the Move List.
I Read Every Move (20)	Win without taking any damage.
Insomniac (20)	Watch all movies in Story mode without skipping any of them.
Jump In (10)	Play a Simple match.
My Fight, My Rules (10)	Create your own online lobby.
Ninja Battle (20)	Clear "Kasumi: Part 2" in Story mode.
On the Edge of Your Seat (10)	Play Spectator mode.
Rival Rampage (30)	Fight online 100 times.
Rival Rumble (20)	Fight online 10 times.
Rivals (20)	Register 5 fighters in your Fight List.
Safety First (10)	Turn Danger Zones off on the Stage Select screen.
Sarah Bryant (20)	Unlock Sarah.
Say Cheese! (10)	Take a photo in Spectator mode.
Survival Cleared (10)	Clear 1 course in Survival mode.
Survival Master (30)	Clear all courses in Survival mode.
Tango Kilo November (20)	Trigger the Special Danger Zone in Hot Zone.
The Curtain Rises (10)	Clear the Prologue in Story mode.
The Fight Never Ends (30)	Fight 100 Versus matches.
The Power of Two (30)	Perform 50 kinds of character-specific tag throws.
The Ultimate Hyper Clone (50)	Get all titles and unlock Alpha-152.
Time Attack Cleared (10)	Clear 1 course in Time Attack mode.
Time Attack Master (30)	Clear all courses in Time Attack mode.
Training Hard (20)	Play Training mode for 1 hour.
You Asked for It! (20)	Fight 10 people through invitations.

UNLOCKABLES

UNLOCKABLE	HOW TO UNLOCK
Character System Voice	Complete a character command training in training mode
Akira Yuki	Defeat him in Story Mode
Alpha-152	Obtain 300 titles

Gen Fu	Clear Eliot's Story Mode Chapter
Pai Chan	Obtain 100 titles
Sarah Bryant	Defeat her in Story Mode

DISHONORED (PLAYSTATION 3)

TROPHIES

UNLOCKABLE	HOW TO UNLOCK
Alive Without Breath (Bronze)	You took possession of a fish
An Unfortunate Accident (Bronze)	You killed Morgan Pendleton with steam
Art Dealer (Silver)	You collected all the Sokolov paintings
Back Home (Bronze)	You grabbed a live grenade and threw it back, killing an attacker
Big Boy (Bronze)	You killed a tallboy using only your sword
Bodyguard (Bronze)	You protected Callista's uncle, Captain Geoff Curnow
Capturing Genius and Madness (Bronze)	You abducted Anton Sokolov, Royal Physician
Child Care (Bronze)	You located Lady Emily Kaldwin, heir to the throne
Clean Hands (Gold)	You completed the game without killing anyone
Cleaner (Bronze)	You fought 5 enemies at once and none of them survived
Creepy Crawly (Bronze)	You used a rat tunnel
Dishonored (Bronze)	You escaped Coldridge Prison
Dunwall in Chaos (Bronze)	You completed the game in high chaos
Excommunication (Bronze)	You eliminated High Overseer Campbell
Faceless (Bronze)	After escaping Coldridge Prison, you completed a mission without alerting anyone
Food Chain (Bronze)	You assassinated an assassin
Gentleman Caller (Bronze)	You completed all the Granny Rags side missions
Ghost (Silver)	You completed all missions after the prologue, alerting or killing no one but key targets
Harm's Way (Bronze)	You caused 5 unintentional suicides
Hornets' Nest (Bronze)	You killed 4 enemies in less than 1 second using the crossbow
Inhabitant (Bronze)	You stayed in possession of others for most of a 3 minute period
Just Dark Enough (Bronze)	You completed the game in low chaos
King of the World (Bronze)	You reached the top of Kaldwin's Bridge
Lights Out (Bronze)	You deactivated at least 5 security systems on Kingsparrow Island
Long Live the Empress (Bronze)	You saved Empress Emily Kaldwin
Manipulator (Bronze)	You made others kill 5 of their own allies
Merchant of Disorder (Bronze)	You acquired 15 equipment upgrades
Mercy is the Mark (Bronze)	You spared Daud's life
Mostly Flesh and Steel (Silver)	You finished the game without purchasing any supernatural powers or enhancements, besides Blink
Occultist (Bronze)	You collected 10 bone charms
Platinum Blades and Dark Corners (Platinum)	You have mastered the City of Dunwall and unlocked all Trophies
Poetic Justice (Gold)	You neutralized all key targets using indirect means
Political Suicide (Bronze)	You brought about the Lord Regent's fall from grace by broadcasting his crimes

Razor Rain (Bronze)	You killed 5 characters with Drop Assassination
Regicide (Bronze)	You assassinated the Lord Regent, Hiram Burrows
Resolution (Gold)	You completed the game
Rogue (Bronze)	You assassinated 10 unaware enemies
Shadow (Silver)	You completed all missions after the prologue without alerting anyone
Specter (Bronze)	After escaping prison, you completed a mission, not alerting anyone and killing less than 5 people
Speed of Darkness (Bronze)	You traveled 30 meters in less than 1 second
Street Conspiracy (Bronze)	You completed all the Slackjaw side missions
Surgical (Silver)	You played from the first mission through Kaldwin's Bridge killing fewer than 10 characters
Tempest (Bronze)	You killed 6 enemies in less than 1 second
The Art of the Steal (Bronze)	You got the Art Dealer's safe combination for Slackjaw, but robbed the safe first
The Escapist (Bronze)	After Coldridge Prison, you eluded 5 pursuers at once without killing them or leaving the map
Thief (Bronze)	You pickpocketed items worth a total of 200 coins
This is Mine (Bronze)	You recovered your belongings
Vanished (Bronze)	You escaped prison and navigated the sewers undetected
Versatile (Bronze)	You killed characters with each weapon and offensive gadget
Wall of Sparks (Bronze)	You killed an enemy with the Wall of Light
Well Mannered (Bronze)	You completed the Boyle Estate mission without spoiling the party

DISHONORED (XBOX 360)

ACHIEVEMENTS

UNLOCKABLE	HOW TO UNLOCK
Alive Without Breath (10)	You took possession of a fish
An Unfortunate Accident (10)	You killed Morgan Pendleton with steam
Art Dealer (50)	You collected all the Sokolov paintings
Back Home (10)	You grabbed a live grenade and threw it back, killing an attacker
Big Boy (20)	You killed a tallboy using only your sword
Bodyguard (10)	You protected Callista's uncle, Captain Geoff Curnow
Capturing Genius and Madness (10)	You abducted Anton Sokolov, Royal Physician
Child Care (10)	You located Lady Emily Kaldwin, heir to the throne
Clean Hands (100)	You completed the game without killing anyone
Cleaner (10)	You fought 5 enemies at once and none of them survived
Creepy Crawly (10)	You used a rat tunnel
Dishonored (5)	You escaped Coldridge Prison
Dunwall in Chaos (50)	You completed the game in high chaos
Excommunication (5)	You eliminated High Overseer Campbell
Faceless (20)	After escaping Coldridge Prison, you completed a mission without alerting anyone
Food Chain (10)	You assassinated an assassin
Gentleman Caller (10)	You completed all the Granny Rags side missions
Ghost (30)	You completed all missions after the prologue, alerting or killing no one but key targets

Harm's Way (10)	You caused 5 unintentional suicides
Hornets' Nest (20)	You killed 4 enemies in less than 1 second using the crossbow
Inhabitant (10)	You stayed in possession of others for most of a 3 minute period
Just Dark Enough (50)	You completed the game in low chaos
King of the World (10)	You reached the top of Kaldwin's Bridge
Lights Out (10)	You deactivated at least 5 security systems on Kingsparrow Island
Long Live the Empress (10)	You saved Empress Emily Kaldwin
Manipulator (10)	You made others kill 5 of their own allies
Merchant of Disorder (20)	You acquired 15 equipment upgrades
Mercy is the Mark (10)	You spared Daud's life
Mostly Flesh and Steel (50)	You finished the game without purchasing any supernatural powers or enhancements, besides Blink
Occultist (20)	You collected 10 bone charms
Poetic Justice (30)	You neutralized all key targets using indirect means
Political Suicide (10)	You brought about the Lord Regent's fall from grace by broadcasting his crimes
Razor Rain (10)	You killed 5 characters with Drop Assassination
Regicide (10)	You assassinated the Lord Regent, Hiram Burrows
Resolution (100)	You completed the game
Rogue (10)	You assassinated 10 unaware enemies
Shadow (30)	You completed all missions after the prologue without alerting anyone
Specter (20)	After escaping prison, you completed a mission, not alerting anyone and killing less than 5 people
Speed of Darkness (10)	You traveled 30 meters in less than 1 second
Street Conspiracy (10)	You completed all the Slackjaw side missions
Surgical (30)	You played from the first mission through Kaldwin's Bridge killing fewer than 10 characters
Tempest (20)	You killed 6 enemies in less than 1 second
The Art of the Steal (10)	You got the Art Dealer's safe combination for Slackjaw, but robbed the safe first
The Escapist (10)	After Coldridge Prison, you eluded 5 pursuers at once without killing them or leaving the map
Thief (20)	You pickpocketed items worth a total of 200 coins
This Is Mine (10)	You recovered your belongings
Vanished (10)	You escaped prison and navigated the sewers undetected
Versatile (20)	You killed characters with each weapon and offensive gadget
Wall of Sparks (10)	You killed an enemy with the Wall of Light
Well Mannered (10)	You completed the Boyle Estate mission without spoiling the party

DMC: DEVIL MAY CRY (PLAYSTATION 3)

TROPHIES

UNLOCKABLE	HOW TO UNLOCK
A man with guts and honor (Bronze)	Reach the end of the descent on Mission 6 having killed all of the enemies
Absolutely crazy about it (Bronze)	Spend 50,000 Red Orbs

Trophy	Requirement
And welcome to Hell! (Gold)	Complete all missions on the Hell and Hell difficulty
And you are set free (Bronze)	Free half of the Lost Souls
Bring it on! (Bronze)	Slay 1,000 Demons
Cleaning up his Dad's mess (Bronze)	Defeat Mundus
Come on Puppy. Let's go! (Bronze)	Defeat your pursuer
Devils never cry (Gold)	Complete all missions on the Dante Must Die difficulty
Dude, the show's over! (Bronze)	Find all of the Keys
Every hero has a weakness (Bronze)	Complete Furnace of Souls without taking damage from the furnace
Fill your dark soul with light (Silver)	Free all of the Lost Souls
Flock off, feather-face! (Bronze)	Survive the encounter with the Tyrant
For Tony Redgrave (Bronze)	Kill 50 enemies using nothing but firearms
He's a demon too (Bronze)	Help Phineas retrieve his eye
Impressive (Bronze)	Slay 100 Demons
In the name of my father (Bronze)	Kill 100 enemies using nothing but Demon weapons
It's got to stay in the family (Bronze)	Acquire Arbiter
It's only the rain (Bronze)	Kill 10 enemies by pushing them into the Hurricane ride on Mission 1
It's showtime. Come on! (Bronze)	Earn 1,500 Style Bonuses
It's time to finish this! (Bronze)	Help Vergil open the Vault
Jackpot! (Gold)	Complete all missions on the Nephilim difficulty with a SSS rank
Keeps getting better and better (Silver)	Gain a 100% completion rank on all missions (difficulty doesn't matter)
Let's rock, baby! (Bronze)	Upgrade Dante's health to maximum
Let's welcome chaos! (Bronze)	Open all of the Secret Doors
Looks like it's your lucky day (Bronze)	Complete a level without taking any damage
Looks like we have a winner (Silver)	Slay 5,000 Demons
More than just a few sparks (Bronze)	Acquire Revenant
No talking! (Bronze)	Acquire Aquila
Now my coat's all charred (Bronze)	Navigate the Sky Bridge on Mission 16 without hitting the lasers
One hell of a party! (Silver)	Complete all of the Secret Missions
Only kind of gift worth giving (Bronze)	Acquire the Angel Boost ability
Platinum Trophy (Platinum)	Collect all DmC Devil May Cry™ Trophies
Power... Give me more power! (Silver)	Purchase all of Dante's combat upgrades
Sensational! (Bronze)	Gain a SSS Style Rank during combat
Stylish! (Bronze)	Complete a mission with a SSS rank
The end? Don't bet on it (Silver)	Complete the final mission on Human, Devil Hunter or Nephilim difficulty
Thing drives me crazy (Bronze)	Acquire Osiris
This baby sure can pack a punch (Bronze)	Acquire Eryx
This is my kind of rain (Bronze)	Spend 10,000 Red Orbs
This is what I live for! (Bronze)	Complete all missions on the Heaven or Hell difficulty
This party's just getting crazy! (Bronze)	Complete 10 Secret Missions
Time to go to work guys! (Bronze)	Purchase your first upgrade

Too easy! (Silver)	Complete all missions on the Son of Sparda difficulty
Whatever, Lady (Bronze)	Defeat Mundus' spawn
Where does the time go? (Bronze)	Complete a level with 2 minutes or less on the clock
You are not a Human, are you? (Bronze)	Acquire the Devil Trigger ability
You can't handle it (Bronze)	Upgrade Dante's Devil Trigger to maximum
You'll never have her fire (Bronze)	Kill 100 enemies using nothing but Angel weapons
You're not going to shoot me (Bronze)	Acquire Kablooey

DMC: DEVIL MAY CRY (XBOX 360)

ACHIEVEMENTS

UNLOCKABLE	HOW TO UNLOCK
A man with guts and honor (10)	You reached the end of the descent on Mission 6 having killed all of the enemies
Absolutely crazy about it (20)	You have Spent 50,000 Red Orbs
And welcome to Hell! (100)	Completed all missions on Hell and Hell difficulty
And you are set free (10)	You have found half of the Lost Souls
Bring it on! (20)	You have slayed 1,000 Demons
Cleaning up his Dad's mess (20)	You have defeated Mundus
Come on Puppy. Let's go! (20)	You have defeated the Hunter
Devils never cry (100)	Completed all missions on the Dante Must Die difficulty
Dude, the show's over! (10)	You have found all 21 Keys
Every hero has a weakness (10)	You completed Furnace of Souls without taking damage from the furnace
Fill your dark soul with light (20)	You have found all of the Lost Souls
Flock off, feather-face! (20)	You have defeated the Tyrant
For Tony Redgrave (10)	You killed 50 enemies using nothing but firearms
He's a demon too (10)	You helped Phineas by retrieving his eye
Impressive (10)	You have slayed 100 Demons
In the name of my father (10)	You killed 100 enemies using nothing but Demon weapons
It's got to stay in the family (10)	You have acquired Arbiter
It's only the rain (10)	You Killed 10 enemies by pushing them into the Hurricane ride
It's showtime. Come on! (20)	You earned 1,500 Style Bonuses
It's time to finish this! (10)	You helped Vergil open the Vault
Jackpot! (80)	Completed all missions on the Nephilim difficultly with a SSS rank
Keeps getting better and better (40)	You have been awarded a 100% completion rank on all missions
Let's rock, baby! (10)	You have upgraded Dante's health to maximum
Let's welcome chaos! (10)	You have opened all 21 Secret Doors
Looks like it's your lucky day (10)	You completed a level without taking any damage
Looks like we have a winner (30)	You have slayed 5,000 Demons
More than just a few sparks (10)	You have acquired Revenant
No talking! (20)	You have acquired Aquila

NEW!

A
B
C
D
E
F
G
H
I
J
K
L
M
N
O
P
Q
R
S
T
U
V
W
X
Y
Z

Now my coat's all charred (10)	You navigated the Sky Bridge without hitting the lasers
One hell of a party! (50)	You have completed all of the Secret Missions
Only kind of gift worth giving (10)	You have acquired the Angel Boost ability
Power... Give me more power! (20)	You have purchased all of Dante's combat upgrades
Sensational! (10)	You gained a SSS Style Rank during combat
Stylish! (10)	Completed a mission with a SSS rank
The end? Don't bet on it (40)	You defeated Vergil on any difficulty
Thing drives me crazy (10)	You have acquired Osiris
This baby sure can pack a punch (20)	You have acquired Eryx
This is my kind of rain (10)	You have spent 10,000 Red Orbs
This is what I live for! (10)	Completed all missions on Heaven Or Hell difficulty
This party's just getting crazy! (20)	You have completed 10 of the Secret Missions
Time to go to work guys! (10)	You purchased your first upgrade
Too easy! (40)	Completed all missions on the Son of Sparda difficulty
Whatever, Lady (20)	You have defeated Mundus' spawn
Where does the time go? (10)	You completed a level in 2 minutes or less
You are not a Human, are you? (10)	You have acquired the Devil Trigger ability
You can't handle it (10)	You have upgraded Dante's Devil Trigger to maximum
You'll never have her fire (10)	You killed 100 enemies using nothing but Angel weapons
You're not going to shoot me (10)	You have acquired Kablooey

DOKURO (PLAYSTATION VITA)

TROPHIES

UNLOCKABLE	HOW TO UNLOCK
A Cornered Rat... (Gold)	Defeat 100 monsters in Skeleton Form
A Hero is Born (Gold)	Defeat 1000 monsters in Hero Form
Apprentice (Bronze)	Complete stages 1 to 4
Aw, Shucks (Bronze)	Pick up the Princess 200 times
Batting 100% (Bronze)	Successfully deflect boomerangs 100 times
Blue Chalk Master (Bronze)	Use blue chalk successfully
Bulging Pockets (Bronze)	Collect 75 coins
Call Me Speedy (Silver)	Complete all areas in a total of 350 minutes or less
Candlelighter (Silver)	Light 4 torches with a single red chalk
Dark Lord's Treasure Complete! (Gold)	Collect all coins
Dark Lord? No Biggie (Silver)	Defeat the Dark Lord without taking any damage
Friends with Death (Bronze)	Die 100 times
Go Big or Go Home (Gold)	Complete stage 14 without taking any damage
Happily Ever After (Silver)	Complete all stages
Hide 'n' Seek (Silver)	Complete stage 11-5 without being discovered once
I'll Just Hold On to These (Bronze)	Collect 10 coins
Knight (Bronze)	Complete stages 9 to 11

Lucky Find (Bronze)	Collect your first coin
Master Knight (Bronze)	Complete stages 12 to 15
Master of the Castle (Gold)	Complete all areas in a total of 250 minutes or less
Moneybags (Silver)	Collect 120 coins
Newby Knight (Bronze)	Complete stages 5 to 8
Numismatist (Bronze)	Collect 25 coins
Old-Mismatist (Bronze)	Collect 50 coins
Red Chalk Master (Bronze)	Use red chalk successfully
Shining Skeleton (Platinum)	Earn all other Dokuro trophies to unlock this platinum trophy
Skydiver (Silver)	Fall from a great height
Treasure Hunter (Silver)	Collect 135 coins
White Chalk Master (Bronze)	Use white chalk successfully
Who Keeps Dropping These? (Silver)	Collect 100 coins
With Friends Like These... (Bronze)	Let the princess get knocked out 100 times

DRAGON BALL Z FOR KINECT (XBOX 360)

ACHIEVEMENTS

UNLOCKABLE	HOW TO UNLOCK
...This Is Super Saiyan 3 (50)	You won without taking any damage in Score Attack mode on Hard.
...We'll Put This Battle On Hold (15)	You battled Majin Vegeta in Score Attack and topped your high score for that stage.
A Shutout Win (40)	You won without ever taking damage from an enemy Super Attack.
All Right! It's Done!! (15)	You battled Frieza Final Form in Score Attack and topped your high score for that stage.
An Awesome Win (40)	You finished the enemy with a Super Attack and won 10 times.
Battle For The Entire Universe (50)	You cleared the Majin Buu Saga in Story Mode for the first time.
Be Reborn As A Good Guy! (15)	You battled Kid Buu 2 in Score Attack and topped your high score for that stage.
Boy, Am I Happy! (15)	You battled Captain Ginyu in Score Attack and topped your high score for that stage.
Cell Games (50)	You cleared the Android Saga in Story Mode for the first time.
Complete Master (30)	You pulled off a 100 hit combo.
Defense Expert (20)	You blocked 10 enemy Super Attacks
Do You Feel Terror? (15)	You battled Android #19 in Score Attack and topped your high score for that stage.
Evasion Expert (20)	You dodged 10 enemy Super Attacks.
Feel The Wrath Of The Namekians! (15)	You battled Frieza 2nd Form in Score Attack and topped your high score for that stage.
Full Power (20)	You stored up the maximum amount of Ki with Ki Charge.
Full-Fledged Adult (10)	You pulled off a 20 hit combo.
Gotta Charge Up My Ki... (15)	You battled Kid Buu in Score Attack and topped your high score for that stage.
Have A Kaioken x3 Kamehameha! (15)	You battled Vegeta in Score Attack and topped your high score for that stage.

I Can Win! I Can Win This!! (15)	You battled Frieza 1st Form in Score Attack and topped your high score for that stage.
I Feel For You... (15)	You battled Captain Ginyu (Goku) in Score Attack and topped your high score for that stage.
It's Your Turn, Gohan!! (15)	You battled Cell Perfect Form in Score Attack and topped your high score for that stage.
Let's Finish This Up (15)	You battled Super Buu (Gohan absorbed) in Score Attack and topped your high score for that stage.
Run!! (15)	You battled Android #17 in Score Attack and topped your high score for that stage.
Serves You Right... (15)	You battled Raditz in Score Attack and topped your high score for that stage.
Show Me Your Perfect Form! (15)	You battled Cell 2nd Form in Score Attack and topped your high score for that stage.
Something Good Before You Die... (20)	You won without taking any damage in Score Attack mode.
Super Attack Beginner (10)	You used 10 Super Attacks.
Super Attack Master (30)	You pulled off 50 Super Attacks.
Super Attack Veteran (20)	You pulled off 20 Super Attacks.
Superior Power (20)	You intercepted the enemy's Super Attack.
Take Care Of Yourself, Trunks... (15)	You battled Majin Buu in Score Attack and topped your high score for that stage.
That Won't Work On Me (30)	You deflected 20 enemy Ki Blasts in a single fight.
The Fruits Of My Training! (15)	You battled Saibamen in Score Attack and topped your high score for that stage.
The Ultimate Decisive Battle (50)	You cleared the Saiyan Saga in Story Mode for the first time.
The Ultimate Power (30)	You won without taking any damage in Score Attack mode on Normal.
Their Final, Greatest Showdown (50)	You cleared the Frieza Saga in Story Mode for the first time.
Veteran Warrior (20)	You pulled off a 50 hit combo.
Welcome To Dragon World (10)	You played Story Mode for the first time.
What Are You, Anyway!? (15)	You battled Cell 1st Form in Score Attack and topped your high score for that stage.
You Can't Win... (15)	You battled Super Buu in Score Attack and topped your high score for that stage.
You Did It, Gohan!! (15)	You battled Perfect Cell in Score Attack and topped your high score for that stage.
You Idiot!! (15)	You battled Full Power Frieza in Score Attack and topped your high score for that stage.
You're Not So Tough (15)	You battled Nappa in Score Attack and topped your high score for that stage.
You're The Best There Is!! (50)	You topped your high score for all Score Attack stages.

TROPHIES

UNLOCKABLE	HOW TO UNLOCK
100% Devotion (Platinum)	You have acquired every Trophy in F1 2012™
Arch-Rival (Bronze)	You have beaten your first rival in Season Challenge.
Austin Power (Bronze)	You beat the lap time of 1:39.635 in Time Trial at the Austin, Texas circuit.
Back to Your Roots (Bronze)	You returned to your starting team in Season Challenge.
Best of the Best (Silver)	You have earned a gold medal in the final scenario in Champions Mode.
Co-op Drivers' World Champion (Silver)	You have won the Drivers' Championship in Co-op.
Constructors' World Champion (Silver)	You have won the Constructors' Championship in Career.
Cut Your Losses (Bronze)	You elected to end R&D on the current season's car in Career.
Domination (Bronze)	You set the fastest lap time in every session of a long race weekend in Career.
Drivers' World Champion (Gold)	You have won the Drivers' Championship in Career on any difficulty.
Earning Your Stripes (Bronze)	You have earned all of the chevrons available in the Young Driver Test.
FORMULA ONE is Back! (Bronze)	You have completed your first Grand Prix in Career or Season Challenge.
FORMULA ONE Pro (Bronze)	You won a race with all driver assists disabled.
From the Front (Bronze)	You won the race from pole position in Career or Season Challenge.
Future Champion (Silver)	You have earned a gold medal in each Young Driver Test.
Gold Rush (Silver)	You have earned a gold medal in all of the Time Attack scenarios.
Golden Delicious (Silver)	You have earned a gold medal in every scenario in Champions Mode.
Graduation Day (Bronze)	You have successfully completed all of the Young Driver Test.
Hardcore (Gold)	You have won the Drivers' Championship in Season Challenge on hard difficulty.
Having a Good Time (Bronze)	You have posted a time in all of the Time Attack scenarios.
Hot Lap (Bronze)	You set the fastest penalty-free race lap in Career or Season Challenge.
Immersion (Bronze)	You have completed a race using only the cockpit camera.
In Demand (Bronze)	During Career, you have had 4 contract offers on the table.
It Takes Two Baby (Silver)	You have won the Constructors' Championship in Co-op.
It's the Taking Part (Bronze)	You have earned a medal in a Champions Mode scenario.
Itchy Feet (Bronze)	You raced for five different teams in Season Challenge in a single season.
Just a Taster (Silver)	You have earned a gold medal in a Young Driver Test.

A B C D E F G H I J K L M N O P Q R S T U V W X Y Z

Keeping it Clean (Bronze)	You have completed a race without colliding with another car or object.
Let's Try That Again (Bronze)	You have successfully used a Flashback during the Young Driver Test.
Made the Papers (Bronze)	You were featured in your first press clipping.
Making the Grade (Bronze)	You passed all of your objectives over a race weekend in Season Challenge.
New Direction (Bronze)	You changed R&D paths mid-season in Career.
One Shot Hero (Silver)	You have taken pole position in One Shot Qualifying.
Online Addiction (Bronze)	You have completed 30 races Online.
Online Dedication (Bronze)	You have completed 15 races Online.
Polesitter (Bronze)	You have taken pole position in Career or Season Challenge.
Proving a Point (Bronze)	You have scored 25,000 points or higher in Season Challenge.
Race to Victory (Bronze)	You have taken your first win in Career or Season Challenge.
Staying Loyal (Bronze)	You stayed with the same team through the whole season in Season Challenge.
Technical (Bronze)	You have won a race using manual gears.
That's My Spot (Bronze)	You beat Vettel's record of 15 pole starts in one full Career season.
The Equipment may be the Same... (Bronze)	You have out-qualified your team mate at every race of a Career or Co-op Season.
The Grass is Greener (Bronze)	You moved to another team mid-season in Career.
The Pressure (Bronze)	You set a valid lap time in One Shot Qualifying.
The Spoils of Victory (Bronze)	You finished a race in the top three in Career or Season Challenge.
Top of the Class (Bronze)	You have beaten four rivals in one season in Season Challenge.
Top Score (Bronze)	You scored maximum points in the Drivers' Championship in Season Challenge.
Trials FORMULA ONE (Bronze)	You have set clean lap times at 5 different circuits in Time Trial.
Winning Ways (Silver)	You have won the Drivers' Championship in Season Challenge.
Zero to Hero (Bronze)	In Career, you qualified outside of the Top 10, but finished on the podium.

F1 2012 (XBOX 360)

ACHIEVEMENTS

UNLOCKABLE	HOW TO UNLOCK
Arch-Rival (15)	You have beaten your first rival in Season Challenge.
Austin Power (10)	You beat the lap time of 1:39.635 in Time Trial at the Austin, Texas circuit.
Back to Your Roots (15)	You returned to your starting team in Season Challenge.
Best of the Best (20)	You have earned a gold medal in the final scenario in Champions Mode.
Co-op Drivers' World Champion (40)	You have won the Drivers' Championship in Co-op.
Constructors' World Champion (50)	You have won the Constructors' Championship in Career.
Cut Your Losses (10)	You elected to end R&D on the current season's car in Career.

Domination (20)	You set the fastest lap time in every session of a long race weekend in Career.
Drivers' World Champion (50)	You have won the Drivers' Championship in Career on any difficulty.
Earning Your Stripes (5)	You have earned all of the chevrons available in the Young Driver Test.
FORMULA ONE is Back! (5)	You have completed your first Grand Prix in Career or Season Challenge.
FORMULA ONE Pro (15)	You won a race with all driver assists disabled.
From the Front (20)	You won the race from pole position in Career or Season Challenge.
Future Champion (40)	You have earned a gold medal in each Young Driver Test.
Gold Rush (20)	You have earned a gold medal in all of the Time Attack scenarios.
Golden Delicious (25)	You have earned a gold medal in every scenario in Champions Mode.
Graduation Day (25)	You have successfully completed all of the Young Driver Test.
Hardcore (45)	You have won the Drivers' Championship in Season Challenge on hard difficulty.
Having a Good Time (10)	You have posted a time in all of the Time Attack scenarios.
Hot Lap (20)	You set the fastest penalty-free race lap in Career or Season Challenge.
Immersion (10)	You have completed a race using only the cockpit camera.
In Demand (15)	During Career, you have had 4 contract offers on the table.
It Takes Two Baby (40)	You have won the Constructors' Championship in Co-op.
It's the Taking Part (10)	You have earned a medal in a Champions Mode scenario.
Itchy Feet (15)	You raced for five different teams in Season Challenge in a single season.
Just a Taster (35)	You have earned a gold medal in a Young Driver Test.
Keeping it Clean (25)	You have completed a race without colliding with another car or object.
Let's Try That Again (5)	You have successfully used a Flashback during the Young Driver Test.
Made the Papers (20)	You were featured in your first press clipping.
Making the Grade (15)	You passed all of your objectives over a race weekend in Season Challenge.
New Direction (10)	You changed R&D paths mid-season in Career.
One Shot Hero (25)	You have taken pole position in One Shot Qualifying.
Online Addiction (20)	You have completed 30 races Online.
Online Dedication (15)	You have completed 15 races Online.
Polesitter (15)	You have taken pole position in Career or Season Challenge.
Proving a Point (15)	You have scored 25,000 points or higher in Season Challenge.
Race to Victory (25)	You have taken your first win in Career or Season Challenge.
Staying Loyal (15)	You stayed with the same team through the whole season in Season Challenge.
Technical (15)	You have won a race using manual gears.

A
B
C
D
E
F
G
H
I
J
K
L
M
N
O
P
Q
R
S
T
U
V
W
X
Y
Z

That's My Spot (20)	You beat Vettel's record of 15 pole starts in one full Career season.
The Equipment may be	You have out-qualified your team mate at every race of a Career or Co-op Season.
The Grass is Greener (15)	You moved to another team mid-season in Career.
The Pressure (5)	You set a valid lap time in One Shot Qualifying.
The Spoils of Victory (20)	You finished a race in the top three in Career or Season Challenge.
Top of the Class (15)	You have beaten four rivals in one season in Season Challenge.
Top Score (30)	You scored maximum points in the Drivers' Championship in Season Challenge.
Trials FORMULA ONE (10)	You have set clean lap times at 5 different circuits in Time Trial.
Winning Ways (30)	You have won the Drivers' Championship in Season Challenge.
Zero to Hero (25)	In Career, you qualified outside of the Top 10, but finished on the podium.

FABLE: THE JOURNEY (XBOX 360)

ACHIEVEMENTS

UNLOCKABLE	HOW TO UNLOCK
A Job for Life (10)	You destroyed a man's livelihood and smashed something up while you were at it. You're a true Hero.
Alas, Poor Nodsy! (20)	You laid to rest the spirits of a platoon of morons. They're another dimension's problem now.
B-B-Q (10)	Roast chicken is the best smell in the world. Unless you're a chicken.
Bam! (20)	There it is! You killed ten creatures with explosive barrels.
Boom-erang (10)	You killed a hobbe with his own bomb. 'Tis the sport to have the enginer hoist with his own petar.
Cartmageddon (20)	A good driver keeps their hands on the reins at all times, apart from when they're killing things.
Chicken Chaser (20)	You purchased ten upgrades. Your powers are beginning to soar. Soar like a chicken.
Don't Stop Believing (100)	You have completed your Journey. The Spire is no more, and a new dawn awaits Albion.
Epic Flail (40)	1,000 kills! That's a lot of killing. You should have a lie down. And a shower.
Fear of Flying (30)	You killed 20 enemies in midair. Flying's fine ・it's landing that hurts. Also, the magic spells.
Five Billion Candle Power (10)	You burned the Corruption from three creatures with one spell. Time to break out the factor 40.
Flail (20)	You killed 500 enemies. The Grim Reaper loves round numbers.
Footloose (20)	You rescued Fergus from a spot of Hobbe bother. Your reward? Singing and beans.
For Every Chest, a Consequence (30)	You opened 15 chests. Now on to the greater mystery: Whose stuff have you been stealing?
Fore! (10)	You killed three enemies with thrown objects. Down in front!
Going Underground (20)	You made it out of Bladebarrow. Most don't.
Great Balls of Fire (10)	You killed three enemies with one Fireball. Goodness gracious.
Happy Camper (20)	You tried your hand at all camp activities. Way to go, cowboy.

Hard Shoulder (10)	You dealt with a travelling enemy by making it crash and die. Ben Hur would be proud.
Heavy Medal (20)	You earned a Bronze Medal in every Arcade Mode challenge.
Hero (30)	You purchased 15 upgrades. Truly, you are a Hero.
Hobbe Juggler (10)	You juggled a hobbe. A career in the circus awaits. A pretty odd circus, admittedly.
I Used to Be an Adventurer (10)	Then I took an arrow to the horse. She's all better now, though.
If I Only Had a Brain (30)	You whiled away the hours, conferring with the flowers. And exploding scarecrows' heads.
In the Palm of Your Hand (20)	The power of the gauntlets is now yours, but so is their burden.
Long Sustained Attacks (30)	You fully upgraded one of your spells. You'll be able to bring down anything now.
Medal Gear Solid (60)	You earned a Gold Medal in every Arcade Mode challenge.
Mind over Matter (20)	The Temptress is no more. Or was it all just a dream?
Mind Your Manas (20)	You dished out a veritable smorgasbord of spell power. Delicious.
No Claims Bonus (20)	You completed The Last Stand without taking any damage.
Off the Chain (20)	You achieved a kill chain of 40 during Arcade Mode.
Off the Menu (20)	The Devourer has been defeated, and Fergus is at rest. There's no turning back now, Hero.
Pedal to the Medal (40)	You earned a Silver Medal in every Arcade Mode challenge.
Pest Control (10)	Ten stingers in five seconds. How long for the other 600,000?
Pimp My Cart (5)	Yo Gabe, we heard you like Heroes so we hung a Hero from your cart so you can Hero while you Hero.
Reflectology (20)	You killed 15 enemies with their own attacks. Reflect on your progress, and feel proud.
Return of the Black Knight (10)	You dismantled a hollow man. It's just a (rotting) flesh-wound!
Roadkill (10)	You ran down an enemy with your cart. Consider investing in a plough.
Saved by the Sun (20)	You escaped the Devourer... for now.
Shardly a Problem (10)	You cast Shards with utmost precision. For your next trick, spear an apple off Seren's head.
Shoo! (20)	You made it to the barn and saw off the White Balverine (with a little help from your friends).
Sparrow (10)	You purchased five upgrades. Your Journey has begun.
Test Your Medal (10)	You earned your first Medal in Arcade Mode.
The Long Road Home (20)	You finally caught up with Katlan. It's you who's needed at the front of the convoy now.
The Open Road (20)	Your story has begun, but where will the road lead you?
The Whites of Their Eyes (10)	You got cosy with a balverine. You must have nerves of steel — and no working olfactory system.
Toasty (10)	Burning through the sky at 200 degrees. That's why they call him Mr. Pushed-in-the-Lava.
Trollololol (20)	You emerged unscathed from a troll fight. Problem?
Wheeee! (5)	You thrust your arms in the air during the minecart ride. Souvenir photo available in the gift shop.
Why the Long Face? (10)	You healed ten wounds on Seren. If she walked into a bar and bruised herself, you'd heal that too.

NEW!

A
B
C
D
E
F
G
H
I
J
K
L
M
N
O
P
Q
R
S
T
U
V
W
X
Y
Z

CODES & CHEATS

UNLOCKABLES

UNLOCKABLE	HOW TO UNLOCK
Fable: The Journey T-Shirt	Fable: The Journey T-Shirt can be unlocked by progressing through your Journey.
Mask of the Devourer	Mask of the Devourer can be unlocked by progressing through your Journey.
Theresa's Blindfold	Theresa's Blindfold can be unlocked by progressing through your Journey.

FAR CRY 3 (PLAYSTATION 3)

TROPHIES

UNLOCKABLE	HOW TO UNLOCK
Aftermarket Junkie (Bronze)	Buy all attachments and paint jobs for one weapon.
Archeology 101 (Silver)	Gather a total of 60 relics.
Artsy Craftsy (Bronze)	Craft 5 upgrades for your equipment.
Bagged and Tagged (Bronze)	Complete a Path of the Hunter quest.
Dead Letters (Silver)	Gather all "Letters of the Lost".
Deep Cover (Bronze)	Complete Riley's interrogation.
Fearless or Stupid (Bronze)	Dive more than 60m (Single Player only).
First Blood (Bronze)	Escape the pirates and survive in the wilderness.
Free Fall (Bronze)	Freefall more than 100m and live (Single Player only).
Full Bars (Silver)	Activate 9 radio towers.
Fully Inked (Gold)	Earn every tattoo by learning all the skills.
Getting Even (Bronze)	Complete "Payback" Co-op map (Online/Offline).
Hands Off My Stoner (Bronze)	Rescue Oliver from the pirates.
Have I Told You? (Silver)	Survive the encounter with Vaas and escape.
Heartless Pyro (Bronze)	Kill 50 enemies with the flamethrower (Single Player only).
Here We Come (Bronze)	Complete "Ready or Not" Co-op map (Online/Offline).
Hide and Seek (Bronze)	Complete "Lights Out" Co-op map (Online/Offline).
Higher Than a Kite (Bronze)	Use your wingsuit to reach the Southern island.
Hunter Hunted (Bronze)	Lure and kill a predator.
Improper Use (Bronze)	Kill an enemy with the Repair Tool (Single Player only).
In Cold Blood (Bronze)	Complete a WANTED Dead quest.
Inked Up (Bronze)	Earn 5 skill tattoos.
Island Liberator (Silver)	Liberate all outposts.
Island Paparazzi (Bronze)	Tag 25 enemies using the camera (Single Player only).
Jungle Journal (Silver)	Unlock 50 entries in the Survivor Guide.
Late Night Pick-up (Bronze)	Complete "Rush Hour" Co-op map (Online/Offline).
Let the Trials Begin (Bronze)	Beat any Trial of the Rakyat score.
Love the Boom (Bronze)	Kill 4 enemies simultaneously with one explosion (Single Player only).
Magic Mushroom (Bronze)	Return to the doctor with the cave mushrooms.
Mastered the Jungle (Platinum)	Obtain all the Trophies.
Memory to Spare (Silver)	Gather all the memory cards.
Money to Burn (Bronze)	Spend $5000 at the shop.

Needle Exchange (Bronze)	Craft 25 syringes.
Never Saw it Coming (Bronze)	Kill an enemy with a takedown from above from a glider, zipline or parachute (Single Player only).
One of Us (Bronze)	Complete the Rakyat initiation.
Poacher (Bronze)	Hunt and skin a rare animal.
Poker Bully (Silver)	Win $1500 playing poker.
Poker Night (Silver)	Kill Hoyt.
Rebel With a Cause (Bronze)	Liberate 3 outposts.
Retake Wallstreet (Bronze)	Rescue Keith from Buck.
Return to Sender (Bronze)	Complete "Sidetracked" Co-op map (Online/Offline).
Road Trip (Bronze)	Complete a Supply Drop quest.
Rock Always Wins (Bronze)	Fully distract 25 enemies with rocks (Single Player only).
Rocking the Boat (Bronze)	Complete "Overboard" Co-op map (Online/Offline).
Say Hi to the Internet (Bronze)	Find the lost Hollywood star.
Taken for Granted (Silver)	Kill Vaas.
The Good Stuff (Bronze)	Craft a special syringe.
Toxophilite (Bronze)	Kill a target from 70m or more with the bow (Single Player only).
Unheard (Bronze)	Liberate an outpost without triggering an alarm.
What a Trip (Gold)	Attend the final ceremony.
Worst Date Ever (Bronze)	Rescue Liza from the burning building.

FAR CRY 3 (XBOX 360)

ACHIEVEMENTS

UNLOCKABLE	HOW TO UNLOCK
Aftermarket Junkie (20)	Buy all attachments and paint jobs for one weapon.
Archeology 101 (20)	Gather a total of 60 relics.
Artsy Craftsy (10)	Craft 5 upgrades for your equipment.
Bagged and Tagged (10)	Complete a Path of the Hunter quest.
Dead Letters (20)	Gather all "Letters of the Lost".
Deep Cover (20)	Complete Riley's interrogation.
Fearless or Stupid (15)	Dive more than 60m (Single Player only).
First Blood (10)	Escape the pirates and survive in the wilderness.
Free Fall (5)	Freefall more than 100m and live (Single Player only).
Full Bars (20)	Activate 9 radio towers.
Fully Inked (30)	Earn every tattoo by learning all the skills.
Getting Even (20)	Complete "Payback" Co-op map (Online/Offline).
Hands Off My Stoner (20)	Rescue Oliver from the pirates.
Have I Told You? (50)	Survive the encounter with Vaas and escape.
Heartless Pyro (10)	Kill 50 enemies with the flamethrower (Single Player only).
Here We Come (20)	Complete "Ready or Not" Co-op map (Online/Offline).
Hide and Seek (20)	Complete "Lights Out" Co-op map (Online/Offline).
Higher Than a Kite (20)	Use your wingsuit to reach the Southern island.
Hunter Hunted (10)	Lure and kill a predator.
Improper Use (5)	Kill an enemy with the Repair Tool (Single Player only).
In Cold Blood (10)	Complete a WANTED Dead quest.
Inked Up (5)	Earn 5 skill tattoos.

A
B
C
D
E
F
G
H
I
J
K
L
M
N
O
P
Q
R
S
T
U
V
W
X
Y
Z

Island Liberator (40)	Liberate all outposts.
Island Paparazzi (15)	Tag 25 enemies using the camera (Single Player only).
Jungle Journal (20)	Unlock 50 entries in the Survivor Guide.
Late Night Pick-up (20)	Complete "Rush Hour" Co-op map (Online/Offline).
Let the Trials Begin (10)	Beat any Trial of the Rakyat score.
Love the Boom (10)	Kill 4 enemies simultaneously with one explosion (Single Player only).
Magic Mushroom (20)	Return to the doctor with the cave mushrooms.
Memory to Spare (20)	Gather all the memory cards.
Money to Burn (15)	Spend $5000 at the shop.
Needle Exchange (15)	Craft 25 syringes.
Never Saw it Coming (20)	Kill an enemy with a takedown from above from a glider, zipline or parachute (Single Player only).
One of Us (20)	Complete the Rakyat initiation.
Poacher (20)	Hunt and skin a rare animal.
Poker Bully (20)	Win $1500 playing poker.
Poker Night (50)	Kill Hoyt.
Rebel With a Cause (10)	Liberate 3 outposts.
Retake Wallstreet (20)	Rescue Keith from Buck.
Return to Sender (20)	Complete "Sidetracked" Co-op map (Online/Offline).
Road Trip (10)	Complete a Supply Drop quest.
Rock Always Wins (10)	Fully distract 25 enemies with rocks (Single Player only).
Rocking the Boat (20)	Complete "Overboard" Co-op map (Online/Offline).
Say Hi to the Internet (10)	Find the lost Hollywood star.
Taken for Granted (50)	Kill Vaas.
The Good Stuff (15)	Craft a special syringe.
Toxophilite (10)	Kill a target from 70m or more with the bow (Single Player only).
Unheard (20)	Liberate an outpost without triggering an alarm.
What a Trip (100)	Attend the final ceremony.
Worst Date Ever (20)	Rescue Liza from the burning building.

FIFA SOCCER 13 (PLAYSTATION 3)

TROPHIES

UNLOCKABLE	HOW TO UNLOCK
1 week (Bronze)	Win all the EAS FC Match Day Games of the Week in a single week
Big Spender (Bronze)	Redeem an item with EAS FC Football Club Credits.
Body Control (Bronze)	Score an off balance shot
Brains and Brawn (Bronze)	Shield the ball out of play for a goal kick
Bronzed (Bronze)	Complete the Bronze stage of all Skills
Bros (Bronze)	Play a Seasons game with a Guest
Building My Club (Bronze)	Claim your first FUT Pack
Challenge Accepted (Silver)	Win a match against the team of the week
Challenging (Silver)	Complete an EA SPORTS Football Club Challenge
Cheeky (Bronze)	Chip the Keeper
Creeping on the Down Low (Bronze)	Wall creep, free kick is blocked by wall
Digi-Me (Bronze)	Start your Player Career with a Created Pro
Division King (Silver)	Win a Division title in Seasons

EASFC Starting 11 (Silver)	Reach level 20 in the EA SPORTS Football Club
EASFC Youth Academy (Bronze)	Reach level 5 in the EA SPORTS Football Club
Filling Cabinets (Silver)	Win a Cup in Seasons
Football Legend (Platinum)	Unlock all other trophies (excluding additional content trophies)
For Country (Bronze)	Become manager of an international team
Get In! (Bronze)	Score a Diving Header
Get Physical (Bronze)	Seal out an attacking player to gain possession of the ball
Getting Real (Bronze)	Play 25 EAS FC Match Day Games
Go Live! (Bronze)	Win an EAS FC Match Day Live Fixture
Good Start (Bronze)	Unlock 10% of the accomplishments with your Online Pro
Hello World (Bronze)	Play your first match with your Online Pro
I Love This Club (Bronze)	Achieve a club value of 85,000,000
Impressive (Silver)	Achieve one of your season objectives as a player at any point in your career
In Form! (Bronze)	Find a team of the week player in a pack
Master Negotiator (Bronze)	Sell a player by getting your counter offer accepted by the CPU
Maxed Out (Bronze)	Reach the daily limit of XP in the EA SPORTS Football Club
Mr. Manager (Bronze)	Take Control of your own FIFA Ultimate Team
National Pride (Silver)	Get called up to the national team as a player
Nice Form (Bronze)	Achieve your match set objective as player at any point in your career
No Goal for You! (Bronze)	Goal Line Clearance
On the Rise (Bronze)	Earn a Promotion in Seasons
One of the Bros (Bronze)	Be part of a Club win
Pack King (Gold)	Open 50 FUT Packs
Packing Bags (Bronze)	Go out on loan or transfer to another club with your Pro in Play as Player
Press Conference (Silver)	Purchase a gold player in the Auction House for 15,000 or more coins using buy it now
Promoted! (Silver)	Earn promotion in FUT Seasons
Road to Mastery (Silver)	Unlock a Skill Challenge
Road to Promotion (Bronze)	Win a FUT Seasons Match
Silverware (Bronze)	Win a Trophy in a FUT Competition
Skill Legend (Gold)	Become Legendary on one of the Skill Challenges
So Euro (Bronze)	Enable European competition in the first season of Career
Still Friends? (Bronze)	Win an Online Friendlies Season
Trolling for Goals (Bronze)	Score on a free kick after running over the ball
Way with Words (Bronze)	Successfully request additional funds from your board in Career
Well on Your Way (Silver)	Unlock 25% of the accomplishments with your Online Pro
Wheeling and Dealing (Bronze)	Complete a Player + cash deal in Career

FIFA SOCCER 13 (PLAYSTATION VITA)

TROPHIES

UNLOCKABLE	HOW TO UNLOCK
A Man Down (Bronze)	Win a game when down one man before half-time.
Against the Odds (Bronze)	Win a Head to Head Ranked Match using a weaker team
All My Own Work (Bronze)	Win a Match with Manual Controls
Back to Back (Gold)	Win consecutive League titles in any top tier League in Manager Mode
Challenging Schedule (Silver)	Complete a Manager Mode Season without simming a game
Classy (Bronze)	Complete 5 Kit & Appearance Accomplishments
Control the Open Space (Bronze)	Make a successful lob pass using the touchscreen in a match
Cup Upset (Silver)	Win a Tournament that starts with sixteen teams with a 1 Star rating team
Custom Sixty Four Winner (Silver)	Win a Created Tournament that starts with sixty four teams
Defiance (Bronze)	Chip the Keeper in a Head to Head Ranked match
Don't Blink (Bronze)	Score within the first 5 minutes of the game in a game vs the CPU
Festive (Silver)	Complete 5 Accomplishments that unlock Celebrations Packs
FIFA Fair Play (Bronze)	Play 5 consecutive matches without getting any cards (Bookings must be enabled in the settings)
Folklore (Silver)	Become a Legend as a player in Career Mode
Football Legend (Platinum)	Unlock all other trophies (excluding additional content trophies)
Fortress (Gold)	Don't lose any matches played at Home in a season.
Good Form (Silver)	Play 5 consecutive Head to Head Ranked Matches without losing
Good Week! (Bronze)	Get yourself selected in the Team of the Week in Career Mode
Great Month! (Bronze)	Win the Manager of the Month award in Career Mode
Hundred and Counting (Gold)	Play 100 Head to Head Ranked Matches
In the Game (Bronze)	Create a Virtual Pro
Massive Signing (Bronze)	Sign a player better than anyone else on your club during the transfer window
Nimble Fingers (Bronze)	Score a touchscreen or rear touch pad goal from a touchscreen pass
No Draw for You! (Bronze)	Score a 90th minute winner in a game vs the CPU
Off the Top of my Hat (Silver)	Score a Hat Trick with your Virtual Pro
One Goal a Season (Bronze)	Score a goal with a defender
Pass Master (Silver)	Make 100 successful passes using the touchscreen
Pinpoint Accuracy (Bronze)	Score a goal using the screen (touchscreen) shot, or a rear touch pad shot
Pressure is On (Bronze)	Score a penalty kick using a touch shot
Ruud boy (Bronze)	Score a goal from a volley
Sharp Shooter (Silver)	Score 50 goals using a touch shot
Sparkly Clean (Silver)	Keep a clean sheet on World Class difficulty or higher
Thread the Needle (Bronze)	Make a successful through pass using the touchscreen

Tiki Taka (Silver)	Make 20 consecutive passes between at least 3 players in the opponent's half
Top of the League? (Bronze)	Win an online Friends League Match
Tour Bus (Bronze)	Complete a match in every stadium
Trait-or (Bronze)	Unlock a trait for your Virtual Pro
Woodwork and In! (Bronze)	Score off the post or cross bar in a match
You Pointing at Me? (Bronze)	Make a successful direct pass using the touchscreen

FIFA SOCCER 13 (XBOX 360)

ACHIEVEMENTS

UNLOCKABLE	HOW TO UNLOCK
1 week (15)	Win all the EAS FC Match Day Games of the Week in a single week
Big Spender (10)	Redeem an item with EAS FC Football Club Credits.
Body Control (5)	Score an off balance shot
Brains and Brawn (15)	Shield the ball out of play for a goal kick
Bronzed (30)	Complete the Bronze stage of all Skills
Bros (15)	Play a Seasons game with a Guest
Building My Club (10)	Claim your first FUT Pack
Challenge Accepted (30)	Win a match against the team of the week
Challenging (10)	Complete an EA SPORTS Football Club Challenge
Cheeky (5)	Chip the Keeper
Creeping on the Down Low (5)	Wall creep, free kick is blocked by wall
Digi-Me (5)	Start your Player Career with a Created Pro
Division King (50)	Win a Division title in Seasons
EASFC Starting 11 (30)	Reach level 20 in the EA SPORTS Football Club
EASFC Youth Academy (10)	Reach level 5 in the EA SPORTS Football Club
Filling Cabinets (30)	Win a Cup in Seasons
For Country (20)	Become manager of an international team
Get In! (15)	Score a Diving Header
Get Physical (5)	Seal out an attacking player to gain possession of the ball
Getting Real (30)	Play 25 EAS FC Match Day Games
Go Live! (15)	Win an EAS FC Match Day Live Fixture
Good Start (30)	Unlock 10% of the accomplishments with your Online Pro
Hello World (5)	Play your first match with your Online Pro
I Love This Club (30)	Achieve a club value of 85,000,000
Impressive (50)	Achieve one of your season objectives as a player at any point in your career
In Form! (20)	Find a team of the week player in a pack
Master Negotiator (10)	Sell a player by getting your counter offer accepted by the CPU
Maxed Out (10)	Reach the daily limit of XP in the EA SPORTS Football Club
Mr. Manager (10)	Take Control of your own FIFA Ultimate Team
National Pride (30)	Get called up to the national team as a player
Nice Form (30)	Achieve your match set objective as player at any point in your career
No Goal for You! (30)	Goal Line Clearance
On the Rise (25)	Earn a Promotion in Seasons

One of the Bros (15)	Be part of a Club win
Pack King (50)	Open 50 FUT Packs
Packing Bags (15)	Go out on loan or transfer to another club with your Pro in Play as Player
Press Conference (30)	Purchase a gold player in the Auction House for 15,000 or more coins using buy it now
Promoted! (30)	Earn promotion in FUT Seasons
Road to Mastery (30)	Unlock a Skill Challenge
Road to Promotion (10)	Win a FUT Seasons Match
Silverware (10)	Win a Trophy in a FUT Competition
Skill Legend (50)	Become Legendary on one of the Skill Challenges
So Euro (5)	Enable European competition in the first season of Career
Still Friends? (30)	Win an Online Friendlies Season
Trolling for Goals (15)	Score on a free kick after running over the ball
Way with Words (5)	Successfully request additional funds from your board in Career
Well on Your Way (50)	Unlock 25% of the accomplishments with your Online Pro
Wheeling and Dealing (15)	Complete a Player + cash deal in Career

FORZA HORIZON (XBOX 360)

ACHIEVEMENTS

UNLOCKABLE	HOW TO UNLOCK
#WINNING! (15)	You've dominated 10 Festival Races.
...and across the line! (10)	You competed in your first race at Horizon.
A Wristed Development (20)	You received your Yellow Wristband.
All Your Race Are Belong to Us (30)	You've won every single race in the game!
Almost Famous (20)	You're the 50th most popular driver at Horizon.
Bargain Shopper (10)	You bagged yourself a nice discount.
Barn This Way (5)	You found your first barn find.
Been There, Done That! (10)	You've fully explored the Horizon Festival Loop.
Black Friday (20)	Never pay for an upgrade again!
Born Slippy (10)	You've won your first Mixed-Surface or Dirt Race.
Close Encounters (20)	You've challenged and beaten 10 festival racers on the spot.
Cruise Club (20)	You've completed 10 free roam challenges online.
Darius Who? (100)	You owned Darius Flynt and became the Horizon Festival champion.
Ding! (5)	You got to Level 5 online.
Domination! (10)	You've sent every Horizon Star packin'.
Exhibitionist (20)	You've won every Showcase Event in the game.
First! (20)	You won your first race at Horizon.
Freshly Squeezed (40)	You received your Orange Wristband.
Gettin' It Done (30)	You rocked every single Festival Event.
Going Green (25)	You received your Green Wristband.
Golden Boy (50)	You received the Golden Wristband.
Hard Driving (10)	You finished in first place on HARD? Nice.
Just Me and the XP (10)	You've reached level 25 online. Did you win a car yet?
Killer Skills (25)	You're the 10th most popular driver at Horizon.

Kudos to You (10)	You've completed 5 Sponsorship challenges.
Lawbreaker (10)	You blasted past 5 speed traps and 5 speed zones.
May The Forza Be With You (10)	You received free cars for being a loyal Forza fan!
Noob No More (20)	25 online races complete... awesome!
Notorious (30)	You're the most popular driver at Horizon.
OMG (5)	You won your first car online.
OMGWT*BBQ!? (20)	You got seriously lucky and won 5 cars online.
One to Watch (10)	You're the 200th most popular driver at Horizon.
Out of the Blue (30)	You received your Blue Wristband.
Playground Games (5)	You completed each of the Playground game types. How fun was that?
Purple Reign (45)	You received your Purple Wristband.
Racing for Pinks (35)	You received your Pink Wristband.
Rave Paint (10)	You created a paintjob and your ride is looking SWEET!
Road Trip (25)	You've driven along every road in the entire game.
Sellout (20)	20 Sponsorship Challenges? Now you're popular and rich!
Still a Noob... (10)	10 online races complete... not bad!
Stuntman (25)	You've completed every Horizon Outpost PR Stunt.
Swings and Roundabouts (20)	You've completed 3 of each Playground game types.
Take Her for a Spin! (15)	You bought a car from the Autoshow. Now take her for a spin!
The Next Big Thing (15)	You're the 100th most popular driver at Horizon.
Vendetta (20)	You've beaten a Rival time in 10 events.
WARNING!!! DANGER TO MANIFOLD (15)	You've won 10 Street Races. Ali would be proud.
Welcome to Horizon (10)	You arrived at Horizon Festival raring to go.
Wheelin' 'n Dealin' (10)	You sold something via your Storefront. KERCHING!
Win Diesel (30)	You cruised past the competition and won every Street Race.
ZOMG! (10)	You've won 3 cars online.

HALO 4 (XBOX 360)

ACHIEVEMENTS

UNLOCKABLE	HOW TO UNLOCK
A Legendary Episode (40)	Completed all chapters in Spartan Ops Episode 1 on Legendary difficulty.
Armorer (5)	Changed your Spartan's armor in the Spartan Armor card.
Badge (5)	Changed your Emblem in the Spartan ID card.
Bromageddon (40)	Completed the Campaign cooperatively on Heroic or harder.
Bropocalypse (10)	Completed any Campaign mission cooperatively on Heroic or harder.
Bros to the Close (20)	Completed mission 4 without one preventable Marine death on Heroic or harder.
Chief, Smash! (20)	Killed 3 Crawlers in one hit with the Gravity Hammer in mission 8.
Composer (10)	Completed mission 7 on any difficulty.
Contact the Domain (10)	Found a Terminal in the Campaign.
Crimson Alone (20)	Completed a Spartan Ops chapter solo on Legendary.

A
B
C
D
E
F
G
H
I
J
K
L
M
N
O
P
Q
R
S
T
U
V
W
X
Y
Z

Dawn (10)	Completed mission 1 on any difficulty.
Dedicated to Crimson (80)	Completed all chapters in the first 5 episodes of Spartan Ops on any difficulty.
Digging up the Past (20)	Found and accessed Chief's record in mission 1.
Explore the Floor (20)	Tricked or forced a Hunter to fall to his demise in mission 6.
Forerunner (10)	Completed mission 3 on any difficulty.
Game Changer (5)	Created and saved a Custom Game type in War Games.
Give Him the Stick (20)	Took out both Hunters using only the Sticky Detonator in mission 7.
Hanging on the Combat Deck (30)	Won 20 War Games matchmaking matches.
I <3 Red vs Blue (15)	Won 5 War Games matchmaking matches.
I Need a Hero (40)	Completed the Campaign on Heroic or harder.
Infinity (10)	Completed mission 4 on any difficulty.
Knight in White Assassination (20)	Assassinated a Knight in any Spartan Ops mission.
Lone Wolf Legend (90)	Completed the Campaign solo on Legendary difficulty.
Midnight (10)	Completed mission 8 on any difficulty.
Midnight Launch (20)	Got significant air in the Warthog at midnight in mission 2.
Mortardom (20)	Hijacked a Wraith and used it to kill at least four enemy Wraiths in mission 5 on Heroic or harder.
Movin' On Up (25)	Ranked up your Spartan-IV to SR-20.
No Easy Way Out (20)	In Ch 1, Ep 5 of Spartan Ops survived the enemy assault during the defense on Normal or harder.
No One Left Behind (20)	Saved at least one Marine in Chapter 3 of Episode 2 of Spartan Ops on Heroic or harder.
Not Some Recruit Anymore (15)	Ranked up your Spartan-IV to SR-5.
Operation Completion (15)	Completed a Spartan Ops Mission on any difficulty.
PWND (5)	Changed your Service Tag in the Spartan ID card.
Reclaimer (10)	Completed mission 5 on any difficulty.
Requiem (10)	Completed mission 2 on any difficulty.
Roses vs Violets (20)	Found one of the RvB Easter Eggs in Spartan Ops.
Sharing is Caring (5)	Uploaded a File to your File Share.
Shutdown (10)	Completed mission 6 on any difficulty.
Skullduggery (15)	Completed any Campaign mission with 3 or more Skulls on Heroic or harder.
Snapshot! (5)	Saved a Screenshot from the Theater.
Terminus (50)	Found all of the Terminals in the Campaign.
The Cartographer (5)	Created and saved a Custom Map in Forge.
The Challenged (10)	Completed a Challenge.
The Challenger (20)	Completed 25 Challenges.
The Director (5)	Saved a Film Clip from the Theater.
The Legend of 117 (70)	Completed the Campaign on Legendary difficulty.
This is my Rifle, This is my Gun (20)	Carried a UNSC weapon all the way through mission 3 on Heroic or harder.
Wake Up, John (20)	Completed the Campaign on Normal or harder.
What a Poser! (5)	Changed your Spartan's pose in the Spartan ID card

.What Power Outage? (20)	Completed Chapter 4, Episode 5 of Spartan Ops without losing a generator on Heroic or harder.

UNLOCKABLES

UNLOCKABLE	HOW TO UNLOCK
Knight Helmet Avatar Award	Unlock the "Knight in White Assassination" achievement to earn this award.
Platinum Mark VI Helmet Avatar Award	Unlock the "Wake Up, John" achievement to earn this award.
UNSC Infinity Hoodie Avatar Award	Unlock the "Not Some Recruit Anymore" achievement to earn this award.

HARLEY PASTERNAK'S HOLLYWOOD WORKOUT (XBOX 360)

ACHIEVEMENTS

UNLOCKABLE	HOW TO UNLOCK
Action Movie Star (20)	Ready your body for those action-packed sequences
Any Time, Any Place (10)	Complete a Single Workout
Beach Cruiser (30)	Pedal far enough to bike from Santa Monica to Venice Beach
Burn, Baby, Burn (10)	Burn 100 calories
Castaway Reality Show Winner (20)	Win those individual competitive challenges
Crab Walk (20)	Sidestep enough times to travel a mile sideways
Dynamo (20)	Burn 1000 calories
Exceed Your Goals (30)	Earn Target Points in an entire Complete Program
Extra Crunchy (20)	Complete all Core Exercises
Freshly Squeezed (30)	Crush enough oranges to make 25 gallons of orange juice
Getting Stronger (20)	Perform strength exercises for 75 minutes
Harley Star (30)	Earn 50000 points
Heavy Lifting (20)	Perform enough push ups to lift a school bus
Hollywood Trainee (30)	Finish a 5-week Complete Program
Inferno (30)	Burn 10000 calories
It's A Bird, It's A Plane (20)	Jump enough distance to leap over the Empire State Building
Kayaked Across Niagara Falls (20)	Row far enough to kayak across the mouth of Niagara Falls
Keep Breathing (20)	Perform 60 minutes of cardio
Limbo Leader (20)	Complete all Lower Body Exercises
Maintain Your Goals (20)	Earn Target Points for a week in a Complete Program
Martial Arts Movie Star (20)	Focus your moves to effectively defend yourself
Move That Body (30)	Perform 200 minutes of cardio
Music Video Idol (20)	Dance for multiple retakes without tiring
No Sweat (10)	Perform 5 minutes of cardio
Olympic Sprinter (20)	Strengthen your legs to run at lightning fast speed
Perfect Program (30)	Miss no days in an entire Complete Program
Perfect Week (20)	Miss no days for a week in a Complete Program
Personal Workout History (10)	View all pages in Workout Journal
Plank Champ (20)	Work your muscles while perpendicular to gravity
Prize Fighter (20)	Get the upper hand on your opponents
Push And Pull (10)	Perform strength exercises for 5 minutes
Red Carpet Body (30)	Complete 15,000 reps. Hollywood, look out!

Rep streak (10)	Perform 5 consecutive reps
Rookie (10)	Earn 1000 points
Scaled The Grand Canyon (30)	Climb high enough to scale up out of the Grand Canyon
Set Your Goals (10)	Earn Target Points in an Exercise
Single-Minded (20)	Complete all Single Workouts
Skating Gold Medalist (20)	Spin and fly across the ice surface
Star Client (40)	Finish a 10-week Complete Program
Superhero Movie Star (20)	Tone your physique in order to squeeze into that superhero outfit
Tight And Toned (30)	Perform strength exercises for 300 minutes
Total Workout (20)	Complete all Exercises
Totally Yodeling (20)	Ski down far enough to descend through the Andes Mountains
Tower Of Power (20)	Complete all Upper Body Exercises
Triathlon Champion (20)	Train your body to endure a grueling race
Veteran (20)	Earn 10000 points
Walked A Mile (20)	Step forward enough times to walk a mile
We're On Our Way (10)	Start a Complete Program

HARRY POTTER FOR KINECT (XBOX 360)

ACHIEVEMENTS

UNLOCKABLE	HOW TO UNLOCK
Advanced Ace (50)	Completed the Advanced Difficulty Mode
Basilisk Basher (15)	Ranked 5 stars in The Chamber Of Secrets
Bridge Bester (15)	Ranked 5 stars in Destroy the Bridge
Burning Day Bystander (10)	Saw Fawkes burst into flames
Caf・Contender (15)	Ranked 5 stars in Luchino Caffe Duel
Casual Conqueror (15)	Completed the Casual Difficulty Mode
Challenge Mode Advanced (30)	Completed the Advanced Challenge Mode
Challenge Mode Casual (15)	Completed the Casual Challenge Mode
Challenge Mode Extreme (50)	Completed the Extreme Challenge Mode
Character Collector (50)	Unlocked all playable characters
Charms Champion (15)	Ranked 5 stars in Charms Class
D.A. Defender (15)	Ranked 5 stars in Room of Requirement
Daring Dodger (30)	Won all blackboard dodging games
Definitive Dueller (15)	Ranked 5 stars in Duelling Club
Dementor Defeater (15)	Ranked 5 stars in Battle The Dementors
Duelling Demon (30)	Won all blackboard duelling groups
Duelling Dervish (25)	Defeated all possible opponents in blackboard duels
Familiar Face (10)	Scanned your face
Greenhouse Guru (15)	Ranked 5 stars in Mandrake Repotting
Hangleton Hero (15)	Ranked 5 stars in Harry vs Voldemort Duel
Inferi Interceptor (15)	Ranked 5 stars in The Locket Horcrux
Maze Master (15)	Ranked 5 stars in Triwizard Tournament Third Task
Ministry Maestro (15)	Ranked 5 stars in Dumbledore vs Voldemort Duel
Multiplayer Master (10)	Played all multiplayer games
Pixie Pesterer (15)	Ranked 5 stars in Cornish Pixies
Potion Perfectionist (40)	Completed all blackboard potions classes
Potions Pro (15)	Ranked 5 stars in Potions Class
Potter Precluder (15)	Ranked 5 stars in Snape vs Harry Duel

Quality Keeper (15)	Ranked 5 stars in Quidditch Match - Keeper
Quirrell Quasher (15)	Ranked 5 stars in The Philosopher's Stone Chamber
Rat Remover (15)	Ranked 5 stars in Catch Scabbers
Snake Slayer (15)	Ranked 5 stars in Nagini Battle
Song Specialist (10)	Listened to all the Sorting Hat's songs
Star Collector (30)	Ranked 5 stars in all games
Stellar Swimmer (15)	Ranked 5 stars in Triwizard Tournament Second Task
Super Spell-caster (15)	Practised all blackboard spells
Superb Seeker (15)	Ranked 5 stars in Quidditch Match - Seeker
Troll Trouncer (15)	Ranked 5 stars in Troll Battle
Ultimate Unlocker (50)	Unlocked all blackboard games
Vault Voyager (15)	Ranked 5 stars in Journey to the Lestrange Vault
Veil Room Victor (15)	Ranked 5 stars in Ministry of Magic Death Eater Battle
Voldemort Vanquisher (15)	Ranked 5 stars in Voldemort Finale
Willow Whiz (15)	Ranked 5 stars in The Whomping Willow
Year Five (20)	Completed Year 5
Year Four (20)	Completed Year 4
Year One (20)	Completed Year 1
Year Seven (20)	Completed Year 7
Year Six (20)	Completed Year 6
Year Three (20)	Completed Year 3
Year Two (20)	Completed Year 2

HISTORY LEGENDS OF WAR: PATTON (XBOX 360)

ACHIEVEMENTS

UNLOCKABLE	HOW TO UNLOCK
Air Support (40)	First aircraft recruited (Campaign Mode)
Armored support (20)	First tank recruited (Campaign Mode)
Assassin! (40)	15 German soldiers killed with knife (Campaign Mode)
Battle Hardened Recruit (30)	First operation completed (Campaign Mode)
Combat veteran (70)	Third operation completed (Campaign Mode)
Destroyer! (20)	50 German units destroyed (Campaign Mode)
First blood! (10)	First mission completed (Campaign Mode)
Full army! (60)	Third Army completed (Campaign Mode)
Heroic (40)	5 heroic victories achieved (Campaign Mode)
Heroic Leader (120)	10 heroic victories achieved (Campaign Mode)
Inspirational General (50)	Max out any of Patton's Skills (Campaign Mode)
New recruit! (10)	Tutorial completed
Retrained! (20)	First upgrade made (Campaign Mode)
Skilled warrior (40)	Second operation completed (Campaign Mode)
Specialist Infantry (10)	First bazooka recruited (Campaign Mode)
Supreme commander (120)	Fourth operation completed without casualties (Campaign Mode)
Their worst nightmare! (40)	100 German units destroyed (Campaign Mode)
War Hero (80)	200 German units destroyed (Campaign Mode)
Weapons Tech (80)	All types of units unlocked (Campaign Mode)
When the war is over (100)	Game completed (Campaign Mode)

HITMAN: ABSOLUTION (PLAYSTATION 3)

TROPHIES

UNLOCKABLE	HOW TO UNLOCK
A Heavy Blow (Bronze)	Assassinate facility leaders
A Personal Contract (Silver)	Assassinate Travis
A Taste for the Game (Bronze)	Complete 10 challenges
Absolution (Gold)	Complete Hitman: Absolution on any professional difficulty
All Bark and no Bite (Bronze)	Assassinate Wade
Blood Money (Bronze)	Complete the Play Contract Tutorial
Catch a Ride (Bronze)	Enter the train in the train station
Chamber of Secrets (Bronze)	Locate room 899
Competitive Spirit (Silver)	Create a contract competition
Contender (Silver)	Participate in a contract competition
Damage Control (Bronze)	Contain a situation gone bad
Destroying Something Beautiful (Bronze)	Assassinate Layla
Faith Can Move Mountains (Bronze)	Defeat Sanchez with your bare hands
First Contract (Bronze)	Complete the Create Contract Tutorial
Forepost (Bronze)	Assassinate Wade's men
Grand Master (Gold)	Complete 100 challenges
Heavy Burden (Bronze)	Assassinate Diana Burnwood
Hour of Reckoning (Bronze)	Approach the church
Inconspicuous (Bronze)	Remain undetected in a whole checkpoint
Information is Power (Silver)	Collect all evidence
It's All in the Wrist (Bronze)	Achieve a lethal throw kill
Jack of All Trades (Silver)	Collect all play styles
Jailbird (Bronze)	Gain access to the jail
Kingslayer (Bronze)	Assassinate the King of Chinatown
Like Stealing Candy From a Baby (Bronze)	Pacify Lenny the Limp
Not Worth It (Bronze)	Leave Lenny in the desert
One of the Guys (Silver)	Blend in successfully
One With the Shadows (Silver)	Escape attention from enemies
Partners in Crime (Silver)	Play a contract created by a friend
Reach for the Stars (Silver)	Complete 50 challenges
Rocksteady (Bronze)	Execute a point shooting with 3 kills
Sandman (Bronze)	Subdue a person
Self-improvement (Bronze)	Buy an upgrade
Set for Life (Silver)	Earn 1 million contract dollars
Signature Weapons (Bronze)	Acquire the Silverballers
Silent Assassin (Silver)	Achieve the rating: Silent Assassin
Step Into the Light (Bronze)	Exit the mines
The Bartender Always Knows (Bronze)	Approach the bartender
The Final Countdown (Bronze)	Assassinate Blake Dexter
The Killing Fields (Bronze)	Eliminate the Saints
The Russian Hare (Bronze)	47 precision headshots using a sniper rifle

Thumbs Up (Silver)	Like a contract
Top of Your Game (Platinum)	Collect all trophies
True Form (Bronze)	Acquire suit & gloves
True Potential (Bronze)	Unlock a technique
Under Wraps (Bronze)	Hide a body
Whoops (Bronze)	Achieve your first accident kill

HITMAN: ABSOLUTION (XBOX 360)

ACHIEVEMENTS

UNLOCKABLE	HOW TO UNLOCK
A Heavy Blow (10)	You assassinated the facility leaders
A Personal Contract (50)	You eliminated Travis and fulfilled Diana's contract
A Taste for the Game (20)	You completed 10 challenges
Absolution (50)	You completed Hitman: Absolution as a professional
All Bark and no Bite (10)	You assassinated Wade
Blood Money (20)	You completed the Contract Basics Tutorial
Catch a Ride (10)	You boarded the train and escaped the Chicago PD
Chamber of Secrets (10)	You located the hotel room number 899
Competitive Spirit (20)	You created a contract competition
Contender (20)	You participated in a contract competition
Damage Control (20)	You contained a situation gone bad
Destroying Something Beautiful (10)	You assassinated Dexter's assistant, Layla
Faith Can Move Mountains (10)	You have defeated Sanchez with your bare hands
First Contract (20)	You completed the Creating Contracts Tutorial
Forepost (10)	You assassinated Wade's men in Chinatown
Grand Master (150)	You completed 100 challenges
Heavy Burden (10)	You infiltrated the mansion and assassinated Diana Burnwood
Hour of Reckoning (10)	You caught up with Skurky
Inconspicuous (20)	You remained undetected throughout a checkpoint
Information is Power (30)	You collected all evidence
It's All in the Wrist (50)	You successfully performed a lethal throw
Jack of All Trades (30)	You collected all 20 play styles
Jailbird (10)	You infiltrated the courthouse and accessed the jail
Kingslayer (10)	You fulfilled Birdie's contract and eliminated The King of Chinatown
Like Stealing Candy From a Baby (10)	You circumvented Lenny's crew and secured Lenny
Not Worth It (10)	You left Lenny in the desert
One of the Guys (20)	You blended in and fooled someone
One With the Shadows (20)	You escaped the attention of an enemy
Partners in Crime (20)	You played a contract made by a friend
Reach for the Stars (50)	You completed 50 challenges
Rocksteady (20)	You executed a point shooting with at least 3 kills
Sandman (20)	You subdued a person
Self-improvement (20)	You bought an upgrade for a weapon
Set for Life (20)	You earned 1 million contracts dollars
Signature Weapons (10)	You re-gained your signature Silverballers

Silent Assassin (20)	You achieved Silent Assassin
Step Into the Light (10)	You found your way through the mines
The Bartender Always Knows (10)	You questioned the bartender
The Final Countdown (10)	You assassinated Blake Dexter
The Killing Fields (10)	You eliminated the Saints
The Russian Hare (20)	You performed 47 headshots using a sniper rifle
Thumbs Up (20)	You liked a contract
True Form (10)	You visited Tommy the Tailor and acquired a new suit and gloves
True Potential (20)	You unlocked a technique
Under Wraps (20)	You hid a body
Whoops (20)	You made a kill look like an accident

KINECT NAT GEO TV (XBOX 360)

ACHIEVEMENTS

UNLOCKABLE	HOW TO UNLOCK
Anteater (20)	In a black bear game, ate 20 ants in 10 seconds (or watched someone do this).
Aspiring Photographer (10)	Successfully took all of the snapshots in a single assignment (or watched someone do this).
Baah-rilliant! (30)	Completed the "Yellowstone Winter" episode with a badge.
Balanced Diet (20)	In a great horned owl game, fed both nests an equal amount of crickets (or watched someone do it).
Beak Streak (30)	In a great horned owl game, didn't let any crickets get away (or watched someone do this).
Bear Brawler (20)	In a Kodiak bear game with rival bears, didn't get hit (or watched someone do this).
Bearing Up Well (30)	Completed the "Expedition Grizzly" episode with a badge.
Bearly Believe It (30)	Completed the "Black Bear Invasion" episode with a badge.
Beekeeper (30)	In a black bear game with bees, didn't get stung (or watched someone do this).
Bird Watcher (30)	In a mountain lion game, got 3 perfect pounces in a row (or watched someone do this).
Bug Free (10)	In a grizzly bear game, ate all of the moths on screen (or watched someone do this).
Butt Out! (20)	Perfectly headbutted all rearing rams without being hit (or watched someone do it).
Catch of the Day (30)	In a Kodiak bear game with pink salmon, didn't let over 2 get away (or watched someone do this).
Chick Guardian (10)	In a great horned owl game, kept all the predators away from the chicks (or watched someone do it).
Cougar-atulations (30)	Completed the "Stalking the Mountain Lion" episode with a badge.
Cozy Critter (15)	Watched what's On Now, Next, and Later all in a row.
Feather Buster (20)	In a mountain lion game, hit 5 or more blue jays in one perfect pounce (or watched someone do this).
Fish Supper (10)	In a Kodiak bear game, ate 6 fish in a row without missing any (or watched someone do this).
For the Winnie (10)	In a black bear game, got honeycombs on both paws at once (or watched someone do this).
Gamesmaster (30)	Earned at least 3 stars in 3 games in Party Animal mode (or watched someone do this).

Hidden Footage (10)	Correctly answered all questions in one Sidetrack (or watched someone do this).
Hornet Herder (30)	In a grizzly bear game with hornets, didn't get stung (or watched someone do this).
Kitten Catcher (10)	In a mountain lion game, dropped 6 cubs into the den and none escaped (or watched someone do this).
Kodiak Moment (30)	Completed the "Project Kodiak" episode with a badge.
Leader of the Pack (30)	Completed the "Inside the Wolf Pack" episode with a badge.
Locked Horns (10)	In a bighorn sheep game, headbutted all charging rams without being hit (or watched someone do it).
Look Ma, No Paws (20)	In a wolverine game, ate 6 pieces of meat without using your paws (or watched someone do this).
Lord of the Weasels (30)	Completed the "Wolverine King" episode with a badge.
Master Photographer (30)	Without ever stopping an episode, earned all of its Snapshot stars (or watched someone do this).
Misbehavin' Ravens (10)	In a grey wolf game with ravens, didn't let them steal any food (or watched someone do this).
Moth Muncher (20)	In a grizzly bear game, ate 30 moths in 10 seconds (or watched someone do this).
On the Hunt (15)	Launched a Nat Geo WILD episode.
Party Time (10)	Earned 3 stars in any game in Party Animal mode (or watched someone do this).
Platinum Performance (100)	Completed any episode with a Platinum Badge.
Six Pack (30)	In a wolverine game, hit 6 wolves in under 6 seconds (or watched someone do this).
Snow Way, Man (10)	In a wolverine game, dodged 3 avalanches in a row (or watched someone do this).
The Biggest Bighorn (30)	In a bighorn sheep game, perfectly headbutted 10 rams in a row (or watched someone do this).
Top Dog (30)	In a grey wolf game, got 10 perfect hits in a row against coyotes (or watched someone do this).
Triple Tracker (30)	Without ever stopping an episode, earned all of its Sidetrack stars (or watched someone do this).
Twit Woo Hoo (30)	Completed the "Yellowstone Spring" episode with a badge.
Wily Coyotes (20)	In a grey wolf game with coyotes, didn't let them steal any food (or watched any player do this).
You're Golden (30)	Completed any episode with a Gold Badge.

KINECT SESAME STREET TV (XBOX 360)

ACHIEVEMENTS

UNLOCKABLE	HOW TO UNLOCK
All the King's Cartons (25)	You found all the egg cartons in Humpty's Big Break!
Bird Buddy (20)	You watched a clip featuring Snuffleupagus!
Bottle Bear (25)	You found all baby bottles in Baby Bear's Baby Doll!
Bubble Pop (35)	You popped all the bubbles in Elmo's World!
Bubble Raider (25)	You found all the golden bubbles in Bubblefest!
Bunny Bash (25)	You found all the white bunnies in Goodbye Pacifier!
Coconut Delivery Monster (6)	You helped Grover get all six of his coconuts back!
Cry Monster (40)	You jumped up and down to play Ernie's gongs!
Day at the Beach (40)	You touched all the fun beach stuff in Elmo's World Beach!
Doggie Do (30)	You helped Abby cut lots of doggie hair!

Dolphin, Dirigible, Dentist (50)	You got the right letters on the Letter D Show! Well clapped!
Eleven - Ah ah ah! (11)	You stood still like a statue so the Count could count to 11!
Elmo Loves You (5)	You watched a clip featuring Elmo!
Fairy School Graduate (30)	You watched 10 episodes of Abby's Flying Fairy School!
Farmer Elmo (40)	You threw Paul Ball to Elmo at the farm!
Fashionista (15)	You stood in front of mirror and Cooper dressed like you!
Feel The Burn! (10)	You watched a clip about exercise!
Float my Boat (25)	You found all the toy boats in Rocco's Boat!
Froggy Fun (15)	You watched a clip featuring Kermit!
Fuzzy and Blue (5)	You watched a clip featuring Grover!
Great Adventurer (30)	You watched 10 episodes of Bert and Ernie's Adventures!
Herd Em Cowboy (40)	You touched all the horses and cows in Elmo's World Horses!
Just For You (5)	You watched a Featured Playlist!
Liftoff (25)	You found all the launchers in Failure to Launch!
Make it a Keeper (18)	You marked a photo or video in the journal as a keeper!
Music Lover (40)	You hit all the notes in Elmo's World Violins!
Om Nom Nom Nom! (10)	You watched a clip featuring Cookie Monster!
One Little Achievement (10)	You watched a clip featuring the Count!
Palindrome (40)	Your jumping made a kayak fall from the Letter Tree!
Pool Playtime (40)	You played with all the toys in the pool in Elmo's World Water!
Rocco's Best Friend (15)	You watched a clip featuring Zoe!
Rooaaarrr! (40)	You touched all the wild animals in Elmo's World Wild Animals!
Ruler Mania (25)	You found all the rulers in Elmozilla!
Scram! (25)	You watched a clip featuring Oscar!
Scribble Hunt (25)	You found all the crayons in Siblings!
Sesame Stalwart (10)	You watched a clip featuring Big Bird!
Sing Along (10)	You watched a clip with a song in it!
Star Spotter (10)	You watched a clip featuring a celebrity!
The Artiste (15)	You watched a clip featuring Baby Bear!
Tingalingaling (40)	You helped Ernie play his bells!
Tree Hugger (10)	You watched a clip about nature!
Viva Piñata (40)	You broke the piñata in Elmo's World!

LEGO THE LORD OF THE RINGS (3DS)

UNLOCKABLES

UNLOCKABLE	CODE
Elrond	A9FB4Q
Gamling	avjii1
Bilbo Baggins	j4337v
Ringwraith White	lyqu1f
Easterling	r7xkdh

LEGO THE LORD OF THE RINGS (PLAYSTATION VITA)

TROPHIES

UNLOCKABLE	HOW TO UNLOCK
And away he goes, Precious! (Silver)	Use Smeagol to defeat Gollum when Gollum is the buddy.
Hobbits really are amazing creatures. (Gold)	Complete all the HUB mini games.
I think I'm quite ready for another adventure! (Silver)	Achieve True Adventurer in every level. (Single Player Only)
It's a dangerous business going out your door. (Bronze)	Complete The Black Rider on the Road.
It's gone... (Gold)	Complete Journey's End.
Let's hunt some Orc! (Bronze)	Complete The Skirmish of Amon Hen.
My precious! (Gold)	Collect every collectible.
Naughty little fly! (Bronze)	Complete Shelob's Lair.
Not with 10,000 men could you do this... (Gold)	Unlock all characters. (Single Player Only)
Of all the inquisitive Hobbits... (Silver)	Collect all the Character Profiles.
On the precious... (Bronze)	Complete The Taming of Gollum.
One does not simply walk into Mordor... (Silver)	Simply walk into Mordor. (Single Player Only)
One Ring to build them all. (Platinum)	Obtain all other Trophies.
Safe is where I'll keep you. (Bronze)	Complete Track the Hobbits.
That is no trinket you carry... (Bronze)	Complete The Camp at Weathertop.
That still only counts as one! (Silver)	Defeat an Oliphaunt as Legolas.
The battle for Middle-earth is about to begin... (Bronze)	Complete The Battle of Helm's Deep.
The day the strength of men failed. (Bronze)	Complete The Battle of the Last Alliance.
The last laugh. (Gold)	Use Tom Bombadil's laugh to destroy Sauron in Free play.
There and back again. (Gold)	Get 100%. (Single Player Only)
There's some good in this world, Mr. Frodo. (Gold)	Deliver all the treasure items.
They have been summoned... (Bronze)	Complete The Paths of the Dead.
This day we fight! (Bronze)	Defeat the Mouth of Sauron.
This is no mine... It's a tomb! (Bronze)	Complete Moria: Balin's Tomb.
What about second breakfast? (Silver)	Complete Weathertop in Free Play.
You and whose army? (Bronze)	Complete The Battle of the Pelennor Fields.
You shall not pass! (Bronze)	Complete Moria: Bridge of Khazad-dûm.

UNLOCKABLES

UNLOCKABLE	CODE
Unlock exclusive Elrond (2nd Age)	A9FB4Q

LEGO THE LORD OF THE RINGS (XBOX 360)

ACHIEVEMENTS

UNLOCKABLE	HOW TO UNLOCK
... And away he goes, Precious! (10)	Defeat Gollum as Gollum.
A link to the elements. (5)	Craft the Fire and Ice Bows. (Single Player Only)
A Wizard should know better! (25)	Complete 'Osgiliath'.
An expected journey. (5)	Travel to Trollshaws as Bilbo.

A
B
C
D
E
F
G
H
I
J
K
L
M
N
O
P
Q
R
S
T
U
V
W
X
Y
Z

Dance of the dead. (10)	Turn an enemy into a skeleton and make them dance.
Delved too greedily... (25)	Collect more than 10,000,000,000 studs. (Single Player Only)
Don't tell the Elf... (10)	Throw Gimli 30 times.
Great! ...Where are we going? (5)	Form The Fellowship of the Ring.
Here's a pretty thing! (30)	Craft every Mithril item. (Single Player Only)
I told you he was tricksy. (30)	Collect all the Red Bricks. (Single Player Only)
I'm glad to be with you. (10)	Complete a level in co-op.
I've always been taller! (10)	Use the Ent Draught on Pippin.
It won't be that easy! (5)	During 'Prologue', jump into the fires of Mount Doom as Isildur.
It's a dangerous business... (25)	Complete 'The Black Rider'.
It's gone. (25)	Complete 'Mount Doom'.
Let's hunt some Orc! (25)	Complete 'Amon Hen'.
My Precious... (50)	Collect all the Mithril Bricks. (Single Player Only)
Naughty little fly... (25)	Complete 'The Secret Stairs'.
Not with 10,000 men... (30)	Unlock all characters. (Single Player Only)
Of all the inquisitive Hobbits. (30)	Unlock all the Map Stones in Middle-earth. (Single Player Only)
On the Precious... (25)	Complete 'Taming Gollum'.
One does not simply... (5)	Walk into Mordor.
Our only wish to catch a fish! (10)	Fish perfectly 20 times by pressing the icon as it flashes.
Pointy-eared Elvish princeling. (10)	Defeat 42 Uruk-hai as Legolas.
Ready for another adventure. (30)	Achieve True Adventurer in every level. (Single Player Only)
Return of the Mushroom King. (5)	Equip Aragorn with the Mushroom Crown.
Safe is where I'll keep you. (25)	Complete 'Track Hobbits'.
Soft and quick as shadows... (25)	Complete 'The Dead Marshes'.
Stinking creatures... (25)	Complete 'Warg Attack'.
Taking the Hobbits to Isengard. (10)	Travel to Isengard as every playable Hobbit.
That is a rare gift. (10)	Reach the top of Amon Hen without being caught once by Boromir. (Single Player Only)
That is no trinket you carry. (25)	Complete 'Weathertop'.
That one counts as mine! (10)	Finish one of Gimli's opponents as Legolas in 'Helm's Deep'.
That still only counts as one! (10)	Defeat an Oliphaunt as Legolas.
The battle is about to begin... (25)	Complete 'Helm's Deep'.
The long way around. (25)	Complete 'The Pass of Caradhras'.
The Lord of the Ring. (30)	Complete the Bonus Level.
The strength of Men failed. (25)	Complete 'Prologue'.
There and Back Again. (75)	Get 100%. (Single Player Only)
There's some good in this world. (50)	Complete all the Fetch Quests in Middle-earth. (Single Player Only)
They have been summoned. (25)	Complete 'The Paths of the Dead'.
This day we fight! (25)	Complete 'The Black Gate'.
This is no mine... it's a tomb. (25)	Complete 'The Mines of Moria'.
We cannot linger. (10)	Complete 'The Mines of Moria' in under 15 minutes.

We did it, Mr. Frodo. (25)	Complete 'Cirith Ungol'.
What about second breakfast? (10)	Complete 2 cooking puzzles.
Worth greater than the Shire. (10)	Dress a character completely in treasure items.
You and whose army? (25)	Complete 'The Battle of Pelennor Fields'.

LIBERATION MAIDEN (3DS)

UNLOCKABLES

UNLOCKABLE	HOW TO UNLOCK
Honor 01	Make preparations for war.
Honor 02	Maneuvered in strafing mode.
Honor 03	Reached the edge of the combat zone.
Honor 04	Attacked with the Liberator's blade.
Honor 05	Completed a Sub Mission.
Honor 06	Used all attack variations.
Honor 07	Cleared Stage 1.
Honor 08	Cleared Stage 2.
Honor 09	Cleared Stage 3.
Honor 10	Cleared Stage 4.
Honor 11	Cleared Stage 5.
Honor 12	Destroyed 300 tanks.
Honor 13	Destroyed 50 battleships.
Honor 14	Destroyed 50 cannons.
Honor 15	Destroyed 30 submaries.
Honor 16	Destroyed 100 walkers.
Honor 17	Destroy 50 supply trains.
Honor 18	Played a total of two hours.
Honor 19	Played a total of four hours.
Honor 20	Completed over 50 chains.
Honor 21	100% Purification in Stage 1.
Honor 22	100% Purification in Stage 2.
Honor 23	100% Purification in Stage 3.
Honor 24	100% Purification in Stage 4.
Honor 25	Completed over 100 chains.
Honor 26	Cleared a stage without taking damage.
Honor 27	Played the game over 10 times in Normal mode.
Honor 28	Played the game over 10 times in Hard mode.
Honor 29	Cleared Stage 1 in Story Mode.
Honor 30	Obtained 100% Approval Rating.
Easy Stage 1: Tokyo	Beat Stage 1 on Easy in Story Mode.
Easy Stage 2: Kagoshima	Beat Stage 2 on Easy in Story Mode.
Easy Stage 3: Osaka	Beat Stage 3 on Easy in Story Mode.
Easy Stage 4: Hokkaido	Beat Stage 4 on Easy in Story Mode.
Easy Stage 5: Mt. Fuji	Beat Stage 5 on Easy in Story Mode.
Hard Stage 1: Tokyo	Beat Stage 1 on Hard in Story Mode.
Hard Stage 2: Kagoshima	Beat Stage 2 on Hard in Story Mode.
Hard Stage 3: Osaka	Beat Stage 3 on Hard in Story Mode.
Hard Stage 4: Hokkaido	Beat Stage 4 on Hard in Story Mode.
Hard Stage 5: Mt. Fuji	Beat Stage 5 on Hard in Story Mode.

Normal Stage 1: Tokyo	Beat Stage 1 on Normal in Story Mode.
Normal Stage 2: Kagoshima	Beat Stage 2 on Normal in Story Mode.
Normal Stage 3: Osaka	Beat Stage 3 on Normal in Story Mode.
Normal Stage 4: Hokkaido	Beat Stage 4 on Normal in Story Mode.
Normal Stage 5: Mt. Fuji	Beat Stage 5 on Normal in Story Mode.

LITTLEBIGPLANET KARTING (PLAYSTATION 3)

TROPHIES

UNLOCKABLE	HOW TO UNLOCK
100% Complete (Platinum)	Earn all the LittleBigPlanet
About Me (Bronze)	Completely populate your profile page
Active Recommendation (Bronze)	Complete a level a friend has written a review for
Aerial Grappler (Bronze)	Chain three different grapples without touching the ground
Arms Creator (Bronze)	Create a custom weapon in Create mode
Battler (Bronze)	Achieve a 5 hit streak in any Story battle level
Better Than You (Bronze) community level	Beat a score posted by a friend on any
Big Combo (Bronze)	Accumulate a 5x score multiplier in a Story level
Building the Imagisphere (Gold)	Spend 24 active hours in Create mode
Celestial Decorator (Bronze)	Create a personalized planet and save it
Complete Eve's Asylum (Bronze)	Complete the main path of Eve's Asylum
Complete Hoard Garage (Bronze)	Complete the main path of Hoard Sweet Hoard
Complete LittleBigPlanet (Bronze)	Complete the main path of LittleBigPlanet
Complete Monster Islands (Bronze)	Complete the main path of Monster Islands
Complete Story Mode (Gold)	Complete the main path of Story mode
Complete The Progress Emporium (Bronze)	Complete the main path of The Progress Emporium
Complete The Space Bass (Bronze)	Complete the main path of The Space Bass
Complete Victoria's Laboratory (Bronze)	Complete the main path of Victoria's Laboratory
Creator Maker (Silver)	Create three cooperative levels and three versus levels
Crowd Pleaser (Silver)	Publish a level and have 10 different players complete the level
Custom Object (Bronze)	Create a custom object inside one of your levels
Dive In! (Silver)	Dive into 25 community levels and complete those levels
Finale Star (Silver)	Star every 'finale' level in the main story
First Impressions (Bronze)	Complete a level with less than 5 playthroughs and leave a review
Flamin' Skid (Bronze)	Drift non-stop for 10 seconds without stopping in any racing Story level
Get Gathering (Bronze)	Invite three other players into your playgroup
Hot Wheels (Bronze)	Change your ride and save it
Interior Decoration (Bronze)	Create a custom pod and save it
Just Getting Started (Bronze)	Spend 30 minutes in Create mode

Kart Mastery (Bronze)	Complete all the tutorials on the first planet, LittleBigPlanet
Makeover (Bronze)	Change your costume and save it
Making The Community (Bronze)	Build and save any level created in Create mode
Online Champ (Silver)	Place 1st in 25 different online levels with other human players
Online Sampler (Silver)	Complete 25 community levels
Planet Star (Bronze)	Star a planet in Story mode
Playing the Popular (Bronze)	Play any level in your Recent Activity
Road Rage (Bronze)	Slap another Sackboy on any level
Save This For Later (Bronze)	Add a level to your queue
Scholar (Bronze)	Watch all of the creation tutorials from start to finish
Showing Who's Boss! (Bronze)	Hit 50 Hoard minions in Story mode with any weapon
Snapper (Bronze)	Publish a photo taken from any level
Story Star (Gold)	Star every level in the Story mode
The Adventures Continue (Gold)	Complete 100 community levels
The Brave Defender! (Bronze)	Defend against 30 attacks from opponents in any level
We Have Good Taste (Bronze)	Complete a level in Team Picks

LITTLEBIGPLANET PS VITA (PLAYSTATION VITA)

TROPHIES

UNLOCKABLE	HOW TO UNLOCK
25 Online Versus Wins (Bronze)	Win 25 Versus community levels against at least one other online player.
40 Yays! (Bronze)	Give positive feedback on 40 community levels.
50 Unique Players (Bronze)	A level you published was played by 50 unique players.
Aced Story Mode (Gold)	Ace the main path of the Story.
Arcade Champion (Gold)	Complete all achievements in all games from The Arcade.
Aspiring Director (Bronze)	Publish a cut scene level.
Balancing Act (Bronze)	Balance another sackperson on an object while lifting it with touch.
Chases The Aces (Bronze)	Complete 10 Story levels in a row without being killed.
Complete 75 Cooperative Levels (Silver)	Complete 75 unique Cooperative community levels.
Complete Coaster Valley (Bronze)	Complete the main path of Coaster Valley.
Complete Jackpot City (Bronze)	Complete the main path of Jackpot City.
Complete La Marionetta (Bronze)	Complete the main path of La Marionetta.
Complete Land of Odd (Bronze)	Complete the main path of Land of Odd.
Complete Spooky Mansion (Bronze)	Complete the main path of Spooky Mansion.
Complete Story Mode (Silver)	Complete the main path of the Story.
Creative Spark (Bronze)	Spend 10 active minutes in Create mode.
Double 11 (Bronze)	Play LittleBigPlanet™ PlayStation®Vita at 11 minutes past 11.
Everyone's A Critic (Bronze)	Submit a review for a level.
Fashionista (Bronze)	Change your costume.

A
B
C
D
E
F
G
H
I
J
K
L
M
N
O
P
Q
R
S
T
U
V
W
X
Y
Z

Finger Cramp (Bronze)	Bash 1000 bonces in 'Bonce Tappin'.
First Among Equals (Bronze)	Win a 4-player game.
Get A Life (Gold)	Spend 1440 active minutes in Create mode.
God Complex (Bronze)	Spin any of the planets 720 degrees with a single flick.
Happy Snapper (Bronze)	· Upload a photo.
Hi Score (Silver)	Collect 1,000,000 points over all story levels you have played.
House Proud (Bronze)	Place 10 stickers or decorations in your pod.
Insert Coin (Bronze)	Complete all achievements in one game from The Arcade.
Just A Scratch (Bronze)	Spin the LP disc in Jackpot City.
Mindful Vandalism (Bronze)	Place a sticker or a decoration on another player's sackperson.
Mr Know-It-All (Bronze)	Watch all the tutorials.
Multiplier x10 (Bronze)	Score a x10 multiplier in a Story level.
Multiplier x15 (Silver)	Score a x15 multiplier in a Story level.
Multiplier x5 (Bronze)	Score a x5 multiplier in a Story level.
Obsessive Collecting (Silver)	Find and collect 100% of the Prize Bubbles in Story levels.
Pianist Pioneer (Bronze)	Play 'Do Re Mi' on the piano in La Marionetta.
Platinum Club (Platinum)	Earn all LittleBigPlanet™ PlayStation®Vita trophies.
Prize Collector (Bronze)	Find and collect 50% of the Prize Bubbles in Story levels.
Queued Up (Bronze)	Play a level that has been added to your Queue.
Quick Badge Job (Bronze)	Publish a level with a custom badge created from a Camera photo or an in-game photo.
Rising Star (Bronze)	Collect 50% of Skill Rewards in Story Mode.
Scoreboard 25% (Silver)	Place in the top 25% of a Story Level scoreboard containing more than 50 scores.
Scoreboard 50% (Bronze)	Place in the top 50% of a Story Level scoreboard containing more than 50 scores.
Share & Share Alike (Bronze)	Publish a level.
Social Animal (Bronze)	Complete a level with more than one player.
The Tourist (Bronze)	Complete a community level.
Time Well Spent (Silver)	Play LittleBigPlanet™ PlayStation®Vita on every day of the week.
Tired Of Life (Bronze)	Accumulate 20 deaths in one Story level.

MADDEN NFL 13 (PLAYSTATION 3)

TROPHIES

UNLOCKABLE	HOW TO UNLOCK
80 Overall (Bronze)	As a created player, achieve a player rating of 80 overall in Connected Careers.
85 Overall (Bronze)	As a created player, achieve a player rating of 85 overall in Connected Careers.
90 Overall (Bronze)	As a created player, achieve a player rating of 90 overall in Connected Careers.
All Madden (Silver)	As a created coach, win 100 games in your first 10 seasons in Connected Careers.
Battle Tested (Gold)	Score 600 points in Online Ranked Head to Head Games.

Belting (Bronze)	Complete a Madden Moments Live situation.
Deion Sanders Award (Silver)	As a created DB, surpass Deion Sanders on Legacy Score in Connected Careers.
Emmitt Smith Award (Silver)	As a created RB, surpass Emmitt Smith on Legacy Score in Connected Careers.
Gronk Spike (Bronze)	Score a TD with Rob Gronkowski (no SuperSim, OTP or co-op).
Hall Of Famer (Gold)	As a created player or coach, get inducted into the Hall of Fame in Connected Careers.
Jerry Rice Award (Silver)	As a created WR, surpass Jerry Rice on Legacy Score in Connected Careers.
Joe Montana Award (Silver)	As a created QB, surpass Joe Montana on Legacy Score in Connected Careers.
Lawrence Taylor Award (Silver)	As a created LB, surpass Lawrence Taylor on Legacy Score in Connected Careers.
Let's Get Physical (Bronze)	Tackle an opponent using the Hit Stick (no SuperSim, OTP or co-op).
Madden NFL 13 Master (Platinum)	Congratulations on earning every Madden NFL 13 trophy!
Made Ya Look (Bronze)	Abort the play action and complete a pass for a TD (no SuperSim, OTP or co-op).
Matt Flynn's Arcade (Bronze)	Score 6 touchdowns with your backup quarterback (no SuperSim, OTP or co-op).
Montana's Mountain (Silver)	As a created QB, win 4 Super Bowls in Connected Careers.
MUT Maniac (Bronze)	Complete 20 MUT games.
MVP! MVP! MVP! (Silver)	Complete the Level 4 season goals in one season in Connected Careers.
Online Level 1 (Bronze)	Score 25 points in Online Ranked Head to Head Games.
Online Level 2 (Bronze)	Score 50 points in Online Ranked Head to Head Games.
Online Level 3 (Bronze)	Score 100 points in Online Ranked Head to Head Games.
Online Level 4 (Bronze)	Score 150 points in Online Ranked Head to Head Games.
Online Level 5 (Bronze)	Score 200 points in Online Ranked Head to Head Games.
Online Level 6 (Bronze)	Score 250 points in Online Ranked Head to Head Games.
Online Level 7 (Bronze)	Score 300 points in Online Ranked Head to Head Games.
Online Level 8 (Bronze)	Score 400 points in Online Ranked Head to Head Games.
Online Level 9 (Bronze)	Score 500 points in Online Ranked Head to Head Games.
Pass the Salsa (Bronze)	Score a TD with Victor Cruz (no SuperSim, OTP or co-op).
Peak Performance (Gold)	As a created player, achieve a player rating of 99 overall in Connected Careers.
Reggie White Award (Silver)	As a created DL, surpass Reggie White on Legacy Score in Connected Careers.
Shannon Sharpe Award (Silver)	As a created TE, surpass Shannon Sharpe on Legacy Score in Connected Careers.
Single Riders Only (Bronze)	Play a MUT game against the CPU.
Tebowing (Bronze)	Tebow Time! Throw a TD with Tim Tebow on the first play in overtime (no SuperSim, OTP or co-op).

NEW!

A
B
C
D
E
F
G
H
I
J
K
L
M
N
O
P
Q
R
S
T
U
V
W
X
Y
Z

The Penitent Man Shall Pass (Bronze)	As a QB, win the game with 4 or fewer completed passes (no SuperSim, OTP or co-op).
This One is Easy. We Promise (Bronze)	Create a MUT team.
This One is Hard 2.0 (Silver)	Build an 85 rated MUT team.
Verizon Scoreboard	Score 50 points in one game (no SuperSim, OTP or co-op).
Vince Lombardi Award (Silver)	As a created coach, surpass Vince Lombardi on Legacy Score in Connected Careers.
Welcome to the Community (Bronze)	Join an Online Community.
You're In the Game (Bronze)	Download A Game Face in Create-a-Player or in Connected Careers.

MADDEN NFL 13 (PLAYSTATION VITA)

TROPHIES

UNLOCKABLE	HOW TO UNLOCK
Arian Foster Award (Bronze)	Rush for 168+ yards with a single player in a game
Buffalo Bills Award (Silver)	Record 10+ sacks as a team in one game
Calvin Johnson Award (Silver)	Gain 244+ yards receiving with one player
Cam Newton Award (Bronze)	Score 3 rushing TDs with a QB in a game
Chopping Block (Bronze)	Complete one season's final cut day in Franchise Mode
Cleveland Browns Award (Silver)	Hold your opponents to 137 or fewer yards of total offense
Cruz 'in the Field (Bronze)	Catch a 90+ yard TD pass with Victor Cruz
Darrelle Revis Award (Gold)	Return an interception for 100+ yards
DeMarco Murray Award (Silver)	Rush for 253+ yards in a game with one player
Demaryius Thomas Award (Bronze)	Catch a game winning TD pass in OT
Devin Hester Award (Silver)	Score a TD on a Kick Return
Drew Brees Award (Silver)	Complete 88% of your passes (minimum 20 attempts)
Future Hall of Famer? (Bronze)	Create an NFL Superstar
Happy 21st EA SPORTS! (Bronze)	Score 21 points in a game
Honing Your Skills (Bronze)	Complete a practice in Superstar Mode
Houston Texans Award (Bronze)	Gain over 100+ yards rushing with 2 HBs in the same game
Jahvid Best Award (Bronze)	Score on an 88+ yard TD run
Madden NFL 13 Master (Platinum)	Congratulations on earning every Madden NFL 13 Trophy!
Matthew Stafford Award (Silver)	Pass for 520+ yards in one game with one player
Maurice Jones-Drew Award (Silver)	Score 4+ rushing TDs in a single game with 1 player
Patrick Peterson Award (Gold)	Return a punt for a TD in OT
Safety Inspector Award (Bronze)	Tackle the ball carrier in their own end zone
Sebastian Janikowski Award (Silver)	Kick a 60+ yard FG
Tactical Masher (Bronze)	Win a player in FA bidding in Franchise Mode
Ted Ginn Jr. Award (Gold)	Score 2+ Kick Return TDs in a single game
Tim Tebow Award (Bronze)	Rush for 118+ yards with your QB

Tom Brady Award (Bronze)	Have a total offense of 519+ yards in a game
Verizon Scoreboard Overload (Gold)	Score 50 points in one game
Vince Wilfork Award (Gold)	Score a fumble recovery TD with a Defensive Linemen
Wes Welker Award (Silver)	Catch 16+ passes in one game with one player

MADDEN NFL 13 (XBOX 360)

ACHIEVEMENTS

UNLOCKABLE	HOW TO UNLOCK
80 Overall (10)	As a created player, achieve a player rating of 80 overall in Connected Careers.
85 Overall (15)	As a created player, achieve a player rating of 85 overall in Connected Careers.
All Madden (100)	As a created coach, win 100 games in your first 10 seasons in Connected Careers.
Battle Tested (20)	Score 600 points in Online Ranked Head to Head Games.
Belting (25)	Complete a Madden Moments Live situation.
Deion Sanders Award (30)	As a created DB, surpass Deion Sanders on Legacy Score in Connected Careers.
Emmitt Smith Award (30)	As a created RB, surpass Emmitt Smith on Legacy Score in Connected Careers.
Gronk Spike (25)	Score a TD with Rob Gronkowski (no SuperSim, OTP or co-op).
Hall Of Famer (100)	As a created player or coach, get inducted into the Hall of Fame in Connected Careers.
Jerry Rice Award (30)	As a created WR, surpass Jerry Rice on Legacy Score in Connected Careers.
Joe Montana Award (30)	As a created QB, surpass Joe Montana on Legacy Score in Connected Careers.
Lawrence Taylor Award (30)	As a created LB, surpass Lawrence Taylor on Legacy Score in Connected Careers.
Let's Get Physical (5)	Tackle an opponent using the Hit Stick (no SuperSim, OTP or co-op).
Made Ya Look (10)	Abort the play action and complete a pass for a TD (no SuperSim, OTP or co-op).
Matt Flynn's Arcade (55)	Score 6 touchdowns with your backup quarterback (no SuperSim, OTP or co-op).
Montana's Mountain (20)	As a created QB, win 4 Super Bowls in Connected Careers.
MUT Maniac (20)	Complete 20 MUT games.
MVP! MVP! MVP! (30)	Complete the Level 4 season goals in one season in Connected Careers.
Online Level 1 (5)	Score 25 points in Online Ranked Head to Head Games.
Online Level 2 (5)	Score 50 points in Online Ranked Head to Head Games.
Online Level 3 (5)	Score 100 points in Online Ranked Head to Head Games.
Online Level 4 (10)	Score 150 points in Online Ranked Head to Head Games.
Online Level 5 (10)	Score 200 points in Online Ranked Head to Head Games.
Online Level 6 (10)	Score 250 points in Online Ranked Head to Head Games.

A
B
C
D
E
F
G
H
I
J
K
L
M
N
O
P
Q
R
S
T
U
V
W
X
Y
Z

Online Level 7 (15)	Score 300 points in Online Ranked Head to Head Games.
Online Level 8 (15)	Score 400 points in Online Ranked Head to Head Games.
Online Level 9 (15)	Score 500 points in Online Ranked Head to Head Games.
Overall 90 (20)	As a created player, achieve a player rating of 90 overall in Connected Careers.
Pass The Salsa (25)	Score a TD with Victor Cruz (no SuperSim, OTP or co-op).
Peak Performance (30)	As a created player, achieve a player rating of 99 overall in Connected Careers.
Reggie White Award (30)	As a created DL, surpass Reggie White on Legacy Score in Connected Careers.
Shannon Sharpe Award (30)	As a created TE, surpass Shannon Sharpe on Legacy Score in Connected Careers.
Single Riders Only (5)	Play a MUT game against the CPU.
Smart Mouth (25)	Complete a successful pre-play adjustment using Kinect (no SuperSim, OTP or co-op).
Tebowing (25)	Tebow Time! Throw a TD with Tim Tebow on the first play in overtime (no SuperSim, OTP or co-op).
The Penitent Man Shall Pass (20)	As a QB, win the game with 4 or fewer completed passes (no SuperSim, OTP or co-op).
This One is Easy. We Promise (5)	Create a MUT team.
This One is Hard 2.0 (15)	Build an 85 rated MUT team.
Verizon Scoreboard Overload (50)	Score 50 points in one game (no SuperSim, OTP or co-op).
Vince Lombardi Award (30)	As a created coach, surpass Vince Lombardi on Legacy Score in Connected Careers.
Welcome to the Community (5)	Join an Online Community.
You're In the Game (10)	Download A Game Face in Create-a-Player or in Connected Careers.

MARVEL AVENGERS: BATTLE FOR EARTH (XBOX 360)

ACHIEVEMENTS

UNLOCKABLE	HOW TO UNLOCK
Adamantium (30)	You obtained an adamantium grade.
Army of One (50)	You won a fight without changing characters in Campaign.
Avengers (5)	You won a battle with Captain America and Iron Man.
Bad Intentions (5)	You won a battle with Super Skrull & Doctor Doom.
Breaker (5)	You used your Breaker to break a Combo.
Brothers (5)	You won a battle with Thor and Loki.
Champion (20)	You won a Tournament.
Closure (100)	You finished the Campaign mode.
Combo (5)	You chained two Super Attacks.
Completist (150)	You finished all character's challenge.
Counter (10)	You countered a Super Attack with another Super Attack.
Dodge this (5)	You dodged a Super Attack.
Earth United (30)	You finished the first part of the Campaign.
Escapist (5)	You performed a Counter Kick.
Experienced (20)	You got 100 000 Experience points.

Fashion (5)	You changed the costume of one of your character.
Fearless (50)	You won a match without dodging in Campaign.
Fire & Ice (5)	You won a battle with Human Torch & Iceman.
Heatwave (5)	You won a battle with Phoenix & Human Torch.
Here I am! (5)	You won your first battle in Campaign.
Impressive feets (5)	You performed a Close-Combat.
King of the Hill (20)	You won the arcade mode once.
Leading Ladies (5)	You won a battle with Scarlet Witch & Storm.
Legend (200)	You unlocked the highest Rank.
Maximum Combo (20)	You chained 4 Super Attacks by switching characters twice.
Need a Doctor? (5)	You won a battle with Doctor Doom & Doctor Strange.
Part of me (5)	You won a battle with Spider-Man & Venom.
Pioneers (5)	You won a battle with Hulk & Iron Man.
Power duo (5)	You won a battle in CO-OP.
Ride the lightning (5)	You won a battle with Thor & Storm.
S.H.I.E.L.D (5)	You won a battle with Hawkeye & Black Widow.
Skrulls (5)	You won a battle with Super-Skrull and Veranke.
Speed and Power (15)	You reached the FAST velocity when doing a Super Attack 5 times in a row.
Student (30)	You finished the Tutorial challenges.
Super charged (5)	You used your ULTRA Attack.
Super Tag Combo (15)	You chained 3 Super Attacks by switching characters twice.
Symbiosis (5)	You performed a 4x Combo in CO-OP.
Tag Combo (10)	You chained two Super Attacks by switching characters.
Team power (10)	You fired projectiles during the ULTRA attack in CO-OP.
The X-Men (5)	You won a battle with Wolverine and Phoenix.
Trialist (50)	You finished every Trial.
Uneasy Alliance (5)	You won a battle with Wolverine & Magneto.
Untouchable (50)	You won a fight without being hit in Campaign.

MEDAL OF HONOR: WARFIGHTER (PLAYSTATION 3)

TROPHIES

UNLOCKABLE	HOW TO UNLOCK
All In (Silver)	Called in Apache support
Back in the Fight (Gold)	Completed one tour with all classes.
Brothers in Arms (Bronze)	Won a round with a friend as a Fire Team Buddy
Class Dismissed (Bronze)	Completed Connect the Dots
Closing Ceremony (Bronze)	Completed Old Friends
Dirty Laundry (Bronze)	Found the grenades in the laundry room in Bump in the Night
Double Header (Bronze)	Killed two enemies with one bullet in the Changing Tides mission
Downrange (Bronze)	Played online for 15 minutes
Extreme Realism (Bronze)	Recovered from near-death 5 times without dying
For Honor For Country (Platinum)	Collected all other Medal of Honor™ Warfighter Trophies

Global Warfighters (Silver)	Unlocked a soldier from each unit
Hardcore (Gold)	Completed the campaign on Hardcore difficulty
Hit the Beach (Bronze)	Completed Shore Leave
Honey Badger (Bronze)	Used your Fire Team buddy to re-arm or heal
It's Dangerous to go Alone! (Bronze)	Requested ammo from an Ally in the Campaign
Jack of all Guns (Silver)	Earn the Marksman Badge for all Weapons
Job done (Bronze)	Complete 3 Combat Mission objectives
Know the Enemy (Bronze)	Completed Through the Eyes of Evil
Lead Farmer (Bronze)	Requested ammo from an Ally 25 times in Campaign
Lean With It (Bronze)	Killed 25 enemies while using peek and lean during the Campaign
Leftover Lead (Bronze)	Completed the sniping section in Shore Leave without missing a shot
Let Him Rot (Bronze)	Completed Shut It Down
Master Locksmith (Bronze)	Used each breaching option at least once
Monsoon Lagoon (Bronze)	Completed Rip Current
MVP (Silver)	MVP in a ranked match
Non-Official Cover (Bronze)	Completed Finding Faraz
On the Clock (Bronze)	Completed the training in Through the Eyes of Evil in under 18 seconds
One Man Mutiny (Bronze)	Completed Bump in the Night
One Shot, Three Kills (Bronze)	Completed Hat Trick
Pedal to the Medal (Bronze)	Completed Hello and Dubai
Peek-a-Boo (Bronze)	Killed an enemy while using peek and lean in the Campaign
Pit and Pin (Bronze)	Completed Hot Pursuit
Preacher's Path (Silver)	Finished all the Preacher Missions
Rain of Terror (Bronze)	Completed Changing Tides
Release the Kraken! (Bronze)	Killed 20 enemies during the boat exfil in Rip Current
Room Service (Bronze)	Unlocked all door breach options
Squad Leader (Bronze)	Unlocked a soldier of each class
Storm Watch (Bronze)	Got through the sandstorm without hitting any vehicles in Hello and Dubai
Stump's No Chump (Silver)	Finished all the Stump Missions
Tactical Toggler (Bronze)	Killed 25 enemies while using Combat Toggle
Tag, You're It (Bronze)	Caught Faraz within 15 minutes in Finding Faraz
Target Practice (Bronze)	Shot down the targets in the training camp caves in Connect the Dots
The Axeman (Bronze)	Killed 25 enemies with melee during the Campaign
There IS an I in Fire Team (Bronze)	Finished a round as part of the top Fire Team
Tier 1 (Silver)	Completed the campaign on Tier 1 difficulty
Tier 1 Imports (Bronze)	Got 50 kills while holding enemy weapons
Unexpected Cargo (Bronze)	Completed Unintended Consequences
Unstoppable (Silver)	Completed a combat mission on Hardest difficulty setting without dying
Vender Bender (Bronze)	Destroyed 90 market stalls in Hot Pursuit
Warchief (Silver)	Unlocked all soldiers in multiplayer

| Warfighter (Silver) | Completed the campaign |

UNLOCKABLES

UNLOCKABLE	HOW TO UNLOCK
Hardcore Mode	Complete the Warfighter Campaign on Hard Difficulty
Tier 1 Mode	Complete the Warfighter Campaign on Hard Difficulty

MEDAL OF HONOR: WARFIGHTER (XBOX 360)

ACHIEVEMENTS

UNLOCKABLE	HOW TO UNLOCK
All In (20)	Called in Apache support
Back in the Fight (50)	Completed one tour with all classes.
Brothers in Arms (20)	Won a round with a Friend as a Fire Team Buddy
Class Dismissed (20)	Completed Connect the Dots
Closing Ceremony (20)	Completed Old Friends
Dirty Laundry (15)	Found the grenades in the laundry room in Bump in the Night
Double Header (10)	Killed two enemies with one bullet in the Changing Tides mission
Downrange (20)	Played online for 15 minutes
Extreme Realism (10)	Recovered from near-death 5 times without dying
Global Warfighters (25)	Unlocked a soldier from each unit
Hardcore (80)	Completed the campaign on Hardcore difficulty
Hit the Beach (15)	Completed Shore Leave
Honey Badger (10)	Used your Fire Team buddy to re-arm or heal
It's Dangerous to go Alone! (5)	Requested ammo from an Ally in the Campaign
Jack of all Guns (20)	Earned the Marksman Pin for all Weapons
Job done (20)	Complete 3 Combat Mission objectives
Know the Enemy (15)	Completed Through the Eyes of Evil
Lead Farmer (10)	Requested ammo from an Ally 25 times in Campaign
Lean With It (15)	Killed 25 enemies while using peek and lean during the Campaign
Leftover Lead (15)	Completed the sniping section in Shore Leave without missing a shot
Let Him Rot (20)	Completed Shut It Down
Master Locksmith (15)	Used each breaching option at least once
Monsoon Lagoon (15)	Completed Rip Current
MVP (20)	Finished in first place in any online match
Non-Official Cover (20)	Completed Finding Faraz
On the Clock (10)	Completed the training in Through the Eyes of Evil in under 18 seconds
One Man Mutiny (20)	Completed Bump in the Night
One Shot, Three Kills (15)	Completed Hat Trick
Pedal to the Medal (20)	Completed Hello and Dubai
Peek-a-Boo (5)	Killed an enemy while using peek and lean in the Campaign
Pit and Pin (20)	Completed Hot Pursuit
Preacher's Path (30)	Finished all the Preacher Missions
Rain of Terror (15)	Completed Changing Tides
Release the Kraken! (15)	Killed 20 enemies during the boat exfil in Rip Current
Room Service (20)	Unlocked all door breach options

Squad Leader (20)	Unlocked a soldier of each class
Storm Watch (10)	Got through the sandstorm without hitting any vehicles in Hello and Dubai
Stump's No Chump (30)	Finished all the Stump Missions
Tactical Toggler (15)	Killed 25 enemies while using Combat Toggle
Tag, You're It (10)	Caught Faraz within 15 minutes in Finding Faraz
Target Practice (10)	Shot down the targets in the training camp caves in Connect the Dots
The Axeman (20)	Killed 25 enemies with melee during the Campaign
There IS an I in Fire Team (15)	Finished a round as part of the top Fire Team
Tier 1 (50)	Completed the campaign on Tier 1 difficulty
Tier 1 Imports (15)	Got 50 kills while holding enemy weapons
Unexpected Cargo (15)	Completed Unintended Consequences
Unstoppable (30)	Completed Shore Leave on Hardcore difficulty
Vender Bender (10)	Destroyed 90 market stalls in Hot Pursuit
Warchief (35)	Unlocked all soldiers in multiplayer
Warfighter (40)	Completed the campaign

UNLOCKABLES

UNLOCKABLE	HOW TO UNLOCK
Hardcore Mode	Complete the Warfighter Campaign on Hard Difficulty
Tier 1 Mode	Complete the Warfighter Campaign on Hard Difficulty

NASCAR THE GAME: INSIDE LINE (PLAYSTATION 3)

TROPHIES

UNLOCKABLE	HOW TO UNLOCK
1%'er (Silver)	Earn a total of 1,000,000Cr.
Action Shot (Bronze)	Take a picture of your car with all four wheels off the track.
Brainiac (Bronze)	Answer 150 trivia questions correctly.
Challenge Complete (Silver)	Complete all the Inside Line Highlight Challenges.
Challenger (Silver)	Complete an Inside Line Highlight Challenge.
Challenging (Silver)	Complete a Head to Head Challenge.
Champion (Gold)	Win the Sprint Cup in Career Mode.
Chase Champion (Bronze)	Win the Sprint Cup in Chase Mode.
Clock Watcher (Bronze)	Earn Gold at a Thunderlap Invitational event.
Collector (Silver)	Purchase everything in the Reward Store.
Consistent (Bronze)	Win a Gauntlet Invitational event.
Contender (Silver)	Win your first Public Online Race.
Day At The Beach (Silver)	Win the Daytona 500.
Director (Bronze)	Save a replay of a race.
Draft Dodger (Bronze)	Draft a total of 1000 yards in a race.
First Steps (Bronze)	Take part in your first Career or Season Race.
Gambler (Bronze)	Run out of fuel and coast into pit road.
Gear Head (Bronze)	Create your own custom setup.
Hustler (Bronze)	Win a Public Online Race after passing 5 cars on the last lap.
In The Chase (Silver)	Make the Chase.
Ironman (Bronze)	Take part in 250 Public Online Races.
Lap It Up (Bronze)	Lap an opponent in a Public Online Race.

Last Man Standing (Bronze)	Win an Eliminator Invitational event.
Long Road Back (Bronze)	Win a Public Online Race after qualifying last.
Mano a Mano (Bronze)	Win a Driver Duel Invitational event.
Maxed Out! (Silver)	Fully upgrade your Career Car.
Miles Away (Bronze)	Win your first Intermediate track race in Career or Season Mode.
Newbie (Bronze)	Take part in your first Public Online Race.
Pass in the Grass (Bronze)	Win a race after overtaking on grass.
Passing The Time (Bronze)	Flip the Track Pass 500 times during loading.
Perfect Day (Silver)	Qualify in pole, lead all laps, win the race.
Photo Finish (Silver)	Win an offline race by less than 0.02 seconds.
Platinum (Platinum)	Unlock every trophy in the game
Polish Victory Lap (Bronze)	Complete a victory lap driving the opposite direction around the track.
Season Champion (Silver)	Win the Sprint Cup in Single Season Mode.
Serious (Bronze)	Win a race with no assists.
Shake & Bake (Bronze)	Slingshot to victory in the final straight.
Short & Sweet (Bronze)	Win your first Short track race in Career or Season Mode.
Slippery (Bronze)	Complete a race without touching another car.
Snap Happy (Bronze)	Take a picture in any Photo Mode.
Speed Star (Bronze)	Win your first Superspeedway track race in Career or Season Mode.
Startin' on Pole (Bronze)	Qualify on pole for the first time in Career or Season Mode.
Taking Care Of Business (Bronze)	Sign a sponsor to each location on the car.
The Intimidator (Bronze)	Spin out an opponent.
The King (Silver)	Win the Sprint Cup in Career Mode while playing on Champion difficulty.
Too Much! (Silver)	Win the race after crossing the finishing line backwards.
Treat Yourself (Bronze)	Purchase an item from the Reward Store.
Trend Setter (Silver)	Finish a race with the fastest lap 100 times.
Turn Right? (Bronze)	Win your first Road Course race in Career or Season Mode.
Upgrade Complete (Bronze)	Purchase your first upgrade.
Van Gogh (Bronze)	Create a custom paint scheme.

NASCAR THE GAME: INSIDE LINE (XBOX 360)

ACHIEVEMENTS

UNLOCKABLE	HOW TO UNLOCK
1%'er (25)	Earned a total of 1,000,000Cr.
Action Shot (15)	Took a picture of the car with all four wheels off the track.
Brainiac (20)	Answered 150 trivia questions correctly.
Challenge Complete (20)	Completed all Inside Line Highlight Challenges.
Challenger (20)	Completed an Inside Line Highlight Challenge.
Challenging (15)	Completed a Head to Head Challenge.
Champion (50)	Won the Sprint Cup in Career Mode.
Chase Champion (15)	Won the Sprint Cup in Chase Mode.
Clock Watcher (25)	Earned Gold at a Thunderlap Invitational event.

A
B
C
D
E
F
G
H
I
J
K
L
M
N
O
P
Q
R
S
T
U
V
W
X
Y
Z

Collector (20)	Purchased everything in the Reward Store.
Consistent (25)	Won a Gauntlet Invitational event.
Contender (20)	Won a Public Online Race.
Day At The Beach (30)	Won the Daytona 500.
Director (5)	Saved a replay of a race.
Draft Dodger (15)	Drafted a total of 1000 yards in a race.
First Steps (5)	Took part in a Career or Season Race.
Gambler (25)	Ran out of fuel and coasted into pit road.
Gear Head (15)	Created a custom setup.
Hustler (25)	Won a Public Online Race after passing 5 cars on the last lap.
In The Chase (25)	Made the Chase.
Ironman (25)	Took part in 250 Public Online Races.
Lap It Up (20)	Lapped an opponent in a Public Online Race.
Last Man Standing (25)	Won an Eliminator Invitational event.
Long Road Back (20)	Won a Public Online Race after qualifying last.
Mano a Mano (25)	Won a Driver Duel Invitational event.
Maxed Out! (25)	Fully upgraded the Career Car.
Miles Away (25)	Won an Intermediate track race in Career or Season Mode.
Newbie (5)	Took part in a Public Online Race.
Pass in the Grass (20)	Won a race after overtaking on grass.
Passing The Time (15)	Flipped the Track Pass 500 times during loading.
Perfect Day (25)	Qualified in pole, led all laps, won the race.
Photo Finish (15)	Won an offline race by less than 0.02 seconds.
Polish Victory Lap (15)	Completed a victory lap driving the opposite direction around the track.
Season Champion (25)	Won the Sprint Cup in Single Season Mode.
Serious (15)	Won a race with no assists.
Shake & Bake (15)	Slingshotted to victory in the final straight.
Short & Sweet (25)	Won a Short track race in Career or Season Mode.
Slippery (25)	Completed a race without touching another car.
Snap Happy (5)	Took a picture in Photo Mode.
Speed Star (25)	Won a Superspeedway race in Career or Season Mode.
Startin' on Pole (15)	Qualified on pole in Career or Season Mode.
Taking Care Of Business (20)	Signed a sponsor to each location on the car.
The Intimidator (10)	Spun out an opponent.
The King (50)	Won the Sprint Cup in Career Mode while playing on Champion difficulty.
Too Much! (25)	Won the race after crossing the finishing line backwards.
Treat Yourself (5)	Purchased an item from the Reward Store.
Trend Setter (20)	Finished a race with the fastest lap 100 times.
Turn Right? (25)	Won a Road Course race in Career or Season Mode.
Upgrade Complete (10)	Purchased an upgrade.
Van Gogh (10)	Created a custom paint scheme.

UNLOCKABLES

UNLOCKABLE	HOW TO UNLOCK
3 New Items	Select "Enter Code" at the Rewards menu, then enter "Godaddy".

NBA 2K13 (PLAYSTATION 3)

TROPHIES

UNLOCKABLE	HOW TO UNLOCK
...One with Everything (Platinum)	Earn every trophy in NBA 2K13
Another Day, Another Win (Bronze)	Win 5 NBA Today matchups
Back to Back to Back (Bronze)	Win 3 Versus matches in a row
Block Party (Bronze)	Record 10 or more blocks with any team in a non-simulated game
Both Feet on the Ground (Bronze)	Sign an endorsement contract with either Nike or Jordan in MyCAREER mode
Buzzer Beater (Bronze)	Make a game winning shot with no time left on the clock in a non-simulated game
Come Fly with Me (Bronze)	Purchase Michael Jordan's dunk package (Historic Jordan) in MyCAREER mode
Dawn of an Era (Silver)	Get drafted as a lottery pick in the NBA draft in MyCAREER mode
Don't Hate the Player (Silver)	Win the championship in an Online Association
Dub-Dub (Bronze)	Record two double doubles with any teammates in the same non-simulated game
Everyone is Special (Bronze)	Purchase and equip 1 Special Ability in MyCAREER mode
Five by Five (Bronze)	Record 5 or more in 5 different stats with any player in a non-simulated game
From the Ground Up (Bronze)	Purchase 15 Boosters in MyTEAM mode
Giveth and Taketh Away (Bronze)	Record 10 or more rebounds and assists with any player in a non-simulated game
Hamilton (Silver)	Win 10 Versus matches total
Hey Mr. DJ (Bronze)	Create a 2K Beats Playlist
Hold the Fat Lady (Bronze)	Start the 4th period losing by 10 or more points and win with any team in a non-simulated game
I'm Here to Stay (Bronze)	Get 1,000,000 fans in MyCAREER mode
Immortality (Gold)	Make the Hall of Fame in MyCAREER mode
It's Raining (Bronze)	Make 15 or more 3-pointers with any team in a non-simulated game
KD Unlimited (Silver)	Score at least 52 points in one game with Kevin Durant to set a new career-high
Lincoln (Bronze)	Win 5 Versus matches total
Maestro (Bronze)	Create a shoe in the 2K Shoe Creator
Man of the People (Silver)	Get 2,000,000 fans in MyCAREER mode
Men of Steal (Bronze)	Record 10 or more steals with any team in a non-simulated game
My All-Star (Silver)	Be named an NBA All-Star in MyCAREER mode
My Every Day Player (Bronze)	Become a starter in the NBA in MyCAREER mode
MyPLAYER of the Game (Bronze)	Be named Player of the Game (in an NBA Game) in MyCAREER mode
NBA Cares (Bronze)	Make a donation to the NBA Cares global community outreach initiative in MyCAREER mode
Not Your Father's Association (Bronze)	Join an Online Association

NEW!

A
B
C
D
E
F
G
H
I
J
K
L
M
N
O
P
Q
R
S
T
U
V
W
X
Y
Z

Now Playing (Bronze)	Purchase a pre-game ritual in MyCAREER mode
On the Road Again (Bronze)	Play a MyPLAYER Blacktop game online
Puppet Master (Bronze)	Adjust your "Total Sim Control" strategy in The Association or Season mode
Raining 3's (Silver)	make at least 9 three-pointers in one non-simulated game with Brandon Jennings to set a new career-high
Remaking History (Bronze)	Play with a historic team online
Runneth Over (Silver)	Obtain a balance of 20,000 VC
Serving Notice (Bronze)	Get 250,000 fans in MyCAREER mode
Shooting Star (Silver)	Win the MVP award in NBA: Creating a Legend mode
Smothering (Bronze)	Hold the opposing team's FG% below 40% with any team in a non-simulated game
Some more Special than Others (Silver)	Purchase and equip 5 Special Abilities simultaneously in MyCAREER mode
Streaking (Bronze)	Win 5 non-simulated games in a row in The Association mode
Swat and Swipe (Bronze)	Record at least 5 blocks and 5 steals with any team in a non-simulated game
The Closer (Bronze)	Hold the opposing team to zero points in the final two minutes of a non-simulated game
The Here and Now (Bronze)	Start an Association using today's date
The Sum of Its Parts (Bronze)	Play a Team-Up Game
This One Counts (Bronze)	Win one online Versus match
Ticker Tape (Silver)	Win an NBA Championship in The Association mode
To Good Use (Bronze)	Play a MyTEAM game online
Trip-Dub (Bronze)	Record a triple double with any player in a non-simulated game
Wire to Wire (Bronze)	Do not allow your opponent to lead the game at any point with any team in a non-simulated game
You're Officially Hot (Silver)	Win 5 Versus matches in a row

NBA 2K13 (XBOX 360)

ACHIEVEMENTS

UNLOCKABLE	HOW TO UNLOCK
Another Day, Another Win (20)	Win 5 NBA Today matchups.
Back to Back to Back (15)	Win 3 Versus matches in a row.
Block Party (20)	Record 10 or more blocks with any team in a non-simulated game.
Both Feet on the Ground (30)	Sign an endorsement contract with either Nike® or Jordan in MyCAREER mode.
Buzzer Beater (20)	Make a game winning shot with no time left on the clock in a non-simulated game.
Come Fly with Me (15)	Purchase Michael Jordan's dunk package (Historic Jordan) in MyCAREER mode.
Dawn of an Era (15)	Get drafted as a lottery pick in the NBA draft in MyCAREER mode.
Don't Hate the Player (30)	Win the championship in an Online Association.
Dub-Dub (20)	Record two double doubles with any teammates in the same non-simulated game.
Everyone is Special (15)	Purchase and equip 1 Special Ability in MyCAREER mode.

Five by Five (20)	Record 5 or more in 5 different stats with any player in a non-simulated game.
From the Ground Up (20)	Purchase 15 Boosters in MyTEAM mode.
Giveth and Taketh Away (20)	Record 10 or more rebounds and assists with any player in a non-simulated game.
Hamilton (20)	Win 10 Versus matches total.
Hey Mr. DJ (10)	Create a 2K Beats Playlist.
Hold the Fat Lady (20)	Start the 4th period losing by 10 or more points and win with any team in a non-simulated game.
I'm Here to Stay (25)	Get 1,000,000 fans in MyCAREER mode.
Immortality (30)	Make the Hall of Fame in MyCAREER mode.
It's Raining (20)	Make 15 or more 3-pointers with any team in a non-simulated game.
KD Unlimited (20)	Score at least 52 points in one game with Kevin Durant to set a new career-high.
Lincoln (15)	Win 5 Versus matches total.
Maestro (15)	Create a shoe in the 2K Shoe Creator.
Man of the People (40)	Get 2,000,000 fans in MyCAREER mode.
Men of Steal (20)	Record 10 or more steals with any team in a non-simulated game.
My All-Star (25)	Be named an NBA All-Star in MyCAREER mode.
My Every Day Player (20)	Become a starter in the NBA in MyCAREER Mode.
MyPLAYER of the Game (20)	Be named Player of the Game (in an NBA game) in MyCAREER mode.
NBA Cares (15)	Make a donation to the NBA Cares global community outreach initiative in MyCAREER mode.
Not Your Father's Association (10)	Join an Online Association.
Now Playing (15)	Purchase a pre-game ritual in MyCAREER mode.
On the Road Again (15)	Play a MyPLAYER Blacktop game online.
Puppet Master (10)	Adjust your "Total Sim Control" strategy in The Association or Season mode.
Raining 3's (20)	Make at least 9 three-pointers in one game with Brandon Jennings to set a new career-high.
Remaking History (15)	Play with an historic team online.
Runneth Over (30)	Obtain a balance of 20,000 VC.
Serving Notice (15)	Get 250,000 fans in MyCAREER mode.
Shooting Star (30)	Win the MVP award in NBA: Creating a Legend mode.
Smothering (20)	Hold the opposing team's FG% below 40% with any team in a non-simulated game.
Some more Special than Others (30)	Purchase and equip 5 Special Abilities simultaneously in MyCAREER mode.
Streaking (25)	Win 5 non-simulated games in a row in The Association mode.
Swat and Swipe (20)	Record at least 5 blocks and 5 steals with any team in a non-simulated game.
The Closer (20)	Hold the opposing team to zero points in the final two minutes of a non-simulated game.
The Here and Now (15)	Begin a "Today" Association.
The Sum of Its Parts (15)	Play a Team-Up Game.
This One Counts (15)	Win one online Versus match.

NEW!

A
B
C
D
E
F
G
H
I
J
K
L
M
N
O
P
Q
R
S
T
U
V
W
X
Y
Z

Ticker Tape (30)	Win an NBA Championship in The Association mode (playing every playoff game).
To Good Use (15)	Play a MyTEAM game online.
Trip-Dub (20)	Record a triple double with any player in a non-simulated game.
Wire to Wire (20)	Do not allow your opponent to lead the game at any point with any team in a non-simulated game.
You're Officially Hot (20)	Win 5 Versus matches in a row.

NBA BALLER BEATS (XBOX 360)

ACHIEVEMENTS

UNLOCKABLE	HOW TO UNLOCK
Ankle Breaker (50)	You have sucessfully executed every skill move in NBA Baller Beats.
Around The World (10)	Successfully perform the Around The World skill move outside of Move School.
Back to Back (5)	Successfully perform two skill moves back to back in Play Now.
Behind The Back Crossover (15)	Successfully perform a Behind The Back Crossover in any direction outside of Move School.
Between The Legs Crossover (10)	Successfully perform a Between The Legs Crossover in any direction outside of Move School.
Boosted (10)	Earn a maximum multiplier in Play Now.
Buzzer Beater (70)	Achieve the 5th star on any non-DLC track with the last Skill Move of a song.
Credit Where It's Due (5)	Watch the credits roll from start to finish.
Crossover Dribble (5)	Successfully complete the Crossover Dribble in any direction outside of Move School.
Dynasty (60)	Purchase all NBA themed items from the NBA Store.
Eclectic (100)	Earn 5 stars for all non-DLC tracks across all difficulties in Play Now.
Flow Dribble (10)	Successfully perform the Flow Dribble in any direction outside of Move School.
Give Us A Wave (5)	Purchase all Wavy Davey skins in the NBA Store
Got Backup (10)	Purchase all runway backings in the NBA Store
Hot Streak (30)	Earn 5 stars on any 5 non-DLC tracks in Play Now.
I Need A Bib (40)	Perform 1,000 successful dribbles in 'Play Now' mode.
I've Lost Count (50)	Reach 250,000 successful dribbles across all game modes.
It's A Religion (25)	Purchase all rewards for a specific team from the NBA Store.
It's Bigger Than Hip Hop (40)	5 star any non-DLC track with the game's sound settings turned down to zero in any game mode.
Johnny Hopkins (20)	Successfully perform any Johnny Hopkins skill move, in any direction, outside of Move School.
Jump Pump Fake (15)	Successfully perform the Jumping Pump Fake skill move in any direction outside of Move School.
Lime Light (5)	Save your pictures to the gallery.
Look At Me Mom! I'm A Baller! (20)	Earn 5 stars in any non-DLC track at Baller difficulty within Play Now.
Mamma Said... (10)	Play your first Baller Beats Versus Battle.
Megastar (30)	Have a total of 500 Reward Stars in the bank
MVP I (20)	Earn 5 stars on all short non-DLC tracks in Rookie difficulty within Play Now.

MVP II (40)	Earn 5 stars on all short non-DLC tracks in Pro difficulty within Play Now.
MVP III (60)	Earn 5 stars on all short non-DLC tracks in Baller difficulty within Play Now.
My Ball (10)	Purchase all Team Balls in the NBA Store
One Better (20)	Beat the high score on any song you previously earned 5 stars on.
Perfection (50)	Hit every dribble and every skill move in a routine within Play Now.
Pull Dribble (15)	Successfully perform the Pull Dribble skill move in any direction outside of Move School.
Pump Fake (5)	Successfully perform the Pump Fake skill move in any direction outside of Move School.
Reward Me (5)	Purchase your first item from the NBA Store.
School's Out (10)	Practice every move in NBA Baller Beats via Move School.
Schooled (5)	Practice a skill in 'Move School'
Side Pass (5)	Successfully perform the Side Pass skill move outside of Move School.
Sign Me Up (10)	Sign in with your Xbox LIVE gamer profile.
Sold Out (10)	Purchase all player posters in the NBA Store
Starry Eyed (20)	Have a total of 50 Reward Stars in the bank
Superstar (25)	Have a total of 250 Reward Stars in the bank
Take It To The Bank (20)	Successfully perform every skill move in a routine via Play Now.
Time Keeper (10)	Hit more than 90% perfectly timed dribbles in any non-DLC track in Play Now.
Track Owner (10)	Earn 5 stars for the same track at Rookie, Pro and Baller

NEED FOR SPEED: MOST WANTED - A CRITERION GAME (PLAYSTATION VITA)

TROPHIES

UNLOCKABLE	HOW TO UNLOCK
After Market (Bronze)	Unlock a mod for a car in Multiplayer
Alpha Dog (Bronze)	Shut down Most Wanted car number 10: Alfa Romeo 4C Concept (Single Player)
Arachnophobic (Bronze)	Shut down Most Wanted car number 5: Porsche 918 Spyder Concept (Single Player)
Battering Ram (Bronze)	Smash through a roadblock without crashing
Beast from the East (Silver)	Escape from the cops in the Marussia B2
Blackout (Bronze)	Shut down Most Wanted car number 8: Mercedes-Benz SL 65 AMG (Single Player)
Cameraman (Bronze)	Trigger every Speed Camera
Charming (Bronze)	Shut down Most Wanted car number 9: Shelby COBRA 427® (Single Player)
Don't Blink (Silver)	Shut down Most Wanted car number 1: Koenigsegg Agera R (Single Player)
Escape Velocity (Bronze)	Jump over 200 yards (182.88 meters) through a Billboard
Fast Forward (Bronze)	Trigger a speed camera at over 200mph (321.97km/h)
Feeling the Need (Bronze)	Empty a full nitrous bar without hitting anything
First Strike (Bronze)	Takedown your first Cop
Fix Me Up (Bronze)	Use a Bodyshop to paint or repair your car for the first time

Gladiator (Silver)	Takedown every racer at least once in a single race
Go Pro or Go Home (Bronze)	Unlock all the Pro mods on a car (Single Player)
Got to Smash Them All (Bronze)	Smash every Billboard
Gotcha (Bronze)	Get Busted for the first time
How Do You Like Me Now? (Bronze)	Beat a friend's Autolog Recommendation
In Your Face (Bronze)	Smash a friend's face on a billboard and beat their jump distance
Iron Boots (Bronze)	Drive over 5 spike strips with re-inflates equipped
Kitchen Sink (Bronze)	Use a Billboard and a Jack Spot to successfully evade a pursuit (Single Player)
Lexus Ranger (Bronze)	Shut down Most Wanted car number 7: Lexus LFA (Single Player)
Licensed to ill (Silver)	Customize your license plate and number in Multiplayer
Love Them and Leave Them (Bronze)	Drive every Car
Main Avent (Bronze)	Shut down Most Wanted car number 4: Lamborghini Aventador (Single Player)
Mauled (Silver)	Wreck 10 cops in a single pursuit in the Ford F-150 SVT Raptor
Mighty Wind (Bronze)	Shut down Most Wanted car number 2: Pagani Huayra (Single Player)
Mix Master (Bronze)	Play a Custom Speedlist you have created (Multiplayer)
Most Wanted Rides (Gold)	Own all the Most Wanted cars (Single Player)
Moving On Up (Bronze)	Move up the Most Wanted List for the first time
Networking (Bronze)	Find every Jack Spot
None More Wanted (Platinum)	Awarded for successfully collecting all Most Wanted trophies
Nothing Personal (Bronze)	Takedown a friend in Multiplayer
Pit Stop (Bronze)	Repair a burst tire at a Bodyshop
Rim Shot (Silver)	Escape the cops with at least one blown tire
Second is Nothing (Gold)	Finish first in every race, in every car (Single Player)
Sidewinder (Bronze)	Do a 250 yard (228.6 meter) drift
Slip the Cuffs (Bronze)	Drive through a roadblock without hitting it
Social Climber (Bronze)	Get 5 or more NFS friends
Switcheroo (Bronze)	Use a Jack Spot in a Pursuit (Single Player)
The Gatecrasher (Bronze)	Break through every Security Gate
The Heat is Off (Silver)	Escape successfully from all Heat levels
The Modfather (Silver)	Unlock 3 Pro Mods in Multiplayer
Track Weapon (Bronze)	Shut down Most Wanted car number 6: McLaren MP4-12C (Single Player)
Troublemaker (Silver)	Takedown 50 Cops
White Gold (Bronze)	Shut down Most Wanted car number 3: Bugatti Veyron Super Sport (Single Player)

NEED FOR SPEED: MOST WANTED - A CRITERION GAME (PLAYSTATION 3)

TROPHIES

UNLOCKABLE	HOW TO UNLOCK
After Market (Bronze)	Unlock a mod for a car in Multiplayer

Alpha Dog (Bronze)	Shut down Most Wanted car number 10: Alfa Romeo 4C Concept (Single Player)
Arachnophobic (Bronze)	Shut down Most Wanted car number 5: Porsche 918 Spyder Concept (Single Player)
Battering Ram (Bronze)	Smash through a roadblock without crashing
Beast from the East (Silver)	Escape from the cops in the Marussia B2
Blackout (Bronze)	Shut down Most Wanted car number 8: Mercedes-Benz SL 65 AMG (Single Player)
Cameraman (Bronze)	Trigger every Speed Camera
Charming (Bronze)	Shut down Most Wanted car number 9: Shelby COBRA 427® (Single Player)
Don't Blink (Silver)	Shut down Most Wanted car number 1: Koenigsegg Agera R (Single Player)
Escape Velocity (Bronze)	Jump over 200 yards (182.88 meters) through a Billboard
Fast Forward (Bronze)	Trigger a speed camera at over 200mph (321.97km/h)
Feeling the Need (Bronze)	Empty a full nitrous bar without hitting anything
First Strike (Bronze)	Takedown your first Cop
Fix Me Up (Bronze)	Use a Bodyshop to paint or repair your car for the first time
Gladiator (Silver)	Takedown every racer at least once in a single race
Go Pro or Go Home (Bronze)	Unlock all the Pro mods on a car (Single Player)
Got to Smash Them All (Bronze)	Smash every Billboard
Gotcha (Bronze)	Get Busted for the first time
How Do You Like Me Now? (Bronze)	Beat a friend's Autolog Recommendation
In Your Face (Bronze)	Smash a friend's face on a billboard and beat their jump distance
Iron Boots (Bronze)	Drive over 5 spike strips with re-inflates equipped
Kitchen Sink (Bronze)	Use a Billboard and a Jack Spot to successfully evade a pursuit (Single Player)
Lexus Ranger (Bronze)	Shut down Most Wanted car number 7: Lexus LFA (Single Player)
Licensed to ill (Silver)	Customize your license plate and number in Multiplayer
Love Them and Leave Them (Bronze)	Drive every Car
Main Avent (Bronze)	Shut down Most Wanted car number 4: Lamborghini Aventador (Single Player)
Mauled (Silver)	Wreck 10 cops in a single pursuit in the Ford F-150 SVT Raptor
Mighty Wind (Bronze)	Shut down Most Wanted car number 2: Pagani Huayra (Single Player)
Mix Master (Bronze)	Play a Custom Speedlist you have created (Multiplayer)
Most Wanted Rides (Gold)	Own all the Most Wanted cars (Single Player)
Moving On Up (Bronze)	Move up the Most Wanted List for the first time
Networking (Bronze)	Find every Jack Spot
None More Wanted (Platinum)	Awarded for successfully collecting all Most Wanted trophies
Nothing Personal (Bronze)	Takedown a friend in Multiplayer
Pit Stop (Bronze)	Repair a burst tire at a Bodyshop

A
B
C
D
E
F
G
H
I
J
K
L
M
N
O
P
Q
R
S
T
U
V
W
X
Y
Z

Rim Shot (Silver)	Escape the cops with at least one blown tire
Second is Nothing (Gold)	Finish first in every race, in every car (Single Player)
Sidewinder (Bronze)	Do a 250 yard (228.6 meter) drift
Slip the Cuffs (Bronze)	Drive through a roadblock without hitting it
Social Climber (Bronze)	Get 5 or more NFS friends
Switcheroo (Bronze)	Use a Jack Spot in a Pursuit (Single Player)
The Gatecrasher (Bronze)	Break through every Security Gate
The Heat is Off (Silver)	Escape successfully from all Heat levels
The Modfather (Silver)	Unlock 3 Pro Mods in Multiplayer
Track Weapon (Bronze)	Shut down Most Wanted car number 6: McLaren MP4-12C (Single Player)
Troublemaker (Silver)	Takedown 50 Cops
White Gold (Bronze)	Shut down Most Wanted car number 3: Bugatti Veyron Super Sport (Single Player)

NEED FOR SPEED: MOST WANTED - A CRITERION GAME (XBOX 360)

ACHIEVEMENTS

UNLOCKABLE	HOW TO UNLOCK
After Market (10)	Unlocked a mod for a car in Multiplayer
Alpha Dog (20)	Shut down Most Wanted car number 10: Alfa Romeo 4C Concept (Single Player)
Arachnophobic (20)	Shut down Most Wanted car number 5: Porsche 918 Spyder Concept (Single Player)
Battering Ram (10)	Smashed through a roadblock without crashing
Beast from the East (30)	Escaped from the cops in the Marussia B2
Blackout (20)	Shut down Most Wanted car number 8: Mercedes-Benz SL 65 AMG (Single Player)
Cameraman (25)	Triggered every Speed Camera
Charming (20)	Shut down Most Wanted car number 9: Shelby COBRA 427® (Single Player)
Don't Blink (45)	Shut down Most Wanted car number 1: Koenigsegg Agera R (Single Player)
Escape Velocity (20)	Jumped over 200 yards (182.88 meters) through a Billboard
Fast Forward (20)	Triggered a speed camera at over 200mph (321.97km/h)
Feeling the Need (5)	Emptied a full nitrous bar without hitting anything
First Strike (5)	Took down your first Cop
Fix Me Up (5)	Used a Bodyshop to paint or repair your car for the first time
Gladiator (25)	Took down every racer at least once in a single race
Go Pro or Go Home (15)	Unlocked all the Pro mods on a car (Single Player)
Got to Smash Them All (25)	Smashed every Billboard
Gotcha (15)	Got Busted for the first time
How Do You Like Me Now? (15)	Beat a friend's Autolog Recommendation
In Your Face (20)	Smashed a friend's face on a billboard and beat their jump distance
Iron Boots (20)	Drove over 5 spike strips with re-inflates equipped

Kitchen Sink (10)	Used a Billboard and a Jack Spot to successfully evade a pursuit (Single Player)
Lexus Ranger (20)	Shut down Most Wanted car number 7: Lexus LFA (Single Player)
Licensed to ill (10)	Customized your license plate and number in Multiplayer
Love Them and Leave Them (30)	Drove every Car
Main Avent (20)	Shut down Most Wanted car number 4: Lamborghini Aventador (Single Player)
Mauled (30)	Wrecked 10 cops in a single pursuit in the Ford F-150 SVT Raptor
Mighty Wind (20)	Shut down Most Wanted car number 2: Pagani Huayra (Single Player)
Mix Master (10)	Played a Custom Speedlist you created (Multiplayer)
Most Wanted Rides (100)	Own all the Most Wanted cars (Single Player)
Moving On Up (10)	Moved up the Most Wanted List for the first time
Networking (25)	Found every Jack Spot
Nothing Personal (15)	Took down a friend in Multiplayer
Pit Stop (10)	Repaired a burst tire at a Bodyshop
Rim Shot (25)	Escaped the cops with at least one blown tire
Second is Nothing (80)	Finished first in every race, in every car (Single Player)
Sidewinder (25)	Did a 250 yard (228 .6 meter) drift
Slip the Cuffs (10)	Drove through a roadblock without hitting it
Social Climber (10)	Have 5 or more NFS friends
Switcheroo (10)	Used a Jack Spot in a Pursuit (Single Player)
The Gatecrasher (25)	Broke through every Security Gate
The Heat is Off (20)	Escaped successfully from all Heat levels
The Modfather (25)	Unlocked 3 Pro Mods in Multiplayer
Track Weapon (20)	Shut down Most Wanted car number 6: McLaren MP4-12C (Single Player)
Troublemaker (30)	Took down 50 Cops
White Gold (20)	Shut down Most Wanted car number 3: Bugatti Veyron Super Sport (Single Player)

NHL 13 (PLAYSTATION 3)

TROPHIES

UNLOCKABLE	HOW TO UNLOCK
Another Direction (Bronze)	Get traded to another team in Be A Pro with a Created Pro
Are You Kidding Me? (Bronze)	Hit the post 3 times in 1 game in Be A Pro with a Created Pro
Best of the Best (Bronze)	Win the Art Ross Trophy in Be A Pro with a Created Pro
Call In The Ringers (Bronze)	Win a GM Connected league game with an OTP partner
Changing Skins (Bronze)	Change the team of a player by using the Change Team item in Hockey Ultimate Team
Chosen One (Bronze)	Assign a captain to your Hockey Ultimate Team using the Assign Captain item
Coast To Coast (Silver)	Starting from behind your net, skate up the ice and score without passing
Come At Me Bro (Bronze)	Change your team's bias to Neutral Zone

Complete Set (Silver)	Collect all player, jersey and logo items for any team in the Collection in Hockey Ultimate Team
Desperate Measures (Silver)	Score a goal with your goalie pulled
EASHL™ Legend (Gold)	Achieve Legend 1 status for your Online Pro
EASHL™ Playoffs (Bronze)	Be a member of an EA SPORTS™ Hockey League team when they participate in a monthly playoff.
EASHL™ Pro (Silver)	Achieve Pro 1 status for your Online Pro
EASHL™ Rookie (Bronze)	Achieve Rookie 1 status for your Online Pro
Fear No Man (Silver)	Complete 30 EA SPORTS™ Hockey League regular matches without receiving a DNF or backout penalty
Firewall (Bronze)	Win the James Norris Memorial Trophy in Be A Pro with a Created Pro
HONDA - 82 Game Grind (Bronze)	Win a regular season NHL Moments Live moment
HONDA - Second Season (Bronze)	Win a playoff NHL Moments Live moment
HONDA - Superstar For A Moment (Bronze)	Win a NHL Moments Live moment on Superstar difficulty
HONDA - Time To Shine (Bronze)	Win a team based NHL Moments Live moment
HONDA - Your Moment Is Now (Bronze)	Win a Be A Pro NHL Moments Live moment
HUT Playoff Winner (Silver)	Win any Hockey Ultimate Team monthly playoff tournament
Kid's Got Talent (Bronze)	Win the Calder Memorial Trophy in Be A Pro with a Created Pro
Lead By Example (Bronze)	As captain or assistant captain, be named one of the 3 stars during an EASHL match
Legend GM (Silver)	Achieve Legendary GM Status in Be A GM
Legend Player (Silver)	Play and win any NHL player trophy in Be A Pro with a Created Pro
Legendary (Gold)	Retire as a Legend in Be A Pro with a Created Pro
Locked and Loaded (Bronze)	Score on a slapshot in Online Ranked Shootout
Mad Scientist (Bronze)	Use the line assistant feature to setup your lines in Hockey Ultimate Team
Memorial Cup (Bronze)	Play and win the Memorial Cup in Be A Pro with a Created Pro
MVP (Bronze)	Win the Hart Memorial Trophy in Be A Pro with a Created Pro
Opportunist (Bronze)	Score on a sprawling goalie
Play Through the Pain (Bronze)	Score a goal while injured in Be A Pro with a Created Pro
Playoff Hero (Bronze)	During the NHL Playoffs, score a goal in OT in Be A Pro with a Created Pro
Pro Contender (Silver)	Win a Hockey Ultimate Team tournament
Promising Start (Bronze)	Get drafted 1st overall to an NHL team in Be A Pro with a Created Pro
Puck Puck Goose Egg (Bronze)	Win the Vezina Trophy in Be A Pro with a Created Pro
Put It On Net (Bronze)	Score while skating full speed
Raise the Cup (Silver)	Play and win the Stanley Cup in Be A Pro with a Created Pro

Raise Your Banner '13 (Platinum)	Acquire all of the Bronze, Silver and Gold trophies
Real Competition (Bronze)	Play in a GM Connected league of 5 Human GMs
Red Light Specialist (Bronze)	Win the Maurice "Rocket" Richard Trophy in Be A Pro with a Created Pro
Savior (Bronze)	While playing as a goalie in an EA SPORTS™ Hockey League match, make a desperation save in OT
Tactical Advantage (Bronze)	Win a GM Connected league game using your Build Your AI file
That's Embarrassing (Bronze)	Score a goal on a goalie who is performing a desperation save in Online Ranked Shootout
Two-Way Threat (Bronze)	Win the Frank J. Selke Trophy in Be A Pro with a Created Pro
Winter Classic (Bronze)	Complete a Winter Classic Match playing with the New York Rangers versus the Philadelphia Flyers
You Are The Champion My Friend (Silver)	Participate in and Win the Stanley Cup game in GM Connected

NHL 13 (XBOX 360)

ACHIEVEMENTS

UNLOCKABLE	HOW TO UNLOCK
Another Direction (10)	Get traded to another team in Be A Pro with a Created Pro
Are You Kidding Me? (15)	Hit the post 3 times in 1 game in Be A Pro with a Created Pro
Best of the Best (15)	Win the Art Ross Trophy in Be A Pro with a Created Pro
Call In The Ringers (10)	Win a GM Connected league game with an OTP partner
Changing Skins (10)	Change the team of a player by using the Change Team item in Hockey Ultimate Team
Chosen One (20)	Assign a captain to your Hockey Ultimate Team using the Assign Captain item
Coast To Coast (30)	Starting from behind your net, skate up the ice and score without passing
Come At Me Bro (5)	Change your team's bias to Neutral Zone
Complete Set (30)	Collect all player, jersey and logo items for any team in the Collection in Hockey Ultimate Team
Desperate Measures (30)	Score a goal with your goalie pulled
EASHL™ Legend (60)	Achieve Legend 1 status for your Online Pro
EASHL™ Playoffs (15)	Be a member of an EA SPORTS™ Hockey League team when they participate in a monthly playoff
EASHL™ Pro (30)	Achieve Pro 1 status for your Online Pro
EASHL™ Rookie (10)	Achieve Rookie 1 status for your Online Pro
Fear No Man (105)	Complete 30 EA SPORTS™ Hockey League regular matches without receiving a DNF or backout penalty
Firewall (15)	Win the James Norris Memorial Trophy in Be A Pro with a Created Pro
HONDA - 82 Game Grind (15)	Win a regular season NHL Moments Live moment
HONDA - Second Season (15)	Win a playoff NHL Moments Live moment
HONDA - Superstar For A Moment (15)	Win a NHL Moments Live moment on Superstar difficulty

HONDA - Time To Shine (15)	Win a team based NHL Moments Live moment
HONDA - Your Moment Is Now (15)	Win a Be A Pro NHL Moments Live moment
HUT Playoff Winner (40)	Win any Hockey Ultimate Team monthly playoff tournament
Kid's Got Talent (15)	Win the Calder Memorial Trophy in Be A Pro with a Created Pro
Lead By Example (20)	As captain or assistant captain, be named one of the 3 stars during an EASHL match
Legend GM (30)	Achieve Legendary GM Status in Be A GM
Legend Player (30)	Play and win any NHL player trophy in Be A Pro with a Created Pro
Legendary (50)	Retire as a Legend in Be A Pro with a Created Pro
Locked and Loaded (15)	Score on a slapshot in Online Ranked Shootout
Mad Scientist (15)	Use the line assistant feature to setup your lines in Hockey Ultimate Team
Memorial Cup (15)	Play and win the Memorial Cup in Be A Pro with a Created Pro
MVP (15)	Win the Hart Memorial Trophy in Be A Pro with a Created Pro
Opportunist (10)	Score on a sprawling goalie
Play Through the Pain (10)	Score a goal while injured in Be A Pro with a Created Pro
Playoff Hero (15)	During the NHL Playoffs, score a goal in OT in Be A Pro with a Created Pro
Pro Contender (30)	Win a Hockey Ultimate Team tournament
Promising Start (10)	Get drafted 1st overall to an NHL team in Be A Pro with a Created Pro
Puck Puck Goose Egg (15)	Win the Vezina Trophy in Be A Pro with a Created Pro
Put It On Net (30)	Score while skating full speed
Raise the Cup (30)	Play and win the Stanley Cup in Be A Pro with a Created Pro
Real Competition (10)	Play in a GM Connected league of 5 Human GMs
Red Light Specialist (15)	Win the Maurice "Rocket" Richard Trophy in Be A Pro with a Created Pro
Savior (15)	While playing as a goalie in an EA SPORTS™ Hockey League match, make a desperation save in OT
Tactical Advantage (10)	Win a GM Connected league game using your Build Your AI file
That's Embarrassing (15)	Score a goal on a goalie who is performing a desperation save in Online Ranked Shootout
Two-Way Threat (15)	Win the Frank J. Selke Trophy in Be A Pro with a Created Pro
Winter Classic (10)	Complete a Winter Classic Match playing with the New York Rangers versus the Philadelphia Flyers
You Are The Champion My Friend (30)	Participate in and Win the Stanley Cup game in GM Connected

ACHIEVEMENTS

UNLOCKABLE	HOW TO UNLOCK
1 Month Club (30)	Complete your first program
10K NikeFuel (30)	Earn 10000 NikeFuel in Nike+ Kinect Training
2 Month Club (40)	Complete two programs
2.5K NikeFuel (15)	Earn 2500 NikeFuel in Nike+ Kinect Training
3 Month Club (50)	Complete three programs
5K NikeFuel (25)	Earn 5000 NikeFuel in Nike+ Kinect Training
A New Challenger Appears (15)	Opt in for a challenge at the end of a program Strength or Weight Training session
Artful Dodger (25)	Survive for 20 seconds in sudden death in a Dodgeball challenge
Beat Your Best (20)	Beat a Personal Best in any drill or challenge (excluding Fitness Challenge)
Break a Dozen (40)	Complete 12 Quick Start training sessions
Break a Sweat (20)	Earn 500 NikeFuel in a single session
Burger Burn (20)	Burned 3000 calories
Check My Stats (10)	Participate in a challenge
Cheer Leader (20)	Cheer a friend
Decathlete (25)	Participate in 10 challenge drills
Dial It In (10)	Get your first Fuel Print
Drill Sergeant (30)	Participate in 5 drills in Take on the World
Extra Round (15)	Choose to do another round during a Strength or Weight Training session
Five Days of Fitness (25)	Complete a session 5 days in a row
Hide in Plain Sight (25)	Survive for 20 seconds in sudden death in a Split Decision challenge
High Stepper (20)	Do 120 or more reps in a High Knee Sprint challenge
In the Zone (15)	Finish a Split Decision or Dodgeball drill or challenge without getting hit
Join the Community (10)	Link or create a Nike+ account
Jump In (15)	Complete a Quick Start training session
Just for Kicks (15)	Hit 4 soccer balls in Dodgeball
Leg It Out (25)	Score 300 or more in a Leg Matrix challenge
Look Before You Leap (15)	Clear 2 hurdles with one jump during a Hurdles Matrix drill or Hardcore Hurdles challenge
Massive Hops (25)	Survive for 20 seconds in sudden death in a Hardcore Hurdles challenge
Metronome (15)	Stay on tempo for the entire duration of a Strength or Weight Training drill
On Your Way (10)	Complete your first workout session
Perfect Attendance (25)	Complete a program without missing a scheduled session
Perfection (25)	Get perfect form on every rep of a drill
Personalized Just for You (10)	Complete the assessment
Pizza Party (30)	Burned 9000 calories
Power Train (30)	Complete a 60 minute Quick Start session
Push It (20)	Do 10 or more perfect reps in a Push Up Power challenge

A
B
C
D
E
F
G
H
I
J
K
L
M
N
O
P
Q
R
S
T
U
V
W
X
Y
Z

Say What? (10)	Rewatch the tutorial for a drill
Serve Notice (20)	Invite a friend to beat your challenge score
Show and Tell (20)	Post to Facebook to let friends know you're starting a workout or challenge
Six Pack (30)	Complete 6 Quick Start training sessions
Strike a Pose (15)	Dodge 2 consecutive walls in Split Decision without moving
The Numbers Don't Lie (25)	Improve your Fuel Print
U Mad? (25)	Beat a friend's challenge score
Workout Buddies (30)	Complete 5 Workouts with a Friend
Workout Warrior (30)	Choose to do an extra round during 5 Strength or Weight Training sessions

PERSONA 4 GOLDEN (PLAYSTATION VITA)

TROPHIES

UNLOCKABLE	HOW TO UNLOCK
A Favor for Marie (Bronze)	Register a Skill Card
A New Quiz King (Bronze)	Win the Miracle Quiz Finals
A Prince Appears (Bronze)	Rescue Yukiko Amagi
A Special Lady (Bronze)	Enter a special relationship with someone
A True Bond (Bronze)	Max out a Social Link
A True Man's Stand (Bronze)	Rescue Kanji Tatsumi
Advantage Mine (Bronze)	Enter a battle with Player Advantage
An Acquired Taste (Bronze)	Drink the coffee at Chagall Cafe
Big Bro is Worried (Bronze)	Visit Nanako in the hospital 3 times
Boarded-Up Lab (Bronze)	Rescue Naoto Shirogane
Bond Maniac (Bronze)	Max out 10 Social Links
Breaking Through the Fog (Bronze)	Secure Tohru Adachi
Bug Hunter (Bronze)	Swing the net with perfect timing
Card Collector (Bronze)	Register 100 Skill Cards
Compulsive Reader (Bronze)	Read all books
Cooking With Gas (Bronze)	Make 5 perfect boxed lunches
Displaying Adaptability (Bronze)	Switch Personas 5 times in 1 battle
Fashion Plate (Bronze)	Fight a battle in costume
Fill Your Hand (Bronze)	Get 50 Sweep Bonuses
Fishing Master (Bronze)	Catch the Sea Guardian
Food Fighter (Bronze)	Finish Aiya's special dish
Fusion Expert (Bronze)	Perform 50 Persona fusions
Game Over (Bronze)	Secure Mitsuo Kubo
Going Nova (Bronze)	Deal over 999 damage in 1 attack
Golden Completed (Platinum)	Earn all trophies
Granter of Your Desires (Bronze)	Buy 5 things from Tanaka's Amazing Commodities
Grasping at Greed (Bronze)	Defeat a Golden Hand
Hardcore Risette Fan (Bronze)	Hear 250 of Rise's navigation lines
Head of the Class (Bronze)	Rank #1 in your class on an exam
It's Working Today (Bronze)	Buy an item from the Capsule Machine
Legend of Inaba (Silver)	Max out all Social Links
Lucky Me! (Bronze)	Win a prize from the vending machine
Moderate Bookkeeper (Silver)	Register over 50% of the Compendium

Movie Buff (Bronze)	Go to 3 movies at 30 Frame
Mr. Perfect (Silver)	Max out all social qualities
One Who Has Proven Their Power (Gold)	Defeat Margaret
Persona Shopper (Bronze)	Buy a Persona from the Compendium
Seize the Moment (Bronze)	Buy a special croquette from Sozai Daigaku
Skilled Commander (Bronze)	Perform 50 All-Out Attacks
Special Fusion Expert (Bronze)	Use 4 or more Personas in a special fusion
Tactical Fighter (Bronze)	Exploit enemy weaknesses 100 times
The Lounge Is Closed (Bronze)	Rescue Rise Kujikawa
The Nose Doesn't Always Know (Bronze)	Experience a fusion accident
The Other Self (Bronze)	Obtain the Persona Izanagi
The Power of Truth (Silver)	Create Izanagi-no-Okami
The Reaper Becomes the Reaped (Silver)	Defeat The Reaper
The Return of the Angels (Bronze)	Rescue Nanako Dojima
The Truth In Your Hands (Gold)	Defeat Izanami
Thorough Bookkeeper (Gold)	Complete the Persona Compendium
Welcome Back (Silver)	Rescue Marie

POKEMON BLACK VERSION 2 (3DS)

UNLOCKABLES

UNLOCKABLE	HOW TO UNLOCK
License	See all Unova Pokedex
Round Charm	Catch all Unova Pokedex
Shining Charm	Catch all National Pokedex

POWER RANGERS SUPER SAMURAI (XBOX 360)

ACHIEVEMENTS

UNLOCKABLE	HOW TO UNLOCK
A Samurai in the making (10)	Create an ID Card
Armed for battle! (20)	Successfully attack Gigertox 3 times in a row during a Megazord Battle
Breaking Training Complete (40)	Complete Levels 1 through 4 in Breaking Challenge single player
Bullzooka Blast! (20)	Use the Bullzooka
Counter Victory (20)	Defeat a MegaMonster using only counterattacks.
Dayu's final song (20)	Defeat Dayu as Pink Ranger
Defuse the situation (10)	Prevent Splitface from exploding during a Ranger mission
Excellente! (20)	Perform 10 or more Excellent moves while Training
Fast, brave and lucky (20)	Successfully attack Deker 3 times in a row during a Ranger Battle
Gold Power (20)	Train with the Gold Ranger
Hold it right there, Nighlok! (10)	Defeat an enemy group that tried to mount a special attack in a Ranger mission
Megazord mobilized! (10)	Have a Megazord or MegaMonster appear during Training

A
B
C
D
E
F
G
H
I
J
K
L
M
N
O
P
Q
R
S
T
U
V
W
X
Y
Z

Megazord perfection (10)	Complete a Megazord Battle without taking damage
Mooger Training... Complete? (40)	Complete all Training Stages with the Nighlok
Now that's teamwork! (20)	Use the 5-Disc Cannon
Perceive that not seen (10)	Don't let the enemies that appeared during the power outage escape
Power Disc (10)	Defeat an enemy group that has an item in a Ranger mission
Power of the Ancestors (40)	Complete all Super Samurai achievements
Quadruple Slash? (40)	Defeat 4 or more enemies with one finishing move
Ranger Training Complete (40)	Complete all Training Stages with all Rangers
Rangers Together, Smile Forever! (20)	Take a photo with all of the Rangers
Read the enemy's moves and react (20)	Avoid Rofer's spin attack three times in a row in a Ranger mission
Samurai Break! (20)	Break more than 7 bricks at once
Samurai Chop! (20)	Perform 5 top-speed chops in Breaking Challenge
Samurai Perfection (10)	Complete a Ranger mission without taking damage
Samurai Victory (10)	Clear Game on Kids Level in Ranger Mode
Shogun Victory (40)	Clear Game on Hard Level in Ranger Mode
Smile, we are united! (20)	Take a photo with all of the Megazords
Spitacular (10)	Defeat a Spitfang with its own fireball in a Ranger Battle
Strike first, finish later (20)	Hit Serrator in a Ranger mission before taking an attack from him
Stroke of Fate (10)	Defeat Serrator
Super Samurai Mode! (40)	Become a Super Samurai
Super Samurai Victory (20)	Clear Game on Normal Level in Ranger Mode
Symbol Master (20)	Complete all the Ranger symbols
Symbol Power! (20)	Write a Samurai symbol for the first time
Tameshiwari Expert (40)	Set a Personal Record above 300 bricks
Team Spirit (20)	Defeat Splitface
The great duel (20)	Defeat Gigertox
The new Red Ranger (20)	Train with a secret Red Ranger
The ultimate duel (20)	Defeat Deker as the Red Ranger
Toxic Evader (20)	Defeat Dayu in a Ranger mission without taking one hit from her poison bullets or mist
Training just went Mega Mode! (10)	Have a Megazord or MegaMonster appear five times during Training
Two Rangers in perfect sync! (20)	Do a Synchronized Attack on a MegaMonster
Untouchable (20)	Avoid all Xandred's attacks in a Megazord Battle
VICTORY IS OURS! (20)	Defeat Master Xandred
You are a true Samurai Ranger! (40)	Collect all badges
You can do anything as a team (20)	Defeat Rofer with Red Ranger and Green Ranger (Co-op)

PRO EVOLUTION SOCCER 2013 (PLAYSTATION 3)

TROPHIES

UNLOCKABLE	HOW TO UNLOCK
Champion Manager (Silver)	Awarded for winning the League Title in any of the Top Leagues featured in [Master League].
Copa Santander Libertadores King (Silver)	Awarded for becoming a [Copa Santander Libertadores] Winner.
Copa Santander Libertadores R16 (Silver)	Awarded for making it through the Group stage in [Copa Santander Libertadores].
Copa Santander Libertadores Win (Bronze)	Awarded for defeating the COM for the first time in [Copa Santander Libertadores].
Cup Winners (Silver)	Awarded for single-handedly guiding a team to Cup glory in [Cup].
European Elite 16 (Silver)	Awarded for making it through the Group stage of the UEFA Champions League in [Master League].
First Glory: Competition (Silver)	Awarded for your first win in an [Online Competition].
First Glory: Exhibition (Bronze)	Awarded for defeating the COM for the first time in [Exhibition].
First Glory: Master League (Silver)	Awarded for your first win in [Master League].
First Win: UEFA Champions League (Bronze)	Awarded for defeating the COM for the first time in [UEFA Champions League].
Kings of Europe (Silver)	Awarded for becoming a UEFA Champions League Winner in [Master League].
League Best Eleven (Silver)	Awarded for being picked for the Team of the Season in [Become a Legend].
League Champions (Silver)	Awarded for winning the League Title in [Become a Legend].
Mr. Versatility (Silver)	Awarded for learning to play in another position in [Become a Legend].
No.1 Club (Gold)	Awarded for being named the No.1 Club in the [Master League] Club Rankings.
Online Debutant (Bronze)	Awarded for completing your debut match in [Online]. No disconnections permitted.
Pride of a Nation (Silver)	Awarded for playing in the International Cup in [Become a Legend].
Promoted (Silver)	Awarded for Winning Promotion to a Top League in [Master League].
Proud Skipper (Silver)	Awarded for being named Club Captain in [Become a Legend].
Super Star (Gold)	Awarded for winning the UEFA Best Player in Europe Award [Become a Legend].
The Debutant (Silver)	Awarded for making a professional debut in [Become a Legend].
The Multi-Talented (Silver)	Awarded for acquiring a New Skill in [Become a Legend].

The Treble Winner (Silver)	Awarded for winning the League, UEFA Champions League and League Cup in a [Master League] season.
UEFA Champions League Debut (Silver)	Awarded for making your UEFA Champions League debut in [Become a Legend].
UEFA Champions League Elite 16 (Silver)	Awarded for making it through the Group stage in [UEFA Champions League].
UEFA Champions League Winner (Silver)	Awarded for becoming a [UEFA Champions League] Winner.
Ultimate Player (Platinum)	Perfect Collection
Wheeler and Dealer (Silver)	Awarded for making your first ever signing in [Master League Online].
World Footballer of the Year (Gold)	Awarded for being named World Footballer of the Year in [Become a Legend].

PRO EVOLUTION SOCCER 2013 (XBOX 360)

ACHIEVEMENTS

UNLOCKABLE	HOW TO UNLOCK
Champion Manager (30)	Awarded for winning the League Title in any of the Top Leagues featured in [Master League].
Copa Santander Libertadores King (40)	Awarded for becoming a [Copa Santander Libertadores] Winner.
Copa Santander Libertadores R16 (20)	Awarded for making it through the Group stage in [Copa Santander Libertadores].
Copa Santander Libertadores Win (10)	Awarded for defeating the COM for the first time in [Copa Santander Libertadores].
Cup Winners (30)	Awarded for single-handedly guiding a team to Cup glory in [Cup].
European Elite 16 (40)	Awarded for making it through the Group stage of the UEFA Champions League in [Master League].
First Glory: Competition (40)	Awarded for your first win in an [Online Competition].
First Glory: Exhibition (5)	Awarded for defeating the COM for the first time in [Exhibition].
First Glory: Master League (10)	Awarded for your first win in [Master League].
First Win: UEFA Champions League (10)	Awarded for defeating the COM for the first time in [UEFA Champions League].
Kings of Europe (50)	Awarded for becoming a UEFA Champions League Winner in [Master League].
League Best Eleven (30)	Awarded for being picked for the Team of the Season in [Become a Legend].
League Champions (20)	Awarded for winning the League Title in [Become a Legend].
Mr. Versatility (20)	Awarded for learning to play in another position in [Become a Legend].
No.1 Club (90)	Awarded for being named the No.1 Club in the [Master League] Club Rankings.
Online Debutant (20)	Awarded for completing your debut match in [Online]. No disconnections permitted.

Pride of a Nation (70)	Awarded for playing in the International Cup in [Become a Legend].
Promoted (20)	Awarded for Winning Promotion to a Top League in [Master League].
Proud Skipper (50)	Awarded for being named Club Captain in [Become a Legend].
Super Star (90)	Awarded for winning the UEFA Best Player in Europe Award [Become a Legend].
The Debutant (5)	Awarded for making a professional debut in [Become a Legend].
The Multi-Talented (20)	Awarded for acquiring a New Skill in [Become a Legend].
The Treble Winner (60)	Awarded for winning the League, UEFA Champions League and League Cup in a [Master League] season.
UEFA Champions League Debut (40)	Awarded for making your UEFA Champions League debut in [Become a Legend].
UEFA Champions League Elite 16 (20)	Awarded for making it through the Group stage in [UEFA Champions League].
UEFA Champions League Winner (40)	Awarded for becoming a [UEFA Champions League] Winner.
Wheeler and Dealer (30)	Awarded for making your first ever signing in [Master League Online].
World Footballer of the Year (90)	Awarded for being named World Footballer of the Year in [Become a Legend].

RATCHET & CLANK: FULL FRONTAL ASSAULT (PLAYSTATION 3)

TROPHIES

UNLOCKABLE	HOW TO UNLOCK
A Night at the Mansion (Silver)	Get 8 transmorphed bunnies to dance on screen at once.
Back to the Basement (Gold)	Complete the campaign.
Crushed Ice (Silver)	Shatter 25 frozen enemies.
Custom Job (Bronze)	Play a custom match.
Defenseless (Gold)	Complete a level other than Zurgo's Lair of Doom without purchasing any base defenses. (Campaign)
Fear Does Not Exist... (Bronze)	Play 5 pvp matches.
Hero Academy (Bronze)	Play a ranked match.
Hoverboot Madness (Bronze)	Cross the gap leading to the Major Weapon Node in Korgon Refinery without touching the moving platforms. (Campaign)
Intergalactic Dance Party (Silver)	Get at least 1 of every enemy in the game to dance by using the Groovitron. (Any Mode)
Ironmadman (Gold)	Hoverboot 112 Miles, Run 26.2 Miles and Hoverboot Glide for 2.4 miles across all game modes.
Let's Set up Camp (Bronze)	The QForce has been re-established, now go save the Galaxy! (Campaign)
No Tank You (Silver)	Defeat a Grungarian tank before it reaches your base in any level. (Any Mode)
Over the Top (Gold)	Beat 3 or more of the Insomniac Challenge Times. (Any Campaign Levels)

A
B
C
D
E
F
G
H
I
J
K
L
M
N
O
P
Q
R
S
T
U
V
W
X
Y
Z

Peace through Ridiculous Firepower (Gold)	Land the killing blow on 10 Grungarian tanks.
QForce Master (Silver)	Unlocked for earning the rank of Master.
QForce, Activate! (Bronze)	Play Co-Op in split screen or online.
Rack 'em and Hack 'em (Silver)	Successfully trigger all bonuses on 5 hacker puzzles in a row.
Ready for Armageddon (Gold)	Upgrade all weapons to level 3. (Campaign)
Save Ammo, Smack a Fool (Gold)	Defeat 50 Grungarian Brawlers using your melee weapon.
Smorgasbord of Destruction (Bronze)	Buy one of each available turret type in any level. (Any mode)
The Collector (Platinum)	Collect all trophies.
Variety is the Spice of Life (Bronze)	Use every weapon in the game at least once.
Zurgo's Revenge (Silver)	Restore all Planetary Defense Centers and discover Zurgo's intentions. (Campaign)

RATCHET & CLANK: FULL FRONTAL ASSAULT (PLAYSTATION VITA)

TROPHIES

UNLOCKABLE	HOW TO UNLOCK
A Night at the Mansion (Silver)	Get 8 transmorphed bunnies to dance on screen at once.
Back to the Basement (Gold)	Complete the campaign.
Crushed Ice (Silver)	Shatter 25 frozen enemies.
Custom Job (Bronze)	Play a custom match.
Defenseless (Gold)	Complete a level other than Zurgo's Lair of Doom without purchasing any base defenses. (Campaign)
Fear Does Not Exist… (Bronze)	Play 5 pvp matches.
Hero Academy (Bronze)	Play a ranked match.
Hoverboot Madness (Bronze)	Cross the gap leading to the Major Weapon Node in Korgon Refinery without touching the moving platforms. (Campaign)
Intergalactic Dance Party (Silver)	Get at least 1 of every enemy in the game to dance by using the Groovitron. (Any Mode)
Ironmadman (Gold)	Hoverboot 112 Miles, Run 26.2 Miles and Hoverboot Glide for 2.4 miles across all game modes.
Let's Set up Camp (Bronze)	The QForce has been re-established, now go save the Galaxy! (Campaign)
No Tank You (Silver)	Defeat a Grungarian tank before it reaches your base in any level. (Any Mode)
Over the Top (Gold)	Beat 3 or more of the Insomniac Challenge Times. (Any Campaign Levels)
Peace through Ridiculous Firepower (Gold)	Land the killing blow on 10 Grungarian tanks.
QForce Master (Silver)	Unlocked for earning the rank of Master.
QForce, Activate! (Bronze)	Play Co-Op in split screen or online.
Rack 'em and Hack 'em (Silver)	Successfully trigger all bonuses on 5 hacker puzzles in a row.
Ready for Armageddon (Gold)	Upgrade all weapons to level 3. (Campaign)
Save Ammo, Smack a Fool (Gold)	Defeat 50 Grungarian Brawlers using your melee weapon.

Smorgasbord of Destruction (Bronze)	Buy one of each available turret type in any level. (Any mode)
The Collector (Platinum)	Collect all trophies.
Variety is the Spice of Life (Bronze)	Use every weapon in the game at least once.
Zurgo's Revenge (Silver)	Restore all Planetary Defense Centers and discover Zurgo's intentions. (Campaign)

RESIDENT EVIL 6 (PLAYSTATION 3)

TROPHIES

UNLOCKABLE	HOW TO UNLOCK
A Revolting Development (Bronze)	Complete Chapter 2 in Jake's campaign.
Ada's Demise (Bronze)	Complete Chapter 4 in Ada's campaign.
After Her! (Bronze)	Complete Chapter 3 in Chris' campaign.
B.O.W.s Are Ugly (Silver)	Defeat 100 enemies that have come out of a chrysalid.
Back in My Day (Silver)	Complete the entire game on Veteran.
Big Trouble in China (Bronze)	Complete Chapter 4 in Leon's campaign.
Bob and Weave (Bronze)	Counter an enemy's attack three times in row.
Bring the Heat (Bronze)	Take down an enemy from 50 meters away with a headshot using the thermal scope.
Buried Secrets (Bronze)	Complete Chapter 2 in Leon's campaign.
Check Out My Dogs (Bronze)	Customize your dog tags.
Counterintelligence (Bronze)	Complete Chapter 2 in Ada's campaign.
Covered in Brass (Silver)	Earn 150 different medals.
Down, Not Out (Bronze)	Defeat an enemy while dying, then recover without any help.
Duty Calls (Bronze)	Complete Chapter 5 in Chris' campaign.
Finish What You Start (Bronze)	Perform a coup de grace on ten enemies.
Flying Ace (Bronze)	Pilot the VTOL without getting a scratch on it.
Get on the Plane (Bronze)	Complete Chapter 3 in Leon's campaign.
Give a Little Push (Bronze)	Knock ten enemies off a high place.
Gone to Hell (Bronze)	Complete Chapter 1 in Leon's campaign.
Green around the Ears (Bronze)	Complete the entire game on Amateur.
Hard Choice (Bronze)	Shoot the helicopter pilot with a Magnum at point-blank range.
Heirlooms (Silver)	Collect all the serpent emblems.
High Voltage (Bronze)	Defeat ten enemies with a stun rod charge attack.
I Prefer Them Alive (Bronze)	Rescue two female survivors at the cathedral.
I Spy (Bronze)	Complete Chapter 1 in Ada's campaign.
J'avo Genocide (Bronze)	Defeat 500 J'avo.
Leave It to the Pro (Gold)	Complete the entire game on Professional.
Let's Blow This Joint (Bronze)	Complete Chapter 3 in Jake's campaign.
Lifesaver (Bronze)	Help or rescue your partner ten times.
Mad Skillz (Gold)	Max out all the skills that allow you to level up.
Money Talks (Bronze)	Complete Chapter 1 in Jake's campaign.
Normal Is Good (Silver)	Complete the entire game on Normal.
One Is Better Than None (Bronze)	Purchase one skill.
Rescue the Hostages (Bronze)	Complete Chapter 1 in Chris' campaign.

A
B
C
D
E
F
G
H
I
J
K
L
M
N
O
P
Q
R
S
T
U
V
W
X
Y
Z

RESIDENT EVIL 6 Platinum Trophy (Platinum)	Congratulations! You've overcome all your fears in RESIDENT EVIL 6!
Rising Up (Silver)	Earn a level-four title.
See You Around (Bronze)	Complete Chapter 5 in Jake's campaign.
Silent Killer (Bronze)	Use a stealth attack to take down five enemies.
Sneaking Around (Bronze)	Get through the aircraft carrier's bridge area without being noticed.
Still on the Run (Bronze)	Complete Chapter 4 in Jake's campaign.
Stuntman (Bronze)	Defeat 20 enemies with the Hydra using a quick shot.
The Longest Night (Bronze)	Complete the tutorial.
The Trouble with Women (Bronze)	Complete Chapter 5 in Leon's campaign.
There's Always Hope (Bronze)	Complete Chapter 4 in Chris' campaign.
They're ACTION Figures! (Bronze)	Collect 3 figures.
This Takes Me Back (Bronze)	Complete Chapter 3 in Ada's campaign.
Titular Achievement (Bronze)	Earn 10 different titles.
Tragedy in Europe (Bronze)	Complete Chapter 2 in Chris' campaign.
Weapons Master (Silver)	Use all the weapons in the game and kill ten enemies with each of them.
What's Next? (Bronze)	Complete Chapter 5 in Ada's campaign.
Zombie Massacre (Bronze)	Defeat 500 zombies.

UNLOCKABLES

UNLOCKABLE	HOW TO UNLOCK
Ada	Complete Ada's Campaign
Carla	Unlock all other characters costumes.
Helena	Finish Urban Chaos Map with a B rank or higher.
Piers	Finish Steel Beast Map with a B rank or higher.
Secret BSAA Soldier	Unlock all other characters and costumes.
Sherry	Finish Mining the Depths map with a B rank or higher.

RESIDENT EVIL 6 (XBOX 360)

ACHIEVEMENTS

UNLOCKABLE	HOW TO UNLOCK
A Revolting Development (15)	Complete Chapter 2 in Jake's campaign.
Ada's Demise (15)	Complete Chapter 4 in Ada's campaign.
After Her! (15)	Complete Chapter 3 in Chris' campaign.
B.O.W.s Are Ugly (30)	Defeat 100 enemies that have come out of a chrysalid.
Back in My Day (30)	Complete the entire game on Veteran.
Big Trouble in China (15)	Complete Chapter 4 in Leon's campaign.
Bob and Weave (15)	Counter an enemy's attack three times in row.
Bring the Heat (15)	Take down an enemy from 50 meters away with a headshot using the thermal scope.
Buried Secrets (15)	Complete Chapter 2 in Leon's campaign.
Check Out My Dogs (15)	Customize your dog tags.
Counterintelligence (15)	Complete Chapter 2 in Ada's campaign.
Covered in Brass (30)	Earn 150 different medals.
Down, Not Out (15)	Defeat an enemy while dying, then recover without any help.
Duty Calls (15)	Complete Chapter 5 in Chris' campaign.

Finish What You Start (15)	Perform a coup de grace on ten enemies.
Flying Ace (15)	Pilot the VTOL without getting a scratch on it.
Get on the Plane (15)	Complete Chapter 3 in Leon's campaign.
Give a Little Push (15)	Knock ten enemies off a high place.
Gone to Hell (15)	Complete Chapter 1 in Leon's campaign.
Green around the Ears (15)	Complete the entire game on Amateur.
Hard Choice (15)	Shoot the helicopter pilot with a Magnum at point-blank range.
Heirlooms (30)	Collect all the serpent emblems.
High Voltage (15)	Defeat ten enemies with a stun rod charge attack.
I Prefer Them Alive (15)	Rescue two female survivors at the cathedral.
I Spy (15)	Complete Chapter 1 in Ada's campaign.
J'avo Genocide (15)	Defeat 500 J'avo.
Leave It to the Pro (90)	Complete the entire game on Professional.
Let's Blow This Joint (15)	Complete Chapter 3 in Jake's campaign.
Lifesaver (15)	Help or rescue your partner ten times.
Mad Skillz (90)	Max out all the skills that allow you to level up.
Money Talks (15)	Complete Chapter 1 in Jake's campaign.
Normal Is Good (30)	Complete the entire game on Normal.
One Is Better Than None (15)	Purchase one skill.
Rescue the Hostages (15)	Complete Chapter 1 in Chris' campaign.
Rising Up (30)	Earn a level-four title.
See You Around (15)	Complete Chapter 5 in Jake's campaign.
Silent Killer (15)	Use a stealth attack to take down five enemies.
Sneaking Around (15)	Get through the aircraft carrier's bridge area without being noticed.
Still on the Run (15)	Complete Chapter 4 in Jake's campaign.
Stuntman (15)	Defeat 20 enemies with the Hydra using a quick shot.
The Longest Night (10)	Complete the tutorial.
The Trouble with Women (15)	Complete Chapter 5 in Leon's campaign.
There's Always Hope (15)	Complete Chapter 4 in Chris' campaign.
They're ACTION Figures! (15)	Collect 3 figures.
This Takes Me Back (15)	Complete Chapter 3 in Ada's campaign.
Titular Achievement (15)	Earn 10 different titles.
Tragedy in Europe (15)	Complete Chapter 2 in Chris' campaign.
Weapons Master (30)	Use all the weapons in the game and kill ten enemies with each of them.
What's Next? (15)	Complete Chapter 5 in Ada's campaign.
Zombie Massacre (15)	Defeat 500 zombies.

SILENT HILL: BOOK OF MEMORIES (PLAYSTATION VITA)

TROPHIES

UNLOCKABLE	HOW TO UNLOCK
Agnostic (Bronze)	Achieve the NEUTRAL ending in every Forsaken Room
Antiquarian (Silver)	Complete your Artifacts Checklist 100%
Apprentice (Bronze)	Level up to LVL 25
Architect (Silver)	Complete your Rooms Checklist 100%

Arms Dealer (Silver)	Complete your Weapons Checklist 100%
Author (Gold)	Defeat the Steel Guardian and complete the game
Beast Master (Bronze)	Defeat any Guardian without taking damage
Beat Maniac (Bronze)	Earn a 30 or greater timed hit combo
Blacksmith (Bronze)	Level up 10 different weapons
Bleeder (Bronze)	Lose more than 400% health in one Zone without dying
Blood Barrage (Bronze)	Use Blood Barrage Karma Ability to kill 5 or more enemies
Blood Beam (Bronze)	Use Blood Beam Karma Ability on 5 or more enemies at once
Blood Burn (Bronze)	Use Blood Burn Karma Ability to damage 4 different enemy types at once
Bouncer (Bronze)	Complete a Zone using only your fists (no weapons)
Brainiac (Bronze)	Complete any 5 puzzles without using the hint lever
Choice Meat (Bronze)	Defeat 25 Butchers with the Great Cleaver
Comatose (Bronze)	Reach Zone 100
Consumer (Bronze)	Make a purchase in Howard's shop
Couch Potato (Silver)	Complete your Broadcasts Checklist 100%
Creator (Bronze)	Create a character
Deep Sleeper (Bronze)	Reach Zone 50
Disorderly Conduct (Bronze)	Defeat 25 Nurses with the Steel Pipe
Emissary (Silver)	Complete Valtiel's missions in Zones 1 through 21
Executioner (Bronze)	Perform a timed execution on 10 enemies in one Zone
Fireman (Bronze)	Defeat the Fire Guardian
Hammer Time (Bronze)	Defeat 25 Bogeymen with the Bogeyman's Hammer
Hyperthymesiac (Platinum)	Earn every trophy in the game
Klutz (Bronze)	Trigger every kind of trap in the game
Librarian (Silver)	Complete your Notes Checklist 100%
Light Heal Me (Bronze)	Use Heal Me Karma Ability to restore 25% or more health
Light Heal Us (Bronze)	Use Heal Us Karma Ability to restore 50% or more health each to 3 players (multiplayer)
Light Heal You (Bronze)	Use Heal You Karma Ability to restore 50% or more health to a friend (multiplayer)
Light Napper (Bronze)	Complete Zone 1
Lumberjack (Bronze)	Defeat the Wood Guardian
Master (Bronze)	Level up to LVL 50
Medic (Bronze)	Drop a health pack after a friend requests one (multiplayer)
Miner (Bronze)	Defeat the Earth Guardian
Moneybags (Bronze)	Spend over 250,000 MR in Howard's shop
Ninja (Bronze)	Complete a Zone without turning on your flashlight
Novice (Bronze)	Level up to LVL 2
Phlebotomist (Bronze)	Defeat the Blood Guardian
Plumber (Bronze)	Defeat the Water Guardian
Power Breaker (Bronze)	Use Weapon Breaker Power Move with a weapon that's about to shatter
Power Charger (Bronze)	Use Charge Tackle Power Move to knock one enemy into another

Power Flasher (Bronze)	Use Flash Burst Power Move to kill 5 or more stunned enemies in a row
Power Inverter (Bronze)	Use Karma Flip Power Move to flip 8 or more enemies at once
Power Repeller (Bronze)	Use Push Force Power Move to knock 8 or more enemies back at once
Power Savior (Bronze)	Use Health Siphon Power Move to bring a dying friend back to life (multiplayer)
Power Switcher (Bronze)	Use 360 Attack Power Move to strike 4 or more enemies at once
Pyramid Scheme (Bronze)	Defeat 25 Pyramid Heads with the Great Knife
Saint (Bronze)	Achieve the LIGHT ending in every Forsaken Room
Sandman (Bronze)	Defeat the Light Guardian
Sinner (Bronze)	Achieve the BLOOD ending in every Forsaken Room
Storyteller (Silver)	Achieve all 6 of the game's endings
Sugar High (Bronze)	Complete a Zone without stopping for more than 30 seconds total
Tommfoolery (Bronze)	Perform every in-game VO clip for one character
Veterinarian (Silver)	Complete your Bestiary Checklist 100%
Wingman (Bronze)	Defeat any Guardian with all four players still alive (multiplayer)

UNLOCKABLES

UNLOCKABLE	HOW TO UNLOCK
Robbie Dolls and Weapon	At the main menu in your character's bedroom, enter Up, Up, Down, Down, Left, Right, Left, Right, Square, Triangle, Start.

SLEEPING DOGS (PLAYSTATION 3)

TROPHIES

UNLOCKABLE	HOW TO UNLOCK
A Big Betrayal (Silver)	Complete Dockyard Heist.
A Slap in the Face (Bronze)	Kill someone with a fish.
Auto Enthusiast (Bronze)	Purchase all vehicles.
Big Smiles All Around (Silver)	Complete Big Smile Lee.
Bounty Hunter (Bronze)	Complete all of Roland's Jobs.
Case Closed (Silver)	Complete all cases.
Central Scavenger (Bronze)	Unlock every lockbox in Central.
Chief Inspector (Gold)	Complete 100% of all missions, cases, favors, events, jobs and races.
Detective (Silver)	Complete 50% of all missions, cases, favors, events, jobs and races.
Environmentalist (Bronze)	Perform 5 unique environmental kills.
Event Driven (Bronze)	Complete half of the open world events.
Event Planner (Bronze)	Complete all of the open world Events.
Fashion Statement (Bronze)	Change all your clothes in your wardrobe or a clothing store.
Fashion Victim (Bronze)	Purchase all clothing.
Foodie (Bronze)	Try 10 different foods or drinks.
Gadgetman (Bronze)	Pick a lock, plant a bug, trace a phone, crack a safe, and take over a spy camera.
Gaining Face (Bronze)	Achieve Face Level 5.
Gold Rush (Bronze)	Achieve 5 Gold Stat Awards.
Golden Touch (Silver)	Achieve 15 Gold Stat Awards.

Great Face (Bronze)	Achieve Face Level 10.
Gun Nut (Bronze)	Use 10 different firearms to defeat enemies.
Hong Kong Legend (Platinum)	Earn all the Sleeping Dogs™ trophies to unlock this platinum trophy.
Hong Kong Super Hacker (Bronze)	Hack every Security Camera in the game.
In With the Gang (Bronze)	Complete Night Market Chase.
Infowlable (Bronze)	Win 50,000 on a single cockfight.
Karaoke Superstar (Bronze)	Achieving 90% and above for all songs at the Karaoke Bars in HK.
Kleptomaniac (Bronze)	Hijack 5 trucks and collect their cargo.
Man Around Town (Bronze)	Visit Aberdeen, Central, Kennedy Town and North Point.
Martial Law (Bronze)	Defeat all 4 Martial Arts Clubs
Minor Face (Bronze)	Achieve Face Level 2.
Mr. Nice Guy (Silver)	Complete all Favors.
North Point Scavenger (Bronze)	Unlock every lockbox in North Point.
Officer (Bronze)	Complete 25% of all missions, cases, favors, events, jobs and races.
Pure Gold (Gold)	Achieve 30 Gold Stat Awards.
Rookie (Bronze)	Complete 10% of all missions, cases, favors, events, jobs and races.
Safe Driver (Bronze)	Cruise for 2 minutes straight without damaging your car.
Sharpshooter (Bronze)	Shoot out a cop's tires while fleeing in a police chase.
Slight Silver (Bronze)	Achieve 5 Silver Stat Awards.
Solid Silver (Silver)	Achieve 30 Silver Stat Awards.
Spiritual Healing (Bronze)	Pray at all of the Health Shrines.
Strike Gold (Bronze)	Achieve 1 Gold Stat Award.
Stuntman (Bronze)	Successfully perform an action hijack.
Substantial Silver (Bronze)	Achieve 15 Silver Stat Awards.
Super Cop (Bronze)	Unlock ten Cop Upgrades.
Take A Bite Out Of Crime (Bronze)	Complete a Case.
That'll Show 'em (Bronze)	Complete Payback.
Tourist (Bronze)	Win a bet on a cockfight.
Ultimate Fighter (Bronze)	Unlock ten Triad Upgrades.
Wei of the Road (Bronze)	Complete all Street Races.
West End Scavenger (Bronze)	Unlock every lockbox in Kennedy Town and Aberdeen.
Whatever's Handy (Bronze)	Use 10 different melee weapons to defeat enemies.

SLEEPING DOGS (XBOX 360)

ACHIEVEMENTS

UNLOCKABLE	HOW TO UNLOCK
A Big Betrayal (35)	Complete Dockyard Heist.
A Slap in the Face (10)	Kill someone with a fish.
Auto Enthusiast (10)	Purchase all vehicles.
Big Smiles All Around (50)	Complete Big Smile Lee.
Bounty Hunter (20)	Complete all of Roland's Jobs.
Case Closed (30)	Complete all cases.

Central Scavenger (20)	Unlock every lockbox in Central.
Chief Inspector (75)	Complete 100% of all missions, cases, favors, events, jobs and races.
Detective (35)	Complete 50% of all missions, cases, favors, events, jobs and races.
Environmentalist (15)	Perform 5 unique environmental kills.
Event Driven (20)	Complete half of the open world events.
Event Planner (15)	Complete all of the open world Events.
Fashion Statement (10)	Change all your clothes in your wardrobe or a clothing store.
Fashion Victim (15)	Purchase all clothing.
Foodie (10)	Try 10 different foods or drinks.
Gadgetman (20)	Pick a lock, plant a bug, trace a phone, crack a safe, and take over a spy camera.
Gaining Face (25)	Achieve Face Level 5.
Gold Rush (10)	Achieve 5 Gold Stat Awards.
Golden Touch (30)	Achieve 15 Gold Stat Awards.
Great Face (50)	Achieve Face Level 10.
Gun Nut (15)	Use 10 different firearms to defeat enemies.
Hong Kong Super Hacker (15)	Hack every Security Camera in the game.
In With the Gang (5)	Complete Night Market Chase.
Infowlable (15)	Win 50,000 on a single cockfight.
Karaoke Superstar (10)	Achieving 90% and above for all songs at the Karaoke Bars in HK.
Kleptomaniac (15)	Hijack 5 trucks and collect their cargo.
Man Around Town (20)	Visit Aberdeen, Central, Kennedy Town and North Point.
Martial Law (15)	Defeat all 4 Martial Arts Clubs
Minor Face (5)	Achieve Face Level 2.
Mr. Nice Guy (30)	Complete all Favors.
North Point Scavenger (20)	Unlock every lockbox in North Point.
Officer (15)	Complete 25% of all missions, cases, favors, events, jobs and races.
Pure Gold (60)	Achieve 30 Gold Stat Awards.
Rookie (10)	Complete 10% of all missions, cases, favors, events, jobs and races.
Safe Driver (20)	Cruise for 2 minutes straight without damaging your car.
Sharpshooter (25)	Shoot out a cop's tires while fleeing in a police chase.
Slight Silver (5)	Achieve 5 Silver Stat Awards.
Solid Silver (35)	Achieve 30 Silver Stat Awards.
Spiritual Healing (15)	Pray at all of the Health Shrines.
Strike Gold (5)	Achieve 1 Gold Stat Award.
Stuntman (5)	Successfully perform an action hijack.
Substantial Silver (15)	Achieve 15 Silver Stat Awards.
Super Cop (15)	Unlock ten Cop Upgrades.
Take A Bite Out Of Crime (10)	Complete a Case.
That'll Show 'em (20)	Complete Payback.
Tourist (10)	Win a bet on a cockfight.
Ultimate Fighter (15)	Unlock ten Triad Upgrades.

NEW!

A
B
C
D
E
F
G
H
I
J
K
L
M
N
O
P
Q
R
S
T
U
V
W
X
Y
Z

Wei of the Road (15)	Complete all Street Races.
West End Scavenger (20)	Unlock every lockbox in Kennedy Town and Aberdeen.
Whatever's Handy (15)	Use 10 different melee weapons to defeat enemies.

STREET FIGHTER X TEKKEN (PLAYSTATION VITA)

TROPHIES

UNLOCKABLE	HOW TO UNLOCK
A Glimmering Light (Bronze)	Activate your Assist Gems 30 times.
A Perfect Victory! (Bronze)	Win a round without getting hit 30 times.
A Splendid Conclusion (Bronze)	Finish a round with a Super Art 30 times.
A Very Special Gift (Bronze)	Connect with 50 Special Moves.
After The Dust Has Settled (Bronze)	Clear Arcade mode on Medium difficulty or higher.
All Star (Bronze)	Use all characters.
All Too Easy (Bronze)	Win by K.O. using Battle Tap.
An Unknown Power (Bronze)	Activate Pandora 50 times.
Any Time, Any Place! (Bronze)	Use Arcade Fight Request 10 times.
Anything Goes (Bronze)	Activate Cross Assault 50 times.
Doused In My Color! (Bronze)	Customize a character's color.
Evangelist Of The "X" (Bronze)	Have your replay downloaded 3 times in My Channel's Broadcast Mode.
Forge Your Own Path (Bronze)	Win 10 matches online.
Fruits of Labor (Bronze)	Go into Training mode 3 times.
Head Of The Dojo (Bronze)	Create a lobby in Endless Battle.
Here's My Shoutout (Bronze)	Customize your player comment.
I'm Just Getting Started! (Bronze)	Swap teams in Arcade Mode.
It's Just For Research! (Bronze)	Access the Store.
Just The Beginning (Bronze)	Clear one trial in Trial mode.
Learn The Fundamentals (Bronze)	Win 5 matches online.
Let's Heat Things Up! (Bronze)	Activate your Boost Gems 30 times.
Love Is Blind (Bronze)	Use a character in battle over 30 times.
Maelstrom Of Combos (Bronze)	Connect with 30 Quick Combos.
Magnanimity (Bronze)	Give 5 character color gifts.
Maturity Through Discipline (Bronze)	Clear all of the lessons in the Tutorial.
Mission Specialist (Bronze)	Clear all of the missions in Mission mode.
My Big First Step (Bronze)	Clear one lesson in the Tutorial.
Observer (Bronze)	View 3 replays in the Replay Channel.
On the Cutting Edge (Bronze)	Fight using Casual Style.
One Down! (Bronze)	Win in a Ranked Match.
Photo Op (Bronze)	Take a photo in the AR Gallery.
Power Consumes All (Bronze)	Finish a round with Pandora 30 times.
Proof Of Your Victory (Silver)	Get to C rank for the first time in Ranked Match.
Signs of Friendship (Bronze)	Fight in Ad Hoc Mode.
Stories to Tell (Silver)	Unlock every item in the Graphic Gallery.
Sturm und Drang (Bronze)	Finish a round with Cross Assault 30 times.
Supersonic (Bronze)	Play the Sound Gallery 3 times.
Ten Down... (Bronze)	Win 10 consecutive Burst Kumite battles.
The Battle Never Ends (Bronze)	Win a match in Endless Battle.

The Chosen Path (Silver)	Win 30 consecutive Burst Kumite battles.
The Cross Revolution (Bronze)	Finish a round with a Cross Art 30 times.
The Crossroads of Tragedy (Bronze)	Fight 30 matches online.
The Endless Road (Bronze)	Fight 100 matches online.
The Excellence of Execution (Bronze)	Clear 100 trials in Trial mode.
The First Mission (Bronze)	Clear one mission in Mission mode.
The Harsh Road (Bronze)	Fight 50 matches online.
The Root Of Chaos (Silver)	Defeat all of the bosses in Arcade mode on the hardest difficulty.
The Stones Guide Me (Bronze)	Customize a Gem Unit.
The Warrior's Road (Bronze)	Fight 10 matches online.
This Is How I Roll (Bronze)	Customize your player Title.
Time For Some Fireworks! (Bronze)	Connect with 50 Launchers.
Title Idol (Silver)	Obtain 300 Titles.
To the Victor Go the Spoils (Bronze)	Obtain a K.O. Monument.
To The Victor... (Silver)	Raise your battle class rank for the first time in Ranked Match.
Trail Of Ruined Dreams (Bronze)	Defeat 5 rival teams in Arcade mode on Medium difficulty or higher.
Transcend All You Know (Bronze)	Win 50 matches online.
Trial Expert (Bronze)	Clear ten trials in Trial mode.
Two Minds, Fighting As One (Bronze)	Connect with 50 Cross Arts.
Your Legend Will Never Die (Gold)	Win 100 matches online.
Zenith (Platinum)	Unlock all Trophies.

TEKKEN TAG TOURNAMENT 2 (PLAYSTATION 3)

TROPHIES

UNLOCKABLE	HOW TO UNLOCK
All Hail, Tekken Incarnate! (Platinum)	You earned everything.
Avoid Flying Heads (Bronze)	You escaped from Alisa's Spam Bomb move.
Bad Date (Bronze)	You dropped a damsel into the pool in the Eternal Paradise stage.
Bazillionaire (Silver)	You earned over 10,000,000G total.
Be Still My Iron Heart (Bronze)	You won a ranked match in Online Mode.
Behold the Tekken Lord! (Gold)	You became Tekken Lord in Offline Mode.
Below the Belt (Bronze)	You pulled off 3 low parries.
Combot, Annihilate! (Bronze)	You cleared Stage 4 in Fight Lab.
Combot, Engage! (Bronze)	You cleared Stage 3 in Fight Lab.
Combot, Move Out! (Bronze)	You cleared Stage 2 in Fight Lab.
Combot, On Standby! (Bronze)	You cleared Stage 1 in Fight Lab.
Combot, Return to Base! (Silver)	You cleared Stage 5 in Fight Lab.
Dance to Your Own Beat (Bronze)	You changed the background music using TEKKEN TUNES.
Dish Best Served Cold (Bronze)	You pulled off 3 reversals.
Doused But Not Out (Bronze)	Your upper body got wet in the Fallen Garden stage.
Enter the Vanquisher! (Silver)	You earned Vanquisher in Offline Mode.
Escape Artist (Bronze)	You successfully completed 10 throw escapes.

NEW!

A B C D E F G H I J K L M N O P Q R S T U V W X Y Z

Fickle Friend (Silver)	You switched places with your partner 765 times.
Flying Butt-Kicker (Bronze)	You pulled off 3 10 hit combos.
Fortunate Fighter (Silver)	You earned 3 Lucky Boxes.
Geronimooo! (Bronze)	You broke a balcony.
GREAT Gladiator (Silver)	You won a GREAT battle.
Impressive Moves (Silver)	You pulled off a GREAT combo.
Insane Juggler (Silver)	You dealt more than 62 damage in a midair combo.
Iron Heartache (Bronze)	You fought 3 times in Online Mode.
Lead Coach (Bronze)	You dealt a total of 1000 damage in Practice in Offline Mode.
Master of the Direct Tag Assault (Bronze)	You pulled off 3 Direct Tag Assaults.
Master of the Tag Assault (Bronze)	You pulled off 10 Tag Assaults.
Master of the Tag Combo (Bronze)	You pulled off 10 Tag Combos.
Master of the Tag Throw (Bronze)	You pulled off 10 Tag Throws.
Movie Buff (Silver)	You unlocked 40 characters' ending movies.
Oodles of Ukemi (Bronze)	You pulled off 3 ukemi.
PERFECT Player (Bronze)	You won a PERFECT battle.
Preeminent Partner (Bronze)	You cleared an Offline Mode arcade battle with a partner.
Proof of Your Existence (Silver)	You won 10 consecutive battles in Survival in Offline Mode.
Renovation Time (Bronze)	You broke a wall.
Secret Weapon (Bronze)	You used an item move.
Solo Warrior (Bronze)	You cleared an Offline Mode arcade battle solo.
Stick It to 'Em (Bronze)	You pulled off 10 homing attacks.
Super Combot DX Complete (Gold)	You unlocked all the content in Fight Lab.
Super-Speed Fists (Bronze)	You cleared Offline Mode Time Attack within 20 minutes.
Tekken Black Belt (Bronze)	You earned 1st dan in Online Mode.
Tenacious Fighter (Bronze)	You won 3 team battles in Offline Mode.
The Best of Friends (Silver)	You pulled off 3 partner-specific Tag Throws.
The Original Bouncer (Bronze)	You pulled off 10 bound combos.
Touch-Up Artist (Bronze)	You customized a character.
True Friendship (Bronze)	You pulled off 3 Tag Crashes.
Tug at My Iron Heart Strings (Bronze)	You won a player match in Online Mode.
Watch Your Step! (Bronze)	You broke a floor.
Who You Gonna Call? (Bronze)	You defeated 30 ghosts.

TEKKEN TAG TOURNAMENT 2 (XBOX 360)

ACHIEVEMENTS

UNLOCKABLE	HOW TO UNLOCK
All Hail, Tekken Incarnate! (10)	You earned everything.
Avoid Flying Heads (15) move.	You escaped from Alisa's Spam Bomb
Bad Date (15) Eternal Paradise stage.	You dropped a damsel into the pool in the

Bazillionaire (30)	You earned over 10,000,000G total.
Be Still My Iron Heart (15)	You won a ranked match in Online Mode.
Behold the Tekken Lord! (45)	You became Tekken Lord in Offline Mode.
Below the Belt (15)	You pulled off 3 low parries.
Combot, Annihilate! (15)	You cleared Stage 4 in Fight Lab.
Combot, Engage! (15)	You cleared Stage 3 in Fight Lab.
Combot, Move Out! (15)	You cleared Stage 2 in Fight Lab.
Combot, On Standby! (15)	You cleared Stage 1 in Fight Lab.
Combot, Return to Base! (30)	You cleared Stage 5 in Fight Lab.
Dance to Your Own Beat (15)	You changed the background music using TEKKEN TUNES.
Dish Best Served Cold (15)	You pulled off 3 reversals.
Doused But Not Out (15)	Your upper body got wet in the Fallen Garden stage.
Enter the Vanquisher! (30)	You earned Vanquisher in Offline Mode.
Escape Artist (15)	You successfully completed 10 throw escapes.
Fickle Friend (30)	You switched places with your partner 765 times.
Flying Butt-Kicker (15)	You pulled off 3 10 hit combos.
Fortunate Fighter (30)	You earned 3 Lucky Boxes.
Geronimooo! (15)	You broke a balcony.
GREAT Gladiator (30)	You won a GREAT battle.
Impressive Moves (30)	You pulled off a GREAT combo.
Insane Juggler (30)	You dealt more than 62 damage in a midair combo.
Iron Heartache (15)	You fought 3 times in Online Mode.
Lead Coach (20)	You dealt a total of 1000 damage in Practice in Offline Mode.
Master of the Direct Tag Assault (20)	You pulled off 3 Direct Tag Assaults.
Master of the Tag Assault (20)	You pulled off 10 Tag Assaults.
Master of the Tag Combo (20)	You pulled off 10 Tag Combos.
Master of the Tag Throw (15)	You pulled off 10 Tag Throws.
Movie Buff (30)	You unlocked 40 characters' ending movies.
Oodles of Ukemi (15)	You pulled off 3 ukemi.
PERFECT Player (20)	You won a PERFECT battle.
Preeminent Partner (15)	You cleared an Offline Mode arcade battle with a partner.
Proof of Your Existence (30)	You won 10 consecutive battles in Survival in Offline Mode.
Renovation Time (15)	You broke a wall.
Secret Weapon (15)	You used an item move.
Solo Warrior (15)	You cleared an Offline Mode arcade battle solo.
Stick It to 'Em (15)	You pulled off 10 homing attacks.
Super Combot DX Complete (45)	You unlocked all the content in Fight Lab.
Super-Speed Fists (15)	You cleared Offline Mode Time Attack within 20 minutes.
Tekken Black Belt (15)	You earned 1st dan in Online Mode.
Tenacious Fighter (15)	You won 3 team battles in Offline Mode.

NEW!

A
B
C
D
E
F
G
H
I
J
K
L
M
N
O
P
Q
R
S
T
U
V
W
X
Y
Z

The Best of Friends (30)	You pulled off 3 partner-specific Tag Throws.
The Original Bouncer (15)	You pulled off 10 bound combos.
Touch-Up Artist (15)	You customized a character.
True Friendship (15)	You pulled off 3 Tag Crashes.
Tug at My Iron Heart Strings (15)	You won a player match in Online Mode.
Watch Your Step! (15)	You broke a floor.
Who You Gonna Call? (20)	You defeated 30 ghosts.

THE TESTAMENT OF SHERLOCK HOLMES (PLAYSTATION 3)

TROPHIES

UNLOCKABLE	HOW TO UNLOCK
A Fine Romance (Silver)	The most winning woman I ever knew was hanged for poisoning. But I digress. You found the letter!
A Very Fine Loafer (Bronze)	There are in you the makings of a very fine loafer.
Anarchy in the UK (Bronze)	There are always some lunatics about. It would be a dull world without them.
Attention to Detail (Silver)	You have a turn for both observation and deduction!
Blackmailer (Bronze)	Your morals don't improve!
Bomb Defuser (Silver)	You never can resist a touch of the dramatic!
Breaking the Law (Silver)	I have a great deal of respect for your judgement. You opened the safe room!
Deduction Apprentice (Bronze)	To a great mind, nothing is little. You completed the first deduction board.
Desperately Seeking Sherlock (Bronze)	I would have made an actor —and a rare one. You deduced my disguise.
Elementary (Silver)	It seems you share my love of all that is bizarre. You recovered the Samoan necklace, well done!
Finders Key-pers (Silver)	You handled that with less than your usual —that is to say, you handled it well. You found the key!
First-Class Chemist (Bronze)	It was the bisulphate of baryta!
Freedom of the Press (Bronze)	The Press is a most valuable institution —if you only know how to use it!
Garden Gumshoe (Bronze)	With your usual happy mixture of cunning and audacity, you recovered all that was stolen!
Hidden Message (Bronze)	See the value of imagination!
Law of Nature (Silver)	One's ideas must be as broad as Nature if they are to interpret Nature. Well done!
Lazarus (Gold)	An isolated phenomenon? A brain without a heart? I trust that you did not judge me so quickly!
Lockpicker (Bronze)	I can see that you are a force to be reckoned with.
Master of Deduction (Silver)	Genius is an infinite capacity for taking pains. Bravo!
Melomania (Silver)	You are a conductor of light! You discovered the hidden code.
Minesweeper (Gold)	Your nerves are fairly proof!

Number Lover (Silver)	With all respect for your natural acumen, you handled that very well. You opened the safe box!
Pea-Souper (Bronze)	Moonshine is a brighter thing than fog, but this is a pea-souper! You asked for Help a great deal.
Prison Break (Bronze)	A trusty comrade is always of use. Well done. And yet one got away...
Safecracker (Bronze)	You would make a highly efficient criminal.
Sherlock Holmes' will (Platinum)	Strength and perseverance to the end
Sleuth-Hound (Gold)	The beautiful, faithful nature of dogs!
Stage Manager (Silver)	A simple trick, but exceedingly effective!
The Brain (Gold)	I never get your limits... there are unexplored possibilities about you.
The Gambler (Bronze)	You have never failed to play the game!
The Holmesian (Silver)	I was sure that I might rely on you. You found all the items from my past adventures.
The Legacy (Gold)	I must compliment you exceedingly upon the zeal and the intelligence which you have shown.
Watson Alone (Bronze)	The one fixed point in a changing age.

THE TESTAMENT OF SHERLOCK HOLMES (XBOX 360)

ACHIEVEMENTS

UNLOCKABLE	HOW TO UNLOCK
A Fine Romance (20)	The most winning woman I ever knew was hanged for poisoning. But I digress. You found the letter!
A Very Fine Loafer (20)	There are in you the makings of a very fine loafer.
Anarchy in the UK (20)	There are always some lunatics about. It would be a dull world without them.
Attention to Detail (30)	You have a turn for both observation and deduction!
Blackmailer (20)	Your morals don't improve!
Bomb Defuser (20)	You never can resist a touch of the dramatic!
Breaking the Law (30)	I have a great deal of respect for your judgement. You opened the safe room!
Deduction Apprentice (20)	To a great mind, nothing is little. You completed the first deduction board.
Desperately Seeking Sherlock (20)	I would have made an actor – and a rare one. You deduced my disguise.
Elementary (30)	It seems you share my love of all that is bizarre. You recovered the Samoan necklace, well done!
Finders Key-pers (30)	You handled that with less than your usual – that is to say, you handled it well. You found the key!
First-Class Chemist (20)	It was the bisulphate of baryta!
Freedom of the Press (20)	The Press is a most valuable institution – if you only know how to use it!
Garden Gumshoe (20)	With your usual happy mixture of cunning and audacity, you recovered all that was stolen!
Hidden Message (20)	See the value of imagination!

Law of Nature (30)	One's ideas must be as broad as Nature if they are to interpret Nature. Well done!
Lazarus (50)	An isolated phenomenon? A brain without a heart? I trust that you did not judge me so quickly!
Lockpicker (20)	I can see that you are a force to be reckoned with.
Master of Deduction (30)	Genius is an infinite capacity for taking pains. Bravo!
Melomania (20)	You are a conductor of light! You discovered the hidden code.
Minesweeper (50)	Your nerves are fairly proof!
Number Lover (20)	With all respect for your natural acumen, you handled that very well. You opened the safe box!
Pea-Souper (10)	Moonshine is a brighter thing than fog, but this is a pea-souper! You asked for Help a great deal.
Prison Break (20)	A trusty comrade is always of use. Well done. And yet one got away...
Safecracker (20)	You would make a highly efficient criminal.
Sleuth-Hound (50)	The beautiful, faithful nature of dogs!
Stage Manager (20)	A simple trick, but exceedingly effective!
The Brain (100)	I never get your limits... there are unexplored possibilities about you.
The Gambler (20)	You have never failed to play the game!
The Holmesian (30)	I was sure that I might rely on you. You found all the items from my past adventures.
The Legacy (150)	I must compliment you exceedingly upon the zeal and the intelligence which you have shown.
Watson Alone (20)	The one fixed point in a changing age.

UNLOCKABLES

UNLOCKABLE	HOW TO UNLOCK
Sherlock Holmes Classic Hat	For realising that not all is lost when faced with innumerable dead-ends: this charming Top Hat.
Sherlock Holmes T-Shirt	Successfully completing the game will earn you this T-Shirt, which is a must for any wardrobe.

TRANSFORMERS: FALL OF CYBERTRON (PLAYSTATION 3)

TROPHIES

UNLOCKABLE	HOW TO UNLOCK
All Hail You! (Gold)	Complete Campaign - Hard
Ballistic Energon Goodie (Bronze)	Return five heads at once in a headhunter game during a public Multiplayer match
Beachcomber (Bronze)	Collect all blueprints
Belly of the Beast (Bronze)	Complete Chapter VII
Car Wash of Doom (Bronze)	Chapter VI: Destroy all of the homing mines chasing Blast Off before they self destruct
Carnage in C-Major (Bronze)	Chapter III: Take out a cluster of five Decepticons using Metroplex's Air Strike
Cassetticon Audiophile (Silver)	Collect all audio logs
Chop Shop (Silver)	Purchase all weapons and perks

Club Con! (Bronze)	Chapter VII: Ram a jet (on the ground or in the air)
Combaticons Combine! (Bronze)	Complete Chapter VIII
Cut and Run (Bronze)	Complete Chapter V
Death from Above (Bronze)	Complete Chapter VI
Defend the Ark (Bronze)	Complete Chapter II
Eye of the Storm (Bronze)	Complete Chapter IV
Full Throttle Scramble Power! (Bronze)	Earn MVP in any game mode during a public Multiplayer match
Fusilateral Quintrocombiner (Bronze)	Chapter VIII: Melee an enemy through the goal post
Grimlock Smash (Bronze)	Complete Chapter XII
Headmaster! (Bronze)	Reach max level in a single class
Heavy Metal War (Bronze)	Kill 6 different opposing players in a TDM game during a public Multiplayer match
I, Robot Master (Bronze)	Chapter IX: Destroy all images of Starscream and his Statues
Internal Affairs! (Bronze)	Chapter XI: Hack all of the security terminals before the Decepticons can activate them
Invisibility Spray (Bronze)	Chapter IV: Sneak through the Trash Compactor Facility undetected
King of the Scrap Heap (Gold)	Reach max level in all four classes
Maccadams Old Oil House (Bronze)	Complete wave 15 in Escalation (DownFall)
Master Builder (Silver)	Fully upgrade all weapons
Megatron Returns (Bronze)	Complete Chapter IX
Metroplex Heeds the Call (Bronze)	Complete Chapter III
Monacus Spender (Bronze)	Spend 250,000 Energon in the Teletraan 1 store
Moonbase One (Bronze)	Personally capture all 3 nodes in a conquest game during a public Multiplayer match
More Than Meets the Eye (Silver)	Complete Campaign - Normal
Octopunch Scavenger (Bronze)	Open fifteen Armory Recreators in Campaign or Escalation
Reconfiguration Matrix (Bronze)	Create a custom character in Multiplayer
Reconstructor (Bronze)	Fully upgrade one weapon
Robotopossum (Bronze)	Complete wave 15 in Escalation (Ignition)
Rust Marks (Bronze)	Complete wave 15 in Escalation (Ancients)
Slap the Grimlock (Bronze)	Chapter XII: Kill a Leaper in the air with an explosive barrel
Space Pirates! (Bronze)	Complete wave 15 in Escalation (Oblivion)
Starscream's Betrayal (Bronze)	Complete Chapter XI
Target Master 2.0 (Bronze)	Chapter V: Shoot a Sniper out of the air with a scoped weapon
Teletraan 1 Regular (Bronze)	Rate all weapons, weapon upgrades, and equipment
The Battle is Far From Over! (Bronze)	Complete Campaign - Easy
The Exodus (Bronze)	Complete Chapter I
The Final Countdown (Bronze)	Complete Chapter X
The Harder They Die (Bronze)	Chapter X: Kill five Autobots with a single hover slam attack

The Last Stand (Bronze)	Chapter II: Save two Autobots when Optimus is downed by the first Leaper
Ultimate Menasor (Bronze)	Capture three flags in a single CTF game during a public Multiplayer match
Ultra Power Master (Silver)	Spend 100,000 credits in Escalation
Vector Sigma Victory (Platinum)	Unlock All Trophies
What Prime Directives? (Silver)	Unlock Prime Mode

TRANSFORMERS: FALL OF CYBERTRON (XBOX 360)

ACHIEVEMENTS

UNLOCKABLE	HOW TO UNLOCK
All Hail You! (100)	Complete Campaign - Hard
Ballistic Energon Goodie (15)	Return five heads at once in a headhunter game during a public Multiplayer match
Beachcomber (25)	Collect all blueprints
Belly of the Beast (10)	Complete Chapter VII
Car Wash of Doom (15)	Chapter VI: Destroy all of the homing mines chasing Blast Off before they self destruct
Carnage in C-Major (15)	Chapter III: Take out a cluster of five Decepticons using Metroplex's Air Strike
Cassetticon Audiophile (25)	Collect all audio logs
Chop Shop (50)	Purchase all weapons and perks
Club Con! (15)	Chapter VII: Ram a jet (on the ground or in the air)
Combaticons Combine! (10)	Complete Chapter VIII
Cut and Run (10)	Complete Chapter V
Death from Above (10)	Complete Chapter VI
Defend the Ark (10)	Complete Chapter II
Eye of the Storm (10)	Complete Chapter IV
Full Throttle Scramble Power! (15)	Earn MVP in any game mode during a public Multiplayer match
Fusilateral Quintrocombiner (15)	Chapter VIII: Melee an enemy through the goal post
Grimlock Smash (10)	Complete Chapter XII
Headmaster! (25)	Reach max level in a single class
Heavy Metal War (15)	Kill 6 different opposing players in a TDM game during a public Multiplayer match
I, Robot Master (15)	Chapter IX: Destroy all images of Starscream and his Statues
Internal Affairs! (15)	Chapter XI: Hack all of the security terminals before the Decepticons can activate them
Invisibility Spray (15)	Chapter IV: Sneak through the Trash Compactor Facility undetected
King of the Scrap Heap (100)	Reach max level in all four classes
Maccadams Old Oil House (15)	Complete wave 15 in Escalation (DownFall)
Master Builder (25)	Fully upgrade all weapons
Megatron Returns (10)	Complete Chapter IX
Metroplex Heeds the Call (10)	Complete Chapter III
Monacus Spender (25)	Spend 250,000 Energon in the Teletraan 1 store

Moonbase One (15)	Personally capture all 3 nodes in a conquest game during a public Multiplayer match
More Than Meets the Eye (50)	Complete Campaign - Normal
Octopunch Scavenger (15)	Open fifteen Armory Recreators in Campaign or Escalation
Reconfiguration Matrix (10)	Create a custom character in Multiplayer
Reconstructor (15)	Fully upgrade one weapon
Robotopossum (15)	Complete wave 15 in Escalation (Ignition)
Rust Marks (15)	Complete wave 15 in Escalation (Ancients)
Slap the Grimlock (15)	Chapter XII: Kill a Leaper in the air with an explosive barrel
Space Pirates! (15)	Complete wave 15 in Escalation (Oblivion)
Starscream's Betrayal (10)	Complete Chapter XI
Target Master 2.0 (15)	Chapter V: Shoot a Sniper out of the air with a scoped weapon
Teletraan 1 Regular (10)	Rate all weapons, weapon upgrades, and equipment
The Battle is Far From Over! (25)	Complete Campaign - Easy
The Exodus (10)	Complete Chapter I
The Final Countdown (10)	Complete Chapter X
The Harder They Die (15)	Chapter X: Kill five Autobots with a single hover slam attack
The Last Stand (15)	Chapter II: Save two Autobots when Optimus is downed by the first Leaper
Till All Are One - (Megatron) (15)	Complete Chapter XIII as Megatron Estimated
Till All Are One - (Optimus) (15)	Complete Chapter XIII as Optimus Prime
Ultimate Menasor (15)	Capture three flags in a single CTF game during a public Multiplayer match
Ultra Power Master (25)	Spend 100,000 credits in Escalation
What Prime Directives? (25)	Unlock Prime Mode

UNLOCKABLES

UNLOCKABLE	HOW TO UNLOCK
High Moon T-Shirt Avatar Award	Complete Chapter I.
Megatron Helmet Avatar Award	Complete Chapter XIII as Megatron.
Optimus Prime Helmet Avatar Award	Complete Chapter XIII as Optimus.

WWE '13 (PLAYSTATION 3)

TROPHIES

UNLOCKABLE	HOW TO UNLOCK
A fresh beginning (Bronze)	Play in an Online match (Player match/Ranked match)
A legend begins (Bronze)	Win at least one match on Hard difficulty or higher (single player).
A man who wastes no opportunity (Silver)	Cash in a Money in the Bank and win using a Custom Superstar in WWE Universe (single player).
A once in a lifetime event (Bronze)	Appear in WrestleMania using a Custom Superstar in WWE Universe (single player)
A Superstar is born! (Bronze)	Win a match using a Custom Superstar in WWE Universe mode (single player).
A winner is you! (Bronze)	Win 10 ranked matches.

A
B
C
D
E
F
G
H
I
J
K
L
M
N
O
P
Q
R
S
T
U
V
W
X
Y
Z

A winning combination! (Bronze)	Use a wake-up taunt, land a Finisher and immediately pin your opponent (single player)
All original baby! (Bronze)	Compete as a Custom Superstar in a Custom Arena for a Custom Championship.
Arena designer (Bronze)	Create an arena in Create an Arena mode.
Awesome! (Bronze)	Take a screenshot in Create a Highlight mode.
Berserker (Bronze)	Break a total of 50 tables, ladders, and chairs by attacking with them (single player).
Check out my Entrance Video! (Bronze)	Create an entrance movie in Create an Entrance mode
Comeback! (Bronze)	Successfully perform a Comeback Move (single player).
Create and destroy (Bronze)	Exhibition (Title Match) - Attack your opponent with a custom belt (single player).
Critic (Bronze)	Review 5 or more user-created content items in Community Creations.
Established veteran (Silver)	Achieve the rank 10 online.
Fighting smart (Bronze)	Exhibition - Attack the same body part 10 or more times in a single match (single player).
Gold standard (Silver)	Earn the WWE, WCW, and ECW Championship belts with a single Superstar.
I just keep evolving! (Bronze)	Exhibition (Legend difficulty) - With a Superstar, defeat his Attitude Era version (single player).
Invincible man (Silver)	Win at least 20 matches on Hard difficulty or higher (single player).
King of the world (Gold)	Achieve the maximum rank online.
Made-up original story (Bronze)	Create a story including a Custom Superstar or a Custom Arena.
Mr. Money in the Bank (Silver)	Win Money in the Bank using a Custom Superstar in WWE Universe mode (single player).
Negotiatior (Bronze)	Exhibition - Force an opponent to quit in an "I Quit" Match (single player).
One of history's greats (Bronze)	Exhibition (Legend difficulty) - Defeat a Superstar with his Attitude Era version (single player).
Paint tool magician (Bronze)	Use the paint tool to create and add an original logo to any original creation.
Platinum (Platinum)	Obtain all other Trophies.
Reached the ropes! (Bronze)	Crawl to the ropes during a submission (Single Player).
Ring hooligan (Bronze)	Break a total of 20 tables, ladders, and chairs by attacking with them (single player).
Rising star (Bronze)	Achieve the rank 5 online.
The champ is here! (Bronze)	Create an original championship belt in the Championship Editor.
The ring is my home! (Bronze)	Play a match in an arena created in Create an Arena mode.

The Streak Ends (Gold)	Beat The Undertaker at WrestleMania with a Custom Superstar on Legend difficulty (single player).
This is special! (Bronze)	Create a front, top-rope, and corner special move.
Welcome to the creators' circle (Bronze)	Your Community Creations content has been reviewed at least 5 times.

WWE '13 (XBOX 360)

ACHIEVEMENTS

UNLOCKABLE	HOW TO UNLOCK
A fresh beginning (5)	Play in an Xbox LIVE match (Player match/Ranked match)
A legend begins (20)	Win at least one match on Hard difficulty or higher (single player).
A man who wastes no opportunity (35)	Cash in a Money in the Bank and win using a Custom Superstar in WWE Universe (single player).
A once in a lifetime event (20)	Appear in WrestleMania using a Custom Superstar in WWE Universe (single player)
A Superstar is born! (10)	Win a match using a Custom Superstar in WWE Universe mode (single player).
A winner is you! (10)	Win 10 ranked matches.
A winning combination! (25)	Use a wake-up taunt, land a Finisher and immediately pin your opponent (single player).
All original baby! (15)	Compete as a Custom Superstar in a Custom Arena for a Custom Championship.
Arena designer (10)	Create an arena in Create an Arena mode.
Austin 3:16 scenario cleared! (15)	Clear the "Austin 3:16" chapter.
Awesome! (5)	Take a screenshot in Create a Highlight mode.
Berserker (25)	Break a total of 50 tables, ladders, and chairs by attacking with them (single player).
Brothers of Destruction cleared! (20)	Clear the "Brothers of Destruction" chapter.
Check out my Entrance Video! (10)	Create an entrance movie in Create an Entrance mode
Comeback! (20)	Successfully perform a Comeback Move (single player).
Create and destroy (15)	Exhibition (Title Match) - Attack your opponent with a custom belt (single player).
Critic (5)	Review 5 or more user-created content items in Community Creations.
Established veteran (30)	Achieve the rank 10 on Xbox LIVE.
Fighting smart (15)	Exhibition - Attack the same body part 10 or more times in a single match (single player).
Gold standard (45)	Earn the WWE, WCW, and ECW Championship belts with a single Superstar.
Holy sh**t!! (40)	Break the ring with an OMG Move (single player).

I just keep evolving! (20)	Exhibition (Legend difficulty) - With a Superstar, defeat his Attitude Era version (single player).
Invincible man (40)	Win at least 20 matches on Hard difficulty or higher (single player).
It's like a car crash! (20)	Exhibition - Break the barricade in 2 places in the same match (single player).
King of the world (50)	Achieve the maximum rank on Xbox LIVE.
Made-up original story (15)	Create a story including a Custom Superstar or a Custom Arena.
Mankind scenario cleared! (30)	Clear the "Mankind" chapter.
Mr. Money in the Bank (30)	Win Money in the Bank using a Custom Superstar in WWE Universe mode (single player).
Negotiatior (15)	Exhibition - Force an opponent to quit in an "I Quit" Match (single player).
Off Script scenario cleared! (45)	Clear the "Off Script" chapter.
Oh my! (15)	Break the announcer table with an OMG Move (single player).
One of history's greats (25)	Exhibition (Legend difficulty) - Defeat a Superstar with his Attitude Era version (single player).
Paint tool magician (10)	Use the paint tool to create and add an original logo to any original creation.
Reached the ropes! (10)	Crawl to the ropes during a submission (Single Player).
Ring hooligan (15)	Break a total of 20 tables, ladders, and chairs by attacking with them (single player).
Rise of D-X scenario cleared! (10)	Clear the "Rise of D-X" chapter.
Rising star (20)	Achieve the rank 5 on Xbox LIVE.
Road to WrestleMania XV cleared! (40)	Clear the "Road to WrestleMania XV" chapter.
The champ is here! (10)	Create an original championship belt in the Championship Editor.
The Great One scenario cleared! (25)	Clear the "The Great One" chapter.
The rattlesnake is coming!? (20)	Win by throwing an opponent through the window in Backstage Brawl (single player).
The ring is my home! (15)	Play a match in an arena created in Create an Arena mode.
The Streak Ends (50)	Beat The Undertaker at WrestleMania with a Custom Superstar on Legend difficulty (single player).
This is special! (10)	Create a front, top-rope, and corner special move.
Watch out! (30)	Successfully reverse a Finisher (single player).
Welcome to the creators' circle (5)	Your Community Creations content has been reviewed at least 5 times.
Yes! Yes! Yes! (10)	Use Daniel Bryan to defeat Sheamus (single player, Exhibition Mode only).
You can't let down your guard (20)	Land a Catch Finisher (single player, Exhibition Mode only).

TROPHIES

UNLOCKABLE	HOW TO UNLOCK
...and Practice (Bronze)	Build a Workshop.
A Continental Fellow (Silver)	Win the game from each of the 5 starting locations.
Ain't No Cavalry Comin' (Silver)	Have a soldier survive every mission in a full game.
All Employees Must Wash Hands... (Bronze)	In a single game, complete every Autopsy.
All Together Now (Bronze)	Get satellite coverage over every country on one continent.
And Hell's Coming With Me (Bronze)	Successfully assault an Overseer UFO.
And So It Begins... (Bronze)	Complete the tutorial mission.
Angel of Death (Bronze)	Kill an alien while flying. Single player only.
As A Scalpel (Bronze)	Earn the "Excellent" rating in every performance category on a terror mission.
Bada Boom (Bronze)	Kill 50 aliens with explosive weapons.
Beyond the Veil (Bronze)	Find a soldier with the Gift.
Combat Ready (Bronze)	Build an item.
Drums in the Deep (Bronze)	Gain access to the lowest level in your base.
Earth First (Silver)	Beat the game on Classic difficulty.
Edison (Bronze)	In a single game, complete every Research Project.
Eye in the Sky (Bronze)	Launch a Satellite.
Flight of the Valkyries (Bronze)	Win a mission with an all-female squad. Single player only.
Happy to Oblige (Bronze)	Fulfill a Council request.
Humanity's Savior (Bronze)	Beat the game on any difficulty.
Hunter/Killer (Bronze)	In a single game, shoot down one of each alien craft.
Lone Wolf (Silver)	Clear a UFO crash site with one soldier on Classic or Impossible difficulty.
Man No More (Bronze)	Build a suit of powered armor.
Meet New People. Then Kill Them. (Bronze)	Win a multiplayer match.
No Looking Back (Gold)	Beat the game in Ironman mode on Classic or Impossible difficulty.
Off My Planet (Silver)	Recover the Hyperwave Beacon.
On the Shoulders of Giants (Bronze)	Build the Gollop Chamber.
One Gun at a Time (Bronze)	Staff the Engineering Department with 80 engineers.
Oppenheimer (Bronze)	Staff the Research Labs with 80 scientists.
Our Finest Hour (Gold)	Beat the game on Impossible difficulty.
Pale Horse (Silver)	Kill 500 aliens.
Poison Control (Bronze)	Cure poison on five soldiers in a single mission. Single player only.
Prisoner of War (Bronze)	Capture a live alien.
Ride the Lightning (Bronze)	Build a Firestorm.
See All, Know All (Bronze)	Build the Hyperwave Relay.
Shooting Stars (Silver)	Shoot down 40 UFOs.

NEW!

A
B
C
D
E
F
G
H
I
J
K
L
M
N
O
P
Q
R
S
T
U
V
W
X
Y
Z

Skunkworks (Bronze)	In a single game, complete every Foundry project.
Tables Turned (Bronze)	Shoot down a UFO.
The Gatekeeper (Bronze)	Stun an Outsider.
The Hardest Road (Silver)	Advance one of your soldiers to Colonel rank.
The Volunteer (Bronze)	Make contact with the Ethereal hive mind.
Theory... (Bronze)	Build a Laboratory.
Up and Running (Bronze)	Build a base facility.
We Happy Few (Bronze)	Complete a mission without losing a soldier.
Welcoming Committee (Bronze)	Kill 150 aliens.
Wet Work (Silver)	Complete a Very Difficult abduction mission in five turns or less on Classic or Impossible difficulty.
What Wonders Await (Bronze)	Complete a Research Project.
Worth Every Penny (Bronze)	Acquire 1000 credits in one month.
X Marks the Spot (Bronze)	Uncover the alien base's location.
Xavier (Silver)	Mind Control an Ethereal. Single player only.
You Have 5 Seconds to Comply (Bronze)	Build a S.H.I.V
You Win (Platinum)	Gain all trophies.

XCOM: ENEMY UNKNOWN (XBOX 360)

ACHIEVEMENTS

UNLOCKABLE	HOW TO UNLOCK
...and Practice (10)	Build a Workshop.
A Continental Fellow (50)	Win the game from each of the 5 starting locations.
Ain't No Cavalry Comin' (50)	Have a soldier survive every mission in a full game.
All Employees Must Wash Hands... (10)	In a single game, complete every Autopsy.
All Together Now (10)	Get satellite coverage over every country on one continent.
And Hell's Coming With Me (10)	Successfully assault an Overseer UFO.
And So It Begins... (15)	Complete the tutorial mission.
Angel of Death (10)	Kill an alien while flying. Single player only.
As A Scalpel (25)	Earn the "Excellent" rating in every performance category on a terror mission.
Bada Boom (10)	Kill 50 aliens with explosive weapons.
Beyond the Veil (10)	Find a soldier with the Gift.
Combat Ready (5)	Build an item.
Drums in the Deep (10)	Gain access to the lowest level in your base.
Earth First (60)	Beat the game on Classic difficulty.
Edison (25)	In a single game, complete every Research Project.
Eye in the Sky (5)	Launch a Satellite.
Flight of the Valkyries (10)	Win a mission with an all-female squad. Single player only.
Happy to Oblige (15)	Fulfill a Council request.
Humanity's Savior (30)	Beat the game on any difficulty.

Hunter/Killer (15)	In a single game, shoot down one of each alien craft.
Lone Wolf (20)	Clear a UFO crash site with one soldier on Classic or Impossible difficulty.
Man No More (10)	Build a suit of powered armor.
Meet New People. Then Kill Them. (25)	Win a multiplayer match.
No Looking Back (100)	Beat the game in Ironman mode on Classic or Impossible difficulty.
Off My Planet (25)	Recover the Hyperwave Beacon.
On the Shoulders of Giants (10)	Build the Gollop Chamber.
One Gun at a Time (20)	Staff the Engineering Department with 80 engineers
Oppenheimer (20)	Staff the Research Labs with 80 scientists.
Our Finest Hour (90)	Beat the game on Impossible difficulty.
Pale Horse (50)	Kill 500 aliens.
Poison Control (10)	Cure poison on five soldiers in a single mission. Single player only.
Prisoner of War (10)	Capture a live alien.
Ride the Lightning (10)	Build a Firestorm.
See All, Know All (10)	Build the Hyperwave Relay.
Shooting Stars (35)	Shoot down 40 UFOs.
Skunkworks (20)	In a single game, complete every Foundry project.
Tables Turned (10)	Shoot down a UFO.
The Gatekeeper (10)	Stun an Outsider.
The Hardest Road (10)	Advance one of your soldiers to Colonel rank.
The Volunteer (10)	Make contact with the Ethereal hive mind.
Theory... (10)	Build a Laboratory.
Up and Running (5)	Build a base facility.
We Happy Few (10)	Complete a mission without losing a soldier.
Welcoming Committee (20)	Kill 150 aliens.
Wet Work (10)	Complete a Very Hard abduction mission in five turns or less on Classic or Impossible difficulty.
What Wonders Await (5)	Complete a Research Project.
Worth Every Penny (20)	Acquire 1000 credits in one month.
X Marks the Spot (10)	Uncover the alien base's location.
Xavier (10)	Mind Control an Ethereal. Single player only.
You Have 5 Seconds to Comply (10)	Build a S.H.I.V.

ZERO ESCAPE: VIRTUE'S LAST REWARD (PLAYSTATION VITA)

TROPHIES

UNLOCKABLE	HOW TO UNLOCK
A Certain Point of View (Gold)	Caught a glimpse of another time.
A Consumate Collection (Gold)	Found ALL the files!
An Eidetic Experience (Bronze)	Found a file.
An Equal and Opposite Reaction (Silver)	Saw Quark's ending.
Arms Race (Silver)	Saw Sigma's ending.
Bachelor of Escapology (Bronze)	Escaped from the elevator.
Behind Blue Eyes (Silver)	Saw Dio's ending.
Best Served Cold (Silver)	Saw Alice's ending.
Classified (Bronze)	Found a secret.

Doctor of Escapology (Silver)	Escaped from sixteen rooms.
Escapest (Gold)	Escaped everything on Hard difficulty.
Escapey (Bronze)	Escaped on Hard difficulty.
Every Ending Begins Somewhere (Bronze)	Saw any of the endings.
Fire and Ice (Gold)	Saw the end. Or maybe the beginning?
Gotta Hand It To You (Bronze)	Opened the third lock.
He Was Convicted of a String of Numbers (Bronze)	Opened the fifth lock.
I Can't Believe It's Not Murder! (Bronze)	Opened the second lock.
If I Told You You Had A Nice Antibody... (Bronze)	Opened the fourth lock.
In Root Beer Veritas (Silver)	Saw Tenmyouji's ending.
Master of Escapology (Bronze)	Escaped from eight rooms.
No Lying Down On the Job (Bronze)	Opened the sixth lock.
Redacted (Gold)	Found ALL the secrets!
Secret Agent Woman (Silver)	Saw Clover's ending.
Some Days You Just Can't Get Rid of a Bomb (Bronze)	Opened the tenth lock.
Tears in the Rain (Silver)	Saw Luna's ending.
That Wasn't Supposed to Happen (Bronze)	Saw any of the bad endings.
Through the Looking Glass (Silver)	Saw K's ending.
Time After Time (Silver)	Saw Phi's ending.
To Each According to His Needle (Bronze)	Opened the first lock.
Virtue's Last Reward (Platinum)	Acquired all trophies.
Who Set Up Us The Bomb, Part 1 (Bronze)	Opened the seventh lock.
Who Set Up Us The Bomb, Part A (Bronze)	Opened the ninth lock.
Why'd You Do That, You Dumas! (Bronze)	Opened the eighth lock.

1942: JOINT STRIKE (XBOX 360)

SECRET PLANE

Beat the game on Wing King Difficulty setting, then select Shinden in the Plane Selection screen by pressing "Y." This enables you to use a black and red version of the Shinden with maxed out power.

300: MARCH TO GLORY (PSP)

Enter this code while the game is paused.

UNLOCKABLE	CODE
25,000 Kleos	⇩, ⇦, ⇩, ⇦, ⇧, ⇦

50 CENT: BLOOD ON THE SAND (PLAYSTATION 3)

UNLOCKABLES

Accessed through the Unlockables menu.

UNLOCKABLE	HOW TO UNLOCK
Infinite Ammo	Earn 52 medals/badges in Story mode.
Infinite Grenades	Earn 56 medals/badges in Story mode.

A BOY AND HIS BLOB (WII)

UNLOCKABLES

UNLOCKABLE	HOW TO UNLOCK
Bonus Content	Complete a Challenge Level to unlock bonus content that is accessible from the hideout.
Challenge Levels	Find all three treasure chests in a regular level to unlock a Challenge Level that is accessible from the hideout.

ACE COMBAT: ASSAULT HORIZON (PLAYSTATION 3)

TROPHY

UNLOCKABLE	HOW TO UNLOCK
Ace of Aces (Silver)	Obtained an A rank for every mission (free mission).
Aerial Sniper (Bronze)	Used DFM to destroy 10 airborne enemies in competitive online.
All Rounder (Silver)	Obtained all MVPs.
Bail Out (Bronze)	Ejected from a damaged aircraft.
Berserker (Bronze)	Destroyed the air defense system, opening the way for allied pilots.
Bomber Master (Bronze)	Defeated a large number of enemies while flying a bomber.
Calamity (Bronze)	Used Trinity to wipe out the enemy (free mission).
Category 5 (Bronze)	Pursued the enemy and shot down Major Illich.
Chain Master (Silver)	Took down 5 hostiles in a row with an assault chain.
Checking In (Bronze)	Flew through the big hotel's gates.
Critical Hit (Silver)	Took down a hostile fighter with a charged homing missile.
Defender of World Heritage (Bronze)	Prevented enemy from using Trinity to destroy Derbent.

UNLOCKABLE	HOW TO UNLOCK
Diverse Strikes (Bronze)	Defeated hostiles with all 3 of the gunship's weapons.
Eagle Eye (Bronze)	Successfully focused on 3 targets.
Emergency (Bronze)	Attempted an emergency landing in a damaged aircraft.
Fearsome Guardian (Bronze)	Protected your allies using the gunship, and led a successful attack on the base.
Fire Hazard (Bronze)	Removed enemy presence from the oil field and the base.
Formation Attack (Silver)	Joined the same DFM with two others and shot down a hostile (mission co-op).
Friendly Fire (Bronze)	Alleviated the attack on Miami and helped Guts bail out.
Ground Pounder (Bronze)	Used ASM to destroy 30 ground enemies in competitive online.
Guardian (Bronze)	Protected Washington D.C. from the threat of Trinity, and returned alive.
Gun Master (Bronze)	Took out a large number of hostiles as the door gunner.
Guns Guns Guns (Bronze)	Destroyed 5 hostile vehicles from the air as the door gunner.
Hard Strike (Bronze)	Wiped out hostile ground forces with ASM.
Hot Pit (Bronze)	Successfully took off to protect allies amid heavy hostile fire.
Interceptor (Bronze)	Used an attack helicopter and destroyed 10 missiles or bombs in competitive online.
Life Saver (Bronze)	Rescued Major Illich from enemy captivity.
Limbo (Bronze)	Flew beneath a falling chimney.
Machine Gun Faithful (Bronze)	Destroyed an enemy aircraft using only the standard machine gun while piloting an aircraft.
Nice Assist (Bronze)	Used DFM support or ASM support to join a flight member.
Nice Kill (Silver)	Shot down a large number of hostile players in competitive online.
Nice Save (Bronze)	Saved an ally being targeted by hostile players in DFM in competitive online.
Nick of Time (Bronze)	Destroyed the ICBMs.
One Million Tons of Scrap Prime Metal (Bronze)	Sank the enemy fleet and saved the Russian Minister.
Patriot (Bronze)	Protected Moscow from destruction, freeing it from enemy control.
Pursuit Master (Bronze)	Successfully pursued 3 enemies with counter maneuvers.
Shot Master (Bronze)	Took down 5 hostiles with a direct shot.
Sierra Hotel (Platinum)	Obtained all Trophies.
Smooth Flight (Silver)	Managed to get Sova 1 to land safely.
Speed Demon (Bronze)	Destroyed all radar missile defense systems in a short period of time.
Stay On Target (Bronze)	Obtained and destroyed 10 enemies in a helicopter.
Steel Hunter (Bronze)	Eliminated enemy threat from the Suez Canal.
Successive Kill (Bronze)	Took down 3 hostiles in a row with an assault chain.
Switch Master (Silver)	Successfully switched from defense to offense 10 times with counter maneuvers.

The Collector (Bronze)	Piloted all aircraft in the game.
Total Annihilation (Bronze)	Disintegrated enemy bombers in mid-air, keeping damage to the city to a minimum.
Veteran Pilot (Silver)	Sortied for 50 hours in competitive online or mission co-op.
Warwolf 1 (Gold)	Cleared all missions.
Warwolf Squadron (Gold)	Cleared all levels in mission co-op.
Welcome to Mission Co-Op (Bronze)	Cleared 1 level in mission co-op.
World Tour (Silver)	Played on all maps in competitive online.

UNLOCKABLE

UNLOCKABLE	HOW TO UNLOCK
Unlock Call Sign - Antares	Obtain a toal of 1,000,000 points
Unlock Call Sign - Aquila	Receive "Survivor" bonus in Mutiplayer
Unlock Call Sign - Burner	Win 20 times in Capital Conquest
Unlock Call Sign - Cougar	Shoot down 100 enemy players in Competitive Multiplayer
Unlock Call Sign - Dragon	Win 10 times in Capital Conquest
Unlock Call Sign - Falco	Receive "Ace Stiker" bonus in Mutiplayer
Unlock Call Sign - Galm	Receive "Ace Pilot" bonus 5 times in Mutiplayer
Unlock Call Sign - Garuda	Complete the Campaign Mode
Unlock Call Sign - Gryphus	Receive "Hero" bonus 5 times in Multiplayer
Unlock Call Sign - Mobius	Receive "Hero" bonus in Multiplayer
Unlock Call Sign - Mohawk	Earn 100,000 points
Unlock Call Sign - Phoenix	Rank first place in Deathmatch
Unlock Call Sign - Racer	Perform DFM support 50 times in Multiplayer
Unlock Call Sign - Renegade	Earn 300,000 points
Unlock Call Sign - Scarface	Receive "Ace Pilot" bonus in Mutiplayer
Unlock Call Sign - Strigon	Receive "Survivor" bonus 5 times in Mutiplayer
Unlock Call Sign - Sweeper	Destroy 50 enemies with helicopter in Multiplayer
Unlock Call Sign - Viking	Earn 20,000 points
Unlock Call Sign - Wardog	Receive "Ace Striker" bonus 5 times in Mutiplayer
Unlock Call Sign - Wildcat	Shoot down 50 enemy players in Multiplayer
Unlock Color 2 for all aircraft	Complete the Campaign Mode
Unlock F-15E Strike Eagle	Complete the Campaign Mode
Unlock Mi-24 (HIND)	Complete the Campaign Mode
Unlock PAK-FA	Complete the Campaign Mode

ADVENTURE ISLAND (WII)

PASSWORDS

PASSWORD	EFFECT
3WSURYXZY763TE	Advanced items/abilities
RMAYTJEOPHALUP	Disable sounds
NODEGOSO000000	Start the game as Hu man
3YHURYW7Y7LL8C	Start the game as Hawk man
3YHURYW7Y7LRBW	Start the game as Lizard man
3YHURYW7Y7LN84	Start the game as Piranha man
3YHURYW7Y7LK88	Start the game as Tiger man

ADVENTURES OF LOLO (WII)

LEVEL PASSWORDS

PASSWORD	EFFECT
BCBT	Level 1-2
BDBR	Level 1-3
BGBQ	Level 1-4
BHBP	Level 1-5
BJBM	Level 2-1
BKBL	Level 2-2
BLBK	Level 2-3
BMBJ	Level 2-4
BPBH	Level 2-5
BQBG	Level 3-1
BRBD	Level 3-2
BTBC	Level 3-3
BVBB	Level 3-4
BYZZ	Level 3-5
BZZY	Level 4-1
CBZV	Level 4-2
CCZT	Level 4-3
CDZR	Level 4-4
CGZQ	Level 4-5
CHZP	Level 5-1
CJZM	Level 5-2
CKZL	Level 5-3
CLZK	Level 5-4
CMZJ	Level 5-5
CPZH	Level 6-1
CQZG	Level 6-2
CRZD	Level 6-3
CTZC	Level 6-4
CVZB	Level 6-5
CYYZ	Level 7-1
CZYY	Level 7-2
DBYV	Level 7-3
DCYT	Level 7-4
DDYR	Level 7-5
DGYQ	Level 8-1
DHYP	Level 8-2
DJYM	Level 8-3
DKYL	Level 8-4
DLYK	Level 8-5
DMYJ	Level 9-1
DPYH	Level 9-2
DQYG	Level 9-3
DRYD	Level 9-4
DTYC	Level 9-5
DVYB	Level 10-1
DYVZ	Level 10-2
DZVY	Level 10-3
GBVV	Level 10-4
GCVT	Level 10-5

LEVEL SKIP

UNLOCKABLE	HOW TO UNLOCK
Level Skip	This only works if you have a password that starts with A, B, C, or D and if the second letter in the password appears earlier in the alphabet than the fourth letter. If so, switch the second and fourth letters in the password. Use the new password to start at a level one higher than the original.

ADVENTURES OF LOLO 2 (WII)

NEW DIFFICULTY LEVELS

PASSWORD	EFFECT
PPHP	Floor 01, Room 1
PHPK	Floor 01, Room 2
PQPD	Floor 01, Room 3
PVPT	Floor 01, Room 4
PRPJ	Floor 01, Room 5
PZPC	Floor 02, Room 1
PGPG	Floor 02, Room 2
PCPZ	Floor 02, Room 3
PLPY	Floor 02, Room 4
PBPM	Floor 02, Room 5
PYPL	Floor 03, Room 1
PMPB	Floor 03, Room 2
PJPR	Floor 03, Room 3
PTPV	Floor 03, Room 4
PDPQ	Floor 03, Room 5
PKPH	Floor 04, Room 1
HPPP	Floor 04, Room 2
HHKK	Floor 04, Room 3
HQKD	Floor 04, Room 4
HVKT	Floor 04, Room 5
HRKJ	Floor 05, Room 1
HBKM	Floor 05, Room 2
HLKY	Floor 05, Room 3
HCKZ	Floor 05, Room 4
HGKG	Floor 05, Room 5
HZKC	Floor 06, Room 1
HYKL	Floor 06, Room 2
HMKB	Floor 06, Room 3
HJKR	Floor 06, Room 4
HTKV	Floor 06, Room 5
HDKQ	Floor 07, Room 1
HKKH	Floor 07, Room 2
QPKP	Floor 07, Room 3
QHDK	Floor 07, Room 4
QQDD	Floor 07, Room 5
QVDT	Floor 08, Room 1
QRDJ	Floor 08, Room 2
QBDM	Floor 08, Room 3
QLDY	Floor 08, Room 4

QCDZ	Floor 08, Room 5
QGDG	Floor 09, Room 1
QZDC	Floor 09, Room 2
QYDL	Floor 09, Room 3
QMDB	Floor 09, Room 4
QJDR	Floor 09, Room 5
QTDV	Floor 10, Room 1
QDDQ	Floor 10, Room 2
QKDH	Floor 10, Room 3
VPDP	Floor 10, Room 4
VHTK	Floor 10, Room 5
VQTD	Last Level

THE ADVENTURES OF TINTIN: THE GAME (PLAYSTATION 3)

TROPHY

UNLOCKABLE	HOW TO UNLOCK
Acrobat reporter (Bronze)	Move along the length of the Karaboudjan using the grappling hook!
Acrobatic duo (Bronze)	Give your partner 5 leg-ups in 'Tintin and Haddock' mode!
Armor expert! (Bronze)	Sir Francis: use the armor to knock out 20 enemies!
Art collector (Bronze)	Knock out 10 enemies with a painting of Sir Francis!
Aviation ace (Bronze)	Finish every level of the three types of PLANE challenges!
Bagghar (Bronze)	Finish chapter 22!
Banana king (Bronze)	Make 15 enemies slip on a banana skin!
Brittany (Bronze)	Finish chapter 28!
Cane and able (Bronze)	Thom(p)sons: get rid of 22 enemies with your stick!
Cane juggler (Bronze)	Bounce 10 objects off Thom(p)son's cane!
Castafiore unlocked (Bronze)	Unlock the Castafiore!
Champion catcher (Silver)	Catch an object in full flight with the grappling hook!
Complete artist (Bronze)	Finish a Tintin & Haddock mode level without losing any coins! (Apart from the side-car levels).
Crab collector (Gold)	Collect all the crabs with golden claws!
Easy Rider (Bronze)	Finish all the SIDECAR challenges!
Ever-dry (Bronze)	In the PLANE challenges, stay near the water for 7 seconds!
Experienced pilot (Bronze)	Get through the storm safely and reach the desert!
Five go bang (Bronze)	Get rid of 2 enemies at the same time with an exploding object!
Football champ (Bronze)	Knock out 2 enemies in a single throw of a ball using a rebound!
Giant Rackham: Take 1 (Bronze)	Beat Giant Rackham a first time!
Giant Rackham: Take 2 (Bronze)	Destroy the galleon!
Giant Rackham: Take 3 (Bronze)	Beat Giant Rackham again!
Giant Rackham: Take 4 (Bronze)	Destroy Giant Rackham and the galleon!

International reporter (Bronze)	Get to Bagghar!
Karaboudjan (Bronze)	Finish chapter 16!
Lights out (Bronze)	Knock out 5 enemies with a chandelier!
Look out below! (Bronze)	Pull five enemies off a ledge you're hanging onto!
Marlinspike (Bronze)	Finish chapter 10!
Marlinspike's heir (Platinum)	Unlock all the game's trophies!
Master rat exterminator (Bronze)	Exterminate 20 rats!
Master treasure hunter (Gold)	Find all the TREASURES in 'Tintin and Haddock' mode!
Metalhead (Bronze)	Throw a pot at an enemy's head!
Motorcycle ace (Bronze)	Finish a SIDECAR challenge without crashing into a wall or obstacle!
Passenger in transit (Bronze)	Change characters in flight with the parrot!
Pilot gold medal (Bronze)	Get gold in all three types of PLANE challenges!
Showered with platinum (Gold)	Finish all the platinum challenges!
Sidecar gold medal (Bronze)	Get gold in all the SIDECAR challenges!
Sir Francis unlocked (Bronze)	Unlock Sir Francis!
Stronger than Diego (Bronze)	Beat Diego the Dreadful!
Stronger than Red Rackham (Silver)	Beat Red Rackham in a sword fight!
Stronger than William (Bronze)	Beat William the Pirate!
Super-sleuth (Silver)	With Snowy, find all the buried objects in 'Tintin and Haddock' mode!
Supersonic parrot (Silver)	Finish 'The mystery of the talking bird' in less than 3 minutes 30 seconds!
Swashbuckler (Bronze)	Finish all the SWORD challenges!
Sword gold medal (Bronze)	Get gold in all the SWORD challenges!
The Castafiore does her turn (Bronze)	Castafiore: do 45 spinning attacks!
The flea market (Bronze)	Finish chapter 4!
Thom(p)sons unlocked (Bronze)	Unlock the Thom(p)sons!
Treasure hunter (Silver)	Find Red Rackham's treasure!
Untouchable (Bronze)	Finish a SWORD challenge without getting a scratch!
Wardrobe full (Bronze)	Buy 30 costumes!

AFTER BURNER CLIMAX (PLAYSTATION 3)

UNLOCKABLE

UNLOCKABLE	HOW TO UNLOCK
Clouds of Twilight	Finish stage 9A or 9B with at least 4 stars.
Golden Valley	Finish stage 5 with at least 4 stars.
After Burner Helmet	Complete your Medal Collection.
After Burner Logo T-Shirt (females)	Unlock all Ex Options.
After Burner Logo T-Shirt (males)	Unlock all Ex Options.

EX OPTIONS

Meet the following conditions during Arcade Mode to unlock these special settings in EX Options. They can only be used in Arcade Mode.

UNLOCKABLE	HOW TO UNLOCK
Aircraft Count: 1	Play a Secret Stage five times.
Aircraft Count: 5	Play a Secret Stage one time.
Aircraft Count: 9	Play a Secret Stage three times.
Aircraft Speed: Fast	Play three different branched stages (A/B).
Aircraft Speed: Slow	Play all eight branched stages (A/B).
Armor: 1%	Get a down rate of over 70% 20 times.
Armor: Half Damage	Get a down rate of over 70% 10 times.
Armor: No Damage	Get a down rate of over 70% 50 times.
Auto-Missiles: On	Reach ending A.
Climax Gauge Recovery: Fast	Activate Climax Mode 50 times.
Climax Gauge Recovery: Free	Activate Climax Mode 200 times.
Climax Gauge Recovery: Slow	Activate Climax Mode 100 times.
Combo Window: Free	Get a combo totaling 3,000.
Combo Window: Long	Get a combo totaling 1,000.
Credits: 5	Get a Game Over one time.
Credits: 7	Get a Game Over three times.
Credits: 9	Get a Game Over five times.
Credits: Free	Get a Game Over 10 times.
Display: No Info	Get a score of over 2,000,000 points in one game.
Display: No Smoke (All)	Get a score of over 1,000,000 points in one game.
Display: No Smoke (Explosions)	Get a score of over 800,000 points in one game.
Display: No Smoke (Missiles)	Get a score of over 600,000 points in one game.
Enemy Attack: 1 Level Down	Shoot down 1,000 enemies.
Enemy Attack: 2 Levels Down	Shoot down 3,000 enemies.
Enemy Attack: 3 Levels Down	Shoot down 5,000 enemies.
Enemy Attack: No Attack	Shoot down 10,000 enemies.
Gun Power: Down	Shoot down 200 enemies with the gun.
Gun Power: Up	Shoot down 50 enemies with the gun.
Lock-On: Auto	Reaching the ending 10 times.
Lock-On: Large Cursor	Reaching the ending one time.
Lock-On: No Cursor	Reaching the ending five times.
Missile Recovery: Free	Fire 5,000 missiles.
Missile Recovery: Off	Fire 2,000 missiles.
Secret Mission: Always	Play Emergency Orders 20 times.

AGE OF EMPIRES: MYTHOLOGIES (DS)

UNLOCKABLES

UNLOCKABLE	HOW TO UNLOCK
Ladon the Lamia	Beat the Greek campaign.
Setekh	Beat the Egyptian campaign.

ALAN WAKE (XBOX 360)

UNLOCKABLES

UNLOCKABLE	HOW TO UNLOCK
Jacket and Scarf (female)	Play the Limited Collector's Edition Bonus Disc.
Jacket and Scarf (male)	Play the Limited Collector's Edition Bonus Disc.
Nightmare Mode	Successfully complete the game.

AIRACE (NDS)

CLASS AND AIRCRAFT UNLOCKABLES

Compete in the Championship mode of the game to unlock the following classes and aircraft.

UNLOCKABLE	HOW TO UNLOCK
Class II—Delta 21 (Vought F4U Corsair)	Complete Class I, Race V
Class II—Fatboy (Brewster F2A Buffalo)	Complete Class I, Race V
Class II—Sky Warrior (Supermarine Spitfire)	Complete Class I, Race V
Class III—Guardian (Mikoyan-Gurevich MiG-17 Fresco)	Complete Class II, Race VI
Class III—Interceptor (Messerschmitt Me-262)	Complete Class II, Race VI
Class III—Razor (Yakovlev Yak-17 Feather)	Complete Class II, Race VI

COURSES

UNLOCKABLE	HOW TO UNLOCK
Amazon River (Backward)	Complete Class I, Race III
City Streets	Complete Class I, Race I
City Streets (Backward)	Complete Class III, Race I
Great Canyon	Complete Class II, Race I
Great Canyon (Backward)	Complete Class II, Race VI
Hangars	Complete Class I, Race V
Hangars (Backward)	Complete Class III, Race II
Land of the Ice	Complete Class I, Race II
Land of the Ice (Backward)	Complete Class II, Race II
Storm Drains (Backward)	Complete Class I, Race IV

AIR CONFLICTS: SECRET WARS (XBOX 360)

ACHIEVEMENT

UNLOCKABLE	HOW TO UNLOCK
Ace-of-Aces (40)	Kill 100 players in multiplayer
All missions (60)	All missions completed
Bird Collector (50)	Unlock all planes in single player campaign
Blue Max (30)	Kill 5 players in multiplayer without dying
Bomber Ace (40)	Destroy 100 ground units in Campaign Game
Bullseye (20)	Long range Rocket Kill in Multiplayer
Cracking Good Show (50)	Place first in Deathmatch with at least 6 players
Fall Blau (40)	Complete Chapter II
Fighter Ace (40)	Shoot down 100 aircraft in Campaign Game
Good Show (30)	Place in top half in Deathmatch with at least 6 players
Great War Officer (40)	Win 5 multiplayer matches with any Great War Team
Liberation of Balkans (50)	Complete Chapter VII
Lucky Shot (50)	Enemy aircraft shot down in single player with rocket at great range
Luftwaffe Officer (40)	Win 5 multiplayer matches with Luftwaffe team
Operation Belt (40)	Complete Chapter IV
Operation Black (40)	Complete Chapter III
Operation Overlord (40)	Complete Chapter V
RAF Officer (40)	Win 5 multiplayer matches with RAF team
Red Air Force Officer (40)	Win 5 multiplayer matches with Red Air Force team
Red Baron (50)	Kill 10 players in multiplayer without dying

Rocket Sniper (50)	Extra long range Rocket Kill in Multiplayer
Siege of Tobruk (40)	Complete Chapter I
Slovak Uprising (50)	Complete Chapter VI
Tally Ho! (30)	Play 50 multiplayer matches

AIR ZONK (WII)

CODES

UNLOCKABLE	HOW TO UNLOCK
Expert Mode	On the Configuration screen, hold ⬆ and press SELECT
Sound Test	Hold ① and ② and SELECT as you turn on the game

AKAI KATANA SHIN (XBOX 360)

ACHIEVEMENTS

UNLOCKABLE	HOW TO UNLOCK
#^&@%&! (5)	Got hit by a bullet in Phantom form, and then died from another bullet immediately afterward.
100 Million and Counting (10)	Earned 100,000,000 points (Origin Mode).
128 Hits! (5)	Earned 128 hits (Origin Mode).
200 Million and Counting (15)	Earned 200,000,000 points (Origin Mode).
256 Hits! (10)	Earned 256 hits (Origin Mode).
400 Million and Counting (10)	Earned 400,000,000 points (Slash Mode).
600 Million and Counting (15)	Earned 600,000,000 points (Slash Mode).
800 Million and Counting (20)	Earned 800,000,000 points (Slash Mode).
Absorption Power (5)	Absorb items into your ship.
Armored Helicopter (25)	Defeated the helicopter mid-boss in Stage 5.
Attack Ships on Fire (5)	Sunk the Fujibara attack ship.
Ayame & Ran of the 10 Suns (45)	Defeated Ayame & Ran.
Back Against the Wall (30)	While in Phantom form, filled up the screen with more than 800 bullets.
Big Catch (5)	Rotated 72 guiding energy items (large) around your ship.
Breaching Submarine (20)	Defeated the Arakashi submarine in Stage 4.
Bullet-proof (30)	Reflected more than 1000 bullets while in Phantom form.
Decay and Dissolution (10)	Lost more than 20 score items that were rotating around your ship during a game.
Destroying the Limit (20)	Earned 3000 hits (Slash Mode).
Emperor Bashou of the 10 Suns (50)	Defeated Emperor Bashou.
Energy Gauge MAX (5)	Filled up your energy gauge.
Heavy Attack Helicopter (35)	Brought down the Himeshikara heavy attack helicopter.
Hiiragi of the 10 Suns (10)	Defeated the 1st stage boss, Hiiragi.
Katana of Justice (30)	Hit a boss with 16 steel orbs.
Katana of Truth (40)	Hit a boss with 16 katanas.
Learning Type 1 (30)	Cleared the game with the Type 1 ship.
Learning Type 2 (30)	Cleared the game with the Type 2 ship.
Learning Type 3 (30)	Cleared the game with the Type 3 ship.
M76 Heavy Tank (10)	Defeated the Goura heavy tank in Stage 2.
Malice Speed Destruction (20)	Destroyed a mid-boss within 2 seconds.
Marigold (30)	Cleared the game using Type 1 without continuing.

Nazuna of the 10 Suns (30)	Defeated the 5th stage boss, Nazuna.
Opening Salvo (5)	Started up the game for the first time.
Orchid (30)	Cleared the game using Type 2 without continuing.
Sakura (30)	Cleared the game using Type 3 without continuing.
Shakunage of the 10 Suns (20)	Defeated the 3rd stage boss, Shakunage.
Shumeigiku of the 10 Suns (15)	Defeated the 2nd stage boss, Shumeigiku.
Summoning (5)	Summoned your Phantom.
Tank Bombardment (15)	Defeated the Gaimon tank in Stage 3.
The Gold Ring (5)	Rotated over 200 score items (large) around your ship while playing as the Phantom.
The Hidden Form (15)	Equipped a total of 16 katanas and 16 steel orbs on your Phantom.
The Phantom (15)	Caused a boss to change forms, or destroyed it while playing as the Phantom.
The Sharpened Blade (20)	Earned 300,000,000 points (Origin Mode).
War Fiend Hiiragi (25)	Defeated the 4th stage boss, War Fiend Hiiragi.

ALEX KIDD IN THE ENCHANTED CASTLE (WII)

SKIP BOSS SEQUENCES

UNLOCKABLE	HOW TO UNLOCK
Skip Boss Sequences	Wait until the conversation with the boss has ended. After that, Press START to get to the Options screen, then press START again and you should skip the sequence.

ALEX RIDER: STORMBREAKER (DS)

Enter the password screen from the main menu and input the following.

PASSWORD	EFFECT
JESSICA PARKER	Allows you to purchase black belt
6943059	Allows you to purchase disk 6 after completing game
VICTORIA PARR	Allows you to purchase M16 badge
RENATO CELANI	Allows you to purchase the fugu
SARYL HIRSCH	Allows you to purchase the sunglasses
9785711	Allows you to select level HARD
4298359	Everything at shop is at half price!
9603717	Gallery is added to Secret mode
5204025	Get 10,000 spy points
6894098	Outfit change is added to Secret mode

ALICE IN WONDERLAND (DS)

DGAMER HONORS + DGAMER AVATAR UNLOCKABLES

Before you begin the game, set up a DGamer profile and create an avatar in off-line mode. Go back to the game once you're done creating your avatar. As you play through the game, you'll unlock "Honors" and gain Alice-themed costumes and gear for your DGamer avatar by completing certain tasks during the game.

UNLOCKABLE	HOW TO UNLOCK
Alice Dress/Alice Armor	Gain all pieces of the Magic Armor.
Caterpillar Outfit	Have Absolem join your team.
Cheshire Outfit	Have the Cheshire Cat join your team.
Dormouse Coat	Enter "3676" at Password screen.
Hatter Outfit	Have the Hatter Join your team.

Living Oraculum	Unlock every chapter.
Puzzle Master	Find every map piece/explore all map locations.
Red Guard Outfit	Defeat one of the tougher, armed Red Guards for the first time.
Rushed Rabbit	Defeat 50 enemies using McTwisp's Slow Down Ability.
Savior of Underland	Beat the Jabberwocky!
Stayne Eyepatch	Defeat Stayne Twice.
Stayne Mantle	Defeat Stayne Once.
Vorpal Sword	Find the Vorpal Sword.
Weird, Wise, Malicious	Gain the remaining three characters in your party.
White Rabbit Jacket	Complete Chapter One.

ALICE: MADNESS RETURNS (XBOX 360)

UNLOCKABLE

Dresses are unlocked after completing each chapter.

UNLOCKABLE	HOW TO UNLOCK
Classic (Regain health when shrunk)	Complete Infernal Train (Chapter 6)
Misstitched (Shrink Sense duration is doubled)	Complete The Dollhouse (Chapter 5)
Royal Suit (Health limited to 4 Roses total)	Complete Queensland (Chapter 4)
Silk Maiden (Enemies drop twice as many Teeth)	Complete Oriental Grove (Chapter 3)
Siren (Enemies drop twice as many Roses)	Complete Deluded Depths (Chapter 2)
Steamdress (Breakables drop more Teeth and Roses)	Complete Hatter's Domain (Chapter 1)
New Game +	Complete the game on any difficulty level.

ALIEN CRUSH (WII)

BONUS

UNLOCKABLE	HOW TO UNLOCK
1 Million Points + Bonus Ball	Get to the bonus round with skulls and green aliens. Kill everything except for one skull. Keep going until a pterodactyl appears. Hit the pterodactyl with the ball to get a million points and a bonus ball once the stage is cleared.

ALIEN VS. PREDATOR (XBOX 360)

SKINS

Reach the indicated rank to unlock each skin.

UNLOCKABLE	HOW TO UNLOCK
Claw (Predator)	Obtain Rank 03.
Connor (Marine)	Obtain Rank 05.
Gibson (Marine)	Obtain Rank 02.
Hunter (Predator)	Obtain Rank 16.
Johnson (Marine)	Obtain Rank 22.
Moss (Marine)	Obtain Rank 13.
Nethead (Alien)	Obtain Rank 34.
Praetorian (Alien)	Obtain Rank 19.
Ridged (Alien)	Obtain Rank 10.
Rookie (Marine)	Obtain Rank 28.
Spartan (Predator)	Obtain Rank 31.
Stalker (Predator)	Obtain Rank 07.
Warrior Dome (Alien)	Obtain Rank 04.
Wolf (Predator)	Obtain Rank 25.

ALONE IN THE DARK: INFERNO (PLAYSTATION 3)

CODES

Enter the following code (combination of Action Buttons and D-Pad) in the game, when in third-person view and without anything in the hands. Entering the same code again will disable the Infinite Ammo Cheat.

EFFECT	CODE
Infinite Ammo Enabled	▲,●,⬓,⬒,■,↑,→,↓,←,▲,■,×,●,↑,←,↓,→

ALTERED BEAST (WII)

CODES

Enter these on the title screen.

UNLOCKABLE	HOW TO UNLOCK
Beast Select	Hold Ⓐ+Ⓑ+Ⓒ+⬛ and then press START
Character Kicks Credits	When the credits are being displayed on the screen after you have beaten the game, you can control your character to kick away the credited names
Continue from Last Stage Played	Hold Ⓐ and press SELECT after a Game Over
Level Select	Press Ⓑ and START
Sound Test	Hold Ⓐ+Ⓒ+⬛ and then press START

THE AMAZING SPIDER-MAN (PLAYSTATION 3)

TROPHY

UNLOCKABLE	HOW TO UNLOCK
A Dash of Spider (Bronze)	Complete all XTreme Race challenges
All Tied Up (Silver)	Defeat 100 enemies by performing Stealth Takedowns
Amazing Spider-Man (Bronze)	Unlock all concept art
Apparent Defeat (Bronze)	Defeat Iguana
Beating the Odds (Bronze)	Clear the second fight against the Hunter robots
Big Apple, Big Worm (Silver)	Defeat the S-02
Call Interrupted (Bronze)	Destroy a Seeker before it can call a Hunter
Car Hopper (Bronze)	Clear all car chases
Clean Victory (Silver)	Defeat a Hunter without using your Web-Shooters
Corporate (Bronze)	Collect all Oscorp Manuals
Deeply Sorry (Bronze)	Defeat Nattie
Does everything a spider can! (Platinum)	Unlock all Trophies
Down for the Count (Bronze)	Defeat Rhino in the sewers
Friendly Neighbor (Bronze)	Save a hostage caught in a petty crime
FYI I'm Spider-Man (Bronze)	Perform 25 Signature Moves
Gladiator (Bronze)	Complete all Oscorp Secret Research Labs
Haymaker (Bronze)	Perform a Web-Rush punch
Heavyweight Champion (Gold)	Defeat 1000 enemies
I'm on a Roll! (Silver)	Achieve a combo streak of 42
Jinxed (Bronze)	Defeat Felicia
Journalist (Bronze)	Collect all audio evidence
Keep It Together (Bronze)	Immobilize 6 enemies simultaneously with web
Librarian (Bronze)	Collect all magazines

Lightweight Champion (Bronze)	Defeat 100 enemies
Middleweight Champion (Silver)	Defeat 500 enemies
Negotiator (Bronze)	Resolve all police deadlocks
On the Fly (Bronze)	Collect all 700 Spider-Man Comic Pages
Peace of Mind (Bronze)	Return all escapees to the police
Pest Control (Bronze)	Defeat Scorpion in the city
Peter Parker (Bronze)	Complete the game on human difficulty
Sanitized (Bronze)	Rescue all infected civilians
Siege Averted (Silver)	Defeat the S-01
Sky Captain (Bronze)	Chain 10 Web-Rushes in the city
Smell You Later (Bronze)	Defeat Vermin
Speed Bump Ahead (Bronze)	Defeat Rhino in the city
Spider-Man (Gold)	Complete the game on super hero difficulty
Stick to the Plan (Bronze) Stealth Takedowns	Defeat 50 enemies by performing
Switched Off (Silver)	Rescue Alistaire Smythe
Tail? You Lose (Bronze)	Defeat Scorpion in quarantine
Tech Savvy (Bronze)	Collect all hidden Tech Pieces
The Camera Loves You (Bronze)	Complete all XTreme Video challenges
The Sky Is the Limit (Silver)	Defeat the S-01 without touching the ground
Tomorrow Is Saved (Silver)	Defeat the S-03
Ultimate Spider-Man (Bronze)	Acquire all upgrades
Vigilante (Silver)	Complete the game on hero difficulty
Welcome Back, Friend (Silver)	Defeat Lizard
Who's the Prey? (Bronze)	Clear the first fight against the Hunter robots

UNLOCKABLE

UNLOCKABLE	HOW TO UNLOCK
1st Black Cat	125 pages of comics collected
1st Gwen Stacy	350 pages of comics collected
1st Iguana	250 pages of comics collected
1st Lizard	15 pages of comics collected
1st Rhino	50 pages of comics collected
1st Scorpion	80 pages of comics collected
1st Smythe	500 pages of comics collected
1st Spider-Man	5 pages of comics collected
Modern Lizard	30 pages of comics collected
Vs. Vermin	175 pages of comics collected
Big Time Suit	In Times Square behind the red bleachers, on the glass.
Classic Black Suit	Under the Gazebo in the narrow park, left of the main Oscorp Building downtown.
Classic Spider-man Costume	Unlocks with the activation of the Rhino Challenge DLC
Cross Species Spider-Man	Complete the game on any setting
Future Foundation Suit	Behind the gas station store in a small alley. One block right of north bridge
Negative Zone Suit	On top of Beenox building, second building inward from Brooklyn Bridge.

New Black Suit	Complete the game 100%
Scarlet Spider (2012) Costume	You need the camera to unlock this costume. Go to Central Park and from the fountain move north away from it until you see a bridge.

THE AMAZING SPIDER-MAN (XBOX 360)

ACHIEVEMENT

UNLOCKABLE	HOW TO UNLOCK
A Dash of Spider (15)	Completed all XTreme Race challenges
All Tied Up (15)	Defeated 100 enemies by performing Stealth Takedowns
Amazing Spider-Man (20)	Unlocked all concept art
Apparent Defeat (20)	Defeated Iguana
Beating the Odds (30)	Cleared the second fight against the Hunter robots
Big Apple, Big Worm (30)	Defeated the S-02
Call Interrupted (15)	Destroyed a Seeker before it could call a Hunter
Car Hopper (15)	Cleared all car chases
Clean Victory (20)	Defeated a Hunter without using your Web-Shooters
Corporate (15)	Collected all Oscorp Manuals
Deeply Sorry (20)	Defeated Nattie
Down for the Count (20)	Defeated Rhino in the sewers
Friendly Neighbor (15)	Saved a hostage caught in a petty crime
FYI I'm Spider-Man (10)	Performed 25 Signature Moves
Gladiator (15)	Completed all Oscorp Secret Research Labs
Haymaker (10)	Performed a Web-Rush punch
Heavyweight Champion (30)	Defeated 1000 enemies
I'm on a Roll! (15)	Achieved a combo streak of 42
Jinxed (20)	Defeated Felicia
Journalist (15)	Collected all audio evidence
Keep It Together (15)	Immobilized 6 enemies simultaneously with web
Librarian (15)	Collected all magazines
Lightweight Champion (15)	Defeated 100 enemies
Middleweight Champion (20)	Defeated 500 enemies
Negotiator (15)	Resolved all police deadlocks
On the Fly (25)	Collected all 700 Spider-Man Comic Pages
Peace of Mind (15)	Returned all escapees to the police
Pest Control (20)	Defeated Scorpion in the city
Peter Parker (25)	Completed the game on human difficulty
Sanitized (15)	Rescued all infected civilians
Siege Averted (30)	Defeated the S-01
Sky Captain (15)	Chained 10 Web-Rushes in the city
Smell You Later (20)	Defeated Vermin
Speed Bump Ahead (20)	Defeated Rhino in the city
Spider-Man (100)	Completed the game on super hero difficulty
Stick to the Plan (15)	Defeated 50 enemies by performing Stealth Takedowns
Switched Off (25)	Rescued Alistaire Smythe
Tail? You Lose (20)	Defeated Scorpion in quarantine
Tech Savvy (15)	Collected all hidden Tech Pieces

The Camera Loves You (15)	Completed all XTreme Video challenges
The Sky Is the Limit (20)	Defeated the S-01 without touching the ground
Tomorrow Is Saved (30)	Defeated the S-03
Ultimate Spider-Man (20)	Acquired all upgrades
Vigilante (50)	Completed the game on hero difficulty
Welcome Back, Friend (30)	Defeated Lizard
Who's the Prey? (30)	Cleared the first fight against the Hunter robots

UNLOCKABLE

UNLOCKABLE	HOW TO UNLOCK
Cross Species Spiderman	Beat on any difficulty.

THE AMAZING SPIDER-MAN (3DS)

ACHIEVEMENT

UNLOCKABLE	HOW TO UNLOCK
Classic Suit	Complete all petty crimes.

AMPED 3 (XBOX 360)

At the Main menu, go into Options, then into the Cheats menu to enter this code.

UNLOCKABLE	CODE
All Sleds	ⓇⓉ, ⊗, ⓁⓉ, ♀, ◇, ⓁⒷ, ⓁⓉ, ⓇⓉ, ♥, ⊗

AR TONELICO QOGA: KNELL OF AR CIEL (PLAYSTATION 3)

TROPHIES

UNLOCKABLE	HOW TO UNLOCK
Bronze - Bad Ending	Fail to defeat MYU before Song Completes.
Bronze - Battle Enthusiast	Fight and win 100 battles.
Bronze - Battle Lover	Fight and win 200 battles.
Bronze - Battle Maniac	Fight and win 300 battles.
Bronze - Chained Finnel	Finnel Cosmosphere L5 Event.
Bronze - Coward	Run from battle 100 times.
Bronze - Destroyer	Empty the Encounter Bar 25 times.
Bronze - Finnel Friendship	30% of Finnel's Cosmosphere Completed.
Bronze - Finnel Love Love	60% of Finnel's Cosmosphere Completed.
Bronze - Finnel Love Love 1	Phase 2 Finnel route Event.
Bronze - Finnel Love Love 2	Phase 3 Finnel route Event. Must have MAXED Hearts!
Bronze - Finnel Normal End	View Finnel's Normal Ending.
Bronze - Finnel's Master	100% of Finnel's Cosmosphere Completed.
Bronze - Frightened	Tilia Binary Field Game L3 Event.
Bronze - Frustration	Collect Max DP for any one of the girls.
Bronze - Game to a certain extent	Clock over 100 hours of game time.
Bronze - Hot Springs Panic!	Phase 2 Event.
Bronze - Longing for	Tilia Binary Field Game L2 and L3 Event.
Bronze - Older Sister Sakiya	Saki Cosmosphere L9 Event.
Bronze - On Stage!	Saki Cosmosphere L4 Event.
Bronze - Phase 1 Clear	Complete Phase 1 of the story.
Bronze - Phase 2 Clear	Complete Phase 2 of the story.
Bronze - Pregnant!?	Saki Cosmosphere L8 Event, Auto if Saki is chosen girl (3 hearts) or accept her love.

Bronze - Reunion with the children	Phase 2 Event.
Bronze - Saki Friendship	30% of Saki's Cosmosphere Completed.
Bronze - Saki Love Love	60% of Saki's Cosmosphere Completed.
Bronze - Saki Love Love 1	Phase 2 Saki route Event.
Bronze - Saki Love Love 2	Phase 3 Saki route Event. Must have MAXED Hearts!
Bronze - Saki Normal End	View Saki's Normal Ending.
Bronze - Saki Strips!	Saki Cosmosphere L3 or L4 Event.
Bronze - Saki's Groom	100% of Saki's Cosmosphere Completed.
Bronze - Salapator's Wedding	Phase 1 Event.
Bronze - Saving often is necessary don't you think?	Save the game 100 times.
Bronze - Singing to create a new world	Finnel Cosmosphere L9 Event.
Bronze - Soma Uninstall	Phase 2 Event.
Bronze - Soma VS Soma	Finnel Cosmosphere L7 Event.
Bronze - Synthesis Beginner	Synthesize 10 unique items
Bronze - Synthesis Expert	Synthesize 60 unique items
Bronze - Synthesis Intermediate	Synthesize 30 unique items
Bronze - The Long Missing Heart	Saki Cosmosphere L6 Event.
Bronze - Tilia Friendship	30% of Tilia's Binary Field Game Completed.
Bronze - Tilia Normal End	View Tilia's Normal Ending.
Bronze - Tilia's Husband	100% of Tilia's Binary Field Game Completed.
Bronze - Tillia Love Love 1	Tilia Phase 3 Event & Accepted her love.
Bronze - Tlia Love Love	60% of Tilia's Binary Field Game Completed.
Bronze - Treasure Hunter	Found and Opened all Treasure Chests.
Bronze - Truth	Tilia Binary Field Game L3 Event.
Bronze - Wailing	Finnel Cosmosphere L8 Event.
Bronze - Wealthy	Obtain Maximum Gold.
Bronze - Yurishica's Great Advance!!	Finnel Cosmosphere L3 Optional Event.
Gold - Purge Festival	In battle, purge heroine 3 levels, and all 3 members have used their super wazas.
Platinum - Ar tonelico thank you once again and next time	Collect all other Trophies
Silver - Breeder	Get to LV99 for all party members.
Silver - Cocona End	View Cocona's Ending.
Silver - Finnel True End	View Finnel's True Ending
Silver - Oyaki Master	Press Select during Cosmosphere dialouge 100 times.
Silver - Saki True End	View Saki's True Ending.
Silver - Tilia True End	View Tilia's True Ending.
Silver - What's wrong with being a pervert!?	Purge heroine 3 levels at once. (On red beat, with animation)

SECRETS

Once you are able to access the Cosmosphere, dive into it. Inside the cosmosphere, Hold L2 and press the triangle button to access the debug menu. In this menu you are able to open flag events, change character levels and parameters, even add money and create clear game files.

ARMORED CORE V (PLAYSTATION 3)

TROPHY

UNLOCKABLE	HOW TO UNLOCK
A Job Well Done (Bronze)	Awarded for successfully completing a job as a mercenary.
AC Wrecker (Bronze)	Awarded for winning a battle against an AC. Any type of mission counts.
Accomplish Territory Mission (Bronze)	Awarded for claiming victory on a Territory Mission.
Air Master (Bronze)	Awarded for destroying Raijin.
Assembler (Bronze)	Awarded for assembling an AC in a workshop.
Big Bird (Platinum)	Awarded for getting all trophies.
Blackbird (Bronze)	Awarded for destroying Exusia.
Charge Master (Bronze)	Awarded for destroying an enemy with a boost charge. Any type of enemy counts.
Color Customizer (Bronze)	Awarded for setting an AC's coloring in a workshop.
Communicator (Bronze)	Awarded for editing a message from the team member list.
Complete Custom Part (Bronze)	Awarded for continuing to use an arm unit to maximize its performance.
Complete Order Missions (Bronze)	Awarded for completing all Order Missions.
Complete Story Missions (Silver)	Awarded for completing all Story Missions.
Conquest Mission Sortie (Bronze)	Awarded for going on a Conquest Mission.
Conquest Mission Victory (Bronze)	Awarded for claiming victory on a Conquest Mission.
Customize Territory (Bronze)	Awarded for acquiring territory and placing gun batteries.
Earth Master (Bronze)	Awarded for destroying Type D No. 5.
Emblem Designer (Bronze)	Awarded for editing an emblem in a workshop.
Emblem Master (Bronze)	Awarded for getting all emblems and emblem pieces by buying them at the shop and/or destroying ACs. (Excludes downloadable emblems.)
Giant Killing (Bronze)	Awarded for destroying LLL.
Mercenary (Bronze)	Awarded for accepting and going on a job as a mercenary.
Migrant (Bronze)	Awarded for raising your money to 10 million Au or more.
MoH (Bronze)	Awarded for wiping out MoH.
Operator (Bronze)	Awarded for leading your team to victory on a Conquest Mission or Territory Mission.
Order Mission (Bronze)	Awarded for completing at least one Order Mission.
Overlord (Bronze)	Awarded for holding ten different territories at the same time.
Perfect Mission (Bronze)	Awarded for completing emergency Territory/Conquest Mission w/four or more members, all surviving.
Rookie (Bronze)	Awarded for joining a team.

Ruler (Gold)	Awarded for holding one territory in all areas at the same time.
Sea Master (Bronze)	Awarded for destroying St Elmo.
Story 00 (Bronze)	Awarded for completing Story Mission 00.
Story 01 (Bronze)	Awarded for completing Story Mission 01.
Story 02 (Bronze)	Awarded for completing Story Mission 02.
Story 03 (Bronze)	Awarded for completing Story Mission 03.
Story 04 (Bronze)	Awarded for completing Story Mission 04.
Story 05 (Bronze)	Awarded for completing Story Mission 05.
Story 06 (Bronze)	Awarded for completing Story Mission 06.
Story 07 (Bronze)	Awarded for completing Story Mission 07.
Story 08 (Bronze)	Awarded for completing Story Mission 08.
Story 09 (Bronze)	Awarded for completing Story Mission 09.
Story Master (Gold)	Awarded for completing all Story Missions with Rank S.
Subquest Master (Gold)	Awarded for completing all Story Mission and Order Mission subquests.
Subquests 30% (Bronze)	Awarded for completing 30% of all Story Mission and Order Mission subquests.
Subquests 50% (Bronze)	Awarded for completing 50% of all Story Mission and Order Mission subquests.
Team Level 10 (Bronze)	Awarded for raising the team level of your team to 10 or higher.
Team Level 50 (Silver)	Awarded for raising the team level of your team to 50 or higher.
Team Sortie (Bronze)	Awarded for going on a Conquest Mission or Territory Mission with four or more team members.
Territorial Claim (Silver)	Awarded for claiming victory and taking territory on a Conquest Mission.
Territory Mission Sortie (Bronze)	Awarded for going on a Territory Mission.
Territory Mission Victory (Silver)	Awarded for claiming victory on a Territory Mission in an emergency state.
Zodiac (Silver)	Awarded for destroying all Zodiac members.

ARMORED CORE V (XBOX 360)

ACHIEVEMENT

UNLOCKABLE	HOW TO UNLOCK
A Job Well Done (10)	Awarded for successfully completing a job as a mercenary.
AC Wrecker (15)	Awarded for winning a battle against an AC. Any type of mission counts.
Accomplish Territory Mission (10)	Awarded for claiming victory on a Territory Mission.
Air Master (30)	Awarded for destroying Raijin.
Assembler (5)	Awarded for assembling an AC in a workshop.
Blackbird (30)	Awarded for destroying Exusia.
Charge Master (5)	Awarded for destroying an enemy with a boost charge. Any type of enemy counts.
Color Customizer (5)	Awarded for setting an AC's coloring in a workshop.
Communicator (5)	Awarded for editing a message from the team member list.

Complete Custom Part (15)	Awarded for continuing to use an arm unit to maximize its performance.
Complete Order Missions (40)	Awarded for completing all Order Missions.
Complete Story Missions (50)	Awarded for completing all Story Missions.
Conquest Mission Sortie (5)	Awarded for going on a Conquest Mission.
Conquest Mission Victory (30)	Awarded for claiming victory on a Conquest Mission.
Customize Territory (10)	Awarded for acquiring territory and placing gun batteries.
Earth Master (30)	Awarded for destroying Type D No. 5.
Emblem Designer (5)	Awarded for editing an emblem in a workshop.
Emblem Master (30)	Awarded for getting all emblems and emblem pieces by buying them at the shop and/or destroying ACs. (Excludes downloadable emblems.)
Giant Killing (30)	Awarded for destroying LLL.
Mercenary (5)	Awarded for accepting and going on a job as a mercenary.
Migrant (20)	Awarded for raising your money to 10 million Au or more.
MoH (30)	Awarded for wiping out MoH.
Operator (15)	Awarded for leading your team to victory on a Conquest Mission or Territory Mission.
Order Mission (10)	Awarded for completing at least one Order Mission.
Overlord (30)	Awarded for holding ten different territories at the same time.
Perfect Mission (30)	Awarded for completing emergency Territory/ Conquest Mission w/four or more members, all surviving.
Rookie (5)	Awarded for joining a team.
Ruler (50)	Awarded for holding one territory in all areas at the same time.
Sea Master (30)	Awarded for destroying St Elmo.
Story 00 (10)	Awarded for completing Story Mission 00.
Story 01 (10)	Awarded for completing Story Mission 01.
Story 02 (10)	Awarded for completing Story Mission 02.
Story 03 (10)	Awarded for completing Story Mission 03.
Story 04 (10)	Awarded for completing Story Mission 04.
Story 05 (10)	Awarded for completing Story Mission 05.
Story 06 (10)	Awarded for completing Story Mission 06.
Story 07 (10)	Awarded for completing Story Mission 07.
Story 08 (10)	Awarded for completing Story Mission 08.
Story 09 (10)	Awarded for completing Story Mission 09.
Story Master (50)	Awarded for completing all Story Missions with Rank S.
Subquest Master (50)	Awarded for completing all Story Mission and Order Mission subquests.
Subquests 30% (20)	Awarded for completing 30% of all Story Mission and Order Mission subquests.

Subquests 50% (20)	Awarded for completing 50% of all Story Mission and Order Mission subquests.
Team Level 10 (15)	Awarded for raising the team level of your team to 10 or higher.
Team Level 50 (40)	Awarded for raising the team level of your team to 50 or higher.
Team Sortie (15)	Awarded for going on a Conquest Mission or Territory Mission with four or more team members.
Territorial Claim (30)	Awarded for claiming victory and taking territory on a Conquest Mission.
Territory Mission Sortie (5)	Awarded for going on a Territory Mission.
Territory Mission Victory (30)	Awarded for claiming victory on a Territory Mission in an emergency state.
Zodiac (40)	Awarded for destroying all Zodiac members.

ARMY CORPS OF HELL (PLAYSTATION VITA)

TROPHY

UNLOCKABLE	HOW TO UNLOCK
Alchemist of Hell (Gold)	Alchemized all possible weapons, armor, and items.
Bastion of Bloodshed (Silver)	Completely filled the Demonic Compendium.
Champion of Courage (Bronze)	Alchemized equipment for spearmen.
Cleanser of Hell (Gold)	Crushed 3,000 foes.
Demon God's Bane (Silver)	Defeated all bosses.
Eternal Reaper (Silver)	Crushed 1,000 foes.
Grim Trailer (Silver)	Achieved an overall platinum rating ten or more times.
Hell's Magi (Bronze)	Cleared a stage between 11 and 20 with magi only.
Hell's Serenader (Bronze)	Achieved the maximum rating (excellent) in one of the musical instrument mini-games.
Hell's Soldiers (Bronze)	Cleared a stage between 11 and 20 with soldiers only.
Hell's Spearmen (Bronze)	Cleared a stage between 11 and 20 with spearmen only.
Infamy of Hell (Bronze)	Cleared a stage between 11 and 20 with an overall platinum rating.
Infamy of Purgatory (Silver)	Cleared a Purgatory stage (21-30) with an overall platinum rating.
Infamy of Tartarus (Gold)	Cleared a Tartarus stage (31-40) with an overall platinum rating.
Lord of Hell (Bronze)	Cleared up to stage 20.
Lord of Purgatory (Silver)	Cleared all Purgatory stages (21-30).
Lord of Tartarus (Gold)	Cleared all Tartarus stages (31-40).
Overlord of the Underworld (Platinum)	Obtained all trophies.
Pinnacle of Gore (Gold)	Exceeded 66,666 jewels in your possession.
Purgatory's Magi (Silver)	Cleared a Purgatory stage (21-30) with magi only.
Purgatory's Soldiers (Silver)	Cleared a Purgatory stage (21-30) with soldiers only.
Purgatory's Spearmen (Silver)	Cleared a Purgatory stage (21-30) with spearmen only.
Resurrection Inceptor (Bronze)	Cleared the first stage.

Ringleader of the Wretched (Bronze)	Alchemized first equipment for magi.
Sage of Antiquity (Bronze)	Alchemized first equipment for soldiers.
Sage of Spears (Silver)	Alchemized all weapons and armor for spearmen.
Sage of Staffs (Silver)	Alchemized all weons and armor for magi.
Sage of Swords (Silver)	Alchemized all weapons and armor for soldiers.
Sage of the Abyss (Bronze)	Alchemized all consumable items.
Sin's Slaughterer (Bronze)	Crushed 100 foes.

CODES

NAME	CODE
Gouls Attack!	G75i8K8a
GxSxD	GUK218Jh
KING'S-EVIL	KB2p3tAs
KNIGHTS OF ROUND	K77w3P5a
Rachel Mother Goose	RJ53z42i
Rebel-Survive	S4R29dlu (l is a capitol "i")
United	U541337k

ARMY OF TWO (PLAYSTATION 3)

CODES

During gameplay press the following:

EFFECT	CODE
Unlimited Life and Ammo	▲, ▲, ✕, ✕, L2, R2, R1, R2, ●, ■

ART OF FIGHTING (WII)

CHARACTER UNLOCKABLES

UNLOCKABLE	HOW TO UNLOCK
Mr. Big	Get to Mr. Big in 1-player mode and lose the match. Restart the game and Mr. Big will now be unlocked in 2-player mode.
Mr. Karate	Get to Mr. Karate in 1-player mode and lose the match. Restart the game and Mr. Karate will now be unlocked in 2-player mode.

ASPHALT: INJECTION (PLAYSTATION VITA)

TROPHY

UNLOCKABLE	HOW TO UNLOCK
1, 2, 3 (Bronze)	Perform 3 knockdowns in 10 seconds
Accomplished (Gold)	Finish every race in Career Mode
Air Time (Bronze)	Hit at least 1 jump in each lap in a single race
Around the world (Gold)	Earn over 1000 drift points in a single drift
Asphalt Domination (Platinum)	Collect all Asphalt trophies
Berserk (Silver)	Perform 5 knockdowns in 20 seconds
Blowout (Bronze)	Finish each lap in first place in a single race
Bouncing Bucket (Bronze)	Jump 1000m in a single race
Brute (Bronze)	Knock down 10 opponents in a race
CARnage! (Silver)	Knock down 15 opponents in a race
Catapulting Clunker (Silver)	Jump 1500m in a single race
Collection Master (Bronze)	Collect more than half of the purple cash items in a Collector race
Contender (Silver)	Win 10 multiplayer races
Drift to the beat (Bronze)	Earn over 500 drift points in a Beat 'em All race
Drift Warrior (Gold)	Knock down an opponent while drifting

Drifter (Bronze)	Earn over 2000 drift points in a single race
First First! (Bronze)	Finish in 1st place!
Get Away From Me! (Bronze)	Complete a Normal Race without touching an opponent
Harasser (Bronze)	Perform at least 3 knockdowns on the same opponent
Legend (Gold)	Win 100 multiplayer races
Lickety Split (Bronze)	Collect 25 Nitro power-ups in a single race
Perfectionist (Silver)	Obtain the maximum amount of stars for all events in a league
Persistant (Bronze)	Complete 50 races
Photo finish (Silver)	Finish 1st in a MP race less than 1s ahead of the 2nd-place finisher
Safety First (Bronze)	Complete a Normal Race without crashing once
Shakedown (Gold)	Knock down each opponent at least once in a single race
Show-off (Bronze)	Cross the finish line while drifting
Spotless (Bronze)	Complete a Normal Race without touching a wall
Survivor (Bronze)	Win an Under Pressure race without crashing once
Three in a Row! (Bronze)	Finish in 1st place 3 times in a row!
Tire-Greater (Silver)	Earn over 3000 drift points in a single race
Too Good (Bronze)	Win a race without using Nitro
Velocius (Silver)	Collect 35 Nitro power-ups in a single race
Veteran (Silver)	Complete 100 multiplayer races

ASSASSIN'S CREED: BROTHERHOOD (XBOX 360)

CAPES

UNLOCKABLE	HOW TO UNLOCK
Auditore Cape	Rebuild Rome
Borgia Cape	Collect all Borgia Flags
Medici Cape	You need to get to Level 30 on the "Assassin's Creed: Project Legacy" Facebook game
Venetian Cape	You need to get to Level 30 on the "Assassin's Creed: Project Legacy" Facebook game

COSTUMES

UNLOCKABLE	HOW TO UNLOCK
Raiden's Costume	Complete all of the tasks in the Animus 2.0 training mode

MEMORY EXTRAS

When you complete a memory sequence, you will be awarded with a cheat that you can activate when you are replaying a completed memory.

UNLOCKABLE	HOW TO UNLOCK
Buns of Steel	100% sync on Sequence 2
Desmond Everywhere	100% sync on Sequence 8
Killing Spree	100% sync on Sequence 3
Ride the Unicorn	100% sync on Sequence 1
Sisterhood	100% sync on Sequence 4
Ultimate Guild	100% sync on Sequence 5
Unlimited Assassin Signals	100% sync on Sequence 6

A
B
C
D
E
F
G
H
I
J
K
L
M
N
O
P
Q
R
S
T
U
V
W
X
Y
Z

GUILD REWARDS

By leveling up with the guilds, you can obtain certain items for Ezio to use. They will appear in Ezio's hideout.

UNLOCKABLE	HOW TO UNLOCK
Assassin's Guild Crest	Complete all Assassins Guild challenges.
Bartolomeo's Axe	Get each guild to Level 3
Courtesans Guild Crest	Get each guild to Level 2
La Volpe's Bite	Get each guild to Level 3
Maria's Dagger	Get each guild to Level 3
Mercenaries Guild Crest	Get each guild to Level 2
Sword of Altair	Complete all Assassins Guild challenges
Thieves Guild Crest	Get each guild to Level 2

UPLAY UNLOCKABLES

UNLOCKABLE	HOW TO UNLOCK
Altair armor skin for Ezio	Obtain 20 Uplay points and use them via Uplay account
Altair skin	Obtain 20 Uplay points and use them via Uplay account
Assassin's Creed Brotherhood Theme	Gain 10 Uplay points and spend them
Florentine Noble in-game skin	Gain 20 Uplay points and spend them
Hellequin (multiplayer character)	Obtain 40 Uplay points
Upgrade hidden pistol ammo capacity	Gain 30 Uplay points and spend them

ASSASSIN'S CREED: REVELATIONS (XBOX 360)

UNLOCKABLE

The following are unlocked as you collect Animus Data Fragments in the game.

UNLOCKABLE	HOW TO UNLOCK
"Capped" Achievement	Collect 100 Fragments
Animus Data Fragments appear on Map	Collect 50 Fragments
Desmond Memory Sequence 1	Collecr 5 Fragments
Desmond Memory Sequence 2	Collect 10 Fragments
Desmond Memory Sequence 3	Collect 15 Fragments
Desmond Memory Sequence 4	Collect 20 Fragments
Desmond Memory Sequence 5	Collect 30 Fragments
Ishak Pasha's Memoir Pages available to buy at Book Shop	Collect 25 Fragments

UNLOCKABLE

Complete the following to unlock these.

UNLOCKABLE	HOW TO UNLOCK
Altair's Sword	Complete the Set 3 Assassin Challenges
Broadsword	Complete the Set 3 Mercenary Challenges
Buns of Steel	Complete Sequence 2 with 100% sync
Calling All Assassins	Complete Sequence 5 with 100% sync
Desmon Miles skin	Complete the Desmond memory gates
Hired Mercenaries stop beggars	Complete the Set 2 Mercenary Challenges
Hired Romanies poison guards	Complete the Set 2 Romani Challenges
Hired Thieves pickpocket akçe	Complete the Set 2 Thief Challenges
Infinite Ammunition	Complete Sequence 7 with 100% sync
Ishak Pasha's Armor	Collect all 10 Memoir Pages

Killing Spree	Complete Sequence 3 with 100% sync
Ottoman Mace	Complete the Set 3 Thief Challenges
Permanent Secrecy	Complete Sequence 6 with 100% sync
Romani Stiletto	Complete the Set 3 Romani Challenges
The Old Eagle Outfit	Complete Sequence 8 with 100% sync
Ultimate Guild	Complete Sequence 4 with 100% sync

ACHIEVEMENT

UNLOCKABLE	HOW TO UNLOCK
A Friend Indeed (20)	Complete all Faction Creed Challenges from a single faction.
Achiever (10)	Complete a Challenge (Multiplayer).
Almost Flying (20)	Parachute directly from the top of the Galata Tower to the golden horn.
Are You Desmond Miles? (20)	Complete Desmond Sequence 5.
Armchair General (20)	Control all cities (except Rhodes) simultaneously in the Mediterranian Defense game.
Best Served Cold (20)	Complete DNA Sequence 1.
Bully (20)	Find and beat up Duccio.
Capped (20)	Collect all animus data fragments.
Craft Maniac (20)	Craft 30 bombs.
Escape To New York (20)	Complete Desmond Sequence 3.
Explorer (20)	Finish a session of each game mode (Multiplayer).
Fast Fingers (20)	Loot 50 dead guards with thief looting.
Fond Memories (20)	Achieve 100% Synchronization in all Sequences.
Holy Wisdom (20)	Complete the Hagia Sofia challenge level.
I can see you (20)	Kill 5 guards while under the cover of a smoke screen bomb.
Iron Curtain (20)	Perform a perfect den defense without using the cannon.
Istanbul and Constantinople (20)	Complete DNA Sequence 2.
Lightning Strikes (20)	Kill 5 guards in 5 seconds using only your hidden blades.
Looking Good (10)	Customize a PERSONA (Multiplayer).
Make the Headlines (30)	Obtain 12 different Accolades (Multiplayer).
Mastering the Art (30)	Earn the INCOGNITO bonus (Multiplayer).
Monster's Dance (20)	Have a guard incapacitate 3 civilians while he's poisoned.
Mosh Pit (20)	Have 10 guards poisoned at the same time.
Mouse Trap (20)	Kill 5 guards with a scaffold after they have been stunned by caltrops.
My Protégé (20)	Have one trainee reach the rank of Master Assassin.
Old Boss, New Boss (20)	Complete DNA Sequence 7.
Overkiller (20)	Assassinate 50 guards with the hidden blade.
Priorities (20)	Complete DNA Sequence 8.
Pyromaniac (20)	Complete all Bomb Missions.
Revelations (50)	Complete DNA Sequence 9.
Sage (20)	Collect all available books.
Seal the Deal (20)	Complete DNA Sequence 3.
Show-Off (20)	Parachute onto a zipline.

Silent But Deadly (20)	Kill three guards simultaneously with only throwing knives.
Spider Assassin (20)	Climb Hagia Sofia, from the ground to the pinnacle, in under 25 seconds.
Successes and Failures (20)	Complete DNA Sequence 6.
Tactician (30)	Score at least 2500 points in a session (Multiplayer).
Tax Evasion (10)	Get your money back from a Templar tax collector.
The Early Years (20)	Complete Desmond Sequence 1.
The Mentor (20)	Have seven trainees reach the rank of Master Assassin.
The Plot Thickens (20)	Complete DNA Sequence 5.
The Prince (20)	Complete DNA Sequence 4.
The Reluctant Assassin (20)	Complete Desmond Sequence 2.
The Rotten Apple (20)	Complete Desmond Sequence 4.
The Way I Like It (20)	Edit your TEMPLAR PROFILE to change your title, emblem, and patron (Multiplayer).
There Is No I in Team (20)	Win a session of a team mode (Multiplayer).
Tools of the Templar (10)	Purchase your first ABILITY in the Abstergo Store (Multiplayer).
True Templar (20)	Reach level 20 (Multiplayer).
Worth A Thousand Words (20)	Collect all of Ishak Pasha's memoir pages.

ASURA'S WRATH (PLAYSTATION 3)

TROPHY

UNLOCKABLE	HOW TO UNLOCK
Platinum (Platinum)	Obtain all trophies.
A Cry of Anger (Bronze)	Activate Burst 50 times.
A Roar of Fury (Bronze)	Activate Burst 100 times.
Hit 'Em Hard (Bronze)	Defeat 100 enemies with a special attack.
Hit 'Em Harder (Bronze)	Defeat 300 enemies with a special attack.
Can't Touch This (Bronze)	Perform 50 counterattacks.
Can't Touch That (Bronze)	Perform 100 counterattacks.
They Don't Stand a Chance (Bronze)	Defeat 50 enemies while in Unlimited Mode.
Unstoppable Force (Bronze)	Defeat 100 enemies while in Unlimited Mode.
Taking Out the Trash (Bronze)	Defeat 300 enemies with heavy attacks and/or lock-on fire.
Quick on the Draw (Bronze)	Achieve 70 EXCELLENT synchronic impact rankings.
Lightning Reflexes (Bronze)	Achieve 150 EXCELLENT synchronic impact rankings.
Be the Fist (Bronze)	Achieve an overall synchronic rate average of 80% on any difficulty.
Pain Is Universal (Bronze)	Accumulate a total of 10000 in damage.
Too Legit to Quit (Bronze)	Continue the game after falling in battle.
Look Ma, No Eyes! (Silver)	Complete the game with the Blind Master gauge equipped.
Who Needs Health? (Gold)	Complete the game with the Mortal gauge equipped.
Ka-ching! (Silver)	Accumulate a total of 120000 Battle points.
View of the Valley (Bronze)	Continue to stare at the hot spring attendant's assets.
Like a Fish (Bronze)	Consume more alcohol than you should.

Sometimes I Feel Like... (Bronze)	Find all the peeping Doji at the hot spring.
Shut Up, Wyzen! (Bronze)	Interrupt Wyzen's monologue.
Shut Up, Kalrow! (Bronze)	Interrupt Kalrow's monologue.
Shut Up, Augus! (Bronze)	Interrupt Augus' monologue.

ASURA'S WRATH (XBOX 360)

ACHIEVEMENT

UNLOCKABLE	HOW TO UNLOCK
A Cry of Anger (15)	Activate Burst a certain number of times.
A Roar of Fury (20)	Activate Burst a certain number of times.
Hit'Em Hard (15)	Defeat a certain number of enemies with a special attack.
Hit'Em Harder (20)	Defeat a certain number of enemies with a special attack.
Can't Touch This (15)	Perform a certain number of counterattacks.
Can't Touch That (20)	Perform a certain number of counterattacks.
They Don't Stand a Chance (15)	Defeat a certain number of enemies while in Unlimited Mode.
Unstoppable Force (20)	Defeat a certain number of enemies while in Unlimited Mode.
Taking Out the Trash (15)	Defeat a certain number of enemies with heavy attacks, lock-on fire, or both.
Quick on the Draw (15)	Achieve a certain number of EXCELLENT synchronic impact rankings.
Lightning Reflexes (20)	Achieve a certain number of EXCELLENT synchronic impact rankings.
Be the Fist (20)	Achieve a certain percentage for your overall synchronic rate average.
Pain Is Universal (15)	Prove that you can take a beating.
Too Legit to Quit (15)	If at first you don't succeed...
Look Ma, No Eyes! (30)	Complete all episodes with a certain gauge equipped.
Who Needs Health? (90)	Complete all episodes with a certain gauge equipped.
Ka-ching! (30)	Accumulate a certain number of battle points.
View of the Valley (15)	When visiting the hot spring, look at the hostess' chest.
Like a Fish (15)	Knock back a few bottles.
Sometimes I Feel Like... (15)	Find all the peeping toms at the hot spring.
Shut Up, Wyzen! (15)	Interrupt the fat one's monologue.
Shut Up, Kalrow! (15)	Interrupt the old one's monologue.
Shut Up, Augus! (15)	Interrupt your former master's monologue.

ATELIER MERURU: THE APPRENTICE OF ARLAND (PLAYSTATION 3)

TROPHY

UNLOCKABLE	HOW TO UNLOCK
A Rich Nation (Silver)	Make Arls rich, developing it into an agricultural powerhouse.
Admission Ceremony (Bronze)	Reach the initial goal and help Arls merge with Arland.
Alchemist! (Gold)	Become an alchemist of Arland and open Atelier Meruru.
All Trophies Earned (Platinum)	Obtain all trophies.
Atelier Totori (Current) (Bronze)	Hear the stories of Miss Totori and her friends.

Boy's Bath (Silver)	Transform Arls into a grand vacation paradise.
Brothers Together (Bronze)	Witness Lias bask in the glow of Rufus's approval.
Castle Life (Silver)	Return to your boring life in the castle.
Certain Sisters (Bronze)	Take a peek at Filly and Esty's intimate sisterhood.
Changing the Past (Bronze)	Bring closure to the tragedy of Arls.
Closer to God (Bronze)	Stare into the abyss and win out against the evil goddess.
Drunkard Legend EX (Bronze)	Suffer the indignity of a drunk's advances at the tavern.
End of the Duel (Bronze)	Encounter a master-pupil showdown between Sterk and Gino.
Finally, As Planned (Silver)	Make friends with the forever-14 Rorolina Frixell.
Friendship, Love (Bronze)	Help Totori and Mimi get along.
Girl's Bath (Bronze)	Visit the hot spring with a group of all girls.
God of the Forest (Bronze)	Put the energetic spirit of the tree into an eternal slumber.
How Do I Look...? (Bronze)	Force Keina to wear some princessly clothes.
Look into the Past (Bronze)	Glimpse Gio lost in thought at the fort.
Masked Man Reappears (Bronze)	Run into Arland's manly masked crusader.
Meruru Statue Complete! (Gold)	Construct a statue of Meruru to mark your achievements.
Miss Popular (Gold)	Gain popularity with everyone.
Now, Go Bravely (Silver)	Arm Arls to the teeth and take command of it all.
Ominous Box (Bronze)	Battle the coffin-bound monster in the mine and emerge victorious.
One from the Sky (Bronze)	Ascend to the ancient city and cast down the ruler of the sky.
One Normal Day (Bronze)	Let Keina help you change at the workshop.
Pie Shop Opens (Bronze)	Construct a Pie Shop and visit with Rorona.
Presence of the Flame (Bronze)	Subdue the Volcano Incarnate.
Resemblance (Bronze)	Find Rufus and Sterk getting along at the tavern.
Rorona Introduction (Bronze)	Watch as a legendary alchemist and her troupe visit the workshop.
Secret Tea Party (Bronze)	Stumble upon Rufus's solitary tea time.
Stars Never Change (Bronze)	Gaze at a starry night sky with Keina and reminisce about the past.
Strongest Princess (Gold)	Become a hero and the land's strongest princess.
Topsy-Turvy (Gold)	Take Arls's population to the limit and turn it into a superpower.
Waterside Encounter (Bronze)	Discover Hanna as she bathes.
Witch's Tea Party (Gold)	Master alchemy and together become feared as the Four Witches.

ATELIER TOTORI: THE ADVENTURER OF ARLAND (PLAYSTATION 3)

TROPHY

UNLOCKABLE	HOW TO UNLOCK
A New Journey (Silver)	See Marc's Ending.
Adventurer BFFs (Silver)	See Mimi's Ending.
Alchemy Restaurant (Gold)	With limitless funding, Totori opens a restaurant.
Ambushed (Silver)	View the event where Melvia and Ceci are cornered.

Arise, McVellion! (Silver)	View the event where McVellion activates.
Aristocratic Love (Silver)	View the event where Mimi tries to cheer Totori up.
Bad End (Bronze)	Watched the bad ending.
Catch of the Day (Bronze)	Haul in a 'fishy fishy' from Alanya.
Chivalrous Defender (Silver)	View the event where Gino learns his strongest skill.
Cuteness Swarm! (Bronze)	See the event detailing Chim's birth.
Fishing Festival (Gold)	Hold the swimsuit contest.
Haunted Doll? (Silver)	Learn the truth about Pamela.
Indecisive Knight (Silver)	See Sterk's Ending.
Legendary 'Fish' (Silver)	Learned the true nature of the 'Guardian.'
Legendary Drunkard (Silver)	Went with Tiffani and Filly to have a drink.
Like the Flash (Bronze)	Get rescued on your way to Arland.
Monstrous Power (Bronze)	View Melvia's introduction.
Normal End (Silver)	Watched the normal ending.
Promises (Silver)	See Melvia's Ending.
Receive All Other Trophies (Platinum)	Received All Other Trophies.
Shouting Match (Bronze)	Witness Cordelia and some other girl arguing.
Still a Child (Silver)	View the event where Ceci embraces Totori.
The Hardest Workers (Silver)	See Chim's Ending.
Tragic Discovery (Gold)	Learn the final whereabouts of Totori's mother.
True End (Gold)	Watched the true ending.
Two Masters (Silver)	See Gino's Ending.
Unlikely Party (Silver)	Reminisce with Rorona and her friends at Iksel's restaurant.
Usual Scenery (Bronze)	Watched the opening event.
Who's the Teacher? (Silver)	See Rorona's Ending.

CODES & CHEATS

B

BAND HERO (XBOX 360)

CODES
Select "Input Cheats" under the Options menu. G = Green, R = Red, Y = Yellow, B = Blue.

EFFECT	CODE
Air Instruments	B,Y,B,R,R,Y,G,Y
All HO/POs	R,G,B,G,B,G,R,G
Always Slide	Y,G,Y,Y,Y,R,B,R
Auto Kick	Y,G,Y,B,B,R,B,R
Electrika Steel Unlocked	B,B,R,Y,R,Y,B,B
Focus Mode	Y,Y,G,G,R,R,B,B
HUD-Free Mode	G,R,G,R,Y,B,G,R
Invisible Characters	G,R,Y,G,Y,B,Y,G
Most Characters Unlocked	B,Y,G,Y,R,G,R,Y
Performance Mode	Y,Y,B,G,B,R,R,R

BONUS CHARACTERS
Complete the mission on Tour to unlock the listed characters.

UNLOCKABLE	HOW TO UNLOCK
Adam Levine	Successfully complete the Maroon 5 "She Will Be Loved" gig.
Adrian Young	Successfully complete the No Doubt "Don't Speak" gig.
Frankenrocker	Successfully complete the Diamond Bonus Challenge for the Fall Out Boy "Sugar, We're Goin' Down" gig.
Gwen Stefani	Successfully complete the No Doubt "Don't Speak" gig.
Shadow Character	Successfully complete the Gold Bonus Challenge for the David Bowie "Let's Dance" gig.
Taylor Swift	Successfully complete the Taylor Swift "Love Story" gig.
Tom Dumont	Successfully complete the No Doubt "Don't Speak" gig.
Tony Kanal	Successfully complete the No Doubt "Don't Speak" gig.

BANJO-KAZOOIE: NUTS & BOLTS (XBOX 360)

UNLOCKABLES
After beating the game, L.O.G. will give you a Banjo Head Vehicle. The Banjo Head Vehicle can be loaded from the L.O.G's choice option.

BASES LOADED (WII)

PASSWORDS

PASSWORD	EFFECT
LFBDJHE	Boston, one game away from the World Series
PFACNHK	DC, one game away from the World Series
CHXAACC	Game 162
LNADJPD	Hawaii, one game away from the World Series
CBIDNEP	Jersey, last game of the World Series
LFADNHH	Jersey, one game away from the World Series
PNCBNHD	Kansas, one game away from the World Series
PFBCNPD	LA, one game away from the World Series

PFCANHK	Miami, one game away from the World Series
PFDAJHH	New York, one game away from the World Series
LNDAJPD	Omaha, one game away from the World Series
JAELECO	Password for Pennant, must have selected "Pennant" option from menu
LFDBJHE	Philly, one game away from the World Series
Select Pennant Mode and Enter JALECO as Password	Skip to the last team
LNCBJPD	Texas, one game away from the World Series
LNBCJPD	Utah, one game away from the World Series

OTHER ACTIONS

ACTION	HOW TO ENACT
Don't Get Ejected During a Fight	Continually press Ⓑ during the fight
Hitter Charges the Mound and Gets Ejected	After the 3rd inning, bean the 3rd or 4th hitter in the lineup

BATMAN: ARKHAM ASYLUM   (PLAYSTATION 3)

UNLOCKABLES

UNLOCKABLE	HOW TO UNLOCK
Armored-suit Batman	Complete the game. Can only be used in Challenge Mode.

BATMAN: ARKHAM CITY   (PLAYSTATION 3)

TROPHY

UNLOCKABLE	HOW TO UNLOCK
50x Combon (Bronze)	Complete a combo of 50 moves (any play mode, any character)
Acid Bath (Bronze)	Save the damsel, but is she in distress?
Aggravated Assault (Bronze)	Stop all assaults in Arkham City
AR Knight (Silver)	Complete all augmented reality training exercises
Bargaining Chip (Bronze)	Reunite the separated couple
Brainteaser (Silver)	Rescue the fifth hostage from Riddler
Broken Toys (Silver)	Destroy it all
Bronze Revenge (Bronze)	Obtain 24 medals on the original Arkham City ranked maps (as Batman)
Campaign Bronze (Bronze)	Obtain 36 medals on the original Arkham City campaigns (as Batman)
Campaign Gold (Silver)	Obtain all 108 medals on the original Arkham City campaigns (as Batman)
Campaign Silver (Bronze)	Obtain 72 medals on the original Arkham City campaigns (as Batman)
Catch (Bronze)	Find someone to play remote Batarang catch with
Chimney Sweep (Bronze)	There is only one way in
Communication Breakdown (Bronze)	Clear the airwaves
Contract Terminated (Silver)	Stop the contract operative
Conundrum (Bronze)	Rescue the first hostage from Riddler
Dial Z For Murder (Silver)	Stop the phone booth killer
Distress Flare (Bronze)	Answer the call for help
Exit Stage Right (Silver)	All the world is a stage
Flawless Freeflow Fighter 2.0 (Bronze)	Complete one combat challenge without taking damage (any character)

Forensic Expert (Bronze)	Collect enough evidence to locate the gun for hire
Freefall (Bronze)	Don't look down
Fully Loaded (Bronze)	Collect all of Batman's gadgets and upgrades
Gadget Attack (Bronze)	Use 5 different Quickfire gadgets in one fight (any play mode)
Genius (Silver)	Rescue all the hostages from Riddler
Ghost Train (Silver)	Fight for survival
Gladiator (Bronze)	Last man standing
Gold Revenge (Silver)	Obtain all 72 medals on the original Arkham City ranked maps (as Batman)
Gotham Base Jumper (Bronze)	Jump off the tallest building in Arkham City and glide for 1 minute without touching the ground.
Hide And Seek (Silver)	A deadly game of hide and seek
I'm Batman (Bronze)	Become the Bat
Intellectual (Bronze)	Rescue the fourth hostage from Riddler
IQ Test (Bronze)	Solve the first riddle
Lost And Found (Bronze)	Uncover the secret of Arkham City
Mastermind (Bronze)	Rescue the second hostage from Riddler
Mystery Stalker (Bronze)	Reveal the mystery watcher
One-Armed Bandit (Bronze)	Hammer the point home
Pay Your Respects (Bronze)	A moment of remembrance
Perfect Freeflow 2.0 (Bronze)	Perform a perfect combo including all of Batman's combat moves (any play mode)
Perfect Knight - Day 2 (Gold)	Complete every challenge in Arkham City - Main Story, Side Missions, Upgrades, Collectables, New Game Plus and Riddlers Revenge (as Batman)
Platinum (Platinum)	Congratulations!
Puzzler (Bronze)	Rescue the third hostage from Riddler
Ring Ring (Bronze)	Answer a ringing phone
Sandstorm (Silver)	We are legion
Savior (Bronze)	Save the medical volunteers
Serial Killer (Silver)	Track down the serial killer
Silver Revenge (Bronze)	Obtain 48 medals on the original Arkham City ranked maps (as Batman)
Stop the Clock (Bronze)	Time is running out
Storyteller (Bronze)	Have 12 murderous dates with Calendar Man
Twice Nightly (Silver)	Complete New Game Plus
Wrecking Ball (Silver)	Stop the unstoppable

BATTLE CITY (WII)

STAGE SELECT

UNLOCKABLE	HOW TO UNLOCK
Stage Select	When you start the game and see the screen with "Stage 1," press Ⓐ and Ⓑ to choose any stage you want.

BATTLEFIELD 3 (XBOX 360)

ACHIEVEMENT

UNLOCKABLE	HOW TO UNLOCK
1st Loser (30)	Finish as 2nd MVP in a ranked match
Army of Darkness (30)	Shoot out the 4 lights with 4 bullets in Night Shift
Army of Two (50)	Complete all co-op missions on Hard

Between a rock and a hard place (15)	Beat Solomon, flawlessly, in The Great Destroyer
Bullseye (20)	Reach and save the hostages without alerting any enemies in Drop 'em Like Liquid
Butterfly (25)	Take down the jet in one attempt in Rock And A Hard Place
Car Lover (20)	Complete the mission without losing a humvee in Operation Exodus
Colonel (50)	Achieve rank 45
Decorated (50)	Obtain one of each ribbon in the game
FlashForward (10)	Completed Semper Fidelis
In the nick of time (20)	Disarm the bomb in under 20 seconds in The Eleventh Hour
Infantry Efficiency (30)	Obtain all 4 weapon efficiency ribbons
Involuntary Euthanasia (25)	Kill the 2 soldiers before the building falls on them in Uprising
It's better than nothing! (30)	Finish as 3rd MVP in a ranked match
Lock 'n' Load (30)	Unlock all unique co-op weapons
M.I.A (20)	Obtain your first enemy Dog Tag
Most Valuable Player (30)	Finish as MVP in a ranked match
Ninjas (20)	Reach the VIP without setting off the alarm in Exfiltration
No Escape (30)	Captured Kaffarov
Not on my watch (25)	Protect Chaffin from the soldiers in the street in Operation Swordbreaker
Ooh-rah! (30)	Complete the campaign story
Practice makes perfect (15)	Headshot each of the targets in the gun range in Kaffarov
Push On (20)	Reach the garage without going into man-down state in Hit and Run
Roadkill (20)	Kick the car to kill the soldiers in Uprising
Scrap Metal (25)	Destroy 6 enemy tanks before reaching the fort in Thunder Run
Semper Fidelis (50)	Complete the campaign story on Hard
Shock Troop (15)	Survived the quake
Support Efficiency (30)	Obtain all 4 support efficiency ribbons
The Professional (30)	Complete the street chase in Comrades in under 2 minutes 30 seconds without dying
This is the end (20)	Failed to prevent the attack
Two-rah! (30)	Complete all co-op missions
Twofor (15)	Take down 2 enemies with 1 bullet in Night Shift
Untouchable (20)	Complete the mission without using the fire extinguisher in Fire From The Sky
Vehicle Warfare (30)	Obtain all 3 vehicle warfare ribbons
Wanted: Dead or Alive (20)	Captured Al Bashir
What the hell *are* you? (20)	Take a russian Dog Tag in the forest ambush in Rock And A Hard Place
Where are the other two? (20)	Found the nuke
You can be my wingman anytime (30)	Complete Going Hunting in a perfect run

NEW!

A
B
C
D
E
F
G
H
I
J
K
L
M
N
O
P
Q
R
S
T
U
V
W
X
Y
Z

BATTLEFIELD: BAD COMPANY (XBOX 360)

FIND ALL FIVE WEAPONS

UNLOCKABLE	HOW TO UNLOCK
Assault Rifle	Register your old *Battlefield* games at http://www.veteran.battlefield.com/.
Light Machine Gun	Sign up for the newsletter at http://www.findallfive.com/.
Semi-Automatic Shotgun	After playing an Online game, login and check your stats at http://www.findallfive.com/.
Sniper Rifle	Pre-order the game from a participating retailer before June 23rd, 2008.
Uzi	Play the "Battlefield: Bad Company Demo" and get to rank 4. (2,300 EXP required to reach rank 4.)

BATTLESHIP (PLAYSTATION 3)

TROPHY

UNLOCKABLE	HOW TO UNLOCK
A Global Force (Platinum)	Collect all Trophies.
Arleigh Burke (Silver)	Destroy 20 enemy ships with the USS John Quincy Adams.
Bombs away! (Bronze)	Downed 5 enemies with one support call.
Brought a Knife to a Gun Fight? (Bronze)	Downed a Thug with the pistol.
Down But Not Out! (Bronze)	Recover 5 ships.
E.O.D. (Bronze)	Disarm or plant 20 charges.
Earth's Hero (Gold)	Complete the game on any Difficulty.
Escort (Silver)	Complete "Retaliation" on any Difficulty.
Extra Credit (Bronze)	Downed 3 or more enemies with one shot from the Railgun.
Fire in the Hole! (Bronze)	Down 40 enemies with Grenades.
Fish In A Barrel (Silver)	Down 40 enemies that are stunned by the LRAD.
High Velocity (Silver)	Down 40 enemies with the Alien Railgun.
Incoming! (Bronze)	Used your first support call.
Infestation (Bronze)	Complete "Overrun" on any Difficulty.
Iowa (Silver)	Destroy 20 enemy ships with the USS Missouri.
Lawnmower (Silver)	Down 40 enemies with the KRAW.
Locked and Loaded (Bronze)	Fully outfit a ship with the maximum number of Wild cards available.
Los Angeles (Silver)	Destroy 20 enemy ships with the USS Laredo.
Mighty Mo (Bronze)	Complete "The Big Guns" on any Difficulty.
Naval Mastery (Bronze)	Occupied all support positions in "Overrun".
Navy Cross (Gold)	Complete the game on Admiral Difficulty.
Navy Distinguished Service (Gold)	Complete the game on Captain Difficulty or higher.
No Man Left Behind (Silver)	Complete "They're Back!" on any Difficulty.
Officer of the Deck (Bronze)	Defeated 40 enemy vessels in Ship Control gameplay.
Oliver Hazard Perry (Silver)	Destroy 10 enemy ships with the USS Chesapeake.
PEGS! (Bronze)	Found all 28 hidden pegs.

Quick Draw (Silver)	Down 40 enemies with the Pistol.
Rain of Fire (Gold)	Down 200 enemies with artillery support calls.
Sharp Shooter (Silver)	Down 40 enemies with the Carbine.
The Bigger They Are... (Silver)	Complete "End Game" on any Difficulty.
The Dome (Bronze)	Complete "Construction" on any Difficulty.
Ticonderoga (Silver)	Destroy 20 enemy ships with the USS Yukon.
Up Close and Personal (Silver)	Down 40 enemies with the Shotgun.
Welcome to the Islands (Bronze)	Complete "The Arrival" on any Difficulty.

BATTLESHIP (XBOX 360)

ACHIEVEMENT

UNLOCKABLE	HOW TO UNLOCK
Arleigh Burke (30)	Destroyed 20 enemy ships with the USS John Quincy Adams.
Bombs away! (15)	Downed 5 enemies with one support call.
Brought a Knife to a Gun Fight? (10)	Downed a Thug with the pistol.
Down But Not Out! (15)	Recovered 5 ships.
E.O.D. (15)	Disarmed or planted 20 charges.
Earth's Hero (60)	Completed the game on any Difficulty.
Escort (40)	Completed "Retaliation" on any Difficulty.
Extra Credit (15)	Downed 3 or more enemies with one shot from the Railgun.
Fire in the Hole! (15)	Downed 40 enemies with Grenades.
Fish In A Barrel (30)	Downed 40 enemies that are stunned by the LRAD.
High Velocity (30)	Downed 40 enemies with the Alien Railgun.
Incoming! (10)	Used your first support call.
Infestation (30)	Completed "Overrun" on any Difficulty.
Iowa (30)	Destroyed 20 enemy ships with the USS Missouri.
Lawnmower (30)	Downed 40 enemies with the KRAW.
Locked and Loaded (20)	Fully outfitted a ship with the maximum number of Wild cards available.
Los Angeles (30)	Destroyed 20 enemy ships with the USS Laredo.
Mighty Mo (30)	Completed "The Big Guns" on any Difficulty.
Navy Cross (100)	Completed the game on Admiral Difficulty.
Navy Distinguished Service (60)	Completed the game on Captain Difficulty or higher.
No Man Left Behind (40)	Completed "They're Back!" on any Difficulty.
Officer of the Deck (20)	Defeated 40 enemy vessels in Ship Control gameplay.
Oliver Hazard Perry (30)	Destroyed 10 enemy ships with the USS Chesapeake.
PEGS! (15)	Found all 28 hidden pegs.
Quick Draw (30)	Downed 40 enemies with the Pistol.
Rain of Fire (50)	Downed 200 enemies with artillery support calls.
Sharp Shooter (30)	Downed 40 enemies with the Carbine.
The Bigger They Are... (40)	Completed "End Game" on any Difficulty.

The Dome (30)	Completed "Construction" on any Difficulty.
Ticonderoga (30)	Destroyed 20 enemy ships with the USS Yukon.
Up Close and Personal (30)	Downed 40 enemies with the Shotgun.
Welcome to the Islands (30)	Completed "The Arrival" on any Difficulty.

BATTLESTATIONS: MIDWAY (XBOX 360)

Enter this code at the mission select screen.

UNLOCKABLE	CODE
Unlock All Levels	Hold ⑱, ■, ↑, ↖ and push ↘

BAYONETTA (XBOX 360)

EXTRA COSTUMES

To unlock the extra costumes, you have to beat all chapters on Normal first. Load your Clear Data, go to "Gates of Hell," and then go to "Rodin's Treasure" menu. You'll see a Super Mirror there, which costs 100,000 Halos. Purchase this, and you'll unlock the rest of the costumes (Couture Bullets). To change costumes, press R1 at the Chapter Start screen, go to "Costume Change," and then choose your costume there.

UNLOCKABLE	HOW TO UNLOCK
d'Arc (Jeanne-like costume)	Purchase "Couture Bullet (d'Arc)" at Gates of Hell for 100.000 Halos.
Nun	Purchase "Couture Bullet (Nun)" at Gates of Hell for 100,000 Halos.
Old	Purchase "Couture Bullet (Old) at Gates of Hell for 100,000 Halos.
P.E. Uniform: Types A, B & C are available	Purchase "Couture Bullet (P.E. Uniform)" at Gates of Hell for 100,000 Halos.
Queen	Purchase "Couture Bullet (Queen)" at Gates of Hell for 100,000 Halos.
Umbra	Purchase "Couture Bullet (Umbra)" at Gates of Hell for 100,000 Halos.
Umbran Komachi (Kimono): Type A, B & C are available	Purchase "Super Mirror" at Gates of Hell for 100,000 Halos.
Various: Type A (Bikini), B (Bikini) & C (Cheerleader) are available	Purchase "Couture Bullet (Various) at Gates of Hell for 100,000 Halos.

BEJEWELED 2 DELUXE (XBOX 360)

MODE UNLOCKABLES

UNLOCKABLE	HOW TO UNLOCK
Remove Background Grid	Hold ⑬ ⑭ ⑮ ⑯ then press ⑧
Change Jewel Types	Hold ⑬ ⑭ ⑮ ⑯ then press ⑨
Unlock Cognito Mode	Finish all the puzzles in Puzzle mode. It is okay to look at hints constantly to solve all the puzzles. Cognito mode is basically Puzzle mode with no hints.
Finity Mode	Complete 280 levels of Endless mode
Hyper Mode	Complete 8 levels of Action mode
Twilight Mode	Complete 17 levels of Classic mode
Original Mode	Go into Play Game when you first load up the game. Select the Classic, Action, Endless, and Puzzle mode buttons (in that order) at the menu screen repeatedly (so you're basically maneuvering the cursor across the screen clockwise). After several rounds, a window will come up saying "Please Wait," and Original mode will load up.

BEN 10: GALACTIC RACING (PLAYSTATION VITA)

TROPHY

UNLOCKABLE	HOW TO UNLOCK
Absolutely Smashing (Bronze)	Successfully bump an opponent by landing on him in Single Player mode.
Air Show (Bronze)	Take out an opponent with a power-up while the opponent is airborne in Single Player mode.
Alien Force (Bronze)	Successfully bump 50 karts in Single Player mode.
Beat the Clock (Bronze)	Escape elimination in an Ultimate Elimination showdown with less than 10 seconds on the clock in Single Player mode.
Beginner's Luck Complete (Bronze)	Complete the Beginner's Luck circuit in third place or higher in Single Player mode.
Big Air (Bronze)	Complete a jump with an air time of 3 seconds in a race in Single Player mode.
Boom! Winning! (Silver)	Successfully hit every opponent in a race at least once with any Power-Up in Single Player mode.
Bumper Karts (Bronze)	Successfully bump 25 karts in Single Player mode.
Close Call (Bronze)	Win a race by less than a second in Single Player mode.
Codon Infusion (Gold)	Unlock all characters in the game.
Counter Measure (Bronze)	Destroy an incoming attack by firing an attack of your own in Single Player mode.
Double Trouble (Bronze)	Complete 10 2X stunt combos while racing in Single Player mode.
Driverus Primus (Bronze)	Beat the Track Best time in a Time Trial on any Primus track.
Freezeway Jungle Complete (Bronze)	Complete the Freezeway Jungle circuit in third place or higher in Single Player mode.
Galactic Racing Champion (Silver)	Win a trophy on every circuit in Single Player mode.
Get My Drift? (Bronze)	Execute a 500-meter drift in a race in Single Player mode.
Give 'Em the Slip (Bronze)	Pass an opponent while drifting in Single Player mode.
Got Skillz (Bronze)	Beat the Track Best time in a Time Trial on any track by 10 seconds or more.
Ice Water Expanse Complete (Bronze)	Complete the Ice Water Expanse circuit in third place or higher in Single Player mode.
Infinity Circuit Complete (Bronze)	Complete the Infinity Circuit in third place or higher in Single Player mode.
Kart Collector (Silver)	Unlock all karts in the game.
Kineceleration (Bronze)	Execute a continuous boost of 8 seconds or more in a race in Single Player mode.
Leapfrog (Bronze)	Pass an opponent by jumping over/past them in Single Player mode.
Missed Me! (Bronze)	Finish a race in first, second, or third place without being affected by an enemy attack in Single Player mode.
Not Even a Scratch (Bronze)	Block/avoid 100 attacks using your Defensive Power in Single Player mode.
Nothin' But Maximum Skill (Silver)	Win a race on any Advanced track without using an Omni-Node or Offensive Power in Single Player mode.

Nothin' But More Skill (Bronze)	Win a race on any Intermediate track without using an Omni-Node or Offensive Power in Single Player mode.
Nothin' But Skill (Bronze)	Win a race on any Basic track without using an Omni-Node or Offensive Power in Single Player mode.
Null Prime Complete (Bronze)	Complete the Null Prime circuit in third place or higher in Single Player mode.
Omni-Node Master (Silver)	Pick up 8 different Omni-Node types in each of 10 different races in Single Player mode.
Omni-Trickster (Silver)	Complete 10 4X stunt combos while racing in Single Player mode.
On the Right Track (Silver)	Unlock all grand prix tracks.
Outta My Way!!!!! (Silver)	Successfully bump 100 karts in Single Player mode.
Prime Drifter (Bronze)	Execute a 750-meter drift in a race in Single Player mode.
Primus Dominus Complete (Bronze)	Complete the Primus Dominus circuit in third place or higher in Single Player mode.
Shattered (Bronze)	Destroy 10 Shard Mines using the EMP power-up in Single Player mode.
Showdowns Galore (Silver)	Unlock all arena tracks.
Snow Drifter (Bronze)	Beat the Track Best time in a Time Trial on any Kylmyys track.
Tag! I'm It! (Bronze)	Win 10 individual Omni-Tag showdowns in Single Player mode.
Tag! We're It! (Bronze)	Win 10 Team Omni-Tag showdowns in Single Player mode.
Trash Truckin' (Bronze)	Beat the Track Best time in a Time Trial on any Vulpin track.
Triple Threat (Bronze)	Complete 10 3X stunt combos while racing in Single Player mode.
Ultimate Alienator (Bronze)	Win 10 Ultimate Alienation showdowns in Single Player mode.
Ultimate Racer! (Platinum)	Earn all trophies in the game.
Ultimate Trophy Room (Gold)	Win a first place trophy on every circuit in Single Player mode.
Unstoppable! (Bronze)	Win a race by tumbling or spinning over the finish line in Single Player mode.
Volcano Void Complete (Bronze)	Complete the Volcano Void circuit in third place or higher in Single Player mode.
Warp Driver (Bronze)	Beat the Track Best time in a Time Trial on any Null Void track.
Wave Runner (Bronze)	Beat the Track Best time in a Time Trial on any Pisciss track.
Way Bigger Air (Bronze)	Complete a jump with an air time of 4 seconds or more in a race in Single Player mode.
Wet Wasteland Complete (Bronze)	Complete the Wet Wasteland circuit in third place or higher in Single Player mode.

BIONICLE HEROES (WII)

SECRET CHARACTER

UNLOCKABLE	HOW TO UNLOCK
Vezon	Complete the game once

BINARY DOMAIN (PLAYSTATION 3)

TROPHY

UNLOCKABLE	HOW TO UNLOCK
A Friend Indeed (Bronze)	Purchase nanomachines for a teammate.
All Members (Bronze)	Add each teammate to the party at least once.
Assault Shooter Killer (Bronze)	Destroy 100 Assault Shooters in Campaign.
Battlemaster (Bronze)	Win an online vs. match with all rule sets.
Challenge Master (Gold)	Clear all online mode challenges.
Craftsman (Bronze)	Fully upgrade one weapon category.
Data Collector (Bronze)	Collect 20 SECURITY-COM in Campaign.
Data Retrieval Complete (Silver)	Collect all SECURITY-COM in Campaign.
First Victory (Bronze)	Win an online vs. match with any rule set.
Hacker (Bronze)	Destroy all enemies with the mobile gun battery.
Headshot Master (Bronze)	Get 50 headshot bonuses in Campaign.
Jackpot (Bronze)	Hit the jackpot on a vending machine.
Jumper (Bronze)	Get onto the Grand Lancer's head.
Lifesaver (Bronze)	Use first-aid kits to revive teammates 10 times.
Multi-Kill Master (Bronze)	Get 50 multi-kill bonuses in Campaign.
One-Shot Master (Bronze)	Get 50 one-shot bonuses in Campaign.
Platinum Trophy (Platinum)	Earn all other trophies in the game.
Resistance Hero (Bronze)	Clear all stages in INVASION mode.
Rust Crew (Silver)	Clear all chapters on SURVIVOR Mode.
Shop Master (Bronze)	Access all shopping terminals.
Skill Master (Silver)	Get all nanomachines within 1 playthrough in Campaign.
Smash Master (Bronze)	Get 50 smash bonuses in Campaign.
Spend 10,000 credits at vending machines	Spend 10,000 credits at vending machines.
Spider Killer (Bronze)	Destroy all of the Spider's legs.
Still Alive (Bronze)	Clear a stage in INVASION mode.
Tactician (Bronze)	Get enemies to kill each other 50 times.
Transport Takedown (Bronze)	Destroy the Iron Whale's four engines.
Veteran Soldier (Silver)	Reach online level 50.
Weapon Crafter (Bronze)	Upgrade a weapon.

BINARY DOMAIN (XBOX 360)

ACHIEVEMENT

UNLOCKABLE	HOW TO UNLOCK
A Friend Indeed (15)	Purchase nanomachines for a teammate.
All Members (20)	Add each teammate to the party at least once.
Assault Shooter Killer (15)	Destroy 100 Assault Shooters in Campaign.
Battlemaster (30)	Win an Xbox LIVE vs. match with all rule sets.
Challenge Master (50)	Clear all Xbox LIVE mode challenges.
Completion (5)	Earn all other achievements in the game.
Craftsman (30)	Fully upgrade one weapon category.
Data Collector (30)	Collect 20 SECURITY-COM in Campaign.
Data Retrieval Complete (30)	Collect all SECURITY-COM in Campaign.
First Victory (15)	Win an online vs. match with any rule set.
Hacker (15)	Destroy all enemies with the mobile gun battery.

Headshot Master (20)	Get 50 headshot bonuses in Campaign.
Jackpot (15)	Hit the jackpot on a vending machine.
Jumper (10)	Get onto the Grand Lancer's head.
Lifesaver (10)	Use first-aid kits to revive teammates 10 times.
Multi-Kill Master (20)	Get 50 multi-kill bonuses in Campaign.
One-Shot Master (20)	Get 50 one-shot bonuses in Campaign.
Resistance Hero (30)	Clear all stages in INVASION mode.
Rust Crew (30)	Clear all chapters on SURVIVOR Mode.
Shop Master (15)	Access all shopping terminals.
Skill Master (30)	Get all nanomachines within 1 playthrough in Campaign.
Smash Master (20)	Get 50 smash bonuses in Campaign.
Spendthrift (15)	Spend 10,000 credits at vending machines.
Spider Killer (15)	Destroy all of the Spider's legs.
Still Alive (15)	Clear a stage in INVASION mode.
Tactician (15)	Get enemies to kill each other 50 times.
Transport Takedown (15)	Destroy the Iron Whale's four engines.
Veteran Soldier (30)	Reach Xbox LIVE level 50.
Weapon Crafter (15)	Upgrade a weapon.

BIRDS OF STEEL (PLAYSTATION 3)

TROPHY

UNLOCKABLE	HOW TO UNLOCK
Bird of Steel (Platinum)	Earn all available Trophies for Birds of Steel.
Blitz Attack (Bronze)	Destroy 6 enemy bombers before they reach the Wake in the mission "Japanese Raid".
Bombshell (Bronze)	Damage destroyer with machine gun fire in the mission "Invasion of Tulagi".
Brave Spirit (Silver)	Win a battle against superior forces in Versus mode.
Choose Your Favorite (Bronze)	Fly in one of each country's planes.
Combat Pilot (Bronze)	Earn the fifth rank.
Coral Sea (Bronze)	Complete the American chapter "Battle of the Coral Sea".
Defender (Bronze)	Destroy 3 enemy bombers in each wave on Realistic difficulty in the "First Carrier Fleet" mission.
Eagle-Eyed (Bronze)	Find the TF-17 carrier fleet in the "Counterattack" mission.
Fast and Furious (Bronze)	Complete the first objective in less than 5 minutes in the "Tulagi Landing" mission.
First Wave (Bronze)	Destroy all vehicles on Wheeler Field in the mission "First Wave".
Formation Keeper (Bronze)	Stay near the flight leader all the way to the enemy fleet in the "American Strike" mission.
From The Far East (Gold)	Complete the Japanese Historical campaign.
Good Start (Silver)	Receive 5 medals.
Guadalcanal (Bronze)	Complete the Japanese chapter "Guadalcanal Campaign".
Half-Way (Silver)	Earn the tenth rank.
Hedgehopper (Bronze)	Destroy 5 light targets on Midway Island on Simulator difficulty in the "Midway Atoll" mission.

It Was Easy (Bronze)	Land on an aircraft carrier.
Killer (Bronze)	Kill 15 enemy infantry units in the "Battle for Henderson Field" mission.
Kuban (Bronze)	Complete any mission in the Single Missions chapter "Battle for the Kuban".
Leader (Silver)	Win a battle in Versus mode as the leader.
Make a Flight (Bronze)	Complete any mission in CO-OP mode.
Malta (Bronze)	Complete any mission in the Single Missions chapter "Siege of Malta".
Midway Atoll (Bronze)	Complete the Japanese chapter "Battle of Midway".
New Decal (Bronze)	Earn any decal for your plane.
New Guinea (Bronze)	Complete any mission in the Single Missions chapter "New Guinea Campaign".
New Record (Silver)	Destroy 100 planes.
New Skin (Bronze)	Earn any skin for your plane.
New Weapon (Silver)	Destroy 100 ground units.
Not a Victim (Bronze)	Destroy two hostile fighters with the rear gunner in the mission "To Scratch One Flat-top".
One of a Few (Bronze)	Land on the Zuikaku at the end of the "Battle of South Pacific" mission on Realistic difficulty.
Pearl Harbor (Bronze)	Complete the Japanese chapter "Attack on Pearl Harbor".
Preparing (Bronze)	Complete the Pre-War chapter.
Return to Oahu (Bronze)	Make "Touch and Go" on Ford Island in the mission "Return to Oahu".
Rookie (Bronze)	Earn the second rank.
Ruhr (Bronze)	Complete any mission in the Single Missions chapter "Battle of Ruhr".
Second Breath (Bronze)	Rearm on the airfield between attacks on hostile ships in the mission "American Counterattack".
Second Wave (Bronze)	Bomb two different targets by one loadout in the mission "Second Wave".
Sentinel (Bronze)	Don't let enemy fighters destroy any bomber of your group in the mission "Attack on Lexington".
Sharp Shooter (Bronze)	Destroy 5 enemy planes on Realistic difficulty in the "Battle of the Eastern Solomons" mission.
Survivor (Bronze)	Land your damaged aircraft on the airfield in the mission "The Two Against Thirty-Nine".
Take-Off (Bronze)	Take off.
The Australian (Silver)	Fly in each Australian plane.
The Italian (Silver)	Fly in each Italian plane.
To The Far East (Gold)	Complete the American Historical campaign.
Total Annihilation (Bronze)	Destroy at least 20 enemy bombers in the "Battle of the Santa Cruz" mission.
Untouchable (Bronze)	Don't die in the mission "Shokaku Defense".
Wake Island (Bronze)	Complete the American chapter "Battle of Wake Island".
Way of the Sun (Bronze)	Complete the 1st secondary mission objective in the "Fate of Hiryu" mission.

Winner (Bronze)	Complete any Dynamic campaign.
You Will Be Ace (Bronze)	Destroy 4 planes in Versus mode.

BIRDS OF STEEL (XBOX 360)

ACHIEVEMENT

UNLOCKABLE	HOW TO UNLOCK
Blitz Attack (10)	Destroy 6 enemy bombers before they reach the Wake in the mission "Japanese Raid".
Bombshell (10)	Damage destroyer with machine gun fire in the mission "Invasion of Tulagi".
Brave Spirit (30)	Win a battle against superior forces in Versus mode.
Choose Your Favorite (30)	Fly in one of each country's planes.
Combat Pilot (40)	Earn the fifth rank
Defender (10)	Destroy 3 enemy bombers in each wave on Realistic difficulty in the "First Carrier Fleet" mission.
Eagle-Eyed (10)	Find the TF-17 carrier fleet in the "Counterattack" mission.
Fast and Furious (10)	Complete the first objective in less than 5 minutes in the "Tulagi Landing" mission.
First Wave (10)	Destroy all vehicles on Wheeler Field in the mission "First Wave".
Formation Keeper (10)	Stay near the flight leader all the way to the enemy fleet in the "American Strike" mission.
From The Far East (50)	Complete the Japanese Historical campaign.
Good Start (40)	Receive 5 medals
Guadalcanal (20)	Complete the Japanese chapter "Guadalcanal Campaign".
Half-Way (20)	Earn the tenth rank
Hedgehopper (10)	Destroy 5 light targets on Midway Island on Simulator difficulty in the "Midway Atoll" mission.
It Was Easy (20)	Land on an aircraft carrier.
Killer (10)	Kill 15 enemy infantry units in the "Battle for Henderson Field" mission.
Kuban (20)	Complete any mission in the Single Missions chapter "Battle for the Kuban".
Leader (30)	Win a battle in Versus mode as the leader.
Make a Flight (30)	Complete any mission in CO-OP mode
Malta (20)	Complete any mission in the Single Missions chapter "Siege of Malta".
Midway Atoll (20)	Complete the Japanese chapter "Battle of Midway".
New Decal (30)	Earn any decal for your plane
New Guinea (20)	Complete any mission in the Single Missions chapter "New Guinea Campaign".
New Record (50)	Destroy 100 planes
New Skin (30)	Earn any skin for your plane
New Weapon (50)	Destroy 100 ground units
Not a Victim (10)	Destroy two hostile fighters with the rear gunner in the mission "To Scratch One Flat-top".
One of a Few (10)	Land on the Zuikaku at the end of the "Battle of South Pacific" mission on Realistic difficulty.
Pearl Harbor (20)	Complete the Japanese chapter "Attack on Pearl Harbor".
Preparing (20)	Complete the Pre-War chapter.
Return to Oahu (10)	Make "Touch and Go" on Ford Island in the mission "Return to Oahu".

Rookie (10)	Earn the second rank
Ruhr (20)	Complete any mission in the Single Missions chapter "Battle of Ruhr".
Second Breath (10)	Rearm on the airfield between attacks on hostile ships in the mission "American Counterattack".
Second Wave (10)	Bomb two different targets by one loadout in the mission "Second Wave".
Sentinel (10)	Don't let enemy fighters destroy any bomber of your group in the mission "Attack on Lexington".
Sharp Shooter (10)	Destroy 5 enemy planes on Realistic difficulty in the "Battle of the Eastern Solomons" mission.
Survivor (10)	Land your damaged aircraft on the airfield in the mission "The Two Against Thirty-Nine".
The Australian (20)	Fly in each Australian plane.
The Coral Sea (20)	Complete the American chapter "Battle of the Coral Sea".
The Italian (20)	Fly in each Italian plane.
To The Far East (50)	Complete the American Historical campaign.
Total Annihilation (10)	Destroy at least 20 enemy bombers in the "Battle of the Santa Cruz" mission.
Untouchable (10)	Don't die in the mission "Shokaku Defense".
Wake Island (20)	Complete the American chapter "Battle of Wake Island".
Way of the Sun (10)	Complete the 1st secondary mission objective in the "Fate of Hiryu" mission.
Winner (20)	Complete any Dynamic campaign
You Will Be Ace (10)	You Will Be Ace

BLACKWATER (XBOX 360)

ACHIEVEMENT

UNLOCKABLE	HOW TO UNLOCK
After Party (5)	Complete all competition maps with 8 players
Alamo Compound (5)	Complete Mission 2
Best in Town (60)	Kill all 6 Foreign Fighters on each difficulty
Blackwater Operator (60)	Reach experience level 56
Bravo! (20)	Get over 100% accuracy in a combat arena
Brought to You By... (5)	Watch the credits from begining to end
Cut the Chatter (10)	Find 5 Death Radios
Don't Cross This Line (10)	Kill 25 melee attackers before they strike
Elite Club (5)	Get Veteran time in a combat arena
Figure It Out (10)	Find 5 Limbano Lions
Foot First (5)	Complete 100 kick quick-time events
Going Pro (10)	Get Pro time in a combat arena
Grenade! (20)	Get 200 grenade kills
Hat-Trick (5)	Kill 3 enemies with one grenade
Here, Hold This... (10)	Get 50 grenade kills
Jumping Jack (5)	Complete 100 jump quick-time events
Just Normal (40)	Complete all missions on Normal
Lion's Den (20)	Find all Limbano Lions
No Mercenaries (10)	Kill 5 Foreign Fighters
No Score in Sight (5)	Get less than 2,000 points in a combat arena
Nothing Thrown (5)	Complete a combat arena without using grenades

A
B
C
D
E
F
G
H
I
J
K
L
M
N
O
P
Q
R
S
T
U
V
W
X
Y
Z

Nothing's Too Hard (60)	Complete all missions on Hard
Off the Air (20)	Find all Death Radios
Over Easy (20)	Complete all missions on Easy
Overwatch (60)	Fully upgrade Eddi
Party Time (5)	Complete a competition map with 8 players
Plan B (5)	Get 5 kills with the pistol
Propaganda (10)	Find 5 Graffiti
Quick Draw (20)	Get 200 kills with the pistol
Recon Expert (20)	Discover 50% of the paths in all combat arenas
Recon Master (60)	Discover ALL of the paths in the game
Recon Recruit (10)	Discover all paths in a combat arena
Recruit (5)	Complete the training map
Rescue Dila (10)	Complete Mission 5
Riding Shotgun (60)	Fully upgrade Smash
Sir, You Forgot Your Hat (20)	Get 200 headshots
Spray and Pray (40)	Fully upgrade Devon
Stop This Madness (20)	Find all Graffiti
The Bridge (5)	Complete Mission 3
The Exiled Leader (5)	Complete Mission 4
The Long Way Back (20)	Complete Mission 6
The Red Barrel (5)	Blow up 50 red barrels
The Right Person (60)	Fully upgrade Baird
This Ain't Your Daddy's Shotgun! (20)	Kill 6 enemies with the shotgun without reloading
Tight-Aim (10)	Get 50 headshots
Tired Yet? (60)	Complete 1,000 quick-time events
Welcome to Harri (5)	Complete Mission 1
What Time? Can't Tell. (40)	Get at least 7,000 points in a combat arena

BLADES OF TIME (PLAYSTATION 3)

TROPHY

UNLOCKABLE	HOW TO UNLOCK
Angry (Bronze)	Kill 100 enemies during your Time Rewind Berserk buff.
Annihilation Kill (Silver)	Kill 10 enemies at the same time.
Big Corpse (Gold)	Defeat Giant Worm.
Brutal Kill (Bronze)	Kill 5 enemies at the same time.
Brutal Lands (Gold)	Kill the Vicar of Chaos.
Clear the Jungle (Silver)	Kill the Shaman Boss.
Collector (Silver)	Find all the notes.
Coral Dash (Bronze)	Get the ability to dash to the corals.
Curious (Bronze)	Find half the notes.
Double Attack (Bronze)	Kill 25 heavy enemies using the Time Rewind double attack.
Dragon (Bronze)	Ayumi receives her Dragon form.
Enemy Dash (Bronze)	Get the ability to dash to enemies.
Experienced (Bronze)	Play 5 Outbreak matches.
Famous Hunter (Bronze)	Kill 1000 enemies in total.
Faster Than You! (Bronze)	Use Counterattack 100 times.
Free to go! (Silver)	Kill the Gateguard.

Gather Chi (Bronze)	Get the ability to gather Chi.
Grasshopper (Bronze)	Use Dash 30 times without touching the ground.
Hard Times Are Over (Gold)	Finish the game on the Hard difficulty level.
I'm Rich (Bronze)	Find all the chests in story mode on the Normal difficulty level.
Keeper Is Dead (Gold)	Finish the game on any difficulty level.
Old Temple (Bronze)	Reach the Sanctuary.
Order Spell (Bronze)	Survive Chaos event.
Out of My Way (Bronze)	Kill an enemy player in an Outbreak match.
Outbreak Hero (Silver)	Kill each Outbreak boss at least once.
Platinum (Platinum)	Awarded for successfully collecting all trophies.
Rain of Bullets (Bronze)	Shoot off Magic Armor from 50 enemies using Time Rewind clones.
Ready To Fight (Bronze)	Find all types of equipment.
Rifle (Bronze)	Find the rifle.
Sky Islands (Gold)	Leave the Sky Islands.
Time Rewind (Bronze)	Get the ability to rewind time.
Too Hot For You (Bronze)	Kill Brutal Maul without being frozen by his shockwave.
Treasure Hunter (Silver)	Find all the chests in story mode on the Hard difficulty level.
Unstoppable (Bronze)	Win any Outbreak match.
World of Order (Silver)	Defeat Skyguard Commander.
Your Fire Is Nothing (Bronze)	Kill the Shaman Boss without taking damage from his massive fire spell.

BLADES OF TIME (XBOX 360)

ACHIEVEMENT

UNLOCKABLE	HOW TO UNLOCK
Angry (15)	Kill 100 enemies during your Time Rewind Berserk buff.
Annihilation Kill (30)	Kill 10 enemies at once.
Brutal Kill (15)	Kill 5 enemies at once.
Collector (30)	Find all notes.
Curious (15)	Find half of the notes.
Double Attack (15)	Kill 25 heavy enemies using the Time Rewind double attack.
Experienced (10)	Play 5 Outbreak matches.
Famous Hunter (15)	Kill 1000 enemies in total.
Faster Than You! (15)	Use Counterattack 100 times.
Grasshopper (15)	Use Dash 30 times without touching the ground.
I'm Rich (15)	Find all the chests in story mode on the Normal difficulty level.
Out of My Way (15)	Kill an enemy player in Outbreak match.
Outbreak Hero (30)	Kill each Outbreak boss at least once.
Rain of Bullets (15)	Shoot off Magic Armor from 50 enemies using Time Rewind clones.
Ready To Fight (15)	Find all types of equipment.
Too Hot For You (15)	Kill Brutal Maul without being frozen by his shockwave.
Treasure Hunter (30)	Find all the chests in story mode on the Hard difficulty level.
Unstoppable (15)	Win any Outbreak match.

BLAZBLUE: CALAMITY TRIGGER (XBOX 360)

UNLOCKABLES

UNLOCKABLE	HOW TO UNLOCK
True Ending	Individually clear each character's Story Mode.
Unlimited Hakumen	Beat Hakumen's Arcade Mode.
Unlimited Rachel	Beat Rachel's Arcade Mode.
Unlimited Ragna	Beat Ragna's Arcade Mode.
Unlimited v-13	Beat v-13's Arcade Mode.

ASTRAL HEAT

Ragna starts with his Astral Heat (finisher), but every other character needs to unlock theirs. Beat their Arcade Mode and they'll get their own.

BLAZBLUE: CONTINUUM SHIFT (XBOX 360)

UNLOCKABLES

UNLOCKABLE	HOW TO UNLOCK
Mu-12	Achieve every character's Clear ending in Story Mode, and complete the True Ending. This also unlocks her stage and theme song for use in various game modes.
True Ending	Beat Ragna's Story, Jin's Story, Noel's Story, Rachel's Story, Tsubaki's Story, Hakumen's Story, and Hazama's story to unlock the True Ending.
Unlimited Characters	To unlock the Unlimited version of a character you must clear Score Attack Mode with that character.

BLAZBLUE: CONTINUUM SHIFT II (3DS)

UNLOCKABLE

UNLOCKABLE	HOW TO UNLOCK
Arcade Mode Credits	Beat Arcade Mode
Console Credits	Complete the True Ending in Story Mode
Extra Story 1: Military Academy	Reach Noel's canon ending in Story Mode.
Extra Story 2: Sector Seven	Reach Tager's bad ending in Story Mode.

UNLOCKABLE

UNLOCKABLE	HOW TO UNLOCK
Illustration Contest Fighting Spirit Award #10: Ianka	Reach Profile Level 6.
Illustration Contest Fighting Spirit Award #11: Siting Zeng	Reach Profile Level 6.
Illustration Contest Fighting Spirit Award #12: Minari	Reach Profile Level 6.
Illustration Contest Fighting Spirit Award #13: Wanda	Reach Profile Level 6.
Illustration Contest Fighting Spirit Award #1: AME	Reach Profile Level 6.
Illustration Contest Fighting Spirit Award #2: Eiji	Reach Profile Level 6.
Illustration Contest Fighting Spirit Award #3: GANCO	Reach Profile Level 6.
Illustration Contest Fighting Spirit Award #4: Kodama Hibiki	Reach Profile Level 6.
Illustration Contest Fighting Spirit Award #5: Shirahira Kousuke	Reach Profile Level 6.
Illustration Contest Fighting Spirit Award #6: Shirai	Reach Profile Level 6.
Illustration Contest Fighting Spirit Award #7: Chigimita	Reach Profile Level 6.
Illustration Contest Fighting Spirit Award #8: Byakuren	Reach Profile Level 6.
Illustration Contest Fighting Spirit Award #9: Fujimachi	Reach Profile Level 6.
Illustration Contest Grand Winner	Reach Profile Level 10.
Illustration Contest Honorable Mention #1	Reach Profile Level 7.
Illustration Contest Honorable Mention #2	Reach Profile Level 7.
Illustration Contest Honorable Mention #3	Reach Profile Level 7.

Illustration Contest Runner-Up #1	Reach Profile Level 9.
Illustration Contest Runner-Up #2	Reach Profile Level 9.
Special CG #03	Reach Profile Level 6.
Special CG #09	Reach Profile Level 6.
Special CG #12	Reach Profile Level 9.
Special CG #13	Reach Profile Level 6.
Special CG #15	Reach Profile Level 10.
Special CG #17	Reach Profile Level 6.
Special CG #18	Reach Profile Level 6.
Special CG #19	Reach Profile Level 6.
Special CG #21	Reach Profile Level 7.
Special CG #23	Reach Profile Level 6.
Special CG #24	Reach Profile Level 7.
Special CG #25	Reach Profile Level 8.
Special CG #26	Reach Profile Level 6.
Special CG #27	Reach Profile Level 6.
Special CG #28	Reach Profile Level 6.
Special CG #29	Reach Profile Level 10.
Special CG #30	Reach Profile Level 10.
Special CG #31	Reach Profile Level 6.
Special CG #35	Reach Profile Level 8.
Special CG #36	Reach Profile Level 7.
Special CG #37	Reach Profile Level 9.
Special CG #38	Reach Profile Level 9.
Special CG #40	Reach Profile Level 11.
Special CG #41	Reach Profile Level 9.
Special CG #42	Reach Profile Level 14.
Special CG #43	Reach Profile Level 15.
Special CG #44	Reach Profile Level 11.
Special CG #45	Reach Profile Level 17.
Special CG #46	Reach Profile Level 6.
Special CG #47	Reach Profile Level 7.
Special CG #48	Reach Profile Level 9.
Special CG #50	Reach Profile Level 6.
Special CG #51	Reach Profile Level 6.
Special CG #52	Reach Profile Level 6.
Special CG #53	Reach Profile Level 7.
Special CG #54	Reach Profile Level 9.
Special CG #55	Reach Profile Level 10.
Special CG #56	Reach Profile Level 11.
Special CG #57	Reach Profile Level 14.
Special CG #58	Reach Profile Level 16.
Special CG #59	Reach Profile Level 17.
Special CG #60	Reach Profile Level 19.
Special CG #61	Reach Profile Level 6.
Special CG #62	Reach Profile Level 6.
Special CG #63	Reach Profile Level 6.
Special CG #64	Reach Profile Level 6.

NEW!
A
B
C
D
E
F
G
H
I
J
K
L
M
N
O
P
Q
R
S
T
U
V
W
X
Y
Z

Special CG #65	Reach Profile Level 6.
Special CG #66	Reach Profile Level 6.
Special CG #67	Reach Profile Level 6.
Special CG #68	Reach Profile Level 8.
Special CG #69	Reach Profile Level 8.
Special CG #70	Reach Profile Level 8.
Special CG #71	Reach Profile Level 8.
Special CG #72	Reach Profile Level 8.
Special CG #73	Reach Profile Level 8.
Special CG #74	Reach Profile Level 8.
Special CG #75	Reach Profile Level 8.
Special CG #76	Reach Profile Level 11.
Special CG #77	Reach Profile Level 11.
Special CG #78	Reach Profile Level 11.
Special CG #79	Reach Profile Level 11.
Special CG #80	Reach Profile Level 11.
Special CG #81	Reach Profile Level 11.
Special CG #82	Reach Profile Level 12.
Special CG #83	Reach Profile Level 12.
Special CG #84	Reach Profile Level 12.
Special CG #85	Reach Profile Level 12.
Special CG #86	Reach Profile Level 13.
Special CG #87	Reach Profile Level 13.
Special CG #88	Reach Profile Level 13.
Special CG #89	Reach Profile Level 13.
Special CG #90	Reach Profile Level 13.
System Voice BBCS Default	Reach Profile Level 15.
System Voice Kakihara Tetsuya A	Reach Profile Level 15.
System Voice Kakihara Tetsuya B	Reach Profile Level 15.
System Voice Saito Chiwa	Reach Profile Level 15.
System Voice Sawashiro Miyuki A	Reach Profile Level 15.
System Voice Sawashiro Miyuki B	Reach Profile Level 15.
Arakune Motion Storyboard	Reach Profile Level 16.
Arcade Version of the BlazBlue Continuum Shift II Poster Illustration	Reach Profile Level 20.
Back Cover Illustration of the BlazBlue Official Comic 1	Reach Profile Level 20.
Back Cover Illustration of the BlazBlue Official Comic 2	Reach Profile Level 20.
Bang Motion Storyboard	Reach Profile Level 16.
Bascule Image Board	Reach Profile Level 17.
BlazBlue Continuum Shift II Illustration Package	Reach Profile Level 20.
Carl Motion Storyboard	Reach Profile Level 16.
Cover Illustration of the BlazBlue Official Comic 1	Reach Profile Level 20.
Cover Illustration of the BlazBlue Official Comic 2	Reach Profile Level 20.
Cover Illustration of the BlazBlue – Phase 0 Novel	Reach Profile Level 20.
Hakumen Motion Storyboard	Reach Profile Level 16.
Hazama 3D Model	Reach Profile Level 18.
Hazama Motion Storyboard	Reach Profile Level 17.
Heritage Museum Image Board	Reach Profile Level 17.
Jin Motion Storyboard	Reach Profile Level 15.

Lambda Motion Storyboard	Reach Profile Level 16.
Litchi Motion Storyboard	Reach Profile Level 16.
Makoto 3D Model	Reach Profile Level 18.
Makoto Motion Storyboard	Reach Profile Level 19.
Mu Motion Storyboard	Reach Profile Level 17.
Noel Motion Storyboard	Reach Profile Level 15.
Nu 3D Model	Reach Profile Level 18.
Platinum 3D Model	Reach Profile Level 18.
Platinum Motion Storyboard	Reach Profile Level 19.
Rachel Motion Storyboard	Reach Profile Level 16.
Ragna Motion Storyboard.	Reach Profile Level 15.
Score Attack Mode Illustration	Reach Profile Level 20.
Tager Motion Storyboard	Reach Profile Level 16.
Taokaka Motion Storyboard	Reach Profile Level 16.
Tsubaki 3D Model	Reach Profile Level 18.
Tsubaki Motion Storyboard	Reach Profile Level 17.
Valkenhayn 3D Model	Reach Profile Level 18.
Valkenhayn Motion Storyboard	Reach Profile Level 19.

UNLOCKABLE

Each character has a special Unlimited version that has unique moves and abilities. To unlock them, you must gain enough points to level up your profile, and then acquire them in the Gallery.

UNLOCKABLE	HOW TO UNLOCK
Unlimited Arakune	Reach Profile Level 7.
Unlimited Bang	Reach Profile Level 6.
Unlimited Carl	Reach Profile Level 6.
Unlimited Hakumen	Reach Profile Level 8.
Unlimited Hazama	Reach Profile Level 8.
Unlimited Jin	Reach Profile Level 7.
Unlimited Lambda	Reach Profile Level 6.
Unlimited Litchi	Reach Profile Level 7.
Unlimited Makoto	Reach Profile Level 6.
Unlimited Mu	Reach Profile Level 8.
Unlimited Noel	Reach Profile Level 7.
Unlimited Platinum	Reach Profile Level 6.
Unlimited Rachel	Reach Profile Level 7.
Unlimited Ragna	Reach Profile Level 8.
Unlimited Tager	Reach Profile Level 6.
Unlimited Taokaka	Reach Profile Level 6.
Unlimited Tsubaki	Reach Profile Level 6.
Unlimited Valkenhayn	Reach Profile Level 7.

BLAZBLUE: CONTINUUM SHIFT EXTEND (PLAYSTATION VITA)

TROPHY

UNLOCKABLE	HOW TO UNLOCK
Wheeze...Just Getting Started (Bronze)	Increased all character stats to 50 in [Abyss] mode.
A Spectacle (Bronze)	Landed Carl's Vivace, Cantabile, and Allegreto during a combo.
Aaaaaand I'm Spent (Bronze)	Used up the Ignis gauge while fighting as Relius.

CODES & CHEATS

About Half Way (Bronze)	Defeated the boss at level 500 of the [Abyss].
Abyssmal Shopaholic (Gold)	Acquired all the items from the shop in [Abyss] mode.
Artwork?! Gimmie! (Bronze)	Unlocked 50% of the items in the [Gallery].
Better Safe Than Sorry (Bronze)	Dished out significantly more damage than the opponent's remaining HP.
Breaking in the New Guys (Bronze)	Finished Makoto's, Valkenhayn's, Platinum and Relius's scenarios in [Story] mode.
Domestic Battery (Bronze)	Using Relius, fight a battle without depleting the Ignis gauge.
Don't Give A Kaka (Silver)	Sucessfully executed jumping D, jumping ?+D and jumping ?+D in the middle of a combo.
Eye of the Tiger (Bronze)	Trained for more than 30 minutes, non-stop.
Fangs for the Memories! (Bronze)	Used Hazama's Rising, Falling and Devouring Fangs during a battle.
Feels Like the First Time (Bronze)	Won your first team [Player Match].
Fight for Survival (Bronze)	Using Tsubaki, executed all of the 'D' versions of her special attacks in a single combo.
Finger on the Button (Bronze)	Defeated an opponent while using the Stylish Layout.
Gallery Guru (Gold)	Unlocked everything there is to see in the [Gallery].
Get Off My Lawn! (Bronze)	Performed a 30+ hit combo using Valkenhayn.
Getting Down to Abyss-ness (Silver)	Defeated the boss at level 999 of the [Abyss].
I can't Stop Winning (Bronze)	Won three [Ranked Matches].
I See What You Did There (Bronze)	Played back replay data over 10 times in [Replay Theater].
Ice Ice Ice Baby (Bronze)	Used all three of Jin's special attacks that freeze opponents in a single combo.
Insecticide (Bronze)	Summoned and used all of Arakune's bugs during a single combo.
Just Getting Used To It (Silver)	Raised any character's PSR to over 200 in a [Ranked Match]
Just How I...*wheeze*...Planned (Bronze)	Using Bang, had Fu-Rin-Ka-Zan activated for more than 30 seconds of the battle.
Just the Beginning (Bronze)	Defeated the boss level at level 100 of the [Abyss].
Kaka-kaze (Bronze)	Have been blown up by the chibi-kakas in [Unlimited Mars] mode.
Level 20 (Bronze)	Reached level 20.
Like a Boss (Bronze)	Fought 100 matches in [Ranked Match].
Lunatic (Bronze)	Equipped all of Luna's weapons during one round.
Mars Need Winnin' (Bronze)	Attempted [Unlimited Mars] mode over 10 times.
Mastered the Basics (Bronze)	Cleared over 50 missions in [Challenge] mode.

Mastered the...Master? (Silver)	Cleared over 100 missions in [Challenge] mode.
Mind on my Money (Bronze)	Accumulated over 100,000P$.
Murakumo...AWAKEN! (Silver)	Defeated the secret boss in [Arcade] mode.
Nooooo...el! (Bronze)	Finished off an opponent with Noel's Nemesis Stabilizer.
Oh—NOW I Get It...! (Bronze)	Finished the Calamity Trigger scenario in [Story] mode.
Over 9000?! (Silver)	Dealt over 10,000 damage to an opponent in a single combo.
Plays Well With Others (Bronze)	Fought ten team [Player Matches].
Power of the Azure (Bronze)	Performed a 90+ hit combo using Ragna.
Sharp Shooter (Silver)	Hit the opponent with all of Litchi's Great Whell attacks.
Shocking... Positively Shocking (Bronze)	Using Rachel, shocked your opponent more than 15 times during a single combo.
Squirrel Power! (Bronze)	Executed Makoto's super, Particle Flare, with only Level 3 punches.
Tager? Don't Even Know Her! (Bronze)	Turned the tide and won a battle using Genesic Emerald Tager Buster.
That Will Suffice (Bronze)	Finished the [Tutorial] mode.
The Beginning of the End (Silver)	Finished [Score Attack] mode.
There's No 'I' In Team (Bronze)	Won a team elimination match without even fighting.
Threat Level... Escalated (Silver)	During the course of one combo, placed all four of Mu's Stein's Gunners.
Time to Hit the Arcades (Bronze)	Finished [Arcade] mode.
To Be Continued—! (Silver)	Witnessed the true ending in [Story] mode.
Un...believable (Platinum)	Mastered BlazBlue Continuum Shift – Extend.
You've Been... Terminated (Bronze)	With Lambda, summoned every type of sword during a single round.

BLAZING ANGELS 2: SECRET MISSIONS OF WWII (PLAYSTATION 3)

CODES

Enter the code for unlocking the planes and missions in the main menu, and enter the other two codes while paused when on a mission.

EFFECT	CODE
Damage Increased/Normal	Hold L2 and press L1, L1, R1. Release L2, hold R2 and press R1, R1, L1.
God Mode Active/Inactive	Hold L2 and press ■, ▲, ▲, ▲. Release L2, hold R2 and press ▲, ■, ■, ▲.
Unlock All Planes and Missions	Hold both R2, L2 then press ■, L1, R1, ▲, ▲, R1, L1, ■.

BLAZING ANGELS: SQUADRONS OF WWII (PLAYSTATION 3)

Enter these codes while the game is paused.

UNLOCKABLE	CODE
Increase Damage of Weapons	Hold L2 and quickly press L1, L1, R1; release L2, then hold R2 and quickly press R1, R1, L1

CODES & CHEATS

Invincibility	Hold L2 and press ■, ▲, ▲, ■; release L2, then hold R2 and quickly press ▲, ■, ■, ▲

Enter this code at the Title menu while holding L2+R2

UNLOCKABLE	CODE
All Campaign Missions and Planes	■, L1, R1, ▲, ▲, R1, L1, ■

BLITZ: OVERTIME (PSP)

PASSWORD
In the main menu in the "extras" option, input these codes to unlock the following.

PASSWORD	EFFECT
ONFIRE	Ball trails always on. Only affects Quick Play mode.
BOUNCY	Beach Ball. Only affects Quick Play mode.
PIPPED	Double unleash icons. Only affects Quick Play mode.
CHAMPS	In Campaign mode, highlight a team but do not select it. Stay on the menu and press ■, ■, ▲, Triangle to instantly win against the selected team.
NOTTIRED	Stamina disabled. Only affects Quick Play mode.
CLASHY	Super Clash mode. Only affects Quick Play mode.
BIGDOGS	Super Unleash Clash mode. Only affects Quick Play mode.
CHUWAY	Two player co-op mode.

BLITZ: THE LEAGUE (XBOX 360)

Enter these passwords in the Code menu under Extras.

UNLOCKABLE	PASSWORD
Ball Trail Always On	ONFIRE
Beach Ball	BOUNCY
Double Unleash Icons	PIPPED
Stamina Off	NOTTIRED
Two Player Co-op	CHUWAY
Unlimited Clash Icons	CLASHY
Unlimited Unleash	BIGDOGS

BLOODY WOLF (WII)

CODES
UNLOCKABLE	HOW TO UNLOCK
10 Flash Bombs	When your strength is at "1," climb a barricade and press ⬇+⬅+RUN+②
10 Super Grenades	When your strength is at "1," climb a barricade and press ⬇+⬅+RUN+②
50 Bazooka Rounds	When your strength is at "2," climb a fence and press ⬇+①+②
50 Flame Thrower Charges	Hold ⬇+①+② and press RUN when parachuting at the start of level 2 or level 5
50 Shotgun Rounds	When your strength is at "2," climb a fence and press ⬇+①+②
Fast Mode	At the title screen, press ⬇, ⬇, ⬇, ⬇, ①, ①, ② SELECT, RUN
Hover Mode (in game, press jump to hover)	At the title screen, press ⬇, ⬇, ⬇, ⬇, ②, ②, ①, SELECT, RUN
Sound Test	At the title screen, press ⬇, then hold ①+②+SELECT

LEVEL SELECT CODES

Press ②, ①, ①, ②, ①, ②, ②, ① at the title screen. Then press the following for the appropriate level.

CODE	EFFECT
Up	Level 1
Up/Right	Level 2
Right	Level 3
Down/Right	Level 4
Down	Level 5
Down/Left	Level 6
Left	Level 7
Up/Left	Level 8

BODYCOUNT (XBOX 360)

ACHIEVEMENT

UNLOCKABLE	HOW TO UNLOCK
2nd place equals death! (15)	Won a Deathmatch
A very bad feeling (20)	Survived K-8 Nemesis Widowmaker encounter
Bad medicine (20)	Medic Population Diminished
Beat the street (10)	Survived the Street siege
Boombastic (5)	Killed 10 enemies with explosives
Bullet dodger (30)	Single player challenge complete on normal
Bullet Repellent (50)	OSB Adrenaline upgraded
Bullet with their name on it (5)	Killed 10 enemies with the last round in your weapon
Distance warfare (20)	Achieved Sniper Distance Kill
Don't call a doctor (10)	Survived the Militarised Compound siege
Easy-peasy (20)	Single player challenge complete on easy
Finger on the pulse (50)	OSB Pulse Wave upgraded
Hitman (5)	Killed 10 enemies with a headshot
Hot potato (5)	Killed 10 enemies with grenades
Kept at bay (10)	Survived the Pirate Bay siege
Killed 'em all (50)	Won 10 Deathmatches of any type
Kilo-killer (50)	1000 online kills
Last breath death (5)	Killed 10 enemies while health is low
Leg frag (5)	Killed 10 enemies with mines
Lighting their fire (50)	OSB Explosive bullets upgraded
Military intelligence (10)	Highest value intel collected following multiple skillkills
Multiboom-doom (10)	Killed 3 enemies at once with a single grenade
Network weapon (50)	Skillkill x10
Never say 'Die' (50)	Achieved 100 co-op kills within a siege
Nowhere to hide (5)	killed 10 enemies through cover
Online can of whoop-ass (30)	Achieved 50 co-op kills within a siege
Out of the darkness (10)	Survived the Mine siege
Planes and flames (50)	OSB Airstrike upgraded
Rain of fire (30)	Killed 5 enemies at once with a single Airstrike
Robert Ford style (5)	Killed 10 enemies from behind
Sleep when I'm dead (50)	Defeated K-8 Nemesis Widowmaker
Stealing is wrong, kids! (20)	Scavenger Population Diminished

Team Bodycount®! (15)	Won a Team Deathmatch
The Professional (50)	Skillkill x25
Under their nose (5)	10 surprise kills executed
Up close and personal (5)	Killed 10 enemies using melee
Warmonger (45)	Single player challenge complete on hard
Welcome to Africa - Tutorial (15)	Induction Completed
Wind of change (50)	Achieved all objectives in Africa
Wishing this was Vegas (30)	Achieved all objectives in Asia
You FTW (30)	Broke down the enemy's door

BOLT (PLAYSTATION 3)

CODES

Enter the "Extras" menu, then select "Cheats." Enter one of the following codes to unlock the corresponding cheat option. To toggle a cheat on or off, pause gameplay and enter the "Cheats" menu.

EFFECT	CODE
Unlimited Invulnerability	↓,↓,↑,←
Unlimited Laser Eyes	←,←,↑,→
Unlimited Stealth Camo	←,↓,↓,↓
Unlimited Enhanced Vision	←,↑,↑,↓
Unlimited Gas Mines	→,←,←,↑,↓,→
Unlimited SuperBark	→,←,←,↑,↓,↑
Level Select	→,↑,←,→,↑,→
All Mini Games	→,↑,→,→
Unlimited Ground Pound	→,↑,→,↑,←,↓

BRAVE: THE VIDEO GAME (PLAYSTATION 3)

TROPHY

UNLOCKABLE	HOW TO UNLOCK
Affluent (Bronze)	Accumulate a total of 5000 currency.
All bunched up (Bronze)	As Merida, defeat 5 enemies with a single charged shot.
Ante up (Bronze)	Purchase an upgrade.
Bowlicious (Silver)	Collect all bows.
Bowsome (Bronze)	Collect a bow.
Breezy (Bronze)	Defeat 100 enemies using the Wind charm.
Brilliant (Bronze)	Solve all triplet puzzles.
Carpet runner (Bronze)	Collect a tapestry piece.
Charge it up (Bronze)	Defeat 100 enemies using charged shot.
Clothes horse (Silver)	Collect all outfits.
Cooling off (Bronze)	Defeat 100 enemies using the Ice charm.
Digging in the dirt (Bronze)	Find the earth charm.
Dirty work (Bronze)	Cleanse the ring of stones.
Domination (Silver)	Defeat 250 enemies using power attack.
Earthquake (Silver)	Defeat 250 enemies using the Earth charm.
Everyone knows it's windy (Bronze)	Find the wind charm.
Full of power (Bronze)	Purchase 15 upgrades.
Gaelic hero (Gold)	Defeat the game on Brave difficulty, without changing it.
Get out of my way (Bronze)	As Elinor, charge 5 enemies with a single charge attack.
Gotta snag 'em all (Silver)	Purchase all upgrades.

Great scot (Gold)	Defeat Mor'du.
Heating up (Bronze)	Defeat 100 enemies using the Fire charm.
Hurricane (Silver)	Defeat 250 enemies using the Wind charm.
Ice cold (Silver)	Defeat 250 enemies using the Ice charm.
Ice to see you (Bronze)	Find the ice charm.
Impressive (Bronze)	As Merida, defeat 15 enemies in a row without taking damage.
Minimum wage (Bronze)	Accumulate a total of 1000 currency.
Mopping up (Bronze)	Defeat the harpy guardian.
Mum's the word (Bronze)	Defeat 100 enemies as Queen Elinor.
My fair lassie (Bronze)	Collect an outfit.
On Fire (Silver)	Defeat 250 enemies using the Fire charm.
Platinum (Platinum)	Earn all other Trophies.
Power hungry (Bronze)	Defeat 100 enemies using power attack.
Ranged only (Bronze)	Complete a level without using your sword.
Super bow (Silver)	Defeat 250 enemies using charged shot.
Swordful (Bronze)	Collect a sword.
Swordtacular (Silver)	Collect all swords.
Taking out the trash (Bronze)	Defeat the rock golem guardian.
Throw rug (Bronze)	Complete a tapestry.
Toasty (Bronze)	Find the fire charm.
Tremble (Bronze)	Defeat 100 enemies using the Earth charm.
Triple H's (Bronze)	Solve a triplet puzzle.
Untouchable (Silver)	As Merida, defeat 30 enemies in a row without taking damage.
Wall to wall carpeting (Silver)	Complete all tapestries.
Wealthy (Silver)	Accumulate a total of 15 000 currency.

BRAVE: THE VIDEO GAME (XBOX 360)

ACHIEVEMENT

UNLOCKABLE	HOW TO UNLOCK
Affluent (25)	Accumulate a total of 5000 currency.
All bunched up (25)	As Merida, defeat 5 enemies with a single charged shot.
Ante up (10)	Purchase an upgrade.
Bowlicious (25)	Collect all bows.
Bowsome (5)	Collect a bow.
Breezy (15)	Defeat 100 enemies using the wind charm.
Brilliant (25)	Solve all triplet puzzles.
Carpet runner (5)	Collect a tapestry piece.
Charge it up (15)	Defeat 100 enemies using charged shot.
Clothes horse (25)	Collect all outfits.
Cooling off (15)	Defeat 100 enemies using the ice charm.
Digging in the dirt (5)	Find the earth charm.
Dirty work (5)	Cleanse the ring of stones.
Domination (25)	Defeat 250 enemies using power attack.
Earthquake (25)	Defeat 250 enemies using the earth charm.
Everyone knows it's windy (20)	Find the wind charm.
Full of power (25)	Purchase 15 upgrades.

NEW!

A
B
C
D
E
F
G
H
I
J
K
L
M
N
O
P
Q
R
S
T
U
V
W
X
Y
Z

CODES & CHEATS

Gaelic hero (100)	Defeat the game on Brave difficulty, without changing it.
Get out of my way (25)	As Elinor, charge 5 enemies with a single charge attack.
Gotta snag 'em all (40)	Purchase all upgrades.
Great scot (50)	Defeat Mor'du.
Heating up (15)	Defeat 100 enemies using the fire charm.
Hurricane (25)	Defeat 250 enemies using the wind charm.
Ice cold (25)	Defeat 250 enemies using the ice charm.
Ice to see you (15)	Find the ice charm.
Impressive (20)	As Merida, defeat 15 enemies in a row without taking damage.
Minimum wage (15)	Accumulate a total of 1000 currency.
Mopping up (35)	Defeat the harpy guardian.
Mum's the word (15)	Defeat 100 enemies as Queen Elinor.
My fair lassie (10)	Collect an outfit.
On Fire (25)	Defeat 250 enemies using the fire charm.
Power hungry (15)	Defeat 100 enemies using power attack.
Ranged only (25)	Complete a level without using your sword.
Super bow (25)	Defeat 250 enemies using charged shot.
Swordful (5)	Collect a sword.
Swordtacular (25)	Collect all swords.
Taking out the trash (20)	Defeat the rock golem guardian.
Throw rug (20)	Complete a tapestry.
Toasty (10)	Find the fire charm.
Tremble (15)	Defeat 100 enemies using the earth charm.
Triple H's (10)	Solve a triplet puzzle.
Untouchable (40)	As Merida, defeat 30 enemies in a row without taking damage.
Wall to wall carpeting (40)	Complete all tapestries.
Wealthy (40)	Accumulate a total of 15000 currency.

BULLETSTORM   (PLAYSTATION 3) (XBOX 360)

UNLOCKABLE
You can unlock the Emerald-colored Leash by beating the Bulletstorm demo then playing the full game. The Leash behaves exactly the same as the Blue Leash, it's just a different color.

UNLOCKABLE	HOW TO UNLOCK
Emerald-colored Leash	Beat the Bulletstorm demo.

BULLY SCHOLARSHIP EDITION   (WII)

UNLOCKABLES
UNLOCKABLE	HOW TO UNLOCK
Black Ninja Suit	Take a picture of all the students of Bullworth.
BMX Helmet	Complete all bike races.
UNLOCKABLE	**HOW TO UNLOCK**
Crash Helmet	Win the first set of Go-Kart races.
Double Carnival Tickets	Collect all G & G cards.
Fireman's Hat	Pull the fire alarm 15 times to unlock the fireman's hat.
Mo-Ped	Buy from carnival for 75 tickets.
Pumpkin Head	Smash all pumpkins either on Halloween or in basement.

Robber Mask	Break into 15 people's lockers without getting caught.
Rubber Band Ball	Collect all rubber bands.

BURNOUT PARADISE (PLAYSTATION 3)

UNLOCKABLE CARS

Acquire an A level license, then insert these codes in the in-game Cheats menu.

UNLOCKABLE	HOW TO UNLOCK
Best Buy Car	Type BESTBUY
Circuit City Car	Type CIRCUITCITY
Game Stop Car	Type GAMESTOP
Wal-Mart Car	Type WALMART

OTHER UNLOCKABLE CARS

Insert this code in the in-game Cheats menu under the "sponsor codes" section.

UNLOCKABLE	HOW TO UNLOCK
Steel Wheels Car	Type: U84D 3Y8K FY8Y 58N6

LICENSES

To unlock licenses, win the corresponding number of events in the game.

UNLOCKABLE	HOW TO UNLOCK
A	26 events
B	16 events
C	7 events
D	2 events
Burnout Paradise	45 events
Elite	110 events

PAINT COLORS

UNLOCKABLE	HOW TO UNLOCK
Gold Paint	Earn the elite license
Platinum Paint	Earn the elite license and achieve 100 percent completion.

BUST-A-MOVE BASH! (WII)

MORE STAGES

UNLOCKABLE	HOW TO UNLOCK
250 More Stages	After completing the first 250 stages in Puzzle mode, return to the Select screen and press Ⓐ with the cursor hovering over Stage Select. The area should be mostly orange now instead of blue, and only the first stage will be available. This is how you access stages 251-500.

CALL OF DUTY: BLACK OPS (WII)

CODES

You have to use the classic controller for this to work. At the Main menu, look down at your hands and press "ZL" and "ZR" a couple of times to break free from the chair. Walk around behind the chair you were in, and you will see a computer. Press and hold the button it says to access the computer. Now you can use the computer like the other systems, but the codes don't work the same way.

EFFECT	CODE
A text-based game that you can plug a USB keyboard into your Wii to play	ZORK
Get a list of commands; it works like an old UNIX or DOS system	HELP
Unlock all the missions in the Mission Select screen in Campaign mode (no Zombie maps)	3ARC UNLOCK
Unlocks all the intel in the game	3ARC INTEL

TERMINAL CODES

Access the Central Intelligence Agency Data System and type the case-sensitive command "login." When you are prompted to log in with an account, enter the following usernames and passwords. Access their documents with the "dir" command or e-mail with the "mail" command.

EFFECT	CODE
Adrienne Smith	Username: asmith; password: roxy
Bruce Harris	Username: bharris; password: goskins
D. King	Username: dking; password: mfk
Frank Woods	Username: fwoods; password: philly
Grigori "Greg" Weaver	Username: gweaver; password: gedeon
J. Turner	Username: Jturner; password: condor75
Jason Hudson	Username: jhudson; password: bryant1950
John F. Kennedy	Username: jfkennedy; password: lancer
John McCone	Username: jmccone; password: berkley22
Vannevar Bush	Username: vbush; password: manhattan

CALL OF DUTY: BLACK OPS (PLAYSTATION 3) (XBOX 360)

CIA DATA SYSTEM ACCOUNTS

When using the computer to access the CIA Data system, you can use the following login IDs and passwords. After logging into an account, you may then browse each user's unique files using the DIR command or read messages with the MAIL command.

EFFECT	CODE
The user account of Alex Mason, already logged in when you first use the terminal	Username: amason; password: PASSWORD
The user account of Bruce Harris	Username: bharris; password: GOSKINS
The user account of D. King	Username: dking; password: MFK
The user account of Dr. Adrienne Smith	Username: asmith; password: ROXY
The user account of Dr. Vannevar Bush	Username: vbush; password: MANHATTAN
The user account of Frank Woods	Username: fwoods; password: PHILLY

The user account of Grigori "Greg" Weaver	Username: gweaver; password: GEDEON
The user account of J. Turner	Username: jturner; password: CONDOR75
The user account of Jason Hudson	Username: jhudson; password: BRYANT1950
The user account of John McCone, director of Central Intelligence, 1961–1965	Username: jmccone; password: BERKLEY22
The user account of Joseph Bowman	Username: jbowman; password: UWD
The user account of President John Fitzgerald Kennedy	Username: jfkennedy; password: LANCER
The user account of President Lyndon Baines Johnson	Username: lbjohnson; password: LADYBIRD
The user account of President Richard Nixon	Username: rnixon; password CHECKERS
The user account of Richard Helms, director of the CIA from 1966 to 1973	Username: rhelms; password: LEROSEY
The user account of Richard Kain	Username: rkain; password: SUNWU
The user account of Ryan Jackson	Username: rjackson; password: SAINTBRIDGET
The user account of T. Walker	Username: twalker; password: RADIO (zero, not "O")
The user account of Terrance Brooks	Username: tbrooks; password: LAUREN
The user account of William Raborn, director of Central Intelligence from 1965–1966	Username: wraborn; password: BROMLOW

TERMINAL CODES

On the Main menu, and press the L2 and R2 buttons repeatedly. After about five times for each button, you'll break free of your interrogation chair. When you get up, walk around behind you to a computer. When you access it, enter the following using the onscreen keyboard.

EFFECT	CODE
Activates Dead Ops Arcade	DOA
Displays a list of system commands in the terminal and Pentagon user e-mail access	HELP
FI FIE FOE	FOOBAR
Get to root of directory and see all codes	cd .. [Enter] cd .. [Enter] cd bin [Enter] ls [Enter]
Gives a list of audio files and pictures that you can open with the CAT command (e.g., CAT NoteX.txt)	DIR
Gives a list of login names for use with the RLOGIN function (but they require a password)	WHO
It will list all of your audio files and pictures	CAT
To List a directory (same as DIR but for LINUX)	LS
To view a file in a directory using the TYPE command "NAMEOFFILE.EXTENSION"	TYPE
Unlocks all Intel in the game for viewing	3ARC INTEL
Unlocks Dead Ops Arcade and Presidential Zombie Mode	3ARC UNLOCK
Unlocks Zork I: The Great Underground Adventure (a text adventure game from 1980) for play in Black Ops	ZORK
Virtual Therapist Software	ALICIA

EASTER EGGS

Nuketown Mannequin Secret

On the multiplayer map Nuketown, if you blow the heads off of all the mannequins in a short amount of time, the song "Sympathy for the Devil" by the Rolling Stones will play in the background.

Play the song "Don't Back Down" by Eminem in Five zombie maps

There are three red phones throughout the pentagon that ring and flash. The first is located where you first start after opening a set of doors in the corner. The second is on the catwalk circling the room after leaving the first elevator. The third is in one of the rooms after leaving the second elevator on the floor the power is on. Just listen for a cell phone ring and follow it to the red rotary phone. Look at them and hold X till the ringing stops and you hear a busy signal. Once you get the third phone, the music starts.

CALL OF DUTY: MODERN WARFARE 2 (XBOX 360)

EXTRA CUSTOM CLASS SLOT

UNLOCKABLE	HOW TO UNLOCK
Extra Custom Class Slot	Obtain level 70 in multiplayer and enter Prestige Mode to unlock a sixth custom class slot.

KILLSTREAK REWARDS

You can unlock the Killstreaks by receiving the amount designated before dying.

UNLOCKABLE	HOW TO UNLOCK
AC130 Gunship (be the gunner of the AC130)	11 Kills
Attack Helicopter	07 Kills
Care Package (drops ammo/Killstreaks)	04 Kills
Chopper Gunner (be the gunner of the Helicopter)	11 Kills
Counter UAV (jams enemy radars)	04 Kills
Emergency Airdrop (4 ammo/Killstreak drops)	08 Kills
EMP (disables electronics)	15 Kills
Harrier Strike (choose bomb location and defending Harrier)	07 Kills
Nuclear Strike (kills everyone on map)	25 Kills
Pave Low (Armored Helicopter)	09 Kills
Precision Airstrike (drop airstrike)	06 Kills
Predator (guided missiles)	05 Kills
Sentry Gun (deployable gun)	05 Kills
UAV (shows enemy location)	03 Kills

PROFESSIONAL PERKS

With each perk you unlock you can upgrade it by completing various requirements.

UNLOCKABLE	HOW TO UNLOCK
Bling Pro (two primary weapon attachments + two secondary weapon attachments)	Get 200 Kills with a weapon with two attachments.
Cold-Blooded Pro (undetectable by UAV, air support, sentries, and thermal imaging + no red crosshair or name when you are targeted)	Destroy 40 enemy Killstreak Rewards with Cold-Blooded Perk.
Commando Pro (increased Melee Distance + no falling damage)	Get 20 Melee Kills using Commando Perk.
Danger Close Pro (increased explosive weapon damage + extra air support damage)	Get 100 Kills with explosives while using Danger Close Perk.
Hardline Pro (Killstreak Rewards require 1 less Kill + Deathstreak Rewards require 1 less death)	Get 40 Killstreaks (two or more in a row without dying) with Hardline Perk.
Last Stand Pro (pull out your pistol before dying + use equipment in last stand)	Get 20 Kills while in last stand.
Lightweight Pro (move faster + quick aim after sprinting)	Run 30 miles with Lightweight Perk.

Marathon Pro (unlimited sprint + climb obstacles faster)	Run 26 miles with Marathon Perk.
Ninja Pro (invisible to heartbeat sensors + your footsteps are silent)	Get 50 close-range Kills using Ninja Perk.
One Man Army Pro (swap classes at any time + swap classes faster)	Get 120 Kills using One Man Army.
Scavenger Pro (resupply from dead enemies + extra mags)	Resupply 100 times with Scavenger Perk.
Scrambler Pro (jam enemy radar near you + delay enemy claymore explosions)	Get 50 close-range Kills using Scrambler Perk.
Sitrep Pro (detect enemy explosives and tactical insertions + louder enemy footsteps)	Destroy 120 detected explosives or tactical insertions with Sitrep Perk.
Sleight of Hand Pro (faster reloading + faster aiming)	Get 120 kills with Sleight of Hand Perk.
Steady Aim Pro (increased hip fire accuracy + longer hold breath duration)	Get 80 hip fire Kills using Steady Aim.
Stopping Power Pro (extra bullet damage + extra damage to enemy vehicles)	Get 300 Kills with Stopping Power Perk.

MODERN WARFARE 2 MUSEUM

The Museum can be selected from the Mission Select screen once you've completed the game.

UNLOCKABLE	HOW TO UNLOCK
An evening with Infinity Ward: Modern Warfare 2 Gallery Exhibit	Complete the campaign.

MULTIPLAYER WEAPONS AND EQUIPMENT

Reach the level indicated to unlock the weapon and/or piece of equipment.

UNLOCKABLE	HOW TO UNLOCK
.44 Magnum (Pistol)	Level 26
AA-12 (Shotgun)	Level 12
ACR (Assault Rifle)	Level 48
AK-47 (Assault Rifle)	Level 70
AT4-HS (Grenade Launcher)	Level 01
AUG HBAR (LMG)	Level 32
Barret .50 Cal (Sniper)	Level 04
Blast Shield	Level 19
C4	Level 43
Claymore	Level 31
Desert Eagle (Pistol)	Level 62
F2000 (Assault Rifle)	Level 60
FAL (Assault Rifle)	Level 28
FAMAS (Assault Rifle)	Level 01
Frag Grenade	Level 01
Glock 18 (Secondary)	Level 22
Intervention (Sniper Rifle)	Level 01
Javelin (Grenade Launcher)	Level 50
L86 LSW (LMG)	Level 01
M1014 (Shotgun)	Level 54
M16A4 (Assault Rifle)	Level 40
M21 EBR (Sniper Rifle)	Level 56
M240 (LMG)	Level 52

NEW!

A
B
C
D
E
F
G
H
I
J
K
L
M
N
O
P
Q
R
S
T
U
V
W
X
Y
Z

M4A1 (Rifle)	Level 04
M9 (Pistol)	Level 46
M93 Raffica (Secondary)	Level 38
MG4 (LMG)	Level 16
Mini Uzi (SMG)	Level 44
MP5K (SMG)	Level 04
P90 (SMG)	Level 24
PP-2000 (Secondary)	Level 01
Ranger (Shotgun)	Level 42
RPD (SMG)	Level 04
RPG-7 (Grenade Launcher)	Level 65
SCAR-H (Assault Rifle)	Level 08
Semtex Grenade	Level 01
SPAS-12 (Shotgun)	Level 01
Stinger (Grenade Launcher)	Level 30
Striker (Shotgun)	Level 34
Tactical Insertion	Level 11
TAR-21 (Assault Rifle)	Level 20
Throwing Knife	Level 07
Thumper (Grenade Launcher)	Level 14
TMP (Secondary)	Level 58
UMP .45 (SMG)	Level 01
USP .45 (Pistol)	Level 01
Vector (SMG)	Level 12
WA2000 (Sniper)	Level 36
Winchester 1887 (Shotgun)	Level 67

CALL OF DUTY: MODERN WARFARE 3 (XBOX 360)

ACHIEVEMENT

UNLOCKABLE	HOW TO UNLOCK
50/50 (20)	Complete a Special Ops Mission Mode game with the same number of kills as your partner.
Arms Dealer (20)	Buy all items from the Survival Weapon Armory.
Back in the Fight (5)	Start the Single Player Campaign on any difficulty.
Back Seat Driver (10)	Track down Volk. Complete "Bag and Drag" on any difficulty.
Bad First Date (10)	Find the girl. Complete "Scorched Earth" on any difficulty.
Birdie (20)	Kill 2 enemy helicopters without getting hit in a Special Ops Survival game.
Brag Rags (10)	Earn 1 star in Special Ops Mission Mode.
Carpe Diem (10)	Escape the mountain safe house. Complete "Persona Non Grata" on any difficulty.
City of Lights (25)	Complete "Bag and Drag" and "Iron Lady" on Veteran difficulty.
Danger Close (20) grenade in "Bag and Drag."	Take down a chopper with an AC-130 smoke
Danger Zone (20)	Buy all items from the Survival Air Support Armory.
Defense Spending (20)	Buy all items from the Survival Equipment Armory.

Diamond in the Rough (10)	Rescue the Russian President. Complete "Down the Rabbit Hole" on any difficulty.
Flight Attendant (20)	Kill all 5 enemies during the zero-g sequence in "Turbulence."
For Whom the Shell Tolls (20)	Destroy all targets during the mortar sequence with only 4 shells in "Back on the Grid."
Frequent Flyer (10)	Defend the Russian President. Complete "Turbulence" on any difficulty.
Get Rich or Die Trying (25)	Have $50,000 current balance in a Special Ops Survival game.
I Live (10)	Survive 1 wave in a Special Ops Survival game.
Informant (20)	Collect 22 Intel Items.
Jack the Ripper (20)	Melee 5 enemies in a row in Single Player or Special Ops.
Kill Box (20)	Kill 20 enemies with the Chopper Gunner in a single run in "Return to Sender."
Ménage à Trois (20)	Destroy 3 tanks with a single 105mm shot in "Iron Lady."
Nein (20)	Kill 9 enemies with A-10 strafing runs in "Scorched Earth."
No Assistance Required (20)	Complete a Special Ops Mission Mode game on Hardened or Veteran with no player getting downed.
One Way Ticket (10)	Make it to Westminster. Complete "Mind the Gap" on any difficulty.
Out of the Frying Pan… (25)	Complete "Persona Non Grata", "Turbulence", and "Back on the Grid" on Veteran difficulty.
Overachiever (40)	Earn 48 stars in Special Ops Mission Mode.
Payback (25)	Complete "Mind the Gap", "Goalpost", and "Return to Sender" on Veteran difficulty.
Requiem (10)	Escape the city. Complete "Blood Brothers" on any difficulty.
Sandstorm! (10)	Assault the shipping company. Complete "Return to Sender" on any difficulty.
Scout Leader (35)	Collect 46 Intel Items.
Serrated Edge (15)	Finish a Juggernaut with a knife in Special Ops.
Storm the Castle (10)	Discover Makarov's next move. Complete "Stronghold" on any difficulty.
Strike! (20)	Kill 5 enemies with a single grenade in Single Player or Special Ops.
Survivor (20)	Reach Wave 10 in each mission of Special Ops Survival mode.
Tactician (20)	Earn 1 star in each mission of Special Ops Mission Mode.
The Best of the Best (100)	Complete the campaign on Hardened or Veteran difficulty.
The Big Apple (25)	Complete "Black Tuesday" and "Hunter Killer" on Veteran difficulty.
The Darkest Hour (25)	Complete "Eye of the Storm", "Blood Brothers", and "Stronghold" on Veteran difficulty.
This Is My Boomstick (20)	Kill 30 enemies with the XM25 in "Black Tuesday."
This is the End (25)	Complete "Scorched Earth", "Down the Rabbit Hole", and "Dust to Dust" on Veteran difficulty.
Too Big to Fail (10)	Destroy the Jamming Tower. Complete "Black Tuesday" on any difficulty.

Unstoppable (40)	Reach Wave 15 in each mission of Special Ops Survival mode.
Up to No Good (10)	Infiltrate the village. Complete "Back on the Grid" on any difficulty.
Vive la Révolution! (10)	Reach the church. Complete "Eye of the Storm" on any difficulty.
We'll Always Have Paris (10)	Escape Paris with Volk. Complete "Iron Lady" on any difficulty.
Welcome to WW3 (10)	Save the US Vice President. Complete "Goalpost" on any difficulty.
Wet Work (10)	Take back New York Harbor. Complete "Hunter Killer" on any difficulty.
What Goes Up… (20)	Destroy all the choppers with only the UGV's grenade launcher in "Persona Non Grata."
Who Dares Wins (40)	Complete the campaign on any difficulty.

CALL OF DUTY: WORLD AT WAR (XBOX 360)

MODES

UNLOCKABLE	HOW TO UNLOCK
Veteran mode	Reach Level 32 to unlock Veteran mode.
Zombie mode	Successfully complete Campaign mode to unlock Zombie mode, which is a four-player co-op mode against endless waves of Nazi zombies.

MULTIPLAYER UNLOCKABLES

Reach a certain rank on online multiplayer to achieve each unlockable.

UNLOCKABLE	HOW TO UNLOCK
.357 Magnum	Reach Level 49
Arisaka	Reach Level 4
BAR	Reach Level 4
Browning M1919	Reach Level 61
Clan Tag	Reach Level 11
Colt M1911	Reach Level 3
Custom Class Slot 10	Reach Prestige Level 10
Custom Class Slot 6	Reach Prestige Level 1
Custom Class Slot 7	Reach Prestige Level 2
Custom Class Slot 8	Reach Prestige Level 4
Custom Class Slot 9	Reach Prestige Level 7
Double-Barreled Shotgun	Reach Level 29
DP-28	Reach Rank 13
FG-42	Reach Rank 45
Gewehr 47	Reach Rank 6
Kar98K	Reach Rank 41
M1 Garand	Reach Rank 17
M1A1 Carbine	Reach Rank 65
M2 Flamethrower	Reach Rank 65
MG-42	Reach Rank 33
Mosin-Nagant	Reach Rank 21
MP-40	Reach Rank 10
Nambu	Reach Rank 1
PPSh 41	Reach Rank 53
PTRS 41	Reach Rank 57
Springfield	Reach Rank 3

STG-44	Reach Rank 37
SVT-40	Reach Rank 1
Thompson	Reach Rank 1
Tokarev TT38	Reach Rank 21
Trench Gun	Reach Rank 2
Type-100	Reach Rank 25
Type-99	Reach Rank 1
Walther P38	Reach Rank 2

MULTIPLAYER PERK UNLOCKABLES

Reach a certain rank on online multiplayer to achieve each unlockable perk.

UNLOCKABLE	HOW TO UNLOCK
Bandolier	Reach Level 40
Bouncing Betty x 2	Reach Level 24
Camouflage	Reach Level 12
Coaxial Machine Gun (vehicle)	Reach Level 40
Dead Silence	Reach Level 52
Double Tap	Reach Level 36
Fireproof	Reach Level 48
Iron Lungs	Reach Level 60
Juggernaut	Reach Level 4
Leadfoot (vehicle)	Reach Level 28
M2 Flamethrower	Reach Level 65
Martydom	Reach Level 20
Ordinance Training (vehicle)	Reach Level 12
Overkill	Reach Level 56
Primary Grenades x 2	Reach Level 44
Reconnaissance	Reach Level 64
Second Chance	Reach Level 9
Shades	Reach Level 32
Sleight of Hand	Reach Level 28
Toss Back	Reach Level 6

CALL OF DUTY 2 (XBOX 360)

Enter this code on the Mission Select screen.

UNLOCKABLE	CODE
Unlock all levels	Hold both the left and right bumpers, then quickly input ♦, ♦, ♦, ♦, ♥, ♥

CALL OF DUTY 3 (XBOX 360)

Enter this code at the Chapter Select screen.

UNLOCKABLE	CODE
Unlock All Levels and Pictures	Hold ♋ then press ♦, ♦, ♦, ♦, ✪, ✪

CALL OF DUTY 3 (WII)

Enter this code in the Chapter Select screen.

UNLOCKABLE	CODE
Unlock All Levels	Hold ⊕ and press ⬅, ⬅, ➡, ➡, ②, ②
Unlock All Extras	At the Chapter Select screen, hold ⊕, and press ⬅, ⬅, ➡, ➡, ②, ②

CODES & CHEATS

CALL OF DUTY 4: MODERN WARFARE (XBOX 360)

ARCADE AND CHEAT OPTIONS

These unlock automatically for completing *Call of Duty 4: Modern Warfare* on any difficulty level. During gameplay, find the Cheat menu in the Options menu.

UNLOCKABLE	HOW TO UNLOCK
Arcade Mode	Complete game on any difficulty
Cheat Menu	Complete game on any difficulty

CHEATS

Unlock cheats by collecting enemy intel (intelligence), which look like laptop computers that are hidden throughout the campaign. Note: Using cheats disables Achievements.

UNLOCKABLE CHEATS

UNLOCKABLE	HOW TO UNLOCK
A Bad Year: When you kill enemies, they explode into tires!	Collect 15 pieces of enemy intel.
Cluster Bombs: After one of your frag grenades explodes, four more explode in a cross-shaped pattern.	Collect 10 pieces of enemy intel.
CoD Noir: Turns all gameplay into black and white.	Collect 2 pieces of enemy intel.
Infinite Ammo: Weapons have unlimited ammo. Doesn't work with Perk 1 abilities such as C4 and Claymores.	Collect 30 pieces of enemy intel.
Photo-Negative: Inverses all of the game's colors.	Collect 4 pieces of enemy intel.
Ragtime Warfare: Gameplay goes black and white, dust and scratches fill the screen, it plays at 2x speed, and the music becomes piano music.	Collect 8 pieces of enemy intel.
Slow-Mo Ability: Use the melee button to change the game to slow-mo and play at half-speed.	Collect 20 pieces of enemy intel.
Super Contrast: Dramatically increases the game's contrast, making the darks much darker and the lights much lighter.	Collect 6 pieces of enemy intel.

Golden weapons are a special camo (or skin) that you unlock when you fully complete all the challenges under the weapon subtype in the barracks (SMG, LMG, etc.). Access them by choosing the camo of the respective weapon. The effect is purely cosmetic and does not enhance the ability of the weapon in any way.

GOLDEN WEAPONS

UNLOCKABLE	HOW TO UNLOCK
Golden AK-47	Complete all Assault Rifle challenges.
Golden Desert Eagle	Get to Level 55.
Golden Dragunov	Complete all Sniper challenges.
Golden M1014	Complete all Shotgun challenges.
Golden M60	Complete all LMG challenges.
Golden Mini-Uzi	Complete all SMG challenges.

MULTIPLAYER UNLOCKABLES

UNLOCKABLE	UNLOCKED AT RANK:
AK-74U Submachine Gun	28
Bandolier Perk Class 1	32
Barret Sniper Rifle	49
Bomb Squad Perk Class 1	13
\Boot Camp Challenges 1	08

NEW!

A
B
C
D
E
F
G
H
I
J
K
L
M
N
O
P
Q
R
S
T
U
V
W
X
Y
Z

Sniper Class Weapon Class	02
UAV Jammer Perk Class 2	10

CALL OF DUTY 4: MODERN WARFARE (PLAYSTATION 3)

Enter this code in the Chapter Select screen.

UNLOCKABLE	CODE
Unlock All Levels	Hold SELECT and press ⇨, ⇨, ⇦, ⇦, ■, ■

Arcade and Cheat Options

These unlock automatically for completing *Call of Duty 4: Modern Warfare* on any difficulty level. During gameplay, find the Cheat menu in the Options menu.

UNLOCKABLE	HOW TO UNLOCK
Arcade Mode	Complete game on any difficulty
Cheat Menu	Complete game on any difficulty

EASTER EGG (HIDDEN MISSION)

Beat the game on any difficulty and let the credits run all the way through. When they finish, you'll start another mission. This mission takes place on a plane that resembles Air Force One, wherein you must fight your way through a horde of baddies, save the V.I.P., and escape the plane in less than two minutes.

CHEATS

Unlock cheats by collecting enemy intel (intelligence), which look like laptop computers that are hidden throughout the campaign. Note: Using cheats disables Achievements.

UNLOCKABLE CHEATS

UNLOCKABLE	HOW TO UNLOCK
A Bad Year: When you kill enemies, they explode into tires!	Collect 15 pieces of enemy intel.
Cluster Bombs: After one of your frag grenades explodes, four more explode in a cross-shaped pattern.	Collect 10 pieces of enemy intel.
CoD Noir: Turns all gameplay into black and white.	Collect 2 pieces of enemy intel.
Infinite Ammo: Weapons have unlimited ammo. Doesn't work with Perk 1 abilities such as C4 and Claymores.	Collect 30 pieces of enemy intel.
Photo-Negative: Inverses all of the game's colors.	Collect 4 pieces of enemy intel.
Ragtime Warfare: Gameplay goes black andwhite, dust and scratches fill the screen, it plays at 2x speed, and the music becomes piano music.	Collect 8 pieces of enemy intel.
Slow-Mo Ability: Use the melee button to change the game to slow-mo and play at half-speed.	Collect 20 pieces of enemy intel.
Super Contrast: Dramatically increases the game's contrast, making the darks much darker and the lights much lighter.	Collect 6 pieces of enemy intel.

Golden weapons are a special camo (or skin) that you unlock when you fully complete all the challenges under the weapon subtype in the barracks (SMG, LMG, etc.). Access them by choosing the camo of the respective weapon. The effect is purely cosmetic and does not enhance the ability of the weapon in any way.

GOLDEN WEAPONS

UNLOCKABLE	HOW TO UNLOCK
Golden AK-47	Complete all Assault Rifle challenges.
Golden Desert Eagle	Get to Level 55.
Golden Dragunov	Complete all Sniper challenges.
Golden M1014	Complete all Shotgun challenges.
Golden M60	Complete all LMG challenges.
Golden Mini-Uzi	Complete all SMG challenges.

MULTIPLAYER UNLOCKABLES

UNLOCKABLE	UNLOCKED AT RANK
Assault Rifle (G3)	Rank 25
Assault Rifle (G36C)	Rank 37
Assault Rifle (M14)	Rank 46
Assault Rifle (M4)	Rank 10
Assault Rifle (MP44)	Rank 52
LMG (M60E4)	Rank 19
Pistol (Desert Eagle)	Rank 43
Pistol (Golden Desert Eagle)	Rank 55
Pistol (M1911)	Rank 16
Shotgun (M1014)	Rank 31
SMG (AK-74U)	Rank 28
SMG (Mini Uzi)	Rank 13
SMG (P90)	Rank 40
Sniper Rifle (Barret)	Rank 49
Sniper Rifle (Dragunov)	Rank 22
Sniper Rifle (M40)	Rank 04
Sniper Rifle (R700)	Rank 34

CALL OF JUAREZ: BOUND IN BLOOD (PLAYSTATION 3)

CODES

From the Main menu go into Exclusive content and enter code.

EFFECT	CODE
Bonus Cash to be able to buy better weapons earlier in the game.	735S653J

CAPCOM CLASSIC COLLECTION REMIXED (PSP)

Enter this code at the Press Start screen.

UNLOCKABLE	CODE
Arts, Tips, and Sound Tests for Every Game	Press ⇦, ⇨ on D-pad, ⇦, ⇨ on Analog stick, ■, ●, ⇧, ⇩

CARS (XBOX 360)

PASSWORDS

PASSWORD	EFFECT
CONC3PT	All art concept
WATCHIT	All movies
R4MONE	All paint jobs
IMSPEED	Super fast start
VROOOOM	Unlimited boost
YAYCARS	Unlock all cars
MATTL66	Unlock all races
IF900HP	Unlock everything in the game

CARS (WII)

Input codes in the password section under the Options menu.

UNLOCKABLE	CODE
All Cars	YAYCARS
All Concept Art	CONC3PT
All Movies	WATCHIT
All Paint Jobs	R4MONE
All Races	MATTL66
All Tracks and Mini-games	IF900HP

Mater's Speedy Circuit and Mater's Countdown Clean Up	TRGTEXC
Super Fast Start	IMSPEED
Unlimited Boost	VROOOOM

CARS 2: THE VIDEO GAME   (XBOX 360)

UNLOCKABLE

Enter these codes at the Cheat menu to unlock features

UNLOCKABLE	HOW TO UNLOCK
Unlock all modes and all tracks	959595
Unlock lazers	123456
Cars 2: The Video Game	Wii

UNLOCKABLE

Enter these codes at the Cheat menu to unlock features

UNLOCKABLE	HOW TO UNLOCK
Unlock all modes and all tracks	959595
Unlock lazers	123456

CASTLEVANIA: ORDER OF ECCLESIA   (DS)

UNLOCKABLES

UNLOCKABLE	HOW TO UNLOCK
Boss Medals	During a boss fight, do not get hit once. After the fight, a treasure chest will appear from the ground to present you with the medal.
New Game+	After finishing the game, go to your file and press right to access the clear sign and start a new game.
Albus Mode	Complete the game after saving all villagers.
Boss Rush Mode	Complete the game after saving all villagers.
Hard Difficulty	Beat the game once.
Hard Mode Level 255	Complete Hard Mode Level 1 OR connect to Castlevania: Judgment
Sound Mode	Complete the game after saving all villagers.

CASTLEVANIA: SYMPHONY OF THE NIGHT   (XBOX 360)

PLAY AS OTHER CHARACTERS AND EXTRAS

You must complete the game as Alucard with 180% or more and have a "CLEAR" Save.

PASSWORD	EFFECT
Enter AXEARMOR as your name	Alucard with Axelord armor
Enter RICHTER as your name	Play as Richter Belmont
Enter X-X!V"Q as your name	Alucard with lower stats and MAX Luck

CASTLEVANIA: THE ADVENTURE REBIRTH   (WII)

LEVEL SELECT

At the title screen, select "Game Start" and hold right on the D-pad for a few seconds. You'll be able to select and play any levels you have previously reached on the same difficulty.

CATHERINE   (PLAYSTATION 3)

TROPHY

UNLOCKABLE	HOW TO UNLOCK
3-Star Man (Bronze) Normal or Hard	Unlock Menhir by earning 3 Gold Prizes on
5-Star Man (Bronze) on Normal or Hard	Unlock the Obelisk by earning 5 Gold Prizes
A God is Born! (Gold)	Conquer the final stage of Babel

A Life Without Regrets… (Bronze)	View the true Freedom ending
A Mystery Within a Puzzle (Bronze)	Uncover the truth behind Rapunzel
A New Look (Bronze)	Help Todd out of his trouble
Altar Conquered! (Bronze)	Complete Stage 1 of Babel
Babel's Calling (Bronze) Normal or Hard	Unlock the Altar by earning 1 Gold Prize on
Beer Baron (Bronze)	Listen to all the beer factoids
Bomberlamb (Bronze)	Hit 15 blocks with a single explosion (Golden Playhouse)
Cheers To You! (Platinum)	Unlock all other Trophies!
Cocktail Connoisseur (Bronze)	Listen to all the cocktail trivia
Crossing the Courtyard (Bronze)	Conquer Stage 5
Dreams Come True (Gold)	View all of the endings
Everyday Hero (Silver)	Help everyone out of their predicaments
Have an Ice Day (Bronze)	Slide an Ice Block 5 or more blocks (Golden Playhouse)
Hit the Road, Vincent (Bronze)	View the bad Cheater ending
I Can Fly! (Silver)	Jump on a Spring Block 3 times in a row (Golden Playhouse)
Just Like Old Times (Bronze)	View the normal Lover ending
Legendary Prince (Silver)	Hear Rapunzel's sad song
Let My Sheep Go (Bronze)	Conquer Stage 3
Lord of the Night (Bronze)	View the true Cheater ending
Love is Patient, Love is Kind (Bronze)	Resolve Daniel's dilemma
Making Legends (Bronze)	Conquer Stage 8
Menhir Conquered! (Bronze)	Complete Stage 2 of Babel
Mother Inferior (Bronze)	Help Archie work through his quandary
Nighty Night (Bronze)	View the bad Lover ending
No One Expects the… (Bronze)	Conquer Stage 4
Obelisk Conquered! (Bronze)	Complete Stage 3 of Babel
One Last Case (Bronze)	Help Morgan clean up his mess
Past a Heap of Puzzles (Bronze)	Beat Stage 64 of Rapunzel
Path to the Altar (Bronze)	Conquer Stage 7
Play It Again, Vince… (Bronze)	Use the jukebox to change the music
Push It to the Limit! (Bronze)	Push 5 blocks at once (Golden Playhouse)
Read All About It! (Bronze)	Get Justin out of his jam
Sake Sensei (Bronze)	Listen to all the sake sound bites
Sleepless Nights (Bronze)	View the normal Cheater ending
Starting a New Life (Bronze)	View the true Lover ending
Take Your Time (Silver)	Move a Dark Block 10 times in a row (Golden Playhouse)
Taking on the Gods (Silver)	Unlock Axis Mundi by earning all Gold Prizes on Normal or Hard
Text Junkie (Bronze)	Reply to at least 20 text messages by the end of the final day
The Golden Child (Gold)	Earn Gold Prizes on all Hard difficulty stages
The Great Escape (Bronze)	Conquer Stage 2
The Nightmares Have Just Begun (Bronze)	Conquer Stage 1
True Freedom! (Silver)	Conquer Stage 9

NEW!

A
B
C
D
E
F
G
H
I
J
K
L
M
N
O
P
Q
R
S
T
U
V
W
X
Y
Z

Welcome to the Colosseum (Bronze)	Unlock the Colosseum mode
What Time is It? (Bronze)	Conquer Stage 6
Whatever, Buddy (Bronze)	View the normal Freedom ending
Whisky Wiseman (Bronze)	Listen to all the whisky minutiae
You Don't Have To Go Home… (Bronze)	Stay in the bar until all the other customers leave

CODE

At the Rapunzel arcade game title screen, enter the code. Enter the code again to disable it.

EFFECT	CODE
Unlocks new Rapunzel stages	↑,↓,↓,↑,↑,↑,↓,↓,↓,↓,→

CODE

At the Title screen where you can select game modes, activate a new mode.

UNLOCKABLE	HOW TO UNLOCK
Very Easy Mode	Highlight Golden Playhouse and hold Select until the screen flashes whilte

UNLOCKABLE

Earn Gold Prizes in the Golden Playhouse to unlock randomized stages in Babel Mode

UNLOCKABLE	HOW TO UNLOCK
Altar	Earn one Gold Prize from the Golden Playhouse on Normal difficulty or higher.
Axismundi	Earn nine Gold Prizes from the Golden Playhouse on Normal difficulty or higher.
Menhir	Earn three Gold Prizes from the Golden Playhouse on Normal difficulty or higher.
Obelisk	Earn five Gold Prizes from the Golden Playhouse on Normal difficulty or higher.

UNLOCKABLE

Unlock a new mode by beating the game.

UNLOCKABLE	HOW TO UNLOCK
Colosseum Mode	Beat the game once.

SECRET

UNLOCKABLE	HOW TO UNLOCK
Skip a Stage	If you clear all the stages in a chapter in Normal or higher difficulty level with a gold trophy on each stage, you get a gold trophy for the chapter. When you replay the chapter, press Start to skip any stage, including the Boss.

CHEW-MAN-FU   (WII)

CODES

UNLOCKABLE	HOW TO UNLOCK
Golden Balls	At the title screen, hold ①+SELECT and press ⬅+➡

PASSWORDS

PASSWORD	EFFECT
573300	Area 1, Round 1 (2nd Playthrough)
344710	Area 1, Round 1 (3rd Playthrough)
274510	Area 1, Round 1 (4th Playthrough)
321310	Area 1, Round 1 (5th Playthrough)
536300	Area 1, Round 1 (6th Playthrough)
301710	Area 1, Round 1 (7th Playthrough)
231510	Area 1, Round 1 (8th Playthrough)

256310	Area 1, Round 1 (9th Playthrough)
441300	Area 1, Round 1 (10th Playthrough)
677261	Area 5, Round 50
075653	Fight enemy opponents only

CHILDREN OF EDEN (PLAYSTATION 3)

TROPHY

UNLOCKABLE	HOW TO UNLOCK
Absolutely Fabulous (Bronze)	Cleared all the Archives on Normal Difficulty and achieved 100% purification.
Automaton (Bronze)	Achieved a 4 Star Clear Rank.
Collector (Bronze)	25% of Extra bonuses unlocked.
Constellation Overdrive (Bronze)	Obtained more than 800,000 points in the Passion Archive on Normal Difficulty.
Crackerjack (Bronze)	Cleared the Evolution Archive on Normal Difficulty and achieved 100% purification.
Dabbler (Bronze)	10% of Extra bonuses unlocked.
Endless Passion (Bronze)	Obtained all items in the Passion Archive.
Evolution Pack Rat (Bronze)	Obtained all items in the Evolution Archive.
Eye Of The Beholder (Bronze)	Obtained all items in the Beauty Archive.
Feel The Beat (Bronze)	Achieved a Perfect Octa-Lock.
Field Of Dreams (Bronze)	Cleared the Beauty Archive on Normal Difficulty Mode.
Figure Eight (Bronze)	Purified an enemy using Octa-Lock.
Fireworks From Heaven (Silver)	Obtained more than 800,000 points in the Beauty Archive on Hard Difficulty.
Flawless Beauty (Bronze)	Obtained more than 800,000 points in the Beauty Archive on Normal Difficulty.
Genius Play (Bronze)	Cleared the Matrix Archive on Normal Difficulty and achieved 100% purification.
Giver Of Life (Bronze) Mode.	Cleared the Journey Archive on Normal Difficulty
Gunslinger (Silver)	Obtained more than 800,000 points in the Journey Archive on Hard Difficulty.
Hierophant (Silver)	Achieved a Gold Star Clear Rank.
Hope Springs Eternal (Silver)	Cleared the Hope Archive.
Hot Shot (Bronze)	Achieved a total of 100 Perfect Octa-Locks.
If The Spirit Moves You (Bronze)	Cleared the Passion Archive on Normal Difficulty Mode.
Impeccable Virtue (Bronze)	Obtained more than 800,000 points in the Journey Archive on Normal Difficulty.
Luminous (Bronze)	Cleared the Passion Archive on Normal Difficulty and achieved 100% purification.
Magnificent Aura (Bronze)	Obtained more than 800,000 points in the Evolution Archive on Normal Difficulty.
Maniac Play (Bronze)	75% of Extra bonuses unlocked.
Master of Eden (Gold)	Cleared all Archives on Normal and Hard Difficulty Mode with a Gold Star Clear Rank.
Matrix Archivist (Bronze)	Cleared the Matrix Archive on Hard Difficulty Mode.
Matrix Completionist (Bronze)	Obtained all items in the Matrix Archive.
Phoenix Rising (Bronze)	Cleared the Evolution Archive on Normal Difficulty Mode.
Pulse-Pounding (Bronze)	Obtained more than 800,000 points in the Matrix Archive on Normal Difficulty.

A
B
C
D
E
F
G
H
I
J
K
L
M
N
O
P
Q
R
S
T
U
V
W
X
Y
Z

Radiant Avalon (Bronze)	Cleared the Journey Archive on Normal Difficulty and achieved 100% purification.
Savant (Bronze)	Achieved a 5 Star Clear Rank.
Shimmering Brightness (Bronze)	Cleared the Beauty Archive on Hard Difficulty Mode
SRSBZNS (Bronze)	50% of Extra bonuses unlocked.
Super Collider (Silver)	100% of Extra bonuses unlocked.
The Calculator (Silver)	Obtained more than 800,000 points in the Evolution Archive on Hard Difficulty.
The Cleaner (Bronze)	All enemy types purified.
The Great Evolution Round-Up (Bronze)	Cleared the Evolution Archive on Hard Difficulty Mode.
The Journey's End (Bronze)	Cleared the Journey Archive on Hard Difficulty Mode.
The Purest Shining Light (Platinum)	Unlocked all Trophies.
The Skills That Pay The Bills (Bronze)	Achieved 10 consecutive Perfect Octa-Locks.
The Thinker (Bronze)	Cleared the Beauty Archive on Normal Difficulty and achieved 100% purification.
The Wireframe Web Expands (Bronze)	Cleared the Matrix Archive on Normal Difficulty. Mode
Time Becomes A Loop (Silver)	Obtained more than 800,000 points in the Matrix Archive on Hard Difficulty.
Total Eclipse Of The Heart (Silver)	Cleared all the Archives on Hard Difficulty and achieved 100% purification.
Total Enlightenment (Bronze)	Euphoria used.
Ultimate Compiler (Gold)	Collected all Reward Items in Lumi's Garden.
Unforgettable Fire (Bronze)	Cleared the Passion Archive on Hard Difficulty Mode.
Wanderer (Bronze)	Obtained all items in the Journey Archive.
You Sure Showed Them (Silver)	Obtained more than 800,000 points in the Passion Archive on Hard Difficulty.

CHINA WARRIOR (WII)

CODES

UNLOCKABLE	HOW TO UNLOCK
Enable Invincibility and Level Select	Press RUN+SELECT to reset the game, keep the buttons held, then release RUN and press ✛ when the title screen is displayed. Release Select and press ✛, ✛, ✛, ✛, ✛, ✛, ✛, ✛, ✛, ✛, ✛, ✛.
Level Skip	Hold ✛ then SELECT+①+② to skip the first level. For the other levels, hold ✛ instead of ✛.
Continue (up to three times) from the Start of the Las Level Played	Hold ①+②+✛ and press RUN, RUN when the phrase "The End" appears after gameplay is over. Alternately, hold ①+2+✛ and press RUN at the title screen after game play is over.

THE CHRONICLES OF NARNIA: THE LION, THE WITCH, AND THE WARDROBE (DS)

Enter these codes at the Main menu.

UNLOCKABLE	CODE
Acquire Armor	Ⓐ, Ⓧ, Ⓨ, Ⓑ, ↑, ↑, ↑, ↓
All Blessings	←, ↑, Ⓐ, Ⓑ, →, ↓, Ⓧ, Ⓨ
All Skills at Maximum	Ⓐ, ←, →, Ⓑ, ↓, ↑, Ⓧ, Ⓧ
Extra Money	↑, Ⓧ, ↑, Ⓧ, ↑, Ⓑ, ↓, Ⓑ
Invincibility	Ⓐ, Ⓨ, Ⓧ, Ⓑ, ↑, ↑, ↑, ↓
Maximum Attributes	←, Ⓑ, ↑, Ⓨ, ↓, Ⓧ, →, Ⓐ

| Restore Health | ←, →, ↑, ↓, Ⓐ, Ⓐ, Ⓐ, Ⓐ |
| Stronger Attacks | Ⓐ, ↑, Ⓑ, ↓, Ⓧ, Ⓧ, Ⓨ, Ⓨ |

CHRONO TRIGGER (DS)

UNLOCKABLE ENDINGS

UNLOCKABLE	HOW TO UNLOCK
Ending 1 "Beyond Time"	Defeat Lavos after reviving Crono at Death Peak.
Ending 10 "Dino Age"	Defeat Lavos after facing Magus, but before facing Azala.
Ending 11 "What the Prophet Seeks"	Defeat Lavos after facing Azala, but before Schala opens the sealed door.
Ending 12 "Memory lane"	Defeat Lavos after Schala opens the sealed door, but before restoring the light to the pendant.
Ending 13 "Dream's Epilogue"	Defeat the Dream Devourer beyond Time's Eclipse
Ending 2 "Reunion"	Defeat Lavos while Crono is dead.
Ending 3 "The Dream Project"	Defeat Lavos in the Ocean Palace or immediately upon starting a new game.
Ending 4 "The successor of Guardia"	Defeat Lavos after saving Leene and Marle, but before visiting the End of Time.
Ending 5 "Good Night"	Defeat Lavos after visiting the End of Time, but before returning to the Middle Ages.
Ending 6 "The Legendary Hero"	Defeat Lavos after arriving in the Middle Ages, but before obtaining the Hero's Badge.
Ending 7 "The Unknown Past"	Defeat Lavos after obtaining the Hero's Badge, but before the Gate key is stolen.
Ending 8 "People of the times"	Defeat Lavos after regaining the gate key, but before giving the Masamune to Frog.
Ending 9 "The Oath"	Defeat Lavos after giving the Masamune to Frog but before fighting Magus.

ITEM DUPLICATION

Once you reach the Arena of Ages, send your monster out to train until it returns back with an item. When it returns, you will see the monster's status window showing the item it brought back. Without closing this window, press the A button to select the option "Train Monster." Then press the A button a second time and you will now be on the Consumables item screen. Press the B button once to return back to the original screen. This will duplicate the item that the monster brought back (though you will not see any evidence of this until you look in your own inventory). You can continue to do this to get 99 of that item. This is a great way to stock up on magic, speed, or strength capsules.

CLONING CLYDE (XBOX 360)

UNLOCK MUTANT CLYDE

UNLOCKABLE	HOW TO UNLOCK
Mutant Clyde	Beat all levels under par time

COMIX ZONE (WII)

UNLOCKABLES

UNLOCKABLE	HOW TO UNLOCK
Fart	In some areas, press ✛.
Sega Plug	At any time during the main game, press START to pause. After a few seconds, Sketch will yell, "Sega!"
Stage Select	Go to the Jukebox mode and place the red checker on the following numbers in order, pressing ✛ at each one: 14, 15, 18, 5, 13, 1, 3, 18, 15, 6. Now, highlight a number from 1 to 6 and press ✛ to warp to the corresponding stage.

Unlimited Health	Go to Jukebox in the Options menu and push ⬇ on these numbers: 3, 12, 17, 2, 2, 10, 2, 7, 7, 11. You hear Sketch say "oh yeah."
View Credits	At the Options mode, press Ⓐ+Ⓑ+Ⓒ.
Paper Airplane	During gameplay press and hold the Punch button. After a second or so Sketch will tear a piece of paper from the background and make a paper airplane out of it. The plane will travel to the edge of the panel and circle back around. The plane does massive damage to all enemies, objects, and Sketch himself, so be careful. You lose a considerable amount of health when creating the plane.

THE CONDUIT (WII)

CODES

Enter the code from the cheats menu

EFFECT	CODE
Custom ASE unlocked	NewASE11
Secret Agent skin unlocked	SuitMP13
Unlock Drone for Single-player	Drone4SP

UNLOCKABLES

These cheats can be unlocked after gaining achievements. Enable the cheats in the Cheats Menu, under Extras.

UNLOCKABLE	HOW TO UNLOCK
Fiery Death: Enemies Die As If They Had Been Killed By A Charged Shot	Complete the "Secret Master" achievement.
Fully Stocked: Infinite Ammo	Complete the "Annihilator Award" achievement.
Stopping Power: One Shot Kill	Complete the "Campaign Award" achievement.

CONDUIT 2 (WII)

CODE

In the Extras option, go to Promotional Codes and type the following codes in.

EFFECT	CODE
Unlock Eye of Ra ASE.	EYEOFRA
Unlock Golden Destroyer armor. (Online only.)	14KARMOR

CONTRA (XBOX 360)

CODES

CODE	EFFECT
⬆⬆⬇⬇⬅➡⬅➡ⒷⒶ	Start game with 30 lives. Your score is not eligible for the High Score Leader Board.

CRASH: MIND OVER MUTANT (XBOX 360)

CODES

While playing story mode, pause the game. Hold guard and press the following buttons on the D-pad very quickly! To deactivate a cheat, enter its code again.

EFFECT	CODE
Crash freeze any enemy he touches	⬇,⬇,⬇,⬆
Crash turns into a shadow	⬅,➡,⬅,➡
Enemies leave behind x4 damage (Boxing glove)	⬆,⬆,⬆,➡
Enemies leave behind Wumpa fruit	➡,➡,➡,⬆
Make different parts of Crash bigger	⬅,⬅,⬅,⬇

CRASH: MIND OVER MUTANT (WII)

CODES

While playing Story Mode, pause the game. Hold guard and press the following buttons on the D-pad very quickly! To deactivate a cheat, enter its code again.

EFFECT	CODE
Crash freezes any enemy he touches	⇧⇧⇧⇧
Crash turns into a shadow	⇩⇩⇩⇩
Enemies leave behind x4 damage (Boxing glove)	⇧⇧⇧⇩
Enemies leave behind Wumpa fruit	⇩⇩⇩⇧
Make different parts of Crash bigger	⇩⇩⇩⇩

CRATERMAZE (WII)

PASSWORDS

PASSWORD	EFFECT
Unlock All Enter	Press RUN on the title screen and select Password.
Normal Levels	this password, then use ① and ② to select a level before pressing RUN. Blue/Left, Blue/Left, Blue/Right, Red/Front
Expert Level Select	Blue/Back, Blue/Back, Red/Right, Blue/Forward

CRESCENT PALE MIST (PLAYSTATION 3)

UNLOCKABLES

UNLOCKABLE	HOW TO UNLOCK
Boss Only mode	Obtain the Mysterious Button from the enemy D'Artagnan on stage 5 (Normal mode and up only)
Fear difficulty	Obtain the terror medallion from one of the three black star enemies on stage 4 (Hard mode only); then beat the game on Hard mode
Music Room	Locate the music room key on stage 6 (Normal mode and up only)
Planeriel difficulty	Obtain the nightmare medallion from the nightmare of legend enemy on stage 3 (Fear mode only); then beat the game on Fear mode

CYBERNATOR (WII)

CODES

UNLOCKABLE	HOW TO UNLOCK
Extra Continues	At the title screen, hold ⇩+⇧+⇩ and then press START.
Napalm Gun	Complete the first level without shooting anything except the boss, then complete level 2 without dying.
Secret Bad Ending	Go through the first level, and do not destroy the boss. Finish the rest of the game to see the failed ending.

D

DANCE CENTRAL 2 (XBOX 360)

ACHIEVEMENT

UNLOCKABLE	HOW TO UNLOCK
All Over the Place (20)	Nail moves in each column on the screen in a Free-4-All.
All That Glitters (10)	Master The Glitterati's routines on Easy skill level.
Biggest Winner (20)	Burn your first 100 calories in Fitness mode.
Bit of a Lu$h (10)	Master Lu$h Crew's routines on Easy skill level.
Bragging Rights (20)	Earn more than 100,000 points in a Free-4-All.
Certified Double Platinum (25)	Get a solo score of at least 2,000,000 points on a song.
Chump to Champ (20)	Go from 2nd place to 1st in a Free-4-All.
Dance Hall Legend (40)	Earn 5 stars on every song in the game.
Dance Machine (10)	Defeated Dr. Tan's army of robots on Easy skill level.
Def to the World (10)	Master Hi-Def's routines on Easy skill level.
Eclectic Taste (20)	Gold Digger (20)
Endless-ish Setlist (15)	Complete a playlist that is 15 minutes in length or longer.
Finishing Touch (20)	Earn a Flawless Finish on a song.
Fitness Fanatic (15)	Complete an entire Fitness Playlist.
Flash in the Pan (15)	Master Flash4wrd's routines on Medium skill level.
For the Record (15)	Get a perfect score on a move after using Video Record in Break It Down mode.
Forward Motion (10)	Master Flash4wrd's routines on Easy skill level.
Friend of Flash4wrd (20)	Master Flash4wrd's routines on Hard skill level.
Friend of Hi-Def (20)	Master Hi-Def's routines on Hard skill level.
Friend of Lu$h Crew (20)	Master Lu$h Crew's routines on Hard skill level.
Friend of Riptide (20)	Master Riptide's routines on Hard skill level.
Full Dance Card (30)	Dance with every original crew member in the game.
Get the Picture (15)	Upload a Photo to Kinect Share.
Getting Ripped (10)	Master Riptide's routines on Easy skill level.
Gold Digger (20)	Earn Gold Stars on a song.
Hard Act to Follow (20)	Earn 3 stars on any song on Hard skill level.
Hi and Mighty (15)	Master Hi-Def's routines on Medium skill level.
In It to Twin It (15)	Master The Glitterati's routines on Medium skill level.
Latest Model (30)	Have your picture taken 1000 times.
Lu$h Fund (15)	Master Lu$h Crew's routines on Medium skill level.
Minion Potential (25)	Defeated Dr. Tan's army of robots on Medium skill level.
Nailed It! (15)	Skip to the next move by nailing a move the first time you see it in Break It Down.

Patience Is a Virtue (10)	Listen to the entire background theme of the game in one sitting.
Perfect Pair (30)	Earn 5 stars on a co-op performance.
Photo Bomb! (20)	Perform a Freestyle section with 3 or more people.
Proved Your Point (20)	Win 3 Dance Battles in a row.
Recapable (20)	Get a perfect score on a Recap in Break It Down mode.
Shop and Lock (30)	Unlock the alternate outfits for the 10 crew members.
Slow Profile (15)	Get a perfect score on a move after using Slo-Mo in Break It Down mode.
Solo and Steady (20)	Earn 5 stars on a solo performance.
Star Quality (25)	Earn over 100 stars.
Survival of the Fittest (20)	Log 5 total hours in Fitness mode.
Targeted Practice (15)	Customize your Break It Down session by using the "Focus on Select Moves" feature.
Teacher's Pet (25)	Earn 5 stars on a song in Perform It immediately after completing it in Break It Down.
The Doctor Will See You Now (50)	Defeated Dr. Tan's army of robots on Hard skill level.
Thrash and Burn (40)	Burn 3500 calories in Fitness mode.
Turn the Tide (15)	Master Riptide's routines on Medium skill level.
Vanquisher (20)	Win 20 Dance Battles.
Working It Out (20)	Survival of the Fittest (20)
Worthy Adversary (20)	Master The Glitterati's routines on Hard skill level

UNLOCKABLE

UNLOCKABLE	HOW TO UNLOCK
Bring It Tee	Play every song in the game in Perform It mode.
Neon Tee	Get a solo score of at least 2,000,000 points on a song.
Ribbon Tee	Earn Gold Stars on a song.

DANTE'S INFERNO   (PLAYSTATION 3)

UNLOCKABLES

UNLOCKABLE	HOW TO UNLOCK
Making the Baby Feature	Beat the game on any difficulty.
Dante's Crusader Costume	Complete the game and start a new game (or Resurrection Mode game); you'll be prompted to choose the costume before the game begins.
Gates of Hell Survival Mode	Complete the game and it will be selectable from the Main menu.
New Game Plus (Resurrection Mode)	Complete the game.
Infernal Difficulty	Beat the game on any other difficulty.

DARK SOULS   (PLAYSTATION 3)

TROPHY

UNLOCKABLE	HOW TO UNLOCK
Art of Abysswalking (Bronze)	Acquire the Art of Abysswalking.
Bond of a Pyromancer (Silver)	Acquire all pyromancies.
Chaos Weapon (Bronze)	Acquire best wpn through chaos reinfrc.
Covenant: Blade of the Darkmoon (Silver)	Discover Blade of the Darkmoon covenant.
Covenant: Chaos Servant (Silver)	Discover Chaos Servant covenant.

Covenant: Darkwraith (Silver)	Discover Darkwraith covenant.
Covenant: Forest Hunter (Silver)	Discover Forest Hunter covenant.
Covenant: Gravelord Servant (Silver)	Discover Gravelord Servant covenant.
Covenant: Path of the Dragon (Silver)	Discover Path of the Dragon covenant.
Covenant: Princess's Guard (Silver)	Discover Princess's Guard covenant.
Covenant: Warrior of Sunlight (Silver)	Discover Warrior of Sunlight covenant.
Covenant: Way of White (Bronze)	Discover Way of White covenant.
Crystal Weapon (Bronze)	Acquire best wpn through crystal reinfrc.
Dark Lord (Gold)	Reach 'The Dark Lord' ending.
Defeat Bed of Chaos (Silver)	Defeat the Soul Lord Bed of Chaos.
Defeat Crossbreed Priscilla (Silver)	Defeat Crossbreed Priscilla, the Lifehunter.
Defeat Gravelord Nito (Silver)	Defeat the Soul Lord Gravelord Nito.
Defeat Seath the Scaleless (Silver)	Defeat Seath the Scaleless, inheritors of souls.
Defeat the Dark Sun Gwyndolin (Silver)	Defeat Dark Sun Gwyndolin, the Darkmoon God.
Defeat the Four Kings (Silver)	Defeat the Four Kings, inheritors of souls.
Divine Weapon (Bronze)	Acquire best wpn through divine reinfrc.
Enchanted Weapon (Bronze)	Acquire best wpn through enchanted reinfrc.
Enkindle (Bronze)	Light bonfire flame.
Estus Flask (Bronze)	Acquire Estes Flask.
Fire Weapon (Bronze)	Acquire best wpn through fire reinfrc.
Knight's Honor (Silver)	Acquire all rare weapons.
Lightning Weapons (Bronze)	Acquire best wpn through lightning reinfrc.
Lordvessel (Silver)	Acquire the Lordvessel.
Magic Weapon (Bronze)	Acquire best wpn through magic reinfrc.
Occult Weapon (Bronze)	Acquire best wpn through occult reinfrc.
Prayer of a Maiden (Silver)	Acquire all miracles.
Raw Weapon (Bronze)	Acquire best wpn through raw reinfrc.
Reach Anor Londo (Silver)	Arrive in Anor Londo.
Reach Lordran (Bronze)	Arrive in Lordran.
Ring the bell (Quelaag's Domain) (Bronze)	Ring Bell of Awakening in Quelaag's domain.
Ring the Bell (Undead Church) (Bronze)	Ring Bell of Awakening at Undead Church.
Rite of Kindling (Bronze)	Acquire the Rite of Kindling.
Strongest Weapon (Bronze)	Acquire best wpn through standard reinfrc.
The Dark Soul (Platinum)	All trophies obtained. Congratulations!
To Link the Fire (Gold)	Reach 'To Link the Fire' ending.
Wisdom of a Sage (Silver)	Acquire all sorceries.

THE DARKNESS (XBOX 360)

SPECIAL DARKLINGS

At any in-game phone, enter the number and you will unlock a special Darkling

PASSWORD	EFFECT
555-GAME	Unlocks Special 2K Darkling
555-5664	Unlocks the European Retailer (Golfer) Special Darkling

THE DARKNESS (PLAYSTATION 3)

PHONE NUMBERS

Go to any phone and enter the 18 phone numbers, in no specific order, to unlock Keeper of Secrets accomplishment. Find these phone numbers throughout the game on posters, graffiti, etc. Out of the 25, you only need 18 to unlock the accomplishment.

PHONE NUMBER	COUNT
555-6118	1/18
555-9723	2/18
555-1847	3/18
555-5289	4/18
555-6667	5/18
555-6205	6/18
555-4569	7/18
555-7658	8/18
555-9985	9/18
555-1233	10/18
555-1037	11/18
555-3947	12/18
555-1206	13/18
555-9562	14/18
555-9528	15/18
555-7934	16/18
555-3285	17/18
555-7892	18/18

THE DARKNESS II (PLAYSTATION 3)

TROPHY

UNLOCKABLE	HOW TO UNLOCK
2 guys 1 Pole (Bronze)	Kill 2 enemies with one javelin
Allies in Strange Places (Bronze)	Escape the asylum with help from the inside
At Home in the Dark (Gold)	Finish all chapters in New Game+ on any difficulty
Back in the Saddle (Bronze)	Rescue Jackie from the Iron Maiden
Bonnie & Clyde wannabes (Bronze)	Kill Jean-Luc Lambert and Amelie Dubois
Burned His Mansion (Bronze)	Kill Luigi Palladino
Carnie Kid (Bronze)	Earn a score of over 1000 in each of the carnival games
Cheque Please! (Bronze)	Survive the hit
Conquered the Darkness (Platinum)	Unlock all trophies
Coward (Bronze)	Kill Cedro Valdez
Cut and Run (Bronze)	Kill 50 enemies with the Demon Arm Slash attack
Dark Akimbo (Bronze)	Kill 100 enemies while dual wielding 2 different guns as Jackie

Dark Ninjutsu (Bronze)	Complete a mission as Inugami
Date Night (Bronze)	Protect Jenny
Decisions, Decisions (Bronze)	Refuse to cooperate with Victor in the Interrogation
Don of Darkness (Gold)	Finish the game on Don difficulty
Embraced the Darkness (Bronze)	In Vendettas, acquire all the talents for one character
Escape the Brotherhood (Bronze)	Survive the interrogation
Executioner (Bronze)	Kill 50 enemies with Executions while playing as Jackie
Free the Mind (Silver)	Finish the game on any difficulty
Hell Hath No Fury... (Bronze)	Complete a mission as Shoshanna
I'm Just Getting Started (Bronze)	Find and interrogate Swifty
Impish Delight (Bronze)	Kill 15 enemies while playing as the Darkling
It's 12pm Somewhere! (Bronze)	Complete a mission as Jimmy
Jackie's Got Talent (Bronze)	Purchase a Talent in the single player campaign
Karma's a Bitch (Bronze)	Kill a shielded enemy with his own shield
Mmmm Essence! (Bronze)	Pick up 5 Relics in the single player campaign
One Flew Over... (Bronze)	Return to reality...?
One Man Army (Bronze)	Kill 25 enemies while being dragged from the restaurant, without dying or restarting checkpoint
Ready for the Big Leagues (Bronze)	Kill 50 enemies with thrown objects
Relic Hunter (Silver)	Find all 29 Relics in the single player campaign
Romantic (Bronze)	Real guys know how to dance
Should Have Called 555-2368... (Silver)	Survive the battle against the Hell Beast
Skeet Shoot (Bronze)	Throw an enemy into the air and kill him with gunfire before he lands
Step into Hell... (Bronze)	Defeat Victor
Storm the Mansion (Bronze)	Take back your mansion
Suck it Up (Bronze)	Kill 50 enemies with Black Hole while playing as Jackie
Sweet Revenge (Bronze)	Avenge your Aunt Sarah
Talent Show (Silver)	Max out all of Jackie's Talent Trees
Technical difficulties (Bronze)	Kill the NewsWatch 6 team of Tom Dawson, Bud Langley and Sara Stephens
That's Why I'm the Boss (Bronze)	Impress Dolfo in two different ways
The Bird is the Word (Bronze)	Avoid being run over in the parking garage
The Brotherhood Crumbles (Gold)	Complete Vendettas Campaign
The Old Gibber (Bronze)	Kill 100 enemies with Gun Channeling while playing as Jackie
The Swarm King (Bronze)	Kill 50 enemies who are swarmed while playing as Jackie
This Kid's Got Potential (Bronze)	Max out 1 of Jackie's Talent Trees
Truly Talented (Bronze)	Max out 3 of Jackie's Talent Trees
Versatile Killer (Bronze)	Kill enemies in 5 different ways within 30 seconds
Voodoo is More Than Dolls (Bronze)	Complete a mission as JP

| Whipping Boy (Bronze) | Kill Frank Marshall |
| You've Made My Hit List (Silver) | Complete 6 Hit List exclusive missions |

THE DARKNESS II (XBOX 360)

ACHIEVEMENT

UNLOCKABLE	HOW TO UNLOCK
2 Guys 1 Pole (25)	Kill 2 enemies with one javelin
Allies in Strange Places (20)	Escape the asylum with help from the inside
At Home in the Dark (50)	Finish all chapters in New Game+ on any difficulty
Back in the Saddle (20)	Rescue Jackie from the Iron Maiden
Bonnie & Clyde Wannabes (20)	Kill Jean-Luc Lambert and Amelie Dubois
Burned His Mansion (20)	Kill Luigi Palladino
Carnie Kid (20)	Earn a score of over 1000 in each of the carnival games
Cheque Please! (10)	Survive the hit
Coward (20)	Kill Cedro Valdez
Cut and Run (10)	Kill 50 enemies with the Demon Arm Slash attack
Dark Akimbo (10)	Kill 100 enemies while dual wielding 2 different guns while playing as Jackie
Dark Ninjutsu (10)	Complete a mission as Inugami
Date Night (25)	Protect Jenny
Decisions, Decisions (5)	Refuse to cooperate with Victor in the Interrogation
Don of Darkness (100)	Finish the game on Don difficulty
Embraced the Darkness (25)	In Vendettas, acquire all the talents for one character
Escape the Brotherhood (25)	Survive the interrogation
Executioner (10)	Kill 50 enemies with Executions while playing as Jackie
Free the Mind (25)	Finish the game on any difficulty
Hell Hath No Fury... (10)	Complete a mission as Shoshanna
I'm Just Getting Started (25)	Find and interrogate Swifty
Impish Delight (10)	Kill 15 enemies while playing as the Darkling
It's 12pm Somewhere! (10)	Complete a mission as Jimmy
Jackie's Got Talent (5)	Purchase a Talent in the single player campaign
Karma's a Bitch (10)	Kill a shielded enemy with his own shield
Mmmm Essence! (10)	Pick up 5 Relics in the single player campaign
One Flew Over... (20)	Return to reality...?
One Man Army (10)	Kill 25 enemies while being dragged from the restaurant, without dying or restarting checkpoint
Ready for the Big Leagues (10)	Kill 50 enemies with thrown objects
Relic Hunter (50)	Find all 29 Relics in the single player campaign
Romantic (5)	Real guys know how to dance
Should Have Called 555-2368... (10)	Survive the battle against the Hell Beast
Skeet Shoot (10)	Throw an enemy into the air and kill him with gunfire before he lands
Step into Hell... (25)	Defeat Victor
Storm the Mansion (25)	Take back your mansion

Suck It Up (10)	Kill 50 enemies with Black Hole while playing as Jackie
Sweet Revenge (25)	Avenge your Aunt Sarah
Talent Show (50)	Max out all of Jackie's Talent Trees
Technical Difficulties (20)	Kill the NewsWatch 6 team of Tom Dawson, Bud Langley and Sara Stephens
That's Why I'm the Boss (15)	Impress Dolfo in two different ways
The Bird is the Word (5)	Avoid being run over in the parking garage
The Brotherhood Crumbles (50)	Complete Vendettas Campaign
The Old Gibber (10)	Kill 100 enemies with Gun Channeling while playing as Jackie
The Swarm King (10)	Kill 50 enemies who are swarmed while playing as Jackie
This Kid's Got Potential (10)	Max out 1 of Jackie's Talent Trees
Truly Talented (25)	Max out 3 of Jackie's Talent Trees
Versatile Killer (20)	Kill enemies in 5 different ways within 30 seconds
Voodoo is More Than Dolls (10)	Complete a mission as JP
Whipping Boy (20)	Kill Frank Marshall
You've Made My Hit List (25)	Complete 6 Hit List exclusive missions

DARKSIDERS (XBOX 360)

CODES
Enter the Pause Screen during gameplay and select "Options." Under Game Options select "Enter Code" from the menu.

EFFECT	CODE
"The Harvester" Scythe	The Hollow Lord

DARKSIDERS (PLAYSTATION 3)

CODES
Enter the Pause Screen during gameplay and select "Options." Under Game Options select "Enter Code" from the menu.

EFFECT	CODE
"The Harvester" Scythe	The Hollow Lord

DEAD MOON (WII)

UNLOCKABLE

UNLOCKABLE	HOW TO UNLOCK
Option Screen	Hold the following: ✛+①+② and press SELECT

DEAD OR ALIVE: DIMENSIONS (3DS)

CODES
When selecting a character, hold the following for costume variants, then select with Ⓐ.

EFFECT	CODE
Kasumi Alpha: Braid	✛ + ⊗
Kasumi Alpha: High Ponytail	✛ + ⊗
Kasumi Alpha: Low Ponytail	✛ + ✛ + ⊗
Kasumi: Braided hair	✛ + ⊗
Kasumi: High Ponytail	✛ + ⊗
Kasumi: Low Ponytail	✛ + ✛ + ⊗
La Mariposa: No Mask	✛ + ⊗
Lei Fang: Side Braids	✛ + ⊗
Lei Fang: Short Ponytail	✛ + ⊗

Random Select: Shiden Costume 1	⬅️ + ⓧ
Random Select: Shiden Costume 2	➡️ + ⓧ
Random Select: Shiden Costume 3	➡️ + ⬅️ + ⓧ

UNLOCKABLE

UNLOCKABLE	HOW TO UNLOCK
Character Menu Voice	Play and win one round of survival mode
Geo-Thermal Plant(Metroid Stage)	Finish all of Arcade mode

DEAD RISING 2 (PLAYSTATION 3)

SUIT OF ARMOR

To get the suit of armor from Ghouls 'n Ghosts, you must gather all 4 pieces. When you wear all 4 pieces at once, your health is doubled, and just like in Ghouls 'n Ghosts, as you take damage, the armor chips away, leaving you in nothing but your underwear.

UNLOCKABLE	HOW TO UNLOCK
Full Beard	In the back of the store "Moe's Migitations" in Royal Flush Plaza.
Knight Armor	Complete the game with the "S" ending.
Knight Boots	Buy at the pawnshop the Platinum Strip.
Knight Helmet	Eliminate Jack in Strip Poker in the "Ante Up" side mission.

CLOTHING

UNLOCKABLE	HOW TO UNLOCK
Champion's Jacket	Win a TIR episode (be the overall top player by the end).
Convicts	Kill 10 psychopaths.
Hockey Mask	Use every melee weapon on zombies.
Tattered Clothes	Kill 1,000 zombies using hand-to-hand combat.
TIR Helmet	Earn $1,000,000 in TIR Online.
TIR Outfit	Earn $5,000,000 in TIR Online.
Willemette Mall Costume	Rescue 50 survivors.

DEAD RISING 2: CASE 0 (XBOX 360)

UNLOCKABLES

UNLOCKABLE	HOW TO UNLOCK
Easy $1,500	In the casino, there is a slot machine with a cow on it. Put in $100 to gamble and you will always win the first 5 times.
Ending A	Save all survivors, give Katey Zombrex, collect all bike parts, and leave.
Ending B	Collect all bike parts, give Katey Zombrex, then leave.
Ending C	Get caught by the military, away from Katey.
Ending D	Get caught by military on your bike.
Ending E	Forget to give Katey Zombrex.
Ending F (alt)	Forget to give Katey zombrex while near her.

DEAD SPACE (XBOX 360)

CODES

Press Start, then insert the following codes. You will hear a chime if you've done it correctly.

EFFECT	CODE
1,000 credits (one time only per playthrough)	ⓧ,ⓧ,ⓨ,ⓨ,ⓧ
10,000 credits (one time only per playthrough)	ⓧ,ⓧ,ⓨ,ⓨ,ⓧ,ⓧ,ⓨ
2 Nodes (one time only per playthrough)	ⓨ,ⓧ,ⓧ,ⓧ,ⓨ
2,000 credits (one time only per playthrough)	ⓧ,ⓧ,ⓧ,ⓨ,ⓧ
5 Nodes (one time only per playthrough)	ⓨ,ⓧ,ⓨ,ⓧ,ⓧ,ⓧ,ⓨ,ⓧ,ⓧ,ⓨ,ⓧ,ⓧ

5,000 credits (one time only per playthrough)	✪,✪,✪,✪,✪,✪
Refill Your Oxygen	✪,✪,✪,✪,✪
Refill Your Stasis and Kinesis Energy	✪,✪,✪,✪,✪

DEAD SPACE (PLAYSTATION 3)

Codes

Press Start, then insert the following codes. You will hear a chime if you've done it correctly.

EFFECT	CODE
1,000 Credits (one time only)	■,■,■,▲,■
2,000 Credits (one time only)	■,■,■,▲,▲
5,000 Credits (one time only)	■,■,■,▲,■,▲
10,000 Credits (one time only)	■,▲,▲,▲,■,■,▲
Adds 2 Power Nodes (one time only)	▲,■,■,■,▲
Adds 5 Power Nodes (one time only)	▲,■,▲,■,■,▲,■,■,▲,■,■,▲
Refill Your Oxygen	■,■,▲,▲,▲
Refill Your Stasis and Kinesis Energy	▲,■,▲,▲,■,▲

DEATH JR. II: ROOT OF EVIL (PSP)

Enter these codes while the game is paused.

UNLOCKABLE	CODE
All Weapon Upgrades	Hold L2 and press ↑, ↑, ↓, ↓, ←, →, ←, →, X, ●
Invincibility	Hold L2 and press ↑, ↑, ↓, ↓, ←, →, ←, →, ■, ▲
Refill Ammunition	Hold L2 and press ▲, ▲, X, X, ■, ●, ■, ●, ↓, ↑
Unlimited Ammunition	Hold L2 and press ▲, ▲, X, X, ■, ●, ■, ●, ↑, ↓

DESPICABLE ME (PSP)

CODES

Input the codes in the Bonus menu while in Gru's Lab.

EFFECT	CODE
Unlocks the Minionettes Costume Set	●,●,■,▲,X
Unlocks the Taffy Web Gun	←,→,X,●,■,X,▲
Unlocks the Village Folk Costume Set	▲,X,X,●,X

DESPICABLE ME: MINION MAYHEM (DS)

CODES

At the Mode Select screen, press Select to bring up the code entry window and enter the following:

EFFECT	CODE
Unlock Despicable Gru Level	B, A, Down, Down, Y
Unlock Minion Mania	L, A, B, B, Y, Up
Unlock Minion Mania EX	L, A, B, B, Y, Down
Unlock the Girls' Room level	B, L, A, B, B, Y
World Level Unlock	B, Up, Down, Down, Y

DEUS EX: HUMAN REVOLUTION (XBOX 360)

ACHIEVEMENT

UNLOCKABLE	HOW TO UNLOCK
Acquaintances Forgotten (10)	Follow Pritchard's lead to uncover the truth.
Balls (5)	Seems you like playing with balls, eh?
Bar Tab (10)	Help the Hive Bartender settle a tab.

Cloak & Daggers (10)	Deal with the man in the shadows.
Consciousness is Over-rated (15)	Knock out 100 enemies in a single playthrough.
Corporate Warfare (10)	Protect a client's interests by performing a less-than-hostile takeover.
Darker Shades (15)	You convinced a fast-talking bartender to let you see Tong Si Hung.
Deus Ex Machina (50)	Experience all the different endings that Deus Ex: Human Revolution has to offer.
Doctorate (50)	Read all 29 unique XP books within a single playthrough.
First Hack (5)	Perform your first Hack successfully.
First Takedown (5)	Perform your first Takedown. Civilians don't count, so be nice.
Foxiest of the Hounds (100)	Complete Deus Ex: Human Revolution without setting off any alarms.
Ghost (15)	You made it through an entire hostile area without so much as a squeak.
Good Soul (15)	Against all odds, you saved Faridah Malik's life.
Guardian Angel (10)	You paid poor Jaya's debt in full. How very... humane... of you.
Gun Nut (20)	Fully upgrade one of your weapons.
Hangar 18 (10)	You found and read the secret message. Now you know too much...
Hax0r1! (15)	Successfully hack 50 devices within the same playthrough.
Kevorkian Complex (10)	You granted a dying man his final request.
Ladies Man (10)	You convinced Mengyao to spill the beans on the mysterious Hyron Project.
Legend (100)	Complete Deus Ex: Human Revolution at its hardest setting without ever changing the difficulty.
Lesser Evil (10)	Deal with Mr. Carella's indiscretion.
Lucky Guess (10)	Next time, Jacob better use a more complex code to arm his bombs.
Motherly Ties (10)	Put a grieving mother's doubts to rest.
Old School Gamer (10)	You found all the hidden story items in Megan's office. Point and Click much?
Opportunist (15)	Perform 50 takedowns within the same playthrough. (Civilians don't count.)
Pacifist (100)	Complete Deus Ex: Human Revolution without anyone dying by your hand. (Boss fights don't count.)
Rotten Business (10)	Help a lady in the oldest of professions clean house.
Sentimental Value (10)	You kept Megan's bracelet for yourself. Apparently, letting go really is the hardest part.
Shanghai Justice (10)	It may take some sleuthing, but justice must be served.
Smash the State (10)	Help Officer Nicholas take out the trash.
Super Sleuth (10)	You really nailed your case against Lee Hong.
Talion A.D. (10)	Descend into the bowels of an urban jungle and confront a warrior-priest.
The Bull (25)	You defeated Lawrence Barrett, elite member of a secret mercenary hit squad.

The D Project (15)	You watched the entire credit list and saw the surprise at the end.
The Desk Job (15)	You convinced Wayne Haas to let you into the morgue.
The End (25)	You defeated Zhao Yun Ru and destroyed the Hyron Project.
The Fall (10)	You sent Diamond Chan on the trip of a lifetime.
The Final Countdown (15)	You showed millionaire Hugh Darrow that his logic was flawed.
The Last Straw (15)	You talked Doctor Isaias Sandoval out of suicide.
The Mantis (25)	You defeated Yelena Fedorova, elite member of a secret mercenary hit squad.
The Snake (25)	You defeated Jaron Namir, Leader of Belltower's Elite Special Operations Unit.
The Take (10)	Greedy bastard. You accepted O'Malley's blood money and let him go.
The Throwdown (15)	You convinced the smooth-talking politician Bill Taggart to tell the truth in public.
Transhumanist (5)	Fully upgrade your first augmentation of choice.
Trooper (50)	Complete Deus Ex: Human Revolution.
Unforeseen Consequence (15)	You convinced Zeke Sanders to let his hostage go.
Up the Ante! (15)	Upgrade your first weapon of choice.
Yes Boss (15)	You had an argument with your boss, David Sarif, and won.

DEVIL MAY CRY 4   (XBOX 360)

UNLOCKABLES

UNLOCKABLE	HOW TO UNLOCK
Bloody Palace Survival Mode	Complete the game on Devil Hunter difficulty or Human difficulty.
Bonus Art and Character Art	Complete the game on Devil Hunter difficulty or Human difficulty.
Gallery	Complete the game on Devil Hunter difficulty or Human difficulty.
History of Devil May Cry	Complete the game on Devil Hunter difficulty or Human difficulty.
Son of Sparda Difficulty	Complete the game on Devil Hunter difficulty.

DEVIL'S CRUSH   (WII)

UNLOCKABLE

UNLOCKABLE	HOW TO UNLOCK
Sound Mode	Press ✛, ✛, ✛ after pausing
Sound Test	Press RUN, SELECT during gameplay to display the High Score screen, then press ✛, ✛, ✛, ✛, ①

PASSWORDS

PASSWORD	EFFECT
EFGHIJKLMB	924,000,000 points and 73 balls
AAAAAAAAAAAAAAAAB	A 2-player game with unlimited balls
THECRUSHEL	Beat the game—launch the ball and once you hit something, the game ends
DAVIDWHITE	Beat the game—launch the ball and once you hit something, the game ends
FFFFFFFEEE	Beat the game—launch the ball and once you hit something, the game ends

NAXATSOFTI	Infinite balls, 206,633,300 points
AAAAAAHAAA	Infinite balls, 734,003,200 points
DEVILSATAN	Infinite balls, 955,719,100 points
THEDEVILSI	Over 145,000,000 points and 70 balls
ONECRUSHME	Over 594,000,000 points and 27 balls
AAAAAAAAAAAAAAABCE	2-player mode—gives player 1 unlimited balls and player 2 32 balls
PPPPPPPPPA	Unlimited balls
CKDEIPDBFM	25 balls and a score of 300,138,400
OJFJGDEJPD	34 balls and a score of 404,330,300
PNBIJOKJNF	38 balls and a score of 533,501,000
CGIAGPECGK	42 balls and a score of 610,523,600
OEHALCBGPF	45 balls and a score of 710,529,000
OLGGGEAPOF	52 balls and a score of 804,379,700
CBEOBLJGHA	62 balls and a score of 900,057,102
PFFMGHGOLK	65 balls and a score of 999,927,400
NLJBCFHGPO	65 balls and a score of 999,999,000
KGCMMCMLBN	65 balls and a score of 999,999,600
OMGANLOIJA	67 balls and a score of 976,769,800

DIRT 3 (XBOX 360, PLAYSTATION 3)

ACHIEVEMENT

UNLOCKABLE	HOW TO UNLOCK
Air Miles (15)	You have won a race in every location
Assistance is Futile (20)	You won a race without the use of any Driver Assists
Battered Battersea (50)	You completed 100% of the Battersea Compound Missions
Burnt Rubber (30)	You completed 75% of the Battersea Compound Missions
California Dreams (20)	You earned yourself a podium finish at the X Games Tournament
Call me Ace! (15)	You have completed a sensational performance in a Gymkhana Championship event
Can't Touch This! (10)	You have survived a round of Outbreak without being infected (Pro Tour & Jam Session)
Cheeze It! (10)	You evaded the cats, won the game and earned the fans
Cool Running (10)	You have beaten the bobsleigh in the DC Bobsleigh Challenge
Crash Proof (10)	You used a flashback to take you to victory after facing defeat.
DC Challenger (30)	You have completed all of the DC Challenges
DC Gold (10)	You earned all gold medals in the DC Challenges
DC Silver (10)	You earned all silver medals in the DC Challenges
Donut Addict (20)	You completed 50% of the Battersea Compound Missions
Driven (20)	You have won DiRT Tour races using vehicles from every discipline
Driving School (10)	You completed all of the Gymkhana tutorials
Eat my DiRT! (50)	You have unlocked Driver Rep level 30
Flag Stealer (10)	You stole the flag from the opposing team 5 times in a game of Transporter (Pro Tour)
From DiRT to Glory (50)	You have achieved first place finishes in all DiRT Tour Events
Gym-Carnage (20)	You scored 500,000 points in a Gymkhana Event

A
B
C
D
E
F
G
H
I
J
K
L
M
N
O
P
Q
R
S
T
U
V
W
X
Y
Z

Gymkhana Aficionado (30)	You completed all Gymkhana Championships in the DiRT Tour
Honorable Driver (10)	You competed via Xbox LIVE and earned a 'Cautious' rating
Hooning Around (10)	You completed 25% of the Battersea Compound Missions
Into the DiRT (10)	You have completed your first DiRT Tour race
Join the Party (20)	You won a game in every party mode
Kick Off the Training Wheels! (20)	You have achieved a podium finish in the Gymkhana Academy
King of the Road (10)	You have won an Xbox LIVE race in hardcore mode
No-bot Wars (20)	You smashed every robot in a Smash Attack DC Challenge
Pace Setter (15)	You have completed time trials using cars from each class of Rally
Perfect Sprint (20)	You gave a flawless performance in a Gymkhana Sprint DC Challenge
Platinum Performance (20) Challenges	You earned all platinum medals in the DC
Rally Evolution (10)	You have experienced key vehicles from Rally history and triumphed
Reputation Boost (10)	You have completed 5 bonus Race Objectives
Rising Talent (10)	You have unlocked Driver Rep level 10
Road Trip (10)	You shared the experience of the Battersea Compound with your friends
Self Preservation Society (10)	You won a race using the Mini Cooper without receiving any damage
Shake and Bake (30)	You have unlocked Driver Rep level 20
Showcase Drifter (20)	You have drifted past 25,000 points in a Drift Showcase DC Challenge
Steer Hunter (10)	You have completed a game of Invasion without any negative points (Pro Tour)
Sub Zero Hero (20)	You earned yourself a podium finish Winter X Games Tournament
Super Star (30)	You earned yourself enough fans to be considered a 'Superstar'
SuperSeries Champion (100)	You won the DC SuperSeries Championship
Taking the Trophy (20)	You have won 10 Xbox LIVE games
Teacher's Pet (20)	You earned a platinum medal in each one of the Gymkhana tutorials
The Extra Mile (20)	You have completed 25 bonus Race Objectives
The Professional (10)	You completed your first Xbox LIVE Pro Tour Race
The Real Thing (10)	You have experienced the thrill of Rally first hand and beat your competitors
The Road Ahead (15)	You have completed 25 Xbox LIVE games
Today's Forecast is... Victory! (20)	You have earned victories in all weather conditions
World Renowned (20)	You have achieved first place finishes and passed the DC Challenge in a World Tour event

UNLOCKABLE

UNLOCKABLE	HOW TO UNLOCK
Racing Gloves	Reach Fan Level 24
Racing Shoes	Reach Fan Level 12
Racing Suit	Complete Season 1
Rally Helmet	Complete Season 2

DISGAEA 3: ABSENCE OF DETENTION (PLAYSTATION VITA)

TROPHY

UNLOCKABLE	HOW TO UNLOCK
10 Piece Combo Meal (Bronze)	Destroy your enemies with evil teamwork!
A Single Step (Bronze)	Welcome to Disgaea 3: Absence of Detention! We welcome new and returning players alike! Enjoy!
All-Pro Receiver (Bronze)	Let's cross this continent!
Arcarnageologist (Gold)	Reaching the 100th floor...in Carnage!
As the World Turns (Bronze)	If it spins, it's only natural to want to spin it.
BGM Lover (Bronze)	How 'bout buying some music for a change?
Call Me Nacho Cinco! (Bronze)	We're going to outer space, baby!
Ch.1 Netherworld Honor Student Complete (Bronze)	I am indeed the No.1 Honor Student!
Ch.2 Mao's Heart Complete (Bronze)	I was supposed to pour salt and pepper on it, instead of hot sauce!
Ch.3 The Freshmen Leader! Complete (Bronze)	Boss! Boss! Boss!
Ch.4 Almaz the Hero Complete (Bronze)	Babuu.
Ch.5 Grand War Complete (Bronze)	Hot Hot Sensitive Tongue Slash! Kiiiiiaaaaahhhhh!
Ch.6 The Reckoning Complete (Bronze)	Hmhmhm.
Ch.7 An Eye for an Eye Complete (Bronze)	Gimme an autograph later!
Combo No. 255 (Bronze)	I won't stop hitting until you stop getting up.
Commando King (Bronze)	Now you're the Class World King!
Cross Fists as Friends (Bronze)	It's a story about a friendship born through fisticuffs.
Demon King: Have It Your Way (Bronze)	Force your will on them, like the demon your are!
Eryngi Baal Slayer (Bronze)	I'm not going to get my "a" back?
Finale Complete (Bronze)	I will...become the Overlord!
Finger Flicking Good (Bronze)	Mooove! My fingers are on fire!!!
First Setback (Bronze)	That was just a warm. Now I'm ready to go!
Giga Damage! (Bronze)	More training! You can do more!
Gotcha! (Bronze)	Yay! You got a new ally!
Hardcore Gamer! (Bronze)	Thanks for playing! But we suggest you take a break.
Hop, Step, Jump (Bronze)	Isn't jumping sooo much fun?
I Got Gummed... (Bronze)	Why me...?
I Had an Axeldent! (Bronze)	Axel never stops working! Even in the Item World!
It's Da Bomb! (Bronze)	Playing with bombs in Homeroom? You're quite an honor student.
Item Spelunker (Bronze)	Congratulations on reaching the 100th floor! You're on the right track to become a hardcore player!
IWCA Flyweight Champion (Bronze)	You are the Item World Champ!
Kneel Before Cat God! (Bronze)	*blush* Oh, you can stand, meow.
Magichangician (Bronze)	Transform! Yeah!

Majin Academy Complete (Bronze)	I shall take over this Academy!
Master of the Chain (Bronze)	Do massive chains! Use your brain to the max!
Mega Damage! (Bronze)	You gotta train! For starters, a million damage!
Omni Bonus! (Bronze)	It's only natural for a demon to take everything.
PE Teacher Destroyer (Silver)	It's always been a dream to defeat a PE teacher...
Platinum Trophy (Platinum)	Congratulations on getting all the trophies!
Playing Favorites (Bronze)	Aren't you happy to be surrounded by your favorite characters?
Puzzle Master (Bronze)	Erase everything! Train that brain!
Raspberyl Version Complete (Bronze)	You all graduate, today!
Reverse Pirates! Everything is Mine! (Gold)	Reverse Pirates, yeah! Nothing is left in our wake...
Reverse Pirates! I Shall Take Your Innocents! (Silver)	Reverse Pirates, yeah! We're taking all the Innocents with us!
Reverse Pirates! Your Treasure is Mine! (Bronze)	Reverse Pirates, yeah! All that treasure's just for me!
Shopping Spree (Bronze)	As a proud demon, I'll buy everything at the store!
Shut Up Already! (Bronze)	I'll never stop talking!
Super Honor Student (Bronze)	The HQ at this school is truly amazing.
Survival Class: Passed (Bronze)	You truly are the Survival Master!
Tera Damage! (Silver)	Even more training! Good job!
The Shamshank Redemon (Bronze)	I'm just testing your loyalty.
The Towertastic Ten (Bronze)	This is the epitome of a tower!
Treasure Hunter (Bronze)	Don't your legs feel stronger from all that jumping?
Trophy Shopper (Bronze)	I've been waiting for you in this Mystery Room!
Almaz's Ending	Win stage 8-4 with Almaz alone and the battle after
Death Institute, Majin Academy Ending	Clear Death Institute, Majin Academy Side Story
Human World Ending	Kill more then 99 allies and clear two alt. stages by stage 7-6
Laharl's Ending	Go to homeroom and propose "Watch a New Ending" and clear the stage
Mao's Ambition Ending	Clear stage 1-9 on 2nd or higher cycle before stage 4-4
Normal Ending	Don't meet any other ending's requirement
Raspberyl Version Ending	Clear Raspberyl Version Side Story
Raspberyl's Ending 1	Lose against Raspberyl on stage 1-5
Raspberyl's Ending 2	Lose against Raspberyl on stage 2-1
Super Hero Ending	Use Mao at Lv 500 or higher to defeat final boss
Aramis	Clear Class World Command Attack with less than 145 commands
Asagi	Beat extra map 4
Axel	Beat extra map 6

Laharl, Etna, and Flonne	Beat extra map 7
Marona	Beat extra map 5
Master Big Star	Beat extra map 1
Pleinair	In Survival, get 7 Level Spheres and wish for the Mascot Character
Prism Red	Beat extra map 3
Salvatore	Beat extra map 2
Super hero Aurum	Finish 3rd Period of 'Raspberyl version'

NEW!

UNLOCKABLE

UNLOCKABLE	HOW TO UNLOCK
Archer	Have a level 15 Valkyrie and Cleric
Armored Knight	Have a level 15 Warrior and Martial Artist
Beast Master	Have a level 15 Valkyrie and Fight Mistress
Berserker	Have a level 40 Armored Knight and Beast Master
Celestial Host	Beat the Item World Command Attack on any difficulty in under 145 commands
Cheerleader	Have a level 25 Wiseman and Cleric
Dragon	Defeat a Dragon in Item World or Class World
Factory Desco	Unlock Desco, pass the, "Create a Final Boss?" bill as Mao
Felynn	Defeat a Felynn in Item World or Class World
Female Samurai	Have a level 35 Valkyrie and Archer
Gunner	Have a level 15 Magician and Thief
Gunslinger	Have a level 15 Witch and Thief
Kunoichi	Have a level 30 Fight Mistress and Witch
Magic Knight	Have a level 25 Warrior/Valkyrie and Magician/Witch
Majin	Get the Normal or Good ending
Masked Hero	Have a level 45 Thief and Gunner/Gunslinger
Ninja	Have a level 30 Martial Artist and Magician
Ranger	Have a level 15 Warrior and Clergy
Samurai	Have a level 35 Warrior and Ranger
Shaman	Have a level 25 Wiseman and Magician/Witch
Wiseman	Having a level 20 Martial Artist/Fight Mistress and Male/Female Cleric

DISGAEA 3: ABSENCE OF JUSTICE (PLAYSTATION 3)

UNLOCKABLE CLASSES

UNLOCKABLE	HOW TO UNLOCK
Archer (Female)	Level 15 Female Fighter and Level 15 Female Healer
Archer (Male)	Level 15 Male Fighter and Level 15 Male Healer
Berserker	Heavy Knight and Monster Tamer Level 40
Cheerleader (Idol)	Geo Master and Healer Level 25
Geo Master	Fist Fighter and Healer Level 20
Gunner Female	Female Thief and Mage Level 15
Gunner Male	Thief and Male Mage Level 15
Heavy Knight	Male Fighter and Fist Fighter Level 15
Magic Knight	Fighter and Mage Level 25
Majin	Clear second play through tutorial
Masked Hero	Thief and Gunner Level 45
Monster Tamer	Female Fighter and Fist Fighter Level 15
Ninja (Female)	Level 30 Female Monk and Level 30 Female Magician

A
B
C
D
E
F
G
H
I
J
K
L
M
N
O
P
Q
R
S
T
U
V
W
X
Y
Z

Ninja (Male)	Level 30 Male Monk and Level 30 Male Magician
Samurai (Female)	Level 35 Female Fighter and Level 35 Female Archer
Samurai (Male)	Level 35 Male Fighter and Level 35 Male Archer
Shaman	Geo Master and Mage Level 25

UNLOCKABLE CAMEO CHARACTERS

UNLOCKABLE	HOW TO UNLOCK
Asagi	Beat extra map 4
Axel	Beat extra map 6
Laharl, Etna, and Flonne	Beat extra map 7
Marona	Beat extra map 5
Master Big Star	Beat extra map 1
Prism Red	Beat extra map 3
Salvatore	Beat extra map 2

UNLOCKABLE ENDINGS

UNLOCKABLE	HOW TO UNLOCK
Almaz's Ending	Win stage 8-4 with Almaz alone and the battle after
Human World Ending	Kill more then 99 allies and clear two alt. stages by stage 7-6
Laharl's Ending	Go to homeroom and propose "Watch a New Ending" and clear the stage
Mao's Ambition Ending	Clear stage 1-9 on 2nd or higher cycle before stage 4-4
Normal Ending	Don't meet any other ending's requirement
Raspberyl's Ending 1	Lose against Raspberyl on stage 1-5
Raspberyl's Ending 2	Lose against Raspberyl on stage 2-1
Super Hero Ending	Use Mao at Level 500 or higher to defeat final boss

UNLOCKABLE DIFFICULTIES

UNLOCKABLE	HOW TO UNLOCK
Samurai Mode	Complete the game at least once.
Tourny Mode	Complete the game on Samurai Difficulty.

DISGAEA: AFTERNOON OF DARKNESS (PSP)

ETNA MODE

Disgaea contains a hidden mode called Etna mode. Normally you have to get this mode by going through the game and reading Etna's diary every chapter, but you can unlock it instantly by entering the following code during the title screen, with the pointer on "New Game." If you're successful, you'll hear Etna's voice.

EFFECT	CODE
Unlock Etna Mode (US)	▲, ■, ●, ▲, ■, ●, ✕

EXTRA CLASSES

UNLOCKABLE	HOW TO UNLOCK
Angel	Female Cleric, Knight, and Archer all at level 100 or higher.
Archer	Level 3 or higher in Bow Weapon Mastery.
EDF Soldier	Level 30 or higher Gun Weapon Mastery.
Galaxy Mage	Level a Prism Mage to Level 50.
Galaxy Skull	Level a Prism Skull to Level 50.
Knight	Female Warrior and Female Mage each at level 10 or higher.
Majin	Male Warrior, Brawler, Ninja, Rogue, and Scout all at level 200 or higher.
Ninja	Male Fighter and Male Warrior with a total level of 10 or higher.
Prism Mage	Level a Star Mage to Level 35.
Prism Skull	Level a Star Skull to Level 35.

Rogue	Both Fighter and Warrior, Males or Females, each at level 5 or higher.
Ronin	Female Warrior and Female Fighter with a total level of 10 or higher.
Scout	Two Fighters/Warriors, Males or Females, each at level 5 or higher.
Star Mage	Get one Fire, Ice, and Wind Mage and level all three of them to level 5.
Star Skull	Get one Fire, Ice, and Wind Skull and level all three of them to level 5.

DISNEY'S CHICKEN LITTLE: ACE IN ACTION (WII)

Input the codes under Cheat option.

UNLOCKABLE	CODE
All Levels Available	⬆, ⬇, ⬆, ⬇, ⬆
All Weapons Available	⬆, ⬇, ⬆, ⬇
Unlimited Shield Available	⬆, ⬇, ⬆, ⬇, ⬆

DISNEY'S KIM POSSIBLE KIMMUNICATOR (DS)

Enter these codes while playing—do not pause. You must hold down
Ⓛ+Ⓡ to enter these codes.

UNLOCKABLE	CODE
9,999 parts	Ⓨ, Ⓨ, Ⓧ, Ⓑ, Ⓐ, Ⓨ
99 lives	Ⓐ, Ⓐ, Ⓐ, Ⓨ, Ⓧ, Ⓨ, Ⓑ, Ⓐ
Don't lose lives	Ⓨ, Ⓨ, Ⓨ, Ⓧ
Extra Life	Ⓐ, Ⓐ, Ⓐ, Ⓨ, Ⓧ, Ⓨ
Full Health	Ⓐ, Ⓐ, Ⓐ, Ⓨ
Invincibility	Ⓨ, Ⓨ, Ⓨ, Ⓧ, Ⓐ, Ⓑ
Unlock all gadgets	Ⓨ, Ⓨ, Ⓧ, Ⓑ, Ⓐ, Ⓨ, Ⓐ
Unlock all missions	Ⓧ, Ⓨ, Ⓧ, Ⓐ, Ⓧ, Ⓑ
Unlock all outfits	Ⓑ, Ⓐ, Ⓧ, Ⓨ, Ⓐ, Ⓑ

DISSIDIA 012: DUODECIM FINAL FANTASY (PSP)

UNLOCKABLE

Complete the following conditions and then purchase them from the
PP Catalog.

UNLOCKABLE	HOW TO UNLOCK
Play as Desperado Chaos	Complete Main Scenario 000.
Play as Gilgamesh	Complete Report 08 (6) with Bartz.
Play as Prishe	Complete Report 08 (2) with Shantotto.

DOUBLE DUNGEONS (WII)

PASSWORDS

At the Password screen, carefully enter the following passwords.

PASSWORD	EFFECT
cHR0EScxgoAq or iky7ihOfeBGe	In front of the last boss door
2R3KD4RG0J9D3YT0664LJ	Beginning of Level 22
YNzYSMChriGlgLV-ih0dfCGe	End of Level 22
Enter either Player01 or Player 02 as a password, with the remaining spaces filled inwith either +'s or -'s	Get 65,535 HP
Enter any working password for player 1, then enter KKKKKKKKKKKKKKKKKKKKKKKKKK as a password for player 2	Player 2 invincibility

DRAGON AGE: ORIGINS (XBOX 360)

EARLY LEVELING EXPLOIT

In Ostargar, there is a mission called Tainted Blood. Collect the three Vials of Darkspawn Blood but do not collect the Grey Warden Treaties. Return to camp, talk to Duncan, and select the option, "We have the blood, but not the scrolls." You will get the experience for the mission. Then go back and repeat this process until you are the level you want, or have reached the Level 25 max.

DRAGON AGE II (PLAYSTATION 3)

UNLOCKABLES

If you have a save of Dragon Age Origins on your hard drive with the Blood Dragon Armor unlocked, it automatically transfers to Dragon Age 2 as well.

UNLOCKABLES

To unlock the armor set, you have to create an EA account first and then link it with your PSN ID. Play Dead Space 2, go the main menu and log into your account. Once you have done that, Dragon Age 2. You can find the set in your special delivery chest at your house.

DRAGON QUEST IX: SENTINELS OF THE STARRY SKIES (PLAYSTATION 3)

ITEM DUPLICATION THROUGH AD-HOC

First, connect your DQIX to someone else. Give them any items you can, then shut your game off WITHOUT leaving their world. Since you never saved after leaving their world, you'll still have the items you traded, and so will they!

MINI MEDAL REWARDS

While playing the game, you will find numerous items called Mini Medals. In the town of Dourbridge, you can give these to a pirate king who lives there, and he will give you rare items in exchange. After you've given him 80 Mini Medals, he will sell you rare items. But you must use Mini Medals to buy them instead of Gold. Three Medals: Prayer Ring; 5 Medals: Elfin Elixir; 8 Medals: Saint's Ashes; 10 Medals: Reset Stone; 15 Medals: Orihalcum; 20 Medals: Pixie Boots.

UNLOCKABLE	HOW TO UNLOCK
Bunny Suit	Reward for giving 13 Mini Medals to Cap'n Max Meddlin
Dragon Robe	Reward for giving 80 Mini Medals to Cap'n Max Meddlin
Jolly Roger Jumper	Reward for giving 18 Mini Medals to Cap'n Max Meddlin
Mercury Bandanna	Reward for giving 8 Mini Medals to Cap'n Max Meddlin
Meteorite Bracer	Reward for giving 50 Mini Medals to Cap'n Max Meddlin
Miracle Sword	Reward for giving 32 Mini Medals to Cap'n Max Meddlin
Rusty Helmet	Reward for giving 62 Mini Medals to Cap'n Max Meddlin
Sacred Armor	Reward for giving 40 Mini Medals to Cap'n Max Meddlin
Thief's Key	Reward for giving 4 Mini Medals to Cap'n Max Meddlin
Transparent Tights	Reward for giving 25 Mini Medals to Cap'n Max Meddlin

SECRET SHOP IN DOURBRIDGE

If you go around to the back of the village shop in Dourbridge, there is a hidden door. Enter it (requires the Ultimate Key), and then you see a flight of stairs. Go down the stairs, and you can get into a secret shop with rare items.

DRAGON QUEST MONSTERS: JOKER 2 (DS)

UNLOCKABLE

UNLOCKABLE	HOW TO UNLOCK
Drakularge	have owned 100 different monsters
Grandpa Slime	have owned 200 different monsters
Great Argon Lizard	have owned 50 different monsters
Metal King Slime	have owned 150 different monsters

| Free Argogreat | Get 50 different owned monsters in the monster library |

UNLOCKABLE

In Dragon Quest VI you must activate Dreamsharing. In Dragon Quest IX you must activate Tag Mode.

UNLOCKABLE	HOW TO UNLOCK
Malevolamp	Tag Dragon Quest VI
Mottle Slime	Tag Dragon Quest VI
Noble Gasbagon	Tag Dragon Quest VI
Overkilling Machine	Tag Dragon Quest VI
Shogum	Tag Dragon Quest IX
Slime Stack	Tag Dragon Quest IX
Teeny Sanguini	Tag Dragon Quest IX

DRAGON SPIRIT (WII)

CODES

UNLOCKABLE	HOW TO UNLOCK
100 Continues	Press ⬇, ⬅, SELECT, ⬇, ②, ⬇, ①, ⬅, SELECT, ⬅, ①, ②, ① at the title screen
Arcade Mode Screen	Hold Select and press RUN 57 times to reset the game for a narrow screen
Sound Test	⬅, ⬅, ⬇, ⬅, SELECT, ⬅ at the title screen
Two Continues	Hold ① and press ② at the title screen

DRAGON'S CURSE (WII)

UNLOCKABLE

UNLOCKABLE	HOW TO UNLOCK
Full Life	After dying, use a potion while holding ②

PASSWORDS

PASSWORD	EFFECT
3YHURYW7Y7LL8C	Start game at beginning with Max. Gold (983,040)/All Equipment/Full Health (8 Hearts)/Max. Stones (99)/All Items/Hawk-Man Status
3YHURYW7Y7LPBS	Start game at beginning with Max. Gold (983,040)/All Equipment/Full Health (8 Hearts)/Max. Stones (99)/All Items/Hu-Man Status
3YHURYW7Y7LRBW	Start game at beginning with Max. Gold (983,040)/All Equipment/Full Health (8 Hearts)/Max. Stones (99)/All Items/Lizard-Man Status
3YHURYW7Y7LM80	Start game at beginning with Max. Gold (983,040)/All Equipment/Full Health (8 Hearts)/Max. Stones (99)/All Items/Mouse-Man Status
3YHURYW7Y7LN84	Start game at beginning with Max. Gold (983,040)/All Equipment/Full Health (8 Hearts)/Max. Stones (99)/All Items/Piranha-Man Status
3YHURYW7Y7LK88	Start game at beginning with Max. Gold (983,040)/All Equipment/Full Health (8 Hearts)/Max. Stones (99)/All Items/Tiger-Man Status
W0CV5ATVKYR1SV	Start with all the necessary transformations and items to enter the final dungeon
MODE FOR 0000 000	Be Hu Man at Start (JP ONLY)
PLAY THE ONGA KUN	Disable door noise (JP ONLY)
NODEGOS0000000	Start as Be Hu Man
3WSURYXZY763TE	Start with advanced abilities and items
RMAYTJEOPHALUP	Take away the noises from doors

CODES & CHEATS

3ZHURYNZY726VH	Start as Hu-Man with 8 hearts, all equipment, all transformations unlocked, and only the final dungeon to beat

DRAGON'S DOGMA (PLAYSTATION 3)

TROPHY

UNLOCKABLE	HOW TO UNLOCK
A New Ally (Bronze)	Summoned your own pawn.
A Queen's Regalia (Bronze)	Dressed a male party member in women's clothing.
Affinity and Beyond (Bronze)	Raised a person's affinity to the maximum.
Closure (Gold)	Put an end to all things.
Come Courting (Bronze)	Attended an audience with the duke.
Destiny (Bronze)	Accepted the Godsbane blade.
Dragon Forged (Silver)	Strengthened equipment in wyrmfire.
Eye Contact (Bronze)	Defeated an evil eye.
Foreign Recruit (Bronze)	Enlisted a pawn to your party from beyond the rift.
Freedom (Bronze)	Escaped the yoke of eternity.
Getting a Head (Bronze)	Earned the approval of the Enlistment Corps.
Headshunter (Bronze)	Defeated a hydra or archydra.
Human Resources (Bronze)	Changed your vocation.
Inhuman Resources (Bronze)	Changed your main pawn's vocation.
Into Dripstone Cave (Bronze)	Entered the azure caverns.
Into Soulflayer Canyon (Bronze)	Entered the Soulflayer Canyon.
Into the Ancient Quarry (Bronze)	Entered the ancient quarry.
Into the Frontier Caverns (Bronze)	Entered the southwestern caves.
Into the Manse (Bronze)	Entered the duke's manse.
It Begins (Bronze)	Completed the prologue.
Local Recruit (Bronze)	Directly enlisted a pawn to your party.
Mercy (Bronze)	Dealt the blow of deliverance.
Onward (Bronze)	Departed from Cassardis.
Peace (Bronze)	Took refuge in an illusion.
Rough Landing (Bronze)	Completed the urgent mission.
Serpents' Bane (Bronze)	Defeated a drake, wyrm, and wyvern.
Servitude (Bronze)	Soar unto a new world.
Solitude (Bronze)	Obtained the almighty power of sovereignty.
The Captain (Bronze)	Enlisted a large number of pawns.
The Coin Collector (Silver)	Earned a total of 10,000,000G.
The Courier (Bronze)	Entered Gran Soren.
The Craftsman (Bronze)	Combined two materials to make an item.
The Escort (Bronze)	Acted as a reliable travel companion.
The Ever-Turning Wheel (Gold)	Completed the adventure a second time.
The Explorer (Silver)	Visited 150 locations.
The Hero (Silver)	Completed all pre-planned, non-notice board quests.
The Knave (Bronze)	Obtained a forgery.
The Laborer (Bronze)	Completed 50 notice board quests.
The Message (Bronze)	Received the duke's commendation.
The Messiah (Gold)	Defeated the Ur-Dragon.
The Patron (Bronze)	Helped Madeleine open her shop.

The Philanthropist (Bronze)	Gave 50 presents.
The Savior (Bronze)	Used a Wakestone to restore the dead to life.
The Specialist (Silver)	Learned all the skills of a single vocation.
The Tourist (Bronze)	Visited 50 locations.
The True Arisen (Platinum)	Collected all other Dragon's Dogma trophies.
The Vagabond (Bronze)	Visited 100 locations.
The Veteran (Bronze)	Defeated 3,000 enemies.
Treacherous (Bronze)	Peered into the very depths of the world.
Well Equipped (Bronze)	Obtained 350 pieces total of weapons and armor.
Writ Large (Bronze)	Received a writ from the castle.

DRAGON'S DOGMA (XBOX 360)

ACHIEVEMENT

UNLOCKABLE	HOW TO UNLOCK
A New Ally (10)	Summoned your own pawn.
A Queen's Regalia (20)	Dressed a male party member in women's clothing.
Affinity and Beyond (10)	Raised a person's affinity to the maximum.
Closure (40)	Put an end to all things.
Come Courting (15)	Attended an audience with the duke.
Destiny (25)	Accepted the Godsbane blade.
Dragon Forged (30)	Strengthened equipment in wyrmfire.
Eye Contact (30)	Defeated an evil eye.
Foreign Recruit (5)	Enlisted a pawn to your party from beyond the rift.
Freedom (10)	Escaped the yoke of eternity.
Getting a Head (15)	Earned the approval of the Enlistment Corps.
Headshunter (30)	Defeated a hydra or archydra.
Human Resources (20)	Changed your vocation.
Inhuman Resources (20)	Changed your main pawn's vocation.
Into Dripstone Cave (10)	Entered the azure caverns.
Into Soulflayer Canyon (15)	Entered the Soulflayer Canyon.
Into the Ancient Quarry (10)	Entered the ancient quarry.
Into the Frontier Caverns (15)	Entered the southwestern caves.
Into the Manse (20)	Entered the duke's manse.
It Begins (5)	Completed the prologue.
Local Recruit (5)	Directly enlisted a pawn to your party.
Mercy (30)	Dealt the blow of deliverance.
Onward (5)	Departed from Cassardis.
Peace (20)	Took refuge in an illusion.
Rough Landing (10)	Completed the urgent mission.
Serpents' Bane (40)	Defeated a drake, wyrm, and wyvern.
Servitude (20)	Soar unto a new world.
Solitude (20)	Obtained the almighty power of sovereignty.
The Artisan (10)	Combined two materials to make an item.
The Captain (15)	Enlisted a large number of pawns.
The Coin Collector (30)	Earned a total of 10,000,000G.
The Courier (10)	Entered Gran Soren.
The Escort (10)	Acted as a reliable travel companion.
The Ever-Turning Wheel (50)	Completed the adventure a second time.

The Explorer (35)	Visited 150 locations.
The Hero (40)	Completed all pre-planned, non-notice board quests.
The Knave (15)	Obtained a forgery.
The Laborer (20)	Completed 50 notice board quests.
The Message (15)	Received the duke's commendation.
The Messiah (50)	Defeated the Ur-Dragon.
The Patron (15)	Helped Madeleine open her shop.
The Philanthropist (15)	Gave 50 presents.
The Savior (10)	Used a Wakestone to restore the dead to life.
The Specialist (40)	Learned all the skills of a single vocation.
The Tourist (10)	Visited 50 locations.
The Vagabond (20)	Visited 100 locations.
The Veteran (35)	Defeated 3,000 enemies.
Treacherous (10)	Peered into the very depths of the world.
Well Equipped (30)	Obtained 350 pieces total of weapons and armor.
Writ Large (10)	Received a writ from the castle.

DREAMCAST COLLECTION (XBOX 360)

CODE

Enter during cutscenes or during non-gameplay segments. This disables all achievements, avatar awards and leaderboards

EFFECT	CODE
All of Ulala's commands are done automatically	Hold **LT** + **RT** then press **B**,**B**, ↑, ←, **A**, ←, **A**, ←, **A**

UNLOCKABLE

Complete the following task

UNLOCKABLE	HOW TO UNLOCK
Crazy Bike	Beat all the Crazy Box challenges.

CODE

Enter the code. You should hear the word "Fish" if you do it correctly.

EFFECT	CODE
Infinite Time	**A**, **B**, **Y**, **X**, **Y**, **A**, **B**, ←, →, **Y**, **X**, **A**, **B**, **A**, **Y**, **X**, **Y** (on pause screen)

UNLOCKABLE

Complete the following tasks.

UNLOCKABLE	HOW TO UNLOCK
Alternate clothing and boat colors	Reach the final tournament in original mode.
Bonus Falls Level (Arcade Mode)	Finish the last 2 tournaments in Consumer Mode
Bonus Palace Level (Arcade Mode)	Finish the first 2 tournaments in Consumer Mode
Extra Practice Levels	Complete the game once in Arcade Mode
Sonic Lure	Complete all 5 tournaments in Consumer Mode

SECRETS

While choosing your lure, press Up or Down to get a different color.

SECRETS

When at the Area Select screen in Arcade Mode, press A + B simultaneously to control the female character.

UNLOCKABLE

Beat the rest of the four courses. Note: Don't delete your your chao data or else you will have to do them again.

UNLOCKABLE

Complete the tasks to unlock these

UNLOCKABLE	HOW TO UNLOCK
Amy	Talk to her in the Casino as Sonic after finishing Sky Chase.
Big	Defeat Chaos 6 as Sonic.
E-102 Gamma	Defeat Gamma after finishing Sky Deck as Sonic or Tails. An alternate way to unlock him is to finish Twinkle Park as Amy and watch the FMAs after it.
Knuckles	Defeat him after finishing Ice cap as Sonic or Tails.
Miles Tails Prower	Finish the C mission of Emerald Coast action stage as Sonic.
Super Sonic	Finish the game as Sonic, Tails, Knuckles, Amy, Big and E-102 Gamma. Super Sonic will be avaliable only in Adventure Mode.
Super Sonic	Complete the game with every character
Ancient Light (Sonic)	On top of a rock on Angel Island
Booster (E-102)	In the Weapon's Armory on the Egg Carrier
Crystal Ring (Sonic)	Walk up the steps in the hotel, press the two buttons and use light speed dash
Fighting Gloves (Knuckles)	On a ledge over Big's house
Jet Anklet (Tails)	In a hole in the ceiling in the sewer behind Twinkle Park
Laser Blaster (E-102)	In the Restricted room on the Egg Carrier after it crashes
Life Belt (Big)	In the entrance to Icecap
Light Speed Shoes (Sonic)	Find it in the sewer (not the onebehind Twinkle Park)
Long Hammer (Amy)	Beat your own high score on Hedgehog Hammer after the Egg Carrier crashes
Long Rod (Big)	Under the bed at Big's hut
Lure Upgrade 1 (Big)	In the sewer behind Twinkle Park
Lure Upgrade 2 (Big)	Under an sheet of ice in IceCap
Lure Upgrade 3 (Big)	In a cave in the forest
Lure Upgrade 4 (Big)	In one of the jail cells on the Egg Carrier
Rhythm Badge (Tails)	In the flashback with Tikal
Shovel Claw (Knuckles)	In the tunnel inside the tunnel where you find the cart to the Mystic Ruins Chao Garden
Warrior Feather (Amy)	Beat Eggman's high-score on Hedgehog Hammer
Easter Egg	Press X immediately before entering the snowboarding portion of the game to get a blue snowboard or B for a yellow snowboard.
Easter Egg	While playing with Sonic in Casinopolis, go to the pinball game with the NiGHTS motif. Hit the three little purple point givers in order to open up an entrance at the top of the board. Then make your way through the secret entrance. You'll now be in another NiGHTS motif pinball game. Whenever you fail to catch Sonic with the bumpers, don't worry about losing a ball. Instead, Sonic will be transported through a world very familiar to the NiGHTS level Splash Garden.

DRIVER: PARALLEL LINES (WII)

PASSWORD

PASSWORD	EFFECT
steelman	Invincibility

DUNGEON EXPLORER (WII)

PASSWORDS

PASSWORD	EFFECT
CHECK NAMEA	Change names
ADGDP-CJLPG	Final Dungeon is open
DEBDE DEBDA then press RUN+①	Invincibility
JBBNJ HDCOG	Play as Princess Aki
IMGAJ MDPAI	Play as the Hermit
HOMING AAAA	Precision guided weapons (smart weapons)

LEVEL SELECT

Enable the "Invincibility" code. Enter one of the following 15 bushes in front of Axis castle to jump to the corresponding location. (Bush 1 is on the left end, bush 15 is on the right end.)

BUSH	LOCATION
1	Natas
2	Balamous Tower
3	Rotterroad (path to Judas)
4	Mistose Dungeon
5	Ratonix Dungeon
6	Reraport Maze
7	Rally Maze
8	Bullbeast
9	Melba Village
10	After Gutworm
11	Nostalgia Dungeon
12	Water Castle
13	Road to Cherry Tower
14	Stonefield
15	Karma Castle

UNLOCKABLES

UNLOCKABLE	HOW TO UNLOCK
Secret Ending	Input the Invincibility code so you can pass through objects. When you take the ORA stone back to the King and he leaves, pass through the blockade to his throne, which initiates the secret ending.
Use the Harmit (Hermit) the hard way	To use the Harmit (sic), level a Bard until you have at least 50 HP. (Go into the second house to the west of Axis Castle.)

DUNGEON HUNTER: ALLIANCE (PLAYSTATION VITA)

TROPHY

UNLOCKABLE	HOW TO UNLOCK
Along Came a Spider... (Bronze)	Defeat Seba the Man-Eater in a single or multiplayer game.
Ashes To Ashes (Bronze)	Defeat the Warlord in a single or multiplayer game.
Assassin (Bronze)	Defeat 300 monsters using only daggers.
Avenge the Fallen (Bronze)	Defeat Jeremo in a single or multiplayer game.
Battle of the Elements (Bronze)	Defeat all five Generals in a single or multiplayer game.
Berserker (Bronze)	Defeat 300 monsters using only axes (1H or 2H).
Big Spender (Bronze)	Purchase at least one item from every merchant.
Blademaster (Bronze)	Defeat 300 monsters using only swords (1H or 2H).
Bloodlust (Bronze)	Defeat 10,000 monsters with one character.

Boss Goblin Go Boom (Bronze)	Defeat the Goblin King in a single or multiplayer game.
Bottoms Up (Bronze)	Drink 200 potions with one character.
Broken Wings (Bronze)	Defeat the Cloud Beast in a single or multiplayer game.
Champion of Gothicus (Platinum)	Earn all trophies in the game.
Chatterbox (Bronze)	Initiate a conversation with every NPC in the game.
Courage And Grace (Bronze)	Complete the game as a rogue.
Crystal Scavenger (Bronze)	Use the fairies to uncover 10 crystals buried underground.
Dead Dog (Bronze)	Defeat the Big Bad Wolf in a single or multiplayer game.
Dragon Lancer (Bronze)	Defeat 300 monsters using only polearms.
Dungeon Explorer (Bronze)	Reach level 50 with one character.
Dungeon Master (Bronze)	Reach level 75 with one character.
Dungeon Raider (Bronze)	Reach level 10 with one character.
Dungeon Seeker (Bronze)	Reach level 25 with one character.
Dungeon Trainee (Bronze)	Reach level 2 with one character.
Dust To Dust (Bronze)	Defeat the Stone Devil in a single or multiplayer game.
Eagle Eye (Bronze)	Defeat 300 monsters using only crossbows.
Eternal Punishment (Bronze)	Defeat Gilgrath Zire in a single or multiplayer game.
Executioner (Bronze)	Defeat a monster with a single blow.
Failure Is Not an Option (Bronze)	Defeat the Corrupted Captain in a single or multiplayer game.
Gladiator (Bronze)	Defeat 300 monsters using only maces.
Good Night, Sweet Prince (Bronze)	Defeat the Bandit Prince in a single or multiplayer game.
Grand Magus (Bronze)	Defeat 500 monsters using Fairy Spells.
Guardian Angel (Bronze)	Resurrect 20 teammates in a multiplayer game.
He Slimed Me (Bronze)	Defeat the Depth Beast in a single or multiplayer game.
Hero Of The People (Bronze)	Complete all quests in Hero difficulty.
Hunter (Bronze)	Defeat 300 monsters using only bows.
Killer Instinct (Gold)	Defeat the Dark Fairy in a single or multiplayer game without taking damage.
Little Women (Silver)	Control the fairies to damage 200 enemies.
Long Live The King (Silver)	Complete the game with all 3 character classes.
Looking For Loot (Bronze)	Open 30 treasure chests with one character.
Night Stalker (Bronze)	Defeat 300 monsters by wielding two daggers at the same time.
Panzer Hand (Bronze)	Defeat 2,000 monsters using only 2H weapons.
Playing with fire (Bronze)	Defeat the Forge Monster in a single or multiplayer game.
Power And Wisdom (Bronze)	Complete the game as a mage.
Pure Skill (Silver)	Defeat a boss using only skills, no basic attacks.
Rest In Peace (Bronze)	Defeat Lord Plenko in a single or multiplayer game.
Rise from Your Grave (Bronze)	Defeat Reldin in a single or multiplayer game.
Shake It! (Bronze)	Recover from Stun, Fear, or Confuse 25 times by shaking the PS Vita system.

Shalandriel's Chosen (Bronze)	Defeat Shalandriel the Eternal Keeper in a single or multiplayer game.
Sorcerer (Bronze)	Defeat 300 monsters using only orbs.
Strength And Honor (Bronze)	Complete the game as a warrior.
The Darkness Defeated (Bronze)	Defeat the Dark Queen in a single or multiplayer game.
The Legend Can Be Told (Silver)	Complete the game on Legend difficulty.
To Catch a Killer (Bronze)	Defeat the Darklin Assassin in a single or multiplayer game.
United We Stand (Gold)	Complete the game in a 4-player multiplayer game on any difficulty level.
Warlock (Bronze)	Defeat 300 monsters using only staffs.
Warmancer (Silver)	Use every skill in the game once.

DYNASTY WARRIORS 6 (XBOX 360)

CHARACTERS

UNLOCKABLE	HOW TO UNLOCK
Cao Cao	Clear Musou mode with three Wei characters.
Cao Pi	Defeat Cao Pi within five minutes on Wu side of He Fei.
Cao Ren	Succeed in Battle Objective 2 on the Lu Bu side of Fan Castle.
Diao Chan	Clear Musou mode with one character from each Kingdom.
Dong Zhuo	Clear Musou mode with Lu Bu.
Gan Ning	Clear Musou mode with one Wu character.
Guan Ping	Succeed in two battle objectives on the Shu side of Fan Castle and finish battle with Guan Ping alive.
Huang Gai	Succeed in Battle Objective 3 on the Wu side of The Battle of Chi Bi.
Huang Zhong	Succeed in one battle objective on the Wei side of Ding Jun Mountain.
Ling Tong	Succeed in Battle Objective 1 on the Wei side of the Battle of Shi Ting.
Liu Bei	Clear Musou mode with three Shu characters.
Lu Bu	Clear Musou mode with Liu Bei, Cao Cao, and Sun Jian.
Lu Meng	Succeed in two battle objectives on the Wei side of He Fei.
Ma Chao	Succeed in two battle objectives on the Wei side of Han Zhong Attack Defense Battle.
Pang Tong	Succeed in three battle objectives at Cheng Du battle and finish battle with Pang Tong alive.
Sun Ce	Succeed in Battle Objective 1 on the Sun Jian side of the Battle of Xia Pi.
Sun Jian	Clear Musou mode with three Wu characters.
Sun Quan	Succeed in Battle Objective 1 on the Lu Bu side of the Battle of Chi Bi.
Taishi Ci	Defeat him in the Battle for Wu Territory.
Wei Yan	Succeed in two battle objectives on the Shu side of WuZhang Plains and finish battle with Wei Yan alive.
Xiahou Yuan	Succeed in one battle objective on the Shu side of Ding Jun Mountain.
Xiao Quio	Succeed in Battle Objective 3 on the Wu side of the Battle of Shi Ting.
Xu Chu	He Fei, Wu side, personally kill Cao Ren and Xu Chu.
Xu Huang	Succeed in two battle objectives on the Wei/Wu side of Fan Castle.
Yuan Shao	As Wei, complete all three targets and capture Wu Chao before completing the stage.
Yue Ying	Succeed in Battle Objective 1 on the Wei side of the Battle of Wu Zhang Plains.

Zhang Jiao	Beat stage while completing all three targets in the Yellow Turban Rebellion. Playable in only Free mode and Challenge mode.
Zhang Liao	Clear Musou mode with one Wei character.
Zhen Ji	Succeed in Battle Objective 1 on the Lu Bu side of the Xu Du Invasion.
Zheng He	Succeed in two battle objectives on the Shu side of Han Zhong Attack Defense Battle.
Zhou Tai	Succeed in three battle objectives on the Shu side of Yi Ling.
Zhuge Liang	Clear Musou mode with one Shu character.

DIFFICULTIES

UNLOCKABLE	HOW TO UNLOCK
Chaos Difficulty	Clear Musou mode with one character from Wu, Shu, Wei, and Other.
Hell Difficulty	Beat Wei, Wu, Shu, and Other Musou mode.
Master Difficulty	Beat any Musou mode on Easy or Normal.
Very Hard Difficulty	Clear Musou mode with any one character.

DYNASTY WARRIORS 7 (PLAYSTATION 3)

UNLOCKABLE

To unlock characters that are not available after the completion of Story Mode, complete the Legendary Battles hex for that character in Conquest Mode. After you complete all the Legendary Battles for that character he or she will become unlocked.

UNLOCKABLE

Complete the following tasks

UNLOCKABLE	HOW TO UNLOCK
Qilin Blade	Completed all Tresure Battles in Conquest Mode.
Silver Stallion	Unlocked 7 capital cities in Conquest Mode.

UNLOCKABLE

Complete the following tasks to unlock guardian animals

UNLOCKABLE	HOW TO UNLOCK
Hex Mark	Complete Champions of Chaos on Conquest Mode.
Red Hare	Complete Battle for Supremacy.
Shadow Runner	Complete Wolves of Chaos on Conquest Mode.

DYNASTY WARRIORS 7 (XBOX 360)

UNLOCKABLE

To unlock characters that are not available after the completion of Story Mode, complete the Legendary Battles hex for that character in Conquest Mode. After you complete all the Legendary Battles for that character he or she will become unlocked.

UNLOCKABLE

Complete the following tasks to unlock guardian animals

UNLOCKABLE	HOW TO UNLOCK
Red Hare	Complete Battle for Supremacy.
Shadow Runner	Beat Wolves of Chaos

DYNASTY WARRIORS NEXT (PLAYSTATION VITA)

TROPHY

UNLOCKABLE	HOW TO UNLOCK
A Land United (Bronze)	Cleared the stage, 'A Land United.'
A Man of Virtue (Bronze)	Cleared the stage, 'A Man of Virtue.'
Ambition Personified (Silver)	Cleared the Conquest Mode a total of 50 times.
An Endless Quest (Bronze)	Cleared the stage, 'An Endless Quest.'

An Everlasting Love (Bronze)	Formed a marriage pact with another officer.
Anti-Dong Zhou Coalition (Bronze)	Cleared the stage, 'Anti-Dong Zhou Coalition.'
Armor Collector (Bronze)	Obtained all of the available armor.
Army of One (Bronze)	Defeated 1,000 enemies in one battle.
Battle of Chibi (Bronze)	Clear the stage, 'Battle of Chibi.'
Benevolent Ruler (Bronze)	Achieved the best possible Governance Rating.
Card Collector (Gold)	Obtained all of the available Officer Cards.
Character Collector (Bronze)	Created 10 Edit Characters.
Coalition Leader (Bronze)	Completed all of the battles within the Coalition Mode.
Combo Master (Bronze)	Completed a 500 hit combo.
Conqueror of Jiangdong (Bronze)	Cleared the stage, 'Conqueror of Jiangdong.'
End of the Road (Bronze)	Completed a five forces map in Conquest Mode.
Equipment Collector (Bronze)	Obtained all of the available growth items.
Eyes in the Back of Your Head (Silver)	Successfully completed all of the Sudden Encounters with the best possible rating.
Family Ties (Gold)	Formed a sworn oath with all of the officers.
Friends to the End (Bronze)	Formed a sworn oath with another officer.
Great Emperor (Silver)	Cleared all of the stages in the game.
Jack of All Trades (Bronze)	Completed Steeplechase, Bastion, Marksman and Calligrapher within the Gala Mode.
Malevolent Ruler (Bronze)	Achieved the worst possible Governance Rating.
Master Matchmaker (Gold)	Formed a marriage pact with all of the officers.
Master of the Kingdom (Bronze)	Earned 100,000 Exp.
Master of the Land (Silver)	Earned 1,000,000 Exp.
Master of the Realm (Bronze)	Earned 500,000 Exp.
Movie Collector (Bronze)	Viewed all of the movies in the game.
New Recruit (Bronze)	Created a save data file.
Orb Collector (Bronze)	Obtained all of the available orbs.
Quiet Ambition (Bronze)	Cleared the stage, 'Quiet Ambition.'
Say Cheese (Bronze)	Took a picture using the Musou Snapshot feature of the Gala Mode.
Seasoned Veteran (Bronze)	Successfully completed all of the Sudden Encounters.
The Goal is Within Sight (Bronze)	Completed a four forces map in Conquest Mode.
The God of War (Silver)	Defeated more than 100,000 enemies.
The Great Creator (Silver)	Obtained all of the available Edit Character parts.
The Journey Begins (Bronze)	Completed a two forces map in Conquest Mode.
The Kingdom in Three (Bronze)	Cleared the stage, 'The Kingdom in Three.'
The Path of Ambition (Bronze)	Cleared the Conquest Mode a total of 5 times.
The Plot Thickens (Bronze)	Completed a three forces map in Conquest Mode.
The Struggle for Power (Bronze)	Cleared the stage, 'The Struggle for Power.'
The Three Visits (Bronze)	Cleared the stage, 'The Three Visits.'
The Tiger's Advance (Bronze)	Cleared the stage, 'The Tiger's Advance.'
True Warrior of the Three Kingdoms (Platinum)	Obtained all trophies.
Unrivaled Warrior (Bronze)	Defeated 3,000 enemies in one battle.
Untouchable (Bronze)	Completed a battle in either Campaign Mode, or Conquest Mode without taking any damage.

Weapons Collector (Silver)	Obtained all of the available weapons.
Yellow Turban Rebellion (Bronze)	Cleared the stage, 'Yellow Turban Rebellion.'
You Can Pursue Lu Bu (Bronze)	Defeated Lu Bu in the Campaign Mode.

UNLOCKABLE

UNLOCKABLE	HOW TO UNLOCK
Chaos Difficulty	Reach Rank 19
Ancient Remedy	Campaign Mode - Conquer "Changsha" in "A Land United" - Hard mode or higher
Art of War	Campaign Mode - Conquer "BeiPing" in "The Tiger's Advance" - Medium mode or higher
Bai Hu's Jewel	Coalition Mode - "Blitz" Kill all 6 enemy general with 4 mins time left
Bear Mount	Campaign Mode - Conquer "Changan" in "Anti-Dong Zhuo Coalition" - Chaos mode
Charge Bracer	Coalition Mode - "Sentinel" protect all 7 bases, clear game with 6 mins time left
Dragon Greaves	Campaign Mode - Conquer "Hefei" in "Conqueror of Jiangdong" - Hard mode or higher
Elephant Mount	Campaign Mode - Conquer "Nanzhong" in "A Man of Virtue" - Medium mode or higher
Hex Mark Saddle	Gala Mode - Complete Steeplechase under 1'30
Jade Earrings	Campaign Mode - Conquer "Jiaozhi" in "The Three Visits" - Easy mode or higher
Master of Musou	Campaign Mode - Conquer "Jiaozhi" in "Quiet Ambition" - Easy mode or higher
Meat Bun Pouch	Campaign Mode - Complete "Yellow Turban Rebellion" - Easy mode or higher
Obsidian Remedy	Campaign Mode - Conquer "Xiangyang" in "Battle of Chibi" - Easy mode or higher
Power Rune	Coalition Mode - Complete "Sudden Death" with the time left more than 24'30s, kill 1500
Red Hare Saddle	Campaign Mode - Complete "The Endless Quest" Hard mode or chaos mode
Shadow Runner Saddle	Campaign Mode - Conquer "Luoyang" in "The Struggle for Power" - Chaos mode
Stimulant Remedy	Coalition Mode - "Marauder" Take all bases (without lose any base to enemy again), kill all enemy general with 25 mins time left
Survival Guide	Campaign Mode - Conquer "Xiangyang" in "The Three Visits" - Chaos mode
Hex Mare	Complete Steeplechase in Gala Mode
Musou Armor	Complete Marksman in Gala Mode
Way of Musou	Complete Calligraphy in Gala Mode under 2 minutes
Wind Scroll	Complete Bastion in Gala Mode

EA SPORTS NBA JAM (XBOX 360)

UNLOCKABLES

UNLOCKABLE	HOW TO UNLOCK
Team Adidas	When entering initials, enter ADI for player 1 and DAS for player 2. This unlocks Team Adidas, which includes Dwight Howard, Derick Rose, and Josh Smith.
Team Jordan	When entering initials, enter JOR for player 1 and DAN for player 2. This unlocks Team Jordan, which includes Dwayne Wade, Chris Paul, and Carmelo Anthony.
Team Sprite	When entering initials, enter SPR for player 1 and ITE for player 2. This unlocks Team Sprite, which includes Yellow and Green Lebron James.
J. Cole and 9th Wonder	Enter the following codes at the Start screen. A sound will confirm correct code entry. Select "Play Now" mode, then press Start at the Team Selection screen to have the corresponding character appear. Press Up, Left, Down, Right, Up, Left, Down, Right, A, B.
Beastie Boys	Enter the following codes at the Start screen. A sound will confirm correct code entry. Select "Play Now" mode, then press Start at the Team Selection screen to have the corresponding character appear. Press Up(2), Down(2), Left, Right, Left, Right, B, A.
Democrats	Enter the following codes at the Start screen. A sound will confirm correct code entry. Select "Play Now" mode, then press Start at the Team Selection screen to have the corresponding character appear. Press Left(13), A.
Michelle Beadle and Colin Cowherd from Sportsnation	In EA Sports NBA Jam for the Wii, you can unlock Colin Cowherd and Michelle Beadle. On the Enter Initials screen, type ESP for player 1 and NSN for player 2. Go to the Select Team screen and you should hear a noise confirming you've unlocked them, and you'll see them in the teams list.
NBA Mascots	On the Enter Initials screen, type MAS for player 1 and COT for player 2. Go to the Select Team screen; you should hear a noise confirming you've unlocked them, and you'll see them in the teams list.
Republicans	Enter the following codes at the Start screen. A sound will confirm correct code entry. Select "Play Now" mode, then press Start at the Team Selection screen to have the corresponding character appear. Press Right(13), A.
Tim Kitzrow (announcer) and Mark Turmell (developer)	On the Enter Initials screen, type MJT for player 1. Go to the Select Team screen and you should hear a noise confirming you've unlocked them, and you'll see them in the teams list.

ECCO: THE TIDES OF TIME (WII)

UNLOCKABLES

UNLOCKABLE	HOW TO UNLOCK
Debug Menu	Pause while Ecco is facing you. Once Ecco is facing you, press Ⓐ, Ⓑ, Ⓒ, Ⓑ, Ⓒ, Ⓐ, Ⓒ, Ⓐ, Ⓑ If you entered the code correctly, a menu will pop up with all sorts of options such as a sound test, level select, tempo, etc. This code can be entered as many times as you'd like, as long as the game is paused while Ecco is facing you.
Hard Mode	In the starting area, break the two shells above you, and then swim through the tunnel to start the game in Hard mode.

PASSWORDS

LEVEL	PASSWORD
Crystal Springs	UEPMCVEB
Fault Zone	OZUNSKZA
Two Tides	KDKINTYA
Skyway	SZXHCLDB
Sky Tides	OZWIDLDB
Tube of Medusa	QSJRYHZA
Skylands	MULXRXEB
Fin to Feather	YCPAWEXA
Eagle's Bay	YCJPDNDB
Asterite's Cave	AOJRDZWA
Four Islands	UOYURFDB
Sea of Darkness	UQZWIIAB
Vents of Medusa	MMVSOPBB
Gateway	KDCGTAHB
Big Water	QQCQRDRA
Deep Ridge	UXQWJIZD
Hungry Ones	WBQHMIUE
Secret Cave	CHGTEYZE
Gravitorbox	UIXBGWXE
Globe Holder	SBFPWWJE
Dark Sea	MXURVMLA
Vortex Queen	OKIMTBPA
Home Bay	CSNCMRUA
Epilogue	CEWSXKPA
Fish City	SGTDYSPA
City of Forever	WSSXZKVA

PASSWORDS FOR HARD MODE
* = New level found only in Hard mode

LEVEL	PASSWORD
Crystal Springs	WPHSAAFB
Fault Zone	CRNPTFZA
Two Tides	QUKGZZYA
Skyway	MCMBPJDB
Sky Tides	OZMRKIDB
Tube of Medusa	ODFADPYA
Aqua Tubeway*	KNHRKJYA
Skylands	WXRDJYEB
Fin to Feather	UQTFBRXA
Eagle's Bay	QSNVMMDB
Asterite's Cave	EGAQRVXA
Maze of Stone*	EUTQQQWA
Four Islands	CZVQNHCB
Sea of Darkness	WFMYIDAB
Vents of Medusa	SHWZZNBB
Gateway	QKLLFPHB
Moray Abyss	YCFSBRAB
The Eye	AGNEXBTE
Big Water	YCBXONIA

NEW!

A
B
C
D
E
F
G
H
I
J
K
L
M
N
O
P
Q
R
S
T
U
V
W
X
Y
Z

Deep Ridge	UPODMUQD
The Hungry Ones	YOHVUVLE
Secret Cave	SPKHKISE
Lunar Bay	WTHXKISE
Black Clouds	USKIKDOE
GraviatorBox	WNQWZMME
Globe Holder	MIPGDOME
New Machine*	GOSTCXJA
Vortex Queen	OOSFBXAA
Home Bay	QNSGAPGA
Epilogue	AXBGKHBA
Fish City	WKGETHCA
City of Forever	WQHFTZHA
"Secret" Password	AVQJTCBA

UNLOCKABLE

UNLOCKABLE	HOW TO UNLOCK
Unlimited Air and Health	Turn Ecco left or right and pause the game while Ecco is facing the screen. Press Ⓐ, Ⓐ, ⬅, Ⓐ, Ⓒ, Ⓐ, ⬆, Ⓐ, Ⓐ, ⬅, Ⓐ and then unpause. You will now never die from lack of air or injuries.

THE ELDER SCROLLS V: SKYRIM (XBOX 360)

ACHIEVEMENT

UNLOCKABLE	HOW TO UNLOCK
Adept (10)	Reach Level 10
Alduin's Wall (20)	Complete "Alduin's Wall"
Apprentice (5)	Reach Level 5
Artificer (10)	Make a smithed item, an enchanted item, and a potion
Bleak Falls Barrow (10)	Complete "Bleak Falls Barrow"
Blessed (10)	Select a Standing Stone blessing
Blood Oath (10)	Become a member of the Circle
Bound Until Death (10)	Complete "Bound Until Death"
Citizen (10)	Buy a house
Daedric Influence (10)	Acquire a Daedric Artifact
Darkness Returns (10)	Complete "Darkness Returns"
Delver (40)	Clear 50 dungeons
Diplomatic Immunity (20)	Complete "Diplomatic Immunity"
Dragon Hunter (20)	Absorb 20 dragon souls
Dragon Soul (10)	Absorb a dragon soul
Dragonslayer (50)	Complete "Dragonslayer"
Elder Knowledge (20)	Complete "Elder Knowledge"
Expert (25)	Reach Level 25
Explorer (40)	Discover 100 Locations
Gatekeeper (10)	Join the College of Winterhold
Glory of the Dead (30)	Complete "Glory of the Dead"
Golden Touch (30)	Have 100,000 gold
Hail Sithis! (30)	Complete "Hail Sithis!"
Hard Worker (10)	Chop wood, mine ore, and cook food
Hero of Skyrim (30)	Capture Solitude or Windhelm
Hero of the People (30)	Complete 50 Misc Objectives

Married (10)	Get married
Master (50)	Reach Level 50
Master Criminal (20)	Bounty of 1000 gold in all nine holds
Oblivion Walker (30)	Collect 15 Daedric Artifacts
One with the Shadows (30)	Returned the Thieves Guild to its former glory
Reader (20)	Read 50 Skill Books
Revealing the Unseen (10)	Complete "Revealing the Unseen"
Sideways (20)	Complete 10 side quests
Skill Master (40)	Get a skill to 100
Snake Tongue (10)	Successfully persuade, bribe, and intimidate
Standing Stones (30)	Find 13 Standing Stones
Take Up Arms (10)	Join the Companions
Taking Care of Business (10)	Join the Thieves Guild
Taking Sides (10)	Join the Stormcloaks or the Imperial Army
The Eye of Magnus (30)	Complete "The Eye of Magnus"
The Fallen (20)	Complete "The Fallen"
The Way of the Voice (20)	Complete "The Way of the Voice"
Thief (30)	Pick 50 locks and 50 pockets
Thu'um Master (40)	Learn 20 shouts
Unbound (10)	Complete "Unbound"
Wanted (10)	Escape from jail
War Hero (10)	Capture Fort Sungard or Fort Greenwall
With Friends Like These... (10)	Join the Dark Brotherhood
Words of Power (10)	Learn all three words of a shout

ELEMENTS OF DESTRUCTION (DS)

CODES

Pause the game and hold the following four buttons simultaneously.

UNLOCKABLE	HOW TO UNLOCK
Unlimited Energy	Ⓨ, Ⓛ, ⏶, +SELECT
Unlimited Time	Ⓧ, Ⓡ, ⏶, +SELECT

ALL LEVELS

Hold down the following buttons during the first cutscene to unlock all levels for the current profile.

UNLOCKABLE	HOW TO UNLOCK
Unlock All Levels	Ⓑ, Ⓛ, +SELECT

ERAGON (XBOX 360)

UNLIMITED FURY MODE

Pause the game while in a level.

UNLOCKABLE	HOW TO UNLOCK
Unlimited Fury Mode	Hold Ⓛ + ⓛⓣ + Ⓡ + Ⓡⓣ and press ⊗ Ⓑ Ⓑ Ⓑ (Note: This makes magic cooldown go much faster.)

ESWAT: CITY UNDER SIEGE (WII)

UNLOCKABLES

UNLOCKABLE	HOW TO UNLOCK
Level Select	Start a game, and the Hero and Mission screen appears. Now hold down Ⓐ+Ⓑ+Ⓒ and press ⏵, ⏴, ⏵, ⏴. Select the level by pressing ⏵/⏴. Then during the ending sequence, press and hold Ⓐ+Ⓐ+Ⓒ+⏵+⏴. Keep holding these and press START until the Sound Test screen appears.

F

F1 2011 (PLAYSTATION VITA)

TROPHY

UNLOCKABLE	HOW TO UNLOCK
April shower (bronze)	Win a race in the wet
Banger racing (silver)	Repair damage to your car in the pits and go on to win the race
Challenger (bronze)	Complete a challenge with a c rank or above
Champion (gold)	Beat sebastian vettel in the challenge mode head to head race
Clean sweep (silver)	Win every grand prix
Complete (platinum)	Congratulations on completing f1 2011
Driving legend (gold)	Beat the real world lap record on any circuit
Endurance (bronze)	Complete a 100% distance race
Flying lap (bronze)	Achieve your first time trial medal
Get noticed (bronze)	Achieve the fastest lap in a grand prix
Go the distance (silver)	Drive 1000 miles (1610km)
Grade a performance (bronze)	Earn an a rank in challenge mode
Grand prix win (bronze)	Win your first grand prix
High roller (silver)	Win the monte carlo grand prix with vehicle damage enabled
Leader of the pack (silver)	Achieve pole on every circuit
Learning to fly (silver)	Post a flying lap to win a time trial medal with all driving aids disabled
Legendary charge! (gold)	Win a race starting from 24th on the grid
Made the cut (bronze)	Reach q3 in qualifying
Manual master (bronze)	Finish a race using only manual gears
Must dash! (gold)	Earn 14 pole positions in a single season
Pole position (bronze)	Achieve pole position
Prancer (silver)	Complete a lap of monza with an average speed greater than 150mph (241 km/h)
Shoe maker (gold)	Earn 149 championship points in a single season
Speed demon (bronze)	Drive faster than 230mph (370km/h)
Stirling performance (silver)	Lap every car in a race in wet conditions
The greatest of all time (silver)	Win eight world championships
Timed to perfection (gold)	Achieve all gold time trial trophies
Toe to toe (bronze)	Win a head to head challenge
Tuned to perfection (bronze)	Take pole position in qualifying with a tuned vehicle
Unassisted (bronze)	Finish a race with all driving aids turned off
Unplugged (silver)	Win a race with all driving aids disabled

FABLE II (XBOX 360)

EASTER EGG

In the side quest "Treasure Island of Doom," the Lionhead Studios Lion can be found when you get to the treasure island. Look at the island in the middle of the lake and you'll see it is in the shape of the Studio's Lionhead logo.

INFINITE EXPERIENCE

Once you have access to Bowerstone Market, walk to Town Square. There is a potion shopkeeper on the left side. Walk around the right side of the buildings there and down an alley to find a house known as Monster Manor. Sleep there to gain its benefit (+1 star of Physique) Once you gain this benefit, go to your abilities list, select physique, and hit Y to unlearn it. The bonus star from the house does not disappear, but the experience is given to you anyway. Repeat this process as many times as you like, the more stars you have in physique the more exp you get each time. This experience is general experience and can be applied to any skills.

INFINITE EXPERIENCE II

Wait until your character is at least somewhat leveled up. Plug in a second controller and begin a co-op game with a second profile. Using the second controller, go to your henchman's abilities and discard all of them, returning the experience to the pool. Then quit out of the co-op game. You should find that all the "leftover" experience has been transferred to your hero. Repeat as often as you like. Note: Your co-op henchman will have the same abilities that you do, so the stronger the hero, the more abilities there are to sell off and thus more experience.

FABLE III (XBOX 360)

AVATAR AWARDS

UNLOCKABLE	HOW TO UNLOCK
Crown	Become the ruler of Albion
Royal Boots	Win the support of the Dwellers
Royal Shirt	Win the support of the Bowerstone
Royal Trousers	Win the support of the Swift Brigade

DUPLICATION (PRE-PATCH)

This glitch allows you to duplicate gold or anything else. With a second controller, join your game. Then use player 1 to "gift" player 2 whatever you want to duplicate, then have player 2 leave player 1's sanctuary. Have player 2 go into his sanctuary and find the gift. Now have him reject the gift to send it back to player 1. Immediately have player 2 leave his sanctuary, then immediately drop him from the game. Now player 1 has a rejected gift in his sanctuary and player 2 will not be saved, meaning when you reload him, he will also have a gift the game didn't save as being rejected. You can dupe up to 100,000 gold at a time using this.

LIONHEAD STUDIO EASTER EGG

Swim out into the ocean in the Driftwood area. Once you hit the border, tilt your camera to look down into the water. There should be a Lionhead Studios logo on the sea floor.

PORTAL EASTER EGG

When going to capture Nigel Ferret (during the Hideout mission of bowerstone) you will come across a room with a silver key. At the far end of the room there is a path around the boxes to the other jail cell. The cell contains a hobbe worshiping the companion cube from Portal and there is of course some cake.

FALLOUT 3 (XBOX 360)

INFINITE XP

You can gain infinite XP if your Speech skill is high enough (approximately level 30). Go Big Town, north of Vault 101. Speak with a girl named Bittercup. She'll tell you about her dating exploits. After speaking with her, go into the house marked "Common House" and speak to a man named Pappy. There should be a speech skill dialogue option that says "You came here with Bittercup, right?" You get XP every time you click it. Continue to do this as long as you like to gain free XP.

EARLY DETECTION

When heading into seemingly hostile territory, try hitting the VATS button over and over again as you make your character turn around, searching all angles. Doing so will alert you to any enemies you may not yet see by zooming in on them in VATS mode. You won't be able to do damage to your foes from such a distance, but it's a good way to spot foes before they spot you so you know what you're getting yourself into.

SANDMAN GLITCH (PRE-PATCH)

This a glitch for getting infinite experience. Steps: Reach Level 10 with a sneak skill of 60 and get the Mr. Sandman perk. Go to Andale (south central part of the map). Wait until around 1 A.M. and go into the Smith house while they are sleeping. Go upstairs and into the kid's bedroom. Use sandman on him (crouch and select him and use the first option). Repeat the last steps. Increase difficulty for more XP.

FALLOUT: NEW VEGAS (XBOX 360)

INFINITE XP GLITCH

With a Speech skill at 50 or higher, you can persuade Old Ben to offer his escort services to the local bar and gain 61 XP if you succeed in the speech challenge. Then follow him back to the bar and wait until he sits down, speak to him again, and redo the speech challenge for as much XP as you like! Old Ben is usually sitting by a fire close to the King's headquarters in Freeside.

INFINITE CAPS GLITCH

First, you must go to the town of Primm. Complete the "My Kind of Town" quest for them by getting a sheriff for the town. After you get them a sheriff, or the NCR's troops, you have to wait 3 to 7 in-game days, and the Vikki and Vance Casino will open again in Primm. Go there, and exchange some caps for some of the casino's chips. Then, turn in the casino's chips for caps. You will notice that when you turn the chips in, you don't have them removed from your inventory; however, you get the payout. You can exploit this for as long as you want.

VATS GLITCH

Obtain the Anti-Material Rifle and equip it with incendiary rounds. With the rifle equipped, target someone in VATS and then close VATS. They should catch fire and lose health. You can also select more than one person in VATS before closing it to burn more people. You will not lose karma or reputation.

MORE XP GLITCH

You need Speech of 30 or the perk Confirmed Bachelor. You must also be on the good side of NCR. Go to HELIOS One and the lady should automatically talk to you. Once she allows you access to HELIOS One, you should be able to start the mission "That Lucky Old Sun." Follow the mission and talk to Fantastic and Ignacio Rivas. While talking to Rivas, make sure you get him to reveal that he's a Follower of the Apocalypse by using Speech or Confirmed Bachelor and agree with his ideals about peace or just say you're neutral. Do the mission regularly until you get to the point where you activate the Mainframe Terminal. Configure the Power Grid to Full Region (Emergency Output Level). Finish the mission by hitting the Reflector Control Panel outside on top of the tower. Go back to Ignacio Rivas and choose the option "I overloaded the plant. No one . . ." The glitch is that the option never disappears, so you can choose to keep pressing it. You get 350 XP, 3 Stimpacks, and 2 Doctor's Bags.

INFINITE XP

This glitch can be found when arriving at the strip for the first time and you are invited into the Lucky 38 casino. Talk with Mr. House and ask about his lifespan (This requires a medicine check of 35). This will award 35 XP. Asking about his age again and reselecting the option "you appear to be more computer than man" will present the medicine check again, granting 35 XP each time (this glitch works in the current patched version of the game).

FALLOUT: NEW VEGAS (PS3)

INFINITE XP IN VAULT 11

Reach the sacrificial chamber and eliminate the robots, then go to the computer terminal through the previously closed wall and enter it. The last option can be pressed repeatedly to gain 500 XP each time. If any of the other options are chosen or if the terminal is exited, then you cannot use this exploit.

INFINITE CAPS

Once Primm obtains a new sheriff, The Vikki and Vance Casino will become available. If you save before each hand in blackjack, you can reload the game if you lose. You can trade in your chips for caps at the register. The NPC will give you the equivalent chips in caps, but will not take any away. This is repeatable.

EASY KILL

Obtain and equip the Anti-Material Rifle and then equip .50MG Incendiary rounds. Target some one in VATS and then close VATS, they should catch fire and lose health. You can also select more then one person in VATS before closing it, burning more people using the right analog. You will not aggro enemies or friendlies. Also you will not lose karma or Reputation with each kill.

INFINITE EXPERIENCE GLITCH

If you have a speech skill of 50 or higher, you can persuade Old Ben to offer his escort services to the local bar. If you succeed in the Speech Challenge, you'll gain 61 XP. If you follow him back to the bar afterwards, waiting until he sits down, you can speak to him again and redo the same Speech Challenge repeatedly for infinite XP! You can find Old Ben sitting by a fire close to The King's headquarters in Freeside.

INFINITE XP

Obtain "Speech" 30 or the perk "Confirmed Bachelor." You must also be friendly with NCR. Go to "HELIOS One" and the lady should automatically talk to you. Once she allows you to access HELIOS One, you will now be able to start the mission "That Lucky Old Sun". Follow the mission and talk to Fantastic and Ignacio Rivas. While speaking with Rivas, make sure you get him to reveal that he's a Follower of the Apocalypse by. This is accomplished by using Speech or Confirmed Bachelor while agreeing with his ideals about peace…or just say you're neutral. Once you get to the point where you activate the Mainframe Terminal, configure the Power Grid to "5 Full Region (Emergency Output Level). Complete the mission by hitting the Reflector Control Panel outside on top of the tower. Go back to Ignacio Rivas and select "I overloaded the plant. No one....." The glitch is that the option never disappears, so you can choose to keep pressing it. You get 350XP, 3 Stimpacks, and 2 Doctor's Bag.

FAR CRY 2 (PLAYSTATION 3)

CODES

In the menu, go to Additional Content, then Promotion Code, and input the code.

EFFECT	CODE
Unlock all missions.	6aPHuswe
Bonus Mission	tr99pUkA
Bonus Mission	THaCupR4
Bonus Mission	tar3QuzU
Bonus Mission	SpujeN7x
Bonus Mission	sa7eSUPR
Bonus Mission	JeM8SpaW
Bonus Mission	Cr34ufrE
Bonus Mission	96CesuHu
Bonus Mission	2Eprunef
Bonus Mission	zUmU6Rup

FAR CRY INSTINCTS PREDATOR (XBOX 360)

To enter these passwords, pause the game and select the Cheat menu. Note that these passwords are case sensitive.

UNLOCKABLE	PASSWORD
Enable Evolutions	FeralAttack
Evolution Game	GiveMeItAll

Heal Yourself	ImJackCarver
Infinite Adrenaline	Bloodlust
Infinite Ammo	UnleashHell
Unlock All Maps	GiveMeTheMaps

FAR CRY VENGEANCE (WII)

PASSWORD

PASSWORD	EFFECT
GiveMeTheMaps	Unlock All Maps

FATAL FURY (WII)

UNLOCKABLE

UNLOCKABLE	HOW TO UNLOCK
Good Ending	Beat the game on Normal or Hard without using a continue

FIFA SOCCER (PLAYSTATION VITA)

TROPHY

UNLOCKABLE	HOW TO UNLOCK
Aerial Threat (Bronze)	Score a header in a match with a player with the Aerial Threat Speciality
Against the Odds (Bronze)	Win a Head to Head Ranked Match using a weaker team
All My Own Work (Bronze)	Win a Match with Manual Controls
Around the World (Silver)	Play a match with a team from every league
Back of the Net (Bronze)	Score 5 goals in the Arena
Control the Open Space (Bronze)	Make a successful lob pass using the touchscreen in a match
Crosser (Bronze)	Create a goal with a cross with a player with the Crosser Speciality
Distance Shooter (Bronze)	Score from outside the box with a player with the Distance Shooter Speciality
Established Keeper (Silver)	Play a season as a goalkeeper in Career Mode
Experimental (Bronze)	Play 5 consecutive Head to Head Ranked Matches with different teams
FIFA for Life (Gold)	Spend 50 hours on the pitch
Folklore (Silver)	Become a Legend as a player in Career Mode
Good Form (Silver)	Play 5 consecutive Head to Head Ranked Matches without losing
Good Week! (Bronze)	Get yourself selected in the Team of the Week in Career Mode
Great Month (Bronze)	Win the Manager of the Month award in Career Mode
Home and Away (Silver)	Play and win every Stadium
Home Maker (Bronze)	Change the Home Stadium of any team
Hundred and Counting (Gold)	Play 100 Head to Head Ranked Matches
In for the Win (Bronze)	Take a Head to Head Ranked Match to extra time with a weaker team
In the game (Bronze)	Create a Virtual Pro
It's in the Blood (Silver)	Go from being a Player to the Manager (or Player Manager) in Career Mode
Mastermind (Bronze)	Have a substitute score a goal in Career Mode
Nimble Fingers (Bronze)	Score a touchscreen or rear touch pad goal from a touchscreen pass
Once in a Lifetime (Silver)	Score as the Goalkeeper in any match

Pass Master (Silver)	Make 100 successful passes using the touchscreen
Perfect Keeping (Bronze)	Play as the Goalkeeper in a Kick-Off match and finish with 100% Saving Accuracy
Pinpoint Accuracy (Bronze)	Score a goal using the screen (touchscreen) shot, or a rear touch pad shot
Playmaker (Bronze)	Create a goal with a player with the Playmaker Speciality
Poacher (Bronze)	Score from inside the box with a player with the Poacher Speciality
Pressure is On (Bronze)	Score a penalty kick using a touch shot
Rising Talent (Silver) Pro	Complete 100 Accomplishments with your Virtual
Safe Hands (Bronze)	Play any match as the Goalkeeper with no assistance
Sharp Shooter (Silver)	Score 50 goals using a touch shot
Soccer Legend (Platinum)	Unlock all other trophies (excluding additional content trophies)
Thread the Needle (Bronze)	Make a successful through pass using the touchscreen
Training Time (Bronze)	Work on your skills in any Arena Practice Mode
Virtual Legend (Gold)	Play 100 matches with your Virtual Pro
Warming the Gloves (Bronze)	Make 10 saves in the Arena
Woodwork and In! (Bronze)	Score off the post or cross bar in a match
You Pointing at Me? (Bronze)	Make a successful direct pass using the touchscreen

FIFA SOCCER 12 (PLAYSTATION 3)

TROPHY

UNLOCKABLE	HOW TO UNLOCK
'Big Cup' Squad (Silver)	Enter an Ultimate Team tournament and finish a match with an overall squad rating of 85 or higher
10 vs 11 (Bronze)	Win from a draw or behind while down a man in a game vs the CPU
3 Points (Bronze)	Win a season game in Head to Head Seasons
All My Own Work (Bronze)	Win a Match with Manual Controls (including Tactical Defending)
Being Social (Bronze)	Play an Online Friendlies Match
Block Party (Bronze)	Manually block 5 shots while defending in a single game
Campaign Complete (Silver)	Complete a Season in Head to Head Seasons
Century of Goals (Silver)	Score 100 goals in FIFA 12 match play
Challenge Accepted (Bronze)	Complete an EA SPORTS Football Club Game Scenario Challenge
Club Legend (Bronze)	Play 100 matches with any player in FIFA 12 Ultimate Team
Comeback Kid (Bronze)	Win after being down 3 goals in the 2nd half in a game vs. the CPU
Don't Blink (Bronze)	Score within the first 5 minutes of a game in a game vs the CPU
EAS FC Starting 11 (Silver)	Reach level 20 in the EA SPORTS Football Club
EAS FC Youth Academy (Bronze)	Reach level 5 in the EA SPORTS Football Club
FIFA for Life (Silver)	Spend 50 hours on the pitch
Football Legend (Platinum)	Unlock all other trophies (excluding additional content trophies)

Friendly (Bronze)	Finish a match against a Friend in FIFA 12 Ultimate Team
Friends now Enemies? (Bronze)	Win an Online Friendlies season
Fully Formed (Silver)	Have three players be in full form at the same time on your club in Career Mode
Growing Club (Bronze)	Achieve a club value of 85,000,000 in FIFA 12 Ultimate Team
Happy 20th EA SPORTS! (Bronze)	Score 20 match goals in FIFA 12 to celebrate 20 years of EA SPORTS!
How Great is that? (Bronze)	Find a team of the week player in an Ultimate Team pack
I'll have that one (Bronze)	Open your first pack in FIFA 12 Ultimate Team
Legendary (Silver)	Win a game vs. the CPU on legendary difficulty against a club of the same or higher star level
Legends start with Victories (Bronze)	Win a match with your FIFA 12 Ultimate Team club
Marquee Signing (Silver)	Purchase a Gold Player from the trade market for 15,000 or more coins using Buy now
Massive Signing (Bronze)	Sign a player better than anyone else on your club during the transfer window
Megged (Silver)	Successfully dribble the ball through a defender's legs
New Club in Town (Bronze)	Create your FIFA 12 Ultimate Team club
No Draw for You! (Bronze)	Score a 90th minute winner in a game vs. the CPU
Pack King (Gold)	Open 100 packs in FIFA 12 Ultimate Team
Path to the Cup (Bronze)	Win a cup game in Head to Head Seasons
Precision Tackler (Bronze)	Obtain a successful tackle percentage of 80% with a minimum of 5 tackles in a game
Procrastinator (Bronze)	Sign a player on Deadline Day in the transfer window in Career Mode
Puppet Master (Bronze)	Talk to the Press in Career Mode
Quickly Now! (Bronze)	Score shortly after a quick throw-in
Riding Bikes (Silver)	Score with a bicycle kick
Ruud Boy (Bronze)	Score a goal on a volley
Sweet Music (Bronze)	Set up some Custom Audio in FIFA 12
Tournament Victory (Bronze)	Win a tournament in FIFA 12 Ultimate Team
Trophy Time (Silver)	Win the league title in any league in Career Mode
Virtual Debut (Bronze)	Play an online Pro Club or Pro Ranked match with your Virtual Pro
Virtual Legend (Silver)	Play 50 Matches with your Virtual Pro
Warrior (Bronze)	Score a goal after suffering a non-contact injury with a player
We'll need a larger trophy case (Silver)	Win your 10th trophy in FIFA 12 Ultimate Team
Youth is Served (Silver)	Sign a player to your youth squad in Career Mode

FIFA STREET (PLAYSTATION 3)

TROPHY

UNLOCKABLE	HOW TO UNLOCK
5 Tool Player (Gold)	Upgrade 5 attributes on a created player to maximum
Are we there yet? (Bronze)	Reach the World Tour map screen for the first time
Attributed Success (Silver)	Upgrade one of your created players attributes to Max
Career Milestone (Silver)	Score 100 goals with your created player in any game modes

Challenge the pros (Bronze)	Win a street challenge against an authentic club team in stage 4 of world tour
European Champion (Silver)	Win stage 3 of World Tour
Friendly Publicity (Bronze)	Watch a video posted by one of your Friends
Geometry was good for something (Bronze)	Score a goal by deflecting the ball off a wall
Globetrotter (Gold)	In any game mode win a match/event in every venue
Got any Nutmeg? (Bronze)	Panna your first Opponent
It's Tricky (Silver)	Unlock 10 tricks on a created player
Local Heroes (Bronze)	Win the final national tournament with at least 8 created players on your team
Making new Friends (Bronze)	Add a new Friend using the Friend Recommendation feature
Mighty Heroes (Silver)	Have a team with at least 8 created players that are level 50 or higher
Mister Entertainment (Silver)	Earn 100,000 Style Points with your created player in any game mode
Moving on up (Silver)	In a street season obtain promotion to the next division
National Street Champion (Silver)	Win stage 2 of World Tour
New Champion (Bronze)	Win a World Tour Tournament for the first time
Online Cup Champion (Silver)	Win any Online Cup
Online Dominance (Gold)	Win all 9 online cups
Online-Enthusiast (Bronze)	Win a game of 5 a side, 6 a side and Futsal online
Regional Street Champion (Bronze)	Win stage 1 of World Tour
Rush Keepers! (Silver)	Score a goal while controlling your Goal Keeper
Shopping Spree (Bronze)	Wear an Unlocked item in any game mode
Sightseer (Silver)	In any game mode win a match/event in 50% of the venues
Street Legend (Silver)	Defeat Messi in a street challenge game
Time to Celebrate (Bronze)	Unlock a created player celebration and perform it in game
Total Street Domination (Platinum)	Collect all FIFA Street Trophies
Ultimate Humiliation (Bronze)	Score a goal with a Panna
Very Entertaining (Silver)	Earn at least 1500 Style Points without losing possession
Video Proof (Bronze)	Upload a saved video
Watching Film (Bronze)	Watch a gameplay tutorial video
Who brought the snacks? (Bronze)	Win a tournament with a local Co-Op player
World Grand Champion (Gold)	Win stage 4 of World Tour
World Tour Around the World (Silver)	Win any World Tour tournament Online

FIFA STREET (XBOX 360)

ACHIEVEMENT

UNLOCKABLE	HOW TO UNLOCK
5 Tool Player (50)	Upgrade 5 attributes on a created player to maximum as the lead profile
Are we there yet? (10)	Reach the World Tour map screen for the first time as the lead profile
Attributed Success (25)	Upgrade one of your created players attributes to Max as the lead profile

Career Milestone (25)	Score 100 goals with your created player in any game modes as the lead profile
Challenge the pros (20)	Win a street challenge against an authentic club team in stage 4 of world tour as the lead profile
European Champion (50)	Win stage 3 of World Tour as the lead profile
Friendly Publicity (15)	Watch a video posted by one of your Friends as the lead profile
Geometry was good for something (20)	Score a goal by deflecting the ball off a wall
Globetrotter (95)	In any game mode win a match/event in every venue as the lead profile
Got any Nutmeg? (15)	Panna your first Opponent
It's Tricky (20)	Unlock 10 tricks on a created player as the lead profile
Local Heroes (25)	Win the final national tournament with at least 8 created players on your team as the lead profile
Making new friends (15)	Add a new Friend using the Friend Recommendation feature as the lead profile
Mighty Heroes (40)	Have a team with at least 8 created players that are level 50 or higher as the lead profile
Mister Entertainment (25)	Earn 100,000 Style Points with your created player in any game mode as the lead profile
Moving on up (25)	In a street season obtain promotion to the next division as the lead profile
National Street Champion (25)	Win stage 2 of World Tour as the lead profile
New Champion (15)	Win a World Tour Tournament for the first time as the lead profile
Online Cup Champion (25)	Win any Online Cup as the lead profile
Online Dominance (100)	Win all 9 online cups as the lead profile
Online Enthusiast (20)	Win a game of 5 a side, 6 a side and Futsal online as the lead profile
Regional Street Champion (20)	Win stage 1 of World Tour as the lead profile
Rush Keepers! (25)	Score a goal while controlling your Goal Keeper
Shopping Spree (10)	Wear an Unlocked item in any game mode as the lead profile
Sightseer (25)	In any game mode win a match/event in 50% of the venues as the lead profile
Street Legend (20)	Defeat Messi in a street challenge game as the lead profile
Time to Celebrate (15)	Unlock a created player celebration and perform it in game as the lead profile
Ultimate Humiliation (15)	Score a goal with a Panna
Very Entertaining (25)	Earn at least 1500 Style Points without losing possession
Video Proof (20)	Upload a saved video as the lead profile
Watching Film (20)	Watch a gameplay tutorial video as the lead profile
Who brought the snacks? (15)	Win a tournament with a local Co-Op player as the lead profile
World Grand Champion (100)	Win stage 4 of World Tour as the lead profile
World Tour Around the World (30)	Win any World Tour tournament Online as the lead profile

FIFA WORLD CUP SOUTH AFRICA - 2010 (XBOX 360)

CELEBRATIONS

In the Main menu, go to EA Extras and then enter the codes below.

EFFECT	CODE
Flying Dive	ZTSMBDRGJLQBUMSA
African Dance	QCZCGTXKWYWBNPJK
Baby Cradle	VXYJZLXTRPBZUXXJ
Side Slide	BNDIPYYTCDZVJCCN
River Dance	NLGAHWCHCCUCTNUH
Prancing Bird	YMEOCBDOIWYUEVQN
Ice Skating	TLHDMYMCUITLAYJL

FIFA WORLD CUP SOUTH AFRICA - 2010 (WII)

UNLOCKABLES

UNLOCKABLE	HOW TO UNLOCK
Play the World Classic XI Team	Get at least a bronze medal against every team in Zakumi's Dream Team Mode.
Use the World Classic XI Team	Beat the World Classic XI Team (Hit the Pitch Mode only).

CELEBRATION PACKS

UNLOCKABLE	HOW TO UNLOCK
Goal Celebration Pack #1	Win the Adidas Golden Boot Award by winning the FIFA World Cup and having one of the members on your team be the top scorer of the World Cup.
Goal Celebration Pack #2	Take the lead by scoring within the first 5 minutes of any match.
Goal Celebration Pack #3	Score within 5 minutes following a goal you just made.
Goal Celebration Pack #4	Score 100 goals.
Goal Celebration Pack #5	Perform a Hat Trick or score three goals with the same player in a single match.

FINAL FANTASY CRYSTAL CHRONICLES: THE CRYSTAL BEARERS (WII)

UNLOCKABLES

UNLOCKABLE	HOW TO UNLOCK
Layle Moogle in Alfitaria Entrance	Start a New Game +
New Game +	Defeat the final boss, then save at the end.

FINAL FANTASY FABLES: CHOCOBO'S DUNGEON (WII)

ADDITIONAL DUNGEONS

UNLOCKABLE	HOW TO UNLOCK
Chocobo's Memories (Standard Dungeon)	Accessed through the Chocobo statue in the park
Croma's Future (Special Dungeon)	Accessed through Croma in Stella's House

JOBS

Jobs are like classes. You begin with the "Natural" job and can unlock nine others during the game.

UNLOCKABLE	HOW TO UNLOCK
Black Mage	Make it to 10F in Guardian of the Flame.
Dancer	Enter "Pirouette" (capital P at the beginning, the rest lowercase, AND a musical note at the end) as a Romantic Phrase.
Dark Knight	Defeat Croma Shade in 30F in Guardian of the Light.
Dragoon	Complete Meja's Memories.
Knight	Complete Freja's Memories.
Ninja	Complete Volg's Memories.

Scholar	Defeat the four elements in 20F Guardian of the Water.
Thief	Steal the item behind Merchant Hero X in any of his dungeon shops.
White Mage	Complete Pastor Roche's Memories.

FINAL FANTASY IV: COMPLETE COLLECTION (PSP)

UNLOCKABLE

UNLOCKABLE	HOW TO UNLOCK
Lunar Ruins	You must beat the final boss with each character atleast once.
Music Player	Beating the game once unlocks the Music Player. It can be accessed under "Extra" on the title screen.
The Cave of Trials	Once you unlock Party Switching and head back to Mysidia, you'll be informed of a new challenge at Mt. Ordeals. A scene will occur once you get there and the Cave of Trials will be accessible.
Easter Egg	The Developers' room is now renamed the 1991 Dev Team Office. To get there, reach the Underworld for the first time. After gaining access to the armory (after beating Golbez in the crystal room) go down to the Weapon/Armor room and go behind the pillar between the two shop desks. From there, go up, you'll then be in the Lali Ho Pub (another secret room). Then, go right to where there's a dark marking on the floor and progress right through the wall and down a stairway. You will now be at the 1991 Dev Team Office entrance, where you can talk to the developers of the original game, complete with their rank back when they worked on the game in 1991.
"1991 Dev Team Office"	The Developers' room is now renamed the 1991 Dev Team Office. To get there, reach the Underworld for the first time. After gaining access to the armory (after beating Golbez in the crystal room) go down to the Weapon/Armor room and go behind the pillar between the two shop desks. From there, go up, you'll then be in the Lali Ho Pub (another secret room). Then, go right to where there's a dark marking on the floor and progress right through the wall and down a stairway. You will now be at the 1991 Dev Team Office entrance, where you can talk to the developers of the original game, complete with their rank back when they worked on the game in 1991.

FINAL FANTASY XIII (XBOX 360, PLAYSTATION 3)

GAMER PICS

UNLOCKABLE	HOW TO UNLOCK
Fang	Obtain the Treasure Hunter (Gold) trophy.
Hope	Obtain the Instrument of Change (Gold) trophy.
Lightning	Obtain the Superstar (Gold)" trophy.
Sazh	Obtain the Lore Master (Gold) trophy.
Serah	Obtain the Ultimate Hero (Platinum) trophy.
Snow	Obtain the L'Cie Paragon (Gold) trophy.
Vanille	Obtain the Instrument of Faith (Silver) trophy.

FINAL FIGHT: DOUBLE IMPACT (PLAYSTATION 3)

STREET FIGHTER CARTOON
Earn 570,000 points in the Uptown stage and you will be able to view the episode of the "Street Fighter Cartoon" in which the Final Fight Characters have cameo roles.

FINAL FIGHT: DOUBLE IMPACT (XBOX 360)

STREET FIGHTER CARTOON
Earn 570,000 points in the Uptown stage and you will be able to view the episode of the "Street Fighter Cartoon" in which the Final Fight Characters have cameo roles.

FINAL SOLDIER (WII)

LEVEL SELECT

UNLOCKABLE	HOW TO UNLOCK
Level Select	Before the demo starts, press ⬅, ⬅, ①, ⬇, ⬆, ②, ⬇, ⬇, ⬇, ⬇

FLATOUT: HEAD ON (PSP)

CODES

At main screen, go to Extras, then to Enter Code.

EFFECT	CODE
All Cars and 1 Million Credits	GIEVEPIX
All Tracks	GIVEALL
Big Rig	ELPUEBLO
Big Rig Truck	RAIDERS
Flatmobile Car	WOTKINS
Mob Car	BIGTRUCK
Pimpster Car	RUTTO
Rocket Car	KALJAKOPPA
School Bus	GIEVCARPLZ

FLOCK (PLAYSTATION 3 , XBOX 360)

UNLOCKABLES

UNLOCKABLE	HOW TO UNLOCK
Blanka Ball	Get a perfect abduction on all single-player levels.
Chicken Trophy	Get at least a Bronze Medal on all single-player levels.
Cow Trophy	Get Gold Medals on all single-player levels.
Infinite Boost	Get Gold Medals on all single-player levels.
Pig Trophy	Get at least a Silver Medal on all single-player levels.
Sheep Trophy	Get a perfect abduction on all single-player levels.

FOLKLORE (PLAYSTATION 3)

SPECIAL FOLKS

UNLOCKABLE	HOW TO UNLOCK
Ellen—Collbrande	Score 150,000 Campaign Points in Dungeon Trial mode.
Ellen—Duergar	Score 30,000 Campaign Points in Dungeon Trial mode.
Ellen—Kaladbolg	Upload a 4,500-point dungeon.
Keats—Alphard	Upload a 4,500-point dungeon.
Keats—Collbrande	Score 150,000 Campaign Points in Dungeon Trial mode.
Keats—Duergar	Score 30,000 Campaign Points in Dungeon Trial mode.
Keats—Valiant	Score 100,000 Campaign Points in Dungeon Trial mode.

FORZA MOTORSPORT 4 (XBOX 360)

ACHIEVEMENT

UNLOCKABLE	HOW TO UNLOCK
Amateur (25)	Complete the first year of Season Play.
Autocrosser (10)	Complete 10 Autocross events without hitting gate cones.
Awesome Drift (20)	Earn a perfect Drift score.
Born Competitor (30)	Post a time in every Rivals mode event.
Bucket List (80)	Finish 1st in every single race in the Event List in Career play mode.
Car Explorer (10)	Fully explore any car in Autovista.

Champion (25)	Complete the ninth year of Season Play.
Clubbed Up (15)	Create or join a Car Club.
Clubman (25)	Complete the second year of Season Play.
Daily Rewards (5)	Visit the Message Center on at least five unique days.
Driver Level 1 (20)	Reach Driver Level 1 in Career mode.
Driver Level 10 (20)	Reach Driver Level 10 in Career mode.
Driver Level 20 (20)	Reach Driver Level 20 in Career mode.
Driver Level 30 (20)	Reach Driver Level 30 in Career mode.
Driver Level 40 (20)	Reach Driver Level 40 in Career mode.
Driver Level 50 (20)	Reach Driver Level 50 in Career mode.
Elite (25)	Complete the eighth year of Season Play.
Entrepreneur (10)	Sell a car tuning, paint job, or vinyl group from your storefront.
Exclusive Taste (50)	Own the five most expensive cars in the game (not including DLC).
Expert (25)	Complete the fifth year of Season Play.
Factory Driver (60)	Get any Car Manufacturer to Affinity level 50.
Ferrari Collector (40)	Own every Ferrari included on Disc 1.
Flat Out (5)	Earn a perfect Speed score.
Forza Faithful (15)	Import a file from Forza Motorsport 3.
Forza World Tourer (60)	Finish a race on every race track in Forza Motorsport 4.
Grease Monkey (10)	Create a car tuning file for your car.
Here's My Card (10)	Create a custom playercard with badges and titles.
Kingpin (5)	Knock down a gold bowling pin in Car Bowling.
Legend (50)	Complete the tenth year of Season Play.
Legendary Battle (15)	Beat a Ferrari 330 P4 in any race while driving a Ford GT40 Mark II.
Look Ma, No Controller! (5)	Use Kinect to drive any car in Free Play.
Masters (25)	Complete the seventh year of Season Play.
My Car is Your Car (10)	Share a car in your garage with your Car Club.
Nice Pass (15)	Earn a perfect Pass score.
On Location (20)	Take a photo of any car in every Home Space.
Outta Time (10)	Reach 88 mph in a DeLorean.
Painter (10)	Create a paint job or vinyl group for your car.
Perfect Turn (15)	Earn a perfect Turn score.
Professional (25)	Complete the sixth year of Season Play.
Rivals Shootout (10)	Race and defeat an opponent in Rivals mode.
Semi-Pro (25)	Complete the fourth year of Season Play.
Show Off (10)	Upload a movie to Forzamotorsport.net.
Slipstreamin' (5)	Earn a perfect Draft score.
Speed Demon (10)	Reach 240 mph in any car.
Sportsman (25)	Complete the third year of Season Play.
Star in a Reasonably Priced Car (10)	Complete a lap around the TopGear Test Track while driving a KIA cee'd.
Unicorn Hunter (10)	Be the winning bidder on any "unicorn" car in the Auction House.
Welcome to Forza Motorsport (15)	Complete the very first race in the game.

UNLOCKABLE

UNLOCKABLE	HOW TO UNLOCK
Autovista T-Shirt	Fully explore any car in Autovista.
Stopwatch Cap	Post a time in every Rivals Mode Event.
1931 Bentley 8 Litre	Complete 9 Autovista Challenges.
Halo 3 Warthog	Complete all Autovista challenges.

FROGGER (XBOX 360)

MAKE FROGGER BIGGER

UNLOCKABLE	HOW TO UNLOCK
Make Frogger Bigger	At the screen where you are selecting to choose One or Two players, enter ⬆ ⬆ ⬇ ⬇ ⬅ ➡ ⬅ ➡ Ⓑ Ⓐ

FRONTLINES: FUEL OF WAR (PLAYSTATION 3)

MORE LEVELS

To unlock two extra single-player levels, insert the following passwords at the in-game Passwords menu.

UNLOCKABLE	HOW TO UNLOCK
Urban Level	sp-street
Village Level	sp-village

FULL AUTO 2: BATTLELINES (PLAYSTATION 3)

In the Option menu, select the Cheats option to enter these codes.

UNLOCKABLE	CODE
Unlock Sceptre and Mini-Rockets	10E6CUSTOMER
Unlock Vulcan and Flamethrower	5FINGERDISCOUNT

FULL AUTO 2: BATTLELINES (PSP)

Enter these codes in the codes section under features.

UNLOCKABLE	CODE
All Cars	⬆, ⬆, ➡, ➡, ⬅, ⬇, ⬆, ➡, ⬇, ⬇, ⬅, ⬇
All Events	START, ⬅, SELECT, ➡, ➡, ▲, ✕, ■, START, R, ⬇, SELECT

CODES & CHEATS

G.I. JOE: THE RISE OF COBRA (XBOX 360)

CODES

Enter the following codes with the D-pad at the Main menu. A sound effect will play if you entered the code correctly.

EFFECT	CODE
Shana "Scarlett" O'Hara Costumae	⬅,⬆,➡,➡,⬇
Duke Costume	⬅,⬆,⬇,⬆,➡,⬇

GAIN GROUN (WII)

LEVEL SELECT

UNLOCKABLE	HOW TO UNLOCK
Level Select	On the Options screen press Ⓐ, ©, Ⓑ, ©

GALAGA '90 (WII)

UNLOCKABLES

UNLOCKABLE	HOW TO UNLOCK
Galactic Bonus	Just stand still (don't move) and don't shoot in the bonus stage.
Red Capsule	Hold ⬆ and press RUN at the title screen. The capsule on the ship will turn red instead of blue to confirm code entry. Shoot the last target on the first level to capture the red capsule and power-up to a triple ship.

GAME OF THRONES (PLAYSTATION 3)

TROPHY

UNLOCKABLE	HOW TO UNLOCK
'Tis but a scratch! (Bronze)	Chapter 9: suffer all the physical abuse during the torture sequence
Am I not merciful? (Bronze)	Chapter 8: save Orys from the City Watch
As high as honor (Bronze)	Finish chapter 12
Bloodhound (Bronze)	Chapter 7: find all the corrupt brothers of the Night's Watch
Clever dog (Bronze)	Gain all the skills linked to the dog with Mors
Collector (Silver)	Seize the three objects of value from the Collector with Alester
Come try me (Bronze)	Finish chapter 11
Dark wings, dark words (Bronze)	Finish chapter 3
Dead men sing no songs (Bronze)	Finish chapter 6
Desecration (Bronze)	Chapter 8: find the key in Alester's father's tomb
Devout follower (Silver)	Find all the statues of the Seven
Disciplinarian (Bronze)	Chapter 1: confront the four recruits during the training session with Mors
End of the line (Bronze)	Chapter 6: don't lose pursuit of the bastard
Endless watch (Silver)	Send 10 recruits to the Wall with Mors
Family is hope... (Bronze)	Finish chapter 2
Family, duty, honor (Bronze)	Finish chapter 8

Fetch! (Silver)	Use Mors' dog's sense of smell to find 5 secret objects
Fire and blood (Bronze)	Finish chapter 10
Golden touch (Silver)	Acquire 1 golden dragon
Great teamwork (Silver)	Finish the game without a single ally (except Mors and Alester) being KO'd
Growing strong (Bronze)	Finish chapter 13
Hear me roar (Bronze)	Finish chapter 4
Here we stand (Bronze)	Finish chapter 7
Know your place (Bronze)	Chapter 2: protect the nobility with Alester
Lesser of two evils (Bronze)	Chapter 14: come to the aid of the Reapers
Man of the people (Bronze)	Chapter 2: protect the people with Alester
Man's best friend (Bronze)	Kill 10 enemies with Mors' dog in skinchanger mode
Master of light and flame (Bronze)	Master of light and flame
Master-at-arms (Bronze)	Learn all skills within a character's stance tree
Merciless (Bronze)	Mete out 5 deathblows
My darkest hour (Bronze)	Chapter 15: execute the judgement passed down on the Westfords
Once more unto the breach (Silver)	Chapter 7: attack the camp without killing the sentries at the start
Pimp (Silver)	Convince Bethany to return to Chataya's brothel with Alester
Platinum trophy (Platinum)	Earn all the trophies in Game of Thrones
Proud to be faithful (Bronze)	Finish chapter 5
Quiet as a shadow (Silver)	Chapter 13: reach Jeyne's room without ever being seen
R'hllor sees all (Silver)	Find 10 secrets with the vision of R'hllor
Red priest of R'hllor (Bronze)	Finish Alester's story
Swift and deadly (Silver)	Chapter 11: bring an end to the trial by combat in under 2 minutes
Sworn brother (Bronze)	Finish Mors' Story
The butcher comes to dinner (Silver)	Chapter 9: kill 6 of Lord Harlton's soldiers during the fight at dinner
The Greatest (Silver)	Emerge triumphant in the final arena combat
The night is dark... (Bronze)	Finish chapter 15
The true face of the Spider (Bronze)	Lose the final battle
Thorough (Gold)	Complete all the secondary objectives of the story
True warrior (Bronze)	Kill 400 enemies
Unbowed, unbent, unbroken (Bronze)	Finish chapter 9
Unrivaled strategist (Silver)	Chapter 12: take back Riverspring with a total victory
Valar morghulis (Bronze)	Finish chapter 14
Warlord (Silver)	Reach the maximum level
Winter is coming (Bronze)	Finish chapter 1

NEW!

A
B
C
D
E
F
G
H
I
J
K
L
M
N
O
P
Q
R
S
T
U
V
W
X
Y
Z

GAME OF THRONES (XBOX 360)

ACHIEVEMENT

UNLOCKABLE	HOW TO UNLOCK
'Tis but a scratch ! (20)	Chapter 9: suffer all the physical abuse during the torture sequence
Am I not merciful? (15)	Chapter 8: save Orys from the City Watch
As high as honor (10)	Finish chapter 12
Bloodhound (25)	Chapter 7: find all the corrupt brothers of the Night's Watch
Clever dog (30)	Gain all the skills linked to the dog with Mors
Collector (30)	Seize the three objects of value from the Collector with Alester
Come try me (10)	Finish chapter 11
Dark wings, dark words (10)	Finish chapter 3
Dead men sing no songs (10)	Finish chapter 6
Desecration (15)	Chapter 8: find the key in Alester's father's tomb
Devout follower (30)	Find all the statues of the Seven
Disciplinarian (10)	Chapter 1: confront the four recruits during the training session with Mors
End of the line (20)	Chapter 6: don't lose pursuit of the bastard
Endless watch (30)	Send 10 recruits to the Wall with Mors
Family is hope... (10)	Finish chapter 2
Family, duty, honor (10)	Finish chapter 8
Fetch! (30)	Use Mors' dog's sense of smell to find 5 secret objects
Fire and blood (10)	Finish chapter 10
Golden touch (30)	Acquire 1 golden dragon
Great teamwork (30)	Finish the game without a single ally (except Mors and Alester) being KO'd
Growing strong (10)	Finish chapter 13
Hear me roar (10)	Finish chapter 4
Here we stand (10)	Finish chapter 7
Know your place (15)	Chapter 2: protect the nobility with Alester
Lesser of two evils (15)	Chapter 14: come to the aid of the Reapers
Man of the people (15)	Chapter 2: protect the people with Alester
Man's best friend (20)	Kill 10 enemies with Mors' dog in skinchanger mode
Master of light and flame (30)	Gain all the skills linked to R'hllor's fire with Alester
Master-at-arms (25)	Learn all skills within a character's stance tree
Merciless (20)	Mete out 5 deathblows
My darkest hour (10)	Chapter 15: execute the judgement passed down on the Westfords
Once more unto the breach (35)	Chapter 7: attack the camp without killing the sentries at the start
Pimp (30)	Convince Bethany to return to Chataya's brothel with Alester
Proud to be faithful (10)	Finish chapter 5
Quiet as a shadow (35)	Chapter 13: reach Jeyne's room without ever being seen
R'hllor sees all (30)	Find 10 secrets with the vision of R'hllor
Red priest of R'hllor (10)	Finish Alester's story

Swift and deadly (35)	Chapter 11: bring an end to the trial by combat in under 2 minutes
Sworn brother (10)	Finish Mors' Story
The butcher comes to dinner (35)	Chapter 9: kill 6 of Lord Harlton's soldiers during the fight at dinner
The Greatest (30)	Emerge triumphant in the final arena combat
The night is dark... (10)	Finish chapter 15
The true face of the Spider (10)	Lose the final battle
Thorough (40)	Complete all the secondary objectives of the story
True warrior (20)	Kill 400 enemies
Unbowed, unbent, unbroken (10)	Finish chapter 9
Unrivaled strategist (35)	Chapter 12: take back Riverspring with a total victory
Valar morghulis (10)	Finish chapter 14
Warlord (30)	Reach the maximum level
Winter is coming (10)	Finish chapter 1

GAUNTLET (XBOX 360)

WALLS BECOME EXITS

UNLOCKABLE	HOW TO UNLOCK
Walls Become Exits	On any level, all players must stand still for 200 seconds. After 200 seconds, all the walls in the level will become exit doors. If players wish to, they can shoot enemies, and change the direction of their shooting, just as long as they do not move. This works on single and multiplayer.

GEARS OF WAR 3 (XBOX 360)

ACHIEVEMENT

UNLOCKABLE	HOW TO UNLOCK
Ain't My First Rodeo (50)	Complete all campaign Acts on Hardcore Difficulty (Standard or Arcade).
All for One, One for All (10)	Earn the Bronze "Force Multiplier" medal.
Anvil Gate's Last Resort (10)	Story Progression in Act 3 Chapter 1 (Standard or Arcade).
Award Winning Tactics (25)	Earn at least one Onyx medal.
Baird's Favorite Kind of Toy (10)	Story Progression in Act 4 Chapter 5 (Standard or Arcade).
Brothers to the End (10)	Story Progression in Act 3 Chapter 5 (Standard or Arcade).
Collector (5)	Recover 5 Campaign Collectibles (any difficulty, Standard or Arcade).
Enriched and Fortified (10)	Complete all 50 waves of Horde mode (any difficulty, any map).
First Among Equals (25)	Earn the Silver "Number 1" medal.
Hoarder (15)	Recover all 42 Campaign Collectibles (any difficulty, Standard or Arcade).
It's All About the Loot! (25)	Earn the Bronze "Loot Courtesan" medal.
Judge, Jury and Executioner (10)	Get a kill with every possible execution finishing move(any mode).
Lambency (50)	Execute an Epic employee, or someone who already has Lambency, in Versus multiplayer (any mode).
Level 10 (10)	Reach level 10.
Level 15 (15)	Reach level 15.

CODES & CHEATS

Level 25 (25)	Reach level 25.
Level 5 (5)	Reach level 5.
Level 50 (50)	Reach level 50.
Look at That, Instant Summer. (10)	Story Progression in Act 5 Chapter 2 (Standard or Arcade).
Lost Your Good Driver Discount (10)	Story Progression in Act 3 Chapter 3 (Standard or Arcade).
Marcus, It's Your Father (5)	Story Progression in Prologue (Standard or Arcade).
My Fellow Gears (50)	Complete all Campaign Acts in Co-op (any difficulty, Standard or Arcade).
My Turf! Cougars Territory! (10)	Story Progression in Act 1 Chapter 5 (Standard or Arcade).
Oh Yeah, It's Pirate Time (10)	Story Progression in Act 2 Chapter 5 (Standard or Arcade).
Ok. Faith. Yeah. Got It. (10)	Story Progression in Act 5 Chapter 5 (Standard or Arcade).
Okay, Now We Find Hoffman (10)	Story Progression in Act 2 Chapter 1 (Standard or Arcade).
Pack Rat (10)	Recover 20 Campaign Collectibles (any difficulty, Standard or Arcade).
Putting it Scientifically… (10)	Story Progression in Act 1 Chapter 6 (Standard or Arcade).
Ready for More (50)	Complete all campaign Acts on Casual or Normal Difficulty (Standard or Arcade).
Remember the Fallen (15)	Recover all 15 COG Tags during the Campaign (any difficulty, Standard or Arcade).
Respect for the Dead (5)	Your respect for the dead earned you access to Griffin's special weapons stash.
Seriously 3.0 (100)	Reach level 100 and earn every Onyx medal.
Socialite (70)	Earn the Onyx "War Supporter" medal.
Swimmin' in Glowie Gravy (10)	Story Progression in Act 1 Chapter 2 (Standard or Arcade).
Thanks For Flying GasBag Airways (10)	Story Progression in Act 2 Chapter 7 (Standard or Arcade).
That's Just Crazy (75)	Complete all campaign Acts on Insane Difficulty (Standard or Arcade).
The Versus Sampler Platter (10)	Complete one match of all six Versus game modes (Standard or Casual).
Think You Can Handle That? (10)	Story Progression in Act 4 Chapter 3 (Standard or Arcade).
Wait, What Time is it? (10)	Earn the maximum Consecutive Match Bonus in Versus multiplayer (Standard or Casual).
Was it Good For You? (10)	Story Progression in Act 3 Chapter 2 (Standard or Arcade).
We Few, We Happy Few… (50)	Complete all Campaign Acts in 4 player Co-op (any difficulty, Standard or Arcade).
We Struck Gold, Son! (10)	Story Progression in Act 1 Chapter 3 (Standard or Arcade).
Welcome To -redacted- (10)	Story Progression in Act 4 Chapter 6 (Standard or Arcade).
Welcome to Arcade Mode (10)	Complete 5 Arcade Campaign chapters in co-op (any difficulty).
Welcome to Beast Mode (10)	Survive all 12 waves of Beast mode (any difficulty, any map).
Welcome to Horde Mode (10)	Survive the first 10 waves of Horde mode (any difficulty, any map).

Welcome to the Big multiplayer. Leagues (0)	Demonstrate your skill in Casual Versus
Welcome to Versus (10)	Kill 10 enemies in Team Deathmatch (Standard or Casual).
Wreaking Locust mode Vengence (10)	Get a kill with every Locust monster in Beast (any difficulty).
You're Dead! Now Stay Dead! (10)	Story Progression in Act 5 Chapter 6 (Standard or Arcade).

UNLOCKABLE

UNLOCKABLE	HOW TO UNLOCK
Aaron Griffin	Receive the Big Money Onyx Medal or "Like" the Gears of War 3 Facebook page to get an unlock code.
Adam Fenix	Preorder code with purchase of the Gears of War 3 Limited or Epic Edition.
Anthony Carmine	Reach Level 75.
Benjamin Carmine	Reach Level 34.
Chairman Prescott	Receive the silver Allfathers medal.
Civilian Anya	Reach Level 45.
Classic Baird	Reach Level 30.
Classic Cole	Reach Level 23.
Classic Dom	Reach Level 17.
Classic Marcus	Receive the silver Veteran medal.
Clayton Carmine	Reach Level 14.
COG Gear	Reach Level 2.
Cole Train	Play the multiplayer beta.
Colonel Hoffman	Reach Level 50.
Commando Dom	Preorder code from GameStop.
Dizzy Wallin	Reach Level 7.
Golden Gear	Receive the bronze War Supporter medal.
Jace Stratton	Reach Level 10.
Mechanic Baird	Preorder code from Best Buy.
Samantha Byrne	Reach Level 4.
Superstar Cole	Receive the gold MVP medal.
Unarmored Marcus	Finish the campaign on any difficulty level.
Beast Rider	Reach Level 5.
Flame Grenadier	Reach Level 26.
Golden Hunter	Receive the gold Master-at-Arms medal.
Golden Miner	Receive the gold Rifleman medal.
Grenadier	Reach Level 39.
Hunter	Reach Level 8.
Hunter Elite	Reach Level 60.
Kantus	Receive the gold Medic medal.
Miner	Reach Level 3.
Savage Grenadier Elite	Preorder code from Walmart.
Savage Kantus	Preorder code from Amazon.com.
Savage Theron Guard	Complete Beast Mode without failing, on all difficulties.
Sniper	Receive the bronze Headshot medal.
Spotter	Reach Level 20.

NEW!

A
B
C
D
E
F
G
H
I
J
K
L
M
N
O
P
Q
R
S
T
U
V
W
X
Y
Z

Theron Guard	Reach Level 12.
Big Explosions	In any mode, unlock the Hail Mary ribbon 100 times.
Big Head	In Horde Mode, unlock the Gold Horder medal.
Comet	In Versus Mode, unlock the Gold Shock Trooper medal.
Enemy Regeneration	In Arcade Mode, unlock the Silver Afficianado medal.
Flower Blood	In Arcade Mode, unlock the Silver King of Cog medal.
Friendly Fire	In Co-op Campaign, complete the co-op campaign with four players.
Infinite Ammo	In Horde Mode, unlock the Combat Engineer ribbon 100 times.
Instagib Melee	In Beast Mode, play as a Wretch and score 200 kills.
Laugh Track	Unlock the Bronze Tour of Duty, For the Horde, I'm a Beast, and Warmonger medals.
Must Active Reload	Unlock the Silver Active Reloader medal.
Pinata	In Beast Mode, unlock the Gold Investor medal.
Super Reload	In Versus Mode, unlock the Bronze Master at Arms medal.
Vampire	In Versus Mode, unlock the Executioner ribbon 100 times.
Horde Shirt	Get the "Welcome to Horde mode" achievement for beating Horde mode.
Locust Drone Mask	Get the "Welcome to Beast Mode" achievement for beating Beast mode.
Marcus' Doo-rag	Beat the campaign on any difficulty.

GENPEI TOUMADEN (WII)

UNLOCKABLE

UNLOCKABLE	HOW TO UNLOCK
Options Menu	At the title screen, press ⬆, ⬇, ⬇, ⬇, ①, ②

GHOSTBUSTERS THE VIDEOGAME (PLAYSTATION 3, XBOX 360)

NES GHOSTBUSTERS ENDING SCREEN

In the Ghostbusters headquarters, one of the monitors on the upstairs desks has the ending screen from the original Ghostbusters game on the NES. The monitor comes complete with all the spelling and punctuation errors.

GHOULS 'N GHOSTS (WII)

UNLOCKABLES

UNLOCKABLE	HOW TO UNLOCK
Japanese Mode	Enter the Options menu. Choose "26" for the music and "56" for sound selections, then hold ⬆+ⓐ+Ⓑ+Ⓒ+START.
Slow-Mo	At the title screen, press ⬆, ⓐ, ⬇, ⓐ, ⬅, ⓐ, ➡, ⓐ. Begin the game, press START to pause, and hold Ⓑ and unpause.

LEVEL SELECT

Press ⬆, ⬇, ⬅, ➡ repeatedly at the title screen. You'll hear a harp if you did it right. Enter one of the following controller actions to select the corresponding level.

EFFECT	CODE
The Execution Place	Press START
The Floating Island	Press ⓐ, START
The Village of Decay	Press ⬆, START

Town of Fire	Press ⬇+Ⓐ, START
Baron Rankle's Tower	Press ⬇, START
Horrible Faced Mountain	Press ⬇+Ⓐ, START
The Crystal Forest	Press ⬇, START
The Ice Slopes	Press ⬇+Ⓐ, START
Beginning of Castle	Press ⬇, START
Middle of Castle	Press ⬇+Ⓐ, START
Loki	Press ⬇, START

DEBUG MODE

While "Press Start Button" is flashing at the title screen, input Ⓐ, Ⓐ, Ⓐ, Ⓐ, ⬇, ⬇, ⬇, ⬇ and you hear a chime. Start the game and you are in debug mode. Three functions can be accessed from the Pause menu now.

CODE	EFFECT
Tap ⬇ During Pause	Frame Advance
Pause, Ⓐ, Pause	Invincibility Toggle (falling is still fatal)
Hold Ⓑ During Pause	Slow Motion

THE GODFATHER (XBOX 360)

CHEAT CODES

CODE	EFFECT
Ⓨ Ⓧ Ⓨ Ⓧ Ⓑ Ⓐ	Full Ammo
Ⓧ Ⓑ Ⓐ Ⓨ Ⓐ ⓛⒷ	Full Health
Ⓨ Ⓧ Ⓧ Ⓧ Ⓨ ⓛⒷ (click)	Film Clips

INFINITE AMMO

UNLOCKABLE	HOW TO UNLOCK
Infinite Ammo	Become Don of NYC

THE GODFATHER: BLACKHAND EDITION (WII)

Enter these codes while the game is paused. For the film clips, enter that clip in the Film Archives screen.

UNLOCKABLE	CODE
$5,000	⊖, ②, ⊖, ⊖, ②, ⬇
Full Ammo	②, ⬇, ②, ⬇, ⊖, ⬇
Full Health	⬇, ⊖, ⬇, ⊖, ②, ⬇
Unlock Film Clips	②, ⊖, ②, ⊖, ⊖, ⬇

THESE CODES MAY ONLY BE ENTERED ROUGHLY EVERY FIVE MINUTES. IF YOU REALLY NEED THE HEALTH OR AMMO BEFORE FIVE MINUTES, PAUSE AND WAIT A FEW MINUTES, THEN ENTER THE GAME.

THE GODFATHER: THE DON'S EDITION (PLAYSTATION 3)

Enter these codes while the game is paused.

UNLOCKABLE	CODE
$5,000	■, ▲, ■, ■, ▲, ⓛ²
Full Ammo	▲, ⬅, ▲, ⬇, ■, Ⓡ①
Full Health	⬅, ■, ⬇, ▲, ⬇, ⓛ²

GOD OF WAR III (PLAYSTATION 3)

BONUS PLAY ITEMS

There are several bonus play items that can be collected throughout the game. Once they have been obtained, they can be used during bonus play (after you have beaten the game once). Note: enabling any bonus play items will disable Trophies.

UNLOCKABLE	HOW TO UNLOCK
Hades' Helm —Max health, magic, item meters	After killing Hades and jumping into the River Styx, swim down and to the right (against the current) and and locate the helm at the bottom of the river.

CODES & CHEATS

Helios' Shield —Triples combo meter	Located to the right of where you kill Helios.
Hera's Chalice —Slowly drains health meter	Located to the left of where Hera falls in the garden.
Hercules' Shoulder Guard —Decrease damage taken by a third.	After finding Hercules floating in the water, swim beneath him to find his Shoulder Guard.
Hermes' Coin—10x red orbs	Located behind the rubble while chasing Hermes.
Poseidon's Conch Shell —Infinite Magic	Located in the chamber where you rescue the Poseidon Princess.
Zeus' Eagle —Infinite Rage of Sparta	Climb the wall to the right of the Heart of Gaia; item is located on the ground in plain view.

UNLOCKABLES

UNLOCKABLE	HOW TO UNLOCK
Challenges of Olympus	Beat the game.
Combat arena	Beat all challenges.
Chaos Difficulty	Complete any difficulty.
Fear Kratos Costume	Complete any difficulty.

GOD OF WAR: GHOST OF SPARTA (PSP)

THE TEMPLE OF ZEUS

The Optional Bonus Temple that allows you to get the Grave Digger's Shovel relic.

UNLOCKABLE	HOW TO UNLOCK
The Temple of Zeus	Complete the game on any difficulty

COSTUMES

UNLOCKABLE	HOW TO UNLOCK
Deimos	Beat the game on Spartan mode (Hard)
Ghost of Sparta	Beat the game on God mode (Very Hard)
God Armor	Beat the game on Spartan mode (Hard)
Grave Digger	Beat Temple of Zeus
Robotos	Purchase for 250,000 in Temple of Zeus

MODES

UNLOCKABLE	HOW TO UNLOCK
Combat Arena	Beat the game.
God (Very Hard)	Beat the game.

SPECIAL ITEMS

These items can be used after finding them and completing the game.

UNLOCKABLE	HOW TO UNLOCK
Aphrodite's Ambrosia: Gain the Might of Sparta attack	Complete the sex minigame in Sparta 3 times.
Athena's Owl: Helps find treasures	After Kratos destroys the Athena statue in a cutscene, search the right side in a pile of debris.
Bonds of Ares: Infinite Magic	After you enter the Domain of Death through the Death Gate in Atlantis, look in the south section of the screen.
Callisto's Armlet: Automatically win context-sensitive minigames.	Right after you beat Callisto, search the ground by the battle.
Grave Digger's Shovel: Play as Zeus in Arena Combat	Unlock everything in the Temple of Zeus and follow the path created.
King's Ring: Collects 10 times the amount of red orbs	After King Midas turns the lava into gold, drop down by the area where he touched it.

GODZILLA: UNLEASHED (WII)

CODES

At the main menu, press Ⓐ and ✛ at the same time.

CODE	EFFECT
31406	Add 90,000 store points.
0829XX	Set day (where the "xx" equals the actual day you wish to set to).
411411	Show monster moves.
787321	Toggle version number.
204935	Unlock everything.

GOLDEN AXE (WII)

UNLOCKABLES

UNLOCKABLE	HOW TO UNLOCK
9 Continues	Hold ✛+Ⓐ+Ⓒ. Release and press START.
Level Select	Select Arcade mode. Hold ✛+Ⓑ and press START at the Character Selection screen. A number that corresponds to the starting level appears in the screen's upper left. Use the D-pad to change it to the level you want.

GOLDEN AXE 2 (WII)

UNLOCKABLES

UNLOCKABLE	HOW TO UNLOCK
Level Select	While the opening screen scrolls, simultaneously hold down Ⓐ+Ⓑ+Ⓒ+START. Still holding Ⓐ, release Ⓑ+Ⓒ and press them again. This brings you to the Options screen. Still holding Ⓐ, let go of the other two, pick "exit," and press Ⓑ+Ⓒ once more. You'll be back at the main menu. Still holding Ⓐ, release Ⓑ+Ⓒ and hit them again to choose the number of players. Keep all the buttons down and press START. Release only START, select your character, then still holding down Ⓐ+Ⓑ+Ⓒ, press ✛ and hit START. You can now select the level you want to play.
Level Select and 8 Credits (ultimate procedure)	With the cursor go to "Options" sign. Now press and hold Ⓐ+Ⓑ+Ⓒ. In the Options screen, release only Ⓑ+Ⓒ. Now configure the game if you want. Use Ⓑ to confirm successive selections, until the warrior selection. For the 8 credits, the cheat is identical, but release only Ⓐ and use START to confirm successive selections.

GRADIUS (WII)

UNLOCKABLES

UNLOCKABLE	HOW TO UNLOCK
10,000 Bonus Points	Get 6 power-ups so that the ? box is selected, then, when the thousands digit of your score is a 5, get a 7th power-up
Continue	At the Game Over Screen, press ✛, ✛, Ⓐ, Ⓑ, Ⓐ, Ⓑ, Ⓐ, START (once per game)
Full Option Command	Press START during the game, then press ✛, ✛, ✛, ✛, ✛, ✛, ✛, ✛, Ⓑ, Ⓐ, START.
Warp to Level 3 (after defeating Core Fighter)	In level 1, when the thousands digit of your score is even, destroy 4 hatches
Warp to Level 4	Destroy Xaerous Core at end of level 2 within 2 seconds of its core turning blue
Warp to Level 5 (after beating level)	Destroy 10 stone heads in level 3

CODES & CHEATS

GRADIUS 2 (WII)

UNLOCKABLES

UNLOCKABLE	HOW TO UNLOCK
30 Lives	At the title screen, press ⬆️⬆️, ⬇️, ⬇️, ⬅️, ➡️, ⬅️, ➡️, Ⓑ, Ⓐ
Max Out Abilities	During game, press ⬆️, ⬆️, ⬇️, ⬇️, ⬅️, ➡️, ⬅️, ➡️, Ⓑ, Ⓐ (once per level)
Sound Test Menu	Hold Ⓐ+Ⓑ and turn on. When the screen comes up, press START, hold Ⓐ+Ⓑ until title screen, then press START again.

GRADIUS 3 (WII)

UNLOCKABLES

UNLOCKABLE	HOW TO UNLOCK
30 Extra Ships	At the title screen, hold ◀ and press 🅨, 🅨, 🅨, START
Arcade Mode	In the Options menu, highlight the Game Level, and rapidly tap Ⓐ until the level turns into ARCADE
Extra Credits	At the title screen, press ⬇️ as many times as you can and then press START before the screen fades out
Easy Final Boss	The final boss, Bacterion, will die whether or not you attack him. Just dodge his blasts, and in 15 or so seconds, he will spontaneously die. Even cheaper, park your ship in the screen's bottom center, and you can't be hit!
Extended Demo Mode	Continue to hold Ⓐ through the initial demo, and you'll see the entire first stage including the boss.
Full Power-Up	Pause the game and press ⬆️,⬆️,⬇️,⬇️,◀,▶,◀,▶,🅨,🅨
Full Power-Up (without using the code)	Choose "speed down" for the "!" option in the Weapon highlight Select screen. If you can get enough power-ups to the last weapon, which will not be visible, and use it without powering up on speed up, you get all four options, missiles, and the shield. But if you have the laser already, it will be taken away.
Random Weapon Select	At the Weapon Select screen, press ▶ to enter Edit mode, then press ⬇️, 🌀, ⬇️, ⬇️, 🌀, 🌀, ⬇️, 🌀
Spread the Options	Activate the R-Option and collect enough power-ups that the option selection is highlighted. Now press and hold Ⓐ.
Suicide	Pause the game and press ⬆️, ⬆️, ⬇️, ⬇️, ◀, ▶, ◀, ▶, 🅨, Ⓐ, START

BONUS STAGES

When you clear a bonus stage, you end up in the next level. That's right, you don't have to fight the boss of the level you were in previously. However, if you get killed in the bonus stage, you go back to the regular level, and cannot reenter the bonus stage.

STAGE	HOW TO UNLOCK
Stage 2	When you see a hole in the wall at the bottom of the screen, fly down there. Prerequisite: None.
Stage 3	When you reach the lower level, a platform in the ceiling drops down. Fly just below the part where the platform was. Prerequisite: Destroy all of the ground targets in the stage up to that point.

STAGE	HOW TO UNLOCK
Stage 4	In the last set of Moai heads (they look like Easter Island heads), one that's lying down lifts up. Fly behind it. Prerequisite: Nothing must be highlighted on your power-up bar.
Stage 5	Fly just below the ceiling before the narrow corridor. Prerequisite: The hundreds digit of your score reads 5, 7, or 3.

Stage 7 Just after the long downward slope in the second half of the level, stay close to the ground and fly into the wall formation shaped like this:

```
........./
........\
____*/
```

(Key: dots are empty space, lines are walls, the asterisk is where your ship should be.) Prerequisite: Unknown.

GRADIUS COLLECTION   (PSP)

CODES

Unlockable	How to Unlock
All Power-ups and Weapons	Pause the game and then insert the famous "Konami Code": ↑,↑,↓,↓,←,→,←,→,←,→

GRAND SLAM TENNIS 2   (PLAYSTATION 3)

TROPHY

UNLOCKABLE	HOW TO UNLOCK
Australian Open Title (Bronze)	Career - Win the Australian Open
Beat Borg at the French Open (Bronze)	Career - Defeat Bjorn Borg at the French Open
Beat Evert at US Open (Bronze)	Career - Defeat Chris Evert in the US Open
Beat Federer at Australian Open (Bronze)	Career - Defeat Roger Federer at the Australian Open
Beat Henin at the French Open (Bronze)	Career - Defeat Justine Henin at the French Open
Beat McEnroe at US Open (Bronze)	Career - Defeat John McEnroe in the US Open
Beat Navratilova at Wimbledon (Bronze)	Career - Defeat Martina Navratilova at Wimbledon
Beat Sampras at Wimbledon (Bronze)	Career - Defeat Pete Sampras at Wimbledon
Beat Serena at Australian Open (Bronze)	Career - Defeat Serena Williams at the Australian Open
Best of 1980's (Silver)	ESPN Grand Slam Classics - Beat all 80's Matches
Best of 1990's (Bronze)	ESPN Grand Slam Classics - Beat all 90's Matches
Best of 2000 (Bronze)	ESPN Grand Slam Classics - Beat all 2000's Matches
Best of All Time (Bronze)	ESPN Grand Slam Classics - Beat all All-Time Matches
Boom Boom (Bronze)	Any Game Mode - Hit four aces in a row
Break Back (Bronze)	Any Game Mode - Break service immediately after being broken
Broke (Bronze)	Any Game Mode - Win a match without being broken
Calendar Year Grand Slam (Gold)	Career - Win all four Grand Slam tournaments consecutively in the same calendar year
Career Grand Slam (Silver)	Career - Win all four Grand Slam tournaments
Clean Break (Bronze)	Any Game Mode - Break Service
Collector (Gold)	Career - Earn all racquets and shoes in Tennis Store
EA SPORTS™ GRAND SLAM TENNIS 2 Platinum Trophy (Platinum)	Collected all other EA SPORTS™ GRAND SLAM TENNIS 2 trophies

Flushing Meadows Big Show (Bronze)	Career - Play Arthur Ashe Stadium at US Open
French Open Title (Bronze)	Career - Win the French Open
Friendly Competition (Bronze)	Online - Win a ranked doubles online match against a Friend
History Buff (Silver)	ESPN Grand Slam Classics - Beat all Fantasy Matches
Melbourne Park Big Show (Bronze)	Career - Play Rod Laver Arena at Australian Open
Never Broken (Bronze)	Career - Win a tournament without being broken
No Set Lost (Bronze)	Career - Win a tournament without losing a set
Non-Calendar Year Grand Slam (Silver)	Career - Win all four Grand Slam tournaments consecutively, but not in the same calendar year
Pair of Aces (Bronze)	Any Game Mode - Hit 2 aces in a row
Popular (Bronze)	Share A Pro - Download a Tennis Player
Rocket (Bronze)	Any Game Mode - Hit a 209 KMH (130 MPH) serve
Roland Garros Big Show (Bronze)	Career - Play Court Philippe Chatrier at French Open
School Master (Silver)	Training - Complete all Tennis School Lessons
Sharer (Bronze)	Share A Pro - Upload a Tennis Player
Silver Set (Bronze)	Any Game Mode - Win a set without losing a game
Small Grand Slam (Silver)	Career - Win three of the four Grand Slam tournaments in the same year
Streak (Silver)	Online - Win 10 matches in a row
The Legend (Gold)	Career - Finish ranked #1
Tie Break Win (Bronze)	Any Game Mode - Win a tiebreak
US Open Title (Bronze)	Career - Win the US Open
Wimbledon Big Show (Bronze)	Career - Play Centre Court at Wimbledon
Wimbledon Title (Bronze)	Career - Win Wimbledon

GRAND SLAM TENNIS 2 (XBOX 360)

ACHIEVEMENT

UNLOCKABLE	HOW TO UNLOCK
Australian Open Title (20)	Career - Win the Australian Open
Beat Borg at the French Open (20)	Career - Defeat Bjorn Borg at the French Open
Beat Evert at US Open (20)	Career - Defeat Chris Evert in the US Open
Beat Federer at Australian Open (20)	Career - Defeat Roger Federer at the Australian Open
Beat Henin at the French Open (20)	Career - Defeat Justine Henin at the French Open
Beat McEnroe at US Open (20)	Career - Defeat John McEnroe in the US Open
Beat Navratilova at Wimbledon (20)	Career - Defeat Martina Navratilova at Wimbledon
Beat Sampras at Wimbledon (20)	Career - Defeat Pete Sampras at Wimbledon

Beat Serena at Australian Open (20)	Career - Defeat Serena Williams at the Australian Open
Best of 1980's (20)	ESPN Grand Slam Classics - Beat all 80's Matches
Best of 1990's (20)	ESPN Grand Slam Classics - Beat all 90's Matches
Best of 2000 (20)	ESPN Grand Slam Classics - Beat all 2000's Matches
Best of All Time (20)	ESPN Grand Slam Classics - Beat all All-Time Matches
Boom Boom (20)	Any Game Mode - Hit four aces in a row
Break Back (20)	Any Game Mode - Break service immediately after being broken
Broke (20)	Any Game Mode - Win a match without being broken
Calendar Year Grand Slam (50)	Career - Win all four Grand Slam tournaments consecutively in the same calendar year
Career Grand Slam (35)	Career - Win all four Grand Slam tournaments
Clean Break (20)	Any Game Mode - Break Service
Collector (50)	Career - Earn all racquets and shoes in Tennis Store
Flushing Meadows Big Show (20)	Career - Play Arthur Ashe Stadium at US Open
French Open Title (20)	Career - Win the French Open
Friendly Competition (20)	Xbox LIVE - Win a ranked doubles Xbox LIVE match against a Friend
History Buff (30)	ESPN Grand Slam Classics - Beat all Fantasy matches
Melbourne Park Big Show (20)	Career - Play Rod Laver Arena at Australian Open
Never Broken (20)	Career - Win a tournament without being broken
No Set Lost (20)	Career - Win a tournament without losing a set
Non-Calendar Year Grand Slam (35)	Career - Win all four Grand Slam tournaments consecutively, but not in the same calendar year
Pair of Aces (20)	Any Game Mode - Hit 2 aces in a row
Popular (20)	Share A Pro - Download a Tennis Player
Rocket (20)	Any Game Mode - Hit a 209 KMH (130 MPH) serve
Roland Garros Big Show (20)	Career - Play Court Philippe Chatrier at French Open
School Master (35)	Training - Complete all Tennis School Lessons
Sharer (20)	Share A Pro - Upload a Tennis Player
Silver Set (20)	Any Game Mode - Win a set without losing a game
Small Grand Slam (35)	Career - Win three of the four Grand Slam tournaments in the same year
Streak (20)	Xbox LIVE - Win 10 matches in a row
The Legend (50)	Career - Finish ranked #1
Tie Break Win (20)	Any Game Mode - Win a tiebreak
US Open Title (20)	Career - Win the US Open

NEW!
A
B
C
D
E
F
G
H
I
J
K
L
M
N
O
P
Q
R
S
T
U
V
W
X
Y
Z

Wimbledon Big Show (20)	Career - Play Centre Court at Wimbledon
Wimbledon Title (20)	Career - Win Wimbledon

GRAND THEFT AUTO 4 (PLAYSTATION 3, XBOX 360)

CODES

During gameplay, pull out Niko's phone and dial these numbers for the corresponding effect. Cheats will affect missions and achievements.

EFFECT	CODE
Change weather	468-555-0100
Get the Ak-47, knife, Molotov Cocktails, pistol, RPG, sniper rifle and Uzi	486-555-0150
Get the baseball bat, grenades, M4, MP5, pistol, RPG, and sniper rifle	486-555-0100
Raise wanted level	267-555-0150
Remove wanted level	267-555-0100
Restore armor	362-555-0100
Restore health	482-555-0100
Spawn a Cognoscenti	227-555-0142
Spawn a Comet	227-555-0175
Spawn a Jetmax	938-555-0100
Spawn a Sanchez	625-555-0150
Spawn a SuperGT	227-555-0168
Spawn a Turismo	227-555-0147
Spawn an Annihilator	359-555-0100
Spawn an FIB Buffalo	227-555-0100
Spawn an NRG-900	625-555-0100

MAP LOCATIONS

Enter the password into any of the in-game computers.

EFFECT	CODE
Weapon, health, armor, vehicle, pigeon, ramp/stunt, and entertainment locations	www.whattheydonotwantyoutoknow.com

UNLOCKABLES

UNLOCKABLE	HOW TO UNLOCK
Annihilator Helicopter	Kill all 200 Flying Rats (Pigeons)

EASTER EGGS

UNLOCKABLE	HOW TO UNLOCK
The Heart of Liberty City	Gain access to Happiness Island. Once you're able to go there legally, find the Helicopter Tours (which is directly east of Happiness Island) and steal a helicopter. Fly over the Statue of Liberty and jump out at the statue's feet. Land on the topmost tier of the statue, which is basically a square platform with a door in the center of each side. Look for a door with a plaque on either side of it that reads, "No Hidden Content Here." Don't try to open the door; just walk through it. Inside, you'll find an empty room with a tall ladder. Climb it, and when you reach the top, look up; there is a gigantic beating heart, held in place by chains.

FRIENDSHIP BONUSES

Gain the following bonuses by gaining the corresponding amount of friendship.

UNLOCKABLE	HOW TO UNLOCK
Boom? (Call Packie for him to make you a car bomb)	Gain 75% friendship with Packie.
Chopper Ride (He will pick you up in his helicopter)	Gain 70% friendship with Brucie.
Discount Guns (Buy weapons at a cheaper price from Little Jacob)	Gain 60% friendship with Little Jacob.

Extra Help (A car of gang members will be sent to help you out)	Gain 60% friendship with Dwayne.
Free Ride (Call for a taxi)	Gain 60% friendship with Roman.
50% Off for All Clothing Stores	Gain 80% Relationship Status with Alex.
Health Boost (Call Carmen and select "Health Boost")	Gain 80% Relationship Status with Carmen.
Remove Up to 3 Wanted Stars (Call Kiki and select "Remove Wanted")	Gain 80% Relationship Status with Kiki.

UNLOCKABLES

UNLOCKABLE	HOW TO UNLOCK
Rastah Color Huntley SUV	Complete 10 Package Delivery missions.
Remove Ammo Limit	Get 100% completion.

GRAND THEFT AUTO 4: THE BALLAD OF GAY TONY (XBOX 360)

CODES

EFFECT	CODE
Akuma (Bike)	625-555-0200
APC(Tank)	272-555-8265
Buzzard(Helicopter)	359-555-2899
Change Weather	468-555-0100
Floater(Boat)	938-555-0150
Health & Armor	362-555-0100
Health, Armor and Advanced Weapons	482-555-0100
Parachute	359-555-7272
Raise Wanted Level	267-555-0150
Remove Wanted Level	267-555-0100
Sniper rifle bullets explode	486-555-2526
Spawn Annihilator	359-555-0100
Spawn Bullet GT	227-555-9666
Spawn Cognoscenti	227-555-0142
Spawn Comet	227-555-0175
Spawn Jetmax	938-555-0100
Spawn NRG-900	625-555-0100
Spawn Sanchez	625-555-0150
Spawn Super GT	227-555-0168
Spawn Turismo	227-555-0147
Spawns a FIB Buffalo	227-555-0100
Super Punch (exploding punches)	276-555-2666
Vader(Bike)	625-555-3273
Weapons (Advanced) (New Weapons)	486-555-0100
Weapons (Poor)	486-555-0150

GRAND THEFT AUTO: CHINATOWN WARS (DS)

CODES

Enter these during gameplay without pausing

EFFECT	CODE
Armor	Ⓛ,Ⓛ,Ⓡ,Ⓑ,Ⓑ,Ⓐ,Ⓐ,Ⓡ
cloud	⬆,⬆,⬆,⬆,Ⓧ,Ⓨ,Ⓛ,Ⓡ
Explosive Pistol Round	Ⓛ,Ⓡ,Ⓧ,Ⓨ,Ⓐ,Ⓑ,⬆,⬆
health	Ⓛ,Ⓛ,Ⓡ,Ⓐ,Ⓐ,Ⓑ,Ⓑ,Ⓡ
Hurricane	⬆,⬆,⬆,⬆,Ⓑ,Ⓨ,Ⓡ,Ⓛ

lots of rain	⇨,⇩,⇦,⇧,Ⓐ,✕,Ⓡ,Ⓛ
rain	⇨,⇩,⇦,⇧,▽,●,Ⓛ,Ⓡ
sunny	⇨,⇩,⇦,⇧,Ⓐ,Ⓑ,Ⓛ,Ⓡ
wanted level down	Ⓡ,✕,Ⓧ,▽,⬇,▽,Ⓛ,Ⓛ
wanted level up	Ⓛ,Ⓛ,Ⓡ,▽,▽,Ⓧ,✕,Ⓡ
weapons 1 (grenade, nightstick, pistol, minigun, assault, micro SMG, stubby shotgun)	Ⓡ,⇨,Ⓑ,⇩,⇦,Ⓡ,Ⓑ,⇧
weapons 2 (molotov, taser, dual pistols, flamethrower, carbine, SMG, dual-barrel)	Ⓡ,⇨,Ⓐ,⇩,⇦,Ⓡ,Ⓐ,⇧
weapons 3 (mine, chainsaw, revolver, flamethrower, carbine, SMG, dual-barrel)	Ⓡ,⇨,▽,⇩,⇦,Ⓡ,▽,⇧
weapons 4 (flashbang, bat, pistol, RPG, carbine, micro SMG, stubby shotgun)	Ⓡ,⇨,Ⓧ,⇩,⇦,Ⓡ,Ⓧ,⇧

GRAND THEFT AUTO: CHINATOWN WARS (PSP)

BONUS MISSION REWARDS

UNLOCKABLE	HOW TO UNLOCK
Ammunition Discount	Score gold medals on all weapons at the Gun-Club.
Bullet Proof Taxis	Complete 15 Taxi Fares in a row (in the same taxi).
Immune to Fire	Complete five waves of Fire Brigade Missions.
increased Body Armor	Complete five waves of Vigilante Missions with a 100% kill rate.
infinite Sprint	Complete five Paramedic Missions.
Regenerating Health	Beat both Noodle Delivery Missions (with a Gold ranking).
Upgraded Delivery Bag	Beat both Mail Courier Missions (with a Gold ranking).

GRAND THEFT AUTO: LIBERTY CITY STORIES (PSP)

Enter these codes during gameplay. Do not pause the game.

UNLOCKABLE	CODE
$250,000	Ⓛ, Ⓡ, ▲, Ⓛ, Ⓡ, ●, Ⓛ, Ⓡ
Aggressive Drivers	■, ■, Ⓡ, ✕, ✕, Ⓛ, ●, ●
All Green Lights	▲, ▲, Ⓡ, ■, ■, Ⓛ, ✕, ✕
All Vehicles Chrome Plated	▲, Ⓡ, Ⓛ, ⬇, ⬇, Ⓡ, Ⓡ, ▲
Black Cars	●, ●, Ⓡ, ▲, ▲, Ⓛ, ■, ■
Bobble Head World	⬇, ⬇, ⬇, ●, ●, ✕, Ⓛ, Ⓡ
Cars Drive On Water	●, ✕, ⬇, ●, ✕, ⬆, Ⓛ, Ⓛ
Change Bike Tire Size	●, ⇨, ✕, ⇧, ⬇, ✕, Ⓛ, ■
Clear Weather	⇧, ⬇, ●, ⇧, ⬇, ■, Ⓛ, Ⓡ
Commit Suicide	Ⓛ, ⬇, ⇦, Ⓡ, ✕, ●, ⇧, ▲
Destroy All Cars	Ⓛ, Ⓛ, ⇦, Ⓛ, Ⓛ, ⇨, ✕, ■
Display Game Credits	Ⓛ, Ⓡ, Ⓛ, Ⓡ, ⇧, ⬇, Ⓛ, Ⓡ
Faster Clock	Ⓛ, Ⓛ, ⇦, Ⓛ, Ⓛ, ⇨, ●, ✕
Faster Gameplay	Ⓡ, Ⓡ, Ⓛ, Ⓡ, Ⓡ, Ⓛ, ⬇, ✕
Foggy Weather	⇧, ⬇, ▲, ⇧, ⬇, ✕, Ⓛ, Ⓡ
Full Armor	Ⓛ, Ⓡ, ●, Ⓛ, Ⓡ, ✕, Ⓛ, Ⓡ
Full Health	Ⓛ, Ⓡ, ✕, Ⓛ, Ⓡ, ■, Ⓛ, Ⓡ
Have Girls Follow You	⬇, ⬇, ⬇, ▲, ▲, ●, Ⓛ, Ⓡ
Never Wanted	Ⓛ, Ⓛ, ▲, Ⓡ, Ⓡ, ✕, ■, ●
Overcast Weather	⇧, ⬇, ✕, ⇧, ⬇, ▲, Ⓛ, Ⓡ
Pedestrians Attack You	Ⓛ, Ⓛ, Ⓡ, Ⓛ, Ⓛ, Ⓡ, ⇧, ▲
Pedestrians Have Weapons	Ⓡ, Ⓡ, Ⓛ, Ⓡ, Ⓡ, Ⓛ, ⇨, ●
Pedestrians Riot	Ⓛ, Ⓛ, Ⓡ, Ⓛ, Ⓛ, Ⓡ, ⇦, ■
Perfect Traction	Ⓛ, ⇧, ⇦, Ⓡ, ▲, ●, ⬇, ✕
Rainy Weather	⇧, ⬇, ■, ⇧, ⬇, ●, Ⓛ, Ⓡ

Raise Media Attention	L, ⇧, ⇨, R, ▲, ■, ⇩, X
Raise Wanted Level	L, R, ■, L, R, ▲, L, R
Random Pedestrian Outfit	L, L, ⇦, L, L, ⇨, ■, ▲
Slower Gameplay	R, ▲, X, R, ■, ●, ⇦, ⇨
Spawn Rhino	L, L, ⇦, L, L, ⇨, ▲, ●
Spawn Trashmaster	▲, ●, ⇩, ▲, ●, ⇧, L, L
Sunny Weather	L, L, ●, R, R, ■, ▲, X
Upside Down Gameplay	⇩, ⇩, ⇩, X, X, ■, R, L
Upside Up	▲, ▲, ▲, ⇧, ⇧, ⇨, L, R
Weapon Set 1	⇧, ■, ■, ⇩, ⇦, ■, ■, ⇨
Weapon Set 2	⇧, ●, ●, ⇩, ⇦, ●, ●, ⇨
Weapon Set 3	⇧, X, X, ⇩, ⇦, X, X, ⇨
White Cars	X, X, R, ●, ●, L, ▲, ▲

GRAND THEFT AUTO: VICE CITY STORIES (PSP)

Enter any of these codes while playing.

UNLOCKABLE	CODE
25% of MP Content	⇧, ⇧, ⇧, ■, ■, ▲, R, L
50% of MP Content	⇧, ⇧, ⇧, ●, ●, X, L, R
75% of MP Content	⇧, ⇧, ⇧, ⇧, X, X, ■, R, L
100% of MP Content	⇧, ⇧, ▲, ▲, ●, L, R
All Cars Are Black	L, R, L, R, ⇧, ●, ⇧, X
Armor	⇧, ⇩, ⇦, ⇨, ■, ■, L, R
Cars Avoid You	⇧, ⇧, ⇨, ⇦, ▲, ●, L, ■
Chrome Cars	⇨, ⇧, ⇩, ⇩, ▲, ▲, L, ■
Clear Weather	⇦, ⇩, R, L, ⇨, ⇧, ⇦, X
Commit Suicide	⇨, ⇨, ●, ●, L, R, ⇩, X
Destroy All Cars	L, R, R, ⇦, ⇨, ■, ⇩, R
Faster Clock	R, L, L, ⇩, ⇧, X, ⇩, L
Faster Gameplay	⇦, ⇦, R, R, ⇧, ▲, ⇩, X
Foggy Weather	⇦, ⇩, ▲, X, ⇨, ⇧, ⇦, L
$250,000	⇧, ⇩, ⇦, ⇨, X, X, L, R
Guys Follow You	⇨, L, ⇩, L, ●, ⇧, L, ■
Health	⇧, ⇩, ⇦, ⇨, ●, ●, L, R
Lower Wanted Level	⇧, ⇨, ▲, ▲, ⇩, ⇦, X, X
Nearest Ped Gets in Your Vehicle (Must Be in a Car)	⇩, ⇧, ⇨, L, L, ■, ⇧, L
Overcast Weather	⇦, ⇩, L, R, ⇨, ⇧, ⇦, ■
Peds Attack You	⇩, ▲, ⇧, X, L, R, L, R
Peds Have Weapons	⇧, L, ⇩, R, ⇦, ●, ⇨, ▲
Peds Riot	R, L, L, ⇩, ⇦, ⇨, ●, ⇩, L
Perfect Traction	⇩, ⇦, ⇧, L, R, ▲, ●, X
Rainy Weather	⇦, ⇩, L, R, ⇨, ⇧, ⇦, ▲
Raise Wanted Level	⇧, ⇨, ■, ■, ⇩, ⇦, ●, ●
Slower Gameplay	⇦, ⇦, ●, ●, ⇩, ⇧, ▲, X
Spawn Rhino	⇧, L, ⇩, R, ⇦, L, ⇨, R
Spawn Trashmaster	⇩, ⇧, ⇨, ▲, L, ▲, L, ▲
Sunny Weather	⇦, ⇩, R, L, ⇨, ⇧, ⇩, ●
Upside Down Mode 1	■, ■, ■, L, L, R, ⇦, ⇨
Upside Down Mode 2	⇦, ⇦, ⇦, R, R, L, ⇨, ⇦
Weapon Set 1	⇦, ⇨, X, ⇧, ⇩, ■, ⇦, ⇨
Weapon Set 2	⇦, ⇨, ■, ⇧, ⇩, ▲, ⇦, ⇨
Weapon Set 3	⇦, ⇨, ▲, ⇧, ⇩, ●, ⇦, ⇨

GRAN TURISMO 5 (PLAYSTATION 3)

LICENSE TESTS

UNLOCKABLE	HOW TO UNLOCK
A License Tests	Reach Level 3 and complete the B license tests
B License Tests	Buy your first car
International A License Tests	Reach Level 12 and complete the International B license tests
International B License Tests	Reach Level 9 and complete the International C license tests
International C License Tests	Reach Level 6 and complete the A license tests
S License Tests	Reach Level 15 and complete the International A license tests

GRAVITY RUSH (PLAYSTATION VITA)

TROPHY

UNLOCKABLE	HOW TO UNLOCK
A Hundred and One Nights (Bronze)	Completed episode 8
A Meeting with Destiny (Bronze)	Completed episode 5
Adreaux On Call (Bronze)	Completed episode 18
All That Glitters (Gold)	Gold-medaled EVERY challenge.
An Unguarded Moment (Bronze)	Completed episode 20
Ancient Game Hunter (Silver)	Defeated the rare Nevi in Rift Planes: The Ruins.
Burning Game Hunter (Silver)	Defeated the rare Nevi in Rift Planes: The Inferno.
Children of the Past (Bronze)	Completed episode 16
Curiosity Killed the Cat (Bronze)	Completed episode 10
Fading Light (Bronze)	Completed episode 17
Falling to Pieces (Bronze)	Completed episode 19
Frequent Flyer (Silver)	Landed 10 gravity kicks without landing or taking damage.
From Oblivion (Bronze)	Completed episode 1
Gem Aficionado (Gold)	Collected a total of 40,000 precious gems.
Gem Collector (Silver)	Collected a total of 20,000 precious gems.
Going Underground (Silver)	Discovered every manhole.
Gold Medalist (Bronze)	Gold-medaled a challenge.
Gravitational Anomaly (Silver)	Defeated 8 enemies with one special attack.
Home Sweet Home (Bronze)	Completed episode 3
Illusory Game Hunter (Silver)	Defeated the rare Nevi in Rift Planes: The Mirage.
It's all Relative (Platinum)	Collected every trophy. Congratulations!
Kids Just Don't Understand (Bronze)	Completed episode 13
Learner's Permit (Bronze)	Mastered the fundamentals of gravity.
Letting Old Ghosts Die (Bronze)	Completed episode 9
Look Out Below (Bronze)	Completed episode 12
Lost in Time and Space (Silver)	Heard the mysterious couple's complete story.
Lost Kat (Bronze)	Awakened in Auldnoir.
Memories of Another World (Bronze)	Completed episode 15
New Challenger (Bronze)	Cleared a challenge.
No Rest for the Virtuous (Gold)	Completed episode 21
Pitching Machine (Silver)	Hurled 10 objects into enemies without missing or taking damage.
Shadows Over the City (Bronze)	Completed episode 2

Silver Lining (Silver)	Earned a silver or better in every challenge.
The Hekseville Phantom (Bronze)	Completed episode 4
The Lost City (Bronze)	Completed episode 6
The Lost Tribe (Bronze)	Completed episode 14
Thick Skin (Bronze)	Completed episode 11
Too Many Secrets (Bronze)	Completed episode 7
Top Cat (Gold)	Raised Kat's reputation to 'Top Cat.'
True Challenger (Bronze)	Cleared EVERY challenge.

GUITAR HERO 5 (XBOX 360, PLAYSTATION 3)

CODES

Enter these codes to activate the following cheats. (G = Green; R = Red; Y = Yellow; B = Blue)

EFFECT	CODE
Air Instruments	R R B Y G G G Y
All HOPOs	G G B G G G Y G
Always Slide	G G R R Y B Y B
AutoKick	Y G R B B B B R
Contest Winner 1	G G R R Y R Y B
Focus Mode	Y G R G Y B G G
HUD-Free Mode	G R G G Y G G G
Invisible Characters	G R Y Y Y B B G
Performance Mode	Y Y B R B G R R
Unlock All Characters	B B G G R G R Y

UNLOCKABLES

UNLOCKABLE	HOW TO UNLOCK
Character: Carlos Santana	Complete the song "No One to Depend On (Live)" on any difficulty, any instrument.
Character: Johnny Cash	Complete the song "Ring of Fire" on any difficulty, any instrument.
Character: Kurt Cobain	Complete the song "Smells Like Teen Spirit" on any difficulty, any instrument.
Character: Matt Bellamy	Complete the song "Plug In Baby" on any instrument on any difficulty.
Character: Shirley Manson	Complete the song "I'm Only Happy When It Rains" on any difficulty, any instrument.
Cheat: All HOPOs (Changes almost every note possible into a HOPO or Hammer-On/Pull-Off note)	As guitarist, whammy sustain notes on the song "Hurts So Good" for 25 seconds total or more (in Club Boson venue).

UNLOCKABLE	HOW TO UNLOCK
Cheat: All Slider Gems (All single notes are changed into slider/tap notes)	As guitarist, hit 230 tap notes on the song "Du Hast" (in Neon Oasis venue).
Cheat: Auto-kick (all kick bass notes are autoplayed)	As drummer, hit 200 non-cymbal notes on "Mirror People" (in Angel's Crypt venue, fills don't count).
Extra: Air Instruments (Instruments will be almost completely invisible, guitar strings will still be visible)	As Guitarist, strum 340 chords or more on the song "Sultans of Swing" (in O'Connel's Corner venue).
Extra: Focus Mode (blacks out background)	As a drummer, hit 265 tom notes on "Brianstorm" (in the Golden Gate venue).
Extra: HUD-Free Mode (removes rock meter, star power gauge, score display)	as a vocalist, get Excellent on 75 consecutive phrases in the rap song "Bring The Noise 20XX" (in Neon Oasis venue).

| Extra: Performance Mode (removes track and HUD) | With two players, get a band multiplier for 42 seconds on "Bleed American" (in the Aqueduct venue). |
| Quickplay Venue "Wormhole" (required for The Grand Tour) | As guitarist, 4X multiplier for 50 seconds on "Play That Funky Music" (in Sideshow venue). |

GUITAR HERO 5 (WII)

CODES

Enter these codes to activate the following cheats. (G = Green; R = Red; Y = Yellow; B = Blue)

EFFECT	CODE
Air Instruments	R R B Y G G G Y
All HOPOs	G G B G G G Y G
Always Slide	G G R R Y B Y B
AutoKick	Y G R B B B B R
Contest Winner 1	G G R R Y R Y B
Focus Mode	Y G R G Y B G G
HUD-Free Mode	G R G G Y G G G
Invisible Characters	G R Y Y Y B B G
Performance Mode	Y Y B R B G R R
Unlock All Characters	B B G G R G R Y

GUITAR HERO: WARRIORS OF ROCK (XBOX 360, PLAYSTATION 3)

CODES

Input at the "Input Cheat" menu.

EFFECT	CODE
Absolutely nothinge	Press Green, Green, Green, Green, Green, Green, Green, Green
Air instruments	Press Yellow, Red, Red, Blue, Yellow, Green, Green, Green
Placebo	Press Green, Green, Green, Blue, Blue, Green, Green, Green
All taps	Press Blue, Green, Green, Red, Red, Yellow, Blue, Yellow
Color shuffle	Press Blue, Green, Blue, Red, Yellow, Green, Red, Yellow
Focus mode	Press Green, Yellow, Green, Red, Green, Yellow, Blue, Green
HUD Free mode	Press Green, Green, Red, Green, Green, Yellow, Green, Green
Invisible rocker	Press Green, Green, Red, Yellow, Yellow, Yellow, Blue, Blue
Note shuffle	Press Blue, Blue, Red, Blue, Green, Green, Red, Green
Performance mode	Press Red, Yellow, Yellow, Blue, Red, Blue, Green, Red
Unlock all characters	Press Blue, Green, Green, Red, Green, Red, Yellow, Blue
Unlock all venues	Press Red, Blue, Blue, Red, Red, Blue, Blue, Red

GUITAR HERO: WARRIORS OF ROCK (WII)

CODES

Input at the "Input Cheat" menu.

EFFECT	CODE
Unlock all characters	Press Blue, Green, Green, Red, Green, Red, Yellow, Blue
Unlock all venues	Press Red, Blue, Blue, Red, Red, Blue, Blue, Red

GUNSTAR HEROES (WII)

UNLOCKABLES

UNLOCKABLE	HOW TO UNLOCK
Hidden Special Move	With either Gunstar Red or Gunstar Blue motion: ⬇, ⬇➡, ➡, ➡⬇, ⬇+shot button to execute a powerful standing slide.
Make the Logo Rotate	Hold ⬇ on controller 1 before the Gunstar Heroes logo appears on the screen in order to rotate it.
Timeron's Secret	During the second Timeron encounter (which is in the Space Battle stage) a timer begins ticking from 00'00"00. As the timer keeps going, the Timeron's attacks change, and every 20 minutes or so, a circular drone appears, accompanied by Smash Daisaku's laughter. Avoid this drone for about 2 minutes until it self-destructs, because a single hit will reduce your health to zero. At about 50'00"00 or so, large blue balls appear. These rebound once against the screen, and do 11 points of damage instead of the normal 10 points from the smaller ones. Once the timer gets up to 99'50"00 or so, don't destroy the Timeron yet. Instead, wait out the remaining 10 seconds while avoiding the Timeron's attacks, but don't stay too close to the Timeron, or you'll get killed by the drone. Once the timer reaches 00'00"00 again, you'll hear that nasty laughter again, but this time, "GIVE UP!!" appears in the middle of the screen, and the Timeron self-destructs, accompanied by the message, "YOU OPENED THE - SATORI MIND -." A bit more of that nasty laughter accompanies the next message, "REPROGRAMMED BY NAMI - 1993." Now, instead of getting a Timer Bonus as you usually would, a Soul Bonus of exactly 930,410 points is added to your score.

HALF-LIFE 2: THE ORANGE BOX (XBOX 360)

HALF-LIFE 2 *CODES*

Enter the code while playing *Half Life 2*. No specific requirements other than the game. Can be entered at any time on any level. Using cheats does not disable Achievements.

CODE	EFFECT
(LB), ○, (RB), ○, (LB), (LB), ○, (RB), (RB), ○	Invincibility
○, ○, ○, ○, ○, ○, ○, ○, ○, ○	Restores health by 25 points
○, ○, ○, ○, (RB), ○, ○, ○, ○, (RB)	Restores ammo for current weapon
○, ○, ○, ○, ○, P, ○, ○, ○, ○, (RB)	Unlocks all levels, which can then be accessed from the new game window

PORTAL CODES

Enter these codes anytime during gameplay.

CODE	EFFECT
○, ○, ○, ○, ○, ○, ○, ○, ○, ○	Create box
(LB), ○, (RB), ○, (LB), (LB), ○, (RB), (RB), ○	Enables invincibility
○, ○, ○, ○, ○, ○, ○, ○, ○, ○	Fire energy ball
○, ○, ○, ○, ○, ○, ○, ○, ○, ○	Portal placement anywhere
○, ○, (LB), (RB), ○, ○, (LB), (RB), (LT), (RT)	Upgrade Portalgun

HALF-LIFE 2: THE ORANGE BOX (PLAYSTATION 3)

HALF-LIFE 2 CODES

Enter the code while playing. Codes can be entered at any time on any level.

EFFECT	CODE
Restore Ammo (for current weapon)	(R1), ▲, ●, ✕, ■, (R1), ▲, ■, ✕, ●, (R1)
Restore Health by 25 Points	↑, ↑, ↓, ↓, ←, →, ←, →, ●, ✕
Unlock All Levels	←, ←, ←, ←, (L1), →, →, →, →, (R1)

PORTAL CODES

Enter these codes any time during gameplay.

EFFECT	CODE
Create a Cube	↓, ●, ✕, ●, ▲, ↓, ●, ✕, ●, ▲
Fire Energy Ball	↑, ▲, ▲, ■, ■, ✕, ✕, ●, ●, ↑
Unlock All Levels	←, ←, ←, ←, (L1), →, →, →, →, (R1)

HALO 3 (XBOX 360)

CODES

The following cheats can be performed during a local match or replay only. Press and hold the corresponding buttons for 3 SECONDS to toggle the effect on / off.

EFFECT	CODE
Toggle Hide Weapon	(LB), (RB), (L3), ○, ○
Toggle Pan-Cam / Normal while Show Coordinates is enabled.	Hold (L3) and (R3) and press ○
Toggle Show Coordinates / Camera Mode	(L3), +, (L3), ○, ○

ARMOR PERMUTATIONS UNLOCKABLES

Body Pieces: Spartan marked with (S) and Elite marked with (E).

UNLOCKABLE	HOW TO UNLOCK
(E) Ascetic Body	Unlock "Up Close and Personal" Achievement
(E) Ascetic Head	Unlock "Steppin' Razor" Achievement
(E) Ascetic Shoulders	Unlock "Overkill" Achievement
(E) Commando Body	Unlock "Triple Kill" Achievement
(E) Commando Head	Unlock "Overkill" Achievement
(E) Commando Shoulders	Unlock "Killing Frenzy" Achievement
(E) Flight Body	Complete Tsavo Highway on Heroic or Legendary
(E) Flight Head	Complete Campaign mode on Heroic
(E) Flight Shoulders	Complete The Ark on Heroic difficulty or higher
(S) EOD Body	Complete Tsavo Highway on Legendary
(S) EOD Head	Complete Campaign mode on Legendary
(S) EOD Shoulders	Complete The Ark on Legendary
(S) EVA Body	Complete Tsavo Highway on Normal or higher
(S) EVA Head	Complete Campaign mode on Normal
(S) EVA Shoulders	Complete The Ark on Normal difficulty or higher
(S) Hayabusa Chest	Collect 5 hidden skulls
(S) Hayabusa Helmet	Collect 13 hidden skulls
(S) Hayabusa Shoulders	Collect 9 hidden skulls
(S) Mark V Head	Unlock "UNSC Spartan" Achievement
(S) ODST Head	Unlock "Spartan Graduate" Achievement
(S) Rogue Head	Unlock "Spartan Officer" Achievement
(S) Scout Body	Unlock "Too Close to the Sun" Achievement
(S) Scout Head	Unlock "Used Car Salesman" Achievement
(S) Scout Shoulders	Unlock "Mongoose Mowdown" Achievement
(S) Security Head	Earn 1,000 Gamerscore points
(S) Security Shoulders	Earn 850 Gamerscore points
Katana	Complete all Achievements (1,000/1,000)

BLACK-EYE SKULL

Effect: Melee hits instantly recharge your shield.

Level: Crow's Nest

Location: As soon as you start the level, head straight up to the higher level. Head toward the door with the red light, then turn around. Jump onto the racks, onto the red metal light holders, then onto the ventilation tube. The skull spawns at the end.

BLIND SKULL

Effect: "Shoot from the hip."

Level: First Stage

Location: When you get to the area where you see the Phantom overhead (one of the marines points it out) jump over the rocks and keep following the path on the right. When you get to the cliff, there's a rock over on the side. The skull is on the end of the rock. Note: This skull has to be activated before you start a Campaign map.

CATCH SKULL

Effect: all enemies have 2 grenades, throw more grenades.

Level: The Storm

Location: From the start, go through until you go outside again. Outside, look straight across to a small round building. The skull is on top. To get up there, either use a warthog as a platform or grenade-jump. DO NOT destroy the wraith near the door or the skull will disappear.

COWBELL SKULL

Effect: Explosive force increased (sputnik from H2).

Level: The Ark

Location: First pick up a grav lift from the small building near where you fight the scarab. Now proceed through the level until you reach the second sloping hallway (stairway). You should see some partitioned risers (platforms) halfway down. The skull is on the top level. Toss the grav-lift on the right side of the hall so it lands on the fourth little green dot from the door. Then run, jump, and use the grav-lift to propel you to the top. You reach a checkpoint just as you enter the room, so if you miss, just try again.

FAMINE SKULL

Effect: "Trust us. Bring a magazine." Dropped weapons have very little ammo compared to normal.

Level: The Ark

Location: When you first go into the valley to the right after the wrecked phantom, look left to see a huge boulder. Use a ghost and get to the side of the boulder closest to the bridge overhead. It is easy to pilot the ghost up the side of the wall using the thrust. To get the skull, pilot 2 ghosts up the wall to the top of the bridge and stack them one on top of another next to the beam where the skull is placed. Simply jump from the top of the ghosts toward the skull and land on the beam.

FOG SKULL

Effect: "You'll miss those eyes in the back of your head." Your motion sensor disappears.

Level: Floodgate

Location: As you are walking down from the anti-air gun you destroyed in the previous mission, you encounter a ramp (next to a missile launcher). Around this ramp, you hit a checkpoint. At this point, you should also hear a marine yelling, "There! Over There!" Look up and to the right, directly at the roof of the building next to the missile launcher. A single flood form (not to be mistaken for the two other flood forms jumping in front of you) holds the skull. Kill him before he jumps, and he drops the skull down to the ground where you can retrieve it. If you shoot too early, and the skull gets stuck on the roof.

GRUNT BIRTHDAY PARTY SKULL

Effect: Headshots on grunts cause heads to explode with confetti.

Level: Crow's Nest

Location: Right after the first objective, while en route to the barracks, you fall onto a pipe. At the end of this pipe, look over the edge to see a small space a few feet below you. Drop over and as quickly as you can, pull back to land under the floor you were just on. The skull is at the end.

IRON SKULL

Effect: When either player dies in Co-Op on any difficulty both players restart at last checkpoint. In single player, you restart the level if you die.

Level: Sierra 117

Location: In the area where you rescue Sarge, behind the prison cell is a large ledge. Go to the far right side and jump on the boxes, then onto the pipes to get up on the ledge. Go to the far end of the ledge, turn two corners, and the skull is at the far end.

IWHBYD SKULL

Effect: "But the dog beat me over the fence." Unlocks bonus dialogue throughout the game. For most, this is the last skull, so this gives you the Hayabusa Helmet as well.

Level: The Covenant

Location: To get this, get to the room where you "fight" the Prophet of Truth. Let the Arbiter kill him, turn around, and kill all the flood here as well. This makes it a lot easier. Then jump through the Halo holograms in this order: 4 6 5 4 5 3 4. When you jump through the final hologram, they all light up in a sequential pattern. The skull is at the end, right before the energy bridge leading to Truth's corpse.

MYTHIC SKULL

Effect: Every enemy on the field now has double the normal amount of health.

Level: Halo

Location: As soon as the mission starts, walk up the hill in front of you and into the cave. Hug the right side of the cave, and after a large boulder you see a path on your right. Take the short path and find it at the end.

THUNDERSTORM SKULL

Effect: "Field promotions for everyone!" Upgrades enemies to their stronger versions.

Level: The Covenant

Location: After you shut down tower 1 and get access to the hornet, fly to tower 2 (the one the Arbiter shut down). While walking up the stairs, go to the middle part that connects both. A stair leads up to a platform where the skull is.

TILT SKULL

Effect: "What was once resistance is now immunity." Enemies have different body parts that may be resistant to certain bullet types.

Level: Cortana

Location: When in the circular type room with all the flood, look for a small structure piece next to two archways. Jump on top of it and up on the rocks to the top left, turn left and jump up again, then do a 180 and jump to the rocks across from you. Follow the rock sticking out and leading up on top of the original circular room. The skull is in a pile of blood.

TOUGH LUCK SKULL

Effect: Enemies do saving throws.

Level: Tsavo Highway

Location: On Tsavo Highway, about halfway through the mission (right after you are forced to walk through a large blue barrier), you will come out of a tunnel on the highway, and see a large pipeline on your left. Drop down in between the two, and run to the wall in front of you. Follow the wall all the way to where it connects with the cliff on your right, and turn to the left. There should be a few ledges—simply crouch-jump from ledge to ledge, and the last one should have the "Tough Luck" skull on it.

THE SEVEN TERMINALS

The Ark:

1. Start the mission and once you enter the first building, take a left into another door and emerge in a curved corridor. On the inside is a Terminal.

2. After activating the bridge to let your comrades across the gap, do a 180 and you should see it. (It does not open until you activate the bridge.)

3. In the third building after defeating the scarab, kill the group of sleeping covenant, then follow the corridor downward. Once you reach a door in front that is locked, immediately on the left there's an open door. Go through and walk straight, then do a 180 to find a secret room. It is in there.

The Covenant:

1. When in the first tower standing on the lift, face the access panel and turn left. Jump over and it's right there.

2. Land your hornet on the second tower, walk toward the entrance, but when you see the locked door, do a 180.

3. When in the third tower standing on the lift, face the access panel and turn right. Jump over.

Halo:

1. After reaching the end of the first cave, hug the right wall and you see a building. Jump up onto the walkway and hang a left once inside.

HALO 3: ODST (XBOX 360)

FIREFIGHT MISSIONS

Complete certain campaign missions to unlock new maps for the Firefight game mode.

UNLOCKABLE	HOW TO UNLOCK
Alpha Site	Complete the ONI Alpha Site campaign mission on any difficulty.
Chasm Ten	Complete the Date Hive campaign mission on any difficulty.
Last Exit	Complete the Coastal Highway campaign mission on any difficulty.
Lost Platoon	Complete the Uplift Reserve campaign mission on any difficulty.

FIREFIGHT UNLOCKABLE CHARACTERS

Perform the task to unlock characters for use in Firefight mode.

UNLOCKABLE	HOW TO UNLOCK
Buck Firefight Character	Complete "Tayari Plaza" on Normal or higher.
Dare Firefight Character	Complete the campaign on Legendary difficulty.
Dutch Firefight Character	Complete "Uplift Reserve" on Normal or higher.
Mickey Firefight Character	Complete "Kizingo Boulevard" on Normal or higher.
Romeo Character	Complete "NMPD HQ" on Normal or higher.

HALO: REACH (XBOX 360)

AVATAR AWARDS

UNLOCKABLE	HOW TO UNLOCK
Carter's Helmet	Clear a Campaign mission on Legendary without dying.
Emile's Helmet	Earned a Bulltrue medal in either multiplayer or Firefight Matchmaking.
Jorge's Helmet	Earn a Killtacular in multiplayer Matchmaking.
Jun's Helmet	Kill 100 enemies in a row without dying in either the Campaign or Firefight.
Kat's Helmet	Avenged a teammate's death in multiplayer Matchmaking.

MULTIPLAYER NAMEPLATES

UNLOCKABLE	HOW TO UNLOCK
Assault Rifle	Played the Halo Reach Beta in May 2010.
Halo 2 logo	Played Halo 2 on Xbox Live before April 15, 2010.
Halo 3 logo	Play any Campaign level in Halo 3 while connected to Xbox Live.
Marathon Durandal symbol	Have Marathon Durandal in your recently played games list and log in at Bungie.net.
MJOLNIR Mk VI helmet logo	Unlock any 4 of the Halo PC, Halo 2, Halo 3, Halo 3: ODST, or Halo Reach Beta nameplates.
ODST logo	Play Halo 3:ODST while connected to Xbox Live.
Original Halo logo	Register your Halo PC product code at Bungie.net.
The Septagon (7th Column symbol)	Join Bungie.net and log in with your Gamertag's e-mail address.

HALO WARS (XBOX 360)

BLACK BOXES

Black boxes in each level unlock new Halo History entries.

UNLOCKABLE	HOW TO UNLOCK
All Others	Win on each Skirmish map and win Skirmish with each leader.
Black Box 01—Alpha Base	Under the last bridge before entering Alpha Base.
Black Box 02—Relic Approach	Top left of the map, behind a Covenant shield.
Black Box 03—Relic Interior	On the small ramp on the left side, right at the start, before going inside the Relic.
Black Box 04—Arcadia City	Just north of the starting point, right next to the skyscraper where you can save Adam.
Black Box 05—Arcadia Outskirts	Go down the first ramp as you are fleeing from the Covenant; it's behind a downed Pelican.
Black Box 06—Dome of Light	Far left of the map, to the left of where you transport the third Rhino tank.
Black Box 07—Scarab	Far right side of the map, in a small alcove with supply crates.
Black Box 08—Anders' Signal	Near the big brute fire line at the start, on a ridge to the right.

Black Box 09—The Flood	Straight out from the base ramp on the other side of the map.
Black Box 10—Shield World	Alongside Bravo platoon, which is the middle platoon you pick up.
Black Box 11—Cleansing	Left rear of the ship, on wings that slant down; you'll need a flying unit.
Black Box 12—Repairs	Left edge of Spirit of Fire, not far from the Power Core building, on the left side.
Black Box 13—Beachhead	On a ledge near the second set of teleporters, near the Covenant base.
Black Box 14—Reactor	Up and left at the top of the first ramp, on the edge of the ramp.
Black Box 15—Escape	Directly opposite the starting point on the north edge of the map, between the Flood and the Covenant base.

SKULLS LOCATIONS/REQUIREMENTS

In each mission, you must meet the requirement before heading to the skull's location.

UNLOCKABLE	HOW TO UNLOCK
Skull Name: Boomstick (Mission 12: Repairs)	Kill 12 Spirit Transports—take a Hawk to the Lower 2 Airlocks and it's right up the little ramp in the air.
Skull Name: Bountiful Harvest (Mission 14: Reactor)	Kill 20 Vampires—head to the second Covenant base and it's in the far corner at the bottom of the next ramp.
Skull Name: Catch (Mission 10: Shield World)	Kill 350 Swarms—get at least 2 Hornets and fly east of you base past the First Tower to a Plateau covered with Flood Eggs; it is in the center.
Skull Name: Cowbell (Mission 3: Relic Interior)	Kill 45 Hunters—take a Grizzly, Anders, Forge and your Marines back to where they were held up on the central pad.
Skull Name: Emperor (Mission 15: Escape)	Kill 3 Scarabs—Head to the very north of the map and it's dead center in the flood.
Skull Name: Fog (Mission 5: Arcadia Outskirts)	Kill 5 Wraiths—get a Warthog and rush back up the tracks to the left of your main base and just keep going straight past the split in the tracks.
Skull Name: Grunt Birthday Party (Mission 2: Relic Approach)	Kill 20 Jackals—head back to Alpha base with a Warthog; it's in the south end of the base.
Skull Name: Look Daddy! (Mission 1: Alpha Base)	Kill 100 Grunts—get a Warthog and rush back to the front gate of Alpha base; the skull is where the Marines were held up.
Skull Name: Pain Train (Mission 13: Beachhead)	Kill 10 Bomber Forms—head back to the beginning of the map by the first teleporter and head down the path to a flood nest; it's right next to it.
Skull Name: Rebel Leader (Mission 9: The Flood)	Kill 20 Flood Stalks—just to the northeast of your main base is a downed Pelican. Just take a Warthog to claim it fast and easy.
Skull Name: Rebel Supporter (Mission 8: Anders' Signal)	Kill 750 Infection Forms—head to north side of the map where you got the Elephant, head toward a cliff. But you'll see a ridge. Go into ridge.
Skull Name: Rebel Sympathizer (Mission 7: Scarab)	Kill 10 Locusts—get a Warthog and take it to the top-left of the map, where there were 2 Locusts and a Power Nod; it's right there.
Skull Name: Sickness (Mission 6: Dome of Light)	Kill 50 Banshees—take a squad of Marines to the hanger behind your base; it's right there.
Skull Name: Sugar Cookies (Mission 11: Cleansing)	Kill 100 Sentinels—take a Hornet to the front end of the Spirit of Fire and it is right on the nose of the ship.

Skull Name: Wuv Woo (Mission 4: Arcadia City)	Kill 50 Elites—where you set up base 2 in the streets there are some stairs next to it leading to a bronze statue. It's next to the statue.

HARRY POTTER AND THE DEATHLY HALLOWS, PART 1 (XBOX 360)

CODES

EFFECT	CODE
Elite Challenges	Y, Up, X, LT, RT, A
Protego Totalum	Y, B, Up, Left, RT, Right
Superstrength potions	X, Left, Right, A, RT, RB

HARRY POTTER AND THE DEATHLY HALLOWS, PART 2 (XBOX 360)

ACHIEVEMENT

UNLOCKABLE	HOW TO UNLOCK
A Good Offence (10)	Defeated 10 enemy wizards before they cast a spell
A Good Start (10)	Defeated 100 enemy wizards, in the Main Story OR Challenges
Accomplished Wizard (150)	Completed the game on Expert
Back to You ... (10)	Defeated 10 enemy wizards with Protego deflections
Best Friend (5)	Played as Ron
Blind Luck (5)	Defeated 10 enemy wizards from cover, without aiming
Boom! (5)	Played as Seamus
Burning Bridges (10)	Completed 'A Job to Do'
Care of the Castle (20)	Escaped Voldemort with minimal damage to Hogwart
Casting from Cover (5)	Defeated an enemy wizard from cover for the first time
Change of Plans (20)	Completed 'A Turn of Events'
Complete Collection (50)	Collected 100% of all items
Confringo! (10)	Defeated 100 enemy wizards with Confringo
Covert Confidence (20)	Defeated 100 enemy wizards from cover
Defiant Daughter (5)	Played as Ginny
Don't Bank on it! (10)	Completed 'Gringotts'
Expelliarmus! (20)	Successfully dispelled 100 Protego shields with Expelliarmus
Expulso! (10)	Defeated 100 enemy wizards with Expulso
Familiar Faces (15)	Completed 'Surrender'
First Rung (10)	Completed your first challenge
Full of Character (40)	Found all characters
Future Auror (50)	Got all achievements, 100% the game!
Getting There ... (20)	Defeated 500 enemy wizards in the Main Story OR Challenges
Got It Covered! (5)	Played as Neville
Having a Blast (5)	Triggered 5 explosive reactions
Hogwarts Burning (15)	Completed 'The Battle of Hogwarts'
Hogwarts Defender (20)	Defeated 1000 enemy wizards in the Main Story OR Challenges
It's All Come Down to This ... (20)	Completed 'Voldemort's Last Stand'
Listen Up (40)	Found all Music Tracks
Lost and Found (15)	Completed 'The Lost Diadem'
Magical McGonagall (5)	Played as McGonagall
Mastering Magic (80)	Completed the game on Advanced

Motherly Love (20)	Completed 'Not My Daughter'
Not a Scratch (5)	Completed a level without being defeated
Now You See Me (10)	Apparated over 100 metres
Petrificus Totalus! (15)	Successfully paralysed 100 enemy wizards using Petrificus Totalus
Protego! (20)	Used Protego against 100 spells
Pulling Teeth (10)	Completed 'The Basilisk Fang'
Shining Example (50)	Completed all challenges at Gold standard
Snape Sacked (10)	Completed 'A Problem of Security'
Stay Away from Her (5)	Played as Molly
Stopped in Their Tracks (10)	Defeated 5 enemy wizards with one Impedimenta cast
Strategic Spell-casting (10)	Defeated 50 enemy wizards using more than one spell
Streets of Hogsmeade (10)	Completed 'The Streets of Hogsmeade'
That Showed Them ... (10)	Defeated 4 enemy wizards with a Confringo cast
The Best Defence ... (10)	Used Protego to defeat 20 enemy wizards at close range
The Bigger They Are ... (15)	Completed 'A Giant Problem'
The Brightest Witch (5)	Played as Hermione
Up to the Challenge (30)	Completed all challenges
Wizard-in-Training (40)	Completed the game on Normal

HARRY POTTER AND THE HALF BLOOD PRINCE (XBOX 360)

UNLOCKABLES

Collect the following number of crests to unlock the corresponding bonuses.

UNLOCKABLE	HOW TO UNLOCK
Two-Player Dueling Pack 4: Paved Courtyard Dueling Arena	113 Hogwarts Crests
More mini-crests with each cast	129 Hogwarts Crests
Two-Player Dueling Pack 2: Training Ground Dueling Arena	14 Hogwarts Crests
Dungbombs in prank boxes around Hogwarts	21 Hogwarts Crests
Two-Player Dueling Pack 2: Crabbe & Goyle	29 Hogwarts Crests
Two-Player Dueling Pack 1: Draco & Luna	3 Hogwarts Crests
Score boost in flying events	38 Hogwarts Crests
Exploding Cauldrons in prank boxes around Hogwarts	48 Hogwarts Crests
Two-Player Dueling Pack 4: The Transfiguration Dueling Arena	59 Hogwarts Crests
Even More health in duels	71 Hogwarts Crests
More health in duels	8 Hogwarts Crests
Two-Player Dueling Pack 5: Ginny & Hermione	84 Hogwarts Crests
Love Potion in Potions Club	98 Hogwarts Crests

HARVEST MOON: THE TALE OF TWO TOWNS (DS)

UNLOCKABLE

UNLOCKABLE	HOW TO UNLOCK
Alpaca	Unlocked in year 2 Fall.
Jersey Cow/Calf	Unlocked in Year 2.
Owl	Unlocked after the 1st tunnel upgrade.
Shetland Horse	Unlocked after you complete the three tunnel upgrades.
Silkie Chicken/Chick	Unlocked in year 2.
Suffolk Sheep/Lamb	Unlocked in year 2.
Throughbred Horse	Unlocked after the first tunnel upgrade.

NEW!

A
B
C
D
E
F
G
H
I
J
K
L
M
N
O
P
Q
R
S
T
U
V
W
X
Y
Z

Alisa	Raise Nathan's friendship to 2 White Flowers, be in Fall of year 2 or later, and then walk to the Mountain Summit between 10:00 pm-3:00 am on sunny.
Dirk	In Summer of your 1st year walk from the Konohana low-mountain area to the Konohana entrance area between 9:00am-8:00 pm on a sunny, snowy to unlocked.
Mikhail	Introduced to you by mayor in Fall 6. He will move into whichever town you are living in at the time.
Nathan	Winter 3, the mayor will introduce you to him he'll be at the church in Bluebell from now on.
Oracle	Walk from the Bluebell Low-Mountain to Bluebell Mid-Mountain area after 8:00 pm starting in year 2 to unlock her.
Cardboard Cart	Raise Oracle's friendship to 2 Flowers and have Request Level rank 4 or higher. You need 1 Mythic Ore, 5 Brown Alpaca Wool, and 30,000,000 G.
Chicken Cart	Available at either Animal shop starting in year 3.
Fancy Cart	Win any Cooking Festival in year 2.
Lion Cart	Available at either Animal shop starting in year 3.
Shrine Cart	Win any Cooking Festival in year 2.
Sled	Own the Shrine Cart and the Fancy Cart and have the tunnel between both towns reconnected, and then win a cooking festival starting in year 2.
UFO Cart	Raise Oracle's friendship to 2 Flowers and have Request Level rank 4 or higher. You need 1 Stone Tablet, 5 White Alpaca Wool, and 19,771,116 G.
Axe	Requested by Sheng in 1st year you need to raise 5,000 FP to unlocked the request needed 8000 G and 10 branches.
Fishing Rod	Given to you by mayor in Summer 1 at 1st Year.
Hammer	Requested by Sheng in Spring 12 at 1st year needed 8 stones.
Master Rod	Requested by Rutger needed 10 old boots and 10 old balls
Skateboard	Requester by Oracle in year 2 needed 10 old balls and 10 material lumber.
Snowboard	Requested by Oracle in year2 needed 10 elli leaves and 10 snow balls.
Stethoscope	Requested by Ash needed 5 milk and 5 egg plus 1,500g

CAPSULES

Capsules contain items that are added to the course. They have no effect on the gameplay, they are just there for show.

UNLOCKABLE	HOW TO UNLOCK
Armored Zombie	Play 20 rounds at Euro Classic G.C. (Regular Tee).
Bear	Play 20 rounds at Highland C.C. (Long Tee).
Blue Whale	Play 20 rounds at The Crown Links (Long Tee).
Child Witch	Play 20 rounds at Euro Classic G.C. (Long Tee).
Glider	Play 20 rounds at The Crown Links (Regular Tee).
Gnome	Play 20 rounds at Silver Peaks G.C. (Regular Tee).
Helicopter	Play 20 rounds at Highland C.C. (Regular Tee).
Jet Formation	Play 20 rounds at Okinawa Golf Resort (Regular Tee).
Lion	Play 20 rounds at Great Safari C.C. (Long Tee).
Manta	Play 20 rounds at Okinawa Golf Resort (Long Tee).
Rhino	Play 20 rounds at Great Safari C.C. (Regular Tee).
Unicorn	Play 20 rounds at Silver Peaks G.C. (Long Tee).

HOT SHOTS GOLF: WORLD INVITATIONAL (PLAYSTATION VITA)

TROPHY

UNLOCKABLE	HOW TO UNLOCK
A True Hot Shots Golfer (Bronze)	Win VS Grace on Pro Rank.
Absolute Class (Bronze)	Purchase a Lv3 club or ball.
All our thanks to Everybody's Golfers! (Platinum)	Get every trophy.
Art Fancier (Bronze)	Purchase every piece of concept art.
Audiophile (Bronze)	Purchase every Music track.
Chaser of the Flame (Silver)	Perform a homing shot in an official round.
Chewing Up Challenges (Bronze)	Win VS Stuart on Bronze Rank.
Courses Complete! (Bronze)	Gain membership to every course.
Daily Participant (Bronze)	Enter a Daily Int'l Tournament and complete the round.
Fancy Dresser (Bronze)	Purchase a costume.
Fear the Receptionist! (Bronze)	Gain access to Amy as a playable character.
Gear Collector (Bronze)	Purchase every type of ball and club.
Gear Master (Silver)	Purchase Lv3 versions of every ball with levels.
Go for the Ace! (Silver)	Score an hole-in-one in an official round.
Greased Lightning (Silver)	Perform a rising shot in an official round.
I Love Everybody! (Gold)	Raise all characters' loyalty to max.
It's a Miracle! (Silver)	Score an albatross in an official round.
Journey's End...? (Silver)	Win VS Pandora on Gold Rank.
King of Kings (Gold)	Collect every crown in Challenge Mode.
Lobby Character Part Collector (Bronze)	Collect over 50% of the normal parts.
Lobby Character Part Lover (Silver)	Collect over 50% of the special parts.
Lobby Character Part Maniac (Gold)	Collect over 50% of the deluxe parts.
My First Birdie (Bronze)	Score a birdie in an official round.
My First Chip-In (Bronze)	Perform a chip-in in an official round.
Overwhelming Power (Bronze)	Hit a drive over 350 yards in an official round.
Perfect Spiral (Silver)	Perform a spiral shot in an official round.
Putting Pro (Bronze)	Sink a putt over 15m long in an official round.
Rockin' Score (Bronze)	Score an eagle in an official round.
Shot Type Selector (Bronze)	Use every shot type in an official round.
So Long, Amateur League (Bronze)	Win VS Pancho on Amateur Rank.
SOLD OUT (Gold)	Purchase every item in the shop.
Starry Night (Silver)	Collect every star in Challenge Mode.
The Challenge Begins (Bronze)	Win VS Isabelle on Beginner Rank.
The Climax! (Bronze)	Win VS Max on Silver Rank.
The Real Ending! (Gold)	Win VS Izzak on Platinum Rank.
True Dedication (Bronze)	Raise one character's loyalty to max.
Watery Wonder (Bronze)	Skip the ball across water three or more times in a row in an official round.

THE HOUSE OF THE DEAD: OVERKILL (WII)

UNLOCKABLES

UNLOCKABLE	HOW TO UNLOCK
Director's Cut mode	Complete Story mode to unlock Director's Cut mode.
Dual Wield mode	Clear Director's Cut.
Handcannon Weapon	Complete Story mode to unlock the handcannon.
Mini-Gun Weapon	Complete all levels in Director's Cut.

HYPERDIMENSION NEPTUNIA MK2 (PLAYSTATION 3)

TROPHY

UNLOCKABLE	HOW TO UNLOCK
5pb. chan (Bronze)	5bp chan joined your party.
Battle Master (Bronze)	Fought over 500 battles.
Blanc (Bronze)	Blanc joined your party.
Brave the Hard (Bronze)	Beat Brave the Hard.
Candidates of Lastation Goddess (Bronze)	Encountered with Uni.
Candidates of Luwian Goddess (Bronze)	Encountered with Rom and Ram.
Chain original combo (Bronze)	Chained your original combo.
Chain the combo (Bronze)	Chained 80+ original combo.
Counter Stop (Silver)	All characters reached level 99.
Create Items (Bronze)	Created items.
Delphinus (Gold)	Beat Delphinus.
Goddess-ize (Bronze)	Watched the event 'Trapped Goddess'
Grave of the industry (Bronze)	Watched the event 'Grave of the industry'
GUST chan (Bronze)	GUST chan joined your party.
Hard-bitten (Bronze)	Fought over 100 battles.
Hot Spring (Bronze)	Watched the event 'Hot Spring'
Judge the Hard (Bronze)	Beat Judge the Hard.
Lastation Ending (Silver)	Watched the 'Lastation' Ending.
Leanbox Ending (Silver)	Watched the 'Leanbox' Ending.
Let's play games (Bronze)	Watched the event 'Let's play games'
Live Stage (Bronze)	Watched the event 'Live Stage'
Lowee Ending (Silver)	Watched the 'Lowee' Ending.
Magic Sword (Bronze)	Obtained the Magic sword.
Magic the Hard (Bronze)	Beat Magic the Hard.
Makers Ending (Silver)	Watched the 'Makers' Ending.
Maximum Power (Bronze)	Dealt maximum 100000+ damage.
Nepgear Start (Bronze)	Started the game.
Nepgear Version Up (Bronze)	Nepgear upgraded.
Neptune (Bronze)	Neptune joined your party.
Nippon Ichi chan (Bronze)	Nippon Ichi chan joined your party.
Noire (Bronze)	Noire joined your party.
Normal Ending (Silver)	Watched the Normal Ending.
PeroPero (Bronze)	Watched the event 'PeroPero'
Planeptune Ending (Silver)	Watched the 'Planeptune' Ending.
Rehabilitation (Bronze)	Fought your first battle.

Release Planeptune (Bronze)	Released Planeputune.
Rescue the Goddess (Bronze)	Watched the event 'Rescue the Goddess'
Rom and Ram Version Up (Bronze)	Rom and Ram upgraded
Ruling Ending (Gold)	Watched the 'Ruling' Ending.
The fateful encounter (Bronze)	Watched the event 'Encounter with Histoire'
Trapped Goddess (Bronze)	Watched the event 'Trapped Goddess'
Trick the Hard (Bronze)	Beat Trick the Hard.
True Ending (Gold)	Watched the True Ending.
Ultimate Neptune Mk2 Master (Platinum)	Acquired all trophies.
Uni Version Up (Bronze)	Uni upgraded
Uranus (Bronze)	Encountered with Uranus.
Vert (Bronze)	Vert joined your party.

NEW!

A
B
C
D
E
F
G
H
I
J
K
L
M
N
O
P
Q
R
S
T
U
V
W
X
Y
Z

ICE AGE: CONTINENTAL DRIFT - ARCTIC GAMES (PLAYSTATION 3)

TROPHY

UNLOCKABLE	HOW TO UNLOCK
Acorn Nut (Bronze)	Collect every Acorn in Glacier Hopping.
Bob Smasher (Bronze)	Finish a Bob-Smashing race in Story Mode.
Bring home the Gold (Gold)	Get a Gold Acorn on every single game event.
Bullseye (Bronze)	Place all your shells on the target in one round of Shell Slide.
Cliffhanger (Bronze)	Collect all acorns and reach the goal in under 1:00 minute in Ice Smash.
Coconut Slinger (Bronze)	Finish a Coconut Slingshot game in Story Mode.
Come on, fraidy cat! (Bronze)	Fall into the water 15 times with either Diego or Shira.
Dream come true (Bronze)	Find the hidden Acorn in the Scrat Cannon event.
Drifting like a sir (Bronze)	Pass through every gate in a single Mountain Drift race.
Further down the road (Bronze)	Reach the end of the level bouncing 20 times or less in Scrat Cannon.
Glacier Hopper (Bronze)	Finish a Glacier Hopping race in Story Mode.
Golden Breaker (Bronze)	Obtain a Gold Acorn time in Ice Smash (Free Play only).
Golden Flyer (Bronze)	Obtain a Gold Acorn score in Scrat Cannon (Free Play only).
Golden Glider (Bronze)	Obtain a Gold Acorn score in Shell Slide (Free Play only).
Golden Hopper (Bronze)	Obtain a Gold Acorn time in Glacier Hopping (Free Play only).
Golden Jumper (Bronze)	Obtain a Gold Acorn score in Style Jump (Free Play only).
Golden Plumber (Bronze)	Obtain a Gold Acorn score in Prehistoric Plumber (Free Play only).
Golden Skier (Bronze)	Obtain a Gold Acorn time in Mountain Drift (Free Play only).
Golden Slider (Bronze)	Obtain a Gold Acorn time in Slip Slide (Free Play only).
Golden Slingshooter (Bronze)	Obtain a Gold Acorn score in Coconut Slingshot (Free Play only).
Golden Smasher (Bronze)	Obtain a Gold Acorn score in Bob-Smashing (Free Play only).
Herd Hero (Gold)	Finish the Story mode while playing on the Herd's side.
Herd Migration (Silver)	Slide down 1000 miles of ice or snow.
Ice Breaker (Bronze)	Finish a Ice Smash game in Story Mode.
Learn to Fly (Silver)	Fly 500 miles over land or sea.
Master Bullseye (Silver)	Place a shell in the exact center of the target, without steering it or hitting any other shell.
Mountain Drifter (Bronze)	Finish a Mountain Drift race in Story Mode.
None left standing (Bronze)	Break every wall of your team without breaking any wall of the opposing team in a Bob-Smashing race.

Oak Forest (Silver)	Collect 1000 acorns.
Pirate Captain (Gold)	Finish the Story mode while playing on the Crew's side.
Platinum Acorn (Platinum)	Obtain every other trophy in the game.
Scrat Cannoneer (Bronze)	Finish a Scrat Cannon game in Story Mode.
Scrat Plumber (Bronze)	Finish a Prehistoric Plumber game in Story Mode.
Sharp Shooter (Silver)	Destroy all targets in Coconut Slingshot.
Shell Slider (Bronze)	Finish a Shell Slide game in Story Mode.
Slip Slider (Bronze)	Finish a Slip Slide race in Story Mode.
Speedster (Bronze)	Finish a Slip Slide race without hitting any snow patches.
Strike the Pose (Bronze)	Successfully complete 8 tricks in a single Style Jump game.
Style Jumper (Bronze)	Finish a Style Jump game in Story Mode.
That treasure is mine! (Silver)	Win a Tournament against a friend.
The most beautiful story ever (Gold)	Finish Story mode without losing a single game event.

ICE AGE: CONTINENTAL DRIFT - ARCTIC GAMES (XBOX 360)

ACHIEVEMENT

UNLOCKABLE	HOW TO UNLOCK
Acorn Nut (15)	Collected every Acorn in Glacier Hopping.
Bob-Smasher (20)	Finished a Bob-Smashing race in Story Mode.
Bring home the Gold (75)	Got a Gold Acorn on every single game event.
Bullseye (15)	Placed all your shells on the target in one round of Shell Slide.
Cliffhanger (15)	Collected all acorns and reached the goal in under 1:00 minute in Ice Smash.
Coconut Slinger (20)	Finished a Coconut Slingshot game in Story Mode.
Come on, fraidy cat! (10)	Fell into the water 15 times with either Diego or Shira.
Dream comes true (20)	Found the hidden Acorn in the Scrat Cannon event.
Drifting like a sir (15)	Passed through every gate in a single Mountain Drift race.
Further down the road (15)	Reached the end of the level bouncing 20 times or less in Scrat Cannon.
Glacier Hopper (20)	Finished a Glacier Hopping race in Story Mode.
Golden Breaker (20)	Obtained a Gold Acorn time in Ice Smash (Free Play only).
Golden Flyer (20)	Obtained a Gold Acorn score in Scrat Cannon (Free Play only).
Golden Glider (20)	Obtained a Gold Acorn score in Shell Slide (Free Play only).
Golden Hopper (20)	Obtained a Gold Acorn time in Glacier Hopping (Free Play only).
Golden Jumper (20)	Obtained a Gold Acorn score in Style Jump (Free Play only).
Golden Plumber (20)	Obtained a Gold Acorn score in Prehistoric Plumber (Free Play only).
Golden Skier (20)	Obtained a Gold Acorn time in Mountain Drift (Free Play only).
Golden Slider (20)	Obtained a Gold Acorn time in Slip Slide (Free Play only).
Golden Slingshooter (20)	Obtained a Gold Acorn score in Coconut Slingshot (Free Play only).

CODES & CHEATS

Golden Smasher (20)	Obtained a Gold Acorn score in Bob-Smashing (Free Play only).
Herd Hero (50)	Finished the Story Mode while playing on the Herd's side.
Herd Migration (40)	Slid down 1000 miles of ice or snow.
Ice Breaker (20)	Finished an Ice Smash game in Story Mode.
Learn to Fly (30)	Flew 500 miles over land or sea.
Master Bullseye (30)	Placed a shell in the exact center of the target, without steering it or hitting any other shells.
Mountain Drifter (20)	Finished a Mountain Drift race in Story Mode.
None left standing (15)	Broke every wall of your team without breaking any wall of the opposing team in a Bob-Smashing race.
Oak Forest (40)	Collected 1000 acorns.
Pirate Cap'n (50)	Finished the Story Mode while playing on the Crew's side.
Scrat Cannoneer (20)	Finished a Scrat Cannon game in Story Mode.
Scrat Plumber (20)	Finished a Prehistoric Plumber game in Story Mode.
Sharp Shooter (30)	Destroyed all targets in Coconut Slingshot.
Shell Slider (20)	Finished a Shell Slide game in Story Mode.
Slip Slider (20)	Finished a Slip Slide race in Story Mode.
Speedster (15)	Finished a Slip Slide race without hitting any snow patches.
Strike the Pose (15)	Successfully struck 8 poses in a single Style Jump game.
Style Jumper (20)	Finished a Style Jump game in Story Mode.
That treasure is mine! (30)	Won a Tournament against a friend.
The most beautiful story ever (75)	Finished Story Mode without losing a single game event.

ICE AGE 2: THE MELTDOWN   (WII)

CODES
Pause the game and press the following codes.

UNLOCKABLE	HOW TO UNLOCK
Unlimited Health	⬆, ⬇, ⬆, ⬇, ⬆, ⬇, ⬆, ⬇

IMAGE FIGHT   (WII)

UNLOCKABLES

UNLOCKABLE	HOW TO UNLOCK
Arcade Mode	Do a reset (START+SELECT), then immediately hold ①
Mr. Heli mode	Highlight song C in Sound Test mode and press ⬆, SELECT, ②+①, then press ① on Mr. Heli and then press RUN
Sound Test	Press SELECT on the title screen

INDIANA JONES AND THE STAFF OF KINGS   (WII)

CODES

EFFECT	CODE
Unlock Fate of Atlantis game	In the main menu, while holding down Ⓩ press: Ⓐ, ⬆, ⬇, Ⓑ, ⬆, ⬇, ⬆, ⬇, ⬇, Ⓑ

INFAMOUS 2   (PLAYSTATION 3)

TROPHY

UNLOCKABLE	HOW TO UNLOCK
A Streetcar Named 'Boom!' (Bronze)	Complete BOOM!
Am I The Daddy? (Bronze)	Complete Nix's New Family.

Ambulance Chaser (Bronze)	Complete Hearts and Minds Campaign.
Arch Villain (Silver)	Earn full negative Karma.
Army Of Me (Bronze)	Defeat 300 enemies.
Back to the Bayou (Bronze)	Return to the swamp blockade.
Behind the Curtain (Bronze)	Collect 50% of the available Dead Drops.
Closed Casket Affair (Bronze)	Give Bertrand what he wants.
Cole' Blooded (Bronze)	Defeat 100 civilians.
Dazed and Defused (Bronze)	Take down the Blast Shard Bomber.
Discerning Taste (Bronze)	Take down a street performer who is imitating a statue.
Don't Fence Me In (Bronze)	Climb a chain link fence and rejoice.
Exposure (Bronze)	Complete Exposing Bertrand.
Express Elevator (Bronze)	Ascend 50 vertical launch poles.
Extreme Makeover (Bronze)	Destroy 30 verandas or other large objects.
Fight the Good Fight (Silver)	Unlock the good ending.
Finish What You Started (Bronze)	Perform 100 finishers or ultra melee combos.
Forging Your Own Path (Silver)	Unlock the evil ending.
Frozen Asset (Bronze)	Complete the ice Conduit side missions.
Get Nix'ed (Bronze)	Choose Nix in Storm the Fort.
Go Long! (Bronze)	Hurl 50 objects using the Kinetic Pulse ability.
Head Hunter (Bronze)	Use the Precision ability to rack up three head shots in rapid succession.
Heavy Hitter (Bronze)	Use your Ionic Powers 30 times.
Hero to the People (Bronze)	Stop 80 crimes in progress.
I'm As Shocked As You Are (Bronze)	Defeat an enemy or civilian by stepping in water.
Incorruptible (Silver)	Earn full positive Karma.
inFAMOUS 2 Platinum Trophy (Platinum)	Collect all other inFAMOUS 2 Trophies
It's My Town, Now (Silver)	Take over the second island in New Marais.
Just One More (Gold)	Pick up all the blast shards scattered around New Marais.
Knockout in the Blackout (Bronze)	Defeat 50 enemies in powered down areas while no missions are active.
Land Lord (Silver)	Take over the first island in New Marais.
Level Up (Bronze)	Create a new mission using the UGC level editor.
Matching Set (Bronze)	Unlock and purchase a power of each type by performing stunts.
Mountaineer (Bronze)	Climb to the top of the 3 tallest buildings in New Marais.
Nothing Can Bring Me Down (Bronze)	Stay off the ground for 130 meters.
Pain Builds Character (Gold)	Finish the game on hard difficulty.
Playing Both Sides (Bronze)	Complete Fooling the Rebels.
Quid Pro Kuo (Bronze)	Complete Leading the Charge.
Return to Sender (Bronze)	Send a Helicopter's rockets back at it using any Blast ability.
Shardcore (Silver)	Pick up 50% of blast shards scattered around New Marais.
Shock and Awe (Bronze)	Thunder drop into a group of 5 or more enemies.
Status Kuo (Bronze)	Choose Kuo in Storm the Fort.
Take Them For A Spin (Bronze)	Hit at least 6 cars in a single Ionic Vortex.

The Cleaner (Bronze)	Complete the assassination side missions.
Thunder Flop (Bronze)	Thunder drop from the highest place in New Marais.
Trail Blazer (Bronze)	Play 5 user-generated missions under the Newest filter.
UGC Curious (Bronze)	Play 10 user-generated missions.
UGC Veteran (Bronze)	Play 25 user-generated missions.
Vehicular Manslaughter (Bronze)	Defeat 25 enemies by throwing cars at them.
Watch That First Step (Bronze)	Defeat an enemy by destroying the object they stand on.
Well inFORMED (Silver)	Collect all Dead drops.
With Great Power Comes Greater Power (Silver)	Unlock and purchase all powers.

UNLOCKABLE

Complete the story twice, once with the Hero route and once as Infamous. Once the credits end after the second playthrough, the post game is available and you have unlocked access to the opposite Karma powers of your current Cole along with the powers of the character with which you didn't transfer. You are also awarded 15,000 XP.

INVERSION (PLAYSTATION 3)

TROPHY

UNLOCKABLE	HOW TO UNLOCK
Ah Gross! (Bronze)	Use the Gravlink to throw a corpse at your friend (Co-op mode)
All Up In Them Guts (Bronze)	Use a Shotgun to gib 25 Lutadore enemies (Any Difficulty)
Brotastic! (Bronze)	Revive a friend online (Co-op mode)
Burn it Down (Bronze)	Set 25 Lutadore enemies on fire with the Lavagun (Any Difficulty)
Chapter Eight (Bronze)	Complete the final checkpoint in Into the Depths on Normal or High Difficulty
Chapter Eleven (Bronze)	Complete the final checkpoint in Red Sky on Normal or High Difficulty
Chapter Five (Bronze)	Complete the final checkpoint in Street Fight on Normal or High Difficulty
Chapter Four (Bronze)	Complete the final checkpoint in Road Home on Normal or High Difficulty
Chapter Nine (Bronze)	Complete the final checkpoint in Enlightenment on Normal or High Difficulty
Chapter One (Bronze)	Complete the final checkpoint in Vanguard Down on Normal or High Difficulty
Chapter Seven (Bronze)	Complete the final checkpoint in Edge of the World on Normal or High Difficulty
Chapter Six (Bronze)	Complete the final checkpoint in Road to Hell on Normal or High Difficulty
Chapter Ten (Bronze)	Complete the final checkpoint in Reveal on Normal or High Difficulty
Chapter Thirteen (Bronze)	Complete the final checkpoint in Reversion on Normal or High Difficulty
Chapter Three (Bronze)	Complete the final checkpoint in Breakout on Normal or High Difficulty
Chapter Twelve (Bronze)	Complete the final checkpoint in Deja Vanguard on Normal or High Difficulty
Chapter Two (Bronze)	Complete the final checkpoint in Caged on Normal or High Difficulty

Dude Bro! (Bronze)	Complete a Campaign level with a Friend (Any Difficulty)
Easy Going (Bronze)	Finish the Campaign on Low Gravity Difficulty
Enforcer (Bronze)	Reach Gold Grav Major Rank
Feats Don't Fail Me Now (Gold)	Complete All Multiplayer Basic Challenges
Fivesome (Silver)	Use the Gravlink to kill 5 Lutadores with one object (Campaign)
Gold Star (Bronze)	Get 1st Place in a Deathmatch game (Matchmaking)
Grand Master Gravity (Platinum)	Unlock all trophies
Grappler (Silver)	Take the Gravlink from the Lutadores
Gravlink Gangsta (Silver)	Use the Gravlink to throw 50 Lutadore Enemies (Campaign)
Gravlink Hustler (Silver)	Use the Gravlink to throw 30 Lutadore Enemies (Campaign)
Gravlink Thug (Bronze)	Use the Gravlink to throw 15 Lutadore Enemies (Campaign)
Half Sack (Bronze)	Reach Silver Grav Sergeant Rank
High G Amateur (Bronze)	Perform 10 Finishing Moves using High Grav Powers (Campaign)
High G Champ (Silver)	Perform 50 Finishing Moves using High Grav Powers (Campaign)
I'm About to Blow (Silver)	Kill 100 Lutadore Enemies with explosives in the Campaign (Grenades, Rockets, Barrels)
I'm Designer (Bronze)	Change your multiplayer character's appearance
Kicking Weightless Ass (Silver)	Escape from a Lurker's grasp 5 times during single player
Low G Amateur (Bronze)	Perform 10 Finishing Moves using Low Grav Powers (Campaign)
Low G Champ (Silver)	Perform 50 Finishing Moves using Low Grav Powers (Campaign)
Man of Mayhem (Bronze)	Reach Diamond Grav Commander Rank
Master Blaster (Silver)	Complete All Multiplayer Weapon Challenges
Meatheads (Bronze)	Finish the Campaign with a Friend (Any Difficulty)
Meet Your Master (Bronze)	Defeat The Prophet Kiltehr (Any Difficulty)
Normal Guy (Silver)	Finish the Campaign on Normal Gravity Difficulty
Rock Hard (Gold)	Finish the Campaign on High Gravity Difficulty
Soldier (Bronze)	Reach Bronze Grav Captain Rank
Spot me Bro! (Bronze)	Have a friend boost you over a ledge (Co-op mode)
Teamster (Bronze)	Be a part of a winning team in Team Deathmatch (Matchmaking)
That's Assault Brotha! (Bronze)	Be a part of a winning team in Assault Mode (Matchmaking)
The Collector (Bronze)	Defeat The Slave Driver (Any Difficulty)
The Great Destroyer (Bronze)	Defeat The Brute (Any Difficulty)
The Tin Man (Bronze)	Defeat The Butcher (Any Difficulty)
Threesome (Bronze)	Use the Gravlink to kill 3 Lutadores with one object (Campaign)
William Tell Routine (Bronze)	Shoot off 100 Lutadore Helmets (Any Difficulty)

INVERSION (XBOX 360)

ACHIEVEMENT

UNLOCKABLE	HOW TO UNLOCK
Ah Gross! (5)	Use the Gravlink to throw a corpse at your friend (Co-op mode)
All Up In Them Guts (25)	Use a Shotgun to gib 25 Lutadore enemies (Any Difficulty)
Brotastic! (5)	Revive a friend online (Co-op mode)
Burn it Down (25)	Set 25 Lutadore enemies on fire with the Lavagun (Any Difficulty)
Chapter Eight (10)	Complete the final checkpoint in Into the Depths on Normal or High Difficulty
Chapter Eleven (10)	Complete the final checkpoint in Red Sky on Normal or High Difficulty
Chapter Five (10)	Complete the final checkpoint in Street Fight on Normal or High Difficulty
Chapter Four (10)	Complete the final checkpoint in Road Home on Normal or High Difficulty
Chapter Nine (10)	Complete the final checkpoint in Enlightenment on Normal or High Difficulty
Chapter One (10)	Complete the final checkpoint in Vanguard Down on Normal or High Difficulty
Chapter Seven (10)	Complete the final checkpoint in Edge of the World on Normal or High Difficulty
Chapter Six (10)	Complete the final checkpoint in Road to Hell on Normal or High Difficulty
Chapter Ten (10)	Complete the final checkpoint in Reveal on Normal or High Difficulty
Chapter Thirteen (10)	Complete the final checkpoint in Reversion on Normal or High Difficulty
Chapter Three (10)	Complete the final checkpoint in Breakout on Normal or High Difficulty
Chapter Twelve (10)	Complete the final checkpoint in Deja Vanguard on Normal or High Difficulty
Chapter Two (10)	Complete the final checkpoint in Caged on Normal or High Difficulty
Dude Bro! (5)	Complete a Campaign level with a Friend (Any Difficulty)
Easy Going (25)	Finish the Campaign on Low Gravity Difficulty
Enforcer (25)	Reach Gold Grav Major Rank
Feats Don't Fail Me Now (50)	Complete All Multiplayer Basic Challenges
Fivesome (50)	Use the Gravlink to kill 5 Lutadores with one object (Campaign)
Gold Star (10)	Get 1st Place in a Deathmatch game (Matchmaking)
Grappler (25)	Take the Gravlink from the Lutadores
Gravlink Gangsta (25)	Use the Gravlink to throw 50 Lutadore Enemies (Campaign)
Gravlink Hustler (15)	Use the Gravlink to throw 30 Lutadore Enemies (Campaign)
Gravlink Thug (10)	Use the Gravlink to throw 15 Lutadore Enemies (Campaign)
Half Sack (5)	Reach Silver Grav Sergeant Rank
High G Amateur (15)	Perform 10 Finishing Moves using High Grav Powers (Campaign)

High G Champ (25)	Perform 50 Finishing Moves using High Grav Powers (Campaign)
I'm About to Blow (25)	Kill 100 Lutadore Enemies with explosives in the Campaign (Grenades, Rockets, Barrels)
I'm Designer (5)	Change your multiplayer character's appearance
Kicking Weightless Ass (10)	Escape from a Lurker's grasp 5 times during single player
Low G Amateur (15)	Perform 10 Finishing Moves using Low Grav Powers (Campaign)
Low G Champ (25)	Perform 50 Finishing Moves using Low Grav Powers (Campaign)
Man of Mayhem (50)	Reach Diamond Grav Commander Rank
Master Blaster (50)	Complete All Multiplayer Weapon Challenges
Meatheads (50)	Finish the Campaign with a Friend (Any Difficulty)
Meet Your Master (15)	Defeat The Prophet Kiltehr (Any Difficulty)
Normal Guy (50)	Finish the Campaign on Normal Gravity Difficulty
Rock Hard (75)	Finish the Campaign on High Gravity Difficulty
Soldier (15)	Reach Bronze Grav Captain Rank
Spot me Bro! (5)	Have a friend boost you over a ledge (Co-op mode)
Teamster (15)	Be a part of a winning team in Team Deathmatch (Matchmaking)
That's Assault Brotha! (15)	Be a part of a winning team in Assault Mode (Matchmaking)
The Collector (10)	Defeat The Slave Driver (Any Difficulty)
The Great Destroyer (10)	Defeat The Brute (Any Difficulty)
The Tin Man (10)	Defeat The Butcher (Any Difficulty)
Threesome (25)	Use the Gravlink to kill 3 Lutadores with one object (Campaign)
William Tell Routine (50)	Shoot off 100 Lutadore Helmets (Any Difficulty)

NEW!

A
B
C
D
E
F
G
H
I
J
K
L
M
N
O
P
Q
R
S
T
U
V
W
X
Y
Z

JONAH LOMU RUGBY CHALLENGE (XBOX 360)

ACHIEVEMENT

UNLOCKABLE	HOW TO UNLOCK
A Gentleman's Game (15)	Do not concede more than 2 penalties in a single match
Bank of Toulon (100)	Collect $100,000 Rugby Dollars
Conversion Point Pro (35)	Score a conversion on pro difficulty
End-To-End (40)	Make a try-scoring run which starts within your own in-goal area
Good Sport (40)	Complete 25 online matches
Hardcore Fan (100)	Complete Career Mode
Lack of Discipline (10)	The ref calls one red card against you
No School Boy Difficulty Here (30)	Get gold medals in every tutorial
Online Captain (125)	Complete 50 online matches
Played for Our Sins (35)	Win a match with 2 players sent off
Possessed (10)	Maintain Over 60% possession in a match
Super, Thanks For Asking (50)	Win the Rugby 15 Competition
Tall as Metcalfe (15)	Win 60% of lineouts in a match that aren't thrown by your team
Team Player (40)	Win 10 matches, each as a different team
That's No Oil Painting, But OK (10)	Create and save a custom player
The Catt Memorial Service (20)	Break through a full back with Jonah Lomu
There's No Forfeiting This One (50)	Win the Top 14 Competition
This is My House (10)	Maintain over 60% territory in a match
Where is Tim Timber? (50)	Win the ITM Cup Competition
Working On My Quads (50)	Win the Quad Nations Competition
World Champ Domination (60)	Win the World Championship Competition without losing or drawing a match

JUICED 2: HOT IMPORT NIGHTS (XBOX 360)

DRIVER DNA CAR UNLOCKABLES

Enter the passwords in the DNA lab to unlock the special challenges. If you win the challenges, you unlock a custom version of the following cars.

UNLOCKABLE	HOW TO UNLOCK
Audi TT 1.8L Quattro	YTHZ
BMW Z4 Roadster	GVDL
Frito-Lay Infiniti G35	MNCH
Holden Monaro	RBSG
Hyundai Coupe 2.7L V6	BSLU
Infiniti G35	MRHC
Koenigsegg CCX	KDTR
Mitsubishi Prototype X	DOPX
Nissan 350Z	PRGN

Nissan Skyline R34 GT-R	JWRS
Saleen S7	WIKF
Seat Leon Cupra R	FAMQ

JURASSIC: THE HUNTED (XBOX 360)

UNLOCKABLE

UNLOCKABLE	HOW TO UNLOCK
Laser Rifle	Beat the game on normal to unlock the Laser Rifle for Hard mode.

JUST CAUSE 2 (XBOX 360)

UNLOCKABLES

UNLOCKABLE	HOW TO UNLOCK
Bubble Blaster	South-Southwest of the Communication Outpost Gurun Lautan Lama Gamma in the Lautan Lama Desert Territory, there is a wide-open field full of trees with white leaves. In the northern part of this field there is a lone bell tower. If you climb to the top of this bell tower you will find a small table with a purple gun on it. You can equip this gun. It is the called the Bubble Blaster.
Lost Easter Egg	If you go to the top-left corner of the map you see an island shaped like a square. If you fly a plane over the island your plane will explode, causing you to parachute down to the beach (if over it). You will see a search sign on the beach with an arrow pointing to the jungle. Go into the jungle and you'll find the hatch from "Lost." It is even said by people that you actually can hear the smoke monster in the background.

JUST DANCE 3 (XBOX 360)

ACHIEVEMENT

UNLOCKABLE	HOW TO UNLOCK
Ace Pair - Bronze (5)	Finish a Duet with 2 players getting at least 3 stars on both choreographies (songs with 2 coaches)
Ace Pair - Gold (35)	Finish any Duet with 2 players getting 5 stars on both choreographies (songs with 2 coaches)
Ace Pair - Silver (25)	Finish a Duet with 2 players getting at least 4 stars on both choreographies (songs with 2 coaches)
Big Band Theory - Bronze (5)	Finish any Dance Crew with all 4 players getting at least 3 stars (songs with 4 coaches)
Big Band Theory - Gold (35)	Finish any Dance Crew with all 4 players getting 5 stars (songs with 4 coaches)
Big Band Theory - Silver (25)	Finish any Dance Crew with all 4 players getting at least 4 stars (songs with 4 coaches)
Choreographer - Bronze (5)	Create a choreography in Just Create
Choreographer - Gold (35)	Create 50 choreographies in Just Create
Choreographer - Silver (25)	Create 25 choreographies in Just Create
Constellation Maker - Bronze (5)	Get at least 3 stars on every choreography in the "Songs" menu
Constellation Maker - Gold (35)	Get 5 stars on every choreography in the "Songs" menu
Constellation Maker - Silver (25)	Get at least 4 stars on every choreography in the "Songs" menu
Dancing with The Devil (25)	Dance between Midnight and 4am
Eyes Closed - Bronze (5)	Get 5 stars on any song after disabling pictograms in the Settings menu (excluding Just Create)
Eyes Closed - Gold (35)	Get 5 stars on 10 songs in a row after disabling pictograms in Settings menu (excluding Just Create)
Eyes Closed - Silver (25)	Get 5 stars on 5 songs in a row after disabling pictograms in Settings menu (excluding Just Create)
Highway to Stars - Bronze (5)	Get 5 stars on 2 songs in a row from the "Songs" menu
Highway to Stars - Gold (35)	Get 5 stars on 10 songs in a row from the "Songs" menu

Highway to Stars - Silver (25)	Get 5 stars on 6 songs in a row from the "Songs" menu
I could do this all night! (25)	Dance every song in the "Songs" menu in a row while in the same game
Just Dance Master! (15)	Play every song in the "Songs" menu at least once
Marathon (25)	Dance for more than 1 hour in Non-Stop Shuffle
Morning Exercise (15)	Get 1000 Sweat Points between 5am and 9am with Sweat Mode activated
Part of the community - Bronze (5)	Play one of your own choreographies
Part of the community - Gold (5)	Upload one of your own choreographies
Part of the community - Silver (5)	Download one Just Create choreography
Perfectionist - Bronze (5)	Finish any song in the "Songs" menu without missing a move
Perfectionist - Gold (35)	Finish any song in the "Songs" menu with at least 90% of "Perfect" moves
Perfectionist - Silver (25)	Finish any song in the "Songs" menu, and score "Good" or better on all moves
Saturday Night Fever (15)	Play at least 3 hours Between 8pm and 3am on a Saturday
Simon's Best - Bronze (5)	Get 3 stars in Simon Says
Simon's Best - Gold (35)	Get 5 stars in Simon Says
Simon's Best - Silver (25)	Get 4 stars in Simon Says
Singer - Bronze (5)	Shout Out at least once in a song
Singer - Gold (35)	Shout Out at least once in 20 different songs
Singer - Silver (25)	Shout Out at least once in 10 different songs
Stylist - Bronze (5)	Get all Styles once (excluding Just Create)
Stylist - Gold (35)	Get all Styles with the same player during one game session! (excluding Just Create)
Stylist - Silver (25)	Get four Dance Styles at the same time! (excluding Just Create)
Super Dancer - Bronze (5)	Play 50 songs (excluding Just Create)
Super Dancer - Gold (35)	Play 200 songs (excluding Just Create)
Super Dancer - Silver (25)	Play 100 songs (excluding Just Create)
Sweat & Score - Bronze (5)	Reach 150 Sweat Points with a 3-star rating on any song with Sweat Mode activated
Sweat & Score - Gold (35)	Reach 350 Sweat Points with a 5-star rating on any song with Sweat Mode activated
Sweat & Score - Silver (25)	Reach 250 Sweat Points with a 4-star rating on any song with Sweat Mode activated
Sweat Me a River - Bronze (5)	Earn 1,000 Sweat Points with Sweat Mode activated
Sweat Me a River - Gold (35)	Earn 20,000 Sweat Points with Sweat Mode activated
Sweat Me a River - Silver (25)	Earn 10,000 Sweat Points with Sweat Mode activated
That's my jam! (5)	Play the same song five times in a row
The Daltons (15)	Get 4 Players to line up side by side from shortest to tallest while in the pre-game Lobby

KIDOU SENSHI GUNDAM SEED: BATTLE DESTINY (PLAYSTATION VITA)

TROPHY

UNLOCKABLE	HOW TO UNLOCK
100 Kills (Bronze)	Shoot down a total of 100 enemy mobile suits.
1000 Kills (Silver)	Shoot down a total of 1000 enemy mobile suits.
150 Kills (Bronze)	Shoot down a total of 150 enemy mobile suits.
1500 Kills (Silver)	Shoot down a total of 1500 enemy mobile suits.
200 Kills (Bronze)	Shoot down a total of 200 enemy mobile suits.
2000 Kills (Silver)	Shoot down a total of 2000 enemy mobile suits.
3000 Kills (Silver)	Shoot down a total of 3000 enemy mobile suits.
400 Kills (Bronze)	Shoot down a total of 400 enemy mobile suits.
50 Kills (Bronze)	Shoot down a total of 50 enemy mobile suits.
500 Kills (Silver)	Shoot down a total of 500 enemy mobile suits.
700 Kills (Silver)	Shoot down a total of 700 enemy mobile suits.
Ace Pilot (Bronze)	Clear 20 missions in story mode with an A-Rank.
Battle Mania (Silver)	Win 100 times in VS mode.
Captain (Bronze)	Clear 20 missions in story mode.
Destiny Clear (Bronze)	Clear the final CE 73 story mission.
Elite Earth Alliance Pilot (Silver)	Clear all of the CE 71 and CE 73 story missions as an Earth Alliance pilot.
Elite Pilot (Bronze)	Clear a story mode mision with an S-Rank.
Elite ZAFT Pilot (Silver)	Clear the CE 71 and CE 73 story missions as a ZAFT pilot.
Ensign (Bronze)	Clear 5 missions in story mode.
Excellent Pilot (Silver)	Clear all of the Hyper Boss Battle extra missions.
Great Pilot (Bronze)	Clear 10 missions in story mode with an S-Rank.
Gundam Seed Freak (Gold)	Clear story mode with all three factions.
Killing-King (Silver)	Shoot down 5000 enemy mobile suits.
Lacus-sama Banzai! (Silver)	Clear all of the CE 71 and CE 73 story missions as an Archangel pilot.
Legendary Pilot (Silver)	Clear 25 missions in story mode with an S-Rank.
Lieutenant (Bronze)	Clear 10 missions in story mode.
MS Collector (Silver)	Obtain 80 mobile suits.
Pilot Collector (Silver)	Collect all 30 pilots.
Recruit (Bronze)	Clear 1 mission in story mode.
Seed Clear (Bronze)	Clear the final CE 71 story mission.
Skill Collector (Silver)	Collect all 40 skills.
Super Ace Pilot (Gold)	Clear the CE 73 story missions, "Another" and, "Battle Destiny."
Trophy Complete (Platinum)	Obtain all other trophies in the game.
Ultimate Pilot (Gold)	Clear all story missions.
Veteran Pilot (Silver)	Clear 30 missions in story mode with an A-Rank.

KILLZONE 3 (PLAYSTATION 3)

TROPHIES

UNLOCKABLE	HOW TO UNLOCK
Aerial Superiority - Kill 5 Helghast while in the air (Bronze)	Killed 5 Helghast while airborne using the Jetpack
Bring It Down - Defeat the MAWLR (Bronze)	Defeated the MAWLR defending the Space Elevator
Cagefighter - Kill 10 Helghast using Brutal Melee (Bronze)	Killed 10 Helaghast using Brutal Melee
Close Quarters Killer - Kill 25 Helghast Brutal Melee (Silver)	Killed 25 Helghast using Brutal **using** Melee
Completist - Destroy everything on the MAWLR (Bronze)	Destroyed every destructible weapon on the MAWLR while on foot and on the Intruder
Double Trouble - Reach the river in Co-op (Bronze)	Made it to the Corinth River in Co-op mode
Eagle Eye - Every Sniper Rifle bullet is a kill (Bronze)	Shot and killed 6 Helghast using the Sniper Rifle without reloading or switching weapons
Evening The Odds - Kill 500 Helghast (Bronze)	Kill 500 Helghast
Excessive Force - Kill a lone Helghast with the WASP secondary fire (Bronze)	Used the secondary fire function of the WASP launcher to kill a single Helghast
Fight To The Last - Kill 1500 Helghast (Silver)	Killed 1500 Helghast
Frag Out - Kill 3 Helghast with 1 Frag Grenade (Bronze)	Killed 3 Helghast using 1 fragmentation grenade
Frazzle Dazzle - Kill 3 Helghast with one) shot from the StA5X Arc Cannon (Bronze	Used the StA5X Arc Cannon to kill 3 Helghast with one shot
Go Down And Stay Down - Destroy the ATAC (Bronze)	Defeated the ATAC outside the Stahl Arms facility
Grand Slam - Win a match in 3 multiplayer (Gold)	Won a match in Operations, **modes** Warzone & Guerrilla Warfare modes
Hand To Hand Master - Kill 50 Helghast Brutal Melee (Silver)	Killed 50 Helghast using Brutal **using** Melee
Handy Man - Repair an object (Bronze)	Repaired an object for the first time
Iced - Destroy all Ice-Saws and Dropships (Bronze)	Destroyed all 4 Helghast Ice-Saws and all 6 Dropships
In Your Face - First Brutal Melee (Bronze)	Performed first Brutal Melee move
Into The Lair - Reach the cable car (Bronze)	Reached the cable car and gained access to Stahl Arms South
Iron Man - Get a kill with the Exo (Bronze)	Killed a player using the Exo in any multiplayer mode
ISA TV - Establish communications (Bronze)	Made contact with Earth
Jail Break - Liberate Narville (Bronze)	Liberated Narville from Stahl Arms South
Let's Go Home - Destroy Stahl's Cruiser (Gold)	Destroyed Stahl's Cruiser and left the planet on any difficulty
Medic! - Revive another player (Bronze)	Revived a friendly player for the first time
Minigunned - Destroy all targets (Bronze)	Destroyed everything while using the Minigun on the Intruder
Mopping Up - Kill 40 Helghast foot soldiers (Bronze)	Killed 40 or more Helghast foot soldiers on the beach
Never There - Sneak past Helghast (Bronze)	Sneaked past all Helghast in the Jungle without alerting any of them
No Witnesses - Destroy all dropships on Highway (Bronze)	Destroy all dropships on the **the** Highway

Now It's Personal - Kill 1000 Helghast (Silver)	Killed 1000 Helghast
Now You See Me - Kill using Cloak (Bronze)	Killed another player while cloaked
One Each - Kill 3 Helghast with Shotgun Pistol, no reloads (Bronze)	Shot and killed 3 Helghast using the Shotgun Pistol without reloading or switching weapons
Pilot's Wings - Mid-air kill (Bronze)	Got a mid-air kill using the Jet Pack in any multiplayer mode
Pinpoint - Kill the Heavy with an StA-14 (Bronze)	Killed the Heavy using the StA-14 rifle
Platinum (Platinum)	Collect all Killzone 3 trophies
Power Spike - Nail a Helghast to an exploding object (Bronze)	Used the Boltgun to nail a Helghast to an exploding object
Quick Exit - Escape the Oil Rig quickly (Bronze)	Got off the 2nd rig within 2 minutes.
Ready For Battle - Complete weapons training (Bronze)	Completed weapons training in Prologue
Save The Intruders - Arc APCs destroyed (Bronze)	Successfully assisted with defeating the Arc APCs
Sawn Off - Destroy all chasing APC's (Bronze)	Destroyed all chasing SawBlade APC's in the Senlin Beach section
Shattered - Destroy all glass in the Labs (Bronze)	Destroy all glass panes in the Stahl Arms South laboratories
Smoking Wrecks - Destroy all Tanks on Senlin Beach (Bronze)	Destroyed all the Helghast Tanks in the Senlin Beach section
Spiky Personality - Kill a Helghast using a Burster (Bronze)	Killed a Helghast by shooting a Burster plant
Spread The Love - Kill 5 Helghast at once using the WASP's secondary fire (Bronze)	Killed 5 Helghast at once using the secondary fire mode of the WASP launcher
Spy Game - Kill using Disguise (Bronze)	Killed another player while disguised
Stranded Together - Reach the Extraction Point in Co-op (Bronze)	Made it to the Extraction Point in Co-op mode
Team Player - Play a match as part of a squad (Bronze)	Joined and completed a match as part of a squad
Time For A Dip - Reach the river (Bronze)	Reached the Corinth River with the convoy
Turf War - Capture a Tactical Spawn Point (Bronze)	Captured a Tactical Spawn Point for the first time
Turn The Tables - Melee Kill a Capture Trooper (Bronze)	Killed a Capture Trooper using melee
Up Close & Personal - Brutal Melee another player (Bronze)	Used the Brutal Melee move against another player
Victory - Complete Campaign on Elite (Gold)	Completed every mission on Elite difficulty
You Drive - Drive the Mobile Factory (Bronze)	Took over the controls of the Mobile Factory

KINECT RUSH: A DISNEY-PIXAR ADVENTURE (XBOX 360)

ACHIEVEMENT

UNLOCKABLE	HOW TO UNLOCK
A Friend Indeed (30)	Open all buddy areas in the game, alone or with a friend.
A New Me! (10)	Complete your first scanning.
A New You! (20)	Unlock your first playable character, alone or with a friend.
Absolute Perfection! (30)	Win your first platinum medal, alone or with a friend.

All Around the World (30)	Unlock all of the episodes in the game, alone or with a friend.
Better the Second Time Around (25)	Unlock all secondary goals in a world, alone or with a friend.
Bronze Away! (10)	Win your first bronze medal, alone or with a friend.
Can I Cook or What? (20)	Complete the Ratatouille world, alone or with a friend.
Checkered Flag (20)	Complete the Cars world, alone or with a friend.
Compliments to the Chef (15)	Play the entire Ratatouille world as Remy, alone or with a friend.
Fast Learner (20)	Complete your first episode, alone or with a friend.
Friends Forever (30)	Unlock all buddy characters, alone or with a friend.
Golden! (25)	Win your first gold medal, alone or with a friend.
Hat Trick (30)	Win three gold medals in a row, alone or with a friend.
I Am Speed (15)	Play the entire Cars world as Lightning McQueen, alone or with a friend.
I Can See in the Dark (20)	Find all night vision areas in the "Omnidroid Bash" episode, alone or with a friend.
Just Like Old Times (15)	Play the entire Incredibles world as Mr. Incredible, alone or with a friend.
Linear Thinking (15)	Jump from zipline to zipline 10 times in the "Free the Birds!" episode, alone or with a friend.
Loyal to the End (15)	Open all buddy areas in all UP episodes, alone or with a friend.
Say It with Rockets (20)	Open all boxes with rockets in the "Daycare Dash" episode, alone or with a friend.
Second Helping (15)	Unlock your first secondary goal, alone or with a friend.
Second to None (30)	Unlock all secondary goals in the game, alone or with a friend.
See What I Did! (15)	Share an award with KinectShare.
See? I Can Do Anything! (20)	Share 10 KinectShare awards.
Senior Wilderness Explorer (15)	Play the entire UP world as RU.S.S.ell, alone or with a friend.
Showtime! (20)	Unlock your first special ability, alone or with a friend.
Silverado! (20)	Win your first silver medal, alone or with a friend.
Simply Super (20)	Complete the Incredibles world, alone or with a friend.
Spirit of Adventure (20)	Complete the UP world, alone or with a friend.
Stay 'Til the Lights Come Up (10)	Watch the credits without skipping.
Steady Drivin' (15)	Complete the entire "Fancy Drivin'" episode without hitting any obstacles.
Super Poise (25)	Slide through the entire "Save Metroville" episode without falling.
Super Teamwork (15)	Open all buddy areas in all of the Incredibles episodes, alone or with a friend.

The Gang's All Here (30)	Unlock all playable characters, alone or with a friend.
The Grand Canyoneer (20)	Survive the entire "Canyon Expedition" episode without falling.
Throw It All Away (15)	Throw 20 tennis balls in the "Floodgates" episode, alone or with a friend.
To Infinity ... and Beyond! (15)	Play the entire Toy Story world as Buzz Lightyear, alone or with a friend.
Top of the Charts (20)	See the leaderboards for an episode, alone or with a friend.
Toys Stick Together (20)	Open all buddy areas in all Toy Story episodes, alone or with a friend.
Traffic Jam (15)	Reach all areas using glide and missiles in all Cars episodes, alone or with a friend.
True Adventurer (20)	Complete your first world, alone or with a friend.
We Belong Together (15)	Unlock your first buddy, alone or with a friend.
We Don't Need Roads (20)	Perform a 100-meter glide in the "Bomb Squad" episode.
We'll Always Have Paris (10)	Open all buddy areas in all Ratatouille episodes, alone or with a friend.
Whip It Good (20)	Open all areas with the whip in the "House Chase" episode, alone or with a friend.
Work/Play Balance (15)	Complete the entire "Daycare Dash" episode without falling.
You ... Are ... a ...TOY! (20)	Complete the Toy Story world, alone or with a friend.
You Can Do It All (30)	Unlock all special abilities, alone or with a friend.
You Will Believe a Rat Can Fly (20)	Perform an 8-second glide in the "Rooftop Run" episode in one try.
You're Not the Boss of Me (40)	Defeat all bosses, alone or with a friend.

KINECT STAR WARS (XBOX 360)

ACHIEVEMENT

UNLOCKABLE	HOW TO UNLOCK
Angry World Traveller (10)	Played any map at level 5 or higher in Rancor Rampage, alone or with a friend.
Arch-Rivals! (10)	Raced with Sebulba's Podracer, alone or with a friend.
Bantha Poodoo (10)	Crossed the finish line last in a race, alone or with a friend.
Ben-Hur, Done That (10)	Completed the Podracing Destiny as a Rookie, alone or with a friend.
Boonta Clause (30)	Completed the Podracing Destiny as a Veteran, alone or with a friend.
Catch-22 (20)	Completed 2 two-player races.
Crowd Control (20)	Knocked down 15 people or droids in one attack, alone or with a friend.
Decapitalized (20)	Destroyed the Subjugator-class Capital ship, alone or with a friend.
Don't Get Cocky (40)	Completed all four Space Combat missions without restarting, alone or with a friend.
Down with the Royals (10)	Destroyed every statue in Theed in Rancor Rampage in 1 session, alone or with a friend.

Duels Mode Unlocked (10)	Completed the Jedi Adventures Duels tutorial, alone or with a friend.
Felucia In a Flash (25)	Completed all Felucia missions in a single session, alone or with a friend.
Fighter Ace (20)	Destroyed 5 TIE fighters in 1 mode in Rancor Rampage.
Going Somewhere, Solo? (50)	Completed "I'm Han Solo" without losing a multiplier, alone or with a friend.
Hot Potato (10)	Made a creature or droid jump to an enemy vehicle in Podracing, alone or with a friend.
I Just Wanna Dance (10)	Completed your first song in co-op mode.
I'm Invincible! (30)	Completed Mos Espa wihout losing a life in Rancor Rampage, alone or with a friend.
It's a Trap! (20)	Completed Providence Mission 1 without your ship being destroyed, alone or with a friend.
Mastering the Juyo Form (20)	Completed any Duel in less than 3 minutes, alone or with a friend.
Now Face the Chosen One (15)	Defeated Ror with a Jedi Knight rating, alone or with a friend.
Now this is Podracing! (10)	Won a race for the first time in the Podracing Destiny, alone or with a friend.
One Buffed Dude (30)	Played any map at level 10 in Rancor Rampage, alone or with a friend.
One Up, Two Down (10)	In Rancor Rampage, leveled a Felucian Heavy Missile Platform in 1 throw, alone or with a friend.
Only a Master of Evil (25)	Completed the Vader Duel with a Jedi Master rating, alone or with a friend.
Rebel Commando (10)	Knocked out the shield of the Imperial garrison in Mos Eisley, alone or with a friend.
Savior of Coruscant (50)	Completed the Jedi Adventures: Dark Side Rising campaign, alone or with a friend.
Sky Walker (20)	Completed the Podracing Destiny as a Professional, alone or with a friend.
Sleemo! (40)	Destroyed 3 enemy Podracers in a single race, alone or with a friend.
Sorry About the Mess (15)	Defeated 13 enemy speeders in the Kashyyyk forest speederbike level, alone or with a friend.
Teras Kasi (10)	Defeated an enemy by kicking them off a ledge, alone or with a friend.
The Chosen One (30)	Scored at least 500,000 points on any song on the Death Star, alone or with a friend.
The Force That Binds (20)	Completed a co-op Jedi Adventures ground combat mission with neither player being knocked out.
The Only Human Who Can Do It (15)	Placed first in 3 Podraces in a row in a single session, alone or with a friend.
The Real Force in the Galaxy (20)	Played the Coloi Rancor, alone or with a friend.
The Shield Is Down! (15)	Disabled the Commerce Guild fortress shield, alone or with a friend.
This Party's Over (40)	Earned 5 stars playing "Celebration" on extended difficulty, alone or with a friend.
To the Rescue (15)	Reached the Jedi training camp on Kashyyyk, alone or with a friend.

Tusken Raider Revenge (20)	Destroyed all Podracers in Mos Espa in Rancor Rampage, alone or with a friend.
Two-For-One Discount (10)	Defeated at least two droids with a single use of Force powers, alone or with a friend.
Unlimited Power! (10)	Used a fully upgraded powerup in Podracing at least once, alone or with a friend.
Untouchable (30)	Completed any Duel without taking a single hit, alone or with a friend.
Very Very Angry (10)	Played Rancor Rampage Fury in co-op mode.
We Got Company! (20)	Earned 5 stars each on a song while playing with another person in co-op mode.
Well, Wookiee There! (10)	Destroyed 10 Trandoshan slave ships while escaping from Kashyyyk, alone or with a friend.
Who's Keeping Score? (25)	Completed all Providence missions in a single session, alone or with a friend.
Witness the Power (10)	Used all special attacks in 1 mode in Rancor Rampage, alone or with a friend.
Wookiee Life Debt (40)	Completed all Kashyyyk missions in a single session, alone or with a friend.
Wookiee Wingman (15)	Teamed up with a friend to complete a speeder bike chase in 2-player co-op mode.
You May Fire When Ready (20)	Destroyed all shield arrays in a single pass on Felucia Mission 5, alone or with a friend.
You Must Have Jedi Reflexes (15)	Won all Destiny races in one sitting, with racing line & drive assist off, alone or with a friend.

THE KING OF FIGHTERS XIII (PLAYSTATION 3)

TROPHY

UNLOCKABLE	HOW TO UNLOCK
After all, you're just trash. (Bronze)	Get an SS at the victory screen
And the final blow...! (Bronze)	Get 50 NEO MAX Super Special Moves Finishes (Arcade, Versus)
Come back later! (Bronze)	Perform 50 Drive Cancels (Arcade, Versus)
Do you understand now? (Silver)	Complete STORY.
Doesn't it feel good? (Bronze)	Win 25 [ranked matches / player matches]
Excellent! (Gold)	Win 100 [ranked matches / player matches]
Go easy on me! (Bronze)	Play your first [ranked match / player match]
Good! (Bronze)	Play 50 [ranked matches / player matches]
Great (Bronze)	Be challenged by "Saiki" and win in ARCADE
Hehe... hot, wasn't it? (Silver)	Play 100 [ranked matches / player matches]
Heheh. Not bad. (Bronze)	Perform 50 MAX Cancels (Arcade, Versus)
Here I come, buddy! (Bronze)	Create 10 characters in Customize
Hey! (Bronze)	Hit 100 times using NEO MAX Super Special Moves (Arcade, Versus)
Hey, hey, hey! (Bronze)	Be challenged by "Billy" and win in ARCADE
Hmph... this is only natural. (Bronze)	Get 10 straight wins (Arcade, Versus)
How was it? (Silver)	Clear ARCADE MODE without continuing
I shall not waver! (Silver)	Play 300 [ranked matches / player matches]
I will execute my mission! (Bronze)	Defeat 3 characters in Survival mode

NEW! A B C D E F G H I J K L M N O P Q R S T U V W X Y Z

CODES & CHEATS

I'm enough for this job! (Silver)	Defeat 35 characters in Survival mode
Isn't this fun, eh? (Silver)	Win 50 [ranked matches / player matches]
It's about time to start! (Bronze)	Register an icon, team and message in Customize
Let's play warrior! (Bronze)	Create 10 rooms
Let's see what you've got... (Bronze)	Clear STORY.
Looks like I was just on time. (Bronze)	Clear Time Attack mode for the first time
Mission Complete! (Bronze)	Perform 50 Super Cancels (Arcade, Versus)
Number 1! (Bronze)	Get 5 consecutive wins in a ranked match
Okay! (Bronze)	Get 2 consecutive wins in a ranked match
Piece of cake! (Bronze)	Perform 50 HD Cancels (Arcade, Versus)
Play time is over! (Bronze)	Perform 50 Super Special Moves Finishes (Arcade, Versus)
Show me what humans are made of... (Bronze)	Perform 10 Target Actions (Arcade)
Spinning! (Bronze)	Hit 100 times using EX Special Moves (Arcade, Versus)
Strength! (Bronze)	Hit 100 times using Special Moves (Arcade, Versus)
That should do it! (Silver)	Complete all trials for 1 character in Trial mode
THE KING OF FIGHTERS (Platinum)	Unlock all trophies.
This is... my victory! (Silver)	Clear ARCADE MODE on VERY HARD
This was just a greeting! (Bronze)	Win 5 [ranked matches / player matches]
Time will soon turn to ashes... (Bronze)	Get an S at the victory screen
What's wrong? (Silver)	Perform 300 Target Actions (Arcade)
Yahoooo! (Bronze)	Hit 100 times using Super Special Moves (Arcade, Versus)
Yay! Perfect! (Bronze)	Perform 10 Perfect Victories (Arcade, Versus)
Yeah! (Bronze)	Win your first [ranked match / player match]
Yeah! I did it! (Silver)	Get 10 consecutive wins in a ranked match
Yeeeeaaah! (Bronze)	Hit 100 times using EX Super Special Moves (Arcade, Versus)
Yes! I'm the best! (Gold)	Clear 200 trials in Trial mode
You can't compare to me. (Silver)	Clear Time Attack mode with 30 characters
You can't win against me! (Bronze)	Be challenged by "Ash" and win in ARCADE
You're not so bad! (Bronze)	Complete the tutorial

CODE

After selecting certain characters, pressing "select" before selecting a color can yield either an alternate costume or a separate color palette.

UNLOCKABLE	CODE
Andy - Ninja Mask	Press "select" before selecting his color.
Elisabeth - KOF XI Outfit	Press "select" before selecting her color.
Joe - Tiger-Striped Boxers	Press "select" before selecting his color.
K' - Dual-Colored Outfit	Press "select" before selecting his color.
Kyo - Orochi Saga Outfit	Press "select" before selecting his color.
Raiden - Big Bear Outfit	Press "select" before selecting his color.

Ralf - Camouflage	Press "select" before selecting his color.
Takuma - Mr. Karate Outfit	Press "select" before selecting his color.
Yuri - Braided Ponytail	Press "select" before selecting her color.

UNLOCKABLE

UNLOCKABLE	HOW TO UNLOCK
Battle Againts Ash	Get 4,000,000 Points before the 6th Stage.
Battle Against Dark Ash (Final Stage)	Defeat True Saiki in stage 6.
Battle Againts True Saiki (stage 7)	Get 2,500,000 after by the end of stage 6
Billy Kane	Perform at least 2 target actions per match in arcade mode. He should then appear as a challenger, defeating him will unlock him
Saiki	Perform at least 5 target actions per match in arcade mode. Saiki should then appear as a challenger, defeating him will unlock him

THE KING OF FIGHTERS XIII (XBOX 360)

ACHIEVEMENT

UNLOCKABLE	HOW TO UNLOCK
After all, you're just trash. (30)	Get an SS at the victory screen
And the final blow...! (20)	Get 50 NEO MAX Super Special Moves Finishes (Arcade, Versus)
Come back later! (20)	Perform 50 Drive Cancels (Arcade, Versus)
Do you understand now? (40)	Complete STORY.
Doesn't it feel good? (20)	Win 25 [ranked matches / player matches]
Excellent! (50)	Win 100 [ranked matches / player matches]
Go easy on me! (10)	Play your first [ranked match / player match]
Good! (20)	Play 50 [ranked matches / player matches]
Great (20)	Be challenged by "Saiki" and win in ARCADE
Hehe... hot, wasn't it? (30)	Play 100 [ranked matches / player matches]
Heheh. Not bad. (10)	Perform 50 MAX Cancels (Arcade, Versus)
Here I come, buddy! (20)	Create 10 characters in Customize
Hey! (10)	Hit 100 times using NEO MAX Super Special Moves (Arcade, Versus)
Hey, hey, hey! (20)	Be challenged by "Billy" and win in ARCADE
Hmph... this is only natural. (10)	Get 10 straight wins (Arcade, Versus)
How was it? (30)	Clear ARCADE MODE without continuing
I shall not waver! (40)	Play 300 [ranked matches / player matches]
I will execute my mission! (10)	Defeat 3 characters in Survival mode
I'm enough for this job! (30)	Defeat 35 characters in Survival mode
Isn't this fun, eh? (30)	Win 50 [ranked matches / player matches]
It's about time to start! (10) Customize	Register an icon, team and message in
Let's play warrior! (10)	Create 10 rooms
Let's see what you've got... (30)	Clear STORY.
Looks like I was just on time. (10)	Clear Time Attack mode for the first time
Mission Complete! (20)	Perform 50 Super Cancels (Arcade, Versus)
Number 1! (30)	Get 5 consecutive wins in a ranked match
Okay! (20)	Get 2 consecutive wins in a ranked match
Piece of cake! (20)	Perform 50 HD Cancels (Arcade, Versus)

Play time is over! (10)	Perform 50 Super Special Moves Finishes (Arcade, Versus)
Show me what humans are made of (20)	Perform 10 Target Actions (Arcade)
Spinning! (10)	Hit 100 times using EX Special Moves (Arcade, Versus)
Strength! (10)	Hit 100 times using Special Moves (Arcade, Versus)
That should do it! (30)	Complete all trials for 1 character in Trial mode
This is... my victory! (40)	Clear ARCADE MODE on VERY HARD
This was just a greeting! (10)	Win 5 [ranked matches / player matches]
Time will soon turn to ashes... (20)	Get an S at the victory screen
What's wrong? (30)	Perform 300 Target Actions (Arcade)
Yahoooo! (10)	Hit 100 times using Super Special Moves (Arcade, Versus)
Yay! Perfect! (10)	Perform 10 Perfect Victories (Arcade, Versus)
Yeah! (10)	Win your first [ranked match / player match]
Yeah! I did it! (40)	Get 10 consecutive wins in a ranked match
Yeeeeaaah! (10)	Hit 100 times using EX Super Special Moves (Arcade, Versus)
Yes! I'm the best! (50)	Clear 200 trials in Trial mode
You can't compare to me. (40)	Clear Time Attack mode with 30 characters
You can't win against me! (20)	Be challenged by "Ash" and win in ARCADE
You're not so bad! (10)	Complete the tutorial

UNLOCKABLE

UNLOCKABLE	HOW TO UNLOCK
Billy Kane	You must do 2+ TAs during each match (At average 6 TAs per stage.) before Stage 4. Defeat him when he challenges you.
Human Saiki	You must do 5+ TAs during each match (At average 15 TAs per stage.) before Stage 4. Defeat him when he challenges you.

KINGDOM HEARTS 3D: DREAM DROP DISTANCE (3DS)

TROPHY

UNLOCKABLE	HOW TO UNLOCK
Badge of Pride	Finish the story on Proud Mode
Critical Praise	Finish the story on Critical Mode
Daring Diver	Score more than 7,500,000 points in Dive Mode
Dream Pleaser	Max out every Spirit's Affinity Level
Frequent Friend	Place at least 30 Link Portals
In the Clear	Finish the story
In the Munny	Amass 5,000 munny
Keyslinger	Take out 2,500 Dream Eaters
King of Rush	Take first place in every Flick Rush cup
Memento Maniac	Save at least 20 photos while bonding with Spirits
Motion Slickness	Defeat 1,000 enemies while in Flowmotion
Portal Champ	Complete every Special Portal and Secret Portal
Pro Linker	Link with your Spirits at least 50 times
Reality Shifter	Defeat 50 enemies using Reality Shift
Spirit Guide	Obtain at least one of every Spirit

Stat Builder	Max out every stat-boosting ability
Stop Drop Roller	Rack up 2,000 Drop Points
Treasure Seeker	Find every last treasure

UNLOCKABLE

UNLOCKABLE	HOW TO UNLOCK
Critical Mode	Finish the game on any difficulty
Secret Message in Glossary	Get all the glowing letters to spell "Secret Message Unlocked" to get an extra item in your glossary.

KINGDOM HEARTS: BIRTH BY SLEEP (PSP)

UNLOCKABLES

UNLOCKABLE	HOW TO UNLOCK
Final Chapter	Acquire all Xehanort Reports
Lingering Spirit Vanitas boss	Clear Final Story
Mysterious Figure boss	Beat Lingering spirit Vanitas at Keyblade Graveyard
Trinity Archives	Complete the story with any character

SECRET MOVIE

To unlock the secret movie, you must do the following:

UNLOCKABLE	HOW TO UNLOCK
On Critical mode	Complete the final episode
On Proud mode	Complete the final episode
On Standard mode	Complete 100% of the Reports Section % and complete the final episode

KINGDOMS OF AMALUR: RECKONING (PLAYSTATION 3)

TROPHY

UNLOCKABLE	HOW TO UNLOCK
A Life of Crime (Bronze)	Got caught committing a crime 25 times.
A Wink and a Smile (Bronze)	You have succeeded at 50 Persuasion attempts.
And Then There Were None (Bronze)	Killed 500 enemies with abilities.
Big Spender (Bronze)	Spent 200,000 gold.
Blades of Glory (Bronze)	Acquired 10 Unique weapons (Special Delivery weapons excluded).
Bookworm (Bronze)	Read 50 books.
Breaking and Entering (Bronze)	Picked 50 locks.
Bull in a China Shop (Bronze)	Smashed 1,000 objects.
Cartographer (Bronze)	Discovered 100 locations.
Cleaning Up the Streets (Bronze)	Killed 50 bandits.
Crime Doesn't Pay (Bronze)	Spent over 10,000 gold in crime bribes.
Destiny Defiant (Silver)	You have defeated Tirnoch, and defied destiny.
Destiny Dominated (Gold)	You have won the game on Hard difficulty.
Diamond in the Rough (Bronze)	Crafted a Pristine Shard.
Elixir of Fate (Bronze)	Made a potion with the Essence of Fate.
Five Finger Discount (Bronze)	Stole and fenced an item.
Foiled Again! (Bronze)	Parried 100 times.
Good as New (Bronze)	Repaired a piece of equipment.
Green Thumb (Bronze)	Harvested 10 of each type of reagent.
Hero of Mel Senshir (Gold)	You have defeated the great Balor.

House of Ballads (Silver)	Completed the House of Ballads storyline quests.
House of Sorrows (Silver)	Completed the House of Sorrows storyline quests.
It Didn't Explode! (Bronze)	Made a stable potion by experimenting.
It is Your Destiny (Bronze)	Unlocked a top tier destiny.
Jack of All Trades (Bronze)	Unlocked a Jack of All Trades destiny.
Jailbreak (Bronze)	You broke out of jail.
Juggler (Silver)	Landed 5 consecutive hits on a launched enemy.
Loremaster (Bronze)	Found all Lorestones.
Master of the Forge (Bronze)	Crafted an item that uses all 5 forge component slots.
Niskaru Slayer (Bronze)	Killed 25 Niskaru.
No Destiny, All Determination (Bronze)	You have met High King Titarion, and have been confronted with the true scope of your powers.
Open Sesame (Bronze)	Dispelled 50 wards.
Out of Your League (Bronze)	Killed an enemy 4 levels higher than you.
Perfectionist (Platinum)	Awarded all trophies.
Reborn (Bronze)	You were reborn from the Well of Souls, and have escaped Allestar Tower.
Reckoning Rampage (Bronze)	Killed 5 enemies with a single Fateshift.
Riposte! (Bronze)	Landed 25 special attacks out of Parry.
Romancing the Gem (Bronze)	Crafted an Epic Gem.
Scholia Arcana (Silver)	Completed the Scholia Arcana storyline quests.
Shock and Awe (Bronze)	Killed 100 enemies with abilities.
Shop Class (Bronze)	Crafted a piece of equipment with Blacksmithing.
Some of This, Some of That (Bronze)	Unlocked a two-class hybrid destiny.
Streaker (Bronze)	You spoke to someone while not wearing clothes.
The Great Detective (Bronze)	Detected 25 hidden things.
They Never Saw it Coming (Bronze)	Backstabbed 20 enemies.
Trapper (Bronze)	Killed 25 enemies with traps.
Travelers (Silver)	Completed the Travelers storyline quests.
Turning the Tide (Silver)	A ruse has baited Octienne into betraying the necromantic nature of his experiments.
Warsworn (Silver)	Completed the Warsworn storyline quests.
Where's My Wallet? (Bronze)	Pickpocketed 20 times.
Would You Like Fries with that? (Bronze)	Landed 100 complete attack chains.

KINGDOMS OF AMALUR: RECKONING (XBOX 360)

ACHIEVEMENT

UNLOCKABLE	HOW TO UNLOCK
A Life of Crime (15)	Get caught committing a crime 25 times.
A Wink and a Smile (15)	Succeed at 50 Persuasion attempts.
And Then There Were None (20)	Kill 500 enemies with abilities.
Big Spender (15)	Spend 200,000 gold.

Blades of Glory (15)	Acquire 10 Unique weapons (Special Delivery weapons excluded).
Bookworm (15)	Read 50 books.
Breaking and Entering (15)	Pick 50 locks.
Bull in a China Shop (15)	Smash 1,000 objects.
Cartographer (20)	Discover 100 locations.
Cleaning Up the Streets (20)	Kill 50 bandits.
Complete the Travelers storyline quests	Complete the Travelers storyline quests.
Crime Doesn't Pay (10)	Spend over 10,000 gold in crime bribes.
Destiny Defiant (75)	You have defeated Tirnoch, and defied destiny.
Destiny Dominated (100)	You have won the game on Hard difficulty.
Diamond in the Rough (10)	Craft a Pristine Shard.
Elixir of Fate (20)	Make a potion with the Essence of Fate.
Five Finger Discount (10)	Steal and fence an item.
Foiled Again! (15)	Parry 100 times.
Good as New (10)	Repair a piece of equipment.
Green Thumb (15)	Harvest 10 of each type of reagent.
Hero of Mel Senshir (75)	You have defeated the great Balor.
House of Ballads (20)	Complete the House of Ballads storyline quests.
House of Sorrows (20)	Complete the House of Sorrows storyline quests.
It Didn't Explode! (10)	Make a stable potion by experimenting.
It is Your Destiny (50)	Unlock a top tier destiny.
Jack of All Trades (10)	Unlock a Jack of All Trades destiny.
Jailbreak (10)	Break out of jail.
Juggler (20)	Land 5 consecutive hits on a launched enemy.
Loremaster (20)	Discover all Lorestones.
Master of the Forge (20)	Romancing the Gem (15)
Niskaru Slayer (20)	Kill 25 Niskaru.
No Destiny, All Determination (15)	You have met High King Titarion, and have been confronted with the true scope of your powers.
Open Sesame (15)	Dispel 50 wards.
Out of Your League (20)	Kill an enemy 4 levels higher than you.
Pickpocket 20 times.	Pickpocket 20 times.
Reborn (10)	You were reborn from the Well of Souls, and have escaped Allestar Tower.
Reckoning Rampage (20)	Kill 5 enemies with a single Fateshift.
Riposte! (10)	Land 25 special attacks out of Parry.
Romancing the Gem (15)	Craft an Epic Gem.
Scholia Arcana (20)	Complete the Scholia Arcana storyline quests.
Shock and Awe (15)	Kill 100 enemies with abilities.
Shop Class (10)	Craft a piece of equipment with Blacksmithing.
Some of This, Some of That (10)	Unlock a two-class hybrid destiny.
Streaker (10)	You spoke to someone while not wearing clothes.

The Great Detective (10)	Detect 25 hidden things.
They Never Saw it Coming (10)	Backstab 20 enemies.
Trapper (15)	Kill 25 enemies with traps.
Turning the Tide (20)	A ruse has baited Octienne into betraying the necromantic nature of his experiments.
Warsworn (20)	Complete the Warsworn storyline quests.
Would You Like Fries with that? (15)	Land 100 complete attack chains.

KNIGHTS IN THE NIGHTMARE (DS)

UNLOCKABLES

UNLOCKABLE	HOW TO UNLOCK
Hard Mode	Beat the game on Normal mode.
Play as Astart	Beat the game.
Nightmare mode	Beat the game on Hard mode.

KUNG FU PANDA (XBOX 360, PLAYSTATION 3)

CODES

From the main menu, select Extras and then select Cheats.

EFFECT	CODE
All Multiplayer Characters	←,↓,←,→,↓
Big Head Mode (Story Mode)	↓,↑,←,→,→
Infinite Chi	↓,→,←,↑,↓
Invulnerability	↓,→,→,↑,←
Dragon Warrior Outfit (Multiplayer Mode)	←,↓,→,←,↑
4x Damage Multiplier	↑,↓,↑,→,←

KUNG FU PANDA (WII)

CODES

From the main menu, select Extras and then select Cheats.

EFFECT	CODE
All Multiplayer Characters	⬅,⬇,⬅,➡,⬇
Big Head Mode (Story Mode)	⬇,⬆,⬅,➡,➡
Infinite Chi	⬇,➡,⬅,⬆,⬇
Invulnerability	⬇,➡,➡,⬆,⬅
Dragon Warrior Outfit (Multiplayer Mode)	⬅,⬇,➡,⬅,⬆
4x Damage Multiplier	⬆,⬇,⬆,➡,⬅

LAIR (PLAYSTATION 3)

PASSWORDS

Enter into the game's Cheat menu:

PASSWORD	EFFECT
chicken	Chicken Curry video
686F7420636F66666565	Hot Coffee video
koelsch	Unlocks Stable option for all levels on the Mission Select screen

LEFT 4 DEAD (XBOX 360)

UNLOCKABLE	HOW TO UNLOCK
Rocket Launcher	Complete the game on any difficulty.

LEGO BATMAN (XBOX 360), (PLAYSTATION 3)

CODES

Enter the codes on the second level of the Batcave at the computer above the outfit changer.

EFFECT	XBOX 360 CODE	PLAYSTATION 3 CODE
Alfred	ZAQ637	ZAQ637
Bat-Tank	KNTT4B	KNTT4B
Batgirl	JKR331	JKR331
Bruce Wayne	BDJ327	BDJ327
Bruce Wayne's Private Jet	LEA664	LEA664
Catwoman (Classic)	M1AAWW	M1AAWW
Catwoman's Motorcycle	HPL826	HPL826
Clown Goon	HJK327	HJK327
Commissioner Gordon	DDP967	DDP967
Fishmonger	HGY748	HGY748
Freeze Girl	XVK541	XVK541
Garbage Truck	DUS483	DUS483
Glideslam	BBD7BY	BBD7BY
Goon Helicopter	GCH328	GCH328
Harbor Helicopter	CHP735	CHP735
Harley Quinn's Hammer Truck	RDT637	RDT637
Joker Goon	UTF782	UTF782
Joker Henchman	YUN924	YUN924
Mad Hatter	JCA283	JCA283
Mad Hatter's Glider	HS000W	HS000W
Mad Hatter's Steamboat	M4DM4N	M4DM4N
Man-Bat	NYU942	NYU942
Military Policeman	MKL382	MKL382
Mr. Freeze's Iceberg	ICYICE	ICYICE
Mr. Freeze's Kart	BCT229	BCT229
Nightwing	MVY759	MVY759

Penguin Goon	NKA238	NKA238
Penguin Goon Submarine	BTN248	BTN248
Penguin Henchman	BJH782	BJH782
Penguin Minion	KJP748	KJP748
Poison Ivy Goon	GTB899	GTB899
Police Bike	LJP234	LJP234
Police Boat	PLC999	PLC999
Police Car	KJL832	KJL832
Police Helicopter	CWR732	CWR732
Police Marksman	HKG984	HKG984
Police Officer	JRY983	JRY983
Police Van	MAC788	MAC788
Police Watercraft	VJD328	VJD328
Riddler Goon	CRY928	CRY928
Riddler Henchman	XEU824	XEU824
Riddler's Jet	HAHAHA	HAHAHA
Robin's Submarine	TTF453	TTF453
S.W.A.T.	HTF114	HTF114
Sailor	NAV592	NAV592
Scientist	JFL786	JFL786
Security Guard	PLB946	PLB946
The Joker (Tropical)	CCB199	CCB199
The Joker's Van	JUK657	JUK657
Two-Face's Armored Truck	EFE933	EFE933
Yeti	NJL412	NJL412
Zoo Sweeper	DWR243	DWR243

EXTRA CODES

EFFECT	XBOX 360 CODE	PLAYSTATION 3 CODE
Always Score Multiply	9LRGNB	9LRGNB
Area Effect	TL3EKT	TL3EKT
Armor Plating	N8JZEK	N8JZEK
Bats	XFP4E2	XFP4E2
Beep Beep	RAFTU8	RAFTU8
Character Studs	DY13BD	DY13BD
Decoy	TQ09K3	TQ09K3
Disguise	GEC3MD	GEC3MD
Extra Toggle	EWAW7W	EWAW7W
Extra Hearts	ML3KHP	ML3KHP
Fast Batarangs	JRBDCB	JRBDCB
Fast Build	GHJ2DY	GHJ2DY
Fast Grapple	RM4PR8	RM4PR8
Fast Walk	ZOLM6N	ZOLM6N
Faster Pieces	EVG26J	EVG26J
Flaming Batarangs (Used with heat batman)	D8NYWH	D8NYWH
Freeze Batarang	XPN4NG	XPN4NG
Ice Rink	KLKL4G	KLKL4G
Immune to Freeze	JXUDY6	JXUDY6
Invincible	WYD5CP	WYD5CP

Minikit Detector	ZXGH9J	ZXGH9J
More Batarang Targets	XWP645	XWP645
More Detonators	TNTN6B	TNTN6B
Piece Detector	KHJ544	KHJ544
Power Brick Detector	MMN786	MMN786
Regenerate Hearts	HJH7HJ	HJH7HJ
Score x2	N4NR3E	N4NR3E
Score x4	CX9MAT	CX9MAT
Score x6	MLVNF2	MLVNF2
Score x8	WCCDB9	WCCDB9
Score x10	18HW07	18HW07
Silhouettes	YK4TPH	YK4TPH
Slam	BBD7BY	BBD7BY
Sonic Pain	THTL4X	THTL4X
Stud Magnet	LK2DY4	LK2DY4

LEGO BATMAN   (WII)

CODES

Enter the codes on the second level of the Batcave at the computer above the outfit changer.

EFFECT	CODE
Bruce Wayne	BDJ327
Commissioner Gordon	DDP967
More Batarang Targets	XWP645
Nightwing	MVY759
Penguin Minion	KJP748
Police Van	MAC788
The Joker (Tropical)	CCB199
Yeti	NJL412

FREE PLAY CODES

EFFECT	CODE
Unlocks Alfred in Free Play	ZAQ637
Unlocks Commissioner Gordon in Free Play	DPP967
Unlocks Free Girl in Free Play	XVK541
Unlocks Harley Quinn's Hammer Truck	RDT637
Unlocks More Batarang Targets	XWP645
Unlocks Penguin Henchman in Free Play	BJH782
Unlocks Yeti in Free Play	NJL412

LEGO BATMAN   (DS)

CODES

Enter the following codes at the main menu. If you enter them correctly you will hear a sound.

EFFECT	CODE
Add 1 Million Studs	X, Y, B, D, Y, X, L, L, R, R, Up, Up, Down, Down, +START, +SELECT
All Characters	X, B, D, Up, Y, +START, Up, R, D, L, R, R, R, Up, Up, Down, Y, Y, Y, +START, +SELECT
All Episodes and Free Play mode	Up, R, B, L, X, Y, Up, Up, B, L, R, L, Up, Up, Down, Y, X, B, B, Up, L, R, +START, +SELECT
All Extras	Up, R, L, R, L, R, Up, B, X, X, Y, Y, B, B, L, Up, Down, L, R, L, R, Up, Up, +START, +SELECT

LEGO BATMAN (PSP)

CODES

Enter the codes on the second level of the Batcave at the computer above the outfit changer.

EFFECT	CODE
Alfred	ZAQ637
Bat-Tank	KNTT4B
Batgirl	JKR331
Bruce Wayne	BDJ327
Bruce Wayne's Private Jet	LEA664
Catwoman (Classic)	M1AAWW
Catwoman's Motorcycle	HPL826
Clown Goon	HJK327
Commissioner Gordon	DDP967
Fishmonger	HGY748
Freeze Girl	XVK541
Garbage Truck	DUS483
Glideslam	BBD7BY
Goon Helicopter	GCH328
Harbor Helicopter	CHP735
Harley Quinn's Hammer Truck	RDT637
Joker Goon	UTF782
Joker Henchman	YUN924
Mad Hatter	JCA283
Mad Hatter's Glider	HS000W
Mad Hatter's Steamboat	M4DM4N
Man-Bat	NYU942
Military Policeman	MKL382
Mr. Freeze's Iceberg	ICYICE
Mr. Freeze's Kart	BCT229
Nightwing	MVY759
Penguin Goon	NKA238
Penguin Goon Submarine	BTN248
Penguin Henchman	BJH782
Penguin Minion	KJP748
Poison Ivy Goon	GTB899
Police Bike	LJP234
Police Boat	PLC999
Police Car	KJL832
Police Helicopter	CWR732
Police Marksman	HKG984
Police Officer	JRY983
Police Van	MAC788
Police Watercraft	VJD328
Riddler Goon	CRY928
Riddler Henchman	XEU824
Riddler's Jet	HAHAHA
Robin's Submarine	TTF453
S.W.A.T.	HTF114
Sailor	NAV592
Scientist	JFL786

Security Guard	PLB946
The Joker (Tropical)	CCB199
The Joker's Van	JUK657
Two-Face's Armored Truck	EFE933
Yeti	NJL412
Zoo Sweeper	DWR243

EXTRA CODES

EFFECT	CODE
Always Score Multiply	9LRGNB
Area Effect	TL3EKT
Armor Plating	N8JZEK
Bats	XFP4E2
Beep Beep	RAFTU8
Character Studs	DY13BD
Decoy	TQ09K3
Disguise	GEC3MD
Extra Toggle	EWAW7W
Extra Hearts	ML3KHP
Fast Batarangs	JRBDCB
Fast Build	GHJ2DY
Fast Grapple	RM4PR8
Fast Walk	ZOLM6N
Faster Pieces	EVG26J
Flaming Batarangs (Used with heat batman)	D8NYWH
Freeze Batarang	XPN4NG
Ice Rink	KLKL4G
Immune to Freeze	JXUDY6
Invincible	WYD5CP
Minikit Detector	ZXGH9J
More Batarang Targets	XWP645
More Detonators	TNTN6B
Piece Detector	KHJ544
Power Brick Detector	MMN786
Regenerate Hearts	HJH7HJ
Score x2	N4NR3E
Score x4	CX9MAT
Score x6	MLVNF2
Score x8	WCCDB9
Score x10	18HW07
Silhouettes	YK4TPH
Slam	BBD7BY
Sonic Pain	THTL4X
Stud Magnet	LK2DY4

LEGO BATMAN 2: DC SUPER HEROES (PLAYSTATION 3)

TROPHY

UNLOCKABLE	HOW TO UNLOCK
Arkham Asylum Antics (Bronze)	Complete story level 3
Asylum Assignment (Bronze)	Complete story level 4
Chemical Crisis (Bronze)	Complete story level 5
Chemical Signature (Bronze)	Complete story level 6

NEW!

A
B
C
D
E
F
G
H
I
J
K
L
M
N
O
P
Q
R
S
T
U
V
W
X
Y
Z

City Slicker (Gold)	Collect all the gold bricks (Single Player Only)
Combo Hero (Bronze)	Do a finishing move
Complete Hero (Platinum)	Collected all of the Trophies
Core Instability (Bronze)	Complete story level 13
Destination Metropolis (Bronze)	Complete story level 8
Down to Earth (Bronze)	Complete story level 10
Dynamic Duo (Bronze)	Play a level in co-op
Extra! Extra! (Bronze)	Collect all the red bricks (Single Player Only)
Girl Power (Silver)	Unlock all female heroes and villains. (Single Player Only)
Gorilla Thriller (Bronze)	Climb to the top of Wayne tower while riding a Gorilla and playing as a female character.
Green Lantern's Light (Bronze)	Defeat Sinestro as Green Lantern
Halfway Through (Silver)	Get 50% (Single Player Only)
Harboring a Criminal (Bronze)	Complete story level 2
Heroes Unite (Bronze)	Complete story level 15
Inferior Machines (Bronze)	With Brainiac, defeat any LexBot
It's A Bird... It's A Plane... (Bronze)	Fly with Superman
Justice League (Silver)	Unlock all Justice League characters (Single Player Only)
Kal-El Last Son of Krypton (Bronze)	Defeat Zod as Superman
Minikit Hero (Gold)	Use all the Minikit vehicles
My Hero (Silver)	Rescue all Citizens in Peril (Single Player Only)
Research and Development (Bronze)	Complete story level 9
Subway Hero (Bronze)	Use the Gotham City Metro
Super Hero (Silver)	Get Super Hero in all levels (Single Player Only)
Super-Villain (Silver)	Unlock all the Bosses (Single Player Only)
Team Building (Gold)	Unlock all characters (Single Player Only)
Test Hero (Silver)	Test a custom character
The End (Gold)	Get 100% (Single Player Only)
The House of Luthor (Silver)	Obtain more than 10,100,000,000 Studs (Single Player Only)
The Next President (Bronze)	Complete story level 12
Theatrical Pursuits (Bronze)	Complete story level 1
Tower Defiance (Bronze)	Complete story level 14
Toy Gotham (Bronze)	Complete the Bonus level
Underground Retreat (Bronze)	Complete story level 11
Unwelcome Guests (Bronze)	Complete story level 7

LEGO BATMAN 2: DC SUPER HEROES (PLAYSTATION VITA)

TROPHY

UNLOCKABLE	HOW TO UNLOCK
A Winning Formula (Bronze)	Complete ACE Chemicals.
A-maze-ing Chase (Bronze)	Complete Arkham Estate.
All Change! (Silver)	Swap characters using Super Freeplay.
Bad Influence (Gold)	Collect all the Villain characters.

Bane of my Life (Bronze)	Take down Batman with Bane. (Single Player Only)
Batter Up! (Silver)	Using the Batman glide ability, spend 5 seconds or more in the air.
Behind Enemy Lines (Bronze)	Complete Attack on LexCorp.
Brick by Brick (Silver)	Collect all the Red Bricks.
Call Shotgun (Silver)	Stun an enemy using Commissioner Gordon's trusty weapon and finish them. (Single Player Only)
Complete Hero (Platinum)	Collect all trophies.
Deconstructive Criticism (Bronze)	Complete The Batcave.
Dishonourably Discharged! (Bronze)	Complete Arkham Asylum.
Double-crossed! (Bronze)	Complete Brawl at City Hall.
Flying Lessons (Bronze)	Complete Assault the VTOL.
Frequent Flyer (Bronze)	Complete Robot Sky Battle.
Happy Daze (Gold)	Stun 100 enemies.
Hero in Train-ing (Bronze)	Complete Gotham Metro.
Hostile Takeover (Bronze)	Complete Wayne Industries.
Justice is Served (Gold)	Win gold in every arena in Justice League Mode.
Justice League, Assemble! (Bronze)	Complete The Final Battle.
MVP (Gold)	Complete every arena in Justice League Mode.
Open Mic Knight (Bronze)	Complete Gotham Theatre.
Road to Ruin (Bronze)	Complete Juggernaut Chase.
Siamese Bat (Silver)	As Catwoman, use the Stealth Takedown ability to attack Batman. (Single Player Only)
Sound Advice (Silver)	Collect all the Sound Bite tokens.
Starter Pack (Silver)	Unlock all the Ability packs for the Character Customiser.
Super Friends (Gold)	Collect all the Hero characters.
Taking the Plunge (Silver)	Help an enemy off a ledge in Wayne Industries.
The Big Brick Theory (Bronze)	Create your first character in the Character Customiser.
The Joke's on you! (Bronze)	Complete The Joker Getaway.
True Hero (Silver)	Achieve a True Hero stud total.
Unbreakable (Gold)	Finish a level without losing all your hearts.

CODE

UNLOCKABLE	HOW TO UNLOCK
Clown Goon	9ZZZBP
Lexbot	W49CSJ
Mime Goon	ZQA8MK
Regenerate Hearts	ZXEX5D
Riddler Goon	Q285LK
Studs X2	74EZUT
Two-Face Goon	95KPYJ

LEGO BATMAN 2: DC SUPER HEROES (XBOX 360)

ACHIEVEMENT

UNLOCKABLE	HOW TO UNLOCK
Arkham Asylum Antics (25)	Complete story level 3
Asylum Assignment (25)	Complete story level 4

NEW!

A
B
C
D
E
F
G
H
I
J
K
L
M
N
O
P
Q
R
S
T
U
V
W
X
Y
Z

Chemical Crisis (25)	Complete story level 5
Chemical Signature (25)	Complete story level 6
City Slicker (35)	Collect all the gold bricks (Single Player Only)
Combo Hero (20)	Do a finishing move
Core Instability (25)	Complete story level 13
Destination Metropolis (25)	Complete story level 8
Down to Earth (25)	Complete story level 10
Dynamic Duo (20)	Play a level in co-op
Extra! Extra! (20)	Collect all the red bricks (Single Player Only)
Girl Power (20)	Unlock all female heroes and villains. (Single Player Only)
Gorilla Thriller (20)	Climb to the top of Wayne tower while riding a Gorilla and playing as a female character.
Green Lantern's Light (20)	Defeat Sinestro as Green Lantern
Halfway Through (50)	Get 50% (Single Player Only)
Harboring a Criminal (25)	Complete story level 2
Heroes Unite (25)	Complete story level 15
Inferior Machines (20)	With Brainiac, defeat any LexBot
It's A Bird... It's A Plane... (20)	Fly with Superman
Justice League (20)	Unlock all Justice League characters (Single Player Only)
Kal-El Last Son of Krypton (20)	Defeat Zod as Superman
Minikit Hero (20)	Use all the Minikit vehicles
My Hero (50)	Rescue all Citizens in Peril (Single Player Only)
Research and Development (25)	Complete story level 9
Subway Hero (20)	Use the Gotham City Metro
Super Hero (50)	Get Super Hero in all levels (Single Player Only)
Super-Villain (20)	Unlock all the Bosses (Single Player Only)
Team Building (50)	Unlock all characters (Single Player Only)
Test Hero (20)	Test a custom character
The End (70)	Get 100% (Single Player Only)
The House of Luthor (20)	Obtain more than 10,100,000,000 Studs (Single Player Only)
The Next President (25)	Complete story level 12
Theatrical Pursuits (25)	Complete story level 1
Tower Defiance (25)	Complete story level 14
Toy Gotham (20)	Complete the Bonus level
Underground Retreat (25)	Complete story level 11
Unwelcome Guests (25)	Complete story level 7

LEGO HARRY POTTER: YEARS 1-4 (XBOX 360), (PLAYSTATION 3), (WII)

GOLD BRICK CODES

Enter the codes upstairs in Wiseacres Wizarding Supplies.

EFFECT	XBOX 360 CODE	PLAYSTATION 3 CODE	WII CODE
Gold Brick 01	QE4VC7	QE4VC7	QE4VC7
Gold Brick 02	FY8H97	FY8H97	FY8H97
Gold Brick 03	3MQT4P	3MQT4P	3MQT4P
Gold Brick 04	PQPM7Z	PQPM7Z	PQPM7Z
Gold Brick 05	ZY2CPA	ZY2CPA	ZY2CPA
Gold Brick 06	3GMTP6	3GMTP6	3GMTP6

Gold Brick 07	XY6VYZ	XY6VYZ	XY6VYZ
Gold Brick 08	TUNC4W	TUNC4W	TUNC4W
Gold Brick 09	EJ42Q6	EJ42Q6	EJ42Q6
Gold Brick 10	GFJCV9	GFJCV9	GFJCV9
Gold Brick 11	DZCY6G	DZCY6G	DZCY6G

MISCELLANEOUS CODES

Enter the codes upstairs in Wiseacres Wizarding Supplies.

EFFECT	XBOX 360 CODE	PLAYSTATION 3 CODE	WII CODE
Carrot Wands	AUC8EH	AUC8EH	AUC8EH
Character Studs	H27KGC	H27KGC	H27KGC
Character Token Detector	HA79V8	HA79V8	HA79V8
Christmas	T7PVVN	T7PVVN	T7PVVN
Disguise	4DMK2R	4DMK2R	4DMK2R
Extra Hearts	J9U6Z9	J9U6Z9	J9U6Z9
Fall Rescue	ZEX7MV	ZEX7MV	ZEX7MV
Fast Dig	Z9BFAD	Z9BFAD	Z9BFAD
Fast Magic	FA3GQA	FA3GQA	FA3GQA
Gold Brick Detector	84QNQN	84QNQN	84QNQN
Hogwarts Crest Detector	TTMC6D	TTMC6D	TTMC6D
Ice Rink	F88VUW	F88VUW	F88VUW
Invincibility	QQWC6B	QQWC6B	QQWC6B
Red Brick Detector	7AD7HE	7AD7HE	7AD7HE
Regenerate Hearts	89ML2W	89ML2W	89ML2W
Score x2	74YKR7	74YKR7	74YKR7
Score x4	J3WHNK	J3WHNK	J3WHNK
Score x6	XK9ANE	XK9ANE	XK9ANE
Score x8	HUFV2H	HUFV2H	HUFV2H
Score x10	H8X69Y	H8X69Y	H8X69Y
Silhouettes	HZBVX7	HZBVX7	HZBVX7
Singing Mandrake	BMEU6X	BMEU6X	BMEU6X
Stud Magnet	67FKWZ	67FKWZ	67FKWZ

SPELL CODES

Enter the codes upstairs in Wiseacres Wizarding Supplies.

EFFECT	XBOX 360 CODE	PLAYSTATION 3 CODE	WII CODE
Accio	VE9VV7	VE9VV7	VE9VV7
Anteoculatia	QFB6NR	QFB6NR	QFB6NR
Calvorio	6DNR6L	6DNR6L	6DNR6L
Colovaria	9GJ442	9GJ442	9GJ442
Engorgio Skullus	CD4JLX	CD4JLX	CD4JLX
Entomorphis	MYN3NB	MYN3NB	MYN3NB
Flipendo	ND2L7W	ND2L7W	ND2L7W
Glacius	ERA9DR	ERA9DR	ERA9DR
Herbifors	H8FTHL	H8FTHL	H8FTHL
Incarcerous	YEB9Q9	YEB9Q9	YEB9Q9
Locomotor Mortis	2M2XJ6	2M2XJ6	2M2XJ6
Multicorfors	JK6QRM	JK6QRM	JK6QRM
Redactum Skullus	UW8LRH	UW8LRH	UW8LRH
Rictusempra	2UCA3M	2UCA3M	2UCA3M
Slugulus Eructo	U6EE8X	U6EE8X	U6EE8X

NEW!

A
B
C
D
E
F
G
H
I
J
K
L
M
N
O
P
Q
R
S
T
U
V
W
X
Y
Z

Stupefy	UWDJ4Y	UWDJ4Y	UWDJ4Y
Tarentallegra	KWWQ44	KWWQ44	KWWQ44
Trip Jinx	YZNRF6	YZNRF6	YZNRF6

LEGO HARRY POTTER: YEARS 1-4 (DS)

GOLD BRICK CODES

Enter the codes upstairs in Wiseacres Wizarding Supplies.

EFFECT	CODE
Gold Brick 01	QE4VC7
Gold Brick 02	FY8H97
Gold Brick 03	3MQT4P
Gold Brick 04	PQPM7Z
Gold Brick 05	ZY2CPA
Gold Brick 06	3GMTP6
Gold Brick 07	XY6VYZ
Gold Brick 08	TUNC4W
Gold Brick 09	EJ42Q6
Gold Brick 10	GFJCV9
Gold Brick 11	DZCY6G

LEGO HARRY POTTER: YEARS 5-7 (PLAYSTATION 3)

TROPHY

Enter the following passwords in the Start Menu under Extras while in game. It's the first option of the Extras menu.

UNLOCKABLE	CODE
Character Studs	H27KGC
Character Token Detector	HA79V8
Christmas (everyone wears Santa hats)	T7PVVN
Collect Ghost Studs	2FLY6B
Extra Hearts	J9U6Z9
Fall Rescue	ZEX7MV
Gold Brick Detector	84QNQN
Hogwarts Crest Detector	TTMC6D
Invincibility	QQWC6B
Red Brick Detector	7AD7HE
Score Multiplier x10	H8X69Y
Score Multiplier x2	74YKR7
Score Multiplier x6	XK9ANE
Score Multiplier x8	HUFV2H
Super Strength (can pull heavy objects w/o potion)	BMEU6X

LEGO HARRY POTTER: YEARS 5-7 (PLAYSTATION VITA)

TROPHY

UNLOCKABLE	HOW TO UNLOCK
A Siriusly Cold Dish (Bronze)	As Sirius, defeat Bellatrix in the Duelling Club
All Finished! (Platinum)	Acquire all trophies.
Beat the Parents (Bronze)	As a custom character, defeat Lily and James Potter in the Duelling club.
Bellatrix Beaten (Silver)	As Molly Weasley, defeat Bellatrix without taking damage in the Final Battle.
Blind as a Basilisk (Bronze)	Blind an enemy creature.

Bonus Category Duelling Champion (Silver)	Defeat all duellers in the Bonus Duelling category.
Bricked! (Silver)	Collect all the Red Bricks.
Complete Collection (Silver)	Collect all the characters.
Creature Confusion (Bronze)	Force any enemy creature to attack another.
Death Eater Category Duelling Champion (Bronze)	Defeat all duellers in the Death Eater Duelling category.
Deathly Hallows - Part 1 Trophy (Silver)	Complete Deathly Hallows - Part 1.
Deathly Hallows - Part 2 Trophy (Silver)	Complete Deathly Hallows - Part 2.
Draco's Disco (Silver)	As Draco Malfoy, cast Tarantallegra at another character.
Dumbledore's Army Category Duelling Champion (Bronze)	Defeat all duellers in the Dumbledore's Army Duelling category.
Falling to Pieces (Bronze)	Fail to put together puzzle pieces after six attempts
Half-Blood Prince Trophy (Silver)	Complete Half-Blood Prince.
Hogwarts Category Duelling Champion (Bronze)	Defeat all duellers in the Hogwarts Duelling category.
I said, bow! (Silver)	As Voldemort, defeat Harry Potter in Duelling Club.
Infer Inferi are Inferior (Silver)	Cause the Inferi to destroy each other in the cave.
Kitted Out (Silver)	Collect all Minikits.
Know Your Enemy (Bronze)	Defeat one of each enemy.
Kreacher Confusion (Bronze)	Cast Confundo on Kreacher in Grimmauld Place
Master Dueller (Gold)	Defeat all duellers in each category.
Ministry of Magic Category Duelling Champion (Bronze)	Defeat all duellers in the Ministry of Magic Duelling category.
Niceties Must be Observed (Gold)	Defeat Voldemort without taking any damage.
Open Category Duelling Champion (Bronze)	Defeat all duellers in the Open Duelling category.
Order of the Phoenix Trophy (Silver)	Complete Order of the Phoenix.
Phoenix Category Duelling Champion (Bronze)	Defeat all duellers in the Order of the Phoenix Duelling category.
Playtime (Silver)	Enjoy all the fun in the playground
Put me down! (Bronze)	Cast Levicorpus on an enemy.
Richer by the Galleon (Bronze)	Bank 10,000,000 studs.
Shield Charm Master (Bronze)	Take no damage when duelling in Duelling Club.
Student Category Duelling Champion (Bronze)	Defeat all duellers in the Student Duelling category.
Suits You! (Bronze)	As Voldemort in a suit, defeat Arthur Weasley in a suit in the Duelling Club.
The Best Offense is a Strong Defense (Silver)	Use only Protego during a duel in the Duelling Club.
The End (Gold)	Complete 100% of the game.
The Enemy Within (Bronze)	As a Death Eater, cast at anyone in the Hogwarts hub.
This is Knuts! (Bronze)	Bank 100,000,000 studs.
Too True (Silver)	Achieve a single True Wizard Stud Total
Trans-figure-ation (Bronze)	Create your own character in the character customiser.
Well Done Draco (Bronze)	As Draco, defeat Dumbledore in the Duelling Club.

NEW!

A
B
C
D
E
F
G
H
I
J
K
L
M
N
O
P
Q
R
S
T
U
V
W
X
Y
Z

LEGO HARRY POTTER: YEARS 5-7 (XBOX 360)

ACHIEVEMENT

Enter the following passwords in the Start Menu under Extras while in game. It's the first option of the Extras menu.

UNLOCKABLE	CODE
Character Studs	H27KGC
Character Token Detector	HA79V8
Christmas	T7PVVN
Extra Hearts	J9U6Z9
Fall Rescue	ZEX7MV
Fall Rescue	ZEX7MV
Ghost Coins	2FLY6B
Gold Brick Detector	84QNQN
Hogwarts Crest Detector	TTMC6D
Invincibility	QQWC6B
Red Brick Detector	7AD7HE
Score x10	H8X69Y
Score x2	74YKR7
Score x6	XK9ANE
Score x8	HUFV2H
Super Strength	BMEU6X

LEGO HARRY POTTER: YEARS 5-7 (WII)

CODE

Enter the following passwords in the Start Menu under Extras while in game. It's the first option of the Extras menu.

UNLOCKABLE	PASSWORD
Carrot Wands	AUC8EH
Character Studs	H27KGC
Character Token Detector	HA79V8
Collect Ghost Studs	2FLY6B
Extra Hearts	J9U6Z9
Fall Rescue	ZEX7MV
Fast Dig	Z9BFAD
Gold Brick Detctor	84QNQN
Hogwarts Crest Detector	TTMC6D
Invinvibility	QQWC6B
Red Brick Detector	7AD7HE
Score x10	H8X69Y
Score x2	74YKR7
Score x6	XK9ANE
Score x8	HUFV2H

CODE

Enter the following password in the Weasleys' Joke Shop in Diagon Alley

UNLOCKABLE	CODE
Immobulus	AAAAAA

LEGO INDIANA JONES: THE ORIGINAL ADVENTURES
(XBOX 360), (PLAYSTATION 3), (WII)

CHARACTER CODES

Enter the codes on the blackboard in the math classroom of Barnett College (the 2nd door on the left in the main hallway).

EFFECT	XBOX 360 CODE	PS3 CODE	WII CODE	PS2 CODE
Bandit	12N68W	12N68W	12N68W	12N68W
Bandit Swordsman	1MK4RT	1MK4RT	1MK4RT	1MK4RT
Barranca	04EM94	04EM94	04EM94	04EM94
Bazooka Trooper (Crusade)	MK83R7	MK83R7	MK83R7	MK83R7
Bazooka Trooper (Raiders)	S93Y5R	S93Y5R	S93Y5R	S93Y5R
Belloq	CHN3YU	CHN3YU	CHN3YU	CHN3YU
Belloq (Jungle)	TDR197	TDR197	TDR197	TDR197
Belloq (Robes)	VEO29L	VEO29L	VEO29L	VEO29L
British Officer	VJ5TI9	VJ5TI9	VJ5TI9	VJ5TI9
British Troop Commander	B73EUA	B73EUA	B73EUA	B73EUA
British Troop Soldier	DJ5I2W	DJ5I2W	DJ5I2W	DJ5I2W
Captain Katanga	VJ3TT3	VJ3TT3	VJ3TT3	VJ3TT3
Chatter Lal	ENW936	ENW936	ENW936	ENW936
Chatter Lal (Thuggee)	CNH4RY	CNH4RY	CNH4RY	CNH4RY
Chen	3NK48T	3NK48T	3NK48T	3NK48T
Colonel Dietrich	2K9RKS	2K9RKS	2K9RKS	2K9RKS
Colonel Vogel	8EAL4H	8EAL4H	8EAL4H	8EAL4H
Dancing Girl	C7EJ21	C7EJ21	C7EJ21	C7EJ21
Donovan	3NFTU8	3NFTU8	3NFTU8	3NFTU8
Elsa (Desert)	JSNRT9	JSNRT9	JSNRT9	JSNRT9
Elsa (Officer)	VMJ5US	VMJ5US	VMJ5US	VMJ5US
Enemy Boxer	8246RB	8246RB	8246RB	8246RB
Enemy Butler	VJ48W3	VJ48W3	VJ48W3	VJ48W3
Enemy Guard	VJ7R51	VJ7R51	VJ7R51	VJ7R51
Enemy Guard (Mountains)	YR47WM	YR47WM	YR47WM	YR47WM
Enemy Officer (Desert)	2MK450	572 E61	572 E61	572 E61
Enemy Officer	572 E61	2MK450	2MK450	2MK450
Enemy Pilot	B84ELP	B84ELP	B84ELP	B84ELP
Enemy Radio Operator	1MF94R	1MF94R	1MF94R	1MF94R
Enemy Soldier (Desert)	4NSU7Q	4NSU7Q	4NSU7Q	4NSU7Q
Fedora	V75YSP	V75YSP	V75YSP	V75YSP
First Mate	0GIN24	0GIN24	0GIN24	0GIN24
Grail Knight	NE6THI	NE6THI	NE6THI	NE6THI
Hovitos Tribesman	H0V1SS	H0V1SS	H0V1SS	H0V1SS
Indiana Jones (Desert Disguise)	4J8S4M	4J8S4M	4J8S4M	4J8S4M
Indiana Jones (Officer)	VJ850S	VJ850S	VJ850S	VJ850S
Jungle Guide	24PF34	24PF34	24PF34	24PF34
Kao Kan	WMO46L	WMO46L	WMO46L	WMO46L
Kazim	NRH23J	NRH23J	NRH23J	NRH23J
Kazim (Desert)	3M29TJ	3M29TJ	3M29TJ	3M29TJ
Lao Che	2NK479	2NK479	2NK479	2NK479

Maharaja	NFK5N2	NFK5N2	NFK5N2	NFK5N2
Major Toht	13NS01	13NS01	13NS01	13NS01
Masked Bandit	N48SF0	N48SF0	N48SF0	N48SF0
Mola Ram	FJUR31	FJUR31	FJUR31	FJUR31
Monkey Man	3RF6YJ	3RF6YJ	3RF6YJ	3RF6YJ
Pankot Assassin	2NKT72	2NKT72	2NKT72	2NKT72
Pankot Guard	VN28RH	VN28RH	VN28RH	VN28RH
Sherpa Brawler	VJ37WJ	VJ37WJ	VJ37WJ	VJ37WJ
Sherpa Gunner	ND762W	ND762W	ND762W	ND762W
Slave Child	0E3ENW	0E3ENW	0E3ENW	0E3ENW
Thuggee	VM683E	VM683E	VM683E	VM683E
Thuggee Acolyte	T2R3F9	T2R3F9	T2R3F9	T2R3F9
Thuggee Slavedriver	VBS7GW	VBS7GW	VBS7GW	VBS7GW
Village Dignitary	KD48TN	KD48TN	KD48TN	KD48TN
Village Elder	4682 E1	4682 E1	4682 E1	4682 E1
Willie (Dinner Suit)	VK93R7	VK93R7	VK93R7	VK93R7
Willie (Pajamas)	MEN4IP	MEN4IP	MEN4IP	MEN4IP
Wu Han	3NSLT8	3NSLT8	3NSLT8	3NSLT8

ITEM CODES

Enter the codes on the blackboard in the math classroom of
Barnett College (the 2nd door on the left in the main hallway).

EFFECT	XBOX 360 CODE	PS3 CODE	WII CODE	PS2 CODE
Artifact Detector	VIKED7	VIKED7	VIKED7	VIKED7
Beep Beep	VNF59Q	VNF59Q	VNF59Q	VNF59Q
Character Treasure	VIES2R	VIES2R	VIES2R	VIES2R
Disarm Enemies	VKRNS9	VKRNS9	VKRNS9	VKRNS9
Disguises	4ID1N6	4ID1N6	4ID1N6	4ID1N6
Fast Build	V83SLO	V83SLO	V83SLO	V83SLO
Fast Dig	378RS6	378RS6	378RS6	378RS6
Fast Fix	FJ59WS	FJ59WS	FJ59WS	FJ59WS
Fertilizer	B1GW1F	B1GW1F	B1GW1F	B1GW1F
Ice Rink	33GM7J	33GM7J	33GM7J	33GM7J
Parcel Detector	VUT673	VUT673	VUT673	VUT673
Poo Treasure	WWQ1SA	WWQ1SA	WWQ1SA	WWQ1SA
Regenerate Hearts	MDLP69	MDLP69	MDLP69	MDLP69
Secret Characters	3X44AA	3X44AA	3X44AA	3X44AA
Silhouettes	3HE85H	3HE85H	3HE85H	3HE85H
Super Scream	VN3R7S	VN3R7S	VN3R7S	VN3R7S
Super Slap	0P1TA5	0P1TA5	0P1TA5	0P1TA5
Treasure Magnet	H86LA2	H86LA2	H86LA2	H86LA2
Treasure x2	VM4TS9	VM4TS9	VM4TS9	VM4TS9
Treasure x4	VLWEN3	VLWEN3	VLWEN3	VLWEN3
Treasure x6	V84RYS	V84RYS	V84RYS	V84RYS
Treasure x8	A72E1M	A72E1M	A72E1M	A72E1M
Treasure x10	VI3PS8	VI3PS8	VI3PS8	VI3PS8

LEGO INDIANA JONES: THE ORIGINAL ADVENTURES (DS)

CODES

EFFECT	CODE
All Characters Unlocked	⊗, ⬆, Ⓑ, ⬇, Ⓨ, ⬅, •START, ⬇, Ⓓ, Ⓡ, Ⓛ, Ⓡ, Ⓑ, ⬇, ⬇, ⬇, Ⓨ, Ⓥ, Ⓨ, •START, •SELECT
All Episodes Unlocked + Free Play	⬇, ⬇, Ⓓ, Ⓛ, ⊗, Ⓥ, ⬇, ⬆, Ⓑ, Ⓛ, Ⓓ, Ⓛ, ⬇, ⬇, ⬇, Ⓥ, Ⓥ, ⊗, Ⓑ, Ⓑ, ⬇, Ⓛ, Ⓡ, •START, •SELECT
All Extras Unlocked	⬇, ⬇, Ⓛ, Ⓓ, Ⓛ, Ⓓ, Ⓛ, ⬆, ⬇, ⬇, ⊗, ⊗, Ⓥ, Ⓥ, Ⓑ, Ⓑ, Ⓛ, ⬇, ⬇, Ⓛ, Ⓓ, Ⓡ, ⬇, •START, •SELECT
Start with 1,000,000 Studs	⊗, Ⓥ, Ⓑ, Ⓑ, Ⓥ, ⊗, Ⓛ, Ⓛ, Ⓓ, Ⓑ, ⬇, ⬇, ⬇, ⬇, •START, •SELECT
Start with 3,000,000 Studs	⬇, ⬇, Ⓑ, ⬇, ⬇, ⊗, ⬇, ⬇, Ⓛ, Ⓓ, Ⓛ, Ⓡ, Ⓑ, Ⓥ, ⊗, •START, •SELECT

LEGO INDIANA JONES: THE ORIGINAL ADVENTURES (PSP)

CHARACTER CODES

Enter the codes on the blackboard in the math classroom of Barnett College(the 2nd door on the left in the main hallway).

EFFECT	CODE
Bandit	12N68W
Bandit Swordsman	1MK4RT
Barranca	04EM94
Bazooka Trooper (Crusade)	MK83R7
Bazooka Trooper (Raiders)	S93Y5R
Belloq	CHN3YU
Belloq (Jungle)	TDR197
Belloq (Robes)	VEO29L
British Officer	VJ5TI9
British Troop Commander	B73EUA
British Troop Soldier	DJ5I2W
Captain Katanga	VJ3TT3
Chatter Lal	ENW936
Chatter Lal (Thuggee)	CNH4RY
Chen	3NK48T
Colonel Dietrich	2K9RKS
Colonel Vogel	8EAL4H
Dancing Girl	C7EJ21
Donovan	3NFTU8
Elsa (Desert)	JSNRT9
Elsa (Officer)	VMJ5US
Enemy Boxer	8246RB
Enemy Butler	VJ48W3
Enemy Guard	VJ7R51
Enemy Guard (Mountains)	YR47WM
Enemy Officer	572 E61
Enemy Officer (Desert)	2MK45O
Enemy Pilot	B84ELP
Enemy Radio Operator	1MF94R
Enemy Soldier (Desert)	4NSU7Q
Fedora	V75YSP
First Mate	0GIN24
Grail Knight	NE6THI
Hovitos Tribesman	H0V1SS

CODES & CHEATS

Indiana Jones (Desert Disguise)	4J8S4M
Indiana Jones (Officer)	VJ85OS
Jungle Guide	24PF34
Kao Kan	WMO46L
Kazim	NRH23J
Kazim (Desert)	3M29TJ
Lao Che	2NK479
Maharaja	NFK5N2
Major Toht	13NS01
Masked Bandit	N48SF0
Mola Ram	FJUR31
Monkey Man	3RF6YJ
Pankot Assassin	2NKT72
Pankot Guard	VN28RH
Sherpa Brawler	VJ37WJ
Sherpa Gunner	ND762W
Slave Child	0E3ENW
Thuggee	VM683E
Thuggee Acolyte	T2R3F9
Thuggee Slavedriver	VBS7GW
Village Dignitary	KD48TN
Village Elder	4682 E1
Willie (Dinner Suit)	VK93R7
Willie (Pajamas)	MEN4IP
Wu Han	3NSLT8

ITEM CODES

Enter the codes on the blackboard in the math classroom of Barnett College(the 2nd door on the left in the main hallway).

EFFECT	CODE
Artifact Detector	VIKED7
Beep Beep	VNF59Q
Character Treasure	VIES2R
Disarm Enemies	VKRNS9
Disguises	4ID1N6
Fast Build	V83SLO
Fast Dig	378RS6
Fast Fix	FJ59WS
Fertilizer	B1GW1F
Ice Rink	33GM7J
Parcel Detector	VUT673
Poo Treasure	WWQ1SA
Regenerate Hearts	MDLP69
Secret Characters	3X44AA
Silhouettes	3HE85H
Super Scream	VN3R7S
Super Slap	0P1TA5
Treasure Magnet	H86LA2
Treasure x2	VM4TS9
Treasure x4	VLWEN3
Treasure x6	V84RYS

| Treasure x8 | A72E1M |
| Treasure x10 | VI3PS8 |

INVINCIBILITY

Enter the code on the blackboard of the math classroom.

EFFECT	CODE
Invincibility	B83EA1

SECRET LEVELS

UNLOCKABLE	HOW TO UNLOCK
Ancient City	Collect all of the artifacts in Temple of Doom.
Warehouse Level	Collect all of the artifacts in The Last Crusade.
Young Indy level	Collect all of the artifacts in Raiders of the Lost Ark.

LEGO INDIANA JONES 2: THE ADVENTURE CONTINUES (XBOX 360), (WII)

CODES

EFFECT	XBOX 360 CODE	WII CODE
Beep Beep	UU3VSC	UU3VSC
Disguise	Y9TE98	Y9TE98
Fast Build	SNXC2F	SNXC2F
Fast Dig	XYAN83	XYAN83
Fast Fix	3Z7PJX	3Z7PJX
Fearless	TUXNZF	TUXNZF
Hot Rod	YLG2TN	YLG2TN
Ice Rink	TY9P4U	TY9P4U
Indiana Jones: 1	PGWSEA	PGWSEA
Indiana Jones: 2	DZFY9S	DZFY9S
Indiana Jones: Desert	M4C34K	M4C34K
Indiana Jones: Disguised	2W8QR3	2W8QR3
Indiana Jones: Kali	J2XS97	J2XS97
Indiana Jones: Officer	3FQFKS	3FQFKS
Invincibility	6JBB65	6JBB65
Lao Che	7AWX3J	7AWX3J
Mola Ram	82RMC2	82RMC2
Mutt	2GK562	2GK562
Poo Money	SZFAAE	SZFAAE
Professor Henry Jones	4C5AKH	4C5AKH
Rene Belloq	FTL48S	FTL48S
Sallah	E88YRP	E88YRP
Score x2	U38VJP	U38VJP
Score x3	PEHHPZ	PEHHPZ
Score x4	UXGTB3	UXGTB3
Score x6	XWJ5EY	XWJ5EY
Score x8	S5UZCP	S5UZCP
Score x10	V7JYBU	V7JYBU
Silhouettes	FQGPYH	FQGPYH
Snake Whip	2U7YCV	2U7YCV
Stud Magnet	EGSM5B	EGSM5B
Willie: Singer	94RUAJ	94RUAJ

LEGO PIRATES OF THE CARIBBEAN (XBOX 360), (PLAYSTATION 3), (WII)

UNLOCKABLE

Enter the following codes at the Unlock section of the main menu.

EFFECT	CODE
Ammand the Corsair	ew8t6t
Angelica (Disguised)	dlrr45
Angry Cannibal	vgf32c
Blackbeard	d3dw0d
Clanker	zm37gt
Clubber	zm37gt
Davy Jones	4djlkr
Governor Weatherby Swann	ld9454
Gunner	y611wb
Hungry Cannibal	64bnhg
Jack Sparrow (Musical)	vdjspw
Jimmy Legs	13glw5
King George	rked43
Koehler	rt093g
Mistress Ching	gdetde
Phillip	wev040
Quartermaster	rx58hu
The Spaniard	p861jo
Twigg	kdlfkd

LEGO PIRATES OF THE CARIBBEAN (DS), (PSP), (3DS)

UNLOCKABLE

At the Main Menu, go to Options, then Codes. Type in the code to unlock these characters.

EFFECT	CODE
Ammand the Corsair	ew8t6t
Angelica (Disguised)	dlrr45
Angry Cannibal	vgf32c
Blackbeard	d3dw0d
Clanker	zm37gt
Clubber	zm37gt
Davy Jones	4djlkr
Governor Weatherby Swann	ld9454
Gunner	y611wb
Hungry Cannibal	64bnhg
Jack Sparrow (Musical)	vdjspw
Jimmy Legs	13glw5
King George	rked43
Koehler	rt093g
Mistress Ching	gdetde
Phillip	wev040
Quartermaster	rx58hu
The Spaniard	p861jo
Twigg	kdlfkd

LEGO ROCK BAND (DS)

UNLOCK GUEST ARTISTS

Complete the following songs in Tour Mode to unlock the corresponding guest artist and their parts for use in your own band.

UNLOCKABLE	HOW TO UNLOCK
Blur	Beat "Song 2" in Tour.
David Bowie	Beat "Let's Dance" in Tour.
Iggy Pop	Beat "The Passenger" in Tour.
Queen	Beat "We Are The Champions" in Tour.

LEGO STAR WARS: THE COMPLETE SAGA (XBOX 360)

CHARACTERS

To use the codes, enter the Cantina, go to the bar, access the codes command, and type in the codes.

CHARACTER	XBOX 360 CODES	PS3 CODE	WII CODE
Admiral Ackbar	ACK646	ACK646	ACK646
Battle Droid Commander	KPF958	KPF958	KPF958
Boba Fett (Boy)	GGF539	GGF539	GGF539
Boss Nass	HHY697	HHY697	HHY697
Captain Tarpals	QRN714	QRN714	QRN714
Count Dooku	DDD748	DDD748	DDD748
Darth Maul	EUK421	EUK421	EUK421
Ewok	EWK785	EWK785	EWK785
General Grievous	PMN576	PMN576	PMN576
Greedo	ZZR636	ZZR636	ZZR636
IG-88	GIJ989	GIJ989	GIJ989
Imperial Guard	GUA850	GUA850	GUA850
Indiana Jones	After you watch the trailer for the upcoming Indiana Jones game in the Bonus Room, Indy will become a playable character.		
Jango Fett	KLJ897	KLJ897	KLJ897
Ki-Adi-Mundi	MUN486	MUN486	MUN486
Luminara	LUM521	LUM521	LUM521
Padmé	VBJ322	VBJ322	VBJ322
R2-Q5	EVILR2	EVILR2	EVILR2
Sandtrooper	CBR954	CBR954	CBR954
Stormtrooper	NBN431	NBN431	NBN431
Super Battle Droid	XZNR21	XZNR21	XZNR21
Taun We	PRX482	PRX482	PRX482
Vulture Droid	BDC866	BDC866	BDC866
Watto	PLL967	PLL967	PLL967
Zam Wesell	584HJF	584HJF	584HJF

SHIPS

UNLOCKABLE SHIPS	XBOX 360 CODES	PS3 CODE	WII CODE
Droid Trifighter	AAB123	AAB123	AAB123
Imperial Shuttle	HUT845	HUT845	HUT845
Slave I	Collect all 10 Minikits on each level.		
TIE Fighter	DBH897	DBH897	DBH897

UNLOCKABLE SHIPS	XBOX 360 CODES	PS3 CODE	WII CODE
TIE Interceptor	INT729	INT729	INT729
Zam's Speeder	UUU875	UUU875	UUU875

SKILLS

UNLOCKABLE SKILLS	XBOX 360 CODES	PS3 CODE	WII CODE
Disguise	BRJ437	BRJ437	BRJ437
Force Grapple Leap	CLZ738	CLZ738	CLZ738

LEGO STAR WARS II: THE ORIGINAL TRILOGY (XBOX 360)

DIFFERENT CHARACTERS

PASSWORD	EFFECT
Beach Trooper	UCK868
Ben Kenobi's Ghost	BEN917
Bespin Guard	VHY832
Bib Fortuna	WTY721
Boba Fett	HLP221
Death Star Trooper	BNC332
Emperor	HHY382
Ewok	TTT289
Gamorean Guard	YZF999
Gonk Droid	NFX582
Grand Moff Tarkin	SMG219
Han Solo with Hood	YWM840
IG-88	NXL973
Imperial Guard	MMM111
Imperial Officer	BBV889
Imperial Shuttle Pilot	VAP664
Imperial Spy	CVT125
Lobot	UUB319
Palace Guard	SGE549
Rebel Pilot	CYG336
Rebel Trooper from Hoth	EKU849
Red Noses on All Characters	NBP398
Santa Hat and Red Clothes	CL4U5H
Skiff Guard	GBU888
Snowtrooper	NYU989
Stormtrooper	PTR345
TIE Fighter	HDY739
TIE Fighter Pilot	NNZ316
TIE Interceptor	QYA828
Ugnaught	UGN694
Unlock Greedo	NAH118
Unlock Jawa	JAW499
Unlock Sandtrooper	YDV451
Unlock Tusken Raider	PEJ821
White Beard Extra	TYH319

LEGO STAR WARS II: THE ORIGINAL TRILOGY (DS)

Enter this password in the Cantina.

UNLOCKABLE	PASSWORD
10 extra studs	4PR28U

LEGO STAR WARS II: THE ORIGINAL TRILOGY (PSP)

PASSWORDS

Enter the following codes at the Mos Eisley Cantina to unlock the character for purchase in Free Play mode.

UNLOCKABLE	HOW TO UNLOCK
Beach Trooper	UCK868
Ben Kenobi's Ghost	BEN917
Bespin Guard	VHY832
Bib Fortuna	WTY721
Boba Fett	HLP221
Death Star Trooper	BNC332
Emperor	HHY382
Ewok	TTT289
Gamorean Guard	YZF999
Gonk Droid	NFX582
Grand Moff Tarkin	SMG219
Han Solo with Hood	YWM840
IG-88	NXL973
Imperial Guard	MMM111
Imperial Officer	BBV889
Imperial Shuttle Pilot	VAP66
Imperial Spy	CVT125
Lobot	UUB319
Palace Guard	SGE549
Rebel Pilot	CYG336
Rebel Trooper from Hoth	EKU849
Red Noses on All Characters	NBP398
Santa Hat and Red Clothes	CL4U5H
Skiff Guard	GBU888
Snow Trooper	NYU989
Stormtrooper	PTR345
TIE Fighter	HDY739
TIE Fighter Pilot	NNZ316
TIE Interceptor	QYA828
Ugnaught	UGN694
White Beard Extra	TYH319

UNLOCKABLE CHARACTERS

Complete challenge by collecting 10 Blue Minikits within the time limit allowed per level.

UNLOCKABLE	HOW TO UNLOCK
R4-P17, PK Droid	Episode 4, Chapter 2
Battle Droid, B. D. (Security), B. D. (Geonosis), B. D. (Commander)	Episode 4, Chapter 4
Chancellor Palpatine, General Grievous, Grievous' Bodyguard	Episode 6, Chapter 5
Clone (Episode III, Pilot)	Episode 4, Chapter 6

Clone (Episode III, Swamp)	Episode 5, Chapter 4
Clone, Clone (Episode III), Commander Cody, Clone (Episode III Walker)	Episode 6, Chapter 3
Disguised Clone, Boba Fett (Boy)	Episode 6, Chapter 1
Droideka	Episode 4, Chapter 5
Geonosian	Episode 5, Chapter 3
Jango Fett	Episode 6, Chapter 2
Luminara, Ki-Adi-Mundi, Kit Fisto, Shaak Ti	Episode 5, Chapter 1
Mace Windu, Mace Windu (Episode 3)	Episode 6, Chapter 6
Padmé (Battle), Padmé (Clawed), Padmé (Geonosis)	Episode 5, Chapter 2
Padmé, Anakin Skywalker (boy)	Episode 4, Chapter 3
Queen Amidala, Royal Guard, Captain Panaka	Episode 5, Chapter 6
Super Battle Droid	Episode 5, Chapter 5
TC-14	Episode 4, Chapter 1
Wookiee, Jar Jar Binks	Episode 6, Chapter 4

LEGO STAR WARS III: THE CLONE WARS (PLAYSTATION 3, (XBOX 360)

UNLOCKABLE

Pause game during play and go to Extras to enter these passwords.

EFFECT	CODE
Character Studs	qd2c31
Dark Side	x1v4n2
Dual Wield	c4es4r
Fast Build	gchp7s
Geonosian Starfighter unlocked.	EDENEC
Glow in the Dark	4gt3vq
Invincibility	j46p7a
Minikit Detector	csd5na
Perfect Deflect	3F5L56
Regenerate Hearts	2d7jns
Score X10	n1ckr1
Score X2	yzphuv
Score X4	43t5e5
Score X6	sebhgr
Score X8	byfsaq
Stud Magnet	6mz5ch
Super Saber Cut	bs828k
Super Speeders	b1d3w3
Unlock Savage Oppress	MELL07
Vulture Droid unlocked	7w7k7s

LEGO STAR WARS III: THE CLONE WARS (WII)

UNLOCKABLE

At the Pause menu, select Extras and enter these passwords at "Enter Code".

EFFECT	CODE
Makes multiplier available - Every stud collected in game is multiplied by the number stated	Yzphuv
Makes Perfect Deflect available - Deflected lasers always hit a target	3f5l56

Unlock Dual Wield	c4es4r
Unlock Fast Build	gchp7s
Unlock Glow in the Dark	4gt3vq
Unlock Invincibility	j46p7a
Unlock Regenerativ Hearts	2d7jns
Unlock Super Saber Cut	bs828k
Unlock Super Speeders	b1d3w3
Unlock the Character Studs	qd2c31
Unlock the Dark Side	x1v4n2
Unlock the Minikit Detector	csd5na
Unlock the Stud Magnet	6mz5ch
Unlock X10 Score Multiplier	n1ckr1
Unlock X4 Score Multiplier	43t5e5
Unlock X6 Score Multiplier	sebhgr
Unlock X8 Score Multiplier	byfsaw
Vulture Droid unlocked	7w7k7s

LIMBO (XBOX 360)

AVATAR AWARDS

UNLOCKABLE	HOW TO UNLOCK
LIMBO Pet	Beat the game.
LIMBO T-shirt	Get your first LIMBO achievement.

LITTLE BIG PLANET 2 (PLAYSTATION 3)

SECRET PINS

These special pins do not appear normally in the pin list (and do not count toward your pin total).

UNLOCKABLE	HOW TO UNLOCK
Amy's Birthday Pressie	Play on Amy's Birthday (July 29)
Festive Spirit	Wear a Christmas costume on Christmas Day
Halloween Hauntings	Wear the Pumpkin Head costume on Halloween
Mm Picked!	Have one of your levels feature in Mm Picks
Mm's Birthday	Play LBP2 on Media Molecule's birthday (January 4)
Royalty	You are awarded a Crown (LBP1 or LBP2)
Thanksgiving Turkey	Wear the Turkey Head costume on Thanksgiving
Who's Who	Watch the credits all the way through

LITTLE DEVIANTS (PLAYSTATION VITA)

TROPHY

UNLOCKABLE	HOW TO UNLOCK
A Head for Heights (Bronze)	Complete Stage 1 of Risky Inclination with at least 30 seconds remaining.
Air Miles And Miles (Bronze)	Fly 1,000,000m.
Blackrust Refinery (Bronze)	Unlock Blackrust Refinery region.
Blink and you'll miss it (Bronze)	Pick up the Star from the secret chamber in Risky Rambler.
Bomb 'Em, Man (Bronze)	Destroy 2 or more Dead 'Uns with one fire attack in Corridor Calamity.
Cat-alouged (Silver)	All Moggers collected.
Cave Brave (Bronze)	Collect at least 120 pickups in a single game of Risky Trails.
Chillrock Gorge (Bronze)	Unlock Chillrock Gorge region.

Cold As Ice (Bronze)	Smash 5 frozen Botz or more in a game of Corridor Complications.
Competent Deviant (Silver)	Win at least a silver spaceship on all games.
Crate Breaker (Bronze)	Break open a crate in under half a second in Rolling Shores.
Day None Patch (Bronze)	Complete Hot Air Hero without patching the balloon once.
Dead 'Un Masher (Bronze)	Splat 6 or more Dead 'Uns with one shot in Rotten Rumble.
Deviant Storm (Bronze)	Boost over the finishing line in Street Speeder.
Devilish Deviant (Gold)	Win a gold spaceship on all games.
Dipped into Deviants (Bronze)	Win your first bronze spaceship.
Exhibitionist (Silver)	All gallery items unlocked.
Fint the Time (Silver)	Collect 1,000 Clocks.
Full Controller (Bronze)	Complete Rolling Pastures with full health at the end of the game.
Fun Deviant (Bronze)	Win at least a bronze spaceship on all games.
Grave Digger (Silver)	Destroy 500 Dead 'Uns.
Heavy Metal (Bronze)	Destroy 20 Botz in Destructor Constructor.
Honor Upheld (Bronze)	Defeat a challenge from a PlayStation Network friend.
I didn't wipe (Bronze)	Complete Botz Blast without wiping any green goo from the screen.
Jump Around (Bronze)	Jump on one platform 5 times in Bouncer Trouncer.
Just made it! (Bronze)	Finish Stage 4 of Depth Avenger with at least 10 seconds remaining.
Kyle says, "Don't touch..." (Bronze)	Score 35,000 points in Shack Shover without hitting a Whoman or a Deviant.
Laaaaaaaaaaaaaa! (Bronze)	Hold a note in Smashing Tune for at least 5 seconds.
Long Way Roller (Bronze)	Roll 500,000m.
Meow! (Bronze)	Collect your first Mogger.
Metroburg (Bronze)	Unlock Metroburg region.
Mmm, hardware (Bronze)	Use each of the PlayStation Vita system's input devices that are featured in Little Deviants.
No-Electro Hero (Bronze)	Complete Corridor Caper without using any EMP pickups.
Over-boinged (Silver)	Bounce a Deviant 1,500 times.
Perfect 12 (Bronze)	In City Shover hit all 12 Number-Botz in sequence.
Scored! (Bronze)	Post a score to the online leaderboard.
Sharpshooter (Bronze)	Destroy 10 Botz without missing a shot in a game of Botz Invasion.
Smooth Mover (Bronze)	Complete Depth Charge without hitting any walls.
Star Barred (Bronze)	Complete Aqua Speeder without picking up more than 20 Stars.
Starry Eyed (Silver)	Collect 5,000 Stars.
Stay on target! (Bronze)	Boost 5 times in a row without crashing in Death Speeder.
Storm Chaser (Bronze)	Hit at least 10 different wind vortices in Depth Dive and still complete the game.
Stream Saver (Bronze)	Complete Neutron Nudger without any Botz damaging the energy sphere.

Surfcrest Bay (Bronze)	Unlock Surfcrest Bay region.
Taste of Victory (Bronze)	Win your first gold spaceship.
Teacher's Pet (Bronze)	Input 3 consecutive codes correctly in Cannon Codes.
Terminated (Silver)	Destroy 2,500 Botz.
The Mighty Boost (Bronze)	Boost through all the rings in any single stage of Cloud Rush.
The right way is the wrong way (Bronze)	Complete Manic Melter by only twisting the platform clockwise.
They mostly come at night, mostly (Bronze)	Play Rolling Horror between 00:00 and 01:00.
Throwdown (Bronze)	Challenge a PlayStation Network friend.
Timeless (Bronze)	Score at least 28,000 points in Chalet Shover without using any Clock pickups.
Trophyumphant (Platinum)	Unlock all other trophies.
Twisty Root Groove (Bronze)	Unlock Twisty Root Grove region.
Watch the Birdy (Bronze)	Collect 3 bird pickups in a single game of Tower of Boing.

LITTLEST PET SHOP: JUNGLE (DS)

CODES

Enter the following code in the options menu under the "Enter Passwords" section.

EFFECT	CODE
Giraffe	LPSTRU

LODE RUNNER (WII)

UNLOCKABLES

UNLOCKABLE	HOW TO UNLOCK
Game Speed	Press SELECT to view current level. Hold SELECT and press ⑧ to decrease game speed, or Ⓐ to increase game speed.
Level Select	Press select to view current level. Press SELECT then press Ⓐ to increase a level and ⑧ to drop one.

LOLLIPOP CHAINSAW (PLAYSTATION 3)

TROPHY

UNLOCKABLE	HOW TO UNLOCK
Accidental Vandalism (Bronze)	Destroyed 300 objects in the game.
Aced Auto-shop Class (Bronze)	Clear all the Kill Car QTE's in a row.
Advanced Zombie Hunter (Silver)	Clear Stage 3, surpassing Dad's score.
Always On The Phone (Bronze)	Collected all telephone messages.
Beginner Zombie Hunter (Silver)	Clear Stage 1, surpassing Dad's score.
Cheerleader Overboard! (Bronze)	Succeed in QTE at edge of Vikke's ship.
Congratulations! Happy Birthday! (Gold)	Watched the happy ending.
Critical UFO Finish (Bronze)	Funk Josey in the last 10 seconds.
Dirty Hippy (Bronze)	Defeated Mariska.
Disco's Dead (Bronze)	Defeated Josey.
Elephant Tamer (Bronze)	Counter Lewis' attack 10 times.
Endorsed by Cordelia (Bronze)	Get 30 headshots.
Excellent Zombie Hunter (Silver)	Clear Stage 5, surpassing Dad's score.
Fingered (Bronze)	Cut off 20 fingers during Killabilly's fight!
Go, Medal Racer, Go! (Bronze)	Picked up all zombie medals on the rooftop with Chainsaw Dash.
Groovy Hunter (Bronze)	Kill 500 zombies.

Gunn Struck (Bronze)	Struck by lightning 10 times.
Horrid Birthday (Bronze)	Watched the bad ending.
I Came, I Saw, I Kicked Its Ass (Bronze)	Defeated Killabilly.
I Swear! I Did It By Mistake! (Bronze)	Peeped under Juliet's skirt once.
Intermediate Zombie Hunter (Silver)	Clear Stage 2, surpassing Dad's score.
International Zombie Hunter (Bronze)	Registered in world leaderboards for all stages.
JULIET51 (Bronze)	51 successful dropkicks.
Leapfrog girl (Bronze)	Leapfrogged 10 times in a row.
Legendary harvester (Bronze)	Harvested all crops in the 1st field with the combine in Stage 3.
Legendary Zombie Hunter (Platinum)	100% Complete! Thank you for playing!
Life Guard (Bronze)	Rescued all classmates in Prologue.
Little Sisters Are The Worst! (Bronze)	Do not get hit by Rosalind's wrecking ball.
Lollipop Addict (Silver)	Collected all lollipop wrappers.
Love Nick (Bronze)	Kissed Nick 100 times.
Master Sushi Chef (Silver)	Collected all combos.
Master Zombie Hunter (Silver)	Clear Stage 6, surpassing Dad's score.
Millionaire Hunter (Silver)	Pick up 10,000 zombie medals.
n00b Zombie Hunter (Silver)	Clear Prologue, surpassing Dad's score.
No Fear Of Heights (Bronze)	Beat the Gondola game without shooting.
OMG, Music Is Soooo Coooool (Silver)	Collected all BGM.
Perfect Body (Silver)	Completely level up Juliet.
Rich Hunter (Bronze)	Pick up 1,000 zombie medals.
Rock'n Roll Isn't Here Anymore (Bronze)	Defeated Lewis LEGEND.
San Romero Knights Savior (Silver)	Rescued All Classmates.
Sparkle Hunting Master (Bronze)	Succeed in 7 zombie Sparkle Hunting.
Super Shopper (Bronze)	Spend 10,000 medals at Chop2Shop. Zom.
Super Zombie Hunter (Silver)	Clear Stage 4, surpassing Dad's score.
Third Eye (Bronze)	Dodge all balloon attacks in Mariska battle.
Unclean and Uncool (Bronze)	Defeated Hazmat in Prologue.
Viking Metal Rules! (Bronze)	Defeated Vikke.
Watch Out For The Balls (Bronze)	Dodge & Counter Zed's Electric Balls 15 times.
Zed's Dead, Baby, Zed's Dead (Bronze)	Defeated Zed.
Zombie Fancier (Silver)	Completed the zombie album.
Zombie Hunter Apprentice (Bronze)	Buy a combo at Chop2Shop.Zom and use it.
Zombie Slayer?! (Silver)	Kill 3,000 zombies.

LOLLIPOP CHAINSAW (XBOX 360)

ACHIEVEMENT

UNLOCKABLE	HOW TO UNLOCK
Accidental Vandalism (15)	Destroyed 300 objects in the game.
Aced Auto-shop Class (15)	Clear all the Kill Car QTE's in a row.
Advanced Zombie Hunter (30)	Clear Stage 3, surpassing Dad's score.
Always On The Phone (30)	Collected all telephone messages.
Beginner Zombie Hunter (30)	Clear Stage 1, surpassing Dad's score.

Cheerleader Overboard! (10)	Succeed in QTE at edge of Vikke's ship.
Congratulations! Happy Birthday! (100)	Watched the happy ending.
Critical UFO Finish (10)	Funk Josey in the last 10 seconds.
Dirty Hippy (15)	Defeated Mariska.
Disco's Dead (15)	Defeated Josey.
Elephant Tamer (10)	Counter Lewis' attack 10 times.
Endorsed by Cordelia (10)	Get 30 headshots.
Excellent Zombie Hunter (30)	Clear Stage 5, surpassing Dad's score.
Fingered (10)	Cut off 20 fingers during Killabilly's fight!
Go, Medal Racer, Go! (15)	Picked up all zombie medals on the rooftop with Chainsaw Dash.
Groovy Hunter (10)	Kill 500 zombies.
Gunn Struck (10)	Struck by lightning 10 times.
Horrid Birthday (15)	Watched the bad ending.
I Came, I Saw, I Kicked Its Ass (15)	Defeated Killabilly.
I Swear! I Did It By Mistake! (10)	Peeped under Juliet's skirt once.
Intermediate Zombie Hunter (30)	Clear Stage 2, surpassing Dad's score.
International Zombie Hunter (15)	Registered in world leaderboards for all stages.
JULIET51 (15)	51 successful dropkicks.
Leapfrog Girl (10)	Leapfrogged 10 times in a row.
Legendary harvester (15)	Harvested all crops in the 1st field with the combine in Stage 3.
Life Guard (15)	Rescued all classmates in Prologue.
Little Sisters Are The Worst! (15)	Do not get hit by Rosalind's wrecking ball.
Lollipop Addict (30)	Collected all lollipop wrappers.
Love Nick (15)	Kissed Nick 100 times.
Master Sushi Chef (30)	Collected all combos.
Master Zombie Hunter (30)	Clear Stage 6, surpassing Dad's score.
Millionaire Hunter (30)	Pick up 10,000 zombie medals.
n00b Zombie Hunter (30)	Clear Prologue, surpassing Dad's score.
No Fear Of Heights (15)	Beat the Gondola game without shooting.
OMG, Music Is Soooo Coooool (30)	Collected all BGM.
Perfect Body (30)	Completely level up Juliet.
Rich Hunter (10)	Pick up 1,000 zombie medals.
Rock'n Roll Isn't Here Anymore (15)	Defeated Lewis LEGEND.
San Romero Knights Savior (30)	Rescued All Classmates.
Sparkle Hunting Master (10)	Succeed in 7 zombie Sparkle Hunting.
Super Shopper (15)	Spend 10,000 medals at Chop2Shop.Zom.
Super Zombie Hunter (30)	Clear Stage 4, surpassing Dad's score.
Third Eye (10)	Dodge all balloon attacks in Mariska battle.
Unclean and Uncool (15)	Defeated Hazmat in Prologue.
Viking Metal Rules! (15)	Defeated Vikke.
Watch Out For The Balls (10)	Dodge & Counter Zed's Electric Balls 15 times.
Zed's Dead, Baby, Zed's Dead (15)	Defeated Zed.
Zombie Fancier (30)	Completed the zombie album.
Zombie Hunter Apprentice (5)	Buy a combo at Chop2Shop.Zom and use it.
Zombie Slayer?! (30)	Kill 3,000 zombies.

NEW!
A
B
C
D
E
F
G
H
I
J
K
L
M
N
O
P
Q
R
S
T
U
V
W
X
Y
Z

CODES & CHEATS

LOST PLANET 2 (XBOX 360)

CODES

From any character customization screen, press Y to bring up the slot machine, then enter the password.

EFFECT	CODE
4Gamer.net Shirt	25060016
Black shirt	63152256
Blue shirt	56428338
Famitsu Weekly Magazine T-Shirt	73154986
Famitsu.com Shirt	88020223
Green shirt with WCP baseball cap T-shirt	18213092
Midnight Live 360 shirt	69088873
Monthly GAMEJAPAN shirt	52352345
Pink JP Playboy shirt	34297758
Purple + tan	65162980
Purple shirt with "D" logo and Japanese characters T-shirt	71556463
Street Jack	12887439
White shirt with blue sleeves with face T-shirt	26797358
White shirt with person holding Gatling gun T-shirt	31354816
Xbox 360 shirt (male and female)	94372143
Yellow shirt	96725729

LOST PLANET 2 (PLAYSTATION 3)

CODES

From any character customization screen, press Y to bring up the slot machine, then enter the password.

EFFECT	CODE
4Gamer.net Shirt	25060016
Black shirt	63152256
Blue shirt	56428338
Famitsu Weekly Magazine T-Shirt	73154986
Famitsu.com Shirt	88020223
Green shirt with WCP baseball cap t-shirt	18213092
Midnight Live 360 shirt	69088873
Monthly GAMEJAPAN shirt	52352345
EFFECT	**CODE**
Pink JP Playboy shirt	34297758
Purple + Tan	65162980
Purple shirt with "D" logo and Japanese characters T-shirt	71556463
Street Jack	12887439
White shirt with blue sleeves with face T-shirt	26797358
White shirt with person holding Gatling gun T-shirt	31354816
Xbox 360 shirt (male and female)	94372143
Yellow shirt	96725729
Man in Uniform	I LOVE A MAN IN UNIFORM
Play as Jack	OH MY SON, MY BLESSED SON
Sharp Dressed Man	DON'T YOU LOOK FINE AND DANDY
Spawn a horse-drawn coach.	NOW WHO PUT THAT THERE?

Spawn a horse	BEAST AND MAN TOGETHER
Unlock all areas	YOU GOT YOURSELF A FINE PAIR OF EYES
Unlock all gang outfits	YOU THINK YOU TOUGH, MISTER?

LOST PLANET: EXTREME CONDITION (XBOX 360)

Enter these codes when the game is paused. They can be used only on Easy mode.

UNLOCKABLE	CODE
500 Thermal Energy	⬆, ⬆, ⬇, ⬇, ⬅, ➡, ⬅, ➡, ✕, ▼, RB, LB
Infinite Ammunition	LB, LT, RT, RB, ▼, ✕, ➡, ⬇, ⬅, LB, LT, RT, LT, LB, RB, ✕, ⬅, ⬇, ✕, RB, LB
Infinite Health	⬇, ⬇, ⬇, ⬆, ✕, ⬆, ⬆, ⬆, ✕, ⬆, ⬆, ⬆, ⬇, ⬇, ✕, ✕, ⬇, ✕, ⬆, ▼, ➡, ✕, ⬅, ⬇, ➡, ✕, RB, LB
Infinite Ammunition	RT, RB, ▼, ✕, ➡, ⬇, ⬅, LB, LT, RT, RB, ▼, ✕, ⬅, ⬇, LB, LT, RT, LT, LB, RB, ✕, ⬅, ⬇, ✕, RB, LB

LUMINES: ELECTRONIC SYMPHONY (PLAYSTATION VITA)

TROPHY

UNLOCKABLE	HOW TO UNLOCK
A Perfect Storm (Bronze)	Use a Chain Block to connect at least 25 blocks.
A True Pioneer (Bronze)	Clear 10 Skins in Voyage Mode.
Avatar Addicts (Bronze)	Use Avatar Abilities 200 times.
Black Belt (Silver)	Unlock Master Zone 5.
Journey's End (Silver)	Clear all Skins in Voyage Mode.
Lucky 5 (Bronze)	Create 5 Squares with 1 Shuffle Block.
New Recruit (Bronze)	Get a total score of 50,000.
Prodigy (Bronze)	Achieve a BONUSx3.
Thank You (Bronze)	Watch through the entire Credits sequence.
The DJ Is In The House (Bronze)	Create, save and then clear 12 Playlists.
Time Stands Still (Silver)	Erase 30 Squares in Stopwatch Mode – 30 Seconds.
True Believer (Bronze)	Play for over 3 hours within 24 hours.
Winner Takes It All (Gold)	Unlock all Skins and all Avatars.

M

MADAGASCAR 3: THE VIDEO GAME   (PLAYSTATION VITA)

TROPHY

UNLOCKABLE	HOW TO UNLOCK
3 Rings of Fun! (Bronze)	Get 5 Stars in any Flaming Rings Act
A Proper Send-Off! (Bronze)	Get 5 Stars in any Trapeze Act
A Rare Sight! (Silver)	Find all 195 Thermometers For Melman
A Real Blast! (Silver)	Find all 195 Cannonball Balloons for Marty
A Sure Hit! (Bronze)	Get 5 Stars in any Cannonball Act
All Aboard for Adventure! (Silver)	Finish Italian Countryside Tutorials
Arrivederci, Rome! (Bronze)	Finish Rome Circus
Au Revoir, Dubois! (Bronze)	Defeat Chantal Dubois
Au Revoir, Paris! (Bronze)	Finish Paris Circus
Aye Aye, Skipper! (Bronze)	Finish A Mission for Skipper
Back to the Big Apple (Bronze)	Get the Gang to New York
Belisima! (Bronze)	Complete the Leaning Tower Publicity Stunt
Biggest Star Under the Big Top! (Silver)	Get 5 Stars in each Circus Act
Boss of the Toss! (Bronze)	Get 5 Stars in any Snack Toss
Ciao, Pisa! (Bronze)	Finish Pisa Circus
Circus Beauty! (Silver)	Find all 195 Flowers for Gloria
Colossal! (Bronze)	Complete the Colosseum Publicity Stunt
Everything! (Platinum)	Earn every Trophy in the game
Farewell, London! (Bronze)	Finish London Circus
For King Julien (Silver)	Complete All King Julien's Tasks
High Wire Highness! (Bronze)	Get 5 Stars in any High Wire Act
International Superstar (Gold)	Get 5 Stars on All City Events
King of the Circus (Bronze)	Finish New York Circus
Lemur Located: London (Bronze)	Find Mort in London
Lemur Located: Paris (Bronze)	Find Mort in Paris
Lemur Located: Pisa (Bronze)	Find Mort in Pisa
Lemur Located: Rome (Bronze)	Find Mort in Rome
Lon-Done! (Bronze)	Finish London City Events
London Circus Superstar (Silver)	Get 5 Stars in all London Circus Acts
London City Superstar (Silver)	Complete all London City events with 5 Stars
Mort is Everywhere! (Bronze)	Find Mort in all Cities
New York Circus Superstar! (Silver)	Get 5 Stars in all New York Circus Acts
Paris Circus Superstar (Silver)	Get 5 Stars in all Paris Circus Acts
Paris City Superstar (Silver)	Complete all Paris City events with 5 Stars
Penguin Problem Solved! (Silver)	Get all the Items Skipper Needs
Pisa Cake! (Bronze)	Finish Pisa City Events
Pisa Circus Superstar (Silver)	Get 5 Stars in all Pisa Circus Acts
Pisa City Superstar (Silver)	Complete all Pisa City events with 5 Stars

Roman Circus Superstar (Bronze)	Get 5 Stars in all Rome Circus Acts
Roman City Superstar (Bronze)	Complete all Rome City events with 5 Stars
Running Things in Rome! (Bronze)	Finish Rome City Events
Scrapwood Surplus! (Bronze)	Find All the Scrap Wood Skipper Needs
The Circus is Coming to Town (Bronze)	Complete All Poster Races
The Ultimate Showman! (Silver)	Find all 195 Stars for Alex
The Whole Frenchilada! (Bronze)	Finish Paris City Events
Ticket to Adventure! (Bronze)	Get 5 Stars in any Ticket Sales
Towering Bridge Star! (Bronze)	Complete the Tower Bridge Publicity Stunt
What an Eye Full! (Bronze)	Complete the Eiffel Tower Publicity Stunt
Wild About the Circus! (Bronze)	Free All Captured Compadres
Yes, Your Highness! (Bronze)	Finish A Mission for King Julien
You Went Bananas! (Bronze)	Get 5 Stars in any Banana Race

MADDEN NFL 10 (WII)

CODES

From the "Extras" menu select "Enter Codes"

EFFECT	CODE
Franchise Mode	TEAMPLAYER
Master Code (unlocks everything)	THEWORKS
Situation Mode	YOUCALLIT
Superstar Mode	EGOBOOST
Unlocks Pro Bowl Stadium	ALLSTARS
Unlocks Super Bowl Stadium	THEBIGSHOW

MADDEN NFL 12 (XBOX 360)

ACHIEVEMENT

UNLOCKABLE	HOW TO UNLOCK
Adrian Peterson Award (25)	Score on an 80+ yard TD run (No OTP or co-op)
Arian Foster Award (25)	Rush for 231+ yards in a game with one player (No OTP or co-op)
Bryan McCann Award (30)	Return an interception 100+ yards (No OTP or co-op)
Dan Carpenter Award (50)	Kick a 60+ yard FG (No OTP or co-op)
Darren McFadden Award (25)	Score 4+ rushing TDs in a single game (No OTP or co-op)
David Bowens Award (50)	Have 2 pick 6's in the same game (No OTP or co-op)
DeAngelo Hall Award (50)	Intercept 4+ passes in one game (No OTP or co-op)
DeSean Jackson Award (25)	Return a punt for a TD (No OTP or co-op)
Happy 20th EA SPORTS! (20)	Score 20 points in a game and celebrate 20 years of EA Sports! (No OTP or co-op)
Hey, Can I Talk to You? (10)	User complete one season's final cut day in Franchise Mode
Jahvid Best Award (25)	Gain 154+ yards receiving with Jahvid Best (No OTP or co-op)
Kenny Britt Award (25)	Gain 225+ yards receiving with one player (No OTP or co-op)
Leon Washington Award (50)	Return 2+ kicks for touchdowns in one game with one player (No OTP or co-op)
Mario Manningham Award (25)	Catch a 92+ yard TD pass (No OTP or co-op)
Matt Schaub Award (25)	Pass for 497+ yards in one game with one player (No OTP or co-op)

Michael Vick Award (30)	Rush for 130+ yards with your QB (No OTP or co-op)
MUT Maniac (40)	Complete 20 MUT Games
New York Giants Award (30)	Record 10+ sacks as a team in one game (No OTP or co-op)
New York Jets Award (25)	Gain over 100+ yards rushing with 2 RBs in the same game (No OTP or co-op)
Oakland Raiders Award (30)	Win by 45 points or more (No OTP or co-op)
Peyton Hillis Award (25)	Rush for 184+ yards in one game with Peyton Hillis (No OTP or co-op)
Put Da Team On My Back (50)	Catch a 99 yard TD pass with Greg Jennings (No OTP or co-op)
Reggie Wayne Award (25)	Catch 14+ passes in one game with one player (No OTP or co-op)
Rob Gronkowski Award (25)	Catch 3+ TD passes with a TE in a game (No OTP or co-op)
San Diego Chargers Award (30)	Hold your opponent to under 67 yds of total offense (minimum 5 min. qtr., no OTP or co-op)
Santonio Holmes Award (25)	Catch a game winning TD pass in OT (No OTP or co-op)
The Next Big Thing (5)	Create an NFL Superstar
This One is Easy (5)	Create a MUT team
This One is Hard (50)	Build an 80 rated MUT team
Tim Tebow Award (30)	Score a 40+ yard TD run with a QB (No OTP or co-op)
Tom Brady Award (25)	Have a passer rating of 149+ in a game (No OTP or co-op)
Ultimate Veteran (20)	Complete 10 MUT Games
Verizon Scoreboard Overload (40)	Score 50 points in one game (No OTP or co-op)
We're Talking About Practice (10)	Complete a practice in Superstar mode
Wheel and Deal (10)	Make a MUT Trade
Winning (10)	Win a FA bidding in Franchise Mode

MAGICIAN'S QUEST: MYSTERIOUS TIMES (DS)

UNLOCKABLES

UNLOCKABLE	HOW TO UNLOCK
Bug Wizard	Catch all bugs.
Evil Wizard	Cause mischief all around town.
Fish Wizard	Catch all fish.
Flower Wizard	Make 200 flowers bloom in your town.
Forgetful Wizard	Don't save four times and get this title.
Gallant Wizard	Talk to everyone for 10 consecutive days.
Love Wizard	Have 10 classmates confess love.
Skull Wizard	Kill 100 ghosts with the flatulence spell.
Wise Wizard	Finish all mystery cases.
Great Wizard	Win some tournaments during extracurricular lessons, then get evaluated by Principal Sol.
Righteous Wizard	Beat Captain Dot 20 Times.
Evil Wizard	Use Prank Magic on your classmates over 100 times.
A La Mode Wizard	Get 12 different hair styles.
Stylish Wizard	Change into four different sets of clothes every day for 10 days.

MAHJONG FIGHT CLUB: SHINSEI ZENKOKU TAISEN HAN (PLAYSTATION VITA)

TROPHY

UNLOCKABLE	HOW TO UNLOCK
100 Dora Breakthrough (bronze)	Use a total of 100 dora bonus tiles
100 National Matches Breakthrough (silver)	Complete 100 online matches (of 2 rounds each)
200 Dora Breakthrough (silver)	Use a total of 200 dora bonus tiles
200 National Matches Breakthrough (gold)	Complete 200 online matches (of 2 rounds each)
50 National Matches Breakthrough (bronze)	Complete 50 online matches (of 2 rounds each)
50,000 pts (hidden bronze)	Finish with a score of 50,000+ points
70,000 pts (hidden silver)	Finish with a score of 70,000+ points
Baiman (bronze)	Win with a baiman hand (8-10 han)
Buttobashi (hidden bronze)	Bust other players a total of ten times
Buttobashi Double (hidden bronze)	Bust two players at the same time
Consecutive Tops (hidden bronze)	Come first in five consecutive matches
Dora 4 (bronze)	Win with four dora bonus tiles
Dora 5 (hidden bronze)	Win with five dora bonus tiles
Dora 6 (hidden bronze)	Win with six dora bonus tiles
Dora 7 (hidden silver)	Win with seven dora bonus tiles
Dora 8+ (hidden silver)	Win with eight or more dora bonus tiles
GII Winner (silver)	Achieve GII
GIII Winner (bronze)	Achieve GIII
Haneman (bronze)	Win with a haneman hand (6-7 han)
Inverted Ron (hidden bronze)	Use the "inverted ron" function to win a hand by ron
Inverted Tsumo (hidden bronze)	Use the "inverted ron" function to win a hand by tsumo
Kouryuu Level 10 (hidden silver)	Achieve Golden Dragon level 10
Kouryuu Level 20 (hidden gold)	Achieve Golden Dragon level 20
Kouryuu Summons (hidden silver)	Enter the Golden Dragon ranks
Mangan (bronze)	Win with a mangan hand (5 han / 4 han with 40+ fu / 3 han with 70+ fu)
Master Summons (silver)	Achieve Master rank
Reverse Touch (hidden bronze)	Use the "reverse touch" function
Sanbaiman (silver)	Win with a sanbaiman hand (11-12 han)
Shijin Index 800 (hidden bronze)	Achieve a rating of 800+ over your past 50 matches
Shijin Index 900 (hidden silver)	Achieve a rating of 900+ over your past 50 matches
Swift Attack (hidden bronze)	Win a hand within six turns
Thunder 100 (gold)	Win 100 hands at any limit (mangan etc)
Thunder 30 (bronze)	Win 30 hands at any limit (mangan etc)
Trophies Complete (platinum)	Collect all other trophies
Yakuman (gold)	Win with a yakuman hand (top limit)

MAJOR LEAGUE BASEBALL 2K8 (XBOX 360)

CODES

Enter the codes in the Codes menu located in the Trading Card Album.

EFFECT	CODE
Unlocks all of the American League Central Classic Jersey Trading Cards.	ALCENTRALCLASSICTHREADS08
Unlocks all of the American League East Classic Jersey Trading Cards.	ALEASTCLASSICTHREADS08
Unlocks all of the American League West Classic Jersey Trading Cards.	ALWESTCLASSICTHREADS08
Unlocks all of the National League Central Classic Jersey Trading Cards.	NLCENTRALCLASSICTHREADS08
Unlocks all of the National League East Classic Jersey Trading Cards.	NLEASTCLASSICTHREADS08
Unlocks all of the National League West Classic Jersey Trading Cards.	NLWESTCLASSICTHREADS08

MAJOR LEAGUE BASEBALL 2K12 (PLAYSTATION 3)

TROPHY

UNLOCKABLE	HOW TO UNLOCK
2-Peat (Silver)	Win Back to Back World Series in My Player Mode.
A Job Well Done (Silver)	Win 100+ games in a season in My Player Mode.
A Pitcher's Best Friend (Bronze)	Turn a double play in a non-simulated game.
A Virtue (Silver)	Face 10 pitches as the batter in a non-simulated game.
Almost There (Bronze)	Hit 37 triples with your user profile.
As Good as a Hit (Silver)	Walk 233 times with your user profile.
Back to the Cage (Bronze)	Get a Golden Sombrero (strikeout 4 times in 1 game) in My Player Mode.
Chicks Dig It (Bronze)	Hit 74 home runs with your user profile.
Count it (Bronze)	Complete and win a ranked match.
Domination (Bronze)	Save 63 games with your user profile.
Don't Call it a Comeback (Bronze)	Win after being down by 4 after the 6th inning in a non-simulated game.
Down But Not Out (Bronze)	Get a hit with 2 strikes in a non-simulated game.
Dual Threat (Bronze)	Steal a base with a pitcher in a non-simulated game.
Fanning the Flames (Bronze)	Strike out 514 batters with your user profile.
Grab Some Pine (Bronze)	Get a strikeout to end the inning in a non-simulated game.
He Taketh Away (Bronze)	Rob a Home Run by climbing the wall in a non-simulated game.
Home, Sweet Home (Bronze)	Score 193 runs with your user profile.
I Came, I Saw... (Bronze)	Hit a Walk-off Home Run in a non-simulated game.
King of the Hill (Bronze)	Get to the top of the Best of the Best ladder in Home Run Derby Mode.
Mr. Consistency (Silver)	Get a hit in all 9 innings in a non-simulated game.
My Fellow Man (Bronze)	Complete and win an online league game.

My Main Squeeze (Bronze)	Bunt the man home in a non-simulated game.
No Hole too Deep (Bronze)	Battle Back: Down 0-2, get walked in a non-simulated game.
One Man Show (Gold)	Throw a No-Hitter in a 9 inning, non-simulated game.
Payback (Bronze)	Hit a home run off a former team in My Player Mode.
Production (Bronze)	Drive in 192 RBI with your user profile.
Productivity (Bronze)	Get 263 hits with your user profile.
Remember Me (Bronze)	Break a record in Franchise Mode. (play at least 20 games)
Set the Table (Bronze)	Hit 68 doubles with your user profile.
State Farm: The Road to Victory (Bronze)	Get 3 consecutive batters on base in a non-simulated game.
Stooges (Bronze)	Strikeout all three hitters in the inning in a non-simulated game.
Take That (Bronze)	Get an RBI after getting brushed back off the plate in a non-simulated game.
The Call (Bronze)	Get called up to the Majors in My Player Mode.
The Champs (Silver)	Win a World Series in Franchise Mode. (play at least 20 games)
The Goal (Bronze)	Accomplish a Team Season Goal in My Player Mode.
The Hall (Silver)	Make the Hall of Fame in My Player Mode.
The Road to Greatness (Bronze)	Complete and win 3 ranked matches in a row.
The Spice of Life (Bronze)	Play 10 ranked matches using 10 different teams.
The Star (Silver)	Make the All-Star team in My Player Mode.
The Start of Something Special (Bronze)	Lead off an inning by hitting a triple in a non-simulated game.
The Team to Beat (Bronze)	Beat the St. Louis Cardinals in a completed online match.
The Top (Silver)	Become the #1 ranked player in your My Player organization.
This is Why I'm Here (Bronze)	Be successful in a major league clutch moment in My Player Mode.
Throw First and Aim Later (Bronze)	Miss your throw to first base with 2 outs in a non-simulated game.
To the Rescue (Bronze)	Get a save with the tying run on base in a non-simulated game.
Upset Alert (Bronze)	Use the Houston Astros in a completed ranked match.
Walk Off (Platinum)	Unlock all Trophies
What's Your Ring Size? (Gold)	Win a World Series in My Player Mode.
You Make Your Own Destiny (Bronze)	Steal 139 bases with your user profile.
You're Special (Bronze)	Win a Season award in Franchise Mode. (play at least 20 games)
Your Day (Bronze)	Win player of the game in an MLB game in My Player Mode.

MAJOR LEAGUE BASEBALL 2K12 (XBOX 360)

ACHIEVEMENT

UNLOCKABLE	HOW TO UNLOCK
2-Peat (25)	Win Back to Back World Series in My Player Mode.
A Job Well Done (25)	Win 100+ games in a season in My Player Mode.
A Pitcher's Best Friend (10)	Turn a double play in a non-simulated game.
A Virtue (20)	Face 10 pitches as the batter in a non-simulated game.
Almost There (10)	Hit 37 triples with your user profile.
As Good as a Hit (40)	Walk 233 times with your user profile.
Back to the Cage (10)	Get a Golden Sombrero (strikeout 4 times in 1 game) in My Player Mode.
Chicks Dig It (10)	Hit 74 home runs with your user profile.
Count it (10)	Complete and win a ranked match.
Domination (20)	Save 63 games with your user profile.
Don't Call it a Comeback (10)	Win after being down by 4 after the 6th inning in a non-simulated game.
Down But Not Out (5)	Get a hit with 2 strikes in a non-simulated game.
Dual Threat (20)	Steal base with pitcher in a non-simulated game.
Fanning the Flames (10)	Strike out 514 batters with your user profile.
Grab Some Pine (5)	Get a strikeout to end the inning in a non-simulated game.
He Taketh Away (20)	Rob a Home Run in a non-simulated game.
Home, Sweet Home (10)	Score 193 runs with your user profile.
I Came, I Saw... (20)	Hit a Walk-off Home Run in a non-simulated game.
King of the Hill (20)	Get to the top of the Best of the Best ladder in Home Run Derby Mode.
Mr. Consistency (20)	Get a hit in all 9 innings in a non-simulated game.
My Fellow Man (10)	Complete and win an online league game.
My Main Squeeze (15)	Bunt the man home in a non-simulated game.
No Hole too Deep (10)	Battle Back: Down 0-2, get walked in a non-simulated game.
One Man Show (80)	Throw a No-Hitter in a 9 inning, non-simulated game.
Payback (15)	Hit a home run off a former team in My Player Mode.
Production (20)	Drive in 192 RBI with your user profile.
Productivity (20)	Get 263 hits with your user profile.
Remember Me (20)	Break a record in Franchise Mode. (play at least 20 games)
Set the Table (15)	Hit 68 doubles with your user profile.
State Farm: The Road to Victory (20)	Get 3 consecutive batters on base in a non-simulated game.
Stooges (10)	Strikeout all three hitters in the inning in a non-simulated game.
Take That (15)	Get an RBI after getting brushed back off the plate in a non-simulated game.

The Call (20)	Get called up to the Majors in My Player Mode.
The Champs (20)	Win a World Series in Franchise Mode. (play at least 20 games)
The Goal (10)	Accomplish a Team Season Goal in My Player Mode.
The Hall (75)	Make the Hall of Fame in My Player Mode.
The Road to Greatness (20)	Complete and win 3 ranked matches in a row.
The Spice of Life (10)	Play 10 ranked matches using 10 different teams.
The Star (40)	Make the All-Star team in My Player Mode.
The Start of Something Special (10)	Lead off an inning by hitting a triple in a non-simulated game.
The Team to Beat (15)	Beat the St. Louis Cardinals in a completed online match.
The Top (30)	Become the #1 ranked player in your My Player organization.
This is Why I'm Here (15)	Be successful in a major league clutch moment in My Player Mode.
Throw First and Aim Later (10)	Miss your throw to first base with 2 outs in a non-simulated game.
To the Rescue (10)	Get a save with the tying run on base in a non-simulated game.
Upset Alert (10)	Use the Houston Astros in a completed ranked match.
What's Your Ring Size? (80)	Win a World Series in My Player Mode.
You Make Your Own Destiny (20)	Steal 139 bases with your user profile.
You're Special (20)	Win a Season award in Franchise Mode. (play at least 20 games)
Your Day (15)	Win player of the game in an MLB game in My Player Mode.

MAN VS. WILD   (XBOX 360)

ACHIEVEMENT

UNLOCKABLE	HOW TO UNLOCK
All God's Creatures (20)	Find all the animals of interest in the Everglades
Animal Kingdom (20)	Locate all Animals of Interest in the Rockies
As I Scan This Wasted Land (100)	Complete the "Sahara" campaign.
Bear Grylls (100)	Reach the Level "Bear Grylls"
Bob's Boats (20)	Find all of Bob McClure's Boats in the Everglades
Born Survivor (100)	Complete all episodes without passing out
Casted Away (20)	Find all the Man Made Items in Deserted Island
Climbing the Rockies (100)	Complete the "Rocky Mountains" campaign.
Down in the Low, Low Land (100)	Complete the "Everglades" campaign.
Flight 815 (20)	Find all the Plane Debris in Deserted Island
Hard to Pronounce, Hard to Find (20)	Find all Five Andiperla Willinkis in Patagonia
Horticulture Grylls (20)	Locate the Rare Plants in the Rockies
How about A Winter's Tale (100)	Complete the "Patagonia" campaign.
Nice Place You Had Here (20)	Locate all the Trash in Patagonia

NEW!

A
B
C
D
E
F
G
H
I
J
K
L
M
N
O
P
Q
R
S
T
U
V
W
X
Y
Z

Only Hope Can Keep Me Together (100)	Complete the "Deserted Island" campaign.
Osteologist Grylls (20)	Find all the Camel Bones in the Sahara
Pack Rat Grylls (20)	Tag all the Junk in the Everglades
Patton Was Here (20)	Find all the WWII Artifacts in the Sahara
Reminders of the Rush (20)	Locate all the Gold Rush Trash in the Rockies
These Belong in a Museum (20)	Find all the Ancient Artifacts in the Sahara
Wild, Man! (40)	Completed the Tutorial in Base Camp

MARVEL: ULTIMATE ALLIANCE 2 (XBOX 360)

CODES

Enter one of the following codes at the indicated screen (saving is disabled).

EFFECT	CODE
Fusion	▷, ▷, ◇, ♡, ◇, ◇, ◁, 🅐
Heroes (All Characters)	◇, ◇, ♡, ♡, ◁, ◁, ◁, 🅐
Hulk (Character)	♡, ◁, ◁, ◁, ◇, ◇, ♡, ◁, 🅐
Jean Grey (Character)	◁, ◁, ▷, ▷, ◇, ♡, ◇, ♡, 🅐
Money	◇, ◇, ♡, ♡, ◇, ◇, ◇, ♡, 🅐
Movies	◇, ◁, ◁, ◇, ◇, ▷, ◇, ◇, 🅐
Skins (Costumes)	◇, ♡, ◁, ▷, ◁, ▷, 🅐
Thor (Character)	◇, ▷, ▷, ♡, ▷, ♡, ◁, ▷, 🅐

TEAM BONUSES

Certain character combinations unlock special boosts.

UNLOCKABLE	HOW TO UNLOCK
Agile Warriors: +2 all Attributes	Daredevil, Spider-Man, Deadpool, Iron Fist
Bruisers: +5 Striking	Juggernaut, Hulk, Thing, Luke Cage, Thor
Classic Avengers: +15% Max Stamina	Hulk, Thor, Iron Man, Captain America
Fantastic Four: +35% Fusion Gain	Mr. Fantastic, Human Torch, Thing, Invisible Woman
Femmes Fatales: +5% Damage	Jean Grey, Storm, Invisible Woman, Ms. Marvel
Martial Artists: +5 Striking	Daredevil, Wolverine, Iron Fist, Deadpool
Masters of Energy: +15% Max Health	Gambit, Iron Fist, Jean Grey, Ms. Marvel, Nick Fury, Penance
Natural Forces +5% Damage inflicted as Health Gain	Storm, Iceman, Thor, Human Torch
New Avengers: +10% to all resistances	Ms. Marvel, Spider-Man, Wolverine, Iron Man, Luke Cage, Iron Fist
Pro-Reg Heroes: +15% Max HP	Iron Man, Mr. Fantastic, Deadpool, Songbird, Ms Marvel, Spider-Man
Secret Avengers: +3 Teamwork	Captain America, Iron Fist, Luke Cage, Invisible Woman, Human Torch, Storm, Spider-Man
Shut Up Already! - 15% Extra Health	Play as a team of Spider-Man, Iceman, Deadpool, and Human Torch.
Think Tank: +15% Max HP	Mr. Fantastic, Iron Man, Green Goblin, Spider-Man, Hulk
Thunderbolts: +5% Damage	Green Goblin, Songbird, Venom, Penance
Weapon Specialists: +5% Criticals	Daredevil, Deadpool, Gambit, Thor, Green Goblin, Captain America
X-Men: +15% Max Stamina	Gambit, Jean Grey, Wolverine, Storm, Ice Man, Juggernaut (interchangeable)

SPECIAL CHARACTERS

Unlock the following characters by performing the actions listed.

UNLOCKABLE	HOW TO UNLOCK
Deadpool	Beat the D.C. Level
Green Goblin and Venom	Beat them at the end of Wakanda Act 3.
Hulk	Collect all five Gamma Regulators.
Iron Fist	Choose the Rebel side when faced with the choice.
Jean Grey	Collect all five M'Kraan Shards.
Ms. Marvel	Beat the NYC Level.
Nick Fury	Beat the game.
Penance	Defeat him in the portal room to the negative zone.
Songbird	Choose the Register side when faced with the choice.
Thor	Collect all five Asgardian Runes.

MARVEL: ULTIMATE ALLIANCE 2 (PLAYSTATION 3)

CODES

Enter one of the following codes at the indicated screen (saving is disabled).

EFFECT	CODE
Diaries	⇦, ⇨, ⇦, ⇦, ⇧, ⇧, ⇨, START
Dossier	⇩, ⇩, ⇦, ⇨, ⇨, ⇩, ⇩, START
Fusion	⇨, ⇨, ⇧, ⇧, ⇧, ⇨, ⇦, START
Heroes (All Characters)	⇧, ⇧, ⇩, ⇩, ⇦, ⇦, ⇦, START
Hulk (Character)	⇩, ⇦, ⇦, ⇧, ⇨, ⇧, ⇩, ⇦, START
Jean Grey (Character)	⇦, ⇦, ⇨, ⇨, ⇨, ⇩, ⇧, ⇧, START
Money	⇧, ⇨, ⇩, ⇩, ⇨, ⇧, ⇨, ⇩, START
Movies	⇧, ⇦, ⇦, ⇧, ⇨, ⇨, ⇧, START
Power	⇧, ⇨, ⇩, ⇩, ⇨, ⇨, ⇨, ⇦, START
Skins (Costumes)	⇧, ⇩, ⇦, ⇨, ⇨, ⇨, START
Thor (Character)	⇧, ⇨, ⇨, ⇩, ⇩, ⇩, ⇦, ⇨, START

TEAM BONUSES

Certain character combinations unlock special boosts.

UNLOCKABLE	HOW TO UNLOCK
Agile Warriors: +2 all Attributes	Daredevil, Spider-Man, Deadpool, Iron Fist
Bruisers: +5 Striking	Juggernaut, Hulk, Thing, Luke Cage, Thor
Classic Avengers: +15% Max Stamina	Hulk, Thor, Iron Man, Captain America
Fantastic Four: +35% Fusion Gain	Mr. Fantastic, Human Torch, Thing, Invisible Woman
Femmes Fatales: +5% Damage	Jean Grey, Storm, Invisible Woman, Ms. Marvel
Martial Artists: +5 Striking	Daredevil, Wolverine, Iron Fist, Deadpool
Masters of Energy: +15% Max Health	Gambit, Iron Fist, Jean Grey, Ms. Marvel, Nick Fury, Penance
Natural Forces +5% Damage inflicted as Health Gain	Storm, Iceman, Thor, Human Torch
New Avengers: +10% to all resistances	Ms. Marvel, Spider-Man, Wolverine, Iron Man, Luke Cage, Iron Fist
Pro-Reg Heroes: +15% Max HP	Iron Man, Mr. Fantastic, Deadpool, Songbird, Ms Marvel, Spider-Man
Secret Avengers: +3 Teamwork	Captain America, Iron Fist, Luke Cage, Invisible Woman, Human Torch, Storm, Spider-Man

Shut Up Already! —15% Extra Health	Play as a team of Spider-Man, Iceman, Deadpool, and Human Torch.
Think Tank: +15% Max HP	Mr. Fantastic, Iron Man, Green Goblin, Spider-Man, Hulk
Thunderbolts: +5% Damage	Green Goblin, Songbird, Venom, Penance
Weapon Specialists: +5% Criticals	Daredevil, Deadpool, Gambit, Thor, Green Goblin, Captain America
X-Men: +15% Max Stamina	Gambit, Jean Grey, Wolverine, Storm, Ice Man, Juggernaut (interchangeable)

SPECIAL CHARACTERS

Unlock the following characters by performing the actions listed.

UNLOCKABLE	HOW TO UNLOCK
Deadpool	Beat the D.C. Level.
Green Goblin and Venom	Beat them at the end of Wakanda Act 3.
Hulk	Collect all five Gamma Regulators.
Iron Fist	Choose the Rebel side when faced with the choice.
Jean Grey	Collect all five M'Kraan Shards.
Ms. Marvel	Beat the NYC Level.
Nick Fury	Beat the game.
Penance	Defeat him in the portal room to the negative zone.
Songbird	Choose the Register side when faced with the choice.
Thor	Collect all five Asgardian Runes.

MARVEL: ULTIMATE ALLIANCE 2 (WII)

CODES

Enter the following codes with the D-Pad

EFFECT	CODE
All Bonus Missions (at Bonus Missions screen)	⇧⇧⇩⇩⇦⇩⇦⇩
All Heroes (at Character Select screen)	⇧⇩⇩⇦⇦⇩⇩⇩
Characters Advance 10 Levels (at Pause menu)	⇩⇩⇩⇦⇦⇦⇩⇩
Fusion Power Always Four Stars	⇩⇩⇦⇩⇩⇩⇩⇩
God Mode (at Pause menu)	⇩⇩⇩⇩⇩⇩⇦⇩

MASS EFFECT 2 (XBOX 360)

UNLOCKABLES

UNLOCKABLE	HOW TO UNLOCK
Bonus 25% Experience	Beat the game on any difficulty
200k Credits	Start New Game after 1 Playthrough
50k of each Resource	Start New Game after 1 Playthrough
New Colors for Party Members	Complete a party member's loyalty mission.
Unlock Loyalty Skills	Complete the Loyalty missions for each of your party members to unlock their individuals skills.

MASS EFFECT 2 (PLAYSTATION 3)

UNLOCKABLE

After you complete a character's Loyalty Mission, the character gains their loyalty power. Research Advanced Training as Shepard at the research terminal in Mordin's lab. You can learn a single loyalty power as a "bonus power". Each time Shepard undergoes Advanced Training, the new power replaces the previous one and the skill points allotted to the old power will transfer to the new bonus power. Any bonus powers gained during previous playthroughs will be available at the start of the new game at character creation aas well as at research terminals.

UNLOCKABLE	HOW TO UNLOCK
Armor Piercing Ammo	Complete Archangel's Loyalty Mission
Barrier	Complete Jacob's Loyalty Mission
Dominate	Side with Morinth in Samara's Loyalty Mission
Flashbang Grenade	Complete Kasumi's Loyalty Mission
Fortification	Complete Grunt's Loyalty Mission
Geth Shield Boost	Complete Legion's Loyalty Mission
Inferno Grenade	Complete Zaeed's Loyalty Mission.
Neural Shock	Complete Mordin's Loyalty Mission.
Reave	Side with Samara in Samara's Loyalty Mission.
Shield Drain	Complete Tali's Loyalty Mission.
Shredder Ammo	Complete Thane's Loyalty Mission.
Slam	Complete Miranda's Loyalty Mission.
Stasis	Complete the Lair of the Shadow Broker DLC.
Warp Ammo	Complete Jack's Loyalty Mission.
25% Experience Boost	Start a new game after beating the game once.
Start with 200,000 Credits	Start a new game after beating the game once.
Start with 50,000 of Each Resource	Start a new game after beating the game once.
New Game+	Clear Suicide Mission

MASS EFFECT 3 (PLAYSTATION 3)

TROPHY

UNLOCKABLE	HOW TO UNLOCK
A Personal Touch (Bronze)	Modify a weapon.
Almost There (Bronze)	Reach level 15 in multiplayer or level 50 in single-player.
Always Prepared (Bronze)	Obtain two non-customizable suits of armor.
Arbiter (Bronze)	Win a political stand-off.
Battle-Scarred (Bronze)	Promote a multiplayer character to the Galaxy at War or import an ME3 character.
Bringer of War (Bronze)	Chase down an assassin.
Bruiser (Bronze)	Kill 100 enemies with melee attacks.
Combined Arms (Silver)	Perform any combination of 50 biotic combos or tech bursts.
Defender (Bronze)	Attain the highest level of readiness in each theater of war.
Driven (Bronze)	Return to active duty.
Enlisted (Bronze)	Start a character in multiplayer or customize a character in single-player.
Executioner (Bronze)	Defeat an old adversary.
Explorer (Bronze)	Complete three multiplayer matches or five N7 missions.
Eye of the Hurricane (Bronze)	Kill a brute while it's charging you.
Fact Finder (Bronze)	Discover an enemy's monstrous origin.
Focused (Bronze)	Evolve any of your powers to rank 6.
Giant Killer (Bronze)	Defeat a Harvester.
Gunsmith (Silver)	Upgrade any weapon to level 10.
Hard Target (Bronze)	Call down an orbital strike.
Hijacker (Bronze)	Hijack an Atlas mech.
Insanity (Gold)	Finish the game on Insanity without changing difficulty after leaving Earth.

NEW!
A
B
C
D
E
F
G
H
I
J
K
L
M
N
O
P
Q
R
S
T
U
V
W
X
Y
Z

Last Witness (Bronze)	Extract ancient technology.
Legend (Silver)	Mission accomplished.
Liberator (Bronze)	Stop a Cerberus kidnapping.
Long Service Medal (Silver)	Complete Mass Effect 3 twice, or once with a Mass Effect 2 import.
Lost and Found (Bronze)	Dispatch 10 probes to retrieve people or resources in Reaper territory.
Mail Slot (Bronze)	Kill 10 guardians with headshots from the front while their shields are raised.
Master and Commander (Silver)	Deliver most of the Galaxy at War assets to the final conflict.
Mobilizer (Bronze)	Bring a veteran officer aboard.
N7 Elite (Platinum)	Acquire all trophies.
Overload Specialist (Bronze)	Overload the shields of 100 enemies.
Paramour (Bronze)	Establish or rekindle a romantic relationship.
Party Crasher (Bronze)	Sabotage a dreadnought.
Pathfinder (Bronze)	Explore a lost city.
Patriot (Bronze)	Make the final assault.
Peak Condition (Bronze)	Reach level 20 in multiplayer or level 60 in single-player.
Problem Solver (Bronze)	Evacuate a scientific facility.
Pyromaniac (Bronze)	Set 100 enemies on fire with powers.
Recruit (Bronze)	Kill 250 enemies.
Saboteur (Bronze)	Disable a group of fighter squadrons.
Shopaholic (Bronze)	Visit a store in the single-player campaign.
Sky High (Bronze)	Lift 100 enemies off the ground with powers.
Soldier (Bronze)	Kill 1,000 enemies.
Tour of Duty (Bronze)	Finish all multiplayer maps or all N7 missions in single-player.
Tourist (Bronze)	Complete one multiplayer match or two N7 missions.
Tunnel Rat (Bronze)	Survive the swarm.
Untouchable (Bronze)	Escape a Reaper in the galaxy map.
Unwavering (Gold)	Finish all multiplayer maps on Gold or all single-player missions on Insanity.
Veteran (Silver)	Kill 5,000 enemies.
Well Connected (Bronze)	Send a warning across the galaxy.
World Shaker (Bronze)	Destroy an Atlas dropped from orbit.

MASS EFFECT 3 (XBOX 360)

ACHIEVEMENT

UNLOCKABLE	HOW TO UNLOCK
A Personal Touch (10)	Modify a weapon.
Almost There (15)	Reach level 15 in multiplayer or level 50 in single-player.
Always Prepared (10)	Obtain two non-customizable suits of armor.
Arbiter (25)	Win a political stand-off.
Battle Scarred (25)	Promote a multiplayer character to the Galaxy at War or import an ME3 character.
Bringer of War (10)	Chase down an assassin.
Bruiser (10)	Kill 100 enemies with melee attacks.
Combined Arms (25)	Perform any combination of 50 biotic combos or tech bursts.

Defender (25)	Attain the highest level of readiness in each theater of war.	
Driven (5)	Return to active duty.	
Enlisted (5)	Start a character in multiplayer or customize a character in single-player.	
Executioner (25)	Defeat an old adversary.	
Explorer (15)	Complete three multiplayer matches or five N7 missions.	
Eye of the Hurricane (10)	Kill a brute while it's charging you.	
Fact Finder (15)	Discover an enemy's monstrous origin.	
Focused (25)	Evolve any of your powers to rank 6.	
Giant Killer (10)	Defeat a harvester.	
Gunsmith (25)	Upgrade any weapon to level 10.	
Hard Target (15)	Call down an orbital strike.	
Hijacker (10)	Hijack an Atlas mech.	
Insanity (75)	Finish the game on Insanity without changing difficulty after leaving Earth.	
Last Witness (25)	Extract ancient technology.	
Legend (50)	Mission accomplished.	
Liberator (15)	Stop a Cerberus kidnapping.	
Long Service Medal (50)	Complete Mass Effect 3 twice, or once with a Mass Effect 2 import.	
Lost and Found (25)	Dispatch 10 probes to retrieve people or resources in Reaper territory.	
Mail Slot (10)	Kill 10 guardians with headshots from the front while their shields are raised.	
Master and Commander (50)	Deliver most of the Galaxy at War assets to the final conflict.	
Mobilizer (15)	Bring a veteran officer aboard.	
Overload Specialist (15)	Overload the shields of 100 enemies.	
Paramour (25)	Establish or rekindle a romantic relationship.	
Party Crasher (15)	Sabotage a dreadnought.	
Pathfinder (15)	Explore a lost city.	
Patriot (25)	Make the final assault.	
Peak Condition (25)	Reach level 20 in multiplayer or level 60 in single-player.	
Problem Solver (15)	Evacuate a scientific facility.	
Pyromaniac (15)	Set 100 enemies on fire with powers.	
Recruit (10)	Kill 250 enemies.	
Saboteur (15)	Disable a group of fighter squadrons.	
Shopaholic (10)	Visit a store in the single-player campaign.	
Sky High (15)	Lift 100 enemies off the ground with powers.	
Soldier (15)	Kill 1,000 enemies.	
Tour of Duty (20)	Finish all multiplayer maps or all N7 missions in single-player.	
Tourist (5)	Complete one multiplayer match or two N7 missions.	
Tunnel Rat (15)	Survive the swarm.	
Untouchable (10)	Escape a Reaper in the galaxy map.	
Unwavering (50)	Finish all multiplayer maps on Gold or all single-player missions on Insanity.	
Veteran (25)	Kill 5,000 enemies.	
Well Connected (15)	Send a warning across the galaxy.	

NEW!

A
B
C
D
E
F
G
H
I
J
K
L
M
N
O
P
Q
R
S
T
U
V
W
X
Y
Z

CODES & CHEATS

World Shaker (15)	Destroy an Atlas dropped from orbit.

UNLOCKABLE

UNLOCKABLE	HOW TO UNLOCK
N7 Helmet Avatar Award	Return to Active Duty.
Omniblade Avatar Award	Kill 25 Enemies with Melee Attacks.

MAX PAYNE 3 (PLAYSTATION 3)

TROPHY

UNLOCKABLE	HOW TO UNLOCK
A Few Hundred Bullets Back (Bronze)	Use Every Weapon In The Game
A License To Kill (Silver)	Collect All Golden Guns
A New York Minute (Gold)	Finish In A New York Minute
All Of The Above (Gold)	Finish All Single Player Grinds
Along For The Ride (Bronze)	Trigger A Bullet Cam On The Zipline [FREE AIM]
Amidst The Wreckage (Bronze)	Destroy All The Models In The Boardroom
An Echo Of The Past (Bronze)	Find All Clues
Colder Than The Devil's Heart (Bronze)	Kill 30 Enemies In 2 Minutes
Dearest Of All My Friends (Bronze)	Kill Someone On Your Friends List
Deathmatch Challenge (Bronze)	Winner In Any Public Deathmatch
Feel The Payne (Bronze)	Story Complete [MEDIUM]
Full Monty (Bronze)	Complete One Of Each Game Mode Including All Gang Wars
Grave Robber (Bronze)	Looted A Body
It Was Chaos And Luck (Bronze)	Get 6 Kills While Riding The Push Cart [FREE AIM]
It's Fear That Gives Men Wings (Bronze)	10 Bullet Time Kills In A Row
Man Of Many Faces (Bronze)	Unlock All Faction Characters
Man Of Many Weapons (Bronze)	Unlock All Weapons
Max Payne Invitational (Bronze)	Invite someone to play through the in-game contact list
Maximum Payne (Gold)	Story Complete [OLD SCHOOL]
One Bullet At A Time (Bronze)	300 Headshots
Out The Window (Bronze)	Get 6 Kills While Diving Through The VIP Window [FREE AIM]
Part I Complete (Bronze)	Complete Part I Of The Story
Part II Complete (Bronze)	Complete Part II Of The Story
Part III Complete (Bronze)	Complete Part III Of The Story
Past The Point Of No Return (Bronze)	Take 100 Painkillers
Payne Bringer (Silver)	Kill 100 Other Players
Payne In The Ass (Bronze)	Story Complete [HARDCORE]
Platinum Trophy (Platinum)	Unlock All Max Payne 3 Trophies
Serious Payne (Silver)	Story Complete [HARD]
So Much For Being Subtle (Bronze)	Get 9 Kills While Being Pulled By A Chain [FREE AIM]
Something Wicked This Way Comes (Bronze)	Get 7 Kills While Jumping From The Rickety Boat [FREE AIM]
Sometimes You Get Lucky (Bronze)	Get A Headshot During The Rooftop Tremors
Sweep (Bronze)	Flawless Team Gang Wars Victory
That Old Familiar Feeling (Bronze)	Clear The Hallway Of Lasers

The Fear Of Losing It (Bronze)	Survive A Level Without Painkillers
The Gambler (Bronze)	Won A Wager
The One Eyed Man Is King (Bronze)	Cover Passos With Perfect Aim
The Only Choice Given (Bronze)	Get 8 Kills While Dangling From A Chain [FREE AIM]
The Road-Kill Behind Me (Bronze)	Total Everything On The Runway
The Shadows Rushed Me (Silver)	Unlock And Complete New York Minute Hardcore
Training Complete (Silver)	Achieve Level Rank 50
Trouble Had Come To Me (Bronze)	Clear Everyone On The Bus Ride
With Practiced Bravado (Bronze)	100 Kills During Shootdodge
You Might Hurt Someone With That (Bronze)	Shoot 10 Airborne Grenades
You Play, You Pay, You Bastard (Bronze)	100 Kills With Melee
You Push A Man Too Far (Bronze)	Don't Shoot The Dis-Armed Man
You Sure Know How To Pick A Place (Bronze)	Discover All Tourist Locations

MAX PAYNE 3 (XBOX 360)

ACHIEVEMENT

UNLOCKABLE	HOW TO UNLOCK
A Few Hundred Bullets Back (20)	Use Every Weapon In The Game
A License To Kill (40)	Collect All Golden Guns
A New York Minute (100)	Finish In A New York Minute
All Of The Above (100)	Finish All Single Player Grinds
Along For The Ride (10)	Trigger A Bullet Cam On The Zipline [FREE AIM]
Amidst The Wreckage (5)	Destroy All The Models In The Boardroom
An Echo Of The Past (35)	Find All Clues
Colder Than The Devil's Heart (15)	Kill 30 Enemies In 2 Minutes
Dearest Of All My Friends (10)	Kill Someone On Your Friends List
Deathmatch Challenge (20)	Winner In Any Public Deathmatch
Feel The Payne (30)	Story Complete [MEDIUM]
Full Monty (10)	Complete One Of Each Game Mode Including All Gang Wars
Grave Robber (5)	Looted A Body
It Was Chaos And Luck (10)	Get 6 Kills While Riding The Push Cart [FREE AIM]
It's Fear That Gives Men Wings (20)	10 Bullet Time Kills In A Row
Man Of Many Faces (25)	Unlock All Faction Characters
Man Of Many Weapons (25)	Unlock All Weapons
Max Payne Invitational (5)	Invite someone to play through the in-game contact list
Maximum Payne (80)	Story Complete [OLD SCHOOL]
One Bullet At A Time (20)	300 Headshots
Out The Window (10)	Get 6 Kills While Diving Through The VIP Window [FREE AIM]
Part I Complete (20)	Complete Part I Of The Story
Part II Complete (20)	Complete Part II Of The Story
Part III Complete (20)	Complete Part III Of The Story
Past The Point Of No Return (10)	Take 100 Painkillers
Payne Bringer (30)	Kill 100 Other Players
Payne In The Ass (20)	Story Complete [HARDCORE]

NEW!

A
B
C
D
E
F
G
H
I
J
K
L
M
N
O
P
Q
R
S
T
U
V
W
X
Y
Z

Serious Payne (50)	Story Complete [HARD]
So Much For Being Subtle (10)	Get 9 Kills While Being Pulled By A Chain [FREE AIM]
Something Wicked This Way Comes (10)	Get 7 Kills While Jumping From The Rickety Boat [FREE AIM]
Sometimes You Get Lucky (5)	Get A Headshot During The Rooftop Tremors
Sure Know How To Pick A Place (10)	Discover All Tourist Locations
Sweep (10)	Flawless Team Gang Wars Victory
That Old Familiar Feeling (10)	Clear The Hallway Of Lasers
The Fear Of Losing It (20)	Survive A Level Without Painkillers
The Gambler (15)	Won A Wager
The One Eyed Man Is King (10)	Cover Passos With Perfect Aim
The Only Choice Given (10)	Get 8 Kills While Dangling From A Chain [FREE AIM]
The Road-Kill Behind Me (10)	Total Everything On The Runway
The Shadows Rushed Me (10)	Unlock And Complete New York Minute Hardcore
Training Complete (25)	Achieve Level Rank 50
Trouble Had Come To Me (15)	Clear Everyone On The Bus Ride
With Practiced Bravado (20)	100 Kills During Shootdodge.
You Might Hurt Someone With That (20)	Shoot 10 Airborne Grenades
You Play, You Pay, You Bastard (20)	100 Kills With Melee
You Push A Man Too Far (5)	Don't Shoot The Dis-Armed Man

MEDAL OF HONOR: AIRBORNE (XBOX 360)

CODES

UNLOCKABLE	HOW TO UNLOCK
Enter Cheat menu	Press ⓡ+ⓛ, then press Ⓧ,Ⓑ,Ⓨ,Ⓐ,Ⓐ
Full Ammo	Press and hold ⓛ+ⓡ then press Ⓑ,Ⓑ,Ⓨ,Ⓧ,Ⓧ,Ⓨ
Full Health	Ⓨ,Ⓧ,Ⓧ,Ⓨ,Ⓐ,Ⓑ

MEDIEVIL RESURRECTION (PSP)

To enter this code, pause the game.

UNLOCKABLE	CODE
Invincibility and All Weapons	Hold Ⓡ, then press ⬇, ⬆, ■, ▲, ▲, ●, ⬇, ⬆, ■, ▲

MEGA MAN (WII)

UNLOCKABLES

UNLOCKABLE	HOW TO UNLOCK
Select Trick	When using a weapon that goes through an enemy, press the SELECT button (this pauses the game without bringing up the weapon menu) when the weapon is making contact with the enemy.
	While the game is paused this way the enemy continues to flash. When the flashing has stopped, press the SELECT button again to un-pause the game and the weapon hits the enemy again, causing
	more damage. You can do this trick repeatedly with many of the bosses, making them very easy to beat.

MEN IN BLACK: ALIEN CRISIS (PLAYSTATION 3)

TROPHY

UNLOCKABLE	HOW TO UNLOCK
100 Enemies - Adorian Crossbow (Bronze)	Defeat 100 enemies with the Adorian Crossbow

200 Enemies - The BANGer (Bronze)	Defeat 200 enemies with the BANGer
250 Enemies - Tribarrel (Bronze)	Defeat 250 enemies with the Tribarrel
350 Enemies - Tribarrel (Silver)	Defeat 350 enemies with the Tribarrel
50 Enemies - Std. Issue 1995 (Bronze)	Defeat 50 enemies with the Std. Issue 1995
60 Enemies - Noisy Cricket (Bronze)	Defeat 60 enemies with the Noisy Cricket
Assert Fail (Silver)	Defeat Khnemu in Story Mode
Brute Force (Bronze)	Achieve a 25x multiplier in a Story Mode
Conqueror (Bronze)	Achieve at least 300,000 points in one V.R. Mission
Demolition Expert (Silver)	Defeat 20 enemies with the Rocket Launcher while flying the car
Dodge and Weave (Bronze)	Dodge the mines placed by Nethera in Story Mode
Duelist (Bronze)	Complete all the Competitive maps in V.R. Missions
Enjoy the Ride (Bronze)	Start playing in Story Mode
Flying Car? Where? (Bronze)	Don't be detected while flying the car
Group Off (Bronze)	Destroy 3 enemy platforms in Story Mode
Hide'n'Seek (Bronze)	Scan 2 hidden aliens in Story Mode
High Score (Bronze)	Successfully finish the Virtual Reality training program in Story Mode
High Standards (Gold)	Defeat Nethera and save Catyana
HOT Streak (Gold)	Defeat 900 enemies
Juggernaut (Bronze)	Use the Refracto Shield to reflect 100 enemy projectiles
Junior Agent (Silver)	Complete Story Mode as an Agent
Keep it Slow (Silver)	Defeat 30 enemies while they're under the effect of Cerebro Accelerator
Kicking and Screaming (Bronze)	Escape Serleena's drag attack
MIB Veteran (Platinum)	Unlock all trophies in game
Own the Road (Bronze)	Defeat 70 bikers in Story Mode
Party Crasher (Bronze)	Crash Chauncey's party in Story Mode
Pest Control (Silver)	Defeat 700 enemies
Road Hog (Bronze)	Defeat 40 bikers in Story Mode
Save the Universe (Gold)	Complete all the missions in Story Mode
Senior Agent (Gold)	Complete Story Mode as an Elite Agent
Shattered Expectations (Bronze)	Freeze 30 enemies with the Icer
Smile for the Camera! (Bronze)	Neuralize 7 humans in Story Mode
Superior Fighter (Bronze)	Achieve at least 150,000 points in one V.R. Mission
Superstar (Bronze)	Achieve at least 200,000 points in one V.R. Mission
The Gatherer (Gold)	Gather 50 upgrade points

The Spice of Life (Bronze)	Defeat enemies using 10 different combos
This Won't Take Long (Bronze)	Defeat Nakkadan Elite Guard in Story Mode
Ugly on the Inside (Bronze)	Defeat Adorian Elite Guard in Story Mode
What Goes Up... (Silver)	Use the Anti-Gravity grenade on 30 enemies

MEN IN BLACK: ALIEN CRISIS (XBOX 360)

ACHIEVEMENT

UNLOCKABLE	HOW TO UNLOCK
100 Enemies - Adorian Crossbow (30)	Defeated 100 enemies with the Adorian Crossbow (P1)
200 Enemies - The BANGer (30)	Defeated 200 enemies with the BANGer (P1)
250 Enemies - Tribarrel (30)	Defeated 250 enemies with the Tribarrel (P1)
350 Enemies - Tribarrel (30)	Defeated 350 enemies with the Tribarrel (P1)
50 Enemies - Std. Issue 1995 (30)	Defeated 50 enemies with the Std. Issue 1995 (P1)
60 Enemies - Noisy Cricket (30)	Defeated 60 enemies with the Noisy Cricket (P1)
Assert Fail (20)	Defeated Khnemu in Story Mode
Brute Force (20)	Achieved a 25x multiplier in Story Mode
Conqueror (25)	Achieved at least 300,000 points in one V.R. Mission (P1)
Demolition Expert (30)	Defeated 20 enemies with the Rocket Launcher while flying the car
Dodge and Weave (20)	Dodged the mines placed by Nethera in Story Mode
Duelist (30)	Completed all the Competitive maps in V.R. Missions (P1)
Enjoy the Ride (20)	Started playing in Story Mode
Flying Car? Where? (20)	Didn't get detected while flying the car
Group Off (20)	Destroyed 3 enemy platforms in Story Mode
Hide'n'Seek (10)	Scanned 2 hidden aliens in Story Mode
High Score (20)	Successfully finished the Virtual Reality training program in Story Mode
High Standards (30)	Defeated Nethera and saved Catyana
HOT Streak (30)	Defeated 900 enemies (P1)
Juggernaut (20)	Used the Refracto Shield to reflect 100 enemy projectiles (P1)
Junior Agent (50)	Completed Story Mode as an Agent
Keep it Slow (20)	Defeated 30 enemies while they were under the effect of the Cerebro Accelerator (P1)
Kicking and Screaming (20)	Escaped Serleena's drag attack
Own the Road (20)	Defeated 70 Bikers in Story Mode
Party Crasher (20)	Crashed Chauncey's party in Story Mode
Pest Control (30)	Defeated 700 enemies (P1)
Road Hog (20)	Defeated 40 bikers in Story Mode
Save the Universe (50)	Completed all the missions in Story Mode

Senior Agent (60)	Completed Story Mode as an Elite Agent
Shattered Expectations (30)	Froze 30 enemies with the Icer (P1)
Smile for the Camera! (20)	Neuralized 7 humans in Story Mode
Superior Fighter (25)	Achieved at least 150,000 points in one V.R. Mission (P1)
Superstar (30)	Achieved at least 200,000 points in one V.R. Mission (P1)
The Gatherer (30)	Gathered 50 upgrade points
The Spice of Life (20)	Defeated enemies using 10 different combos (P1)
This Won't Take Long (20)	Defeated the Nakkadan Elite Guard in Story Mode
Ugly on the Inside (20)	Defeated the Adorian Elite Guard in Story Mode
What Goes Up… (20)	Used the Anti-Gravity grenade on 30 enemies (P1)

MERCENARIES 2: WORLD IN FLAMES (XBOX 360)

UNLOCKABLE COSTUMES

To unlock costumes, you must complete Level 3 of a weapon challenge, which can be done by talking to Fiona at your PMC. Each time you complete a Level 3 weapon challenge, you receive one of three costumes.

METAL GEAR ACID (PSP)

Enter the following in the Passwords menu through the Main menu.

CARD	PASSWORD
Gives Card No. 173 - Viper	Viper
Gives Card No. 178 - Mika Slayton	Mika
Gives Card No. 182 - Karen Houjou	Karen
Gives Card No. 184 - Jehuty	Jehuty
Gives Card No. 199 - XM8	Xmeight
Gives Card No. 200 - Kosaka Yuka	Kobe
Gives Card No. 201 - Asaki Yoshida	umeda
Gives Card No. 202 - Yu Saito	YEBISU
Gives Card No. 203 - Shibuya Eri	Roppongi

METAL GEAR ACID 2 (PSP)

Enter these passwords at the password screen. You'll obtain them as you load your saved games.

PASSWORD	EFFECT
Ronaldsiu	Banana Peel Card
Dcy	Card No. 203—Decoy Octopus
SONOFSULLY	Card No. 291—Jack
Vrs	Card No. 046—Strain (JP Version only)
Cct	Card No. 099—Gijin-san (JP Version only)
Konami	Card No. 119—Reaction Block
Viper	Card No. 161—Viper
Mika	Card No. 166—Mika Slayton
Karen	Card No. 170—Karen Houjou
Jehuty	Card No. 172—Jehuty
Xmeight	Card No. 187—XM8
Signt	Card No. 188—Mr. Sigint
Sgnt	Card No. 188—SIGINT (JP Version only)
Hrrr	Card No. 197—Sea Harrier (JP Version only)

Dcyctps	Card No. 203—Decoy Octopus (JP Version only)
Rgr	Card No. 212—Roger McCoy (JP Version only)
Xx	Card No. 281—Hinomoto Reiko (JP Version only)
Kinoshitaa	Card No. 285—Kinoshita Ayumi (JP Version only)
Shiimeg	Card No. 286—Ishii Meguru (JP Version only)
Nonat	Card No. 287—Sano Natsume (JP Version only)
No Place	Card No. 288—MGS4 (JP Version only)
Snake	Card No. 294—Solid Snake (MGS4)
Otacon	Card No. 295—Otacon (MGS4)
shrrr	Card No. 197 Sea Harrier (US version)
Ginormousj	Emma's Parrot Card
Gekko	Gekko (US Version)
NEXTGEN	Get MGS4 card
shinta	Gives you card Gijin-san
nojiri	Gives you card Strand
mgr	Ishii Meguru
aym	Kinoshita Ayumi
mk2	Metal Gear MK. II (MGS4) Card unlocked
smoking	No Smoking card (US Version)
thespaniard	Possessed Arm card
gcl	Reaction Block 119 (Japanese version only)
tobidacid	Solid Eye card (US/UK Version)
ntm	Unlocks Natsume Sano Card an Solid Eye Video
Hnmt	Unlocks Reiko Hinomoto card
Mccy	Unlocks the Roger McCoy card

CARD PACK UPGRADES

Complete the game once. Load your finished game save and play
through the game again. At the points where you received the card
packs, they will be upgraded into newer versions.

UNLOCKABLE	HOW TO UNLOCK
Chronicle Unlimited Pack	Upgrade Chronicle Pack
MGS1 Integral Pack	Upgrade MGS1 Pack
MGS2 Substance Pack	Upgrade MGS2 Pack
MGS3 Subsistence Pack	Upgrade MGS3 Pack

UNLOCKABLE CARDS

Complete the game on any difficulty and get a certain rare card.

UNLOCKABLE	HOW TO UNLOCK
"E-Z Gun" Card	Beat 6 levels in Arena mode on Easy setting
"G36C" Card	Beat 6 levels in Arena mode on Extreme setting
"Stealth Camo" Card	Beat 6 levels in Arena mode on Normal setting
Metal Gear RAY	Beat Campaign mode twice
Metal Gear Rex	Complete game on Normal
MGS4	Complete game on Easy
Running Man Card	Complete 6 rounds in the Arena on Hard setting

METAL GEAR SOLID 2: SONS OF LIBERTY (PLAYSTATION VITA)

TROPHY

UNLOCKABLE	HOW TO UNLOCK
A Cut Above (Gold)	Beat the Tanker and Plant chapters on any difficulty
Animal Control (Bronze)	Collect a dog tag
Another Snake Bites the Dust (Bronze)	Defeat Solidus Snake

Beagle (Bronze)	Get the brown wig	
Bohemian Candidate (Bronze)	Meet President James Johnson	
Bomb Squad (Bronze)	Learn how to defuse C4 bombs from Peter Stillman	
Bye Bye Big Brother (Bronze)	Destroy 15 cameras	
Complete Stealth (Gold)	Clear the game without entering alert mode (not including events where alert mode is mandatory)	
Don't Taze Me, Bro (Bronze)	Tranquilize 100 enemies	
Down in Smoke (Bronze)	Disorient an enemy with a cloud of smoke from a fire extinguisher	
Extremely Solid (Platinum)	Collect all trophies	
Great Dane (Gold)	Collect all dog tags in the Plant chapter to obtain the Blue Wig	
Hurt Locker (Bronze)	Put an enemy in a locker	
I Think You Need a Hug, E (Bronze)	Find Emma Emmerich	
In It To Win It (Silver)	Place first in 50 different VR/Alternative Missions	
Johnny on the Spot (Bronze)	Hear Johnny's bowel noises in two locations	
Kissing Booth (Bronze)	Kiss a poster in a locker	
Lights Out (Bronze)	Defeat Olga Gurlukovich	
Love Hurts (Bronze)	Watch Rose kill Raiden on a rooftop	
Moving Day (Silver)	Collect all boxes	
No Boss of Mine (Silver)	Complete Boss Survival	
No Ray, José (Bronze)	Defeat Metal Gear RAY	
No-Fly Zone (Bronze)	Destroy the AV-88 Harrier II	
Nothing Personal (Bronze)	Break the neck of 30 enemies	
Party's Over (Bronze)	Defeat Fatman	
Photo Finish (Bronze)	Acquire the digital camera	
Piece of Cake (Bronze)	Complete a VR or Alternative mission	
Poodle (Bronze)	Get the Tanker stealth suit	
Rent Money (Bronze)	Beat 30 enemies unconscious	
Sexting (Bronze)	Send Otacon a picture of the marine with no pants	
Sharing Is Caring (Bronze)	Befriend Olga Gurlukovich	
Shiba Inu (Bronze)	Get the Plant stealth suit	
Silence is Golden (Bronze)	Shoot 10 enemy radios	
Snake Beater (Bronze)	Get caught by Otacon stimulating yourself	
Spaghetti Cinema (Bronze)	Meet Revolver	
St. Bernard (Bronze)	Get the orange wig	
Steamed (Bronze)	Kill 5 enemies with pipe steam	
Steel Grip (Bronze)	Attain grip level 3	
Tell Me a Tale (Silver)	Complete all Snake Tales	
Thanks, Ames (Bronze)	Learn the location of the president	
To Catch a Predator (Bronze)	Lure a guard with a girlie magazine	
Vamp Eyer (Bronze)	Catch a glimpse of Vamp standing in the streets of New York during the end cinematic	
Vampire Slayer (Bronze)	Defeat Vamp	
Virtually Impossible (Gold)	Complete alL VR and Alternative missions	

NEW!

A
B
C
D
E
F
G
H
I
J
K
L
M
N
O
P
Q
R
S
T
U
V
W
X
Y
Z

CODES & CHEATS

Who Ya Gonna Call? (Silver)	Take a clear photograph of the ghost image in Hold No. 2
Yorkie (Bronze)	Get the bandana

UNLOCKABLE

UNLOCKABLE	HOW TO UNLOCK
Bandana (gives you infinite ammo)	Beat the game. Select Tanker. Get over 30 dog tags.
Blue Wig (gives you infinite 02)	Collect all the dog tags.
Brown Wig (unlimited ammo for Raiden)	Beat normal mode with more than 100 dog tags
Orange Wig (infinite grip)	Beat the game with 150 dog tags.
Shaver	Grip yourself over behind the caged fence when you start with Raiden.
Stealth Camo	Beat the game. Select "Tanker". Get more than 60 dog tags.
Stealth Camo #2	Beat the game with 120 dog tags.
Ranking: Bat - Normal Difficulty	Tanker: 1 alert, Plant: 2 alerts, Tanker-Plant: 3 alerts
Ranking: Big Boss - Extreme Difficulty (Tanker-Plant)	Radar off, under 3hr clear, Damage: under 10.5, Shots Fired: under 700, under 3 alerts, 0 kills, 0 continues, 0 rations, 0-8 saves, no special items
Ranking: Capybara - Normal Difficulty	Tanker: 5+ hours, Plant: 25+ Hours, Tanker-Plant: 30+ Hours

UNLOCKABLE	HOW TO UNLOCK
Tanker-Plant: 100 + saves	
Ranking: Chicken - Very Easy/ Easy Difficulty	Radar: off, 250+ alerts, 250+ kills, 60+ continues, 31+ rations used, 100+ saves
Ranking: Cow - All Difficulty Levels	Tanker: 50+ Alerts, Plant: 200+ alerts, Tanker-Plant: 250+ alerts
Ranking: Deer - Normal Difficulty	Tanker: 25+ saves, Plant: 75+ saves, Tanker-Plant: 100 + saves
Ranking: Doberman - Hard Difficulty (Tanker-Plant)	Under 3hr clear, under 3 alerts, 0 kills, 0 escapes, 0 continues, 0-3 rations, no special items
Ranking: Doberman - Normal Difficulty (Tanker-Plant)	Radar off, under 3hr clear, Damage: under 10.5, Shots Fired: under 700, under 3 alerts, 0 kills, 0 continues, 0 rations, 0-8 saves, no special items
Ranking: Eagle - Extreme Difficulty	Tanker: 18 minutes or less, Plant: 2hrs 45 min or less, Tanker-Plant: 3hrs or less
Ranking: Elephant - Normal Difficulty	31 Rations used
Ranking: Falcon - Normal Difficulty	Tanker: 18 minutes or less, Plant: 2hrs 45 min or less, Tanker-Plant: 3hrs or less
Ranking: Flying Fox - Hard Difficulty	Tanker: 1 alert, Plant: 2 alerts, Tanker-Plant: 3 alerts
Ranking: Flying Squirrel - Very Easy/ Easy Difficulty	Tanker: 1 alert, Plant: 2 alerts, Tanker-Plant: 3 alerts
Ranking: Fox - Extreme Difficulty (Tanker-Plant)	Under 3hr clear, under 3 alerts, 0 kills, 0 escapes, 0 continues, 0-3 rations, no special items
Ranking: Fox - Hard Difficulty (Tanker-Plant)	Radar off, under 3hr clear, Damage: under 10.5, Shots Fired: under 700, under 3 alerts, 0 kills, 0 continues, 0 rations, 0-8 saves, no special items
Ranking: Gazelle - All Difficulty Levels	Tanker: 50+ Clearing Escapes, Plant: 100+ clearing escapes, Tanker-Plant: 150+ Clearing Escapes

Ranking: Giant Panda - Extreme Difficulty	Tanker: 5+ hours, Plant: 25+ Hours, Tanker-Plant: 30+ Hours
Ranking: Hawk - Hard Difficulty	Tanker: 18 minutes or less, Plant: 2hrs 45 min or less, Tanker-Plant: 3hrs or less
Ranking: Hippopotamus - Extreme Difficulty	Tanker: 25+ saves, Plant: 75+ saves, Tanker-Plant: 100 + saves
Ranking: Hound - Easy Difficulty (Tanker-Plant)	Radar off, under 3hr clear, Damage: under 10.5, Shots Fired: under 700, under 3 alerts, 0 kills, 0 continues, 0 rations, 0-8 saves, no special items
Ranking: Hound - Normal Difficulty (Tanker-Plant)	Under 3hr clear, under 3 alerts, 0 kills, 0 escapes, 0 continues, 0-3 rations, no special items
Ranking: Jaws - Hard Difficulty	Tanker: 50+ Enemies killed, Plant: 200+ Enemies killed, Tanker-Plant: 250+ Enemies killed
Ranking: Koala - Very Easy/Easy Difficulty	Tanker: 5+ hours, Plant: 25+ Hours, Tanker-Plant: 30+ Hours
Ranking: Mammoth - Hard Difficulty	31 Rations used
Ranking: Mouse - Normal Difficulty	Radar: off, 250+ alerts, 250+ kills, 60+ continues, 31+ rations used, 100+ saves
Ranking: Night Owl - Extreme Difficulty	Tanker: 1 alert, Plant: 2 alerts, Tanker-Plant: 3 alerts
Ranking: Orca - Extreme Difficulty	Tanker: 50+ Enemies killed, Plant: 200+ Enemies killed, Tanker-Plant: 250+ Enemies killed
Ranking: Ostrich - Extreme Difficulty	Radar: off, 250+ alerts, 250+ kills, 60+ continues, 31+ rations used, 100+ saves
Ranking: Pig - Very Easy/Easy Difficulty	31 Rations used
Ranking: Pigeon - All Difficulty Levels	No Enemies Killed
Ranking: Piranha - Very Easy/Easy Difficulty	Tanker: 50+ Enemies killed, Plant: 200+ Enemies killed, Tanker-Plant: 250+ Enemies killed
Ranking: Rabbit - Hard Difficulty	Radar: off, 250+ alerts, 250+ kills, 60+ continues, 31+ rations used, 100+ saves
Ranking: Sea Louce - All Difficulty Levels	Beat the game with a Sea Louce in your inventory
Ranking: Shark - Normal Difficulty	Tanker: 50+ Enemies killed, Plant: 200+ Enemies killed, Tanker-Plant: 250+ Enemies killed
Ranking: Sloth - Hard Difficulty	Tanker: 5+ hours, Plant: 25+ Hours, Tanker-Plant: 30+ Hours
Ranking: Swallow - Very Easy/Easy Difficulty	Tanker: 18 minutes or less, Plant: 2hrs 45 min or less, 3hrs or less
Ranking: Whale - Extreme Difficulty	31 Rations used
Ranking: Zebra - Hard Difficulty	Tanker: 25+ saves, Plant: 75+ saves, Tanker-Plant: 100 + saves
Grip Gauge Level 2	Do 100 Pull-ups
Grip Gauge Level 3	Do 100 Pull-ups after unlocking Grip Gauge Level 2

METAL GEAR SOLID 3: SNAKE EATER (PLAYSTATION VITA)

TROPHY

UNLOCKABLE	HOW TO UNLOCK
A Bird in the Hand... (Bronze)	Collect every type of bird
A Good Man Is Hard to Find (Bronze)	Achieve a camouflage index of 100%
Beekeeper (Bronze)	Use bees to harass an enemy

CODES & CHEATS

Believe It or Not (Silver)	Catch a Tsuchinoko (mythical serpent)
Can I Keep It? (Bronze)	Capture any animal alive
Charmer (Bronze)	Collect every type of snake
Close Shave (Bronze)	CQC Slit an enemy's throat
Don't Touch The Sides (Bronze)	Use a knife to remove a bullet
Everything Is in Season (Bronze)	Collect every type of fruit
Fashionista (Silver)	Find every type of camouflage
Fungus Among Us (Bronze)	Collect every type of mushroom
Grounded (Bronze)	Defeat Volgin in a fist fight
Houston, We HAD a Problem (Bronze)	Defeat The Fury
I Can Totally See You (Bronze)	Achieve a camouflage index of +90%
If It Bleeds, We Can Kill It (Bronze)	Defeat The Fear
It Ain't Easy Being Green (Gold)	Find all 64 Kerotans
Just Because (Bronze)	Blow up a munitions shed with TNT
Just What the Doctor Ordered (Bronze)	Collect every type of medicinal plant
King of the Jungle (Gold)	Obtain the title of MARKHOR
Like a Boss (Gold)	Finish the game on any difficulty
Mama Said (Bronze)	CQC Slam a guard and knock him out
Mostly Dead (Bronze)	Use the Fake Death Pill
Only Skin Deep (Silver)	Find every type of face paint
Pain Relief (Bronze)	Defeat The Pain
PEACE WALKER (Gold)	Finish the game without killing anyone
Prince Charming (Bronze)	Shoot a kerotan for the first time
Problem Solved, Series Over (Bronze)	Create the Ocelot Time Paradox
Ralph Called (Bronze)	Make Snake throw up
River of Pain (Bronze)	Defeat The Sorrow
Serenity Now (Bronze)	Call one Healing Radio frequency
Shagadelic (Bronze)	Defeat Shagohod
Snake Bit (Bronze)	Poison a guard
Snake Eaten (Platinum)	Collect all trophies
Snake Eater (Bronze)	Eat a snake of any type
Snake Eyes (Bronze)	See all of the first-person views that are not indicated by the R button icon
Tall Tale (Bronze)	Collect every type of fish
Tell Me Where the Bomb Is (Bronze)	CQC Interrogate an enemy
The Cat's out of the Bag (Bronze)	Catch a glimpse of Ocelot, who's seen behind the president when he tries to shake Snake's hand
The Early End (Silver)	Kill The End before the boss battle
The End (Bronze)	Defeat The End
The Patriot (Bronze)	Defeat The Boss
Them's Good Eatin' (Bronze)	Collect every type of frog
Tune-In Tokyo (Bronze)	Call every Healing Radio frequency
You Snooze, You Lose (Silver)	Sneak up on The End and hold him up
Young Gun (Bronze)	Submit Ocelot

UNLOCKABLE

UNLOCKABLE	HOW TO UNLOCK
Animals	Beat Ocelot
Cold War	Beat Volgen

Fire	Beat The Fury
Hornet Stripe	Beat The Pain
Moss	Hold up The End
Snake	Beat The Boss
Spider	Beat The Fear
DPM Camouflage	Beat Special Duel Mode
Green Face Paint	Beat Normal Duel Mode
"Box" Conversation	Equip a Box and call Sigint. (Very Funny)
"Chocolate Chip" Conversation	Wear "Choco Chip" Camo and call Sigint
"Glowcap" Conversation	Eat a Glowcap and Call Para-Medic
"Granin" Conversation	Call Sigint after speakng to Granin
"Patriot" Conversation	Call Sigint with the Patriot equiped
"Pretty" Convo	Call Para-Medic after catching a Green Tree Python
"Tsuchinoko" Conversation	Catch a Tsuchinoko and Call Para-Medic
Funny Conversation	Wear "Naked" Camo and call Sigint
Raiden conversation	Call Major Zero after obtaining the Officer camo, with the mask and Officer camo equipped
Sigint's nightmare conversation	Call Sigint after waking up from nightmare (the nightmare appears when you load a save file while in the prison cell)
Banana Camouflage	Get the highest record time in every stage of Snake vs. Monkey
Colt Single Action Army	Choose the gun on the right during the final duel.
Extreme Difficulty Mode	Complete the game once
Intro movie on title screen	Complete Virtuous Mission
Mechanic Uniform	In Second Locker on Far Right in Groznjy Grad (Near the locker where you put Major Raikov at)
Mosin Nagant	Defeat The End/MK22 only
Moss Camo	Defeat The End by sneaking up behind him during battle and pointing a gun at him. He will lay on the ground. Point the gun at his head three times, aiming elsewhere when he speaks.
Patriot	Complete the game once
Snake vs. Monkey levels 4 and 5	Complete the game once
Sneaking Suit	In Locker you put Major Raikov in (Second time you go to Groznjy Grad)
Stealth Camouflage	Find and shoot all 64 Kerotan frogs that are scatter through out the whole game.
Stealth Camouflage (alternate method)	Beat the game with no alerts
Tuxedo Camouflage	Complete the game once
Camo Chocolate Chip	Bolshaya Past South.
Camo Ga-Ko	Chyornyj Prud, underwater in northeast.
Camo Grenade	Download it to your memory card.
Camo Mummy	Download it to your memory card.
Camo Rain Drop	Dremuchij North, under the rope bridge on the far side.
Camo Santa	Download it to your memory card.
Camo Snow	Peschera Cave, on the right branch before the Pain.

NEW!

A
B
C
D
E
F
G
H
I
J
K
L
M
N
O
P
Q
R
S
T
U
V
W
X
Y
Z

Camo Splitter	Bolshaya Past South.
Camo Valentine	Download it to your memory card. (JP and EU versions)
Camo Water	Bolshaya Past Base.
Facepaint Desert	Ponizovje Warehouse.
Facepaint Kabuki	Tikhogornyj, at the bottom of the pool before the waterfall.
Facepaint Oyama	Graniny Gorky Lab, Exterior. In the air duct.
Facepaint Snow	Bolshaya Past Base, In the fox hole on the left side of the middle building
Facepaint Water	After talking to Granin and fighting The Fear, go all the way back to the beginning of Ponizovje South.
Facepaint Zombie	Rassvet during snake eater mission. Behind the building.
Fly Camouflage	In the third bathroom stall on the second floor of the building where Granin is (it's locked so break the door down).
Infinity Face Paint	Beat the game with the Foxhound Rank
Infinity Face Paint (alternate method)	Catch a live Tsuchinoko before torture scene. After you get your weapons, go back and capture it again just outside. Finish the game with it alive.
Monkey Mask	Complete every level in Snake vs. Monkeys
Spirit camouflage	Last all the way through Sorrow's river
Uniform Maintenance	Groznyj Grad Weapons Lab: East Wing in locker. Same time as the Sneaking Suit.
Uniform Officer	Steal it from Raikov.
Uniform Scientist	Given to you by Eva.
Uniform Sneaking Suit	Groznyj Grad Weapons Lab: East Wing. In the locker with the red stripe.
Peep Show Movie.	Collect all the Movies in Demo Theatre.
Alligator - Any Difficulty	81-249 Alerts, 41 or more Continues, 101-299 Kills
Bat - Normal Ranking	No Alerts
Capybara - Normal Ranking	Play Time over 30 hours
Cat - Easy and Very Easy Ranking	Save over 100 times
Centipede - Any Difficulty	1-20 Alerts, 41 or more continues, 1-100 kills
Chicken - Easy and Very Easy Difficulties	Alert Mode over 300 times, Kill over 300 people, Eat more than 31 Meals, Play Time over 30 hours, Continue over 60 times, Save over 100 times
Cow - Special Ranking	Alert Mode raised over 300 times
Crocodile - Any Difficulty	81-249 Alerts, 0-40 Continues, 101-299 Kills
Deer - Normal Ranking	Save over 100 times
Doberman - Extreme Ranking	No Special Item used, 1 Alert, 0 Kills, Under 3 Life Meds, Under 5:15 play time, 0 continues
Doberman - Hard Ranking	No Special Item used, 0 Alerts, 0 Kills, 0 Life Meds, Under 5:00 play time, under 50 saves, 0 continues
Doberman - Normal Ranking	No Special Item used, 0 Alerts, Under 10 Life Bars of Damage, 0 Kills, 0 Life Meds, Under 5:00 play time, under 25 saves, 0 continues

Eagle - Extreme Ranking	Play Time under 5:00
Elephant - Normal Ranking	Over 31 Meals Eaten
Falcon - Normal Ranking	Play Time under 5:00
Flying Fox - Hard Ranking	No Alerts
Flying Squirrel - Easy and Very Easy Ranking	No Alerts
Fox - Extreme Ranking	No Special Item used, 0 Alerts, 0 Kills, 0 Life Meds, Under 5:00 play time, under 50 saves, 0 continues
Fox - Hard Ranking	No Special Item used, 0 Alerts, Under 10 Life Bars of Damage, 0 Kills, 0 Life Meds, Under 5:00 play time, under 25 saves, 0 continues
Foxhound - Extreme Ranking	No Special Item used, 0 Alerts, Under 10 Life Bars of Damage, 0 Kills, 0 Life Meds, Under 5:00 play time, under 25 saves, 0 continues
Giant Panda - Extreme Ranking	Play Time over 30 hours
Hawk - Hard Ranking	Play Time under 5:00
Hippopotamus - Extreme Ranking	Save over 100 times
Hound - Easy Ranking	No Special Item used, 0 Alerts, Under 10 Life Bars of Damage, 0 Kills, 0 Life Meds, Under 5:00 play time, under 25 saves, 0 continues
Hound - Extreme Ranking	No Special Item used, 2 Alerts, 0 Kills, Under 5:00 play time, under 25 saves, 0 continues
Hound - Hard Ranking	No Special Item used, 1 Alert, 0 Kills, Under 3 Life Meds, Under 5:15 play time, 0 continues
Hound - Normal Ranking	No Special Item used, 0 Alerts, 0 Kills, 0 Life Meds, Under 5:00 play time, under 50 saves, 0 continues
Hyena - Any Difficulty	51-80 Alerts, 41 or more Continues, 101-299 Kills
Iguana - Any Difficulty	81-249 Alerts, 0-40 Continues, 1-100 Kills
Jackal - Any Difficulty	51-80 Alerts, 0-40 Continues, 1-100 Kills
Jaguar - Any Difficulty	21-50 Alerts, 0-40 Continues, 1-100 Kills
Kerotan - Special Ranking	Shoot all 64 Kerotan Frogs
Koala - Easy and Very Easy Ranking	Play Time over 30 hours
Komodo Dragon - Any Difficulty	81-249 Alerts, 41 or more Continues, 1-100 Kills
Leech - Special Ranking	Clear the Game with Leech attached
Leopard - Any Difficulty	21-50 Alerts, 41 or more Continues, 1-100 Kills
Mammoth - Hard Ranking	Kill over 300 Humans
Markhor - Special Ranking	Every Plant and Animal Captured, Cure Supply Plant, and non animal-plant item (RC Mate, Noodles, etc.)
Mongoose - Any Difficulty	51-80 Alerts, 41 or more Continues, 1-100 Kills
Mouse - Normal Difficulty	Alert Mode over 300 times, Kill over 300 people, Eat more than 31 Meals, Play Time over 30 hours, Continue over 60 times, Save over 100 times
Night Owl - Extreme Ranking	No Alerts
Orca - Extreme Ranking	Kill 250 or more Humans

Ostrich - Extreme Difficulty	Alert Mode over 300 times, Kill over 300 people, Eat more than 31 Meals, Play Time over 30 hours, Continue over 60 times, Save over 100 times
Panther - Any Difficulty	21-50 Alerts, 0-40 Continues, 101-299 Kills
Pig - Easy and Very Easy Ranking	Over 31 Meals Eaten
Pigeon - Special Ranking	No Kills
Piranha - Easy and Very Easy Ranking	Kill over 300 Humans
Puma - Any Difficulty	21-50 Alerts, 41 or more Continues, 101-299 Kills
Rabbit - Hard Difficulty	Alert Mode over 300 times, Kill over 300 people, Eat more than 31 Meals, Play Time over 30 hours, Continue over 60 times, Save over 100 times
Scorpion - Any Difficulty	1-20 Alerts, 0-40 continues, 1-100 kills
Shark - Normal Ranking	Kill over 300 Humans
Sloth - Hard Ranking	Play Time over 30 hours
Spider - Any Difficulty	1-20 Alerts, 41 or more continues, 101-299 kills
Swallow - Easy and Very Easy Ranking	Play Time under 5:00
Tarantula - Any Difficulty	1-20 Alerts, 0-40 continues, 101-299 kills
Tasmanian Devil - Any Difficulty	51-80 Alerts, 0-40 Continues, 101-299 Kills
Tsuchinoko - Special Ranking	Clear game with living Tsuchinoko captured
Whale - Extreme Ranking	Kill over 300 Humans
Zebra - Hard Ranking	Save over 100 times

METAL GEAR SOLID 4: GUNS OF THE PATRIOTS (PLAYSTATION 3)

BONUS WEAPONS

UNLOCKABLE	HOW TO UNLOCK
Bandanna	Complete a single-player session, on any difficulty, without killing anyone (including bosses).
Desert Eagle, Long Barrel	Earn the Fox emblem on a single-player session.
Digital Camera	In the Nomad vehicle during the mission intermission; you can unlock a special photo by picking up this item in stage 4 instead of earlier.
Patriot Future Assault Weapon	Earn the Big Boss emblem on a single-player session.
Race (Ricochet) Gun	Clear the single-player game once.
Scanning Plug S	Log more than 10 hours of Metal Gear Online play time on the same profile as your Metal Gear 4 game. You purchase this from Drebin.
Solar Gun	Collect the five statues (those of the four Battle Beauties and the Frog Soldier/Haven Troopers in stage 1) using non-lethal means on their respective idols.
Stealth Item	Complete a single-player session without instigating a single alert (caution is okay, but not alert). You can do this on any difficulty.
Thor 45-70	Earn the Fox Hound emblem on a single-player session.
World War I Pistol	Earn the Hound emblem on a single-player session.

COMPLETION UNLOCKABLES

UNLOCKABLE	HOW TO UNLOCK
Big Boss Extreme Difficulty	Complete the single-player mode once (and saving the cleared data).
New Combat Vests	Clear the single-player game once.

COSTUMES

UNLOCKABLE	HOW TO UNLOCK
Altair	Obtain the Assassin emblem.
Civilian Disguise	Start Eastern Europe level.
Corpse Camo	Get 41 continues or more in a single playthrough to unlock this Octocamo.
Middle East Militia Disguise	Middle East in the Militia Safe House.
South American Rebel Disguise	South America (Cove Valley Village).
Suit	Clear the game once.

DOLLS/STATUES

UNLOCKABLE	HOW TO UNLOCK
Crying Wolf Doll/Statue	In a side of a building just where you start after killing her beast form
Frog Soldier Doll/Statue	At the garage at the end of the battle
Laughing Beast Doll/Statue	On a bed in a little room
Raging Raven Doll/Statue	On the upper floor on a corner
Screaming Mantis Doll/Statue	On the corridor where you started

FACE PAINT

UNLOCKABLE	HOW TO UNLOCK
Big Boss's	Earn the Big Boss emblem on a single-player session.
Crying Wolf	Defeat the Battle Beauty (human form) Crying Wolf by non-lethal means.
Drebin	Purchase and keep more than 60 different weapons.
FaceCamo	Defeat the Battle Beauty Laughing Octopus (the overall battle, no specifics involved).
Laughing Octopus	Defeat the Battle Beauty (human form) Laughing Octopus by non-lethal means.
Otacon	Shock Dr. Emmerich using the Metal Gear II during the intermission scene.
Raging Raven	Defeat the Battle Beauty (human form) Raging Raven by non-lethal means.
Raiden Mask A	Shock Sunny using the Metal Gear II during the intermission scene.
Raiden Mask B	Shock Dr. Naomi Hunter using the Metal Gear II during the intermission scene.
Roy Campbell	Shock Colonel Campbell using the Metal Gear II during the intermission scene.
Screaming Mantis	Defeat the Battle Beauty (human form) Screaming Mantis by non-lethal means.
Young Snake	Beat Act 2.
Young Snake with Bandana	Beat Act 2.

IPOD TUNES

Snake's iPod can download specific tunes throughout the course of the game. Some songs have an additional "secret" effect when it is played in the game.

UNLOCKABLE	HOW TO UNLOCK
Beyond the Bounds (increases power stun damage done by Snake from non-lethal weapons)	Stage 4 Shadow Moses, Tank Hangar. After is restored, backtrack to the upper catwalk and explore all rooms.

CODES & CHEATS

Big Boss (increases stun damage and increases Snake's accuracy when played)	Earn the Big Boss emblem.
Bio Hazard	Frisk the resistance fighter in Easter Europe.
Bio Hazard (cause soldiers held by Snake to scream in terror)	Stage 3 Europe, Midtown.
Boktai 2 Theme	Act 2, Mission Briefing, upstairs in the Nomad.
Bon Dance	Act 2, Marketplace.
Destiny's Call (causes soldiers held by Snake to go enraged)	A random gift from a militia or rebel soldier if Snake gives them a healing item.
Flowing Destiny (causes soldiers held by Snake to weep like a little girl)	Stage 4 Shadow Moses, Canyon. Before leaving the canyon area, examine the rocky walls for a hole hiding this item.
Fury, The (causes soldiers held by Snake to go enraged)	Stage 2 South America, Cove Valley Village. Inside the fire ravaged house.
Inorino Uta	Act 1, Mission Briefing.
Level 3 Warning	Act 1, Advent Palace.
Lunar Knights Main Theme	Act 4, Mission Briefing, upstairs in the Nomad.
Metal Gear 20 Years History: Part 2	Act 4, Warhead Storage Building B2.
Metal Gear 20 Years History: Part 3	Act 2, South America Confinement Facility. In room with beds inside the house.
Metal Gear Solid Main Theme (The Document Remix)	Act 5, under hatch to the left at the beginning of area.
MGS 4 Love Theme / Action (causes soldiers held by Snake to weep like a little girl)	A random gift from a militia or rebel soldier if Snake gives them a healing item.
On Alert	Act 3, Midtown N Sector.
One Night in Neo Kobe City (causes soldiers held by Snake to laugh)	Act 3, Midtown, hold-up PMC.
Opening—Old L.A. 2040 (increases Snake's accuracy)	Stage 4 Shadow Moses, Nuclear Warhead Storage B2. Input 78925 into Otacon's lab computer.
Policenaughts Ending (causes soldiers held by Snake to fall asleep on touch)	Stage 4 Shadow Moses, Nuclear Warhead Storage B2. Input 13462 into Otacon's lab computer.
Rock Me (increases Snake's amount of life recovered from items and other means)	Stage 2 South America, Confinement Facility. Island in the southeastern quadrant.
Sailor (increases Snake's amount of life recovered from items and other means)	Stage 2 South America, Vista Mansion. Between the east wall and a cargo container
Shin Bokura no Taiyou Theme	Act 3, Mission Briefing, upstairs in the Nomad.
Show Time (causes soldiers held by Snake to scream in terror)	A random gift from a militia or rebel soldier if Snake gives them a healing item.
Snake Eater (increase the life recovery rate of Snake through items and other actions)	Unlocked by earning all 40 game clear emblems.
Subsistence (increase Snake's accuracy)	Play at least one game of Metal Gear Online. You must start the match with at least two players.
Test Subject's Duality	Act 3, Midtown S Sector.
The Best Is Yet To Come	Act 4, Snow Field. Just before the "Disc Change" Codec scene.
The Essence of Vince	Act 3, Echo's Beacon.

The Fury	Act 2, in the Cave Valley Village in badly burned building.
Theme of Solid Snake	Act 1, Millennium Park.
Theme of Tara	Act 1, Militia Safehouse. Just before seeing the unmanned flying-bomber on the table.
Warhead Storage	Act 4, Tank Hanger. Upper floor ventilation shaft.
Yell (Dead Cell)	Act 4, Casting Facility North.
Zanzibarland Breeze	Act 1, Urban Ruins before cutscene.

UNLOCKABLE EMBLEMS

UNLOCKABLE	HOW TO UNLOCK
Ant Emblem	Shake 50 enemies for items.
Assassin's Emblem	Beat the game with 50+ knife kills, 50+ CQC holds, and 25 or less alerts.
Bear Emblem	Choke 100 enemies to death.
Bee Emblem	Use the Scanning Plug S or Syringe on 50 enemies.
Big Boss Emblem	Beat the game on the highest difficulty with no deaths, no alerts, no kills, no recovery items, no stealth suit, no bandana items, in under 5 hours.
Blue Bird Emblem	Give friendly soldiers 50 items.
Centipede	Get less than 75 alert phases, less than 250 kills, and over 25 continues.
Chicken	Get over 150 alert phases, over 500 kills, over 50 continues, use over 50 recovery items and finish the game in over 35 hours.
Cow	Activate over 100 alerts.
Crocodile	Have over 400 kills.
Eagle Emblem	Get 150 headshots.
Fox Emblem	Beat the game on Normal or higher with no deaths, 5 or less alerts, no kills, no recovery items, no stealth suit, no bandana items, in under 6 hours.
Fox Hound Emblem	Beat the game on Hard or higher with no deaths, 3 or less alerts, no kills, no recovery items, no stealth suit, no bandana items, in under 5.5 hours.
Frog Emblem	Dive or roll 200 times.
Gecko Emblem	Press against walls for a total of 1 hour.
Giant Panda Emblem	Complete the game after 30 cumulative hours of play.
Gibbon Emblem	Hold up 50 enemies.
Hawk Emblem	Be admired by 25 friendly soldiers.
Hog Emblem	Get 10 combat highs.
Hound Emblem	Beat the game on hard or higher with no deaths, 3 or less alerts, no kills, no recovery items, no stealth suit, no bandana items, in under 6.5 hours.
Hyena Emblem	Pick up 400 dropped weapons.
Inch Worm Emblem	Crawl on the ground for a total of 1 hour.
Jaguar	Get over 75 alert phases, less than 250 kills, and less than 25 continues.
Leopard	Get over 75 alert phases, less than 250 kills, and over 25 continues.
Little Gray Emblem	Collect all 69 weapons.
Lobster Emblem	Spend a total of 2.5 hours crouching.
Mantis	Finish the game with no alerts activated; no continues; no rations, noodles, or regains used; and in under 5 hours.
Octopus	Beat the game without activating any alert phases.

Panther	Get over 75 alert phases, over 250 kills, and less than 25 continues.
Pig	Use more than 50 recovery items.
Pigeon	Beat the game without killing a single person (Gekkos and Dwarf Gekkos don't count).
Puma	Get over 75 alert phases, over 250 kills, and over 25 continues.
Rabbit	Flick through 100 *Playboy* pages.
Rabbit Emblem	Look at 100 *Playboy* pages.
Raven	Beat the game in under 5 hours.
Scarab	Perform over 100 rolls.
Scorpion	Get less than 75 alert Phases, less than 250 kills, and less than 25 continues.
Spider	Get less than 75 alert phases, over 250 kills, and over 25 continues.
Tarantula	Get less than 75 alert phases, over 250 kills, and less than 25 continues.
Tortoise	Spend more than 60 minutes inside the drum can or cardboard box (this can be done throughout the game, not all at once),
Wolf	Beat the game with no continues and no rations, regains, or noodles used.

METAL MARINES (WII)

CODES

CODE	EFFECT
Enter CSDV as a password	Start with more Money and Energy for each level
HBBT	Level 02
PCRC	Level 03
NWTN	Level 04
LSMD	Level 05
CLST	Level 06
JPTR	Level 07
NBLR	Level 08
PRSC	Level 09
PHTN	Level 10
TRNS	Level 11
RNSN	Level 12
ZDCP	Level 13
FKDV	Level 14
YSHM	Level 15
CLPD	Level 16
LNVV	Level 17
JFMR	Level 18
JCRY	Level 19
KNLB	Level 20

MICHAEL JACKSON THE EXPERIENCE (DS)

UNLOCKABLE

Collect the required nubmer of coins to unlock a tour set list. Here are the requirements for each tour set list.

UNLOCKABLE	HOW TO UNLOCK
Tour Set List 2 (Heal The World & Bad)	Collect 6 coins in Tour Mode.
Tour Set List 3 (The Way You Make Me Feel, Don't Stop 'Til You Get Enough & Black or White)	Collect 13 coins in Tour Mode.

| Tour Set List 4 (Wanna Be Startin' Somethin', Streetwalker, Leave Me Alone & Smooth Criminal) | Collect 25 coins in Tour Mode. |
| Tour Set List 5 (Beat It) | Collect 41 coins in Tour Mode. |

MICHAEL JACKSON THE EXPERIENCE HD (PLAYSTATION VITA)

TROPHY

UNLOCKABLE	HOW TO UNLOCK
A Glove for Any Occasion! (Gold)	Unlock all the Gloves in the game.
A Smooth Criminal... (Silver)	Hold a Max Combo Level for 90 seconds on Smooth Criminal (Medium difficulty)
Feelin' Good! (Silver)	Complete 150 Perfect moves on The Way You Make Me Feel (Medium difficulty)
Figure Collector (Gold)	Unlock all the Michael Jackson Figures in the game
Freeway Dancer! (Bronze)	Complete Speed Demon 6 times
Going Hollywood... (Gold)	Perform 50 Perfect moves in a row on Hollywood Tonight (Expert difficulty)
Legendary (Gold)	Become Legend (Level 20)
Not Alone (Bronze)	Unlock, equip and dance with the alternate costume on Leave Me Alone
Out on the Dance floor (Bronze)	Draw only lines and spins during Freestyle on Blood on The Dance Floor
Papparazzi! (Bronze)	Score at least 80,000 on Billie Jean
Perfect Expert (Gold)	Perform 30 Perfect moves in a row on Thriller (Expert difficulty)
Remember the Sequence! (Silver)	Perform the secret freestyle sequence on Remember The Time
Rock The Night Away! (Silver)	Don't miss a single move on Rock With You (Medium difficulty)
Still Not Enough! (Bronze)	Win 3 multiplayer Battles on Don't Stop 'Til You Get Enough
Supernatural! (Silver)	Perform 250 Perfect moves on Ghosts
The Negiotiator (Gold)	Score 145,000 Points on Beat It
The Setlist (Bronze)	Complete every song once
The Spectator (Bronze)	Watch any song in the "On demand Performance" Mode
The Tour Begins... (Bronze)	Become a Trainee (Level 2)
The Tour Continues... (Silver)	Become a Dance Fanatic (Level 10)
Thriller Tonight! (Bronze)	Get a B grade or better on Thriller (Medium difficulty)
Top of the World! (Silver)	Get the highest score in the leaderboard on Black or White
Unbreakable (Platinum)	Obtain all the trophies in Michael Jackson The Experience HD
Wardrobe! (Silver)	Unlock, equip and dance with an alternate costume for the first time
Who's Bad? (Silver)	Get an A grade on Bad (Medium difficulty)
Zombie Dance (Bronze)	Perform the special Thriller move during Freestyle

UNLOCKABLE

UNLOCKABLE	HOW TO UNLOCK
Black Armguard	Draw 50 Perfect Shapes in a Row on Hollywood Tonight on Expert Difficulty
Emerald Glove	Draw 45 Perfect Shapes in a Row on Smooth Criminal

CODES & CHEATS

Golden Glove	Reach the top position on the leaderboard for "Leave Me Alone"
Red Ruby Glove	Wear the Alternate Outfit on Ghosts.
Star Sapphire Glove	Score 145,000 Points on Beat It

MILITARY MADNESS (WII)

UNLOCKABLES

UNLOCKABLE	HOW TO UNLOCK
Alternate Colors	Power on the system, and hold SELECT to reset. While continuing to hold SELECT, choose the 1-player continue option and enter a map name.
Play as Axis	Select the new game or 1-player continue option on the title screen, then hold SELECT and press ①.
Switch Sides	Hold SELECT and press RUN before choosing the 1-player continue option.

PASSWORDS

PASSWORD	EFFECT
REVOLT	Level 01
ICARUS	Level 02
CYRANO	Level 03
RAMSEY	Level 04
NEWTON	Level 05
SENECA	Level 06
SABINE	Level 07
ARATUS	Level 08
GALIOS	Level 09
DARWIN	Level 10
PASCAL	Level 11
HALLEY	Level 12
BORMAN	Level 13
APOLLO	Level 14
KAISER	Level 15
NECTOR	Level 16
MILTON	Level 17
IRAGAN	Level 18
LIPTUS	Level 19
INAKKA	Level 20
TETROS	Level 21
ARBINE	Level 22
RECTOS	Level 23
YEANTA	Level 24
MONOGA	Level 25
ATTAYA	Level 26
DESHTA	Level 27
NEKOSE	Level 28
ERATIN	Level 29
SOLCIS	Level 30
SAGINE	Level 31
WINNER	Level 32
ONGAKU	Sound Test

MILON'S SECRET CASTLE (WII)

UNLOCKABLES

UNLOCKABLE	HOW TO UNLOCK
Continue Game	Hold down left and press START when you die after getting the first crystal

MLB 12: THE SHOW (PLAYSTATION 3)

TROPHY

UNLOCKABLE	HOW TO UNLOCK
"RESPECT THE GAME!" (Bronze)	In any game mode, enter a game with a mismatching uniform.
A Year in the Life (Silver)	Play through one season (5 games) in Diamond Dynasty mode.
Back, Back, Back, Back, Back... (Bronze)	Hit a home run of 490ft or more in Home Run Derby.
Boom Goes the Dynamite (Bronze)	In any game mode, hit a home run with your first batter of the game.
Collector (Gold)	In Diamond Dynasty mode, acquire one of every card type. (Bronze, Silver, Gold, Platinum, MLB)
Congratulations! (Platinum)	You got all of the MLB 12 The Show Trophies!
Contact Killer (Silver)	In any mode excluding RttS, play an entire 9 inning game without striking out. Must be done in a full, uninterrupted, 9 inning game against a CPU control
Cruzball (Bronze)	Playing as the pitcher in any game mode, intentionally walk a batter, then turn a double play. Must be done against a CPU controlled team.
Deep Dish (Bronze)	Hit a home run into the Bullpen Sports Grill in rightfield at U.S. Cellular Field. (CWS)
Don't Phase Me Bro (Silver)	In any game mode, hit a home run off a 100+ MPH pitch. Must be done against a CPU controlled team.
Don't Try That Again (Bronze)	On defense, throw a runner out at 3B or home plate from the outfield. Must be done against a CPU controlled team.
Early Exit (Silver)	In any game mode, knock out the opponent's starting pitcher before the end of the 3rd inning. Must be done against a CPU controlled team.
Everyone's a Winner (Gold)	Win a game with every MLB team. Must be done in full, uninterrupted, 9-inning games.
Fish off a Barrel (Bronze)	Hit the aquarium behind home plate at Marlins Park. (MIA)
Free Baseball (Bronze)	In any game mode, win a game in extra innings.
Go Chasin' Waterfalls (Bronze)	Hit a home run into a waterfall at Kauffman Stadium. (KC)
In The Bag! (Bronze)	As the batter, hit 1st, 2nd, or 3rd base with the ball. Trophy is not achievable in Home Run Derby or Challenge of the Week.
King Slayer (Gold)	In Exhib. Mode, beat team that's ranked 1st overall in team select screen w/Pitching & Batting dif. set Legend. Be done in full, uninterrupted, 9 inning game
Loud and Clear (Bronze)	Hit a home run into the speaker in center field at Dodger Stadium. (LAD)

Masterpiece (Bronze)	Create a Diamond Dynasty team and custom logo including at least 20 layers.
Meatball Buffet (Silver)	Bat around in an inning. Must be comple. on All-Star or higher Batting diff.Must be done in a full, uninterrupted, 9 inning game against a CPU control
Million Dollar Arm (Gold)	In any game mode, throw a perfect game against a CPU contolled team. Must be done in a full, uninterrupted, 9 inning game.
Plowman (Bronze)	As a baserunner, plow the catcher. Must be done against a CPU controlled team.
Pulsating (Bronze)	With the pitching difficulty set to All-Star or higher, use Pulse Pitching to strike out the side. Must be done against a CPU controlled team.
Quality Start (Silver)	Throw more than 70% first pitch strikes in a complete game victory. Must be done in a full, uninterrupted, 9 inning game against a CPU controlled team
Run Benjie, Run! (Bronze)	Steal a base with a player whose primary position is Catcher. Must be done against a CPU controlled team.
Slinging in the Rain (Silver)	Play a full game in the rain without making an error.
Sombrero Dealer (Bronze)	In any mode, strike out the same player four times in a game. Must be done against a CPU controlled team.
Squeezeball (Silver)	In any game mode, win the game with an RBI bunt. Must be done in a full, uninterrupted, 9 inning game against a CPU controlled team.
Texas Two-Step (Bronze)	Hit a home run onto Greene's Hill in CF at Rangers Ballpark In Arlington. (TEX)
The Old Fashioned Way (Bronze)	In any mode, earn a save by having your reliever pitch last 3 innings of a win. Must be done in full,uninterrupted,9 inning game against a CPU control
Vulture a Win (Bronze)	In any mode, blow a save and get the win with the same pitcher. Must be done in a full, uninterrupted, 9 inning game against a CPU controlled team.
Winning (Gold)	Hit 10 consecutive home runs in Home Run Derby.
You Blew It (Bronze)	In any mode, blow your opponents save opportunity. Must be done against a CPU controlled team.
Zone Plus Analog Blast (Bronze)	With hitting difficulty set to All-Star or harder, hit a home run using Zone Plus Analog controls.This trophy is not unlockable in Home Run Derby modes

MLB 12: THE SHOW (PLAYSTATION VITA)

TROPHY

UNLOCKABLE	HOW TO UNLOCK
'RESPECT THE GAME!' (Bronze)	In any game mode, enter a game with a mismatching uniform.
Back, Back, Back, Back, Back... (Bronze)	Hit a home run of 490ft or more in Home Run Derby.
Congratulations (Platinum)	You got all of the MLB 12 The Show Trophies!
Contact Killer (Silver)	In any mode,excluding RttS,play an entire 9 inning game w/o striking out.Must be done in full,uninterrupted,9 inning game against CPU controlled team.

Cruzball (Bronze)	Playing as the pitcher in any game mode, intentionally walk a batter, then turn a double play. Must be done against a CPU controlled team.
Deep Dish (Bronze)	Hit a home run into the Bullpen Sports Grill in rightfield at U.S. Cellular Field. (CWS)
Don't Phase Me Bro (Silver)	In any game mode, hit a home run off a 100+ MPH pitch. Must be done against a CPU controlled team.
Don't Try That Again (Bronze)	On defense, throw a runner out at 3B or home plate from the outfield. Must be done against a CPU controlled team.
Early Exit (Silver)	In any game mode, knock out the opponent's starting pitcher before the end of the 3rd inning. Must be done against a CPU controlled team.
Fish off a Barrel (Bronze)	Hit the aquarium behind home plate at Marlins Park. (MIA)
For the Greater Good (Silver)	In any game mode, get a broken bat base hit.
Go Chasin' Waterfalls (Bronze)	Hit a home run into a waterfall at Kauffman Stadium. (KC)
In The Bag! (Bronze)	As the batter, hit 1st, 2nd, or 3rd base with the ball. Trophy is not achievable in Home Run Derby.
King Slayer (Gold)	In Exhib Mode,beat team ranked 1st overall in team select screen w/Pitching&Batting difficulties to Legend.Must be done in full,uninterrupted,9 inning
Loud and Clear (Bronze)	Hit a home run into the speaker in center field at Dodger Stadium. (LAD)
Meatbull Buffet (Silver)	Bat around in inning.Must be completed on All-Star or higher Batting difficulty.Must be done in full,uninterrupted,9 inning game against CPU control
Million Dollar Man (Gold)	In any game mode, throw a perfect game against a CPU controlled team. Must be done in a full, uninterrupted, 9 inning game.
Mr. 300 (Silver)	Reach 300 XP in online play.
On The Beach (Bronze)	Hit a home run into the sand area in Petco Park. (SD)
Plowman (Bronze)	As a baserunner, plow the catcher. Must be done against a CPU controlled team.
Pulsating (Bronze)	With the pitching difficulty set to All-Star or higher, use Pulse Pitching to strike out the side. Must be done against a CPU controlled team.
Quality Start (Silver)	Throw > 70% 1st pitch strikes in complete game victory.Must be done in full, uninterrupted, 9 inning game against CPU controlled team.
Rally Killer (Silver)	In any game mode, hit into 2 double plays in a game with the same player. Must be done against a CPU controlled team.
Run Benjie, Run! (Bronze)	Steal a base with a player whose primary position is Catcher. Must be done against a CPU controlled team.
Solid D (Silver)	Using Pure Analog Throwing,w/throwing difficulty to All-Star or higher,complete 9 inning game w/o error.Must be done against CPU controlled team.
Sombrero Dealer (Bronze)	In any mode, strike out the same player four times in a game. Must be done against a CPU controlled team.

NEW!

A
B
C
D
E
F
G
H
I
J
K
L
M
N
O
P
Q
R
S
T
U
V
W
X
Y
Z

Sooo Close! (Gold)	Lose your shot at a perfect game or no hitter in the 9th inning. Must be done against a CPU controlled team.
Squeezeball (Bronze)	In any game mode, win the game with an RBI bunt. Must be done in a full, uninterrupted, 9 inning game against the CPU controlled team.
Take Out Your Rival (Bronze)	In any mode, hit the opposing pitcher with a pitch.
Texas Two-Step (Bronze)	Hit a home run onto Greene's Hill in CF at Rangers Ballpark In Arlington. (TEX)
The Old Fashioned Way (Bronze)	In any mode, earn save by having your reliever pitch last 3 innings of a win. Must be done in full, uninterrupted, 9 inning game against CPU controlled
Vulture a Win (Bronze)	In any mode, blow save & get win w/ same pitcher Must be done in full, uninterrupted, 9 inning game against the CPU controlled team.
Winning (Gold)	Hit 10 consecutive home runs in Home Run Derby(TM).
You Blew It (Bronze)	In any mode, blow your opponents save opportunity. Must be done against a CPU controlled team.
You're the Man! (Gold)	Reach 500 XP in online play.
Zone Plus Analog Blast (Bronze)	W/ hitting difficulty set to All-Star or harder, hit home run using Zone Plus Analog controls. This trophy isn't unlockable in Home Run Derby modes.

MODNATION RACERS: ROAD TRIP   (PLAYSTATION VITA)

TROPHY

UNLOCKABLE	HOW TO UNLOCK
Aggro Racer (Bronze)	Sideswipe 75 opponents
Anonymous (Bronze)	Play an Ad Hoc race
Beat Down (Bronze)	Win your first Ad Hoc action race on a particular published track
Bonus Tour Winner (Silver)	Get 1st place overall in the Bonus Tour
Bonus! (Silver)	Complete all 5 Tours and pass the Career Stat thresholds
Bruiser (Bronze)	Get a total of 200 takedowns
Busting Ghosts (Bronze)	Beat one ghost in Time Trial
Cashing In (Bronze)	Cash in an Item Pod 50 times
Dominator (Gold)	Come 1st in every race in the career
Dresser (Bronze)	Create a Mod in Mod Studio
Drifting Superstar (Bronze)	Earn 100,000 drift points in one drift
Fast Learner (Bronze)	Complete all the race tutorials
Fill 'Er Up (Bronze)	Fill your boost meter
Headspinner (Bronze)	Do a 1080 spin and land successfully
Hoarder (Silver)	Collect all the tokens in the single player career
Join the Team (Silver)	Beat all 30 developer best lap times in career
Knockin' Boost (Bronze)	Drive over 100 boost pads
Level of Merit (Silver)	Complete all the career challenges
Mechanic (Bronze)	Create a kart in Kart Studio
ModNation Legend (Platinum)	Earn all the ModNation Racers: Road Trip trophies to unlock this platinum trophy
ModNation Superstar (Gold)	Achieve level rank 28

Offering Opinions (Bronze)	Rate 10 tracks, 10 Mods, and 10 karts
Pacifist (Bronze)	Win an action race in Career without firing any weapons
Pioneer Racer (Bronze)	Post the first Time Trial time on a published track
Post Cards for Everyone (Bronze)	Create a Post Card
Remixer (Bronze)	Remix a Mod, a kart, and a track
Say Cheese! (Bronze)	Use photo mode in a race or studio
Sculptor (Bronze)	Create a track in Track Studio
Sharing Karts (Bronze)	Publish a kart and have at least 10 people download it
Sharing Mods (Bronze)	Publish a Mod and have at least 10 people download it
Sharing Splines (Bronze)	Publish a track and have at least 10 people download it
Shields Up! (Bronze)	Successfully defend yourself with your shield 20 times
Shopping Spree (Bronze)	Enter the Shop
Slow and Steady (Bronze)	Win an action race in Career without using any boost or boost pads of any type
Star Creator (Gold)	Earn at least 50,000 Create XP
Startline Booster (Bronze)	Successfully boost off the line 20 times
Taster Session (Bronze)	Try all the game modes in Single Player Race
The Drifter (Bronze)	Drift 1,000 times in total
Third Eye (Bronze)	Hit 5 opponents with mines in a Career Race
Time Stamp (Bronze)	Post your time while in a time trial
Top of the Ladder (Silver)	Place first on a time trial leaderboard
Tour 1 Winner (Bronze)	Get 1st place overall in Tour 1
Tour 2 Winner (Bronze)	Get 1st place overall in Tour 2
Tour 3 Winner (Bronze)	Get 1st place overall in Tour 3
Tour 4 Winner (Bronze)	Get 1st place overall in Tour 4
Tour 5 Winner (Silver)	Get 1st place overall in Tour 5
Trigger Happy (Bronze)	Use all the weapons in the game

MONSTER TALE   (DS)

CODES

Enter the code at the title screen

UNLOCKABLE	HOW TO UNLOCK
New color palette (Yellow Clothes) for Ellie and 5% off on item	Press ⬆, ⬆, ⬆, ⬆, ⬆, ⬆, ⬆, ⬆, •SELECT

MORTAL KOMBAT   (PLAYSTATION 3)

CODE

UNLOCKABLE	HOW TO UNLOCK
Original / Classic Stage Music	During Player Select, go to the Arena Select Menu, and hit the Start button on the arena music you want to select.

CODE

At the versus screen before the match starts, Player 1 enters the first 3 digits while Player 2 enters the last 3.

EFFECT	CODE
Armless Kombat	P1: 9-1-1 P2: 9-1-1
Blocking Disabled	P1: 0-2-0 P2: 0-2-0

CODES & CHEATS

Breakers Disabled	P1: 0-9-0 P2: 0-9-0
Dark Kombat	P1: 0-2-2 P2: 0-2-2
Double Dash	P1: 3-9-1 P2: 1-9-3
Dream Kombat	P1: 2-2-2 P2: 5-5-5
Enhance Moves Disabled	P1: 0-5-1 P2: 1-5-0
Explosive Kombat	P1: 2-2-7 P2: 2-2-7
Foreground Objects Disabled	P1: 0-0-1 P2: 0-0-1
Headless Kombat	P1: 8-0-8 P2: 8-0-8
Health Recovery	P1: 0-1-2 P2: 0-1-2
Hyper Fighting	P1: 0-9-1 P2: 0-9-1
Invisible Kombat	P1: 7-7-0 P2: 7-7-0
Jumping Disabled	P1: 8-3-1 P2: 8-3-1
Kombos Disabled	P1: 9-3-1 P2: 9-3-1
No Blood	P1: 9-0-0 P2: 9-0-0
Player 2 Half Health	P1: 0-0-0 P2: 1-1-0
Power Bars Disabled	P1: 4-0-4 P2: 4-0-4
Psycho Kombat	P1: 7-0-7 P2: 7-0-7
Quick Uppercut Recovery	P1: 3-0-3 P2: 3-0-3
Rainbow Kombat	P1: 2-3-4 P2: 2-3-4
Sans Power	P1: 0-4-4 P2: 4-4-0
Silent Kombat	P1: 3-0-0 P2: 3-0-0
Specials Disabled	P1: 7-3-1 P2: 7-3-1
Super Recovery	P1: 1-2-3 P2: 1-2-3
Throwing Disabled	P1: 1-0-0 P2: 1-0-0
Throwing Encouraged	P1: 0-1-0 P2: 0-1-0
Tournament Mode	P1: 1-1-1 P2: 1-1-1
Unlimited Super Meter	P1: 4-6-6 P2: 4-6-6
Vampire Kombat	P1: 4-2-4 P2: 4-2-4
X-Rays Disabled	P1: 2-4-2 P2: 2-4-2
Zombie Kombat	P1: 6-6-6 P2: 6-6-6

UNLOCKABLE

These secret battles can only be unlocked in Arcade Mode.

UNLOCKABLE	HOW TO UNLOCK
Secret "Jade" Battle	Get a double flawless victory and perform a fatality on Shang Tsung when battling against him.
Secret "Noob Saibot" Battle	When you see Noob in "The Temple" stage's background win that battle without using the R2 (Block) button.
Secret "Reptile" Battle	On "The Pit 2 (Night)" stage wait until a shadowy figure flies across the moon, then get a double flawless victory and perform a stage fatality.
Secret "Smoke" Battle	On "The Living Forest" stage wait until Smoke appears behind one of the trees. On that moment press Down + Select repeatedly.

UNLOCKABLE

UNLOCKABLE	HOW TO UNLOCK
Mileena's Fleshpit Costume (Third costume)	Complete the last level (Level 300) of the Challenge Tower.
Play as Cyber Sub-Zero	Complete Chapter 13 in Story Mode. From then on he will be selectable on the Character Selection screen.
Play as Quan Chi	Complete all chapters in Story Mode. From then on he will be selectable on the Character Selection screen.

SECRET

Highlight the character you want to play as and press "START." Press "×" to get the original color, press "START" again to get the alternate color

MORTAL KOMBAT (PLAYSTATION VITA)

TROPHY

UNLOCKABLE	HOW TO UNLOCK
A For Effort (Bronze)	Complete Tutorial Mode
Arcade Champion (Silver)	Complete Arcade Ladder with All Fighters
Back In Time... (Silver)	Complete Story Mode 100%
Balancing Act (Bronze)	Complete all Test Your Balance mini-game challenges
Best...Alternate...Ever! (Bronze)	Unlock Mileena's 3rd Alternate Costume
Block This! (Bronze)	Perform a 10-hit combo with any fighter
Brotherhood of Shadow (Bronze)	Discover and fight Hidden Kombatant 4 in Arcade Ladder
Complet-ality (Bronze)	Perform 1 of each type of "-ality"
Cyber Challenger (Bronze)	Complete 100 Versus Matches
Dim Mak! (Bronze)	Complete all Test Your Strike mini-game challenges
Don't Jump! (Bronze)	Win A Ranked Online Match without jumping
e-X-cellent! (Bronze)	Successfully land every playable fighter's X-Ray
Fatality! (Bronze)	Perform a Fatality!
Finish Him? (Bronze)	Perform any fighter's hidden finishing move
Finish What You Start! (Bronze)	Perform a Fatality with all playable fighters
Halfway There! (Bronze)	Complete Story Mode 50%
Hide and Seek (Bronze)	Discover and fight Hidden Kombatant 2 in Arcade Ladder
Humiliation (Bronze)	Get a Flawless Victory in a Versus Match
I "Might" Be the Strongest (Bronze)	Complete all Test Your Might mini-game challenges
Ladder Master (Bronze)	Complete Arcade Ladder on max difficulty without using a continue
License to Kill (Bronze)	Complete Fatality Trainer
Luck Be A Lady (Bronze)	Get all MK Dragons in Test Your Luck
My Kung Fu Is Strong (Silver)	Gain Mastery of 1 Fighter
My Kung Fu Is Stronger (Gold)	Gain Mastery of All Fighters
Outstanding! (Silver)	Win 10 Ranked Online Matches in a row
Pit Master (Bronze)	Discover and fight Hidden Kombatant 3 in Arcade Ladder
Platinum Trophy (Platinum)	You've unlocked all Trophies!
Robots Rule! (Bronze)	Win Arcade Tag Ladder with robot Sektor and Cyrax
Slice of Life (Bronze)	Swipe your way through a set of all-new mini-game challenges
Tag, You're It! (Bronze)	Perform and land a Tag Combo
The Fall Guy! (Bronze)	Discover all the deathtraps in Test Your Balance
The Grappler (Bronze)	Perform every fighter's forward and backwards throws
The Krypt Keeper (Silver)	Unlock 100% of the Krypt

There Will Be Blood! (Bronze)	Spill 10000 pints of blood
These Aren't My Glasses! (Bronze)	Complete all Test Your Sight mini-game challenges
Three's Company (Silver)	Unlock Kenshi, Skarlet, and Rain Alternate Costumes
Throws Are For Champs (Bronze)	Perform 8 throws in an Online Ranked Match
Touch and Go (Bronze)	Perform 1 "-ality" using the PlayStation®Vita system touchscree
Tough Guy! (Bronze)	Win a Versus Match
Tower Apprentice (Bronze)	Complete 25 Tower missions
Tower Champion (Silver)	Complete 100 bonus tower missions
Tower God (Gold)	Complete all 150 bonus tower missions
Tower Master (Silver)	Complete all Tower missions
Tower Recruit (Bronze)	Complete 50 bonus tower missions
Ultimate Humiliation (Silver)	Perform every fighter's hidden finishing move
Undertaker (Bronze)	Unlock 50% of the Krypt
Wavenet... (Silver)	Win 100 total Versus Matches
What Does This Button Do?? (Bronze)	Complete Arcade Ladder without blocking (allowed to continue)
Where's The Arcade? (Bronze)	Complete Arcade Ladder with Any Fighter
You Found Me! (Bronze)	Discover and fight Hidden Kombatant 1 in Arcade Ladder
You've Got Style! (Bronze)	Unlock all Alternate Costumes

MORTAL KOMBAT (XBOX 360)

CODE

After selecting a character at the Character select screen in Ladder Mode, hold down 🔲 while selecting difficulty. The game will default to include Goro, rather than Kintaro in the boss fight.

UNLOCKABLE	HOW TO UNLOCK
Always fight Goro in Ladder Mode	Hold down 🔲 when selecting difficulty mode

UNLOCKABLE

These secret battles can only be unlocked in Arcade Mode.

UNLOCKABLE	HOW TO UNLOCK
Secret "Jade" Battle	Get a double flawless victory and perform a fatality on Shang Tsung when battling against him.
Secret "Noob Saibot" Battle	When you see Noob in "The Temple" stage's background win that battle without using the R2 (Block) button.
Secret "Reptile" Battle	On "The Pit 2 (Night)" stage wait until a shadowy figure flies across the moon, then get a double flawless victory and perform a stage fatality.
Secret "Smoke" Battle	On "The Living Forest" stage wait until Smoke appears behind one of the trees. On that moment press 🔲 + Select repeatedly.

UNLOCKABLE

UNLOCKABLE	HOW TO UNLOCK
Mileena's Fleshpit Costume (Third costume)	Complete the last level (Level 300) of the Challenge Tower.
Play as Cyber Sub-Zero	Complete Chapter 13 in Story Mode. From then on he will be selectable on the Character Selection screen.

Play as Quan Chi	Complete all chapters in Story Mode. From then on he will be selectable on the Character Selection screen.

CODE

At the versus screen before the match starts, Player 1 enters the first 3 digits while Player 2 enters the last 3.

UNLOCKABLE	HOW TO UNLOCK
Armless Kombat	P1: 9-1-1 P2: 9-1-1
Blocking Disabled	P1: 0-2-0 P2: 0-2-0
Breakers Disabled	P1: 0-9-0 P2: 0-9-0
Dark Kombat	P1: 0-2-2 P2: 0-2-2
Double Dash	P1: 3-9-1 P2: 1-9-3
Dream Kombat	P1: 2-2-2 P2: 5-5-5
Enhance Moves Disabled	P1: 0-5-1 P2: 1-5-0
Explosive Kombat	P1: 2-2-7 P2: 2-2-7
Foreground Objects Disabled	P1: 0-0-1 P2: 0-0-1
Headless Kombat	P1: 8-0-8 P2: 8-0-8
Health Recovery	P1: 0-1-2 P2: 0-1-2
Hyper Fighting	P1: 0-9-1 P2: 0-9-1
Invisible Kombat	P1: 7-7-0 P2: 7-7-0
Jumping Disabled	P1: 8-3-1 P2: 8-3-1
Klassik Music	P1: 1-0-1 P2: 1-0-1
Kombos Disabled	P1: 9-3-1 P2: 9-3-1
No Blood	P1: 9-0-0 P2: 9-0-0
Power Bars Disabled	P1: 4-0-4 P2: 4-0-4
Psycho Kombat	P1: 7-0-7 P2: 7-0-7
Quick Uppercut Recovery	P1: 3-0-3 P2: 3-0-3
Rainbow Kombat	P1: 2-3-4 P2: 2-3-4
Sans Power	P1: 0-4-4 P2: 4-4-0
Silent Kombat	P1: 3-0-0 P2: 3-0-0
Specials Disabled	P1: 7-3-1 P2: 7-3-1
Super Recovery	P1: 1-2-3 P2: 1-2-3
Throwing Disabled	P1: 1-0-0 P2: 1-0-0
Throwing Encouraged	P1: 0-1-0 P2: 0-1-0
Tournament Mode	P1: 1-1-1 P2: 1-1-1
Unlimited Super Meter	P1: 4-6-6 P2: 4-6-6
Vampire Kombat	P1: 4-2-4 P2: 4-2-4
X-Rays Disabled	P1: 2-4-2 P2: 2-4-2
Zombie Kombat	P1: 6-6-6 P2: 6-6-6

SECRET

When selecting a stage in Versus Mode, press " Q START " and you hear a laugh. Now the stage soundtrack will be replaced with a song from one of the previous Mortal Kombat titles.

SECRET

To select an alternate color for your character, go to the character select screen, then select your character by pressing Q START , then press Q START again on either costume 1 or 2 to get the corresponding alternative color.

MORTAL KOMBAT VS. DC UNIVERSE (XBOX 360)

UNLOCKABLES

Both of these characters can be unlocked by beating story mode with a certain side. Hold down ⒭Ⓑ on character select.

UNLOCKABLE	HOW TO UNLOCK
Darkseid	Beat the DC side of story mode.
Shao Kahn	Beat the MK side of story mode.

MORTAL KOMBAT VS. DC UNIVERSE (PLAYSTATION 3)

UNLOCKABLES

Both of these characters can be unlocked by beating story mode with a certain side. To play as these characters, hold down ⒭⒈ on character select.

UNLOCKABLE	HOW TO UNLOCK
Darkseid	Beat the DC side of story mode.
Shao Kahn	Beat the MK side of story mode.

MOTOGP 10/11 (XBOX 360)

ACHIEVEMENTS

UNLOCKABLE	HOW TO UNLOCK
125cc Elite (30)	Win a 125cc class season on Insane difficulty. Not unlockable by Co-riders.
125cc World Champion (15)	Win a 125cc class season. Not unlockable by Co-riders.
1st Servic (30)	Ride over 1000 miles. Not unlockable by Co-riders.
A Class (15)	Obtain an 'A' rating in all sessions of a race weekend in Career Mode. Not unlockable by Co-riders.
Addicted (15)	Earn first place 20 times in any mode. Not unlockable in Splitscreen Mode or by Co-riders.
Admired (15)	Obtain a reputation level of 15 in Career Mode. Not unlockable by Co-riders.
Bedded In (15)	Ride over 400 miles. Not unlockable by Co-riders.
Been Practicing (30)	Win any race on Insane difficulty. Not unlockable in Splitscreen Mode or by Co-riders.
Big Business (15)	Hire a full complement of staff in Career Mode. Not unlockable by Co-riders.
Collected (15)	Obtain a full complement of sponsors. Not unlockable by Co-riders.
Consistency (15)	Earn first place 10 times in any mode. Not unlockable in Splitscreen Mode or by Co-riders.
Dedicated (15)	Use your own Career Mode motorbike and rider in a multiplayer race.
DING (15)	Obtain a reputation level of 1 in Career Mode. Not unlockable by Co-riders.
Dinner with Friends (15)	Win a race against a full grid of human riders.
DIY (15)	Customise every aspect of your bike and rider. Not applicable to co-riders.
Fixed Overheads (15)	Spend over 100,000 on staff wages in one pay day. Not unlockable by Co-riders.
Hardcore (90)	Complete a full Challenge Mode season without using a continue.
Hoarder (30)	Amount 100,000 in savings in Career Mode. Not unlockable by Co-riders.
Hometown Champion (15)	Win on your home circuit in Career Mode. Not unlockable by Co-riders.
Leader of the Pack (15)	Qualify for pole position. Not unlockable by Co-riders.

Methodical (15)	Get every type of time bonus within the same lap on Challenge Mode.
Moto2 Elite (30)	Win a Moto2 class season on Insane difficulty. Not unlockable by Co-riders.
New Kid on the Block (15)	Obtain a reputation level of 5 in Career Mode. Not unlockable by Co-riders.
Oil Change (15)	Ride over 200 miles. Not unlockable by Co-riders.
Online Dominator (15)	Win 21 races online.
Piggy Bank Full (15)	Amount 50,000 in savings in Career Mode. Not unlockable by Co-riders.
Professional (15)	Obtain a reputation level of 20 in Career Mode. Not unlockable by Co-riders.
Ride your way (10)	Host a multiplayer race.
Running on economy (15)	Spend a total of 10 minutes slipstreaming in Challenge Mode.
Savvy (25)	Spend over 100,000 on upgrades. Not unlockable by Co-riders.
Self Sufficient (15)	Obtain a reputation level of 10 in Career Mode. Not unlockable by Co-riders.
Show off (15)	Do a wheelie lasting at least 500 feet on a motorbike. Not unlockable by Co-riders.
Spick and Span (15)	Win with no penalties, all clean sections, no crashes, no collisions. Not unlockable by Co-riders.
Stabilisers are off (15)	Ride over 100 miles. Not unlockable by Co-riders.
Staff Liability (30)	Spend over 200,000 on staff wages in one pay day. Not unlockable by Co-riders.
Star (30)	Obtain a reputation level of 25 in Career Mode. Not unlockable by Co-riders.
Superstar (90)	Obtain a reputation level of 30 in Career Mode. Not unlockable by Co-riders.
The G.O.A.T. (30)	Win a MotoGP class season on Insane difficulty. Not unlockable by Co-riders.
Time Hoarder (15)	Finish a race with more time than you started with without using any continues in Challenge Mode.
Untouchable (30)	Earn first place 30 times in any mode. Not unlockable in Splitscreen Mode or by Co-riders.
Victory (5)	Your first win. Not unlockable by Co-riders.
Voltaire (15)	Successfully perform every type of dynamic objective. Not unlockable by Co-riders.
World Champion (90)	Win a MotoGP class season. Not unlockable by Co-riders.

MOTORSTORM (PLAYSTATION 3)

Enter this code at the main menu.

UNLOCKABLE	CODE
Unlock Everything	Hold L1, L2, R1, R2, R2 pushed up, L2 pushed down

Enter this code while the game is paused.

UNLOCKABLE	CODE
Big Head on ATVs and Bikes	Hold L1, L2, R1, R2, R2 pushed right, L1 pushed left

MVP BASEBALL (PSP)

Under the "My MVP" menu, create a player named "Dan Carter." Once you do this, there will be a message indicating that the code was successful.

MX VS. ATV REFLE (XBOX 360)

CODES

Enter codes in Cheat Code screen.

EFFECT	CODE
Unlocks KTM's and Justin Brayton	READYTORACE
Unlocks all AI guys	allai
Unlocks all ATVs	couches
Unlocks all boots	kicks
Unlocks all gear	gearedup
Unlocks all goggles	windows
Unlocks all helmets	skullcap
Unlocks all locations	whereto

MX VS. ATV UNLEASHED (PLAYSTATION 2)

Enter in the Cheats menu.

UNLOCKABLE	CODE
50cc Bikes	Minimoto
Unlock all freestyle tracks	Huckit
Unlock Everything	Toolazy

MX VS. ATV UNTAMED (XBOX 360), (PLAYSTATION 3), (PLAYSTATION 2)

UNLOCKABLES

Type in the following codes in the Cheats menu to unlock the gear.

UNLOCKABLE	HOW TO UNLOCK
All Handlebars	NOHANDS
FOX Riding Gear	CRAZYLIKEA

MX VS. ATV UNTAMED (WII)

CODES

Go to the Options screen and go to the Cheat Code input screen.

EFFECT	CODE
1 Million Store Points	MANYZEROS
50cc Bike Class	LITTLEGUY
All Bikes	ONRAILS
All Challenges	MORESTUFF
All Gear	WELLDRESSED
All Machines	MCREWHEELS
All Riders	WHOSTHAT
Freestyle Tracks	FREETICKET
Paralyzer Monster Truck	PWNAGE
Unlock Everything	YOUGOTIT

MYSIMS (WII)

CODES

While running around town, pause the game, then push the following buttons on the Wiimote to get to the hidden password system: ⓐ,①,⬇,⬆,⬇,⬆,⬇,⬆,⬇. A keyboard appears to allow you to type in the following case-sensitive codes.

UNLOCKABLE	HOW TO UNLOCK
Bunk Bed (Furniture)	F3nevr0
Camouflage Pants	N10ng5g
Diamond Vest (Outfit)	Tglg0ca
Genie Outfit	Gvsb3k1

Hourglass Couch	Ghtymba
Kimono Dress (Outfit)	I3hkdvs
Modern Couch	T7srhca
Racecar Bed (Furniture)	Ahvmrva
Rickshaw Bed	Itha7da
White Jacket	R705aan

TOOLS

Once you reach a certain level, you get a message saying you've earned the following new tools.

UNLOCKABLE	HOW TO UNLOCK
Blow Torch	Have your town reach four stars.
Crowbar	Have your town reach one star.
Pickaxe	Have your town reach three stars.
Saw	Have your town reach two stars.
Town Monument Blueprint	Have a five-star town.

UBER-SIMS

After getting your interest level to 100% in any of the six categories, you get a message about a special guest waiting for you in the hotel. Check the next day and find the following Sims.

UNLOCKABLE	HOW TO UNLOCK
Amazing Daryl	100% Fun Town
Chancellor Ikara	100% Tasty Town
Hopper	100% Cute Town
Mel	100% Spooky Town
Samurai Bob	100% Studious Town
Star	100% Geeky Town

MYSIMS KINGDOM (WII)

CODES

From the Pause menu enter the following codes to get the desired effect.

EFFECT	CODE
Detective outfit	⬆⬇⬆⬇⬆⬇⬆
Tattoo Vest outfit	©,Ⓩ,©,Ⓩ,Ⓑ,Ⓐ,Ⓑ,Ⓐ
Swordsman outfit	⬆⬆⬆⬆⬆⬆⬆⬆

MYSIMS PARTY (WII)

UNLOCKABLES

UNLOCKABLE	HOW TO UNLOCK
New inhabitants	Get at least 60 points in the minigame they're hosting.
New playable characters	Get at least 80 points in the minigame they're hosting.

MYSIMS RACING (WII)

CODES

From the main menu go to Extras, then to Cheats. After entering the code a message will appear telling you that a new car part has been unlocked. Go to "Story Mode" and enter the garage to equip your new car part.

EFFECT	CODE
Unlocks Butterflies (Wheels)	z74hsv
Unlocks Holstein (Hood Ornament)	36mj5v
Unlocks Mega Spoiler (Rear Accessory)	k4c2sn

N+ (DS)

CODES
Hold Ⓛ and Ⓡ and insert the following code at the Unlockables menu.

EFFECT	CODE
Unlocks Atari Bonus Levels	Ⓐ,Ⓑ,Ⓐ,Ⓑ,Ⓐ,Ⓐ,Ⓑ

N+ (PSP)

CODES
Hold Ⓛ and Ⓡ and insert the following code at the Unlockables menu.

EFFECT	CODE
Unlocks Atari Bonus Levels	✕,●,✕,●,✕,✕,●

NAMCO MUSEUM ESSENTIALS (PLAYSTATION 3)

DIG DUG UNLOCKABLES
UNLOCKABLE	HOW TO UNLOCK
Carrot	Grab the Carrot.
Complete Dig	Successfully dig the whole entire level.
Cucumber	Grab the Cucumber.
Eggplant	Grab the Eggplant.
Green Pepper	Grab the Green Pepper.
Mushroom	Grab the Mushroom.
No Dig	Complete the level without digging.
Pineapple	Grab the Pineapple.
Quad Squash	Successfully squash four enemies with one rock.
Tomato	Grab the Tomato.
Turnip	Grab the Turnip.
Watermelon	Grab the Watermelon.

DRAGON SPIRIT UNLOCKABLES
UNLOCKABLE	HOW TO UNLOCK
Earthquake	Collect the Earthquake power-up.
Endurance	Successfully survive against a boss under a timed limit without killing him.
Fire Breath	Collect the Fire Breath power-up.
Homing Fire	Collect the Homing Fire power-up.
Incubation	Collect the Incubation power-up.
Maximum	Successfully get three heads and six fire power orbs without getting hit.
Over The Jungle	Get to the Jungle Area.
Power Down	Collect the Power Down power-up.
Power Wing	Collect the Power Wing power-up.
Small Dragon	Collect the Small Dragon power-up.
Small N Wide	Collect the Small Dragon, followed by Wide Fire without getting hit.
Wide Fire	Collect the Wide Fire power-up.

GALAGA UNLOCKABLES

UNLOCKABLE	HOW TO UNLOCK
Blue Spaceship	Destroy the Blue Spaceship.
Boss Alien	Destroy the Boss Alien.
Destroy Fighter	Successfully destroy your captured ship.
Dragonfly	Destroy the Dragonfly.
Dual Fighter	Successfully destroy the enemy holding your ship captive.
Maple	Destroy the Maple.
Perfect	Win a perfect game in the Challenging Stage.
Scorpion	Destroy the Scorpion.
Stage 10	Reach Stage 10.
Stage 20	Reach Stage 20.
Stage 30	Reach Stage 30.
Stingray	Destroy the Stingray.

NARUTO: CLASH OF NINJA REVOLUTION (WII)

CHARACTERS

To unlock the following characters, beat the Mission mode at least once, then do the following:

UNLOCKABLE	HOW TO UNLOCK
Gaara	Beat Single Player mode with Naruto and Shikamaru.
Guy	Clear Mission 13.5.
Hinata Hyuuga	Beat Single Player mode with Neji.
Ino Yamanaka	Beat Single Player mode with Sakura.
Itachi Uchiha	Beat Mission "Rematch Itachi vs. Saskue," after unlocking all other starting characters plus Guy and Kankuro.
Kankuro	Clear Mission mode once.
Kisame	Beat Single Player mode with Naruto, Sasuke, Kakashi, Guy, and Jiraiya.
Orochimaru	Beat Single Player mode with Naruto, Sasuke, Kakashi, and Jiraiya.
Shino Aburame	Beat Arcade mode with Kankuro.
Temari	Beat Shikamaru's Single Player mode.
Tenten	Clear Mission 20.
Tsunade	Beat Single Player mode with Jiraiya.

NARUTO SHIPPUDEN: SHINOBI RUMBLE (DS)

UNLOCKABLE

After fulfilling the requirements to unlock a character, their mark will appear in the Kuchiyose menu. Select their mark and copy it onto the grid on the bottom screen using the stylus, taking care to use the proper stroke order. Correctly drawing a character's mark will unlock them, even if their mark hasn't been acquired.

UNLOCKABLE	HOW TO UNLOCK
Deidara	Complete Arcade Mode with Itachi
Fukusaku & Shima	Complete Arcade Mode with all characters
Itachi	Complete Story Mode
Jiraiya	Complete Arcade Mode with Naruto
Jugo	Complete Arcade Mode with Karin
Karin	Complete Arcade Mode with Suigetsu
Konan	Complete Arcade Mode with Jiraiya
Orochimaru	Complete Arcade Mode with Jugo

| Pain | Complete Arcade Mode with Konan |
| Suigetsu | Complete Arcade Mode with Sasuke |

UNLOCKABLE

You can unlock additional jutsus for each character by playing Mission Mode. As you complete missions, depending on the mission's difficulty, you will gain either 1, 2, or 3 marks on that character's Bingo Sheet. When a row, column, or diagnol is complete, a new ability will be unlocked for that character, until the entire Bingo Sheet has been completed. A character's ability set can be customized after selecting the character in Battle, Arcade, and Mission Modes.

NARUTO SHIPPUDEN: ULTIMATE NINJA IMPACT (PSP)

UNLOCKABLE

UNLOCKABLE	HOW TO UNLOCK
Sakura Hauno	Beat "A Test of Strength" in Ultimate Road

NARUTO SHIPPUDEN: ULTIMATE NINJA STORM GENERATIONS (PLAYSTATION 3)

TROPHY

UNLOCKABLE	HOW TO UNLOCK
10 Down (Silver)	You've defeated 10 opponents in Ultimate Survival.
Advanced Survivor! (Bronze)	You've completed all of Advanced Survival.
Akatsuki Tournament Champ! (Bronze)	You've completed the Akatsuki Tournament.
Beginner Survivor! (Bronze)	You've completed all of Beginner Survival.
Boy's Life Tournament Champ! (Bronze)	You've completed the Boy's Life Tournament.
First Ninja Tool Edit! (Bronze)	You've edited a ninja tool set for the first time.
First S Rank! (Bronze)	You've earned your first S Rank in a battle.
First Shopping! (Bronze)	You've done your first shopping.
Five Kage Tournament Champ! (Bronze)	You've completed the Five Kage Tournament.
I'm the greatest ninja! (Platinum)	You've acquired all trophies.
Image Master (Bronze)	Images collected: 80%
Intermediate Survivor! (Bronze)	You've completed all of Intermediate Survival.
Introductory Stage Survivor! (Bronze)	You've completed all of Introductory Survival.
Leaf Chunin Tournament Champ! (Bronze)	You've completed the Leaf Chunin Tournament.
Leaf Genin Tournament Champ! (Bronze)	You've completed all Leaf Genin Tournament battles.
Leaf Higher-Up Tournament Champ! (Bronze)	You've completed the Leaf Higher-Up Tournament.
New Team Seven Tournament Champ! (Bronze)	You've completed the New Team Seven Tournament.
Ninja Info Card Collector (Bronze)	Ninja Info Card images collected: 50%
Ninja Tool Master (Bronze)	Ninja Tools collected: 80%
Peerless Ninja Tournament Champ! (Bronze)	You've completed the Peerless Ninja Tournament.

Sand Genin Tournament Champ! (Bronze)	You've completed the Sand Genin Tournament.
Shippuden Tournament Champ! (Bronze)	You've completed the Shippuden Tournament.
Substitution Jutsu Master (Bronze)	Substitution Jutsu collected: 80%
Tale of Naruto Uzumaki complete (Bronze)	Completed Tale of Naruto Uzumaki.
Tale of Sasuke Uchiha complete (Bronze)	Completed Tale of Sasuke Uchiha.
Tale of Young Naruto complete (Bronze)	Completed Tale of Young Naruto.
Team Seven Tournament Champ! (Bronze)	You've completed the Team Seven Tournament.
Ultimate Jutsu Movie Master (Bronze)	Ultimate Jutsu scenes collected: 80%
Ultimate Ninja Tournament Champ! (Bronze)	You've completed the Ultimate Ninja Tournament.
Wealthy Ninja (Silver)	You've earned a total of 1,000,000 Ryo.

NARUTO SHIPPUDEN: ULTIMATE NINJA STORM GENERATIONS (XBOX 360)

ACHIEVEMENT

UNLOCKABLE	HOW TO UNLOCK
10 Down (30)	You've defeated 10 opponents in Ultimate Survival.
Advanced Survivor! (15)	You've completed all of Advanced Survival.
Akatsuki Tournament Champ! (15)	You've completed the Akatsuki Tournament.
Alias Master (100)	Titles collected: 80%
Beginner Survivor! (15)	You've completed all of Beginner Survival.
Boy's Life Tournament Champ! (15)	You've completed the Boy's Life Tournament.
Card Collection Master (100)	Ninja Info Card images collected: 80%
First Ninja Tool Edit! (5)	You've edited a ninja tool set for the first time.
First S Rank! (5)	You've earned your first S Rank in a battle.
First Shopping! (5)	You've done your first shopping.
Five Kage Summit (5)	All Kage at the Five Kage Summit can now be used.
Five Kage Tournament Champ! (15)	You've completed the Five Kage Tournament.
Game Master! (30)	You've played for a total of over 30 hours.
Gimme a hand! (5)	You can now use all support characters.
I'm the greatest ninja! (0)	You've unlocked all achievements.
Image Master (15)	Images collected: 80%
Intermediate Survivor! (15)	You've completed all of Intermediate Survival.
Introductory Stage Survivor! (15)	You've completed all of Introductory Survival.
Leaf Chunin Tournament Champ! (15)	You've completed the Leaf Chunin Tournament.
Leaf Genin Tournament Champ! (15)	You've completed all Leaf Genin Tournament battles.

CODES & CHEATS

Leaf Higher-Up Tournament Champ! (15)	You've completed the Leaf Higher-Up Tournament.
Master Survivor! (30)	You've completed all of Survival Mode.
New Team Seven Tournament Champ! (15)	You've completed the New Team Seven Tournament.
Ninja Info Card Collector (5)	Ninja Info Card images collected: 50%
Ninja Lover! (50)	You've used all leader characters.
Ninja Tool Master (15)	Ninja Tools collected: 80%
Past Hokages (5)	You can now use all past Hokages.
Peerless Ninja Tournament Champ! (15)	You've completed the Peerless Ninja Tournament.
Sand Genin Tournament Champ! (15)	You've completed the Sand Genin Tournament.
Shippuden (15)	You can use all the characters from Shippuden.
Shippuden Tournament Champ! (15)	You've completed the Shippuden Tournament.
Substitution Jutsu Master (15)	Substitution Jutsu collected: 80%
Tale of Gaara complete (15)	Completed Tale of Gaara.
Tale of Itachi Uchiha complete (15)	Completed Tale of Itachi Uchiha.
Tale of Jiraiya complete (15)	Completed Tale of Jiraiya.
Tale of Kakashi Hatake complete (15)	Completed Tale of Kakashi Hatake.
Tale of Killer Bee complete (15)	Completed Tale of Killer Bee.
Tale of Madara Uchiha complete (15)	Completed Tale of Madara Uchiha.
Tale of Minato Namikaze complete (15)	Completed Tale of Minato Namikaze.
Tale of Naruto Uzumaki complete (15)	Completed Tale of Naruto Uzumaki.
Tale of Sasuke Uchiha complete (15)	Completed Tale of Sasuke Uchiha.
Tale of Young Naruto complete (15)	Completed Tale of Young Naruto.
Tale of Zabuza and Haku complete (15)	Completed Tale of Zabuza Momochi and Haku.
Team Seven Tournament Champ! (15)	You've completed the Team Seven Tournament.
Tournament Champ! (30)	You've completed all Challenge Tournaments.
Ultimate Jutsu Movie Master (15)	Ultimate Jutsu scenes collected: 80%
Ultimate Ninja Gathering (50)	You can now use all characters.
Ultimate Ninja Tournament Champ! (15)	You've completed the Ultimate Ninja Tournament.
Wealthy Ninja (50)	You've earned a total of 1,000,000 Ryo.
Younger Version (15)	You can use all the characters of the Young Version.

NASCAR 09 (XBOX 360)

CODES

EFFECT	CODE
Unlocks All Fantasy Drivers	CHECKERED FLAG
Unlocks Walmart Track (Chicago Pier) and the Walmart Car	Walmart Everyday

NASCAR KART RACING (WII)

CODES

EFFECT	CODE
Joey Logano as a driver	426378

NAUGHTY BEAR (XBOX 360)

UNLOCKABLES

UNLOCKABLE	HOW TO UNLOCK
Cop Naughty (hat)	Get Gold on Episode 1.
Epic Naughty (hat)	Get Gold on all Top Hat Challenges.
Naughticorn	Get a Total Score of 100,000,000.
Naughty the Party Animal (hat)	Complete Chapter 1.

NBA 09: THE INSIDE (PLAYSTATION 3)

UNLOCK NEW JERSEYS

From Main Menu choose Progression, go to Extras, then Jerseys, press left or right to get to nba.com tab and press Square to enter code.

UNLOCKABLE	CODE
Eastern All-Stars 09 Jersey	SHPNV2K699
L.A. Lakers Latin Night Jersey	NMTWCTC84S
Miami Heat Latin Night Jersey	WCTGSA8SPD
Phoenix Suns Latin Night Jersey	LKUTSENFJH
San Antonio Spurs Latin Night Jersey	JFHSY73MYD
Western All-Stars 09 Jersey	K8AV6YMLNF

NBA 2K10 (XBOX 360)

CODES

Go into the Options menu and select the Codes section to enter these codes.

EFFECT	CODE
2K Sports team	2ksports
ABA ball	payrespect
Blazers "Rip City" Jersey	ycprtii
Cavs, Jazz, Magic, Raptors, T'Wolves, Trail Blazers, Warriors Hardwood Classic Jerseys Unlocked	wasshcicsl
Grizzlies, Hawks, Mavericks, and Rockets secondary road jerseys	eydonscar
Unlock the 2K China team	2kchina
Unlock the 2K development team	nba2k
Unlock visual concepts team	vcteam

NBA 2K10 (PLAYSTATION 3)

CODES

Go into the Options menu and select the Codes section to enter these codes.

EFFECT	CODE
2K Sports team	2ksports
ABA ball	payrespect
Blazers "Rip City" Jersey	ycprtii
Cavs, Jazz, Magic, Raptors, T'Wolves, Trail Blazers, Warriors Hardwood Classic Jerseys Unlocked	wasshcicsl
Grizzlies, Hawks, Mavericks, and Rockets secondary road jerseys	eydonscar
Unlock the 2K China team	2kchina
Unlock the 2K development team	nba2k
Unlock visual concepts team	vcteam

NBA 2K10 (WII)

CODES

Go into the Options menu and select the Codes section to enter these codes.

EFFECT	CODE
2K Sports team	2ksports
ABA ball	payrespect
Blazers "Rip City" Jersey	ycprtii
Cavs, Jazz, Magic, Raptors, T'Wolves, Trail Blazers, Warriors Hardwood Classic Jerseys Unlocked	wasshcicsl
Grizzlies, Hawks, Mavericks, and Rockets secondary road jerseys	eydonscar
Unlock the 2K China team	2kchina
Unlock the 2K development team	nba2k
Unlock visual concepts team	vcteam

NBA 2K11 (PSP)

CODES

Accessed in the cheat menu under "features."

EFFECT	CODE
2K Development Team	nba2k
2K Sports China Team	2kchina
2K Sports team	2ksports
ABA Ball	payrespect
Bobcats Nascar Racing Uniform	agsntrccai
Cavs Cavfanatic Uniform	aifnaatccv
Hardwood Classics Uniforms (7 teams only)	wasshcicsl
Hornets Mardi Gras Uniform	asrdirmga
Secondary Road Uniforms (Grizzlies, Hawks, Mavs, and Rockets)	eydonscar
St Patrick's Day Uniforms (Bulls, Celtics, Knicks, and Raptors)	riiasgerh
Trail Blazers Rip City Uniform	ycprtii
Visual Concepts Team	vcteam

NBA 2K11 (XBOX 360)

CODES

Accessed in the cheat menu under "features."

EFFECT	CODE
2k Sports team	2Ksports
2k China team	2kchina
ABA Ball	payrespect
MJ: Creating a Legend	icanbe23
NBA2k Development Team	nba2k
Visual Concepts Team	vcteam

NBA 2K11 (PLAYSTATION 3)

CODES

Accessed in the cheat menu under "features."

EFFECT	CODE
2k Sports team	2Ksports
2k China team	2kchina
ABA Ball	payrespect

MJ: Creating a Legend	icanbe23
NBA2k Development Team	nba2k
Visual Concepts Team	vcteam

NBA 2K12 (PLAYSTATION 3)

CODE

UNLOCKABLE	CODE
Unlock 2K Sports team	2ksports
Unlock All Retro Jordan Shoes	23
Unlock NBA 2K Development Team	nba2k
Unlock Visual Concepts Team	vcteam
Unlocks 2K China team	2kchina
Unlocks ABA Basketball (toggle)	payrespect

NBA BALLERS: REBOUND (PSP)

Enter these passwords in the Phrase-ology under Inside Stuff.

UNLOCKABLE	PASSWORD
All Alternate Gear, Players, and Movies	NBA Ballers True Playa
Allen Iverson's Recording Studio	The Answer
Alonzo Mourning Alternate Gear	Zo
Ben Gordon's Yacht	Nice Yacht
Chris Weber's Alternate Gear	24 Seconds
Clyde Drexler's Alternate Gear	Clyde The Glide
Dikembe Mutumbo's Alternate Gear	In The Paint
Emanuel Ginobli Alternate Gear	Manu
Jerry Stackhouse Alternate Gear	Stop Drop And Roll
Julius Irving Alternate Gear	One On One
Kevin McHale Alternate Gear	Holla Back
Lebron James' Alternate Gear	King James
Magic Johnson Alternate Gear	Laker Legends
Nene's Hilarios Alternate Gear	Rags To Riches
Pete Maravich's Alternate Gear	Pistol Pete
Rasheed Wallace Alternate Gear	Bring Down The House
Rick Hamilton's Alternate Gear	Rip
Stephon Marbury's Alternate Gear	Platinum Playa
Steve Francis Alternate Gear	Ankle Breaker
Steve Francis' Alternate Gear	Rising Star
Tim Duncan Alternate Gear	Make It Take It
Wilt Chamberlain's Alternate Gear	Wilt The Stilt

NBA JAM (XBOX 360)

CHARACTERS

UNLOCKABLE	HOW TO UNLOCK
Allen Iverson	Elusive // Perform 10 successful shove counters.
Beastie Boys Team	3 The Hard Way // Defeat the Beastie Boys team in Remix Tour.
Bill Laimbeer, Isiah Thomas	Central Division Represent // Beat the Central Division Legend Team in Classic Campaign.
Brad Daugherty	Double Up // Beat the CPU in a 2V2 game by doubling their score or better.
Bryant Reeves	100 Club // Win 100 games.
Chris Mullin, Tim Hardaway	Pacific Division Represent // Beat the Pacific Division Legend Team in Classic Campaign.
Chuck Person	Fired Up // Get on Fire 4 times in a single game.

Clyde Drexler	NBA Domination // Beat Classic Campaign with a team from each division in the NBA.
Dan Majerle	Century Scorer // Score 100 points in one game.
Danny Manning	Grand Scorer // Score 1,000 points.
Patrick Ewing and John Starks	Beat Atlantic Legend Team in Classic Campaign

NBA LIVE 10 (XBOX 360, PLAYSTATION 3)

ALTERNATE JERSEYS

Go to the Main menu, My NBA Live 10, EA Sports Extras, NBA Codes and then input the code.

CODE	EFFECT
ndnba1rooaesdc0	Unlocks alternate jerseys.

NBA LIVE 10 (XBOX 360)

CODES

Go to Main menu, My NBA Live 10, EA Sports Extras, NBA Codes, then type the code.

EFFECT	CODE
Unlock the Blazers, Cavaliers, Jazz, Magic, Raptors, Timberwolves, and Warriors Hardwood Retro Jerseys.	hdogdrawhoticns

EFFECT	CODE
Unlock the Rockets, Mavericks, Hawks, and Grizzlies alternate jerseys	ndnba1rooaesdc0
Nike Air Max LeBron VII's 1	ere1nbvlaoeknii
Nike Air Max LeBron VII's 2	2ovnaebnkrielei
Nike Air Max LeBron VII's 3	3rioabeneikenvl
Nike Huarache Legion	aoieuchrahelgn
Nike KD 2	kk2tesaosepinrd
Nike Zoom Flip'n	epfnozaeminolki
Nike Zoom Kobe V's 1	ovze1bimenkoko0
Nike Zoom Kobe V's 2	m0kveokoiebozn2
Nike Zoom Kobe V's 3	eev0nbimokk3ozo
Nike Zoom Kobe V's 4	bmo4inozeeo0kvk

NBA LIVE 10 (PLAYSTATION 3)

CODES

Go to Main menu, My NBA Live 10, EA Sports Extras, NBA Codes, then type the code.

EFFECT	CODE
Second set of secondary jerseys for Cleveland, Golden State, Minnesota, Orlando, Philadelphia, Portland, Toronto, Utah, and Washington	hdogdrawhoticns
Bobcats NASCAR Race Day Jersey	ceobdabacarstcy
Mavericks, Rockets, Grizzlies, Hawks secondary road jerseys	Ndnba1rooaesdc0
Hornets Mardi Gras Jersey	nishrag1rosmad0
Jordan CP3 III	iaporcdian3ejis
Jordan Melo M6	emlarmeoo6ajdsn
Jordan Sixty Plus	aondsuilyjrspxt
Nike Air Max LeBron VII	ivl5brieekaeonn
Nike Air Max LeBron VII	n6ieirvalkeeobn
Nike Air Max LeBron VII	ri4boenanekilve

Nike Air Max LeBron VII	3rioabeneikenvl
Nike Air Max LeBron VII	2ovnaebnkrielei
Nike Air Max LeBron VII	ere1nbvlaoeknii
Nike Huarache Legion	aoieuchrahelgn
Nike KD 2	kk2tesaosepinrd
Nike Zoom Flip	epfnozaeminolki
Nike Zoom Kobe V	m0kveokoiebozn2
Nike Zoom Kobe V	eev0nbimokk3ozo
Nike Zoom Kobe V	bmo4inozeeo0kvk
Nike Zoom Kobe V	ovze1bimenkoko0

NBA LIVE 10 (PSP)

CODES

Go to My NBA Live, go to Options, and select Codes. Now type the codes.

EFFECT	CODE
Unlock additional Hardwood Classics Nights for the Cleveland Cavaliers, Golden State Warriors, Minnesota Timberwolves, Orlando Magic, Philadelphia 76e	hdogdrawhoticns

EFFECT	CODE
Unlock the Adidas Equations.	adaodqauieints1
Unlock the Adidas TS Creators with ankle braces.	atciadsstsdhecf
Unlock the Charlotte Bobcats' 2009/2010 Race Day alternate jerseys.	ceobdabacarstcy
Unlock the Jordan CP3 IIIs.	iaporcdian3ejis
Unlock the Jordan Melo M6s.	emlarmeoo6ajdsn
Unlock the Jordan Sixty Pluses.	aondsuilyjrspxt
Unlock the new alternate jerseys for the Atlanta Hawks, Dallas Mavericks, Houston Rockets and Memphis Grizzlies.	ndnba1rooaesdc0
Unlock the New Orleans Hornets' 2009/2010 Mardi Gras alternate jerseys.	nishrag1rosmad0
Unlock the Nike Huarache Legions.	aoieuchrahelgn
Unlock the Nike KD 2s.	kk2tesaosepinrd
Unlock the Nike Zoom Flip'Ns.	epfnozaeminolki
Unlock the TS Supernatural Commanders.	andsicdsmatdnsr
Unlock TS Supernatural Creators.	ard8siscdnatstr

NCAA FOOTBALL 10 (XBOX 360)

UNLOCKABLE

UNLOCKABLE	HOW TO UNLOCK
All 34 Championship Trophies—In 1 Dynasty!	Play Dynasty Mode through to the postseason. When you get to Week 1 of the Bowl Season, play and win each bowl game with any team. These will count on your profile, and when you finish every bowl (including the National Championship), you will get the Trophy!

NCAA FOOTBALL 13 (PLAYSTATION 3)

TROPHY

UNLOCKABLE	HOW TO UNLOCK
And the Winner Is... (Bronze)	Win the Heisman Memorial Trophy® in single team Dynasty Mode, Road to Glory Mode, or Heisman Challenge Mode.
Best Class Ever (Bronze)	Have the #1 ranked recruiting class in a season in single team Dynasty Mode.

Don't Run Home to Mamma (Bronze)	In Dynasty, convince a homesick player to stay at your school instead of transferring.
Dream Job (Silver)	Become the head coach of your alma mater in Dynasty (Coach Contracts on).
Dual Threat Coach (Gold)	Win the BCS Championship & have the #1 recruiting class in a single season as head coach in Dynasty.
Earn My Trust (Silver)	Reach the max coach trust in Road to Glory Mode.
Future Star (Bronze)	Become a 5-star prospect in Road to Glory Mode.
Go Ahead, Ask me Anything (Bronze)	Earn a minimum of 75 recruiting points on a Prospect Choice topic.
Go for Broke (Bronze)	Complete a pass for 50 or more yards (excludes Co-Op).
Heisman Performance (Platinum)	Congratulations for unlocking all trophies in NCAA® Football 13!
High School Champ (Bronze) Game in any state.	Play and win the High School Championship
Highlight of the Year (Bronze)	Upload a photo or video to EASports.com.
Hometown Hero (Gold)	Lead your alma mater to a National Championship as a head coach in Dynasty (Coach Contracts on).
I am Andre Ware (Silver)	Win the Heisman with Andre Ware.
I am Barry Sanders (Silver)	Win the Heisman with Barry Sanders.
I am Carson Palmer (Silver)	Win the Heisman with Carson Palmer.
I am Charlie Ward (Silver)	Win the Heisman with Charlie Ward.
I am Desmond Howard (Silver)	Win the Heisman with Desmond Howard.
I am Doug Flutie (Silver)	Win the Heisman with Doug Flutie.
I am Eddie George (Silver)	Win the Heisman with Eddie George.
I am Herschel Walker (Silver)	Win the Heisman with Herschel Walker.
I am Marcus Allen (Silver)	Win the Heisman with Marcus Allen.
I am RG III (Silver)	Win the Heisman with Robert Griffin III.
Keep 'em Honest (Bronze)	Gain 200 rushing yards and 200 passing yards in the same game (excludes Co-Op and Road to Glory).
Let's Do it Again (Silver)	As a head coach in Dynasty, sign an extension to stay at the same school (Coach Contracts on).
Living Legend (Gold)	Reach a coach prestige of A+ with a created coach in Dynasty (Coach Contracts on).
Look at the Game Tape! (Bronze)	Unlock 5 attributes on a single scouting session.
My Two Cents (Bronze)	In Online Dynasty, write a comment on a Dynasty Wire story.
No Regrets (Bronze)	Convince a player to stay for their senior year using only one promise to get their degree.
Pick Up 20 (Bronze)	Break off a 20 yard run (excludes Co-Op).
Put Your Helmet On (Bronze)	Become a starter in Road to Glory Mode.
Read and React (Bronze)	Intercept a pass while using Reaction Time.
Take What's Mine (Silver)	Win a position battle in Road To Glory Mode.
Tire Fire Offense (Silver)	Win a game without scoring an offensive touchdown and gaining less than 200 yards (excludes Co-Op).
Unstoppable (Bronze)	Win a game by 35+ points on Heisman difficulty (excludes Co-Op).

Up the Gut for the Score (Bronze)	Score a touchdown handing off to the fullback on a triple option play (excludes Co-Op).
Welcome to the Club (Silver)	Win the National Championship in year 1 of Dynasty with either UMASS, UTSA, or Texas State.

NCAA FOOTBALL 13 (XBOX 360)

ACHIEVEMENT

UNLOCKABLE	HOW TO UNLOCK
And the Winner Is... (15)	Win the Heisman Memorial Trophy® in single team Dynasty, Road to Glory, or Heisman Challenge Mode.
Best Class Ever (15)	Have the #1 ranked recruiting class in a season in single team Dynasty Mode.
Don't Run Home to Mamma (20)	In Dynasty, convince a homesick player to stay at your school instead of transferring.
Dream Job (35)	Become the head coach of your alma mater in Dynasty (Coach Contracts on).
Dual Threat Coach (160)	Win the BCS Championship & have the #1 recruiting class in a single season as head coach in Dynasty.
Earn My Trust (25)	Reach the max coach trust in Road to Glory Mode.
Future Star (15)	Become a 5-star prospect in Road to Glory Mode.
Go Ahead, Ask me Anything (15)	Earn a minimum of 75 recruiting points on a Prospect Choice topic.
Go for Broke (20)	Complete a pass for 50 or more yards (excludes Co-Op).
High School Champ (15)	Play and win the High School Championship Game in any state.
Highlight of the Year (10)	Upload a photo or video to EASports.com.
Hometown Hero (50)	Lead your alma mater to a National Championship as a head coach in Dynasty (Coach Contracts on).
I am Andre Ware (30)	Win the Heisman with Andre Ware.
I am Barry Sanders (30)	Win the Heisman with Barry Sanders.
I am Carson Palmer (30)	Win the Heisman with Carson Palmer.
I am Charlie Ward (30)	Win the Heisman with Charlie Ward.
I am Desmond Howard (30)	Win the Heisman with Desmond Howard.
I am Doug Flutie (30)	Win the Heisman with Doug Flutie.
I am Eddie George (30)	Win the Heisman with Eddie George.
I am Herschel Walker (30)	Win the Heisman with Herschel Walker.
I am Marcus Allen (30)	Win the Heisman with Marcus Allen.
I am RG III (30)	Win the Heisman with Robert Griffin III.
Keep 'em Honest (15)	Gain 200 rushing yards and 200 passing yards in the same game (excludes Co-Op and Road to Glory).
Let's Do It Again (20)	As a head coach in Dynasty, sign an extension to stay at the same school (Coach Contracts on).
Living Legend (50)	Reach a coach prestige of A+ with a created coach in Dynasty (Coach Contracts on).
Look at the Game Tape! (20)	Unlock 5 attributes on a single scouting session.
My Two Cents (10)	In Online Dynasty, write a comment on a Dynasty Wire story.

No Regrets (20)	Convince a player to stay for their senior year using only one promise to get their degree.
Pick Up 20 (20)	Break off a 20 yard run (excludes Co-Op).
Put Your Helmet On (15)	Become a starter in Road to Glory Mode.
Read and React (20)	Intercept a pass while using Reaction Time.
Take What's Mine (20)	Win a position battle in Road To Glory Mode.
Tire Fire Offense (30)	Win a game without scoring an offensive touchdown and gaining less than 200 yards (excludes Co-Op).
Unstoppable (15)	Win a game by 35+ points on Heisman difficulty (excludes Co-Op).
Up the Gut for the Score (10)	Score a touchdown handing off to the fullback on a triple option play (excludes Co-Op).
Welcome to the Club (40)	Win the National Championship in year 1 of Dynasty with either UMASS, UTSA, or Texas State.

NEED FOR SPEED: MOST WANTED   (XBOX 360)

All codes should be entered at the Start screen.

UNLOCKABLE	CODE
Unlocks Burger King Challenge Event (#69)	↑, ↓, ↓, ↓, ←, →, ←, →
Unlocks Free Engine Upgrade Bonus Marker (Can be used in the backroom of the customization shops)	↑, ↑, ↑, ↓, ←, →, →, ↑, ↓
Unlocks Special Edition Castrol Ford GT (Which is added to your bonus cars)	←, →, ←, →, ↑, ↓, ↑, ↓

NEED FOR SPEED: PROSTREET   (PLAYSTATION 3, XBOX 360)

CODES

Go to the "Enter Codes" section of the Career menu and enter the following codes.

UNLOCKABLE	HOW TO UNLOCK
Extra $2,000	1MA9X99
Extra $4,000	W2i0LLO1
Extra $8,000	L1iS97A1
Extra $10,000	1Mi9K7E1
Extra $10,000	REGGAME
Extra $10,000	CASHMONEY
Extra $10,000 and Castrol Syntec Bonus Vinyl	CASTROLSYNTEC
5 Repair Tokens	SAFETYNET
Audi TT 3.2 Quattro (In Garage)	ITSABOUTYOU
Bonus Energizer Lithium Vinyl	ENERGIZERLITHIUM
Dodge Viper (In Garage)	WORLDSLONGESTLASTING
K&N Bonus Vinyl	HORSEPOWER
Lancer Evo (In Garage)	MITSUBISHIGOFAR
Pre-tuned Grip Coke Zero Golf GTI (In Garage) and Bonus Coke Zero Vinyl	ZEROZEROZERO
Re-Locks Everything Unlocked by "Unlockallthings"	LEIPZIG
Unlocks Everything (maps, cars, parts)	UNLOCKALLTHINGS

NEED FOR SPEED: PROSTREET (WII)

CODES

Go to the "Enter Codes" section of the Career menu and enter the following codes.

UNLOCKABLE	HOW TO UNLOCK
Audi TT 3.2 Quattro (In Garage)	ITSABOUTYOU
Bonus Energizer Lithium Vinyl	ENERGIZERLITHIUM
Dodge Viper (In Garage)	WORLDSLONGESTLASTING
Extra $2,000	1MA9X99
Extra $4,000	W2iOLLO1
Extra $8,000	L1iS97A1
Extra $10,000	1Mi9K7E1
Extra $10,000	REGGAME
Extra $10,000	CASHMONEY
Extra $10,000 and Castrol Syntec Bonus Vinyl	CASTROLSYNTEC
Five Repair Tokens	SAFETYNET
K&N Bonus Vinyl	HORSEPOWER
Lancer Evo (In Garage)	MITSUBISHIGOFAR
Pre-tuned Grip Coke Zero Golf GTI (In Garage) and Bonus Coke Zero Vinyl	ZEROZEROZERO
Re-Locks Everything Unlocked by "Unlockallthings"	LEIPZIG
Unlocks Everything (maps, cars, parts)	UNLOCKALLTHINGS

NEED FOR SPEED: UNDERCOVER (XBOX 360, PLAYSTATION 3)

CODES

EFFECT	CODE
$10,000 in-game currency	$EDSOC
Die-Cast Lexus IS F bonus car	0;5M2;
Die-Cast Nissan 240SX (S13) bonus car	?P:COL
Die-Cast Volkswagen R32 bonus car	!2ODBJ;
NeedforSpeed.com Lotus Elise bonus car	-KJ3=E

NEUTOPIA II (WII)

EVERYTHING COLLECTED

PASSWORD	EFFECT
At the Password screen, enter the following passwords: IbnoBJt$ AyUkJ7Wa XACpGDjm q1j1uR1Q M8ozNOQa cPUM&XcX	Puts you in the Town of Oasis ready to tackle the last dungeon, The Atra Labyrinth
Music_From_Neutopia	Sound Test
Thats_Entertainment_Neutopia	View Enemies

NEVERDEAD (PLAYSTATION 3)

TROPHY

UNLOCKABLE	HOW TO UNLOCK
A pain in the ass! (Bronze)	Defeat the Sword Pig.
Antiquarian (Bronze)	Destroy less than 25% of the museum exhibits.
Big Spender (Gold)	Purchase all abilities.
Boulder Dodge (Bronze)	Dodge the boulders.
BryceBQ (Bronze)	Kill an enemy with Fire.
Completist (Bronze)	Unlock all Prestige Badges.
Criminal Damages (Silver)	Destroy $1,000,000 worth of objects.

Curiosity Killed the Cat (Bronze)	Explore all of Arcadia's Apartment.
De-Cyphered (Bronze)	Take a trip down memory lane...
Don't Stop, Look or Listen (Bronze)	Dodge the traffic on the bridge.
Easter Bunny (Bronze)	Win an Egg Hunt challenge.
Endangered Species (Silver)	Kill 8 panda bears.
Evacuation Plan (Bronze)	Get all the civilians to the chopper.
Ever Dead (Silver)	Complete the game on easy difficulty.
Explosive Personality (Bronze)	Blow up 35 enemies in the Asylum using barrels.
Eye for an eye (Bronze)	Defeat Astaroth, King of Hell.
Four-to-one Odds (Bronze)	Defeat Quad Jaw.
Frail Friend (Bronze)	Win a Fragile Alliance challenge.
Funky Dunker (Bronze)	Put head through all basketball hoops.
Group Hug (Silver)	Kill 5 enemies with a single limb explosion.
Hop, Skip and Jump (Bronze)	Hop, roll and jump...
I'll bite your legs off! (Platinum)	Get all trophies.
Insurance Fraud (Bronze)	Destroy $100,000 worth of objects.
Let There be Light (Bronze)	Light all the sewer barrels.
Level Up (Silver)	Purchase 50% of the abilities.
Mind the gap (Bronze)	Lure Panda Bear in front of a train.
Never Dead (Gold)	Complete the game on hardcore difficulty.
Onslaughter (Bronze)	Complete an Arena Onslaught Challenge.
Out of the Frying Pan (Bronze)	Lure Panda Bear into lava.
Premature Evacuation (Bronze)	You win some, you lose some...
Rarely Dead (Silver)	Complete the game on normal difficulty.
Runner (Bronze)	Complete an Onslaught Challenge.
Sangria, on ice (Bronze)	Defeat Sangria, Duke of Hell.
Saviour (Bronze)	Complete a Search and Rescue challenge.
Serve and Protect (Bronze)	Save Nikki.
Shock and Awe (Bronze)	Kill an enemy with Electricity.
Swiss Army Bryce (Bronze)	Kill an enemy with every weapon.
The Great Collector (Gold)	Find all Major Collectibles.
There can be only one! (Bronze)	Defeat your nemesis.
Tower'n Inferno (Bronze)	Take down the water tower.
Tumble Dried (Bronze)	Get caught up in the whirlwind.
Womb with a view (Bronze)	Defeat Sullivan.
You and whose army? (Silver)	Shoot 50 enemies with dismembered limbs.

NEVERDEAD (XBOX 360)

ACHIEVEMENT

UNLOCKABLE	HOW TO UNLOCK
A pain in the ass! (20)	Defeat the Sword Pig.
Antiquarian (25)	Destroy less than 25% of the museum exhibits.
Big Spender (50)	Purchase all abilities.
Boulder Dodge (20)	Dodge the boulders.
BryceBQ (20)	Kill an enemy with Fire.
Completist (50)	Unlock all Prestige Badges.
Criminal Damages (25)	Destroy $1,000,000 of objects.
Curiosity Killed the Cat (20)	Explore all of Arcadia's Apartment.

De-Cyphered (20)	Take a trip down memory lane.
Don't Stop, Look or Listen (20)	Dodge the traffic on the bridge.
Easter Bunny (20)	Win an Egg Hunt challenge.
Endangered Species (20)	Kill 8 panda bears.
Evacuation Plan (20)	Get all the civilians to the chopper.
Ever Dead (40)	Complete the game on easy difficulty.
Explosive Personality (20)	Blow up 35 enemies in the Asylum using barrels.
Eye for an eye (20)	Defeat Astaroth, King of Hell.
Four-to-one Odds (20)	Defeat Quad Jaw.
Frail Friend (20)	Win a Fragile Alliance challenge.
Funky Dunk (30)	Put head through all basketball hoops.
Group Hug (20)	Kill 5 enemies with a single arm explosion
Hop, Skip and Jump (10)	Hop, roll and jump...
Insurance Fraud (10)	Destroy $100,000 worth of objects.
Let There be Light (20)	Light all the sewer barrels.
Level Up (25)	Purchase 50% of the abilities.
Mind the gap (20)	Lure Panda Bear in front of a train.
Never Dead (50)	Complete the game on hardcore difficulty.
Onslaughter (20)	Complete an Arena Onslaught Challenge.
Out of the Frying Pan (20)	Lure Panda Bear into lava.
Premature Evacuation (5)	You win some, you lose some...
Rarely Dead (45)	Complete the game on normal difficulty.
Runner (20)	Complete an Onslaught Challenge.
Sangria, on ice (20)	Defeat Sangria, Duke of Hell.
Saviour (20)	Complete a Search and Rescue challenge.
Serve and Protect (20)	Save Nikki.
Shock and Awe (20)	Kill an enemy with Electricity.
Swiss Army Bryce (20)	Kill an enemy with every weapon.
The Great Collector (50)	Find all Major Collectibles.
There can be only one! (20)	Defeat your nemesis.
Tower'n Inferno (20)	Take down the water tower.
Tumble Dried (20)	Get caught up in the whirlwind.
Womb with a view (20)	Defeat Sullivan
You and whose army? (25)	Shoot 50 enemies with dismembered arms.
Unlock Assault Bowguns	Beat the game on any difficulty

NEW ADVENTURE ISLAND (WII)

UNLOCKABLES

UNLOCKABLE	HOW TO UNLOCK
Level Select	Press ⬇, ⬆, ①, ⬅, ⬇, ②, ➡, ⬆, ⬇, ⬇
Level Skip	Insert a NEC Avenue 6 pad in 6-button mode into port 1

NHL 10 (XBOX 360), (PLAYSTATION 3)

CODES

Enter the following code at the EA Extras screen

EFFECT	CODE
Unlocks third jerseys	rwyhafwh6ekyjcmr

NHL 12 (PLAYSTATION 3)

TROPHY

UNLOCKABLE	HOW TO UNLOCK
A Smash Hit (Bronze)	Break a pane of glass with a hit on a CPU player
Amateur Contender (Bronze)	Qualify for a Hockey Ultimate Team Amateur monthly playoff tournament
Benched! (Bronze)	Check an opposing player into the benches
Complete Set (Silver)	Collect all player, jersey and logo cards for any team in the Collection
EASHL Hero (Bronze)	Score the OT winner in an EA Sports Hockey League match
EASHL Legend (Gold)	Achieve Legend 1 status for your online Pro
EASHL Playoffs (Bronze)	Be a member of an EA SPORTS Hockey League team when they participate in a monthly playoff
EASHL Pro (Silver)	Achieve Pro 1 status for your online Pro
EASHL Rookie (Bronze)	Achieve Rookie 1 status for your online Pro
EAUHL 24/7 Victory (Bronze)	Win a match against a downloaded Hockey Ultimate Team
Elite Contender (Silver)	Qualify for a Hockey Ultimate Team Elite monthly playoff tournament
Every Man (Bronze)	Play as every skater position while completing EA SPORTS Hockey League matches
From the Office (Bronze)	Have 7 assists in a single NHL Be A Pro game with a created Pro on Pro difficulty or higher
Happy 20th EA SPORTS! (Bronze)	Play & get 20 goals in a Be A Pro CHL season with a created Pro to celebrate 20 years of EA SPORTS
Hats Off To You (Bronze)	Be the player that scores 3 goals consecutively in an EA SPORTS Hockey League match
High Flying (Bronze)	Score a goal after completing a jump deke in a Ranked Online Shootout match
HUT Playoff Winner (Silver)	Win any Hockey Ultimate Team monthly playoff tournament
King of the Crease (Bronze)	Win a goalie versus goalie fight
Le Magnifique (Bronze)	Earn 8 points in a single NHL Be A Pro playoff game with a created Pro on Pro difficulty or higher
Legend GM (Silver)	Achieve Legendary GM Status
Legend Player (Silver)	Play and win any NHL player trophy in Be A Pro with a created Pro
Lost His Lid (Bronze)	Knock the helmet off an opposing player's head
Magnificent Mario (Bronze)	Score goals 5 different ways in a NHL Be A Pro game with a created Pro on Pro difficulty or higher
Magnificently Great (Bronze)	Score 4 goals in one period of a NHL Be A Pro game as a created Pro on Pro difficulty or higher
Memorial Cup (Bronze)	Play and win the Memorial Cup in Be A Pro with a created Pro
Mr. Hockey (Bronze)	Complete a Gordie Howe Hat Trick (Goal/Assist/Fight) in a Be A Pro NHL game with a created Pro
On Bended Knee (Bronze)	Score with a one knee one timer
One Great Career (Gold)	Earn 2,858 NHL career points in Be A Pro with a created Pro on Pro difficulty or higher
One Great Season (Silver)	Earn 216 NHL career points in a single Be A Pro season with a created Pro on at least Pro difficulty

Past Their Potential (Bronze)	Train a player past their potential
PP Powerhouse (Silver)	Have 30 PP goals in 2 different NHL Be A Pro seasons with a created Pro on Pro difficulty or higher
Pro Contender (Silver)	Qualify for a Hockey Ultimate Team Pro monthly playoff tournament
Raise the Cup (Silver)	Play and win the Stanley Cup in Be A Pro with a created Pro
Raise Your Banner '12 (Platinum)	Acquire all of the Bronze, Silver and Gold trophies
Russian Rocket (Bronze)	Score a goal after completing a skate-to-stick deke in a Ranked Online Shootout match
Superstar (Bronze)	Have 4 five goal games in a NHL Be A Pro career with a created Pro on Pro difficulty or higher
Taking Shots (Bronze)	Play as the goalie while completing an EA SPORTS Hockey League match
Team Doctor (Bronze)	Use a Healing card to heal an injured player in Hockey Ultimate Team
The Comeback Kid (Bronze)	Have three 8 point games in a NHL Be A Pro career with a created Pro on Pro difficulty or higher
The Great One (Silver)	Score 93 goals in a single NHL Be A Pro season with a created Pro on Pro difficulty or higher
Top Prospect (Bronze)	Qualify for and complete the CHL Top Prospects game in Be A Pro with a created Pro
Unlucky for Some (Silver)	Score 14 shorthanded goals in a NHL Be A Pro season with a created Pro on Pro difficulty or higher
Versus Legend (Silver)	Reach level 25 of online Versus
Versus Pro (Silver)	Reach level 10 of online Versus
Versus Rookie (Bronze)	Reach level 5 of online Versus
Winter Classic (Bronze) WSH	Complete a NHL Winter Classic Match with PIT versus

NHL 2K6 (XBOX 360)

Enter this as a profile name. Case Sensitive.

UNLOCKABLE	PASSWORD
Unlock everything	Turco813

NHL 2K9 (XBOX 360), (PLAYSTATION 3)

UNLOCKABLES

Go to Features, and enter the code into the Code menu.
The code is case sensitive.

EFFECT	CODE
Unlocks the third jerseys	R6y34bsH52

NHL 2K10 (XBOX 360), (WII)

CODES

In the cheats/password option located in the extras menu enter the following codes.

EFFECT	CODE
2K/Visual Concepts developer teams	vcteam
The five alternates for this season	G8r23Bty56

NINJA GAIDEN (WII)

UNLOCKABLES

UNLOCKABLE	HOW TO UNLOCK
Sound Test	When the screen says Techmo Presents 1989: Hold Ⓐ+Ⓑ+⇦+⇨+SELECT, and press START
Extra Lives	In Area 5-3, there's a 1UP on the third floor of the tower. Go back down the ladder to the second floor, and then back up to the third floor. The 1UP has returned. You can do this as many times as you want.

NINJA GAIDEN II (XBOX 360)

UNLOCKABLES

UNLOCKABLE	HOW TO UNLOCK
Black Jaguar Costume	Complete Path of Mentor.
Camouflage Ninja Outfit	Complete the game on Warrior.
Gamerpic of Ryu	Complete the game on Path of the Master Ninja.
Gamerpic	Collect all 30 crystal skulls.
Golden Ninja Costume	Complete the game on Path of The Master Ninja.
Music Test	Clear the game on any difficulty.
New Game +	Complete the game and save after Credit Scroll.
Old Film Filter	Beat the game.
Path of the Master Ninja	Beat Path of the Mentor.
Path of the Mentor	Beat Path of the Warrior.
Red Ninja Outfit	Complete the game on Acolyte.

EASTER EGGS: HIDDEN SILVER XBOX

At the bottom of the Statue of Liberty diagonally across from where the save point there is a false wall. Inside of the breakable wall is a silver Xbox that will regenerate Ryu's health.

NINJA GAIDEN 3 (PLAYSTATION 3)

TROPHY

UNLOCKABLE	HOW TO UNLOCK
Abysmal Creations (Bronze)	Escape from the Chimera Disposal Facility.
Advent of the Goddess (Bronze)	Finish Day 7.
Ahab (Bronze)	Attack the Black Narwhal.
An Honorable Death (Bronze)	Perform harakiri.
Antediluvian Slumber (Bronze)	Finish Day 3.
Atonement (Bronze)	One more death to make amends.
Beyond the Flames (Bronze)	Make it through the fire.
Brothers (Bronze)	The sibling rivalry comes to an end.
Bumpy Ride (Bronze)	Finish Day 2.
Evil Twin (Bronze)	Defeat the Epigonos.
Falcon Dive (Bronze)	Learn the Falcon Dive.
Flying Bird Flip (Bronze)	Learn the Flying Bird Flip.
Guardian of the Village (Bronze)	Play the Hidden Village stage 10 times.
Hayabusa Style Grand Master (Bronze)	Reach level 50.
Hero (Silver)	Clear the game on Hero.
I Got Your Back (Bronze)	Play a Co-op Ninja Trial with a partner.
Inferno (Bronze)	Learn Ninpo.
Initiate (Bronze)	Clear 10 Acolyte Trials.
Initiation (Bronze)	Play a Clan Battle.
Izuna Drop (Bronze)	Learn the Izuna Drop.
Kunai Climb (Bronze)	Learn the Kunai Climb.

Lone Ninja (Silver)	Clear 10 Solo Ninja Trials.
Master Ninja (Gold)	Clear the game on Master Ninja.
Master of the Katana (Bronze)	Raise the katana to level 10.
Master of the Secret Arts (Platinum)	Obtain all trophies.
Mentor (Silver)	Clear the game on Hard.
Mind the Gap (Bronze)	Escape from the monorail.
Observer (Bronze)	Play the Watchtower stage 10 times.
One Against the World (Bronze)	Win a battle royale match.
Overlord (Silver)	Clear 5 Master Ninja Trials.
Prestige (Bronze)	Clear 5 Leader Trials.
Rope Crossing (Bronze)	Learn how to cross a rope.
Shady (Bronze)	Perform a betrayal.
Shinobi (Silver)	Clear the game on Normal.
Sliding (Bronze)	Learn how to slide.
Sneaky (Bronze)	Perform a ghost kill.
Snowman (Bronze)	Play the Snowfield stage 10 times.
Steel on Bone (Bronze)	Cut down 100 enemies with Steel on Bone attacks.
Steel on Steel (Bronze)	Destroy the Steel Spider.
Teamwork (Bronze)	Win 10 team battles.
The Acolyte (Bronze)	Successfully clear the Sanji event in Hayabusa Village.
The Great Escape (Bronze)	Finish Day 4.
The Grip of Murder (Bronze)	Finish Day 1.
The Karma of a Shinobi (Bronze)	Finish Day 5.
The Spice of Life (Bronze)	Get 10 customization parts.
Ultimate Ninja (Gold)	Clear 3 Ultimate Ninja Trials.
Ultimate Technique (Bronze)	Learn the Ultimate Technique.
Veteran (Bronze)	Clear 10 Mentor Trials.
Waiting (Bronze)	Finish Day 6.
Walking Dictionary (Silver)	Get 100 kanji.
Wall Run (Bronze)	Learn the Wall Run.

NINJA GAIDEN 3 (XBOX 360)

ACHIEVEMENT

UNLOCKABLE	HOW TO UNLOCK
Abysmal Creations (15)	Escaped from the Chimera Disposal Facility.
Advent of the Goddess (15)	Finish Day 7.
Ahab (15)	Land on the Black Narwhal.
An Honorable Death (10)	Perform harakiri.
Antediluvian Slumber (15)	Finish Day 3.
Atonement (15)	Defeated Theodore.
Beyond the Flames (15)	Made it through the fire.
Brothers (15)	Defeated Cliff.
Bumpy Ride (10)	Finish Day 2.
Evil Twin (15)	Defeated the Epigonos.
Falcon Dive (10)	Learn the Falcon Dive.
Flying Bird Flip (10)	Learn the Flying Bird Flip.
Guardian of the Village (10)	Play the Hidden Village stage 10 times.

Hayabusa Style Grand Master (15)	Reached level 50.
Hero (50)	Cleared the game on Hero.
I Got Your Back (10)	Play a Co-op Ninja Trial with a partner.
Inferno (10)	Learned Ninpo.
Initiate (10)	Cleared 10 Acolyte Trials.
Initiation (10)	Play a Clan Battle.
Izuna Drop (10)	Learn the Izuna Drop.
Kunai Climb (10)	Learn the Kunai Climb.
Lone Ninja (50)	Cleared 10 Solo Ninja Trials.
Master Ninja (100)	Cleared the game on Master Ninja.
Master of the Katana (15)	Raised the katana to level 10.
Mentor (60)	Cleared the game on Hard.
Mind the Gap (10)	Escaped from the monorail.
Observer (10)	Play the Watchtower stage 10 times.
One Against the World (10)	Win a battle royale match.
Overlord (50)	Cleared 5 Master Ninja Trials.
Prestige (10)	Cleared 5 Leader Trials.
Rope Crossing (10)	Learn how to cross a rope.
Shady (10)	Perform a betrayal.
Shinobi (50)	Cleared the game on Normal.
Sliding (10)	Learn how to slide.
Sneaky (10)	Perform a ghost kill.
Snowman (10)	Play the Snowfield stage 10 times.
Steel on Bone (10)	Cut down 100 enemies with Steel on Bone attacks.
Steel on Steel (10)	Destroyed the Steel Spider.
Teamwork (10)	Win 10 team battles.
The Acolyte (15)	Successfully responded to Sanji's ambush.
The Great Escape (15)	Finish Day 4.
The Grip of Murder (10)	Finish Day 1.
The Karma of a Shinobi (15)	Finish Day 5.
The Spice of Life (10)	Get 10 customization parts.
Ultimate Ninja (100)	Cleared 3 Ultimate Ninja Trials.
Ultimate Technique (10)	Learn the Ultimate Technique.
Veteran (10)	Cleared 10 Mentor Trials.
Waiting (15)	Finish Day 6.
Walking Dictionary (50)	Get 100 kanji.
Wall Run (10)	Learn the Wall Run.

NINJA GAIDEN SIGMA PLUS (PLAYSTATION VITA)

TROPHY

UNLOCKABLE	HOW TO UNLOCK
Cleared 10 Trials	Clear Secrets of Fighting, Military Destruction, Descent of the Fiends, and Captivating Goddesses (Bronze)
Cleared 14 Trials	Clear Desperation, Fateful Confrontation, Battlefield of the Abyss, and Giants of the Underworld (Bronze)
Cleared 2 Trials (Bronze)	Clear all Ninja Tutorials and Path to the Ultimate Ninja.

Cleared 6 Trials(Bronze)	Clear Unrivalef Meeting, Nightmarish Phantasms, Abysmal Lair, and Secrets of shooting
Cleared all Trials. (Bronze)	Clear Unearthed Challenge and Eternal Legend
Cleared Hard	Finish all chapters of the game on Hard (Bronze)
Cleared Master Ninja	Finish all chapters of the game on Master Ninja (Gold)
Cleared Tairon Under Alert	Completed Chapter 10 (Bronze)
Cleared The Caverns	Completed Chapter 15 (Bronze)
Cleared The Fiend Hunter	Completed Chapter 5 (Bronze)
Cleared The Way of the Ninja (Bronze)	Completed Chapter 1.
Cleared Very Hard	Finish all chapters of the game on Very Hard (Bronze)
Coin Aficionado(Silver)	clear 50 missions in ninja trials
Coin Collector	Get coins in all Ninja Trials (Silver)
Coin Master	Get platinum coins in all Ninja Trials (Gold)
Dabilahro Master (Bronze)	Defeat 1000 enemies with the Dabilahro.
Dragon Sword Master (Bronze)	Defeat 1000 enemies with the Dragon Sword.
Dual Kitana Master (Bronze)	Defeat 1000 enemies with the Dual Kitana.
Feat of Ultimate Destruction (Bronze)	Use the strongest Ultimate Technique on 100 enemies.
Fire Wheels Master (Bronze)	Use Fire Wheels successfully 100 times.
First Clear(Bronze)	Finish all chapters of the game.
Guillotine Throw Master (Bronze)	Use the Guillotine Throw on 100 enemies.
Heroes Never Give Up	Activate Hero Mode 100 times (Bronze)
Ice Storm Master (Bronze)	Use Ice Storm successfully 100 times.
Inazuma Master (Bronze)	Use Inazuma successfully 100 times.
Inferno Master (Bronze)	Use Inferno successfully 100 times.
Izuna Drop Master (Bronze)	Use the Izuna Dro on 100 enemies.
Just Put Me on(Bronze)	Hold/keep up to 99,999 Yellow Essence
Kitetsu Master (Bronze)	Defeat 1000 enemies with the Kitetsu.
Lead Scarab Hunter(Bronze)	find 10 scarabs.
Legendary Scarab Hunter(Silver)	Find all scarabs.
Lunar Staff Master (Bronze)	Defeat 1000 enemies with the Lunar Staff.
Master Scarab Hunter(Bronze)	find 30 scarabs.
Ninja Carnage	Kill every enemy in an Ambush (Bronze)
Ninja Massacre	Kill every enemy in all Ambushes (Silver)
Ninja Slaughter	Kill every enemy in 6 Ambushes (Bronze)
Over 10,000,000 Karma(Bronze)	In ninja trials get this score. best way to get this trophy is playing mission 2 of Unrivaled Meeting
Over 50,000,000 Karma	Get 50,000,000 Karma (Silver)
Projectile Weapons (Bronze)	Defeat 100 enemies with projectile weapons.
Rachel Master	Defeat 500 enemies with Rachel (Bronze)
Rookie Scarab Hunter(Bronze)	find 1 scarab.
Sorcery Master	Use Ice Storm successfully 100 times. (Bronze)
Thanks for Finding Me!(Bronze)	Find all the Team Ninja logos in story mode.
Thanks for playing! -from) Team NINJA (Gold	Get Master on all chapters on Master Ninja.
The Journey to Master Ninja (Bronze)	Get Master Ninja on all chapters.

NEW!

A
B
C
D
E
F
G
H
I
J
K
L
M
N
O
P
Q
R
S
T
U
V
W
X
Y
Z

The Long Journey to Master Ninja (Bronze)	Get Master Ninja on all chapters on Hard.
The Really Long Journey to Master Ninja (Bronze)	Get Master Ninja on all chapters on Very Hard.
True Ultimate Ninja (Platinum)	Collect all trophies.
Vigoorian Flail Master (Bronze)	Defeat 1000 enemies with the Vigoorian Flail.
War Hammer Master (Bronze)	Defeat 1000 enemies with the War Hammer (Hayabusa).
Wooden Sword/Unlabored Flawlessness Master (Bronze)	Defeat 1000 enemies with the Wooden Sword/ Unlabored Flawlessness.

UNLOCKABLE

UNLOCKABLE	HOW TO UNLOCK
Master Ninja	Clear the game on Very Hard
Ninja Dog	Die 3 times while playing on Normal
Very Hard	Clear the game on Hard
Biker (Rachel)	Clear the game on Hard
Doppelganger (Ryu)	Clear the game on Normal
Formal Attire (Rachel)	Clear the game on Normal
Legendary Ninja (Ryu)	Clear the game on Normal
The Grip of Murder (Ryu)	Clear the game on Very Hard difficulty setting.

NO MORE HEROES 2: DESPERATE STRUGGLE (WII)

UNLOCKABLES

UNLOCKABLE	HOW TO UNLOCK
Bitter Mode	Complete the game on Mild.
BJ5 Video	Beat BJ5 game, then select from TV menu.
Deathmatch (Boss Rush)	Beat the game, then select from Main menu.
E3 Trailer	Beat the game, then select from TV menu.
No Jacket	Complete all the "Revenge" missions.
New Game +	Beat the game and save your data. When you start No More Heroes 2 again you will be brought to the intro fight where you have all of your old equipment and items from the previous game.

OKAMIDEN (DS)

UNLOCKABLE

Your final end-of-game evaluation based on what you did in the game will determine what you get once you beat the game.

UNLOCKABLE	HOW TO UNLOCK
Dark Sun (Dark Chibi)	Beat the game
First Sunrise (Chibi Shiranui)	Complete everything
Karmic Returner (Original Amaterasu)	Beat the game
Moon's Legacy (Made of Ice)	Complete the Treasure Tome
Painter's Legend (Ishaku's armor)	Complete the Bestiary

UNLOCKABLE

Complete the story, save your game when prompted, and select Continue on the title screen to begin a new game with all the health and ink pots earned in the previous save, as well as bonus items you might have earned.

ONSLAUGHT (WII)

STAGES

In addition to the three difficulty settings available from the start, there are two unlockable difficulty settings.

UNLOCKABLE	HOW TO UNLOCK
Expert difficulty	Finish the game on Hard difficulty.
Ultra difficulty	Finish the game on Expert difficulty.

UPGRADE LOCATIONS

Each weapon has 2 upgrades that count as additional weapons.

UNLOCKABLE	HOW TO UNLOCK
2nd level Assault Rifle	Box in Mission 5.
2nd level Grenades	Clear Missions 1, 2, and 3 in Normal difficulty (S rank).
2nd level Rocket Launcher	Clear Missions 9, 10, and 11 in Normal difficulty (S rank).
2nd level Shotgun	Box in Mission 11.
2nd level SMG	Box in Mission 3.
2nd level Whip	Clear Missions 5, 6, and 7 in Normal difficulty (S rank).
3rd level Assault Rifle	Beat the game in Ultra difficulty.
3rd level Grenades	Clear Missions 1 to 8 in Hard difficulty (S rank).
3rd level Rocket Launcher	Clear Missions 1 to 12 in Ultra difficulty (S rank).
3rd level Shotgun	Beat the game in Expert difficulty.
3rd level SMG	Beat the game in Hard difficulty.
3rd level Whip	Clear Missions 1 to 8 in Expert difficulty (S rank).

OPEN SEASON (WII)

UNLOCKABLE MINIGAMES

UNLOCKABLE	HOW TO UNLOCK
Duck Chorus	Complete "Crazy Quackers"
Flowers for My Deer	Complete "Meet the Skunks"
Rise, Rise to the Top!	Complete "Beaver Damage"

| Shake That Butt! | Complete "Hunted" |
| Wild Memory | Complete "Shaw's Shack" |

OPERATION FLASHPOINT: DRAGON RISING   (XBOX 360)

CODES

EFFECT	CODE
Unlocks "Ambush" mission	AmbushU454
Unlocks "Close Quarters" mission	CloseQ8M3
Unlocks "Coastal Stronghold" mission	StrongM577
Unlocks "F.T.E." mission	BLEEDINGBADLY
Unlocks "Night Raid" mission	RaidT18Z
Unlocks "Debris Field" mission	OFPWEB2
Unlocks "Encampment" mission	OFPWEB1

OPOONA   (WII)

UNLOCKABLES

UNLOCKABLE	HOW TO UNLOCK
Fifth Citizen Ranking Star	Acquire the Five-Star Landroll Ranger License. Must be done before talking to woman for Sixth Star.
Five-Star Landroll Ranger License	Win 100 battles in the Intelligent Sea server room.
Sixth Citizen Ranking Star	Talk to a woman on the bottom floor of the Moon Forest Tokione Hotel after spending the night.

ORDYNE   (WII)

UNLOCKABLES

UNLOCKABLE	HOW TO UNLOCK
Continue Game	While falling, hold ① and press RUN
Princess Mode	At the title screen, hold ① for about 10 seconds
Secret Test Mode	At the title screen, hold down RUN while pressing SELECT, SELECT, SELECT, SELECT, SELECT, then release. Hold down ①+②+⬆+⬇, then press RUN. Press SELECT and RUN simultaneously to reach each part of the Secret Test mode. You can access a Sound Test, select your starting stage and your starting number of ships, among other things.

PAC-MAN WORLD 3 (PSP)

Enter this code at the main menu.

UNLOCKABLE	CODE
Unlock levels and mazes	⇐, ⇒, ⇐, ⇒, ⇐, ●, ⇑

PATAPON 2 (PSP)

UNLOCKABLES

Complete the following tasks to gain the corresponding miracles.

UNLOCKABLE	HOW TO UNLOCK
Attack Miracle	Beat invincible Dragon Majidonga Level 3
Blizzard Miracle	Finish Watchtower and Two Karmen Mission.
Defense Miracle	Beat Fearful Tentacle Monster Darachura Level 3.
Earthquake Miracle	Beat Living Fortress Cannodears Level 3.
Rain Miracle	Finish Mushroom shroom shroom Nyokiri Swamp Mission in the Second Time.
Storm Miracle	Beat God General of Staff Hookmen.
Tailwind Miracle	Finish Mystery of the Desert's Sandstorm Mission in the Second Time.

PATAPON 3 (PSP)

UNLOCKABLE

Complete the following requirements to unlock these shops.

UNLOCKABLE	HOW TO UNLOCK
Hoshipon Shop	Achieve a team goal.
Meden Mart	Complete the Cave of Valour.

PERSONA 4 ARENA (PLAYSTATION 3)

TROPHY

UNLOCKABLE	HOW TO UNLOCK
Action! (Bronze)	You performed 100 Furious Actions in Arcade Mode or online.
All-Out Attack to the MAX! (Bronze)	You finished an All-Out Attack with a Fatal Counter in Arcade Mode or online.
Amazing, Sensei! (Bronze)	You've earned your first online victory! You've bear-ly scratched the surface.
BAM! (Bronze)	You used every character's Instant Kill move in Arcade Mode or online!
Belt Collector (Gold)	You completed Arcade Mode with all characters.
Black Belt (Silver)	You have reached Grade C in Ranked Matches.
C'est Magnifique! (Gold)	You completed Score Attack Mode with all characters.
Calm Down. (Bronze)	You suffered a Persona Break in Arcade Mode or online. It happens to everybody...
Champion! (Bronze)	You completed Arcade Mode with one character.
Combo Crazy (Gold)	You have completed all the Challenges! Funky Student would be proud.
Combo Master (Silver)	You have completed 300 Challenges.

Die for Me! (Bronze)	You performed 30 Fatal Counters in Arcade Mode or online.
Halfway There (Bronze)	You completed Stage 6 in Score Attack.
I am Thou... (Platinum)	You have mastered P4A.
I Learned a Few Moves (Bronze)	You have completed 150 Challenges.
I Mastered that One (Silver)	You have completed all of one character's Challenges!
Meat Dimension (Bronze)	You defeated an opponent in Arcade Mode or online before he Awakened! Now, that's a real challenge!
Null Physical (Bronze)	You performed 50 Instant Blocks in Arcade Mode or online.
One More! (Bronze)	You performed 20 One More Bursts in Arcade Mode or online.
Per...so......na...! (Bronze)	Have you burned your dread? Or reached out to the truth?
Perfect! (Bronze)	You had a perfect victory in Arcade Mode or online.
Persona Breaker (Bronze)	You created 10 Persona Breaks in Arcade Mode or online.
Replay Reviewer (Bronze)	You watched a Replay in the Theater. Are you as good as you remember?
School's Out (Bronze)	You've aced all the tests.
Serious Gamer (Silver)	You have reached Level 30 by playing online matches!
Speak with Your Fists! (Bronze)	You've battled against every character in online matches. You're a grizzly'd warrior now!
Stylish! (Bronze)	You performed 100 Auto Combos in Arcade Mode or online.
The Angel (Bronze)	Aigis' Story chapter has been told.
The Beast (Bronze)	Teddie's Story chapter has been told.
The Boxer (Bronze)	Akihiko's Story chapter has been told.
The Captain (Bronze)	Yosuke's Story chapter has been told.
The Carnivore (Bronze)	Chie's Story chapter has been told.
The Detective (Bronze)	Naoto's Story chapter has been told.
The Emperor (Bronze)	Kanji's Story chapter has been told.
The Kingpin (Bronze)	Yu's Story chapter has been told.
The Queen (Bronze)	Mitsuru's Story chapter has been told.
The Unconquerable (Bronze)	Yukiko's Story chapter has been told.
They Call Me... (Bronze)	You've created a Title for your online matches.
Time for the All-Out Attack! (Bronze)	You performed 100 All-Out Attacks in Arcade Mode or online.
Trained in Seclusion (Bronze)	You spent 30 minutes in Training in one sitting. Now take it to the streets!
Tres Bien! (Bronze)	You completed Score Attack Mode with one character.
Veteran (Bronze)	You have completed 100 online matches, win or lose. No bear puns here. Congrats.
Victory Cry (Bronze)	You won 30 Rounds in Arcade Mode or Online by using SP Skills or Awakened SP Skills.
Wild (Bronze)	You have used all the characters in Arcade Mode or Online. Variety is good for you!
You know the Midnight Channel? (Bronze)	Tuned In
You Should Leave Him Be... (Bronze)	You were afflicted with every ailment in Arcade Mode or online. Not even Mr. Edogawa can help you.

PERSONA 4 ARENA (XBOX 360)

ACHIEVEMENT

UNLOCKABLE	HOW TO UNLOCK
Action! (10)	You performed 100 Furious Actions in Arcade Mode or online.
All-Out Attack to the MAX! (10)	You finished an All-Out Attack with a Fatal Counter in Arcade Mode or online.
Amazing, Sensei! (20)	You've earned your first online victory! You've bear-ly scratched the surface.
BAM! (30)	You used every character's Instant Kill move in Arcade Mode or online!
Belt Collector (80)	You completed Arcade Mode with all characters.
Black Belt (40)	You have reached Grade C in Ranked Matches.
C'est Magnifique! (80)	You completed Score Attack Mode with all characters.
Calm Down. (10)	You suffered a Persona Break in Arcade Mode or online. It happens to everybody...
Champion! (10)	You completed Arcade Mode with one character.
Combo Crazy (80)	You have completed all the Challenges! Funky Student would be proud.
Combo Master (40)	You have completed 300 Challenges.
Die for Me! (10)	You performed 30 Fatal Counters in Arcade Mode or online.
Halfway There (20)	You completed Stage 6 in Score Attack.
I Learned a Few Moves (20)	You have completed 150 Challenges.
I Mastered that One (40)	You have completed all of one character's Challenges!
Meat Dimension (20)	You defeated an opponent in Arcade Mode or online before he Awakened! Now, that's a real challenge!
Null Physical (20)	You performed 50 Instant Blocks in Arcade Mode or online.
One More! (10)	You performed 20 One More Bursts in Arcade Mode or online.
Per...so......na...! (10)	Have you burned your dread? Or reached out to the truth?
Perfect! (10)	You had a perfect victory in Arcade Mode or online.
Persona Breaker (10)	You created 10 Persona Breaks in Arcade Mode or online.
Replay Reviewer (10)	You watched a Replay in the Theater. Are you as good as you remember?
School's Out (10)	You've aced all the tests.
Serious Gamer (40)	You have reached Level 30 by playing online matches!
Speak with Your Fists! (30)	You've battled against every character in online matches. You're a grizzly'd warrior now!
Stylish! (10)	You performed 100 Auto Combos in Arcade Mode or online.
The Angel (10)	Aigis' Story chapter has been told.
The Beast (10)	Teddie's Story chapter has been told.
The Boxer (10)	Akihiko's Story chapter has been told.
The Captain (10)	Yosuke's Story chapter has been told.
The Carnivore (10)	Chie's Story chapter has been told.
The Detective (10)	Naoto's Story chapter has been told.

The Emperor (10)	Kanji's Story chapter has been told.
The Kingpin (10)	Yu's Story chapter has been told.
The Queen (10)	Mitsuru's Story chapter has been told.
The Unconquerable (10)	Yukiko's Story chapter has been told.
They Call Me... (10)	You've created a Title for your online matches.
Time for the All-Out Attack! (10)	You performed 100 All-Out Attacks in Arcade Mode or online.
Trained in Seclusion (10)	You spent 30 minutes in Training in one sitting. Now take it to the streets!
Tres Bien! (30)	You completed Score Attack Mode with one character.
u003e You Should Leave Him Be... (10)	You were afflicted with every ailment in Arcade Mode or online. Not even Mr. Edogawa can help you.
Veteran (30)	You have completed 100 online matches, win or lose. No bear puns here. Congrats.
Victory Cry (20)	You won 30 Rounds in Arcade Mode or Online by using SP Skills or Awakened SP Skills.
Wild (10)	You have used all the characters in Arcade Mode or Online. Variety is good for you!
You know the Midnight Channel? (10)	Tuned In

PHANTOM BREAKER (XBOX 360)

ACHIEVEMENT

UNLOCKABLE	HOW TO UNLOCK
Aerial Combat! (25)	Landed a total of 25 hits during clock-up with overdrive in one round.
All I've got (20)	Unlocked by using a Critical-Burst.
Break free! (15)	Perform at least 30 successful counter-attacks in one round [Story, Arcade, and Online matches only]
Brick wall defense! (10)	Blocked a total of 15 hits during clock-up with overdrive in one round.
Clocked-in power?! (10)	Executed a total of 40 hits during clock-up with overdrive in one round.
Cocoa (30)	Story Mode: Viewed the ending for Cocoa.
Count your sins! (10)	Fin has arrived!
Counter master (30)	Broke through a total of 3,000 counter-attacks.
Didn't even need it (5)	In burst gauge MAX mode, chose weak attack to win.
Don't stop me now! (25)	Unlocked after fighting 50 ranked matches.
Escape artist (25)	Broke through slip shift a total of 250 times.
Flash! (5)	Use Overdrive mode while the fight style is set to Quick [Story, Arcade, and Online matches only]
Going slightly mad! (10)	Use a Counter-Burst. [Story, Arcade, and Online matches only]
I won't be caught (10)	Succeeded in escaping a throw.
I'll kill your illusions (10)	Rimi has arrived!
I'll open your head (10)	Kurisu has arrived!
I'm not your damn maid. (20)	Unlocked Kurisu.
Itsuki (30)	Story Mode: Viewed the ending for Itsuki.
Keep blocking (15)	Used protection 15 times in one round.
Keep escaping (15)	Used slip shift 15 times in one round.

Keep yourself alive! (15)	Unlocked after winning ranked matches twice in a row.
Locked up! (15)	Unlocked by using a deadly technique for the deadly technique cancel enforcement.
M (30)	Story Mode: Viewed the ending for M.
Mei (30)	Story Mode: Viewed the ending for Mei.
Mikoto (35)	Story Mode: Viewed the ending for Mikoto.
Nailed it! (15)	Successfully executed a throw combo.
Now I have to use it (15)	Unlocked by using an ultra deadly technique.
Now I'm here! (5)	Unlocked after winning a ranked match for the first time.
Phantom breaker maniacs (10)	Saving Phantom Breaker demo version data, or cancelling all performance records.
Phantom Breaking (50)	Broke through a total of 500 blocks.
Quit dreaming! (20)	Unlocked Rimi.
Ren (30)	Story Mode: Viewed the ending for Ren.
Revival (20)	Unlocked by launching Imagine Mode in one round.
Ria (30)	Story Mode: Viewed the ending for Ria.
Rock you! (5)	Use Overdrive mode while the fight style is set to Hard. [Story, Arcade, and Online matches only]
Rushing headlong! (15)	Unlocked after fighting 25 ranked matches.
Save me! (10)	Unlocked when emergency is used.[Story, Arcade, and Online matches only]
Schroedinger's Cat! (20)	Unlocked Fin.
Textbook fighter (5)	Read all of the game reference.
The neverending one (20)	Unlocked Infinity.
Think you just captured me?! (15)	Succeeded in escaping a just throw.
To be continued...? (30)	Story Mode: Viewed the ending for Fin.
Tokiya (30)	Story Mode: Viewed the ending for Tokiya.
Uke artist (25)	Broke through protection a total of 250 times.
Under pressure? (10)	Unlocked when guard break is applied [Story, Arcade, and Online matches only]
Waka (30)	Story Mode: Viewed the ending for Waka.
Wasn't expecting an uppercut... (15)	Unlocked by using a cross Counter-Burst.
Yodame Cantabile (60)	Achieve an attack damage of 65,536 points.
You are the champion! (30)	Unlocked when arcade mode is completed on any difficulty.
Yuzuha (30)	Story Mode: Viewed the ending for Yuzuha.

PHINEAS AND FERB: ACROSS THE 2ND DIMENSION (PLAYSTATION VITA)

TROPHY

UNLOCKABLE	HOW TO UNLOCK
Agh, Bees! (Bronze)	Run through the bee path in under 38 seconds.
Balloon Gold (Silver)	Collect all of the gold tokens in the balloon dimension.
Barging Through (Bronze)	Ride the entire balloon barge without falling once.
Charging Goozim (Bronze)	Make the Goozim charge into all the gnome village wreckage.
Chiptastic (Silver)	Collect every upgrade,effect,and mod chip in the game.

CODES & CHEATS

Commander Counselor (Bronze)	Defeat 3 Dooftron Commanders in the level. (The giant buildings.)
Cruiser Destroyer (Bronze)	Don't let any cruisers get away. (Shoot them all down.)
Cruising through Crushers (Bronze)	Get through all the crushers without getting hit.
Dimensional Gold Claim (Gold)	Collect all of the gold tokens across all the dimensions.
Evil Doof's Gold (Silver)	Collect all of the gold tokens assaulting Evil Doof's HQ.
Evil Vanquisher (Bronze)	Beat all the levels in the game.
Fantasy Gold (Silver)	Collect all of the gold tokens in the gnome dimension.
Figure Madman (Gold)	Collect Every Figure in the game.
First Gadget (Bronze)	Collect all the parts and construct your first gadget.
Gelatin Freedom-Fighter (Bronze)	Beat all the gelatin dimension levels.
Gelatin Gold (Silver)	Collect all of the gold tokens in the gelatin dimension.
Gelatin Revolution (Bronze)	Defeat the Gelatin Monster in under 180 seconds.
Gnome Toppler (Bronze)	Complete all the gnome dimension levels.
Grand Slam (Silver)	Use only the Baseball Launcher to defeat the Doof-Robot.
I'm A-levelin' Mah Gadgets! (Bronze)	Get each and every gadget up to maximum level.
Just Bouncy (Bronze)	Climb up the gelatin mountain but never bounce more than once on the same bouncy pad.
Laser Tracer (Silver)	Avoid 4 quad-laser attacks in a row.
Let's Play Dress-Up (Gold)	Unlock all 17 additional skins
Lifetime Accomplishment Award (Platinum)	Collect every trophy in the game.
Modtacular (Bronze)	Collect all the mod chips in the game.
Old Timey Winds (Silver)	Go across the windy canyon without falling down once.
Padfoot (Bronze)	Don't trip any turret shots by stepping on the laser sensors.
Platform Walker (Bronze)	Stay on the moving platforms for at least 60 seconds. (Don't touch solid ground.)
Quick and Timely Champion (Bronze)	Don't miss any button prompts during the giant robot fight.
Robot Rioter (Bronze)	Complete all the robot factory levels.
Robotic Gold (Silver)	Collect all of the gold tokens in the robot factory.
Rush to the Sewers (Bronze)	Get from the treehouse all the way into the sewers as quickly as possible.
That Old Timey Life (Bronze)	Complete all the old timey dimension levels.
The Full Cast (Silver)	Unlock every single playable character (Baljeet, Isabella, Pinky, Peter).
There's Gold in Them Thar Hills (Silver)	Collect all of the gold tokens in the old timey dimension.
Ticket Stockpiler (Silver)	Have 500 tickets in your posession at once.
Up, Up and Away... (Bronze)	Complete all the balloon dimension levels.
Version 2.0 (Silver)	Install half of the upgrade chips in the game.
Weekend at the Arcade (Bronze)	Earn 2000 tickets in the course of the game.
What the Boulder's Cooking (Silver)	Defeat 3 enemies with boulders.

PIKMIN 2 (WII)

UNLOCKABLE

UNLOCKABLE	HOW TO UNLOCK
Challenge Mode	Defeat the Beady Long Legs at the bottom of the Spider Citadle, and bring the key to the recon drone thing.
Cinemas and Credits	Collect 10,000 pocos
Gold Ship	Collect 10,000 pokos
Louie's Cooking Notes	Rescue Louie from Titan Dweevil at Dream Den
Louie's Dark Secret movie	Complete all 30 Challenge Mode Arenas obtaining pink flowers (ie no Pikmin deaths).
Sales Pitch	Collect all items in any series
Shacho	Collect 10,000 pocos to save Hokotate Intergalactic Delivery, then choose to continue.
Treasure Completion Movie	Collect all the pieces and rescue Looie.
Awakening Wood Level	Collect the sphere map in Emergence Cave.
Perplexing Pool Level	Collect the exploration map in the Awakening Wood.
Wistful Wild Level	Repay the 10,000 pokos of your company's debt.

PINBALL HALL OF FAME (PSP)

Enter these passwords on the Password screen.

UNLOCKABLE	PASSWORD
999 Credits	JAT
Freeplay on Big Shot	UJP
Freeplay on Black Hole	LIS
Freeplay on Goin' Nuts	PHF
Freeplay on Love Meter	HOT

Enter these passwords on the Password screen.

UNLOCKABLE	PASSWORD
Freeplay on Tee'd Off	PGA
Freeplay on Xolten	BIG
Unlocks Payout mode	WGR
Unlocks Aces High for freeplay	UNO
Unlocks Central Park for freeplay	NYC
Unlocks custom balls in Options	CKF
Unlocks freeplay on Strikes 'N Spares	PBA
Unlocks optional tilt in Options	BZZ
Unlocks Play Boy table for freeplay	HEF

PIRATES OF THE CARIBBEAN: AT WORLD'S END (DS)

UNLOCKABLES

UNLOCKABLE	HOW TO UNLOCK
Secret Cove	Collect all 7 Secret Map Fragments in Shipwreck Cove.

PIRATES PLUNDARRR (WII)

UNLOCKABLE CHARACTERS

UNLOCKABLE	HOW TO UNLOCK
Amazon	Defeat Tecciztecatl, Witch Doctor.
Spectral	Defeat Nanauatl, Hero of the Sun.

PIXELJUNK EDEN (PLAYSTATION 3)

CUSTOM SOUNDTRACK

Find all 50 spectra to unlock in-game custom soundtrack.

PLANTS VS. ZOMBIES (XBOX 360)

CODES

To enter a cheat code, press LB, RB, LT, RT in game; some codes require a tall enough tree of wisdom.u.

EFFECT	CODE
A shower of candy when a zombie dies	pinata
Alternate lawn mower appearance	trickedout
Gives zombies futuristic shades	future
Mustaches for zombie	mustache
Once zombies are killed, they leave small daisies behind	daisies
Toggles the zombie's call for brains sound	sukhbir
Zombies dance	dance

POKÉMON BLACK (DS)

UNLOCKABLE

UNLOCKABLE	HOW TO UNLOCK
National Dex	Beat the Elite Four once and upon leaving your house after the credits Professor Juniper's Dad will reward you with a National Dex.

UNLOCKABLE

Get new wallpapers for beating the elite four for the first time, then some more when you beat them the second time.

UNLOCKABLE	HOW TO UNLOCK
Wallpapers	Beat the Elite Four twice.

UNLOCKABLE

The color of your Trainer Card changes as you complete certain objectives.

UNLOCKABLE	HOW TO UNLOCK
Color Change	Complete the National Pokedex
Color Change	Obtain all Entralink Powers
Color Change	Obtain all Pokemon Musical Items
Color Change	Get a 49 Streak in both Super Single and Super Double Subway lines in the Battle Subway (Good Luck)
Color Change	Deafeat the Elite 4

POKÉMON HEARTGOLD (DS)

UNLOCKABLES

UNLOCKABLE	HOW TO UNLOCK
National Dex	Beat the Elite Four once and go to the S.S Aqua ship in Olivine City to get the National Dex.
Beautiful Beach	Obtain 200 Watts.
Beyond the Sea	Obtain a foreign Pokémon via use of the GTS.
Big Forest	Obtain 40,000 Watts and own the National Dex.
Blue Lake	Obtain 2,000 Watts.
Dim Cave	Obtain 1,000 Watts.
Hoenn Field	Obtain 5,000 Watts and own the National Dex.
Icy Mountain Rd.	Obtain 30,000 Watts and own the National Dex.
Night Sky's Edge	Trade a fateful-encounter Jirachi onto your HG or SS.
Noisy Forest	Available from the start.
Quiet Cave	Obtain 100,000 Watts and own the National Dex.

Refreshing Field	Available from the start.
Resort	Obtain 80,000 Watts and own the National Dex.
Rugged Road	Obtain 50 Watts.
Scary Cave	Obtain 20,000 Watts and own the National Dex.
Sinnoh Field	Obtain 25,000 Watts and own the National Dex.
Stormy Beach	Obtain 65,000 Watts and own the National Dex.
Suburban Area	Obtain 500 Watts.
Town Outskirts	Obtain 3,000 Watts.
Tree House	Obtain 15,000 Watts and own the National Dex.
Volcano Path	Obtain 10,000 Watts and own the National Dex.
Warm Beach	Obtain 7,500 Watts and own the National Dex.
White Lake	Obtain 50,000 Watts and own the National Dex.

POKÉMON RUMBLE BLAST (3DS)

CODE

Use these codes to unlock special Pokémon in the specified levels. Speak to Munna in Easterly Town to enter a code. You must defeat them to add them to your collection.

UNLOCKABLE	HOW TO UNLOCK
Gallade (in 4-2 Everspring Valley) 3535-6928	
Gliscor (in 4-3 Sunny Seashore) 9625-7845	
Heat Stamp Emboar (in 1-3 Echo Valley) 8902-7356	
Oshawott (in 2-4 Shimmering Lake) 7403-2240	
Pikachu (in 3-2 Volcanic Slope) 7746-3878	
Tornadus (in 3-2 Volcanic Slope) 0250-7321	

UNLOCKABLE

As you meet people with the game on Street Pass, you'll be able to find new Legendary Pokemon on different areas.

UNLOCKABLE	HOW TO UNLOCK
Azelf [Shimmering Lake: Lake Area]	Meet 10 People
Celebi [Everspring Valley: Forest Area]	Meet 60 People
Jirachi [Firebreathing Mountain: Tower Area]	Meet 40 People
Manaphy [Rugged Flats: Beach Area]	Meet 20 People
Mesprit [Soothing Shore: Lake Area]	Meet 5 People
Mew [Sunny Seashore: Factory Area]	Meet 80 People
Phione [Rugged Flats: Beach Area]	Meet 20 People
Shaymin (Land Forme) [World Axle Underground 2F: Ice Area]	Meet 100 People
Shaymin (Sky Forme) [World Axle Underground 1F: Forest Area]	Meet 120 People
Uxie [Sun-Dappled Bank: Lake Area]	Meet 2 People
Victini [World Axle Underground 2F: Tower Area]	Meet 150 People

POKÉMON SOULSILVER (DS)

UNLOCKABLES

UNLOCKABLE	HOW TO UNLOCK
National Dex	Beat the Elite Four once and go to the S.S. Aqua ship in Olivine City to get the National Dex.
Amity Meadow	Unreleased to all versions.
Beautiful Beach	Collect 200 Watts.

Beyond the Sea	Trade for an International Pokémon in the GTS in Goldenrod City.
Big Forest	Collect 40,000 Watts + National Dex.
Blue Lake	Collect 2,000 Watts.
Dim Cave	Collect 1,000 Watts.
Hoenn Field	Collect 5,000 Watts + National Dex.
Icy Mountain Road	Collect 30,000 Watts + National Dex.
Night Sky's Edge	Obtain the PokéDex Data for Jirachi.
Quiet Cave	Collect 100,000 Watts + National Dex.
Rally	Unreleased to U.S. versions.
Rugged Road	Collect 50 Watts.
Scary Cave	Collect 20,000 Watts + National Dex.
Sightseeing	Unreleased to U.S. versions.
Sinnoh Field	Collect 25,000 Watts + National Dex.
Stormy Beach	Collect 65,000 Watts + National Dex.
Suburban Area	Collect 500 Watts.
The Resort	Collect 80,000 Watts + National Dex.
Town Outskirts	Collect 3,000 Watts.
Treehouse	Collect 15,000 Watts + National Dex.
Volcano Path	Collect 10,000 Watts + National Dex.
Warm Beach	Collect 7,500 Watts + National Dex.
White Lake	Collect 50,000 Watts + National Dex.

POKEMON WHITE (DS)

UNLOCKABLE
After beating the game, leave your house and Professor Juniper's Father will upgrade your Pokedex to National Mode.

UNLOCKABLE
Get new wallpapers for beating the elite four for the first time, then some more when you beat them the second time.

UNLOCKABLE	HOW TO UNLOCK
Wallpapers	Beat the Elite Four twice.

PORTAL: STILL ALIVE (XBOX 360)

UNLOCKABLES
UNLOCKABLE	HOW TO UNLOCK
Portal Gamer picture	In test chamber 17, incinerate the companion cube.
Portal Gamer picture (2)	Defeat GLaDOS and escape

PORTAL 2 (XBOX 360)

UNLOCKABLE
UNLOCKABLE	HOW TO UNLOCK
Alternate Title Screen	Beat the game to get a different title screen

UNLOCKABLE
Complete the task to earn an item for your avatar.

UNLOCKABLE	HOW TO UNLOCK
Companion Cube	Complete Portal 2 Single Player.
Love Shirt	Hug 3 friends in Portal 2 Coop.
Portal 2 Hat	Survive the manual override.
Portal 2 Shirt	Complete Portal 2 Coop
Turret Shirt	Complete Test Chamber 10 in under 70 seconds.

EASTER EGG

UNLOCKABLE	HOW TO UNLOCK
Singing Turrets	Look for a turret in a ventilation shaft in one of the test chambers at the very beginning. Use the laser and reflector cube to destroy it, then go through the new opening to find singing turrets.

PRINCE OF PERSIA: CLASSIC (XBOX 360)

PASSWORDS

PASSWORD	EFFECT
73232535	Level 2
96479232	Level 3
53049212	Level 4
51144526	Level 5
18736748	Level 6
42085223	Level 7
98564243	Level 8
51139315	Level 9
53246739	Level 10
32015527	Level 11
44153123	Level 12
96635134	Level 13
75423134	Level 14
89012414	End

PRO EVOLUTION SOCCER 2012 (PLAYSTATION 3)

TROPHY

UNLOCKABLE	HOW TO UNLOCK
Champion Chairman (Silver)	Awarded for winning a Top Flight League Title in [Club Boss].
Champion Manager (Silver)	Awarded for winning the League Title in any of the Top Leagues featured in [Master League].
Copa Santander Libertadores King (Silver)	Awarded for becoming a [Copa Santander Libertadores] Winner.
Copa Santander Libertadores R16 (Bronze)	Awarded for making it through the Group stage in [Copa Santander Libertadores].
Copa Santander Libertadores Win (Bronze)	Awarded for defeating the COM for the first time in [Copa Santander Libertadores].
European Elite 16 (Bronze)	Awarded for making it through the Group stage of the UEFA Champions League in [Master League].
First Glory: Club Boss (Bronze)	Awarded for your first win as a Club Owner in [Club Boss].
First Glory: Competition (Bronze)	Awarded for your first win in an [Online Competition].
First Glory: Exhibition (Bronze)	Awarded for defeating the COM for the first time in [Exhibition].
First Glory: Master League (Bronze)	Awarded for your first win in [Master League].
First Glory: Quick Match (Bronze)	Awarded for winning your first [Quick Match]. No disconnections permitted.
First Win: UEFA Champions League (Bronze)	Awarded for defeating the COM for the first time in [UEFA Champions League].
International Champion (Silver)	Awarded for winning a National Team Competition in [League/Cup].
Kings of Europe (Silver)	Awarded for becoming a UEFA Champions League Winner in [Master League].

League Best Eleven (Silver)	Awarded for being picked for the Team of the Season in [Become a Legend].
League Champion (Silver)	Awarded for single-handedly winning a League Title in [League/Cup].
League Champions (Silver)	Awarded for winning the League Title in [Become a Legend].
Mr. Versatility (Bronze)	Awarded for learning to play in another position in [Become a Legend].
No.1 Club (Gold)	Awarded for being named the No.1 Club in the [Master League] Club Rankings.
No.1 Owner (Gold)	Awarded for being the Greatest Owner within the Beautiful Game in [Club Boss].
Online Debutant (Bronze)	Awarded for completing your debut match in [Online]. No disconnections permitted.
Pride of a Nation (Silver)	Awarded for playing in the International Cup in [Become a Legend].
Promoted (Bronze)	Awarded for Winning Promotion to a Top League in [Master League].
Proud Skipper (Bronze)	Awarded for being named Club Captain in [Become a Legend].
Super Star (Gold)	Awarded for winning the UEFA Club Footballer of the Year Award [Become a Legend].
The Community Associate (Silver)	Awarded for joining your first [Online Community].
The Debutant (Bronze)	Awarded for making a professional debut in [Become a Legend].
The Highlight Show (Bronze)	Awarded for watching Highlight Footage in [Final Highlights].
The Multi-Talented (Bronze)	Awarded for acquiring a New Skill in [Become a Legend].
The Treble Winner (Silver)	Awarded for winning the League, UEFA Champions League and League Cup in a [Master League] season.
Theatre Connoisseur (Bronze)	Awarded for watching a Highlight Reel uploaded by another user in the [Theatre of Legends].
UEFA Champions League Debut (Silver)	Awarded for making your UEFA Champions League debut in [Become a Legend].
UEFA Champions League Elite 16 (Bronze)	Awarded for making it through the Group stage in [UEFA Champions League].
UEFA Champions League Winner (Silver)	Awarded for becoming a [UEFA Champions League] Winner.
Ultimate Player (Platinum)	Perfect Collection
Wheeler and Dealer (Bronze)	Awarded for making your first ever signing in [Master League Online].
World Footballer of the Year (Gold)	Awarded for being named World Footballer of the Year in [Become a Legend].

PRO WRESTLING (WII)

UNLOCKABLES

UNLOCKABLE	HOW TO UNLOCK
Battle the Great Puma	Once you are VWA Champion, defend your title for 10 matches. Then you will have a match with the Great uma.

PROFESSOR LAYTON AND THE DIABOLICAL BOX (DS)

UNLOCKABLES

After beating the game, go to the Top Secret section of the Bonuses menu to access the following unlockables.

UNLOCKABLE	HOW TO UNLOCK
Art Gallery	Beat the game.
Character Profiles List	Beat the game.
Layton's Challenges: The Sweetheart's House	Beat the game.

PROTOTYPE (XBOX 360)

CODES

Select "Extras" from the Main menu and go to "Cheats."

EFFECT	CODE
Unlock Body Surf Ability	➡,➡,⬅,⬇,⬇,⬆,⬆,⬇

PROTOTYPE (PLAYSTATION 3)

CODES

Select "Extras" from the Main Menu and go to "Cheats."

EFFECT	CODE
Unlock Body Surf Ability	→,→,←,↓,↑,↑,↑,↓

PROTOTYPE 2 (PLAYSTATION 3)

TROPHY

UNLOCKABLE	HOW TO UNLOCK
//BLACKNET Hacker (Silver)	Complete all //BLACKNET dossiers.
All Growed Up (Silver)	Fully upgrade Heller.
All Together Now (Bronze)	10 or more kills with a single Black Hole attack.
Anger Management (Silver)	Destroy 5 vehicles using a Finisher.
Arcade Action (Bronze)	Karate kick a helicopter.
Back Atcha! (Bronze)	Deflect 5 missiles at enemies using Shield Block.
Cannonball! (Bronze)	20 or more kills with a single Hammerfist dive attack.
Compulsive Eater (Bronze)	5 consumes in 10 seconds or less.
Do the Evolution (Bronze)	Acquire 5 Mutations.
Eating Your Way to the Top (Silver)	Acquire 30 upgrades through Consumes.
Finally Full (Gold)	Acquire all 46 upgrades through Consumes.
Follow Your Nose (Silver)	Find all BlackBoxes.
Hard to Please (Silver)	Acquire a Mutation in each of the 5 categories.
Hijack Be Nimble (Bronze)	Stealth hijack 5 tanks or APCs.
I Caught a Big One! (Bronze)	Mount a helicopter using Whipfist.
I Want Some More (Bronze)	Complete RESURRECTION.
Icarus (Bronze)	Reach the highest point in the world.
It's an Epidemic (Bronze)	Complete MEET YOUR MAKER.
Just a Flesh Wound (Bronze)	Dismember a Brawler.
Lair to Rest (Bronze)	Destroy a single Lair.
Master Prototype (Silver)	Complete the game on HARD difficulty.
Murder your Maker? (Gold)	Complete the game.
One by One (Bronze)	Stealth Consume 50 Blackwatch troopers.
Over-Equipped (Bronze)	Weaponize 10 vehicles.

Platinum Trophy (Platinum)	Unlock all Trophies.
Project Closed (Bronze)	Complete a //BLACKNET operation.
Religious Experience (Bronze)	Meet Father Guerra.
Road Rage (Silver)	Destroy 10 Blackwatch tanks, APCs or helicopters using a single hijacked tank or APC.
Sic 'em! (Bronze)	Destroy 5 helicopters using Pack Leader.
So Above It All (Silver)	Spend at least 25 consecutive seconds in the air (helicopters don't count).
Something to Live For (Silver)	Complete FALL FROM GRACE.
Spindler's Search (Silver)	Destroy all Lairs.
Strike, You're Out. (Bronze)	Destroy a Strike Team in 15 seconds or less.
The Best Offense (Bronze)	Counter enemy attacks 20 times using Shield.
The Floor is Lava (Bronze)	Travel a half mile using only Wall Run, Glide, Jump and Air Dash.
The Mad Scientist (Silver)	Complete NATURAL SELECTION.
This is a Knife (Bronze)	Acquire a Prototype Power.
Two for the Price of One (Bronze)	Simultaneously kill 2 Brawlers using a single Devastator.
Up to No Good (Silver)	Defeat all Field Ops teams.
Vitamin B-rains (Bronze)	Acquire 10 upgrades through Consumes.
Wanted Man (Bronze)	Trigger 50 alerts.
What a Bitch (Silver)	Complete LABOR OF LOVE.
Who Watches the Watchers? (Silver)	Consume 10 //BLACKNET targets.
You're the Bomb (Bronze)	10 or more kills using a single Bio-Bomb.

UNLOCKABLE

UNLOCKABLE	HOW TO UNLOCK
New Game +	Complete the game on any difficulty
Insane Mode	Complete the game on any difficulty

PROTOTYPE 2 (XBOX 360)

ACHIEVEMENT

UNLOCKABLE	HOW TO UNLOCK
//BLACKNET Hacker (40)	Completed all //BLACKNET dossiers.
All Growed Up (50)	Fully upgraded Heller.
All Together Now (20)	10 or more kills with a single Black Hole attack.
Anger Management (20)	Destroyed 5 vehicles using a Finisher.
Arcade Action (10)	Karate kicked a helicopter.
Back Atcha! (20)	Deflected 5 missiles at enemies using Shield Block.
Cannonball! (10)	20 or more kills with a single Hammerfist dive attack.
Compulsive Eater (10)	5 consumes in 10 seconds or less.
Do the Evolution (20)	Acquired 5 Mutations.
Eating Your Way to the Top (30)	Acquired 30 upgrades through Consumes.
Finally Full (50)	Acquired all 46 upgrades through Consumes.
Follow Your Nose (30)	Found all BlackBoxes.
Hard to Please (20)	Acquired a Mutation in each of the 5 categories.

Hijack Be Nimble (15)	Stealth hijacked 5 tanks or APCs.
I Caught a Big One! (10)	Mounted a helicopter using Whipfist.
I Want Some More (10)	Complete RESURRECTION.
Icarus (15)	Reached the highest point in the world.
It's an Epidemic (10)	Complete MEET YOUR MAKER.
Just a Flesh Wound (10)	Dismembered a Brawler.
Lair to Rest (15)	Destroyed a single Lair.
Master Prototype (50)	Completed the game on HARD difficulty.
Murder your Maker? (100)	Complete the game.
One by One (20)	Stealth Consumed 50 Blackwatch troopers.
Over-Equipped (20)	Weaponized 10 vehicles.
Project Closed (20)	Completed a //BLACKNET mission.
Religious Experience (10)	Meet Father Guerra.
Road Rage (20)	Destroyed 10 Blackwatch tanks, APCs or helicopters using a single hijacked tank or APC.
Sic 'em! (20)	Destroyed 5 helicopters using Pack Leader.
So Above It All (20)	Spend at least 25 consecutive seconds in the air (helicopters don't count).
Something to Live For (30)	Complete FALL FROM GRACE.
Spindler's Search (40)	Destroyed all Lairs.
Strike, You're Out. (10)	Destroyed a Strike Team in 15 seconds or less.
The Best Offense (20)	Countered enemy attacks 20 times using Shield.
The Floor is Lava (15)	Traveled a half mile using only Wall Run, Glide, Jump and Air Dash.
The Mad Scientist (30)	Complete NATURAL SELECTION.
This is a Knife (20)	First Prototype Power aquired.
Two for the Price of One (20)	Simultaneously killed 2 Brawlers using a single Devastator.
Up to No Good (30)	Defeated all Field Ops teams.
Vitamin B-rains (10)	Acquired 10 upgrades through Consumes.
Wanted Man (20)	Triggered 50 alerts.
What a Bitch (30)	Complete LABOR OF LOVE.
Who Watches the Watchers? (20)	Consumed 10 //BLACKNET targets.
You're the Bomb (10)	10 or more kills using a single Bio-Bomb.

UNLOCKABLE

UNLOCKABLE	HOW TO UNLOCK
Avatar Award: Alex Mercer Outfit	With RADNET activated, access the Events Screen for unlock details.
Avatar Award: Heller Hoodie	With RADNET activated, access the Events Screen for unlock details.
Avatar Award: James Heller Outfit	With RADNET activated, access the Events Screen for unlock details.
Avatar Award: Shield	With RADNET activated, access the Events Screen for unlock details.
Avatar Award: T-Shirt	With RADNET activated, access the Events Screen for unlock details.

PULSEMAN (WII)

UNLOCKABLES

UNLOCKABLE	HOW TO UNLOCK
Level SELECT	At the Sega logo, press (in joystick 2): Ⓐ, Ⓑ, Ⓒ, Ⓒ, Ⓑ, Ⓐ. After this, go to Options and use the Map option.

PUYO POP FEVER (DS)

To enter this code, go into Options, then Gallery, then highlight Cutscene Viewer.

UNLOCKABLE	CODE
Unlock all characters and cutscenes	Hold Ⓧ and press ↑, ↓, ←, →

QUAKE 4 (XBOX 360)

To enter these codes, press the Back button while playing.

UNLOCKABLE	CODE
Ammo Refill for All Weapons	Ⓑ, Ⓐ, Ⓧ, Ⓨ, ◌, ◌, ◌
Full Health Refill	Ⓑ, Ⓐ, Ⓑ, Ⓐ, ◌, ◌, ◌, Ⓧ

QUANTUM REDSHIFT (XBOX)

Enter Cheat as your name, then in the Options menu, select the Cheats menu to enter these codes. Codes are case sensitive.

UNLOCKABLE	CODE
All Characters	Nematode
All Speeds	zoomZOOM
Infinite Turbo	FishFace
Infinite Shields	ThinkBat
Upgrade All Characters	RICEitup

R-TYPE (WII)

UNLOCKABLES

UNLOCKABLE	HOW TO UNLOCK
Extra Credits	Set the turbo switch for I to full. Then, hold SELECT+① and press RUN on the title screen.

PASSWORDS

PASSWORD	EFFECT
CPL-3590-CM	Hard mode

R-TYPE 2 (WII)

PASSWORDS

PASSWORD	EFFECT
JJL-6589-MB	All items and 99 lives

R-TYPE 3 (WII)

UNLOCKABLES

UNLOCKABLE	HOW TO UNLOCK
Level Select	At the continue screen, press ⬆, ⬆, ⬆, ⬆, ⬆, ⬆, ⬆, ⬆, ⬆, ⬆ then press ⬆ one or more times, then press START (the number of times L is pressed dictates the level you skip to

RAGNAROK DS (DS)

MIRAGE TOWER

Mirage Tower consists of 50 floors with random monsters. This dungeon allows you to play online with other Ragnarok Online DS players. This dungeon is found at the lower-right portal of the North Sograt Desert

UNLOCKABLE	HOW TO UNLOCK
Mirage Tower	Complete the main quest till quest 25.

RAIDEN FIGHTERS JET (XBOX 360)

SECRET PLANES

UNLOCKABLE	HOW TO UNLOCK
Fairy	On the ship select screen hold B on Miclus and then press A (B must still be held down).
Slave	On the ship select screen Hold B on any ship except Miclus and then press A (while B is still held down).

RAMPAGE: TOTAL DESTRUCTION (WII)

At the main menu, press the ⊖+⊕ to open the Password screen.

UNLOCKABLE	PASSWORD
All Monsters Unlocked	141421
Demo Mode with Two Random Monsters	082864
Disable All Active Codes	000000
Display Game Version	314159
Instant Demo Mode with Two Random Monsters	874098
Invincible to Military Attacks, Bombers, Infantry, Tanks, Etc.	986960

Obtain All Ability Upgrades	011235
One Hit Destroys a Building	071767
Unlock All Cities	271828
View Credits	667302
View Ending Theme	667301
View Opening Theme	667300

RAYMAN ORIGINS (PLAYSTATION VITA)

TROPHY

UNLOCKABLE	HOW TO UNLOCK
B Side! (Bronze)	Played an Unlocked Character in any map.
Back At You! (Bronze)	You Bubblized a Hunter with his own live missile!
Beautiful Beats! (Bronze)	Holly Luya, the Music Nymph is Free!
Betilla's Back! (Bronze)	Head Nymph Betilla is Free!
Blue Baron! (Silver)	Beat the Giant Eel within 60 Seconds in 'Aim for the Eel.'
Boing! Boing! Boing! (Bronze)	Bounce-Bubblized 11 Enemies without landing in 'Polar Pursuit!'
Bubble Wrap Maniac! (Bronze)	Popped 100 Item Bubbles with tap
Clear Sighted (Bronze)	You found 30 Relics
Crush Combo! (Bronze)	Simultaneously crushed 4 enemies.
Crusher! (Bronze)	Crushed 50 Enemies.
Dr. Lividstone, I presume? (Gold)	You found ALL hidden cages.
Eagle Eyed (Silver)	You found all Relics.
Electoon Friend (Bronze)	Completed 10 Medallions.
Electoon Hero (Silver)	Completed 25 Medallions.
Electoon Legend (Gold)	Completed ALL Medallions.
Explorer (Silver)	You found 25 hidden cages.
Feed the Fairy! (Bronze)	Edith Up, the Gourmet Fairy is Free!
Fisher King! (Bronze)	Swam a Marathon!
Full Mouth (Silver)	Earned 5 Skull Teeth.
Grim Reaper (Bronze)	Popped 50 Enemy Bubbles with tap
Hover Happy! (Bronze)	One hour of flight time!
Hyperspeed! (Bronze)	Sprinted for an Entire Level!
I'm Back! (Bronze)	Replayed any completed map.
Kung Fu Combo! (Bronze)	Perform a swipe-to-air Kick Combo!
Merm-Aid! (Bronze)	Annetta Fish, the Ocean Nymph is Free!
Milk Tooth (Bronze)	Earned 1 Skull Tooth.
Nitro! (Gold)	Earned ALL speed trophies!
No Panic! (Bronze)	Saved ALL Darktooned Wizards in 'Port 'O Panic'.
Nothing Lasts Forever... (Gold)	Ding, Dong, the Livid Boss is Dead!
Nymphs Rock! (Bronze)	Helena Handbasket, the Mountain Nymph is Free!
Painless! (Bronze)	Completed a level without taking a hit!
Scout (Bronze)	You found 10 hidden cages.
Speedy! (Bronze)	Earned 5 speed trophies.
Sprinter! (Bronze)	Sprinted a Marathon!
Survivor (Bronze)	Survived a Piranha Pond without a scratch!
Sweet Dreams! (Platinum)	Won ALL trophies in the game! SICK!
The Bubblizer! (Bronze)	Chain-Bubblized 4 Enemies.
The Jaw (Gold)	Earned ALL Skull Teeth.

| Turbo! (Silver) | Earned 15 speed trophies! |
| Vacuum Snack! (Bronze) | Inhaled 50 things on Moskito-back. |

RAYMAN ORIGINS (XBOX 360)

ACHIEVEMENT

UNLOCKABLE	HOW TO UNLOCK
B Side! (15)	Played an Unlocked Character in any map.
Back At You! (15)	You Bubblized a Hunter with his own live missile!
Beautiful Beats! (15)	Holly Luya, the Music Nymph is Free!
Betilla's Back! (15)	Head Nymph Betilla is Free!
Blue Baron! (35)	Beat the Giant Eel within 60 Seconds in "Aim for the Eel."
Boing! Boing! Boing! (15)	Bounce-Bubblized 11 Enemies without landing in "Polar Pursuit!"
Crush Combo! (15)	Simultaneously crushed 4 enemies.
Crusher! (15)	Crushed 50 Enemies.
Dr. Lividstone, I presume? (80)	You found ALL hidden cages.
Electoon Friend (15)	Completed 10 Medallions.
Electoon Hero (35)	Completed 25 Medallions.
Electoon Legend (80)	Completed ALL Medallions.
Explorer (35)	You found 25 hidden cages.
Feed the Fairy! (15)	Edith Up, the Gourmet Fairy is Free!
Fisher King! (20)	Swam a Marathon!
Full Mouth (35)	Earned 5 Skull Teeth.
Hover Happy! (20)	One hour of flight time!
Hyperspeed! (35)	Sprinted for an Entire Level!
I'm Back! (15)	Replayed any completed map.
Kung Fu Combo! (15)	Perform a swipe-to-air Kick Combo!
Merm-Aid! (15)	Annetta Fish, the Ocean Nymph is Free!
Milk Tooth (15)	Earned 1 Skull Tooth.
Nitro! (80)	Earned ALL speed trophies!
No Panic! (15)	Saved ALL Darktooned Wizards in "Port 'O Panic".
Nothing Lasts Forever... (80)	Ding, Dong, the Livid Boss is Dead!
Nymphs Rock! (15)	Helena Handbasket, the Mountain Nymph is Free!
Painless! (15)	Completed a level without taking a hit!
Pop! Pop! BOOM! (15)	Popped 50 Enemy Bubbles.
Scout (15)	You found 10 hidden cages.
Speedy! (15)	Earned 5 speed trophies!
Sprinter! (20)	Sprinted a Marathon!
Survivor! (15)	Survived a Piranha Pond without a scratch!
The Bubblizer! (15)	Chain-Bubblized 4 Enemies.
The Jaw! (80)	Earned ALL Skull Teeth.
Turbo! (35)	Earned 15 speed trophies!
Vacuum Snack! (15)	Inhaled 50 things on Moskito-back.

UNLOCKABLE

UNLOCKABLE	HOW TO UNLOCK
Land of the Livid Dead	Collect all ten Skull Teeth.

REALITY FIGHTERS (PLAYSTATION VITA)

TROPHY

UNLOCKABLE	HOW TO UNLOCK
Advanced Survival (Silver)	Win 20 combats in survivor mode in a single run
Against the Clock (Bronze)	Reach Bronze score in all Time Attack Challenges
Ballerina Master (Bronze)	Perform all the moves for the Ballerina fight style in a single fight
Basic Survival (Bronze)	Win 10 combats in survivor mode in a single run
Beat Reality Fighters (Platinum)	Get all Gold, Silver and Bronze trophies
Boxing Master (Bronze)	Perform all the moves for the Boxing fight style in a single fight
Break Dance Master (Bronze)	Perform all the moves for the Break Dance fight style in a single fight
Capoeira Master (Bronze)	Perform all the moves for the Capoeira fight style in a single fight
Cowboy Master (Bronze)	Perform all the moves for the Cowboy fight style in a single fight
Disco Master (Bronze)	Perform all the moves for the Disco fight style in a single fight
Extreme Survival (Gold)	Win 30 combats in survivor mode in a single run
Karate Master (Bronze)	Perform all the moves for the Karate fight style in a single fight
Kung Fu Master (Bronze)	Perform all the moves for the Kung Fu fight style in a single fight
Love Challenge IV (Gold)	Discover the Disco Inferno and the Dancing Dino costumes
Lovely Challenge I (Silver)	Discover the Space Cowboy and the Fisher King costumes
Lovely Challenge II (Silver)	Discover the Lord of the Gnomes and the Handyman costumes
Lovely Challenge III (Gold)	Discover the Rocket Rocker and the Thumbling Stone costumes
Master of Time (Gold)	Achieve Gold score in all Time Attack challenges
Muay Thai Master (Bronze)	Perform all the moves for the Muay Thai fight style in a single fight
Perfect combat (Bronze)	Defeat an enemy receiving no damage at all
Rodeo Drive (Gold)	Buy all clothing, weapons and fight styles
Rush hour (Silver)	Beat five different friends in Infrastructure in less than one hour
Samurai Master (Bronze)	Perform all the moves for the Samurai fight style in a single fight
Sorcerer Master (Bronze)	Perform all the moves for the Sorcerer fight style in a single fight
Super Hero Master (Bronze)	Perform all the moves for the Super Hero fight style in a single fight
Super Heroine Master (Bronze)	Perform all the moves for the Super Heroine fight style in a single fight
The New Sensei (Gold)	Complete the story mode
Time Warrior (Silver)	Reach silver score in all Time Attack challenges
Wrestling Master (Bronze)	Perform all the moves for the Wrestling fight style in a single fight
Zombie Master (Bronze)	Perform all the moves for the Zombie fight style in a single fight

RED DEAD REDEMPTION (PS3)

CODES

Enabling a code will permanently prevent the game from being saved and trophies from being earned.

EFFECT	CODE
Become a nobody	HUMILITY BEFORE THE LORD
Decrease Bounty	THEY SELL SOULS CHEAP HERE
Diplomatic Immunity	I WISH I WORKED FOR UNCLE SAM
Enable the Sepia filter	THE OLD WAYS IS THE BEST WAYS
Fame	I AM ONE OF THEM FAMOUS FELLAS
Get $500	THE ROOT OF ALL EVIL, WE THANK YOU!
Good Guy	IT AINT PRIDE. IT'S HONOR
Gun Set 1	IT'S MY CONSTITUTIONAL RIGHT
Gun Set 2	I'M AN AMERICAN. I NEED GUNS
Infinite ammo	ABUNDANCE IS EVERYWHERE
Infinite Dead Eye	I DON'T UNDERSTAND IMNFINITY
Infinite Horse Stamina	MAKE HAY WHILE THE SUN SHINES
Invincibility	HE GIVES STRENGTH TO THE WEAK
Man in Uniform	I LOVE A MAN IN UNIFORM
Play as Jack	OH MY SON, MY BLESSED SON
Sharp Dressed Man	DON'T YOU LOOK FINE AND DANDY
Spawn a horse-drawn coach	NOW WHO PUT THAT THERE?
Spawn a horse	BEASTS AND MAN TOGETHER
Unlock all areas	YOU GOT YOURSELF A FINE PAIR OF EYES
Unlock all gang outfits	YOU THINK YOU TOUGH, MISTER?

RED DEAD REDEMPTION (XBOX 360)

CODES

Enabling a code will permanently prevent the game from being saved and achievements from being earned.

EFFECT	CODE
Become a nobody	HUMILITY BEFORE THE LORD
Decrease Bounty	THEY SELL SOULS CHEAP HERE
Diplomatic Immunity	I WISH I WORKED FOR UNCLE SAM
Enable the Sepia filter	THE OLD WAYS IS THE BEST WAYS
Fame	I AM ONE OF THEM FAMOUS FELLAS
Get $500	THE ROOT OF ALL EVIL, WE THANK YOU!
Good Guy	IT AINT PRIDE. IT'S HONOR
Gun Set 1	IT'S MY CONSTITUTIONAL RIGHT
Gun Set 2	I'M AN AMERICAN. I NEED GUNS
Infinite ammo	ABUNDANCE IS EVERYWHERE
Infinite Dead Eye	I DON'T UNDERSTAND IMNFINITY
Infinite Horse Stamina	MAKE HAY WHILE THE SUN SHINES
Invincibility	HE GIVES STRENGTH TO THE WEAK

RED FACTION: GUERRILLA (XBOX 360)

CODES

Fom the main menu select "Options," then "Extras," then enter code.

EFFECT	CODE
Bonus multiplayer map pack featuring four maps	MAPMAYHEM
Unlocks golden sledgehammer for single-player use	HARDHITTER

A B C D E F G H I J K L M N O P Q R S T U V W X Y Z

RED FACTION: GUERRILLA (PLAYSTATION 3)

CODES

Fom the main menu select "Options," then "Extras," then enter code.

EFFECT	CODE
Bonus multiplayer map pack featuring four maps	MAPMAYHEM
Unlocks golden sledgehammer for single-player use	HARDHITTER

RED STEEL 2 (WII)

CODES

Go to the Extras menu then to "Preorder" and enter the codes.

EFFECT	CODE
Barracuda	3582880
Nihonto Hana Sword (alternate code)	58855558
Sora Katana of the Katakara Clan	360152
Tataro Magnum	357370402
The Lost Blade of the Kusagari Clan	360378

RESIDENT EVIL 5 (PLAYSTATION 3)

REGENERATE ITEMS

In Chapter 2-1, take all the items at the beginning and then quit the game. Resume the game by pressing "Continue" to start Chapter 2-1 again. This time you will have items you got before you quit the game in your inventory, however, new sets of the items are there for you to collect. Repeat the process to get as many as you like. This glitch is also available in Chapter 3-1.

RESIDENT EVIL 5: LOST IN NIGHTMARES (XBOX 360)

UNLOCKABLES

UNLOCKABLE	HOW TO UNLOCK
Jill Valentine playable character	Complete Lost in Nightmares
Figures	Beat the game to unlock figurines. Viewable in the Bonus Gallery.
Old-School Resident Evil Camera Mode:	When the chapter starts, turn around and try to open the front door. Do this three times and a "?" will appear. Click to activate classic camera!

RESIDENT EVIL: OPERATION RACCOON CITY (PLAYSTATION 3)

TROPHY

UNLOCKABLE	HOW TO UNLOCK
A Gun by Any Other Name (Bronze)	Kill an enemy with each weapon type including special weapons.
A Hero Spared! (Bronze)	Attempt "The Rescue" and survive.
Baker's Dozen (Bronze)	Kill 13 zombified teammates.
Betrayal (Bronze)	Complete the fifth mission of the U.S.S. campaign.
Bloody Good Time (Bronze)	Kill 5 enemies with Blood Frenzy in a single campaign game or multiplayer match.
By Trail Of Dead (Bronze)	Kill 50 opponents in Versus. (lifetime)
Chaos Averted (Bronze)	Kill an infected teammate with a headshot before they become a zombie in any mode.
Choices Aplenty (Bronze)	Purchase 15 weapons.
Clingy (Bronze)	13 Parasite Zombies killed (lifetime)
Corrupted (Bronze)	Complete the second mission of the U.S.S. campaign.

Danger, High Voltage! (Bronze)	Complete the third mission of the U.S.S. campaign.
Died Trying (Bronze)	Attempt "The Rescue" and fail
Down Boy (Bronze)	Kill 13 zombie dogs (lifetime)
Down in the Labs (Bronze)	Complete the sixth mission of the U.S.S. campaign.
Epic Standards (Silver)	Upgrade all abilities for all characters to its maximum level.
Fallen Idols (Silver)	In Heroes mode, eliminate 4 Heroes in one game.
Feelin' Stronger Every Day (Bronze)	Fully upgrade an ability.
Great Success (Gold)	Gain S+ on all U.S.S. missions on Veteran or Professional difficulty
Green Thumb (Bronze)	Heal with 101 Green Herbs (lifetime)
Hat Trick (Bronze)	3 Tyrants Killed (lifetime)
Like a Bee (Silver)	Kill 10 enemy players in one multiplayer game with CQC.
Like a Butterfly (Bronze)	Kill 100 zombies with CQC (lifetime)
Look What I Can Do (Bronze)	Purchase all abilities for one character class.
Mr. Death (Platinum)	Get all Trophies.
No Sample For You (Bronze)	Force 25 enemies to drop G-Virus Samples in Biohazard (lifetime).
Now That's G (Bronze)	Collect 3 G-Virus Samples in one match.
On A Roll (Bronze)	Achieve a 5 kill streak in a Versus match.
One Trick Pony (Bronze)	Purchase an ability.
Only Hurts For A While (Bronze)	Infected 13 times (lifetime)
Organic Shield (Silver)	Kill 5 enemies while using a zombie as a shield.
Outbreak Survivalist (Silver)	Complete all U.S.S. missions on Veteran.
Quite The Collection (Silver)	Purchase all available weapons.
Raccoon City Cleanser (Gold)	Complete all U.S.S. missions on Professional.
Raccoon City Mascot (Bronze)	Collect all 7 Raccoons
Ready To Dominate (Bronze)	Fully upgrade all abilities for one character class.
Revival (Silver)	Revive 31 teammates (lifetime)
Rogue's Gallery (Bronze)	Complete the fourth mission of the U.S.S. campaign.
Sampler (Bronze)	Play at least one match in every game mode type.
Skill... Or Luck? (Silver)	Achieve a 10 kill streak in a Versus match.
So Hot Right Now (Bronze)	Kill 103 enemies with incendiary rounds (lifetime)
So Many Choices (Silver)	Purchase all abilities for all character classes.
Stop Squirming (Bronze)	17 Hunters Killed (lifetime)
Success (Silver)	Complete all U.S.S. missions with an S Rank.
Supreme Survivors (Bronze)	In Survivors mode, have all 4 players on your team Survive the game.
The Loyalists (Bronze)	Follow orders and defeat all liabilities.
These Will Do (Bronze)	Purchase 5 weapons.
This Place Crawls (Bronze)	31 Parasites killed (lifetime)

NEW!

A
B
C
D
E
F
G
H
I
J
K
L
M
N
O
P
Q
R
S
T
U
V
W
X
Y
Z

Tongue Tied (Bronze)	Free teammate from Licker grapple.
Up Close and Personal (Bronze)	Kill 5 players in one multiplayer game with CQC Kills.
Witness (Bronze)	Witness the beginning of the Raccoon City outbreak.
You Love to Hate My 98 (Silver)	Complete 98 versus games

RESIDENT EVIL: OPERATION RACCOON CITY (XBOX 360)

ACHIEVEMENT

UNLOCKABLE	HOW TO UNLOCK
A Gun by Any Other Name (15)	Kill an enemy with each weapon type including special weapons.
A Hero Spared! (15)	Attempt "The Rescue" and survive.
Baker's Dozen (30)	Kill 13 zombified teammates.
Betrayal (20)	Complete the fifth mission of the U.S.S. campaign.
Bloody Good Time (20)	Kill 5 enemies by causing Blood Frenzy in a single campaign game or multiplayer match.
By Trail Of Dead (10)	50 Versus opponents killed (lifetime)
Chaos Averted (5)	Kill an infected teammate with a headshot before they become a zombie in any mode.
Choices Aplenty (15)	Purchase 15 weapons.
Clingy (10)	13 Parasite Zombies killed (lifetime)
Corrupted (20)	Complete the second mission of the U.S.S. campaign.
Danger, High Voltage! (20)	Complete the third mission of the U.S.S. campaign.
Died Trying (15)	Attempt "The Rescue" and fail
Down Boy (15)	Kill 13 zombie dogs (lifetime)
Down in the Labs (20)	Complete the sixth mission of the U.S.S. campaign.
Epic Standards (40)	Upgrade all abilities for all characters to its maximum level.
Fallen Idols (30)	In Heroes mode, eliminate 4 Heroes in one game.
Feelin' Stronger Every Day (15)	Fully upgrade an ability.
Great Success (45)	Gain S+ on all U.S.S. mission on Professional/ Veteran difficulty
Green Thumb (25)	Heal with 101 Green Herbs (lifetime)
Hat Trick (15)	3 Tyrants Killed (lifetime)
Like a Bee (20)	Kill 10 enemy players in one Versus game with CQC.
Like a Butterfly (15)	Kill 100 zombies with CQC (lifetime)
Look What I Can Do (20)	Purchase all abilities for one character class.
No Sample For You (30)	Force 25 enemies to drop G-Virus Samples in Biohazard (lifetime).
Now That's G (15)	Collect 3 G-Virus Samples in one Biohazard match.
On A Roll (15)	Achieve a 5 kill streak in a Versus match.
One Trick Pony (10)	Purchase an ability.
Only Hurts For A While (10)	Infected 13 times (lifetime)
Organic Shield (20)	Kill 5 enemies consecutively while using a zombie as a shield.
Outbreak Survivalist (25)	Complete all U.S.S. missions on Veteran.
Quite The Collection (30)	Purchase all available weapons.

Raccoon City Cleanser (35)	Complete all U.S.S. missions on Professional.
Raccoon City Mascot (15)	Collect all 7 Raccoons.
Ready To Dominate (20)	Fully upgrade all abilities for one character class.
Revival (20)	Revive 31 team mates (lifetime)
Rogue's Gallery (20)	Complete the fourth mission of the U.S.S. campaign.
Sampler (20)	Play at least one match in every Versus game type
Skill... Or Luck? (25)	Achieve a 10 kill streak in a Versus match.
So Hot Right Now (15)	Kill 103 enemies with incendiary rounds (lifetime)
So Many Choices (30)	Purchase all abilities for all character classes.
Stop Squirming (10)	17 Hunters Killed (lifetime)
Success (30)	Complete all U.S.S. missions with an S Rank.
Supreme Survivors (20)	In Survivors mode, have all 4 players on your team Survive the game.
The Loyalists (15)	Stop Squirming (10)
These Will Do (10)	Purchase 5 weapons.
This Place Crawls (15)	31 Parasites killed (lifetime)
Tongue Tied (10)	Kill a Licker that is grappling a Teammate.
Up Close and Personal (10)	Kill 5 players in one multiplayer game with CQC Kills.
Witness (20)	Witness the beginning of the Raccoon City outbreak.
You Love to Hate my 98 (50)	Complete 98 Versus games

RESIDENT EVIL: REVELATIONS (3DS)

UNLOCKABLE

UNLOCKABLE	HOW TO UNLOCK
Chris, outfit 1 (Snow)	Clear episode 1-3 in the main game
Chris, outfit 2 (Ship)	Reach player level 30
Jessica, outfit 1 (Snow)	Reach player level 10
Jessica, outfit 2 (Ship)	Clear every stage on Trench difficulty
Jessica, outfit 3 (Terragrigia)	Reach player level 40
Jill, outfit 1 (Ship)	Clear episode 1-3 in the main game
Jill, outfit 2 (Beach)	Reach player level 5
Keith, outfit 1 (Snow)	Clear episode 4-6 in the main game
Keith, outfit 2 (HQ)	Clear 50 missions
Morgan	Find the real exit on stage 21
Norman	Obtain all rare weapons
O'Brian	Clear every stage on Abyss difficulty
Parker, outfit 1 (Ship)	Clear episode 1-3 in the main game
Parker, outfit 2 (Beach)	Reach player level 20
Parker, outfit 3 (Terragrigia)	Obtain one rare weapon
Quint, outfit 1 (Snow)	Clear 100 missions
Quint, outfit 2 (HQ)	Reach player level 50
Raymond	Clear every stage on Chasm difficulty
Trench Difficulty	Complete all Raid Mode stages on Chasm Difficulty
Abyss Difficulty	Complete all Raid Mode stages on Trench Difficulty
Raid Mode Bonus Stage 21	Clear the game
Raid Mode Stages 1-7	Clear Episodes 1-3

Raid Mode Stages 13-17	Clear Episodes 7-9
Raid Mode Stages 18-20	Clear episodes 10-12
Raid Mode Stages 8-12	Clear Episodes 4-6
Hell Difficulty	Complete the game once on normal
Hydra Shotgun	Complete the game on Normal difficulty or higher
Infinite Rocket Launcher	Complete the Game on Hell difficulty
New Game+	Complete the game once on any difficulty.

RESISTANCE: BURNING SKIES (PLAYSTATION VITA)

TROPHY

UNLOCKABLE	HOW TO UNLOCK
Axed (Silver)	Kill 50 Chimera with Riley's axe in the Single Player Campaign
Boom (Silver)	Kill 100 Chimera with headshots in the Single Player Campaign
Combine (Silver)	Upgrade both slots of a weapon in the Single Player Campaign
Conversion Tower (Bronze)	Successfully complete level 6
Customize (Gold)	Upgrade all weapons in the Single Player Campaign
Dangerous (Bronze)	Kill 250 Chimera in the Single Player Campaign
Deadly (Silver)	Kill 500 Chimera in the Single Player Campaign
Ellis Island (Bronze)	Successfully complete level 4
Executed (Silver)	Kill an Executioner
G-man (Gold)	Kill Gorrell
George Washington Bridge (Bronze)	Successfully complete level 3
Giant (Gold)	Kill any combination of 18 Impalers or Executioners
Impaled (Silver)	Kill an Impaler
Incite (Gold)	Complete one round of multiplayer
Indiscriminate (Bronze)	Kill an enemy with every weapon in the Single Player Campaign
Inhuman (Gold)	Kill the Leviathan
Lethal (Gold)	Kill 1000 Chimera in the Single Player Campaign
Military Ocean Terminal (Bronze)	Successfully complete level 2
Overheat (Silver)	Kill 50 Chimera by detonating their heatstacks in the Single Player Campaign
Platinum (Platinum)	Earn all trophies
Protection Camp (Bronze)	Successfully complete level 5
Staten Island (Bronze)	Successfully complete level 1
Unnatural (Gold)	Kill the Abomination
Upgrade (Bronze)	Upgrade a weapon in the Single Player Campaign
Variety (Bronze)	Use the secondary fire of each weapon in the Single Player Campaign

RESISTANCE 3 (PLAYSTATION 3)

TROPHY

UNLOCKABLE	HOW TO UNLOCK
Access Denied (Bronze)	Absorb 1000 damage with Auger Shields
Archivalist (Silver)	Collect all journals
Backstabber (Bronze)	Kill 20 enemies with melee while they are idle
BARF! (Bronze)	Make 6 Wardens puke at the same time in the prison

Bloodborne (Bronze)	Kill 3 enemies simultaneously using a single mutated body
Body Count (Bronze)	Kill 1000 enemies
Bookworm (Bronze)	Collect 50% of the journals
Boomstick (Bronze)	Use the upgraded Rossmore secondary fire to set 6 enemies on fire at once
Bouncer (Bronze)	Keep Chimeran forces from entering the Brewpub
Brutal (Gold)	Complete Campaign Mode on Superhuman
Buckshot (Bronze)	Kill 2+ enemies with one Rossmore blast
Bull in a China Shop (Bronze)	Freeze and melee kill 3 Ravagers
Calm Under Pressure (Bronze)	Defeat the Brawler in the Post Office in under 2 minutes
Chamber Full of Death (Bronze)	Kill 5+ Hybrids at once by using the HE .44 Magnum secondary fire
Cheap Shots (Bronze)	Kill 25 enemies firing the Auger through an object
Collector (Bronze)	Collect 10 journals
Corpse Wagon (Bronze)	Detonate fallen Leeches to kill 25 enemies
Counter-Sniper (Bronze)	Use the Deadeye to kill 20 snipers
Electric Avenue (Bronze)	Use the EMP to take down 25 drones
Expert Sniper (Bronze)	Get 50 headshot kills in Campaign Mode
Feeling Lucky, Punk (Bronze)	Detonate multiple Magnum rounds to kill 2+ enemies at once, 5 times
Fireworks (Bronze)	Use the Wildfire secondary fire to kill 6 enemies in one shot
Frickin' Laser Beams (Bronze)	Get to the first mineshaft without being hit by sniper fire in Mt. Pleasant, PA
From the Hip (Bronze)	Kill 50 enemies with the Bullseye or Marksman while moving, without using zoom
Gardener (Bronze)	Destroy 100 blast roots
Good Fences (Bronze)	Don't allow any counter-attackers into the Washington Square base
Grasshopper Unit (Bronze)	Kill 5 Longlegs in mid-jump
Grenadier (Bronze)	Kill 3 or more Military Chimera with a single Grenade
Hello Driver (Bronze)	Kill 5 drivers without destroying their vehicle
Helping Hands (Bronze)	Revive a Co-op partner 20 times
In This Together (Bronze)	Defeat the Widowmaker in Times Square without killing a single Hybrid
Irresistible Force (Silver)	Complete Campaign Mode on any difficulty
Juggler (Bronze)	Simultaneously burn, freeze and poison 4 separate enemies
Land, Sea, and Air (Bronze)	Travel in 3 different vehicles on your journey
Master Mechanic (Silver)	Fully upgrade all weapons in Campaign Mode
Medusa (Bronze)	Freeze 5 enemies at once and destroy them with a blast of the Cryogun's secondary fire
No Escape (Bronze)	Destroy all Warden vehicles in the Motorpool
Nothing But Net (Bronze)	Score a basket by lobbing a grenade through a basketball hoop
One Eyed Jack (Bronze)	Find and kill 'Jack' in Graterford Prison
Opportunity Knocks (Bronze)	Kill 20 enemies with environmental objects
Overload (Bronze)	Use the EMP to take down 10 Steelhead Auger shields

NEW!

A
B
C
D
E
F
G
H
I
J
K
L
M
N
O
P
Q
R
S
T
U
V
W
X
Y
Z

Platinum Trophy (Platinum)	Obtain all Gold, Silver, and Bronze Trophies for Resistance 3
Raining Limbs (Bronze)	Kill 25 Grims using only grenades
Roops! (Bronze)	Knock a Hybrid off the cliffs in Mt. Pleasant, PA
Sandman (Bronze)	Kill 5 Grims in a row using only headshots
Shoe Leather (Bronze)	Travel 30 km on foot
Short Out (Bronze)	Defeat the Stalker in under 60 seconds
Silent Partner (Silver)	Damage the same enemy in Cooperative Mode for 100 kills
Slaybells (Bronze)	Make Santa and his reindeer fly
Snipe Hunt (Bronze)	Collect all Deadeye rifles without dying while fighting the Widowmaker in St. Louis
Tag, You're It (Bronze)	Kill 40 Bullseye tagged enemies
This is my Rifle (Bronze)	Fully upgrade one weapon in Campaign Mode
Toast (Bronze)	Use the upgraded Deadeye secondary fire to kill 2+ enemies, 5 times
Up Your Arsenal (Bronze)	Get a kill with every weapon in your arsenal
Vehicular Manslaughter (Bronze)	Destroy 10 Warden vehicles while on the train
Warp Speed (Bronze)	Use the Atomizer secondary fire to kill 30 enemies
Waste Not (Bronze)	Get 5 headshot kills with one Deadeye clip
Weaponsmith (Bronze)	Upgrade 5 weapons in Campaign Mode
Zookeeper (Silver)	Kill the Brawler in Haven without taking any damage

RIDGE RACER (PLAYSTATION VITA)

TROPHY

UNLOCKABLE	HOW TO UNLOCK
Accomplished (Silver)	Your Skill Grade has increased to Level 10. You can proudly claim to have earned a rank among the top ridge racers of the world.
Been Around the Block (Bronze)	You raced at least once in every race mode.
Capable (Bronze)	Your Skill Grade has increased to Level 2. Your rivals will be equally tougher. Make it a worthwile victory.
Claim to Fame VIP (Silver)	You've been selected as today's Spotlight VIP for your team.
Divinity (Silver)	You beat the legendary Angel Car in all races.
Dynamic and Dangerous (Bronze)	You placed first in a race with the most Dynamic drift settings.
Ectoplasmed (Bronze)	You submitted your race to Ghost Battle. Now they're out to get you!
Electronic Warfare (Bronze)	You obtained Hacker Kit and Data Jammer for hi-tech electronic tactics.
Exorcist (Silver)	You beat the legendary Devil Car in all races.
Filthy VIP (Silver)	You ranked high in Credit Ranking and earned the title of VIP.
Free Agent (Gold)	You obtained over 30,000 CR, meaning you can transfer to a new team after watching Team Vision.
Friend or Foe? (Bronze)	You raced with a Friend in an Online Battle.
Generous at Heart (Bronze)	You uploaded 100 Victory Points to your team through Team Vision.
Ghost Contender (Bronze)	You beat a Ghost that is higher than 10 G.

Ghost Hunter (Bronze)	You beat over 50 races in Ghost Battle.
Gift from Beyond (Bronze)	You received the Devil's Gift and now Ridge Racer and Reiko took on a whole new look...
Journeyman (Bronze)	You raced on all 3 courses— Southbay Docks, Highland Cliffs, and Harborline 765 (including R courses). So which did you like best?
Machine Junkie (Bronze)	You raced at least once with each of the 5 machines (BISARGENTO, RAUNA, FIERA, EO, SYNCi). So which driving style and design did you like best?
Mad Mechanic (Bronze)	You reached the first branch-off point in the Machine Upgrade Map. Every great invention has its roots in risk.
Mild and Menacing (Bronze)	You placed first in a race with the most Mild drift settings.
Nitrous Master (Silver)	You obtained all types of Nitrous kits on the Machine Upgrade Map. Learn to take advantage of each one's unique properties.
Nitrous-Free (Bronze)	You placed first without using any Nitrous.
Parting Gift (Bronze)	You regifted the Devil's Gift to another racer on PlayStationNetwork.
Platinum Ridge Racer (Platinum)	You earned all the trophies in RIDGE RACER.
Practice Makes Perfect (Bronze)	You raced in over 50 Spot Races. That same commitment will pay off in the World Races, too.
Prodigy (Bronze)	Your team sponsor acknowledges your steady efforts, and has upgraded your machine's specs to the next level. Keep up the good work.
Rocketeer (Bronze)	You successfully pulled off a rocket start.
Single Lap Spirit (Bronze)	You raced more than 200 laps in Lap Time Attack.
Skillful (Bronze)	Your Skill level has increased to level 5. You're making your way to being a top ridge racer!
Socialite (Bronze)	You raced in over 50 Face-to-Face Battles.
Solid Foundation (Bronze)	You've maxed-out your machine's basic specs. All that's left is letting your choice of upgrade kits and driving technique determine the winner.
Speed Demon (Bronze)	You reached the maximum speed with a maxed-up machine, and added a maximum nitrous.
Steal the Spotlight (Bronze)	You raced against a VIP racer in an Online Battle.
Stellar (Gold)	Your Skill Grade has increased to Level 16. You can now claim the title of "ultimate racer."
Stop and Smell the Roses (Bronze)	You stopped by that special spot on the Harborline 765 course.
Switching Sides (Silver)	You transferred teams.
Tech Tree Climber (Gold)	You completed the Machine Upgrade Map.
Technician (Bronze)	You mastered the paddle shift in a race.
Tinkerer (Bronze)	You took the first momentous step toward developing an upgrade kit on the Machine Upgrade Map.
Top Dog VIP (Silver)	You ranked high in Score Ranking and earned the title of VIP.
Triple Lap Trickster (Bronze)	You raced in Total Time Attack over 50 times.
Triple Threat (Bronze)	You equipped an upgrade kit from Groups A through C for the first time.
Welcome to Circlite Racing! (Bronze)	You signed with Circlite Racing.
Welcome to Squaris GP! (Bronze)	You signed with Squaris GP.
Welcome to Trianchor Alliance! (Bronze)	You signed with Trianchor Alliance.

Welcome to Xealot Motorspot! (Bronze)	You signed with Xealot Motorsport.
Wind Whipper (Bronze)	You obtained Super Slipstream and Zero Slipstream for controlling the effects of slipstreaming.
World Racer (Bronze)	You raced in over 50 Online Battles.

RIDGE RACER UNBOUNDED (PLAYSTATION 3)

TROPHY

UNLOCKABLE	HOW TO UNLOCK
Award Collector (Bronze)	Get all Race Awards.
Award Hogger (Silver)	Receive 20 awards in one race.
Best In The World (Gold)	Win all 5 events in any 8 player City Domination match.
Bombardment (Bronze)	Frag a total of 10 racers while airborne.
Boost Scrooge (Bronze)	Finish 1st in any 8 player multiplayer race without using boost.
Can't Touch This (Bronze)	Finish 1st in 10 Domination Races without crashing or getting fragged.
Challenger (Bronze)	Dominate 10 challenge events.
Champion (Bronze)	Finish 1st in 20 Domination Races.
City Creator (Bronze)	Publish a city with 5 events.
City Demolisher (Bronze)	Destroy 10 city targets in one race.
City-Wide Destruction (Bronze)	Destroy 100 City Targets.
Creative Destruction (Silver)	Destroy 25 targets in one event.
Dealing with Rage Issues (Silver)	Destroy all targets and frag 5 racers in one race.
Domination Incarnate (Silver)	Dominate all districts in Shatter Bay.
Drift Master (Bronze)	Get three domination stars from all Shatter Bay Drift Attacks.
Drift to Win (Bronze)	Finish 1st with 2,000 m/yd of total Drifting in any 8 player Domination Race.
Fanboy's Revenge (Bronze)	Win an 8 player multiplayer race with the Crinale.
Flashing Fury (Bronze)	Frag a total of 200 police cars in Frag Attack events.
Frag Capacitor (Bronze)	Frag 10 racers in one race.
Frag Master (Bronze)	Get three domination stars from all Shatter Bay Frag Attacks.
Fragging Ball (Silver)	Multiplayer. Frag 10 cars in one 8 player Domination Race.
Garage Hoarder (Bronze)	Unlock all cars.
Getting Creative (Bronze)	Create a track that uses Advanced Editor.
GG HF (Bronze)	Complete the Shatter Bay career.
High Flyer (Bronze)	Get 10,000 m/yd of total Airtime.
Homage (Bronze)	Unlock the Nakamura Racer '70.
I Just Want to Sing! (Bronze)	Finish 1st in 20 Domination Races with 0 frags.
I Know You! (Bronze)	Frag same racer three times in one multiplayer race.
Interceptor (Bronze)	Frag a racer just before the finish line.
Learning The Ropes (Bronze)	Complete Domination Race tutorial.
Litterbug (Bronze)	Cause $10,000 worth of collateral damage in one race.
Mechanic's Nightmare (Bronze)	Get your own car destroyed 100 times.

Model Citizen (Silver)	Finish in top three without causing any collateral damage.
My City (Bronze)	Publish a city.
Not Easy Being Mean (Bronze)	Frag 20 cars in one race.
Nothing but Wreck (Bronze)	Frag 200 racers in total.
Platinum Trophy (Platinum)	You've earned all Trophies
Public Enemy (Bronze)	Cause $100,000 worth of collateral damage in total.
Pure Racing Blood (Bronze)	Finish 1st in any 8 player multiplayer race without fragging anyone.
Race Dominator (Bronze)	Finish 1st in 50 Domination Races.
Race Master (Gold)	Finish 1st in every Shatter Bay Domination Race.
Shattered Bay (Silver)	Destroy one of every City Target in the game.
Sideslammer (Bronze)	Frag any racer a total of 10 times while drifting.
Super Drifter (Bronze)	Get 50,000 m/yd of total Drifting.
Tail Chaser (Bronze)	Get 35,000 m/yd of total Chasing.
Time Lord (Silver)	Get three domination stars in all Time Attack events.
Ultimate Dominator (Bronze)	Reach rank 30.
Unbeatable (Bronze)	Finish 1st in 50 multiplayer races.
Unbounded Gang Member (Bronze)	Reach rank 10.
Winning! (Bronze)	Finish 1st in 150 Domination Races.
World Domination (Bronze)	Dominate 50 challenge events.

RIDGE RACER UNBOUNDED (XBOX 360)

ACHIEVEMENT

UNLOCKABLE	HOW TO UNLOCK
Award Collector (15)	Get all Race Awards.
Award Hogger (25)	Receive 20 awards in one race.
Best In The World (100)	Win all 5 events in any 8 player City Domination match.
Bombardment (15)	Frag a total of 10 racers while airborne.
Boost Scrooge (15)	Finish 1st in any 8 player multiplayer race without using boost.
Can't Touch This (15)	Finish 1st in 10 Domination Races without crashing or getting fragged.
Challenger (15)	Dominate 10 challenge events.
Champion (15)	Finish 1st in 20 Domination Races.
City Creator (15)	Publish a city with 5 events.
City Demolisher (15)	Destroy 10 city targets in one race.
City-Wide Destruction (15)	Destroy 100 City Targets.
Creative Destruction (25)	Destroy 25 targets in one event.
Dealing with Rage Issues (25)	Destroy all targets and frag 5 racers in one race.
Domination Incarnate (25)	Dominate all districts in Shatter Bay.
Drift Master (15)	Get three domination stars from all Shatter Bay Drift Attacks.
Drift to Win (15)	Finish 1st with 2,000 m/yd of total Drifting in any 8 player Domination Race.
Fanboy's Revenge (15)	Win an 8 player multiplayer race with the Crinale.
Flashing Fury (15)	Frag a total of 200 police cars in Frag Attack events.
Frag Capacitor (15)	Frag 10 racers in one race.

NEW!

A
B
C
D
E
F
G
H
I
J
K
L
M
N
O
P
Q
R
S
T
U
V
W
X
Y
Z

Frag Master (15)	Get three domination stars from all Shatter Bay Frag Attacks.
Fragging Ball (25)	Frag 10 cars in one 8 player Domination Race.
Garage Hoarder (15)	Unlock all cars.
Getting Creative (15)	Create a track that uses Advanced Editor.
GG HF (15)	Complete the Shatter Bay career.
High Flyer (15)	Get 10,000 m/yd of total Airtime.
Homage (15)	Unlock the Nakamura Racer '70.
I Just Want to Sing! (15)	Finish 1st in 20 Domination Races with 0 frags.
I Know You! (15)	Frag the same racer three times in one multiplayer race.
Interceptor (15)	Frag a racer just before the finish line.
Learning The Ropes (15)	Complete Domination Race tutorial.
Litterbug (15)	Cause $10,000 worth of collateral damage in one race.
Mechanic's Nightmare (15)	Get your own car destroyed 100 times.
Model Citizen (25)	Finish in top three without causing any collateral damage.
My City (15)	Publish a city.
Not Easy Being Mean (15)	Frag 20 cars in one race.
Nothing but Wreck (15)	Frag 200 racers in total.
Public Enemy (15)	Cause $100,000 worth of collateral damage in total.
Pure Racing Blood (15)	Finish 1st in any 8 player multiplayer race without fragging anyone.
Race Dominator (15)	Finish 1st in 50 Domination Races.
Race Master (100)	Finish 1st in every Shatter Bay Domination Race.
Shattered Bay (25)	Destroy one of every City Target in the game.
Sideslammer (15)	Frag any racer a total of 10 times while drifting.
Super Drifter (15)	Get 50,000 m/yd of total Drifting.
Tail Chaser (15)	Get 35,000 m/yd of total Chasing.
Time Lord (25)	Get three domination stars in all Time Attack events.
Ultimate Dominator (15)	Reach rank 30.
Unbeatable (15)	Finish 1st in 50 multiplayer races.
Unbounded Gang Member (15)	Reach rank 10.
Winning! (15)	Finish 1st in 150 Domination Races.
World Domination (15)	Dominate 50 challenge events.

RIDGE RACER 3D (3DS)

UNLOCKABLE

Complete the following events in Grand Prix mode to unlock these.

UNLOCKABLE	HOW TO UNLOCK
Age Solo Petit500 (Special Cat. 1 Machine)	Finish Expert Grand Prix Event No. 44
Catagory 1 Machines	Finish Advanced Grand Prix Event No. 26
Catagory 2 Machines & Advanced Grand Prix	Finish Beginner Grand Prix Event No. 18
Catagory 3 Machines	Finish Beginner Grand Prix Event No. 08
Expert Grand Prix	Finish Advanced Grand Prix Event No. 36
Kamata ANGL Concept (Special Cat. 1 Machine)	Finish Expert Grand Prix Event No. 42

Lucky & Wild Madbull (Special Cat. 1 Machine)	Finish Expert Grand Prix Event No. 45
Mirrored & Mirrored Reverse Courses	Finish Expert Grand Prix Event No. 48
Namco New Rally-X (Special Cat. 1 Machine)	Finish Expert Grand Prix Event No. 47
Namco Pacman (Special Cat. 1 Machine) & Pacman Music CD	Finish Expert Grand Prix Event No. 46
Soldat Crinale (Special Cat. 1 Machine)	Finish Expert Grand Prix Event No. 43

RISEN (XBOX 360)

GLITCH

Seek out Rhobart in the Bandit Camp and then go and collect the 10 reeds of Brugleweed he asks for. When you return to him with the reeds, he will give you 70 gold and 50 XP. Attack him until he is unconscious but do not kill him. Loot his body and retrieve the Brugleweed you just gave him. When he gets up, give him the pilfered Brugleweed for additional gold and XP. Repeat as often as you like (will go faster with higher amounts of Brugleweed).

RISEN 2: DARK WATERS (PLAYSTATION 3)

TROPHY

UNLOCKABLE	HOW TO UNLOCK
100% (Platinum)	Earn all Risen 2 trophies to unlock the platinum trophy
All-Rounder (Silver)	Learned each skill once
Bane of the Beasts (Silver)	Killed 500 monsters
Beginner (Bronze)	Killed 10 monsters
Big Game Hunter (Silver)	Killed 2000 monsters
Birdbrain (Bronze)	Used parrot 5 times
Blademaster (Bronze)	Learned everything about blades
Captain (Silver)	'A New Ship' completed
Cash Cow (Silver)	Acquired 100,000 gold
Cheese Knife (Bronze)	'The Cunning Captain' completed
Crab Catcher (Bronze)	Killed 10 giant crabs
Crack Shot (Bronze)	Hit 10 times in one game in the shooting mini-game
Deep Sea Fisherman (Bronze)	Killed 50 sea monsters
Digger (Bronze)	Dug up 50 treasures
Drunkard (Bronze)	Won drinking duel mini-game 10 times
Friend of the Gnomes (Bronze)	'The Gnome Eater' completed
Gunslinger (Bronze)	Learned everything about firearms
Harpooner (Bronze)	'The Titan Weapon' completed
Just a little tipple... (Bronze)	Drank first rum
Kleptomaniac (Bronze)	Picked 100 locks
Knight in Shining Armour (Bronze)	'Rescue Patty!' completed
Legendary Hero (Bronze)	Collected 20 legendary items
Liberator (Bronze)	'Free Hawkins' completed
Made of Money (Silver)	Acquired 300,000 gold
Mr Industrious (Gold)	Completed 250 quests
Necromancer (Bronze)	'The Split Soul' completed
Pet Cemetery (Bronze)	Killed 20 ambient animals
Protector (Bronze)	Won duel against Severin

Provisions Master (Bronze)	'Ship's Equipment' completed
Rogue (Bronze)	Learned everything about cunning
Skinflint (Bronze)	Acquired 1000 gold
Storyteller (Bronze)	Collected 10 legendary items
The Hand of God (Bronze)	'The Greedy Captain' completed
The Right Hand (Bronze)	'Chaka Datu's Legacy' completed
Tour Guide (Bronze)	At least 5 crew members on the ship
Treasure Hunter (Bronze)	Found first treasure in the game
Tub Captain (Bronze)	'Build a Raft' completed
Voodoo Pirate (Bronze)	'The Ancestors' Blessing' completed
Voodoo Wizard (Bronze)	Learned everything about voodoo

RISEN 2: DARK WATERS (XBOX 360)

ACHIEVEMENT

UNLOCKABLE	HOW TO UNLOCK
All-Rounder (30)	Learned each skill once
Artefact Hunter (20)	'Steelbeard's Artefact' completed
Bane of the Beasts (30)	Killed 500 monsters
Beginner (10)	Killed 10 monsters
Big Game Hunter (50)	Killed 2000 monsters
Birdbrain (10)	Used parrot 5 times
Blademaster (20)	Learned everything about blades
Bookworm (20)	'Following Garcia's Trail' completed
Captain (30)	'A New Ship' completed
Cash Cow (30)	Acquired 100,000 gold
Cheese Knife (20)	'The Cunning Captain' completed
Crab Catcher (10)	Killed 10 giant crabs
Crack Shot (10)	Hit 10 times in one game in the shooting mini-game
Deep Sea Fisherman (10)	Killed 50 sea monsters
Detective (20)	'Garcia's Masquerade Uncovered' completed
Digger (10)	Dug up 50 treasures
Drunkard (10)	Won drinking duel mini-game 10 times
Friend of the Gnomes (20)	'The Gnome Eater' completed
Ghost Pirate (20)	'The Journey to the Underworld' completed
Gunslinger (20)	Learned everything about firearms
Harpooner (20)	'The Titan Weapon' completed
He Really Exists! (20)	'Find Steelbeard' completed
Just a little tipple... (10)	Drank first rum
Kleptomaniac (10)	Picked 100 locks
Knight in Shining Armour (10)	'Rescue Patty!' completed
Legendary Hero (20)	Collected 20 legendary items
Liberator (10)	'Free Hawkins' completed
Lord of the Tentacle (50)	'Defeat the Kraken' completed
Made of Money (50)	Acquired 300,000 gold
Monkey Dance (10)	Used monkey 20 times
Mr Industrious (50)	Completed 250 quests
Necromancer (20)	'The Split Soul' completed
Pet Cemetery (10)	Killed 20 ambient animals

Pirate (20)	'Become a Pirate' completed
Pirate with Muskets (20)	'Four Muskets against Crow' completed
Protector (10)	Won duel against Severin
Provisions Master (20)	'Ship's Equipment' completed
Rogue (20)	Learned everything about cunning
Seafarer (10)	Travelled by ship 20 times
Skinflint (10)	Acquired 1000 gold
Storyteller (10)	Collected 10 legendary items
The Curse Is Broken! (50)	'Kill Mara' completed
The Hand of God (20)	'The Greedy Captain' completed
The Right Hand (20)	'Chaka Datu's Legacy' completed
Tough Bastard (20)	Learned everything about toughness
Tour Guide (10)	At least 5 crew members on the ship
Treasure Hunter (10)	Found first treasure in the game
Tub Captain (20)	'Build a Raft' completed
Voodoo Pirate (20)	'The Ancestors' Blessing' completed
Voodoo Wizard (20)	Learned everything about voodoo

RISTAR (WII)

PASSWORDS

PASSWORD	EFFECT
STAR	A shooting star goes across the background (JP)
MUSEUM	Boss Rush mode
XXXXXX	Clears/Deactivates the current password
AGES	Copyright info is displayed
MIEMIE	Hidden items' grab points are shown with a blue star
FEEL	ILOVEU, MIEMIE, CANDY active all at once (JP)
CANDY	Invincibility (JP)
MACCHA	Mentions Miyake color (JP)
MASTER	Mentions next game (JP)
AAAAAA	No Continue limit (JP)
MAGURO	Onchi Music mode and credits music in sound test
HETAP	Reverses the high score in Demo mode (JP)
VALDI	Shows the solar system (JP)
ILOVEU	Stage select
SUPERB	Super Difficulty mode
SUPER	Super Hard mode
DOFEEL	Time Attack mode

RIVER CITY RANSOM (WII)

PASSWORDS

PASSWORD	EFFECT
XfMdZTHwiR3 jaj6jfRUDEt tilm2tWRo8b	Final Boss, with Max Stats, Dragon Feet, Stone Hands, GrandSlam, and Texas Boots
XfMdZTHUPR3 rztzPeQUCTt 61lxhtWRo2b	Final Boss, with Max Stats, Stone Hands, Dragon Feet, Acro Circus, Grand SlaM, 4 Karma Jolts, and $999.99 cash
t1izvpdOZnZ JxNkJp7Cpub XMPQgXErSMF	Ivan Beaten, High School Open
w412ysgtMqc MUSjKm2PqtE UJMNdUTGOQC	Power Up

| jrYplfTgbdj nOorLTlYXwR SjTuqpilUHP cash | Start with all abilities and $500 in |
| fHUFBbvcnpa MS8iPpICZJP VKNOeVRQPDD | Strange item in inventory that gives stat increases |

UNLOCKABLES

UNLOCKABLE	HOW TO UNLOCK
Change Character Names	On the Character Select screen, press SELECT on the controller to go to a screen where you can change Alex and Ryan's names to whatever you want.
Merlin's Mystery Shop	To find Merlin's Mystery Shop go to the Armstrong Thru-Way. Once inside, press up at the top wall and the wall opens. Inside you can buy the best items in the game.

ROCK BAND (XBOX 360)

UNLOCK ALL

Enter quickly at the "Rock Band" title screen (disables saving).

CODE	EFFECT
Red, Yellow, Blue, Red, Red, Blue, Blue, Red, Yellow, Blue	Unlock All Songs

ROCK BAND (WII)

CODES

Using the colored fret buttons on the guitar, enter these codes QUICKLY on the title screen.

EFFECT	CODE
Unlock All Songs (Disable Saving)	R, Y, B, R, R, B, B, R, Y, B

ROCK BAND 2 (XBOX 360)

CODES

Go to the "Extras" option in the main menu. Choose "Modify Game," then input the following codes. All codes disable saving.

EFFECT	CODE
Awesome Detection	Yellow, Blue, Orange, Yellow, Blue, Orange, Yellow, Blue, Orange
Stage Mode	Blue, Yellow, Red, Blue, Yellow, Red, Blue, Yellow, Red

EFFECT	CODE
Unlock All Songs	Red, Yellow, Blue, Red, Red, Blue, Blue, Red, Yellow, Blue
Venue Select: Unlock All Venues	Blue, Orange, Orange, Blue, Yellow, Blue, Orange, Orange, Blue, Yellow

ROCK BAND 3 (XBOX 360)

CODES

Enter the following codes at the Main menu of the game.

EFFECT	CODE
Ovation D-2010 Guitar	Orange, Blue, Orange, Orange, Blue, Blue, Orange, Blue
Stop! Guitar unlocked	Orange, Orange, Blue, Blue, Orange, Blue, Blue, Orange
Unlocks Guild X-79 Guitar in Customization Options	Blue, Orange, Orange, Blue, Orange, Orange, Blue, Blue

SECRET INSTRUMENTS

UNLOCKABLE	HOW TO UNLOCK
Baroque Stage Kit	Expert Hall of Fame induction in Pro Drums: Expert Song Progress
Clear Microphone Song	Expert Hall of Fame induction in Vocal Harmony: Expert Progress

Cthulhu's Revenge	Expert Hall of Fame induction in Pro Guitar: Expert Song Progress
DKS-5910 Pro-Tech High Performance Kit	Expert Hall of Fame Induction in Drums: Expert Song Progress
Gold Microphone	Expert Hall of Fame induction in Vocals: Expert Song Progress
Gretsch Bo-Diddley	Expert Hall of Fame induction in Guitar: Expert Song Progress
Gretsch White Falcon	Expert Hall of Fame induction in Bass: Expert Song Progress
The Goat Head	Expert Hall of Fame induction in Pro Bass: Expert Song Progress
The Green Day Guitar	Welcome to Paradise in Guitar: Green Day: Rock Band
VOX Continental	Expert Hall of Fame induction in Keys: Expert Song Progress
Yamaha CS-50	Expert Hall of Fame induction in Pro Keys: Expert Song Progress

ROCK BAND 3 (PS3)

CODES

Enter the following codes at the Main menu of the game.

EFFECT	CODE
Ovation D-2010 Guitar	Orange, Blue, Orange, Orange, Blue, Blue, Orange, Blue
Unlocks Guild X-79 Guitar n Customization Options	Blue, Orange, Orange, Blue, Orange, Orange, Blue, Blue

UNLOCKABLE

UNLOCKABLE	HOW TO UNLOCK
Play Keys on Guitar	Achieve the Guitar Immortal goal 5* 50 Medium Rock Band 3 Songs (or 3* on a higher difficulty)

ROCK BAND 3 (WII)

CODES

Enter the following codes at the Main menu of the game.

EFFECT	CODE
Ovation D-2010 Guitar	Orange, Blue, Orange, Orange, Blue, Blue, Orange, Blue
Unlocks Guild X-79 Guitar in Customization Options	Blue, Orange, Orange, Blue, Orange, Orange, Blue, Blue

THE BEATLES: ROCK BAND (WII)

CODES

Enter quickly at The Beatles Rock Band title screen

EFFECT	CODE
Unlocks set of bonus photos	Blue, Yellow, Orange, Orange, Orange, Blue, Blue, Blue, Yellow, Orange

ROCKSMITH (XBOX 360)

ACHIEVEMENT

UNLOCKABLE	HOW TO UNLOCK
All Rounder (20)	Beat 100,000 points in a Combo Arrangement
Art + Functionality (30)	Collect all guitars
Batter Up (5)	Play the Guitarcade game: Big Swing Baseball
Beat Harmonics (20)	Beat 1,000,000 points in the Guitarcade game: Harmonically Challenged
Beneficial Friends (20)	Play multiplayer with 2 guitars
Better Than An Encore? (20)	Qualify for a Double Encore
Cente-beater (10)	Beat a 100 Note Streak
Challenge Harmonics (5)	Play the Guitarcade game: Harmonically Challenged
Chordinated (20)	Beat 100,000 points in a Chord Arrangement

D-licious (10)	Use the Tuner to tune to Drop-D
Duck Hunter (5)	Play the Guitarcade game: Ducks
Ducks x 6 (5)	Play the Guitarcade game: Super Ducks
Elite Guitarist (60)	Reach Rank 9
Fret Fast (20)	Beat 10,000,000 points in the Guitarcade game: Ducks
Furious Plucker (20)	Beat 5,000,000 points in the Guitarcade game: Quick Pick Dash
Giant! (20)	Beat 2,000,000 points in the Guitarcade game: Big Swing Baseball
Guitardead (20)	Beat 1,000,000 points in the Guitarcade game: Dawn of the Chordead
Half-K (25)	Beat a 500 Note Streak
Happy Shopper (5)	Visit the shop
Hear Me Now (10)	Use the Amp
International Headliner (40)	Reach Rank 8
International Support Act (40)	Reach Rank 7
Just Awesome (40)	Beat a 750 Note Streak
Just Singing? (10)	Using a mic, sing along and achieve Nice Singing
Just Super! (20)	Beat 150,000,000 points in the Guitarcade game: Super Ducks
Local Headliner (10)	Reach Rank 4
Local Support Act (10)	Reach Rank 3
My 1st Encore (10)	Qualify for an Encore
My 1st Gig (5)	Play an Event
National Headliner (20)	Reach Rank 6
National Support Act (20)	Reach Rank 5
New Act (5)	Reach Rank 2
No Dischord (20)	Beat a 25 Chord Streak
OK, I Learned (20)	Beat 200,000 points in Master Mode
Rocksmith (100)	Reach Rank 11
Scales Owned (20)	Beat 50,000,000 points in the Guitarcade game: Scale Runner
Singles Rock (20)	Beat 100,000 points in a Single Note Arrangement
Slide Puzzle (5)	Play the Guitarcade game: Super Slider
Slide to Victory (20)	Beat 15,000,000 points in the Guitarcade game: Super Slider
Solo Foundations (5)	Play the Guitarcade game: Scale Runner
Stage Ready (40)	Complete a Master Event
Strummer (5)	Beat a 5 Chord Streak
Super Elite Guitarist (60)	Reach Rank 10
The Basics (5)	Complete Soundcheck (Reach Rank 1)
The One With Zombies (5)	Play the Guitarcade game: Dawn of the Chordead
The Rocksmith Method (20)	Earn all Bronze Technique Medals
Tone is My Avatar (10)	Create and save a custom tone
Tone Peddler (30)	Collect 50 effects pedals
Tutorials My Axe (30)	Earn all Gold Technique Medals
Where Rainbows Come From (5)	Play the Guitarcade game: Quick Pick Dash

ROCKSTAR GAMES PRESENTS TABLE TENNIS (WII)

UNLOCKABLE SHIRTS

UNLOCKABLE	HOW TO UNLOCK
Carmen's blue/green/gray Shirt	Win a match using a heavy leftspin shot.
Carmen's dark blue shirt	Win a match using a heavy topspin shot.
Carmen's grey shirt	Shut out the CPU in at least one game in the match.
Cassidy's brown shirt	Win a match using a heavy backspin shot.
Cassidy's dark blue shirt	Win a match using a heavy rightspin shot.
Cassidy's yellow/white shirt	Win a match by making the ball bounce 2or more times on the CPU's side of the table.
Liu Ping's green shirt	Win a match using a late swing.
Liu Ping's red/white shirt	Win a match by returning a shot from the CPU that dropped short.
Liu Ping's yellow shirt	Win a match using a forehand shot.
Solayman's dark blue shirt	Win a match with a 4-point deficit comeback.
Solayman's green shirt	Win a match using a backhand shot.
Solayman's gray shirt	Win a match using a smash shot.

RUNE FACTORY 2: A FANTASY HARVEST MOON (DS)

UNLOCKABLES

These are only accessible in the Second Generation, from the dresser on the left side of the second floor of the house.

UNLOCKABLE	HOW TO UNLOCK
Handsome Armor	Win the Adventure Contest.
Monster Costume	Win the Monster Taming Contest.

RUSH 'N ATTACK (XBOX 360)

CODES

A meow confirms that the code was entered correctly.

CODE	EFFECT
At the main menu, using the D-pad, press ⟰/⟰/⟱/⟱/⟲/⟳/⟲/⟳/🅑/🅐	Alternate Sound FX

A B C D E F G H I J K L M N O P Q R S T U V W X Y Z

'SPLOSION MAN (XBOX 360)

UNLOCKABLES

UNLOCKABLE	HOW TO UNLOCK
'Splosion Man Gamer Pic	Beat Single Level 1–4
'Splosion Man Premium Theme	Beat Single Level 3–18
Scientist Gamer Pic	Beat Multiplayer Level 1–4
Cowards' Way Out (Level skip feature)	Kill yourself repeatedly by holding right trigger until it unlocks.

SAINTS ROW (XBOX 360, PLAYSTATION 3)

CODES

Dial the following phone numbers in the phone book to get the corresponding effects.

EFFECT	XBOX 360 CODE	PLAYSTATION 3 CODE
12 Gauge	#cashmoneyz	#2274666399
1,000 dollars	#920	#920
.44 Cal	#921	#921
Add Gang Notoriety	#35	#35
Add Police Notoriety	#4	#4
Annihilator RPG	#947	#947
AR-200	#922	#922
AR-50	#923	#923
AR-50 with Grenade launcher	#924	#924
AS14 Hammer	#925	#925
Baseball Bat	#926	#926
Car Mass Increased	#2	#2
Chainsaw	#927	#927
Clear Sky	#sunny	—
Crowbar	#955	#955
Drunk Pedestrians	#15	#15
Everybody Is Shrunk	#202	#202
Evil Cars	#16	#16
Fire Extinguisher	#928	#928
Flame Thrower	#929	#929
Flashbang	#930	#930
Full Health	#1	#1
GAL 43	#931	#931
GDHC	#932	#932
Get Horizon	#711	#711
Get Snipes 57	#712	#712
Get Tornado	#713	#713
Get Wolverine	#714	#714
Giant	#200	#200

Grenade	#933	#933
Gyro Daddy Added to Garage	#4976	#4976
Heaven Bound	#12	#12
Itty Bitty	#201	#201
K6	#935	#935
Knife	#936	#936
Kobra	#934	#934
Lighting Strikes	#666	#666
Low Gravity	#18	#18
Machete	#937	#937
McManus 2010	#938	#938
Milk Bones	#3	#3
Mini-Gun	#939	#939
Molotov	#940	#940
Never Die	#36	#36
Nightstick	#941	#941
No Cop Notoriety	#50	#50
No Gang Notoriety	#51	#51
NR4	#942	#942
Pedestrian Wars	#19	#19
Pepper Spray	#943	#943
Pimp Slap	#969	#969
Pimpcane	#944	#944
Pipe Bomb	#945	#945
Player Pratfalls	#5	#5
Raining Pedestrians	#20	#20
RPG	#946	#946
Samurai Sword	#948	#948
Satchel Charge	#949	#949
Shock Paddles	#950	#950
SKR-9	#951	#951
Sledge Hammer	#952	#952
Stun Gun	#953	#953
Super Explosions	#7	#7
Super Saints	#8	#8
TK3	#954	#954
Tombstone	#956	#956
Unlimited Ammo	#11	#11
Unlimited Clip	#9	#9
Unlimited Sprint	#6	#6
Unlock D-STROY UFO	#728237	#728237
Unlock Peewee Mini Bike	#7266837	#7266837
Vice 9	#957	#957
XS-2 Ultimax	#958	#958

SAINTS ROW: THE THIRD (PLAYSTATION 3)

CODE

Enter one of the following codes in your phone (press select -> Extras -> Cheats) to activate the corresponding cheat function.

UNLOCKABLE	CODE
Add Gang Notoriety	lolz
Add police notoriety	pissoffpigs
Bloody Mess	notrated
Cloudy Weather	overcast
Give D4TH Blossom (SMG)	giveblossom
Give GL G20 (grenade launcher)	givelauncher
Gives $100,000 in cash	cheese
Gives a full suite of weapons	letsrock
Gives Flamethrower	giveflamethrower
Gives respect	whatitmeanstome
Heaven Bound	fryhole
Infinite Sprint	runfast
No Gang Notoriety	oops
No police notoriety	goodygoody
One hit kill	goldengun
Pedestrians Are Drunk	dui
Pedestrians Are Mascots	mascot
Pedestrians are Pimps & Prostitutes	hohoho
Pedestrians are Zombies	brains
Rainy Weather	lightrain
Repair damage to your vehicle	repaircar
Spawn Air Strike	giveairstrike
Spawn Ambulance	giveembulance
Spawn Anchor	giveanchor
Spawn Apocafists	giveapoca
Spawn AS3 Ultimax	giveultimax
Spawn Attrazione	giveattrazione
Spawn Bootlegger	givebootlegger
Spawn Chainsaw	givechainsaw
Spawn Challenger	givechallenger
Spawn Commander	givecommander
Spawn Condor	givecondor
Spawn Cyber Blaster	givecybersmg
Spawn Cyber Buster	givecyber
Spawn Drone	givedrone
Spawn Eagle	giveeagle
Spawn Electric Grenade	giveelectric
Spawn Estrada	giveestrada
Spawn F69 VTol	givevtol
Spawn Gatmobile	givegatmobile
Spawn Grenade	givegrenade
Spawn Hammer	givehammer
Spawn K-8 Krukov	givekrukov
Spawn Kanada	givekanada

Spawn Kenshin	givekenshin
Spawn Knoxville	giveknoxville
Spawn Kobra KA-1	givekobra
Spawn Krukov	givekrukov
Spawn McManus 2015	givesniper
Spawn Miami	givemiami
Spawn Minigun	giveminigun
Spawn Molotov	givemolotov
Spawn Municipal	givemunicipal
Spawn Nforcer	givenforcer
Spawn Nocturne	givesword
Spawn Peacemaker	givepeacemaker
Spawn Phoenix	givephoenix
Spawn Quasar	givequasar
Spawn Reaper	givereaper
Spawn RPG	giverpg
Spawn Sandstorm	givesandstorm
Spawn Satchel Charge	givesatchel
Spawn Shark	giveshark
Spawn Sheperd	givesheperd
Spawn Shock Hammer	giverocket
Spawn Specter	givespecter
Spawn Status Quo	givestatusquo
Spawn Taxi	givetaxi
Spawn Tek Z-10	givetek
Spawn The Penetrator	givedildo
Spawn Titan	givetitan
Spawn Toad	givetoad
Spawn Tornado	givetornado
Spawn Viper Laser Rifle	giveslm8
Spawn Vortex	givevortex
Spawn Vulture	givevulture
Spawn Widowmaker	givewidowmaker
Spawn Woodpecker	givewoodpecker
Sunny Weather	clearskies
Vehicle Smash	isquishyou
Very Rainy Weather	heavyrain
Your vehicle is immune to damage	vroom

UNLOCKABLE

Alternate gang styles can be unlocked by completing certain in-game tasks. Gang styles can be changed at cribs or strongholds.

UNLOCKABLE	HOW TO UNLOCK
Cops / SWAT	complete all instances of SNATCH for Kinzie
Deckers	complete mission 37
Hos	complete all instances of SNATCH for Zimos
Luchadores	complete mission 43
Mascots	complete all instances of Prof. Genki S.E.R.C.
Morningstar	complete mission 29
National Guard	complete all instances of TANK MAYHEM

Space Saints	complete mission 47
Strippers	complete all instances of ESCORT for Zimos
Wrestlers	complete all instances of TIGER ESCORT
Wraith and X2 Phantom (Tron Bike)	Complete the hard level of Trail Blazing in Deckers territory.

SAINTS ROW: THE THIRD (XBOX 360)

CODE

Enter one of the following codes in your phone (press select -> Extras -> Cheats) to activate the corresponding cheat function.

UNLOCKABLE	CODE
Add Gang Notóriety (+1 star)	lolz
Add Police Notoriety (+1 shield)	pissoffpigs
Bloody Mess (everyone killed explodes into blood)	notrated
Clear Skies (change weather)	clearskies
Drunk Pedestrians	dui
Give 45 Sheperd	givesheperd
Give Apoca-Fists	giveapoca
Give AR 55	givear55
Give AS3 Ultimax	giveultimax
Give Baseball Bat	givebaseball
Give Cash ($100,000)	cheese
Give Chainsaw	givechainsaw
Give Cyber Blaster	givecybersmg
Give Cyber Buster	givecyber
Give D4TH Blossom	giveblossom
Give Electric Grenade	giveelectric
Give Flamethrower	giveflamethrower
Give Flashbang	giveflashbang
Give GL G20	givelauncher
Give Grave Digger	givedigger
Give Grenade	givegrenade
Give K-8 Krukov	givekrukov
Give KA-1 Kobra	givekobra
Give McManus 2015	givesniper
Give Mini-Gun	giveminigun
Give Molotov	givemolotov
Give Nocturne	givesword
Give RC Possesor	givercgun
Give Reaper Drone	givedrone
Give Respect	whatitmeanstome
Give Riot Shield	giveshield
Give S3X Hammer	givehammer
Give SA-3 Airstrike	giveairstrike
Give Satchel Charges	givesatchel
Give Shock Hammer	giverocket
Give Sonic Boom	givesonic
Give Stun Gun	givestungun
Give TEK Z-10	givetek

Give The Penetrator	givedildo
Give Viper Laser Rifle	giveslm8
Golden Gun (one-shot gun kills)	goldengun
Heaven Bound (dead bodies float into the air)	fryhole
Heavy Rain (changes weather)	heavyrain
Infinite Sprint	runfast
Light Rain (changes weather)	lightrain
Mascots (all pedestrians are mascots)	mascot
No Cop Notoriety	goodygoody
No Gang Notoriety	oops
Overcast (changes weather)	overcast
Pimps and Hos (all pedestrians are pimps and hos)	hohoho
Repair Car (fully repairs vehicle)	repaircar
Spawns Ambulance	giveambulance
Spawns Anchor	giveanchor
Spawns Attrazione	giveattrazione
Spawns Bootlegger	givebootlegger
Spawns Challenger	givechallenger
Spawns Commander	givecommander
Spawns Condor	givecondor
Spawns Eagle	giveeagle
Spawns Estrada	giveestrada
Spawns Gat Mobile	givegatmobile
Spawns Kaneda	givekaneda
Spawns Kenshin	givekenshin
Spawns Knoxville	giveknoxville
Spawns Miami	givemiami
Spawns Municipal	givemunicipal
Spawns NForcer	givenforcer
Spawns Peacemaker	givepeacemaker
Spawns Phoenix	givephoenix
Spawns Quasar	givequasar
Spawns Reaper	givereaper
Spawns Sandstorm	givesandstorm
Spawns Shark	giveshark
Spawns Specter	givespecter
Spawns Status Quo	givestatusquo
Spawns Taxi	givetaxi
Spawns Titan	givetitan
Spawns Toad	givetoad
Spawns Tornado	givetornado
Spawns Vortex	givevortex
Spawns VTOL	givevtol
Spawns Vulture	givevulture
Spawns Widowmaker	givewidowmaker
Spawns Woodpecker	givewoodpecker

NEW!

A
B
C
D
E
F
G
H
I
J
K
L
M
N
O
P
Q
R
S
T
U
V
W
X
Y
Z

Vehicles No Damage (your vehicle is immune to damage)	vroom
Vehicles Smash (your vehicle crushes other vehicles)	isquishyou
Weapons (gives a full compliment of weapons)	letsrock
Zombies (all pedestrians become zombies)	brains

UNLOCKABLE

UNLOCKABLE	HOW TO UNLOCK
Oversized Gat Mask?	Completed the mission "When Good Heists…"
Saints Logo Shirt	Earned the "Flash the Pan" Achievement.
SR:TT Logo Shirt	Created and uploaded your first character to the community site!
Decker outfit	Assassinate Lucas by putting on the outfit kinze gives you

SCHIZOID (XBOX 360)

ACHIEVEMENTS

UNLOCKABLE	HOW TO UNLOCK
21st Century Schizoid Man (15)	Complete level 21 ("Tyger Tyger") either in Local Co-Op, Xbox LIVE, or Uberschizoid.
Barber of Schizzville (20)	Shave the Orbiddles from 8 Astramoebas on a level, without destroying Astramoebas or losing a life.
Corpus Callosum Severed (20)	Complete level 119 ("Ragnarok") in Uberschizoid mode.
Flitt Breeder (10)	Get a gold medal on level 5 ("My Man Flitt") without destroying any Flitts.
Huevos Done Naked (20)	Gold level 47 ("Los Huevos") without activating any power-ups.
One Mind, Two Goals (20)	Earn 20 silver or gold medals in Uberschizoid mode.
Playing the Field (15)	Play a game in each mode: Xbox LIVE, Local Co-Op, Wingman Bot Training, and Uberschizoid.
Schiz Hunter (20)	Destroy 30 Schizzes on a single level, using power-ups and without losing any lives.
Schizoid Sensei (20)	Earn 10 medals (any combination of gold, silver, and bronze) over Xbox LIVE.
Seafood Buffet (20)	Destroy 2,500 Scorpios.
Sploderific (10)	Destroy all enemies on level 12 ("Smartbomb") with a single smartbomb.
Wired (10)	Destroy an enemy with a razorwire.

SCOTT PILGRIM VS. THE WORLD (PLAYSTATION 3))

UNLOCKABLES

UNLOCKABLE	HOW TO UNLOCK
Nega-Scott	Beat the game using Kim, Stills, Ramona, and Scott.

SCRAP METAL (XBOX 360)

UNLOCKABLES

UNLOCKABLE	HOW TO UNLOCK
Scrap Metal RC car	Complete all missions in the single-player game.
Scrap Metal T-Shirt	Complete first race.

SCRIBBLENAUTS (DS)

GOLD STAR RANKING

After you've completed a given puzzle, you'll be awarded a Silver Star on the puzzle selection screen to indicate your success. However, you can get a higher ranking. Retrying the same puzzle activates Advance Mode, which is a bonus challenge. You have to beat the same level three times in a row, and with different objects each time. If you restart, you'll have to begin the challenge from the beginning. If you successfully complete the Advance Mode version of a puzzle, you'll be awarded a Gold Star on the selection screen.

MERITS

Merits are awards/achievements you can earn by doing different things in a given level. However, you need to complete the level to get them.

UNLOCKABLE	HOW TO UNLOCK
5th Cell	Spawn a 5th Cell employee.
All New	Complete a level with objects you've never used before.
Architect	Write two buildings.
Arrrrr	Attach the Jolly Roger to a flagpole.
Audiophile	Write two or more instruments or audio objects.
Bioterrorist	Introduce the plague and infect two or more people.
Botanist	Write two or more plants.
Chauffeur	Drive a vehicle with more than one passenger.
Chef	Write two or more foods.
Closet	Write two or more clothes.
Combo	Combine any two objects together.
Cupid	Shoot a humanoid with Cupid's arrow.
Decorator	Write two furniture objects.
Electrolysis	Shock someone with electricity.
Elemental	Write more than one element.
Entertainer	Write two or more entertainment objects.
Entomologist	Spawn two or more insects.
Environmentalist	Write two or more environmental objects.
Explosive	Spawn two or more objects that explode.
Exterminator	Two or more humanoids or animals start a level and are destroyed.
Fantasynovel	Write two fantasy objects.
Fashion Designer	Clothe Maxwell's head, body, legs, feet and give him an accessory.
Firefighter	Put out at least two fires.
Genius	Complete a level twice in a row.
Glutton	Feed someone or something three times in a row.
Gold Digger	Spawn three or more precious stones.
Grab and Go	Write two or more grabbing tool objects.
Haxxor	Write five or more developers.
Healer	Spawn two or more medical objects.
Herpetologist	Write two or more reptiles.
Humanitarian	Write two or more humans.
Infected	Spawn a zombie and make it infect at least two humanoids.
Janitor	Spawn two or more cleaning objects.
Jockey	Use an animal as a vehicle.
Joust	Defeat a knight while Maxwell is mounted.
Knight School	Kill a dragon using a melee weapon.
Luddite	Short out three or more objects.
Lumberjack	Cut down three or more trees.
Mad Hatter	Place a hat on four or more humanoids or animals.
Magician	Use the magic wand to turn something into a toad.
Marine Biologist	Write two or more fish.
Mechanic	Jump-start a vehicle.

Messiah	Turn a humanoid into a deity.
Militant	Use two weapons and one weaponized vehicle.
Miner 49er	Dig a massive hole.
Miser	Obtain a total of 300,000 or more Ollars.
New Object	Write a completely new item.
No Weapons	Don't write a weapon to complete a level.
Novice Angler	Catch a fish with a fishing pole.
Old School	Write two or more classic video game objects.
Organ Donor	Spawn two or more organs.
Ornithologist	Write two or more birds.
Paleontologist	Spawn two ore more dinosaurs.
Pariah	Make three humanoids or animals flee.
Pi	Earn exactly 314 Ollars in a level.
Picasso	Write two or more drawing object tools.
Pilot	Spawn two or more aircraft.
Prodigy	Complete a level three times in a row.
Pyromaniac	Set at least four objects on fire in a level.
Reanimator	Bring a corpse back to life.
Roped In	Write two or more rope objects.
Russian Doll	Place an object inside another object, and then place that object into a third object.
Savior	Two or more humanoids or animals start and finish a level alive.
Sea Two	Write two or more sea vehicles.
Series of Tubes	Spawn "tube" five times.
Shoveler	Spawn two or more digging objects.
Smasher	Write two or more melee weapons.
Smuggler	Hide an item in a container.
Split Personality	Write two or more cutting or splitting tool objects.
Stealth	Destroy a security camera.
Sweet Tooth	Write two or more junk foods.
Tooling Around	Write two or more tool objects.
Washington	Chop down a cherry tree.
Water Jockey	Use a sea animal as a vehicle.
Whisperer	Ride a hostile animal.
Zookeeper	Write two or more animals.

HIDDEN LEVELS

If you spawn a teleporter and use it, it takes you to one of three secret levels.

GLITCH

Challenge Mode encourages you to get creative by not allowing you to use the same words in three separate trials. If you are feeling uncreative, you can take advantage of The Great Adjective Exploit to bypass this entirely: just add an adjective (or gibberish) in front of a word and the game will give you a free pass to use it again. You can clear a stage three times by typing "Wings" the first time, "Big Wings" the second time and "Small Wings" the third time; you'll simply get the Wings all three times, but the game will register three different words and will allow it.

BACKGROUND SCREEN

When you're at the title screen (Sandbox Mode), you can unlock 14 more backgrounds by typing words that fall into certain categories. These are some words that unlock the backgrounds.

UNLOCKABLE	HOW TO UNLOCK
Background 02	Type "cat."
Background 03	Type "car."
Background 04	Type "bee."

Background 05	Type "tree."
Background 06	Type "woman."
Background 07	Type "coffin."
Background 08	Type "vibes."
Background 09	Type "coin."
Background 10	Type "chair."
Background 11	Type "zombie."
Background 12	Type "court."
Background 13	Type "rain" and select "rain(water)."
Background 14	Type "it."
Background 15	Type "pc."

SECTION 8 (XBOX 360)

CODES

At the main menu go to dropship and enter the following codes. Entering the Captain's Armor code twice disables the code.

EFFECT	CODE
Chrome Assault Rifle	68432181
Unlock Black Widow auto-pistol	13374877
Unlock Captain's Armor	17013214

SHADOW LAND (WII)

SECRET PASSWORD SCREEN

UNLOCKABLE	HOW TO UNLOCK
Password Screen	At the title screen hold ①+②+SELECT and press RUN

PASSWORDS

PASSWORD	EFFECT
PC-ENGINE	(message)
NAMCO	(message)
NAMCOT	(message)
6502	(message)
6809	(message)
68000	(message)
756-2311	(message)
YAMASHITA	(message)
AKIRA	(message)
KOMAI	(message)
KAZUHIKO	(message)
KAWADA	(message)
SPEED-UP (4 way split screen)	Reset after entering the password
S.62.08.22 (Start from level 5)	Reset after entering the password

SHIFT 2 UNLEASHED: NEED FOR SPEED (XBOX 360)

ACHIEVEMENT

UNLOCKABLE	HOW TO UNLOCK
Amateur (5)	Reached Driver Level 5
Badge Collector (50)	Earned 100 Badges
Badge Earner (5)	Earned 10 Badges
Badge Hunter (10)	Earned 50 Badges
Bounty Hunter (20)	Earned $10,000,000 total during your career
Competition License (10)	Won 50 Career events on Medium difficulty or higher

Cub Scout (10)	Won your first Event Set badge
Day Walker (50)	Mastered every location in day or dusk
Dialled In (10)	Used On-Track Tuning to save a Tuning Setup for a car
Dominator (100)	Beaten all the Rivals
Elitist (10)	Placed 1st in an event using Elite handling model
Globetrotter (20)	Competed at every location in the game
Going the extra mile (25)	Completed 250 Event Objectives
Grass Roots (10)	Completed JR's Grass Roots event
GT1 Champion (100)	Beat Jamie Campbell-Walter and won the FIA GT1 World Championship
GT3 Champion (50)	Beat Patrick Soderlund and won the FIA GT3 European Championship
I'm Going To Hollywood! (10)	Got through the Qualifying round in the Driver Duel Championship
I. Am. Iron Man. (10)	Placed 1st in 5 consecutive Online events
In The Zone (10)	Won an Online event from helmet cam
Intercept & Pursue (10)	Completed an Online Catchup Pack and Online Catchup Duel event
King of the Hill (10)	Won your first Driver Duel Championship crown
Leno would be proud (10)	Have at least one car from each manufacturer in your garage
Nailed It (10)	Track Mastered your first location
Night Rider (100)	Mastered every location at night
Notorious (25)	Played Online for over 10 hours total
Paparazzi (5)	Shared a photo or replay with others
Pro (50)	Reached Driver Level (15)
Proving Grounds (10)	Won JR's GTR Challenge
Race License (50)	Won 75 Career events on Hard difficulty
Recommended (5)	Completed an event recommended by a friend
Road to Glory (10)	Beaten your first Rival
Semi-Pro (10)	Reached Driver Level 10
Sizzlin' (10)	Beaten the 1st Target Time in a Hot Lap event
Sports License (10)	Won 25 Career events on Easy difficulty or higher
The Driver's battle (5)	Completed an event purely from helmet cam
The World is my Oyster (10)	Unlocked the FIA GT1 Branch
Tic Tac Toe (10)	Own a Modern, Retro, and Muscle car
Veteran (75)	Reached Driver Level 20
Workaholic (10)	Upgraded 3 vehicles to Works spec
Works Champion (50)	Beat Mad Mike Whiddett and won the Works Championship

SHINING FORCE (WII)

UNLOCKABLES

UNLOCKABLE	HOW TO UNLOCK
Control All Opponents (JP Version Only)	When the battle begins, quickly tap Ⓐ, Ⓑ, Ⓒ, ✛, Ⓐ, Ⓒ, Ⓐ, Ⓑ, Ⓐ
Fight Any Battle (JP Version Only)	Hold START on controller 2 then reset the system. Let go of START and hold Ⓐ+Ⓑ on controller 2. Select continue and wait until the girl says good luck. At that instant hold Ⓐ on controller 1 while continuing to hold Ⓐ+Ⓑ on controller 2.

| Name Characters | Start a new game (must have completed game first) and go to the Name Your Character screen. Put the cursor on end and hold START+ⓐ+ⓑ+ⓒ on controller 2 while holding: START+ⓐ+ⓒ on controller 1. You will see another character. Continue this to name all characters. |

OTHER UNLOCKABLES

UNLOCKABLE	HOW TO UNLOCK
2 Jogurts	If you put jogurt in your army and kill an enemy with him, you get a jogurt ring item. Use this in battle on any character to make that character look like a jogurt! Repeat as many times as you want, but you will have to get another ring when it breaks.
Anri's Alternate Costume	During the Laser Eye battle in Chapter 3, search to the left of the three dark elves. You'll receive a hidden item called Kitui Huku ("tight clothes" in Japanese). Give it to Anri and she'll have a new outfit.
Tao's Alternate Costume	In Chapter 3, after fighting the first battle to get the Moon Stone, go inside the cave and search the walls for a secret item called the Sugoi Mizugi. Give it to Tao and she will have an alternate costume.

SHINOBIDO 2: REVENGE OF ZEN (PLAYSTATION VITA)

TROPHY

UNLOCKABLE	HOW TO UNLOCK
Alchemical Aspirations (Bronze)	Use alchemy to create an original ninja tool.
Alchemical Genius (Silver)	Create the symbol of an Alchemical Genius.
Apprentice Ninja (Bronze)	Beat the game on Easy Difficulty.
Assassin's Pedigree (Silver)	Perform all the special Chimatsuri Sappo successfully.
Bandit Buster (Bronze)	Leave no bandit alive.
Chimatsuri Sappo (Bronze)	Perform a Chimatsuri Sappo successfully.
Counter Puncher (Bronze)	Perform a Mikiri successfully.
Covert Ninja (Bronze)	A true ninja always goes unseen.
Cutie Kaede (Bronze)	Kaede is so cute! I wish I could play as her...
Familiar Faces (Bronze)	You met some familiar ninja from bygone days.
First Class Ninja (Silver)	Beat the game on Hard difficulty.
Flying the Night Skies (Bronze)	Use the Fukurou to fly.
Full-fledged Ninja (Bronze)	Beat the game on Normal difficulty.
Gaga for Greens (Silver)	Collect every type of weed.
Gears and Springs (Bronze)	I love wind-up toys!!
Gecko Hunter (Silver)	Collect every type of gecko.
Grapple Hook King (Bronze)	Throw that grapple hook!!
Hard Worker (Bronze)	Complete all the tutorials.
Headhunter (Bronze)	Perform a Zankoku successfully.
Ichijo's Peace (Bronze)	View Ichijo's ending event.
Jack-of-All-Trades (Silver)	Versatility is part of being a ninja.
Kazama is Never Satisfied (Bronze)	View Kazama's ending event.
Kihan's New Journey (Bronze)	View Kihan's ending event.
Killing Spree (Bronze)	Kill 2 enemies with a single Zankoku.
King of the Beasts (Silver)	Encounter a bear like none other.
Legendary Ninja (Gold)	Beat the game on Deadly difficulty.
Mikiri Maestro (Bronze)	Find fortune in peril.
Moneymaker (Silver)	A true ninja also knows how to save.
Mushroom Village (Silver)	Collect every type of mushroom.
Ninja Hunter (Silver)	Every ninja must die.

NEW!

A
B
C
D
E
F
G
H
I
J
K
L
M
N
O
P
Q
R
S
T
U
V
W
X
Y
Z

CODES & CHEATS

Ninja Initiation (Bronze)	Level up for the first time.
Ninja Tool Craftsman (Bronze)	Become a connoisseur of alchemical ninja tools.
Obsession (Bronze)	Finish Chapter 3.
One Flower (Bronze)	View the "One Flower" ending.
Onigami (Silver)	Become a master of using Chimatsuri Sappo.
Person of Power (Bronze)	You gave it your all to wipe the enemy out.
Recovery Elixir Popper (Bronze)	Coming back from the brink of death is part of being a ninja.
Reflections (Bronze)	View the "Reflections" ending.
Reunion (Bronze)	Finish Chapter 2.
Saint (Silver)	A ninja loves all without bias.
Salmon, Salmon, and More Salmon (Bronze)	You really like salmon, don't you?
Scattered Petals, Burning Petals (Bronze)	Finish Chapter 1.
Shinobido Mastery (Platinum)	Acquire every trophy.
Shuriken Sharpshooter (Bronze)	Prove the strength of the shuriken.
Sticky Fingers (Bronze)	Did you steal something?
The First Step (Bronze)	Complete the first mission succesfully.
The Only One I Love (Bronze)	Finish Chapter 4.
The Silencer (Bronze)	Silence every witness to your deeds.
The Zankoku One (Bronze)	Become a master of using Zankoku.
Two Flowers (Bronze)	View the "Two Flowers" ending.
Uzumbi Artisan (Bronze)	It's their fault for stepping on it.

SILENT HILL: DOWNPOUR (PLAYSTATION 3)

TROPHY

UNLOCKABLE	HOW TO UNLOCK
Art Appreciation (Bronze)	Completed "The Art Collector" side quest.
Ashes, Ashes (Bronze)	Collected 3 pages of the rhyme book.
Birdman (Bronze)	Completed the "Bird Cage" side quest.
Broken Cycle (Bronze)	Defeated The Bogeyman.
Calling All Cars (Bronze)	Completed the "All Points Bulletin" side quest.
Capital Punishment (Gold)	Completed the game on the hard game difficulty setting, any ending.
Cutting Room Floor (Bronze)	Completed the "Cinéma Vérité" side quest.
Dust to Dust (Bronze)	Completed the "Ashes to Ashes" side quest.
Ending A (Silver)	Achieved "Forgiveness" ending.
Ending B (Silver)	Achieved "Truth & Justice" ending.
Ending C (Silver)	Achieved "Full Circle" ending.
Ending D (Silver)	Achieved "Execution" ending.
Ending E (Silver)	Achieved "Surprise!" ending.
Fight or Flight? (Silver)	Escaped from 20 monsters.
Found a Friend! (Bronze)	Met DJ Ricks in the Radio Station.
Going off the Rails (Bronze)	Escaped from Devil's Pit.
Good Behavior (Silver)	Completed the game on any difficulty without killing any monsters.
Gun Control (Bronze)	Killed 25 monsters with the Pistol or Shotgun.
Hypochondriac (Bronze)	Used 20 First Aid Kits.

Lockdown (Silver)	Killed or incapacitated 10 Prisoner Minions.
Long Walk, Short Pier (Bronze)	Completed the "Ribbons" side quest.
Neighborhood Watch (Bronze)	Completed the "Stolen Goods" side quest.
No Turning Back (Bronze)	Reached Overlook Penitentiary.
Now You're Cooking... (Bronze)	Survived the Diner Otherworld.
Out of the Frying Pan (Bronze)	Rode the Sky Tram to Devil's Pit.
Piñata Party (Silver)	Killed or incapacitated 10 Weeping Bats.
Puzzle Master (Gold)	Completed the game on the hard puzzle difficulty setting, any ending.
Rain Maker (Platinum)	Collected all trophies.
Shadow Boxer (Silver)	Killed or incapacitated 10 Dolls.
Silence is Golden (Silver)	Killed or incapacitated 10 Screamers.
Silent Alarm (Bronze)	Completed "The Bank" side quest.
Silent Hill Historic Society (Silver)	Completed Murphy's Journal with all Mysteries.
Silent Hill Tour Guide (Gold)	Completed all side quests.
Spot the Difference (Bronze)	Completed the "Mirror, Mirror" side quest.
Stay of Execution (Silver)	Incapacitated 20 monsters without killing them.
Telltale Heart (Bronze)	Completed the "Dead Man's Hand" side quest.
The Bigger They Are... (Silver)	Killed or incapacitated 10 Prisoner Juggernauts.
Turn Back Time (Bronze)	Completed "The Gramophone" side quest.
Useless Trinkets (Bronze)	Completed the "Digging up the Past" side quest.
What's Your Sign? (Bronze)	Completed the "Shadow Play" side quest.
Whatever Doesn't Kill You... (Bronze)	Escaped the Radio Station Otherworld.
Will Work For Food (Bronze)	Completed the "Homeless" side quest.

UNLOCKABLE

UNLOCKABLE	HOW TO UNLOCK
Unlock Nail Gun and Double Axe	When you reach a green locker type in 171678 to unlock.

SILENT HILL: DOWNPOUR (XBOX 360)

ACHIEVEMENT

UNLOCKABLE	HOW TO UNLOCK
Art Appreciation (5)	Completed "The Art Collector" side quest.
Ashes, Ashes (10)	Collected 3 pages of the rhyme book.
Birdman (5)	Completed the "Bird Cage" side quest.
Broken Cycle (10)	Defeated The Bogeyman.
Calling All Cars (5)	Completed the "All Points Bulletin" side quest.
Capital Punishment (100)	Completed the game on the hard game difficulty setting, any ending.
Cutting Room Floor (5)	Completed the "Cinéma Vérité" side quest.
Dust to Dust (5)	Completed the "Ashes to Ashes" side quest.
Ending A (50)	Achieved "Forgiveness" ending.
Ending B (50)	Achieved "Truth & Justice" ending.
Ending C (50)	Achieved "Full Circle" ending.
Ending D (50)	Achieved "Execution" ending.
Ending E (70)	Achieved "Surprise!" ending.

Fight or Flight? (20)	Escaped from 20 monsters.
Found a Friend! (10)	Met DJ Ricks in the Radio Station.
Going off the Rails (10)	Escaped from Devil's Pit.
Good Behavior (50)	Completed the game on any difficulty without killing any monsters.
Gun Control (25)	Killed 25 monsters with the Pistol or Shotgun.
Hypochondriac (10)	Used 20 First Aid Kits.
Lockdown (20)	Killed or incapacitated 10 Prisoner Minions.
Long Walk, Short Pier (5)	Completed the "Ribbons" side quest.
Neighborhood Watch (5)	Completed the "Stolen Goods" side quest.
No Turning Back (10)	Reached Overlook Penitentiary.
Now You're Cooking... (10)	Survived the Diner Otherworld.
Out of the Frying Pan (10)	Rode the Sky Tram to Devil's Pit.
Piñata Party (20)	Killed or incapacitated 10 Weeping Bats.
Puzzle Master (100)	Completed the game on the hard puzzle difficulty setting, any ending.
Shadow Boxer (20)	Killed or incapacitated 10 Dolls.
Silence is Golden (20)	Killed or incapacitated 10 Screamers.
Silent Alarm (5)	Completed "The Bank" side quest.
Silent Hill Historic Society (50)	Completed Murphy's Journal with all Mysteries.
Silent Hill Tour Guide (100)	Completed all side quests.
Spot the Difference (5)	Completed the "Mirror, Mirror" side quest.
Stay of Execution (25)	Incapacitated 20 monsters without killing them.
Telltale Heart (5)	Completed the "Dead Man's Hand" side quest.
The Bigger They Are... (20)	Killed or incapacitated 10 Prisoner Juggernauts.
Turn Back Time (5)	Completed "The Gramophone" side quest.
Useless Trinkets (5)	Completed the "Digging up the Past" side quest.
What's Your Sign? (5)	Completed the "Shadow Play" side quest.
Whatever Doesn't Kill You... (10)	Escaped the Radio Station Otherworld.
Will Work For Food (5)	Completed the "Homeless" side quest.

SILENT HILL: SHATTERED MEMORIES   (WII)

UFO ENDING

UNLOCKABLE	HOW TO UNLOCK
UFO ending	Photograph 13 hidden UFOs.

EASTER EGG

Press 1 on the Wii Remote, go to "Hints," click on "Cell Phone Calls," on the picture of Harry's phone with a number. Dial the number on your phone to call Konami Customer Service. Unfortunately, they are unable to help you due to the fact you're in Silent Hill.

SIMCITY DS   (DS)

PASSWORDS

At the main menu, go to "Museum" then select "Landmark Collection," and finally "Password," then enter the following codes.

UNLOCKABLE	CODE
Anglican Cathedral (UK)	kipling
Arc de Triomphe (France)	gaugin
Atomic Dome (Japan)	kawabata

Big Ben (UK)	orwell
Bowser Castle (Nintendo)	hanafuda
Brandenburg Gate (Germany)	gropius
Coit Tower (USA)	kerouac
Conciergerie (France)	rodin
Daibutsu (Japan)	mishima
Edo Castle (Japan)	shonagon
Eiffel Tower (France)	camus
Gateway Arch (USA)	twain
Grand Central Station (USA)	f.scott
Great Pyramids (Egypt)	mahfouz
Hagia Sofia (Turkey)	ataturk
Helsinki Cathedral (Finland)	kivi
Himeji Castle (Japan)	hokusai
Holstentor (Germany)	durer
Independence Hall (USA)	mlkingjr
Jefferson Memorial (USA)	thompson
Kokkai (Japan)	soseki
LA Landmark (USA)	hemingway
Lincoln Memorial (USA)	melville
Liver Building (UK)	dickens
Melbourne Cricket Ground (Australia)	damemelba
Metropolitan Cathedral (UK)	austen
Moai (Chile)	allende
Mt. Fuji (Japan)	hiroshige
National Museum (Taiwan)	yuantlee
Neuschwanstein Castle (Germany)	beethoven
Notre Dame (France)	hugo
Palace of Fine Arts (USA)	bunche
Palacio Real (Spain)	cervantes
Paris Opera (France)	daumier
Parthenon (Greece)	callas
Pharos of Alexandria (Egypt)	zewail
Rama IX Royal Park (Thailand)	phu
Reichstag (Germany)	goethe
Sagrada Famillia (Spain)	dali
Shuri Castle (Japan)	basho
Smithsonian Castle (USA)	pauling
Sphinx (Egypt)	haykal
St. Paul's Cathedral (UK)	defoe
St. Basil's Cathedral (Russia)	tolstoy
St. Stephen's Cathedral (Austria)	mozart
Statue of Liberty (USA)	pollack
Stockholm Palace (Sweden)	bergman
Sydney Opera House Landmark # 12 (Australia)	bradman
Taj Mahal (India)	tagore
Tower of London (UK)	maugham
Trafalgar Square (UK)	joyce
United Nations (USA)	amnesty
United States Capitol (USA)	poe
Washington Monument (USA)	capote
Westminster Abbey (UK)	greene
White House (USA)	steinbeck

UNLOCKABLE BUILDINGS FROM POPULATION GROWTH

When your city reaches a certain number of people, Dr. Simtown unlocks buildings that help your city.

UNLOCKABLE	HOW TO UNLOCK
Center for the Arts	Reach a population of 100,000.
Court House	Reach a population of 25,000.
Mayor's House	Reach a population of 5,000.
Medical Research Lab	Have a population of 80,000 when you reach year 1999.
Museum	Reach a population of 3,000.
Post Office	Reach a population of 100.

THE SIMS 3 (DS)

KARMA POWERS

Karma Powers can be unlocked after you have accumulated enough Lifetime Happiness for each one. To trigger Karma Powers, go to the locations that follow and click on the object described.

UNLOCKABLE	HOW TO UNLOCK
Bless This Mess	Garden Gnome outside Landgraab house
Casanova	Dance Club, near the restrooms
Cosmic Curse	Graveyard at night only
Epic Fail	Statue at Goth's house
Giant Jackpot	Bench near the Lighthouse
Muse	Painting in the Art Museum
Super Satisfy	Wrought Iron Trellis off path near Lighthouse
The Riddler	Jet statue near Military Base
Winter Wonderland	Alcove near the Stadium
Wormhole	Potted flower outside Poet's Abode

THE SIMS 2: PETS (WII)

UNLOCKABLES

UNLOCKABLE	HOW TO UNLOCK
10,000 Simoleons	Hold ⑱, press ⬆, ⬅, ⬇, ➡
Advance 6 Hours	⬆, ⬇, ⬆, ⬇, ⬆, ⬇
Change Skills	⬇, ⬇, ⬇, ⬇, ⬇, ⬆

SKATE 2 (XBOX 360)

CODES

Enter the code in the code entry screen in the "Extras" menu. The code for 3-D requires that you have 3-D glasses.

EFFECT	CODE
Turns the Game 3-D	Strangeloops
Unlocks Big Black as a playable character	letsdowork

UNLOCKABLES

UNLOCKABLE	HOW TO UNLOCK
GvR Plaza	Complete all Street Challenges to unlock the Etnies GvR Plaza.
King of the Mountain Crown	Beat all of the Races in Career mode (not the bonus races, though).
Legend Crown	Reach Legend level online.
Monster Skate Park	Get Sponsored and complete Team Film Challenges until you get a demo session with Rob Drydek; after completing this earn $200,000 to buy the park.
S.V. Dam	Complete all the Thrasher Mag challenges to drain the dam.

S.V. Stadium	Complete all Tranny Contests to unlock the S.V. Mega-Ramp Stadium.
S.V. Summit	Complete all the Death Races to unlock the peak of Cougar Mountain.
Training Park	Complete all Team Film Challenges to unlock the Training Park.

SKATE 2 (PLAYSTATION 3)

CODES

Enter the code in the code entry screen in the "Extras" menu. The code for 3-D requires that you have 3-D glasses.

EFFECT	CODE
Turns The Game 3-D	Strangeloops
Unlocks Big Black as a playable character	letsdowork

SKATE 3 (XBOX 360)

CODES

Activate the codes by pressing Start, Options, then Extras, and then entering them.

EFFECT	CODE
Enables Mini-Skater Mode	miniskaters
Enables Zombie Mode Pedestrians chase you; screen goes yellowish	zombie
Hoverboard Mode Trucks and wheels disappear from your deck	mcfly
Resets all objects in every area back to their original positions	streetsweeper
Unlocks Isaac from Dead Space as a playable skater	deadspacetoo

SKATE 3 (PLAYSTATION 3)

CODES

Pause the game, go to Options, Extras, and then enter the following codes.

EFFECT	CODE
Enables Mini-Skater Mode	miniskaters
Enables Zombie Mode	zombie
Hoverboard Mode	mcfly
Resets all objects in every area back to their original positions	streetsweeper
Unlocks Isaac from Dead Space as a playable skater	deadspacetoo

SMALL ARMS (XBOX 360)

UNLOCKABLES

UNLOCKABLE	HOW TO UNLOCK
Shooting Range Practice	Beat Mission mode
Billy Ray Logg	Beat him in Mission mode with any character
ISO-7982	Complete Mission mode
Mousey McNuts	Beat him in Mission mode with any character
Professor Von Brown	Beat him in Mission mode with any character

SMASH T (XBOX 360)

INVINCIBILITY

CODE	EFFECT
Press Ⓐ+Ⓨ	Become invincible. This code must be entered in every room. You can move around and change the angle of your shooting. If you stop shooting, the code deactivates. Don't stop shooting unless you want to pick up a new weapon or prize.

SNIPER ELITE V2 (PLAYSTATION 3)

TROPHY

UNLOCKABLE	HOW TO UNLOCK
Apprentice Sniper (Bronze)	Destroy the V2 Facility and escape to safety
Bedpan Commando (Bronze)	Resuscitate your partner in coop 10 times
Bomb Happy (Bronze)	Survive 10 Games of bombing run
Can Do! (Silver)	Complete all co-op Overwatch Missions
Cooking Off (Bronze)	Snipe a grenade on an enemy's webbing from 100m
Deadeye (Bronze)	Snipe an enemy through his eye
Detonator (Silver)	Career total of 50 shots on explosives
Double Dose (Bronze)	Snipe 2 people with one shot
Ear Plugs (Bronze)	Snipe an enemy while your rifle fire is masked by a loud sound
Expert Sniper (Bronze)	Eliminate Müller
Feared Sniper (Bronze)	Destroy the V2 rocket
Fish Tank (Bronze)	Send the tank into the river by blowing up the bridge
Front and Center (Bronze)	Get a scoped headshot over 150m
Fuel Tank (Bronze)	Destroy a tank by sniping the fuel supply
Get Off the ground (Bronze)	Kill everyone in the convoy from ground level, except for Kreidl
Go the Distance (Silver)	Get a cumulative sniped kill distance of a marathon
Gold Rush (Silver)	Find and retrieve all the stolen gold bars
Gung Ho (Silver)	Snipe 100 moving targets
Head Honcho (Silver)	Get 100 sniped headshots
Hide and Hope (Silver)	Complete a level without being shot a single time
High and Mighty (Bronze)	Wipe out the Elite Russian Sniper Team from the rooftops
Iron Lung (Silver)	Hold your breath for a cumulative time of half an hour
Journeyman Sniper (Bronze)	Hold off the Russian advance
Jungle Juice (Gold)	Find and snipe all the hidden bottles throughout the game
Kilroy was Here (Bronze)	Make it through the tower to the winch room without being spotted
Legendary Sniper (Silver)	Prevent Wolff from escaping
Make Every Bullet Count (Silver)	Complete a level with 100% accuracy, using only rifles
Master Sniper (Bronze)	Uncover Wolff's plan
Mousetrap Fuse (Bronze)	Use a trip mine to kill an enemy who is trying to assault your position
Novice Sniper (Bronze)	Stop the convoy
Pass the Buck (Silver)	Get a sniped ricochet headshot
Platinum Trophy (Platinum)	Win all other trophies to take your place as the world's greatest sniper
Potato Masher (Silver)	Kill 100 enemies with explosives
Pro Sniper (Bronze)	Collect intel from the church and make it out alive
Silent but deadly (Bronze)	Covertly kill 25 unaware enemies
Skilled Sniper (Bronze)	Stop the execution

Sniper Elite (Gold)	Complete all missions on highest difficulty
Target Eliminated! (Silver)	As a sniper in Overwatch, snipe 50 enemies tagged by your partner
Target Spotted! (Silver)	As a spotter in Overwatch, tag 50 enemies
Trainee Sniper (Bronze)	Escape the German assault
Veteran Sniper (Bronze)	Discover the location of the V2 launch site
World Record (Silver)	Get 506 cumulative sniper kills

SNIPER ELITE V2 (XBOX 360)

ACHIEVEMENT

UNLOCKABLE	HOW TO UNLOCK
Apprentice Sniper (20)	Destroy the V2 Facility and escape to safety
Bedpan Commando (20)	Resuscitate your partner in coop 10 times
Bomb Happy (20)	Survive 10 Games of bombing run
Can Do! (20)	Complete all co-op Overwatch Missions
Cooking Off (20)	Snipe a grenade on an enemy's webbing from 100m
Deadeye (10)	Snipe an enemy through his eye
Detonator (20)	Career total of 50 shots on explosives
Double Dose (20)	Snipe 2 people with one shot
Ear Plugs (10)	Snipe an enemy while your rifle fire is masked by a loud sound
Expert Sniper (20)	Eliminate Müller
Feared Sniper (20)	Destroy the V2 rocket
Fish Tank (15)	Send the tank into the river by blowing up the bridge
Front and Center (10)	Get a scoped headshot over 150m
Fuel Tank (10)	Destroy a tank by sniping the fuel supply
Get Off the ground (15)	Kill everyone in the convoy from ground level, except for Kreidl
Go the Distance (20)	Get a cumulative sniped kill distance of a marathon
Gold Rush (50)	Find and retrieve all the stolen gold bars
Gung Ho (20)	Snipe 100 moving targets
Head Honcho (20)	Get 100 sniped headshots
Hide and Hope (50)	Complete a level without being shot a single time
High and Mighty (15)	Wipe out the Elite Russian Sniper Team from the rooftops
Iron Lung (20)	Hold your breath for a cumulative time of half an hour
Journeyman Sniper (20)	Hold off the Russian advance
Jungle Juice (50)	Find and snipe all the hidden bottles throughout the game
Kilroy was Here (15)	Make it through the tower to the winch room without being spotted
Legendary Sniper (65)	Prevent Wolff from escaping
Make Every Bullet Count (25)	Complete a level with 100% accuracy, using only rifles
Master Sniper (20)	Uncover Wolff's plan
Mousetrap Fuse (10)	Use a trip mine to kill an enemy who is trying to assault your position
Novice Sniper (20)	Stop the convoy
Pass the Buck (30)	Get a sniped ricochet headshot
Potato Masher (20)	Kill 100 enemies with explosives

NEW!

A
B
C
D
E
F
G
H
I
J
K
L
M
N
O
P
Q
R
S
T
U
V
W
X
Y
Z

Pro Sniper (20)	Collect intel from the church and make it out alive
Silent but deadly (10)	Covertly kill 25 unaware enemies
Skilled Sniper (20)	Stop the execution
Sniper Elite (100)	Complete all missions on highest difficulty
Target Eliminated! (30)	As a sniper in Overwatch, snipe 50 enemies tagged by your partner
Target Spotted! (30)	As a spotter in Overwatch, tag 50 enemies
Trainee Sniper (20)	Escape the German assault
Veteran Sniper (20)	Discover the location of the V2 launch site
World Record (30)	Get 506 cumulative sniper kills

SNOOPY FLYING ACE (XBOX 360)

UNLOCKABLES

Use the Avatar Costumes/Shirts by downloading them from the "Download Avatar Awards" option in the Help & Options menu after completing the requirements below.

UNLOCKABLE	HOW TO UNLOCK
Snoopy Gamer Pic	Obtain 5,000 Online Points.
Woodstock Gamer Pic	Reach level 20.
Red Baron Avatar Costume	Reach the rank of Flying Ace.
Snoopy Avatar Shirt	Receive at least one medal on all missions.

SOLDIER BLADE (WII)

CODES

EFFECT	CODE
Level Select	Hold ⬇, press SELECT, hold ⬇, press SELECT, hold ⬆, press SELECT, hold ⬆, press SELECT

SOLDNER-X 2: FINAL PROTOTYPE (PLAYSTATION 3)

UNLOCKABLES

UNLOCKABLE	HOW TO UNLOCK
Stage 5	Collect at least 4 keys from any stage
Stage 6	Collect at least 4 keys from any 3 stages
Stage 7	Collect at least 4 keys from stages 1–6
Final Ship	Complete the Challenge "Assassin"
Extra Hard difficulty	Complete the game on Hard difficulty
Hard difficulty	Complete the game on Normal difficulty

SOLOMON'S KEY (WII)

UNLOCKABLES

UNLOCKABLE	HOW TO UNLOCK
Continue Game	At the "Game Deviation Value" screen, hold ⬇+Ⓐ+Ⓑ

SONIC 3D BLAST (WII)

UNLOCKABLES

UNLOCKABLE	HOW TO UNLOCK
Level Select	Go to the Press Start screen and enter Ⓑ, Ⓐ, ⬇, Ⓐ, Ⓒ, ⬇, ⬇, Ⓐ (or baracuda). You're taken to the main screen. Press the Start option and the level select appears.
Quick Emerald Gain	Enter the Level Select code twice, and go to a level/act with Knuckles or Tails in it. Enter one of their bonus levels by collecting 50 rings. When the bonus level begins, press Ⓐ+ START and you will receive the emerald for the bonus level.
Skip Levels	Do the Level Select code and start the game in any level. To skip levels, pause the game and press Ⓐ.

| Stage Select (Alternative) | Beat the entire game with all the Chaos Emeralds. After the credits, the stage select is on. |

SONIC GENERATIONS (XBOX 360)

CODE

When in the Collection Room, hold down the Back button until Sonic jumps down through a black hole. This lets you access the Secret Statue Room. Input the following codes to unlock different character statues.

UNLOCKABLE	CODE
Aero-Cannon	329 494
Amy Rose	863 358
Big The Cat	353 012
Blaze The Cat	544 873
Booster	495 497
Buzz Bomber	852 363
Capsule	777 921
Chao	629 893
Chaos Emeralds	008 140
Charmy Bee	226 454
Chip	309 511
Chopper	639 402
Classic Dr. Robotnik	103 729
Classic Sonic The Hedgehog	171 045
Classic Tails	359 236
Cop Speeder	640 456
Crab Meat	363 911
Cream The Rabbit	332 955
Dark Chao	869 292
E-123 Omega	601 409
Egg Chaser	200 078
Egg Fighter	851 426
Egg Launcher	973 433
Egg Pawn	125 817
Egg Robo	360 031
Espio The Chameleon	894 526
Flickies	249 651
Goal Plate	933 391
Goal Ring	283 015
Grabber	275 843
GUN Beetle	975 073
GUN Hunter	668 250
Hero Chao	507 376
Iblis Biter	872 910
Iblis Taker	513 929
Iblis Worm	711 268
Item Box	209 005
Jet The Hawk	383 870
Knuckles The Echidna	679 417
Metal Sonic	277 087

Modern Dr. Eggman	613 482
Modern Sonic The Hedgehog	204 390
Modern Tails	632 951
Moto Bug	483 990
Omochao	870 580
Ring	390 884
Rouge The Bat	888 200
Sand Worm	548 986
Shadow The Hedgehog	262 416
Silver The Hedgehog	688 187
Spinner	530 741
Spiny	466 913
Spring	070 178
Spring 2	537 070
Vector The Crocodile	868 377

UNLOCKABLE

UNLOCKABLE	HOW TO UNLOCK
Classic Eggman Suit (Bottoms)	Defeat all rivals on Hard Mode.
Classic Eggman Suit (Head)	Defeat the final boss on Hard Mode.
Classic Eggman Suit (Tops)	Defeat all bosses on Hard Mode.
Super Sonic	Defeat the Final Boss

SONIC GENERATIONS (PLAYSTATION 3)

CODE

In the Collection room position Sonic to the right of the Movie Chair located to the left of the Art painting, Hold down Select to enter a hole which takes you to the Statue Room. Once there, press Select to bring up a code screen. Enter these codes to unlock statues.

UNLOCKABLE	CODE
008 140	Chaos Emerald
070 178	Spring (Yellow)
103 729	Classic Eggman
125 817	Egg Pawn
171 045	Classic Sonic
200 078	Egg Chaser
204 390	Sonic the Hedgehog
209 005	Item Box
226 454	Charmy Bee
249 651	Cucky/Picky/Flicky/Pecky
262 416	Shadow the Hedgehog
275 843	Grabber
277 087	Metal Sonic
283 015	Goal Ring
309 511	Chip
329 494	Aero-Cannon
332 955	Cream the Rabbit
353 012	Big the Cat
359 236	Classic Tails
360 031	Eggrobo
363 911	Crabmeat
383 870	Jet the Hawk

390 884	Ring
466 913	Spiny
483 990	Moto Bug
495 497	Booster
507 376	Hero Chao
513 929	Iblis Taker
530 741	Spinner
537 070	Spring (Red)
544 873	Blaze the Cat
548 986	Sandworm
601 409	E-123 Omega
613 482	Dr. Eggman
629 893	Chao
632 951	Miles "Tails" Prower
639 402	Chopper
640 456	Cop Speeder
668 250	Gun Hunter
679 417	Knuckles the Echidna
688 187	Silver the Hedgehog
711 268	Iblis Worm
777 921	Capsule
851 426	Egg Fighter
852 363	Buzz Bomber
863 358	Amy Rose
868 377	Vector the Crocodile
869 292	Dark Chao
870 580	Omochao
872 910	Iblis Biter
888 200	Rouge the Bat
894 526	Espio the Chameleon
933 391	Goal Plate
973 433	Egg Launcher
975 073	Gun Beetle

UNLOCKABLE

After unlocking the classic Sonic the Hedgehog game, load the game. After Sonic appears on the title screen press these buttons in order to select your level.

UNLOCKABLE	HOW TO UNLOCK
Level Select	↑, ↓, ←, →, ✕

UNLOCKABLE

At the shop to the left of the Green Hill Zone, buy the Sega controller, then take it to the Sega console at the top left section of the Green Hill Zone.

UNLOCKABLE	HOW TO UNLOCK
Original Sonic the Hedgehog	

SONIC RUSH ADVENTURE (DS)

UNLOCKABLES

UNLOCKABLE	HOW TO UNLOCK
Blaze the Cat	Defeat the Kraken boss in Coral Cave to unlock Blaze as a playable character.
Deep Core: Final extra boss stage	Collect all Sol Emeralds and Chaos Emeralds.

SONIC SPINBALL (WII)

UNLOCKABLES

UNLOCKABLE	HOW TO UNLOCK
Level Select	Access the Options from the title screen, take controller 1, and press: Ⓐ, ⬇, Ⓑ, ⬇, Ⓒ, ⬇, Ⓐ, Ⓑ, ⬇, Ⓐ, Ⓒ, ⬇, Ⓑ, Ⓒ, ⬇. If you did it correctly, you hear a special sound. Go back to the title screen and hold Ⓐ and press START to begin on Level 2, Ⓑ and press START for Level 3, and ⬇ and press START for level 4.
Multi-Ball Stage	Collect every ring in any stage.
Stop the Platform in The Machine	In Level 3, The Machine, a moving platform takes you to either side of the area. Stand on the platform and press up or down to make the platform stop, allowing you to get a good look around or plan your jump carefully.

SONIC THE HEDGEHOG (PLAYSTATION 3)

UNLOCKABLE	HOW TO UNLOCK
Last Episode	Beat Sonic's Episode, Shadow's Episode, and Silver's Episode
Audio Room	Complete Sonic, Shadow, or Silver's story 100%
Theater Room	Complete Sonic, Shadow, or Silver's story 100%
Shadow the Hedgehog	Complete "Crisis City" with Sonic
Silver the Hedgehog	Complete "Silver the Hedgehog" boss battle with Sonic

SONIC THE HEDGEHOG (WII)

UNLOCKABLES

UNLOCKABLE	HOW TO UNLOCK
Config Mode	There is a code called Control mode, which is required before activating this code. To activate Control mode, press ⬇, Ⓒ, ⬇, Ⓒ, ⬇, Ⓒ, Ⓒ at the title screen, but before pressing START to begin the game, hold Ⓐ as you hit START. Now, rather than just being in Control mode, you can enable Config mode by pressing Ⓑ. Sonic will morph into a ring, and the arrows can move him anywhere, even in the air, or through obstacles such as walls, floors, or even ceilings. You can change the item Sonic appears as by hitting Ⓐ while in Config mode. Ⓑ makes Sonic normal again, and ⬇ will place the sprite that you have selected for Sonic to appear as. For example, you press Ⓑ, and Sonic becomes a ring, press ⬇ to make a ring appear exactly where the ring icon is. WARNING!: This distorts several different things, such as the score, time, and other various icons throughout the game such as the finish signs at the end of the first two acts of each zone that spin when Sonic shoots past them, and the small score icons that appear whenever Sonic jumps high enough after finishing a level.
Drunk Sonic	During the demo, hold ⬇. Sonic will crash into walls and get hit by enemies.
Level Select	At the title screen, press ⬇, ⬇, ⬇, ⬇. You should hear a noise like a ring being collected. Then, hold Ⓐ and press START for a level select!
Secret Game Message	At the title screen, press Ⓒ, Ⓒ, Ⓒ, Ⓒ, Ⓒ, Ⓒ, ⬇, ⬇, ⬇, ⬇. When the demo starts, hold Ⓐ+Ⓑ+Ⓒ+⬇ then press START. Instead of the Sonic Team logo, you will see a list of the game's evelopers in Japanese. When the title screen appears, a flashing "Press Start Button" will be there under Sonic's head.
Different Ending	Beat game with all Chaos Emeralds.

SONIC THE HEDGEHOG 2 (XBOX 360)

CODE	EFFECT
17	Play Invincibility Music
65	Plays a Shifting Sound

| 09 | Plays Casino Night Zone 1-Player Music |
| 19 | Plays Sonic 2 Theme |

SONIC THE HEDGEHOG 2 (Wii)

UNLOCKABLES

UNLOCKABLE	HOW TO UNLOCK
Level Select	Some other cheats require you to enable this one first. Go to the Options menu from the main screen. From there, head to the Sound Select menu and play the following sounds: 19, 65, 09, 17. Once you have played each (1 time only), press ⬆ and then press START to be brought back to the title screen. Now, when you see Sonic and Tails (Miles) appear on screen, hold Ⓐ and press START to finish off the code. You're brought to a menu where you have access to any level in the game, whether you've completed the level or not.
14 Continues	Go to the sound test (not the one on the level select) and put in 19, 65, 09, 17, 01, 01, 02, 04 (press Ⓐ after each one). There won't be a confirmation sound. Start the game by pressing START on the first option (character select) and you have 14 continues.
All 7 Chaos Emeralds	This code only works for Sonic. First, do the Level Select cheat. In the Level Select menu, go to Sound Test and play the sounds 04, 01, 02, 06. If done correctly, you'll hear a Chaos Emerald sound effect. Now, select any stage from this menu and you can turn into Super Sonic with 50 rings plus you'll get Sonic's second ending after beating Death Egg Zone.
Change Tails' Name to Miles	Press ⬆, ⬆, ⬆, ⬇, ⬇, ⬇, ⬇ at the title screen.
Debug Mode	First enter the Level Select code. Now, go to Sound Test option, and play the following tunes: 01, 09, 09, 02, 01, 01, 02, 04. It should make a ring sound when track 4 is played to signify you've entered it correctly. Now select the stage you want to go to, and press START while holding Ⓐ until the stage starts, and you'll have debug activated. Press Ⓑ to turn Debug on/off, Ⓐ to switch object, and ⬆ to put down object selected. Pressing Ⓐ while the game is paused will cause the game to reset.
Debug Mode (Alternate)	At Sound Test, enter: 19, 65, 09, 17, then press Ⓐ+START, then when Sonic and Tails pop up, press Ⓐ+START to go to the Level Select screen. On the Sound Test area, enter 01, 09, 09, 02, 01, 01, 02, 04, and then press Ⓐ+START.
Debug Mode and All Emeralds (when locked-on to Sonic and Knuckles)	First activate and go to the Stage Select. Play the following tracks in Sound Test with Ⓑ: 01, 09, 09, 04, 01, 00, 01, 08. This enables the Debug code, and you should hear a ring chime if the code is entered correctly. Start the selected level with Ⓐ+START. To get all 7 Chaos Emeralds, input this code the same way: 01, 06, 07, 07, 07, 02, 01, 06. You should hear the Emerald chime. Note: this code may not work without the Debug code.
Enable Super Sonic	First, head to the Options menu from the title screen, and then into the Sound Select menu from there. Play the following sounds in this order: 19, 65, 09, 17. After that, press ⬆, START. You will be taken back to the title screen. Now, when you see Sonic and Tails (Miles) appear on the screen, press and hold Ⓐ and press START to be taken to the Level Select menu. From this menu, enter the Sound Test feature, and play the following sounds: 04, 01, 02, 06. If done correctly, a familiar tune plays. Exit this menu and start the game as normal. Once you collect a minimum of 50 coins in any level, Jump (Press Ⓐ) to activate the Super Sonic code.

Get Super Sonic on Emerald Hill	First, enter the Stage Select code, shown above. Then you go into the Special Stage in the Stage Select menu. Every time you finish the special stage, press reset and go back to the special stage. Keep doing this until you get the sixth emerald. Then don't press reset. It zaps you with your 6 emeralds into Emerald Hill. Get the last emerald on Emerald Hill, get 50 rings, and jump to be Super Sonic. Don't run out of rings or you will change into Sonic again. The rings start disappearing when you are Super Sonic.
Infinite Lives	First, enable the Level Select cheat and the Debug mode. Choose Sonic and Tails as the players. After entering the codes, choose any stage from the Level Select menu (preferably stage 1). As soon as you can move Sonic, hold ⬇ and press Ⓐ (don't let go of down on the D-pad). This activates Sonic's spin; Tails will copy the Sonic spin also. Press Ⓑ and Sonic will become the Debug cursor. (Tails will be locked in the Sonic spin move). Press Ⓐ until the debug cursor displays an enemy sprite, like the monkey or that bee robot. Now that the debug cursor displays an enemy sprite, move the debug cursor to where Tails is, and repeatedly tap ⬇. This produces enemies where Tails is, and because Tails is locked in the Sonic spin move, he destroys the enemies. As Tails destroys enemies in this position, press ⬇ more until the score for destroying an enemy increases from 100 to 8,000 to a 1Up. Once you have enough 1Ups, press Ⓑ again to revert to Sonic.
Level Select (When Locked-On to Sonic and Knuckles)	At the title screen, press ⬇, ⬇, ⬇, ⬇, ⬇, ⬇, ⬅, ⬅, ⬅, ⬅. Then, hold Ⓐ and press START to be taken to the Level Select menu.
Night Mode	Activate level select and hold ⬇ while selecting a stage to darken the level. The effect wears off when you die or when you beat the level.
Level Select Screen	At the title screen, select Options. Highlight Sound Test then play the following music and sounds: 19, 65, 09, and 17. You hear a ring-collecting sound for correct code entry. Then press START to return to the title screen. Highlight 1-Player, hold Ⓐ, and press START. You are directed to Level Select screen. Choose a level then press START to begin.
Slow Motion	First, enter the Level Select code. Then start your game in any level. When you start, press pause. Then hold Ⓑ and try to do anything with Sonic. The game plays in slow motion as long as you hold down Ⓑ.
Oil Ocean Music Forever	Go to the Sound Test in the Options menu and put in the sounds, 02, 01, 02, 04, and hold Ⓐ and press START. The Oil Ocean music will now be playing constantly, no matter what stage.
Pseudo Super Sonic	In Oil Ocean Zone, if you manage to take a hit and end up landing in one of those green-and-gold checkered cannons, you'll fall right out, but you'll be moving at twice your normal speed as well as jumping twice your normal height (with twice as much gravity). A good place for doing this would be in Oil Ocean Zone, Act 2, near the first set of pop-tops and cannons. Just jump into the semi-hidden bed of spikes on the right and land in the cannon. Note: Moving at twice normal velocity can often get you stuck in a wall. Also, this wears off if you Super Spin Dash or Spin Dash. It also only lasts for that act.
Super Tails	Normally, when you turn into Super Sonic you lose Tails behind you all the time. Well, after you put in the debug cheat and have started a level (preferably Emerald Hill), turn yourself into a box and place it somewhere on the floor while you are Super Sonic. It should be a switch places box. Hit it and Tails has a permanent invincible circle around him. He stays like this through the whole level.
Unlimited Speed Shoes in 2-Player vs. Mode	In 2-Player vs. mode, get speed shoes and die (while you still have them) and you get to keep your speed shoes until the end of the level.

CODES

CODE	EFFECT
17	Play Invincibility Music
65	Plays a Shifting Sound
09	Plays Casino Night Zone 1-Player Music
19	Plays Sonic 2 Theme

SONIC THE HEDGEHOG 3 (WII)

UNLOCKABLES

UNLOCKABLE	HOW TO UNLOCK
All 7 Chaos Emeralds and Super Sonic	To get all 7 Chaos Emeralds without having to complete their Special Stages, first enter the Level Select and Sound Test codes. Go to the Sound Test and play the following tunes in order: 02, 04, 05, 06. You will hear an emerald sound if the code is entered correctly. To get Super Sonic after entering the previous code, just select any level from the level select and start it. Once you acquire 50 Rings, do a double-jump to become Super Sonic.
Control Tails in a 1-Player Game	Start a 1-player game with Sonic and Tails as the characters. With controller 2, you can take control of Tails while also using Sonic.
Hidden Special Stage	On the Level Select menu, play sounds 01, 03, 05, 07. Highlight Special Stage 2 and press Ⓐ+START.
Infinite Lives	Get up to Launch Base Zone. Sound any of the alarms, so that the Kamikaze birds come after you. Charge up a Super Sonic Dash in between the alarm, but do not let go of the button. The birds continually crash into you. After about 30 seconds, you have gained enough points to get an extra life. Continue the process for as many lives as you want.
Level Select (When Locked-On to Sonic and Knuckles)	Start a game and go to Angel Island Zone, Act 1. Go to one of the swings that you hang from and grab on. While Sonic is swinging, press ⇧, ⇧, ⇧, ⇧, ⇧, ⇧, ⇧, ⇧. You will hear a ring if you entered the code correctly. Pause the game and press Ⓐ to take you back to the title screen. Press ⇧, ⇧ to find the newly unlocked Sound Test menu. Enter it, where you can play all of the sounds/music in the game and warp to any level.
Turn into Super Sonic	After entering the Level Select and Debug code, you can use the debug to turn yourself into Super Sonic without getting all of the Chaos Emeralds. With the debug on, go into any level and press Ⓑ to turn yourself into a ring. Then press Ⓐ to turn yourself into a monitor. Now, press ⇧ to duplicate the monitor, and then Ⓑ again to change back into Sonic. Jump on the monitor and you will become Super Sonic.
Level Select	When the "SEGA" screen fades, quickly press ⇧, ⇧, ⇧, ⇧, ⇧, ⇧, ⇧, ⇧. If you have done this right, you should be able to scroll down to "Sound Test" below "Competition."
Sonic and Knuckles Mini-Boss Music	Get to the end of Act 1 of Hydrocity Zone (Zone 2). When facing the mini-boss, keep yourself underwater until the water warning music plays. Then jump out of the water. The game should now be playing the mini-boss music from Sonic and Knuckles, which wasn't out at the time (the music was evidently included in Sonic 3 to make the backward compatibility feature easier).
Walk Thru Walls	In the Icecap Zone, Act 1, when you come to a wall that only Knuckles can bust through, hold ⇧ until Sonic or Tails looks down, and the screen pans all the way down. Then press ⇧ and jump at the same time. The screen starts to rotate. Walk in the direction of the wall and you will walk right through it.
100,000 Points	Beat a stage at with your time at exactly 9:59.
Frame by Frame	When playing a level after enabling the Level Select cheat, pause the game, then press ⇧ to advance the game by one frame.

| Slow Motion Mode | When playing any level that you have accessed using the Cheat menu, pause the game and hold ⑧. While ⑧ is held down, the game plays in Slow Motion mode. |

CODES

CODE	EFFECT
Hold ⑧ and press ⬆	Your character shows all of his sprite animations
Hold ⑧ and press ⬆ again	Your character stops the sprite show if it is activated

SONIC THE HEDGEHOG 4: EPISODE I (PLAYSTATION 3)

SUPER SONIC

Complete all 7 special stages by collecting the Chaos Emerald at the end. Then enter any level, collect 50 rings, and press the Square button or Triangle button to transform into Super Sonic.

SONIC THE HEDGEHOG 4: EPISODE I (XBOX 360)

AVATAR AWARDS

UNLOCKABLE	HOW TO UNLOCK
Sonic Costume (Body)	After collecting the 7 Chaos Emeralds, defeat the final boss one more time.
Sonic Costume (Head)	Collect all rings during the ending of the final stage.

SOULCALIBUR IV (XBOX 360)

ITEMS/WEAPONS

UNLOCKABLE	HOW TO UNLOCK
Advanced Equipment	Achieve 20 achievements.
All Weapons for a Character	Clear Story mode with that character.
Animal Head Equipment	Achieve 25 achievements.
Basic Equipment	Achieve 5 achievements.
Intermediate Equipment	Achieve 15 achievements.
Leviathan and Voodoo Equipment	Achieve 30 achievements.
More Equipment	Achieve 10 achievements.

CHARACTERS

UNLOCKABLE	HOW TO UNLOCK
Algol	Beat Story mode with a character that faces him as the last boss (Mitsurugi, Taki, etc.).
Amy	Purchase her in the Character Creation for 4,000 gold.
Angol Fear	Defeat her in Story mode.
Ashlotte	Defeat her in Story mode.
Cervantes	Purchase him in the Character Creation for 4,000 gold.
Hong Yun-seong	Purchase him in the Character Creation for 4,000 gold.
Kamikirimusi	Defeat her in Story mode.
Lizardman	Buy for 4,000 gold.
Rock	Purchase him in the Character Creation for 4,000 gold.
Scheherazade	Defeat her in Story mode.
Seong Mi Na	Highlight and purchase for 4,000 gold.
Setsuka	Highlight and purchase for 4,000 gold.
Shura	Defeat her in Story mode.
Sophitia	Purchase her in the Create a Soul mode for 4,000 Gold.
Talim	Buy her for 4,000 gold in Character Creation mode.
The Apprentice	Beat Arcade mode with Yoda.
Yoshimitsu	Highlight and purchase for 4000 gold.
Zasalamel	Buy him for 4,000 gold in Character Creation mode.

TOWER OF LOST SOULS HIDDEN ITEMS (ASCENDING)

UNLOCKABLE	HOW TO UNLOCK
01f Soldier's Hat	Clear stage while taking no damage.
02f Warrior Trousers	Clear stage with no ring outs from either side.
03f Pauldron	Switch with ally more than 2 times.
04f Warlord's Belt	Perform 3 attack throws.
05f Clergy Clothes	Defeat an enemy with a ring out.
06f Wonder Jacket	Throw an opponent.
07f Warrior Trousers	Clear the stage without missing any attacks.
08f Armor Ring: Ice Mirror	Switch characters twice.
09f Scarlett Blossoms	Guard against the opponent's attack 3 times in a row.
10f Silver Boots	Guard the opponent's attack 10 times in a row.
11f Grim Horn	Defeat all enemies with a critical finish.
12f Magus Cloth	Defeat all enemies with ring outs.
13f Pegasus Sallet	Destroy all the walls.
14f Stage: Phantom Pavilion Seesaw	Perform guard impact more than 3 times.
15f Submissions Belt	Clear the stage using only the A and G buttons.
16f Warlord's Belt	Clear the stage with 0 time remaining.
17f Arm Bandages	Execute a 5+ combo.
18f Kouchu Kabuto	Stand on all corners of the stage.
19f Longhua Qippo	Switch with ally more than 5 times.
20f Life Gem: Sun	Clear the stage with a critical finish.
21f Longhua Qippo	Voluntarily ring yourself out.
22f Honor Boots	Perform more than 4 counter hits.
23F Frilled Skirt	Guard more than 3 times in a row.
24f Protect Gem: Cardinal Directions	Perform a combo with more than 240 damage.
25f Zhuque Changpao	Throw more than 5 times.
26f Warthog Cuirass	Execute a 10+ combo.
27f Iron Gauntlets	Clear the stage with no damage taken.
28F Aculeus Suit	Opponent guards a guard break attack at least twice.
29f Menghu Boots	Switch with ally 5+ times.
30f Spirit Gem: Noniple Heads	Clear stage without guarding.
31f Longming Qippo	Perform 5+ Just Inputs.
32f Vane Mask	Perform a low throw.
33f Battle Dress	Perform 3 attack throws.
34f Power Gem: Warrior Princess	Perform guard impact 3+ times.
35f Warthog Pauldrons	Clear without switching.
36f Parlor Blouse	Clear stage with 0 time remaining.
37f Siren's Helm	Defeat all enemies with critical finishes.
38f Gorgon Fauld	Defeat all enemies with ring out.
39f Kingfisher Greaves	Clear the stage without changing position.
40f Deer Head	Execute a 5+ combo.
41f Minotaur	Perform 5+ Just Inputs.
42f Demonic Gloves	Clear the stage without letting opponents invoke a skill.
43f Repel Gem: Iron Shell	Perform an over the back throw.
44f War Cloak	No ring outs either side.
45f Tiger Lily Kabuto	Defeat enemies without using any skills.

46f Butterfly Salet	Defeat enemies without using any skills.
47f Succubus Boots	Throw 5 times.
48f Life Dem: Jade	Clear stage with a character equipped with the "invisible" skill.
49f Horns of Calamity	Clear stage with no attacks missing.
50f Tiger Lily Breastplates	Execute a 10+ combo.
51f Tiger Lily Fauld	Perform more than 4 counter hits.
52f Feathered Wings	Clear stage with a critical finish.
53f Blade Ring: Demon Lord	Defeat all enemies with a ring out.
54f Leviathan Pauldron	Destroy all the walls.
55f Priestess Kimono	Perform 3 attack throws.
56f Leviathan Burgonet	Perform a combo with more than 240 damage.
57f Voodoo Armlets	Voluntarily perform a ring out.
58f Tiger Pauldrons	Defeat all enemies without any skills equipped.
59f Voodoo Greaves	Guard an enemy's attack 10 times in a row.
60f Voodoo Breastplate	Clear the stage without switching character.

TOWER OF LOST SOULS REWARD ITEMS (DESCENDING)

UNLOCKABLE	HOW TO UNLOCK
B05	Dark Knight's Cloak
B10	Blade Ring: Raging Thunder
B15	Lapin Chapeau
B20	Repel Gem: Fox Demon
B25	Succubus Gauntlets
B30	Demonic Armor
B35	Demonic Pauldrons
B40	Voodoo Crown

CREATE-A-SOUL ITEMS/WEAPONS

UNLOCKABLE	HOW TO UNLOCK
Advanced Equipment	Achieve 20 achievements.
All Weapons for a Character	Clear Story mode with that Character.
Animal Head Equipment	Achieve 25 achievements.
Basic Equipment	Achieve 5 achievements.
Intermediate Equipment	Achieve 15 achievements.
Leviathan and Voodoo Equipment	Achieve 30 achievements.
More Equipment	Achieve 10 achievements.

EASTER EGGS

UNLOCKABLE	HOW TO UNLOCK
Metallic Characters	At the Character Select screen, hold down ⑭ and choose a character by pressing Ⓐ. When the battle begins, your character is metallic.

SOULCALIBUR V (PLAYSTATION 3)

TROPHY

UNLOCKABLE	HOW TO UNLOCK
A Soul Coalesces (Bronze)	Edited a player license.
Adored by Heaven (Bronze)	Performed 20 grapple breaks.
Alluring Kaleidoscope (Bronze)	Landed brave edge 100 times.
Awakened to Violence (Bronze)	Reached E4 rank in ranked match.
Beginning of Destiny (Bronze)	Registered 3 rivals.
Black Sword of Death (Bronze)	K.O. with critical edge 30 times.

Carry Out Your Beliefs (Bronze)	Won 5 times in one style on PlayStationNetwork.
Colorful Illusion (Bronze)	Creation: took a thumbnail by manually setting a decoration frame and background.
Conqueror of the Arena (Gold)	Won 50 times on PlayStationNetwork.
Courageous Warrior (Silver)	Won 20 times on PlayStationNetwork.
Fancy of a Mad King (Bronze)	Guard bursted 30 times.
Fetal Soul (Bronze)	Player level reached 5.
First Step of a Legend (Silver)	Reached D1 rank in ranked match.
Footprints of Soldiers (Bronze)	Defeated 100 male characters.
Gale Forces (Bronze)	K.O. the opponent 25 times with an attack after a quick move.
Give in to Temptation (Bronze)	Defeated 100 female characters.
Hands of the Abyss (Bronze)	Won by ring out 50 times.
Hero Carved in History (Silver)	Fought 100 times on PlayStationNetwork.
History Repeats (Bronze)	Battled in SOULCALIBUR V for the first time (excluding training and VS battle).
Home is Faraway (Gold)	Story: cleared final episode.
Like a Flowing Stream (Bronze)	Successfully performed a just guard 5 times.
Lively Pub (Bronze)	Changed the BGM in options.
Mask Another's Memory (Bronze)	Arcade: cleared a ranking route with a record better than your rival.
Mercenary of War (Bronze)	Fought 30 times on PlayStationNetwork.
Momentary Pleasure (Bronze)	Successfully performed an impact 100 times.
Never Ending Effort (Bronze)	Landed an attack 20,000 times.
No-hitter (Silver)	Ranked Match: won 10 times with Ezio.
Notes on Rivals (Bronze)	Play backed another player's replay.
Parrier of Swords (Bronze)	Perfect won 50 times.
Passionate Artist (Bronze)	Creation: created a character with full-on coordination (used everything except for height).
Path to Glory (Bronze)	Quick Battle: defeated 50 warriors.
Perfect Trainee (Bronze)	Arcade: cleared Asia route.
Proof of a Fighter (Bronze)	Won consecutive matches on PlayStationNetwork.
Purge of the Holy (Bronze)	Story: cleared episode 1.
Pursuit of Obsession (Bronze)	Quick Battle: defeated Harada TEKKEN.
Reason to Fight For (Bronze)	Reached E1 rank in ranked match.
Resurrection of Order (Silver)	Story: cleared episode 16.
Road to the Duel (Bronze)	Quick Battle: defeated 150 warriors.
Shields Come Together (Bronze)	Story: cleared episode 8.
Sings Own Praise (Bronze)	Uploaded a replay of your win.
Skills for Duels (Silver)	Legendary Souls: won with brave edge.
Soul Fulfilled (Silver)	Player level reached maximum.
Stalwart Barbarian (Bronze)	Performed a wall hit 50 times.
Strategist of War (Silver)	Fought 75 times on PlayStationNetwork.
Sudden Temptation (Silver)	Quick Battle: defeated all warriors.
Synchronize DNA (Bronze)	Used Ezio in a player match.
Throbbing Soul (Bronze)	Player level reached 50.
Unwritten History (Platinum)	Obtained all trophies.

Usurped True Name (Bronze)	Quick Battle: won against 10 players with titles and used the obtained title on the player license.
War Veteran (Silver)	Arcade: cleared any route with difficulty set on hard.
Wind of Battle (Bronze)	Reached over 87,600 m in total movement distance in battle.

UNLOCKABLE

UNLOCKABLE	HOW TO UNLOCK
Algol	Defeat him in either Legendary Souls / Quick Battle (As Teramos) / Arcade Mode. Or, reach Player Level 31.
Alpha Patroklos	Complete Episode 12 in Story Mode or reach Player Level 15.
Edge Master	Complete Episode 16 in Story Mode or reach Player Level 19.
Elysium	Beat Story Mode or reach Player Level 27.
Kilik	Beat Him In Either Legendary Souls or Arcade Mode, or reach Player Level 9.
Pyrrha Omega	Complete Episode 19 in Story Mode or reach Player Level 23.
Soul Of Devil Jin Fighting Style	Reach Player Level 5
Ancient Citadel: Peacetime	Finish Episode 4 in Story mode or Player level 7
Astral Chaos: Pathway	Player level 25
Conqueror's Coliseum: Underground Fight	Player level 13
Denever Castle: Eye of Chaos	Unlock Omega Pyrrha
Denever Castle:Assault	Finish Episode 18 in Story mode or Player level 18
Last Rites on the Battleground	Finish Episode 18 in Story mode or Player 40
Penitentiary of Destiny	Unlock Kilik
Tower of Glory: Most Holy Dichotomy	Unlock Angol
Tower of Glory: Spiral of Good and Evil	Unlock Edgemaster
Unknown Forest: Dark Night	Finish Episode 7 in Story mode or Player level 21
Utopia of the Blessed	Unlock Elysium

SOULCALIBUR V (XBOX 360)

ACHIEVEMENT

UNLOCKABLE	HOW TO UNLOCK
A Soul Coalesces (5)	Edit a player license.
Adored by Heaven (10)	Perform 20 grapple breaks.
Alluring Kaleidoscope (10)	Land a brave edge 100 times.
Awakened to Violence (10)	Reach E4 rank in ranked match.
Beginning of Destiny (5)	Register 3 rivals.
Black Sword of Death (10)	K.O. with critical edge 30 times.
Carry Out Your Beliefs (10)	Win 5 times in one style on Xbox LIVE.
Colorful Illusion (10)	Creation: take a thumbnail by manually setting a decoration frame and background.
Conqueror of the Arena (100)	Win 50 times on Xbox LIVE.
Courageous Warrior (25)	Win 20 times on Xbox LIVE.
Fancy of a Mad King (15)	Guard burst 30 times.
Fetal Soul (5)	Player level reaches 5.

First Step of a Legend (30)	Reach D1 rank in ranked match.
Footprints of Soldiers (10)	Defeat 100 male characters.
Gale Forces (20)	K.O. the opponent 25 times with an attack after a quick move.
Give in to Temptation (10)	Defeat 100 female characters.
Hands of the Abyss (10)	Win by ring out 50 times.
Hero Carved in History (50)	Fight 100 times on Xbox LIVE.
History Repeats (5)	Battle in SOULCALIBUR V for the first time (excluding training and VS battle).
Home is Faraway (80)	Story: clear final episode.
Like a Flowing Stream (10)	Successfully perform a just guard 5 times.
Lively Pub (5)	Change the BGM in options.
Mask Another's Memory (20)	Arcade: clear a leaderboard route with a record better than your rival.
Mercenary of War (20)	Fight 30 times on Xbox LIVE.
Momentary Pleasure (15)	Successfully perform an impact 100 times.
Never Ending Effort (10)	Land an attack 20,000 times.
No-hitter (30)	Ranked Match: win 10 times with Ezio.
Notes on Rivals (5)	Play back another player's replay.
Parrier of Swords (20)	Perfect win 50 times.
Passionate Artist (20)	Creation: create a character with full-on coordination (used everything except for height).
Path to Glory (10)	Quick Battle: defeat 50 warriors.
Perfect Trainee (20)	Arcade: clear Asia route.
Proof of a Fighter (15)	Win consecutive matches on Xbox LIVE.
Purge of the Holy (10)	Story: clear episode 1.
Pursuit of Obsession (15)	Quick Battle: defeat Harada TEKKEN.
Reason to Fight For (20)	Reach E1 rank in ranked match.
Resurrection of Order (30)	Story: clear episode 16.
Road to the Duel (20)	Quick Battle: defeat 150 warriors.
Shields Come Together (20)	Story: clear episode 8.
Sings Own Praise (10)	Upload a replay of your win.
Skills for Duels (50)	Legendary Souls: win with brave edge.
Soul Fulfilled (30)	Player level reaches maximum.
Stalwart Barbarian (10)	Perform a wall hit 50 times.
Strategist of War (25)	Fight 75 times on Xbox LIVE.
Sudden Temptation (40)	Quick Battle: defeat all warriors.
Synchronize DNA (5)	Use Ezio in a player match.
Throbbing Soul (15)	Player level reaches 50.
Usurped True Name (20)	Quick Battle: win against 10 players with titles and use the obtained title on the player license.
War Veteran (40)	Arcade: clear any route with difficulty set on hard.
Wind of Battle (10)	Reach over 87,600 m in total movement distance in battle.

UNLOCKABLE

UNLOCKABLE	HOW TO UNLOCK
"The Master"	Reach Player Level 25
Algol	Defeat in Arcade or Legendary Souls Mode
Alpha Patroklos	Clear Story Mode
Arcarde Route: "Extra"	Reach Player Level 17

Astral Chaos: Pathway	Fight against Alpha Patroklos in Quick Battle
Devil Jin Style	Reach player level 5
Edge Master	Clear Story Mode
Elysium	Clear Story Mode
Kilik	Defeat in Arcade or Legendary Souls Mode
Pyrrha Omega	Clear Story Mode
Stage: Denever Castle: Eye of Chaos	Defeat Pyrrha Omega in Story Mode
Stage: Penitentiary of Destiny	Defeat Kilik in Legendary Souls Mode or Arcade Mode
Stage: Tower of Glory: Most Holy Dichotomy	Defeat Algol Fear in Legendary Souls Mode or Arcade Mode
Stage: Tower of Glory: Spiral of Good & Evil	Defeat Edge Master in Legendary Souls Mode or Arcade Mode
Stage: Utopia of the Blessed	Defeat Elyssia in Story Mode
Weapon set 8 (Joke Weapons)"	Reach player Level 53

SPEC OPS: THE LINE (PLAYSTATION 3)

TROPHY

UNLOCKABLE	HOW TO UNLOCK
A Bridge Too Far (Bronze)	The end of the line.
A Farewell To Arms (Bronze)	You are relieved.
A Line, Crossed (Bronze)	Choose vengeance.
A Line, Held (Bronze)	Choose restraint.
A Man of Action (Bronze)	Play it loose.
A Man of Patience (Bronze)	Play it smart.
Adapt and Overcome (Bronze)	Blow up 10 explosive objects, killing at least one enemy each time. (campaign only)
Aim High (Bronze)	Kill 250 enemies with headshots. (campaign only)
Airspace Control (Bronze)	Kill 10 enemies while they use zip lines or are rappelling. (campaign only)
All You Can Be (Bronze)	Complete any chapter with 60%+ accuracy without dying or reloading a checkpoint.
Applied Force (Bronze)	Hit 10 enemies with your melee attack. (campaign only)
Army of One (Bronze)	Kill 3 enemies with a single grenade. (campaign only)
Battle Management (Bronze)	Kill 50 enemies using only the Attack Command. (campaign only)
Blind Luck (Bronze)	Kill 5 enemies using blind fire. (campaign only)
Boot (Bronze)	Complete game on "Walk on the Beach" difficulty.
Close Combat Carnage (Bronze)	Kill 4 enemies with a shotgun in 10 seconds or less. (campaign only)
Damn Close (Bronze)	Kill an Edged Weapon Expert while he is up to 5 meters away. (campaign only)
Damned if You Do (Bronze)	Follow your orders.
Damned if You Don't (Bronze)	Buck the chain of command.
Deer Hunter (Bronze)	Kill an oryx. (campaign only)
Desert Storm (Bronze)	Engineer an exit strategy.
Friendly Fire (Bronze)	Show mercy.

Good Training (Bronze)	Sprint into cover 10 times while under fire. (campaign only)
In Your Face (Bronze)	Kick an enemy by vaulting over a cover. (campaign only)
Intel Operative (Gold)	Recover all Intel Items.
Legion of Merit (Platinum)	Unlock all Trophies.
Marksman - Grenade (Bronze)	Kill 50 enemies with grenades. (campaign only)
Marksman - Heavy Arms (Bronze)	Kill 150 enemies with any heavy weapon. (campaign only)
Marksman - Rifle (Bronze)	Kill 350 enemies with any rifle. (campaign only)
Marksman - Shotgun (Bronze)	Kill 75 enemies with any shotgun. (campaign only)
Marksman - Small Arms (Bronze)	Kill 100 enemies with any pistol or SMG. (campaign only)
Marksman - Sniper (Bronze)	Kill 50 enemies with any sniper rifle. (campaign only)
MFWIC (Gold)	Complete game on "FUBAR" difficulty.
Preventive Diplomacy (Bronze)	Kill an enemy just as they are throwing a grenade. (campaign only)
Recon (Silver)	Recover 12 Intel Items.
Sierra Hotel (Silver)	Complete three chapters in a row without being killed or reloading a checkpoint.
Situational Awareness (Bronze)	Stun an enemy by dumping sand on their head. (campaign only)
Spotter (Bronze)	Recover one Intel Item.
The Devil's Disciple (Gold)	Complete game on "Suicide Mission" difficulty.
The Great Escape (Bronze)	Get out of here!
The Horror (Bronze)	Face the horrors of war.
The Human Factor (Bronze)	Kill an enemy by tagging him with a sticky grenade. (campaign only)
The Lost Battalion (Bronze)	We have contact.
The Road Back (Silver)	Live and let live.
The Road To Glory (Silver)	Live and let die.
They Live (Bronze)	What's lost is found.
Three Kings (Bronze)	Stand united.
Too Late The Hero (Bronze)	Carry on, soldier.
Treacherous Ground (Bronze)	Look out below.
Unfriendly Fire (Bronze)	Save a bullet.
We Were Soldiers (Silver)	Complete game on "Combat Op" difficulty.

SPEC OPS: THE LINE (XBOX 360)

ACHIEVEMENT

UNLOCKABLE	HOW TO UNLOCK
A Bridge Too Far (10)	The end of the line.
A Farewell To Arms (30)	You are relieved.
A Line, Crossed (10)	Choose vengeance.
A Line, Held (10)	Choose restraint.
A Man of Action (10)	Play it loose.
A Man of Patience (10)	Playing it smart.
Adapt and Overcome (20)	Blow up 10 explosive objects, killing at least one enemy each time. (campaign only)

CODES & CHEATS

Aim High (20)	Kill 250 enemies with headshots. (campaign only)
Airspace Control (20)	Kill 10 enemies while they use zip lines or are rappelling. (campaign only)
All You Can Be (20)	Complete any chapter with 60%+ accuracy without dying or reloading a checkpoint.
Applied Force (20)	Hit 10 enemies with your melee attack. (campaign only)
Army of One (20)	Kill 3 enemies with a single grenade. (campaign only)
Battle Management (20)	Kill 50 enemies using only the Attack Command. (campaign only)
Blind Luck (20)	Kill 5 enemies using blind fire. (campaign only)
Boot (15)	Complete game on "Walk on the Beach" difficulty.
Close Combat Carnage (20)	Kill 4 enemies with a shotgun in 10 seconds or less. (campaign only)
Damn Close (20)	Kill an Edged Weapon Expert while he is up to 5 meters away. (campaign only)
Damned if You Do (10)	Follow your orders.
Damned if You Don't (10)	Buck the chain of command.
Deer Hunter (20)	Kill an oryx. (campaign only)
Desert Storm (10)	Engineer an exit strategy.
Friendly Fire (10)	Show mercy.
Good Training (20)	Sprint into cover 10 times while under fire. (campaign only)
In Your Face (20)	Kick an enemy by vaulting over a cover. (campaign only)
Intel Operative (50)	Recover all Intel Items.
Marksman - Grenade (25)	Kill 50 enemies with grenades. (campaign only)
Marksman - Heavy Arms (25)	Kill 150 enemies with any heavy weapon. (campaign only)
Marksman - Rifle (25)	Kill 350 enemies with any rifle. (campaign only)
Marksman - Shotgun (25)	Kill 75 enemies with any shotgun. (campaign only)
Marksman - Small Arms (25)	Kill 100 enemies with any pistol or SMG. (campaign only)
Marksman - Sniper (25)	Kill 50 enemies with any sniper rifle. (campaign only)
MFWIC (50)	Complete game on "FUBAR" difficulty.
Preventive Diplomacy (20)	Kill an enemy just as they are throwing a grenade. (campaign only)
Recon (25)	Recover 12 Intel Items.
Sierra Hotel (50)	Complete three chapters in a row without being killed or reloading a checkpoint.
Situational Awareness (20)	Stun an enemy by dumping sand on their head. (campaign only)
Spotter (10)	Recover one Intel Item.
The Devil's Disciple (30)	Complete game on "Suicide Mission" difficulty.
The Great Escape (10)	Get out of here!
The Horror (10)	Face the horrors of war.
The Human Factor (20)	Kill an enemy by tagging him with a sticky grenade. (campaign only)
The Lost Battalion (10)	We have contact.
The Road Back (30)	Live and let live.

The Road To Glory (30)	Live and let die.
They Live (10)	What's lost is found.
Three Kings (10)	Stand united.
Too Late The Hero (30)	Carry on, soldier.
Treacherous Ground (10)	Look out below.
Unfriendly Fire (10)	Save a bullet.
We Were Soldiers (20)	Complete game on "Combat Op" difficulty.

SPEED RACER (WII)

CODES

Enter the following codes in the "Enter Code" section of the "Options" menu. Enter the codes again to disable them.

EFFECT	CODE
Aggressive Opponents	⬇️⬅️⬇️⬅️⬇️⬆️⬇️
Granite Car	Ⓑ⬅️➖⊕①⬇️⊕
Helium	➖⬇️➖②➖⬇️➖
Invulnerability	Ⓐ,Ⓑ,Ⓐ,⬇️,⬅️,⬇️,⬅️
Monster Truck	Ⓑ,⬅️,➖,②,Ⓑ,⬇️,➖
Moon Gravity	⬇️⊕⬇️⬅️➖⬇️➖
Overkill	Ⓐ,➖,⊕,⬇️,⬅️,⊕,①
Pacifist Opponents (other racers don't attack you)	⬇️⬅️⬇️⬅️⬇️⬅️⬇️
Psychedelic	⬅️,Ⓐ,⬅️,⬇️,Ⓑ,⬇️,➖
Tiny Opponents	Ⓑ,Ⓐ,⬅️,⬇️,➖,⬇️,➖
Unlimited Boost	Ⓑ,Ⓐ,⬇️,⬅️,Ⓑ,Ⓐ,⬇️
Unlock the Last 3 Cars	①,②,①,②,Ⓑ,Ⓐ,⊕

UNLOCKABLES

Complete the championships with a ranking of 3rd or higher to unlock the corresponding racer.

UNLOCKABLE	HOW TO UNLOCK
Booster Mbube	Complete Class 2, Championship 6.
Colonel Colon	Complete Class 3, Championship 4.
Delila	Complete Class 3, Championship 3.
Denise Mobile	Complete Class 3, Championship 6.
Esther "Rev" Reddy	Complete Class 3, Championship 7.
Gothorm Danneskjblo	Complete Class 3, Championship 2.
Grey Ghost	Complete Class 1, Championship 3.
Kellie "Gearbox" Kalinkov	Complete Class 2, Championship 4.
Mariana Zanja	Complete Class 3, Championship 5.
Nitro Venderhoss	Complete Class 2, Championship 5.
Pitter Pat	Complete Class 3, Championship 1.
Prince Kabala	Complete Class 2, Championship 3.
Rosey Blaze	Complete Class 1, Championship 1.
Snake Oiler	Complete Class 1, Championship 2.
Sonic "Boom Boom" Renaldi	Complete Class 2, Championship 2.
Taejo Togokahn	Complete Class 2, Championship 1.

SPIDER-MAN: EDGE OF TIME (XBOX 360)

CODE

At the main menu, use the D-pad to enter the code. Select the new costume from the bonus gallery.

UNLOCKABLE	CODE
Big Time Costume is unlocked	➡️⬇️⬇️⬅️➡️⬇️⬇️➡️

CODE

Select a saved game, then enter this code. Select the costume at the bonus gallery.

UNLOCKABLE	CODE
Unlock Future Foundation Costume	← ↓ ← ↓ ← → → ←

SPIDER-MAN: EDGE OF TIME (WII)

CODE

Select a save game and then enter the code at the main menu using the D-pad.

UNLOCKABLE	CODE
Big Time Costume	right down down up left down down right

CODE

Start a new game with Spider-Man: Shattered Dimension data, the find new outfits in the "Alternate Suits Menu."

UNLOCKABLE	CODE
8 Spiderman Outfits	Spider-Man: Shattered Dimension data

SPIDER-MAN: FRIEND OR FOE (XBOX 360)

CODES

Venom and new Green Goblin (from the movie) can be unlocked by entering the following codes using the d-pad when standing in the Helicarrier in between levels. You hear a tone if you entered the code correctly, and they are then be selectable from the sidekick select console.

CODE	EFFECT
↑, ↑, ↓, ↓, ←, →	Gain 5,000 upgrade points
→, ↓, →, →, ↓, ←	New Green Goblin
←, →, →, ↑, ↓, ↓	Venom

SPIDER-MAN: FRIEND OR FOE (WII)

CODES

CODE	EFFECT
5,000 Tech Tokens, One Time Only	⬇, ⬅, ⬇, ⬇, ⬅, ⬇
Unlock New Goblin	⬅, ⬇, ⬇, ⬇, ⬇, ⬇
Unlock Sandman	⬇, ⬇, ⬇, ⬅, ⬇, ⬇
Unlock Venom	⬇, ⬇, ⬇, ⬇, ⬇, ⬇

SPIDER-MAN 2 (PSP)

Go to Options, Special, and Cheats on the Main menu, and then type in the following passwords.

UNLOCKABLE	PASSWORD
All Levels Unlocked	WARPULON
All Moves Purchased	MYHERO
All Movies Unlocked	POPPYCORN
Enemies Have Big Heads and Feet	BAHLOONIE
Infinite Health	NERGETS
Infinite Webbing	FILLMEUP
Spidey Has Big Head and Feet	HEAVYHEAD
Tiny Spider-Man	SPIDEYMAN
Unlock All Production Art	SHUTT
Unlock Storyboard Viewer	FRZFRAME

SPIDER-MAN 3 (WII)

UNLOCKABLES

UNLOCKABLE	HOW TO UNLOCK
Collect all 50 Spider Emblems	Unlock black suit Spider-man after you destroy the suit

SPLATTERHOUSE (WII)

UNLOCKABLES

UNLOCKABLE	HOW TO UNLOCK
Hard Mode	At the title screen, hold SELECT until "HARD" appears on the screen
Sound Test	First enter the code to access the Stage Select option. When the screen comes up and asks you to select what stage you want to start on, press and hold the select button. After a second or two, the Stage Select option becomes a Sound Test menu, allowing you to listen to various "songs" and sound effects. Hold select again to change it back to the Stage Select menu.
Stage Select	When the prologue starts up and there's a house in the rain, press SELECT, SELECT, SELECT, hold ✛ and then press ① or ②. It brings up the option to select a level.

SPLATTERHOUSE (XBOX 360)

UNLOCKABLE CLASSIC SPLATTERHOUSE GAMES

UNLOCKABLE	HOW TO UNLOCK
Splatterhouse	Finish Phase 2: "The Doll That Bled"
Splatterhouse 2	Finish Phase 4: "The Meat Factory"
Splatterhouse 3	Finish Phase 8: "Reflections in Blood"

SPLATTERHOUSE (PS3)

UNLOCKABLES

UNLOCKABLE	HOW TO UNLOCK
Splatterhouse	Finish Phase 2: "The Doll That Bled"
Splatterhouse 2	Finish Phase 4: "The Meat Factory"
Splatterhouse 3	Finish Phase 8: "Reflections in Blood"
Unlock PS3 Exclusive Mask	Complete the Splatterhouse Story mode

SPONGEBOB SQUAREPANTS: CREATURE FROM THE KRUSTY KRAB (WII)

PASSWORDS

PASSWORD	EFFECT
ROCFISH	30,000 Z-Coins
HOVER	Alternate Plankton hovercraft
ROBOT	Astronaut suit for Plankton in Revenge of the Giant Plankton
LASER	Extra laser color in Revenge of the Giant Plankton level
ROCKET	Extra rocket for Patrick in Hypnotic Highway level
PILOT	Get Aviator SpongeBob costume
BRAIN	Get Exposed-Brain SpongeBob costume
INVENT	Get Inventor Plankton costume
SPIN	Get Patrick's different POW! effect
BUNRUN	Get Patrick's purple rocket
SAFARI	Get Safari Patrick costume
BONES	Get Skeleton Patrick costume
KRABBY	Get Skeleton SpongeBob costume
FLAMES	Get SpongeBob's flame effect color
HYPCAR	Get SpongeBob's Hypnotic car skin
DUCKGUN	Get SpongeBob's Squeaky Duck Gun
GASSY	Infinite Fuel (in Flying levels)
VIGOR	Infinite Health (in platforming levels)
SCOOTLES	Obtain all sleepy seeds
TISSUE	Obtain Sleepy Seed Detector

PIRATE	Play as Pirate Patrick in Rooftop Rumble level
SPONGE	Play as Punk SpongeBob in Diesel Dreaming level
PANTS	Play as SpongeBob Plankton in Super-Size Patty level
HOTROD	Unlock a bonus vehicle in the Diesel Dreaming level
PORKPIE	Unlock all bonus games
GUDGEON	Unlock all levels
SPACE	Unlock bonus ship in the Rocket Rodeo level
PATRICK	Unlock tuxedo for Patrick in Starfishman to the Rescue

SPYBORGS   (WII)

UNLOCKABLES

UNLOCKABLE	HOW TO UNLOCK
Infinite Arena	Complete the game on any difficulty level.

SSX   (PLAYSTATION 3)

TROPHY

UNLOCKABLE	HOW TO UNLOCK
Around The World (Bronze)	Ride with all three Pilots with each member of Team SSX
Buried Alive (Silver)	Survive Avalanche Deadly Descent without equipping armor (in World Tour)
Caution Low Visibility (Silver)	Survive Whiteout Deadly Descent without equipping pulse goggles (in World Tour)
Do You See What I See (Silver)	Survive Darkness Deadly Descent without equipping a headlamp or pulse goggles (in World Tour)
Gear Pack (Silver)	Collect all Gear Badges
Gear Up! (Bronze)	Make your first Gear Purchase
Grindage (Bronze)	Grind your first rail (not achievable in Tutorial)
Heart Of Gold (Silver)	Earn your 1st Gold in a Survive Event (in Explore)
I Ain't Afraid of Snow Ghost (Silver)	Beat a Friend's Rival Ghost in every Range (in Explore)
I Am A Ghost (Bronze)	Upload your first personal ghost
I Need A Boost (Bronze)	Make your first Mod Purchase
I'm Alive! (Bronze)	Rewind out of Death for the First Time (not achievable in Tutorial)
I'm Flying! (Bronze)	Deploy your wingsuit for the first time (not achievable in Tutorial)
Ice To See You (Silver)	Survive Ice Deadly Descent without equipping ice axes (in World Tour)
It's Cold Out Here (Silver)	Survive Cold Deadly Descent without equipping a solar panel (in World Tour)
Leave No One Behind (Bronze)	Earn a Bronze in a Survive Event with every member of Team SSX (in Explore)
Pass The Baton (Bronze)	Earn a Bronze in a Race Event with every member of Team SSX (in Explore)
Pass The Board Wax (Bronze)	Make your first Board Purchase
Peak-A-Boo (Bronze)	Participate in a Global Event in every Peak
Playing Favorites (Silver)	Reach level 10 with any character
Rocky Road (Silver)	Survive Rock Deadly Descent without equipping armor (in World Tour)
Survival Guide (Silver)	Collect all Survive Badges

Tag Team (Bronze)	Earn a Bronze in a Trick Event with every member of Team SSX (in Explore)
Team SSX (Bronze)	Unlock every member of Team SSX through World Tour (or purchase in Explore or Global Events)
That Was Easy (Bronze)	Unlock all Game Modes
The Apple Theory (Silver)	Survive Gravity Deadly Descent without equipping a wingsuit (in World Tour)
The Finish Line (Silver)	Collect all Race Badges
The Gold Miner (Gold)	Collect all Explore Badges
The Gold Spender (Gold)	Collect all Global Events Badges
The Gold Standard (Silver)	Earn your 1st Gold in a Race Event (in Explore)
The Golden Campaign (Gold)	Collect all World Tour Badges
The Golden Trick IT (Silver)	Earn your 1st Gold in a Trick Event (in Explore)
The SSX Standard (Platinum)	Earn All Trophies
The Tricker (Silver)	Collect all Tricky Badges
Tree Hugger (Silver)	Survive Trees Deadly Descent without equipping armor (in World Tour)
Uberlesscious (Silver)	Earn a Bronze Medal on a Trick Event in Explore without landing any Super Übers
Who Needs Boost (Silver)	Earn a Bronze Medal on a Race Event in Explore without using any boost

SSX (XBOX 360)

ACHIEVEMENT

UNLOCKABLE	HOW TO UNLOCK
Around The World (10)	Ride with all three Pilots with each member of Team SSX
Buried Alive (25)	Survive Avalanche Deadly Descent without equipping armor (in World Tour)
Caution Low Visibility (25)	Survive Whiteout Deadly Descent without equipping pulse goggles (in World Tour)
Do You See What I See (25)	Survive Darkness Deadly Descent without equipping a headlamp or pulse goggles (in World Tour)
Gear Up! (5)	Make your first Gear Purchase
Grindage (5)	Grind your first rail (not achievable in Tutorial)
Heart Of Gold (10)	Earn your 1st Gold in a Survive Event (in Explore)
I Ain't Afraid of Snow Ghost (10)	Beat a Friend's Rival Ghost in every Range (in Explore)
I Am A Ghost (5)	Upload your first personal ghost
I Need A Boost (5)	Make your first Mod Purchase
I'm Alive! (5)	Rewind out of Death for the First Time (not achievable in Tutorial)
I'm Flying! (5)	Deploy your wingsuit for the first time (not achievable in Tutorial)
Ice To See You (25)	Survive Ice Deadly Descent without equipping ice axes (in World Tour)
It's Cold Out Here (25)	Survive Cold Deadly Descent without equipping a solar panel (in World Tour)
Leave No One Behind (10)	Earn a Bronze in a Survive Event with every member of Team SSX (in Explore)

Pass The Baton (10)	Earn a Bronze in a Race Event with every member of Team SSX (in Explore)
Pass The Board Wax (5)	Make your first Board Purchase
Peak-A-Boo (10)	Participate in a Global Event in every Peak
Playing Favorites (25)	Reach level 10 with any character
Rocky Road (25)	Survive Rock Deadly Descent without equipping armor (in World Tour)
Tag Team (10)	Earn a Bronze in a Trick Event with every member of Team SSX (in Explore)
Team SSX (10)	Unlock every member of Team SSX through World Tour (or purchase in Explore or Global Events)
That Was Easy (5)	Unlock all Game Modes
The Apple Theory (25)	Survive Gravity Deadly Descent without equipping a wingsuit (in World Tour)
The Bronze Badger (10)	Collect all Bronze Tricky Badges
The Bronze Campaign (10)	Collect all Bronze World Tour Badges
The Bronze Finish (10)	Collect all Bronze Race Badges
The Bronze Miner (10)	Collect all Bronze Explore Badges
The Bronze Spender (10)	Collect all Bronze Global Events Badges
The Bronze Survival Guide (10)	Collect all Bronze Survive Badges
The Gold Finish (50)	Collect all Gold Race Badges
The Gold Miner (50)	Collect all Gold Explore Badges
The Gold Spender (50)	Collect all Gold Global Events Badges
The Gold Standard (10)	Earn your 1st Gold in a Race Event (in Explore)
The Golden Campaign (50)	Collect all Gold World Tour Badges
The Golden Survival Guide (50)	Collect all Gold Survive Badges
The Golden Trick It (10)	Earn your 1st Gold in a Trick Event (in Explore)
The Golden Tricker (50)	Collect all Gold Tricky Badges
The Silver Boarder (25)	Collect all Silver Tricky Badges
The Silver Campaign (25)	Collect all Silver World Tour Badges
The Silver Finish (25)	Collect all Silver Race Badges
The Silver Miner (25)	Collect all Silver Explore Badges
The Silver Spender (25)	Collect all Silver Global Events Badges
The Silver Survival Guide (25)	Collect all Silver Survive Badges
This Gear Is Bronze (10)	Collect all Bronze Gear Badges
This Gear Is Golden (50)	Collect all Gold Gear Badges
This Gear Is Silver (25)	Collect all Silver Gear Badges
Tree Hugger (25)	Survive Trees Deadly Descent without equipping armor (in World Tour)
Who Needs Boost (20)	Earn a Bronze Medal on a Race Event in Explore without using any boost
Überlesscious (20)	Earn a Bronze Medal on a Trick Event in Explore without landing any Super Übers

SSX BLUR (WII)

In the Options menu, select Cheat to enter this code.

UNLOCKABLE	CODE
All Characters Unlocked	NoHolds

STAR OCEAN: THE LAST HOPE INTERNATIONAL (PLAYSTATION 3)

UNLOCKABLES

UNLOCKABLE	HOW TO UNLOCK
Chaos difficulty	Beat the game on Universe Mode.
Universe difficulty	Beat the game on Galaxy Mode.
Additional Battle Voices, Set 1	Obtain 30% of the character's Battle Trophies.
Additional Battle Voices, Set 2	Obtain 75% of the character's Battle Trophies.
Level cap increase	Obtain 50% of the character's Battle Trophies.
More CP	Obtain 100% of the character's Battle Trophies.

STAR SOLDIER (WII)

UNLOCKABLES

UNLOCKABLE	HOW TO UNLOCK
Powered Up Ship	At the title screen, press SELECT 10 times on controller 1. Then, hold ⬆+⬇ on controller 2. Then, hold ⬆+⬇+Ⓐ+Ⓑ on controller 1, finally press START, START on controller 1.

STAR TREK: LEGACY (XBOX 360)

UNLOCKABLE	HOW TO UNLOCK
Unlock the U.S.S. Legacy	To unlock the secret ship (and receive the achievement), beat the game once on any difficulty, then load your game. When you do, you should be on the ship buying screen right before the final mission. From there, sell and/or buy ships to make sure you have 3 Sovereign-class ships. The final ship you buy will be the U.S.S. Legacy.

STAR WARS BATTLEFRONT II (PSP)

Pause the game and enter this code.

UNLOCKABLE	CODE
Invincibility	⬆, ⬆, ⬆, ⬅, ⬇, ⬇, ⬇, ⬅, ⬆, ⬆, ⬆, ⬅, ➡

STAR WARS: THE CLONE WARS—REPUBLIC HEROES (XBOX 360)

ULTIMATE LIGHTSABER

EFFECT	CODE
Unlock Ultimate Lightsaber	➡,♀,♀,♂,⬅,♂,♂,♀

STAR WARS: THE FORCE UNLEASHED (XBOX 360), (PLAYSTATION 3)

CODES

Input the following codes at the "Input Code" screen.

EFFECT	CODE
All Databank Entries Unlocked	OSSUS
All Force Push Ranks Unlocked	EXARKUN
All Saber Throw Ranks Unlocked	ADEGAN
All Talents Unlocked	JOCASTA
Combo Unlock	RAGNOS
Incinerator Trooper	PHOENIX
Makes Levels Mirrored	MINDTRICK
New Combo	FREEDON
New Combo	LUMIYA
New Combo	MARAJADE
New Combo	MASSASSI
New Combo	SAZEN
New Combo	YADDLE
Proxy Skin Code	PROTOTYPE

Shadowtrooper Costume	BLACKHOLE
Snowtrooper	SNOWMAN
Stormtrooper Commander Costume	TK421BLUE
Unlock All Lightsaber Crystals	HURRIKANE
Unlock Emperor Costume	MASTERMIND
Unlocks All 32 Costumes	SOHNDANN
Unlocks All Force Combos	MOLDYCROW
Unlocks Bail Organa Costume	VICEROY
Unlocks Deadly Saber	LIGHTSABER
Unlocks Kashyyyk Trooper Costume	TK421GREEN
Unlocks Maximum Force Powers	KATARN
Unlocks Maximum Force Repulse Ranks	DATHOMIR
Unlocks Scout Trooper Costume	FERRAL
Unlocks Sith Master difficulty	SITHSPAWN
Unlocks Stormtrooper Costume	TK421WHITE
Unlocks the Aerial Ambush Combo	VENTRESS
Unlocks the Aerial Assault Combo	EETHKOTH
Unlocks the Ceremonial Jedi Robes	DANTOOINE
Unlocks the Devastating Lightsaber Impale	BRUTALSTAB
Unlocks the Drunken Kota Costume	HARDBOILED
Unlocks the Jedi Adventure Robes	HOLOCRON
Unlocks the Master Kento Costume "The Apprentice's Father"	WOOKIEE
Unlocks the Rahm Kota Costume	MANDALORE
Unlocks the Saber Slam Combo	PLOKOON
Unlocks the Saber Sling Combo	KITFISTO
Unlocks the Sith Slash Combo	DARAGON
Unlocks the Sith Stalker Armor	KORRIBAN

STAR WARS: THE FORCE UNLEASHED (WII)

CODES

From the "Extras" menu inside the Rogue Shadow, select "Cheat Codes" and enter the following codes.

EFFECT	CODE
1,000,000 Force Points	SPEEDER
God Mode	CORTOSIS
Max All Force Powers	KATARN
Max Combos	COUNTDOOKU
Unlimited Force Power	VERGENCE
Unlock All Force Powers	TYRANUS
Your Lightsaber One Hit Kills All Normal Enemies	LIGHTSABER

SKIN CODES

EFFECT	CODE
Aayla Secura	AAYLA
Admiral Ackbar	ITSATWAP
Anakin Skywalker	CHOSENONE
Asajj Ventress	ACOLYTE
Chop'aa Notimo	NOTIMO
Classic Stormtrooper	TK421
Clone Trooper	LEGION

Count Dooku	SERENNO	
Darth Desolus	PAUAN	
Darth Maul	ZABRAK	
Darth Phobos	HIDDENFEAR	
Darth Vader	SITHLORD	
Drexl Roosh	DREXLROOSH	
Emperor Palpatine	PALPATINE	
Episode IV Luke Skywalker	YELLOWJCKT	
Episode VI Luke Skywalker	T16WOMPRAT	
Imperial Shadow Guard	INTHEDARK	
Juno Eclipse	ECLIPSE	
Kleef	KLEEF	
Lando Calrissian	SCOUNDREL	
Mace Windu	JEDIMASTER	
Mara Jade	MARAJADE	
Maris Brood	MARISBROOD	
Navy Commando	STORMTROOP	
Obi-Wan Kenobi	BENKENOBI	
PROXY	HOLOGRAM	
Qui-Gon Jinn	MAVERICK	
Rahm Kota	MANDALORE	
Shaak Ti	TOGRUTA	

EXTRA COSTUMES

EFFECT	CODE
Ceremonial Jedi Robes	DANTOOINE
Kento Marek's Robes	WOOKIEE
Sith Stalker Armor	KORRIBAN
Unlocks All Costumes	GRANDMOFF

STAR WARS: THE FORCE UNLEASHED (DS)

CODES

From the main menu select "Extras," then "Unleashed Codes," and then enter the codes.

EFFECT	CODE
Uber Lightsaber	lightsaber
Rahm Kota's costume	mandalore
Sith Robes	holocron
Starkiller's Father's Robes	wookiee

STAR WARS: THE FORCE UNLEASHED (PSP)

CODES

From the "Extras" menu inside the Rogue Shadow, select "Cheat Codes" and enter the following codes. Specific skin codes are not necessary after you enter the "Unlock All Costumes" code.

EFFECT	CODE
1,000,000 Force Points	SPEEDER
All Combos at Maximum Level	COUNTDOOKU
All Force Powers	TYRANUS
All Force Powers at Maximum Level	KATARN
Amplified Lightsaber Damage	LIGHTSABER
Immunity to All Damage	CORTOSIS

| Unlimited Force Power | VERGENCE |
| Unlock All Costumes | GRANDMOFF |

SKIN CODES

EFFECT	CODE
501st Legion	LEGION
Aayla Secura	AAYLA
Admiral Ackbar	ITSATWAP
Anakin Skywalker	CHOSENONE
Asajj Ventress	ACOLYTE
Ceremonial Jedi Robes	DANTOOINE
Chop'aa Notimo	NOTIMO
Classic Stormtrooper	TK421
Count Dooku	SERENNO
Darth Desolous	PAUAN
Darth Maul	ZABRAK
Darth Phobos	HIDDENFEAR
Darth Vader	SITHLORD
Drexl Roosh	DREXLROOSH
Emperor Palpatine	PALPATINE
General Rahm Kota	MANDALORE
Han Solo	NERFHERDER
Heavy Trooper	SHOCKTROOP
Juno Eclipse	ECLIPSE
Kento's Robe	WOOKIEE
Kleef	KLEEF
Lando Calrissian	SCOUNDREL
Luke Skywalker	T16WOMPRAT
Mace Windu	JEDIMASTER
Mara Jade	MARAJADE
Maris Brood	MARISBROOD
Navy Commando	STORMTROOP
Obi-Wan Kenobi	BENKENOBI
PROXY	HOLOGRAM
Qui-Gon Jinn	MAVERICK
Shaak Ti	TOGRUTA
Shadowtrooper	INTHEDARK
Sith Robes	HOLOCRON
Sith Stalker Armor	KORRIBAN
Twi'lek	SECURA
Yavin Luke	YELLOWJCKT

STAR WARS: THE FORCE UNLEASHED II (WII)

CODES

Enter Story mode and go to the corresponding menu for the code you intend to input. Hold Z until you hear a sound, then press buttons on your Wii Remote:

EFFECT	CODE
Unlocks all costumes (Costume menu)	Hold down Z (until you hear a sound) then press LEFT, RIGHT, C, LEFT, RIGHT, C, UP, DOWN

UNLOCKABLE

UNLOCKABLE	HOW TO UNLOCK
Unlimited Force Energy	Upgrade all force powers to max level
Unlimited Health	Find all of the holocrons

STAR WARS: THE FORCE UNLEASHED II (XBOX 360)

CODES

In the "Options" selection of the Pause Game menu, select the "Cheat Codes" option, then enter the following codes.

EFFECT	CODE
Dark Green Lightsaber Crystal (healing)	LIBO
Experimental Jedi Armor	NOMI
Jedi Mind Trick	YARAEL
Jumptrooper Costume	AJP400
Lightsaber Throw	TRAYA
Play as a Neimoidian	GUNRAY
Play as Boba Fett	Mandalore
Stormtrooper character skin	TK421
Force Repulse	MAREK
Dark Apprentice costume	VENTRESS
Saber guard outfit	MORGUKAI
Sith acolyte costume	HAAZEN
General Kota costume	RAHM
Rebel trooper costume	REBELSCUM
Terror trooper costume	SHADOW
Wisdom Lightsaber crystals	SOLARI

UNLOCKABLE

UNLOCKABLE	HOW TO UNLOCK
General Kota costume	Achieve Silver medal in "Deadly Path Trial" Challenge
Saber guard costume	Achieve Silver medal in "Cloning Spire Trial" Challenge
Terror trooper costume	Achieve Silver Medal in "Terror Trial" Challenge
Ceremonial Jedi robes	Have a Force Unleashed save file with the Light Side ending unlocked
Sith stalker armor	Have a Force Unleashed save file with the Dark Side ending unlocked
Sith training gear	Have a Force Unleashed save file in your hard drive
Guybrush Threepkiller Costume	On the second level after the casino type rooms, you'll come to a room with a Jabba the Hutt hologram and some golden Guybrush Threepwood statues. Unlock the costume by destroying the three machines in the room.

STEEL BATTALION: HEAVY ARMOR (XBOX 360)

ACHIEVEMENT

UNLOCKABLE	HOW TO UNLOCK
Acrophiliac (30)	Complete "King of the Hill" and leave no Uncles to talk about it.
Air Superiority (10)	Complete the November 2082 campaign.
Angel of War (50)	Guide Bravo 1 through the entire war without sustaining a single casualty.
Auspicious June (30)	Guide Bravo 1 through the June 2082 campaign without sustaining a single casualty.
Bad Nephew (10)	Take down your first enemy combatant.
Bombs Away (15)	Give the signal to a friendly bomber.
Bridge Blowout (30)	Complete "Bridge Blowout" and leave no Uncles to talk about it.
Brother in Arms (15)	Survive the war with an inseparable friend.
By the Dawn's Early Light (10)	Complete the April 2084 campaign.

Choices, Choices (20)	Obtain 11 pieces of equipment for your vertical tank.
Corporal Punishment? (15)	Teach your subcom a valuable lesson.
CQC (10)	Take out an enemy soldier in close quarters.
Dark Destrier (20)	Destroy 100 enemy vertical tanks.
Davy Jones (20)	Send 3 armed freighters to the bottom of the sea.
Evidence Eraser (30)	Complete "Crash Site" and leave no Uncles to talk about it.
Family Portrait (40)	After the war, complete Bravo 1's platoon photo by reversing the fate of its fallen members.
Fortunate July (30)	Guide Bravo 1 through the July 2083 campaign without sustaining a single casualty.
Four by Four (20)	Create a platoon with three other players and complete a mission without any player casualties.
Gatecrasher (10)	Complete the January 2084 campaign.
Gift to the Future (15)	Save the most precious of lives.
Golden January (30)	Guide Bravo 1 through the January 2084 campaign without sustaining a single casualty.
Happy November (30)	Guide Bravo 1 through the November 2082 campaign without sustaining a single casualty.
Home Veet Home (40)	Obtain 21 pieces of equipment for your vertical tank.
Iron Coffin (10)	Prevent being gunned down by closing the armored shutter.
Jewel of the Nihil (15)	Find a valuable vacuum tube in the middle of nowhere.
Joyful October (30)	Guide Bravo 1 through the October 2083 campaign without sustaining a single casualty.
Lemmings to Lemonade (30)	Complete "Lemmings" and leave no Uncles to talk about it.
Lights Out, Berlin (30)	Complete "Berlin After Dark" and leave no Uncles to talk about it.
Lucky August (30)	Guide Bravo 1 through the August 2082 campaign without sustaining a single casualty.
Metal of Honor (20)	Destroy an HVT (heavy vertical tank).
Multitasker (10)	Double up as a loader.
New Toy (10)	Obtain your first piece of vertical tank equipment.
Octa-gone (10)	Knock out 8 enemy soldiers with a single HEAT round.
Officer and a Gentleman (15)	Give a generous share of food to your mechanic.
One-way Ticket (10)	Complete the October 2083 campaign.
Perfect April (30)	Guide Bravo 1 through the April 2084 campaign without sustaining a single casualty.
Pirouette (15)	Perform a pivot turn in high-speed mode to take out an enemy behind you.
Port Authority (10)	Complete the August 2082 campaign.
Reach for the Sky! (20)	Knock an enemy bomber out of the skies.
Repatriation (10)	Complete the June 2082 campaign.
Sign of Life (15)	Celebrate a victory with your loader.
Surgeon General (10)	Successfully purge the cockpit of smoke.
The Graduate (10)	Complete basic training.
Uncle Slam (20)	Take down 1000 enemy soldiers.
Urban Warrior (30)	Complete "Urban Warfare" and leave no Uncles to talk about it.

Watch and Learn (10)	Create a platoon with another player and complete a successful mission.
Waterside Wipeout (30)	Complete "Waterside Warehouse" and leave no Uncles to talk about it.
What a Shot! (20)	Hit an enemy using rear ammo.
With You in Spirit (10)	Join another player's platoon and fall in battle while the commanding unit fights on.
World Traveler (10)	Complete the July 2083 campaign

STRANGLEHOLD (PLAYSTATION 3)

DIFFICULTIES

UNLOCKABLE	HOW TO UNLOCK
Hard Boiled Difficulty	Complete the game on Casual mode once to unlock this difficulty.

EASTER EGGS

UNLOCKABLE	HOW TO UNLOCK
Movie Theater Trailers	In the first chapter in the Hong Kong Marketplace, go into the Ambushed section. When you finish killing everyone, go into the building. Break the door, and follow the corridor until you reach a movie theater. The screen is showing trailers for *Wheelman* and *Blacksite*.

STREET FIGHTER X TEKKEN (PLAYSTATION 3)

TROPHY

UNLOCKABLE	HOW TO UNLOCK
A Glimmering Light (Bronze)	Activate your Assist Gems 100 times.
A Perfect Victory! (Bronze)	Win a round without getting hit 100 times.
A Splendid Conclusion (Bronze)	Finish a round with a Super Art 300 times.
A Very Special Gift (Bronze)	Connect with 500 Special Moves.
After The Dust Has Settled (Bronze)	Clear Arcade mode on Medium difficulty or higher.
An Unknown Power (Bronze)	Activate Pandora 500 times.
Any Time, Any Place! (Bronze)	Use Arcade Fight Request 30 times.
Anything Goes (Bronze)	Activate Cross Assault 500 times.
Blink Of An Eye (Bronze)	Connect with 500 EX Special Moves.
Doused In My Color! (Bronze)	Customize a character's color.
Evangelist Of The "X" (Bronze)	Have your replay downloaded 20 times in My Channel's Broadcast Mode.
Forge Your Own Path (Bronze)	Win 10 matches online.
Fruits of Labor (Bronze)	Go into Training mode 10 times.
Head Of The Dojo (Bronze)	Create 10 lobbies in Endless Battle.
Here's My Shoutout (Bronze)	Customize your player comment.
It's Just For Research! (Bronze)	Access the Store.
Just The Beginning (Bronze)	Clear one trial in Trial mode.
Learn The Fundamentals (Bronze)	Win 5 matches online.
Let's Heat Things Up! (Bronze)	Activate your Boost Gems 100 times.
Love Is Blind (Bronze)	Use a character in battle over 300 times.
Maelstrom Of Combos (Bronze)	Connect with 100 Quick Combos.
Maturity Through Discipline (Bronze)	Clear all of the lessons in the Tutorial.
Mission Specialist (Silver)	Clear all of the missions in Mission mode.
My Big First Step (Bronze)	Clear one lesson in the Tutorial.
Observer (Bronze)	View 50 replays in the Replay Channel.
One Down! (Bronze)	Win in a Ranked Match.
Power Consumes All (Bronze)	Finish a round with Pandora 300 times.

NEW!

A

B

C

D

E

F

G

H

I

J

K

L

M

N

O

P

Q

R

S

T

U

V

W

X

Y

Z

Proof Of Your Victory (Gold)	Get to C rank for the first time in Ranked Match.
Sturm und Drang (Bronze)	Finish a round with Cross Assault 300 times.
The Battle Never Ends (Bronze)	Win a match in Endless Battle.
The Cross Revolution (Bronze)	Finish a round with a Cross Art 300 times.
The Crossroads of Tragedy (Bronze)	Fight 100 matches online.
The Endless Road (Gold)	Fight 500 matches online.
The Excellence of Execution (Bronze)	Clear 300 trials in Trial mode.
The First Mission (Bronze)	Clear one mission in Mission mode.
The Harsh Road (Silver)	Fight 300 matches online.
The Root Of Chaos (Silver)	Defeat all of the bosses in Arcade mode on the hardest difficulty.
The Stones Guide Me (Bronze)	Customize a Gem Unit.
The Trump Card (Bronze)	Connect with 500 Super Arts.
The Warrior's Road (Bronze)	Fight 50 matches online.
This Is How I Roll (Bronze)	Customize your player Title.
Time For Some Fireworks! (Bronze)	Connect with 500 Launchers.
Title Idol (Silver)	Obtain 300 Titles.
To The Victor... (Silver)	Raise your battle class rank for the first time in Ranked Match.
Trail Of Ruined Dreams (Bronze)	Defeat 5 rival teams in Arcade mode on Medium difficulty or higher.
Transcend All You Know (Silver)	Win 50 matches online.
Trial Expert (Bronze)	Clear ten trials in Trial mode.
Two Minds, Fighting As One (Bronze)	Connect with 500 Cross Arts.
Your Legend Will Never Die (Gold)	Win 100 matches online.
Zenith (Platinum)	Unlock all Trophies.

STREET FIGHTER X TEKKEN (XBOX 360)

ACHIEVEMENT

UNLOCKABLE	HOW TO UNLOCK
A Glimmering Light (10)	Activate your Assist Gems 100 times.
A Perfect Victory! (50)	Win a round without getting hit 100 times.
A Splendid Conclusion (30)	Finish a round with a Super Art 300 times.
A Very Special Gift (10)	Connect with 500 Special Moves.
After The Dust Has Settled (10)	Clear Arcade mode on Medium difficulty or higher.
An Unknown Power (10)	Activate Pandora 500 times.
Any Time, Any Place! (10)	Use Arcade Fight Request 30 times.
Anything Goes (10)	Activate Cross Assault 500 times.
Blink Of An Eye (10)	Connect with 500 EX Special Moves.
Doused In My Color! (10)	Customize a character's color.
Evangelist Of The "X" (30)	Have your replay downloaded 20 times in My Channel's Broadcast Mode.
Forge Your Own Path (20)	Win 10 matches over Xbox LIVE.
Fruits of Labor (10)	Go into Training mode 10 times.
Head Of The Dojo (20)	Create 10 lobbies in Endless Battle.
Here's My Shoutout (10)	Customize your player comment.
It's Just For Research! (10)	Access the Store.
Just The Beginning (10)	Clear one trial in Trial mode.
Learn The Fundamentals (10)	Win 5 matches over Xbox LIVE.

Let's Heat Things Up! (10)	Activate your Boost Gems 100 times.
Love Is Blind (30)	Use a character in battle over 300 times.
Maelstrom Of Combos (10)	Connect with 100 Quick Combos.
Maturity Through Discipline (10)	Clear all of the lessons in the Tutorial.
Mission Specialist (30)	Clear all of the missions in Mission mode.
My Big First Step (10)	Clear one lesson in the Tutorial.
Observer (30)	View 50 replays in the Replay Channel.
One Down! (10)	Win in a Ranked Match.
Power Consumes All (30)	Finish a round with Pandora 300 times.
Proof Of Your Victory (50)	Get to C rank for the first time in Ranked Match.
Sturm und Drang (30)	Finish a round with Cross Assault 300 times.
The Battle Never Ends (10)	Win a match in Endless Battle.
The Cross Revolution (30)	Finish a round with a Cross Art 300 times.
The Crossroads of Tragedy (20)	Fight 100 matches over Xbox LIVE.
The Endless Road (50)	Fight 500 matches over Xbox LIVE.
The Excellence of Execution (30)	Clear 300 trials in Trial mode.
The First Mission (10)	Clear one mission in Mission mode.
The Harsh Road (30)	Fight 300 matches over Xbox LIVE.
The Root Of Chaos (30)	Defeat all of the bosses in Arcade mode on the hardest difficulty.
The Stones Guide Me (10)	Customize a Gem Unit.
The Trump Card (10)	Connect with 500 Super Arts.
The Warrior's Road (10)	Fight 50 matches over Xbox LIVE.
This Is How I Roll (10)	Customize your player Title.
Time For Some Fireworks! (10)	Connect with 500 Launchers.
Title Idol (50)	Obtain 300 Titles.
To The Victor... (30)	Raise your battle class rank for the first time in Ranked Match.
Trail Of Ruined Dreams (20)	Defeat 5 rival teams in Arcade mode on Medium difficulty or higher.
Transcend All You Know (30)	Win 50 matches over Xbox LIVE.
Trial Expert (20)	Clear ten trials in Trial mode.
Two Minds, Fighting As One (10)	Connect with 500 Cross Arts.
Your Legend Will Never Die (50)	Win 100 matches over Xbox LIVE.
Zenith (0)	Unlock all Achievements.

STREETS OF RAGE (WII)

UNLOCKABLES

UNLOCKABLE	HOW TO UNLOCK
Bad Ending	Choose to be Mr. X's righthand man the first time you meet him. Then complete the game.
Extra Continues	Press ◀, ◀, B, B, B, C, C, C, START at the title screen.
Final Boss Duel	When you get to the final boss in 2-player mode, have one player choose "yes" and the other choose "no." You duel against each other.
Level and Lives Select	Go to the main menu. Hold A+B+C+▲ on controller 2 while selecting Options on controller 1 (best if done with two people). You can now select how many lives you start with and which stage to start on.

STREETS OF RAGE 2 (WII)

UNLOCKABLES

UNLOCKABLE	HOW TO UNLOCK
Level and Lives Select	Go to the main menu. Hold Ⓐ+Ⓑ on controller 2 while selecting Options. Now select how many lives you start with (up to 9), choose your starting stage, and play at the Very Easy and Mania difficulty levels.
Same Character in 2 Player	At the title screen, hold ⬇+Ⓑ on controller 1 and hold ⬇+Ⓐ on controller 2. Press ⬇ on controller 2 with everything else still held down. Now both players can be the same person in 2 Player!

STREETS OF RAGE 3 (WII)

UNLOCKABLES

UNLOCKABLE	HOW TO UNLOCK
Ending 1	Rescue the Chief in Stage 6 before his health runs out. Then, at the end of Stage 7, defeat Robot Y before the time limit runs out.
Ending 2	Rescue the Chief before his health runs out in Stage 6. Then, in Stage 7, defeat Robot Y but let the time limit run out.
Ending 3	Let the Chief's health run out in Stage 6. When you go to Stage 7, you will see that it is changed. Make it to the last boss and defeat him.
Ending 4	Set the difficulty to Easy and beat Robot X in Stage 5.
Extra Lives Select	Go to the Options screen and select the "Lives" option. Press and hold ⬇+Ⓐ+Ⓑ+Ⓒ on controller 2, and press ⬇ or ⬇ on controller 1 to select the number of lives you can start the game with. You can now select 9 lives, instead of the default max of 5.
Play as Ash	To select Ash, defeat him, then hold Ⓐ on controller 1. After losing all of your lives, continue, and you can choose Ash as your character.
Play as Roo	When you fight the clown and Roo, defeat the clown first and Roo should hop away off the screen. When you lose all your lives and continue, cycle through the characters and Roo is now available.
Play as Roo	At the title screen, hold ⬇+Ⓑ, then press START. A kangaroo named Roo is now available at the Character Select screen.
Play as Shiva	After beating Shiva in the first stage when you get the last hit, hold Ⓑ+START. When the continue screen comes up, you can play as Shiva. (He is weaker than his *Streets of Rage 2* character).
Play as Super Axel	Press ⬇ to select a player, then quickly hold Ⓐ and sweep the D-pad in a clockwise circle until Axel appears. Then press Ⓐ.
THIS CHEAT IS VERY HARD TO GET WORKING.	
Play as Super Skate	Pick Skate. As the first level starts, lose your first life having 0 points. You will now be Super Skate, with a much more powerful combo.
Play as the Same Character	Hold ⬇+Ⓒ on controller 2 as you enter 2-player mode with controller 1.
Secret Items	In Stage 1, at the Warehouse area, go to the bottom-left region blocked by the crates in the background and press Ⓑ. You get 5,000 points and a 1-UP. Stage 7, (City Hall) also contains lots of hidden items. Search in areas blocked off by the background such as lampposts, flower pots, etc.
Secret Passageways	On Stage 5, in the first room with all the ninjas, there are three secret routes that you can access by killing all enemies here. These rooms have more items than the normal rooms. Route 1: Above the door where you follow your normal route, notice a white wall with cracks near the top. Punch it to access Secret Route 1. Route 2: Go to the bottom center of this room and punch a few times. You eventually bust a hole in the floor leading you to the basement of Stage 5 and also Secret Route 2. Route 3: Go to the top of the screen and go up to the

red walls. A certain red wall has a few cracks in it. Punch it to access Secret Route 3. There are a lot of enemies here, so be careful.

| Stage Select | Hold ⑱+⬇, then press START. Stage Select appears on the Options screen. |

SUPER C (WII)

UNLOCKABLES

UNLOCKABLE	HOW TO UNLOCK
10 Lives (Player 1)	On the title screen, press ➡, ⬅, ⬇, ⬆, Ⓐ, ⑱, then START
10 Lives (Player 2)	On the title screen, press ➡, ⬅, ⬇, ⬆, Ⓐ, ⑱, SELECT, then START
Access Sound Test	On the title screen, hold down Ⓐ+⑱ then press START
Retain Old Score and # of Lives on New Game	On the title screen, after you've beaten the game, press Ⓐ, and then START
Retain Old Score on New Game	On the title screen, after you've beaten the game, press Ⓐ, ⑱, then START

SUPER CASTLEVANIA IV (WII)

UNLOCKABLES

UNLOCKABLE	HOW TO UNLOCK
Higher Difficulty	Heart, Axe, Space, Water. Axe, Space, Space, Heart. Space, Axe, Space, Space. Space, Heart, Space, Space.

DIFFICULT LEVEL PASSWORDS

Use these passwords to get to stages on the Difficult setting. You need to use a blank name.

PASSWORD	EFFECT
Space, Axe, Space, Space. Water, Water, Space, Space. Space, Heart, Space, Axe. Water, Axe, Space, Space.	Difficult mode Stage 6 level 1
Space, Axe, Space, Heart. Water, Heart, Space, Space. Space, Space, Space, Water. Space, Axe, Space, Space.	Difficult mode Stage 7 level 1
Space, Axe, Space, Space. Water, Water, Space, Space. Space, Heart, Space, Water. Water, Water, Space, Space.	Difficult mode Stage 8 level 1

STAGE PASSWORDS

WHEN YOU COME TO "ENTER YOUR NAME," LEAVE THE SPACE BLANK OR THESE PASSWORDS WON'T WORK.

PASSWORD	EFFECT
Space, Space, Space, Space. Firebombs, Space, Space, Space. Space, Space, Space, Firebombs. Space, Space, Space	Level 2

PASSWORD	EFFECT
Space, Space, Space, Heart. Firebombs, Space, Space, Space. Space, Space, Space, Space. Heart, Space, Space, Space	Level 3
Space, Space, Space, Firebombs. Firebombs, Firebombs, Space, Space. Space, Firebombs, Space, Axe. Space, Space, Space, Space	Level 4
Space, Space, Space, Space. Firebombs, Space, Space, Space. Space, Space, Space, Axe. Firebombs, Axe, Space, Space	Level 5
Space, Space, Space, Firebombs. Firebombs, Firebombs, Space, Space. Space, Firebombs, Space, Axe. Firebombs, Axe, Space, Space	Level 6
Space, Space, Space, Firebombs. Firebombs, Hart, Space, Space. Space, Heart, Space, Firebombs. Space, Heart, Space, Space	Level 7
Space, Space, Space, Space. Firebombs, Firebombs, Space, Space. Space, Firebombs, Space, Firebombs. Firebombs, Firebombs, Space, Space	Level 8

NEW!
A
B
C
D
E
F
G
H
I
J
K
L
M
N
O
P
Q
R
S
T
U
V
W
X
Y
Z

CODES&CHEATS

Space, Space, Space, Heart. Firebombs, Firebombs, Space, Space. Space, Firebombs, Space, Firebombs. Heart, Firebombs, Space, Space	Level 9
Space, Space, Space, Axe. Firebombs, Space, Space, Space. Space, Space, Space, Heart. Heart, Heart, Space, Space	Level B
Space, Space, Space, Firebombs. Firebombs, Firebombs, Space, Space. Space, Firebombs, Space, Space. Space, Heart, Axe, Space	Level B (Dracula)

UNLOCKABLES

UNLOCKABLE	HOW TO UNLOCK
Full Arsenal	In the last stage, before you climb the stairs to Dracula, jump down to land on an invisible platform. Move all the way left and you will get full health, 99 hearts, a cross, a fully upgraded whip, and a III stone.

HIDDEN ROUTES

There are three hidden branches from the main path.

UNLOCKABLE	HOW TO UNLOCK
Hidden Route 1	In stage 3-1, when you must descend a short vertical shaft, halfway down here is a wall of pillars to the left. Demolish these, and you find a small side room containing hearts, cash bags, and some Roast.
Hidden Route 2	The second secret, which is an actual hidden Block, is in stage 6-2. At the very beginning you pass a hallway with Axe Knights and falling chandeliers. The third archway has a chandelier but no guard. Hit the floor a couple of times and it'll crumble, revealing a stairwell into a secret area.
Hidden Route 3	The last one is in Block 9-2. You jump across a bed of spikes at the beginning. After this you see several whirlwind tunnels and some coffins. The last upper platform on the right has a coffin and a tunnel. Let the tunnel suck you in and you'll find a hidden area full of bonuses.

SUPER CONTRA (XBOX 360)

UNLOCKABLE	HOW TO UNLOCK
Unlimited Lives and Super Machine Gun	On the main menu, select Arcade Game, and then enter the following code: (using the D-Pad) ⬆, ⬆, ⬇, ⬇, ⬅, ➡, ⬅, ➡, ⬅, ➡, Ⓑ, Ⓐ. If done correctly, the game will start up instead of backing out to the main menu. You will begin with 5 lives that never decrease when killed, and you will have a super machine gun weapon equipped at all times! Using this code disables all Achievements and you cannot upload scores to Xbox Live Leaderboards. The code remain active until you exit the game using the Exit Game option in the Pause menu.

SUPER GHOULS 'N GHOSTS (WII)

UNLOCKABLES

UNLOCKABLE	HOW TO UNLOCK
Level Select	Highlight "Exit" on the Option screen with controller 1. Hold L + START on controller 2 and press START on controller 1.
Professional Mode	Beat the game on Normal mode.

SUPER MONKEY BALL: BANANA SPLITZ (PLAYSTATION VITA)

TROPHY

UNLOCKABLE	HOW TO UNLOCK
100UP (Bronze)	You got 100 extra monkeys in Monkey Ball!
Advanced Course World 1 Clear (Bronze)	Cleared Monkey Ball Advanced Course World 1!
Advanced Course World 2 Clear (Bronze)	Cleared Monkey Ball Advanced Course World 2!
Advanced Course World 3 Clear (Bronze)	Cleared Monkey Ball Advanced Course World 3!

Advanced Course World 4 Clear (Bronze)	Cleared Monkey Ball Advanced Course World 4!
Advanced Course World 5 Clear (Silver)	Cleared Monkey Ball Advanced Course World 5!
Banana Bandit (Bronze)	You stole 15 bananas in Monkey Rodeo!
Banana Boycott (Bronze)	You cleared a Monkey Ball stage without collecting any bananas!
Banana Master (Gold)	Collected all bananas in all Monkey Ball stages!
Banana Sheriff (Bronze)	You got 30 bananas in Monkey Rodeo!
Banana Splitz (Platinum)	You earned all other trophies!
Beginner Course World 1 Clear (Bronze)	Cleared Monkey Ball Beginner Course World 1!
Bingo! (Bronze)	You got a bingo in Monkey Bingo!
Bingo! Bingo! (Bronze)	You got two bingos in a single game of Monkey Bingo!
Bumper Boss (Bronze)	You crashed into a 100 bumpers!
Countdown Competitor (Bronze)	You cleared 10 Monkey Ball stages in the last 10 seconds!
Edit Anniversary (Bronze)	You created 100 edit stages!
Editor-in-Chief (Bronze)	You've saved as many edited stages as possible!
Excellent Point (Bronze)	You landed a 500-point location in Monkey Target!
Falling Monkey (Bronze)	You fell off 100 times in Monkey Ball!
Funky Baby Monkey (Bronze)	You played Monkey Ball with Baby 250 times!
Go Go GonGon (Bronze)	You played Monkey Ball with GonGon 250 times!
Goal Anniversary (Bronze)	Cleared 100 Monkey Ball stages!
Good Hustle (Bronze)	You dropped two balls in one shot in Battle Billiards!
Hard Shaker (Bronze)	You shook a lot in Edit Mode!
Hide-and-Seek Monkey (Silver)	Passed through all Monkey Ball warp goals!
Hustle King (Bronze)	You sunk one monkey ball from each team in a match of Battle Billiards!
I Love AiAi (Bronze)	You played Monkey Ball with AiAi 250 times!
I My MeeMee (Bronze)	You played Monkey Ball with MeeMee 250 times!
Just-in-Time Monkey (Bronze)	Reached the goal in a Monkey Ball stage with 0 seconds left!
Magic Touch (Bronze)	You got 50 correct in one round of Number Ball!
Monkey Express (Bronze)	You ran at top speed for 5 seconds in Monkey Ball!
Monkey Master (Silver)	Cleared Monkey Ball Master Course!
Motion Simian (Gold)	Clear all Monkey Ball stages in Beginner, Normal and Advanced using motion sensor controls!
Mountain Climber (Bronze)	You uploaded a high score!
My Monkey and Me (Bronze)	Both characters reached the goal simultaneously in Love Maze!
Never Give Up (Bronze)	You retried 10 times in Monkey Ball!
Normal Course World 1 Clear (Bronze)	Cleared Monkey Ball Normal Course World 1!
Normal Course World 2 Clear (Bronze)	Cleared Monkey Ball Normal Course World 2!
Normal Course World 3 Clear (Silver)	Cleared Monkey Ball Normal Course World 3!
Perfect Primate (Bronze)	You got to ten in a row in Number Ball without any mistakes!

NEW!
A
B
C
D
E
F
G
H
I
J
K
L
M
N
O
P
Q
R
S
T
U
V
W
X
Y
Z

Photographer (Bronze)	You retook pictures in Edit Mode 5 times!
Picture Perfect (Bronze)	You got 10 pixies to appear in one shot in Pixie Hunt!
Pixie Hunter (Bronze)	You got a chain of 10 or more in Pixie Hunt!
Pro Irregubowler (Bronze)	You got a turkey in an abnormal lane in Monkey Bowling!
Pro Monkey Bowler (Bronze)	You got a turkey in a regular lane in Monkey Bowling!
Super Monkey Master (Gold)	Cleared all Monkey Ball stages with no continues!
Supersonic Monkey (Silver)	You cleared 10 stages in 10 seconds or less in Monkey Ball!
Target Master (Bronze)	You got 1000 points in a single round of Monkey Target!
Through Thick and Thin (Bronze)	You got a synchronization rating of 200% in Love Maze!
Travelogue (Bronze)	You saved 10 instances of Monkey Ball replay data!

SUPER STAR SOLDIER (WII)

CHEAT MENU

Following code unlocks a Cheat menu where you can mess with all the options for the game such as level selection and enemy difficulty. Input at the title screen.

UNLOCKABLE	HOW TO UNLOCK
Unlock Cheat Menu	Press ⬇, ②, ⬆, ②, ⬅, ②, ➡②②, ⬅, ①, ⬆, ①, ➡, ①, ⬇, ①, ①+② x8, ①+SELECT x8

SUPER STREET FIGHTER IV (XBOX 360), (PLAYSTATION 3)

CHARACTER ICONS AND TITLES

There are a number of character specific icons and titles that are unlocked by clearing Arcade Mode and through each character's unique set of trials.

UNLOCKABLE	HOW TO UNLOCK
Blue Character Title	Clear Arcade with the character on any difficulty.
Character Icon #1	Complete any trial with the character.
Character Icon #2	Complete eight different trials with the character.
Character Icon #3	Complete 16 different trials with the character.
Character Icon #4	Complete all trials with the character.
Gold Character Title #1	Complete 12 different trials with the character.
Gold Character Title #2	Complete 14 different trials with the character.
Gold Character Title #3	Complete 18 different trials with the character.
Gold Character Title #4	Complete 20 different trials with the character.
Gold Character Title #5	Complete 22 different trials with the character.
Red Character Title	Clear Arcade with the character on the hardest difficulty.
Silver Character Title #1	Complete two different trials with the character.
Silver Character Title #2	Complete three different trials with the character.
Silver Character Title #3	Complete four different trials with the character.
Silver Character Title #4	Complete six different trials with the character.
Silver Character Title #5	Complete 10 different trials with the character.

ADDITIONAL COLORS AND TAUNTS (PERSONAL ACTIONS)

For each match you use a character on, you will unlock a new color and Personal Action or Taunt.

UNLOCKABLE	HOW TO UNLOCK
Color #10	Play 16 matches with the character.
Color #11	Start a game with a Street Fighter IV save file.
Color #12	Start a game with a Street Fighter IV save file.
Color #3	Play two matches with the character.
Color #4	Play four matches with the character.
Color #5	Play six matches with the character.
Color #6	Play eight matches with the character.
Color #7	Play 10 matches with the character.
Color #8	Play 12 matches with the character.
Color #9	Play 14 matches with the character.
Taunt #10	Play 16 matches with the character.
Taunt #2	Play one match with the character.
Taunt #3	Play three matches with the character.
Taunt #4	Play five matches with the character.
Taunt #5	Play seven matches with the character.
Taunt #6	Play nine matches with the character.
Taunt #7	Play 11 matches with the character.
Taunt #8	Play 13 matches with the character.
Taunt #9	Play 15 matches with the character.

UNLOCKABLES

UNLOCKABLE	HOW TO UNLOCK
Barrel Buster Bonus Stage	Beat Arcade Mode in any difficulty.
Car Crusher Bonus Stage	Beat Arcade Mode in any difficulty.
Color 11	Have saved data from Street Fighter IV.
Color 12	Have saved data carry over from the original Street Fighter IV.
Japanese Voices	Beat Arcade Mode in any difficulty.
Remixed Character BGM for Use in Battles	Earn "It Begins" achievement.

FIGHT GOUKEN IN ARCADE MODE

The following requirements must be met while playing Arcade Mode to fight Gouken, who will appear after the battle with Seth (in default settings, i.e., three rounds):

* Do not lose a single round.

* Perform five Super or Ultra Combo Finishes.

* Score two Perfect Rounds (not get hit a single time during a round)

* Connect 10 "First Hits" (when you're the first to connect a strike during a round).

SUPER STREET FIGHTER IV: 3D EDITION (3DS)

CODE

Codes must be entered case-sensitve in the Figure Collection Menu

EFFECT	CODE
Bronze Lv6 Adon	jeNbhRXbFR
Golden Abel Figurine	wRqsWklbxT
Golden Blanka Figurine	DmdkeRvbxc
Golden Chun-Li Figurine	zAAkcHVbHk
Golden Guile Figurine	qeJkznDbKE
Golden Lv. 7 Seth	PkwkDjqbja
Golden M.Bison Figurine	CglsQNWbHu (I = uppercase i)

Golden Rufus Figurine	nnhksyvbZy
Golden Ryu Figurine	KjckTnSbwK
Golden Zangief Figurine	hinsVnebTu
Level 7 Silver Sagat	QWzkDXWbeH
Obtain a Platinum Level 7 Chun-Li Figurine	hjekwnEbxG
Platinum C. Viper	xopknDzbqS
Platinum Cammy Figurine	dfukkvGbdt
Platinum Dee Jay	DaRkBPubLf
Platinum El Fuerte Figurine	mhikghwbsf
Platinum Fei Long Figurine	MzisXzabBF
Platinum Guy	AjtsAbWbBD
Platinum Level 7 Ryu	DPrkMnybCd
Platinum M.Bison	EebkxqWbYJ
Silver Akuma Figurine	RYSsPxSbTh
Silver Balrog Figurine	PqUswOobWG
Silver Chun-Li Figurine	tLWkWvrblz
Silver Cody Figurine	naMkEQgbQG
Silver Dan Figurine	rDRkkSIbqS (I = uppercase i)
Silver E. Honda Figurine	uUDsTImbUN
Silver Ibuki Figurine	ilMsRBabpB
Silver Juri Figurine	OfQkARpbJR
Silver Ken Figurine	NyosHgybuW
Silver Lv. 6 Dudley	ZRhsNTMbIA (upper case i)
Silver Lv. 6 Hakan	rLPbyLgbUy
Silver LV. 7 T. Hawk Figurine	tWEsvzubiz
Silver Makoto Figurine	GHakWCTbsl
Silver Rose Figurine	GKkkXXtbSe
Silver Sakura Figurine	uzTsXzIbKn (I = uppercase i)
Special Akuma Figurine	uQHkWgYbJC
Unlock Silver Lv. 5 Dhalsim	JKbsOVHbVC

UNLOCKABLE

Clear Arcade mode and complete each unique character's set of trials.

UNLOCKABLE	HOW TO UNLOCK
Blue Character Title	Clear Arcade with the character on any difficulty.
Character Icon #1	Complete any trial with the character.
Character Icon #2	Complete 8 different trials with the character.
Character Icon #3	Complete 16 different trials with the character.
Character Icon #4	Complete all trials with the character.
Gold Character Title #1	Complete 12 different trials with the character.
Gold Character Title #2	Complete 14 different trials with the character.
Gold Character Title #3	Complete 18 different trials with the character.
Gold Character Title #4	Complete 20 different trials with the character.
Gold Character Title #5	Complete 22 different trials with the character.
Red Character Title	Clear Arcade with the character on the hardest difficulty.
Silver Character Title #1	Complete 2 different trials with the character.
Silver Character Title #2	Complete 3 different trials with the character.
Silver Character Title #3	Complete 4 different trials with the character.
Silver Character Title #4	Complete 6 different trials with the character.
Silver Character Title #5	Complete 10 different trials with the character.

SECRETS

UNLOCKABLE	HOW TO UNLOCK
Fight Akuma	Beat arcade mode without continuing and recieve at least one perfect. After defeating Seth, Akuma appears to challenge you. Defeat him to recieve the "Akuma Killer" title.
Fight Gouken in Arcade mode	Aafter the battle with Seth, Gouken appears. You can't lose a single round. Perform 5 Super or Ultra Combo Finishes, Score 2 Perfect Rounds, and Connect 10 First Hits.
Fight Your 2nd Rival (Arcade Mode)	During Arcade Mode, when "Fight Your Rival" flashes on the screen, hold the R button.

SUPER THUNDER BLADE (WII)

LEVEL SELECT

Press these controller actions at the title screen to begin at the desired level.

CODE	EFFECT
Press Ⓐ, ⬇, ⬇, ⬅, ⬅, ⬅, ⬅, ⬅, ⬅, START	Level 2
Press Ⓐ, Ⓐ, ⬇, ⬇, ⬅, ⬅, ⬅, ⬅, ⬅, ⬅, START	Level 3
Press Ⓐ, Ⓐ, Ⓐ, ⬇, ⬇, ⬅, ⬅, ⬅, ⬅, ⬅, ⬅, START	Level 4
Press Ⓐ, Ⓐ, Ⓐ, Ⓐ, ⬇, ⬇, ⬅, ⬅, ⬅, ⬅, ⬅, ⬅, START	Level 5

UNLOCKABLES

UNLOCKABLE	HOW TO UNLOCK
Avoid Enemy Fire	Begin the game with Hard difficulty. Stay in the upper right or left corners and fire your weapon continuously in levels 1 through 3.
Extra Lives	Enable the Level Select code and get a continue. Highlight "Option" and hold Ⓐ+Ⓑ+Ⓒ and press START. A picture of a panda appears on the "Player" selection to confirm the code.

SUPERMAN RETURNS (XBOX 360)

CHEAT CODES

Anytime during gameplay after the Gladiator Battle first set, pause the game. Enter the following buttons to unlock the cheats. A chime confirms that the code has been entered correctly.

UNLOCKABLE	HOW TO UNLOCK
Infinite Health (Metropolis)	Ⓨ, ➡, Ⓨ, ➡, Ⓐ, ➡, ➡, Ⓨ
Infinite Stamina	Ⓐ, Ⓐ, Ⓨ, Ⓨ, ➡, ➡, ➡, ➡, Ⓨ, Ⓧ
Unlock All Costumes, Trophies, and Theater Items Unlock All Moves	➡, Ⓐ, ➡, Ⓧ, Ⓨ, Ⓨ, Ⓧ, Ⓐ, ➡, Ⓧ, ➡, Ⓨ, ➡, Ⓧ, Ⓨ, Ⓧ, Ⓐ, Ⓨ, Ⓧ, Ⓧ, Ⓧ

UNLOCKABLES

UNLOCKABLE	HOW TO UNLOCK
Bizarro	Ⓐ, ➡, Ⓨ, Ⓐ, ➡, Ⓐ, ➡, Ⓨ, Ⓐ (Enter it when you load your game, at the menu that lets you choose Metropolis or Fortress of Solitude before you start the game you loaded.)
Golden Age Superman Suit	Save Metropolis from the tornadoes
Pod Suit	Beat Bizarro

SUPREMACY MMA: UNRESTRICTED (PLAYSTATION VITA)

TROPHY

UNLOCKABLE	HOW TO UNLOCK
Adrenaline Rush (Silver)	Complete 50 challenges
Apply Yourself (Bronze)	Complete 10 challenges.
Blood. Sweat. Fear. (Gold)	Complete 90 challenges.
Contender (Silver)	Win 5 ranked matches.
Diversity (Bronze)	Attain Level 5 with all fighters.
Domination (Silver)	Complete 80 challenges.

CODES & CHEATS

Double or Nothing (Gold)	Win 10 Revenge matches.
Every Fighter has a Story (Gold)	Complete all fighter stories.
Future Champ (Gold)	Win 10 ranked matches.
Getting the Hang of This (Bronze)	Attain Level 5 with any fighter.
I Let You Win (Bronze)	Win 1 Final Fight match.
In the Zone (Bronze)	Complete 30 challenges
Keep'em Coming (Bronze)	Complete 20 challenges.
Last Laugh (Silver)	Win 5 Final Fight matches.
Legend (Gold)	Complete 100 challenges.
Master (Gold)	Attain Level 15 with any fighter.
Multitalented (Silver)	Attain Level 10 with all fighters.
Rampage (Silver)	Complete 70 challenges.
Relentless (Bronze)	Complete 40 challenges.
Rematch! (Bronze)	Win 1 Revenge match.
Rookie (Bronze)	Win 1 ranked match.
Run It Back (Silver)	Win 5 Revenge matches.
Sandbagger (Gold)	Win 10 Final Fight matches.
Supremacy (Platinum)	Obtain all Trophies.
Unstoppable (Silver)	Complete 60 challenges

SURF'S UP (PLAYSTATION 3)

PASSWORDS

PASSWORD	EFFECT
MYPRECIOUS	All Boards
FREEVISIT	All championship locations
GOINGDOWN	All leaf sliding locations
MULTIPASS	All multiplayer levels
NICEPLACE	Art gallery
ASTRAL	Astral board
TOPFASHION	Customizations for all characters
MONSOON	Monsoon board
IMTHEBEST	Plan as Tank Evans
TINYBUTSTRONG	Play as Arnold
SURPRISEGUEST	Play as Elliot
SLOWANDSTEADY	Play as Geek
KOBAYASHI	Play as Tatsuhi Kobayashi
THELEGEND	Play as Zeke Topanga
TINYSHOCKWAVE	Tine shockwave board
WATCHAMOVIE	Video Gallery

SURF'S UP (WII)

PASSWORDS

PASSWORD	EFFECT
NICEPLACE	Unlocks all art galleries
MYPRECIOUS	Unlocks all boards
GOINGDOWN	Unlocks all leaf-sliding locations
MULTIPASS	Unlocks all multiplayer levels
FREEVISIT	Unlocks all the locales
WATCHAMOVIE	Unlocks all video Galleries
TINYBUTSTRONG	Unlocks Arnold

ASTRAL	Unlocks Astral's board
DONTFALL	Unlocks bonus missions
TOPFASHION	Unlocks character customization
SURPRISEGUEST	Unlocks Elliot
SLOWANDSTEADY	Unlocks Geek
MONSOON	Unlocks Monsoon Board
IMTHEBEST	Unlocks Tank Evans
KOBAYASHI	Unlocks Tatsuhi Kobayashi
TINYSHOCKWAVE	Unlocks Tiny Shockwave board
THELEGEND	Unlocks Zeke Topanga

UNLOCKABLES

UNLOCKABLE	HOW TO UNLOCK
Arnold	Obtain 30,000 points in Shiverpool 2
Big Z	Obtain 100,000 points in Legendary Wave
Elliot	Obtain 40,000 points in Pen Gu North 3
Geek	Obtain 60,000 points in Pen Gu South 4
Tank	Obtain 40,000 points in the Boneyards
Tatsuhi	Obtain 15,000 points in Pen Gu South 2

SWORD OF VERMILION (WII)

UNLOCKABLES

UNLOCKABLE	HOW TO UNLOCK
Quick Cash	In Keltwick, when Bearwulf gives you the dungeon key to get to Malaga, sell it. It's worth 1,000 kims and Bearwulf has an unlimited number of them. Just go back, talk to him, and he'll say "Did you lose the key? I have another one." He'll give it to you, and you can repeat the process as much as you want.
Test Menu	Any time during the game, hold Ⓐ+Ⓑ+Ⓒ and press START on controller 2. A test menu appears with Input, Sound, and C.R.T. tests. And when you exit, it sends you back to the SEGA logo screen.

SYNDICATE (PLAYSTATION 3)

TROPHY

UNLOCKABLE	HOW TO UNLOCK
Platinum (Platinum)	Obtain all trophies.
Syndicated (Bronze)	Complete the game on any difficulty (given at the end of Datacore).
Business Is War (Gold)	Complete all chapters which track difficulty, on hard difficulty.
All Aboard (Bronze)	Complete chapters 2, 3, 4 and 5 on normal or hard difficulty.
Campaign: EuroCorp (Bronze)	Complete chapters 7 and 8 on normal or hard difficulty.
Campaign: La Ballena (Bronze)	Complete chapters 10 and 11 on normal or hard difficulty.
Campaign: Downzone (Bronze)	Complete chapters 12, 13, 14 and 15 on normal or hard difficulty.
Welcome to EuroCorp (Bronze)	Complete Wakeup Call.
See No Evil (Gold)	Defeat Kris without making him visible using EMP or DART Overlay, on normal or hard difficulty.
Revival Meeting (Bronze)	Defeat the final boss without allowing any agent to be revived, on normal or hard difficulty.

Missile Command (Bronze)	Breach an entire barrage of five missiles in the Ramon boss fight, on normal or hard difficulty.
Top Marks (Bronze)	Achieve a perfect result in all the Tutorial challenges.
Golden Handshake (Bronze)	Achieve CEO ranking on any level.
Little Black Box (Bronze)	Find all business cards (unlock all the business card infobank entries).
Wetware Integrity Policy (Bronze)	Don't kill any EuroCorp civilians with the minigun in chapter 8.
Gaggle of Guidance (Bronze)	Use the Swarm's multi-target lock-on firing mode to kill 3 UAV drones with one volley.
Augmented Reality (Bronze)	Kill 3 specters in chapter 14 without using EMP effects on them, on normal or hard difficulty.
Cover Lover (Bronze)	Make it past the conveyor belt without taking any damage from the turret.
Make Them Watch (Gold)	Kill Agent Crane before you kill his two sidekicks, on normal or hard difficulty.
Ambassador of Peace (Bronze)	Kill enemy soldiers of two different syndicates fast enough to receive a rampage energy bonus.
Mastermind (Bronze)	Unlock the Datacore in the minimum number of breaches.
Linked In (Bronze)	Obtain a health bonus from network connect links from your upgrade choices (single player only).
With Friends Like These (Bronze)	Kill an enemy from the explosion of a reactive armor unit.
Deny Everything (Bronze)	Find all propaganda tags (unlock all propaganda tag infobank entries).
Every Bullet Counts (Bronze)	Defeat Tatsuo without restocking your ammunition from the UAVs, on normal or hard difficulty.
Shocking (Bronze)	Kill 3 or more enemies from the electricity discharge of a dying electro armor unit.
Greed is Good (Bronze)	Achieve CEO ranking on all combat levels on hard difficulty.
Shield Breaker (Bronze)	Successfully sprint tackle 25 riot shield units.
Initiation Complete (Bronze)	Complete all Co-Op maps on any difficulty.
High Value Asset (Bronze)	Complete all Co-Op maps on expert difficulty.
Initial Public Offering (Bronze)	Be a member of a Syndicate consisting of at least 4 people.
Hostile Takeover (Bronze)	Defeat an enemy agent squad.
Mace Ace (Bronze)	Save a team member that is stunned by an electron mace.
Super Soldier (Bronze)	Complete a mission without going down.
Highly Adaptable (Bronze)	Kill 4 enemies in 4 different ways within 1 minute.
Field Surgeon (Bronze)	Heal 3 team members for at least 50% of their health within 1 minute.
Oh no you don't! (Bronze)	Complete 10 Contracts against members of your syndicate.
High Flyer (Bronze)	Score a 2,000 points combo.
Employee of the Month (Bronze)	Complete a mission after earning a team savior score.

In The Name of Science (Bronze)	Finish your first research.
Application Manager (Bronze)	Do 10,000 points of damage to enemies and heal or block 10,000 points of damage on team members using applications.
Middle Management (Bronze)	50% completion (level, research and challenges).
CEO (Gold)	100% completion (level, research and challenges).
The Professional (Bronze)	Kill 50 enemies with all the weapons in the game.
Hurt Locker (Bronze)	Breach 873 grenades.
Warpath (Bronze)	Get the rampage bonus up to 5 sequential kills.
Make It Snappy (Bronze)	Kill 50 enemies with melee executions.
Nowhere To Hide (Bronze)	Use a penetration weapon to kill 500 enemies through cover, while in DART Overlay.
Half-Millionaire (Bronze)	Collect 500,000 energy.
Hacker (Bronze)	Use breach abilities 300 times.
Rampageous (Bronze)	Do 250 rampage kills/kill streaks.

SYNDICATE (XBOX 360)

ACHIEVEMENT

UNLOCKABLE	HOW TO UNLOCK
Syndicated (20)	Complete the game on any difficulty (given at the end of Datacore).
Business Is War (50)	Complete all chapters which track difficulty, on hard difficulty.
All Aboard (20)	Complete chapters 2, 3, 4 and 5 on normal or hard difficulty.
Campaign: EuroCorp (20)	Complete chapters 7 and 8 on normal or hard difficulty.
Campaign: La Ballena (20)	Complete chapters 10 and 11 on normal or hard difficulty.
Campaign: Downzone (20)	Complete chapters 12, 13, 14 and 15 on normal or hard difficulty.
Welcome to EuroCorp (5)	Complete Wakeup Call.
See No Evil (30)	Defeat Kris without making him visible using EMP or DART Overlay, on normal or hard difficulty.
Revival Meeting (30)	Defeat the final boss without allowing any agent to be revived, on normal or hard difficulty.
Missile Command (30)	Breach an entire barrage of five missiles in the Ramon boss fight, on normal or hard difficulty.
Top Marks (15)	Achieve a perfect result in all the Tutorial challenges.
Golden Handshake (5)	Achieve CEO ranking on any level.
Little Black Box (30)	Find all business cards (unlock all the business card infobank entries).
Wetware Integrity Policy (20)	Don't kill any EuroCorp civilians with the minigun in chapter 8.
Gaggle of Guidance (5)	Use the Swarm's multi-target lock-on firing mode to kill 3 UAV drones with one volley.
Augmented Reality (15)	Kill 3 specters in chapter 14 without using EMP effects on them, on normal or hard difficulty.
Cover Lover (10)	Make it past the conveyor belt without taking any damage from the turret.

NEW!

A
B
C
D
E
F
G
H
I
J
K
L
M
N
O
P
Q
R
S
T
U
V
W
X
Y
Z

Make Them Watch (30)	Kill Agent Crane before you kill his two sidekicks, on normal or hard difficulty.
Ambassador of Peace (15)	Kill enemy soldiers of two different syndicates fast enough to receive a rampage energy bonus.
Mastermind (5)	Unlock the Datacore in the minimum number of breaches.
Linked In (5)	Obtain a health bonus from network connect links from your upgrade choices (single player only).
With Friends Like These (15)	Kill an enemy from the explosion of a reactive armor unit.
Deny Everything (30)	Find all propaganda tags (unlock all propaganda tag infobank entries).
Every Bullet Counts (30)	Defeat Tatsuo without restocking your ammunition from the UAVs, on normal or hard difficulty.
Shocking (10)	Kill 3 or more enemies from the electricity discharge of a dying electro armor unit.
Greed is Good (35)	Achieve CEO ranking on all combat levels on hard difficulty.
Shield Breaker (10)	Successfully sprint tackle 25 riot shield units.
Initiation Complete (10)	Complete all Co-Op maps on any difficulty.
High Value Asset (25)	Complete all Co-Op maps on expert difficulty.
Initial Public Offering (10)	Be a member of a Syndicate consisting of at least 4 people.
Hostile Takeover (10)	Defeat an enemy agent squad.
Mace Ace (5)	Save a team member that is stunned by an electron mace.
Super Soldier (10)	Complete a mission without going down.
Highly Adaptable (10)	Kill 4 enemies in 4 different ways within 1 minute.
Field Surgeon (10)	Heal 3 team members for at least 50% of their health within 1 minute.
Oh no you don't! (10)	Complete 10 Contracts against members of your syndicate.
High Flyer (15)	Score a 2,000 points combo.
Employee of the Month (10)	Complete a mission after earning a team savior score.
In The Name of Science (5)	Finish your first research.
Application Manager (20)	Do 10,000 points of damage to enemies and heal or block 10,000 points of damage on team members using applications.
Middle Management (50)	50% completion (level, research and challenges).
CEO (100)	100% completion (level, research and challenges).
The Professional (20)	Kill 50 enemies with all the weapons in the game.
Hurt Locker (30)	Breach 873 grenades.
Warpath (5)	Get the rampage bonus up to 5 sequential kills.
Make It Snappy (10)	Kill 50 enemies with melee executions.
Nowhere To Hide (30)	Use a penetration weapon to kill 500 enemies through cover, while in DART Overlay.
Half-Millionaire (30)	Collect 500,000 energy.
Hacker (30)	Use breach abilities 300 times.
Rampageous (15)	Do 250 rampage kills/kill streaks.

TALES OF GRACES F (PLAYSTATION 3)

TROPHY

UNLOCKABLE	HOW TO UNLOCK
A Gentlemanly Triumph (Silver)	Defeated a true Gentleman. Good show!
A Pact Fulfilled (Gold)	Completed Chapter 8.
A Throne Reclaimed (Bronze)	Completed Chapter 3.
Appellatrix (50 titles) (Bronze)	Acquired 50 different titles for Pascal.
Bryce in 60 Seconds (Bronze)	Defeated that jerk with the claw in a minute or less.
Captain Ephinea (100 titles) (Bronze)	Acquired 100 different titles for Malik.
Captain First Class (50 titles) (Bronze)	Acquired 50 different titles for Malik.
Childhood's End (Bronze)	Completed Chapter 1.
Dispaters in 60 Seconds (Bronze)	Defeated the monsters Richard sicced on you in a minute or less.
Emboldened (50 titles) (Bronze)	Acquired 50 different titles for Hubert.
Empowered (100 titles) (Bronze)	Acquired 100 different titles for Hubert.
Entitled (20 titles) (Bronze)	Acquired 20 different titles for Hubert.
Epithetologist (100 titles) (Bronze)	Acquired 100 different titles for Pascal.
First Flower (20 Titles) (Bronze)	Acquired 20 different titles for Sophie.
Flower Power (100 Titles) (Bronze)	Acquired 100 different titles for Sophie.
Fodra Queen in 60 Seconds (Silver)	Defeated the Fodra Queen in a minute or less.
Full Flower (50 Titles) (Bronze)	Acquired 50 different titles for Sophie.
Gagonged! (Silver)	Defeated the Rockgagong.
Game Clear: Chaos (Bronze)	Completed the game on the Chaos difficulty setting.
Game Clear: Evil (Bronze)	Completed the game on the Evil difficulty setting.
Game Clear: Hard (Bronze)	Completed the game on the Hard difficulty setting.
Game Clear: Moderate (Bronze)	Completed the game on the Moderate difficulty setting.
Kurt in 60 Seconds (Bronze)	Ended your fateful battle with Kurt in a minute or less.
Lambda Angelus in 60 Seconds (Gold)	Defeated Lambda in the final battle in a minute or less.
Lambda in 60 Seconds (Silver)	Defeated the materialized Lambda in a minute or less.
Lineage & Legacies (Silver)	Completed Chapter 9. Next up: the Zhonecage! The what? Look to the skits for a hint!
Lionhearted (100 titles) (Bronze)	Acquired 100 different titles for Cheria.
Mixer Maxed (Silver)	Maxed out your Eleth Mixer by boosting its eleth capacity to 9999.

One with Oblivion (Silver)	Defeated Lambda Theos. Impressive!
Openhearted (20 titles) (Bronze)	Acquired 20 different titles for Cheria.
Polycarpus in 60 Seconds (Silver)	Defeated the guardian of the ruins in a minute or less.
Queen Slime in 60 Seconds (Bronze)	Defeated the ruler of all oozes in a minute or less.
Richard in 60 Seconds (Bronze)	Defeated the friend who betrayed you in a minute or less.
Richard the Radiant (20 Titles) (Bronze)	Acquired 20 different titles for Richard.
Richard the Redeemed (80 Titles) (Bronze)	Acquired 80 different titles for Richard.
Richard the Righteous (50 Titles) (Bronze)	Acquired 50 different titles for Richard.
Sobriquetian (20 titles) (Bronze)	Acquired 20 different titles for Pascal.
Terma-nated (Silver)	Defeated Solomus and the Terma Ten.
The Fallen Eden (Bronze)	Completed Chapter 7.
The Infiltration of Fendel (Bronze)	Completed Chapter 5.
The Lord of Lhant (Bronze)	Completed Chapter 2.
The Other Side of the Sky (Bronze)	Completed Chapter 6.
The Sands of Strahta (Bronze)	Completed Chapter 4.
Title Fighter (20 Titles) (Bronze)	Acquired 20 different titles for Asbel.
Title Holder (50 Titles) (Bronze)	Acquired 50 different titles for Asbel.
Title Master (100 Titles) (Bronze)	Acquired 100 different titles for Asbel.
Training Captain (20 titles) (Bronze)	Acquired 20 different titles for Malik.
True Grace (Platinum)	Acquired all trophies. Amazing!
Who Were Those Guys, Again? (Silver)	Defeated Veigue, Reala, and Amber.
Wholehearted (50 titles) (Bronze)	Acquired 50 different titles for Cheria.

TALES OF THE ABYSS (3DS)

UNLOCKABLE

UNLOCKABLE	HOW TO UNLOCK
Game Record	Available at the title screen after beating the game
Grade Shop	Save a clear file after beating the game, and you will be able to start your new game+ file with the grade shop with your cleared file.
Sound Test	Available at the title screen after beating the game
Unknown Mode	Beat the game once
Very Hard Mode	Beat the game once
The Abyss Replica Facility	This is a secret dungeon that can only be unlocked while playing a second playthrough. To gain access, you need to have saved Shiba and completed the Ortion Cavern(East) side quest. Go to Sheridan and talk to the two men in the northwest part of town, then Shiba, and you will at last be taken to the dungeon.
Secret Shop(Brillante)	Complete the Collector's Book

TATSUNOKO VS. CAPCOM: ULTIMATE ALL STARS (WII)

UNLOCKABLES

UNLOCKABLE	HOW TO UNLOCK
Hold the partner button during the character introduction sequence prior to the start of a match to start the match with your second character.	
Frank West	Get three different Capcom characters' Arcade endings.
Joe the Condor	Get six different Tatsunoko characters' Arcade endings.

Tekkaman Blade	Get three different Tatsunoko characters' Arcade endings.
Yatterman-2	Get Frank West, Zero, Tekkaman Blade, and Joe the Condor's Arcade endings.
Zero	Get six different Capcom characters' Arcade endings.
Special Illustration #2	Beat Survival Mode and buy it from shop.
Fourth Color	Clear stage 8 (final boss) of Arcade Mode.
Third Color	Clear stage 4 (giant opponent) of Arcade Mode.
Opening Movie 2	Unlock Yatterman-2
Secret Movie	Beat the game with Frank West, Zero, Tekkaman Blade, Joe the Condor, and Yatterman-2.

TEENAGE MUTANT NINJA TURTLES (WII)

UNLOCKABLES

UNLOCKABLE	HOW TO UNLOCK
Restore Power	Find a doorway that has a pizza slice or full pizza right at the beginning. Enter, grab the pizza, and exit. The pizza regenerates when you reenter. Use this to restore power to all your turtles.
Remove Crushers in Level 3	Hop in the Party Wagon. Whenever you see a pesky Crusher, press SELECT. You exit the car, and the Crusher vanishes.
Share Boomerangs	When you get the boomerangs, throw up to 3 of them in the air, then switch turtles, and have the new turtle catch them. The new turtle can use those boomerangs without having picked up a boomerang icon.

TEENAGE MUTANT NINJA TURTLES (PSP)

CODES
Enter this in the Mission Briefing screens.

CODE	EFFECT
♣, ♣, ♣, ♣, ♣, ♣, ♣, ♣, ×	Unlocks a Fantasy Costume

TEENAGE MUTANT NINJA TURTLES 2: THE ARCADE GAME (WII)

UNLOCKABLES

UNLOCKABLE	HOW TO UNLOCK
Extra Lives and Stage Select	At the title screen, press B, A, B, A, ⬆, ⬆, B, A, ⬆, ⬆, B, A, START
Extra Lives Without Stage Select	On the title screen, press ⬆, ⬆, ⬆, ⬆, ⬆, ⬆, ⬆, ⬆, ⬆, ⬆, B, A, START
Stage Select	On the title screen, press ⬆, ⬆, ⬆, ⬆, ⬆, ⬆, ⬆, ⬆, ⬆, ⬆, ⬆, B, A, START
Easier Battle with Shredder	During the final battle against Shredder, Shredder splits up into two forms. They're identical in appearance, but only one is real and the other is fake. However, both forms use the lightning attack that instantly kills you by turning you into a normal turtle. However, when either form is weakened to near death, his helmet flies off. As you're beating up on the two forms of Shredder, one of them loses his helmet very quickly. When this happens, leave him alone. This Shredder is the fake, and he cannot use the lightning attack without his helmet on. Only the real Shredder can use the attack, but because it's only him using it, you can avoid it and slowly beat him down with ease. For the rest of the fight, ignore the fake. If you kill him, the real Shredder releases another fake.

TEST DRIVE: FERRARI RACING LEGENDS (PLAYSTATION 3)

TROPHY

UNLOCKABLE	HOW TO UNLOCK
40th Anniversary (Bronze)	Complete this Silver Era Mission.

430 Redline (Bronze)	Complete this Modern Era Mission.
50th Anniversary (Bronze)	Complete this Modern Era Mission.
512 Pro Championship (Bronze)	Complete this Silver Era Mission.
A Good Foundation (Bronze)	Complete this Golden Era Mission.
All Time Great (Gold)	Complete all the Eras.
Celebration Tour (Bronze)	Complete this Golden Era Mission.
Challenge Stradale (Bronze)	Complete this Modern Era Mission.
Champ's Day 68 (Bronze)	Complete this Golden Era Mission.
Champs Day 84 (Bronze)	Complete this Silver Era Mission.
Competizione (Bronze)	Complete this Silver Era Mission.
Dino Challenge (Bronze)	Complete this Golden Era Mission.
Driver For Hire (Bronze)	Complete this Silver Era Mission.
Drivers Training 101 (Bronze)	Complete this Golden Era Mission.
F355 Pro-Trofeo (Bronze)	Complete this Modern Era Mission.
F50 GT Supercup (Bronze)	Complete this Modern Era Mission.
Foot in the door (Bronze)	Complete this Golden Era Mission.
Freelance Driver, Chapter 1 (Bronze)	Complete this Modern Era Mission.
Freelance Driver, Chapter 2 (Bronze)	Complete this Modern Era Mission.
Freelance Driver, Chapter 3 (Bronze)	Complete this Modern Era Mission.
FXX Invitationals (Bronze)	Complete this Modern Era Mission.
Game Complete (Platinum)	All Trophies unlocked
GTO Pro Challenge (Bronze)	Complete this Silver Era Mission.
Mid Life Master (Silver)	Complete the Silver Era.
Modern Ferrari World (Bronze)	Complete this Modern Era Mission.
Modern Miracle (Silver)	Complete the Modern Era.
Old Timer (Silver)	Complete the Golden Era.
Prototype (Bronze)	Complete this Modern Era Mission.
Prototype Sports Cup (Bronze)	Complete this Modern Era Mission.
Quattrovalvole Cup (Bronze)	Complete this Silver Era Mission.
Ranked Ace (Gold)	Reach the rank of Ace.
Ranked Amateur (Bronze)	Reach the rank of Amateur.
Ranked Champ (Gold)	Reach the rank of Champ.
Ranked Legend (Gold)	Reach the rank of Legend.
Ranked Pro (Silver)	Reach the rank of Pro.
Ranked Semi-Pro (Silver)	Reach the rank of Semi-Pro.
Scuderia Spec (Bronze)	Complete this Modern Era Mission.
Season 74 (Bronze)	Complete this Silver Era Mission.
Season 79 (Bronze)	Complete this Silver Era Mission.
Season 90 (Bronze)	Complete this Silver Era Mission.
Seasonal Changes (Bronze)	Complete this Golden Era Mission.
The 250 Challenge (Bronze)	Complete this Golden Era Mission.
The Big League (Bronze)	Complete this Golden Era Mission.
The Enzo Tribute (Bronze)	Complete this Modern Era Mission.
The Nordschleife (Bronze)	Complete this Modern Era Mission.
The Rookies (Bronze)	Complete this Golden Era Mission.

TEST DRIVE: FERRARI RACING LEGENDS (XBOX 360)

ACHIEVEMENT

UNLOCKABLE	HOW TO UNLOCK
40th Anniversary (10)	Complete this Silver Era Mission.
430 Redline (10)	Complete this Modern Era Mission.
50th Anniversary (10)	Complete this Modern Era Mission.
512 Pro Championship (10)	Complete this Silver Era Mission.
A Good Foundation (10)	Complete this Golden Era Mission.
All Time Great (100)	Complete all the Eras.
Celebration Tour (10)	Complete this Golden Era Mission.
Challenge Stradale (10)	Complete this Modern Era Mission.
Champ's Day 68 (10)	Complete this Golden Era Mission.
Champ's Day 84 (10)	Complete this Silver Era Mission.
Competizione (10)	Complete this Silver Era Mission.
Dino Challenge (10)	Complete this Golden Era Missipn.
Driver For Hire (10)	Complete this Silver Era Mission.
Drivers Training 101 (10)	Complete this Golden Era Mission.
F355 Pro-Trofeo (10)	Complete this Modern Era Mission.
F50 GT Supercup (10)	Complete this Modern Era Mission.
Foot In The Door (10)	Complete this Golden Era Mission.
Freelance Driver, Chapter 1 (10)	Complete this Modern Era Mission.
Freelance Driver, Chapter 2 (10)	Complete this Modern Era Mission.
Freelance Driver, Chapter 3 (10)	Complete this Modern Era Mission.
XX Invitationals (10)	Complete this Modern Era Mission.
GTO Pro Challenge (10)	Complete this Silver Era Mission.
Mid Life Master (60)	Complete the Silver Era.
Modern Ferrari World (10)	Complete this Modern Era Mission.
Modern Miracle (60)	Complete the Modern Era.
Old Timer (60)	Complete the Golden Era.
Prototype (10)	Complete this Modern Era Mission.
Prototype Sports Cup (10)	Complete this Modern Era Mission.
Quattrovalvole Cup (10)	Complete this Silver Era Mission.
Ranked Ace (80)	Reach the rank of Ace.
Ranked Amateur (20)	Reach the rank of Amateur.
Ranked Champ (70)	Reach the rank of Champ.
Ranked Legend (100)	Reach the rank of Legend.
Ranked Pro (60)	Reach the rank of Pro.
Ranked Semi-Pro (40)	Reach the rank of Semi-Pro
Scuderia Spec (10)	Complete this Modern Era Mission.
Season 74 (10)	Complete this Silver Era Mission.
Season 79 (10)	Complete this Silver Era Mission.
Season 90 (10)	Complete this Silver Era Mission.
Seasonal Changes (10)	Complete this Golden Era Mission.
The 250 Challenge (10)	Complete this Golden Era Mission.
The Big League (10)	Complete this Golden Era Missipn.
The Enzo Tribute (10)	Complete this Modern Era Mission.
The Nordschleife (10)	Complete this Modern Era Mission.
The Rookies (10)	Complete this Golden Era Mission.

TEKKEN 6 (XBOX 360)

UNLOCKABLES

UNLOCKABLE	HOW TO UNLOCK
Arena	Clear Southern Woodlands
Kigan Island stage	Go to Abyss Gate on Hard difficulty and defeat a man with straw hat and grab his loot. Then exit to world map.
Medium and Hard difficulty	Clear Azazel's Temple, Central Corridor.
Mishima Industries, Biotech Research Station Ruins stage	Go right at the first junction in Seahorse Grand Hotel, defeat the kangeroo and clear the stage.
Nightmare Train stage	Clear Azazel's Temple, Central Corridor.
Play as Anna in Arena	Defeat her in G Corporation, Millennium Tower.
Play as Armour King in Arena	Defeat him in Lost Cemetery.
Play as Asuka in Arena	Defeat her in Kazama-Style Traditional Martial Arts Dojo.
Play as Baek in Arena	Defeat him in West Coast Canal Industrial Complex.
Play as Bob in Arena	Defeat him in Central District, 11th Avenue.
Play as Bruce in Arena	Defeat him in G Security Service, Operations Headquarters.
Play as Bryan in Arena	Defeat him in Southern Woodlands.
Play as Christie in Arena	Defeat her in Seahorse Grand Hotel.
Play as Devil Jin	Defeat him in Nightmare Train.
Play as Dragunov in Arena	Defeat him in container Terminal 7.
Play as Eddy in Arena	Defeat him in Tekken Force 4th Special Forces Operation Group Compound.
Play as Feng in Arena	Defeat him in Deserted Temple.
Play as Ganryu in Arena	Defeat him in Aranami Stable.
Play as Hwoarang in Arena	Defeat him in Industrial Highway 357.
Play as in Heihachi Arena	Defeat him in Mshima Estate.
Play as Jack-6 in Arena	Defeat him in Container Terminal 3.
Play as Jin	Defeat him in Azazel's Temple, Central Corridor.
Play as Julia in Arena	Defeat all enemies in G Science and Technology, Research Building 3.
Play as Kazuya in Arena	Defeat him in G Corporation, Millennium Tower Heliport.
Play as King in Arena	Defeat him with Marduk in Mixed Martial Arts Gym "Wild Kingdom."
Play as Kuma or Panda in Arena	Defeat Kuma in North Nature Park.
Play as Law in Arena	Defeat him in West District, Chinatown.
Play as Lee in Arena	Defeat him in Violet Systems.
Play as Lei in Arena	Defeat all enemies in ICPO Branch Office.
Play as Leo in Arena	Defeat it in 16th Archaeological Expedition's Excavation Site.
Play as Lili in Arena	Defeat her in Queen's Harbour.
Play as Marduk in Arena	Defeat him with King in Mixed Martial Arts Gym "Wild Kingdom."
Play as Miguel in Arena	Defeat him in South Bay Warehouse Area.
Play as Mokujin	Defeat it in Subterranean Pavilion.
Play as Nina in Arena	Defeat her in Mishima Zaibatsu, Central Subway Line.
Play as Paul in Arena	Defeat him in West District, 13th Avenue.

Play as Raven in Arena	Defeat him in Secret Underground Passage.
Play as Roger Jr. in Arena	Defeat it in Mishima Industries, Biotech Research Station Ruins.
Play as Steve in Arena	Defeat him in Abyss Gate.
Play as Wang in Arena	Defeat him in Fujian Tulou.
Play as Xiaoyu in Arena	Defeat her in Mishima Polytechnic.
Play as Yoshimitsu	Defeat him in Kigan Island.
Play as Zafina	Defeat all enemies in Mystic's Village.
Subterranean Pavilion stage	Clear 16th Archaeological Expedition's Excavation Site on Hard difficulty.

WIN POSE

Just before the win sequence plays at the end of a match, hold left punch, right punch, left kick, or right kick to select your win pose. Some characters may have more win poses than others.

While the game is paused, enter code on the second controller.

UNLOCKABLE	CODE
View Score Status	■, ■, ⇩, ⇩, ⇧, ⇧

THE 3RD BIRTHDAY (PSP)

UNLOCKABLE

Complete the tasks to unlock the following.

UNLOCKABLE	HOW TO UNLOCK
Countless Ammo	Beat the game ten times in any mode
Free Cross Fire	Beat the game in any mode
High Regen	Beat the game in any mode
Extra Ending Scene after Credits	Clear the game twice
Deadly Mode	Beat the game in Hard Mode
Genocide Mode	Beat the game in Deadly Mode
Music files mode.	Successfully complete the game twice in any
Blaze Edge	Complete the game once in any mode and have at least 7 Stamps on Square-Enix Member Site
M240B	Beat the game twice in Hard Mode
M249	Beat the game in any mode
Mk.46 Mod0	Beat the game in Normal Mode
Pile Bunker	Unlock and purchase all weapons and weapon parts in the game.
Apron Dress Costume	Complete the game on Easy Mode.
Business Suit Costume	Complete the game once on any mode. The Costume is found in the CTI Building in the left hand locker room.
China Dress Costume	Complete the game on Normal Mode.
Knight Armor Costume	Complete the game on Deadly Mode.
Lightning Custom Costume	Complete the game once on any mode and have at least 7 Stamp on Square-Enix Member Site
OD Suit Costume	Complete the game once on any Mode and have at least 1 Stamp on Square-Enix Member Site.
Santa Soldier Costume	Complete the game once on any Mode. You'll find it in Maeda's Base, down the stairs to the lockers, check the left one for the Costume.
Swim Wear Costume	Complete the game on Hard Mode.
Titanium Bunny Costume	Complete the game on Genocide Mode.

THEATRHYTHM FINAL FANTASY (3DS)

UNLOCKABLE

UNLOCKABLE	HOW TO UNLOCK
Aerith (FFVII)	Gather 8 Pink Crystal Fragments
Ashe (FFXII)	Gather 8 Crimson Crystal Fragments
Cid (FFIII)	Gather 8 Yellow Crystal Fragments
Cosmos (Dissidia)	Gather 8 Rainbow Crystal Fragments
Faris (FFV)	Gather 8 Red Crystal Fragments
Kain (FFIV)	Gather 8 Navy Blue Crystal Fragments
Locke (FFVI)	Gather 8 Blue Crystal Fragments
Minwu (FFII)	Gather 8 Silver Crystal Fragments
Princess Sarah (FFI)	Gather 8 Gold Crystal Fragments
Prish (FFXI)	Gather 8 Purple Crystal Fragments
Rydia (FFIV)	Gather 8 Emerald Crystal Fragments
Seifer (FFVIII)	Gather 8 Grey Crystal Fragments
Sephiroth (FFVII)	Gather 8 Black Crystal Fragments
Snow (FFXIII)	Gather 8 White Crystal Fragments
Vivi (FFIX)	Gather 8 Orange Crystal Fragments
Yuuna (FFX)	Gather 8 Sapphire Crystal Fragments

PASSWORD

UNLOCKABLE	HOW TO UNLOCK
01 Warrior of Light	Warrior of Light
01 Warrior of Light	Class Change
02 Firion	Wild Rose
04 Cecil	Dark Knight
06 Terra	Magitek Armor
06 Terra	Flowered tights
07 Cloud	Lifestream
08 Squall	Lionheart
09 Zidane	Zidane Tribal
09 Zidane	Tantalus
09 Zidane	Beloved Dagger
10 Tidus	Jecht Shot
13 Lightning	Serah's sister
14 Princess Sarah	Cornelia
15 Minwu	White Mage
16 Cid	The Enterprise
18 Faris	Princess of Tycoon
20 Aerith	Cetra
21 Seifer	Disciplinary Committee
22 Vivi	Master Vivi
22 Vivi	Black Mage
23 Yuna	Y.R.P.
23 Yuna	Eternal Calm
24 Prishe	Feed me
25 Ashe	Amalia?
26 Snow	Do-rag
26 Snow	Sis!

27 Kain	Cecil's best friend
27 Kain	Son of Richard
28 Sephiroth	Masamune
28 Sephiroth	One-winged angel
28 Sephiroth	Black Materia
29 Cosmos	Goddess of Harmony
30 Chocobo	Gysahl Greens
30 Chocobo	Fat Chocobo
31 Moogle	Red pompom
31 Moogle	Bat wings
32 Shiva	Ice Queen
32 Shiva	Diamond Dust
32 Shiva	Heavenly Strike
33 Ramuh	Judgment Bolt
34 Ifrit	Hellfire
35 Odin	Zantetsuken
36 Bahamut	Mega Flare
36 Bahamut	Rat tail
37 Goblin	Goblin Punch
40 Malboro	Bad Breath
42 Black Knight	Yoichi Bow
42 Black Knight	Sun Blade
44 Hein	Barrier Shift
45 Ahriman	Good at magic
46 Xande	Libra!
50 Barbariccia	Maelstrom
53 Tonberry	Everyone's Grudge
53 Tonberry	Knife and lantern
54 Gilgamesh	Big Bridge
54 Gilgamesh	Bartz's rival
55 Enikdu	White Wind
56 Omega	Wave Cannon
57 Shinryu	Ragnarok
57 Shinryu	Tidal Wave
58 Cactaur	1000 Needles
58 Cactaur	10000 Needles
58 Cactaur	Gigantuar
59 Hill Gigas	Magnitude 8
60 Ultros	Mr. Typhon
62 Kefka	I just can't believe it!
62 Kefka	Heartless Angel
63 Ultima Weapon	Shadow Flare
64 Jenova Synthesis	Countdown to Ultima
64 Jenova Synthesis	Mother
65 Safer Sephiroth	Pale Horse
65 Safer Sephiroth	Super Nova
66 Esthar Soldier	Shotgun
66 Esthar Soldier	Terminator

NEW!
A
B
C
D
E
F
G
H
I
J
K
L
M
N
O
P
Q
R
S
T
U
V
W
X
Y
Z

67 Gesper	Degenerator
68 Pupu	Elixir please!
68 Pupu	UFO?
69 Black Waltz No. 3	Triple time
71 Anima	Pain
74 Shadow Lord	Implosion
74 Shadow Lord	Xarcabard
74 Shadow Lord	The Crystal War
76 Mandragoras	Sochen Cave Palace
77 Judge	Gabranth
77 Judge	Judge Magister
78 Psicom Enforcer	The Hanging Edge
79 Manasvin Warmech	Targeting
79 Manasvin Warmech	Crystal Rain
80 Adamantoise	Trapezohedron
80 Adamantoise	Earth Shaker
80 Adamantoise	Platinum Ingot
81 Chaos	God of Discord
81 Chaos	Demonsdance

UNLOCKABLE

UNLOCKABLE	HOW TO UNLOCK
Hard Mode Series Setlists	clear that Series' three songs in the Challenge section on hard difficulty

THRILLVILLE (PSP)

CODES

Enter these while in a park. You hear a chime if it worked.

UNLOCKABLE	HOW TO UNLOCK
Add $50,000	■, ●, ▲, ■, ●, ▲, ✕
Mission Complete	■, ●, ▲, ■, ●, ▲, ●
Unlock All Parks	■, ●, ▲, ■, ●, ▲, ■
Unlock All Rides in Park	■, ●, ▲, ■, ●, ▲, ▲

TIGER WOODS PGA TOUR 12: THE MASTERS (XBOX 360)

ACHIEVEMENT

UNLOCKABLE	HOW TO UNLOCK
1 Is The Loneliest Number (10)	Be the #1 Ranked Golfer for 10 consecutive weeks.
2005 Masters Champion (25)	Win the 2005 Historic Masters Event (Tiger at the Masters)
A New Generation (25)	Break the top 10 in the EA SPORTS Golf Rankings
Ad Wizard (25)	Play in a Major with Callaway Golf® Level 4 Sponsorship equipped
Aspiring Amateur (10)	Complete the EA SPORTS™ AM TOUR
Bling my Tag (15)	Apply 3 pins to your Bag Tag
Born with Skillz (25)	Master 8 courses
Broken Record (40)	Hold down the #1 spot on the EA SPORTS Golf Rankings for more than 281 weeks
Caddie with a Master's Degree (50)	Master 16 Courses
Choke Artist (15)	Land within 1 yard of the flagstick using a choked approach shot from at least 50 yards out.
Commercial Icon (35)	Play in a Major with Nike Level 4 Sponsorship equipped

Course Master (10)	Master 1 course	
Drop and give me 15 (25)	Earn 15 pins	
Earned my Card! (20)	Complete Q-School	
Egg on the Dance Floor (10)	Sink a 30ft putt without boosting the green read	
FIR (5)	Land the ball on the Fairway after your tee shot. FIR = Fairway in Regulation	
First Time EVER! (35)	Win both the Par 3 and the Masters on the same week in the Road to the Masters mode.	
Flowering Crab Apple in 1! (10)	Hole in one on Hole 4 of Augusta (only one hole in one has ever been recorded on this hole)	
GamerNet Tourist (10)	Earn 2,500 Player Points in EA SPORTS™ GamerNet	
GIR (5)	Land the ball on the Green with at least 2 fewer strokes than par. GIR = Green in Regulation	
Give me the Goodies! (10)	Win a Sponsored Challenge Event in the Road to the Masters mode.	
Great Suggestion (15)	Sink a Hole in One using a Caddie Recommendation	
HAMMERhead Swag (65)	Equip a HAMMERhead Prototype Outfit	
History is Yours (15)	Compete in a Historic Masters Event (Tiger at the Masters)	
Hold my bag as I post my clip (5)	Post an EA SPORTS™ GamerNet Challenge	
I AM CADDIE! (15)	Accept and follow thru 25 Caddie Suggestions in an 18 hole round of golf	
I Got This (15)	From the Fairway, land within 1 yard of the flagstick from 100 yards out using a Custom shot.	
Masters Legend (75)	Win the Green Jacket for a Record 7 times in the Road to the Masters mode.	
Masters Master (15)	Master Augusta National & Augusta Par 3 (Gold Course Mastery)	
New Record Holder! (15)	Beat the course record of 63 at the Masters (In Road to the Masters)	
On the Radar (10)	Break the top 50 in the EA SPORTS Golf Rankings	
On top of the World (50)	Become #1 in the EA SPORTS Golf Rankings	
Online Participation (10)	Play a Live Tournament	
Pin Collector (50)	Earn All Pins	
Ping Pitchman (15)	Play in a Major with PING® Level 4 Sponsorship equipped	
Road to the Masters (35)	Win the Green Jacket in the Road to the Masters mode.	
Shark Attack! (65)	Equip a HAMMERhead Prototype Club	
Short But Sweet (15)	Beat the course record of 20 at Augusta Par 3	
Sponsorship is Calling (10)	Play in a Major with Cleveland Golf Level 4 Sponsorship equipped	
The Presidents Cup Champion (15)	Win The Presidents Cup	
Tiger Quickness (10)	Use the new Speed Play option in game	
Tournament Pro (10)	Complete an 18 hole round under par with Tournament Difficulty turned ON	
Training Wheels (10)	Win a training event in the Road to the Masters mode.	
We've Only Just Begun (15)	Compete in a Nationwide Tour event	
Who's your Caddie?! (5)	Complete the Prologue	
Winner! And Still... (25)	Defend your title in any Major	

NEW!

A B C D E F G H I J K L M N O P Q R S T U V W X Y Z

TIGER WOODS PGA TOUR 13 (PLAYSTATION 3)

TROPHY

UNLOCKABLE	HOW TO UNLOCK
Amateur Years (Bronze)	Complete the Amateur Years in Tiger Legacy Challenge
Can you give me a Boost? (Bronze)	Play an 18 hole round with Boost Pins equipped
Check out my Custom Settings (Bronze)	Complete an 18 hole round using a Custom Difficulty
Dig Deep (Silver)	Land within 1 yard of the flagstick from a bunker
Don't quit your day job (Bronze)	Win the Masters as an amateur
Early Years (Bronze)	Complete the Early Years in Tiger Legacy Challenge
From the Ladies Tees (Bronze)	Complete an 18 hole round using the Red Tees
Going Green with a Hybrid (Bronze)	Land on the green from over 175 yards away using a Hybrid
He's going the distance (Bronze)	Hit a drive over 400 yards
I Finally Belong! (Bronze)	Create or Join a Country Club in Game
I Need a Commitment (Bronze)	Earn a Four Day loyalty Bonus
I Own this Place (Silver)	Defend your title in any Major
Internal Conflict (Silver)	Compete with a teammate in a head-to-head match launched from the Clubhouse lobby
It's a Start (Bronze)	Master 1 course
It's all in the Hips (Bronze)	Sink a 40ft putt
Junior Years (Bronze)	Complete the Junior Years in Tiger Legacy Challenge
King of the Hill (Bronze)	Become #1 in the EA SPORTS Golf Rankings
Like a Boss (Gold)	Master 16 Courses
Like a Homing Pigeon (Bronze)	From the Fairway, land within 1 yard of the flagstick from 150 yards out
Like a Metronome (Bronze)	Complete 10 perfect Tempo Swings with TOUR Pro Difficulty or better
Live from your couch (Bronze)	Play in a Live Tournament
Members Only (Bronze)	Play in a Country Club Tournament
Never leave home without it (Bronze)	Earn PGA TOUR card
No Handouts Please (Bronze)	Actually get a hole in 1 in the 1982 First Hole in One event in Tiger Legacy Challenge
Now we're talking (Bronze)	Master 8 courses
One Small Step for Mankind (Bronze)	Win the Green Jacket in Career Mode
Play Date (Bronze)	Play a Four Player online match with all players using toddlers
Present Day (Silver)	Complete the Present Day in Tiger Legacy Challenge
Pro Gamer (Platinum)	Congratulations for unlocking all trophies in Tiger Woods PGA TOUR® 13!
Pro Years (Bronze)	Complete the Pro Years in Tiger Legacy Challenge
Putt from the rough (Bronze)	Make a putt from the rough
Rookie Years (Bronze)	Complete the Rookie Years in Tiger Legacy Challenge
Shouting at Amen Corner (Silver)	Complete Amen Corner (Augusta 11,12,13) with a birdie or better on each in a single round

Small Tiger, Big Bite (Bronze)	Complete an 18 hole online head-to-head match with toddler Tiger
So Much Easier than Putting (Silver)	Make a hole in one
That was GIRrrreat! (Bronze)	Complete an 18 hole round with a 100 percent GIR. GIR = Green in Regulation
The Future (Bronze)	Complete the Future in Tiger Legacy Challenge
Tiger Slam (Bronze)	Complete the Tiger Slam in Tiger Legacy Challenge
Tigers have FIR (Bronze)	Complete an 18 hole round with a 100 percent FIR. FIR = Fairway in Regulation
Toddler Years (Bronze)	Complete Toddler Years in Tiger Legacy Challenge
Top 10 Hits (Bronze)	Break the top 10 in EA SPORTS Golf Rankings
Top 50 Countdown (Bronze)	Break the top 50 in EA SPORTS Golf Rankings
Unstoppable! (Bronze)	Win the Green Jacket for a Record 7 times in Career Mode
When do we get paid? (Bronze)	Compete in an amateur championship

TIGER WOODS PGA TOUR 13 (XBOX 360)

ACHIEVEMENT

UNLOCKABLE	HOW TO UNLOCK
Amateur Years (15)	Complete the Amateur Years in Tiger Legacy Challenge
Can you give me a Boost? (15)	Play an 18 hole round with Boost Pins equipped
Check out my Custom Settings (15)	Complete an 18 hole round using a Custom Difficulty
Child's Play (15)	Complete an 18 hole round with toddler Ricky
Dig Deep (15)	Land within 1 yard of the flagstick from a bunker
Don't quit your day job (15)	Win the Masters as an amateur
Early Years (15)	Complete the Early Years in Tiger Legacy Challenge
From the Ladies Tees (15)	Complete an 18 hole round using the Red Tees
Going Green with a Hybrid (30)	Land on the green from over 175 yards away using a Hybrid
He's going the distance (30)	Hit a drive over 400 yards
I Finally Belong! (15)	Create or Join a Country Club in Game
I Need a Commitment (15)	Earn a Four Day loyalty Bonus
I Own this Place (25)	Defend your title in any Major
Internal Conflict (15)	Compete with a teammate in a head-to-head match launched from the Clubhouse lobby
It's a Start (15)	Master 1 Course
It's all in the Hips (15)	Sink a 40ft putt
Junior Years (15)	Complete the Junior Years in Tiger Legacy Challenge
King of the Hill (50)	Become #1 in the EA SPORTS Golf Rankings
Like a Boss (60)	Master 16 Courses
Like a Homing Pigeon (15)	From the Fairway, land within 1 yard of the flagstick from 150 yards out
Like a Metronome (15)	Complete 10 perfect Tempo Swings with TOUR Pro Difficulty or better

CODES & CHEATS

Live from your couch (25)	Play in a Live Tournament
Members Only (15)	Play in a Country Club Tournament
Never leave home without it (15)	Earn PGA TOUR card
No Handouts Please (10)	Actually get a hole in 1 in the 1982 First Hole in One event in Tiger Legacy Challenge
Now we're talking (30)	Master 8 Courses
One Small Step for Mankind (35)	Win the Green Jacket in Career Mode
Play Date (15)	Play a Four Player online match with all players using toddlers
Present Day (30)	Complete the Present Day in Tiger Legacy Challenge
Pro Years (20)	Complete the Pro Years in Tiger Legacy Challenge
Putt from the rough (15)	Make a putt from the rough
Rookie Years (15)	Complete the Rookie Years in Tiger Legacy Challenge
Shouting at Amen Corner (10)	Complete Amen Corner (Augusta 11,12,13) with a birdie or better on each in a single round.
Small Tiger, Big Bite (15)	Complete an 18 hole online head-to-head match with toddler Tiger
So Much Easier than Putting (30)	Make a hole in one
Swing and a miss (10)	Whiff the ball
That was Easy (30)	Beat the course record of 63 at the Masters (In Career Mode)
That was GIRrrreat! (15)	Complete an 18 hole round with a 100 percent GIR. GIR = Green in Regulation
The Future (30)	Complete the Future in Tiger Legacy Challenge
Tiger Slam (20)	Complete the Tiger Slam in Tiger Legacy Challenge
Tigers have FIR (30)	Complete an 18 hole round with a 100 percent FIR. FIR = Fairway in Regulation
Toddler Years (15)	Complete Toddler Years in Tiger Legacy Challenge
Top 10 Hits (30)	Break the top 10 in EA SPORTS Golf Rankings
Top 50 Countdown (15)	Break the top 50 in EA SPORTS Golf Rankings
Unstoppable! (75)	Win the Green Jacket for a Record 7 times in Career Mode
When do we get paid? (15)	Compete in an amateur championship

TMNT (XBOX 360)

CODES

At the main menu screen, hold ⬅ and enter the code, then release ⬅. You should hear a sound to confirm you entered the code right.

CODE	EFFECT
AABA	Unlocks challenge map 2
BYAX	Unlocks Don's big head goodie

TMNT (WII)

UNLOCKABLES

At the main menu, hold ⓩ on the Nunchuk and enter the following codes. Release ⓩ after each code to hear a confirmation sound.

UNLOCKABLE	CODE
Unlock Don's Big Head Goodie	①, Ⓐ, Ⓒ, ②
Unlock Challenge Map 2	Ⓐ, Ⓐ, Ⓐ, ①, Ⓐ

TOEJAM AND EARL (WII)

UNLOCKABLES

UNLOCKABLE	HOW TO UNLOCK
Free Presents	Sneak up on Santa Claus before he takes off and he gives you a few presents.
Level 0	On Level 1, on the bottom left side, a small hole leads to level 0, which has hula dancers in a tub and a lemonade man who gives you another life.
Present Island	At the top right of the map on level 1, there is a hidden island with a load of presents for the taking. You need rocket skates, an inner-tube, or icarus wings to get there.
Ultimate Cheat	Pause the game, then press the following button combinations: ✛+Ⓐ+Ⓑ+©, ✛+Ⓐ, ✛+Ⓑ, ✛+©. You hear a sound if you entered the code correctly. Unpause the game, and you have all but one of the ship pieces collected. The last piece will always be located on the next level.

TOEJAM AND EARL IN PANIC ON FUNKOTRON (WII)

PASSWORDS

PASSWORD	EFFECT
R-F411W9Q986	Level 3
PJ04EK-5WT82	Level 5
MW0WEE6JRVF7	Level 7
VANDNEHF9807L	Level 9
MWAAK!8MDT76	Level 11
F!!NEHNW0Q73	Level 15
T0EJAMTEARL!	View Credits

HIGH FUNK PASSWORDS

Enter these passwords at the password screen to go to your desired level with lots of Funk.

PASSWORD	EFFECT
RWJ21EW1R80X	Level 03 with 37 Funk
VJW6EK21-J07	Level 05 with 80 Funk
P0W09KAN-VQ	Level 07 with 95 Funk
VDJF7M2DyT6L	Level 09 with 99 Funk
VYJF73TH1PQQ	Level 11 with 99 Funk
DKYQHX4!EV!7	Level 13 with 89 Funk
J11L3R4C13H7	Level 15 with 49 Funk

TOM CLANCY'S ENDWAR (XBOX 360)

CODES

Under Community and Extras, press "Y" on Downloadable Content. Battalions can be used in Theater of War mode.

EFFECT	CODE
Unlock upgraded European Federation (EFEC) Battalion	EUCA20
Unlock upgraded Joint Strike Force (JSF) Battalion	JSFA35
Unlock upgraded Spetznaz (Russian) Battalion	SPZT17
Unlock upgraded Spetznaz (Russian) Battalion	SPZA39

TOM CLANCY'S ENDWAR (PLAYSTATION 3)

CODES

Go to the Community & Extras screen on the Main Menu, highlight the VIP option and press the Triangle button to input the special codes.

EFFECT	CODE
European Enforcer Corps	EUCA20

CODES & CHEATS

Russian Spetsnaz Guard Brigade	SPZA39
U.S. Joint Strike Force	JSFA35
Unlocks the special Spetsnaz Battalion	SPZT17

TOM CLANCY'S GHOST RECON: ADVANCED WARFIGHTER (XBOX 360)

When the game is paused, enter these codes while holding 🅀, ⒧, ⒭.

UNLOCKABLE	CODE
Full Life	⒧, ⒧, ⒭, ⓧ, ⒭, ⓨ
Scott Mitchell Invincible	ⓨ, ⓨ, ⓧ, ⒭, ⓧ, ⒧
Team Invincible	ⓧ, ⓧ, ⓨ, ⒭, ⓨ, ⒧
Unlimited Ammo	⒭, ⒭, ⒧, ⓧ, ⒧, ⓨ

Enter this code on the Mission Select screen while holding 🅀, ⒧, ⒭.

UNLOCKABLE	CODE
All Levels	ⓨ, ⒭, ⓨ, ⒭, ⓧ

TOM CLANCY'S GHOST RECON: ADVANCED WARFIGHTER 2 (XBOX 360)

Enter this password as a name.

UNLOCKABLE	CODE
FAMAS in Quick Missions Only (works in Australian version only)	GRAW2QUICKFAMAS

TOM CLANCY'S GHOST RECON: FUTURE SOLDIER (PLAYSTATION 3)

TROPHY

UNLOCKABLE	HOW TO UNLOCK
...I Can Do Better (Bronze)	Complete 20 Daily Friend Challenges in Quick Matches
...Must Come Down (Bronze)	Destroy the plane with the weapons system on board while it is in flight
Actionable Intel (Bronze)	Complete 10 Coordinated Kills in Quick Matches
Advanced Warfighter (Silver)	Complete the campaign in Veteran
Anything You Can Do... (Bronze)	Complete a Daily Friend Challenge through all return fire volleys in Quick Matches
Armorer (Silver)	Spend 25 attachment credits with each role
Backup (Bronze)	Assist a teammate 5 times who is taking fire, suppressed, or has called for help in Quick Matches
Battle Buddies (Bronze)	Complete the campaign in Co-op
Blood Brother (Bronze)	Rescue the Georgian Spec Ops
Breathing Room (Bronze) artillery	Destroy the second piece of enemy
Call, Answered (Silver)	Earn all Tour of Duty Trophies
Conflict Domination (Bronze)	Be part of a squad match where your team wins by a margin of 5 points or more
Coordinated Assault (Bronze)	Use the Coordination System to reach an objective in a Quick Match
Counter-Intelligence (Bronze)	Interrupt enemy data hacks on teammates 5 times by killing or stunning them in Quick Matches
Cross Trained (Bronze)	Reach Level 10 on one Rifleman, one Scout, and one Engineer character
Decoy Domination (Bronze)	Be part of 5 squad matches where your team completes the true objective first
Doing Work (Bronze)	Kill 1000 enemies while in Guerrilla mode
EOD (Bronze)	Destroy the Russian weapons transfer station

Field Tested (Bronze)	Play 5 MP matches of each game type in Quick Matches
Fuel for the Fire (Bronze)	Secure the drilling ships and complete the mission
Future Soldier (Gold)	Complete the campaign in Elite
Good Effect on Target (Bronze)	Kill more than 5 enemies with an airstrike
Good Enough for Government Work (Bronze)	Have a Ghost Skill of 80% for all missions
High Speed, Low Drag (Gold)	Reach Level 50 on any character
High-Value Target (Bronze)	Kill 5 High-Value Targets in Quick Matches
Just a Box (Bronze)	While in Guerrilla mode, complete an infiltration sequence without being detected
Just Another Day at the Office (Silver)	Complete the campaign
Kitted Out (Bronze)	Spend attachment credits to customize 1 weapon at all external attachment points
Loose Thread (Bronze)	Secure Gabriel Paez
Master Tactician (Silver)	Complete 100% of the tactical challenges
Mod Pro (Silver)	Spend 50 Attachment points to add attachments to various guns
Mod Rookie (Bronze)	Spend an attachment credit to add an attachment to any gun
No Loose Ends (Bronze)	Eliminate the leader of the Raven's Rock faction
Platinum Trophy (Platinum)	Platinum Trophy
Precious Cargo (Bronze)	Secure the VIP and transfer him to the exfiltration team
Qualified (Bronze)	Have a Ghost Skill of 90% for a single mission
Quality Beats Quantity (Silver)	Defeat all 50 enemy waves on Guerilla mode (any difficulty, any map)
Recon Specialist (Bronze)	Complete 5 Intel Assists in Quick Matches
Relieved of Command (Bronze)	Kill the general commanding the Moscow defenses
Saboteur Domination (Bronze)	Be part of a squad match where your team takes the objective into the enemy base in under 2 minutes
Siege Domination (Bronze)	Be part of a squad match where your team captures the objective in under 2 minutes
Source Control (Bronze)	Secure the VIPs and transfer them to the exfiltration team
Special Election (Bronze)	Rescue Russian President Volodin from the prison camp
Tactician (Bronze)	Complete 50% of the tactical challenges
Total Domination (Bronze)	Earn all of the Domination Trophies
Tour of Duty: Arctic (Bronze)	Win 3 Quick Matches of any game type on each: Buried, Milled, and Alpha maps
Tour of Duty: Nigeria (Bronze)	Win 3 Quick Matches of any game type on each: Depleted, Abandoned, Blinded, and Collapsed maps
Tour of Duty: North Sea (Bronze)	Win 3 Quick Matches of any game type on each: Harbored, Hijacked, and Rigged maps
True Ghost (Bronze)	Get 10 consecutive kills in one Quick Match without dying

CODES&CHEATS

| Tuned Up (Bronze) | Spend attachment credits to customize all the internal parts of one weapon |
| What Goes Up... (Bronze) | Shoot down the cargo plane |

TOM CLANCY'S GHOST RECON: FUTURE SOLDIER (XBOX 360)

ACHIEVEMENT

UNLOCKABLE	HOW TO UNLOCK
...I Can Do Better (5)	Complete 20 Daily Friend Challenges
...Must Come Down. (20)	Destroy the plane with the weapons system on board while it is in flight
Actionable Intel (10)	Complete 10 Coordinated Kills
Advanced Warfighter (40)	Complete the campaign in Veteran
Anything You Can Do... (20)	Complete a Daily Friend Challenge through all return fire volleys
Armorer (35)	Spend 25 Attachment Credits with each role
Backup (5)	Complete 5 Savior Kills in Quick Matches
Battle Buddies (30)	Complete the campaign in Co-op
Blood Brother (20)	Rescue the Georgian Spec Ops
Breathing Room (20)	Destroy the second piece of enemy artillery
Call, Answered (35)	Complete all Tours of Duty
Conflict Domination (10)	Be part of a squad match where your team wins by a margin of 500 points or more
Coordinated Assault (5)	Use the Coordination System to reach an objective
Counter-Intelligence (10)	Interrupt an enemy's attempt to data hack a teammate 5 times, by killing or stunning the enemy
Cross-trained (10)	Reach Level 10 on one Rifleman, one Scout, and one Engineer character
Decoy Domination (10)	In squad matches your team completes the key objective first, five times.
Doing Work (10)	Kill 1000 enemies while in Guerrilla mode
EOD (20)	Destroy the Russian weapons transfer station
Field Tested (5)	Play 5 MP matches of each game type
Fuel for the Fire (20)	Secure the drilling ships and complete the mission
Future Soldier (50)	Complete the campaign in Elite
Good Effect on Target (10)	In Guerrilla mode, kill more than 5 enemies with an airstrike
Good Enough for Government Work (10)	Achieve a Ghost skill rating above 80% for all missions
High Speed, Low Drag (50)	Reach Level 50 on any character
High-Value Target (5)	Kill a member of the dev team, or kill someone who has
Just a Box (10)	While in Guerrilla mode, complete an infiltration sequence without being detected
Just Another Day at the Office (30)	Complete the campaign for the first time
Kitted Out (25)	Customize 1 weapon with an external attachment at every attachment point
Loose Thread (20)	Secure Gabriel Paez
Master Tactician (25)	Complete 100% of the Tactical challenges
Mod Pro (40)	Spend 50 Attachment Credits to add attachments to various guns
Mod Rookie (5)	Add an attachment to any gun

No Loose Ends (20)	Eliminate the leader of the Raven's Rock faction
Precious Cargo (20)	Secure the VIP and transfer him to the exfiltration team
Qualified (25)	Achieve a Ghost skill rating of above 90% on one mission
Quality Beats Quantity (30)	Defeat all 50 enemy waves on Guerrilla mode (any difficulty, any map)
Recon Specialist (25)	Complete 5 Intel Assists in Quick Matches
Relieved of Command (20)	Kill the general commanding the Moscow defenses
Saboteur Domination (10)	Be part of a squad match where your team takes the bomb into the enemy base in under 2 minutes
Siege Domination (10)	Be part of a squad match where your team captures the objective in under 2 minutes
Source Control (20)	Secure the VIP and transfer them to the exfiltration team
Special Election (20)	Rescue Russian President Volodin from the prison camp
Tactician (10)	Complete 50% of the Tactical challenges
Total Domination (40)	Complete all of the Domination achievements
Tour of Duty: Arctic (25)	Win 3 MP matches of any game type on each: Underground, Mill, and Alpha maps
Tour of Duty: Nigeria (25)	Win 3 MP of any game type on each: Pipeline, Market, Sand Storm, and Overpass maps
Tour of Duty: North Sea (25)	Win 3 MP matches of any game type on each: Harbor, Cargo, and Rig maps
True Ghost (10)	Get 10 consecutive kills in one Quick Match without dying
Tuned Up (25)	Customize all the internal parts of one weapon
What Goes Up... (20)	Shoot down the cargo plane

TOM CLANCY'S HAWX (XBOX 360)

CODES

Go to the hangar screen, then enter the codes to unlock the corresponding aircraft.

Unlocks A-12 Avenger II	Hold ⬛ and enter ⊗, ⓁⒷ, ⊗, ⓇⒷ, Ⓨ, ⊗
Unlocks F-18 HARV	Hold ⬛ and enter ⓁⒷ, Ⓨ, ⓁⒷ, Ⓨ, ⓁⒷ, ⊗
Unlocks FB-22	Hold ⬛ and enter ⓇⒷ, ⊗, ⓇⒷ, ⊗, ⓇⒷ, Ⓨ

TOM CLANCY'S HAWX (PLAYSTATION 3)

CODES

Go to the hangar screen, then enter the codes to unlock the corresponding aircraft.

EFFECT	CODE
Unlocks A-12 Avenger II	Hold ⟨L2⟩ and press ■, ⟨L1⟩, ■, ⟨R1⟩, ▲, ■
Unlocks F-18 HARV	Hold ⟨L2⟩ and press ⟨L1⟩, ▲, ⟨L1⟩, ▲, ⟨L1⟩, ■
Unlocks FB-22	Hold ⟨L2⟩ and press ⟨R1⟩, ■, ⟨R1⟩, ■, ⟨R1⟩, ▲

TOM CLANCY'S RAINBOW SIX VEGAS 2 (XBOX 360)

CODES

During gameplay, pause the game, hold the right shoulder button, and enter the following codes.

UNLOCKABLE	HOW TO UNLOCK
GI John Doe Mode	ⓁⒷ, ⓁⒷ, Ⓐ, ⓇⒷ, ⓇⒷ, Ⓑ, ⓁⒷ, ⓁⒷ, ⊗, ⓇⒷ, ⓇⒷ, Ⓨ

CODES & CHEATS

| Super Ragdoll | Ⓐ,Ⓐ,Ⓑ,Ⓑ,Ⓧ,Ⓧ,Ⓨ,Ⓨ,Ⓐ,Ⓑ,Ⓨ |
| Third Person Mode | Ⓧ,Ⓑ,Ⓧ,Ⓑ,(L3),(L3),Ⓨ,Ⓐ,Ⓨ,Ⓐ,(R3),(R3) |

WEAPONS

When you are customizing your character, hold down the right bumper and insert the following code.

UNLOCKABLE	HOW TO UNLOCK
AR-21 Assault Rifle	↓,↓,↑,↑,Ⓧ,Ⓑ,Ⓧ,Ⓑ,Ⓨ,↑,↑,Ⓨ

COMCAST MULTIPLAYER MAP

At the main menu, go to the Extras menu, select Comcast Gift, then enter the following password.

PASSWORD	EFFECT
Comcast faster	Comcast multiplayer map

TOM CLANCY'S RAINBOW SIX VEGAS 2 (PLAYSTATION 3)

CODES

At the Title screen, hold R1 and press the following.

UNLOCKABLE	HOW TO UNLOCK
M468 Assault Rifle	↑,▲,↓,×,←,■,→,●,←,←,→,■
MTAR-21 Assault Rifle	↓,↓,↑,↑,■,●,■,●,▲,↑,↑,▲

SINGLE PLAYER CODES

During gameplay, pause the game, hold R1, and insert the following codes.

UNLOCKABLE	HOW TO UNLOCK
Red and Blue Tracers (also works online, host must enter code)	(L3),(L3),×,(R3),(R3),●,(L3),(L3),■,(R3),(R3),▲
Third-Person View	■,●,■,●,(L3),(L3),▲,×,▲,×,(R3),(R3)
Super Ragdoll Mode	×,×,●,●,■,■,▲,▲,×,●,■,▲

COMCAST MULTIPLAYER MAP

At the game's main menu, go to the Extras menu, select Comcast Gift, then enter the following password.

PASSWORD	EFFECT
Comcast faster	Comcast multiplayer map

TOM CLANCY'S SPLINTER CELL: ESSENTIALS (PSP)

BONUS MISSION CODES

Enter the following at the bonus mission screen (you have to enter the code each time you want to play the mission).

UNLOCKABLE	HOW TO UNLOCK
Unlock the Heroin Refinery Mission	Hold Select and press L+R three more times
Unlock the Paris-Nice Mission	Hold Select and press L+R 12 more times
Unlock the Television Free Indonesia Mission	Hold Select and press L+R three times

TOMB RAIDER LEGENDS (XBOX 360)

Enter these codes in game. Codes can not be used until they are unlocked.

UNLOCKABLE	CODE
Bulletproof	Hold LT press Ⓐ,RT,Ⓨ,RT,Ⓧ,LB
Draw enemies' health	Hold LT press Ⓧ,Ⓑ,Ⓐ,LB,RT,Ⓨ
Excalibur	Hold LB press Ⓨ,Ⓐ,Ⓑ,RT,Ⓨ,LT
Infinite Assault Ammo	Hold LB press Ⓐ,Ⓑ,Ⓐ,LT,Ⓧ,Ⓨ
Infinite Grenade Launcher Ammo	Hold LB press LT,Ⓨ,RT,Ⓑ,LT,Ⓧ
Infinite Shotgun Ammo	Hold LB press RT,Ⓑ,Ⓧ,LT,Ⓧ,Ⓐ
Infinite SMG Ammo	Hold LB press Ⓑ,Ⓨ,LT,RT,Ⓐ,Ⓑ
One Shot Kills	Hold LT press Ⓨ,Ⓐ,Ⓨ,Ⓧ,LB,Ⓑ

| Soul Reaver | Hold ⦿ press Ⓐ, ⓇⒷ, Ⓑ, ⓇⒷ, ⓁⒷ, ⓧ |
| Textureless Mode | Hold ⓁⒷ press ⦿, Ⓐ, Ⓑ, Ⓐ, Ⓨ, ⓇⒷ |

TOMB RAIDER: LEGENDS (PSP)

CODES

Enter these codes while playing a level, but they only work once you have unlocked them.

CODE	EFFECT
Bulletproof	Hold Ⓛ, then: ×, Ⓡ, ▲, Ⓡ, ■, Ⓡ
Draw Enemy Health	Hold Ⓛ, then: ■, ●, ×, Ⓡ, Ⓡ, ▲
Infinite Assault Rifle Ammo	Hold Ⓛ, then: ×, ●, ×, Ⓡ, ■, ▲
Infinite Grenade Launcher	Hold Ⓛ, then: Ⓡ, ▲, Ⓡ, ●, Ⓡ, ■
Infinite Shotgun Ammo	Hold Ⓛ, then: Ⓡ, ●, ■, Ⓡ, ■, ×
Infinite SMG Ammo	Hold Ⓛ, then: ●, ▲, Ⓡ, Ⓡ, ×, ●
One Shot Kill	Hold Ⓛ, then: ▲, ×, ▲, ■, Ⓡ, ●
Wield Excalibur	Hold Ⓛ, then: ▲, ×, ●, Ⓡ, ▲, Ⓡ
Wield Soul Reaver	Hold Ⓛ, then: ×, Ⓡ, ●, Ⓡ, Ⓡ, ■
Zip	Collect 20% of all bronze rewards

TOMB RAIDER: UNDERWORLD (XBOX 360)

UNLOCKABLES

UNLOCKABLE	HOW TO UNLOCK
Lara's bathing suit	Complete the game on any difficulty setting and this becomes unlocked in Treasure Hunt mode when you revisit the Mediterranean Sea Expedition.
Treasure Hunt mode	Complete the game on any difficulty to unlock Treasure Hunt mode, which allows you to revisit all levels to claim Treasures/Relics missed through storm.

TONY HAWK'S AMERICAN WASTELAND (XBOX 360)

In the Options menu, select the Cheats menu and enter these passwords. (Note: case sensitive)

UNLOCKABLE	PASSWORD
Matt Hoffman	the_condor
Perfect Grinds	grindXpert
Perfect Manuals	2wheels!

CODES

Enter codes in the Options menu under "codes."

EFFECT	CODE
Helps you keep balance when grinding	grindXpert
Hitch a ride on the back of cars	h!tchar!de
Lil John	hip2DHop
Moon Gravity	2them00n
Perfect manuals	2wheels!
Play as Jason Ellis	sirius-DJ
Play as Mindy	help1nghand
Unlock legendary skater Matt Hoffman	the_condor

TONY HAWK'S DOWNHILL JAM (WII)

Enter these passwords in the Cheats menu.

UNLOCKABLE	PASSWORD
Always Special	PointHogger
Chipmunk Voices	HelloHelium

Demon Skater	EvilChimneySweep
Display Coordinates	DisplayCoordinates
Enables Manuals	IMISSMANUALS
Extreme Car Crashes	WatchForDoors
First Person Skater	FirstPersonJam
Free Boost	OotbaghForever
Giganto-Skater	IWannaBeTallTall
Invisible Skater	NowYouSeeMe
Large Birds	BirdBirdBirdBird
Mini Skater	DownTheRabbitHole
Perfect Manual	TightRopeWalker
Perfect Rail	LikeTiltingAPlate
Perfect Stats	IAmBob
Picasso Skater	FourLights
Power of the Fish!	TonyFishDownhillJam
Shadow Skater	ChimneySweep
Tiny People	ShrinkThePeople
Unlock All Boards and Outfits	RaidTheWoodshed
Unlock All Events	AdventuresOfKwang
Unlock All Movies	FreeBozzler
Unlock All Skaters	ImInterfacing

TONY HAWK'S PROJECT 8 (XBOX 360)

Enter these passwords in the Cheats menu.

UNLOCKABLE	PASSWORD
All decks unlocked and free except for inkblot deck and Gamestop deck	needaride
All specials in shop	yougotitall
Travis Barker	plus44
Grim Reaper (Freeskate)	enterandwin
Jason Lee	notmono
Anchor Man	newshound
Big Realtor	shescaresme
Christian Hosoi	hohohosoi
Colonel and Security Guard	militarymen
Inkblot Deck	birdhouse
Kevin Staab	mixitup
Nerd	wearelosers
Photographer Girl and Filmer	themedia
Zombie	suckstobedead
Dad and Skater Jam Kid	strangefellows

TONY HAWK'S PROJECT 8 (PLAYSTATION 3)

In the Options menu, select Cheats to enter these passwords.

UNLOCKABLE	PASSWORD
Big Realtor	shescaresme
Christian Hosoi	hohohosoi
Colonel and Security Guard	militarymen
Dad and Skater Jam Kid	strangefellows
Full Air Stats	drinkup
Grim Reaper	enterandwin

Inkblot Deck	birdhouse
Jason Lee	notmono
Kevin Staab	mixitup
Mascot	manineedadate
Most Decks	needaride
Nerd	wearelosers
Photographer and Cameraman	themedia
Travis Barker	plus44
Unlock Specials in Skate Shop	yougotitall

TONY HAWK'S PROVING GROUND (PLAYSTATION 3)

CHEATS

Enter the codes in the options menu of the main menu

UNLOCKABLE	HOW TO UNLOCK
100% Branch Completion (NTT)	FOREVERNAILED
Invisible Man	THEMISSING
Mini Skater	TINYTATER
No Bails	ANDAINTFALLIN
No Board	MAGICMAN
Perfect Manual	STILLAINTFALLIN
Perfect Rail	AINTFALLIN
Super Check	BOOYAH
Unlimited Focus	MYOPIC
Unlimited Slash Grind	SUPERSLASHIN
Unlock Judy Nails	LOVEROCKNROLL

ITEMS

UNLOCKABLE	HOW TO UNLOCK
50 Extra Skill Points	NEEDSHELP
All CAS Items	GIVEMESTUFF
All Decks	LETSGOSKATE
All Fun Items	OVERTHETOP
All Game Movies	WATCHTHIS
All Lounge Bling Items	SWEETSTUFF
All Lounge Themes	LAIDBACKLOUNGE
All Rigger Pieces	IMGONNABUILD
All Special Tricks Available	LOTSOFTRICKS
All Video Editor Effects	TRIPPY
All Video Editor Overlays	PUTEMONTOP
Full Stats	BEEFEDUP

LEVELS

UNLOCKABLE	HOW TO UNLOCK
Unlock Air & Space Museum	THEINDOORPARK
Unlock FDR	THEPREZPARK
Unlock Lansdowne	THELOCALPARK

SKATERS

UNLOCKABLE	HOW TO UNLOCK
Boneman	CRAZYBONEMAN
Bosco	MOREMILK
Cam	NOTACAMERA

CODES & CHEATS

Cooper	THECOOP
Eddie X	SKETCHY
El Patinador	PILEDRIVER
Eric	FLYAWAY
Mad Dog	RABBIES
MCA	INTERGALACTIC
Mel	NOTADUDE
Rube	LOOKSSMELLY
Shayne	MOVERS
Spence	DAPPER
TV Producer	SHAKER

TONY HAWK'S PROVING GROUND (WII)

ITEMS

UNLOCKABLE	HOW TO UNLOCK
50 Extra Skill Points	NEEDSHELP
All CAS Items	GIVEMESTUFF
All Decks	LETSGOSKATE
All Fun Items	OVERTHETOP
All Game Movies	WATCHTHIS
All Rigger Pieces	IMGONNABUILD
All Special Tricks Available	LOTSOFTRICKS
Full Stats	BEEFEDUP

LEVELS

UNLOCKABLE	HOW TO UNLOCK
Unlock Air and Space Museum	THEINDOORPARK
Unlock FDR	THEPREZPARK
Unlock Lansdowne	THELOCALPARK

SKATERS

UNLOCKABLE	HOW TO UNLOCK
Boneman	CRAZYBONEMAN
Bosco	MOREMILK
Cam	NOTACAMERA
Cooper	THECOOP
Eddie X	SKETCHY
El Patinador	PILEDRIVER
Eric	FLYAWAY
Mad Dog	RABBIES
MCA	INTERGALACTIC
Mel	NOTADUDE
Rube	LOOKSSMELLY
Shayne	MOVERS
Spence	DAPPER
TV Producer	SHAKER

TONY HAWK'S PROVING GROUND (DS)

CHEATS

Enter the codes in the Options menu of the main menu.

UNLOCKABLE	HOW TO UNLOCK
100% Branch Completion (NTT)	FOREVERNAILED
Invisible Man	THEMISSING

Mini Skater	TINYTATER
No Bails	ANDAINTFALLIN
No Board	MAGICMAN
Perfect Manual	STILLAINTFALLIN
Perfect Rail	AINTFALLIN
Super Check	BOOYAH
Unlimited Focus	MYOPIC
Unlimited Slash Grind	SUPERSLASHIN
Unlock Judy Nails	LOVEROCKNROLL

ITEMS

UNLOCKABLE	HOW TO UNLOCK
50 Extra Skill Points	NEEDSHELP
All CAS Items	GIVEMESTUFF
All Decks	LETSGOSKATE
All Fun Items	OVERTHETOP
All Game Movies	WATCHTHIS
All Lounge Bling Items	SWEETSTUFF
All Lounge Themes	LAIDBACKLOUNGE
All Rigger Pieces	IMGONNABUILD
All Special Tricks Available	LOTSOFTRICKS
All Video Editor Effects	TRIPPY
All Video Editor Overlays	PUTEMONTOP
Full Stats	BEEFEDUP

LEVELS

UNLOCKABLE	HOW TO UNLOCK
Unlock Air & Space Museum	THEINDOORPARK
Unlock FDR	THEPREZPARK
Unlock Lansdowne	THELOCALPARK

SKATERS

UNLOCKABLE	HOW TO UNLOCK
Boneman	CRAZYBONEMAN
Bosco	MOREMILK
Cam	NOTACAMERA
Cooper	THECOOP
Eddie X	SKETCHY
El Patinador	PILEDRIVER
Eric	FLYAWAY
Mad Dog	RABBIES
MCA	INTERGALACTIC
Mel	NOTADUDE
Rube	LOOKSSMELLY
Shayne	MOVERS
Spence	DAPPER
TV Producer	SHAKER

TONY HAWK'S UNDERGROUND 2 REMIX (PSP)

Go to Game Options, then Cheat Codes and enter the following codes.

UNLOCKABLE	CODE
Perfect Rail Balance	Tightrope
Unlock Tony Hawk from Tony Hawk Pro Skater 1	Birdman

TOSHINDEN (WII)

UNLOCKABLE CHARACTERS

UNLOCKABLE	HOW TO UNLOCK
Dan	Beat Story Mode on hard difficulty
Lilith	Beat Story Mode on any difficulty.
Moritz	Beat Story Mode on any difficulty.
Shouki	Beat Story Mode on hard difficulty.

TOUCH MY KATAMARI (PLAYSTATION VITA)

TROPHY

UNLOCKABLE	HOW TO UNLOCK
Congratulations! (Bronze)	Completed all Requests.
Connoisseur (Silver)	Collected all objects within the Curio Collection.
Fanatic (Gold)	Obtained the ultimate fashion item.
Hoarder (Silver)	Collected all Presents.
Katamari Aficionado (Bronze)	Collected all songs.
Katamari Fan Damacy (Bronze)	Obtained a Fan Damacy for the first time.
Katamari Noob (Bronze)	Completed "Make It Big: Playtime".
Long Live Katamari! (Bronze)	Unlocked Eternal and Katamari Drive modes for all Requests.
Sweet Talker (Silver)	Used 3 Candy Tickets at the same time.
The King of Style (Silver)	Collected all of the King's fashion items.
We Love Cousins (Bronze)	Rolled up all Cousins.

TOUCH THE DEAD (DS)

CODES

Enter the following code at the main menu. A zombie will moan if you enter the code successfully and the Logo Screen will turn red. After that you will have access to all missions, all modes, and all bonuses. You will also be able to use the L and R shoulder buttons to switch to the next/previous camera.

EFFECT	CODE
Unlocks everything, allows camera switching	Ⓧ,Ⓨ,⬇,⬇,Ⓧ

TOWER OF DRUAGA (WII)

CODES

Enter this code at the title screen. If entered properly, the word "DRUA-GA" will turn green. The game is now harder and the levels require different solutions.

CODE	EFFECT
⬇,⬇,⬇,⬇,⬇,⬇,⬅,⬅,⬆,⬆,⬅,⬅,➡	Another Druaga (Second Quest)

TOY SOLDIERS (XBOX 360)

UNLOCKABLES

UNLOCKABLE	HOW TO UNLOCK
Gas Mask (Avatar Item)	Buy the game and play the first level on campaign.
Allied Toy Soldier Gamerpic	Play the first level after buying the game.
Central Toy Soldier Gamerpic	Destroy all 24 golden cubes.

TRANSFORMERS: REVENGE OF THE FALLEN (XBOX 360)

CODES

Enter with the D-Pad in the "Cheat Codes" option in the Main menu. Note: These characters will only be playable in multiplayer.

EFFECT	CODE
Always in Overdrive Mode	⒧,Ⓑ,⒧,Ⓐ,Ⓧ,⒭

Effect	Code
Extra Energon (ex: 4x from defeated enemies)	Y, X, B, R3, A, Y
Golden Megatron	↓, ↑, →, →, ←, ↑
Golden Optimus Prime	↑, ↓, →, ←, →, ↓
Increased Enemy Accuracy	Y, Y, B, B, X, LB
Increased Enemy Damage	LB, Y, A, Y, R3, R3
Increased Enemy Health	B, X, LB, B, R3, Y
Increased Weapon Damage in Root Form	Y, Y, R3, A, LB, Y
Increased Weapon Damage in Vehicle Form	Y, B, RB, X, R3, LB
Invincibility	R3, A, X, LB, X, X
Lower Enemy Accuracy	X, LB, R3, LB, R3, RB
Melee Instant Kills	R3, A, LB, B, R3, LB
No Special Cool Down Time	R3, X, R3, R3, X, A
No Weapon Overheat	LB, X, A, LB, Y, LB
Play as Autobot Protectobot Scout MP in Autobot-based Single-player (only when mission begins, not in character select) Does not work in Deep 6.	R3, LB, LB, Y, X, A
Plays as Decepticon Seeker Warrior MP in Decepticon-based Single-player (only when mission begins, not in character select)	X, Y, X, LB, A, LB
Special Kills Only Mode (Cannot kill enemies except with special kills)	B, B, RB, B, A, LB
Unlimited Turbo	B, LB, X, B, A, Y
Unlock all Cairo Missions and Zones	R3, Y, A, Y, LB, LB
Unlock All Deep Six Missions and Zones	X, RB, Y, B, A, LB
Unlock All East Coast Missions and Zones	R3, LB, RB, A, B, X
Unlock All Shanghai Missions and Zones	Y, LB, LB, B, Y, A
Unlock All West Coast Missions and Zones	LB, RB, R3, Y, RB, B
Unlock and activate ALL Upgrades	LB, Y, LB, B, X, X
Unlocks Generation 1 Starscream	B, A, B, RB, Y, RB

TRANSFORMERS: REVENGE OF THE FALLEN (PLAYSTATION 3)

CODES

From the Main Menu go to Cheat Codes and enter the codes there.

EFFECT	CODE
Always in Overdrive Mode	L1, ●, L1, X, ■, R3
Extra Energon (ex: 4x from defeated enemies)	▲, ■, ●, R3, X, ▲
G1 Colors Ironhide (single-player only)	L1, R1, R1, X, ●, ▲
G1 Starscream	●, X, ●, R1, ▲, R1
Gold Megatron	↓, ↑, →, →, ←, ↑
Gold Optimus Prime	↑, ↓, ←, ←, →, ↓
Increased Enemy Accuracy	▲, ▲, ●, X, ■, L1
Increased Enemy Damage	L1, ▲, X, ▲, R3, R3
Increased Enemy Health	●, ■, L1, ●, R3, ▲
Increased Weapon Damage in Robot Form	▲, ▲, R3, X, L1, ▲
Increased Weapon Damage in Vehicle Form	▲, ●, R1, ■, R3, L3
Invincibility	R3, X, ■, L3, ■, ■
Lower Enemy Accuracy	■, L3, R3, L3, R3, R1
Melee Instant Kills	R3, X, L1, ●, B, L1
No Special Cooldown Time	R3, ■, R3, R3, ■, X
No Weapon Overheat	L3, ■, X, L3, ▲, L3

545

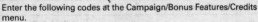

CODES & CHEATS

Play as Autobot Protectobot Scout MP in Autobot-based single-player (only when mission begins, not in character select) Does not work in Deep 6.	[R3], [L1], [L1], ▲, ■, ✕
Plays as Decepticon Seeker Warrior MP in Decepticon-Based single-player (only when mission begins, not in character select)	■, ▲, ■, [L1], ✕, [L1]
Special Kills Only Mode (Cannot kill enemies except with special kills)	●, ●, [R1], ●, ✕, [L3]
Unlimited Turbo	●, [L3], ■, ✕, ▲
Unlock all Cairo Missions and Zones	[R3], ▲, ✕, ▲, [L3], [L1]
Unlock All Deep Six Missions and Zones	■, [R1], ▲, ●, ✕, [L1]
Unlock All East Coast Missions and Zones	[R3], [L3], [R1], ✕, ●, ■
Unlock All Shanghai Missions and Zones	▲, [L3], [R1], [L1], ▲, ✕
Unlock All West Coast Missions and Zones	[L1], [R1], [R3], ▲, [R3], ●
Unlock and activate ALL Upgrades	[L1], ▲, [L1], ●, ■, ■

TRANSFORMERS: THE GAME   (XBOX 360)

CODES

Enter codes at the "Campaign/Bonus Features" main menu. Enter codes for each character during one of their missions. This changes the character's appearance to their Generation 1 skin. Note: Using these cheats prevents you from achieving gamerscore!

CODE	EFFECT
♀, ◁, ◁, ♀, ▷, ▷, ◇	Generation 1 Skin Megatron
◇, ▷, ◁, ◇, ♀, ♀, ◁	Generation 1 Skin Prime
◁, ◇, ♀, ♀, ◁, ◇, ▷	Generation 1 Skin Jazz
♀, ♀, ◇, ◇, ▷, ◁, ▷	Generation 1 Skin Optimus Prime
▷, ♀, ◁, ◁, ♀, ◇, ◇	Generation 1 Skin Starscream
◁, ◁, ◇, ◇, ▷, ♀, ◁	Infinite Health—Invincible
◇, ♀, ◁, ▷, ◇, ◇, ♀	No Ammo Reload
▷, ◁, ◇, ◁, ◇, ◁, ◇	No Military or Police
♀, ◇, ◁, ◇, ▷, ◁, ◇, ♀	Unlock All mission including 2 special mission
▷, ◇, ◇, ♀, ▷, ◁, ◁	Unlocks the two Cybertron missions.

UNLOCKABLES

UNLOCKABLE	HOW TO UNLOCK
G1 Megatron	Collect all the Transformer Shields in the Decepticons Story mode
G1 Optimus Prime (Cartoon Model)	Find all the Autobot faction symbols during the Autobot campaign.
G1 Robo-vision Optimus	Finish the Autobot campaign.
Jazz G1 Repaint	Complete all of the "challenge" sub-missions in both Autobot and Decepticon campaigns.
Starscream G1 repaint	Complete Decepticon Story mode.

TRANSFORMERS: THE GAME   (WII)

CODES

Enter the following codes at the Campaign/Bonus Features/Credits menu.

CODE	EFFECT
⬇, ⬆, ⬇, ⬇, ⬇, ⬇, ⬆, ⬇	Unlock all missions
⬇, ⬆, ⬇, ⬇, ⬇, ⬆, ⬇	Infinite health—invincible
⬇, ⬇, ⬇, ⬇, ⬇, ⬇, ⬇, ⬆	No vehicles running on the street and no tanks/ cops attack
⬇, ⬆, ⬇, ⬆, ⬇, ⬇, ⬆, ⬇	Unlock Cybertron missions

CODE	EFFECT
⇧, ⇧, ⇧, ⇧, ⇧, ⇧, ⇧	Unlock G1 Optimus Prime
⇧, ⇩, ⇩, ⇩, ⇧, ⇩, ⇩	Unlock Generation 1 Jazz Repaint
⇧, ⇧, ⇧, ⇧, ⇧, ⇧, ⇧	Unlock Generation 1 Starscream Repaint
⇧, ⇧, ⇧, ⇧, ⇧, ⇩, ⇩	Unlock Robovision Optimus Prime
⇧, ⇧, ⇧, ⇧, ⇧, ⇧, ⇧	Unlock G1 Megatron

UNLOCKABLES

UNLOCKABLE	HOW TO UNLOCK
G1 Jazz Repaint	Clear all sub-missions in Autobot and Decepticon Story modes
G1 Megatron	Collect all of the Decepticon icons on all of the maps
G1 Optimus Prime	Collect all of the Autobot Icons on all of the maps
G1 Starscream Repaint	Beat the Decepticon's Story mode
Robovision Optimus Prime	Beat the Autobot's Story mode

TRINITY UNIVERSE (WII)

UNLOCKABLES

UNLOCKABLE	HOW TO UNLOCK
Unlock EX form characters	Get 10 or more wins in Survival mode in Single Battle. To use a character's EX form, press left or right on the Character Select screen.
Unlock images from Gallery mode	Beat Story mode using two characters from the same franchise to unlock the first three rows of images. To obtain the other images, beat Story mode using the same method but in their EX form.
Unlockable narrators (system voices)	Beat All Battle mode with any character to unlock their voice in the System Voice option in the Sound Settings.

TRON EVOLUTION (PSP)

CODES

Enter the codes on the Code menu. These codes are case sensitive.

EFFECT	CODE
Unlock Rectifier Disc Battle Arena for Quickplay	Endofline

TRON EVOLUTION: BATTLE GRIDS (WII)

CODES

These are typed in the Cheat Code menu.

EFFECT	CODE
Makes your lightcycle trails taller	lctalltrails
Sharp sliding turns for light cycle arena	lcsupersharpslide

TWISTED METAL (PLAYSTATION 3)

TROPHY

UNLOCKABLE	HOW TO UNLOCK
...and I thank you for playing Twisted Metal. (Bronze)	Complete the Story mode on any difficulty
60 to 0 (Bronze)	Kill a player with full health in one shot.
A la Mode (Silver)	Win 10 Ranked games in each game type.
All sales are final (Bronze)	Win at least 1 Ranked Online game per day for 30 straight days
Am I not merciful? (Bronze)	Kill 100 flaming gunners and/or drivers in campaign mode.
Another Level (Silver)	Win 10 Ranked games in each map. Map size does not matter.

Any car will do (Gold)	Earn 50 Kills with Each Vehicle in Online Ranked Games
Because I care (Bronze)	Complete a campaign game without hitting a single pedestrian.
Birth Control (Bronze)	Defeat the semi before a single enemy is spawned in Juggernaut DM - Watkyn's Harbor.
Blah, Blah, Blah, Gimme the trophy (Bronze)	Play and finish the "Live Training" tutorial mode
Calypso (Bronze)	Achieve the Highest Online Rank
Cookie Party (Bronze)	Kill 3 enemies in a single game using drop mines.
Fire in the sky (Bronze)	Shoot down an enemy missile 1 time in a ranked game of NUKE.
Grace Under Fire (Bronze)	Beat Metro Square Electric Cage on HARD MODE with 5 SECONDS LEFT in your GRACE PERIOD meter. Cooperative Story is allowed.
Grimm's Dark Trip Back (Bronze)	Complete the Grimm story on any difficulty.
He's not heavy (Bronze)	As Talon, pick up teammate (ranked, unranked, split screen, campaign co-op).
I am Sweet Tooth (Platinum)	All Trophies
I h8 poachers (Bronze)	Finish a ranked game with the most damage done and fewest kills overall
In your Face (Bronze)	Hit a statue with a Nuke.
Make up your mind (Bronze)	Use the garage 25 times.
Medic! (Bronze)	Heal a teammate.
Old School (Bronze)	Play a 2,3,4 player split screen local game
Point, Shoot, Kill (Gold)	Kill 100 enemies with every missile during Ranked games.
Racing? In a Twisted Metal game?! (Silver)	Don't miss any gates and win the battle in Race #2, one player only.
Remote Nuke (Silver)	Kill 3 players with a single remote bomb.
Right Place, Right Time (Bronze)	Kill a player less than 5 seconds after you respawn, in an online game
So much anger... (Bronze)	Discover the secret of Sophie Kane
Tantric Twisted (Gold)	Reach 50 cars killed by yourself in Endurance mode
That. Just. Happened. (Bronze)	Kill yourself with a freeze cheap shot in ranked DM or LMS, or in any unranked or offline play
The most dangerous game (Bronze)	Be The Hunted/Stay the Hunted- in ranked, unranked, or split screen local-HUNTED GAME MODE for at least 4 minutes.
The One That Got Away (Bronze)	Complete the Sweet Tooth story on any difficulty.
TMA (Gold)	Complete Story mode without dying or switching cars in the garage.
Tradin' Paint (Bronze)	Ram 5 players to death in a single online game.
Truly Twisted (Silver)	Complete the Story mode on Twisted Difficulty
Twisted Gold (Gold)	Earn a gold medal in every campaign event and boss fight on Twisted difficulty
Twofer (Bronze)	Kill two enemies with a single rat rocket.
Up, Up and Away (Bronze)	Launch a Nuke

Watch Me Shine! (Bronze)	Complete the Doll Face story on any difficulty.
We buy gold! (Bronze)	Earn a gold medal on every campaign event in any difficulty mode including co-op.
You think this game made itself? (Bronze)	Watch the credits, start to finish

TWISTED METAL HEAD ON (PSP)

Input these codes during gameplay.

UNLOCKABLE	CODE
Invulnerability	→, ←, ↓, ↑ and finally press L1 + R1
Infinite Weapons	▲, ▲, ↓, ↓, L1 + R1

TWO WORLDS II (XBOX 360)

CODES

Hold down LB + RB, then while still holding it, press and release buttons in the following order: ▢ -> ♦ -> ▢ -> ♥. The console box appears. Press ✗ to bring up an in-game keyboard and type in the following codes. Using these cheats will disable Achievements on this game save permanently. If you want to earn achievements later, you must restart the game from the dashboard and use a non-cheated game save.

EFFECT	CODE
Add Auras (Currency)	addgold # (Replace # with any positive number)
Add skill points	AddSkillPoints #
Adds parameter points to spend (Strength, Accuracy etc.)	AddParamPoints # (replace # with any positive number)
Enables console cheats	TWOWORLDSCHEATS
Gain Experience Points	AddExperiencePoints # (# is any positive number)
God mode off	GOD 0
God Mode on (Maxes all stats and abilities)	GOD 1
Invisible To Enemies	Player.InvisibleForEnemies 1
Jump Height/Gravity (use a negative number)	ms.Grav #
Run Speed	Hero.Move.FastRunSpeed #
Set time of day (0-255, with 0=midnight, 40=dawn, 20=sunset, 255=just before midnight)	Time #
Sets player level	ec.dbg levels # (replace # with any positive number)
Turns off immortality	IMMORTAL 0
Turns on immortality (Unkillable)	IMMORTAL 1
Walk Up Any Rock or Mountain (use a big negative number)	Physx.Char.SlopeLimit.Rock #
Walk Up Any Slope (use a big negative number)	Physx.Char.SlopeLimit #
With equipped weapon, kill selected enemy	KILL

UNLOCKABLE

Pause the game and enter the code at "Enter Bonus Code".

EFFECT	CODE
Anathros Sword	6770-8976-1634-9490

Axe	1775-3623-3298-1928
Black Legion Ax	4802-6468-2848-6286
Dragon Armor	4149-3083-9823-6545
Dragon Scale Armor	9199-0035-9610-2338
Dusty Scroll	8233-3296-3311-2976
Elexorie	3542-3274-8350-6064
Elexorien Sword	4677-1553-6730-1272
Hammer	6231-1890-4345-5988
Lucienda Sword	9122-5287-3591-0927
Scroll	6972-5760-7685-8477

TWO WORLDS II   (PLAYSTATION 3)

CODES

During the game, hold ⬜L1 + ⬜R1 and press ⬜START, ✛, ⬜START, ✛. You should see the debug menu appear. Enter the following codes for the desired effect. This will disable Trophies.

EFFECT	CODE
Activation Code	TWOWORLDSCHEATS
Add Experience Points	AddExperiencePoints X - Experience points, where X is a number between 0 and 255
Add Gold	Addgold X - Gold, where X is a number between 0 and 255
Add Skill Points	AddSkillPoints X - Skill points, where X is a number between 0 and 255
God Mode	GOD X - Toggle God Mode, , where X is a number is 0 or 1
Set attributes to 1000	ec.dbg iamcheater
Unlock all Skills	ec.dbg skills

UNLOCKABLE

Select the "Bonus Code" option, then enter one of the following codes to get the corresponding item

EFFECT	CODE
Anathros sword	6770-8976-1634-9490
Axe	1775-3623-3298-1928
Dragon scale armor	4149-3083-9823-6545
Elexorien two-handed sword	3542-3274-8350-6064
Hammer	6231-1890-4345-5988
Labyrinth Level	1797-3432-7753-9254
Lucienda sword	9122-5287-3591-0927
Luciendar Sword	6624-0989-0879-6383
Scroll bonus map	6972-5760-7685-8477
Two-handed hammer	3654-0091-3399-0994

UEFA EURO 2012 (PLAYSTATION 3)

TROPHY

UNLOCKABLE	HOW TO UNLOCK
Collector (Silver)	Collect all mosaic pieces in Expedition
Creating History Together (Bronze)	Win UEFA EURO 2012 with more than 1 user playing for the same team in all 6 matches
Expeditionary Nature (Silver)	Defeat all 53 nations in Expedition
Glory Moment (Bronze)	Win Online UEFA EURO 2012
Make It Possible (Bronze)	Succeed in a Challenge
My Euro (Silver)	Win a match in each UEFA EURO 2012 game mode
National Pride (Bronze)	Win an Expedition match with all starting 11 from the same nation
On All Fronts (Bronze)	Defeat one team from each group in Expedition
One Down (Bronze)	Defeat all possible teams from a group in Expedition
We Are The Champions (Bronze)	Win UEFA EURO 2012

UEFA EURO 2012 (XBOX 360)

ACHIEVEMENT

UNLOCKABLE	HOW TO UNLOCK
Collector (50)	Collect all mosaic pieces in Expedition
Creating History Together (30)	Win UEFA EURO 2012 with more than 1 user playing for the same team in all 6 matches
Expeditionary Nature (40)	Defeat all 53 nations in Expedition
Glory Moment (30)	Win Online UEFA EURO 2012
Make It Possible (10)	Succeed in a Challenge
My Euro (40)	Win a match in each UEFA EURO 2012 game mode
National Pride (10)	Win an Expedition match with all starting 11 from the same nation
On All Fronts (10)	Defeat one team from each group in Expedition
One Down (10)	Defeat all teams from a group in Expedition
We Are The Champions (20)	Win UEFA EURO 2012

UFC UNDISPUTED 3 (PLAYSTATION 3)

TROPHY

UNLOCKABLE	HOW TO UNLOCK
A Quarter Down, Three to Go (Silver)	Clear 25% or more of all game modes.
Artiste (Bronze)	Create a Logo and apply it to a CAF as a Tattoo.
Bragging Rights (Bronze)	Create a Highlight Reel.
Breaking your Best Toys (Silver)	Win against a CAF that obtained Career Hall of Fame in Exhibition on Expert Difficulty or higher.

Breaking your Toys (Bronze)	Win a match against the COM on Experienced Difficulty while using a CAF in Exhibition Mode.
Brute Force (Bronze)	Submission Slam or Stomp Escape the COM in Exhibition on Advanced Difficulty or Higher
Chopping 'em Down (Bronze)	Get the TKO win by damaging the opponent's legs.
Determined Champion (Silver)	Clear Title Mode without any interruption.
Dual Division Champion (Silver)	Use 1 fighter in Career Mode to win the UFC championship in 2 weight divisions.
Even Rocky Had a Montage (Silver)	Create a Highlight Reel with 10 or more different fighters.
Everyone's a Critic (Bronze)	Rate contents created by other players in Content Sharing.
Exhibition Excellence (Bronze)	Win 5 ranked Online matches in a row.
Extracurricular (Bronze)	Join an Online camp.
Fight Camp Frenzy (Silver)	Win 10 consecutive Fight Camp Exhibition matches.
Finish the Fight (Gold)	After a KO or TKO, land 4 finishing blows and win the match.
First of Many! (Bronze)	Win a ranked Online match for the first time.
Getting A Leg Up (Silver)	Defeat a COM on Advanced or higher in Exhibition or Tournament Mode with each Leg Submission.
GOOOAAL!!! (Silver)	KO the opponent with a soccer kick.
Hall of famer (Silver)	Enter the Hall of Fame with a fighter in Career Mode.
History is Best Both Ways (Silver)	Obtain a 100% completion score with both fighters in a fight in Ultimate Fights Mode.
Making it Rain (Bronze)	10,000 or more shop points accumulated.
Online Amateur (Bronze)	Play 10 or more Online matches.
Online Journeyman (Silver)	Play 500 or more ranked Online matches.
Platinum (Platinum)	Obtain all trophies
Pound for Pound (Silver)	Win in each division in Exhibition with Advanced Difficulty or higher.
Practice Makes Perfect (Bronze)	Play an Online Fight Camp Sparring match.
Prepared to Win! (Bronze)	Play through each Training Game with a fighter in Career Mode.
PRIDE of a champion (Bronze)	Win 25 fights consecutively in Title Defense Mode.
Prime Time Fighting (Bronze)	Play and complete a 6, 7 or 8 card event in Event Mode.
Prolific Champion (Gold)	Use 1 fighter in Career Mode and win the WFA Championship, UFC Championship, and PRIDE Grand Prix.
Punching is Hard Work (Bronze)	Win a match on Ultimate in Exhibition or Tournament Mode with the Simulation Energy Settings.
Puppeteer (Bronze)	Create a CAF and modify the face with CREATE A FIGHTER.

Storied Career (Bronze)	Complete Career Mode with a CAF or Roster Fighter.
Training Expertise (Silver)	Obtain a 4-star score in a Training Game with a fighter in Career Mode.
Triple Threatening (Silver)	Obtain any level 3 move for 1 fighter in Career Mode.
Willingness (Bronze)	Select a guided tutorial

UFC UNDISPUTED 3 (XBOX 360)

ACHIEVEMENT

UNLOCKABLE	HOW TO UNLOCK
A Quarter Down, Three to Go (50)	Clear 25% or more of all game modes.
All About the Show (10)	Watch a PRIDE entrance in Exhibition once without skipping.
Bragging Rights (5)	Create a Highlight Reel.
Breaking your Best Toys (30)	Win against a CAF that obtained Career Hall of Fame in Exhibition on Expert Difficulty or higher.
Breaking your Toys (10)	Win a match against the COM on Experienced Difficulty while using a CAF in Exhibition Mode.
Brute Force (15)	Submission Slam or Stomp Escape the COM in Exhibition on Advanced Difficulty or Higher
Chopping 'em Down (5)	Get the TKO win by damaging the opponent's legs.
Determined Champion (30)	Clear Title Mode without any interruption.
Dual Division Champion (30)	Use 1 fighter in Career Mode to win the UFC championship in 2 weight divisions.
Even Rocky Had a Montage (50)	Create a Highlight Reel with 10 or more different fighters.
Everyone's a Critic (5)	Rate contents created by other players in Content Sharing.
Exhibition Excellence (30)	Win 5 ranked Xbox LIVE matches in a row.
Extracurricular (10)	Join an Xbox LIVE Fight Camp.
Fight Camp Frenzy (35)	Win 10 consecutive Fight Camp Exhibition matches.
Finish the Fight (100)	After a KO or TKO, land 4 finishing blows and win the match.
First of Many! (10)	Win a ranked Xbox LIVE match for the first time.
Getting A Leg Up (45)	Defeat a COM on Advanced or higher in Exhibition or Tournament Mode with each Leg Submission.
GOOOAAL!!! (15)	KO the opponent with a soccer kick.
Hall of famer (30)	Enter the Hall of Fame with a fighter in Career Mode.
History is Best Both Ways (30)	Obtain a 100% completion score with both fighters in a fight in Ultimate Fights Mode.
Making it Rain (15)	10,000 or more shop points accumulated.
Online Amateur (10)	Play 10 or more ranked Xbox LIVE matches.
Online Journeyman (30)	Play 500 or more ranked Xbox LIVE matches.
Pound for Pound (50)	Win in each division in Exhibition with Advanced Difficulty or higher.
Practice Makes Perfect (5)	Play an Xbox LIVE Fight Camp Sparring match.

Prepared to Win! (10)	Play through each Training Game with a fighter in Career Mode.
PRIDE of a champion (20)	Win 25 fights consecutively in Title Defense Mode.
Prime Time Fighting (15)	Play and complete a 6, 7 or 8 card event in Event Mode.
Prolific Champion (100)	Use 1 fighter in Career Mode and win the WFA Championship, UFC Championship, and PRIDE Grand Prix.
Punching is Hard Work (5)	Win a match on Ultimate in Exhibition or Tournament Mode with the Simulation Energy Settings.
Puppeteer (5)	Create a CAF and modify the face with CREATE A FIGHTER.
Storied Career (15)	Complete Career Mode with a CAF or Roster Fighter.
Training Expertise (50)	Obtain a 4-star score in a Training Game with a fighter in Career Mode.
Triple Threatening (30)	Obtain any level 3 move for 1 fighter in Career Mode.
Willingness (5)	Select a guided tutorial

UFC 2009 UNDISPUTED (XBOX 360, PLAYSTATION 3)

UNLOCKABLE

UNLOCKABLE	HOW TO UNLOCK
Unlock Punkass	To unlock the TapOut crew member Punkass as a fighter, obtain a Sponsorship from TapOut during Career mode.
Unlock Mask	In Career mode, get 3 consecutive wins by tapout/ submission. He will then be selectable in exhibition matches in the light heavyweight weight class.

ULTIMATE MARVEL VS. CAPCOM 3 (PLAYSTATION 3)

TROPHY

UNLOCKABLE	HOW TO UNLOCK
A Friend in Need (Bronze)	Perform 100 Crossover Assists. (Arcade/Online only)
A Warrior Born (Bronze)	Earn 5,000 Player Points (PP).
Above Average Joe (Bronze)	Land a Viewtiful Combo. (Arcade/online only)
Advancing Guardian (Bronze)	Perform 100 Advancing Guards. (Arcade/Online only)
Assemble! (Bronze)	Participate in an 8 player Lobby online.
Big Bang Theory (Bronze)	Perform 30 Hyper Combo Finishes. (Arcade/online only)
Brave New World (Bronze)	Participate in any mode online.
Comic Collector (Gold)	Unlock all items in the Gallery.
Crazy Good (Bronze)	Surpass the rank of Fighter.
Defender (Bronze)	Block 100 times. (Arcade/Online only)
Devil with a Blue Coat (Bronze)	Earn 30,000 Player Points (PP).
Divine Brawler (Silver)	Earn 100,000 Player Points (PP).
Dominator (Silver)	Collect 100 titles.
Dreaded Opponent (Bronze)	Participate in 200 matches online.
Fighting Machine (Silver)	Win 100 battles in Ranked Match.
First Strike (Bronze)	Land 50 First Attacks. (Arcade/Online only)
Forged From Steel (Silver)	Participate in 300 matches online.

Full Roster (Silver)	Battle against all characters online.
Gravity? Please... (Bronze)	Land 50 Team Aerial Combos. (Arcade/Online only)
Hard Corps (Bronze)	Perform 30 Crossover Combination Finishes. (Arcade/online only)
Hellbent (Bronze)	Participate in 100 matches online.
High-Score Hero (Silver)	Earn 500,000 points in Arcade mode.
Hotshot (Bronze)	Win 10 battles in Ranked Match.
Incredible (Bronze)	Win without calling your partners or switching out in an online match.
Master of Tasks (Silver)	Clear 480 missions in Mission mode.
Mega Buster (Bronze)	Use 1,000 Hyper Combo Gauge bars. (Arcade/online only)
Mega Good (Silver)	Surpass the 6th rank of any class.
Mighty Teamwork (Bronze)	Land 30 Team Aerial Counters. (Arcade/Online only)
Missions? Possible. (Bronze)	Clear 120 missions in Mission mode.
Mutant Master (Bronze)	Land an Uncanny Combo. (Arcade/online only)
Need a Healing Factor	Win without blocking in an online match. (Bronze)
Noble Effort (Bronze)	Get a 5-game win streak in Ranked Match.
Passport to Beatdown Country (Bronze)	Fight in all of the stages.
Perfect X-ample (Bronze)	Use X-Factor 50 times. (Arcade/Online only)
Quick Change-Up (Bronze)	Perform 50 Crossover Counters. (Arcade/Online only)
Rivals Welcome (Silver)	Play in Online Mode for over 30 hours.
Savage Playing (Bronze)	Perform 50 Snap Backs. (Arcade/Online only)
Saving My Quarters (Bronze)	Beat Arcade mode without using any continues.
Seductive Embrace (Bronze)	Play in Online Mode for over 5 hours.
Slam Master (Bronze)	Win 50 battles in Ranked Match.
The Best There Is (Bronze)	Beat Arcade mode on the hardest difficulty.
The Points Do Matter (Bronze)	Earn 400,000 points in Arcade mode.
The Ultimate (Platinum)	Obtain all Trophies.
Training in Isolation (Silver)	Play in Offline Mode for over 30 hours.
Training Montage (Bronze)	Play in Offline Mode for over 5 hours.
Up To The Challenge (Silver)	Clear 240 missions in Mission mode.
Waiting for the Trade (Gold)	View all endings in Arcade mode.

CODE

UNLOCKABLE	CODE
Play as Galactus	L1+Select+X while highlighting arcade mode
Galactus	Earn 30,000 points on your player card.

ULTIMATE MARVEL VS. CAPCOM 3 (PLAYSTATION VITA)

TROPHY

UNLOCKABLE	HOW TO UNLOCK
A Friend in Need (Bronze)	Perform 100 Crossover Assists. (Arcade/Online only)
A Warrior Born (Bronze)	Earn 5,000 Player Points (PP).
Above Average Joe (Bronze)	Land a Viewtiful Combo. (Arcade/online only)
Advancing Guardian (Bronze)	Perform 100 Advancing Guards. (Arcade/Online only)

NEW!

A B C D E F G H I J K L M N O P Q R S T U V W X Y Z

Assemble! (Bronze)	Participate in an 8 player Lobby online.
Big Bang Theory (Bronze)	Perform 30 Hyper Combo Finishes. (Arcade/online only)
Brave New World (Bronze)	Participate in any mode online.
Comic Collector (Gold)	Unlock all items in the Gallery.
Crazy Good (Bronze)	Surpass the rank of Fighter.
Defender (Bronze)	Block 100 times. (Arcade/Online only)
Devil with a Blue Coat (Bronze)	Earn 30,000 Player Points (PP).
Divine Brawler (Silver)	Earn 100,000 Player Points (PP).
Dominator (Silver)	Collect 100 titles.
Dreaded Opponent (Bronze)	Participate in 200 matches online.
Fighting Machine (Silver)	Win 100 battles in Ranked Match.
First Strike (Bronze)	Land 50 First Attacks. (Arcade/Online only)
Forged From Steel (Silver)	Participate in 300 matches online.
Full Roster (Silver)	Battle against all characters online.
Gravity? Please... (Bronze)	Land 50 Team Aerial Combos. (Arcade/Online only)
Hard Corps (Bronze)	Perform 30 Crossover Combination Finishes. (Arcade/online only)
Hellbent (Bronze)	Participate in 100 matches online.
High-Score Hero (Silver)	Earn 500,000 points in Arcade mode.
Hotshot (Bronze)	Win 10 battles in Ranked Match.
Incredible (Bronze)	Win without calling your partners or switching out in an online match.
Master of Tasks (Silver)	Clear 480 missions in Mission mode.
Mega Buster (Bronze)	Use 1,000 Hyper Combo Gauge bars. (Arcade/online only)
Mega Good (Silver)	Surpass the 6th rank of any class.
Mighty Teamwork (Bronze)	Land 30 Team Aerial Counters. (Arcade/Online only)
Missions? Possible. (Bronze)	Clear 120 missions in Mission mode.
Mutant Master (Bronze)	Land an Uncanny Combo. (Arcade/online only)
Need a Healing Factor (Bronze)	Win without blocking in an online match.
Noble Effort (Bronze)	Get a 5-game win streak in Ranked Match.
Passport to Beatdown Country (Bronze)	Fight in all of the stages.
Perfect X-ample (Bronze)	Use X-Factor 50 times. (Arcade/Online only)
Quick Change-Up (Bronze)	Perform 50 Crossover Counters. (Arcade/Online only)
Rivals Welcome (Silver)	Play in Online Mode for over 30 hours.
Savage Playing (Bronze)	Perform 50 Snap Backs. (Arcade/Online only)
Saving My Quarters (Bronze)	Beat Arcade mode without using any continues.
Seductive Embrace (Bronze)	Play in Online Mode for over 5 hours.
Slam Master (Bronze)	Win 50 battles in Ranked Match.
The Best There Is (Bronze)	Beat Arcade mode on the hardest difficulty.
The Points Do Matter (Bronze)	Earn 400,000 points in Arcade mode.
The Ultimate (Platinum)	Obtain all Trophies.
Training in Isolation (Silver)	Play in Offline Mode for over 30 hours.
Training Montage (Bronze)	Play in Offline Mode for over 5 hours.

Up To The Challenge (Silver)	Clear 240 missions in Mission mode.
Waiting for the Trade (Gold)	View all endings in Arcade mode.

ULTIMATE MARVEL VS. CAPCOM 3 (XBOX 360)

ACHIEVEMENT

UNLOCKABLE	HOW TO UNLOCK
A Friend in Need (20)	Perform 100 Crossover Assists. (Arcade/Xbox LIVE)
A Warrior Born (10)	Earn 5,000 Player Points (PP).
Above Average Joe (10)	Land a Viewtiful Combo. (Arcade/Xbox LIVE)
Advancing Guardian (10)	Perform 100 Advancing Guards. (Arcade/Xbox LIVE)
Assemble! (15)	Participate in an 8 player Lobby over Xbox LIVE.
Big Bang Theory (15)	Perform 30 Hyper Combo Finishes. (Arcade/Xbox LIVE)
Brave New World (10)	Participate in any mode over Xbox LIVE.
Comic Collector (50)	Unlock all items in the Gallery.
Crazy Good (10)	Surpass the rank of Fighter.
Defender (10)	Block 100 times. (Arcade/Xbox LIVE)
Devil with a Blue Coat (15)	Earn 30,000 Player Points (PP).
Divine Brawler (50)	Earn 100,000 Player Points (PP).
Dominator (30)	Collect 100 titles.
Dreaded Opponent (20)	Participate in 200 matches in Xbox LIVE.
Fighting Machine (40)	Win 100 battles in Ranked Match.
First Strike (10)	Land 50 First Attacks. (Arcade/Xbox LIVE)
Forged From Steel (30)	Participate in 300 matches in Xbox LIVE.
Full Roster (30)	Battle against all characters over Xbox LIVE.
Gravity? Please... (10)	Land 50 Team Aerial Combos. (Arcade/Xbox LIVE)
Hard Corps (15)	Perform 30 Crossover Combination Finishes. (Arcade/Xbox LIVE)
Hellbent (20)	Participate in 100 matches in Xbox LIVE.
High-Score Hero (30)	Earn 500,000 points in Arcade mode.
Hotshot (15)	Win 10 battles in Ranked Match.
Incredible (20)	Win without calling your partners or switching out in a Xbox LIVE match.
Master of Tasks (40)	Clear 480 missions in Mission mode.
Mega Buster (20)	Use 1,000 Hyper Combo Gauge bars. (Arcade/Xbox LIVE)
Mega Good (40)	Surpass the 6th rank of any class.
Mighty Teamwork (10)	Land 30 Team Aerial Counters. (Arcade/Xbox LIVE)
Missions? Possible. (20)	Clear 120 missions in Mission mode.
Mutant Master (10)	Land an Uncanny Combo. (Arcade/Xbox LIVE)
Need a Healing Factor (20)	Win without blocking in an Xbox LIVE match.
Noble Effort (15)	Get a 5-game win streak in Ranked Match.
Passport to Beatdown Country (10)	Fight in all of the stages.
Perfect X-ample (10)	Use X-Factor 50 times. (Arcade/Xbox LIVE)
Quick Change-Up (10)	Perform 50 Crossover Counters. (Arcade/Xbox LIVE)
Rivals Welcome (30)	Play on Xbox LIVE for over 30 hours.

NEW!

A
B
C
D
E
F
G
H
I
J
K
L
M
N
O
P
Q
R
S
T
U
V
W
X
Y
Z

Savage Playing (10)	Perform 50 Snap Backs. (Arcade/Xbox LIVE)
Saving My Quarters (10)	Beat Arcade mode without using any continues.
Seductive Embrace (20)	Play on Xbox LIVE for over 5 hours.
Slam Master (20)	Win 50 battles in Ranked Match.
The Best There Is (10)	Beat Arcade mode on the hardest difficulty.
The Points Do Matter (20)	Earn 400,000 points in Arcade mode.
The Ultimate (50)	Unlock all achievements.
Training in Isolation (30)	Play in Offline Mode for over 30 hours.
Training Montage (20)	Play in Offline Mode for over 5 hours.
Up To The Challenge (30)	Clear 240 missions in Mission mode.
Waiting for the Trade (50)	View all endings in Arcade mode.

CODE

UNLOCKABLE	CODE
Galactus	Earn 30,000 points on your player card.

ULTIMATE MORTAL KOMBAT 3 (XBOX 360)

CODES

Enter codes at the VS screen.

CODE	EFFECT
Player 1: LPx9, BLx8, LKx7; Player 2: LPx6, BLx6, LKx6	"Hold Flippers During Casino Run" Message
Player 1: LPx7, BLx1, LKx1; Player 2: LPx3, BLx1, LKx3	"Rain Can Be Found in the Graveyard" Message
Player 1: LPx1, BLx2, LKx3; Player 2: LPx9, BLx2, LKx6	"There Is No Knowledge That Is Not Power" Message
Player 1: LKx4; Player 2: LPx4	"Whatcha Gun Do?" Message
Player 1: BLx2; Player 2: BLx2	Blocking Disabled
Player 1: LPx6, BLx8, LKx8; Player 2: LPx6, BLx8, LKx8	Dark Kombat
Player 1: LPx1, BLx2, LKx2; Player 2: LPx2, BLx2, LKx1	Display "Skunky !!" Message
Player 1: LPx4, BLx4, LKx8; Player 2: LPx8, BLx4, LKx4	Don't Jump at Me
Player 1: LPx2, BLx2, LKx7; Player 2: LPx2, BLx2, LKx7	Explosive Combat (2 on 2 only)
Player 1: LPx6, BLx8, LKx8; Player 2: LPx4, BLx2, LKx2	Fast Uppercut Recovery Enabled
Player 1: BLx9, BLx1; Player 2: LPx1, BLx9	Kombat Zone: Bell Tower
Player 1: LPx3, BLx3; Player 2: BLx3, LKx3	Kombat Zone: Jade's Desert
Player 1: LKx4; Player 2: BLx7	Kombat Zone: Kahn's Kave
Player 1: LPx8, BLx8; Player 2: LPx2, BLx2	Kombat Zone: Kahn's Tower
Player 1: LPx6; Player 2: BLx4	Kombat Zone: Kombat Temple
Player 1: BLx5; Player 2: BLx5	Kombat Zone: Noob Saibot Dorfen
Player 1: LKx2; Player 2: LKx3	Kombat Zone: River Kombat
Player 1: LPx3, BLx4, LKx3; Player 2: LPx3, BLx4, LKx3	Kombat Zone: Rooftop
Player 1: LPx9, BLx3, LKx3	Kombat Zone: Scislac Busorez
Player 1: LPx6, BLx6, LKx6; Player 2: LPx4, BLx4, LKx4	Kombat Zone: Scorpion's Lair
Player 1: LPx1, BLx2, LKx3; Player 2: LPx9, BLx2, LKx1	Kombat Zone: Soul Chamber
Player 1: BLx7, LKx9; Player 2: BLx3, LKx5	Kombat Zone: Street
Player 1: LPx8, BLx8; Player 2: BLx8, LKx8	Kombat Zone: Subway

Player 1: BLx7, LKx7; Player 2: BLx2, LKx2	Kombat Zone: The Bridge
Player 1: LPx6, BLx6, LKx6; Player 2: LPx3, BLx3, LKx3	Kombat Zone: The Graveyard
Player 1: LPx8, BLx2; Player 2: BLx2, LKx8	Kombat Zone: The Pit 3
Player 1: LPx2, LPx8, LKx2; Player 2: LPx2, BLx8, LKx2	No Fear = EB Button, Skydive, Max Countdown
Player 1: LPx9, BLx8, LKx7; Player 2: LPx1, BLx2, LKx3	No Powerbars
Player 1: BLx3, LKx3	Player 1 Half Power
Player 1: LPx7, LKx7	Player 1 Quarter Power
Player 2: BLx3, LKx3	Player 2 Half Power
Player 2: LPx7, LKx7	Player 2 Quarter Power
Player 1: LPx4, BLx4, LKx4; Player 2: LPx4, BLx4, LKx4	RandPer Kombat (Method 1)
Player 1: LPx4, BLx6; Player 2: LPx4, BLx6	RandPer Kombat (Method 2)
Player 1: LPx9, BLx9, LKx9; Player 2: LPx9, BLx9, LKx9	Revision
Player 1: LPx5, BLx5; Player 2: LPx5, BLx5	See the Mortal Kombat LiveTour !!
Player 1: LPx3; Player 2: LPx3	Silent Kombat
Player 1: LPx1; Player 2: LPx1	Throwing Disabled
Player 1: LPx6, BLx2, LKx2; Player 2: LPx4, BLx6, LKx8	Two-Player Minigame of Galaga
Player 1: BLx4, LKx4; Player 2: LPx4, BLx4	Unikoriv Referri: Sans Power
Player 1: LPx4, BLx6, LKx6; Player 2: LPx4, BLx6, LKx6	Unlimited Run
Player 1: LPx9, BLx6, LKx9; Player 2: LPx1, BLx4, LKx1	Winner of this round battles Motaro
Player 1: BLx3, LKx3; Player 2: LPx5, BLx6, LKx4	Winner of this round battles Shao Kahn
Player 1: LPx2, LKx5; Player 2: LPx2, BLx4, LKx5	Winner of this round battles Smoke
Player 1: LPx7, BLx6, LKx9; Player 2: LPx3, BLx4, LKx2	Winner of this round battles Noob Saibot

UNLOCK AND SAVE HIDDEN CHARACTERS

Choose Arcade mode, lose a match. Then let the timer run out. You have 10 seconds to enter the ultimate kombat code for the character, one at a time. After unlocking them in Arcade mode, get to the Character Select screen. Pause, then exit the game. You'll have them for the rest of that play session. Now, very important, when you start the game up the next time around, you need to first go to the Arcade mode. This loads the characters you unlocked. Just wait and get to the Character Select screen, then exit. Now you can play with the characters online. If you do not go to the Arcade mode first, you will erase the characters. Just load and exit, then play online

UNCHARTED: DRAKE'S FORTUNE (PLAYSTATION 3)

DRAKE'S JERSEY

To unlock a baseball jersey for Drake, go to the Costume section of the game, and input the following code.

| UNLOCKABLE | HOW TO UNLOCK |
| Baseball Jersey | ←,→,↓,↑,▲,R1,L1,■ |

SECRET VIDEOS

To unlock secret videos in the Making a Cutscene section of the game, input the following codes.

UNLOCKABLE	HOW TO UNLOCK
Video for Grave Robbing	←,R2,→,↑,L2,▲,■,↓
Video for Time's Up	L1,→,■,↓,←,▲,R3,↑

CONCEPT ART

Go to the Rewards section of the game, and insert the following codes.

UNLOCKABLE	HOW TO UNLOCK
More Art	■, L1, →, ←, ↓, R2, ▲, ↑
Video	L2, →, ↑, ■, ←, ▲, R1, ↓

UNCHARTED: GOLDEN ABYSS (PLAYSTATION VITA)

TROPHY

UNLOCKABLE	HOW TO UNLOCK
100 Headshots (Bronze)	Defeat 100 enemies with headshots.
200 Kills: GAU - 19 (Bronze)	Defeat 200 enemies with the GAU - 19.
250 Headshots (Silver)	Defeat 250 enemies with headshots.
30 Kills: Desert - 5 (Bronze)	Defeat 30 enemies with the Desert - 5.
30 Kills: Mk - NDI (Bronze)	Defeat 30 enemies with the Mk - NDI.
30 Kills: Moss - 12 (Bronze)	Defeat 30 enemies with the Moss - 12.
30 Kills: RPG - 7 (Bronze)	Defeat 30 enemies with the RPG - 7.
30 Kills: Wes - 44 (Bronze)	Defeat 30 enemies with the Wes - 44.
50 Kills: 92FS - 9mm (Bronze)	Defeat 50 enemies with the 92FS - 9mm.
50 Kills: Dragon Sniper (Bronze)	Defeat 50 enemies with the Dragon Sniper.
50 Kills: GP32 - BND (Bronze)	Defeat 50 enemies with the GP32 - BND.
50 Kills: M79 (Bronze)	Defeat 50 enemies with the M79.
50 Kills: Micro - 9mm (Bronze)	Defeat 50 enemies with the Micro - 9mm.
70 Kills: FAL (Bronze)	Defeat 70 enemies with the FAL.
70 Kills: M4 (Bronze)	Defeat 70 enemies with the M4.
70 Kills: SAS - 12 (Bronze)	Defeat 70 enemies with the SAS - 12.
Bare-knuckle Slugger (Silver)	Defeat 50 enemies with hand-to-hand combat.
Bounty: Arcana (Bronze)	Complete the bounty set.
Bounty: Cádiz (Bronze)	Complete the bounty set.
Bounty: Gemstones (Bronze)	Complete the bounty set.
Bounty: Pieces of Silver (Bronze)	Complete the bounty set.
Charted! - Crushing (Gold)	Finish the game in Crushing Mode.
Charted! - Easy (Bronze)	Finish the game in Easy Mode.
Charted! - Hard (Gold)	Finish the game in Hard Mode.
Charted! - Normal (Silver)	Finish the game in Normal Mode.
Hangman (Bronze)	Defeat 20 enemies with gunfire by aiming while hanging.
Master Ninja (Silver)	Defeat 50 enemies with stealth attacks.
Odessa Mining Company (Bronze)	Complete the Mystery.
Paparazzo (Bronze)	Complete all photographs.
Platinum (Platinum)	Collect all other 55 Trophies for this Trophy.
Poisoned Powder (Bronze)	Complete the Mystery.
Proof of Life (Bronze)	Complete the Mystery.
Puzzle Master (Bronze)	Complete all puzzles.
Relic Finder (Bronze)	Find the strange relic.
Rub One Out (Bronze)	Complete all rubbings.
Ruffle My Feathers (Bronze)	Force José Parrot to squawk out 8 unique quips.
Run-and-Gunner (Bronze)	Defeat 20 enemies by shooting from the hip (without aiming).
Secrets of the Kuna (Bronze)	Complete the Mystery.

Steel Fist Expert (Silver)	Defeat 10 enemies in a row with a single punch, after softening them up with gunfire.
Steel Fist Master (Bronze)	Defeat 20 enemies with a single punch, after softening them up with gunfire.
Survivor (Bronze)	Defeat 75 Enemies in a row without dying.
The Circle of Heaven (Bronze)	Complete the Mystery.
The Collector (Bronze)	Collect first treasure or mystery.
The Conquistadors (Bronze)	Complete the Mystery.
The Friar's Pilgrimage (Bronze)	Complete the Mystery.
The Lost Civilization (Bronze)	Complete the Mystery.
The Revolution (Bronze)	Complete the Mystery.
The Ring of Earth (Bronze)	Complete the Mystery.
The Sete Cidades (Bronze)	Complete the Mystery.
Touch My Rear (Bronze)	Use the rear touch pad to climb a rope or chain.
Trail of Vincent Perez (Bronze)	Complete the Mystery.
Treasure: Jade Carvings (Bronze)	Complete the treasure set.
Treasure: Minor Deities (Bronze)	Complete the treasure set.
Treasure: The Menagerie (Bronze)	Complete the treasure set.
Treasure: Turquoise Glyphs (Bronze)	Complete the treasure set.

UNCHARTED 2: AMONG THIEVES (PLAYSTATION 3)

UNLOCKABLES

UNLOCKABLE	HOW TO UNLOCK
Crushing Difficulty	Beat the game on Hard difficulty to unlock.
Genghis Khan Villain Skin	Beat Crushing difficulty. Cost: 1,500,000
Marco Polo Hero Skin	Get the Platinum trophy. Cost: Free.

FREE IN-GAME MONEY

In Uncharted 2: Among Thieves, you'll have the option to hit the Square button when in the store to check for Uncharted: Drake's Fortune save data. If you have any save data you get cash! The cash can be used in both single-player, and multiplayer stores.

$20,000 In-Game Cash	Have a saved game of Uncharted: Drake's Fortune.
$80,000 In-Game Cash	Have a saved game of Uncharted: Drake's Fortune with the story completed at least once.

MULTIPLAYER BOOSTERS

Boosters give your character more tools to use in multiplayer. Unlock them by reaching certain levels (for the most part you unlock a booster every two levels), then purchase them from the multiplayer store. There are two different booster slots you can use.

UNLOCKABLE	HOW TO UNLOCK
Bandoleer (Booster Slot 2)	Reach Level 4; Costs $2,000
Break Up (Booster Slot 1)	Reach Level 10; Costs $11,250
Come Get Some (Booster Slot 2)	Reach Level 58; Costs $2,000,000
Deposit (Booster Slot 2)	Reach Level 40; Costs $98,250
Down the Irons (Booster Slot 1)	Reach Level 14; Costs $18,750
Evasion (Booster Slot 1)	Reach Level 50; Costs $210,000
Explosive Expert (Booster Slot 2)	Reach Level 20; Costs $32,250
Fleet Foot (Booster Slot 2)	Reach Level 16; Costs $23,250
From the Hip (Booster Slot 1)	Reach Level 6; Costs $5,000
Glass Jaw (Booster Slot 1)	Reach Level 56; Costs $1,500,000
Half Loaded (Booster Slot 2)	Reach Level 54; Costs $400,000

Hell Blazer (Booster Slot 1)	Reach Level 18; Costs $27,750
Invalid (Booster Slot 1)	Reach Level 52; Costs $350,000
Juggler (Booster Slot 1)	Reach Level 38; Costs $94,500
Keep Firing (Booster Slot 2)	Reach Level 12; Costs $14,250
Launch Man (Booster Slot 2)	Reach Level 28; Costs $58,500
Monkey Man (Booster Slot 2)	Reach Level 32; Costs $72,000
Point and Shoot (Booster Slot 1)	Reach Level 2; Costs $2,000
Rapid Hands (Booster Slot 1)	Reach Level 42; Costs $111,000
Revenge (Booster Slot 2)	Reach Level 48; Costs $134,250
Rocket Man (Booster Slot 2)	Reach Level 44; Costs $120,000
Scavenger (Booster Slot 2)	Reach Level 8; Costs $8,250
Scoped In (Booster Slot 2)	Reach Level 36; Costs $87,000
Situational Awareness (Booster Slot 1)	Reach Level 46; Costs $129,000
Sure Foot (Booster Slot 2)	Reach Level 26; Costs $52,500
Sure Shot (Booster Slot 1)	Reach Level 30; Costs $64,500
Treasure Bearer (Booster Slot 2)	Reach Level 24; Costs $43,500
Turtle (Booster Slot 1)	Reach Level 22; Costs $40,500
Veiled (Booster Slot 1)	Reach Level 51; Costs $300,000
Walk Softly (Booster Slot 1)	Reach Level 34; Costs $79,500

MULTIPLAYER SKINS

These skins that can be purchased in the multiplayer store after you reach certain levels.

UNLOCKABLE	HOW TO UNLOCK
Cameraman Jeff	Reach Level 30; Costs $100,000
Doughnut Drake	Reach Level 60; Costs $2,000,000
Genghis Khan Villain Skin	Beat Crushing Difficulty. Cost: 1,500,000
Harry Flynn	Reach Level 20; Costs $50,000
Heist Drake	Reach Level 10; Costs $20,000
Heist Flynn	Reach Level 20; Costs $50,000
Karl Schafer	Reach Level 50; Costs $1,000,000
Lieutenant Draza	Reach Level 50; Costs $1,000,000
Marco Polo Hero Skin	Get the Platinum trophy. Cost: Free.
Skelzor	Reach Level 60; Costs $2,000,000
Winter Chloe	Reach Level 20; Costs $50,000
Winter Drake	Reach Level 40; Costs $250,000
Winter Elena	Reach Level 30; Costs $100,000
Winter Flynn	Reach Level 30; Costs $100,000
Zoran Lazarevic	Reach Level 40; Costs $250,000
Zorskel	Reach Level 10; Costs $20,000

MULTIPLAYER TAUNTS

UNLOCKABLE	HOW TO UNLOCK
Flex Taunt	Reach Level 20; Costs $50,000
Flurry Taunt	Reach Level 30; Costs $100,000
Kiss Taunt	Reach Level 10; Costs $10,000
Pump Taunt	Reach Level 53; Costs $500,000
Yes Taunt	Reach Level 40; Costs $250,000

GLITCH

This glitch is to enable "tweaks" on difficulties that have not been completed. First, start a game on a difficulty you haven't finished and play through until you have a real gun. Next, go to in-game options and set the difficulty where you have unlocked the tweaks. Enable your tweaks, then select "Save and quit". Finally, go to main menu and set the difficulty back to the one you where you just got a real gun. Start the game on that difficulty and enjoy.

UNCHARTED 3: DRAKE'S DECEPTION (PLAYSTATION 3)

TROPHY

UNLOCKABLE	HOW TO UNLOCK
100 Headshots (Silver)	Defeat 100 enemies with headshots
20 Headshots (Bronze)	Defeat 20 enemies with headshots
30 Kills: Arm Micro (Bronze)	Defeat 30 enemies with the Arm Micro
30 Kills: Dragon Sniper (Bronze)	Defeat 30 enemies with the Dragon Sniper
30 Kills: G-MAL (Bronze)	Defeat 30 enemies with the G-MAL
30 Kills: KAL 7 (Bronze)	Defeat 30 enemies with the KAL 7
30 Kills: M9 (Bronze)	Defeat 30 enemies with the M9
30 Kills: Mag 5 (Bronze)	Defeat 30 enemies with the Mag 5
30 Kills: Mk-NDI (Bronze)	Defeat 30 enemies with the Mk-NDI
30 Kills: PAK-80 (Bronze)	Defeat 30 enemies with the PAK-80
30 Kills: RPG7 (Bronze)	Defeat 30 enemies with the RPG-7
30 Kills: SAS-12 (Bronze)	Defeat 30 enemies with the SAS-12
30 Kills: T-Bolt Sniper (Bronze)	Defeat 30 enemies with the T-Bolt Sniper
30 Kills: TAU Sniper (Bronze)	Defeat 30 enemies with the Tau Sniper
Adept Fortune Hunter (Bronze)	Find 60 treasures
Apprentice Fortune Hunter (Bronze)	Find 10 treasures
Bare-knuckle Brawler (Bronze)	Defeat 20 enemies with hand-to-hand combat
Bare-knuckle Slugger (Bronze)	Defeat 50 enemies with hand to hand combat
Blindfire Marksman (Bronze)	Defeat 20 enemies by blind-firing while in cover (without aiming with L1)
Brute Beater (Bronze)	Successfully counter all of a Brute's damage-giving attacks
Buddy System (Bronze)	Complete one Cooperative Multiplayer game
Charted! - Crushing (Gold)	Finish the game in Crushing Mode
Charted! - Easy (Bronze)	Finish the game in Easy Mode
Charted! - Hard (Silver)	Finish the game in Hard Mode
Charted! - Normal (Silver)	Finish the game in Normal Mode
Combat Leapfrog (Silver)	Defeat 10 enemies in a row, alternating hand-to-hand combat and gunplay
Drop the Bomb Headshot (Bronze)	Make 5 enemies drop their grenades by shooting them
Dyno-Might Master (Silver)	Defeat four enemies with one explosion
Expert Fortune Hunter (Bronze)	Find 80 treasures
Expert Ninja (Silver)	Defeat 5 enemies in a row using stealth attacks
First Treasure (Bronze)	Find one treasure
Grenade Hangman (Bronze)	Defeat 10 enemies with grenades while hanging
Hangman (Bronze)	Defeat 20 enemies with gunfire by aiming while hanging
He's Gonna Need a Sturgeon (Bronze)	Hit three enemies with fish in the market
Headshot Expert (Bronze)	Defeat 5 enemies in a row with headshots

Land Shark (Bronze)	Defeat 20 enemies while swimming
Marco Solo (Bronze)	Play in the swimming pool on the Cruise Ship
Master Fortune Hunter (Silver)	Find 100 treasures
Master Ninja (Bronze)	Defeat 50 enemies with stealth attacks
Pro-Pain (Bronze)	Defeat 10 enemies with propane of acetylene tank explosions
Quick Study (Bronze)	Inspect every display case in the Cartagena Museum
Relic Finder (Bronze)	Find the Strange Relic
Reload Master (Silver)	Defeat 50 enemies in a row without auto-reloading
Ride the Crocodile (Bronze)	Stand on the crocodile in the Secret Library
Riot Rocker (Bronze)	Defeat 5 Riot Shield enemies by running over their shield
Rolling Ammo Master (Silver)	20 times in a row, pick up ammo while rolling
Run-and-Gunner (Bronze)	Defeat 20 enemies by shooting from the hip (without aiming with L1)
Side Arm Master (Bronze)	Defeat 30 enemies in a row with your side arm
Skilled Fortune Hunter (Bronze)	Find 40 treasures
Survivor (Silver)	Defeat 75 enemies in a row without dying
Thrillseeker (Bronze)	Complete one Competitive Multiplayer game
Throwback (Bronze)	Kill 10 enemies with thrown-back grenades
Throwback Master (Bronze)	Throw back a grenade and defeat two enemies at once
Truck Brawler (Bronze)	Defeat 10 enemies using hand-to-hand combat on the back of the convoy trucks

UNLOCKABLE

UNLOCKABLE	HOW TO UNLOCK
Crushing Mode	Beat the game on any difficulty.

UNIT 13 (PLAYSTATION VITA)

TROPHY

UNLOCKABLE	HOW TO UNLOCK
13 Squared (Bronze)	Eliminate 169 enemies over the course of your career.
13-Star General (Platinum)	Obtain all Bronze, Silver, and Gold trophies in Unit 13.
Action Hero (Silver)	Complete all Direct Action operations.
Adapt and Overcome (Bronze)	Complete a Daily Challenge operation.
Anti-Venom (Silver)	Eliminate VIPER.
Badass and Bulletproof (Bronze)	Eliminate 13 enemies without taking damage.
Blast from the Past (Bronze)	Find an homage to what has come before...
Brainstorm (Bronze)	Score 13 headshots in a single operation.
By Strength and Guile (Bronze)	Reach level 10 with RINGO.
Ch13f Op3r471v3 (Silver)	Complete all Elite operations.
Cloud Nine (Gold)	Eliminate all High Value Targets.
Crowd Control Jr. (Bronze)	Eliminate 2 enemies with a single grenade.
De Oppresso Liber (Bronze)	Reach level 10 with ANIMAL.
Dead Winger (Silver)	Eliminate PHOENIX.
Doublecrossed (Silver)	Eliminate GRIFTER.
Extra Credit(S) (Bronze)	Watch the credits.

Facit Omnia Voluntas (Bronze)	Reach level 10 with ZEUS.
Fangdango (Silver)	Eliminate VAMPIRE.
Fat Chance (Silver)	Eliminate BIG SLICK.
Finish Him! (Silver)	Eliminate SCORPION.
Friendly Rivalry (Bronze)	Get a higher mission score than someone on your friends list.
Honneur et Fidélité (Bronze)	Reach level 10 with CHUCKLES.
It Pays to be a Winner (Bronze)	Reach level 10 with PYTHON.
L337 $0LD13R (Bronze)	Complete an Elite operation.
Lamplighter (Bronze)	Complete a Covert operation.
Last Laugh (Silver)	Eliminate HYENA.
Less Me, More We (Bronze)	Complete an operation in co-op.
Life of the Party (Bronze)	Show your enemy that you get down with the best of 'em.
Lucky 13 (Silver)	Achieve a 5-star rating in 13 operations.
Master Ninja (Silver)	Complete all Covert operations.
New Recruit (Bronze)	Complete the Unit 13 Training Course.
One Shot, One Kill (Bronze)	Reach level 10 with ALABAMA.
Sine Labore Nihil (Gold)	Max out all operatives.
Snakechaser (Bronze)	Complete a Direct Action operation.
Speed Demon (Bronze)	Complete a Deadline operation.
Sworded Out (Silver)	Eliminate SCIMITAR.
Time Killer (Silver)	Complete all Deadline operations.
Trick Shot (Bronze)	Eliminate an enemy by setting off a mine.
Twin Foiled (Bronze)	Eliminate 2 enemies with a single melee attack.
Two For One (Bronze)	Eliminate 2 enemies with a single bullet.
Unstoppable (Silver)	Achieve the highest score multiplier.
Variety is the Spice of Life (Silver)	Complete 13 different Dynamic missions.
Witchiker (Silver)	Eliminate WIZARD.
World Peace in 36 Easy Steps (Silver)	Complete all Covert, Deadline, Direct Action, and Elite operations.

VANDAL HEARTS: FLAMES OF JUDGMENT (PLAYSTATION 3)

UNLOCKABLES

Optional battle map stages. In case you miss any, all stages can be returned to once you reach Act 4. You can go back to get any of the optional maps up until you board the ship to the research facility.

UNLOCKABLE	HOW TO UNLOCK
Avery Fields	Examine the well at the top of the Church of Restoration on your second visit.
Foreign Quarter	Examine the barrel at the beginning of the Biruni University stage to your left.
Four Swordsman Spring	Examine the hollowed out tree at the dry riverbed.
Gillbari's Gardens	Examine the skeleton on the side of the central tree opposite from the chest in Timion Vale.
Halls of Atonement	Examine the king's throne in the Royal Courtyard.
Keliask's Tomb	Examine the glimmering tablet on the ground in the ancient ruins.
Ragnar's Gorge	Examine one of the crates during the mission in Tolby.
Trivishim's Corridor	Use the second mine cart in Dread to open up a cave entrance.

VANQUISH (XBOX 360)

UNLOCKABLES

UNLOCKABLE	HOW TO UNLOCK
Unlock God Hard Difficulty	Rotate right analog stick clockwise 20 times at the title screen.

VECTORMAN (WII)

UNLOCKABLES

UNLOCKABLE	HOW TO UNLOCK
Blow Up SEGA Logo	At the SEGA screen, move Vectorman slightly to the right of the logo. Aim upward and shoot. There is a hidden TV monitor there. Once it is broken, grab and use an orb power-up. The SEGA logo goes dark and the background stops moving.
Debug Mode	On the Options screen press Ⓐ, Ⓑ, Ⓑ, Ⓐ, ⬆, Ⓐ, Ⓑ, Ⓑ, Ⓐ. A menu then offers health, lives, level select, and weapon options.
Full Health	Pause the game and press Ⓐ, Ⓑ, ⬆, Ⓐ, Ⓒ, Ⓐ, ⬆, Ⓐ, Ⓑ, ⬆, Ⓐ.
Invisibility and Invincibility	First grab a bomb morph, and detonate Vectorman. Pause the game while Vectorman is still exploding and enter CALLACAB (Ⓒ, Ⓐ, ⬆, ⬆, Ⓐ, Ⓒ, Ⓐ, Ⓑ). Unpause the game. Pause again and enter the CALLACAB code. Unpause it, and Vectorman is invisible and invincible. Reenter the CALLACAB code to turn it off. No bomb morph is needed to disable it.
Level Warp	When you turn on the game, you can move Vectorman around on the SEGA screen. Shoot the SEGA logo 24 times, jump and hit the SEGA logo with Vectorman's head 12 times, and the letters S, E, G, and A start falling. Catch 90 to 110 letters to start on Stage 5, catch more than 110 letters to start on Day 10.
Light Bulbs	During gameplay, pause and enter Ⓐ, Ⓑ, Ⓐ, Ⓒ, Ⓐ, Ⓑ and press pause. A group of lights should be around you. The four lights that surround Vectorman indicate the field of collision detection. The light at the bottom indicates the collision detection of Vectorman's jets.

Slow Motion	This code slows down the game whenever you're hit. While playing, pause and press ⬆, ⬅, Ⓐ, Ⓒ, ⬇, ⬅, Ⓐ. Turn it off by entering the code again.
Stage Select	Ⓑ, Ⓐ, Ⓐ, Ⓑ, ⬇, Ⓑ, Ⓐ, Ⓐ, Ⓑ
Taxi Mode	Pause and press Ⓒ, Ⓐ, ⬅, ⬅, Ⓐ, Ⓒ, Ⓐ, Ⓑ (Call a Cab). You turn into a small cursor/arrow and can travel anywhere in the level. Enemies can also be killed by coming in contact with them. Bosses cannot be killed this way. To return to normal, pause and enter the code again.

VIRTUA TENNIS 3 (XBOX 360)

Enter these codes at the main menu.

UNLOCKABLE	CODE
Unlock All Courts	⬆, ⬆, ⬇, ⬇, ⬅, ⬅, ⬅, ➡
Unlock King & Duke	⬆, ⬆, ⬇, ⬇, ⬅, ➡, ⬅, ➡
Unlock All Gear	⬅, ➡, ⬇, ➡, ⬇, ⬅, ⬆, ⬇
Test End Sequence (win one match to win tournament)	⬇, ⬅, ⬇, ➡, ⬆, ⬆, ⬇, ⬇

VIRTUA TENNIS 4: WORLD TOUR EDITION (PLAYSTATION VITA)

TROPHY

UNLOCKABLE	HOW TO UNLOCK
Accomplished (Silver)	Become: Accomplished
Arcade Beginner (Bronze)	Clear a stage in Arcade Mode
Balloon Popper (Bronze)	Pop 30 balloons in Practice Mode
Best Stroker (Bronze)	Win 100 points with ground strokes
Big Hitter (Silver)	Hit 250 MAX Serves
Bomb Fiend (Bronze)	Detonate 20 bombs in the opponent's court in Bomb Match
Breakthrough (Bronze)	Win 10 games as the receiving player
Classic Photographer (Bronze)	Take a classic photo with VT CAM
Doubles Beginner (Bronze)	Clear a stage in Arcade Mode Doubles
Doubles Grand Slammer (Bronze)	Clear Doubles Mode
Emergency Stop (Bronze)	Stop the ships 10 times in Rock the Boat
Endless Rally! (Bronze)	Sustain a rally for 30 shots
Exhibitionist (Bronze)	Play 10 Exhibition Matches
Famous (Bronze)	Become: Famous
First Online Victory (Bronze)	Win a match online
Full Swing! (Bronze)	Hit 50 MAX power shots
Future Champion (Bronze)	Win the final tournament of the Tour Break
Grand Slammer (Bronze)	Clear Singles Mode
Great King (Silver)	Defeat the King in Arcade Mode Singles
Great Sniper (Bronze)	Achieve a 5x Combo in Clay Shooting
Hat Tricker (Bronze)	Score 3 goals in a row in Ace Striker
In Your Face Tennis! (Bronze)	Win 5 VR matches
International Traveler (Bronze)	Play an online visitor 10 times
Jack of all Trades (Gold)	Take lessons for all play styles
Look Alike (Bronze)	Create a player by taking a picture
Loving It! (Bronze)	Win 10 Love games
Marathon Runner (Bronze)	Run 42km (26mi)
Moneybags (Bronze)	Collect 1000 coins in Coin Match
Mother Hen (Bronze)	Deliver at least 10 chicks simultaneously to their mother in Egg Collector
Online Debut (Bronze)	Play online with a customised character

CODES & CHEATS

Online Master (Gold)	Reach Rank A
Online Streak (Bronze)	Win three consecutive matches online
Poker Face (Silver)	Get 10 royal straight flushes in Royal Poker
Power Smash! (Silver)	Hit 250 smashes
Pro-Tennis Fan (Bronze)	Play using all the real tennis players
Regular Customer (Bronze)	Stop at the Management Office 30 times
Screen Sharer (Bronze)	Play a Touch VS game
Shopeholic (Bronze)	Purchase 50 types of items in the Kit Catalouge
Super Player (Silver)	Hit 100 super shots
Swing Machine (Bronze)	Swing 5000 times
Tennis God (Platinum)	Collect every trophy
Ticket to the SPT Finals (Gold)	Make it to the playoffs
Top Condition (Silver)	Reach a Condition level of 20
Turkey Bowler (Bronze)	Get a turkey in Pin Crusher
Tycoon (Bronze)	Earn 1,000,000 in total prize money
Volley Master (Bronze)	Win 100 points with volleys
Wall Whiz (Bronze)	Hit a wall 5 times with the ball in one Wall Match
Wind Master (Bronze)	Pop 3 balloons in one Wind Match
World Tour Cleared! (Bronze)	Clear the game

VIRTUA TENNIS WORLD TOUR (PSP)

Enter these codes at the Main menu while holding R3.

UNLOCKABLE	CODE
All Racquets and Clothing A vailable in the Home Screen	⇨, ⇦, ⇨, ⇨, ⇧, ⇧, ⇧
Begin World Tour mode with $1,000,000	⇧, ⇩, ⇨, ⇩, ▲, ▲, ▲
Earn $2000 Every Week in World Tour mode	⇧, ⇩, ⇨, ⇩, ■, ▲, ▲
Unlock All Stadiums	⇧, ⇩, ⇦, ⇨, ■, ■, ■
Unlock the players King & Queen	⇧, ⇩, ⇧, ⇩, ■, ▲, ■

VIVA PIÑATA (XBOX 360)

Enter these passwords as names for your garden.

UNLOCKABLE	PASSWORD
Five Extra Accessories at the Pet Shop	chewnicorn
Items for Your Piñatas to Wear	goobaa nlock
Items for Your Piñatas to Wear	Bullseye
YMCA Gear	Kittyfloss

WALL-E (XBOX 360)

CHEATS

Enter the following codes in the cheat section of the Bonus Features menu.

EFFECT	CODE
All Bonus Features Unlocked	WALL-E, Auto, EVE, ZPM
All Game Contents Unlocked	M-O, Auto, ZPM, EVE
Costumes	ZPM, WALL-E, M-O, Auto
Gives WALL-E Super Laser Blaster	WALL-E, Auto, EVE, Mo
Invincibility	WALL-E, M-O, Auto, M-O
Make Any Cube Any Time	Auto, M-O, Auto, M-O

WALL-E (WII)

CHEATS

In the password screen enter the codes for the following effects. ZPM = Zero Point Mover.

EFFECT	CODE
All Bonus Features Unlocked	WALL-E, Auto, EVE, ZPM
All Game Content Unlocked	M-O, Auto, ZPM, EVE
All Holiday Costumes Unlocked	Auto, Auto, ZPM, ZPM
All Multiplayer Costumes Unlocked	ZPM, WALL-E, M-O, Auto
All Multiplayer Maps Unlocked	EVE, M-O, WALL-E, Auto
All Single Player Levels Unlocked	Auto, ZPM, M-O, WALL-E
EVE Permanent Super Laser Upgrade	EVE, WALL-E, WALL-E, Auto
Infinite Health	WALL-E, M-O, Auto, M-O
WALL-E & EVE Laser Gun Any Time	ZPM, EVE, M-O, WALL-E
WALL-E & EVE Make Any Cube Any Time	M-O, ZPM, EVE, EVE
WALL-E Always Has Super Laser	WALL-E, Auto, EVE, M-O
WALL-E Makes Any Cube Any Time	Auto, M-O, Auto, M-O
WALL-E with Laser Gun Any Time	WALL-E, EVE, EVE, WALL-E

WALL-E (PSP)

CHEATS

Enter the following codes in the Cheats menu in the corresponding code slot.

EFFECT	CODE
Code 1: Kills or Stuns Everything within Range	BOTOFWAR
Code 2: Can Move Undetected by any Enemy	STEALTHARMOR
Code 3: Laser Switches Color Continuously	RAINBOWLASER
Code 4: Every Cube Is a Explosive Cube	EXPLOSIVEWORLD
Code 5: Lights Dark Areas	GLOWINTHEDARK
Code 6: Wears Ski Goggles	BOTOFMYSTERY
Code 7: WALL-E has Golden Tracks	GOLDENTRACKS

WANTED: WEAPONS OF FATE (XBOX 360)

CODES

Enter these at the "Secret Codes" screen in the Main menu.

EFFECT	CODE
Unlocks Airplane Bodyguard	01010111
Unlocks Cinematic Mode	01110100
Unlocks Close Combat Mode	01100101
Unlocks Cross	01010100
Unlocks Health Improvement	01001100
Unlocks Infinite Adrenaline	01101101
Unlocks Infinite Ammo	01101111
Unlocks Janice	01000100
Unlocks One Shot One Kill	01110010
Unlocks Special Suit	01100001
Unlocks Super Weapons	01001111
Unlocks Wesley	01000011

WANTED: WEAPONS OF FATE (PLAYSTATION 3)

CODES

Enter these at the "Secret Codes" screen in the "Main Menu."

EFFECT	CODE
Unlocks Airplane Bodyguard	01010111
Unlocks Cinematic Mode	01110100
Unlocks Close-Combat Mode	01100101
Unlocks Cross	01010100
Unlocks Health Improvement	01001100
Unlocks Infinite Adrenaline	01101101
Unlocks Infinite Ammo	01101111
Unlocks Janice	01000100
Unlocks One Shot One Kill	01110010
Unlocks Special Suit	01100001
Unlocks Super Weapons	01001111
Unlocks Wesley	01000011

WATER WARFARE (WII)

UNLOCKABLES

By clearing single player mission mode you can unlock new characters to play as.

UNLOCKABLE	HOW TO UNLOCK
Biker Ben	Beat Biker Ben on the Training Level 6.
Cavegirl Carmen	Beat Cavegirl Carmen on Mission 8 of the Nature Park.
Rabid Rabbit	Beat Rabid Rabbit on Mission 8 of the Playground.
Snorkel Jane	Beat Snorkel Jane on Mission 8 of the Beach.
Trooper Tim	Beat Trooper Tim on Mission 8 of the Plaza.

WHERE THE WILD THINGS ARE (XBOX 360)

UNLOCKABLES

These are unlockable cheats that can be activated once you have completed the requirements.

UNLOCKABLE	HOW TO UNLOCK
Infinite Health	Collect all skulls (60).

Kill enemies in one hit	Collect all turtles (60).
The Wild Things won't eat you	Collect all beehives (60).
Treasures show up when holding the back button	collect all geodes (60).
Your ship doesn't take damage	Collect all seeds (60).

WIPEOUT 2048 (PLAYSTATION VITA)

TROPHY

UNLOCKABLE	HOW TO UNLOCK
1 Down, 19 To Go (Bronze)	Complete your first Online Multiplayer Level
2048 Champion (Bronze)	Complete the 2048 season
2048 Elite 1 (Bronze)	Get an ELITE PASS on the C Class Time Trial on Capital Reach in 2048
2048 Elite 2 (Bronze)	Get an ELITE PASS on Empire Climb Zone Mode in 2048
2048 Elite 3 (Bronze)	Get an ELITE PASS on the C Class Combat Event on Metro Park in 2048
2048 Speed Pads (Silver)	Hit a total of 2048 Speed Pads
2049 Champion (Bronze)	Complete the 2049 season
2049 Elite 1 (Bronze)	Get an ELITE PASS on the B Class Race on Unity Square 2049
2049 Elite 2 (Bronze)	Get an ELITE PASS on the A Class Time Trial on Metro Park in 2049
2049 Elite 3 (Bronze)	Get an ELITE PASS on Downtown Zone Mode in 2049
2050 Champion (Bronze)	Complete the 2050 season
2050 Elite 1 (Bronze)	Get an ELITE PASS on Queens Mall Zone Mode in 2050
2050 Elite 2 (Bronze)	Get an ELITE PASS on the A Class Race on Empire Climb in 2050
50 Kills (Bronze)	Destroy 50 ships in Online Multiplayer
50 MP Events (Silver)	Finish 50 Online Multiplayer events
Beat Zico (Gold)	Altima, C Class, Speed Lap, Pir-hana Speed – beat 52.00 seconds
Completist (Silver)	Complete all events in the Single Player Campaign
Elite Completist (Gold)	ELITE PASS every event in the Single Player Campaign
Halfway There (Silver)	Complete 10 Online Multiplayer Levels
Mach 1.5 (Gold)	Reach Zone 65 in any Zone Event
Multiplayer Begins (Bronze)	Finish an Online Multiplayer event
Multiplayer Completist (Gold)	Complete all nodes in the Online Multiplayer Campaign
Multiplayer Finished (Gold)	Finish the Online Multiplayer Campaign
Perfect Pir-hana (Silver)	Get a Perfect Lap in the Pir-hana Prototype, in the A Class, Unity Square, Speed Lap
Prototype (Silver)	ELITE PASS all Prototype Ship Challenges
Rank 25 (Silver)	Reach Rank 25
Rank 50 (Gold)	Reach Rank 50
Speed Thrills (Silver)	ELITE PASS any A+ Class Challenge
The Unlucky 7 (Silver)	Destroy 7 opposition ships in any Race in the Single Player Campaign
This is WipEout! (Platinum)	Obtain every Trophy in WipEout 2048
AG-Systems: Agility	Successfully complete the 2048 Ship unlock event

AG-Systems: Fighter	Reach Rank 7
AG-Systems: Prototype	Successfully complete the Prototype challenge unlocked at Rank 26.
Auricom: Agility	Reach Rank 9
Auricom: Fighter	Reach Rank 46
Auricom: Prototype	Successfully complete the Prototype challenge unlocked at Rank 20.
Auricom: Speed	Reach Rank 41
Feisar: Agility	Reach Rank 13
Feisar: Prototype	Successfully complete the Prototype challenge unlocked at Rank 10.
Pir-Hana: Agility	Reach Rank 17
Pir-Hana: Fighter	Reach Rank 35
Pir-Hana: Prototype	Successfully complete the Prototype challenge unlocked at Rank 50.
Pir-Hana: Speed	Successfully complete the 2050 ship unlock event
Quirex: Fighter	Successfully complete the 2049 ship unlock event
Quirex: Prototype	Successfully complete the Prototype challenge unlocked at Rank 30.
Quirex: Speed	Reach Rank 24

THE WITCHER 2: ASSASSINS OF KINGS (XBOX 360)

ACHIEVEMENT

UNLOCKABLE	HOW TO UNLOCK
Alea Iacta Est (10)	Complete Chapter 2.
Apprentice (10)	Use alchemy to brew five potions or oils.
Artful Dodger (30)	Cut off a tentacle using the kayran trap.
Avenger (30)	Finish the game by killing Letho.
Backbone (20)	Craft a suit of armor from elements of the kayran's carapace.
Being Witcher George (20)	Kill the dragon.
Black Ops (20)	Sneak through the lower camp without raising the alarm.
Craftsman (10)	Hire a craftsman to create an item.
Dragonheart (20)	Spare or save Saskia.
Eagle Eye (10)	Hit Count Etcheverry using the ballista.
Fat Man (15)	Kill the draug.
Focus (30)	Perform three successful ripostes in a row.
Friend of Trolls (15)	Spare all trolls in the game.
Gambler (15)	Win an arm wrestling match, a dice poker game and a fist fight.
Gladiator (15)	Defeat all opponents in the Kaedweni arena.
Guru (50)	Achieve character level 35.
Heartbreaker (10)	Seduce Ves.
Intimidator (15)	Intimidate someone.
Journeyman (10)	Achieve character level 10.
Kayranslayer (10)	Kill the kayran.
Kingmaker (15)	Help Roche rescue Anais from the Kaedweni camp.
Last Man Standing (15)	Survive your 30th fight in the Arena
Librarian (30)	Find all additional information about the insane asylum's history.

Madman (100)	Finish the game while playing at the Dark difficulty level.
Man of the Shadows (15)	Successfully sneak through Loredo's garden and find the component of the kayran trap.
Master Alchemist (10)	Acquire the Mutant ability.
Master of Magic (10)	Acquire the Sense of Magic ability.
Miser (10)	Collect 10000 orens.
Mutant! (30)	Enhance abilities using mutagens at least five times.
Necromancer (50)	Relive all of Auckes's memories in Dethmold's vision.
Old Friends (30)	Finish the game by sparing Letho.
Once Ain't Enough (15)	Complete Chapter 3.
Perfectionist (15)	Kill 10 foes in a row without losing any Vitality.
Pest Control (20)	Finish all quests involing the destruction of monster nests.
Poker! (30)	Roll five-of-a-kind at dice poker.
Reasons of State (15)	Stop Roche from killing Henselt.
Ricochet (10)	Kill a foe by deflecting his own arrow at him.
Sensitive Guy (10)	Save Síle from dying in the unstable portal.
Spellbreaker (15)	Help Iorveth find the dagger needed to free Saskia from the spell that holds her.
Swordmaster (10)	Acquire the Combat Acumen ability.
The Butcher of Blaviken (30)	Kill 500 foes.
The Fugitive (5)	Complete the Prologue.
Threesome (15)	Kill three foes at once by performing a group finisher.
To Aedirn! (5)	Complete Chapter 1.
To Be Continued... (50)	Finish the game at any difficulty level.
Torn Asunder! (15)	Kill more than one opponent using a single exploding bomb.
Tourist (10)	Tour the camp with Zyvik.
Tried-and-True (10)	Survive your 5th fight in the Arena
Trollslayer (30)	Kill all the trolls in the game.
Witch Hunter (10)	Leave Síle to die in the unstable portal.

WOLFENSTEIN (XBOX 360)

UNLOCKABLES

UNLOCKABLE	HOW TO UNLOCK
Cheats	Beat the game on any difficulty. Activating cheats will disable achievements.

WONDER BOY IN MONSTER WORLD (WII)

UNLOCKABLES

UNLOCKABLE	HOW TO UNLOCK
Stay at the Inn for Free	Any Inn throughout the game will let you spend the night, even if you don't have enough gold. They just take whatever You have, even if you don't have any gold at all.

WORLD SERIES OF POKER: TOURNAMENT OF CHAMPIONS (WII)

UNLOCKABLES

UNLOCKABLE	HOW TO UNLOCK
All Locations	Input ✛, ✛, ✛, ✛, ✛ at the main menu

CODES & CHEATS

WRC: FIA WORLD RALLY CHAMPIONSHIP (PSP)

Enter these passwords as Profile names.

UNLOCKABLE	PASSWORD
Bird camera	dovecam
Enables Supercharger cheat	MAXPOWER
Extra avatars	UGLYMUGS
Ghost car	SPOOKY
Reverses controls	REVERSE
Time trial ghost cars	AITRIAL
Unlock everything	PADLOCK

WRECKING CREW (WII)

UNLOCKABLES

UNLOCKABLE	HOW TO UNLOCK
Gold Hammer	In Phase 6, there are five bombs, 2 on the bottom, 2 in the middle of the level, and 1 on the top. Hit the 2 bombs on the bottom and then hit the middle left bomb. In a few seconds, a hammer appears. Hit it to obtain it. You now have the gold hammer. The music changes and you can hit enemies. You have the hammer until you die.

WWE '12 (XBOX 360)

CODE

At the main menu, select "My WWE", "Options", then "Cheat Codes".

UNLOCKABLE	CODE
Unlock the WWE Attitude Era Heavyweight Championship.	OhHellYeah!

UNLOCKABLE

Unlock these in g Road to Wrestlemania or Universe Mode

UNLOCKABLE	HOW TO UNLOCK
Arn Anderson's Civilian Attire	Hero Story Scene 5-1
Dashing Cody Rhodes	Villain Story Scene 4-1
Drew McIntyre Suit Attire	Villain Story Scene 13-2
Edge Entrance Attire	Villain Story 15-2
HHH Street Attire	Outsider Story Cutscene
John Cena Entrance Attire	Villain Story 1-4
John Cena Purple Attire & John Cena with T-Shirt	Play two different Wrestlemania Matches featuring Cena in Universe
Kevin Nash Suit Attire	Hero Story 14-1
Mr.McMahon Suit Attire	Hero Story Cutscene
Randy Orton without Beard	Go into a Wretlemania Match with Randy in Universe
Sheamus Suit Attire	Villain Story 18-1
Sheamus T-Shirt Attire	Villain Story 5-4
Undertaker Hooded Attire	Go into a Wretlemania Match with Undertaker in Universe
Wade Barrett Suit Attire	Villain Story 19-2
William Regal Suit Attire	Villain Story 8-5
Bragging Rights	Win a match in this ppv in Universe
Clash of Champions	Hero Story Cutscene at PPV
Extreme Rules	Win a match in this ppv in Universe
Fatal 4-Way	Win a match in this ppv in Universe
Hell in a Cell	Win a match in this ppv in Universe

Money in the Bank	Win a match in this ppv in Universe
Night of Champions	Win a match in this ppv in Universe
NXT Arena	Hero Story Cutscene
Over the Limit	Win a match in this ppv in Universe
Starrcade	Hero Story Cutscene
Survivor Series	Win a match in this ppv in Universe
TLC	Win a match in this ppv in Universe
Tribute to the Troops	Finish a year of Universe
WCW Monday Nitro	Hero Story 21-1
Jacob Cass Entrance	Hero Story Cutscene 2-1
King of Kings Theme	Outsider Story Cutscene
Mr. McMahon Entrance	Hero Story Cutscene
Undertaker Entrance	Win with Undertaker at Wrestlemania in Universe
United Kingdom Entrance	Villain Story Cutscene
Champion of Champions Title	Win a title at Night of Champions
Classic Intercontinental Title	Win the Intercontinental Title
ECW Title	Win a title at Extreme Rules
European Title	Villain Story 10-1
Hardcore Title	Win a title in a falls count anywhere match
Light Heavyweight Title	Win a title with Mysterio
Million Dollar Title	With a title with Ted DiBiase
WCW Spray Painted World Heavyweight Title	Hero Story Cutscene 13-1
WCW Spray Painted WWE Title	Hero Story Cutscene
WCW Title	Hero Story Cutscene
World Tag Team Title	With the titles on SmackDown
WWE Attitude Era Title	Win the WWE title with Stone Cold
WWE Tag Team Title	Win the titles on Raw
WWE Undisputed Title	Win the WWE title with HHH at a PPV
Arn Anderson	Viillain Story Cutscene
Booker T	Hero Story Cutscene 8-1
Brock Lesnar	Win a singles match in Universe
Demolition	Win the Undisputed Tag Titles in Universe
Eddie Guerrero	Hero Story 7-1
Edge	Villain Cutscene
Goldust	Win the Intercontinental Championship as Cody Rhodes in WWE Universe
Kevin Nash	Outsider Story Cutscene 5-2
Michelle McCool	Win Divas Title in Universe
Ricky Steamboat	Hero Story Cutscene
Road Warriors	Hero Story Cutscene 10-1
Stone Cold	Complete Villain Story or Defend WWE Title in Universe Mode
Vader	Hero Story Cutscene 6-2
Vince McMahon	Hero Story Cutscene

A
B
C
D
E
F
G
H
I
J
K
L
M
N
O
P
Q
R
S
T
U
V
W
X
Y
Z

WWE ALL STARS (PLAYSTATION 3)

UNLOCKABLE

Input the following codess during the Main Menu to unlock features

EFFECT	CODE
All Wrestlers, Arenas, Attires	←, ▲, ↓, ←, ▲, ■, ←, ■, ▲, ↓, →, ■, ←, ↑, ■, →
Austin & Punk Attires	←, ←, →, →, ↑, ↓, ↑, ↓
Roberts & Orton Attires	↑, ↓, ←, →, ↑, ↑, ↓, ↓
Savage & Morrison Attires	↓, ←, ↑, →, →, ↑, ←, ↓

UNLOCKABLE

Complete the tasks to unlock.

UNLOCKABLE	HOW TO UNLOCK
Classic Smackdown Arena	Complete a Path Of Champions With Your Created Superstar
Summerslam Arena	Win 10 Matches With Yor Created Superstar
WWE All-Stars Arena	Create a WWE Superstar

UNLOCKABLE

Complete the tasks to unlock

UNLOCKABLE	HOW TO UNLOCK
Drew McIntyre	Win the Fantasy Warfare Match with him against Roddy Piper
Eddie Guerrero	Win the Fantasy Warfare Match with him against Rey Mysterio Jr.
Edge	Win the Fantasy Warfare Match with him against Bret Hart
Jack Swagger	Win the Fantasy Warfare Match with him against Sgt. Slaughter
Jimmy Snuka	Win the Fantasy Warfare Match with him against Kane
Kane	Win the Fantasy Warfare Match with him against Jimmy Snuka
Mr. Perfect	Win the Fantasy Warfare Match with him against The Miz
Sgt. Slaughter	Win the Fantasy Warfare Match with him against Jack Swagger
Shawn Micheals	Win the Fantasy Warfare Match with him against The Undertaker
The Miz	Win the Fantasy Warfare Match with him against Mr. Perfect

WWE ALL STARS (XBOX 360)

UNLOCKABLE

Input the following codess during the Main Menu to unlock features

UNLOCKABLE	HOW TO UNLOCK
All Wrestlers, Arenas, Attires	←, Ⓨ, ↓, ←, Ⓨ, Ⓧ, ←, Ⓧ, Ⓨ, ↓, →, Ⓧ, ←, ↑, Ⓧ, →
Austin & Punk Attires	←, ←, →, →, ↑, ↓, ↑, ↓
Roberts & Orton Attires	↑, ↓, ←, →, ↑, ↑, ↓, ↓
Savage & Morrison Attires	↓, ←, ↑, →, →, ↑, ←, ↓

UNLOCKABLE

Complete the tasks to unlock

UNLOCKABLE	HOW TO UNLOCK
Classic Smackdown Arena	Complete a Path Of Champions With Your Created Superstar
Summerslam Arena	Win 10 Matches With Yor Created Superstar
WWE All-Stars Arena	Create a WWE Superstar

UNLOCKABLE

Complete the tasks to unlock

UNLOCKABLE	HOW TO UNLOCK
Drew McIntyre	Win the Fantasy Warfare Match with him against Roddy Piper
Eddie Guerrero	Win the Fantasy Warfare Match with him against Rey Mysterio Jr.

Edge	Win the Fantasy Warfare Match with him against Bret Hart
Jack Swagger	Win the Fantasy Warfare Match with him against Sgt. Slaughter
Jimmy Snuka	Win the Fantasy Warfare Match with him against Kane
Kane	Win the Fantasy Warfare Match with him against Jimmy Snuka
Mr. Perfect	Win the Fantasy Warfare Match with him against The Miz
Sgt. Slaughter	Win the Fantasy Warfare Match with him against Jack Swagger
Shawn Micheals	Win the Fantasy Warfare Match with him against The Undertaker
The Miz	Win the Fantasy Warfare Match with him against Mr. Perfect

WWE ALL STARS (WII)

UNLOCKABLE
Complete any Path of Superstars with each WWE Legend or Superstar to unlock their 2nd attire. Complete another path again with Andre the Giant, Hulk Hogan, John Cena, Rey Mysterio, and Randy Savage to unlock their 3rd attire

UNLOCKABLE
Complete the tasks to unlock

UNLOCKABLE	HOW TO UNLOCK
Drew McIntyre	Win the Fantasy Warfare Match with him against Roddy Piper
Eddie Guerrero	Win the Fantasy Warfare Match with him against Rey Mysterio Jr.
Edge	Win the Fantasy Warfare Match with him against Bret Hart
Jack Swagger	Win the Fantasy Warfare Match with him against Sgt. Slaughter
Jimmy Snuka	Win the Fantasy Warfare Match with him against Kane
Kane	Win the Fantasy Warfare Match with him against Jimmy Snuka
Mr. Perfect	Win the Fantasy Warfare Match with him against The Miz
Sgt. Slaughter	Win the Fantasy Warfare Match with him against Jack Swagger
Shawn Micheals	Win the Fantasy Warfare Match with him against The Undertaker
The Miz	Win the Fantasy Warfare Match with him against Mr. Perfect

WWE SMACKDOWN VS. RAW 2010 (XBOX 360) (PLAYSTATION 3)

CODES
Go to "options" then "cheat codes"; the codes are case-sensitive.

EFFECT	CODE
Unlock Dirt Sheet Set and Mr. McMahon's Office backstage areas.	BonusBrawl
Unlock The Rock	The Great One

ROAD TO WRESTLEMANIA UNLOCKABLES

UNLOCKABLE	HOW TO UNLOCK
The Million Dollar Man Ted DiBiase	In "Randy Orton's RTWM," beat Ted DiBiase Jr. at Wrestlemania and KO "The Million Dollar Man" after the match.
Alternate Attire for Chris Jericho	Week 6 of "HBK's RTWM," Make Jericho bleed.
Alternate Attire for Edge	Week 6 of "Edge's RTWM," Win in under 3 minutes.
Alternate Attire for JBL	Week 8 of "HBK's RTWM," win the match in under 4 minutes.
Alternate Attire for Mickie James	Week 6 of "Mickie James' RTWM," beat Michelle McCool in under 3 minutes.
Alternate Attire for Mr. Kennedy	In "Edge's RTWM," eliminate Mr. Kennedy from the Royal Rumble Match.
Alternate attire for Mr. McMahon (suit)	Week 5 of "Create-A-Superstar's RTWM," spend at least one minute of the match outside the ring.

Alternate Attire for Natalya	Week 9 of "Mickie James' RTWM," choose Kendrick over Natalya. Then at week 10, win the match suffering minimal damage.
Alternate Attire for Santino Marella (Street clothes)	Week 12 of "Create-A-Superstar's RTWM," make a successful diving attack from the top of the ladder.
Alternate Attire for Shawn Michaels	Week 4 of "HBK's RTWM," hit both opponents with Sweet CHIN Music.
Alternate Attire for Shawn Michaels (DX) (Option 1)	Week 10 of "HBK's RTWM," accept the Retirement Match. Then at Week 11, have your partner be the legal man longer.
Alternate Attire for Shawn Michaels (DX) (Option 2)	Week 10 of "HBK's RTWM," decline the Retirement Match, then at Week 11, execute three Double Team attacks.
Alternate Attire for The Brian Kendrick	Week 9 of 'Mickie James' RTWM," choose Natalya over Kendrick. Then at week 12, win the match without using a signature move or finisher.
Alternate Attire for Vince McMahon (Chicken Head)	Win the WrestleMania Match in "Create-A-Superstar's RTWM."
Alternate Attires for Miz and Morrison (Street clothes) & Dirt Sheet area for Backstage Brawl	Week 11 of "Brand Warfare's RTWM," win the handicap match as either Triple H or John Cena.
Champion of Champions title belt	Win at Wrestlemania in "Brand Warfare's RTWM."
Cowboy Bob Orton	Week 9 of "Randy Orton's RTWM," don't use any strikes in your match.
Dusty Rhodes	In "Randy Orton's RTWM," beat Cody Rhodes at WrestleMania and KO Dusty after the match.
Eve	Week 2 of "Mickie James' RTWM," pin or submit Maryse
Ezekiel Jackson	Week 3 of "Create-A-Superstar's RTWM," throw each opponent out of the ring at least once.
Green and Red Dummies as Playable Characters	Week 3 of "Randy Orton's RTWM," refuse Cody's help and then reverse three of Batista's attacks.
Interview Room for Backstage	Complete Shawn Michaels RTW.
Jesse	Week 2 of "Edge's RTWM," hit every opponent with a finisher.
John Cena Alternate Attire (Street Clothes)	Week 4 of "Brand Warfare's RTWM," you must put Kane through a table in less than 2:30 as John Cena.
Locker Room Backstage area	In "Edge's RTWM," at No Way Out, drag Mr. Kennedy on top of the Big Show and count the pinfall.
Mr. McMahon (Playable Character)	Week 11 of "Edge's RTWM," Put Triple H through an announcer table.
Randy Orton's Alternate Attire	In "Randy Orton's RTWM," at No Way Out, RKO Dusty Rhodes.
Road to Wrestlemania Event Skip Feature	Week 12 of "Randy Orton's RTWM," spend less than 2 minutes in the ring as the legal superstar.
Santino Marella Story Designer story	Week 11 of "Create-A-Superstar's RTWM," reach 500 degrees at least four times.
The Hardys, DX, & Morrison and The Miz Tag Entrances	Week 2 of "Brand Warfare's RTWM," you must win the battle royal as either Triple H or John Cena.
The Rock	Complete Edge's Road to Wrestlemania.
Triple H Alternate Attire (DX)	Week 6 of "Brand Warfare's RTWM," win your match in under 3 minutes as Triple H.
Trish Stratus	Complete Mickie's Road to Wrestlemania
Vince's Office in Backstage Brawl	Week 6 of "Create-A-Superstar's RTWM," win your match.

UNLOCKABLE ABILITIES

UNLOCKABLE	HOW TO UNLOCK
Durability	Must get Durability Attribute score of 85.
Exploder Turnbuckle Attack	Must get your speed attribute score of 75.
Fan Favorite	Must get charisma score of 80.
Fired Up	Must get an overall rating of 90.
Hardcore Resurrection	Must get hardcore score of 90.
Kip Up	Must get a technical score of 85.
Lock Pick	Must get a submission score of 80.
Object Specialist	Must get a hardcore score of 70.
Resiliency	Must get an overall rating of 92.
Strong Strike	Must get a strike score of 75.

WWE SMACKDOWN VS. RAW 2010 (PSP)

CODES

Go to "options" then "cheat codes," the codes are case-sensitive.

EFFECT	CODE
Unlock Dirt Sheet Set and Mr. McMahon's Office backstage areas.	BonusBrawl
Unlock The Rock	The Great One

WWE SMACKDOWN VS. RAW 2011 (WII)

CODES

You can access the cheat code menu by going to "My WWE," then "Options," then "Cheat Codes."

EFFECT	CODE
John Cena Street Fight gear and Avatar T-Shirt	SLURPEE
Randy Orton Alternate Attire	apexpredator
"Tribute to the Troops" arena	8thannualtribute

WWE SMACKDOWN VS. RAW 2011 (XBOX360)

CODES

You can access the cheat code menu by going to "My WWE," then "Options," then "Cheat Codes."

EFFECT	CODE
John Cena Street Fight gear and Avatar T-Shirt	SLURPEE
Randy Orton Alternate Attire	apexpredator
"Tribute to the Troops" arena	8thannualtribute

UNLOCKABLES

UNLOCKABLE	HOW TO UNLOCK
ECW Create Modes Content	Hold 10 matches in Exhibition Mode
Edge/Christian custom entrance (as seen in Christian's RTWM)	In Christian's RTWM, between Weeks 10 and 12, cash in the money in the bank against Edge and win
Backlash	Win once at Backlash with any superstar (WWE Universe, select match, not custom)
Bragging Rights	Win once at Bragging Rights with any superstar (WWE Universe, select match, not custom)
Breaking Point	Win once at Breaking Point with any superstar (WWE Universe, select match, not custom)
Druid Arena	Complete all 5 RTWMs
ECW	Win once at SummerSlam with any superstar (WWE Universe, select match, not custom)

NEW!

A
B
C
D
E
F
G
H
I
J
K
L
M
N
O
P
Q
R
S
T
U
V
W
X
Y
Z

Extreme Rules	Win once at Extreme Rules with any superstar (WWE Universe, select match, not custom)
Hell In A Cell	Win once at Hell In A Cell with any superstar (WWE Universe, select match, not custom)
Judgment Day	Win once at Royal Rumble with any superstar (WWE Universe, select match, not custom)
Night of Champions	Win once at Night of Champions with any superstar (WWE Universe, select match, not custom)
Survivor Series	Win once at Survivor Series with any superstar (WWE Universe, select match, not custom)
The Bash	Win once at the Bash with any superstar (WWE Universe, select match, not custom)
TLC	Win once at TLC with any superstar (WWE Universe, select match, not custom)
Tribute to the Troops	Win once at WrestleMania XXVI with any superstar (WWE Universe, select match, not custom)
Batista (Civilian)	In Jericho's RTWM, win against Kofi, Henry, and Batista in Week 8
Edge (Civilian)	In Christian's RTWM, defeat Big Show in a locker room area during Elimination Chamber
Jake the Snake Roberts	In week 9 of the vs Undertaker RTWM, win your match with minimal damage taken
Masked Kane Attire	In week 11 of the vs Undertaker RTWM, win your match
Mickie James	When Vince McMahon says you have to wrestle Mickie James after you've won a match, defeat Mickie James and she'll be unlocked for play.
MVP (Civilian)	In Cena's RTWM, win both Week 5 and Week 7 Tag Team Challenge Match against R-Truth and Mike Knox.
Paul Bearer	In week 12 of the vs Undertaker RTWM, knock him out backstage in less than 90 seconds.
Play as Finlay	When Vince McMahon says you have to wrestle Finlay after you've won a match, defeat Finlay and he'll be unlocked for play.
Play as Vladimir Kozlov	When Vince McMahon says you have to wrestle Kozlov after you've won a match, defeat Kozlov and he'll be unlocked for play.
Ricky "The Dragon" Steambot	In week 12 of Jericho's RTWM, defeat him in a singles match.
Rob Van Dam	Complete Rey Mysterio's RTWM
Superfly Jimmy Snuka	In week 10 of the vs Undertaker RTWM, win your match in less than 3 minutes.
Ted DiBiase (T-Shirt)	In Cena's RTWM, defeat Ted DiBiase to win the Week 11 Tag Team Challenge against Ted DiBiase and Cody Rhodes.
Terry Funk	Defeat him at Wrestlemania in Rey Mysterio's RTWM.
The Rock	In week 12 of the vs Undertaker RTWM, you can find the Rock in the food room, and you have to win the match against him to get him.
Todo Americano attire for Jack Swagger	Perform your finisher against him in Rey Mysterio's RTWM
Triple H (Civilian)	In Jericho's RTWM, during Week 6, escape to the parking lot without losing to Triple H.
Zack Ryder	Win a Falls Count Anywhere Match in WWE Universe.

X-BLADES (XBOX 360)

UNLOCKABLES

UNLOCKABLE	HOW TO UNLOCK
New Costumes	Beat the game once to unlock two new costumes: A health Regeneration outfit, and an Armored outfit.
Pro Mode	You can unlock the Pro difficulty by completing the game.

X-BLADES (PLAYSTATION 3)

NEW COSTUMES

Complete the game on HARD difficulty to unlock both secret costumes at once.

UNLOCKABLE	HOW TO UNLOCK
Armored Costume	Beat game on Hard mode.
Regeneration Costume	Beat game on Hard mode.

X-MEN: DESTINY (XBOX 360)

ACHIEVEMENT

UNLOCKABLE	HOW TO UNLOCK
Ace In The Hole (15)	Defeat Gambit.
Alpha Level Mutant (50)	Finish the game on X-Man difficulty.
An Unstoppable Force (15)	Defeat Magneto and Juggernaut.
Another Shrimp on the Barbie (15)	Stop Pyro from being mind-controlled.
Archivist (30)	Collect 15 dossiers.
At Least It's Aerodynamic... (10)	Equip your first suit.
Beginner's Luck (10)	Complete your first Great combo.
Beta Level Mutant (50)	Finish the game on New Mutant difficulty.
Better than the Best (15)	Defeat more enemies than Wolverine in the Prime Enforcer factory.
Broken Glass, Everywhere... (20)	Break 30 Combat Text Pop Ups.
Can I Get A Valkyrie? (0)	You were defeated 100 times.
Choose Wisely (20)	Make second power destiny choice.
Cleaned up the City (30)	Destroy 25 pieces of propaganda.
Completionist (50)	Complete all 15 unique challenge missions.
David Beats Goliath (15)	Defeat Sublime.
Destiny Begins (15)	Select a Power.
Diamond in the Rough (15)	Help Emma Frost defend mutant civilians from Purifier attacks.
Fight Terror with Terror (20)	Defeat 10 enemies with one Ultra power.
Fist of the... (15)	Stop Northstar from being mind-controlled.
Flash Fire (15)	Help Pyro, Juggernaut and Quicksilver defeat the Purifiers.
Four of a Kind (20)	Equip a complete X-Gene set and suit.
Fully Evolved (30)	Fully level up all powers.

CODES & CHEATS

Garbage Collection (10)	Destroy your first piece of propaganda.
Got My Eye on You (30)	Join Cyclops and the X-Men.
How Strong Could It Be? (20)	Trigger X-Mode.
I've Got the Power (20)	Fully level up a power.
It's a Secret to Everybody (15)	Find the U-Men secret lab.
Logan's Run (15)	Help Emma Frost turn Wolverine back to normal.
Magneto Is Right (30)	Join Magneto and the Brotherhood.
Mechageddon (20)	Defeat 20 Purifier Stalker Mechs.
Mutant Tracker (15)	Rescue Caliban.
Omega Level Mutant (50)	Finish the game on X-treme difficulty.
Profiler (10)	Collect your first dossier.
Purify the Purifiers (20)	Defeat 2000 Purifiers.
Reinforced (20)	Defeat 20 Prime Enforcers.
Satellite Interference (15)	Interrupt the transmission.
Shock and Awe (15)	Defeat Cameron Hodge.
Side-tracked (10)	Complete your first challenge mission.
Splicer (10)	Equip your first X-Gene.
Stay Frosty (15)	Help Iceman, Cyclops and Emma Frost defeat the Purifiers.
Taking Every Opportunity (25)	Complete 10 unique challenge missions.
Teleport This! (15)	Help Nightcrawler rescue mutants.
The Choice Is Made (20)	Make third power destiny choice.
The Goon Squad (20)	Defeat 500 MRD Troops.
The Roof, the Roof... (15)	Help Pyro set the roof on fire.
Things Look So Bad Everywhere... (15)	Survive Magneto's attack on the Purifiers.
Think About It... (20)	Make first power destiny choice.
This can't be happening! (20)	Complete your first Insane combo.
U Mad, Bro? (20)	Defeat 30 U-Men in the Secret Lab.
Why Do They Keep Coming? (15)	

CODE

Enter the code at the "X START" screen on the menu.

UNLOCKABLE	CODE
Emma Frost's costume	Hold (⑬+⑭) and press ↑, ↓, →, ←, ⑧, ⑦
Juggernaut Suits	Hold ⑬+⑭, press ↓, →, ↑, ←, ⑦, ⑧

X-MEN LEGENDS 2: RISE OF APOCALYPSE (PSP)

These codes must be entered on the pause screen.

UNLOCKABLE	CODE
1-Hit Kills with Punches	⇦, ⇦, ⇨, ⇨, ⇨, ⇨, [START]
God Mode	⇩, ⇩, ⇧, ⇧, ⇨, ⇨, ⇦, ⇦,
Super Speed	⇧, ⇧, ⇧, ⇧, ⇧, ⇧, [START]
Unlimited XTreme Power	⇦, ⇩, ⇩, ⇩, ⇧, ⇧, ⇩, ⇧, [START]

Enter these at Forge or Beast's equipment screen.

UNLOCKABLE	CODE
100,000 techbits	⇧, ⇧, ⇧, ⇩, ⇨, ⇨, [START]

Enter these codes at the team management screen.

UNLOCKABLE	CODE
All Characters	⇨, ⇦, ⇦, ⇨, ⇧, ⇧, ⇧, [START]
All Character Skins	⇩, ⇧, ⇦, ⇨, ⇧, ⇧, [START]

All Skills	⇦, ⇨, ⇦, ⇨, ⇩, ⇧, START
Level 99 Characters	⇧, ⇩, ⇧, ⇩, ⇦, ⇧, ⇦, ⇨, START

Enter these in the Review menu.

UNLOCKABLE	CODE
All Comic Books	⇨, ⇦, ⇦, ⇨, ⇧, ⇧, ⇨, START
All Concept Art	⇦, ⇨, ⇦, ⇨, ⇧, ⇧, ⇩, START
All Game Cinematic	⇦, ⇨, ⇨, ⇦, ⇩, ⇩, ⇦, START

Enter this in the Danger Room.

UNLOCKABLE	CODE
All Danger Room Courses	⇨, ⇨, ⇦, ⇦, ⇧, ⇩, ⇧, ⇩, START

X-MEN ORIGINS: WOLVERINE   (XBOX 360)

CODES

Enter the following codes during gameplay. Activating the cheats disables Achievements. The costume will be available from the Main menu.

EFFECT	CODE
Unlock classic Wolverine costume	X, A, B, A, A, Y, A, Y, A, X, B, B, RB
Faster Enemy Reflex (Every kill you'll gain double reflex)	A, A, X, X, Y, Y, B, B, Y, X, X, A, A, RB
Infinite Rage	Y, X, X, Y, B, B, Y, X, A, A, Y, RB
Undying (You will lose health but you'll never die)	X, A, A, X, Y, X, X, B, B, X, RB

X-MEN ORIGINS: WOLVERINE   (PLAYSTATION 3)

CODES

Enter the following codes during gameplay. Activating the cheats disables Trophies. The costume will be available from the main menu.

EFFECT	CODE
Unlocks classic Wolverine costume	×, ■, ●, ×, ▲, ×, ▲, ×, ■, ●, ●, ■, R3
Doubles enemy reflex points	×, ×, ■, ■, ▲, ▲, ●, ●, ▲, ▲, ■, ■, ×, ×, R3,
Infinite rage	▲, ■, ■, ▲, ●, ●, ▲, ×, ▲, ▲, R3,
Undying (health goes down but you never die)	■, ×, ×, ■, ▲, ▲, ■, ●, ●, ■, R3,

YAKUZA: DEAD SOULS (PLAYSTATION 3)

TROPHY

UNLOCKABLE	HOW TO UNLOCK
A Weapon Freak is Born (Bronze)	Create at least one weapon from each category.
Akiyama Trophy (Silver)	Land 100 head shots with Akiyama.
All Units, Report! (Bronze)	Train at Gary's Boot Camp with all four protagonists.
Amon's Vanquisher (Gold)	Defeat Amon.
Brainiac (Bronze)	Win at mahjong and shogi once each.
Casino Master (Bronze)	Play each casino game once.
Getting Some Action (Bronze)	Fight zombies together with a hostess.
Goda Trophy (Silver)	Destroy 100 wield-able objects with Goda.
Golden Brown (Bronze)	Defeat 50 zombies with fire.
Hasegawa's Right Hand (Bronze)	Cumulative point total from Hasegawa's directives hit 5,000.
Heavily Armed Bank (Bronze)	Amass over 10 million yen.
Indoor Sportsman (Bronze)	Go batting, bowling, and play table tennis three times each.
Kamurocho Spelunker (Bronze)	Initiate the Kamurocho Subterranea mission.
Kiryu Trophy (Silver)	Defeat 100 mutant variants with Kiryu.
Life of the Party (Bronze)	Play every song at karaoke.
Lounge Lizard (Bronze)	Play darts and pool five times each.
Majima Trophy (Silver)	Defeat 100 enemies using Heat Sniping with Majima.
Mission Complete! (Bronze)	Clear a directive from Hasegawa.
My Eyes! (Bronze)	Daze 50 zombies with stun grenades.
My First Mod (Bronze)	Mod one weapon or piece of armor.
Nice Try (Bronze)	Shoot down an enemy projectile with a Heat Snipe.
Official Sponsor (Bronze)	Fully upgrade Kamiyama's truck.
Oh, the Humanity! (Bronze)	Successfully Heat Snipe a gas tanker.
Old-School (Bronze)	Defeat 10 zombies using wield-able objects.
Outdoorsman (Bronze)	Go golfing and fishing once each.
Pachinko Wizard (Bronze)	Obtain the "trophy" prize at the Volcano Prize Exchange counter.
Part I Complete (Bronze)	Complete the four chapters of Part I.
Part II Complete (Bronze)	Complete the four chapters of Part II.
Part III Complete (Bronze)	Complete the four chapters of Part III.
Part IV Complete (Bronze)	Complete the four chapters of Part IV.
Platinum Trophy (Platinum)	Earn all other trophies in the game.
Pro Gambler (Bronze)	Play each Japanese gambling game once.

Recycler (Bronze)	Collect 100 items in battle.
Road Rage (Bronze)	Run over 10 zombies with a forklift or bulldozer.
Savior of Kamurocho (Gold)	Complete Dead Souls Mode.
Social Butterfly (Bronze)	Have all 14 partner characters available.
Start of Something Good (Bronze)	Befriend your first Perfect Partner character.
Steamed Vegetable (Bronze)	Kill a Hermit with fire while it is still armored.
Substory 20 (Bronze)	Finish 20 substories.
Substory 4 (Bronze)	Finish 4 substories.
Substory 40 (Bronze)	Finish 40 substories.
Thanks for Playing! (Gold)	Complete the Final Chapter.
The True Ending (Silver)	Complete Extra Hard Mode.
Underground Kings (Silver)	Clear 50 floors in the Endless Subterranea.
Unsurpassed Power (Silver)	Reach the maximum character level.
Vigilante Gourmet (Bronze)	Order from every restaurant at least once.
Welcome to SEGA (Bronze)	Play each game in Club SEGA.
Zombie Collector (Bronze)	Defeat each type of mutant variant.
Zombie Hunter (Bronze)	Defeat 100 zombies.

YAKUZA 4 (PLAYSTATION 3)

UNLOCKABLES

Complete the tasks to unlock these

UNLOCKABLE	HOW TO UNLOCK
1000000 yen bonus	Clear Easy mode
2000000 yen bonus	Clear Normal mode
3000000 yen bonus	Clear Hard mode
5000000 yen bonus	Clear EX-Hard mode
Asagao Special Torso Wrap	Have an existing Ryuu ga Gotoku 3 system file
Bell of Gion	Have an existing Ryuu ga Gotoku Kenzan! save file
EX-Hard Mode	Clear Hard mode
Premium Adventure	Clear the game on any difficulty
Premium New Game	Clear the game on any difficulty
Reminiscence (Kaisou)	Clear the game on any difficulty
Ultimate Competition (Kyuukyoku Tougi)	Clear the game on any difficulty
Underground SP Championship	Clear the game on any difficulty. Enter Naomi no Yakata located on Tenkaichi Street. Talk to Utsunomiya Bob A.

YOU DON'T KNOW JACK (XBOX 360)

UNLOCKABLE

Complete the following to unlock these awards

UNLOCKABLE	HOW TO UNLOCK
A Bald-Headed Ski Mask	Play episode 58 score over $0.
A Beautiful Ladies' Pant (Female)	Play episode 9 and score over $0.
A Classy Men's T-Shirt (Male)	Play any episode and score over $0.
A Fashionable Men's Pant (Male)	Play episode 9 and score over $0.
A Trenty Ladies' T-Shirt (Female)	Play any episode and score over $0.
Billy O'Brien Replica Dummy	Find the episode 73 wrong answer of the game.

YU-GI-OH! 5D'S WORLD CHAMPIONSHIP 2010 REVERSE OF ARCADIA (DS)

CLOTHES AND DUEL DISKS

UNLOCKABLE	HOW TO UNLOCK
Academia Disk (Blue)	Buy for five star chips from Chihiro.
Academia Disk (Red)	Buy for five star chips from Chihiro.
Academia Disk (Yellow)	Buy for five star chips from Chihiro.
Black Bird Disk	Beat Crow 10 times in Turbo Duels.
Black Chain Disk	Defeat each level of the single tournament once.
Black Jail Disk	Win all levels of Tournament Mode.
Career Suit	Box item found in the southwest room of the Securities building.
Dark magician outfit	Defeat the duel runner owners 10 times.
Dark Singer	Buy for 15 star chips from Chihiro after beating the main story.
Dark Singer Disk	Buy for 10 star chips from Chihiro after beating the main story.
Denim Jacket	Buy for five Star Chips from Chihiro if male.
K.C. Mass Production Disk	Buy for five star chips from Chihiro.
King Replica Model	Beat Jack 10 times in both duels and Turbo Duels.
Leo's Custom Disk	Beat Leo and Luna in 10 Tag Duels.
Luna's Custom Disk	End three duels in a draw.
One-piece	Buy for five star chips from Chihiro if female.
Race Queen	Buy for five star chips from Chihiro if female.
Rock N' Roller	Box item found inside the third duel gang's hideout if male.
Rose Disk	Box item found in the southwest room of the Securities building.
Rough Style	Box item found in the basement of the first duel gang's hideout.
Sailor Uniform	Box item found inside Zeman's castle if female.
Security Disk	Securities' building, northeast room
Security Helmet	60% card completion
Security Uniform	Given to you by Crow during Chapter 2.
Stuffed Collar Uniform	Box item found inside Zeman's castle if male.
Tag Force Set	100% card completion
The Enforcers	Unlocked automatically at the start of Chapter 2.
Wheel of Fortune (Disk)	Beat Jack 10 times in both duels and Turbo Duels.
Wild Style	Buy for five Star Chips from Chihiro if male.
Witch's dress	Defeat Akiza 10 times in a Turbo Duel.

UNLOCKABLE	HOW TO UNLOCK
Worn-out Clothes	Box item found inside the third duel gang's hideout if female.
Yusei Jacket	Beat Yusei 10 times in Turbo Duels.
Yusei's Hybrid Disk	Beat Yusei 10 times.

CPU OPPONENTS

Fulfill the following conditions to unlock CPU opponents for World Championship Mode. Teams not listed are either unlocked from the start, or unlocked by progressing through Story Mode.

UNLOCKABLE	HOW TO UNLOCK
Ancient Gear Gadjiltron Dragon	Summon Ancient Gear Gadjiltron Dragon.

Archlord Kristya	Beat "Green Baboon, Defender of the Forest" three times.	**NEW!**
Blackwing-Vayu the Emblem of Honor	Summon Blackwing-Silverwind the Ascendant.	
Blue-Eyes White Dragon	Beat "Darklord Desire" three times.	
Chaos Sorcerer	Beat "Solar Flare Dragon" three times.	**A**
Crusader of Endymion	Activate Mega Ton Magical Cannon.	
Cyber Eltanin	Beat "B.E.S. Big Core MK-2" three times.	**B**
Dark Simorgh	Beat "Great Shogun Shien" three times.	**C**
Darkness Neosphere	Play for 100 hours.	
Destiny End Dragoon	Beat "Underground Arachnid" three times.	**D**
Dragunity Knight-Gadearg	Beat "Ancient Fairy Dragon" three times.	
Earthbound Immortal Wiraqocha Rasca	Win with by using the effect of Final Countdown.	**E**
Elemental Hero Absolute Zero	Beat "Fabled Leviathan" three times.	**F**
Elemental Hero Neos	Beat "Ancient Sacred Wyvern" three times.	**G**
Explosive Magician	Beat "Ally of Justice Decisive Armor" three times.	
Fabled Ragin	Beat "Evil Hero Dark Gaia" three times.	**H**
Fossil Dyna Pachycephalo	Have 666 or more Summons.	**I**
Garlandolf, King of Destruction	Play for 50 hours.	
		J
Gigaplant	Summon Perfectly Ultimate Great Moth.	
Gladiator Beast Gyzarus	Summon Gladiator Beast Heraklinos.	**K**
Gravekeeper's Visionary	Beat "Jurrac Meteor" three times.	
Green Gadget	Beat "Power Tool Dragon" three times.	**L**
Harpie Queen	Win by using the effect of Vennominaga the Deity of Poisonous Snakes.	**M**
Hundred Eyes Dragon	Beat "Ojama Yellow" three times.	
Judgment Dragon	Summon Judgment Dragon.	**N**
Locomotion R-Genex	Summon Flying Fortress Sky Fire.	**O**
Lonefire Blossom	Beat "Gungnir, Dragon of the Ice Barrier" three times.	
Majestic Red Dragon	Summon Majestic Red Dragon.	**P**
Naturia Beast	Beat "Reptilianne Vaskii" three times.	
Raiza the Storm Monarch	Beat "Lava Golem" three times.	**Q**
Stardust Dragon /Assault Mode	Unlock 50% or more Duel Bonuses.	**R**
Supersonic Skull Flame	Beat "Mist Valley Apex Avian" three times.	**S**
Swap Frog	Beat "The Dark Creator" three times.	
UNLOCKABLE	**HOW TO UNLOCK**	**T**
The Immortal Bushi	Beat "Naturia Landoise" three times	
Worm Zero	Highest damage is 10,000 or more.	**U**
XX-Saber Hyunlei	Win 10 duels in a row.	**V**

TAG TEAMS

Fulfill the following conditions to unlock CPU Teams for Tag Duel in World Championship Mode. Teams not listed are either unlocked from the start, or unlocked automatically as you progress through Story Mode.

UNLOCKABLE	HOW TO UNLOCK	
Child of Chaos	Beat Team "Water & Fire" three times.	**X**
Cyber Regeneration	Beat Team "Angels & The Fallen" three times.	**Y**
Dragon & Dragon	Summon Five-Headed Dragon.	
		Z

Dual Duel	Beat Team "Removal Guys" three times.
Duel Ritual	Complete 300 Single Duels.
E & D Impact	Beat Team "Darkness + Fiends" three times.
Earthbound Crystal	Summon Rainbow Dragon.
Fish-the-World	Have 200 Spells and Traps activated.
Gadget Emperor	Complete 150 Tag Duels.
Grinder Summoning	Beat Team "Explosive Tag" three times.
Legend's Anniversary	Beat Team "Love Reptiles " three times.
Lo and Behold	Beat Team "Protect & Burn" three times.
Mausoleum's Legend	Beat Team "Order in Chaos" three times.
Simochi Study	Beat Team "Cyber Dragunity" three times.
Storm of Darkness	Beat Team "Fusion & Synchro" three times.
To the Graveyard	Complete 75 Turbo Duels.
Trago Genex	Summon VWXYZ-Dragon Catapult Cannon.
Zombie Path	Win by attacking with Skull Servant.

DUEL RUNNERS

UNLOCKABLE	HOW TO UNLOCK
Blackbird (crow's d-wheel)	Unlock every other frame.
Chariot Frame	Beat the headless ghost in a duel (speak to Trudge after completing Story Mode).
Giganto L (Kalins duel runner)	Buy for 40 star chips from Chihiro after beating the main story.
Wheel of Fortune D-Wheel Frame	Clear all Duel Runner Race battles courses with S Rank.
Yusei D-Wheel Frame	Clear all Duel Runner Race Time courses with S Rank.

YU-GI-OH! 5D'S WORLD CHAMPIONSHIP 2011: OVER THE NEXUS (DS)

UNLOCKABLE

Fulfill the following conditions to unlock different booster packs in the game.

UNLOCKABLE	HOW TO UNLOCK
Absolute Powerforce	Win 3 consecutive Rental Duels in the Daimon Area
Acceleration Finish	Start the final chapter
Acceleration Next	Start Chapter VI
Acceleration Start	Turbo Duel with Toru in Chapter IV
All Cards at Random	Collect 95% of all available cards
Ancient Prophecy	Defeat Torunka and Regulus 3 times each
Champion of Chaos!!	Defeat Heitmann, Hans, and Nicholas 3 times each in single and Tag Duels
Charge of Genex!!	Defeat Chief, Syd, Lawton, Ramon, and Malcolm 3 times each
Crimson Crisis	Start the final chapter
Crossroads of Chaos	Start Chapter V
Cyberdark Impact	200 single duels
Cybernetic Revolution	Duel Jack in Chapter II
Dragunity Hurricane!!	Defeat Trudge, Akiza, Leo, and Luna 3 times each in single, Tag, and Tag Turbo Duels
Duelist Revolution	Defeat Andre in the final chapter
Elemental Energy	100 single duels
Enemy of Justice	Defeat Reimi, Lillie, Hayakawa, Masaki, Gordon, and Kuroe 3 times each
Extra Pack	Clear the side event in your apartment building in the Daimon Area

Extra Pack 2	Clear Toru's side event	
Extra Pack 3	Clear Misaki's side event	**NEW!**
Fabled Revival!!	Defeat Carly, Mina, and Stephanie 3 times each in single duels and Tag Duels	
Flaming Eternity	Get the parts for Toru in Chapter II	
Force of the Breaker	Defeat Rossi, Kazuhiro, Honda, Yanagigaura, Helio, Angie, Nelson, Figaro, and Corse 3 times each	A
Gladiator's Assault	Defeat Lenny, Hunter Pace, Lug, Larry and Randsborg 3 times each	B
Invasion of Worms!!	Available from the start	C
Judgment of Omega!!	Defeat Toru and Misaki 3 times each in single, Tag, Turbo, and Tag Turbo duels	D
Justice Strikes Back!!	Available from the start	
Light of Destruction	Defeat Lazar, Sherry, and Elsworth 3 times each	E
Power of the Duelist	Start Chapter III	F
Pulse of Trishula!!	Duel all of the shop workers	G
Raging Battle	Clear the side event where you defeat Team Satisfaction (the Enforcers) in a race	
Rise of Destiny	50 single duels	H
Shadow of Infinity	Start Chapter III	
Soul of the Duelist	Start Chapter II	I
Stardust Overdrive	Clear a side event in which you duel 3 members of Team 5Ds in Rental Duels	J
Starstrike Blast	Defeat Yusei, Jack, and Crow, 3 times each in single duels, Tag Duels, and Tag Turbo Duels	K
Steelswarm Invasion!!	Complete all of Nico and the Bootleg owner's puzzles	L
Storm of Ragnarok	Defeat Team Ragnarok 3 times each in single duels, Tag Duels, and Tag Turbo Duels	
Strike of Neos	Duel Virgil in Chapter III	M
Synchro, Awaken!!	Available from the start	N
Tactical Evolution	Start Chapter IV	
The Duelist Genesis	Start Chapter VI	O
The Lost Millenium	Defeat Bronson, Minegishi, Gemma, Virgil, Zeruga, Scotch, and Clint 3 times each	P
The Shining Darkness	Defeat Nico, West, Sergio, Barbara, and Kalin 3 times each	
Vylon Descends!!	Defeat all single duelists 3 times each	Q
WC Edition 1	Defeat the 6 CPU Duel opponents available at the start 3 times each	R
WC Edition 10	Unlock 8 CPU Tag Turbo Duel opponents	S
WC Edition 11	Unlock 9 CPU Tag Turbo Duel opponents	
WC Edition 2	Unlock 36 CPU Duel opponents	T
WC Edition 3	Unlock 48 CPU Duel opponents	
WC Edition 4	Unlock 7 CPU Tag Duel opponents	U
WC Edition 5	Unlock 12 CPU Tag Duel opponents	
WC Edition 6	Unlock 16 CPU Tag Duel opponents	V
WC Edition 7	Unlock 12 CPU Turbo Duel opponents	
WC Edition 8	Unlock 16 CPU Turbo Duel opponents	W
WC Edition 9	Unlock 7 CPU Tag Turbo Duel opponents	X

UNLOCKABLE

Fulfill the following conditions to unlock CPU opponents.

UNLOCKABLE	HOW TO UNLOCK	
Archlord Kristya	Beat [Guardian Eatos] 3 times	Z

CODES & CHEATS

Blackwing- Zephyrus the Elite	Summon [Blackwing - Silverwind the Ascendant]
Bountiful Artemis	Beat [Deep Sea Diva] 3 times
Dark Simorgh	Beat [Vylon Omega] 3 times
Dragunity Arma Leyvaten	Have 666 Total Summons
Ehren, Lightsworn Monk	Summon [Judgment Dragon]
Elemental Hero The Shining	Summon [Vylon Omega]
Evil Hero Dark Gaia	50 Hours Total Play Time
Gladiator Beast Gyzarus	Have 10 Consecutive Wins
Guardian Eatos	100 Hours Total Play Time
Infernity Doom Dragon	Win with [Final Countdown]'s effect
Junk Destroyer	Summon [Shooting Star Dragon]
Legendary Six Samurai - Shi En	Summon [Gladiator Beast Heraklinos]
Machina Fortress	Summon [Odin, Father of the Aesir]
Malefic Paradox Dragon	Summon [Malefic Paradox Dragon]
Master Hyperion	Beat [Tiki Curse] 3 times
Meklord Emperor Granel Infinity	Beat [Earthbound Immortal Ccapac Apu] 3 times
Power Tool Dragon	Beat [Wynnda, Priestess of Gusto] 3 times
Queen Angel of Roses	Beat [Flamvell Baby] 3 times
Red-Eyes Darkness Metal Dragon	Summon [Red Nova Dragon]
Stardust Dragon/Assault Mode	Beat [Great Maju Garzett] 3 times
Thestalos the Firestorm Monarch	Have 50% of all Bonuses
Thunder King Rai-Oh	Beat [Gravekeeper's Visionary] 3 times
X-Saber Souza	Have 10000 Max Damage

UNLOCKABLE

Fullfill the following requirements to get these items

UNLOCKABLE	HOW TO UNLOCK
5D's Standard Disk	Complete the Game
Blackbird	S Rank on all Battle Royale
Different Facial Expressions	Duel Torunka and Win
Duel Phantom (Duel Runner Frame)	Talk to the broken Ghost with Misaki as your partner
DWE-CG	Talk to Klaus post-game
DWE-X	Talk to Jack and complete his event
Golden Shield Disk	Talk to Ransborg post-game, and complete his event
King Replica Model	Talk to Jack Post-game
KPC-000	4th Floor of Apartment, must have Lucky Key
Lambda Frame	Talk to Mina with Misaki as your partner and complete her event postgame
Leather Top and Bottom Set (Yusei's Outfit)	Found behind Team 5D's Garage
Leo's Custom Disk	Outside of Sector Security
Lucky Key	Talk to the guy behind Team 5D's garage and choose the right box
Luna's Custom Disk	Outside Securities building (Female only)
Missing Ring	See Spirit World
Speed Spell - Deceased Synchron	Can be found as a Blue card on Battle Royal Race
Stuffy Collar Shirt	See Spirit World
Suit Style	4th Floor of Apartment, must have Lucky Key

The Spirit World	To Access the Spirit World, Duel all 3 Computer Ghosts
Waiter Outfit	Talk to Stephanie and complete her event
Wheel of Fortune	S Rank on all Battle Races
Yusei-Go	S Rank on all Time Races

UNLOCKABLE

Fulfill the following conditions to unlock different structure decks in the game.

UNLOCKABLE	HOW TO UNLOCK
Curse of Darkness	Duel Gordon in Chapter II
Dinosaur's Rage	Start Chapter II
Dragunity Legion	Start Chapter VI
Fury From The Deep	Play in the Rental Deck Tournament in Chapter I
Invincible Fortress	Play in the Rental Deck Tournament in Chapter I
Lord of the Storm	Start Chapter II
Lost Sanctuary	Start Chapter VI
Machina Mayhem	Start Chapter V
Machine Re-Volt	Start Chapter II
Rise of the Dragon Lords	Start Chapter III
Spellcaster's Command	Start Chapter V
Spellcaster's Judgment	Play in the Rental Deck Tournament in Chapter I
Surge of Radiance	Duel Gordon in Chapter II
The Dark Emperor	Start Chapter III
Warrior's Strike	Start Chapter IV
Warrior's Triumph	Play in the Rental Deck Tournament in Chapter I
Zombie World	Start Chapter IV

ZOMBIE APOCALYPSE (XBOX 360)

UNLOCKABLE

UNLOCKABLE	HOW TO UNLOCK
Chainsaw Only Mode	Complete a day with only a chainsaw.
Hardcore Mode	Survive for seven consecutive days.
Turbo Mode	Achieve a multiplier over 100.

ZOMBIE APOCALYPSE (PLAYSTATION 3)

UNLOCKABLE

UNLOCKABLE	HOW TO UNLOCK
Chainsaw Only Mode	Complete a day with only a chainsaw.
Hardcore Mode	Survive for seven consecutive days.
Turbo Mode	Achieve a multiplier over 100.

ZOMBIE PANIC IN WONDERLAND (WII)

UNLOCKABLE

UNLOCKABLE	HOW TO UNLOCK
Alice	Beat Story Mode twice
Bunny Girl Snow White	Beat Story Mode three times.
Dorothy	Reach Stage 2-1 in Story Mode.
Little Red Riding Hood	Beat Story Mode four times.
Snow White	Reach Stage 3-2 in Story Mode.
Survival Stage in Arcade Mode (Pirate Ship)	Beat Story Mode once.